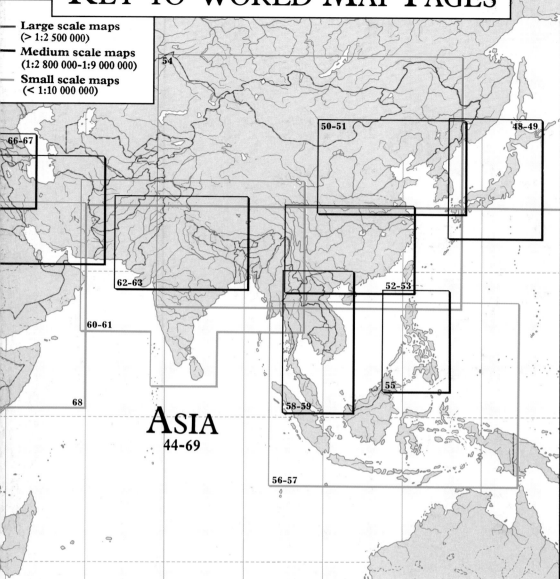

KEY TO WORLD MAP PAGES

- **Large scale maps** (> 1:2 500 000)
- **Medium scale maps** (1:2 800 000–1:9 000 000)
- **Small scale maps** (< 1:10 000 000)

54

50–51

48–49

66–67

62–63

60–61

68

52–53

55

58–59

56–57

ASIA
44-69

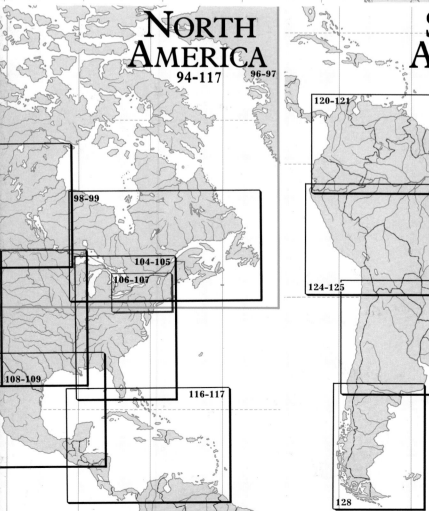

NORTH AMERICA
94-117

96–97

98–99

104–105

106–107

108–109

116–117

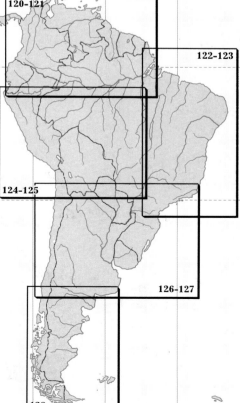

SOUTH AMERICA
118-128

120–121

122–123

124–125

126–127

128

COUNTRY INDEX

Country	Page	Country	Page
Afghanistan	60	Kuwait	64–65
Albania	38–39		
Algeria	74–75	Laos	58
Angola	80–81	Latvia	40
Argentina	126, 128	Lebanon	69
Armenia	67	Lesotho	85
Australia	88–91	Liberia	78
Austria	19, 20–21	Libya	73
Azerbaijan	67	Lithuania	40
		Luxembourg	17
Bahamas	116–117		
Bahrain	65	Macedonia	38–39
Bangladesh	61	Madagascar	85
Barbados	117	Malawi	83
Belgium	17	Malaysia	55–56
Belize	116	Mali	78–79
Belorussia	40	Malta	37
Benin	79	Mauritania	78
Bhutan	61	Mauritius	71
Bolivia	124–125	Mexico	114–115
Bosnia-		Moldavia	42
Herzegovina	21	Mongolia	54
Botswana	84–85	Morocco	74
Brazil	120–127	Mozambique	83
Brunei	56		
Bulgaria	38–39	Namibia	84
Burkina Faso	78–79	Nepal	63
Burma	61	Netherlands	16–17
Burundi	82	New Zealand	87
		Nicaragua	116
Cambodia	58–59	Niger	79
Cameroon	82	Nigeria	79
Canada	96–101	Northern Ireland	15
Central African		Norway	8–9
Republic	82		
Chad	73	Oman	68
Chile	126, 128		
China	50–54	Pakistan	62
Colombia	120	Panama	116
Congo	80	Papua New Guinea	86
Costa Rica	116	Paraguay	126–127
Croatia	21	Peru	124
Cuba	116–117	Philippines	55
Cyprus	37	Poland	20
Czech Republic	20–21	Portugal	30–31
		Puerto Rico	117
Denmark	11		
Djibouti	68	Qatar	65
Dominican			
Republic	117	Romania	38
		Russia	40–45
Ecuador	120	Rwanda	82
Egypt	76		
El Salvador	116	Saudi Arabia	68
England	12–13	Scotland	14
Equatorial Guinea	80	Senegal	78
Eritrea	76–77	Sierra Leone	78
Estonia	40	Singapore	59
Ethiopia	68, 77	Slovak Republic	20–21
		Slovenia	33
Fiji	87	Somali Republic	68
Finland	8–9	South Africa	84–85
France	24–27	Spain	28–31
French Guiana	121	Sri Lanka	60
		Sudan	77
Gabon	80	Surinam	121
Gambia	78	Swaziland	85
Georgia	43	Sweden	8–9
Germany	18–19	Switzerland	22–23
Ghana	78–79	Syria	67
Greece	39		
Greenland	4	Taiwan	53
Guatemala	116	Tajikistan	44
Guinea	78	Tanzania	82–83
Guinea-Bissau	78	Thailand	58–59
Guyana	121	Togo	79
		Trinidad and	
Haiti	117	Tobago	117
Honduras	116	Tunisia	75
Hong Kong	53	Turkey	66–67
Hungary	21	Turkmenistan	44
Iceland	8	Uganda	82
India	60–63	Ukraine	42
Indonesia	56–57	United Arab Emirates	65
Iran	64–65	United Kingdom	12–15
Iraq	64–65	USA	102–113
Irish Republic	15	Uruguay	126–127
Israel	69	Uzbekistan	44
Italy	32–35		
Ivory Coast	78	Venezuela	120–121
		Vietnam	58–59
Jamaica	116		
Japan	48–49	Wales	12–13
Jordan	69		
		Yemen	68
Kazakhstan	44	Yugoslavia	38–39
Kenya	82		
Kirghizia	44	Zaïre	80–81
Korea, North	51	Zambia	83
Korea, South	51	Zimbabwe	83

PHILIP'S

CONCISE WORLD ATLAS

This edition published 1994
by BCA by arrangement with
George Philip Limited,
an imprint of Reed Consumer Books Limited

Cartography by Philip's

Printed in Great Britain

PHILIP'S

CONCISE WORLD ATLAS

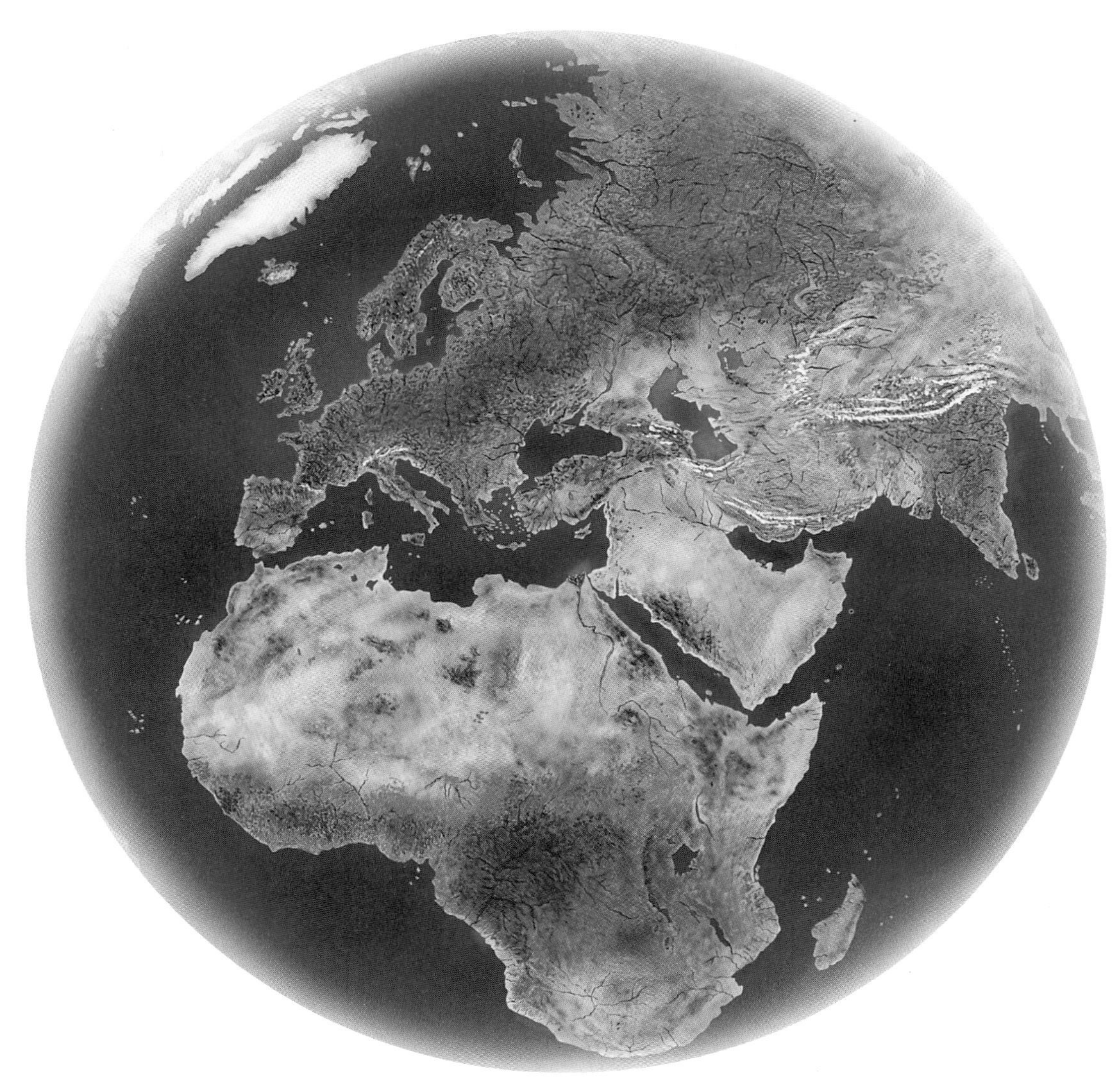

BCA

LONDON   NEW YORK   SYDNEY   TORONTO

CONTENTS

WORLD STATISTICS

Countries vi
Physical
Dimensions vii
Philip's World Maps viii

WORLD MAPS

1–128

Map Symbols
1

The World: Political
1:71 100 000
2–3

Arctic Ocean 1:31 100 000
4

Antarctica 1:31 100 000
5

EUROPE

Europe: Physical
1:17 800 000
6

Europe: Political
1:17 800 000
7

Scandinavia and the
Baltic Lands 1:4 400 000

8–9

Denmark and Southern
Sweden 1:2 200 000

10–11

England and Wales
1:1 800 000
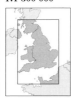
12–13

Scotland 1:1 800 000

14

Ireland 1:1 800 000

15

Netherlands, Belgium and
Luxembourg 1:1 100 000
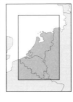
16–17

Germany 1:2 200 000

18–19

Middle Europe 1:3 100 000

20–21

Switzerland 1:900 000

22–23

Northern France 1:2 200 000

24–25

Southern France 1:2 200 000

26–27

Eastern Spain 1:2 200 000

28–29

Western Spain and
Portugal 1:2 200 000

30–31

Northern Italy, Slovenia
and Croatia
1:2 200 000
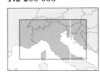
32–33

Southern Italy 1:2 200 000

34–35

Balearics, Canaries and
Madeira 1:900 000 / 1:1 800 000

36

Malta, Crete, Corfu,
Rhodes and Cyprus
1:900 000 / 1:1 200 000

37

The Balkans 1:3 100 000

38–39

Western Russia,
Belorussia and the Baltic
States 1:4 400 000

40–41

Ukraine, Moldavia
and the Caucasus
1:4 400 000

42–43

ASIA

Russia and Central Asia
1:17 800 000

44–45

Asia: Physical
1:44 400 000
46

Asia: Political
1:44 400 000
47

Japan 1:4 400 000

48–49

Northern China and Korea
1:5 300 000

50–51

Southern China 1:5 300 000

52–53

China 1:17 800 000

54

Philippines 1:6 700 000

55

Indonesia 1:11 100 000

56–57

Mainland South-East Asia
1:5 300 000

58–59

South Asia 1:8 900 000

60–61

The Indo-Gangetic Plain
1:5 300 000

62–63

The Middle East 1:6 200 000

64–65

Turkey 1:4 400 000

66–67

Arabia and the Horn of Africa 1:13 300 000

68

The Near East 1:2 200 000

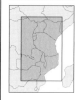

69

AFRICA

Africa: Physical
1:36 000 000
70

Africa: Political
1:36 000 000
71

Northern Africa 1:13 300 000

72–73

North-West Africa
1:7 100 000

74–75

The Nile Valley 1:7 100 000
The Nile Delta 1:3 600 000

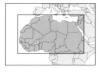

76–77

West Africa 1:7 100 000

78–79

Central and Southern Africa 1:13 300 000

80–81

East Africa 1:7 100 000

82–83

Southern Africa 1:7 100 000
Madagascar 1:7 100 000

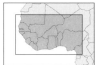

84–85

AUSTRALIA AND OCEANIA

Australia and Oceania: Physical and Political
1:36 000 000
86

New Zealand 1:5 300 000

87

Western Australia
1:7 100 000

88–89

Eastern Australia 1:7 100 000

90–91

Pacific Ocean 1:48 000 000
92–93

NORTH AMERICA

North America: Physical
1:31 100 000
94

North America: Political
1:31 100 000
95

Canada 1:13 300 000
Alaska 1:26 700 000

96–97

Eastern Canada 1:6 200 000

98–99

Western Canada 1:6 200 000

100–101

United States 1:10 700 000
Hawaii 1:8 900 000

102–103

Eastern United States
1:5 300 000

104–105

North-Eastern United States 1:2 200 000

106–107

Middle United States
1:5 300 000

108–109

Western United States
1:5 300 000

110–111

Central and Southern California and Washington 1:2 200 000

112–113

Mexico 1:7 100 000

114–115

Central America and the West Indies 1:7 100 000

116–117

SOUTH AMERICA

South America: Physical
1:26 700 000
118

South America: Political
1:26 700 000
119

South America – North-West 1:7 100 000

120–121

Eastern Brazil 1:7 100 000

122–123

South America – West
1:7 100 000

124–125

Central South America
1:7 100 000

126–127

Southern Chile and Argentina 1:7 100 000

128

INDEX TO WORLD MAPS
129–224

World Statistics: Countries

This alphabetical list includes all the countries and territories of the world. If a territory is not completely independent, then the country it isassociated with is named. The area figures give the total area of land, inland water and ice. Units for areas and populations are thousands. The annual income is the Gross National Product per capita in US dollars. The figures are the latest available, usually 1993.

Country/Territory	Area km² Thousands	Area miles² Thousands	Population Thousands	Capital	Annual Income US $
Adélie Land (Fr.)	432	167	0.03	–	–
Afghanistan	648	250	19,062	Kabul	450
Albania	28.8	11.1	3,363	Tirana	1,000
Algeria	2,382	920	26,346	Algiers	1,980
American Samoa (US)	0.20	0.08	50	Pago Pago	6,000
Amsterdam Is. (Fr.)	0.05	0.02	0.03	–	–
Andorra	0.45	0.17	58	Andorra la Vella	–
Angola	1,247	481	10,609	Luanda	620
Anguilla (UK)	0.09	0.04	9	The Valley	–
Antigua & Barbuda	0.44	0.17	66	St John's	4,770
Argentina	2,767	1,068	33,101	Buenos Aires	2,790
Armenia	29.8	11.5	3,677	Yerevan	2,150
Aruba (Neths)	0.19	0.07	62	Oranjestad	6,000
Ascension Is. (UK)	0.09	0.03	1.5	Georgetown	–
Australia	7,687	2,968	17,529	Canberra	17,050
Australian Antarctic Territory	6,120	2,363	0	–	–
Austria	83.9	32.4	7,884	Vienna	20,140
Azerbaijan	86.6	33.4	7,398	Baku	1,670
Azores (Port.)	2.2	0.87	260	Ponta Delgada	–
Bahamas	13.9	5.4	262	Nassau	11,750
Bahrain	0.68	0.26	533	Manama	7,130
Bangladesh	144	56	119,288	Dacca	200
Barbados	0.43	0.17	259	Bridgetown	6,630
Belau (US)	0.46	0.18	16	Koror	–
Belgium	30.5	11.8	9,998	Brussels	18,950
Belize	23	8.9	198	Belmopan	2,010
Belorussia	207.6	80.1	10,297	Minsk	3,110
Benin	113	43	4,889	Porto-Novo	380
Bermuda (UK)	0.05	0.02	62	Hamilton	25,000
Bhutan	47	18.1	1,612	Thimphu	180
Bolivia	1,099	424	7,832	La Paz/Sucre	650
Bosnia-Herzegovina	51.2	19.8	4,366	Sarajevo	–
Botswana	582	225	1,373	Gaborone	2,590
Bouvet Is. (Nor.)	0.05	0.02	0.02	–	–
Brazil	8,512	3,286	156,275	Brasilia	2,940
British Antarctic Terr. (UK)	1,709	660	0.3	Stanley	–
British Indian Ocean Terr. (UK)	0.08	0.03	3	–	–
Brunei	5.8	2.2	270	Bandar Seri Begawan	6,000
Bulgaria	111	43	8,963	Sofia	1,840
Burkina Faso	274	106	9,490	Ouagadougou	290
Burma (Myanmar)	679	262	43,668	Rangoon	500
Burundi	27.8	10.7	5,786	Bujumbura	210
Cambodia	181	70	9,054	Phnom Penh	300
Cameroon	475	184	12,198	Yaoundé	850
Canada	9,976	3,852	27,562	Ottawa	20,440
Canary Is. (Spain)	7.3	2.8	1,700	Las Palmas/Santa Cruz	–
Cape Verde Is.	4	1.6	384	Praia	750
Cayman Is. (UK)	0.26	0.10	29	Georgetown	–
Central African Republic	623	241	3,173	Bangui	390
Chad	1,284	496	5,961	Ndjamena	220
Chatham Is. (NZ)	0.96	0.37	0.05	Waitangi	–
Chile	757	292	13,599	Santiago	2,160
China	9,597	3,705	1,187,997	Beijing (Peking)	370
Christmas Is. (Aus.)	0.14	0.05	2.3	The Settlement	–
Cocos (Keeling) Is. (Aus.)	0.01	0.005	0.70	–	–
Colombia	1,139	440	33,424	Bogotá	1,260
Comoros	2.2	0.86	585	Moroni	500
Congo	342	132	2,368	Brazzaville	1,120
Cook Is. (NZ)	0.24	0.09	17	Avarua	900
Costa Rica	51.1	19.7	3,099	San José	1,850
Croatia	56.5	21.8	4,764	Zagreb	1,800
Crozet Is. (Fr.)	0.51	0.19	35	–	–
Cuba	111	43	10,822	Havana	3,000
Cyprus	9.3	3.6	716	Nicosia	8,640
Czech Republic	78.9	30.4	10,299	Prague	2,370
Denmark	43.1	16.6	5,170	Copenhagen	23,700
Djibouti	23.2	9	467	Djibouti	1,000
Dominica	0.75	0.29	72	Roseau	2,440
Dominican Republic	48.7	18.8	7,471	Santo Domingo	950
Ecuador	284	109	10,741	Quito	1,020
Egypt	1,001	387	55,163	Cairo	620
El Salvador	21	8.1	5,396	San Salvador	1,070
Equatorial Guinea	28.1	10.8	369	Malabo	330
Eritrea	94	36	3,500	Asmera	–
Estonia	44.7	17.3	1,542	Tallinn	3,830
Ethiopia	1,128	436	55,117	Addis Ababa	120
Falkland Is. (UK)	12.2	4.7	2	Stanley	–
Faroe Is. (Den.)	1.4	0.54	47	Tórshavn	23,660
Fiji	18.3	7.1	739	Suva	1,930
Finland	338	131	5,042	Helsinki	23,980
France	552	213	57,372	Paris	20,380
French Guiana (Fr.)	90	34.7	104	Cayenne	2,500
French Polynesia (Fr.)	4	1.5	207	Papeete	6,000
Gabon	268	103	1,237	Libreville	3,780
Gambia, The	11.3	4.4	878	Banjul	360
Georgia	69.7	26.9	5,471	Tbilisi	1,640
Germany	357	138	80,569	Berlin	23,650
Ghana	239	92	15,400	Accra	400
Gibraltar (UK)	0.007	0.003	31	–	4,000
Greece	132	51	10,300	Athens	6,340
Greenland (Den.)	2,176	840	57	Godthåb	6,000
Grenada	0.34	0.13	91	St George's	2,180
Guadeloupe (Fr.)	1.7	0.66	400	Basse-Terre	7,000
Guam (US)	0.55	0.21	139	Agana	6,000
Guatemala	109	42	9,745	Guatemala City	930
Guinea	246	95	6,116	Conakry	450
Guinea-Bissau	36.1	13.9	1,006	Bissau	190
Guyana	215	83	808	Georgetown	430
Haiti	27.8	10.7	6,764	Port-au-Prince	370
Honduras	112	43	5,462	Tegucigalpa	570
Hong Kong (UK)	1.1	0.40	5,801	–	13,430
Hungary	93	35.9	10,313	Budapest	2,720
Iceland	103	40	260	Reykjavik	23,170
India	3,288	1,269	879,548	Delhi	330
Indonesia	1,905	735	191,170	Jakarta	610
Iran	1,648	636	56,964	Tehran	2,170
Iraq	438	169	19,290	Baghdad	2,000
Ireland	70.3	27.1	3,547	Dublin	11,120
Israel	27	10.3	4,946	Jerusalem	11,950
Italy	301	116	57,782	Rome	18,580
Ivory Coast	322	125	12,910	Abidjan	690
Jamaica	11	4.2	2,469	Kingston	1,480
Jan Mayen Is. (Nor.)	0.38	0.15	0.06	–	–
Japan	378	146	124,336	Tokyo	26,920
Johnston Is. (US)	0.002	0.0009	0.30	–	–
Jordan	89.2	34.4	4,291	Amman	1,060
Kazakhstan	2,717	1,049	17,038	Alma Ata	7,570
Kenya	580	224	26,985	Nairobi	340
Kerguelen Is. (Fr.)	7.2	2.8	0	–	–
Kermadec Is. (NZ)	0.03	0.01	0	–	–
Kirghizia	198.5	76.6	4,472	Bishkek	4,000
Kiribati	0.72	0.28	74	Tarawa	750
Korea, North	121	47	22,618	Pyongyang	900
Korea, South	99	38.2	43,663	Seoul	6,340
Kuwait	17.8	6.9	1,970	Kuwait City	16,380
Laos	237	91	4,469	Vientiane	230
Latvia	65	25	2,632	Riga	3,410
Lebanon	10.4	4	2,838	Beirut	2,000
Lesotho	30.4	11.7	1,836	Maseru	580
Liberia	111	43	2,580	Monrovia	500
Libya	1,760	679	4,875	Tripoli	5,800
Liechtenstein	0.16	0.06	28	Vaduz	33,000
Lithuania	65.2	25.2	3,759	Vilnius	2,710
Luxembourg	2.6	1	390	Luxembourg	31,780
Macau (Port.)	0.02	0.006	374	–	2,000
Macedonia	25.3	9.8	2,174	Skopje	–
Madagascar	587	227	12,827	Antananarivo	210
Madeira (Port.)	0.81	0.31	280	Funchal	–
Malawi	118	46	8,823	Lilongwe	230
Malaysia	330	127	18,181	Kuala Lumpur	2,520
Maldives	0.30	0.12	231	Malé	460
Mali	1,240	479	9,818	Bamako	280
Malta	0.32	0.12	359	Valletta	6,630
Mariana Is. (US)	0.48	0.18	22	Saipan	–
Marshall Is.	0.18	0.07	49	Dalap-Uliga-Darrit	–
Martinique (Fr.)	1.1	0.42	368	Fort-de-France	4,000
Mauritania	1,025	396	2,143	Nouakchott	510
Mauritius	1.9	0.72	1,084	Port Louis	2,420
Mayotte (Fr.)	0.37	0.14	84	Mamoundzou	–
Mexico	1,958	756	89,538	Mexico City	3,030
Micronesia, Fed. States	0.70	0.27	110	Palikir	–
Midway Is. (US)	0.005	0.002	0.45	–	–
Moldavia	33.7	13	4,458	Kishinev	2,170
Monaco	0.002	0.0001	30	–	20,000
Mongolia	1,567	605	2,310	Ulan Bator	400
Montserrat (UK)	0.10	0.04	11	Plymouth	–
Morocco	447	172	26,318	Rabat	1,030
Mozambique	802	309	14,872	Maputo	80
Namibia	825	318	1,562	Windhoek	1,460
Nauru	0.02	0.008	10	Yaren	–
Nepal	141	54	20,577	Katmandu	180
Netherlands	41.5	16	15,178	Amsterdam	18,780
Neths Antilles (Neths)	0.99	0.38	175	Willemstad	6,000
New Caledonia (Fr.)	19	7.3	173	Nouméa	4,000
New Zealand	269	104	3,414	Wellington	12,350
Nicaragua	130	50	4,130	Managua	460
Niger	1,267	489	8,252	Niamey	300
Nigeria	924	357	88,515	Lagos/Abuja	340
Niue (NZ)	0.26	0.10	2	Alofi	–
Norfolk Is. (Aus.)	0.03	0.01	2	Kingston	–
Norway	324	125	4,286	Oslo	24,220
Oman	212	82	1,637	Muscat	6,120
Pakistan	796	307	115,520	Islamabad	400
Panama	77.1	29.8	2,515	Panama City	2,130
Papua New Guinea	463	179	4,056	Port Moresby	820
Paraguay	407	157	4,519	Asunción	1,270
Peru	1,285	496	22,454	Lima	1,070
Peter 1st Is. (Nor.)	0.18	0.07	0	–	–
Philippines	300	116	64,259	Manila	740
Pitcairn Is. (UK)	0.03	0.01	0.06	Adamstown	–
Poland	313	121	38,356	Warsaw	1,790
Portugal	92.4	35.7	9,846	Lisbon	5,930
Puerto Rico (US)	9	3.5	3,580	San Juan	6,470
Qatar	11	4.2	453	Doha	15,860
Queen Maud Land (Nor.)	2,800	1,081	0	–	–
Réunion (Fr.)	2.5	0.97	624	St-Denis	4,000
Romania	238	92	23,185	Bucharest	1,390
Ross Dependency (NZ)	435	168	0	–	–
Russia	17,075	6,592	149,527	Moscow	3,220
Rwanda	26.3	10.2	7,526	Kigali	260
St Christopher & Nevis	0.36	0.14	42	Basseterre	3,960
St Helena (UK)	0.12	0.05	7	Jamestown	–
St Lucia	0.62	0.24	137	Castries	2,500
St Paul Is. (Fr.)	0.007	0.003	0	–	–
St Pierre & Miquelon (Fr.)	0.24	0.09	6	St-Pierre	–
St Vincent & Grenadines	0.39	0.15	109	Kingstown	1,730
San Marino	0.06	0.02	23	San Marino	–
São Tomé & Príncipe	0.96	0.37	124	São Tomé	350
Saudi Arabia	2,150	830	15,922	Riyadh	7,820
Senegal	197	76	7,736	Dakar	720
Seychelles	0.46	0.18	72	Victoria	5,110
Sierra Leone	71.7	27.7	4,376	Freetown	210
Singapore	0.62	0.24	2,812	Singapore	14,210
Slovak Republic	49	18.9	5,297	Bratislava	1,650
Slovenia	20.3	7.8	1,996	Ljubljana	–
Solomon Is.	28.9	11.2	342	Honiara	690
Somalia	638	246	9,204	Mogadishu	150
South Africa	1,219	471	39,790	Pretoria	2,560
South Georgia (UK)	3.8	1.4	0.05	–	–
South Sandwich Is. (UK)	0.38	0.15	0	–	–
Spain	505	195	39,085	Madrid	12,460
Sri Lanka	65.6	25.3	17,405	Colombo	500
Sudan	2,506	967	26,656	Khartoum	310
Surinam	163	63	438	Paramaribo	3,610
Svalbard (Nor.)	62.9	24.3	4	Longyearbyen	–
Swaziland	17.4	6.7	792	Mbabane	1,060
Sweden	450	174	8,678	Stockholm	25,110
Switzerland	41.3	15.9	6,905	Bern	33,610
Syria	185	71	12,958	Damascus	1,160
Taiwan	36	13.9	20,659	Taipei	6,600
Tajikistan	143.1	55.2	5,465	Dushanbe	2,980
Tanzania	945	365	27,829	Dar es Salaam	100
Thailand	513	198	57,760	Bangkok	1,580
Togo	56.8	21.9	3,763	Lomé	410
Tokelau (NZ)	0.01	0.005	2	Nukunonu	–
Tonga	0.75	0.29	97	Nuku'alofa	1,100
Trinidad & Tobago	5.1	2	1,265	Port of Spain	3,620
Tristan da Cunha (UK)	0.11	0.04	0.33	Edinburgh	–
Tunisia	164	63	8,410	Tunis	1,510
Turkey	779	301	58,775	Ankara	1,820
Turkmenistan	488.1	188.5	3,714	Ashkhabad	1,700
Turks & Caicos Is. (UK)	0.43	0.17	13	Grand Turk	–
Tuvalu	0.03	0.01	12	Funafuti	600
Uganda	236	91	18,674	Kampala	160
Ukraine	603.7	233.1	52,200	Kiev	2,340
United Arab Emirates	83.6	32.3	1,629	Abu Dhabi	20,140
United Kingdom	243.3	94	57,848	London	16,550
United States of America	9,373	3,619	255,020	Washington	22,240
Uruguay	177	68	3,131	Montevideo	2,860
Uzbekistan	447.4	172.7	21,627	Tashkent	1,350
Vanuatu	12.2	4.7	157	Port Vila	1,120
Vatican City	0.0004	0.0002	1	–	–
Venezuela	912	352	20,249	Caracas	2,730
Vietnam	332	127	69,306	Hanoi	200
Virgin Is. (UK)	0.15	0.06	17	Road Town	–
Virgin Is. (US)	0.34	0.13	107	Charlotte Amalie	12,000
Wake Is.	0.008	0.003	0.30	–	–
Wallis & Futuna Is. (Fr.)	0.20	0.08	14	Mata-Utu	–
Western Sahara	266	103	250	El Aaiún	–
Western Samoa	2.8	1.1	161	Apia	960
Yemen	528	204	11,282	Sana	540
Yugoslavia	102.3	39.5	10,469	Belgrade	2,940
Zaire	2,345	906	39,882	Kinshasa	230
Zambia	753	291	8,638	Lusaka	460
Zimbabwe	391	151	10,583	Harare	650

World Statistics: Physical Dimensions

Each topic list is divided into continents and within a continent the items are listed in size order. The order of the continents is as in the atlas, Europe through to South America. Certain lists down to this mark > are complete; below they are selective. The world top ten are shown in square brackets; in the case of mountains this has not been done because the world top 30 are all in Asia. The figures are rounded as appropriate.

World, Continents, Oceans

	km²	miles²	%
The World	509,450,000	196,672,000	–
Land	149,450,000	57,688,000	29.3
Water	360,000,000	138,984,000	70.7
Asia	44,500,000	17,177,000	29.8
Africa	30,302,000	11,697,000	20.3
North America	24,241,000	9,357,000	16.2
South America	17,793,000	6,868,000	11.9
Antarctica	14,100,000	5,443,000	9.4
Europe	9,957,000	3,843,000	6.7
Australia & Oceania	8,557,000	3,303,000	5.7
Pacific Ocean	179,679,000	69,356,000	49.9
Atlantic Ocean	92,373,000	35,657,000	25.7
Indian Ocean	73,917,000	28,532,000	20.5
Arctic Ocean	14,090,000	5,439,000	3.9

Mountains

Europe

		m	ft
Mont Blanc	*France/Italy*	4,807	15,771
Monte Rosa	*Italy/Switz.*	4,634	15,203
Dom	*Switzerland*	4,545	14,911
Weisshorn	*Switzerland*	4,505	14,780
Matterhorn/Cervino	*Italy/Switz.*	4,478	14,691
Mt Maudit	*France/Italy*	4,465	14,649
Finsteraarhorn	*Switzerland*	4,274	14,022
Aletschhorn	*Switzerland*	4,182	13,720
Jungfrau	*Switzerland*	4,158	13,642
Barre des Ecrins	*France*	4,103	13,461
Schreckhorn	*Switzerland*	4,078	13,380
Gran Paradiso	*Italy*	4,061	13,323
Piz Bernina	*Italy/Switz.*	4,049	13,284
Ortles	*Italy*	3,899	12,792
Monte Viso	*Italy*	3,841	12,602
Grossglockner	*Austria*	3,797	12,457
Wildspitze	*Austria*	3,774	12,382
Weisskügel	*Austria/Italy*	3,736	12,257
Balmhorn	*Switzerland*	3,709	12,169
Dammastock	*Switzerland*	3,630	11,909
Tödi	*Switzerland*	3,620	11,877
Presanella	*Italy*	3,556	11,667
Monte Adamello	*Italy*	3,554	11,660
Mulhacén	*Spain*	3,478	11,411
Pico de Aneto	*Spain*	3,404	11,168
Posets	*Spain*	3,375	11,073
Marmolada	*Italy*	3,342	10,964
Etna	*Italy*	3,340	10,958
> Olympus	*Greece*	2,917	9,570
Galdhöpiggen	*Norway*	2,469	8,100
Pietrosul	*Romania*	2,305	7,562
Hvannadalshnúkur	*Iceland*	2,119	6,952
Narodnaya	*Russia*	1,894	6,214
Ben Nevis	*UK*	1,343	4,406

Asia

		m	ft
Everest	*China/Nepal*	8,848	29,029
Godwin Austen (K2)	*China/Kashmir*	8,611	28,251
Kanchenjunga	*India/Nepal*	8,598	28,208
Lhotse	*China/Nepal*	8,516	27,939
Makalu	*China/Nepal*	8,481	27,824
Cho Oyu	*China/Nepal*	8,201	26,906
Dhaulagiri	*Nepal*	8,172	26,811
Manaslu	*Nepal*	8,156	26,758
Nanga Parbat	*Kashmir*	8,126	26,660
Annapurna	*Nepal*	8,078	26,502
Gasherbrum	*China/Kashmir*	8,068	26,469
Broad Peak	*India*	8,051	26,414
Gosainthan	*China*	8,012	26,286
Disteghil Sar	*Kashmir*	7,885	25,869
Nuptse	*Nepal*	7,879	25,849
Masherbrum	*Kashmir*	7,821	25,659
Nanda Devi	*India*	7,817	25,646
Rakaposhi	*Kashmir*	7,788	25,551
Kanjut Sar	*India*	7,760	25,459
Kamet	*India*	7,756	25,446
Namcha Barwa	*China*	7,756	25,446
Gurla Mandhata	*China*	7,728	25,354
Muztag	*China*	7,723	25,338
Kongur Shan	*China*	7,719	25,324
Tirich Mir	*Pakistan*	7,690	25,229
Saser	*Kashmir*	7,672	25,170
> K'ula Shan	*Bhutan/China*	7,543	24,747
Pik Kommunizma	*Tajikistan*	7,495	24,590
Aling Gangri	*China*	7,314	23,996
Elbrus	*Russia*	5,633	18,481
Demavend	*Iran*	5,604	18,386
Ararat	*Turkey*	5,165	16,945
Gunong Kinabalu	*Borneo*	4,101	13,455
Yu Shan	*Taiwan*	3,997	13,113
Fuji-san	*Japan*	3,776	12,388
Rinjani	*Indonesia*	3,726	12,224
Mt Rajang	*Philippines*	3,364	11,037
Pidurutalagala	*Sri Lanka*	2,524	8,281

Africa

		m	ft
Kilimanjaro	*Tanzania*	5,895	19,340
Mt Kenya	*Kenya*	5,199	17,057
Ruwenzori	*Uganda/Zaïre*	5,109	16,762
Ras Dashan	*Ethiopia*	4,620	15,157
Meru	*Tanzania*	4,565	14,977
Karisimbi	*Rwanda/Zaïre*	4,507	14,787
Mt Elgon	*Kenya/Uganda*	4,321	14,176
Batu	*Ethiopia*	4,307	14,130
Guna	*Ethiopia*	4,231	13,882
Toubkal	*Morocco*	4,165	13,665
Irhil Mgoun	*Morocco*	4,071	13,356
Mt Cameroon	*Cameroon*	4,070	13,353
Amba Ferit	*Ethiopia*	3,875	13,042
Teide	*Spain (Tenerife)*	3,718	12,198
Thabana Ntlenyana	*Lesotho*	3,482	11,424
Emi Kussi	*Chad*	3,415	11,204

Oceania

		m	ft
Puncak Jaya	*Indonesia*	5,029	16,499
Puncak Trikora	*Indonesia*	4,750	15,584
Puncak Mandala	*Indonesia*	4,702	15,427
Mt Wilhelm	*Papua N. Guinea*	4,508	14,790
> Mauna Kea	*USA (Hawaii)*	4,205	13,796
Mauna Loa	*USA (Hawaii)*	4,170	13,681
Mt Cook	*New Zealand*	3,753	12,313
Mt Balbi	*Solomon Is.*	2,439	8,002
Mt Kosciusko	*Australia*	2,237	7,339

North America

		m	ft
Mt McKinley	*USA (Alaska)*	6,194	20,321
Mt Logan	*Canada*	6,050	19,849
Citlaltepetl	*Mexico*	5,959	19,551
Mt St Elias	*USA/Canada*	5,489	18,008
Popocatepetl	*Mexico*	5,452	17,887
Mt Foraker	*USA (Alaska)*	5,304	17,401
Ixtaccihuatl	*Mexico*	5,286	17,342
Lucania	*Canada*	5,227	17,149
Mt Steele	*Canada*	5,073	16,644
Mt Bona	*USA (Alaska)*	5,005	16,420
Mt Blackburn	*USA (Alaska)*	4,996	16,391
Mt Sanford	*USA (Alaska)*	4,940	16,207
Mt Wood	*Canada*	4,848	15,905
Nevado de Toluca	*Mexico*	4,670	15,321
Mt Fairweather	*USA (Alaska)*	4,663	15,298
Mt Whitney	*USA*	4,418	14,495
Mt Elbert	*USA*	4,399	14,432
Mt Harvard	*USA*	4,395	14,419
Mt Rainier	*USA*	4,392	14,409
Blanca Peak	*USA*	4,372	14,344
Long's Peak	*USA*	4,345	14,255
Nevado de Colima	*Mexico*	4,339	14,235
Mt Shasta	*USA*	4,317	14,163
Tajumulco	*Guatemala*	4,220	13,845
> Gannett Peak	*USA*	4,202	13,786
Mt Waddington	*Canada*	3,994	13,104
Mt Robson	*Canada*	3,954	12,972
Chirripó Grande	*Costa Rica*	3,837	12,589
Pico Duarte	*Dominican Rep.*	3,175	10,417

South America

		m	ft
Aconcagua	*Argentina*	6,960	22,834
Illimani	*Bolivia*	6,882	22,578
Bonete	*Argentina*	6,872	22,546
Ojos del Salado	*Argentina/Chile*	6,863	22,516
Tupungato	*Argentina/Chile*	6,800	22,309
Pissis	*Argentina*	6,779	22,241
Mercedario	*Argentina/Chile*	6,770	22,211
Huascaran	*Peru*	6,768	22,204
Llullaillaco	*Argentina/Chile*	6,723	22,057
Nudo de Cachi	*Argentina*	6,720	22,047
Yerupaja	*Peru*	6,632	21,758
N. de Tres Cruces	*Argentina/Chile*	6,620	21,719
Incahuasi	*Argentina/Chile*	6,600	21,654
Ancohuma	*Bolivia*	6,550	21,489
Sajama	*Bolivia*	6,520	21,391
Coropuna	*Peru*	6,425	21,079
Ausangate	*Peru*	6,384	20,945
Cerro del Toro	*Argentina*	6,380	20,932
Ampato	*Peru*	6,310	20,702
Chimborasso	*Ecuador*	6,267	20,561
> Cotopaxi	*Ecuador*	5,896	19,344
S. Nev. de S. Marta	*Colombia*	5,800	19,029
Cayambe	*Ecuador*	5,796	19,016
Pico Bolivar	*Venezuela*	5,007	16,427

Antarctica

	m	ft
Vinson Massif	4,897	16,066
Mt Kirkpatrick	4,528	14,855

Ocean Depths

Atlantic Ocean

	m	ft
Puerto Rico (Milwaukee) Deep [7]	9,220	30,249
Cayman Trench [10]	7,680	25,197
Gulf of Mexico	5,203	17,070
Mediterranean Sea	5,121	16,801
Black Sea	2,211	7,254
North Sea	660	2,165
Baltic Sea	463	1,519
Hudson Bay	258	846

Indian Ocean

	m	ft
Java Trench	7,450	24,442
Red Sea	2,635	8,454
Persian Gulf	73	239

Pacific Ocean

	m	ft
Mariana Trench [1]	11,022	36,161
Tonga Trench [2]	10,882	35,702
Japan Trench [3]	10,554	34,626
Kuril Trench [4]	10,542	34,587
Mindanao Trench [5]	10,497	34,439
Kermadec Trench [6]	10,047	32,962
Peru-Chile Trench [8]	8,050	26,410
Aleutian Trench [9]	7,822	25,662
Middle American Trench	6,662	21,857

Arctic Ocean

	m	ft
Molloy Deep	5,608	18,399

Land Lows

		m	ft
Caspian Sea	*Europe*	–28	–92
Dead Sea	*Asia*	–400	–1,312
Lake Assal	*Africa*	–156	–512
Lake Eyre North	*Oceania*	–16	–52
Death Valley	*N. America*	–86	–282
Valdés Peninsula	*S. America*	–40	–131

Rivers

Europe

		km	miles
Volga	*Caspian Sea*	3,700	2,300
Danube	*Black Sea*	2,850	1,770
Ural	*Caspian Sea*	2,535	1,574
Dnepr	*Volga*	2,285	1,420
Kama	*Volga*	2,030	1,260
Don	*Volga*	1,990	1,240
Petchora	*Arctic Ocean*	1,790	1,110
Oka	*Volga*	1,480	920
Belaya	*Kama*	1,420	880
Dnestr	*Black Sea*	1,400	870
Vyatka	*Kama*	1,370	850
Rhine	*North Sea*	1,320	820
N. Dvina	*Arctic Ocean*	1,290	800
Desna	*Dnieper*	1,190	740
Elbe	*North Sea*	1,145	710
> Vistula	*Baltic Sea*	1,090	675
Loire	*Atlantic Ocean*	1,020	635
W. Dvina	*Baltic Sea*	1,019	633

Asia

		km	miles
Yangtze [3]	*Pacific Ocean*	6,380	3,960
Yenisey-Angara [5]	*Arctic Ocean*	5,550	3,445
Huang He [6]	*Pacific Ocean*	5,464	3,395
Ob-Irtysh [7]	*Arctic Ocean*	5,410	3,360
Mekong [9]	*Pacific Ocean*	4,500	2,795
Amur [10]	*Pacific Ocean*	4,400	2,730
Lena	*Arctic Ocean*	4,400	2,730
Irtysh	*Ob*	4,250	2,640
Yenisey	*Arctic Ocean*	4,090	2,540
Ob	*Arctic Ocean*	3,680	2,285
Indus	*Indian Ocean*	3,100	1,925
Brahmaputra	*Indian Ocean*	2,900	1,800
Syr Darya	*Aral Sea*	2,860	1,775
Salween	*Indian Ocean*	2,800	1,740
Euphrates	*Indian Ocean*	2,700	1,675
Vilyuy	*Lena*	2,650	1,645
Kolyma	*Arctic Ocean*	2,600	1,615
Amu Darya	*Aral Sea*	2,540	1,575
Ural	*Caspian Sea*	2,535	1,575
Ganges	*Indian Ocean*	2,510	1,560
> Si Kiang	*Pacific Ocean*	2,100	1,305
Irrawaddy	*Indian Ocean*	2,010	1,250
Tigris	*Indian Ocean*	1,900	1,180
Angara	*Yenisey*	1,830	1,135
Yamuna	*Indian Ocean*	1,400	870

Africa

		km	miles
Nile [1]	*Mediterranean*	6,670	4,140
Zaïre/Congo [8]	*Atlantic Ocean*	4,670	2,900
Niger	*Atlantic Ocean*	4,180	2,595
Zambezi	*Indian Ocean*	3,540	2,200
Oubangi/Uele	*Zaïre*	2,250	1,400
Kasai	*Zaïre*	1,950	1,210
Shaballe	*Indian Ocean*	1,930	1,200
Orange	*Atlantic Ocean*	1,860	1,155
Cubango	*Okavango*	1,800	1,120
Limpopo	*Indian Ocean*	1,600	995
> Senegal	*Atlantic Ocean*	1,600	995
Volta	*Atlantic Ocean*	1,500	930
Benue	*Niger*	1,350	840

Australia

		km	miles
Murray-Darling	*Indian Ocean*	3,750	2,330
Darling	*Murray*	3,070	1,905
Murray	*Indian Ocean*	2,575	1,600
Murrumbidgee	*Murray*	1,690	1,050

North America

		km	miles
Mississ.-Missouri [4]	*Gulf of Mexico*	6,020	3,740
Mackenzie	*Arctic Ocean*	4,240	2,630
Mississippi	*Gulf of Mexico*	3,780	2,350
Missouri	*Mississippi*	3,780	2,350
Yukon	*Pacific Ocean*	3,185	1,980
Rio Grande	*Gulf of Mexico*	3,030	1,880
Arkansas	*Mississippi*	2,340	1,450
Colorado	*Pacific Ocean*	2,330	1,445
Red	*Mississippi*	2,040	1,270
Columbia	*Pacific Ocean*	1,950	1,210
Saskatchewan	*Lake Winnipeg*	1,940	1,205
Snake	*Columbia*	1,670	1,040
Churchill	*Hudson Bay*	1,600	990
Ohio	*Mississippi*	1,580	980
Brazos	*Gulf of Mexico*	1,400	870
> St Lawrence	*Atlantic Ocean*	1,170	730

South America

		km	miles
Amazon [2]	*Atlantic Ocean*	6,450	4,010
Paraná-Plate	*Atlantic Ocean*	4,500	2,800
Purus	*Amazon*	3,350	2,080
Madeira	*Amazon*	3,200	1,990
São Francisco	*Atlantic Ocean*	2,900	1,800
Paraná	*Plate*	2,800	1,740
Tocantins	*Atlantic Ocean*	2,750	1,710
Paraguay	*Paraná*	2,550	1,580
Orinoco	*Atlantic Ocean*	2,500	1,550
Pilcomayo	*Paraná*	2,500	1,550
Araguaia	*Tocantins*	2,250	1,400
Juruá	*Amazon*	2,000	1,240
Xingu	*Amazon*	1,980	1,230
Ucayali	*Amazon*	1,900	1,180
Maranón	*Amazon*	1,600	990
> Uruguay	*Plate*	1,600	990
Magdalena	*Caribbean Sea*	1,540	960

Lakes

Europe

		km²	miles²
Lake Ladoga	*Russia*	17,700	6,800
Lake Onega	*Russia*	9,700	3,700
Saimaa system	*Finland*	8,000	3,100
Vänern	*Sweden*	5,500	2,100
Rybinsk Res.	*Russia*	4,700	1,800

Asia

		km²	miles²
Caspian Sea [1]	*Asia*	371,800	143,550
Aral Sea [6]	*Kazakh./Uzbek.*	36,000	13,900
Lake Baykal [9]	*Russia*	30,500	11,780
Tonlé Sap	*Cambodia*	20,000	7,700
Lake Balkhash	*Kazakhstan*	18,500	7,100
> Dongting Hu	*China*	12,000	4,600
Issyk Kul	*Kirghizia*	6,200	2,400
Lake Urmia	*Iran*	5,900	2,300
Koko Nur	*China*	5,700	2,200
Poyang Hu	*China*	5,000	1,900
Lake Khanka	*China/Russia*	4,400	1,700
Lake Van	*Turkey*	3,500	1,400
Ubsa Nur	*China*	3,400	1,300

Africa

		km²	miles²
Lake Victoria [3]	*E. Africa*	68,000	26,000
Lake Tanganyika [7]	*C. Africa*	33,000	13,000
Lake Malawi [10]	*E. Africa*	29,600	11,430
Lake Chad	*C. Africa*	25,000	9,700
Lake Turkana	*Ethiop./Kenya*	8,500	3,300
Lake Volta	*Ghana*	8,500	3,300
Lake Bangweulu	*Zambia*	8,000	3,100
Lake Rukwa	*Tanzania*	7,000	2,700
Lake Mai-Ndombe	*Zaïre*	6,500	2,500
> Lake Kariba	*Zamb./Zimbab.*	5,300	2,000
Lake Mobutu	*Uganda/Zaïre*	5,300	2,000
Lake Nasser	*Egypt/Sudan*	5,200	2,000
Lake Mweru	*Zambia/Zaïre*	4,900	1,900
Lake Kyoga	*Uganda*	4,400	1,700
Lake Tana	*Ethiopia*	3,630	1,400

Australia

		km²	miles²
Lake Eyre	*Australia*	8,900	3,400
Lake Torrens	*Australia*	5,800	2,200

North America

		km²	miles²
Lake Superior [2]	*Canada/USA*	82,350	31,800
Lake Huron [4]	*Canada/USA*	59,600	23,010
Lake Michigan [5]	*USA*	58,000	22,400
Great Bear Lake [8]	*Canada*	31,800	12,280
Great Slave Lake	*Canada*	28,500	11,000
Lake Erie	*Canada/USA*	25,700	9,900
Lake Winnipeg	*Canada*	24,400	9,400
Lake Ontario	*Canada/USA*	19,500	7,500
Lake Nicaragua	*Nicaragua*	8,200	3,200
Lake Athabasca	*Canada*	8,100	3,100
> Smallwood Res.	*Canada*	6,530	2,520
Reindeer Lake	*Canada*	6,400	2,500
Lake Winnipegosis	*Canada*	5,400	2,100
Nettilling Lake	*Canada*	5,500	2,100

South America

		km²	miles²
Lake Titicaca	*Bolivia/Peru*	8,300	3,200
Lake Poopo	*Peru*	2,800	1,100

Islands

Europe

		km²	miles²
Great Britain [8]	*UK*	229,880	88,700
Iceland	*Atlantic*	103,000	39,800
Ireland	*Ireland/UK*	84,400	32,600
Novaya Zemlya (N.)	*Russia*	48,200	18,600
W. Spitzbergen	*Norway*	39,000	15,100
Novaya Zemlya (S.)	*Russia*	33,200	12,800
Sicily	*Italy*	25,500	9,800
Sardinia	*Italy*	24,000	9,300
N. E. Spitzbergen	*Norway*	15,000	5,600
Corsica	*France*	8,700	3,400
Crete	*Greece*	8,350	3,200
Zealand	*Denmark*	6,850	2,600

Asia

		km²	miles²
Borneo [3]	*S. E. Asia*	744,360	287,400
Sumatra [6]	*Indonesia*	473,600	182,860
Honshu [7]	*Japan*	230,500	88,980
Celebes	*Indonesia*	189,000	73,000
Java	*Indonesia*	126,700	48,900
Luzon	*Philippines*	104,700	40,400
Mindanao	*Philippines*	101,500	39,200
Hokkaido	*Japan*	78,400	30,300
Sakhalin	*Russia*	74,060	28,600
Sri Lanka	*Indian Ocean*	65,600	25,300
Taiwan	*Pacific Ocean*	36,000	13,900
Kyushu	*Japan*	35,700	13,800
Hainan	*China*	34,000	13,100
Timor	*Indonesia*	33,600	13,000
Shikoku	*Japan*	18,800	7,300
Halmahera	*Indonesia*	18,000	6,900
Ceram	*Indonesia*	17,150	6,600
Sumbawa	*Indonesia*	15,450	6,000
Flores	*Indonesia*	15,200	5,900
Samar	*Philippines*	13,100	5,100
> Negros	*Philippines*	12,700	4,900
Bangka	*Indonesia*	12,000	4,600
Panay	*Philippines*	11,500	4,400
Sumba	*Indonesia*	11,100	4,300
Mindoro	*Philippines*	9,750	3,800
Bali	*Indonesia*	5,600	2,200
Cyprus	*Mediterranean*	3,570	1,400
Wrangel Is.	*Russia*	2,800	1,000

Africa

		km²	miles²
Madagascar [4]	*Indian Ocean*	587,040	226,660
Socotra	*Indian Ocean*	3,600	1,400
Réunion	*Indian Ocean*	2,500	965
Tenerife	*Atlantic Ocean*	2,350	900
Mauritius	*Indian Ocean*	1,865	720

Oceania

		km²	miles²
New Guinea [2]	*Ind./Pap. NG*	821,030	317,000
New Zealand (S.)	*New Zealand*	150,500	58,100
New Zealand (N.)	*New Zealand*	114,700	44,300
Tasmania	*Australia*	67,800	26,200
New Britain	*Papua NG*	37,800	14,600
New Caledonia	*Pacific Ocean*	19,100	7,400
Viti Levu	*Fiji*	10,500	4,100
Hawaii	*Pacific Ocean*	10,450	4,000
Bougainville	*Papua NG*	9,600	3,700
Guadalcanal	*Solomon Is.*	6,500	2,500
> Vanua Levu	*Fiji*	5,550	2,100
New Ireland	*Papua NG*	3,200	1,200

North America

		km²	miles²
Greenland [1]	*Greenland*	2,175,600	839,800
Baffin Is. [5]	*Canada*	508,000	196,100
Victoria Is. [9]	*Canada*	212,200	81,900
Ellesmere Is. [10]	*Canada*	212,000	81,800
Cuba	*Cuba*	110,860	42,800
Newfoundland	*Canada*	110,680	42,700
Hispaniola	*Atlantic Ocean*	76,200	29,400
Banks Is.	*Canada*	67,000	25,900
Devon Is.	*Canada*	54,500	21,000
Melville Is.	*Canada*	42,400	16,400
> Vancouver Is.	*Canada*	32,150	12,400
Somerset Is.	*Canada*	24,300	9,400
Jamaica	*Caribbean Sea*	11,400	4,400
Puerto Rico	*Atlantic Ocean*	8,900	3,400
Cape Breton Is.	*Canada*	4,000	1,500

South America

		km²	miles²
Tierra del Fuego	*Argent./Chile*	47,000	18,100
Falkland Is. (E.)	*Atlantic Ocean*	6,800	2,600
South Georgia	*Atlantic Ocean*	4,200	1,600
Galapagos (Isabela)	*Pacific Ocean*	2,250	870

PHILIP'S WORLD MAPS

The reference maps which form the main body of this atlas have been prepared in accordance with the highest standards of international cartography to provide an accurate and detailed representation of the Earth. The scales and projections used have been carefully chosen to give balanced coverage of the world, while emphasizing the most densely populated and economically significant regions. A hallmark of Philip's mapping is the use of hill shading and relief colouring to create a graphic impression of landforms: this makes the maps exceptionally easy to read. However, knowledge of the key features employed in the construction and presentation of the maps will enable the reader to derive the fullest benefit from the atlas.

Map sequence

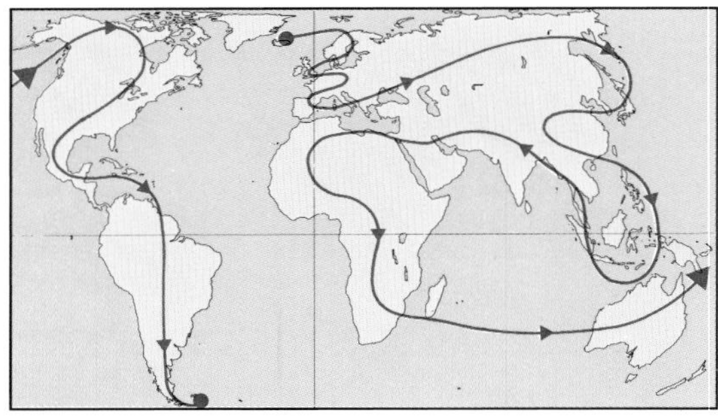

The atlas covers the Earth continent by continent: first Europe; then its land neighbour Asia (mapped north before south, in a clockwise sequence), then Africa, Australia and Oceania, North America and South America. This is the classic arrangement adopted by most cartographers since the 16th century. For each continent, there are maps at a variety of scales. First, physical relief and political maps of the whole continent; then a series of larger-scale maps of the regions within the continent, each followed, where required, by still larger-scale maps of the most important or densely populated areas. The governing principle is that by turning the pages of the atlas, the reader moves steadily from north to south through each continent, with each map overlapping its neighbours. A key map showing this sequence, and the area covered by each map, can be found on the endpapers of the atlas.

Map presentation

With very few exceptions (e.g. for the Arctic and Antarctic), the maps are drawn with north at the top, regardless of whether they are presented upright or sideways on the page. In the borders will be found the map title; a locator diagram showing the area covered and the page numbers for maps of adjacent areas; the scale; the projection used; the degrees of latitude and longitude; and the letters and figures used in the index for locating place names and geographical features. Physical relief maps also have a height reference panel identifying the colours used for each layer of contouring.

Map symbols

Each map contains a vast amount of detail which can only be conveyed clearly and accurately by the use of symbols. Points and circles of varying sizes locate and identify the relative importance of towns and cities; different styles of type are employed for administrative, geographical and regional place names. A variety of pictorial symbols denote landscape features such as glaciers, marshes and reefs, and man-made structures including roads, railways, airports, canals and dams. International borders are shown by red lines. Where neighbouring countries are in dispute, for example in the Middle East, the maps show the *de facto* boundary between nations, regardless of the legal or historical situation. The symbols are explained on the first page of the World Maps section of the atlas.

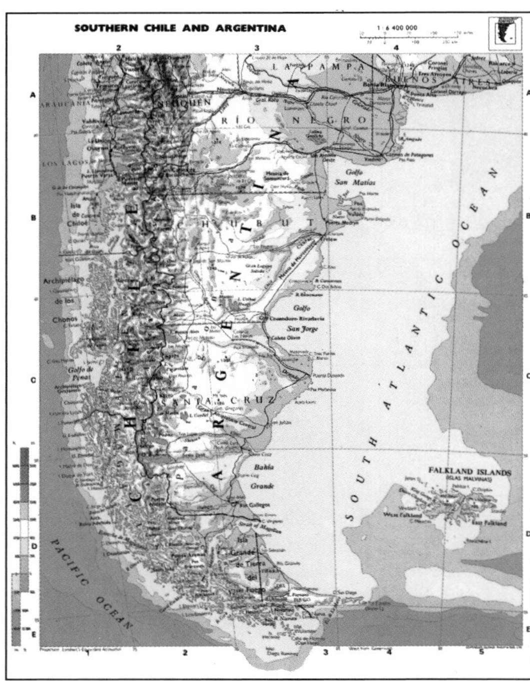

Map scales

1: 16 000 000
1 inch = 252 statute miles

The scale of each map is given in the numerical form known as the 'representative fraction'. The first figure is always one, signifying one unit of distance on the map; the second figure, usually in millions, is the number by which the map unit must be multiplied to give the equivalent distance on the Earth's surface. Calculations can easily be made in centimetres and kilometres, by dividing the Earth units figure by 100 000 (i.e. deleting the last five 0s). Thus 1:1 000 000 means 1 cm = 10 km. The calculation for inches and miles is more laborious, but 1 000 000 divided by 63 360 (the number of inches in a mile) shows that 1:1 000 000 means approximately 1 inch = 16 miles. The table below provides distance equivalents for scales down to 1:50 000 000.

LARGE SCALE		
1: 1 000 000	1 cm = 10 km	1 inch = 16 miles
1: 2 500 000	1 cm = 25 km	1 inch = 39.5 miles
1: 5 000 000	1 cm = 50 km	1 inch = 79 miles
1: 6 000 000	1 cm = 60 km	1 inch = 95 miles
1: 8 000 000	1 cm = 80 km	1 inch = 126 miles
1: 10 000 000	1 cm = 100 km	1 inch = 158 miles
1: 15 000 000	1 cm = 150 km	1 inch = 237 miles
1: 20 000 000	1 cm = 200 km	1 inch = 316 miles
1: 50 000 000	1 cm = 500 km	1 inch = 790 miles
SMALL SCALE		

Measuring distances

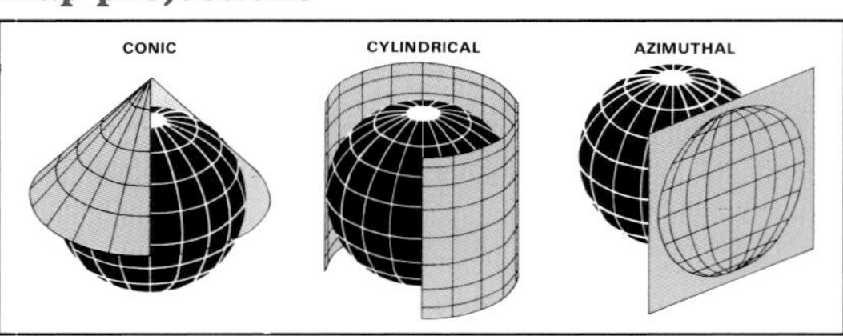

Although each map is accompanied by a scale bar, distances cannot always be measured with confidence because of the distortions involved in portraying the curved surface of the Earth on a flat page. As a general rule, the larger the map scale (i.e. the lower the number of Earth units in the representative fraction), the more accurate and reliable will be the distance measured. On small-scale maps such as those of the world and of entire continents, measurement may only be accurate along the 'standard parallels', or central axes, and should not be attempted without considering the map projection.

Map projections

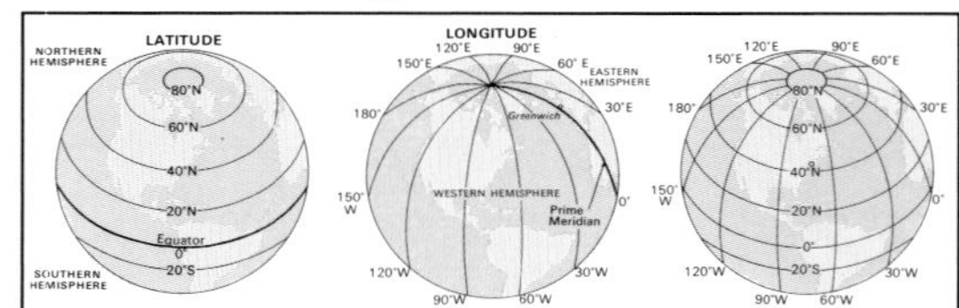

Unlike a globe, no flat map can give a true scale representation of the world in terms of area, shape and position of every region. Each of the numerous systems that have been devised for projecting the curved surface of the Earth on to a flat page involves the sacrifice of accuracy in one or more of these elements. The variations in shape and position of landmasses such as Alaska, Greenland and Australia, for example, can be quite dramatic when different projections are compared.

For this atlas, the guiding principle has been to select projections that involve the least distortion of size and distance. The projection used for each map is noted in the border. Most fall into one of three categories – conic, cylindrical or azimuthal – whose basic concepts are shown above. Each involves plotting the forms of the Earth's surface on a grid of latitude and longitude lines, which may be shown as parallels, curves or radiating spokes.

Latitude and longitude

Accurate positioning of individual points on the Earth's surface is made possible by reference to the geometrical system of latitude and longitude. Latitude *parallels* are drawn west–east around the Earth and numbered by degrees north and south of the Equator, which is designated 0° of latitude. Longitude *meridians* are drawn north–south and numbered by degrees east and west of the *prime meridian*, 0° of longitude, which passes through Greenwich in England. By referring to these co-ordinates and their subdivisions of minutes (⅟₆₀th of a degree) and seconds (⅟₆₀th of a minute), any place on Earth can be located to within a few hundred yards. Latitude and longitude are indicated by blue lines on the maps; they are straight or curved according to the projection employed. Reference to these lines is the easiest way of determining the relative positions of places on different maps, and for plotting compass directions.

Name forms

For ease of reference, both English and local name forms appear in the atlas. Oceans, seas and countries are shown in English throughout the atlas; country names may be abbreviated to their commonly accepted form (e.g. Germany, not The Federal Republic of Germany). Conventional English forms are also used for place names on the smaller-scale maps of the continents. However, local name forms are used on all large-scale and regional maps, with the English form given in brackets only for important cities – the large-scale map of Russia and Central Asia thus shows Moskva (Moscow). For countries which do not use a Roman script, place names have been transcribed according to the systems adopted by the British and US Geographic Names Authorities. For China, the Pin Yin system has been used, with some more widely known forms appearing in brackets, as with Beijing (Peking). Both English and local names appear in the index, the English form being cross-referenced to the local form.

WORLD MAPS

MAP SYMBOLS

SETTLEMENTS

⬠ PARIS ▣ Berne ◉ Livorno ⦿ Brugge ◎ Algeciras ⊙ Fréjus ○ Oberammergau ○ Thira

Settlement symbols and type styles vary according to the scale of each map and indicate the importance of towns on the map rather than specific population figures

∴ Ruins or Archæological Sites ⌣ Wells in Desert

--- ADMINISTRATION ---

──── International Boundaries

─ ─ ─ International Boundaries (Undefined or Disputed)

─·─·─ Internal Boundaries

National Parks

Country Names

NICARAGUA

Administrative Area Names

K E N T

C A L A B R I A

International boundaries show the *de facto* situation where there are rival claims to territory

--- COMMUNICATIONS ---

──── Principal Roads

⌒ Other Roads

‒‒‒ Trails and Seasonal Roads

≍ Passes

✧ Airfields

⌒ Principal Railways

‒‒‒‒ Railways Under Construction

⌒ Other Railways

⊒---⊏ Railway Tunnels

·········· Principal Canals

--- PHYSICAL FEATURES ---

⌇ Perennial Streams

·····‒ Intermittent Streams

⬭ Perennial Lakes

⬮ Intermittent Lakes

Swamps and Marshes

Permanent Ice and Glaciers

▲ 8848 Elevations in metres

▼ 8050 Sea Depths in metres

1134 Height of Lake Surface Above Sea Level in metres

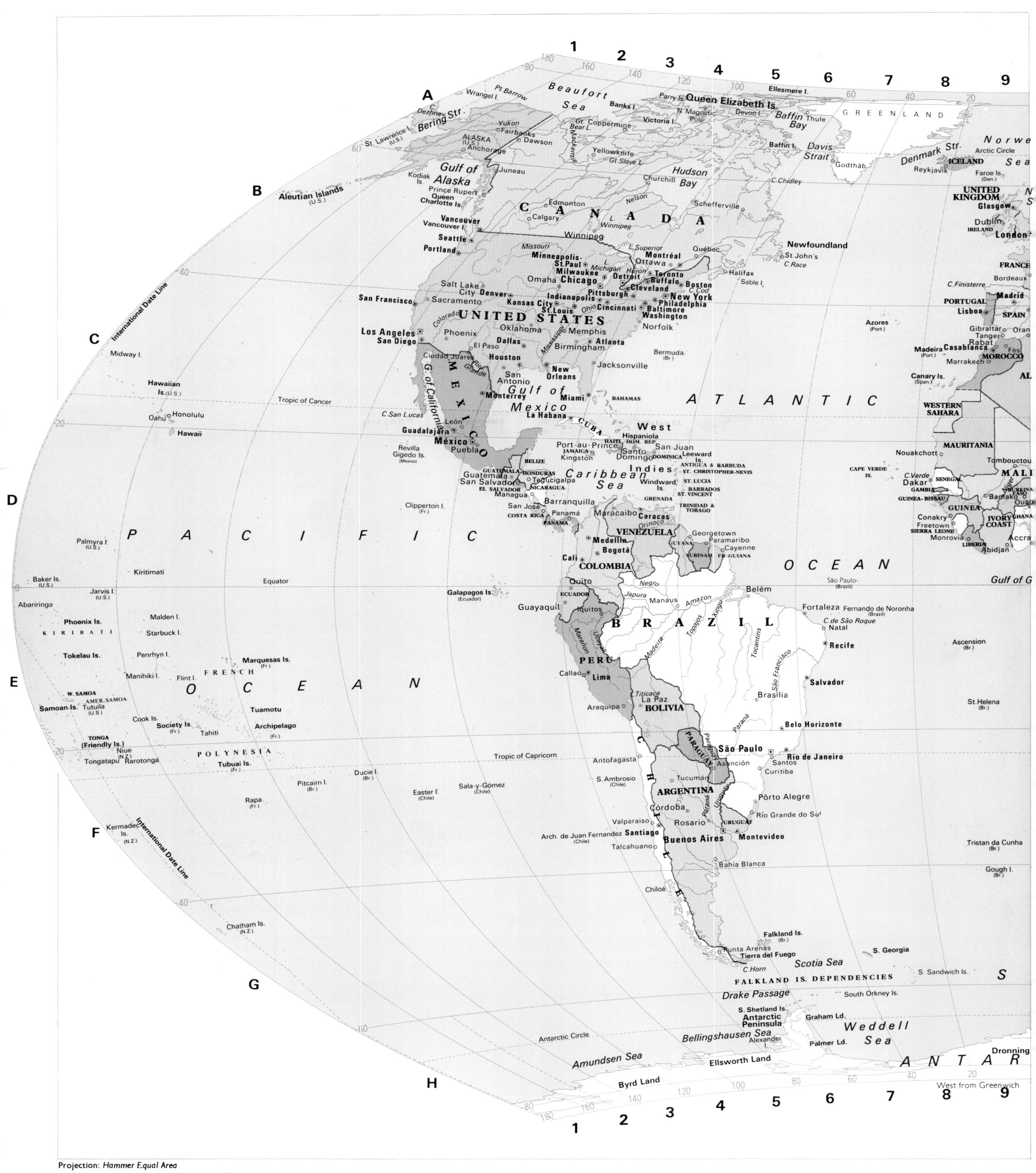

Projection: *Hammer Equal Area*

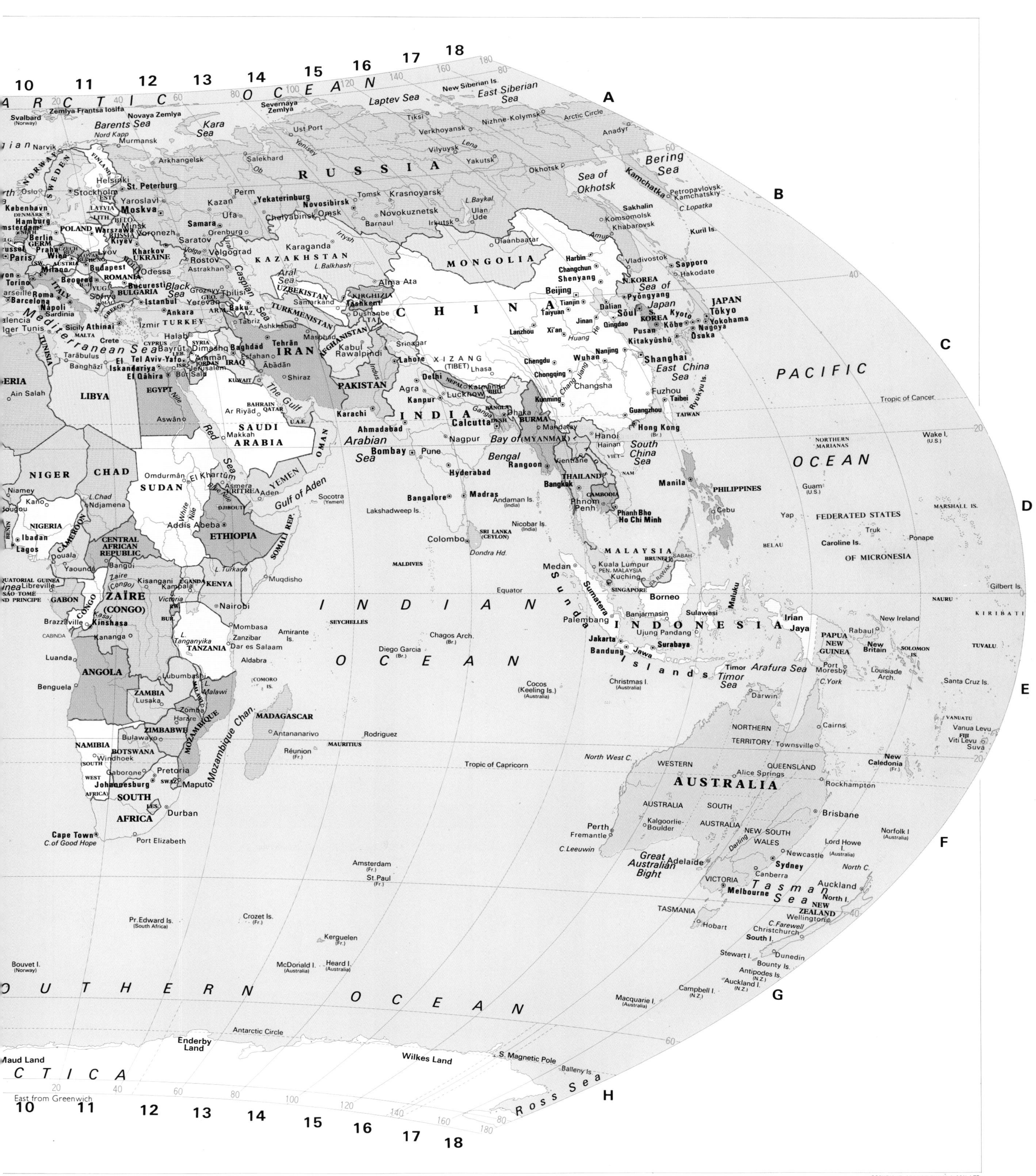

10
11
12
13
14
15
16
17
18
A
B
C
D
E
F
G
H
ARCTIC OCEAN
Svalbard (Norway)
Zemlya Frantsa Iosifa
Novaya Zemlya
Barents Sea
Nord Kapp
Murmansk
Kara Sea
Severnaya Zemlya
Laptev Sea
New Siberian Is.
East Siberian Sea
Ust Port
Tiksi
Verkhoyansk
Nizhne-Kolymsk
Arctic Circle
Anadyr
Vilyuysk
Lena
Yenisey
Yakutsk
Bering Sea
Narvik
Arkhangelsk
Salekhard
Ob
RUSSIA
Okhotsk
Sea of Okhotsk
Kamchatka
Petropavlovsk-Kamchatskiy
C. Lopatka
Oslo
Helsinki
St. Peterburg
Stockholm
Yaroslavl
Perm
Yekaterinburg
Novosibirsk
Tomsk
Krasnoyarsk
L. Baykal
Ulan Ude
Sakhalin
Komsomolsk
Khabarovsk
København
Moskva
Kazan
Ufa
Chelyabinsk
Omsk
Novokuznetsk
Barnaul
Irkutsk
Kuril Is.
Hamburg
Berlin
Praha
Wien
Paris
POLAND
Warszawa
Minsk
Kiyev
Voronezh
Samara
Saratov
Orenburg
Volgograd
Karaganda
Irtysh
Ulaanbaatar
Amur
Kharkov
UKRAINE
Lvov
Budapest
Odessa
Rostov
Astrakhan
KAZAKHSTAN
L. Balkhash
MONGOLIA
Harbin
Vladivostok
Sapporo
Hakodate
Changchun
Shenyang
Torino
Milano
Roma
Barcelona
Napoli
Sardinia
ROMANIA
Bucuresti
BULGARIA
Black Sea
Istanbul
Caspian Sea
Tbilisi
Yerevan
Baku
Aral Sea
UZBEKISTAN
Samarkand
Toshkent
KIRGHIZIA
Alma Ata
Dushanbe
TURKMENISTAN
Beijing
Tianjin
Taiyuan
Dalian
N. KOREA
Pyŏngyang
Sea of Japan
JAPAN
Tōkyō
Yokohama
Kyoto
Kōbe
Nagoya
Ōsaka
Sŏul
S. KOREA
Pusan
Kitakyūshū
Qingdao
Jinan
Xi'an
Lanzhou
CHINA
Huang He
Mediterranean Sea
Sicily
Athinai
Izmir
TURKEY
Ankara
Tabriz
Ashkhabad
Mashhad
Tunis
MALTA
Crete
CYPRUS
Halab
SYRIA
Dimashq
Baghdad
Tehrān
IRAN
AFGHANISTAN
Kabul
Rawalpindi
Srinagar
Lahore
Delhi
XIZANG (TIBET)
Lhasa
NEPAL
Katmandu
Chengdu
Chongqing
Wuhan
Nanjing
Shanghai
East China Sea
Ryukyu Is.
Tarābulus
Banghāzī
Tel Aviv-Yafo
Amman
Jerusalem
IRAQ
Esfahan
Abādān
Shiraz
El Iskandarīya
El Qâhira
Bûr Sa'îd
LIBYA
EGYPT
Nile
KUWAIT
The Gulf
BAHRAIN
QATAR
Ar Riyād
PAKISTAN
Indus
Agra
Kanpur
Lucknow
INDIA
Ganga
BANGLADESH
Dhaka
Calcutta
Karachi
Ahmadabad
Kunming
Chang Jiang
Changsha
Fuzhou
Taibei
TAIWAN
Guangzhou
Hong Kong (Br.)
PACIFIC OCEAN
Tropic of Cancer
Aswân
Red Sea
SAUDI ARABIA
Makkah
U.A.E.
OMAN
Arabian Sea
Bombay
Pune
Nagpur
Bay of Bengal
BURMA (MYANMAR)
Mandalay
Rangoon
Hanoi
Hainan
VIETNAM
South China Sea
Vientiane
THAILAND
Bangkok
CAMBODIA
Phnom Penh
Phanh Bho Ho Chi Minh
NORTHERN MARIANAS
Wake I. (U.S.)
NIGER
CHAD
Omdurmân
El Khartûm
SUDAN
Asmera
ERITREA
YEMEN
Aden
Gulf of Aden
Socotra (Yemen)
Hyderabad
Madras
Bangalore
Lakshadweep Is.
Andaman Is. (India)
Manila
PHILIPPINES
Cebu
Guam (U.S.)
Yap
FEDERATED STATES OF MICRONESIA
MARSHALL IS.
Niamey
Kano
L. Chad
Ndjamena
NIGERIA
Ibadan
Lagos
CAMEROON
CENTRAL AFRICAN REPUBLIC
White Nile
Blue Nile
DJIBOUTI
Addis Abeba
ETHIOPIA
SOMALI REP.
Nicobar Is. (India)
SRI LANKA (CEYLON)
Colombo
Dondra Hd.
Truk
Ponape
BELAU
Caroline Is.
Douala
Yaoundé
Bangui
L. Turkana
MALDIVES
Medan
MALAYSIA
SABAH
BRUNEI
Kuala Lumpur
PEN. MALAYSIA
Kuching
SARAWAK
SINGAPORE
Borneo
Libreville
GABON
SÃO TOMÉ AND PRINCIPE
Kisangani
Kampala
UGANDA
KENYA
Muqdisho
Zaïre (Congo)
ZAÏRE (CONGO)
Victoria
RWANDA
BURUNDI
Nairobi
INDIAN OCEAN
Equator
Sumatera
Sunda Islands
Maluku
Gilbert Is.
NAURU
KIRIBATI
Brazzaville
Kinshasa
CONGO
Kasai
CABINDA
Mombasa
Zanzibar
Dar es Salaam
Amirante Is.
SEYCHELLES
Chagos Arch. (Br.)
Palembang
Banjarmasin
Sulawesi
INDONESIA
Irian Jaya
Ujung Pandang
New Ireland
Rabaul
PAPUA NEW GUINEA
New Britain
SOLOMON IS.
TUVALU
Kananga
L. Tanganyika
TANZANIA
Diego Garcia (Br.)
Jakarta
Bandung
Surabaya
Jawa
Luanda
Aldabra
COMORO IS.
ANGOLA
Lubumbashi
MALAWI
L. Malawi
Benguela
ZAMBIA
Lusaka
Zomba
Harare
Cocos (Keeling Is.) (Australia)
Christmas I. (Australia)
Timor
Timor Sea
Arafura Sea
Port Moresby
C. York
Louisiade Arch.
Santa Cruz Is.
Darwin
MOZAMBIQUE
Mozambique Chan.
MADAGASCAR
Antananarivo
ZIMBABWE
Bulawayo
NAMIBIA
BOTSWANA
Windhoek
Rodriguez
MAURITIUS
Réunion (Fr.)
NORTHERN TERRITORY
Cairns
Townsville
VANUATU
Vanua Levu
FIJI
Viti Levu
Suva
(SOUTH WEST AFRICA)
Gaborone
Pretoria
SWAZILAND
Johannesburg
Maputo
Tropic of Capricorn
North West C.
WESTERN AUSTRALIA
QUEENSLAND
Alice Springs
AUSTRALIA
New Caledonia (Fr.)
Rockhampton
SOUTH AFRICA
LESOTHO
Durban
SOUTH AUSTRALIA
Brisbane
Cape Town
C. of Good Hope
Port Elizabeth
Kalgoorlie-Boulder
Perth
Fremantle
C. Leeuwin
NEW SOUTH WALES
Darling
Lord Howe I. (Australia)
Norfolk I. (Australia)
Newcastle
Sydney
Canberra
Great Australian Bight
Adelaide
North C.
VICTORIA
Melbourne
Tasman Sea
Auckland
North I.
NEW ZEALAND
Wellington
TASMANIA
Hobart
C. Farewell
Christchurch
South I.
Amsterdam (Fr.)
St. Paul (Fr.)
Pr. Edward Is. (South Africa)
Crozet Is. (Fr.)
Kerguelen (Fr.)
Bouvet I. (Norway)
McDonald I. (Australia)
Heard I. (Australia)
Stewart I.
Dunedin
Bounty Is.
Antipodes Is. (N.Z.)
Auckland I. (N.Z.)
Campbell I. (N.Z.)
Macquarie I. (Australia)
SOUTHERN OCEAN
Antarctic Circle
Enderby Land
Maud Land
ANTARCTICA
Wilkes Land
S. Magnetic Pole
Balleny Is.
Ross Sea
East from Greenwich

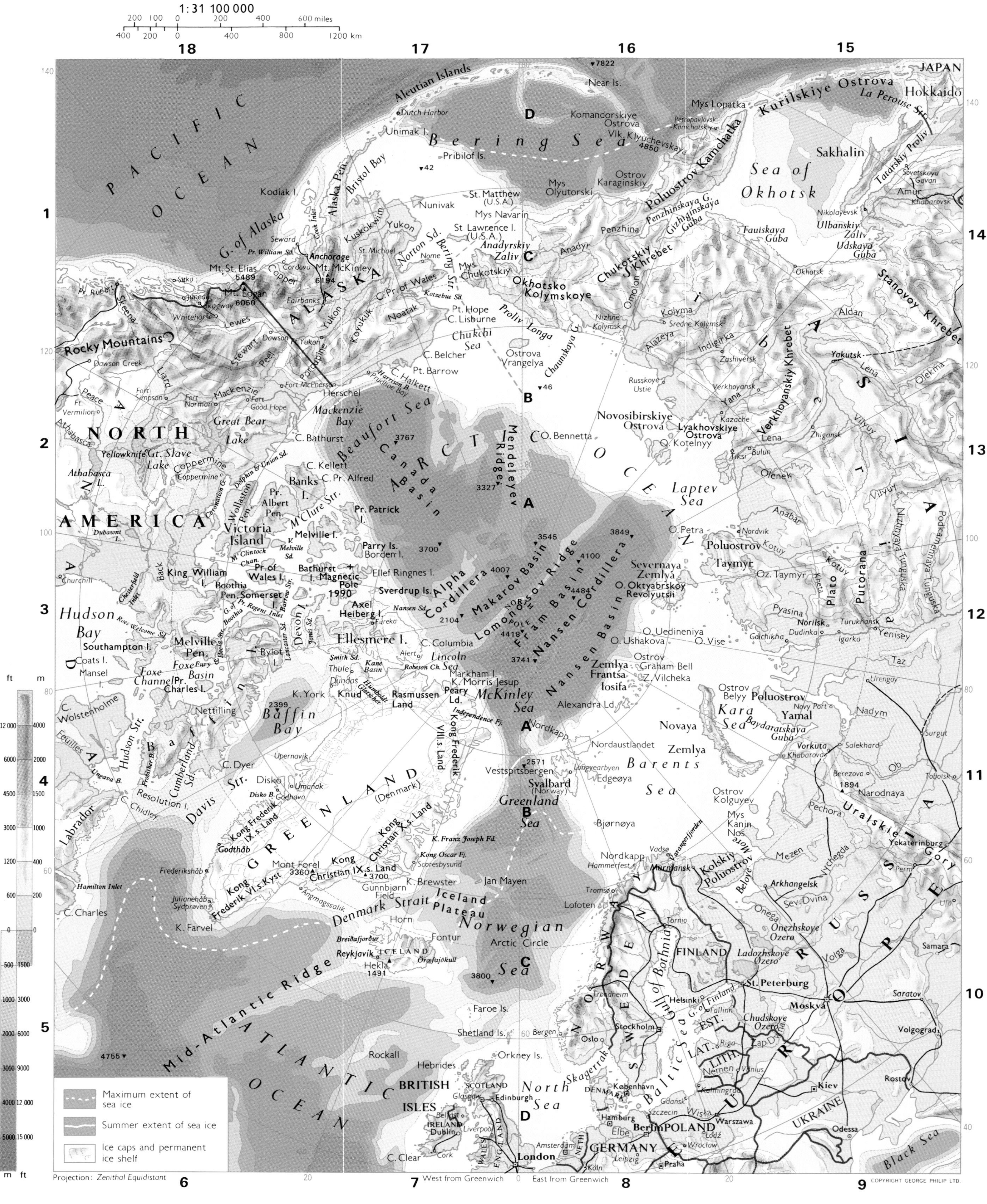

1 : 31 100 000

Projection: Zenithal Equidistant

6 West from Greenwich 7 East from Greenwich 8 9 COPYRIGHT GEORGE PHILIP LTD.

Legend:
- Maximum extent of sea ice
- Summer extent of sea ice
- Ice caps and permanent ice shelf

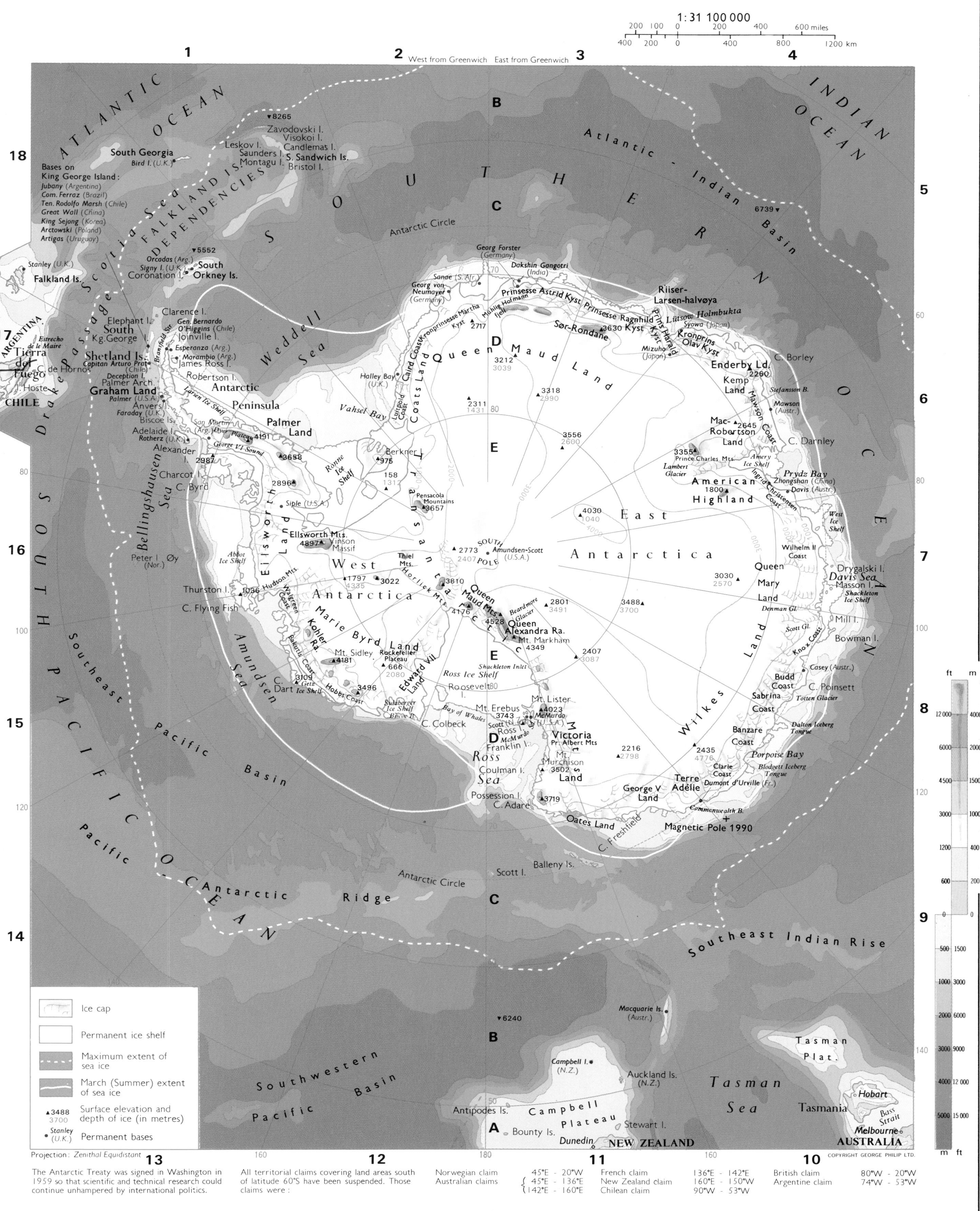

1 : 31 100 000

| | 200 | 100 | 0 | | 200 | | 400 | | 600 miles |
| 400 | 200 | 0 | | 400 | | 800 | | 1200 km |

West from Greenwich | East from Greenwich

Legend

Ice cap

Permanent ice shelf

Maximum extent of sea ice

March (Summer) extent of sea ice

▲3488 / 3700 Surface elevation and depth of ice (in metres)

• Stanley (U.K.) Permanent bases

Projection: *Zenithal Equidistant*

The Antarctic Treaty was signed in Washington in 1959 so that scientific and technical research could continue unhampered by international politics.

All territorial claims covering land areas south of latitude 60°S have been suspended. Those claims were:

Norwegian claim	45°E - 20°W	French claim	136°E - 142°E	British claim	80°W - 20°W
Australian claims	45°E - 136°E	New Zealand claim	160°E - 150°W	Argentine claim	74°W - 53°W
	142°E - 160°E	Chilean claim	90°W - 53°W	

COPYRIGHT GEORGE PHILIP LTD.

Elevation scale (ft / m)

ft	m
12 000	4000
6000	2000
4500	1500
3000	1000
1200	400
600	200
0	0
500	1500
1000	3000
2000	6000
3000	9000
4000	12 000
5000	15 000

m ft

Bases on King George Island:
Jubany (Argentina)
Com. Ferraz (Brazil)
Ten. Rodolfo Marsh (Chile)
Great Wall (China)
King Sejong (Korea)
Arctowski (Poland)
Artigas (Uruguay)

1 : 17 800 000

100   0   100   200   300   400 miles
100   0   100 200 300 400   500   600 km

ATLANTIC OCEAN

NORWEGIAN SEA

NORTH SEA

BALTIC SEA

MEDITERRANEAN SEA

ADRIATIC SEA

BLACK SEA

CASPIAN SEA   -28

Ionian Sea

Tyrrhenian Sea

Ligurian Sea

Aegean Sea

Sea of Azov

White Sea

Iceland   Hekla 1491   Öræfa 2119

British Isles

Great Britain

Ireland

Scandinavia

Kjölen

Lapland

Finland   L. Saimaa

Tundra

Ural Mountains

Volga Uplands

Central Russian Uplands

Ukraine

Carpathians   Transylvanian Alps

Alps   Mont Blanc 4807

Pyrenees   Pico de Aneto 3404

Apennines

Balkan Peninsula

Pindus

Caucasus   Elbrus 5633

Kurdistan

Armenia   Ararat 5165

Anatolia   Erciyas 3170

Iberian Peninsula

Meseta

Sierra Morena

Sierra Nevada   3478

Andalusia

New Castile

Old Castile

Cantabrian Mts.

Maritime Atlas

Plateau of the Shotts

Crete

Cyprus 1951

Corsica

Sardinia

Sicily   Etna 3263

Malta

Balearic Is.

North Cape

Nordkinn

Kola Peninsula

Kanin Peninsula

Pechora

Shetland Is.

Orkney Is.

Hebrides

Faroe Is.

Rockall

Dogger Bank

Fisher Bank

Helgoland

Gotland

Bornholm

Öland

Bay of Biscay

English Channel

Irish Sea

G. of Bothnia

G. of Finland

G. of Riga

G. of Lions

Str. of Gibraltar   C. Trafalgar   C. Spartel

Str. of Otranto

Str. of Messina

C. Matapan   5121

Volga

Don

Dnepr (Dnieper)

Dnestr (Dniester)

Danube

Rhine

Elbe

Weser

Oder (Odra)

Wisła (Vistula)

Niemen

N. Dvina

S. Dvina

Pechora

Mezen

Onega

Oka

Ural

Kama

Loire

Garonne

Rhône

Po

Tagus

Ebro

Seine

Thames

Snowdon 1085

Ben Nevis 1343

Projection: Bonne   West from Greenwich 0 East from Greenwich

1 : 17 800 000

100 0 100 200 300 400 miles
100 0 100 200 300 400 500 600 km

COPYRIGHT GEORGE PHILIP & SON LTD

Projection: Bonne   West from Greenwich 0 East from Greenwich

LONDON Capital Cities

ICELAND
Reykjavik

UNITED KINGDOM
IRELAND   Dublin
SCOTLAND   Edinburgh   Aberdeen   Dundee   Glasgow
ENGLAND   Newcastle   Leeds   Hull   Sheffield   Manchester   Liverpool   Birmingham   Bristol   London   Southampton   Plymouth
WALES   Cardiff   Swansea
Belfast   Cork   C. Clear
Shetland Is.   Orkney Is.   Hebrides   Faroe Is. (Den.)
Isle of Man   Is. of Scilly
English Channel

NORWAY   Oslo   Bergen   Stavanger   Trondheim   Tromsö   Hammerfest   Narvik   Sogne Fd.   Hardanger Fd.
SWEDEN   Stockholm   Göteborg   Malmö   Uppsala   Gävle   Kiruna   L. Vänern   L. Vättern
FINLAND   Helsinki   Tampere   Oulu
DENMARK   COPENHAGEN   Aarhus   Aalborg   Odense
Kattegat   Skagerrak   Gulf of Bothnia   BALTIC SEA   NORTH SEA

ESTONIA   Tallinn
LATVIA   Riga
LITHUANIA   Vilnius   Kaunas
Kaliningrad
BELORUSSIA   Minsk
POLAND   WARSAW   Gdańsk   Poznań   Łódź   Wrocław   Kraków   Katowice   Szczecin   Bydgoszcz   Lublin
GERMANY   BERLIN   Hamburg   Bremen   Hanover   Cologne   Dortmund   Essen   Dresden   Leipzig   Frankfurt   Stuttgart   Munich   Nuremberg   Magdeburg   Halle   Chemnitz   Kiel   Wiesbaden   Elbe   Oder
NETHERLANDS   Amsterdam   The Hague   Rotterdam   Groningen
BELGIUM   Brussels   Antwerp   Lille
LUX.
CZECH REP.   PRAGUE
SLOVAK REP.   Bratislava
AUSTRIA   VIENNA   Graz   Salzburg   Linz
SWITZERLAND   Bern   Zürich   Basel   Geneva
LIECH.

FRANCE   PARIS   Nantes   Bordeaux   Toulouse   Marseille   Lyons   Nice   Strasbourg   Le Havre   Rouen   Limoges   St. Etienne   Toulon   Dijon   Grenoble   Seine   Loire   Garonne   Rhône   Brest   Ushant   Monaco
BAY OF BISCAY

SPAIN   MADRID   Barcelona   Valencia   Sevilla   Zaragoza   Málaga   Murcia   Bilbao   Córdoba   Granada   Valladolid   Alicante   Gijón   Oviedo   Ebro   Tagus   Guadiana   Guadalquivir   Balearic Is.   Mallorca (Majorca)   Menorca   Palma   Gibraltar (Br.)
PORTUGAL   Lisbon   Oporto   Vigo   Douro   C. Finisterre   La Coruña
Str. of Gibraltar

ITALY   Rome   Milan   Naples   Turin   Genoa   Palermo   Florence   Bologna   Venice   Trieste   Bari   Messina   Catania   Tiber   Sardinia   Sicily   Corsica   Pantelleria (It.)   Cagliari   Taranto
MALTA   Valletta
Tyrrhenian Sea   ADRIATIC SEA   Ionian Sea   MEDITERRANEAN SEA

SLOVENIA   Ljubljana
CROATIA   Zagreb
BOSNIA-HERZ.   Sarajevo
YUGOSLAVIA   Belgrade   **SERBIA**   Niš
HUNGARY   BUDAPEST   Miskolc   Debrecen
ROMANIA   BUCHAREST   Cluj-Napoca   Timişoara   Braşov   Galaţi   Danube
MOLDAVIA   Kishinev
BULGARIA   Sofia   Plovdiv   Varna
ALBANIA   Tiranë
MACEDONIA   Skopje
GREECE   ATHENS   Thessaloníki   Piraeus   Pátras   Crete   Iráklion
CYPRUS   Limassol

R U S S I A   MOSCOW   St. Petersburg   Nizhniy Novgorod   Samara   Kazan   Perm   Ufa   Saratov   Volgograd   Voronezh   Yaroslavl   Tula   Ivanovo   Tver   Tambov   Penza   Orel   Kursk   Smolensk   Vitebsk   Orenburg   Ryazan   Kostroma   Vologda   Rybinsk   Kirov   Vyatka   Yekaterinburg   Nizhniy Tagil   Magnitogorsk   Chelyabinsk   Murmansk   Arkhangelsk   Astrakhan   Rostov   Krasnodar   Stavropol   Sevastopol   Volga   Don   Ural   N. Dvina   L. Onega   L. Ladoga   White Sea
KAZAKHSTAN   Guryev   Uralsk
UKRAINE   Kiev   Kharkov   Dnepropetrovsk   Donetsk   Odessa   Zaporozhye   Krivoy Rog   Kherson   Nikolayev   Chernigov   Zhitomir   Lvov   Dnepr (Dnieper)   Dnestr (Dniester)   Bug
Gomel   Mogilev   Pripyat (Pripet)   Białystok   Ostrava
S. of Azov   BLACK SEA   Constanţa

GEORGIA   Tbilisi
ARMENIA   Yerevan
AZERBAIJAN   Baku

TURKEY   Ankara   Istanbul   Izmir   Bursa   Adana   Konya   Kayseri   Erzurum   Samsun   Diyarbakır   Antalya   Aleppo
SYRIA   Homs
IRAQ   Baghdad   Mosul   Tigris   Euphrates
IRAN   Tabriz   Araks
CASPIAN SEA   Makhachkala

ATLANTIC OCEAN   Arctic Circle

MOROCCO   Rabat   Fès   Meknès   Tangier
ALGERIA   Algiers   Oran   Constantine   Annaba (Bône)
TUNISIA   Tunis   Sousse

SCANDINAVIA AND THE BALTIC LANDS

NORWEGIAN SEA

ICELAND
on the same scale
as general map

Reykjavík Akranes Keflavík Hafnarfjörður Vatnajökull Hekla Mýrdalsjökull Langjökull Hofsjökull Snæfell 1833 Vopnafjörður Seyðisfjörður Egilsstaðir Akureyri Siglufjörður Sauðárkrókur Húsavík Dettifoss Grímsey Mývatn Skjálfandafljót

Arctic Circle

Horn Ísafjarðardjúp Ísafjörður Breiðafjörður Faxaflói Snæfellsjökull

Lofoten Vesterålen Vestfjorden Moskenstraumen

Tromsø Narvik Hammerfest Nordkapp Vadsø Vardø Kirkenes Tanafjorden Laksefjorden Porsangen Varangerfjorden

Kiruna Gällivare Luleå Boden Piteå Skellefteå Umeå Örnsköldsvik Härnösand Sundsvall

NORRBOTTEN VÄSTERBOTTEN ÅNGERMANLAND JÄMTLAND

Rovaniemi Kemi Torneå Haparanda Oulu Kokkola Vaasa Kristinestad Jakobstad

LAPPI LAPPLAND FINNMARK TROMS NORDLAND

Namsos Steinkjer Levanger Trondheim N-TRØNDELAG SØR-TRØNDELAG Kristiansund Molde Ålesund

Mo i Rana Mosjøen Bodø Svartisen Saltfjellet

ARCTIC CIRCLE

Östersund Storsjön

1 : 4 400 000

50   0   50   100 miles
50 0 50   100   150 km

F | G | H | J | K

FINLAND

Mikkeli
Heinola
Lovisa
Kotka
Helsinki (Helsingfors)
Porvoo
Tampere
Hämeenlinna
Turku (Åbo)
Pori
Rauma
Uusikaupunki
Hangö (Hanko)
Mariehamn (Maarianhamina)
Åland (Ahvenanmaa)

ESTONIA
Tallinn
Haapsalu
Pärnu
Viljandi
Valga
Hiiumaa (Dagö)
Saaremaa (Ösel)
Kuressaare
Ruhnu

GULF OF FINLAND

BALTIC SEA

LATVIA
Riga
Rīgas Jūras Līcis (Gulf of Riga)
Valmiera
Cēsis
Tukums
Jelgava
Ventspils
Liepāja
Šiauliai

LITHUANIA
Vilnius
Kaunas
Klaipėda
Sovetsk
Kaliningrad
Chernyakhovsk

RUSSIA
BELO-RUSSIA
Grodno
Białystok
Łomża
Ostrołęka
Olsztyn
Elbląg
Malbork
Torún
Grudziądz
Bydgoszcz

POLAND
Gdynia
Gdańsk
Zatoka Gdańska

SWEDEN
STOCKHOLM
Uppsala
Gävle
Söderhamn
Hudiksvall
Borlänge
Falun
Västerås
Eskilstuna
Södertälje
Nyköping
Norrköping
Linköping
Örebro
Karlstad
Motala
Jönköping
Nässjö
Växjö
Kalmar
Oskarshamn
Västervik
Karlskrona
Karlshamn
Kristianstad
Halmstad
Helsingborg
Malmö
Göteborg
Borås
Uddevalla
Trollhättan
Varberg
Falkenberg
Landskrona
Ängelholm

GOTLAND
Visby
Fårö
Öland
Borgholm

ÖSTERGÖTLAND
VÄSTMANLAND
SÖDERMANLAND
KALMAR
BLEKINGE
KRONOBERG
JÖNKÖPING
HALLAND
ÄLVSBORG
GÖTEBORGS OCH BOHUS
VÄRMLAND
ÖREBRO
KOPPARBERG
GÄVLEBORG

NORWAY
OSLO
Drammen
Bergen
Stavanger
Kristiansand
Lillehammer
Hamar
Skien
Larvik
Arendal
Grimstad
Lillesand
Haugesund
Flekkefjord
Farsund
Mandal
Egersund (Eigersund)

TELEMARK
AUST-AGDER
VEST-AGDER
ROGALAND
BUSKERUD
OPPLAND
HEDMARK
SOGN OG FJORDANE

Skagerrak

DENMARK
København (Copenhagen)
Roskilde
Helsingør
Køge
Næstved
Korsør
Slagelse
Odense
Svendborg
Nyborg
Aalborg
Randers
Århus
Horsens
Vejle
Fredericia
Kolding
Esbjerg
Herning
Viborg
Silkeborg
Holstebro
Thisted
Hjørring
Frederikshavn
Sjælland
Fyn
Lolland
Falster
Bornholm
Rønne

Kattegat
The Sound
Store Bælt
Lille Bælt
Limfjorden

GERMANY
Hamburg
Bremen
Lübeck
Kiel
Rostock
Schwerin
Wilhelmshaven
Bremerhaven
Cuxhaven
Oldenburg
Flensburg
Emden

NETHERLANDS
Groningen

East from Greenwich

Projection: Conical with two standard parallels

COPYRIGHT GEORGE PHILIP & SON LTD.

ft   m
6000 2000
4500 1500
3000 1000
1200   400
600   200
0   0
200   600

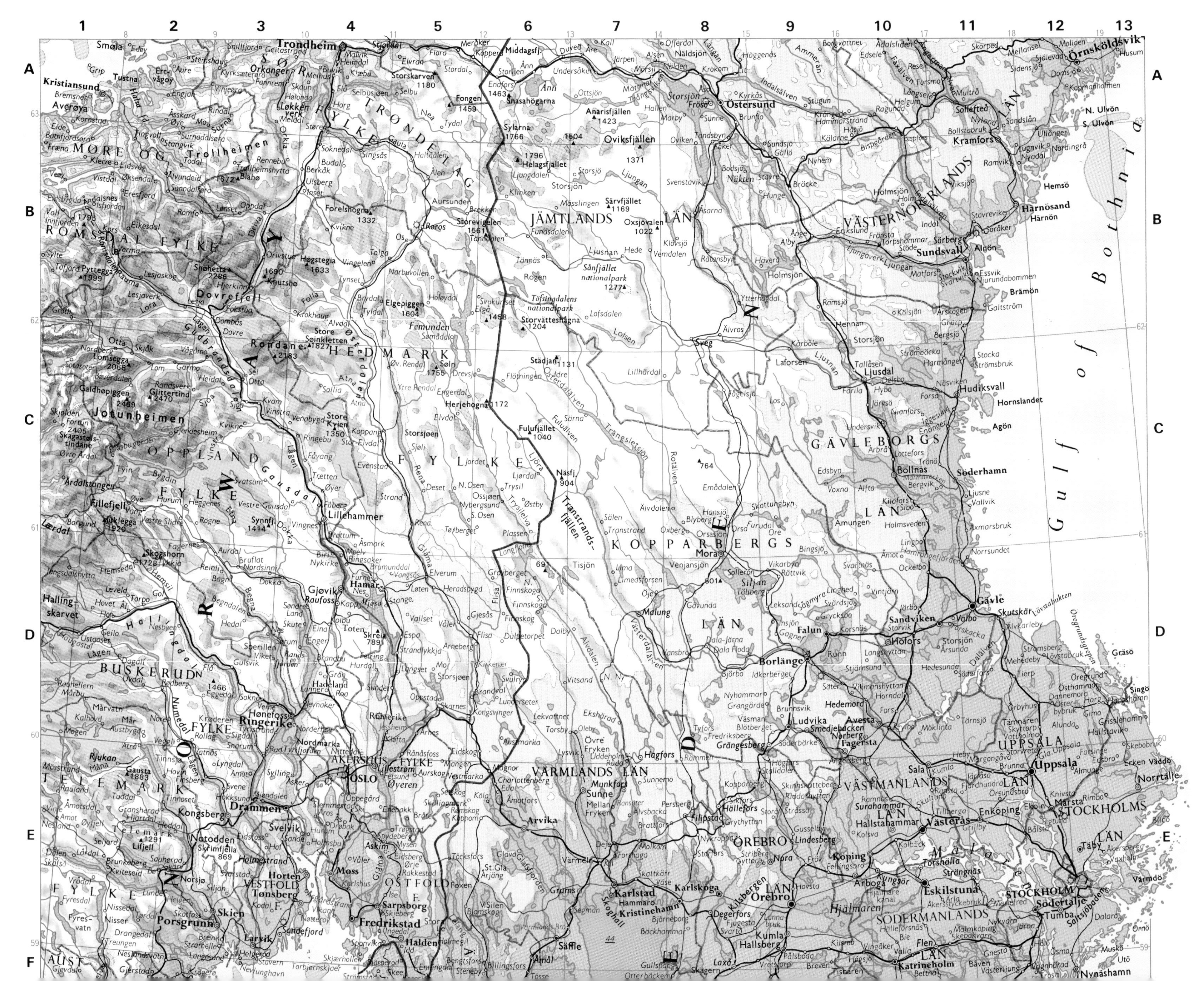
Gulf of Bothnia
Trondheim
Östersund
Sundsvall
Härnösand
Örnsköldsvik
Gävle
Uppsala
Stockholm
Västerås
Eskilstuna
Örebro
Karlstad
Falun
Borlänge
Mora
Oslo
Drammen
Hamar
Lillehammer
Gjøvik
Kongsberg
Skien
Porsgrunn
Larvik
Tønsberg
Horten
Moss
Fredrikstad
Sarpsborg
Halden
Kristiansund
Røros
JÄMTLANDS LÄN
VÄSTERNORRLANDS LÄN
GÄVLEBORGS LÄN
KOPPARBERGS LÄN
UPPSALA LÄN
STOCKHOLMS LÄN
VÄSTMANLANDS LÄN
SÖDERMANLANDS LÄN
ÖREBRO LÄN
VÄRMLANDS LÄN
HEDMARK FYLKE
OPPLAND FYLKE
BUSKERUD FYLKE
TELEMARK FYLKE
VESTFOLD
ØSTFOLD
AKERSHUS FYLKE
SØR TRØNDELAG FYLKE
MØRE OG ROMSDAL FYLKE
Jotunheimen
Dovrefjell
Hjälmaren

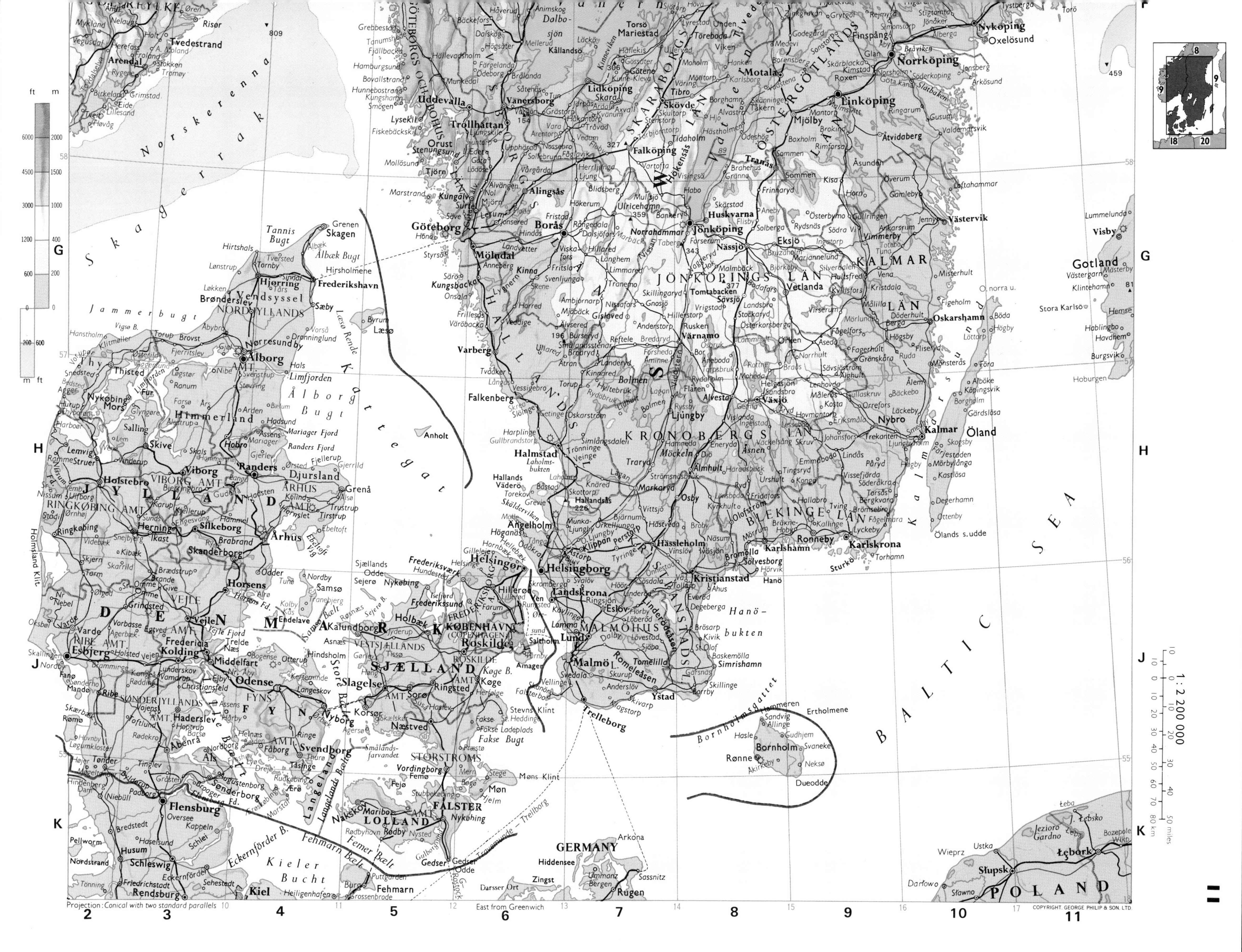

1 : 2 200 000
miles
km
Projection: Conical with two standard parallels
East from Greenwich
COPYRIGHT, GEORGE PHILIP & SON, LTD.
BALTIC SEA
Skagerrak
Kattegat
Norskerenna
Jammerbugt
Ålborg Bugt
Kieler Bucht
Hanöbukten
Bornholmsgattet
Kalmarsund
GERMANY
POLAND
JYLLAND
SJÆLLAND
FYN
LOLLAND
FALSTER
DENMARK
SWEDEN
Gotland
Öland
Bornholm
KØBENHAVN
Göteborg
Malmö
Helsingborg
Jönköping
Norrköping
Linköping
Kalmar
Karlskrona
Ålborg
Århus
Odense
Esbjerg
Flensburg
Kiel
Växjö
Visby

NORTH SEA

IRISH SEA

North Channel

SCOTLAND

Fife Ness
Anstruther
Crail
Kinross
Kirkcaldy
Kinghorn
Leven
Burntisland
Dunfermline
Alloa
Stirling
Forth
L. Lomond
Ben Lomond 974
Helensburgh
Dumbarton
Clydebank
Greenock
Port Glasgow
Gourock
Dunoon
Paisley
Glasgow
Rutherglen
Hamilton
Motherwell
Wishaw
Coatbridge
Airdrie
Falkirk
Linlithgow
Musselburgh
Edinburgh
Leith
Haddington
Dunbar
St. Abb's Hd.
Eyemouth
Berwick-upon-Tweed
Holy I.
Farne Is.
Bamburgh
Alnwick
Coquet
Ashington
Morpeth
Blyth
Tynemouth
Newcastle
Gateshead
South Shields
Sunderland
Houghton-le-Spring
Consett
Durham
Bishop Auckland
Hexham
Allendale
Darlington
Stockton
Billingham
Hartlepool
Middlesbrough
Redcar
CLEVELAND
TEESSIDE
Whitby
Scarborough
Filey
Flamborough Hd.
Bridlington
Hornsea
Withernsea
Spurn Hd.
Mablethorpe
Skegness
The Wash

Pentland Hills
Peebles
Moorfoot Hills
Lammermuir Hills
Galashiels
Selkirk
Hawick
Kelso
Coldstream
Jedburgh
Flodden
Tweed
The Cheviot 816
Cheviot Hills
NORTHUMBERLAND
N. Tyne
S. Tyne
Haltwhistle
Cross Fell 893
PENNINES
Appleby
Brough
CUMBRIA
Penrith
Carlisle
Skiddaw 931
Keswick
Derwent
Helvellyn 950
Ullswater
Ambleside
Windermere
Kendal
Cumbrian Mts.
Sca Fell 978
NORTH YORKSHIRE
Northallerton
Thirsk
Ripon
Wensleydale
Richmond
N. York Moors
Pickering
Malton
Driffield
York
Beverley
Holderness
HUMBERSIDE
Hull
Humber
Grimsby
Cleethorpes
Immingham
Goole
Scunthorpe
Doncaster
Gainsborough
Market Rasen
Louth
Alford
Horncastle
LINCOLN
Lincoln
Newark
Retford
Worksop
Mansfield
Sutton-in-Ashfield
Sherwood Forest
Nottingham
Grantham
Sleaford
Boston
Spalding
Bourne
The Fens

Leadhills
Sanquhar
Nith
Annan
Leadhills
SOUTHERN UPLANDS
Moffat
Dumfries
Lockerbie
Langholm
Dalbeattie
Castle Douglas
Kirkcudbright
Solway Firth
Silloth
Maryport
Workington
Whitehaven
St. Bees Hd.
Millom
Barrow
Walney I.
Morecambe Bay
Morecambe
Heysham
Fleetwood
Cleveleys
Blackpool
Lytham-St. Annes
Southport
Formby Pt.
Ormskirk
Preston
Lancaster
Forest of Bowland
Settle
Skipton
Keighley
Colne
Nelson
Burnley
Accrington
Blackburn
Bradford
Leeds
Harrogate
Knaresborough
Wetherby
Halifax
Huddersfield
Dewsbury
WEST YORKSHIRE
Wakefield
Pontefract
Castleford
Barnsley
SOUTH YORKSHIRE
Sheffield
Rotherham
Chesterfield
DERBY
Matlock
Belper
Ilkeston
Heanor
Derby
Burton-on-Trent
Ashby-de-la-Zouch
Loughborough

Dumfries
Newton Stewart
Cree
Merrick 843
Galloway
Wigtown
Wigtown Bay
Whithorn
Luce Bay
Mull of Galloway
Port Erin
ISLE OF MAN
Snaefell 620
Douglas
Castletown
Ramsey
Peel
Pt. of Ayre
Calf of Man

Jura
Sound of Jura
Kintyre
Campbeltown
Gigha
Mull of Kintyre
Inveraray
Loch Fyne
Arran
Goat Fell 874
Ailsa Craig
Saltcoats
Irvine
Kilmarnock
Ayr
Girvan
Firth of Clyde

Belfast
Belfast Lough
Bangor
Donaghadee
Newtownards
Larne
Magee
Portpatrick
Stranraer
Strangford L.
Downpatrick
Ardglass

Irish Sea

WALES
Anglesey
Amlwch
Holyhead
Holy I.
Sterries
Beaumaris
Bangor
Caernarfon
Menai Strait
Nefyn
Pwllheli
Braich-y-Pwll
Bardsey I.
Porthmadog
Blaenau Ffestiniog
Snowdon 1085
GWYNEDD
Barmouth
L. Bala
Conwy
Llandudno
Colwyn Bay
Great Orme's Hd.
Rhyl
Prestatyn
CLWYD
Denbigh
Ruthin
Mold
Flint
Wrexham
Llangollen
Welshpool
Oswestry

CHESHIRE
Chester
Ellesmere Port
Birkenhead
Wallasey
Bootle
Liverpool
MERSEYSIDE
St. Helens
Widnes
Runcorn
Northwich
Crewe
Nantwich
Newcastle-under-Lyme
Stoke-on-Trent
Leek
Macclesfield
Buxton
Stockport
Manchester
Salford
Oldham
Rochdale
Bury
Bolton
Wigan
Warrington
Altrincham
STAFFORD
Stafford
Stone
Uttoxeter
Rugeley
Cannock

Great Yarmouth
Cromer
The Broads
NORFOLK
Hunstanton
Wells
Fakenham
Sandringham
Kings Lynn
North Walsham
Bure

R. Tweed
R. Eden
R. Lune
R. Ribble
R. Mersey
R. Dee
R. Trent
R. Wear
R. Tees
R. Swale
R. Ure
R. Nidd
R. Wharfe
R. Aire
R. Derwent
R. Ouse

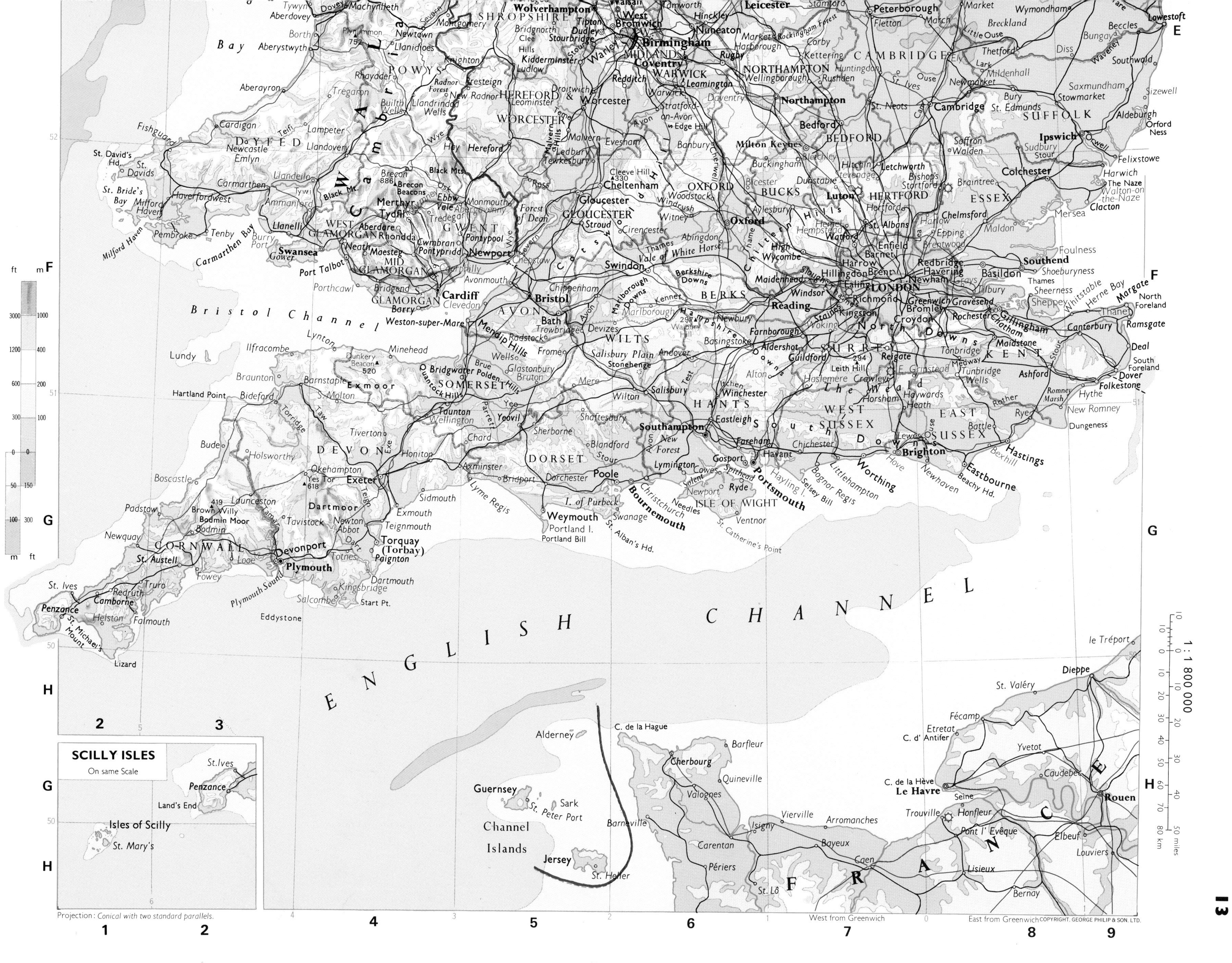
1 : 1 800 000
10 0 10 20 30 40 50 miles
10 0 10 20 30 40 50 60 70 80 km
ENGLISH CHANNEL
Bristol Channel
Carmarthen Bay
Channel Islands
Guernsey
Alderney
Sark
Jersey
FRANCE
CORNWALL
DEVON
DORSET
SOMERSET
AVON
WILTS
HANTS
ISLE OF WIGHT
WEST SUSSEX
EAST SUSSEX
KENT
SURREY
ESSEX
SUFFOLK
CAMBRIDGE
NORTHAMPTON
BEDFORD
HERTFORD
BUCKS
BERKS
OXFORD
GLOUCESTER
HEREFORD & WORCESTER
WARWICK
SHROPSHIRE
POWYS
GWENT
DYFED
WEST GLAMORGAN
MID GLAMORGAN
SOUTH GLAMORGAN
WALES
LONDON
SCILLY ISLES
On same Scale
Isles of Scilly
St. Mary's
Land's End
Penzance
St. Ives
Projection: Conical with two standard parallels.
West from Greenwich
East from Greenwich
COPYRIGHT, GEORGE PHILIP & SON, LTD.

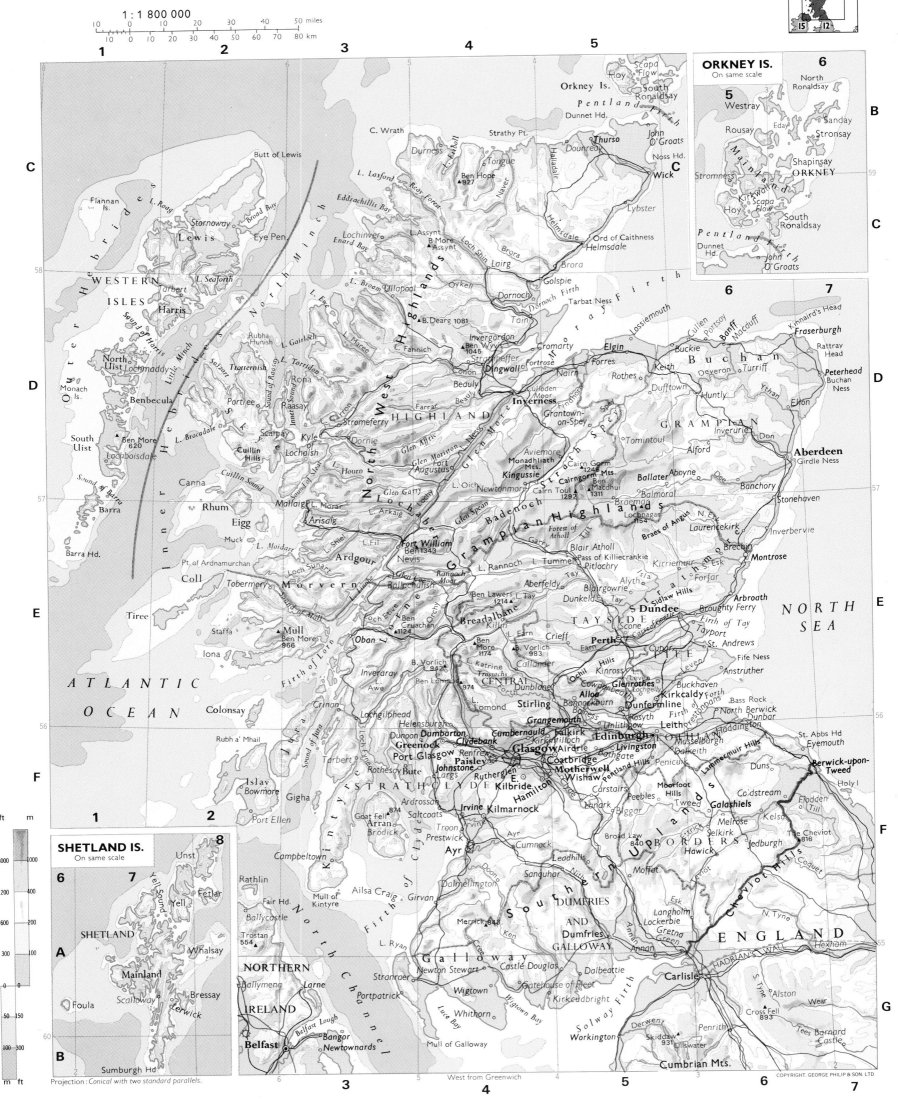

1 : 1 800 000

SHETLAND IS.
On same scale

Projection: Conical with two standard parallels.

COPYRIGHT. GEORGE PHILIP & SON. LTD

West from Greenwich

1 : 1 800 000

| 10 | 0 | 10 | 20 | 30 | 40 | 50 miles |

| 10 | 0 | 10 | 20 | 30 | 40 | 50 | 60 | 70 | 80 km |

ATLANTIC OCEAN

NORTHERN IRELAND

IRELAND

IRISH SEA

St. George's Channel

North Channel

Towns underlined in Northern Ireland give their
names to the Districts in which they stand

The remaining Districts are:—

1	Fermanagh	5	Castlereagh
2	Moyle	6	Ards
3	Newtownabbey	7	Down
4	North Down	8	Newry & Mourne

Projection: Conical with two standard parallels.

West from Greenwich

COPYRIGHT. GEORGE PHILIP & SON. LTD.

ft m

3000 1000

1200 400

600 200

300 100

0 0

100 300

200 600

m ft

N O R T H   S E A

O S T F R I E S I S C H E   I N S E L N

W A D D E N E I L A N D E N

W A D D E N Z E E

IJSSELMEER

Markermeer

Texel
Vlieland
Terschelling
Ameland
Schiermonnikoog

Den Helder
Alkmaar
Haarlem
AMSTERDAM
'S GRAVENHAGE
(DEN HAAG)
(THE HAGUE)
'S-Gravenhage
ROTTERDAM
Dordrecht
Leiden
Utrecht
Hilversum
Zwolle
Leeuwarden
Groningen
Emden
Deventer
Apeldoorn
Arnhem
Nijmegen
Enschede
Hengelo
Almelo
Zutphen
Emmen
Hoogeveen
Meppel
Assen

FRIESLAND
GRONINGEN
DRENTE
OVERIJSSEL
GELDERLAND
FLEVOLAND
Noordoostpolder
Oostelijk-Flevoland
Zuidelijk-Flevoland
Lelystad

Ems
Dollart
Lauwers

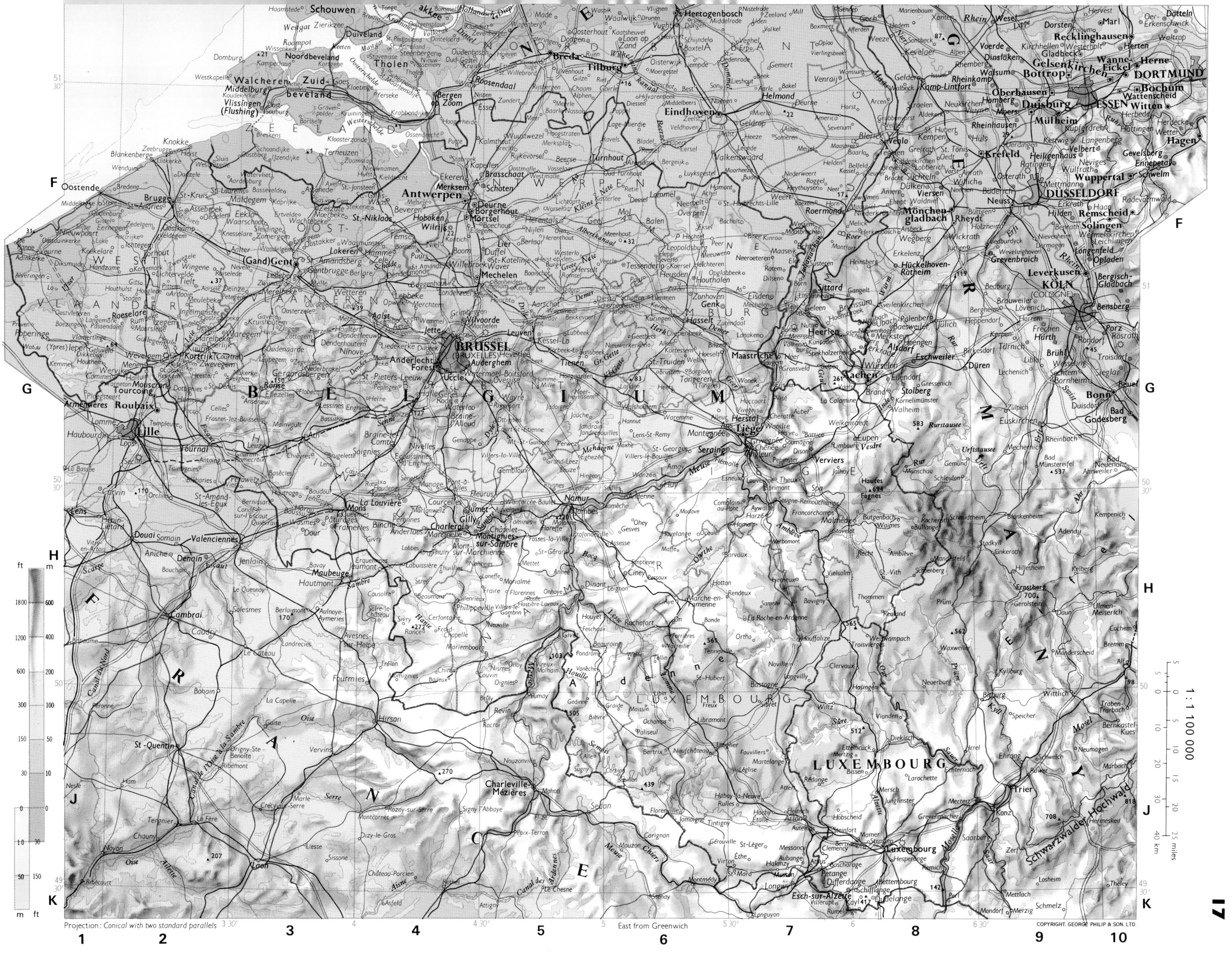
1 : 1 100 000
miles
km
BELGIUM
LUXEMBOURG
GERMANY
FRANCE
NEDERLAND
BRUSSEL
(BRUXELLES)
Antwerpen
(Gand) Gent
Brugge
Oostende
Liège
Namur
Charleroi
Mons
Mechelen
Leuven
Hasselt
Maastricht
Eindhoven
Tilburg
Breda
's-Hertogenbosch
Aachen
KÖLN
(COLOGNE)
DÜSSELDORF
ESSEN
DORTMUND
Duisburg
Bonn
Trier
Luxembourg
Lille
Roubaix
Tourcoing
Valenciennes
Cambrai
St-Quentin
Laon
Charleville-Mézières
Sedan
Verviers
Vlissingen
(Flushing)
ZEELAND
VLAANDEREN
Ardenne
Meuse
Moselle
Schwarzwalder Hochwald
Projection: Conical with two standard parallels
East from Greenwich
COPYRIGHT, GEORGE PHILIP & SON, LTD.

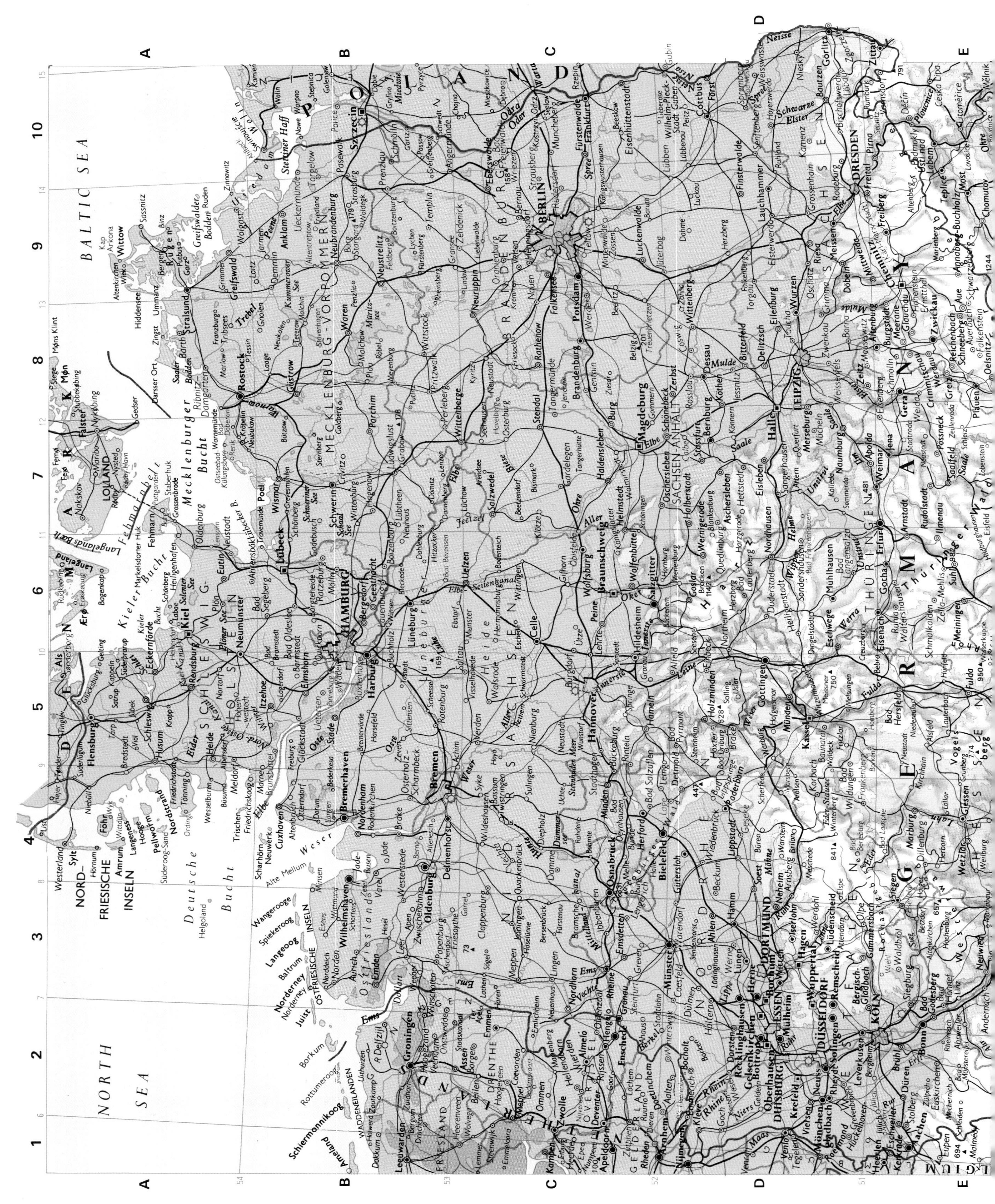
BALTIC SEA
NORTH SEA
DEUTSCHE BUCHT
MECKLENBURGER BUCHT
KIELER BUCHT
POLAND
DENMARK
NORD-FRIESISCHE INSELN
OSTFRIESISCHE INSELN
SCHLESWIG-HOLSTEIN
MECKLENBURG-VORPOMMERN
NIEDERSACHSEN
BRANDENBURG
SACHSEN-ANHALT
THÜRINGEN
SACHSEN
NORDRHEIN-WESTFALEN
HAMBURG
BERLIN
BREMEN
HANNOVER
KIEL
ROSTOCK
SZCZECIN
MAGDEBURG
LEIPZIG
DRESDEN
DORTMUND
DÜSSELDORF
ESSEN
KÖLN
DUISBURG
Lüneburger Heide
Elbe
Weser
Ems
Oder
Rhein
A B C D E
1 2 3 4 5 6 7 8 9 10

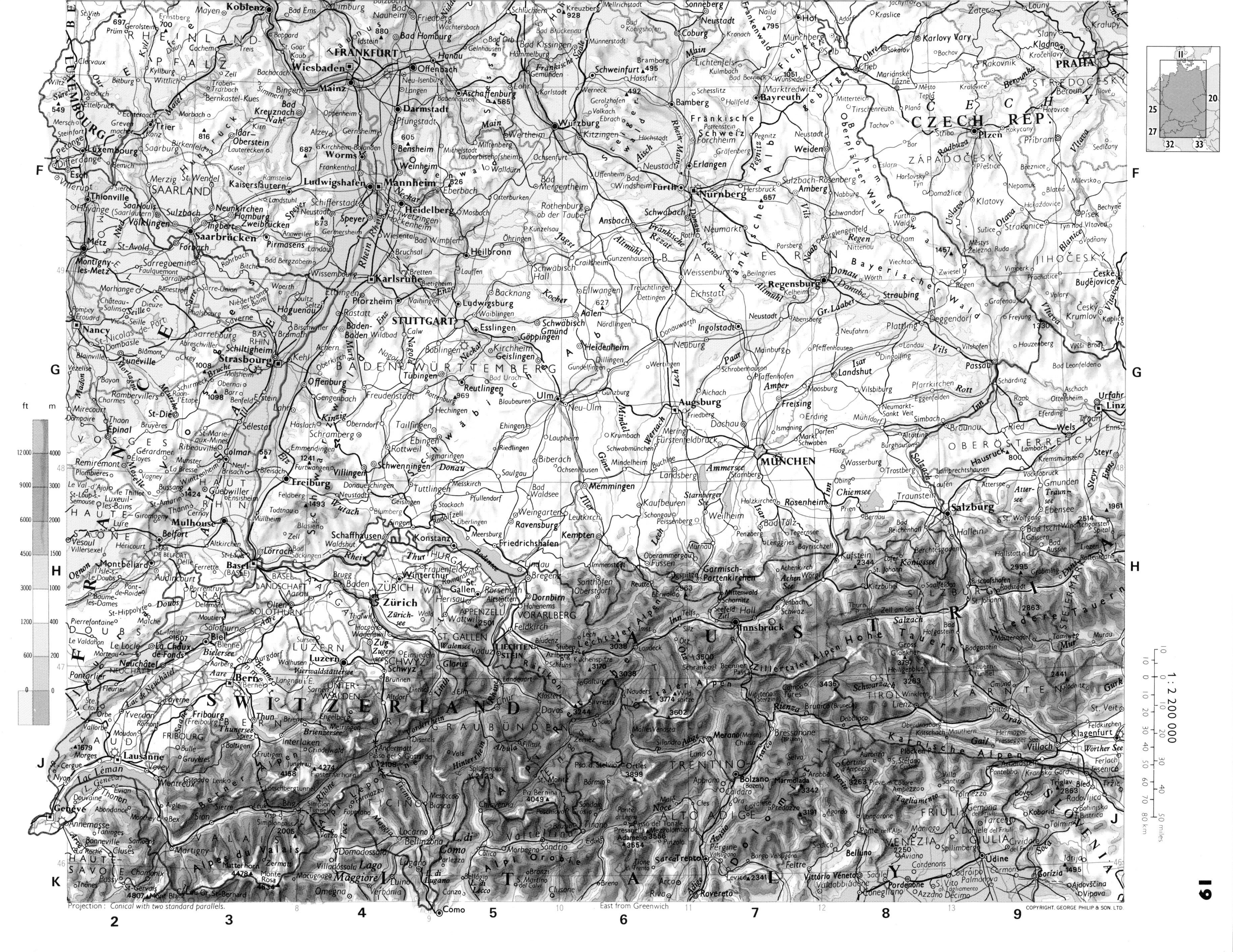
1 : 2 200 000
10 0 10 20 30 40 50 miles
10 0 10 20 30 40 50 60 70 80 km
Projection: Conical with two standard parallels.
East from Greenwich
COPYRIGHT, GEORGE PHILIP & SON, LTD.
CZECH REP.
PRAHA
SWITZERLAND
LUXEMBOURG
MÜNCHEN
STUTTGART
FRANKFURT
Zürich
Bern
Innsbruck
Salzburg
Strasbourg
Nürnberg
Regensburg
Augsburg
Mannheim
Karlsruhe
Basel
Luzern
Lausanne
Genève
Linz
Plzeň
Udine
Bolzano
Metz
Nancy
Mulhouse
Freiburg
Ulm
Würzburg
ft
m
12 000
9000
6000
4500
3000
1200
600
0
4000
3000
2000
1500
1000
400
200
0

BALTIC SEA

DENMARK

LITHUANIA

(RUSSIA)

Kaliningrad (Königsberg)

BELORUSSIA

UKRAINE

GERMANY

POLAND

CZECH REP.

SLOVENSKÉ REP.

BERLIN

POTSDAM

DRESDEN

LEIPZIG

WARSZAWA (Warsaw)

ŁÓDŹ

WROCŁAW (Breslau)

POZNAŃ

KRAKÓW

PRAHA (PRAGUE)

BRNO

Gdańsk (Danzig)

Gdynia

Szczecin (Stettin)

Bydgoszcz

Toruń

Białystok

Lublin

Radom

Grodno

Brest

L'vov

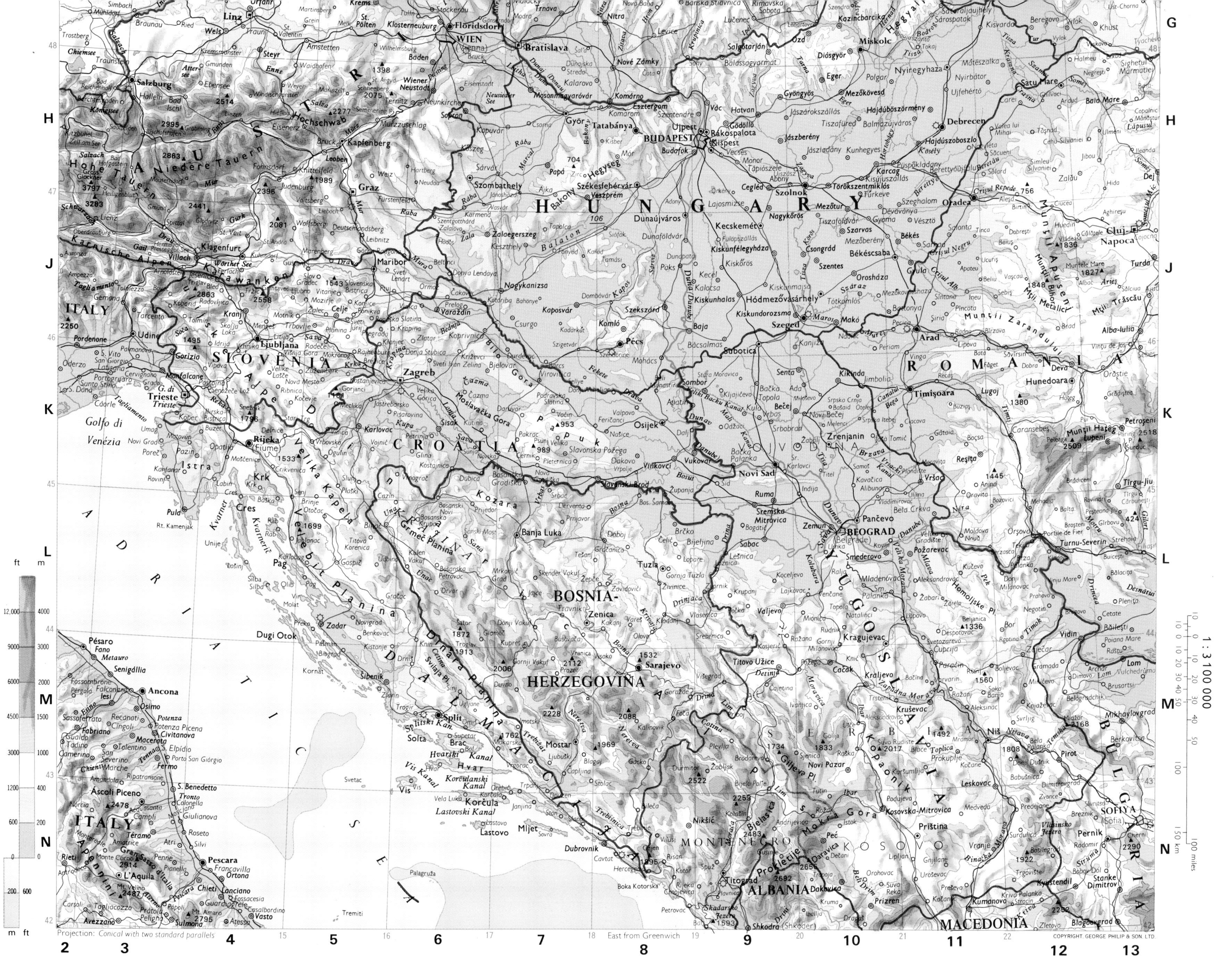

1 : 3 100 000

100 miles

150 km

COPYRIGHT GEORGE PHILIP & SON LTD

Projection: Conical with two standard parallels

25 19
25
27 32
32

1 2 3 4 5 6

A

HAUTE-SAÔNE
Vesoul
Luxeuil-les-Bains
St-Sauveur
Lure
Belfort
BELFORT
MULHOUSE
HAUT RHIN
Sundgau
Schwarzwald
Müllheim
Lörrach
Waldshut
Rheinfelden
Säckingen

F R A N C E

Montbéliard
Audincourt
A J U R A
Delémont
BASEL (BASLE)
Pratteln
Liestal
Aarau
Olten
Zofingen
Langenthal
Sursee

B

BESANÇON
DOUBS
Maîche
Franches Montagnes
Saignelégier
Tramelan
Moutier
Solothurn
Grenchen
Biel (Bienne)
Biberist
Ober-Aargau
LUZERN
Burgdorf

La Chaux-de-Fonds
St-Imier
Le Locle
Morteau
NEUCHÂTEL
Bielersee
Aarberg
Lyss
Schüpfen

47

Pontarlier
Neuchâtel
Lac de Neuchâtel
Payerne
Fribourg (Freibourg)
BERN (BERNE)
Worb
Münsingen
Köniz
Mittelland
EMMENTAL
Langnau i.E.
Signau
Entlebuch

C

Champagnole
Ste-Croix
Yverdon
Orbe
FRIBOURG
Gruyère
Thun
Steffisburg
Thunersee
Brienzersee
Brienz
Meiringen
OBWALDEN

Vallorbe
Le Sentier
Mt.Tendre 1679
Bulle
Gruyères
Spiez
Frutigen
Grindelwald
Schreckhorn 4078
Finsteraarhorn 4274

D

Morez
St-Claude
La Côte
Nyon
Thonon-les-Bains
LAUSANNE
Morges
Lutry
Vevey
Montreux
Villeneuve
Aigle
Les Diablerets
Gstaad
BERNER ALPEN
Lenk
Adelboden
Kandersteg
Jungfrau 4158

GENÈVE (GENEVA)
Annemasse
HAUTE-SAVOIE
Léman (L. Geneva)
Évian-les-Bains
Monthey
St-Maurice
Sion
Sierre
VALAIS
Brig
Simplon
Matterhorn 4478

Bellegarde-s.-V.
Pays de Gex
Oyonnax

E

Annecy
Lac d'Annecy
Chamonix-Mont-Blanc
Martigny
Orsières
Col du Gd-St-Bernard
VALLE D'AOSTA
Aosta
Monte Rosa 4634
Zermatt

Aix-les-Bains
Albertville
SAVOIE
Petit St-Bernard
VALLE D'AOSTA

ft m
9000 3000
6000 2000
4500 1500
3000 1000
1200 500
600 200

Projection: Conical with two standard parallels

1 2 3 4 5

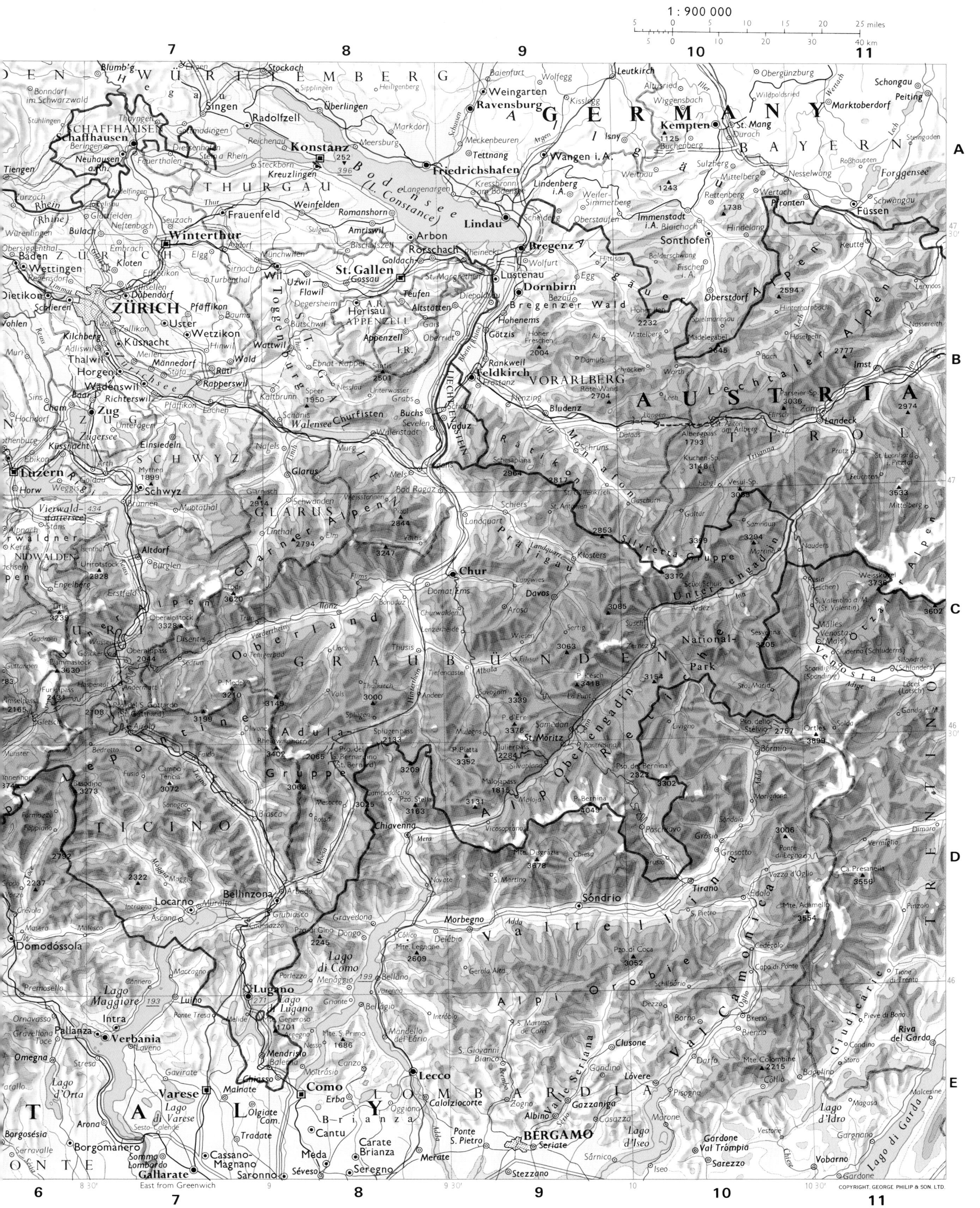
1 : 900 000
5 0 5 10 15 20 25 miles
5 0 10 20 30 40 km
GERMANY
AUSTRIA
ITALY
ZÜRICH
Bodensee (L. Constance)
Konstanz
Friedrichshafen
Bregenz
Winterthur
St. Gallen
Luzern
Chur
Vaduz
LIECHTENSTEIN
Feldkirch
Landeck
Lugano
Como
Lecco
Bergamo
Sóndrio
Bellinzona
Locarno
Varese
Lago Maggiore
Lago di Como
Kempten
Füssen
Davos
St. Moritz
GRAUBÜNDEN
TICINO
LOMBARDIA
TIROL
VORARLBERG
COPYRIGHT, GEORGE PHILIP & SON, LTD.

ENGLAND

English Channel

CHANNEL ISLANDS
Alderney
Guernsey
St. Peter Port
Herm
Sark
Jersey
St. Helier

Baie de la Seine

Golfe de St-Malo

Mer d'Iroise

Baie de Bourgneuf

Pertuis Breton
Pertuis d'Antioche

NORMANDIE
BRETAGNE
ANJOU
MAINE
PERCHE
POITOU
AUNIS
ANGOUMOIS

Cherbourg · Le Havre · Rouen · Caen · Bayeux · Lisieux · Évreux · Dreux
Alençon · Le Mans · Angers · Tours · Blois
Rennes · St-Brieuc · Morlaix · Brest · Quimper · Lorient · Vannes · Nantes · St-Nazaire
La Roche-sur-Yon · Les Sables-d'Olonne · Niort · La Rochelle · Rochefort · Saintes · Cognac · Angoulême · Poitiers · Châtellerault · Limoges

Plymouth · Exeter · Torquay · Bournemouth · Southampton · Portsmouth · Brighton · Eastbourne · Hastings · Penzance · Newquay · Truro

ft   m
12 000   4000
9000   3000
6000   2000
4500   1500
3000   1000
1200   400
600   200
0   0
200   600
2000   6000
m   ft

DÉPARTEMENTS IN THE PARIS AREA
1 Ville de Paris   3 Val-de-Marne
2 Seine-St-Denis   4 Hauts-de-Seine

Projection: Conical with two standard parallels

West from Greenwich   East from Greenwich

1 : 2 200 000

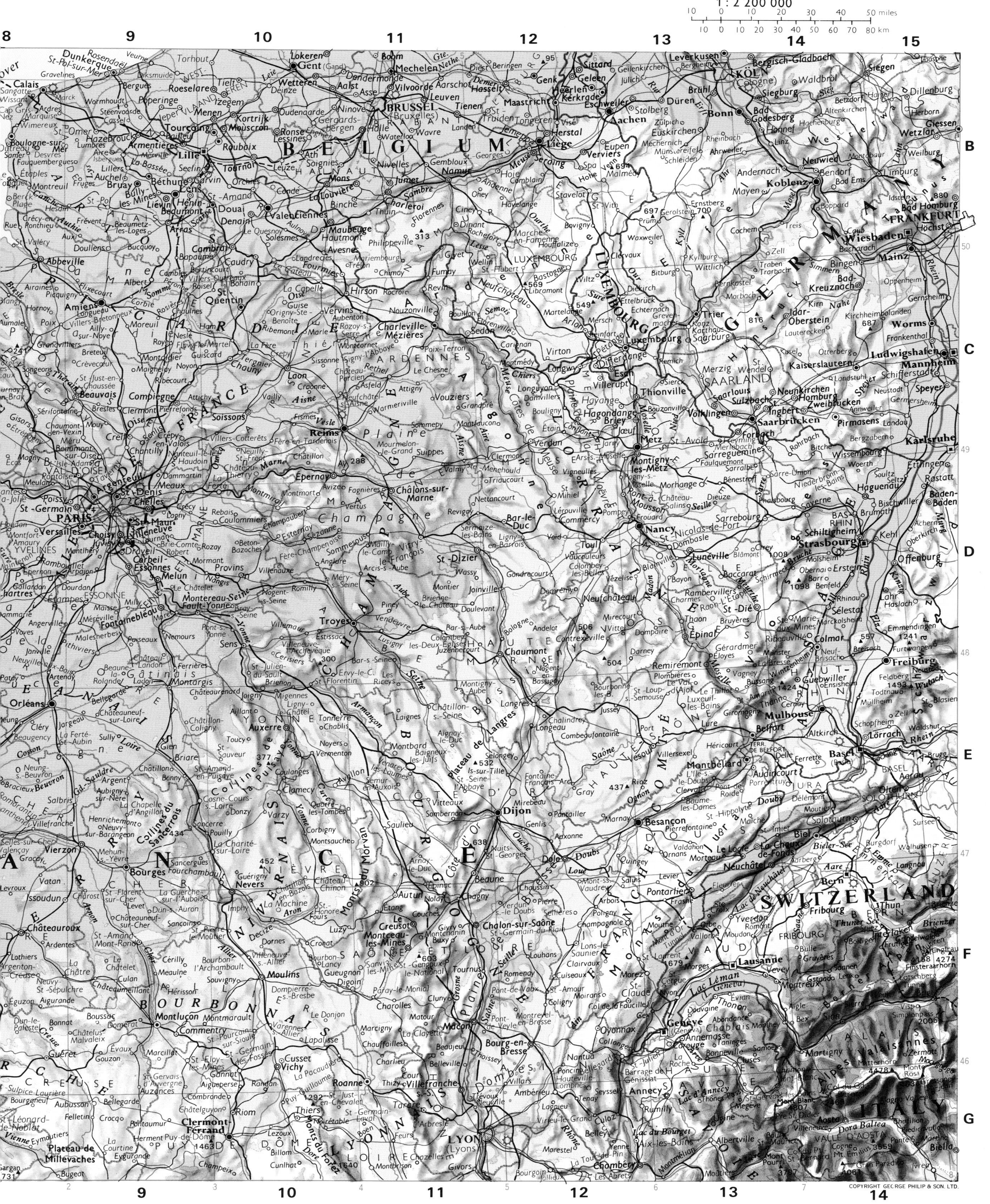
10 0 10 20 30 40 50 miles
10 0 10 20 30 40 50 60 70 80 km
8
9
10
11
12
13
14
15
B
C
D
E
F
G
BELGIUM
LUXEMBOURG
GERMANY
FRANCE
SWITZERLAND
ITALY
PICARDIE
CHAMPAGNE
ARDENNES
LORRAINE
BOURGOGNE
FRANCHE COMTÉ
NIVERNAIS
BOURBONNAIS
SAARLAND
BAS RHIN
HAUT RHIN
Calais
Dunkerque
Gent
Brussel
Liège
Lille
Amiens
Reims
PARIS
Versailles
Orléans
Troyes
Dijon
Nancy
Metz
Strasbourg
Mulhouse
Besançon
Basel
Bern
Lausanne
Genève
Annecy
Chambéry
Lyon
Clermont-Ferrand
Vichy
Moulins
Bourges
Nevers
Auxerre
Luxembourg
Saarbrücken
Trier
Koblenz
Köln
Bonn
Aachen
Maastricht
Frankfurt
Wiesbaden
Mainz
Mannheim
Karlsruhe
Freiburg
Lac Léman
Plateau de Langres
Plateau de Millevaches
Monts du Morvan
Dombes
Champagne
Bourbonnais

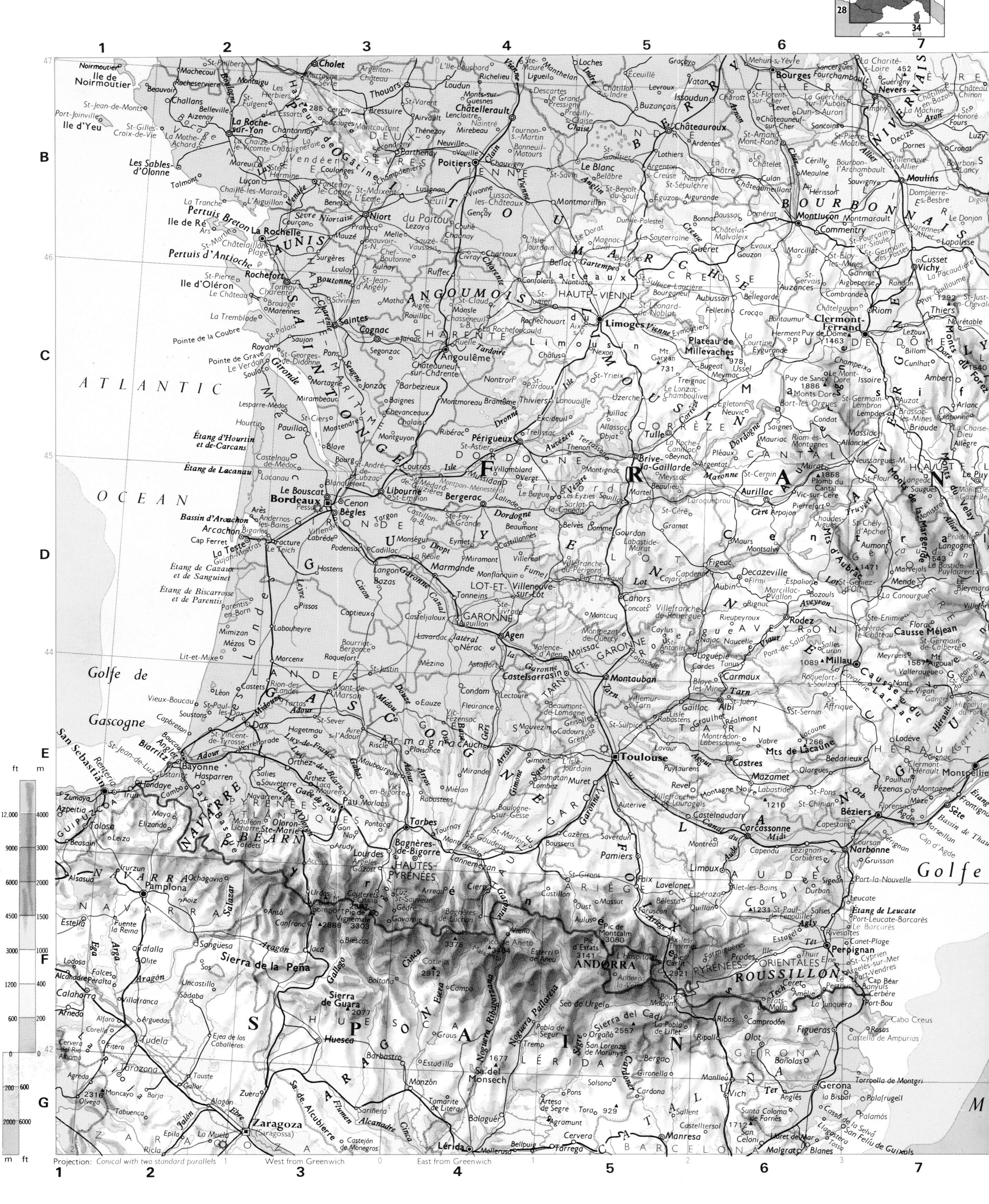

ATLANTIC
OCEAN
Golfe de Gascogne
Golfe
Pertuis Breton
Pertuis d'Antioche
Ile de Noirmoutier
Ile d'Yeu
Ile de Ré
Ile d'Oléron
Étang d'Hourtin et de Carcans
Étang de Lacanau
Bassin d'Arcachon
Étang de Cazaux et de Sanguinet
Étang de Biscarrosse et de Parentis
Étang de Leucate
AUNIS
SAINTONGE
ANGOUMOIS
LIMOUSIN
MARCHE
BERRY
BOURBONNAIS
NIVERNAIS
AUVERGNE
GUYENNE
GASCOGNE
LANDES
BÉARN
NAVARRE
LANGUEDOC
FOIX
ROUSSILLON
ANDORRA
SPAIN
NAVARRA
ARAGÓN
CATALUÑA
Plateau de Millevaches
Monts Dore
Monts du Cantal
Causse Méjean
Mts de Lacaune
Sierra de la Peña
Sierra de Guara
Sierra del Cadí
Pic de Vignemale 3303
Pic d'Aneto 3404
Pic d'Estats 3141
Puy de Dôme 1463
Puy de Sancy 1886
Nantes
Cholet
Poitiers
Bourges
Nevers
Châteauroux
La Rochelle
Rochefort
Niort
Angoulême
Limoges
Montluçon
Moulins
Vichy
Clermont-Ferrand
Bordeaux
Périgueux
Brive-la-Gaillarde
Tulle
Aurillac
Cahors
Agen
Montauban
Toulouse
Albi
Rodez
Millau
Mende
Bayonne
Biarritz
Pau
Tarbes
Lourdes
Carcassonne
Narbonne
Béziers
Montpellier
Sète
Perpignan
San Sebastián
Pamplona
Huesca
Zaragoza
Lérida
Gerona
Manresa
Projection: Conical with two standard parallels
West from Greenwich
East from Greenwich

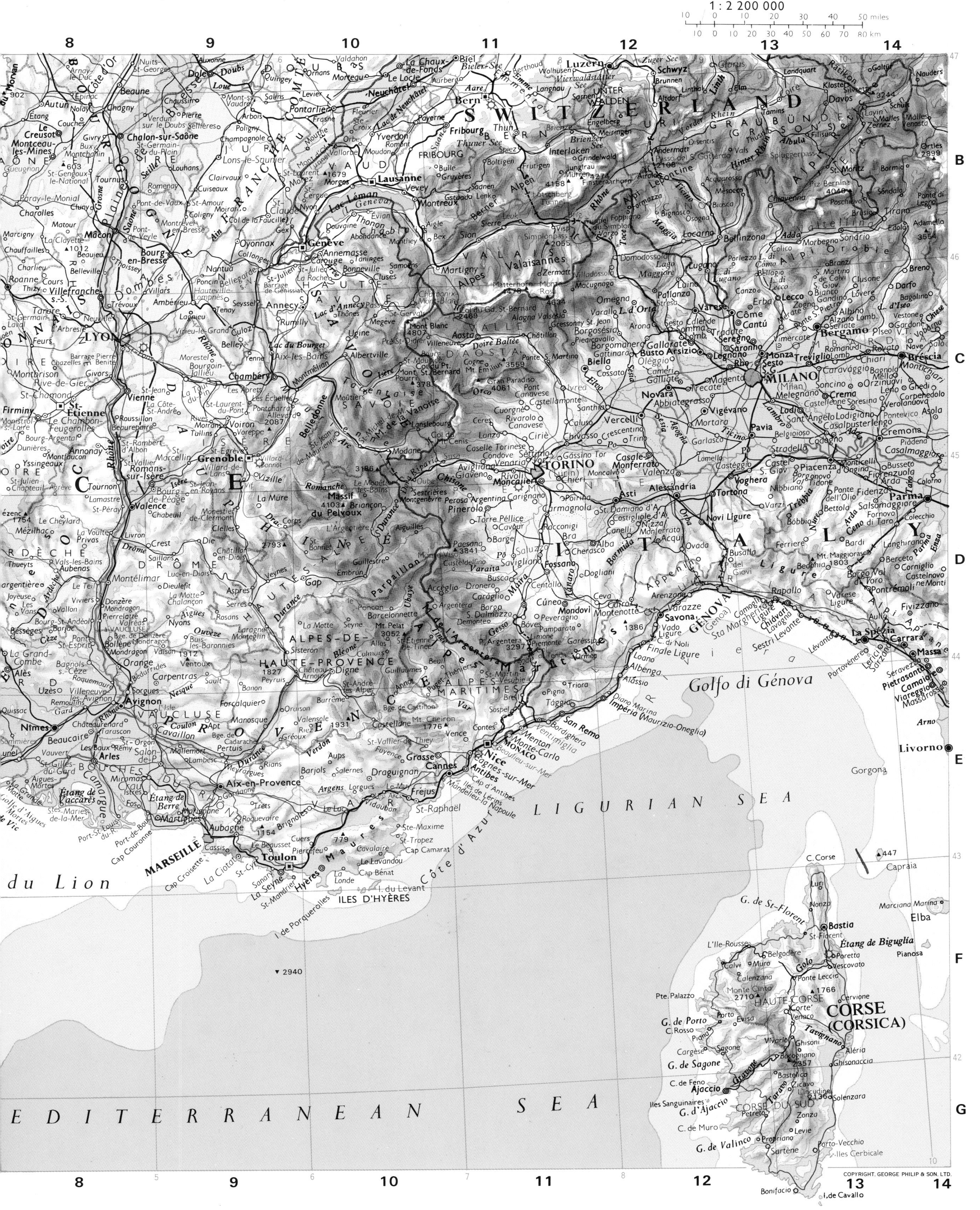

1 : 2 200 000
10 0 10 20 30 50 miles
10 0 10 20 30 40 50 60 70 80 km
8 9 10 11 12 13 14
B
C
D
E
F
G
SWITZERLAND
ITALY
LIGURIAN SEA
MEDITERRANEAN SEA
Golfo di Génova
du Lion
CORSE (CORSICA)
HAUTE-CORSE
CORSE-DU-SUD
ILES D'HYÈRES
ALPES-DE-HAUTE-PROVENCE
ALPES-MARITIMES
VAUCLUSE
PROVENCE
SAVOIE
HAUTE-SAVOIE
DRÔME
ISÈRE
VAUD
FRIBOURG
VALAIS
JURA
LYON
Genève
Lausanne
Bern
Luzern
Grenoble
Chambéry
Annecy
Valence
Avignon
Nîmes
Arles
Aix-en-Provence
MARSEILLE
Toulon
Nice
Cannes
Antibes
Monaco
Monte-Carlo
San Remo
Impéria
Savona
GENOVA (Genoa)
La Spezia
TORINO (Turin)
MILANO (Milan)
Novara
Pavia
Alessandria
Asti
Cúneo
Bergamo
Brescia
Cremona
Parma
Piacenza
Como
Lugano
Bellinzona
Aosta
Mont Blanc 4807
Matterhorn 4478
Gran Paradiso 4061
Massif du Pelvoux
Ajaccio
Bastia
Corte
Calvi
Porto-Vecchio
Bonifacio
Livorno
Elba
Capraia
Gorgona
Massa
Carrara
Saint-Étienne
Villefranche-s.-S.
Mâcon
Chalon-sur-Saône
Bourg-en-Bresse

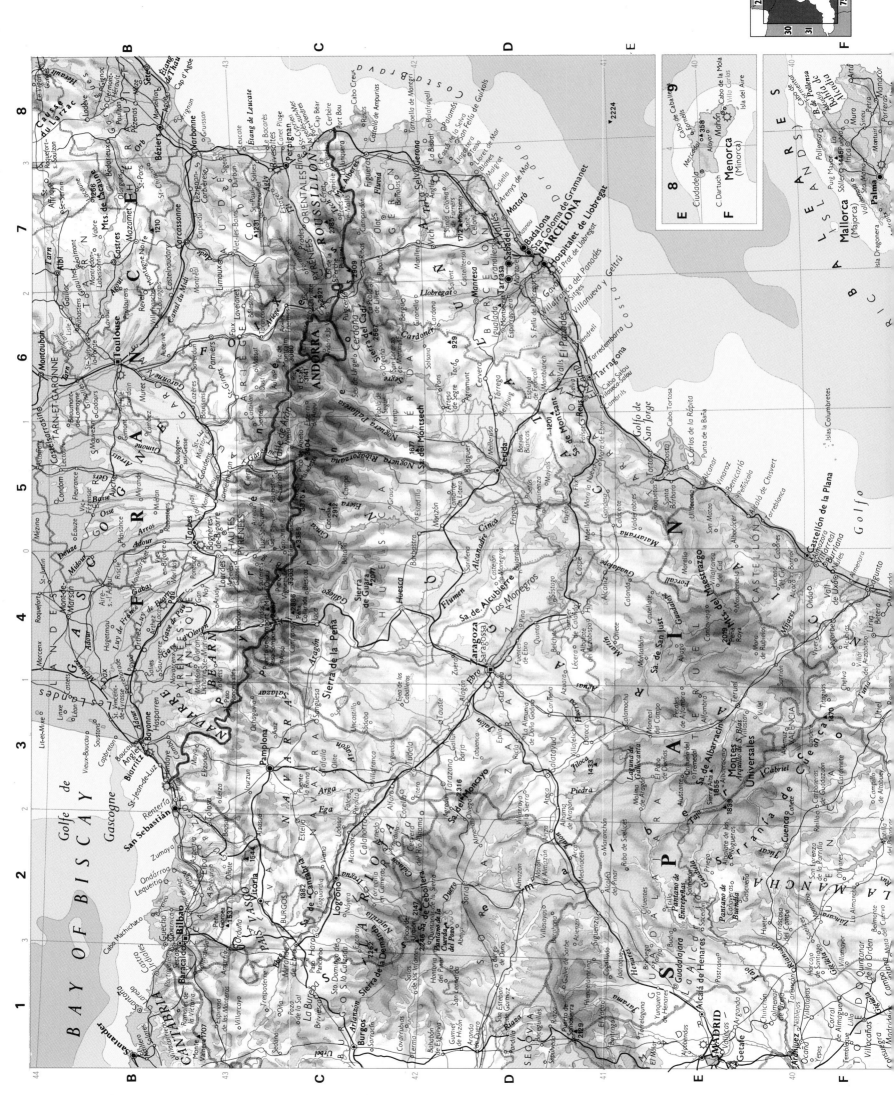

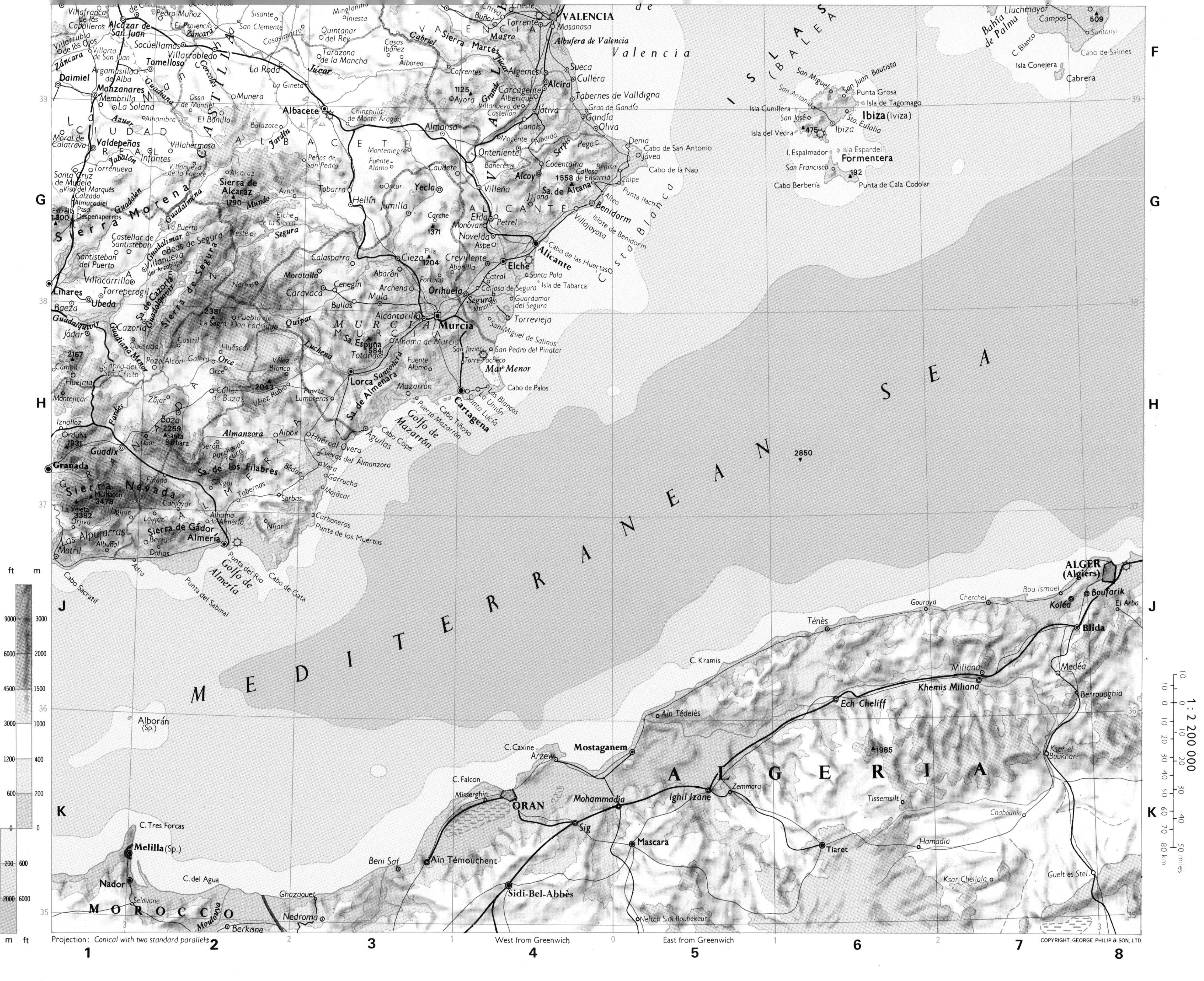

1 : 2 200 000

10   10   20   30   40   50 miles
10 0 10 20 30 40 50 60 70 80 km

Projection: Conical with two standard parallels

East from Greenwich

West from Greenwich

F G H J K

8 7 6 5 4 3 2 1

ALGER (Algiers)
Boufarik
El Arba
Blida
Koléa
Bou Ismael
Medéa
Berrouaghia
Ksar el Boukhari
Cherchel
Miliana
Khemis Miliana
Hamadia
Gouraya
Ech Cheliff
Tissemsilt
Ténès
C. Kramis
1985
Tiaret
C. Caxine
Arzeu
Mostaganem
Ighil Izane
Zemmora
Mascara
Mohammadia
Sig
ORAN
Sidi-Bel-Abbès
C. Falcon
Arzew
Beni Saf
Aïn Témouchent
Ghazaouet
Nedroma
Berkane
C. Tres Forcas
Melilla (Sp.)
Nador
C. del Agua

A L G E R I A

M O R O C C O

M E D I T E R R A N E A N   S E A

B A L E A R I C   I S L A N D S

Ibiza (Iviza)
Formentera
San Antonio
San José
Isla del Vedra
Cabo Berbería
Punta de Cala Codolar
I. Espalmador
San Francisco
Isla Conejera
Cabrera
Cabo de Salinas
Cabo Blanco
Campos
Lluchmayor
Bahía de Palma

Valencia

VALENCIA
Torrente
Sueca
Cullera
Játiva
Alcira
Gandía
Denia
Jávea
Cabo de San Antonio
Cabo de la Nao
Benidorm
Villajoyosa
Alicante
Elche
Santa Pola
Torrevieja
Mar Menor
Cartagena
Golfo de Mazarrón
Cabo de Palos
Cabo de Gata
Golfo de Almería
Almería
Sierra Nevada
Mulhacén 3478
Granada
Guadix
Sierra de Gádor
Albolote
Motril
Adra

2850

192

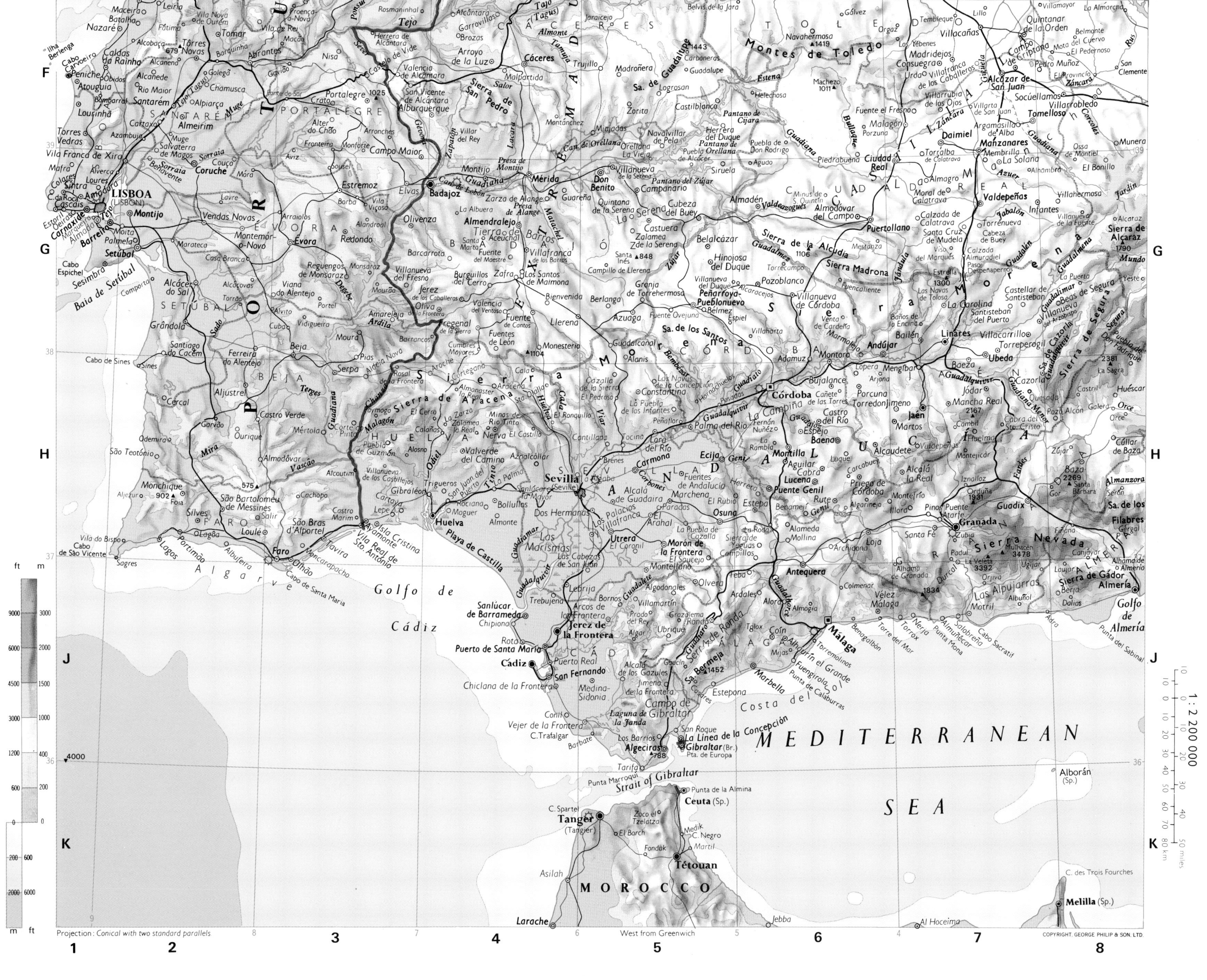
1 : 2 200 000
10 0 10 20 30 40 50 miles
10 0 10 20 30 40 50 60 70 80 km
MEDITERRANEAN
SEA
Golfo de Cádiz
Algarve
Costa del Sol
Strait of Gibraltar
MOROCCO
Montes de Toledo
Sierra Nevada
Sierra Madrona
Sierra de la Alcudia
Campo de Gibraltar
Playa de Castilla
Las Marismas
LISBOA (LISBON)
Setúbal
Évora
Badajoz
Mérida
Cáceres
Ciudad Real
Puertollano
Sevilla
Córdoba
Granada
Málaga
Jaén
Linares
Úbeda
Almería
Golfo de Almería
Huelva
Cádiz
Jerez de la Frontera
Puerto de Santa María
San Fernando
Algeciras
Gibraltar (Br.)
La Línea de la Concepción
Marbella
Antequera
Faro
Ceuta (Sp.)
Tanger (Tangier)
Tétouan
Larache
Melilla (Sp.)
Alborán (Sp.)
West from Greenwich
Projection: Conical with two standard parallels
COPYRIGHT, GEORGE PHILIP & SON, LTD.
ft m
9000 3000
6000 2000
4500 1500
3000 1000
1200 400
600 200
0 0
200 600
2000 6000
m ft

SWITZERLAND

FRANCHE-COMTÉ

SAVOIE

DAUPHINÉ

PROVENCE

VAL D'AOSTA

PIEMONTE

LOMBARDIA

EMILIA

TOSCANA

Milano (Milan)
Torino (Turin)
Genova (Genoa)
Lyon (Lyons)
Marseille (Marseilles)
Grenoble
Bern
Luzern
Lausanne
Genève (Geneva)
Livorno (Leghorn)
Parma
Reggio
Modéna
Brescia
Bergamo
Monza
Cremona
Mántova
Piacenza
Pavia
Novara
Vercelli
Asti
Alessandria
Cúneo
La Spezia
Massa
Carrara
Pisa
Lucca
Pistoia
Toulon
Nice
Cannes
Monaco
Monte Carlo
Aix-en-Provence
Avignon
Valence
Vienne
Chambéry
Annecy
Aosta

L I G U R I A N   S E A

Golfo di Génova

C O R S E
(C O R S I C A)

HAUTE-CORSE
CORSE-DU-SUD

Bastia
Ajaccio
Elba
Montecristo
Pianosa
Capraia
Gorgona

Arcipelago Toscano

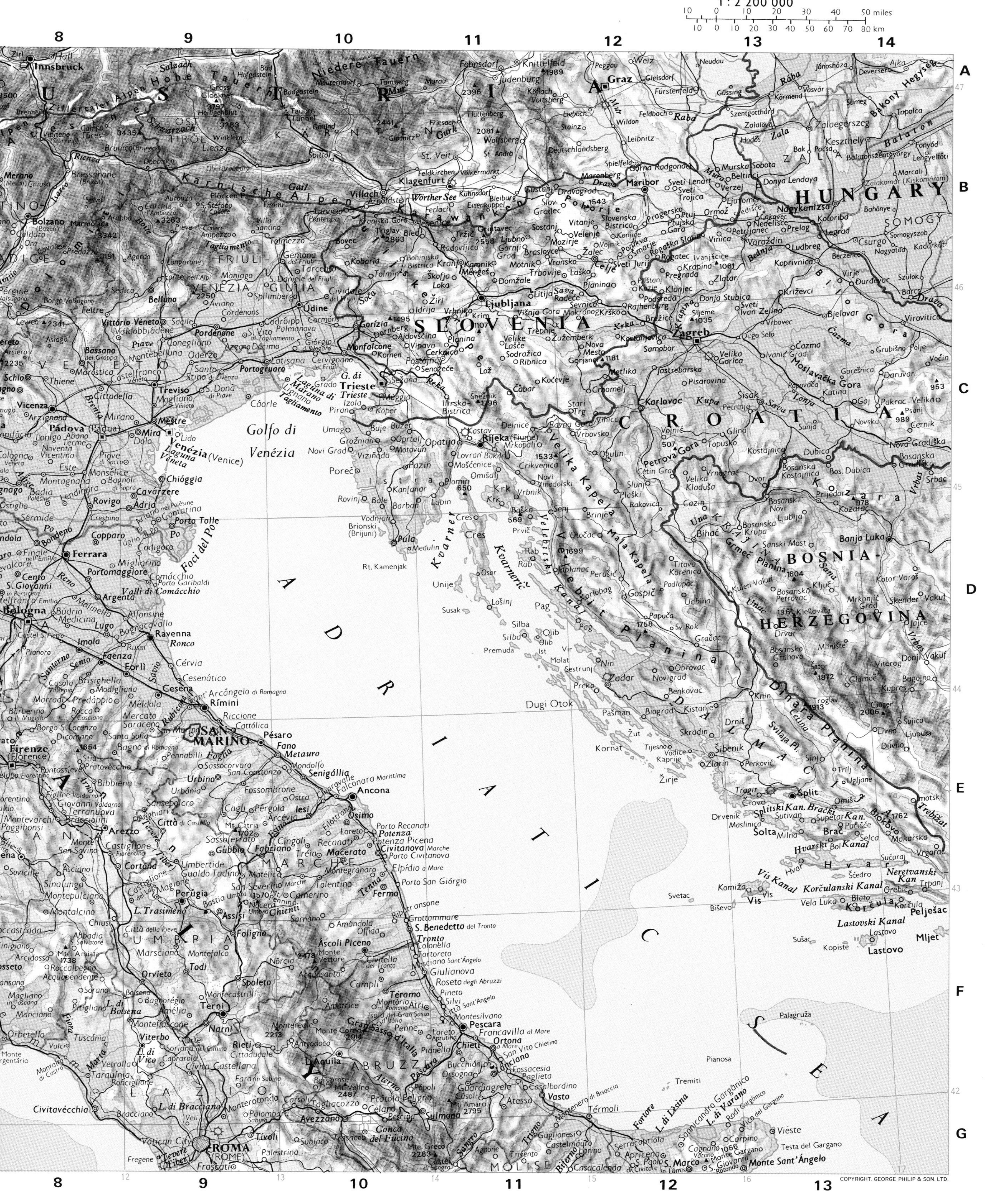
1 : 2 200 000
10 0 10 20 30 40 50 miles
10 0 10 20 30 40 50 60 70 80 km
8 9 10 11 12 13 14
A B C D E F G
AUSTRIA
SLOVENIA
CROATIA
HUNGARY
BOSNIA-HERZEGOVINA
ITALIA
ADRIATIC SEA
Golfo di Venézia
SAN MARINO
Innsbruck
Graz
Maribor
Klagenfurt
Villach
Ljubljana
Zagreb
Karlovac
Rijeka (Fiume)
Trieste
Udine
Venézia (Venice)
Pádova (Padua)
Vicenza
Treviso
Verona
Bolzano
Ferrara
Bologna
Ravenna
Rímini
Pésaro
Ancona
Firenze (Florence)
Perúgia
Pescara
L'Aquila
ROMA (ROME)
Vatican City
Split
Zadar
Šibenik
Pula
Banja Luka
Bihać
Zalaegerszeg
Nagykanizsa
Keszthely
Balaton
Niedere Tauern
Hohe Tauern
Karnische Alpen
Karawanken
Julijske Alpe
Velebit
Dinara Planina
Kvarner
Kvarnerić
Dalmacija
Gran Sasso d'Italia
ABRUZZI
MARCHE
UMBRIA
LAZIO
MOLISE
VENETO
FRIULI-VENEZIA GIULIA
Istra
Dugi Otok
Lastovo
Mljet
Vis
Palagruža
Tremiti
Pianosa

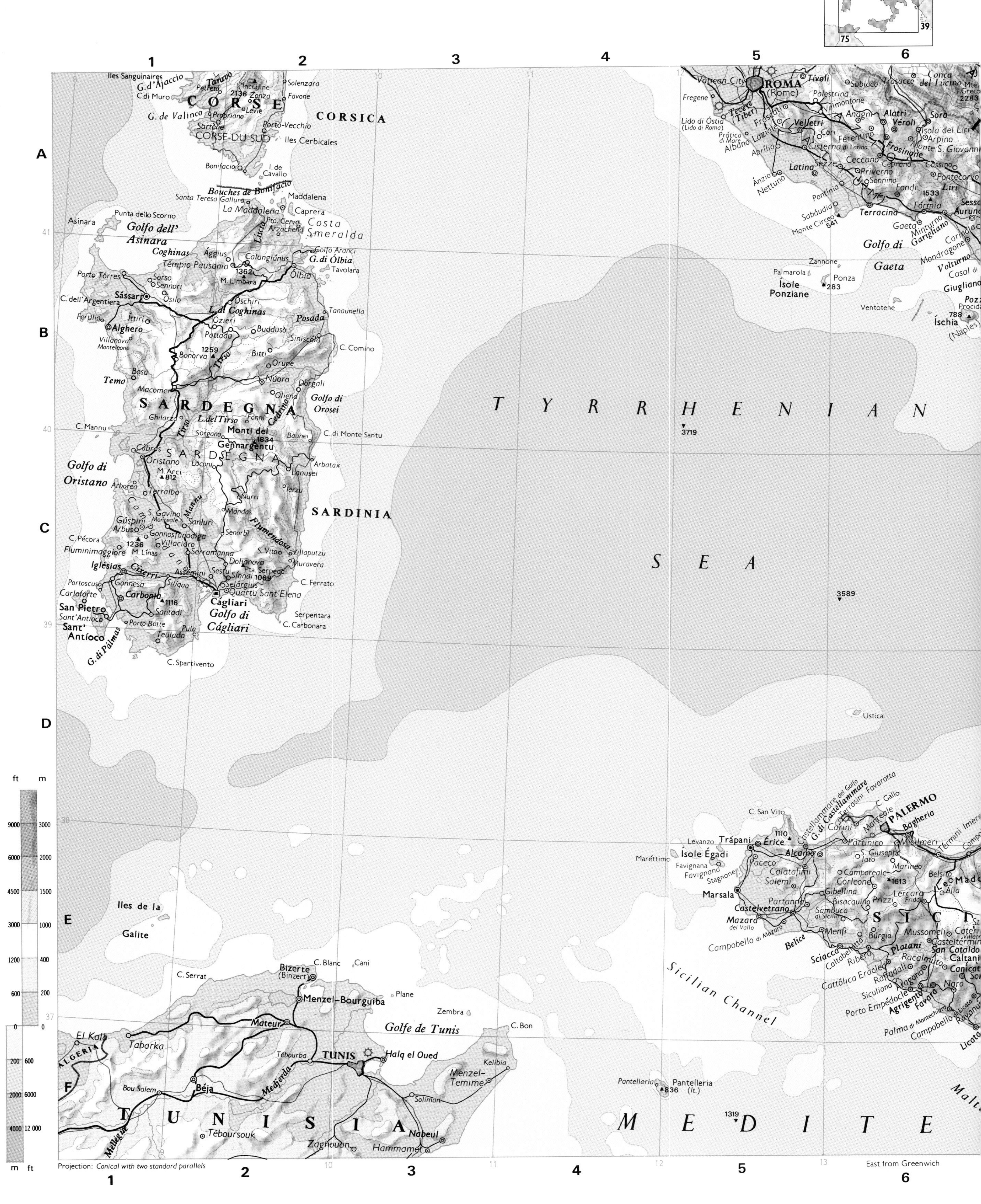

CORSE / CORSICA

Iles Sanguinaires
G. d'Ajaccio
Petreto
Taravo
Tavera
2136 Zonza
Levie
Solenzara
Favone
C. di Muro
G. de Valinco
Propriano
Sartène
Porto-Vecchio
CORSE-DU-SUD
Iles Cerbicales
Bonifacio
I. de Cavallo
Bouches de Bonifacio
Maddalena
Santa Teresa Gallura
Caprera
Punta dello Scorno
La Maddalena
Pto. Cervo
Arzachena
Costa Smeralda

Asinara
Golfo dell' Asinara
Coghinas
Ággius
Calangiánus
Golfo Aranci
G. di Ólbia

Porto Tórres
Sorso
Sennori
Tempio Pausánia
1362
M. Limbara
Ólbia
Tavolara

Sássari
Ósilo
Oschiri
Buddusò
Posada
Tanaunella

Fertilia
Ittiri
L. di Coghinas
Ozieri
Siniscóla

Álghero
Villanova Monteleone
Bonorva
1259
Pattada
Bitti
Orune
C. Comino

Bosa
Temo
Macomer
Núoro
Orune
Dorgali

SARDEGNA
Ghilarza
L. del Tirso
Fonni
Oliena
Golfo di Orosei

C. Mannu
Sórgono
Monti del Gennargentu 1834
Baunei
C. di Monte Santu

Golfo di Oristano
Oristano
M. Arci 812
SARDEGNA
Láconi
Lanusei
Arbatax

Arborea
Terralba
Nurri
Jerzu

S. Gavino
Monreale
Sanluri
Mándas
Villaputzu

Gúspini
Arbus
1236
M. Línas
Serramanna
S. Vito
Muravera

Fluminimaggiore
Gonnosfanádiga
Villacidro
Dolianova
C. Ferrato

Iglésias
Siliqua
Assémini
Sestu
Sínnai 1069
C. Ferrato

Portoscuso
Gonnesa
Carbónia
Siliqua
Selárgius
Quartu Sant'Elena

Carloforte
San Pietro
Santadi 1116
Cágliari
Serpentara

Sant'Antíoco
Porto Botte
Pula
Golfo di Cágliari
C. Carbonara

Sant' Antíoco
G. di Palmas
Teulada
C. Spartivento

CORSICA
SARDINIA

TYRRHENIAN SEA

3719

3589

Ustica

ROMA (Rome)
Vatican City
Tívoli
Subiaco
Trevi
Conca del Fúcino

Fregene
Palestrina
Valmontone
Alatri
Sora
2283

Lido di Óstia (Lido di Roma)
Cori
Ferentino
Véroli
Monte S. Giovanni

Prática di Mare
Cisterna di Latina
Frosinone
Arpino

Albano Laziale
Aprília
Sezze
Ceccano
Ceprano
Pontecorvo

Ánzio
Nettuno
Latina
1533
Fondi
Liri

Pontínia
Sonnino
Sabáudia
Gaeta
Mintúrno
Aurunci

Monte Círceo 541
Terracina
Fórmia
Sessa

Zannone
Golfo di Gaeta
Volturno
Carinola

Palmarola
Ponza
Mondragone
Casal di

Ísole Ponziane
283
Giugliano

Ventotene
788 Ischia (Naples)
Prócida
Pozz

PALERMO

Castellammare del Golfo
Favarotta

C. San Vito
G. di Castellammare
Bagheria

Levanzo
Trápani
Érice 1110
Monreale
Misilmeri

Ísole Égadi
Alcamo
S. Giuseppe
Términi Imerese

Maréttimo
Favignana
Páceco
Calatafimi
Iato
Mad

Marsala
Salemi
Corleone
1613
Lércara
Friddi

Castelvetrano
Partanna
Gibellina
Bisacquino
Prizzi
Alia

Mazara del Vallo
Menfi
Sambuca di Sicília
Búrgio
SICI

Campobello di Mazara
Belice
Sciacca
Mussomeli
Cateri
Caltani

Sicilian Channel
Ribera
Platani
San Cataldo

Cáttolica Eráclea
Racalmuto
Aragona
Naro
Canica

Porto Empédocle
Agrigento
Favara
Licata

Palma di Montechiaro
Campobello di Licata
Ravanu

Pantelleria
836
Pantelleria (It.)

1319

MEDITE

Malt

TUNISIA

Iles de la Galite

Bizerte (Binzert)
C. Blanc
Cani

Menzel-Bourguiba
Plane
Zembra

Mateur
Golfe de Tunis
C. Bon

C. Serrat
El Kala
Tabarka
Tébourba
TUNIS
Halq el Oued
Kelibia

ALGERIA
Bou Salem
Béja
Medjerda
Menzel-Temime

Méliègue
Téboursouk
Soliman

Medjerda
Nabeul

TUNISIA
Zaghouan
Hammamet

ft m
9000 3000
6000 2000
4500 1500
3000 1000
1200 400
600 200
0 0
200 600
2000 6000
4000 12.000
m ft

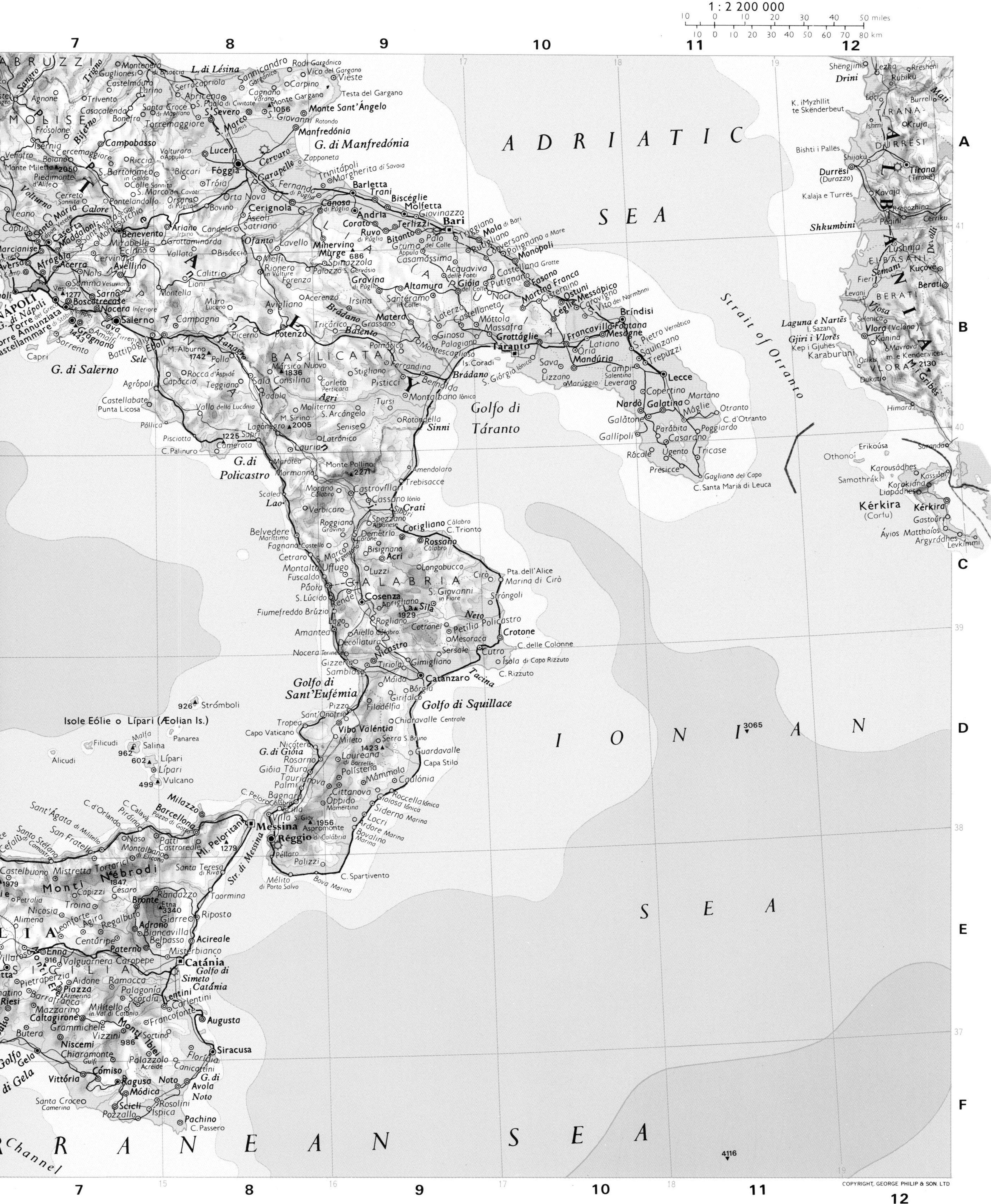

1 : 2 200 000

10   0   10   20   30   40   50 miles
10 0 10 20 30 40 50 60 70 80 km

ABRUZZI

MOLISE

A D R I A T I C

S E A

Shëngjini
Lezha Rrësheni
Rubikü
Drini
K. iMyzhllit
te Skënderbeut

T I R A N A
Durrësi
(Durazzo)
Tirana
(Tiranë)
Kavaja
Kalaja e Turrës
Shkumbini
Peqin

A L B A N I A

Bishti i Pallës
Shijaku
Ishm
Kruja
Burreli

E L B A S A N I
Lushnja Kuçovë
Fieri Semani
Levani Berati
B E R A T I
Seleniçe

Vlora (Valona)
Kanina
Oriku
m. e Kendervices
2130
Himarë

Laguna e Nartës
I. Sazan
Gjiri i Vlorës
Kep i Gjuhes
Karaburuni

V L O R A

Dukati

Strait of Otranto

Erikoúsa
Othonoí
Karousádhes
Kassiópi
Samothráki
Korakiána
Liapádhes
Kérkira
(Corfu)
Kérkira
Gastoúri
Áyios Ematthaíos
Argyrádhes
Levkimmi

G. di Manfredónia

A D R I A T I C

S E A

Golfo di
Táranto

I O N I A N

S E A

S E A

Isole Eólie o Lípari (Æolian Is.)

926 Strómboli
Filicudi Panarea
Alicudi Malfa
Salina
602 Lípari
499 Vulcano

4116

COPYRIGHT, GEORGE PHILIP & SON LTD

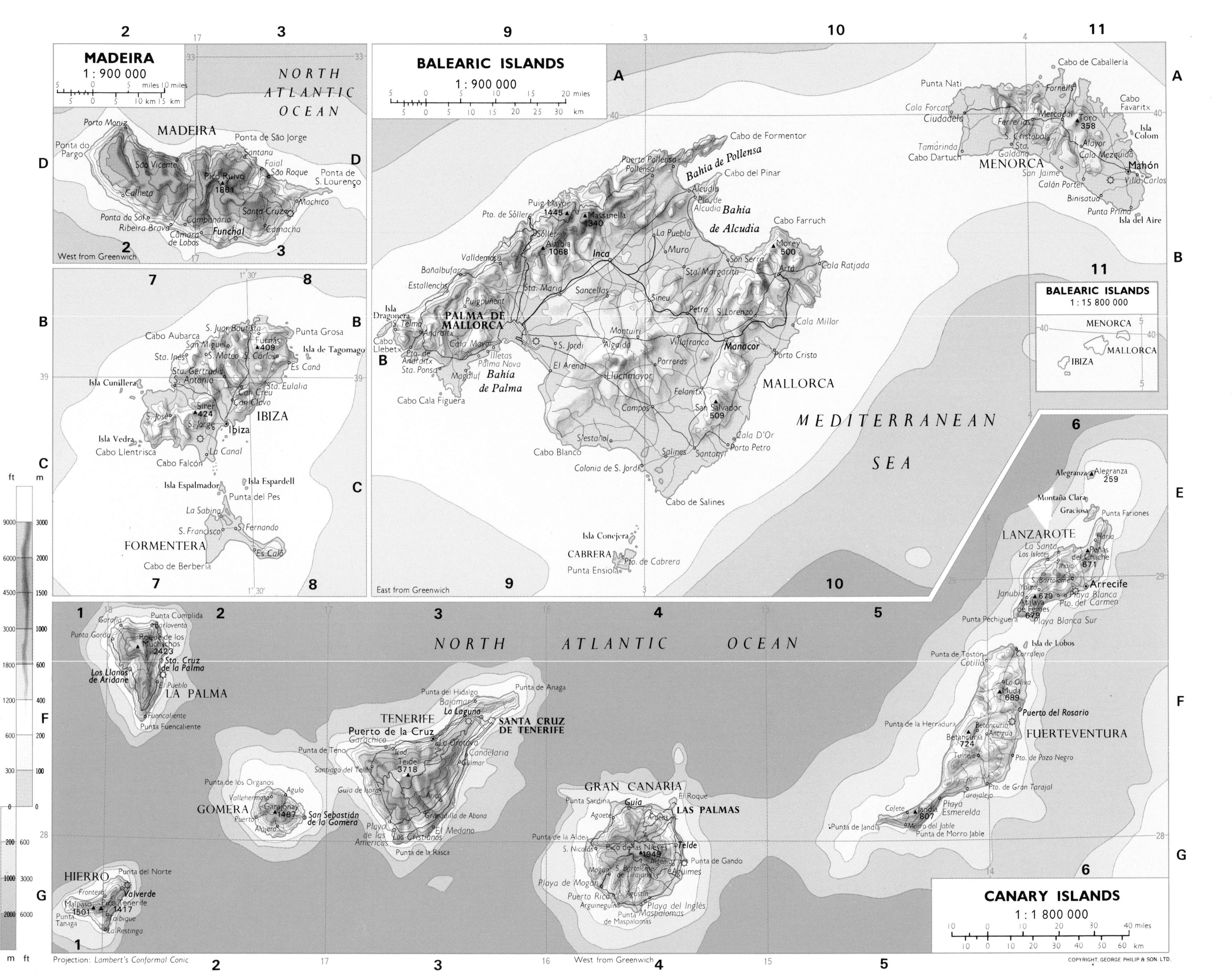

BALEARIC ISLANDS
1 : 900 000

BALEARIC ISLANDS
1 : 15 800 000

MENORCA

MALLORCA

IBIZA

MENORCA

Cabo de Caballería
Punta Nati
Cala Forcat
Ciudadela
Tamarinda
Cabo Dartuch
Fornells
Ferrerías
Sta.
Galdana
Mercadal
Toro
358
Alayor
Cabo Mezquida
Cabo Primo
Mahón
Villa Carlos
Isla Colom
Cabo Favaritx
Isla del Aire
Punta Prima
San Jaime
Calán Porter
Binisalú

MALLORCA

MEDITERRANEAN   SEA

Cabo de Formentor
Cabo de Pollensa
Cabo del Pinar
Bahía de Pollensa
Puerto Pollensa
Pollensa
Pto. de Sóller
Sóller
Puig Mayor
1445
Alfabía
1340
Inca
Cabo de Formentor
Morey
500
Artá
San Serra
Sta. Margarita
Cala Ratjada
Cala Millor
Porto Cristo
Porto Petro
Cala D'Or
Cabo Farruch
MALLORCA
Manacor
San Lorenzo
Petra
Villafranca
San Salvador
509
Felanitx
Santany
Cabo de Salines
Cabo Blanco
Bahía
de Alcudia
Alcudia
La Puebla
Muro
Sta. María
Sineu
Montuiri
Algaida
Lluchmayor
Campos
Salines
S'Estañol
El Arenal
Colonia de S. Jordi
S. Jordi
Cabo Salinas
S. Jordi

Valldemosa
Estellenchs
Bañalbufar
Andraitx
Puigpuñent
Esporlas
S. María
Palma Nova
Magaluf
PALMA DE MALLORCA
Bahía de Palma
Cabo Cala Figuera
Isla Dragonera
Cabo de Andraitx
Sta. Ponsa
Lluebol

CABRERA
Isla Conejera
Pta. de Cabrera
Isla Ensiola
Punta Ensiola

MADEIRA
1 : 900 000

NORTH   ATLANTIC   OCEAN

MADEIRA
Ponta de São Jorge
Ponta de S. Lourenço
Porto Moniz
Ponta do Pargo
Ponta do Sol
Ribeira Brava
Câmara
de Lobos
Funchal
Pico Ruivo
1861
Santana
Faial
São Roque
Machico
Caniçal
Santa Cruz
Camacha
Calheta
São Vicente

Ponta de São Jorge

West from Greenwich

IBIZA

Cabo Aubarca
Punta Grossa
S. Juan Bautista
San Miguel
San Mateo
Sta. Inés
Sta. Gertrudis
S. Antonio
San José
San Jorge
IBIZA
Ibiza
Sta. Eulalia
S. Carlos
Isla de Tagomago
Es Caná
Isla del Pes
Punta de la Canal
Cabo Falcón
Isla Espardell
Es Calo

FORMENTERA
Isla Vedrá
Cabo Llentrisca
Isla Cunillera
Cabo de Berbería
La Sabina
S. Francisco
S. Fernando
La Canal
Isla Espalmador

CANARY ISLANDS
1 : 1 800 000

COPYRIGHT GEORGE PHILIP & SON LTD.

NORTH   ATLANTIC   OCEAN

LANZAROTE
Alegranza
Alegranza   259
Graciosa
Montaña Clara
La Santa
Los Islotes
Jameo
Haría
Arrecife
Tinajo
Janubio
Punta Pechiguera
Yaiza
Playa Blanca
Isla de Lobos

FUERTEVENTURA
Corralejo
Punta de Tostón
Cotillo
La Oliva
Tindaya
Muda
689
Puerto del Rosario
Punta de la Herradura
Betancuria
807
Tuineje
Pta. de Gran Tarajal
Colete
Pozo Negro
Esmerelda
Playa
Morro Jable
Punta del Jable
Punta de Jandía

GRAN CANARIA
Las Palmas
El Roque
Pico de las Nieves
1949
Guía
Gáldar
Agaete
Telde
Punta de Gando
Punta de la Aldea
S. Nicolás
Tejeda
Aguimes
Playa del Inglés
Puerto Rico
Maspalomas
Punta de Maspalomas

TENERIFE
Punta de Anaga
SANTA CRUZ DE TENERIFE
La Laguna
Puerto de la Cruz
Garachico
Teide
3718
Tenerife
Candelaria
Güimar
Icod
Guía de Isora
Granadilla de Abona
Playa de los Cristianos
Punta de la Rasca
El Medano

GOMERA
Punta del Hidalgo
Bajamar
Hermigua
Agulo
Vallehermoso
San Sebastián de la Gomera
1487
Chipude
Playa de Santiago

LA PALMA
Punta Cumplida
Barlovento
Roque de los Muchachos
2423
Sta. Cruz de la Palma
El Paso
Los Llanos de Aridane
Fuencaliente
Punta Fuencaliente
Punta Gorda

HIERRO
Punta del Norte
Valverde
Malpaso
1501
Frontera
Punta de la Restinga

MEDITERRANEAN
SEA

East from Greenwich

Projection: Lambert's Conformal Conic

m   ft
9000
6000
4500
3000
1800
1200
600
300
0
200
2000
6000

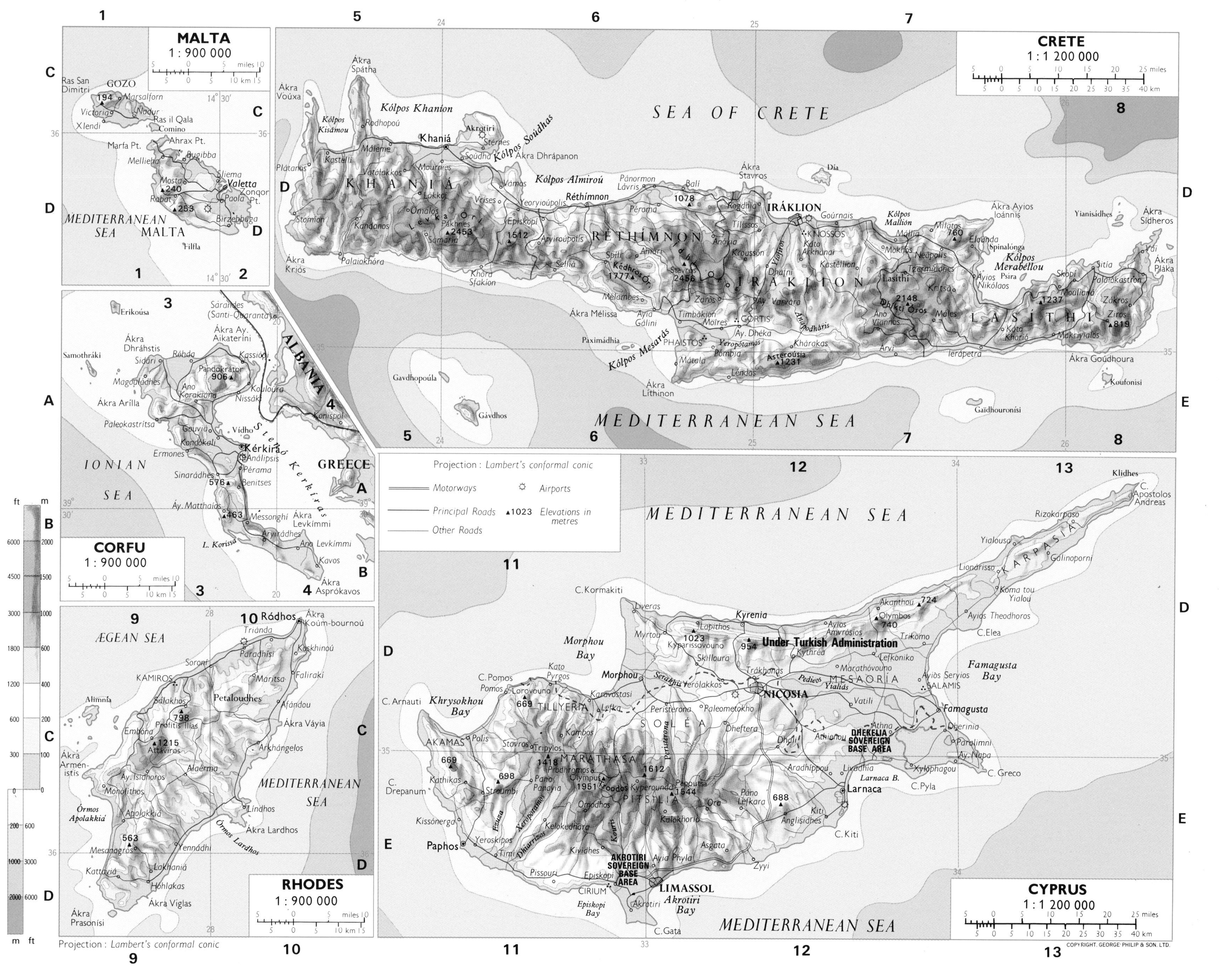
MALTA
1 : 900 000
CRETE
1 : 1 200 000
SEA OF CRETE
MEDITERRANEAN SEA
CORFU
1 : 900 000
IONIAN SEA
ALBANIA
GREECE
RHODES
1 : 900 000
ÆGEAN SEA
CYPRUS
1 : 1 200 000
MEDITERRANEAN SEA
Projection : Lambert's conformal conic
Motorways
Principal Roads
Other Roads
Airports
Elevations in metres
Under Turkish Administration
AKROTIRI SOVEREIGN BASE AREA
DHEKELIA SOVEREIGN BASE AREA
COPYRIGHT, GEORGE PHILIP & SON, LTD.

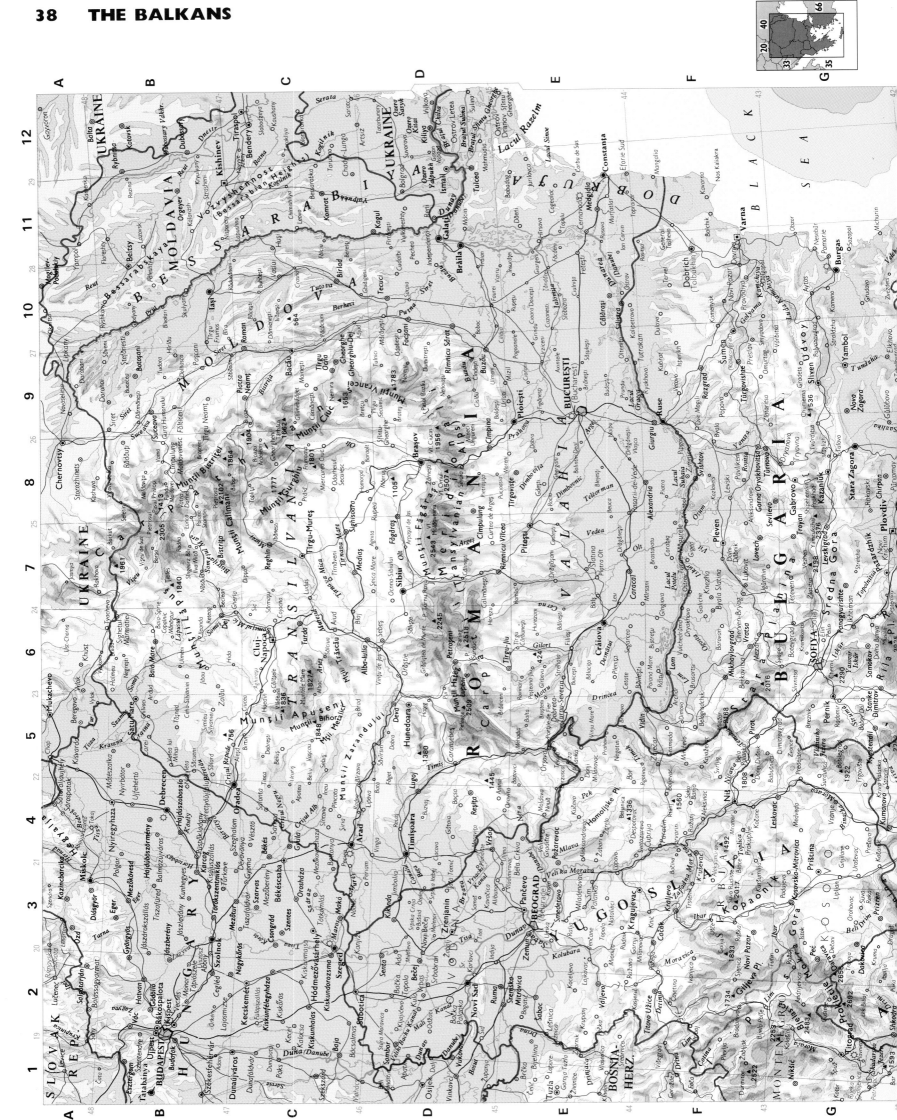

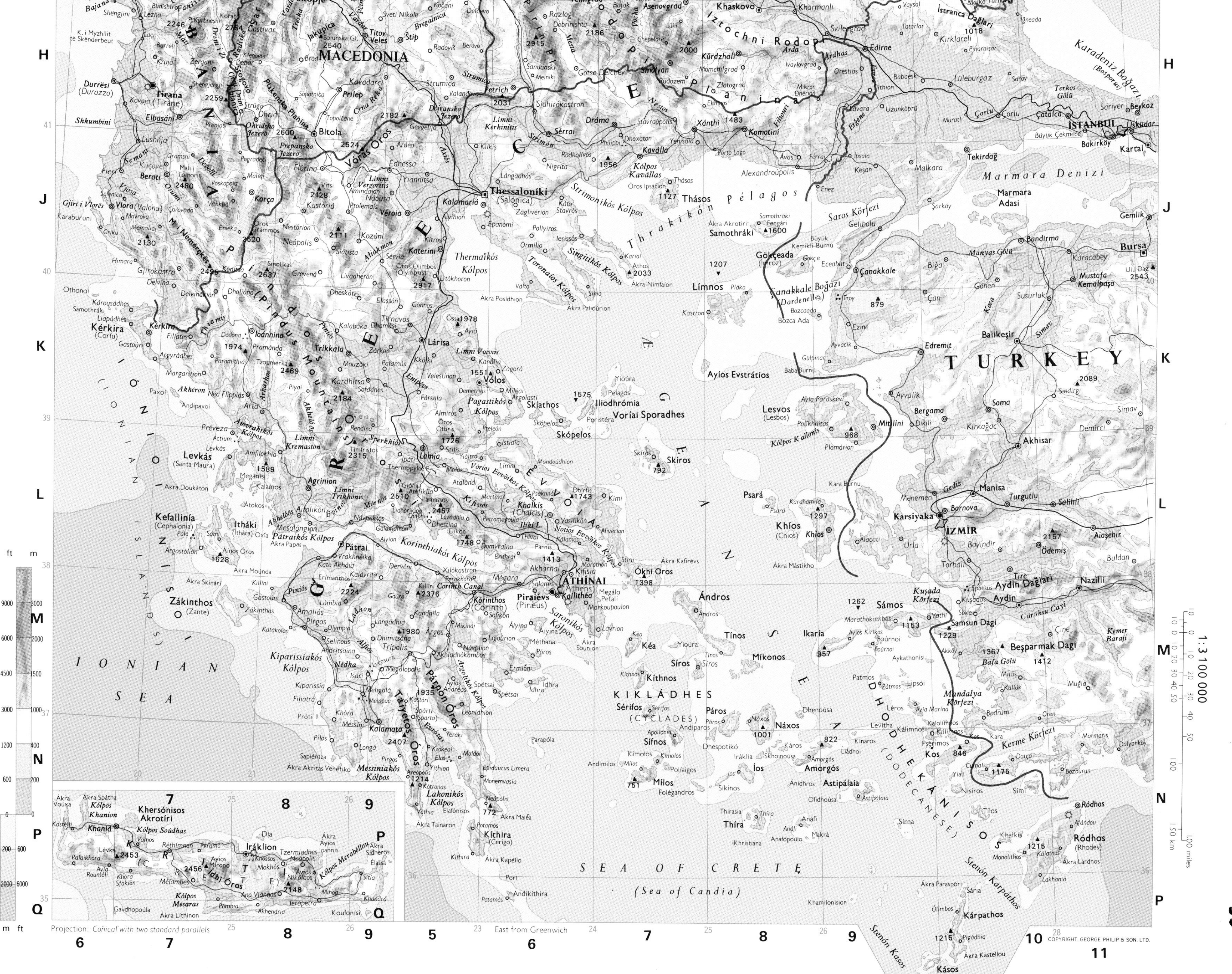

1 : 3 100 000

10   0   10   20   30   40   50   100 miles
10 0 10 20 30 40 50   100   150 km

Projection: Conical with two standard parallels

COPYRIGHT GEORGE PHILIP & SON LTD.

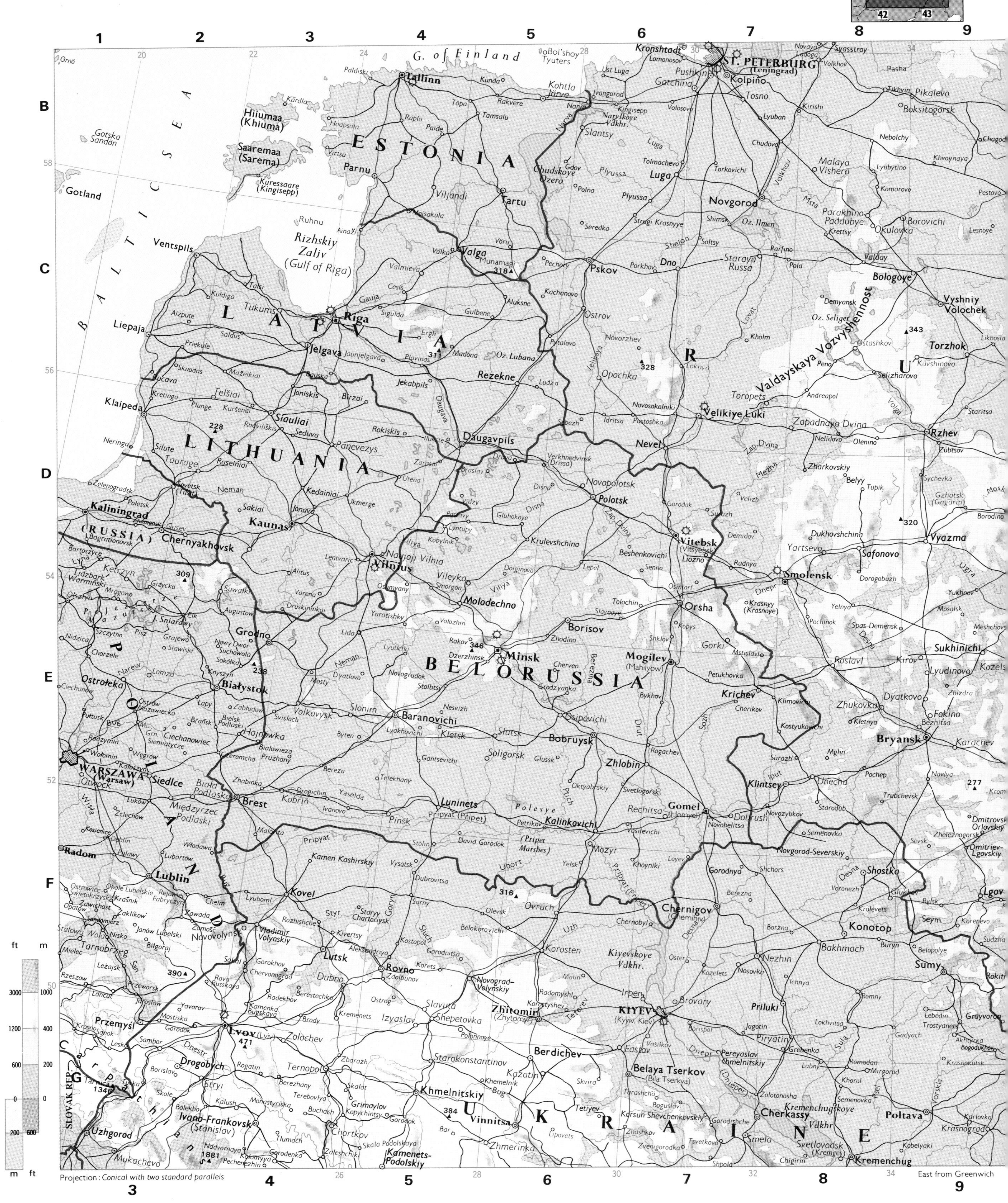

East from Greenwich

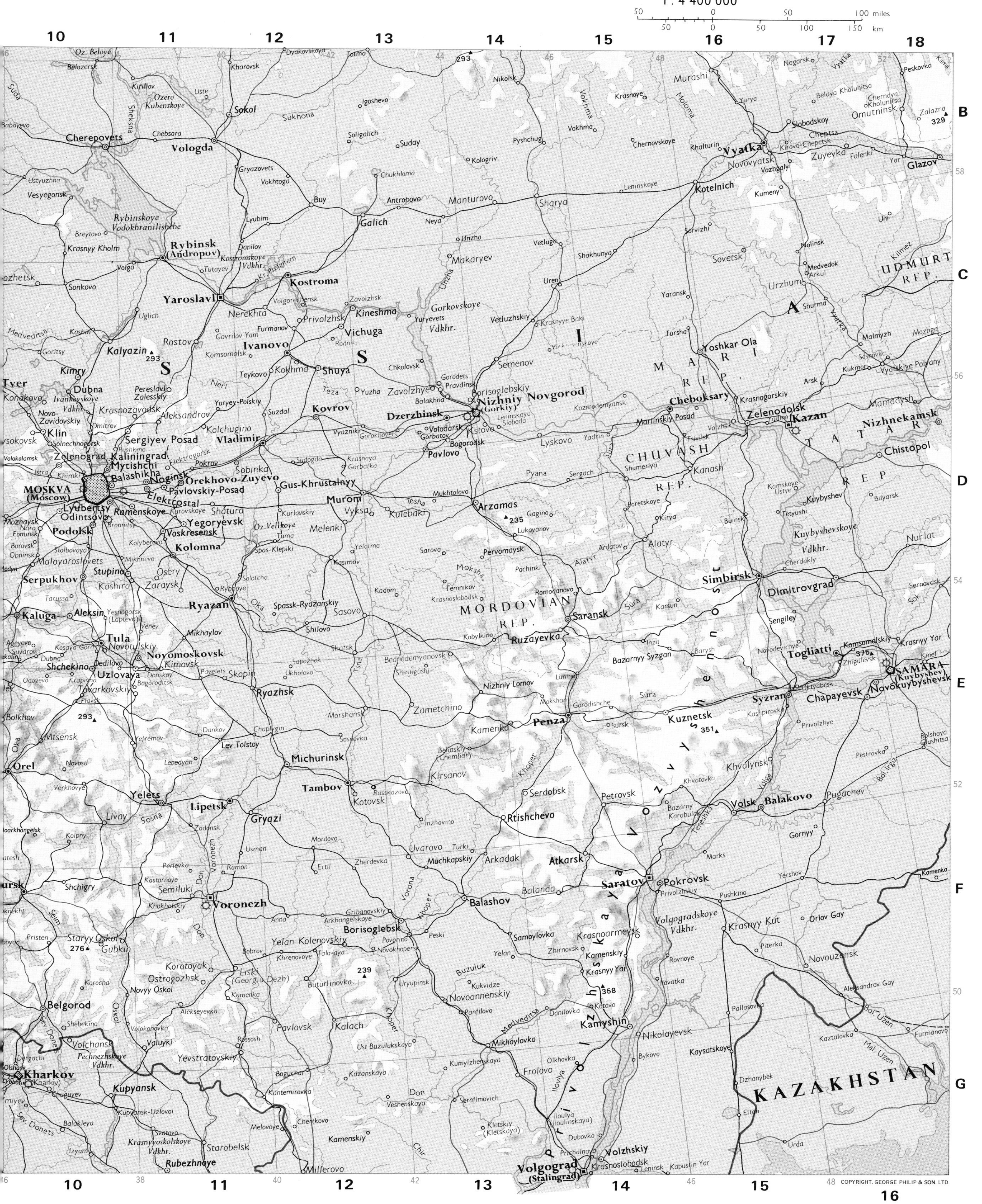
1 : 4 400 000
50 0 50 100 miles
50 0 50 100 150 km
10 11 12 13 14 15 16 17 18
B C D E F G
Cherepovets
Vologda
Sokol
Belozersk
Kirillov
Ozero Kubenskoye
Sukhona
Igoshevo
Soligalich
Suday
Kologriv
Nikolsk
Vokhma
Vokhma
Krasnoye
Pyshchug
Chernovskoye
Murashi
Moloma
Khalturin
Vyatka
Novovyatsk
Slobodskoy
Belaya Kholunitsa
Omutninsk
Zalazna
329
Kirovo-Chepetsk
Zuyevka
Falenki
Glazov
Peskovka
Kama
Yurya
Nagorsk
Vyatka
Chebsara
Ustyuzhna
Vesyegonsk
Gryazovets
Vokhtoga
Chukhloma
Buy
Antropovo
Manturovo
Sharya
Leninskoye
Kotelnich
Kumeny
Rybinskoye Vodokhranilishche
Breytovo
Krasnyy Kholm
Lyubim
Galich
Neya
Unzha
Vetluga
Shakhunya
Sovetsk
Nolinsk
Medvedok
Arkul
Kilmez
UDMURT REP.
Rybinsk (Andropov)
Danilov
Kostromskoye Vdkhr.
Tutayev
Volga
Sonkovo
Kostroma
Yaroslavl
Makaryev
Uren
Yaransk
Urzhum
Shurma
Uglich
Nerekhta
Zavolzhsk
Kineshma
Gorkovskoye Vdkhr.
Yuryevets
Privolzhsk
Vichuga
Vetluzhskiy
Krasnyye Baki
Tursha
Yoshkar Ola
Malmyzh
Mozhga
Medveditsa
Kashin
Kalyazin
293
Rostov
Gavrilov Yam
Furmanov
Ivanovo
Rodniki
Komsomolsk
Teykovo
Kokhma
Shuya
Chkolovsk
Gorodets
Pravdinsk
Semenov
MARI REP.
Kukmor
Vyatskiye Polyany
Arsk
Kimry
Dubna
Tver
Konakovo
Ivankovskoye Vdkhr.
Pereslavl Zalesskiy
Neri
Yuryev-Polskiy
Teza
Yuzha
Zavolzhye
Balakhna
Borisoglebskiy
Nizhniy Novgorod (Gorkiy)
Kozmodemyansk
Cheboksary
Krasnogorskiy
Zelenodolsk
Kazan
Mamadysh
Nizhnekamsk
Novo-Zavidovskiy
Krasnozavodsk
Aleksandrov
Suzdal
Kovrov
Dzerzhinsk
Leninskaya Sloboda
Marlinskiy Posad
Volzhsk
Klin
Dmitrov
Kolchugino
Sergiyev Posad
Vladimir
Vyazniki
Gorokhovets
Volodarsk
Gorbatov
Kstovo
Bogorodsk
Lyskovo
Yadrin
Tsivilsk
TATAR REP.
Volokolamsk
Solnechnogorsk
Zelenograd
Kaliningrad
Pushkino
Mytishchi
Elektrogorsk
Pokrov
Sobinka
Sudogda
Krasnaya Gorbatka
Pavlovo
Pyana
Sergach
Shumerlya
CHUVASH REP.
Kanash
Chistopol
Istra
Khimki
Balashikha
Noginsk
Orekhovo-Zuyevo
Pavlovskiy-Posad
Gus-Khrustalnyy
Mukhtolovo
MOSKVA (Moscow)
Elektrostal
Shatura
Murom
Tesha
Arzamas
Kamskoye Ustye
Kuybyshev
Bilyarsk
Mozhaysk
Lyubertsy
Ramenskoye
Odintsovo
Kurovskoye
Kurlovskiy
Vyksa
Kulebaki
Poretskoye
Naro Fominsk
Bronnitsy
Yegoryevsk
Oz. Velikoye
Melenki
235
Gagino
Kirya
Tetyushi
Buinsk
Podolsk
Voskresensk
Tuma
Lukoyanov
Kuybyshevskoye Vdkhr.
Nurlat
Borovsk
Obninsk
Kolyberovo
Kolomna
Spas-Klepiki
Yelatma
Sarova
Pervomaysk
Ardatov
Alatyr
Maloyaroslavets
Mikhnevo
Kasimov
Cherdakly
Serpukhov
Stupino
Osery
Zaraysk
Splotcha
Moksha
Pachinki
Alatyr
Simbirsk
Dimitrovgrad
Kashira
Rybnoye
Kadom
Temnikov
Krasnoslobodsk
Romodanovo
Sernovdsk
Sok
Tarussa
Ryazan
Oka
Spassk-Ryazanskiy
MORDOVIAN REP.
Saransk
Sura
Karsun
Kaluga
Aleksin
Yesnogorsk (Laptevo)
Sasovo
Venev
Shilovo
Sengiley
Tula
Mikhaylov
Novotulskiy
Kobylkino
Ruzayevka
Inza
Krasnyy Yar
Kosaya Gora
Suvorov
Novomoskovsk
Shatsk
Novodevichye
Komsomolskiy
Dubna
Shchekino
Dedilovo
Kimovsk
Sapozhok
Bednodemyanovsk
Bazarnyy Syzgan
Barysh
Togliatti
375
Zhigulevsk
SAMARA (Kuybyshev)
Kinel
Uzlovaya
Pavelets
Skopin
Ukholovo
Shiringushi
Lunino
Odoyevo
Krapivna
Donskoy
Bogoroditsk
Tsna
Nizhniy Lomov
Oktyabrsk
Chapayevsk
Novokuybyshevsk
Tovarkovskiy
Ryazhsk
Sura
Syzran
Plavsk
Morshansk
Zametchino
Mokshan
Gorodishche
Kuznetsk
Kashpirovka
293
Bolkhov
Kamenka
Penza
Sursk
351
Mtsensk
Dankov
Chaplygin
Privolzhye
Yefremov
Sosnovka
Lev Tolstoy
Belinskiy (Chembar)
Bolshaya Glushitsa
Oka
Novosil
Lebedyan
Michurinsk
Pestravka
Orel
Kirsanov
Khoper
Khvalynsk
Bol. Irgiz
Verkhovye
Tambov
Rasskazovo
Serdobsk
Khvatovka
Yelets
Kotovsk
Petrovsk
Pugachev
Livny
Lipetsk
Bazarny Karabulak
Volsk
Balakovo
Sosna
Inzhavino
Rtishchevo
Terechka
Volga
Arkhangelsk
Zadonsk
Gryazi
Kolpny
Mordovo
Gornyy
Usman
Uvarovo
Turki
Muchkapskiy
Arkadak
Atkarsk
Voronezh
Ertil
Zherdevka
Marks
Perlevka
Ramon
Don
Vorona
Kamenka
Kastornoye
Semiluki
Balanda
Saratov
Pokrovsk
Yershov
Kursk
Shchigry
Voronezh
Khokholskiy
Balashov
Privolzhskiy
Pushkino
Anna
Gribanovskiy
Arkhangelskoye
Khoper
Volgogradskoye Vdkhr.
Orlov Gay
Seim
Pristen
Staryy Oskol
Gubkin
276
Borisoglebsk
Povorino
Novokhopersk
Peski
Samoylovka
Krasnoarmeysk
Krasnyy Kut
Yelan-Kolenovskiy
Talovaya
Zhirnovsk
Kamenskiy
Bobrov
Khrenovoye
Yelan
Rovnoye
Piterka
Novouzensk
Korotoyak
Liski (Georgiu-Dezh)
239
Krasnyy Yar
Ostrogozhsk
Buturlinovka
Uryupinsk
Buzuluk
Kukvidze
Lavatka
358
Korocha
Novyy Oskol
Kamenka
Novoannenskiy
Aleksandrov Gay
Belgorod
Oskol
Alekseyevka
Panfilovo
Kotovo
Pallasovka
Shebekino
Volokonovka
Medveditsa
Danilovka
Kamyshin
Bol. Uzen
Sev. Donets
Valuyki
Rossosh
Pavlovsk
Kalach
Nikolayevsk
Furmanovo
Volchansk
Pechnezhskoye Vdkhr.
Khoper
Mikhaylovka
Kaztalovka
Dergachi
Olshany
Kharkov
Yevstratovskiy
Ust Buzulukskaya
Bykovo
Kaysatskoye
Mal. Uzen
Kumylzhenskaya
Olkhovka
Kupyansk
Boguchar
Kazanskaya
Frolovo
Dzhanybek
KAZAKHSTAN
Chuguyev
Kantemirovka
Don
Ilovlya
Veshenskaya
Serafimovich
Kupyansk-Uzlovoi
Ilovlya (Ilovlinskaya)
Elton
Balakleya
Svatovo
Chertkovo
Kletskiy (Kletskaya)
Izyum
Krasnyyoskolskoye Vdkhr.
Melovoye
Dubovka
Kamenskiy
Chir
Starobelsk
Urda
Prichalnaya
Volzhskiy
Rubezhnoye
Millerovo
Volgograd (Stalingrad)
Krasnoslobodsk
Leninsk
Kapustin Yar
RUSSIA
Privolzhskaya Vozvyshennost
58 56 54 52 50
38 40 42 44 46 48 50 52
COPYRIGHT, GEORGE PHILIP & SON, LTD.

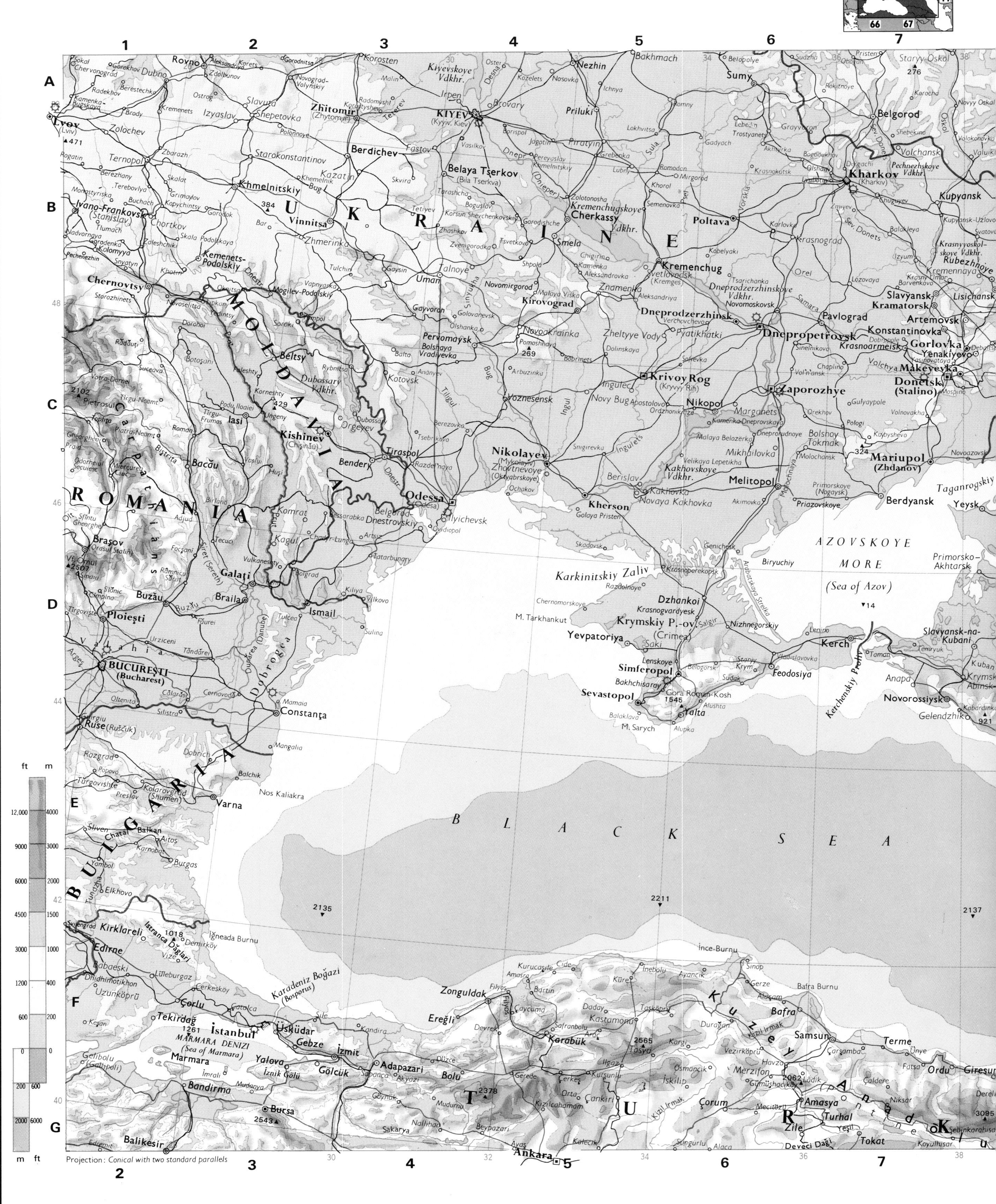
40
41
38
44
66
67
1
2
3
4
5
6
7
A
B
C
D
E
F
G
U K R A I N E
MOLDAVIA
ROMANIA
BULGARIA
T U R K E Y
BLACK SEA
AZOVSKOYE MORE
(Sea of Azov)
Lvov
(Lviv)
Rovno
Dubno
Kremenets
Izyaslav
Slavuta
Shepetovka
Zhitomir
(Zhytomir)
Korosten
Kiyevskoye Vdkhr.
KIYEV
(Kyyiv, Kiev)
Brovary
Nezhin
Bakhmach
Priluki
Sumy
Belgorod
Kharkov
(Kharkiv)
Volchansk
Kupyansk
Zolochev
Ternopol
Starokonstantinov
Berdichev
Fastov
Belaya Tserkov
(Bila Tserkva)
Khmelnitskiy
Vinnitsa
Ivano-Frankovsk
(Stanislav)
Kolomyya
Chortkov
Kamenets-Podolskiy
Zhmerinka
Uman
Talnoye
Smela
Cherkassy
Kremenchugskoye Vdkhr.
Kremenchug
Poltava
Krasnograd
Izyum
Rubezhnoye
Lisichansk
Slavyansk
Kramatorsk
Artemovsk
Konstantinovka
Gorlovka
Yenakiyevo
Makeyevka
Donetsk
(Stalino)
Pavlograd
Dnepropetrovsk
Dneprodzerzhinsk
Novomoskovsk
Krasnoarmeisk
Zaporozhye
Kirovograd
Novomirgorod
Pervomaysk
Chernovtsy
Mogilev-Podolskiy
Beltsy
Dubossary Vdkhr.
Kotovsk
Kishinev
(Chişinău)
Iasi
Bendery
Tiraspol
Odessa
Ilyichevsk
Belgorod-Dnestrovskiy
Voznesensk
Krivoy Rog
Nikopol
Nikolayev
(Mykolayiv)
Kherson
Kakhovka
Novaya Kakhovka
Kakhovskoye Vdkhr.
Melitopol
Mariupol
(Zhdanov)
Berdyansk
Taganrogskiy
Yeysk
Primorsko-Akhtarsk
Karkinitskiy Zaliv
Dzhankoi
Krymskiy P.-ov.
(Crimea)
Yevpatoriya
Simferopol
Sevastopol
Yalta
Feodosiya
Kerch
Kerchenskiy Proliv
Anapa
Novorossiysk
Gelendzhik
Kuban
Slavyansk-na-Kubani
Gora Roman-Kosh
1545
M. Tarkhankut
M. Sarych
Bacău
Braşov
Galaţi
Braila
Buzău
Ploieşti
BUCUREŞTI
(Bucharest)
Constanţa
Ismail
Tulcea
Ruse (Ruščuk)
Dobrich
Varna
Burgas
Yambol
Edirne
Kirklareli
Tekirdağ
İstanbul
Üsküdar
Gebze
İzmit
Karadeniz Boğazi
(Bosporus)
MARMARA DENIZI
(Sea of Marmara)
Marmara
Yalova
Bandirma
Bursa
Balikesir
Adapazari
Gölcük
Bolu
Zonguldak
Ereğli
Karabük
Kastamonu
Çankiri
Çorum
Merzifon
Amasya
Samsun
Bafra
Sinop
İnce-Burnu
Terme
Ordu
Giresun
Tokat
Turhal
Zile
Ankara
Kuzey Anadolu
2135
2211
2137
14
Projection: Conical with two standard parallels

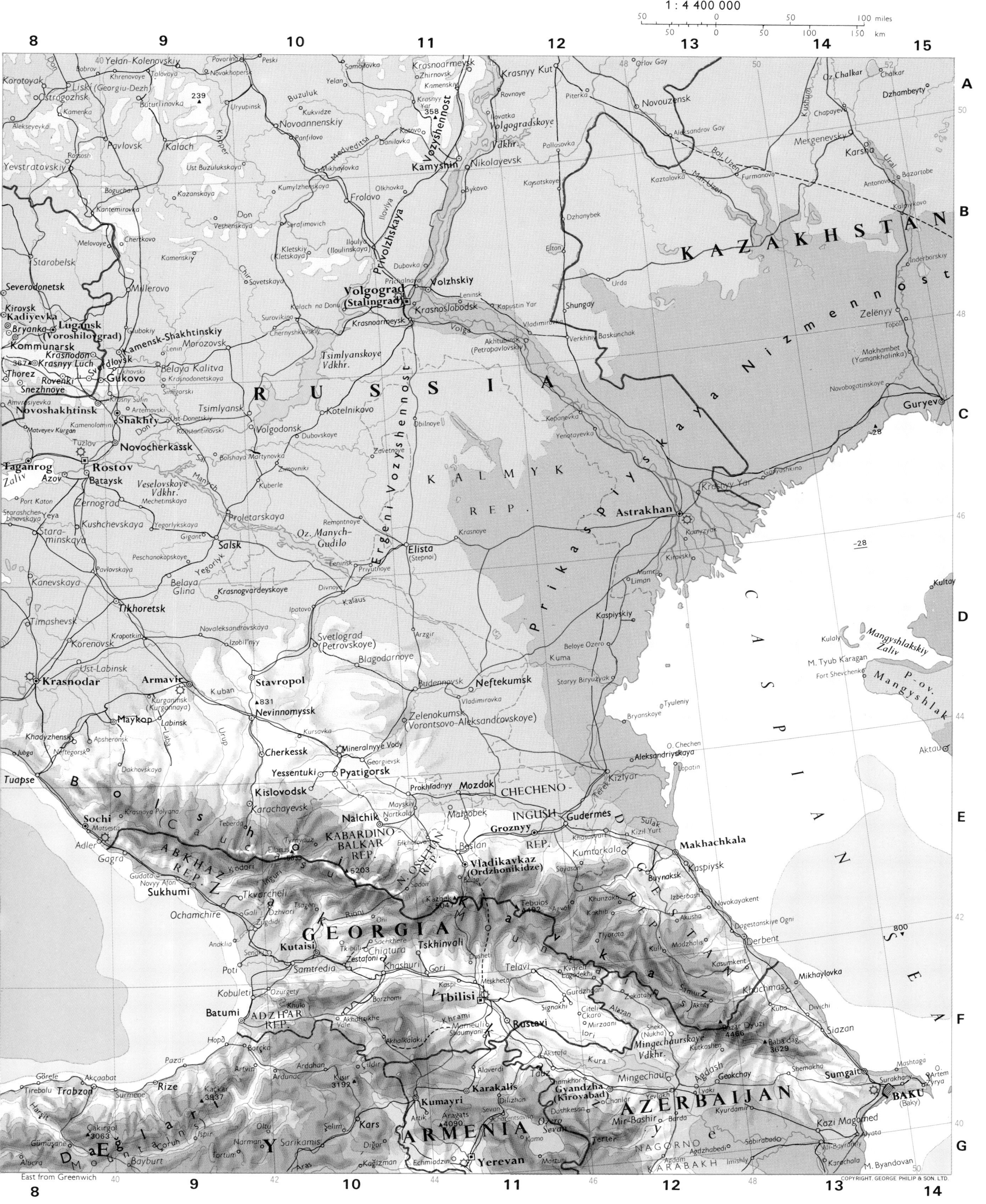
1 : 4 400 000
RUSSIA
KAZAKHSTAN
GEORGIA
ARMENIA
AZERBAIJAN
CASPIAN SEA
Volgograd (Stalingrad)
Astrakhan
Rostov
Krasnodar
Stavropol
Elista
Tbilisi
Yerevan
BAKU
Makhachkala
Groznyy
Vladikavkaz (Ordzhonikidze)
Kutaisi
Batumi
Sukhumi
Sochi
Guryev
Prikaspiyskaya Nizmennost
KALMYK REP.
CHECHENO - INGUSH REP.
DAGESTAN REP.
KABARDINO BALKAR REP.
N. OSSETIAN REP.
ABKHAZ REP.
ADZHAR REP.
NAGORNO KARABAKH
East from Greenwich
COPYRIGHT. GEORGE PHILIP & SON. LTD.

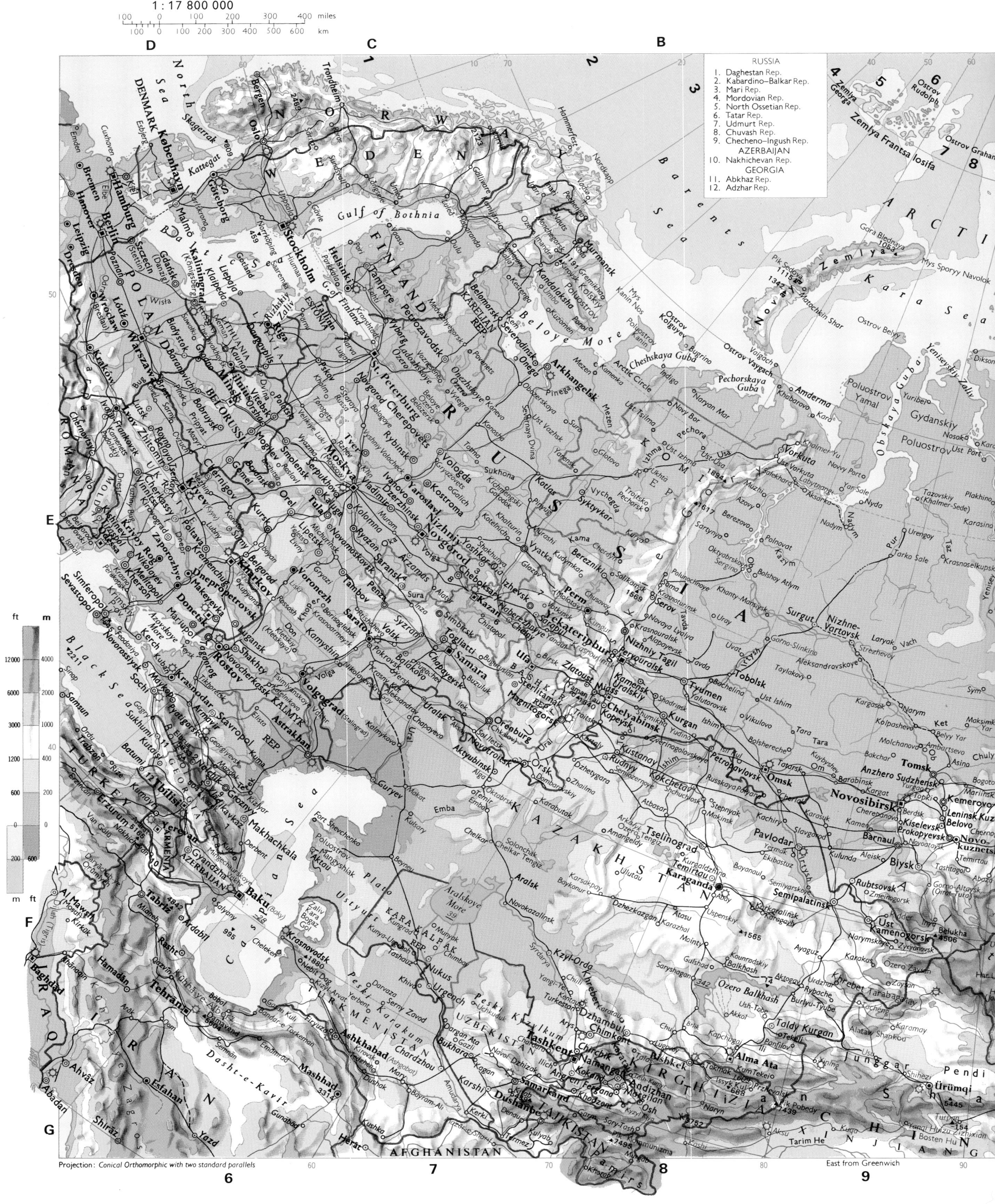
1 : 17 800 000
miles
km
RUSSIA
1. Daghestan Rep.
2. Kabardino–Balkar Rep.
3. Mari Rep.
4. Mordovian Rep.
5. North Ossetian Rep.
6. Tatar Rep.
7. Udmurt Rep.
8. Chuvash Rep.
9. Checheno–Ingush Rep.
AZERBAIJAN
10. Nakhichevan Rep.
GEORGIA
11. Abkhaz Rep.
12. Adzhar Rep.
Barents Sea
Kara Sea
Gulf of Bothnia
Black Sea
Caspian Sea
Aralskoye More
Beloye More
NORWAY
SWEDEN
FINLAND
POLAND
BELORUSSIA
UKRAINE
ROMANIA
TURKEY
IRAQ
IRAN
AFGHANISTAN
KAZAKHSTAN
TURKMENISTAN
UZBEKISTAN
TAJIKISTAN
KIRGHIZIA
RUSSIA
Moskva
St. Petersburg
Kiyev
Minsk
Stockholm
Helsinki
Tallinn
Riga
Vilnius
Warszawa
København
Berlin
Tbilisi
Yerevan
Baku
Tehran
Ashkhabad
Tashkent
Dushanbe
Bishkek
Alma Ata
Omsk
Novosibirsk
Yekaterinburg
Chelyabinsk
Samara
Volgograd
Arkhangelsk
Murmansk
Ürümqi
Projection: Conical Orthomorphic with two standard parallels
East from Greenwich

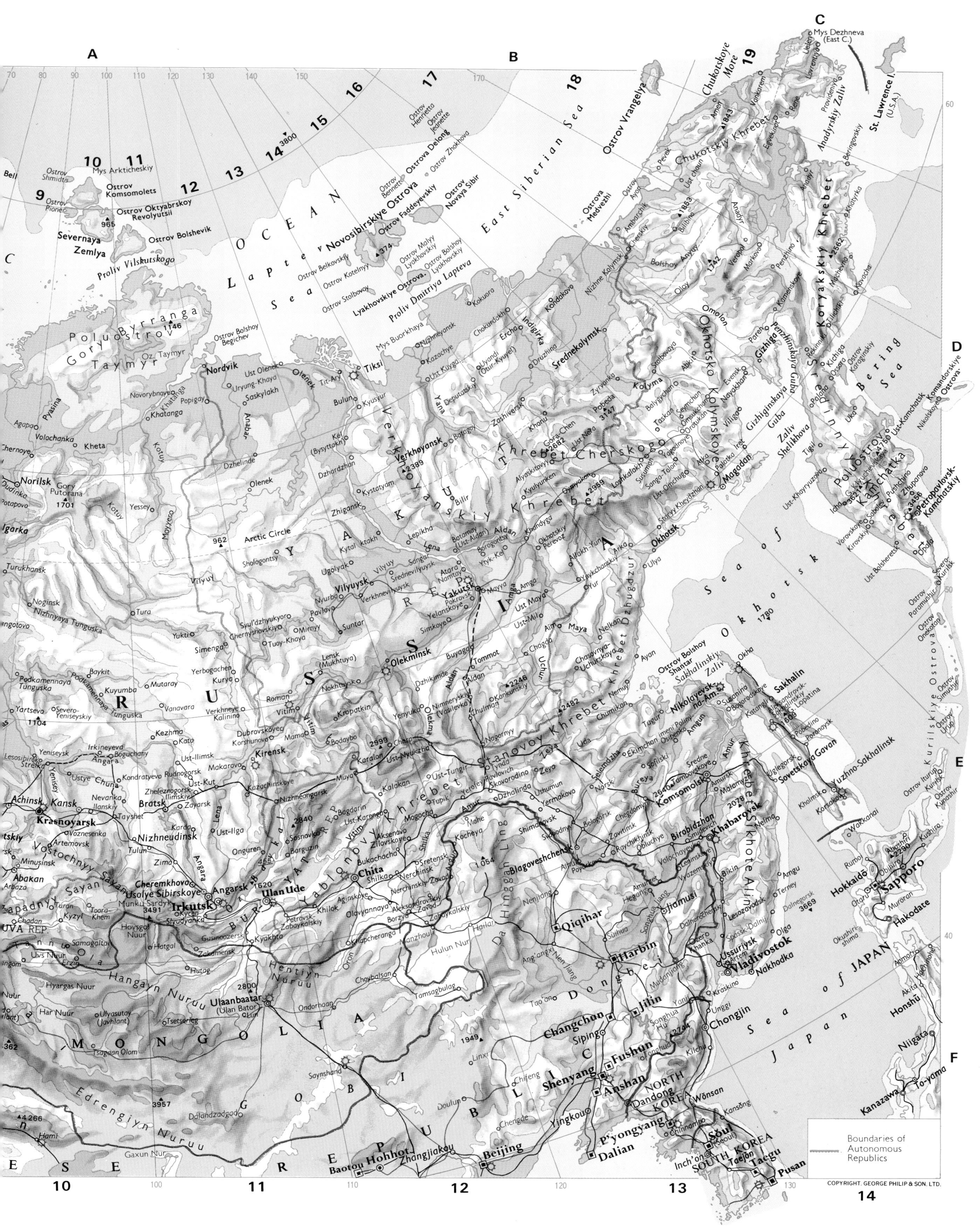

OCEAN
Laptev Sea
East Siberian Sea
Chukotskoye More
Sea of Okhotsk
Bering Sea
Sea of JAPAN
Japan Sea
Severnaya Zemlya
Ostrov Komsomolets
Ostrov Oktyabrskoy Revolyutsii
Ostrov Bolshevik
Proliv Vilkitskogo
Poluostrov Taymyr
Gory Byrranga
Novosibirskiye Ostrova
Ostrov Kotelnyy
Ostrov Faddeyevskiy
Ostrov Novaya Sibir
Lyakhovskiye Ostrova
Proliv Dmitriya Lapteva
Ostrov Vrangelya
Mys Dezhneva (East C.)
St. Lawrence I. (U.S.A.)
Anadyrskiy Zaliv
Chukotskiy Khrebet
Koryakskiy Khrebet
Poluostrov Kamchatka
Petropavlovsk-Kamchatskiy
Komandorskiye Ostrova
Kurilskiye Ostrova
Sakhalin
Yuzhno-Sakhalinsk
Sovetskaya Gavan
Nikolayevsk-na-Amure
Khrebet Cherskogo
Verkhoyanskiy Khrebet
Stanovoy Khrebet
Khrebet Dzhugdzur
Yablonovyy Khrebet
Khrebet Sikhote Alin
Kolymskoye Nagorye
Arctic Circle
Norilsk
Nordvik
Tiksi
Verkhoyansk
Srednekolymsk
Magadan
Okhotsk
Yakutsk
Vilyuysk
Olekminsk
Kirensk
Bratsk
Krasnoyarsk
Achinsk
Kansk
Nizhneudinsk
Angarsk
Irkutsk
Ulan Ude
Chita
Blagoveshchensk
Khabarovsk
Komsomolsk
Birobidzhan
Vladivostok
Nakhodka
Harbin
Qiqihar
Jilin
Changchun
Shenyang
Fushun
Anshan
Dalian
Beijing
Hohhot
Baotou
Zhangjiakou
Ulaanbaatar (Ulan Bator)
Hangayn Nuruu
Hentiyn Nuruu
MONGOLIA
Da Hinggan Ling
NORTH KOREA
SOUTH KOREA
P'yongyang
Sŏul
Pusan
Taegu
Chongjin
Hokkaidō
Sapporo
Hakodate
Honshū
Niigata
Kanazawa
Boundaries of Autonomous Republics

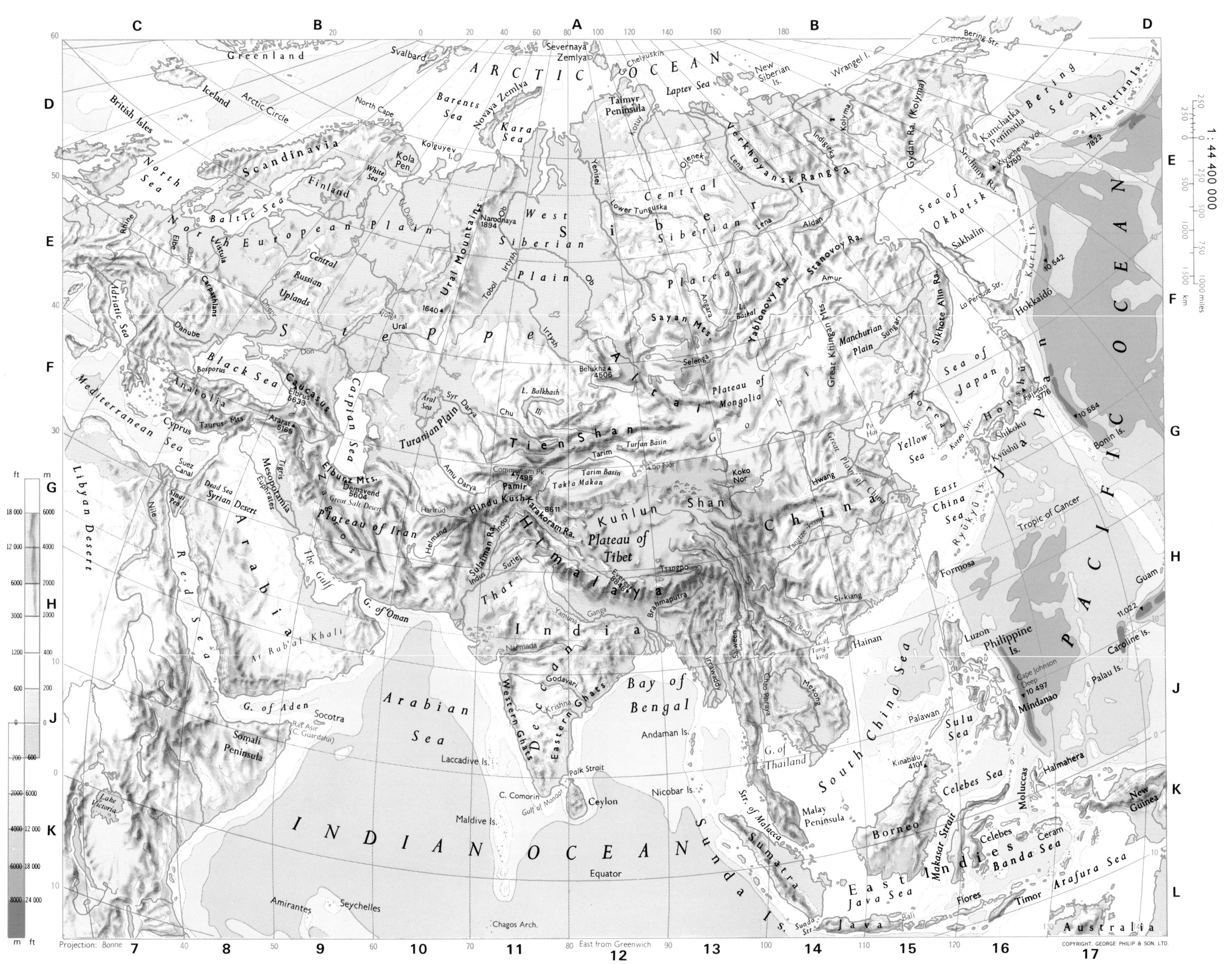

1 : 44 400 000

COPYRIGHT GEORGE PHILIP & SON, LTD.

Projection: Bonne

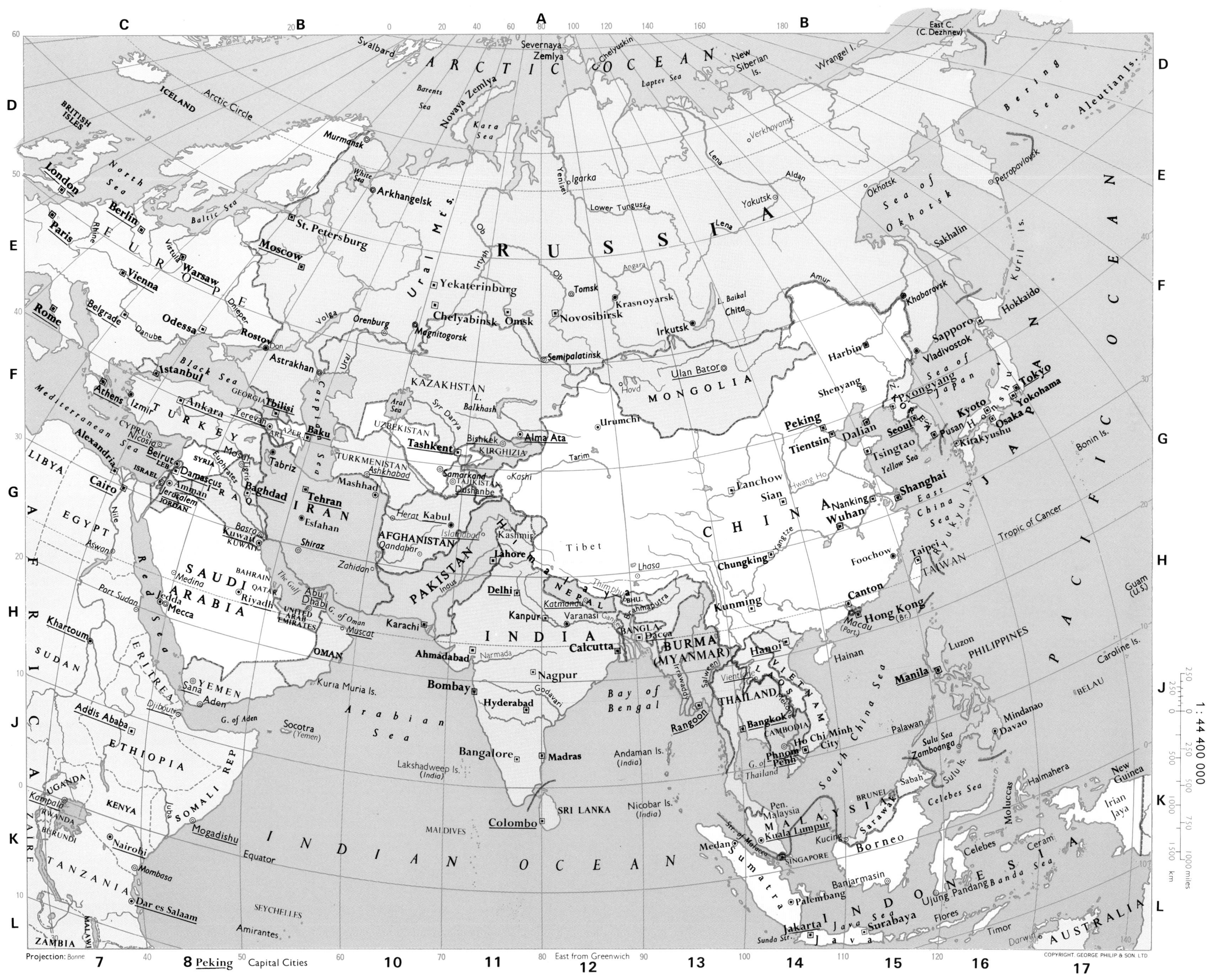

1 : 44 400 000

Projection: Bonne

COPYRIGHT GEORGE PHILIP & SON LTD

8 Peking 50 Capital Cities

East from Greenwich

Grid references (top)
B C D E F

12 11 10 9 8 7 6 5

Grid references (left/bottom)
A B C D E

46 44 42 40

132 134 136 138 140 142 144

SEA OF OKHOTSK

HOKKAIDO

SAPPORO

HONSHU

TOHOKU

CHŪBU

SEA OF JAPAN

RUSSIA

CHINA

NORTH KOREA

Sakhalin

La Pérouse Strait
(Sōya-Kaikyō)

Ostrov Kunashir
Nemuro-Kaikyō

Abashiri-Wan
Kushiro
Obihiro
Hidaka-Sammyaku

Wakkanai
Rishiri-Tō
Rebun-Tō
Teshio
Esashi
Ōmu
Mombetsu
Yūbetsu
Kitami
Asahigawa
Sammyaku
Ishikari-Wan
(Otaru-Wan)
Otaru
Ebetsu
Iwamizawa
Tomakomai
Shikotu-Ko
Uchiura Wan
Muroran
Hakodate
Tsugaru-Kaikyō
Okushiri-Tō

Esan-Misaki
Shiriya-Zaki
Mutsu-Wan
Aomori
Hachinohe
Misawa
Hirosaki
Towada-Ko
Odate
Noshiro
Oga-Hantō
Akita
Hiraizumi
Morioka
Kamaishi
Kesennuma
Ishinomaki
Sendai-Wan
Sendai
Yamagata
Yonezawa
Niigata
Sado
Shibata

Svetlaya
Amgu
Velikaya Kema
Terney
Plastun
Dalnegorsk
Kavalerovo
Olga
Margaritovo
Valentin
Preobrazheniye
Nakhodka
Vladivostok
Artem
Ussuriysk
Spassk-Dalniy
Lesozavodsk
Dalnerechensk
Bikin
Ozero Khanka

Zaliv Petra Velikogo
Slavyanka
Najin
Chongjin

Shuangyashan
Jiamusi
Hamust
Songhua
Wusuli Jiang

SIKHOTE ALIN

Sōya-Misaki
Shiretoko-Misaki

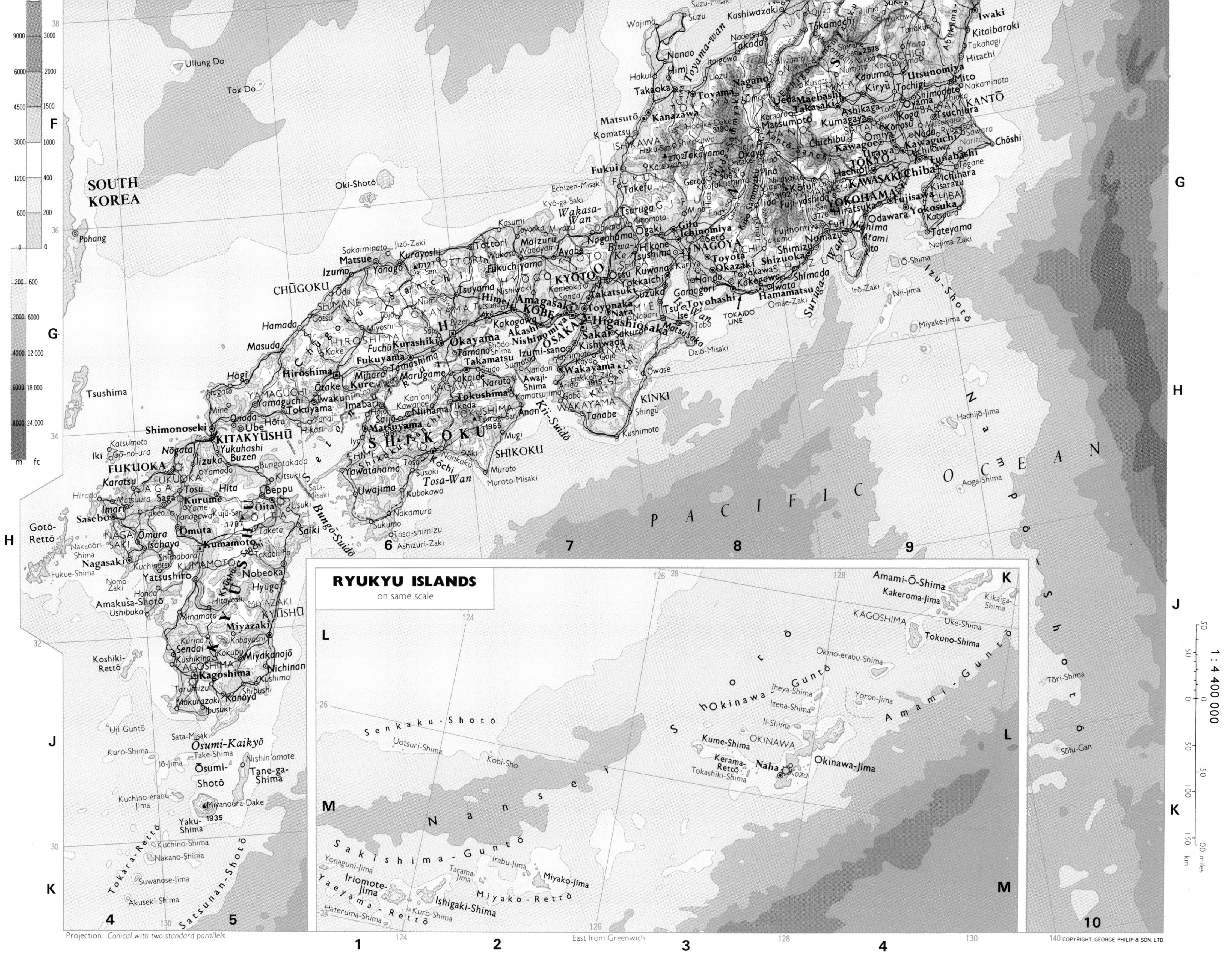

RYUKYU ISLANDS
on same scale

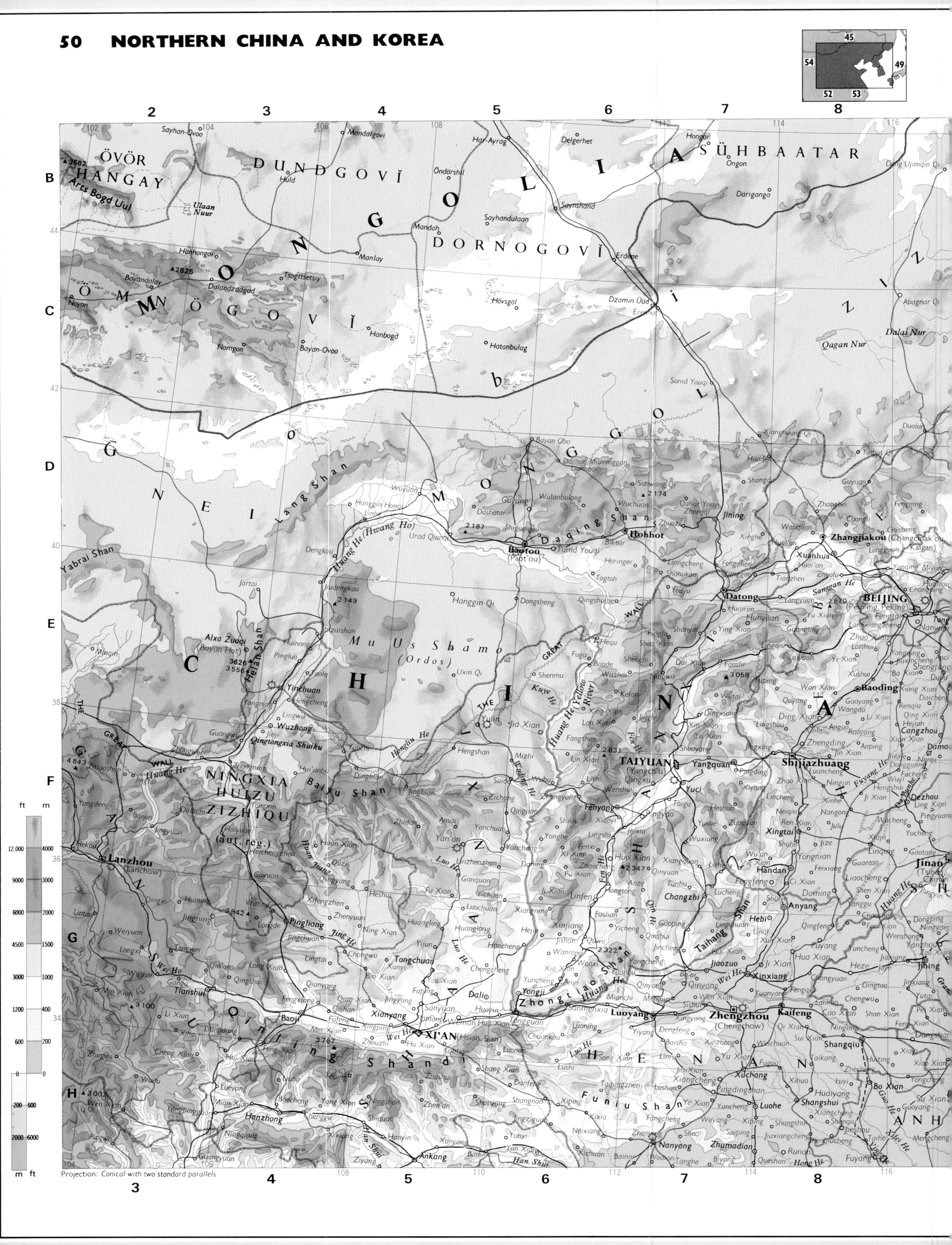

ft m
12,000 4000
9000 3000
6000 2000
4500 1500
3000 1000
1200 400
600 200
0 0
200 600
2000 6000
m ft

Projection: Conical with two standard parallels

ÖVÖR HANGAY
Arts Bogd Uul
▲3582

D U N D G O V Ĭ

M O N G O L I A

S Ü H B A A T A R

Sayhan-Ovoo
Mandalgovi
Har-Ayrag
Delgerhet
Ongon
Hongor
Dariganga
Dzüünmod

Hüld
Öndörshil
Darhan Muminggan

Ulaan Nuur
Ö M N Ö G O V Ĭ
Hanhongor
▲2825
Dalandzadgad
Tsogttsetsiy
Manlay
Mandah
Sayhandulaan
Seynshand
Erdene
Dzamin Üüd
Ereen
Hatanbulag
Sonid Youqi
Abagnar Qi
Qagan Nur
Dalai Nur
Duolun

Noyon
Bayandalay
Nomgon
Bayan-Ovoo
Hovsgol

N E I
G

Langshan
Bayan Obo
Siziwang Qi
Xianghuang Qi
Zhangbei
Fengning

M O N G O L

Huang He (Hwang Ho)
Wuyuan
Hanggin Houqi
Linhe
Dashetai
▲2187
Guyang
Wulanbulang
Wuchuan
▲2174
Qahar Youyi Zhongqi
Shangdu
Guyuan

Dengkou
Urad Qianqi
Baotou (Paot'ou)
Daqing Shan
Hohhot
Jining
Xinghe
Wanquan
Zhangjiakou (Changchiak'ou) Kalgan
Longguan

Jartai
Judengkou
▲2149
Hanggin Qi
Dongsheng
Qingshuihe
Togtoh
Horinger
Liangcheng
Shahukou
Youyu
Datong
Huairen
Tianzhen
Yangyuan
Xuanhua
Huai'an
Yanqing
Xuanhua
BEIJING (Peiping, Peking)

Alxa Zuoqi (Bayan Hot)
▲3626
3556
Yinchuan
Hengcheng
Yongning
M u   U s   S h a m o (Ordos)
Uxin Qi
Shenmu
Wuzhai
Dai Xian
▲3058
Wutai
Fanshi
Lingqiu
Quyang
Baoding

Huinong
Pingluo
Taole
Hengshan
Kelan
Xing Xian
Jingle
Xin Xian
Lingshou
Zhengding
Cangzhou

Wuzhong
Qingtongxia Shuiku
Guangwu
Hengshan
Hongliu He
Yulin
Jia Xian
Lan Xian
Fanzhi
Shouyang
Yangquan
Pingding
Shijiazhuang

▲4843
THE GREAT WALL
Zhongning
Baiyu Shan
Jingbian
Zizhou
Mizhi
Suide
Lin Xian
▲2831
TAIYUAN (Yangch'ü)
Yuci
Huoxian
Handan

N I N G X I A   H U I Z U   Z I Z H I Q U (aut. reg.)
Yanchi
Dingbian
Zhidan
Ansai
Yanchuan
Yonghe
Lishi
Fenyang
Qingxu
Taigu
Yushe
Xingtai

Zhongwei
Tongxin
Huan Xian
Yan'an
Yanchang
Xi Xian
Fenxi
Lingshi
Wuxiang
Jize
Yongnian

Lanzhou (Lanchow)
Hekou
Huining
Dingxi
Qingyang
Ganquan
Fu Xian
Ji Xian
Linfen
Xiangning
Qinyuan
Tunliu
Changzhi
Lucheng
Anyang
Hebi

Weiyuan
Jingyuan
▲2942
Pingliang
Zhenyuan
Heshui
Luochuan
Yichuan
Fushan
Quwo
Yicheng
Jincheng
Gaoping
Qinyang
Jiaozuo
Xinxiang

Longxi
Tangwei
Jingning
Huangling
Huanglong
Hancheng
▲2322
Wanrong
Yangcheng
Hui Xian
Jiaozuo
Huojia

Min Xian
Gangu
Tianshui
Qingshui
Qian Xian
Long Xian
Lingtai
Chongwu
Yijun
Liu He
Hancheng
Xia Xian
Wenxi
Yuncheng
Yongji
Mianchi
Luoyang (Chengchow)
Zhengzhou
Kaifeng

▲3100
Li Xian
Didao
Fengxiang
Qishan
Jingyang
Baoji
Tongchuan
Yao Xian
Chengcheng
Dali
Huayin
Sanmenxia
Zhongtiao Shan
Luoyang

Zhugqu
Wudu
Lüeyang
▲3300
Wen Xian
Mian Xian
▲3767
Zhouzhi
XI'AN (Hsian, Sian)
Weinan
Hua Xian
Tongguan
Song Xian

Hanzhong
Yangbingguan
Baocheng
Zhen'an
Shanyang
Xixia
Lushi
Luoning
Dengfeng
Xuchang

S H A A N X I
S H A N X I
H E B E I
S H A N D O N G
H E N A N
A N H U I

Jinan (Tsinan)
Jining
Puyang
Shangqiu
Bo Xian

Nanyang
Funiu Shan
Luohe
Zhumadian
Queshan
Fuyang

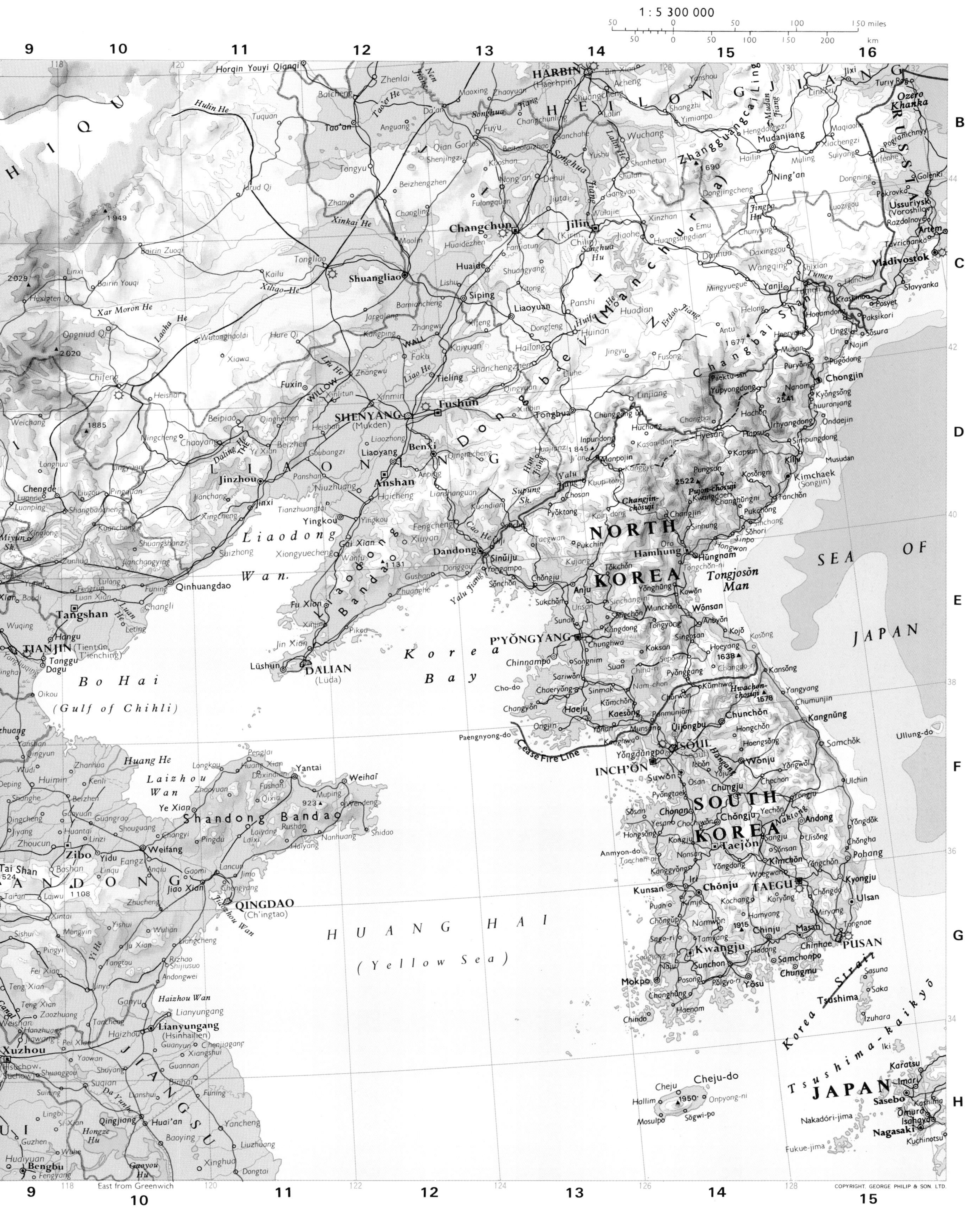
1 : 5 300 000
50 0 50 100 150 miles
50 0 50 100 150 200 km
9 10 11 12 13 14 15 16
B C D E F G H
HARBIN
(Haerhpin)
HEILONGJIANG
JILIN
LIAONING
RUSSIA
Vladivostok
Ussuriysk
(Voroshilov)
Changchun
Jilin
(Kirin)
Shuangliao
Siping
Liaoyuan
SHENYANG
(Mukden)
Fushun
Benxi
Liaoyang
Anshan
Jinzhou
Dandong
Yingkou
DALIAN
(Lüda)
Lüshun
Liaodong Bandao
Liaodong Wan
Bo Hai
(Gulf of Chihli)
TIANJIN (Tientsin, T'ienching)
Tangshan
Qinhuangdao
Shandong Bandao
Laizhou Wan
Yantai
Weihai
QINGDAO
(Ch'ingtao)
Zibo
Weifang
Lianyungang
Xuzhou
JIANGSU
HUANG HAI
(Yellow Sea)
Korea Bay
NORTH KOREA
P'YŎNGYANG
Chongjin
Hamhung
Hŭngnam
Wŏnsan
Tongjosŏn Man
Sinŭiju
Cease Fire Line
SŎUL
(Seoul)
INCH'ŎN
SOUTH KOREA
Taejŏn
TAEGU
PUSAN
Kwangju
Chŏnju
Mokpo
Cheju-do
SEA OF JAPAN
Korea Strait
Tsushima
Tsushima-kaikyō
JAPAN
Sasebo
Nagasaki
Changbai Shan
Paektu-san
Manchuria
Yalu Jiang
Songhua Jiang
Mudanjiang
Ozero Khanka
Ulleung-do
East from Greenwich

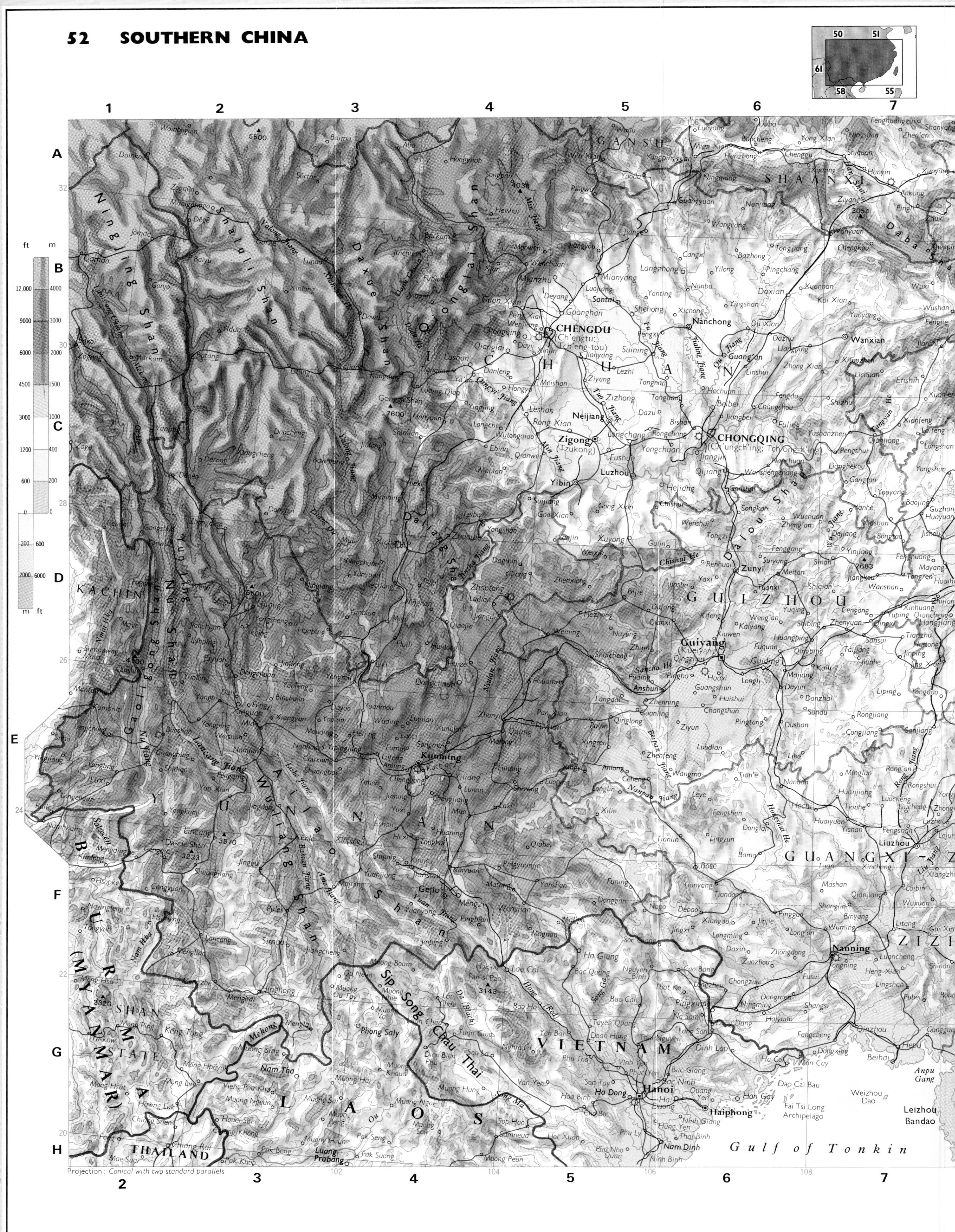

50
51
61
58
55
1
2
3
4
5
6
7
A
B
C
D
E
F
G
H
ft
m
12,000
9000
6000
4500
3000
1200
600
0
4000
3000
2000
1500
1000
400
200
0
200
2000
600
6000
GANSU
SHAANXI
SICHUAN
GUIZHOU
YUNNAN
GUANGXI-Z
VIETNAM
LAOS
THAILAND
BURMA (MYANMAR)
SHAN STATE
KACHIN
CHENGDU
(Ch'engtu; Tch'eng-tou)
CHONGQING
(Ch'ungch'ing; Tch'ong-k'ing)
Kunming
Guiyang
(Kueiyang)
Nanning
Hanoi
Haiphong
Zigong
(Tzukong)
Neijiang
Luzhou
Yibin
Nanchong
Wanxian
Zunyi
Gejiu
Liuzhou
Mianyang
Guang'an
Nam Dinh
Ha Dong
Phong Saly
Nam Tha
Luang Prabang
Lao Cai
Ningjing Shan
Shaluli Shan
Daxue Shan
Qionglai Shan
Daliang Shan
Dalou Shan
Daba Shan
Nu Shan
Yun Ling
Gaoligong Shan
Wuliang Shan
Ailao Shan
Sip Song Chau Thai
Gongga Shan
7600
5500
6500
4038
3054
2683
3143
3570
3233
2320
Min Jiang
Jinsha Jiang
Yalong Jiang
Lancang Jiang
Nu Jiang
Mekong
Hong (Red)
Da (Black)
Chishui He
Hongshui He
Nanpan Jiang
Gulf of Tonkin
Leizhou Bandao
Weizhou Dao
Fai Tsi Long Archipelago
Dao Cai Bau
Anpu Gang
Projection: Conical with two standard parallels
98
100
102
104
106
108
32
30
28
26
24
22
20

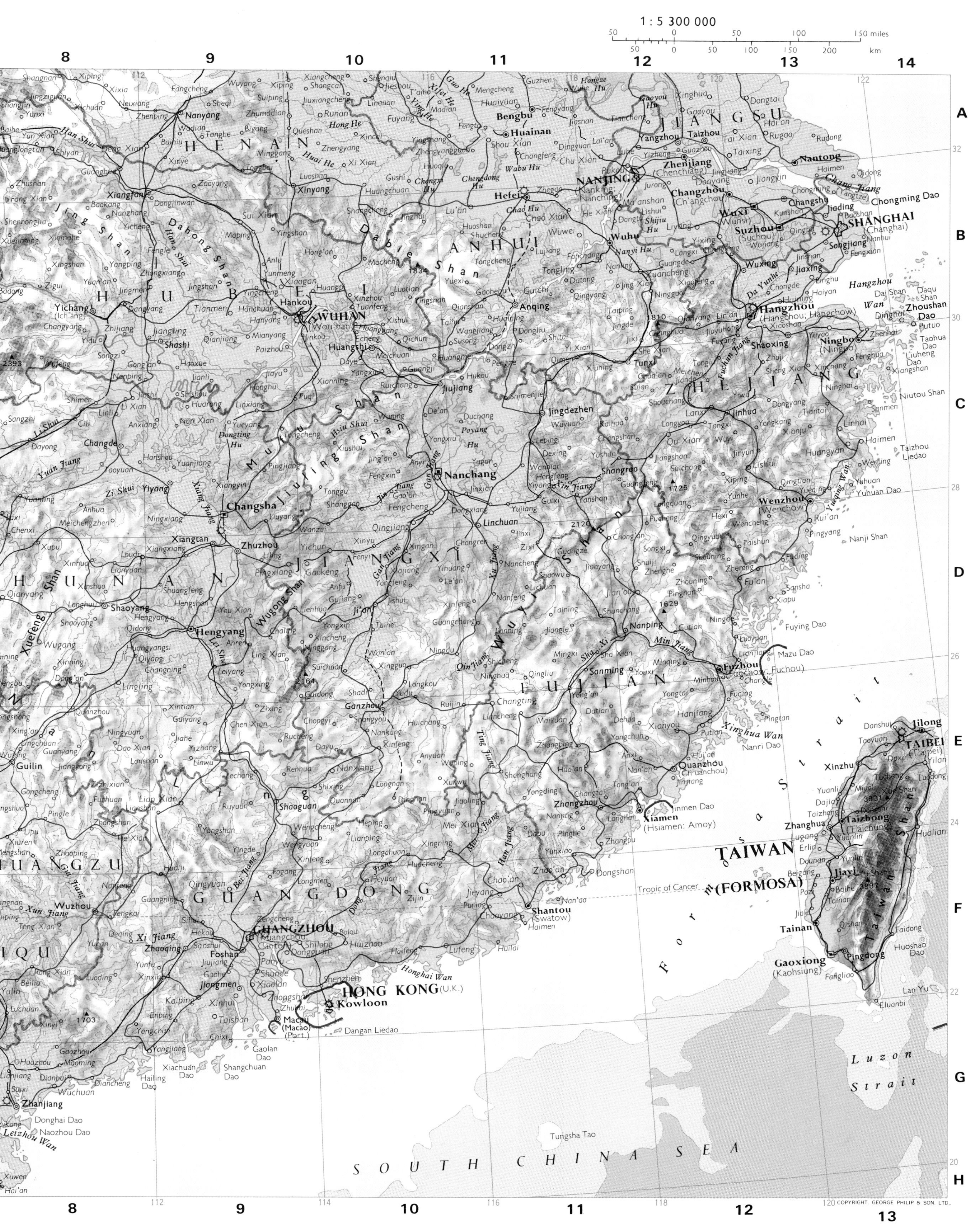
1 : 5 300 000
50 0 50 100 150 miles
50 0 50 100 150 200 km
8
9
10
11
12
13
14
A
B
C
D
E
F
G
H
HENAN
HUBEI
ANHUI
JIANGSU
ZHEJIANG
JIANGXI
HUNAN
FUJIAN
GUANGDONG
TAIWAN (FORMOSA)
Nanyang
Xinyang
Bengbu
Huainan
Hefei
NANJING (Nanking; Nanching)
Zhenjiang (Chenchiang)
Yangzhou
Nantong
Changzhou (Ch'angchou)
Wuxi (Wuhsi)
Suzhou (Suchou)
SHANGHAI (Changhai)
Chongming Dao
Wuhu
Hangzhou (Hangchou; Hangchow)
Hangzhou Wan
Zhoushan Dao
Ningbo (Ningpo)
Shaoxing
Yichang (Ich'ang)
Shashi
Xiangfan
Hankou
WUHAN (Wou-han)
Huangshi
Anqing
Jiujiang
Jingdezhen
Poyang Hu
Nanchang
Changsha
Xiangtan
Zhuzhou
Changde
Dongting Hu
Hengyang
Shaoyang
Guilin
Wuzhou
Shaoguan
Ganzhou
Linchuan
Shangrao
Wenzhou (Wenchow)
Fuzhou (Foochow; Fuchou)
Nanping
Sanming
Quanzhou (Ch'uanchou)
Xiamen (Hsiamen; Amoy)
Zhangzhou
Shantou (Swatow)
GUANGZHOU (Kuangchou; Canton)
Foshan
Jiangmen
HONG KONG (U.K.)
Kowloon
Macau (Macao) (Port.)
Zhanjiang
TAIBEI (T'aipei)
Jilong
Xinzhu
Taizhong (T'aichung)
Jiayi
Tainan
Gaoxiong (Kaohsiung)
Formosa Strait
Tropic of Cancer
Luzon Strait
SOUTH CHINA SEA
Tungsha Tao
Leizhou Wan
Dabie Shan
Wuyi Shan
Taiwan Shan
COPYRIGHT GEORGE PHILIP & SON LTD.

1 : 17 800 000

100   0   100   200   300   400 miles
100 0 100 200 300 400 500 600 km

A   B   C   D   E

COPYRIGHT GEORGE PHILIP & SON LTD

RUSSIA

KAZAKHSTAN

KIRGHIZIA

MONGOLIA

Ulaanbaatar

XINJIANG UYGUR

Urumqi

Tarim Pendi

Junggar Pendi

TIBET (XIZANG)

Lhasa

Kunlun Shan

Altun Shan

QINGHAI

Qilian Shan

GANSU

NINGXIA

Lanzhou

NEPAL

Kathmandu

BHUTAN

BANGLADESH

Dhaka

INDIA

CALCUTTA

DELHI

Lucknow

Kanpur

Varanasi

Patna

Allahabad

BURMA (MYANMAR)

Mandalay

THAILAND

LAOS

VIETNAM

HANOI

Haiphong

Kunming

YUNNAN

GUIZHOU

Guiyang

CHONGQING

SICHUAN

CHENGDU

SHAANXI

HUBEI

WUHAN

HUNAN

Changsha

JIANGXI

Nanchang

FUJIAN

GUANGDONG

GUANGXI

GUANGZHOU

Hong Kong

Kowloon

Macao

Haikou

HAINAN

Hainan Dao

SOUTH CHINA SEA

G. of Tonkin

BAY OF BENGAL

HEBEI

HENAN

Zhengzhou

SHANXI

TAIYUAN

Shijiazhuang

BEIJING

TIANJIN

Hohhot

Baotou

Datong

SHANDONG

Jinan

QINGDAO

YELLOW SEA

Bo Hai

DALIAN

LIAONING

SHENYANG

Anshan

JILIN

Changchun

HEILONGJIANG

HARBIN

Qiqihar

NORTH KOREA

P'yongyang

SOUTH KOREA

Seoul

Taegu

Pusan

JAPAN

Fukuoka

Nagasaki

EAST CHINA SEA

TAIWAN (FORMOSA)

Taibei

Gaoxiong

RYUKYU-RETTO

PHILIPPINES

LUZON

Batan Is.

Bashi Channel

JIANGSU

NANJING

SHANGHAI

ZHEJIANG

Hangzhou

Ningbo

Wenzhou

ANHUI

Hefei

Vladivostok

Khabarovsk

L. Baikal (Ozero Baikal)

Irkutsk

Ulan-Ude

Chita

Tarim

Huang (Yellow R.)

Chang (Yangtze)

Great Wall

Mu Us Shamo

Projection: Bonne   East from Greenwich

m 6000 4000 3000 2000 1500 1000 400 200 0 ft
ft 18 000 12 000 9000 6000 4500 3000 1200 600 0 m

1 : 6 700 000

50 0 50 100 150 200 miles
50 0 50 100 150 200 250 300 km

53
56 57

| | 1 | 2 | 3 | 4 | 5 | 6 | 7 | 8 |

A

116 118 120 122 124 126 128

Itbayat
Batanes Is.
Batan

20

Balintang Channel

B

Calayan
Dalupiri Babuyan Camiguin
Islands
Fuga
Mayraira Pt. Babuyan Channel
Claveria Aparri
Bacarra Bangui Ballesteros Port San Vicente
San Nicolas ● Laoag Kabugao Gonzaga
18 Batuc ▲ 2360 Gattaran Tuguegarao
Cabagao Banna Tudo Chico
Vigan Bangued Cagayan
Santa Chico Cresta
Maria Lubuagan ▲ 1672
Candon Roxas Nagan
Tagudin Bontoc San Mateo Palanan Pt.

C

Luna Santiago Palanan
San Fernando Cordon
Lingayen Gulf Pulog Solano
Bolinao Baguio ● ▲ 2929 Bayombong
16 Alaminos Rosario Anacuao
Lingayen ● Dagupan ▲ 1850 C. San Ildefonso
San Carlos San Manuel Baler Bay
Santa Cruz Bayambang ● San Jose Baler
Camiling Cuyapo Victoria Dingalan
Palauig Tarlac Cabanatuan
Iba Capas ▲ 2038 Gapan **LUZON**

D

Sapangbato Angeles Polillo Is.
San Narciso San Fernando Polillo Str.
San Antonio Malaban Patnanongan
Olongapo Ortni Caloocan Jomalig
14 Bataan Manila **Quezon City** Larap Paracale
Cavite ● **MANILA** Lamon Bay Pandan
Trece Martires Pasay Santa Cruz
Nasugbu Tagaytay Lucban Daet
Balayan Lipa ● San Pablo Arimonan
Lemery Batangas Lucena Lopez Naga ● Iriga
Verde I. Tayabas Bay Catanauan Nabua Catanduanes
C. Calavite Pass Boac Tablas Marin- Virac
Memburao duque Burias Ligaos ● Tabaco Rapu Rapu

E

MINDORO Baco Sibuyan Legazpi ● Sorsogon
▲ 2488 Pingmalayan Sea Donsol Gubat
Sablayan Bongabong Romblon Bulan San Bernardino Str.
12 Roxas Tablas Sibuyan Bugui Irosin
San Jose Odiongan Pt. Ticao Laoang
Busuanga Ilin Mandaon ● Masbate Mondragon Gamay
Calamian Masbate Calbayog Catarman Arteche
Group Milagros Oras
Semirara Is. Placer SAMAR
Linapacan Str. Pandan Catbalogan Wright Borongan
Libro Pt. Kalibo Roxas Biliran Villa Real General MacArthur

F

Linapacan Sigma VISAYAN Carigara Sta. Rita San Antonio
Cuyo West Pass ▲ 2117 SEA Palompon Guiuan
Cuyo Is. Tibiao Ajuy Estancia Tacloban
Taytay **PANAY** Pototan Bantayan Carcar **LEYTE** ● Ormoc Dulag
Cuyo Cuyo East Pass **Iloilo** Cadiz Camotes Is. Abuyog Leyte Gulf
Bugasong San Jose Silay Bogo Baybay Homonhon
de Buenavista **Victorias** Danao Sogod
PALAWAN Guimaras **Bacolod** ▲ 2465 **Cebu** Camotes
Dumaran Hinigaran San Carlos Maasin Dinagat
Cagayan La Calamba Mandaue Matalom Siargao
10 Irahuan Carlota Bohol Panaon ▼ 10 497
Honda B. Binalbagan Caliling Argao Surigao Bucas Grande
Puerto Princesa Himamaylan Kabankalan **Bohol** Carrascal
Sipalay Basa Tagbilaran Bacuag
NEGROS Tanjay Lanuza
Bayawan Oslob BOHOL Nasipi L. Mainit Tandag
Dumaguete ▲ 1837 Tago

G

Mantalingajan Siquijor SULU Camiguin Hilonghilong
▲ 2085 Bonawan Zamboanguita SEA Talisayan ● Butuan San Juan
8 C. Bulilayan Dapitan Balingasag Lianga
Bugsuk Dipolog ● Manucan Esperanza Marihatag
Oroquieta Iligan Opol Balatan
Balabac Sindangan Bay Ozamiz ● Iligan ● **Cagayan de Oro** Malaybalay Mangagoy
Balambangan Labason Tubod ● Marawi ▲ 2896 Apayao Bunawan Cateel
Bangel Ticoy Kabasalan **MINDANAO** Bislig
Kudat Jambongan Pagadian L. Lanao Panabo
SABAH Siocon Malabang ▲ 2815 Parang ▲ 2954 Baganga
Cagayan Sulu Margosatubig Illana Midsayap Apo Tagum
Suba Talan Bay Cotabato Pikit **Davao**
Sibuco Parang Datu Piang Mati
Zamboanga Olutanga Talayan Digos Manay
Basilan Str. Moro Gulf Salaman Lebok Davao Botobato
Isabela Pilas Lamitan Kronadal Gulf
Pangutaran Basilan Milbuk Malita
Group Samales ▲ 2346 **General** C. San Agustin
Jolo ● Jolo Group Kiamba **Santos**
Laparan Parang Lahing Lahing Sarangani Bay

H

SOUTH CHINA SEA

SULU SEA

PACIFIC OCEAN

Mindanao Trench

J

Kota Belud Tuaran Menggatal Crocker Range
Kota Kinabalu ▲ 4101 Penampang Papar
Beaufort Keningau Tenom Melalap Kemabong
Brassey Range Sapulut
CELEBES SEA

Tawitawi Sibutu Tinaca Pt. Sarangani Is.
Group Kawio Is. Talaud Is.

ft m
9000 3000
6000 2000
4500 1500
3000 1000
1200 400
600 200
0 0
200 600
4000 12 000
8000 24 000
m ft

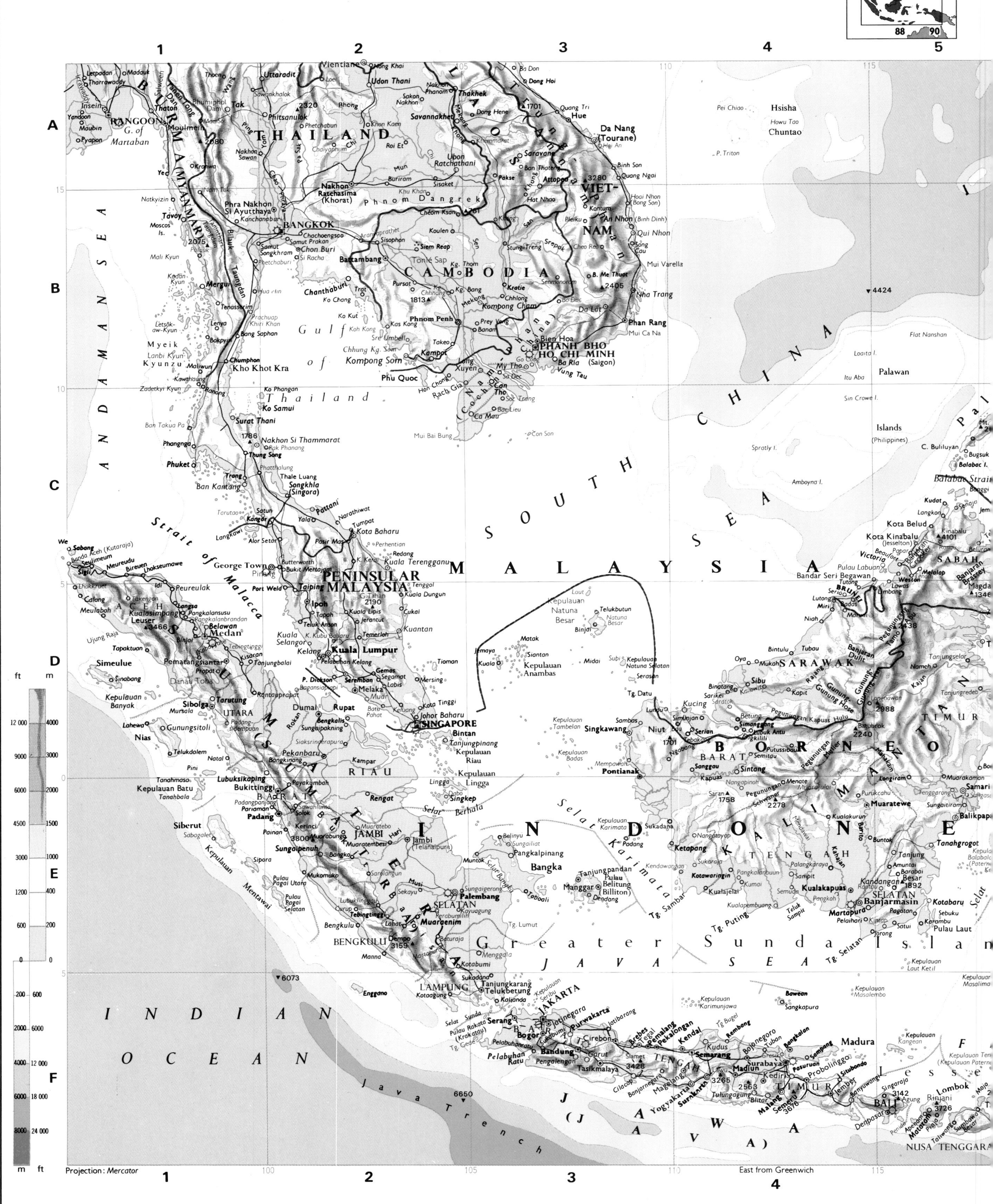

THAILAND
CAMBODIA
LAOS
VIET-NAM
BURMA (MYANMAR)
MALAYSIA
PENINSULAR MALAYSIA
SINGAPORE
BRUNEI
SARAWAK
SABAH
BORNEO
KALIMANTAN
INDONESIA
SUMATERA
JAWA (JAVA)
BALI
NUSA TENGGARA
BANGKOK
RANGOON
PHNOM PENH
PHANH BHO HO CHI MINH (Saigon)
Kuala Lumpur
JAKARTA
Palembang
Medan
Padang
Pontianak
Banjarmasin
Bandung
Semarang
Surabaya
Kuching
Da Nang (Tourane)
Hue
Vientiane
Gulf of Thailand
SOUTH CHINA SEA
ANDAMAN SEA
INDIAN OCEAN
JAVA SEA
Greater Sunda Islands
Strait of Malacca
Selat Karimata
Java Trench
G. of Martaban
Kepulauan Natuna Besar
Kepulauan Anambas
Kepulauan Riau
Kepulauan Lingga
Bangka
Pulau Belitung (Billiton)
Madura
Lombok
Simeulue
Nias
Siberut
Kepulauan Mentawai
Enggano
Palawan
Spratly I.
Projection: Mercator
East from Greenwich
ft
m

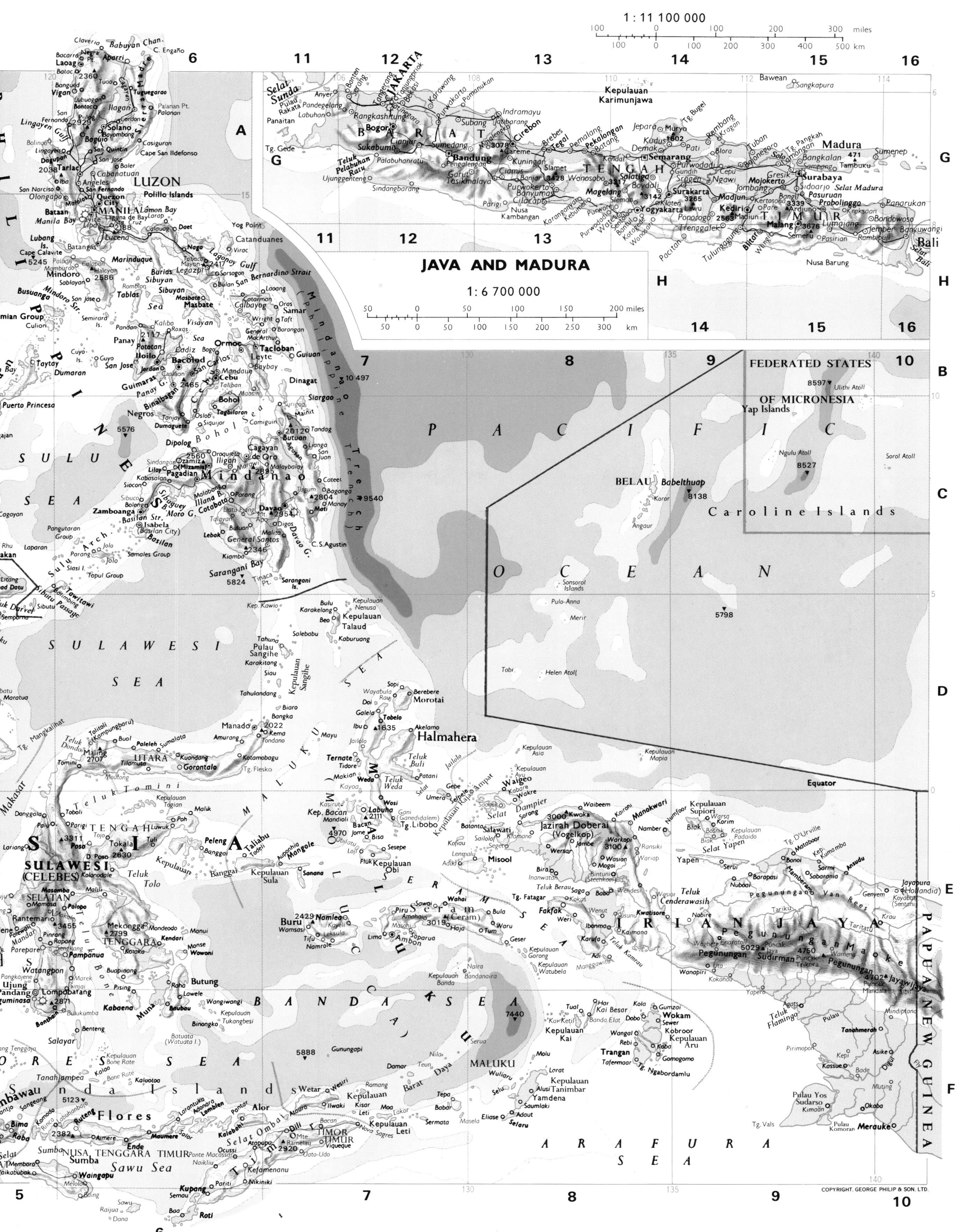
1 : 11 100 000
100 0 100 200 300 miles
100 0 100 200 300 400 500 km
JAVA AND MADURA
1: 6 700 000
50 0 50 100 150 200 miles
50 0 50 100 150 200 250 300 km
JAKARTA
Bogor
Bandung
Cirebon
Semarang
Surabaya
Madura
Yogyakarta
Surakarta
Malang
Kediri
Bali
Kepulauan Karimunjawa
Selat Sunda
Selat Madura
Nusa Barung
Bawean
LUZON
Polillo Islands
MANILA
Manila Bay
Quezon City
Mindoro
Marinduque
Sibuyan Sea
Masbate
Samar
Panay
Negros
Cebu
Leyte
Bohol
Bohol Sea
Visayan Sea
Mindanao
Davao
Zamboanga
Sulu Arch.
SULU SEA
SULAWESI SEA
Mindanao Trench (Philippine Trench)
10 497
9540
PACIFIC OCEAN
FEDERATED STATES OF MICRONESIA
Yap Islands
Caroline Islands
BELAU
Babelthuap
Equator
Halmahera
Morotai
Manado
Gorontalo
SULAWESI (CELEBES)
Teluk Tomini
Teluk Bone
Kepulauan Sula
Buru
Seram (Ceram)
Ambon
BANDA SEA
MALUKU
MALUKU SEA
Kepulauan Kai
Kepulauan Aru
Kepulauan Tanimbar
Misool
Waigeo
Jazirah Doberai (Vogelkop)
Teluk Cenderawasih
IRIAN JAYA
Pegunungan Sudirman
Puncak Jaya
Jayapura (Hollandia)
Merauke
PAPUA NEW GUINEA
ARAFURA SEA
FLORES SEA
Sunda Islands
Flores
Sumba
Sumbawa
Sawu Sea
Timor
NUSA TENGGARA TIMUR
TIMOR TIMUR
Dili
Kupang
Roti
COPYRIGHT, GEORGE PHILIP & SON, LTD.

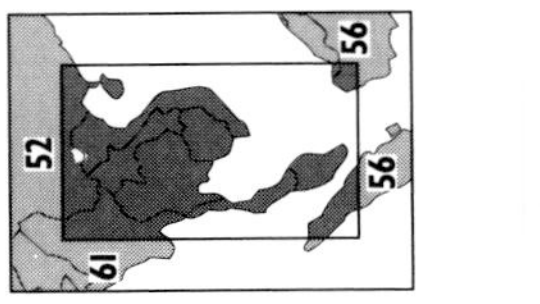
52
56
61

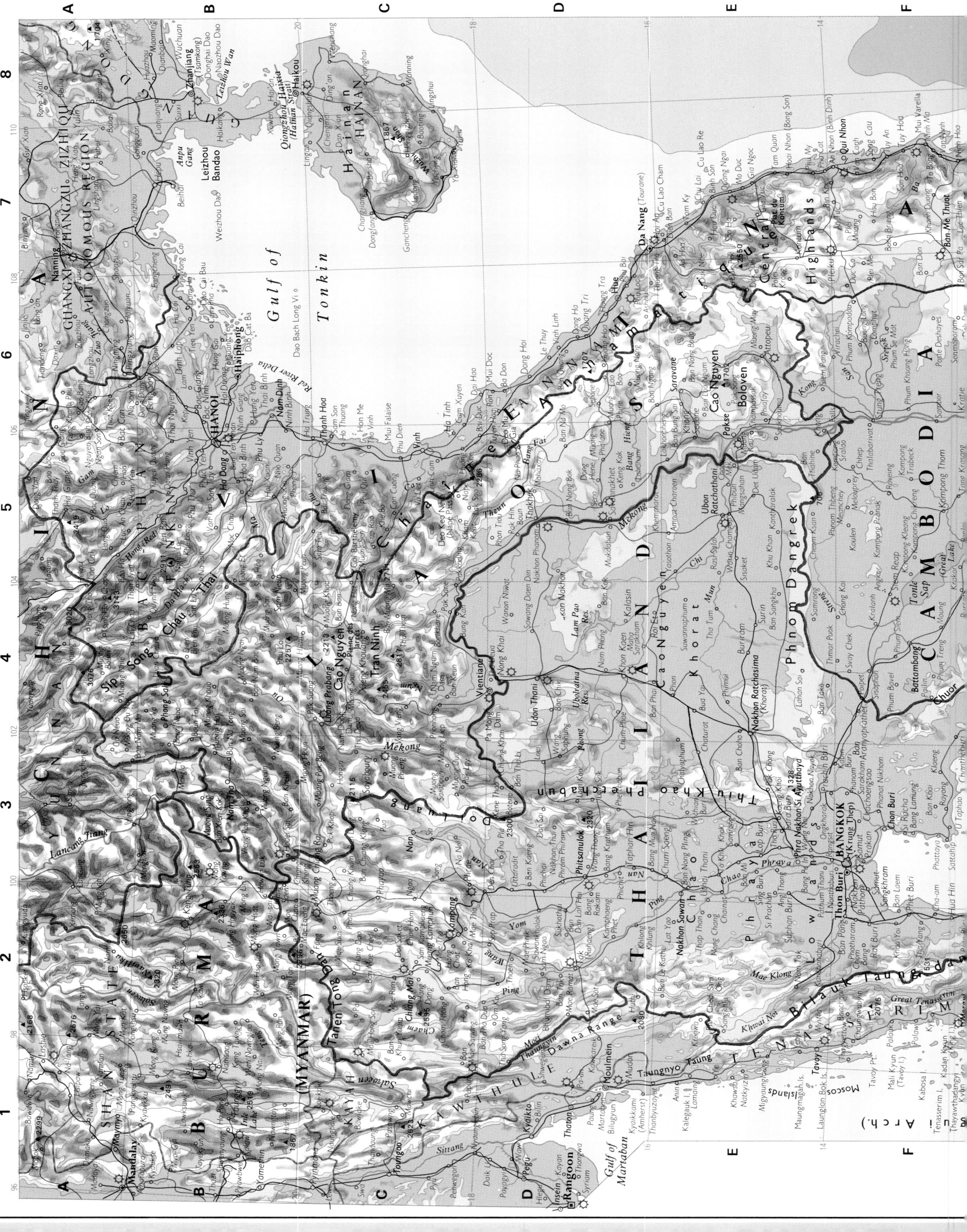
Gulf of Tonkin
Hainan
HAINAN
Haikou
Zhanjiang
Nanning
GUANGXI ZHUANGZU ZIZHIQU AUTONOMOUS REGION
YUNNAN
HANOI
Haiphong
Nam Dinh
Thanh Hoa
Vinh
Hue
Da Nang
Qui Nhon
Vientiane
Luang Prabang
Udon Thani
Ubon Ratchathani
Nakhon Ratchasima
BANGKOK
Chiang Mai
Mandalay
Rangoon
Moulmein
Gulf of Martaban
BURMA (MYANMAR)
CAMBODIA
Tonle Sap
Mekong
Phnom Dangrek
Khorat
Central Highlands
Dawna Range
Tanen Tong

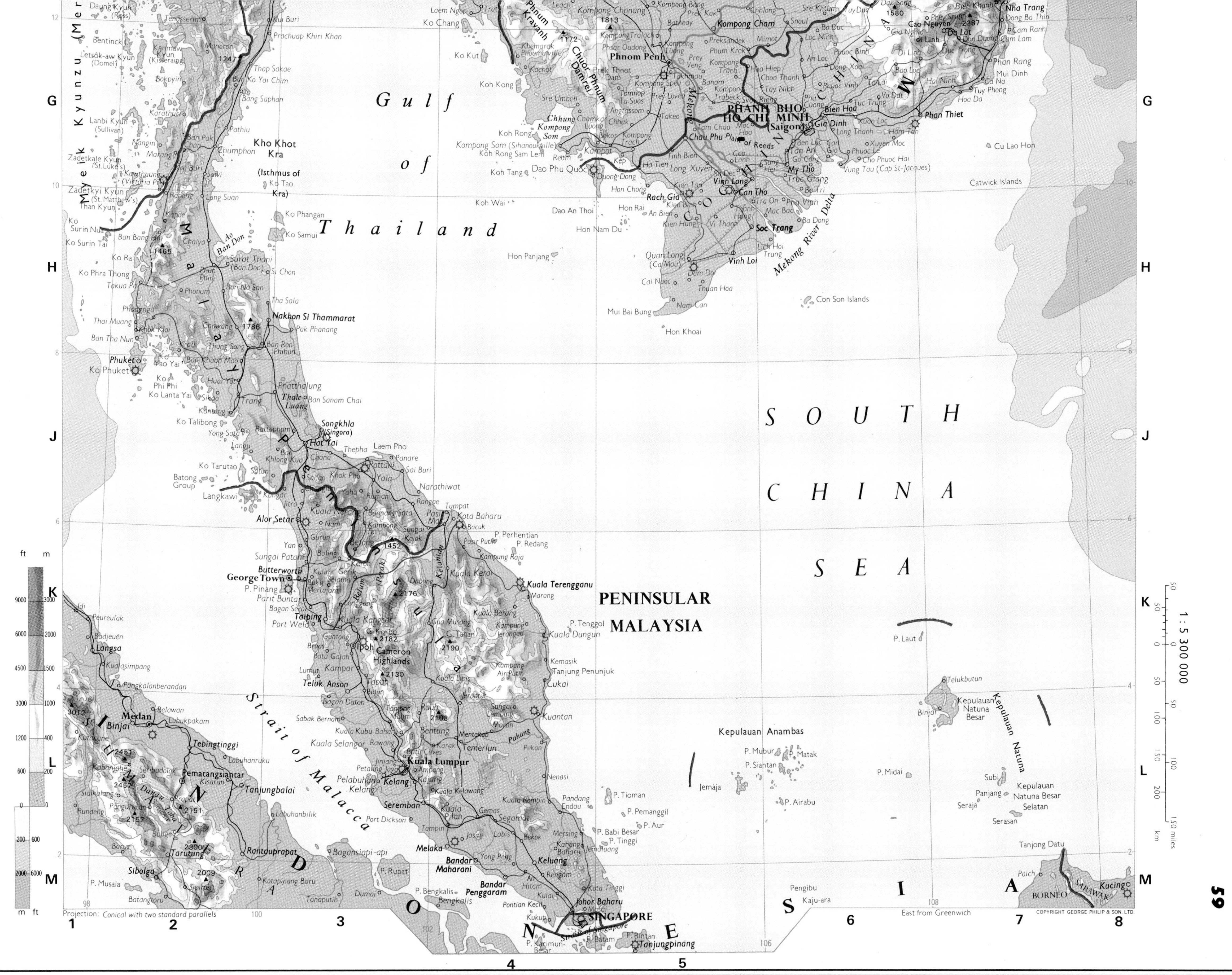

1 : 5 300 000

50   0   50   100   150 miles
50   0   50   100   150   200   km

East from Greenwich

Projection: Conical with two standard parallels

SOUTH CHINA SEA

Gulf of Thailand

Strait of Malacca

PENINSULAR MALAYSIA

Thailand

Malay

Isthmus of Kra
Kho Khot Kra

Kepulauan Natuna
Kepulauan Natuna Besar
Natuna Besar
Selatan
Serasan
Subi
Panjang
Seraja

Kepulauan Anambas
P. Mubur
Matak
P. Santan
Jemaja

BORNEO
SARAWAK
Kuching
Tanjong Datu

Mekong River Delta
PHNOM PENH
Phnom Penh
HO CHI MINH
Saigon
Nha Trang
Phan Rang
Phan Thiet
Bien Hoa
Gia Dinh
Can Tho
Soc Trang
Vinh Long
Rach Gia

Con Son Islands

Kompong Cham
Kompong Chhnang
Kompong Som
Chuor Phnum Damrei
Phnum Kravanh

Ko Chang
Ko Kut
Koh Kong
Ko Phangan
Ko Samui
Ko Tao
Nakhon Si Thammarat
Songkhla (Singora)
Hat Yai
Phatthalung
Trang
Phuket
Ko Phuket
Ko Tarutao
Langkawi
Batong Group

Alor Setar
Butterworth
George Town
P. Pinang
Taiping
Port Weld
Ipoh
Cameron Highlands
Kuala Lumpur
Kelang
Pelabuhan Kelang
Seremban
Melaka
Teluk Anson
Port Dickson

Kuala Terengganu
P. Perhentian
P. Redang
Kota Bharu
Kuala Krai
P. Tenggol
Kuala Dungun
Kuantan
Pekan
P. Tioman
P. Pemanggil
P. Aur
P. Babi Besar
P. Tinggi

Johor Baharu
SINGAPORE
Johor Baharu
Kota Tinggi
P. Karimun Besar
Tanjungpinang
Bintan
Batam

Bandar Maharani
Bandar Penggaram
Kukup
Pontian Kechil

Medan
Belawan
Binjai
Tebingtinggi
Pematangsiantar
Rantauprapat
Tanjungbalai
Labuhanbilik
Sibolga

Kho Khot Kra

m   ft
9000
6000
4500
3000
1500
600
200
0
200
2000
6000

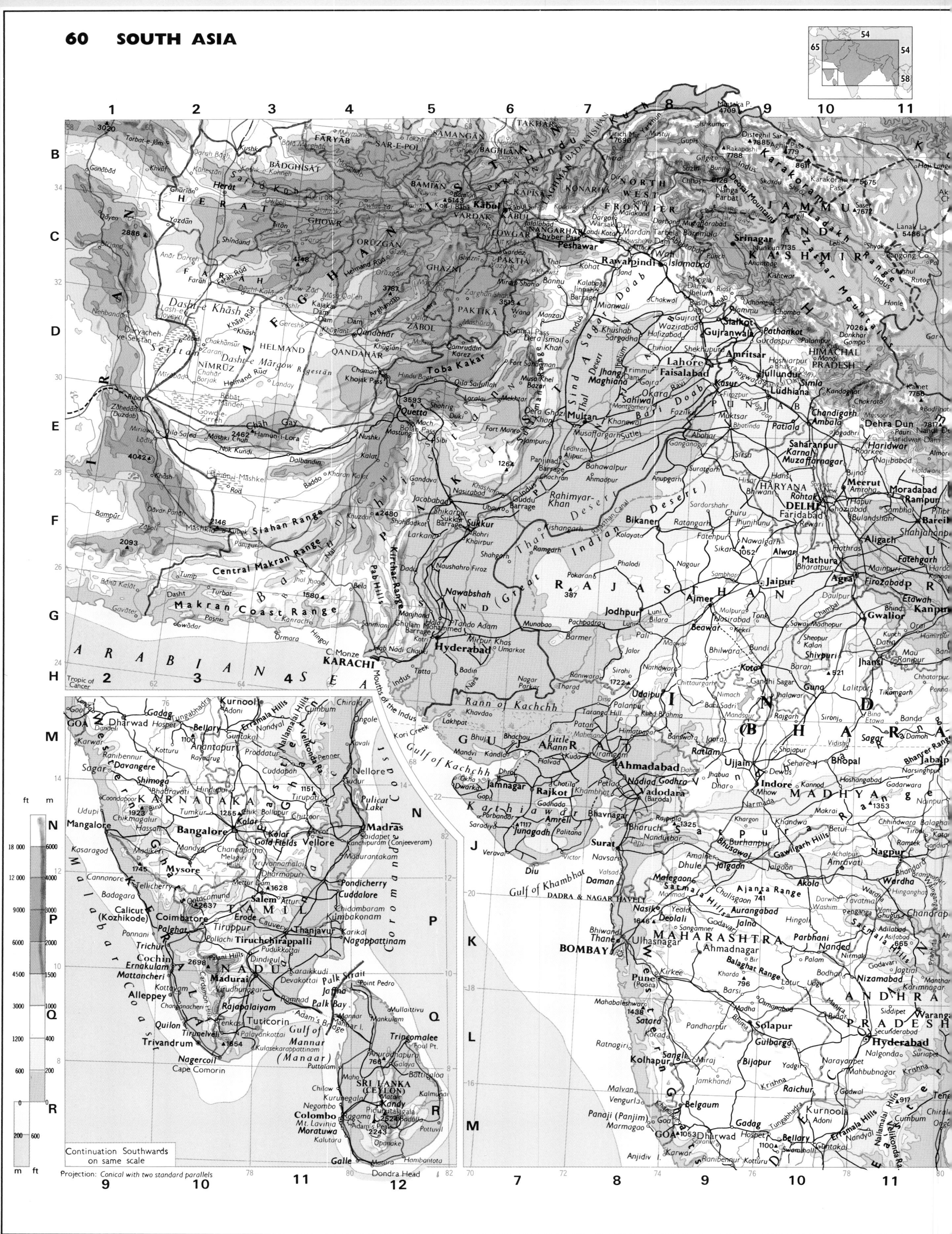
ARABIAN SEA
Tropic of Cancer
Makran Coast Range
Central Makran Range
Siahan Range
Toba Kakar
Dasht-e Khāsh
Dasht-e Mārgow
Seistan
Sulaiman Range
Thar Desert (Great Indian Desert)
Rann of Kachchh
Gulf of Kachchh
Gulf of Khambhat
Mouths of the Indus
Karakoram Pass
Karakoram
Ladakh Range
Zaskar Mountains
Hindu Kush
JAMMU AND KASHMIR
NORTH WEST FRONTIER
HIMACHAL PRADESH
PUNJAB
HARYANA
RAJASTHAN
MADHYA PRADESH
MAHARASHTRA
ANDHRA PRADESH
KARNATAKA
TAMIL NADU
KERALA
SRI LANKA (CEYLON)
DADRA & NAGAR HAVELI
Satpura Range
Vindhya Range
Western Ghats
Eastern Ghats
Malabar Coast
Coromandel Coast
Palk Strait
Palk Bay
Gulf of Mannar (Manaar)
Adam's Bridge
Cape Comorin
Dondra Head
Kābul
Herāt
Qandahār
Quetta
Peshawar
Rawalpindi
Islamabad
Srinagar
Lahore
Faisalabad
Multan
Hyderabad
KARACHI
Sukkur
Amritsar
Ludhiana
Jullundur
Simla
Chandigarh
DELHI
Meerut
Agra
Aligarh
Jaipur
Jodhpur
Ajmer
Bikaner
Ahmadabad
Vadodara (Baroda)
Rajkot
Jamnagar
Surat
BOMBAY
Pune (Poona)
Nagpur
Indore
Ujjain
Bhopal
Gwalior
Jhansi
Aurangabad
Nasik
Solapur
Kolhapur
Belgaum
Hyderabad
Bangalore
Mysore
Mangalore
Madras
Pondicherry
Cuddalore
Salem
Coimbatore
Madurai
Tiruchchirappalli
Thanjavur
Nagappattinam
Calicut (Kozhikode)
Cochin
Ernakulam
Alleppey
Quilon
Trivandrum
Nagercoil
Tuticorin
Jaffna
Trincomalee
Kandy
Colombo
Moratuwa
Galle
Continuation Southwards on same scale
Projection: Conical with two standard parallels

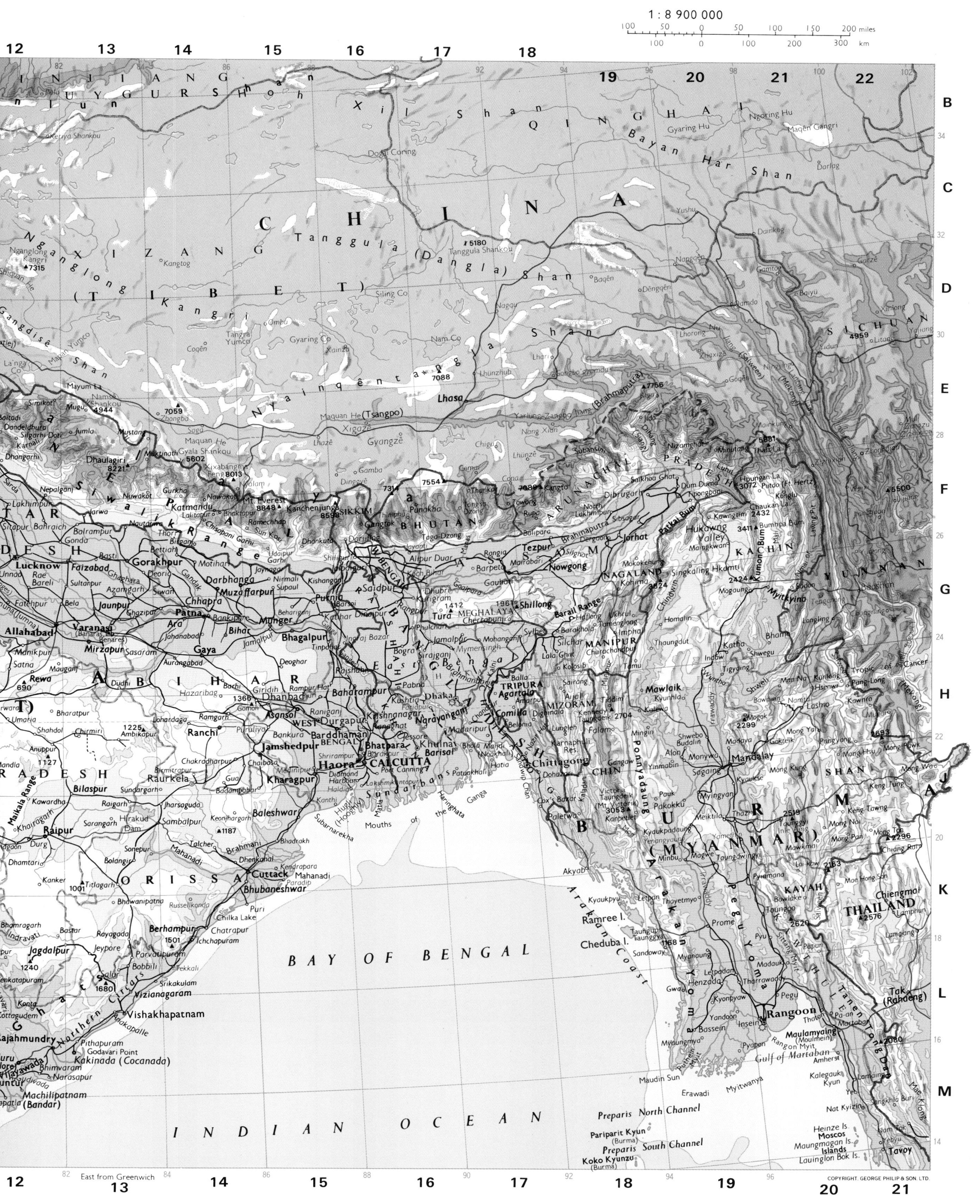

1 : 8 900 000

B

C

X I N J I A N G
U Y G U R S H A N
Xil Shan
Q I N G H A I
Gyaring Hu Ngoring Hu Maqên Gangri
Dogai Coring Bayan Har Shan
Doring
34

C

C H I N A
Yushu Gutzê
32

5180
Tanggula (Dangla) Shan
Nagqu Dêngqên
X I Z A N G Tanggula Shankou
Kangtog Siling Co Baqên
Bayi
(T I B E T) K a n g r i
Lhasa
S I C H U A N
4959
30
D

Nganglong Kangri
7315
La'nga Co Mapam Yumco
7059 Zhongba
Gyaring Co Xainza Nam Co
Nyainqêntanglha Shan 7088
Lhünzhub
Maquan He (Tsangpo)
Xigazê Gyangzê
Yarlung Zangbo Jiang (Brahmaputra) 7758
5500
28
E

Namse
4944 Mustang
Dhaulagiri 8221 5602
Everest 8848 8013
Kanchenjunga 8598
7314 7554 70801 Kangto
7088 Lhünze
ARUNACHAL PRADESH 3072 Putao (Ft. Hertz)
26
F

N E P A L Katmandu Patan
SIKKIM
Gangtok
Thimphu Punakha
BHUTAN
Taga-Dzong
Tezpur S M 5881 Thai La
KACHIN
2432
Hukawng Valley 3411
Myitkyina
Y U N N A N
G

U T T A R
Lucknow Faizabad Gorakhpur
D E S H
Allahabad Varanasi (Banaras) Patna
Darbhanga Muzaffarpur
WEST BENGAL
Shillong MEGHALAYA Barail Range
1412 1961 Silchar
NAGALAND Kohima 3824
MANIPUR Imphal
2424
H

B I H A R Gaya
Bhagalpur Munger
Dhanbad Asansol Durgapur
WEST BENGAL Krishnanagar
Dhaka Narayanganj
BANGLADESH
Comilla TRIPURA Agartala
MIZORAM 2704
Mawlaik 2299
B U R M A (MYANMAR)
Mandalay
S H A N
24

22
H

M A D H Y A
P R A D E S H
Raipur
O R I S S A Cuttack
Bhubaneshwar
Jamshedpur Kharagpur
Haora CALCUTTA
Barisal Khulna
Chittagong CHIN
Akyab
Ramree I.
Magwe
K A Y A H
THAILAND
20

18
K

B A Y O F B E N G A L
Cheduba I.
Arakan Coast
Prome
Rangoon
Maulamyaing (Moulmein)
Gulf of Martaban
16
L

Vishakhapatnam
Machilipatnam (Bandar)
Bassein
Amherst
Tavoy
14
M

I N D I A N O C E A N
Preparis North Channel
Pariparit Kyun (Burma)
Preparis South Channel
Koko Kyunzu (Burma)
Maungmagan Is.
Lauington Bok Is.

East from Greenwich

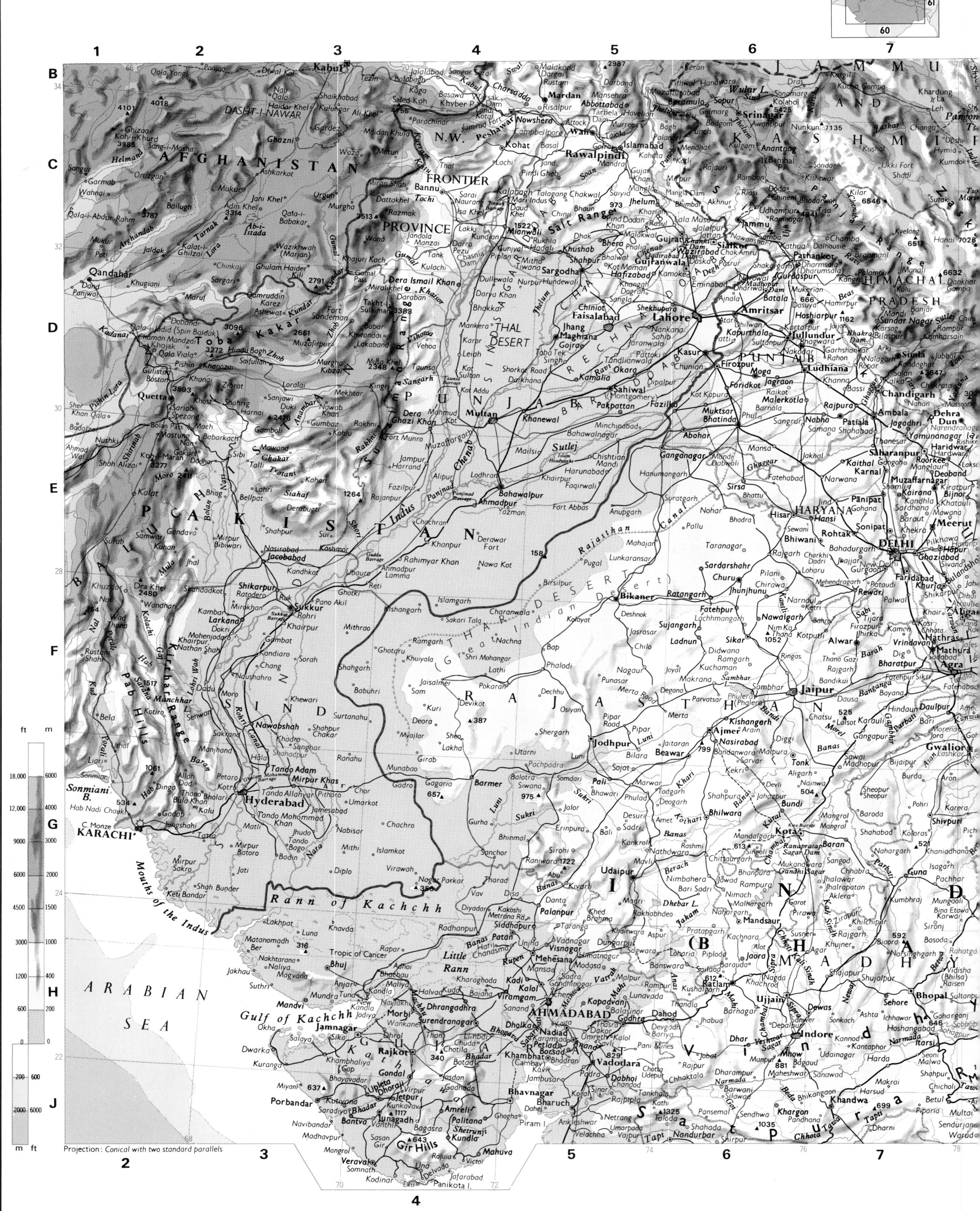

AFGHANISTAN
PAKISTAN
N.W. FRONTIER PROVINCE
PUNJAB
SIND
BALUCHISTAN
RAJASTHAN
HARYANA
HIMACHAL PRADESH
JAMMU AND KASHMIR
MADHYA PRADESH
GUJARAT
THAR DESERT
(Great Indian Desert)
THAL DESERT
ARABIAN SEA
Gulf of Kachchh
Rann of Kachchh
Little Rann
Mouths of the Indus
Tropic of Cancer
Kabul
Peshawar
Rawalpindi
Islamabad
Lahore
Amritsar
Multan
Quetta
Qandahar
Hyderabad
KARACHI
Sukkur
Bahawalpur
Faisalabad
Jammu
Srinagar
Chandigarh
Simla
Ludhiana
Jullundur
DELHI
Meerut
Agra
Jaipur
Bikaner
Jodhpur
Ajmer
Udaipur
Kota
Gwalior
Bhopal
Ujjain
Indore
AHMADABAD
Vadodara
Rajkot
Jamnagar
Bhavnagar
Junagadh
Bhuj
Salt Range
Toba Kakar
Kirthar Range
Pab Hills
Gir Hills
Indus
Chenab
Jhelum
Ravi
Sutlej
Beas
Luni
Narmada
Tapi
Chambal
Rajasthan Canal
Projection: Conical with two standard parallels

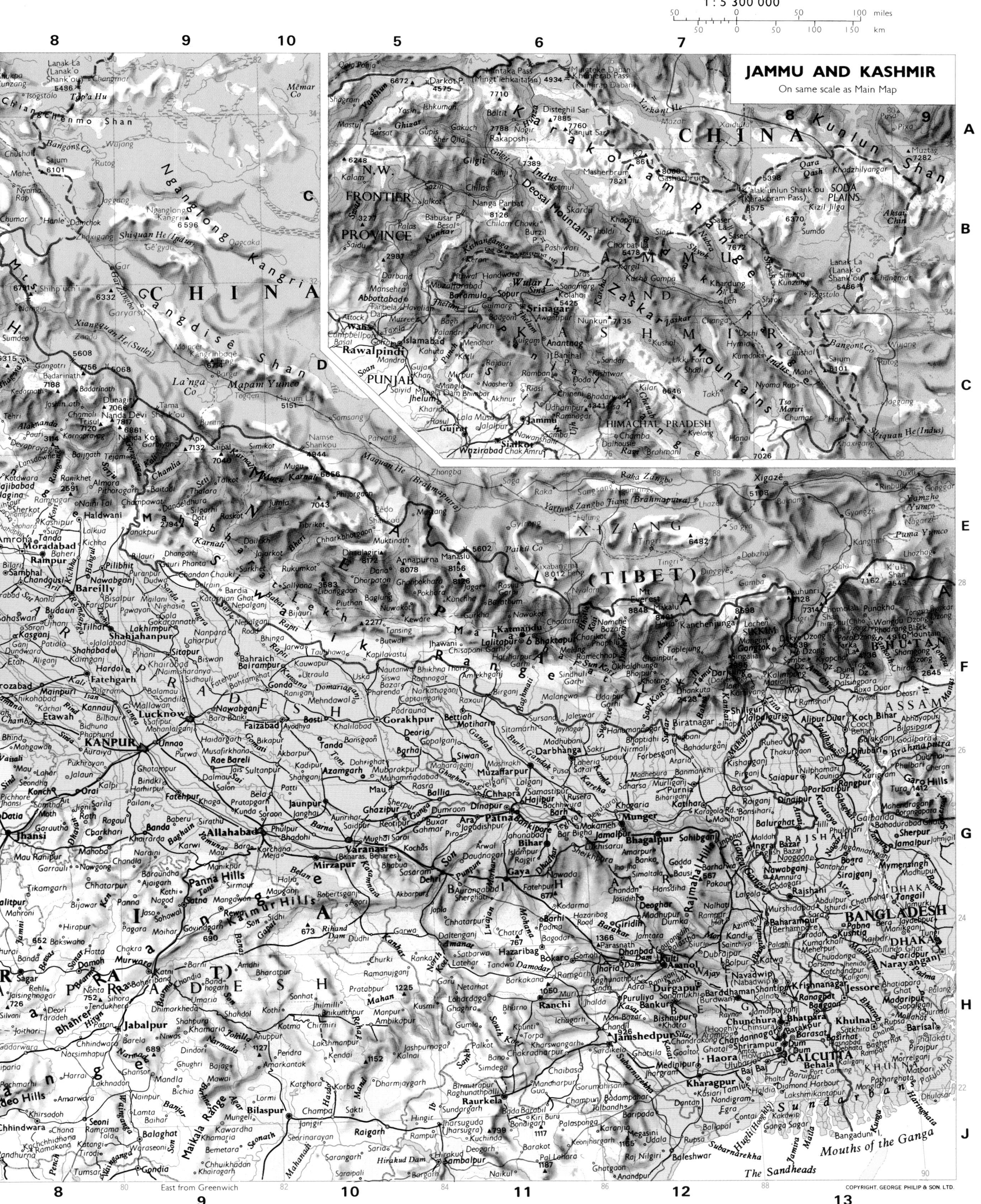

1 : 5 300 000

JAMMU AND KASHMIR
On same scale as Main Map

East from Greenwich

COPYRIGHT. GEORGE PHILIP & SON. LTD.

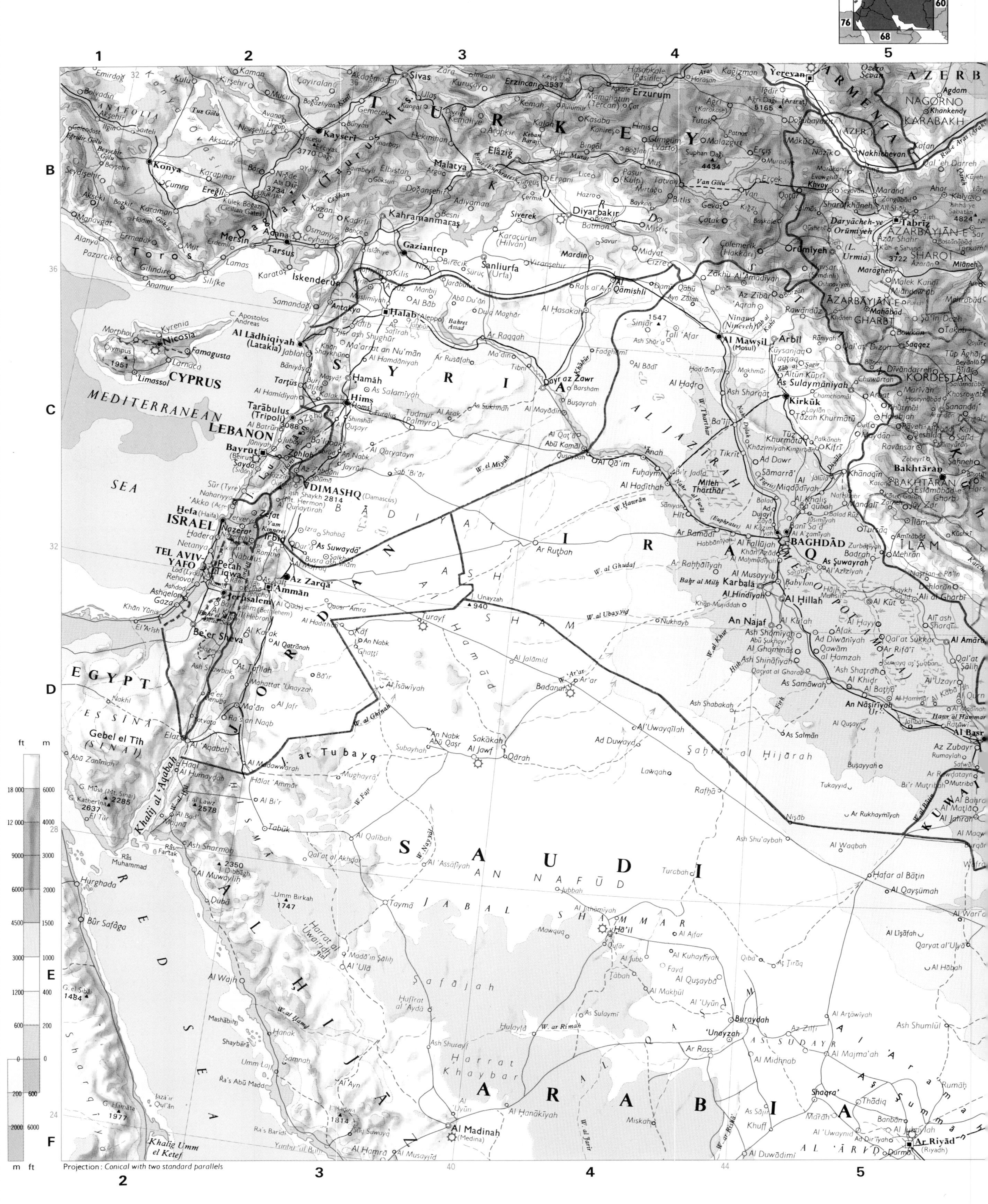
1
2
3
4
5
B
C
D
E
F
TURKEY
SYRIA
IRAQ
JORDAN
LEBANON
ISRAEL
CYPRUS
EGYPT
SAUDI ARABIA
ARMENIA
KUWAIT
MEDITERRANEAN SEA
RED SEA
AN NAFŪD
AL JAZĪRAH
BĀDIYAT ASH SHAM
AL ḤIJĀZ
JABAL SHAMMAR
MESOPOTAMIA
Ṣaḥrā' al Ḥijārah
Harrat Khaybar
Ṣafājah
AS SUDAYR
AL 'ĀRID
Gebel el Tih (SINAI)
ES SÎNÂ
ANATOLIA
Toros
Khalīj al 'Aqabah
Yerevan
Sivas
Erzurum
Kayseri
Konya
Malatya
Elâzığ
Diyarbakır
Adana
Mersin
Tarsus
Iskenderun
Gaziantep
Kahramanmaraş
Sanliurfa
Mardin
Antakya
Ḥalab (Aleppo)
Al Lādhiqīyah (Latakia)
Nicosia
Famagusta
Limassol
Larnaca
Ḥamāh
Ḥimṣ (Homs)
Ṭarābulus (Tripoli)
Bayrūt (Beirut)
Ṣaydā (Sidon)
DIMASHQ (Damascus)
Ḥefa (Haifa)
TEL AVIV-YAFO
Jerusalem
Be'er Sheva
'Ammān
Az Zarqā'
Irbid
Al 'Aqabah
Elat
Ma'ān
Tabūk
Tabrīz
Orūmīyeh
Daryācheh-ye Orūmīyeh
Al Mawṣil (Mosul)
Arbīl
Kirkūk
As Sulaymānīyah
BAGHDĀD
Karbalā'
An Najaf
Al Ḥillah
Al Kūt
An Nāṣirīyah
Al Baṣrah
Ar Ramādī
Ar Ruṭbah
Dayr az Zawr
Ar Raqqah
Al Qāmishlī
Al Ḥasakah
Bakhtarān
Ḥā'il
Buraydah
'Unayzah
Al Madīnah (Medina)
Ar Riyāḍ (Riyadh)
Al Jawf
Sakākah
Ḥafar al Bāţin
Projection: Conical with two standard parallels

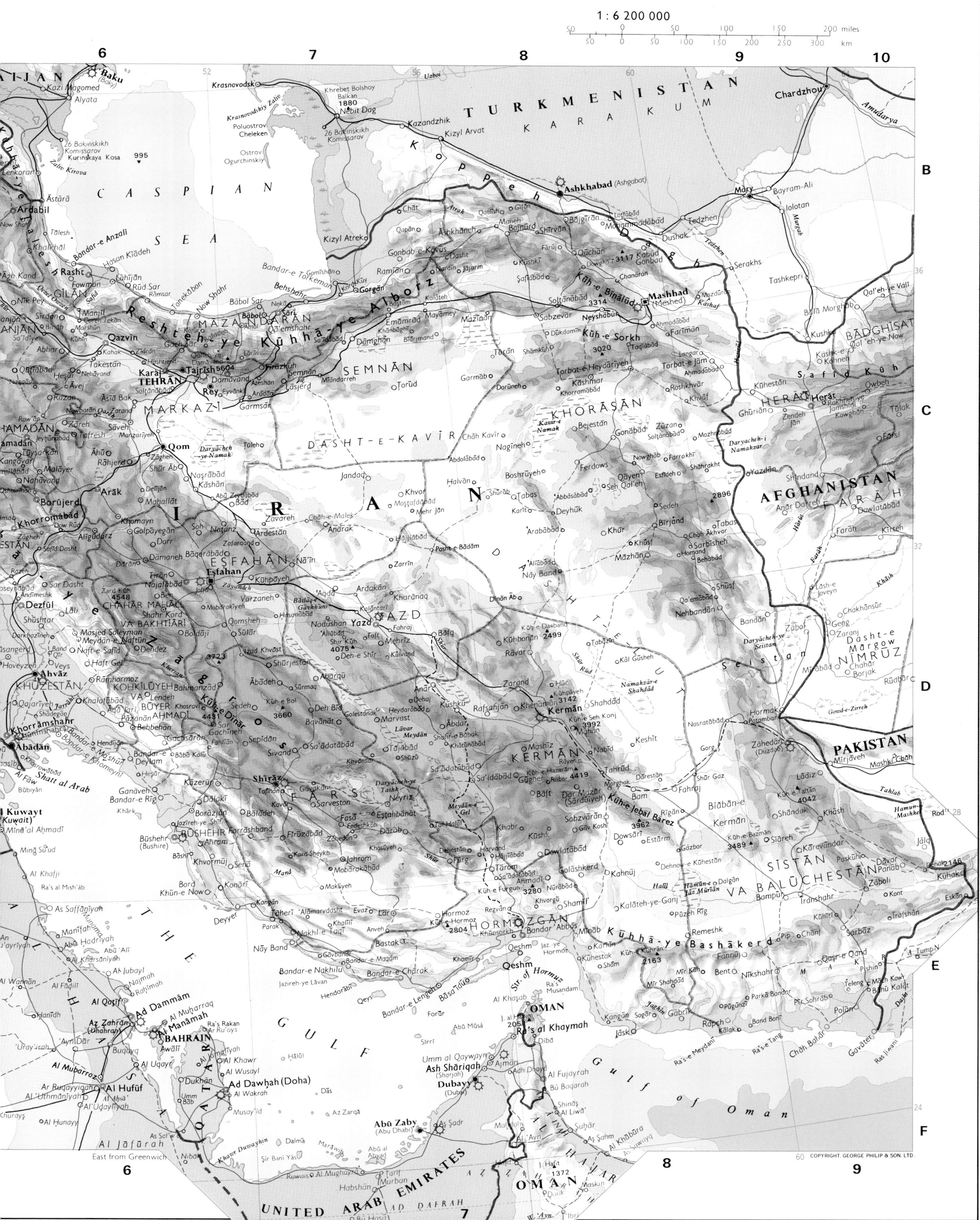

1 : 6 200 000
miles
km
TURKMENISTAN
KARA KUM
CASPIAN SEA
IRAN
AFGHANISTAN
PAKISTAN
OMAN
UNITED ARAB EMIRATES
QATAR
BAHRAIN
THE GULF
Gulf of Oman
Str. of Hormuz
Reshteh-ye Kūhhā-ye Alborz
Kopet Dagh
Zagros
DASHT-E-KAVĪR
DASHT-E-LUT
Kūhhā-ye Bashākerd
KHORĀSĀN
SEMNĀN
MAZANDARAN
GĪLĀN
MARKAZI
ESFAHĀN
YAZD
KERMĀN
FARS
BUSHEHR
HORMOZGĀN
SĪSTĀN VA BALŪCHESTĀN
KHUZESTĀN
KOHKĪLŪYEH VA BŪYER AHMADĪ
CHAHĀR MAHALL VA BAKHTĪĀRĪ
TEHRĀN
Tajrīsh
Rey
Karaj
Qom
Esfahān
Shīrāz
Yazd
Kermān
Mashhad (Meshed)
Ashkhabad (Ashgabat)
Baku (Bakı)
Krasnovodsk
Chardzhou
Mary
Herāt
Zāhedān (Duzdab)
Ahvāz
Ābādān
Khorramshahr
Bandar Abbās
Qeshm
Ad Dammām
Al Manāmah
Ad Dawḥah (Doha)
Abū Ẓaby (Abu Dhabi)
Dubayy (Dubai)
Ash Shāriqah (Sharjah)
Ra's al Khaymah
Kuwayt (Kuwait)
Shatt al Arab
Al Jāfūrah
East from Greenwich
COPYRIGHT. GEORGE PHILIP & SON. LTD.

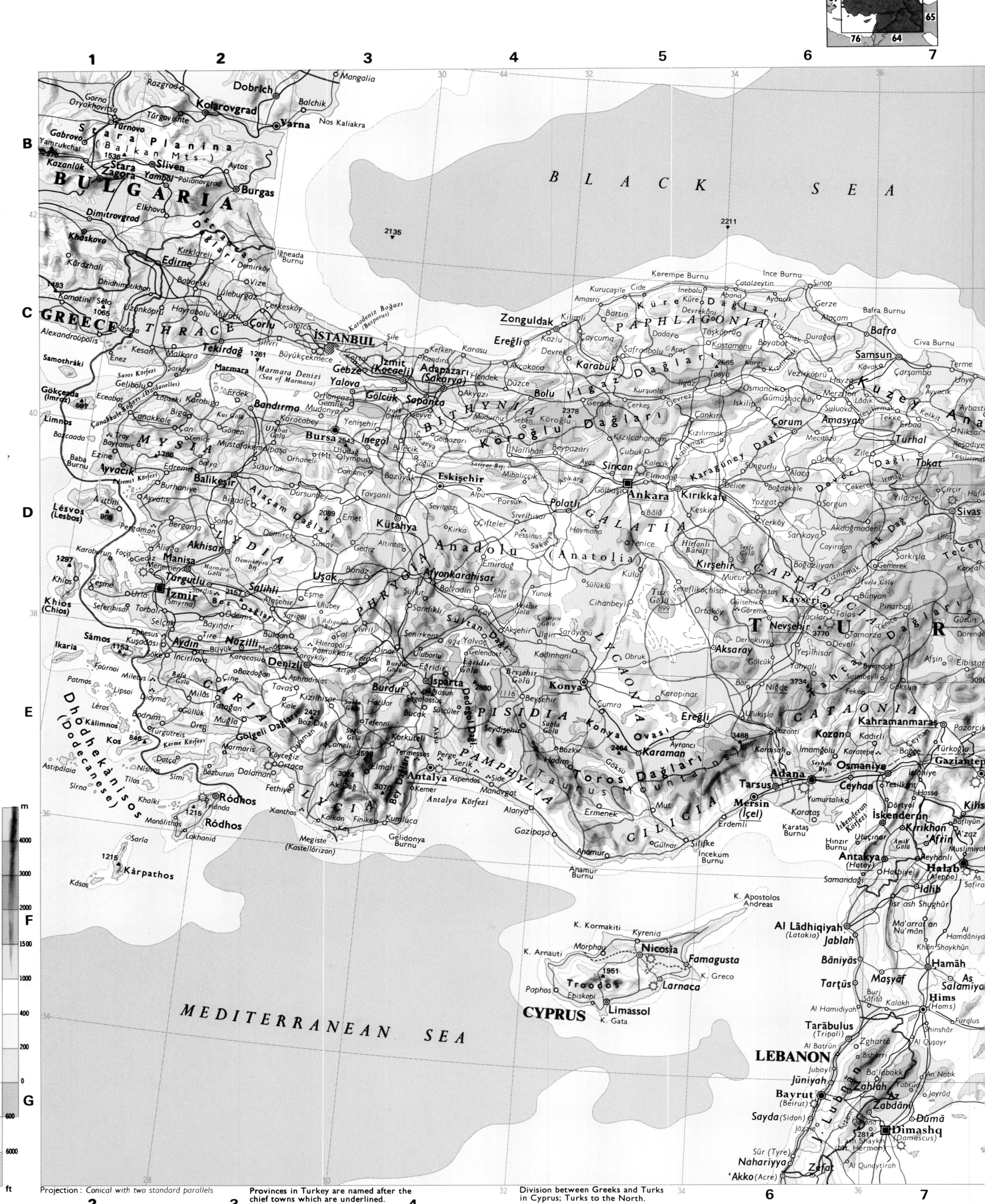

Projection: *Conical with two standard parallels*

Provinces in Turkey are named after the chief towns which are underlined.

Division between Greeks and Turks in Cyprus; Turks to the North.

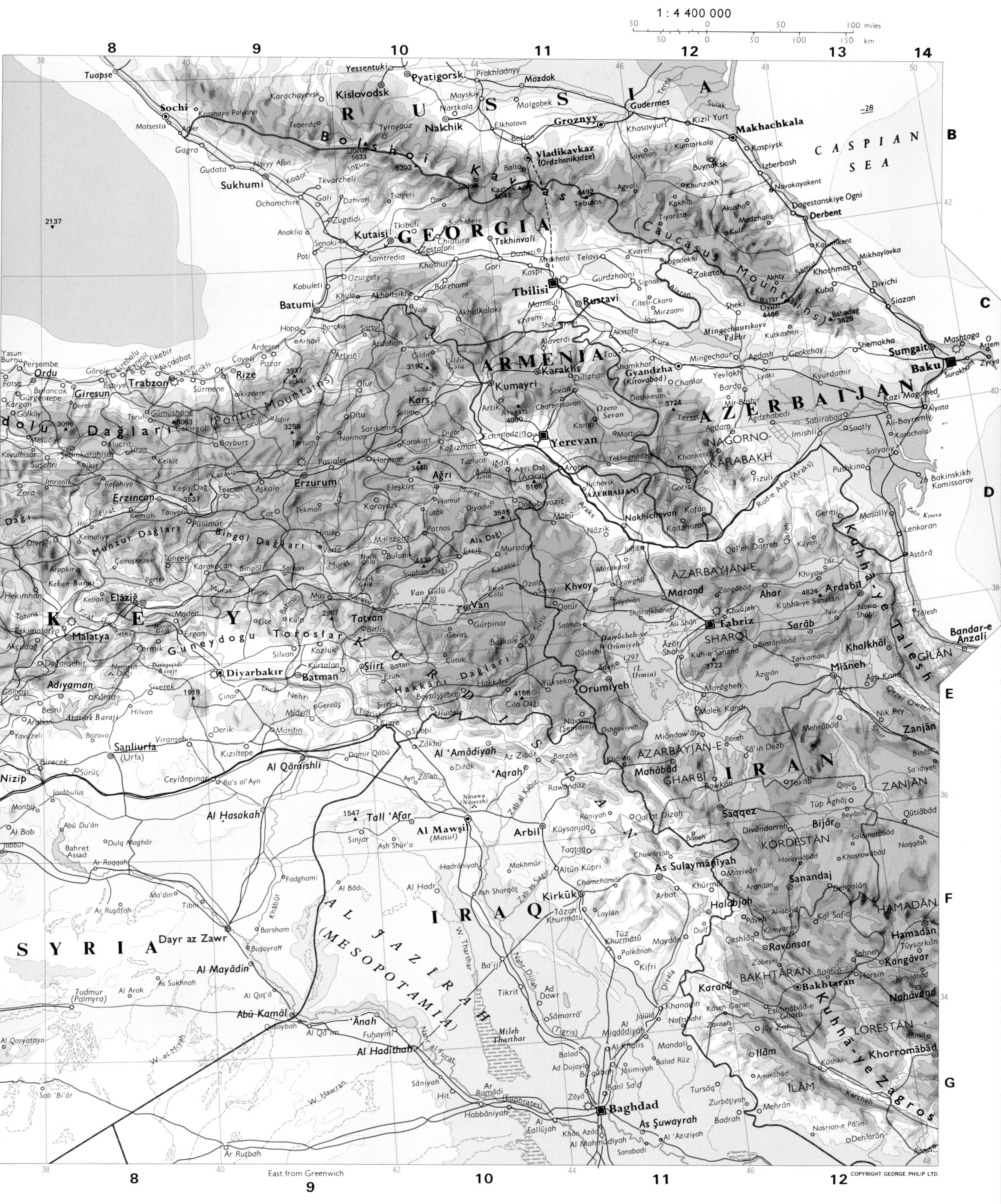
1 : 4 400 000
50 0 50 100 miles
50 0 50 100 150 km
8
9
10
11
12
13
14
B
C
D
E
F
G
East from Greenwich
RUSSIA
GEORGIA
ARMENIA
AZERBAIJAN
AZERBAIJAN
NAGORNO-KARABAKH
TURKEY
KURDISTAN
IRAQ
IRAN
SYRIA
CASPIAN SEA
Bolshoi Kavkas
Caucasus Mountains
Pontic Mountains
Güneydogu Toroslar
Hakkâri Dağlari
Munzur Dağlari
Bingöl Dağlari
Kuhha-ye Talesh
Kuhha-ye Zagros
AL JAZIRAH
(MESOPOTAMIA)
ĀZARBAYJĀN-E SHARQI
ĀZARBAYJĀN-E GHARBI
KORDESTĀN
BAKHTARAN
LORESTĀN
ĪLĀM
HAMADĀN
ZANJĀN
GĪLĀN
Tuapse
Sochi
Matsesta
Adler
Gagra
Gudata
Sukhumi
Ochamchire
Anaklia
Poti
Kobuleti
Batumi
Kutaisi
Zestafoni
Samtredia
Khashuri
Gori
Tskhinvali
Tbilisi
Rustavi
Telavi
Borzhomi
Akhaltsikhe
Akhalkalaki
Yessentuki
Pyatigorsk
Kislovodsk
Mozdok
Nalchik
Vladikavkaz
(Ordzhonikidze)
Groznyy
Gudermes
Khasavyurt
Makhachkala
Kaspiysk
Izberbash
Derbent
Elbrus 5633
Kazbek 5047
Tebulos 4492
Bazar Dyuzi 4466
Babadag 3629
Sumgait
Baku
Kumayri
Karaklis
Yerevan
Sevan
Ozero Sevan
Gyandzha
(Kirovabad)
Mingechaur
Yevlakh
Shemakha
Lenkoran
Astārā
Nakhichevan
Kafan
Goris
Stepanakert
Fizuli
Aragats 4090
Ağrı Dağı (Ararat) 5165
Ordu
Giresun
Trabzon
Rize
Artvin
Ardahan
Kars
Erzurum
Erzincan
Ağrı
Doğubayazit
Van Gölü
Van
Tatvan
Bitlis
Siirt
Batman
Diyarbakır
Elâzığ
Malatya
Adıyaman
Şanliurfa
(Urfa)
Mardin
Cizre
Khvoy
Marand
Tabriz
Ardabīl
Ahar
Sarāb
Orumiyeh
Daryācheh-ye Orūmiyeh
Mahābād
Miāneh
Zanjān
Saqqez
Bijār
Sanandaj
Bakhtarān
Hamadān
Kangāvar
Nahāvand
Khorramābād
Īlām
Bandar-e Anzali
Al Qāmishli
Al Ḩasakah
Dayr az Zawr
Al Mayādin
Abū Kamāl
Tudmur
(Palmyra)
Tall 'Afar
Al Mawşil
(Mosul)
Arbil
Kirkūk
As Sulaymānīyah
Halabjah
Tikrit
Sāmarrā'
Baghdad
Al Fallūjah
Ar Ramādi
Al Hadithah
'Ānah
Ba'qūbah
As Şuwayrah
Ar Ruţbah
COPYRIGHT GEORGE PHILIP LTD.

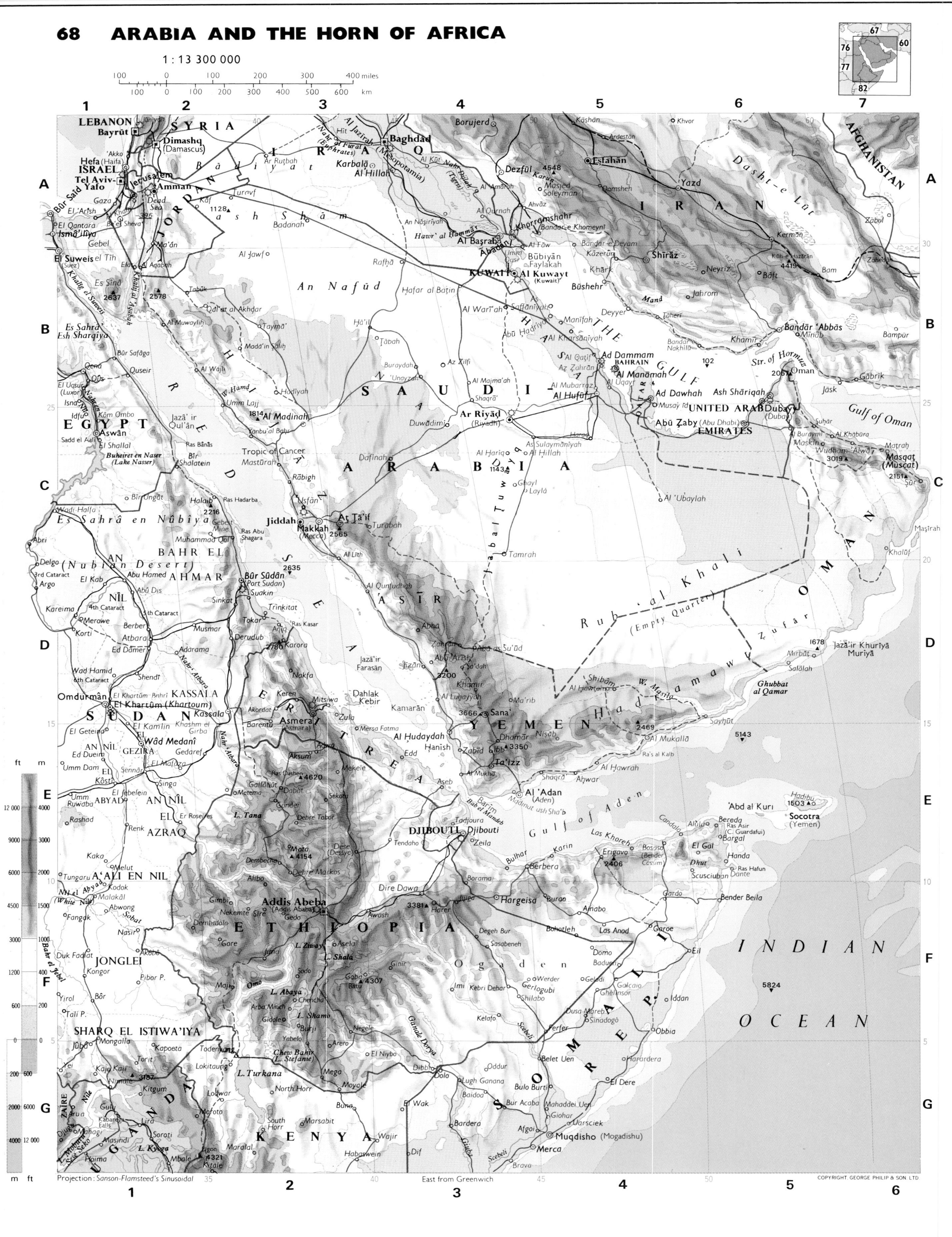
68 ARABIA AND THE HORN OF AFRICA
1 : 13 300 000
100 0 100 200 300 400 miles
100 0 100 200 300 400 500 600 km
LEBANON
Bayrût
SYRIA
Dimashq (Damascus)
Baghdad
IRAQ
Hefa (Haifa)
ISRAEL
Tel Aviv-Yafo
Jerusalem
Amman
JORDAN
Bâdiyat ash Shâm
Karbalā
Al Hillah
Dezfūl
Eşfahān
IRAN
Dasht-e Lūt
Yazd
Kermān
Shīrāz
AFGHANISTAN
Al Başrah
Abadan
Khorramshahr
KUWAIT
Al Kuwayt (Kuwait)
Būshehr
Bandar 'Abbās
Str. of Hormuz
THE GULF
Ad Dammam
BAHRAIN
Al Manāmah
QATAR
Ad Dawhah
UNITED ARAB EMIRATES
Abū Ẓaby (Abu Dhabi)
Dubayy (Dubai)
Ash Shāriqah
Gulf of Oman
Masqat (Muscat)
OMAN
Bûr Saîd
Ismâ'îlîya
El Suweis (Suez)
Es Sînâ
An Nafūd
SAUDI ARABIA
Ar Riyāḍ (Riyadh)
Al Madīnah
Jiddah
Makkah (Mecca)
Aṭ Ṭā'if
Tropic of Cancer
RED SEA
Rub' al Khali (Empty Quarter)
EGYPT
Aswân
Buheiret en Naser (Lake Nasser)
Es Sahrâ en Nûbîya (Nubian Desert)
Bûr Sûdân (Port Sudan)
BAHR EL AHMAR
NÎL
KASSALA
Omdurmân
El Khartûm (Khartoum)
SUDAN
Wâd Medanî
GEZIRA
ERITREA
Asmera (Asmara)
YEMEN
Sana'
Al Ḥudaydah
Al 'Adan (Aden)
Ḥaḍramawt
Gulf of Aden
Socotra (Yemen)
DJIBOUTI
Djibouti
Addis Abeba (Addis Ababa)
ETHIOPIA
L. Tana
Ogaden
Hargeisa
SOMALI REP.
Muqdisho (Mogadishu)
INDIAN OCEAN
KENYA
L. Turkana
UGANDA
JONGLEI
SHARQ EL ISTIWA'IYA
Projection: Sanson-Flamsteed's Sinusoidal
East from Greenwich
COPYRIGHT. GEORGE PHILIP & SON. LTD

1 : 2 200 000

10 0 10 20 30 40 50 miles
10 0 10 20 30 40 50 60 70 80 km

CYPRUS

Paphos
Episkopi
Episkopi Bay
Limassol
Akrotiri Bay
C. Gata

M E D I T E R R A N E A N

S E A

Al Hamidiyah
Tall Kalakh
Hims (Homs)
1075
Furqlus

Al Minā'
Halbā
ASH SHAMĀL
Al Quşayr
HIMS
Tarābulus (Tripoli)
Zgharta
Qurnat as Sawdā'
3088
Al Hirmil
An Nabk
Bi'r Ghadir

Al Batrūn
Dūmā
Bega'a Valley
Al Buray'
Al Qaryatayn

Jubayl
Qurtadā
246
Az Zabādāni
2616
Ba'labakk
Yabrūd
Yabrūdā

Jūniyah
Ibrāhim
2628
SYRIA
J. az Zubaydīyah 1406

BAYRŪT (Beirut)
Bikfayyā
2420
Ash Sham
Al Qutayfah
Alayh
Zahlah
Jabal

Ash Shuwayfāt
Khirbat Qanāfār al Bārūk
1942
DIMASHQ
Dūmā
Khān Abū Shāmāt

LEBANON
Saydā (Sidon)
Jazzin
An Nabatiyah at Tahta
Ash Shaykh (Jt. Hermon) 2814
DIMASHQ (Damascus)
Qatanā
Darayyā
A'waj
Al Hijānah

AL JANŪB
Sūr (Tyre)
Al Khiyām
Al Kiswah
Burāq

Qiryat Shemona
1977
Al Qunaytirah
Rafid
As Sanamayn
DARĀ
As Safa

Nahariyya
Me'ona
HAZOR
Golan Hts.
As Suwaydā
Shahba

Akko (Acre)
Zefat
Hagalil
Yam
Saham al Jawlān
W. al Harir
AS SUWAYDĀ

Mifraz Hefa
Sakhnin
Migdal
Dar'ā
As Suwaydā
1800
Sālah

Hefa (Haifa)
Qiryat Yam
Qiryat Ata
Teverya (Tiberias)
Kinneret
Yarmūk
DARĀ
Salkhad
As Safa

Tirat Karmel
Nazerat (Nazareth)
Al Ramthā
Salkhad
Umm al Qittayn

Dāliyat el Karmel
HEFA
'Afula
Bet She'an
Irbid
Jusrā ash Shām

TEL MEGIDDO
HAZAFON
Aijūn
ad Darā
Al Mafraq
IRBID

CAESAREA
Umm el Fahm
Jenin
1247
Jarash

Hadera
Pardes Hanna
Shōmrōn
Zarqā
AL 'ĀSIMAH

ISRAEL
Netanya
NABULUS
SAMARIA
Az Zarqā'

HAMERKAZ
Tulkarm
W. az Zarqā'
AMMĀN

Herzliyya
Under Israeli Administration
As Salt
AL BALQA'

Benē Beraq
SHILO
Wadi as Sir
At Tunayb

Tel Aviv-Yafo
Petah Tiqwa
Ramat Gan
WEST BANK
Tell 'Asur
AMMĀN

Bat Yam
Lod
1016
Mādabā

Rishon le Ziyyon
N. Soreq
Ramla
AL QUDS
'Aliya (Jericho)
Mādabā

Rehovot
Ram Allāh
Arihā
W. al Haydān
Dhibān

Ashdod
Yavne
Bet Shemesh
Jerusalem (Yerushalayim) (Al Quds)
W. al Mawjib

Qiryat Mal'akhi
Bet Lahm (Bethlehem)
Al Khalil (Hebron)
1065

Ashqelon
TEL LAKHISH
Az Zāhiriya
Al Qatrānah

Qiryat Gat
AL KHALIL
'Arad
Al Karak
981

Gaza
N. Shiqma
Sederot
JORDAN
AL KARAK

Gaza Strip
Be'er Sheva
El Daheir
Bor Mashash
1305
W. al Hasa

Bûr Sa'id (Port Said)
Khān Yūnis
Rafah
Dimona
682
At Tafilah
W. al Ghadaf
W. al Mukhrug

Bûr Fu'ad
Khalīg el Tina
Sabkhet el Bardawil
Râs Burûn
El 'Arish
-333
AL KARAK
Bā'ir

Qanâ el Suweis
Ismâ'ilîya
Bîr el Garārāt
Qezi'ot
Bir'an
-121
W. Bā'ir

Khamsa
Bîr Qatia
Bîr el Abd
Bîr Kaseiba
HADAROM
1072
W. ash Shawmari

El Qantara
Wâhid
Muweilih
El Qunaima
Nijil
Mahattat 'Unayzah

El Buheirat el Murrat el Kubra (Gt. Bitter L.)
Bîr el Mâlhi
892
Mizpe Ramon
Hanegev (Negev Desert)
Bi'r ad Dabbāghāt
Ruim Tal'at al Jamā'ah
1736
W. Abū Safar

Gineifa
Bîr Hasana
G. Yi 'Allaq 1094
Bîr Beida
N. Paran
MA'ĀN
Qa' el Jafr

EL SUWEIS
EGYPT
Bîr el Thamâda
W. el Brûk
W. Qiratya
El 'Agrûd
N. Higyon
PETRA
Al Jafr

875
El Suweis (Suez)
Taufiq
'Ain Sudr
W. el Saheira
W. el 'Aqaba
W. Mahasham
Yotvata
Ma'ān
Bi'r al Mārī

Uyûn Mûsa
Nakhl
El Quntilla
Ra's an Naqb
Mahattat ash Shidiyah

Bîr Bad'
S I N A I
W. Giddi
'En 'Avrona
Ra's an Naqb 1435
Bi'r al Qattara

Ghubbet el Bûs
948 G. el Kabrit
Gebel el Tîh
El Thamad
Bîr Abu Muhammad
Bi'r al Butayyih

Bîr Abu Sandīq
1272
Sinai Peninsula
W. Abu Ga'da
W. el Gaiîr
1592
Al 'Aqabah
952

SAUDI ARABIA

Bîr el Biârt
Bîr Tâba
Khalig al 'Aqaba
W. an Nuwayfi
J. at Tubayq

1165

- - - 1949 Armistice Line, 1967 and 1974 Cease Fire Lines

ft m
9000 3000
6000 2000
4500 1500
3000 1000
1200 400
600 200
0 0
200 600
2000 6000
m ft

1 : 36 000 000

200   0   200   400   600   800   1000 miles
200   0   200   400   600   800 1000 1200 1400 1600 km

1 2 3 4 5 6 7 8 9 10

ATLANTIC OCEAN

British Isles
Bay of Biscay
Carpathians
Black Sea
Caucasus   Elbrus 5633
Aral Sea
Caspian Sea
Alps   Mt. Blanc 4807
Pyrenees
Apennines
Dinaric Alps
Adriatic Sea
Anatolia
Iberian Peninsula
Corsica
Sardinia
6576
Madeira
Str. of Gibraltar
C. Bon   Sicily   5121   Crete   Cyprus   Levant   Mesopotamia   Tigris
Mediterranean Sea
Malta
High plateaus
Middle Atlas   High Atlas   Saharan Atlas
Chott Djerid
G. of Gabes
G. of Sidra
Syrian Desert   Euphrates
The Gulf
Tripolitania   Cyrenaica
Anti Atlas   Toubkal 4165
Canary Is.   3718
Tenerife
Dra
Igidi
Tuat
Tasili Plateau
Fezzan
Siwa
Egypt   Nile
Kufra
El Kharga
Libyan Desert
Arabian Desert   Sinai 2642
Hejaz
Red Sea
Arabia
Tropic of Cancer
Bahrain I.
Ras Nouadhibou
Sahara
El Djouf
Hoggar
Nubian Desert
Nubia
Rub' al Khali
Cape Verde Is.
Adrar
Aïr
Tibesti 3415
Bilma
Socotra
C. Vert
Senegal
Senegambia
Gambia
Fouta Djalon
Niger (Joliba)
Volta
Niger
L. Chad
Wadai   Darfur   Kordofan
White Nile   Blue Nile
Atbara
Ras Dashan 4620   L. Tana
Perim I.
Str. of Bab el Mandeb
Gulf of Aden
Ras Asir
Sudan
Ethiopian Highlands
Somali Peninsula
Guinea
Grain Coast
Gold Coast   Slave Coast
Ivory Coast
Bight of Benin
C. Palmas
Bioko   6363
Adamawa Highlands
Cameroon Peak 4070
Chari
Benue
Ubangi
Dar Banda
Bahr el Ghazal
Ghazal   Bel Jebel
Uele
Turkana
Shabeli
Gulf of Guinea
São Tomé
Principe
C. Lopez
Annobón
Congo
Zaire (Congo)
Ogoue
Chutes Boyoma
L. Mobutu Sese Seko
Ruwenzori 5109
Elgon 4321
Kenya 5199
Equator
Basin
Kasai
Sankuru
Lualaba
L. Edward
L. Kivu
Victoria
Kilimanjaro 5895
INDIAN OCEAN
Ascension
St. Helena
Pool Malebo
Kwango
Kasai
L. Tanganyika
Pemba
Zanzibar
Guanza
Cubango
Luapula
Mweru
Rungwe 2961
L. Nyasa
Ruvuma
C. Delgado
Aldabra Is.
Comoros Is.
ATLANTIC OCEAN
Bié Plateau
L. Bangweulu
Shabal
Malawi
Mozambique Channel
Madagascar   2643
C. Fria
Cunene
Cubango
Cuando
Zambezi
Shire   Mlanje 3000
Walvis Bay
Namib Desert
Victoria Falls
Kalahari
Limpopo
Tropic of Capricorn
Maur
Réunion
Orange
High Veld
Drakensberg 3482
Delagoa Bay
Compass B 2505
Nieuveldberge   Gt. Karoo   Swartberg
Orange
Algoa Bay
C. of Good Hope
C. Agulhas
Agulhas Bank

ft   m
12 000   4000
9000   3000
6000   2000
4500   1500
3000   1000
1200   400
600   200
0   0
600   200
2000   6000
4000   12 000
6000   18 000
m   ft

Projection: Zenithal Equidistant.
10   West from Greenwich   0   East from Greenwich   10   20   30   40   50
COPYRIGHT. GEORGE PHILIP & SON LTD.

1 2 3 4 5 6 7 8 9

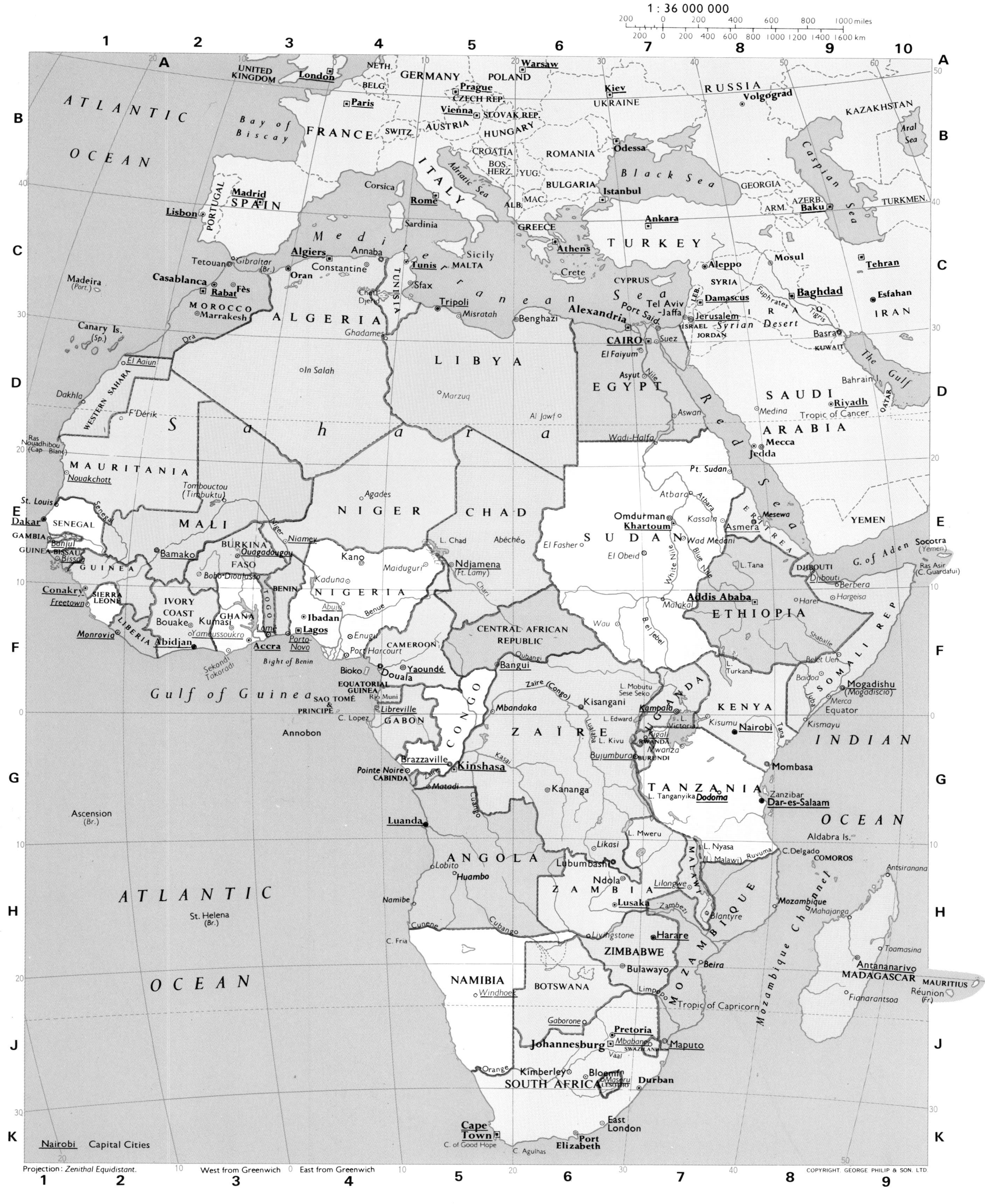

1 : 36 000 000

200   0   200   400   600   800   1000 miles
200   0   200 400 600 800 1000 1200 1400 1600 km

Projection: *Zenithal Equidistant.*

Nairobi   Capital Cities

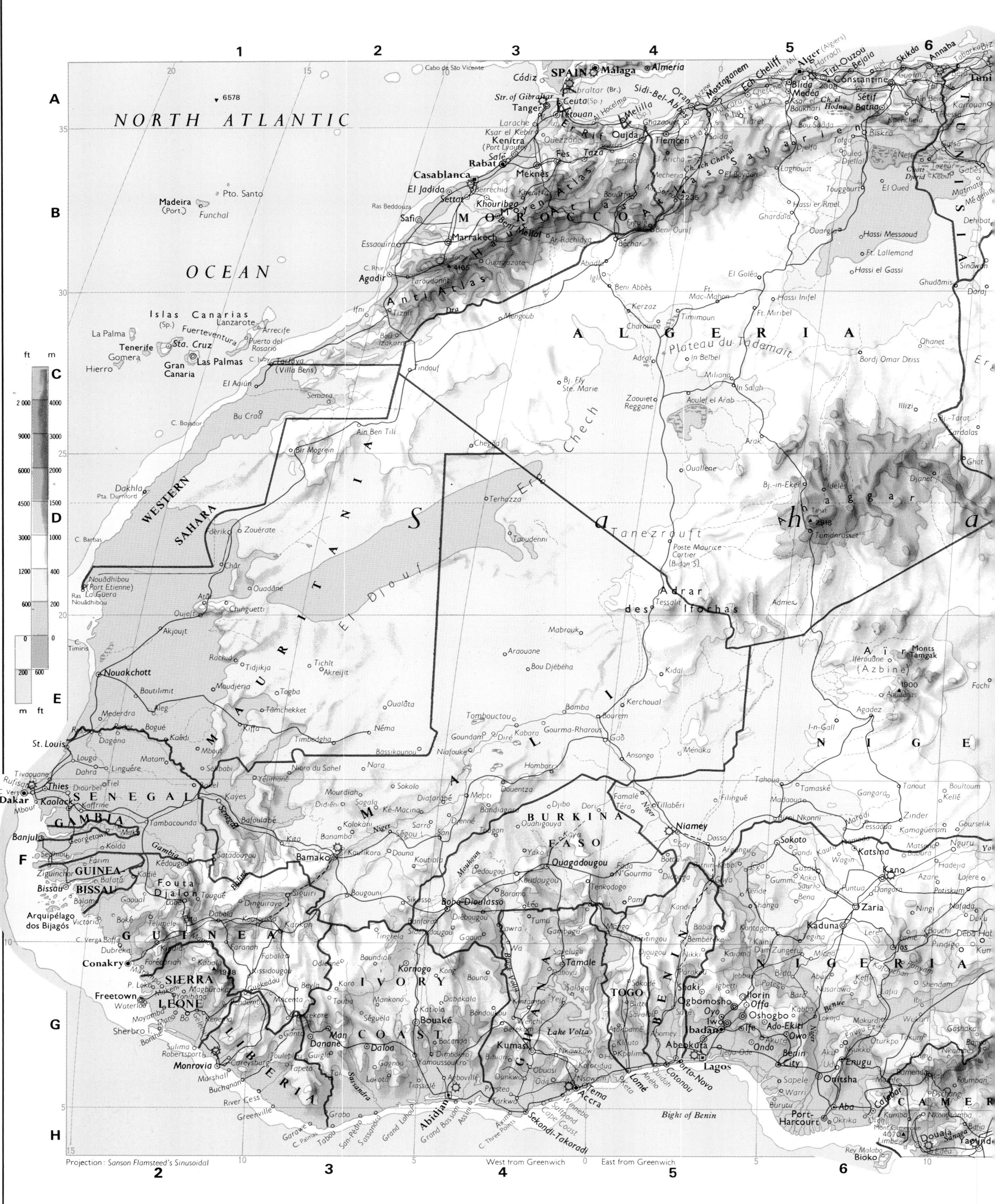
NORTH ATLANTIC
OCEAN
Madeira (Port.)
Funchal
Pto. Santo
Islas Canarias (Sp.)
Lanzarote
Fuerteventura
La Palma
Tenerife
Gomera
Hierro
Gran Canaria
Las Palmas
Sta. Cruz
SPAIN
Málaga
Almeria
Cádiz
Str. of Gibraltar
Gibraltar (Br.)
Tanger
Ceuta (Sp.)
Tétouan
Melilla (Sp.)
Oujda
Tlemcen
Oran
Sidi-Bel-Abbès
Mostaganem
Ech Cheliff
Alger (Algiers)
Blida
Médéa
Tizi-Ouzou
Bejaia
Skikda
Annaba
Constantine
Sétif
Batna
Biskra
Touggourt
Laghouat
Ghardaïa
Ouargla
Hassi Messaoud
Ft. Lallemand
Hassi el Gassi
El Goléa
Larache
Kenitra
Rabat
Salé
Fès
Taza
Meknès
Casablanca
El Jadida
Settat
Khouribga
Safi
Marrakech
Essaouira
Agadir
Ouarzazate
Ar-Rachidya
Béchar
Beni Abbès
MOROCCO
Anti Atlas
Haut Atlas
Moyen Atlas
Er Rif
Tindouf
Tarfaya (Villa Bens)
El Aaiún
Semara
Bu Craa
C. Bojador
Dakhla
WESTERN SAHARA
C. Barbas
Nouâdhibou (Port Etienne)
Ras Nouâdhibou
ALGERIA
Plateau du Tademait
Adrar
In Salah
Timimoun
Reggane
Hassi Inifel
Bordj Omar Driss
Illizi
Djanet
Ahaggar
Tamanrasset
Tanezrouft
Poste Maurice Cortier (Bidon 5)
Adrar des Iforhas
Tessalit
Kidal
Bj. Fly Ste. Marie
Chech
Erg
Taoudenni
Terhazza
Chegga
Bir Mogrein
Zouérate
F'dérik
Atâr
Chinguetti
Ouadâne
Akjoujt
Nouakchott
Tidjikja
Tichît
Néma
Kiffa
Aleg
Rosso
Boutilimit
Kaédi
MAURITANIA
El Djouf
Araouane
Bou Djébéha
Mabrouk
Tombouctou
Gao
Bourem
Kerchoual
Ménaka
Ansongo
MALI
Mopti
Ségou
Bamako
Kayes
Sikasso
Niono
Nioro du Sahel
St. Louis
Dakar
Thies
Kaolack
SENEGAL
GAMBIA
Banjul
Tambacounda
Ziguinchor
GUINEA-BISSAU
Bissau
Arquipélago dos Bijagós
Fouta Djalon
GUINEA
Conakry
Kankan
Labé
SIERRA LEONE
Freetown
LIBERIA
Monrovia
IVORY COAST
Bouaké
Abidjan
Daloa
Man
Korhogo
BURKINA FASO
Ouagadougou
Bobo-Dioulasso
GHANA
Kumasi
Tamale
Lake Volta
Accra
Tema
Sekondi-Takoradi
TOGO
Lomé
BENIN
Porto-Novo
Cotonou
Niamey
NIGER
Agadez
Aïr (Azbine)
Monts Tamgak
Zinder
Maradi
Tahoua
NIGERIA
Sokoto
Kano
Katsina
Zaria
Kaduna
Jos
Ilorin
Ogbomosho
Oshogbo
Ibadan
Abeokuta
Lagos
Benin City
Onitsha
Enugu
Port Harcourt
Aba
Calabar
Bight of Benin
Bioko
Douala
Yaoundé
CAMEROON
TUNISIA
Ghudāmis
Projection: Sanson Flamsteed's Sinusoidal
West from Greenwich
East from Greenwich

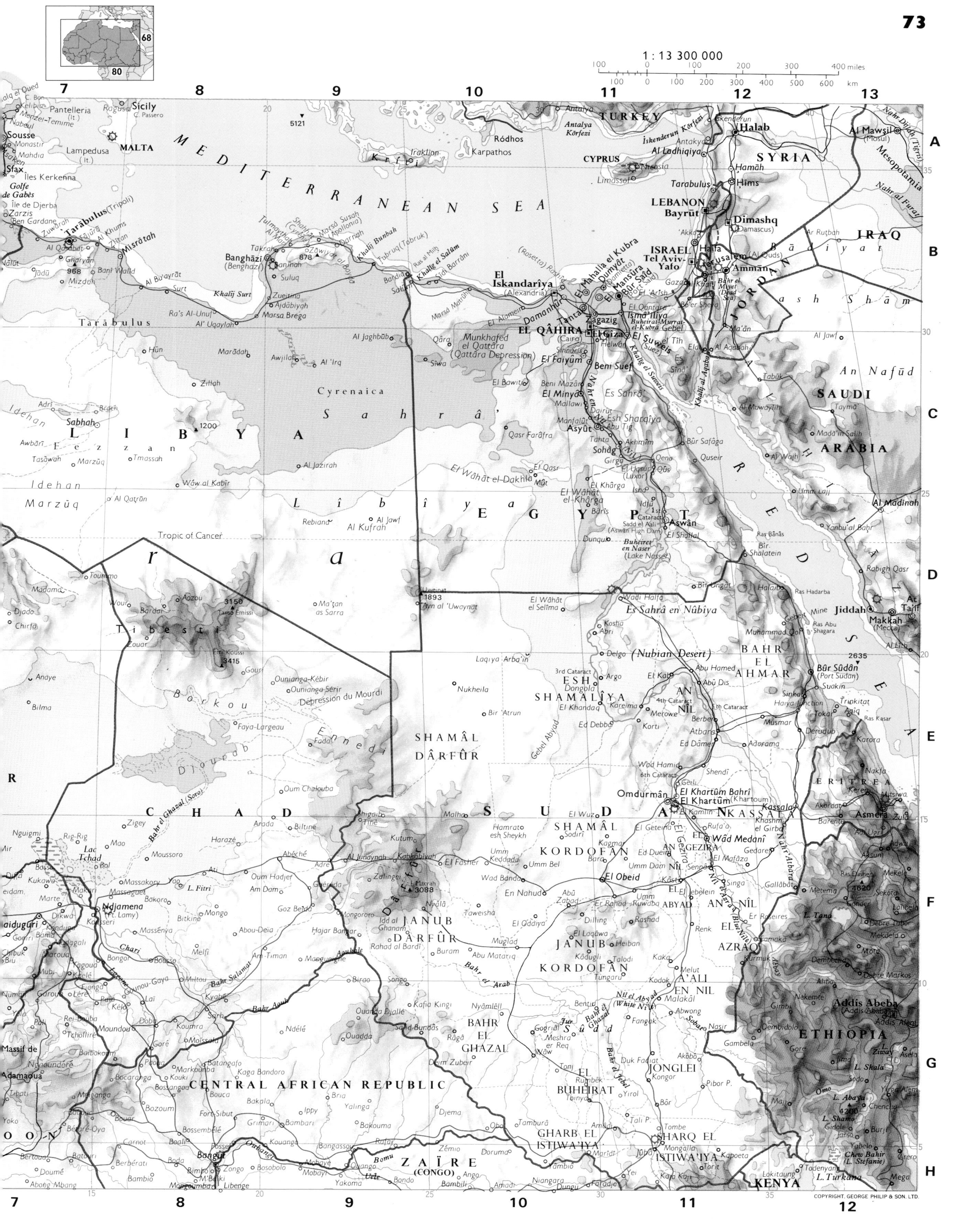
1 : 13 300 000
miles
km
MEDITERRANEAN SEA
TURKEY
SYRIA
LEBANON
IRAQ
ISRAEL
JORDAN
CYPRUS
MALTA
Sicily
Pantelleria
Lampedusa
Ródhos
Karpathos
Kríti
Iráklion
Antalya
Antalya Körfezi
Iskenderun Körfezi
Halab
Al Mawsil
(Mosul)
Mesopotamia
Al Lādhiqīya
Hamāh
Hims
Tarābulus
Bayrūt
Dimashq
(Damascus)
Haifa
Tel Aviv-Yafo
Jerusalem
(Al Quds)
'Ammān
Bahr el Miyet
(Dead Sea)
Bādiyat ash Shām
SAUDI ARABIA
An Nafūd
Al Jawf
Tabūk
Al Madīnah
Yanbu' al Bahr
Jiddah
Makkah
(Mecca)
At Tā'if
Rābigh
LIBYA
Tarābulus(Tripoli)
Misrātah
Banghāzī
(Benghazi)
Khalīj Surt
Surt
Cyrenaica
Sahrâ' Lîbîya
Fezzan
Sabhah
Marzūq
Ideha Marzūq
Al Kufrah
Al Jawf
Tropic of Cancer
Tibesti
Emi Koussi
3415
3150
Borkou
Ennedi
Djourab
CHAD
Ndjamena
(Ft. Lamy)
Lac Tchad
EGYPT
El Iskandarîya
(Alexandria)
EL QÂHIRA
(Cairo)
El Gîza
Port Said
Bûr Sa'îd
El Suweis
(Suez)
Munkhafed el Qattâra
(Qattâra Depression)
Sîwa
El Faiyûm
Beni Suef
El Minya
Asyût
Sohâg
Qena
El Uqsur
(Luxor)
Aswân
Buheiret en Naser
(Lake Nasser)
El Wâhât el-Dakhla
El Wâhât el-Khârga
Es Sahrâ en Nûbîya
(Nubian Desert)
Wadi Halfa
RED SEA
BAHR EL AHMAR
Bûr Sûdân
(Port Sudan)
SUDAN
ESH SHAMALÎYA
SHAMÂL DÂRFÛR
JANUB DÂRFÛR
SHAMÂL KORDOFÂN
JANUB KORDOFÂN
BAHR EL GHAZAL
JONGLEI
EL BUHEIRAT
GHARB EL ISTIWA'IYA
SHARQ EL ISTIWA'IYA
KASSALA
EL GEZIRA
Omdurmân
El Khartûm
(Khartoum)
El Khartûm Bahrî
Wad Medanî
El Obeid
El Fasher
Atbara
Kassala
ERITREA
Asmera
ETHIOPIA
Addis Abeba
L. Tana
L. Turkana
KENYA
CENTRAL AFRICAN REPUBLIC
Bangui
ZAÏRE
(CONGO)
COPYRIGHT, GEORGE PHILIP & SON, LTD.

73
78 79

1   **2**   **3**

A

NORTH

ATLANTIC

Sanlúcar de Barramede
SPAIN
Cádiz
C. Trafalgar
Algeciras
Gibraltar (Br.)
Strait of Gibraltar
C. Spartel
Ceuta (Sp.)
Tanger
Ras Tarf
Asilah
Martil
Tétouan
Larache
Ksar el Kebir
Chechaouen
Ouezzane
Souk el Arba du Rharb
Mechra-bel-Ksiri
Allal-Tazi
Kenitra (Port Lyautey)
Sidi Slimane
Sidi Kacem
Salé
RABAT
MEKNES
Volubilis
FES
Sefrou

B

Madeira (Port.)
Porto Moniz
SãoVicente
Santana
Machico
Funchal
I. de Porto Santo
Ilhas Desertas

Mohammedia (Fedala)
CASABLANCA
Azemmour
Bir Jdid
Ben Slimane
Berrechid
Benahmed
El Jadida (Mazagan)
Sidi Smail
Khouribga
Khemisset
El Hajeb
Azrou
Oulmes
Settat
Oued Zem
Fkih ben Salah
Ksiba
Beni Mellal
Safi
Youssoufia
El Kelâa
O. Oum er Rbia
Tadla
MOROCCO
Essaouira (Mogador)
C. Sim
MARRAKECH
Chichaoua
Demnate
Azilal
Tamanar
Amizmiz
Asni
Taroudannt
Ouarzazate
Djebel Sarhro
Cap Rhir
Tamri
Agadir
Inezgane
Taliouine
Tafraout

C

Islas Canarias (Sp.)
La Palma
Sta. Cruz de la Palma
Los Llanos de Aridane
Tenerife
La Laguna
Santa Cruz de Tenerife
La Orotava
Icod
S. Sebastian de la G.
Gomera
Granadilla de Abona
Valverde
Hierro
Gran Canaria
Las Palmas
Pta. de Maspalomas

Alegranza
Graciosa
Lanzarote
Arrecife
La Oliva
I. de Lobos
Fuerteventura
Puerto del Rosario
C. Juby
Tarfaya (Villa Bens)
Hasi Tafraut
El Aaiún
Daora
Hagunia
El Masat
Tucat
Tindouf
Hamada Tounassine

Saguia el Hamra
Smara
WESTERN SAHARA
C. Bojador
El Hasian
Bu Craa
El Hadeb
Aridal
Tifarati
MAURITANIA

D

Dakhla (Villa Cisneros)
Pta. Durnford
El Argub
Bir Enzarân
Tiris
Zemmur
Agmar
Bir Bel Guerdâne
Sebkhet Iguetti
G. de Cintra
Pta. Negra
Sebkhet Oumm ed Droûs Telli
Sebkhet Oumm ed Droûs Guebli
Sidi Emhamed
MAURITANIA
C. Barbas
Sebkhet Ijill
Fdérik
Kédiet Ijill 915
Zouïrât
Tourine
C. Corbeiro
Uad Tenouaur
Bir Gandús
Tichla
Zug
Aguenit
Meleizem
Bir Amrâne
Agada

E

La Güera
Nouâdhibou (Port Etienne)
Râs Nouâdhibou
Dakhlet Nouâdhibou
Bir el Gâreb
Ahmeyim
Agouifa
Amsaga
Oujeft
Chinguetti
Bollé
MALI
Et Tidra
Râs Timiris
Nouâmghâr
Bennichâb
Akjoujt
Ogueilet en Nmâdi
Ouadâne

1   **2**   **3**   **4**

West from Greenwich

ft m
12,000 — 4000
9000 — 3000
6000 — 2000
4500 — 1500
3000 — 1000
1200 — 400
600 — 200
0 — 0
200 — 600
2000 — 6000
4000 — 12,000
m ft

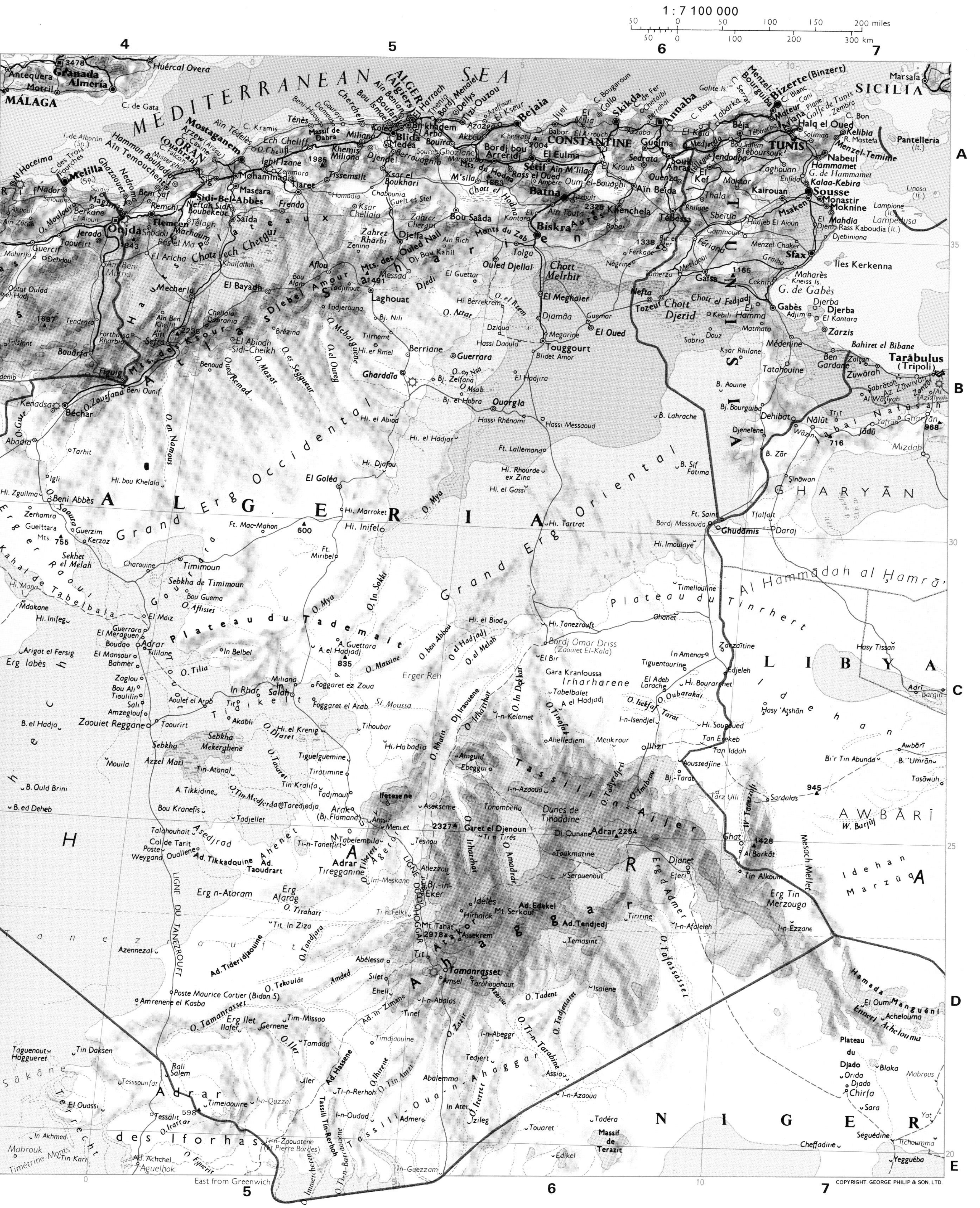

MEDITERRANEAN SEA

SICILIA

MÁLAGA

ALGERIA

LIBYA

TUNISIA

NIGER

1 : 7 100 000

East from Greenwich

COPYRIGHT. GEORGE PHILIP & SON. LTD.

THE NILE DELTA
1:3 600 000

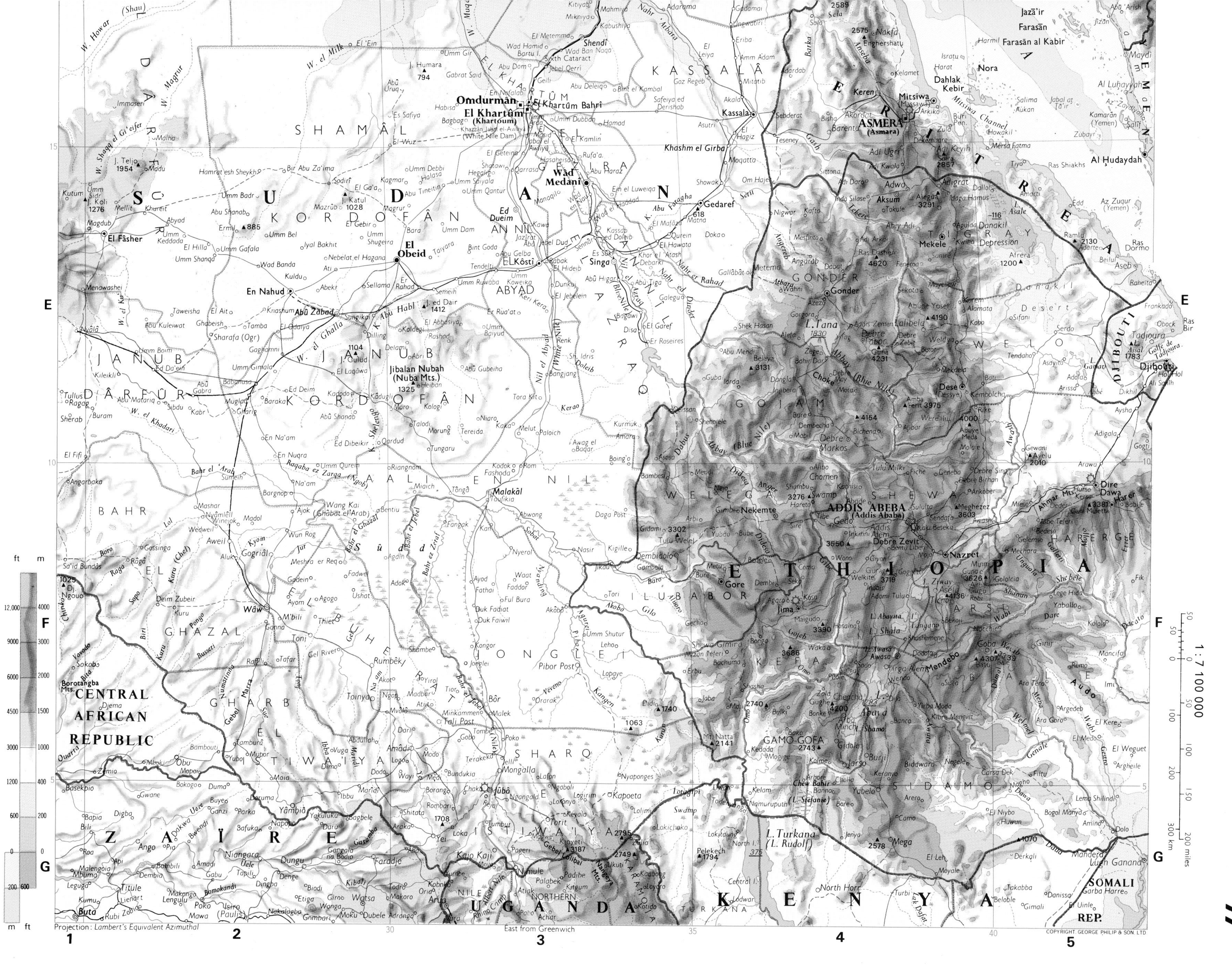

1 : 7 100 000

Projection: Lambert's Equivalent Azimuthal

COPYRIGHT GEORGE PHILIP & SON LTD

72
72
80

MAURITANIA

Nouakchott · Akjoujt · Oujeft · Ouâdâne · Chinguetti

Et Tidra · Râs Tîmirist · Nouâmghâr · Bennichâb

Sebkhet Te-n-Dghâmcha · Boû Rjeimât · Idîni

Tidjikja · 420 · Gâneb · Tichît · Aratâne · Akreijit · Sidi Moktar

Moudjéria · 522 · Letflatat · Tâmchekket · Aoukâr · Tagourâret · Oualâta

Mederdra · Boutilimit · Aleg · Môl · Togba · Tî n Ahmer

Rosso · Bogué · El Ghabra · Kiffa · Tintâne · 'Ayoûn el 'Atroûs · Néma

SENEGAL

St. Louis · Sénégal · Louga · Thiès · DAKAR · Rufisque · Diourbel · Mbour · Fatick · Kaolack

Linguère · Matam · Bakel · Kayes · Kidira

Tambacounda · Kolda · Ziguinchor

GAMBIA
Banjul

GUINEA-BISSAU
Bissau · Arquipélago dos Bijagós · Bolama · Bafatá · Gabú

GUINEA
Conakry · Kindia · Boké · Télimélé · Labé · Fouta Djalon · Mamou · Dabola · Dinguiraye · Siguiri · Kankan · Kérouané · Kissidougou · Macenta · Nzérékoré · Faranah

SIERRA LEONE
Freetown · Waterloo · Port Loko · Makeni · Magburaka · Bo · Kenema · NORTHERN · EASTERN · SOUTHERN · WESTERN

LIBERIA
Monrovia · Buchanan · Greenville · Harper · Careysburg · Paynesville · Gbarnga · Tapeta · Zwedru

MALI
Bamako · Ségou · Koulikoro · Kita · Nioro du Sahel · Nara · Sokolo · Mopti · Bafoulabé · Kayes

IVORY COAST
Abidjan · Bouaké · Daloa · Man · Korhogo · Ferkéssédougou · Odienné · Séguéla · Bondoukou · Gagnoa · Divo · Abengourou · Agboville · Grand Bassam · San-Pédro

BURKINA FASO
Bobo Dioulasso · Banfora

Grain Coast · Ivory Coast · Cape Palmas · Cape Three Points · GULF OF GUINEA

West from Greenwich

Projection: Lambert's Equivalent Azimuthal

ft m — 12 000 / 4000 · 9000 / 3000 · 6000 / 2000 · 4500 / 1500 · 3000 / 1000 · 1200 / 400 · 600 / 200 · 0 / 0 · 200 / 600 · 2000 / 6000 · 4000 / 12 000 · 6000 / 18 000

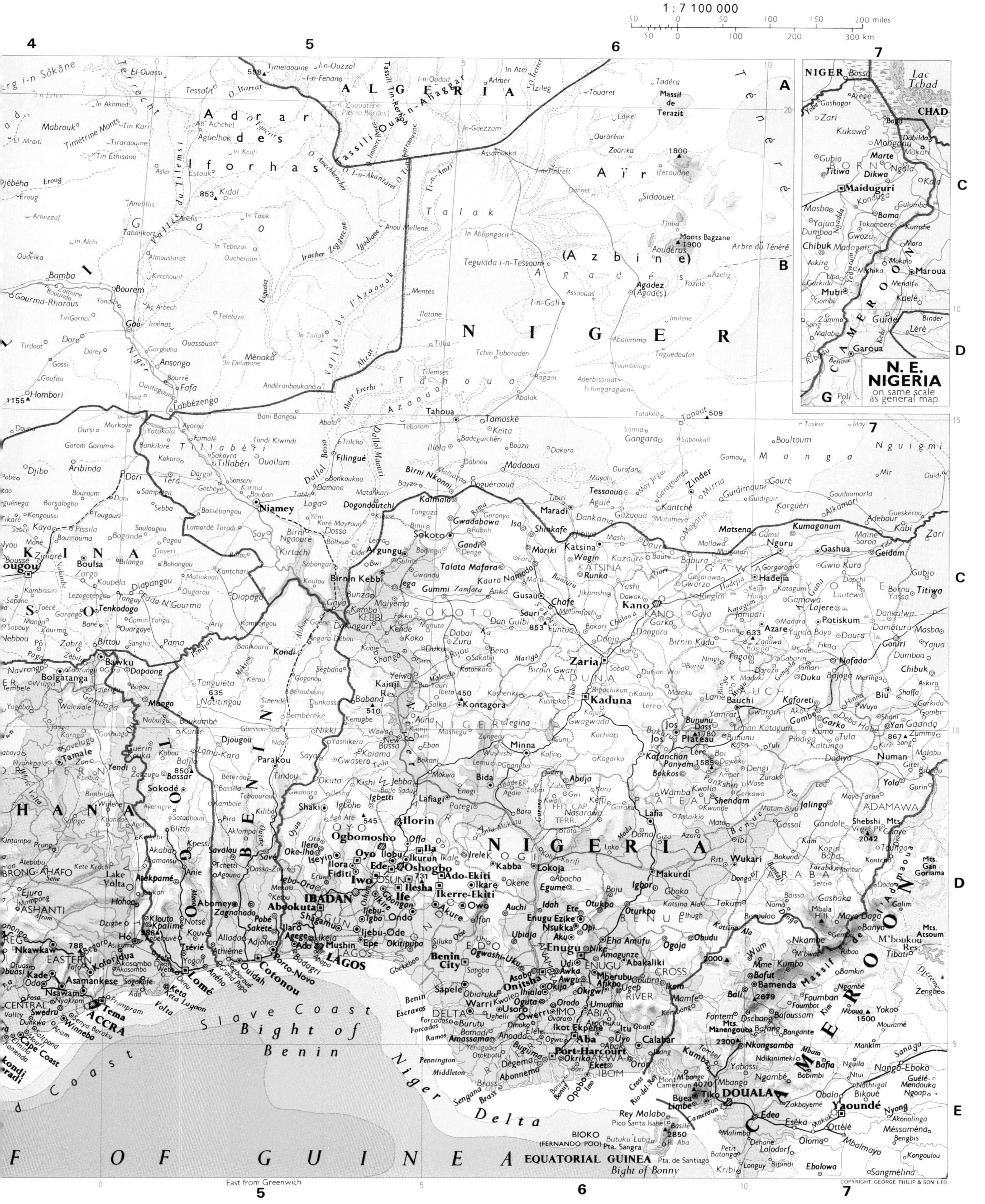
1 : 7 100 000
NIGER
ALGERIA
NIGERIA
BENIN
TOGO
GHANA
CAMEROON
CHAD
EQUATORIAL GUINEA
N. E. NIGERIA
on same scale
as general map
Bight of Benin
Slave Coast
Niger Delta
Bight of Bonny
OF GUINEA
East from Greenwich

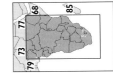

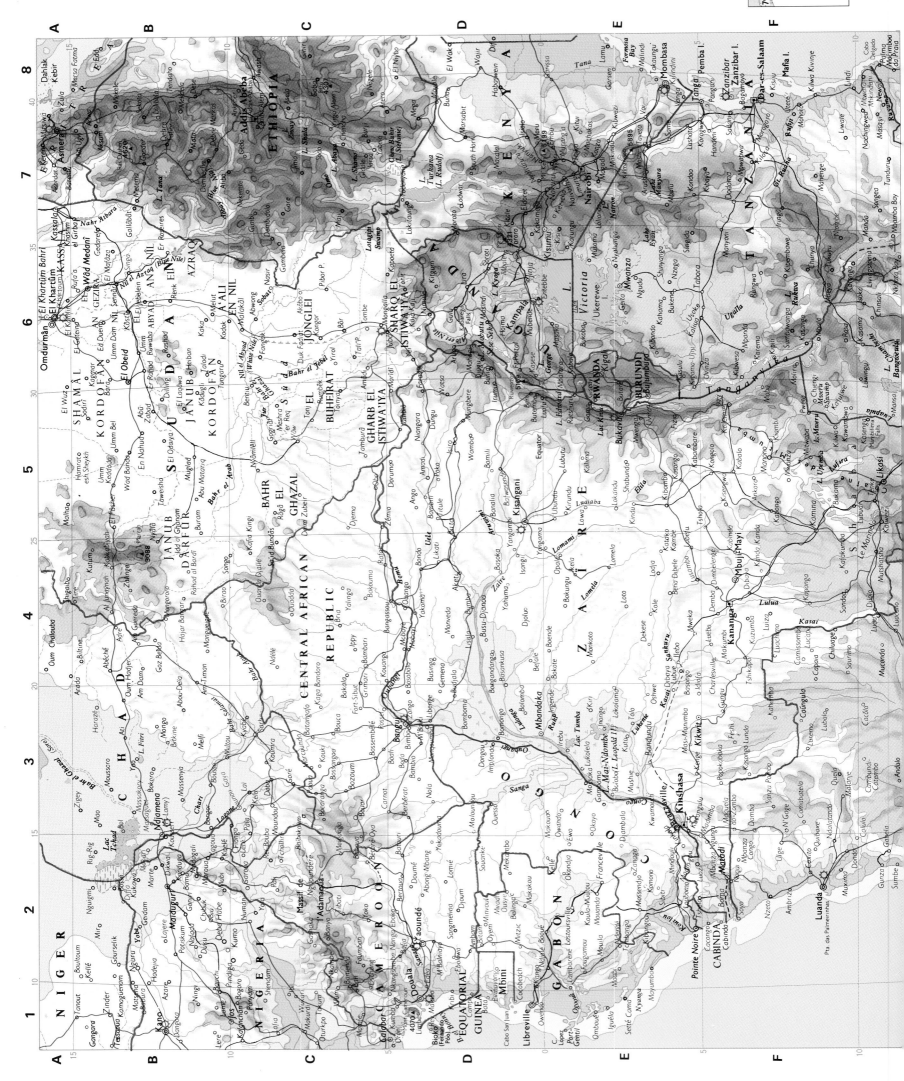

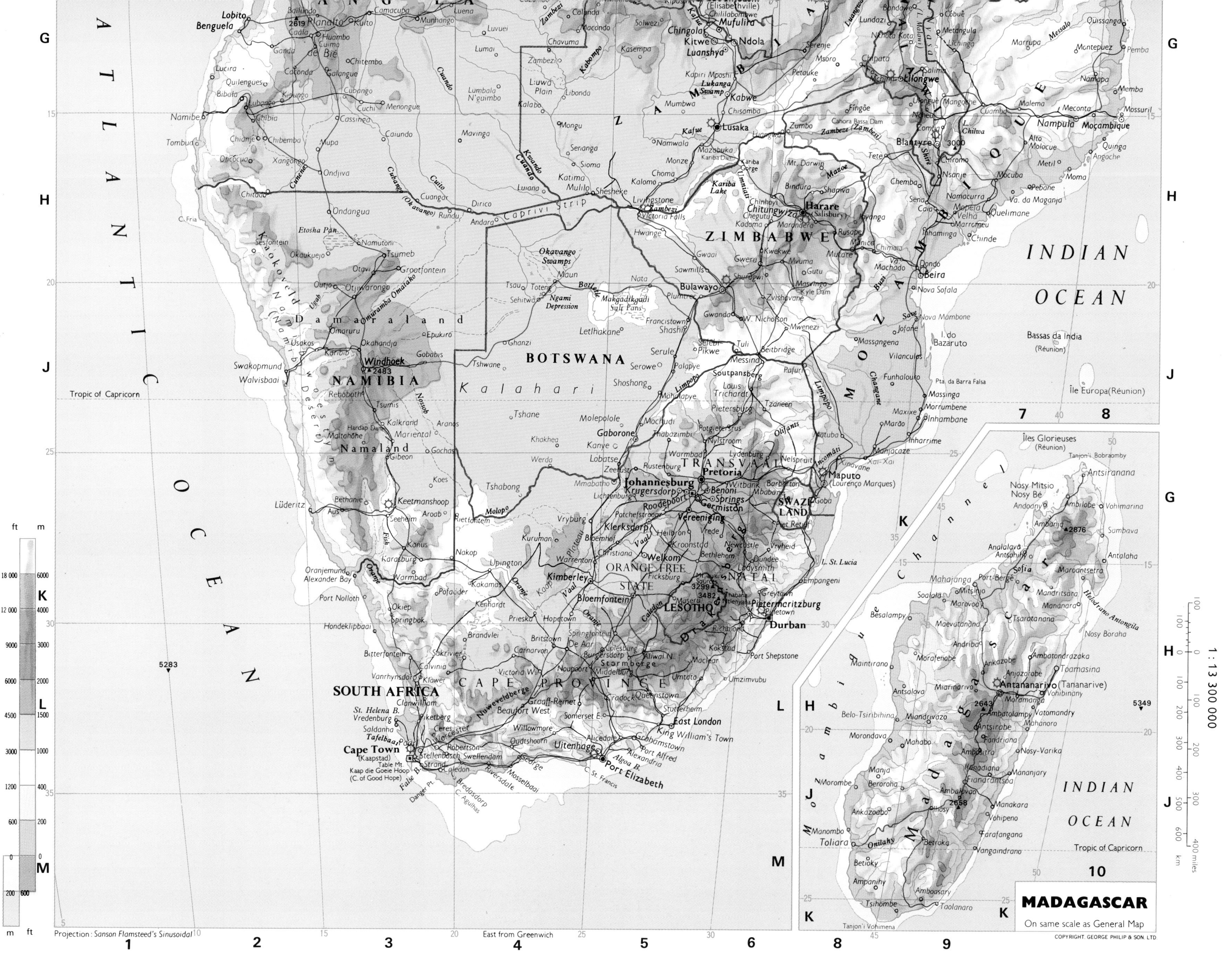

1 : 13 300 000

MADAGASCAR
On same scale as General Map

COPYRIGHT GEORGE PHILIP & SON LTD

Projection: Sanson Flamsteed's Sinusoidal

SOMALI REP.

ETHIOPIA

KENYA

UGANDA

TANZANIA

SUDAN

RWANDA

BURUNDI

CENTRAL AFRICAN REPUBLIC

ZAIRE

Lake Victoria

L. Tanganyika

L. Turkana (L. Rudolf)

L. Albert

L. Kivu

Nairobi

Mombasa

Zanzibar

Dar es Salaam

Kisangani

Kampala

Entebbe

Jinja

Dodoma

Tabora

Arusha

Pemba I.

Mafia I.

EQUATOR

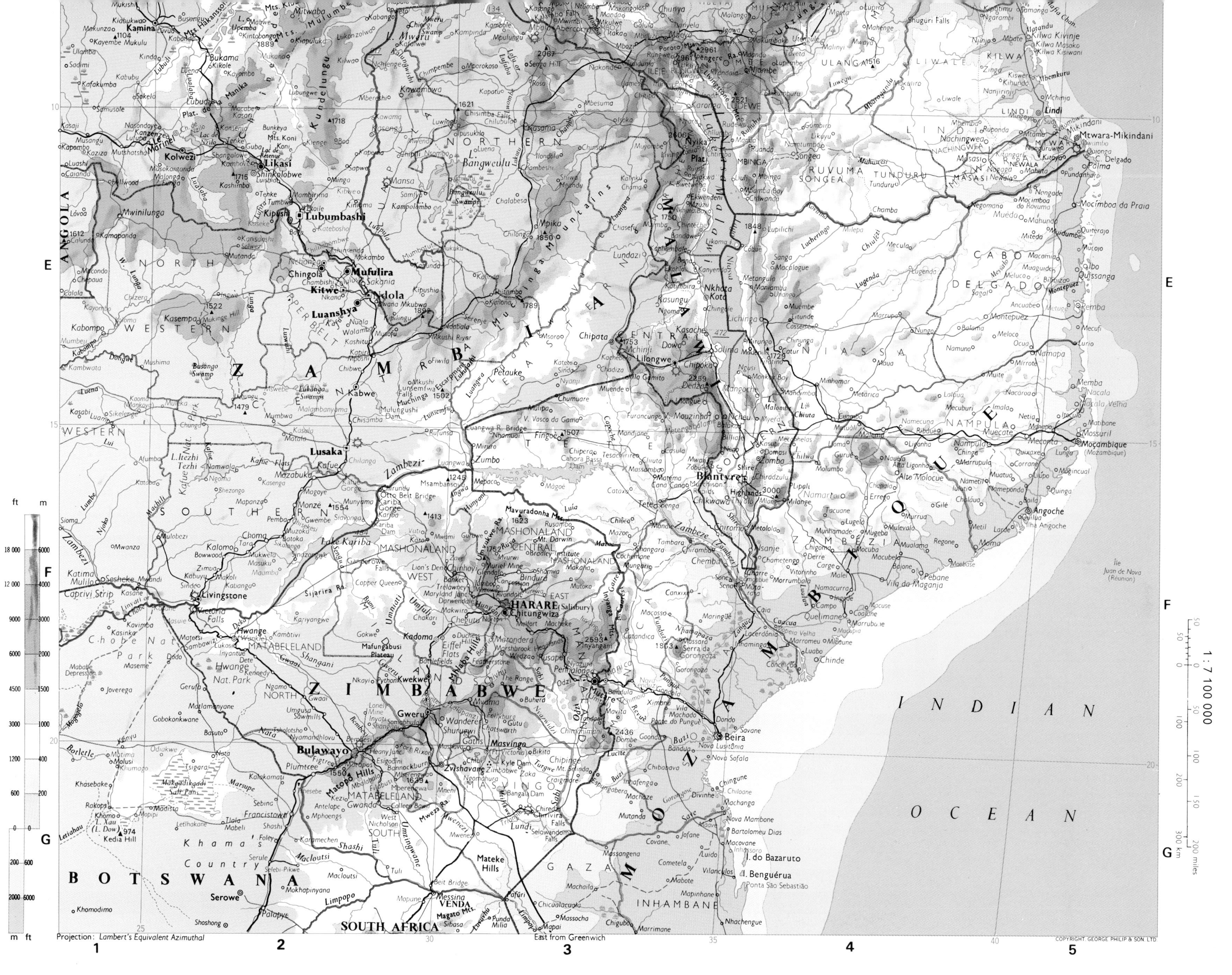

1 : 7 100 000

Projection: Lambert's Equivalent Azimuthal

East from Greenwich

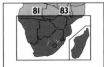

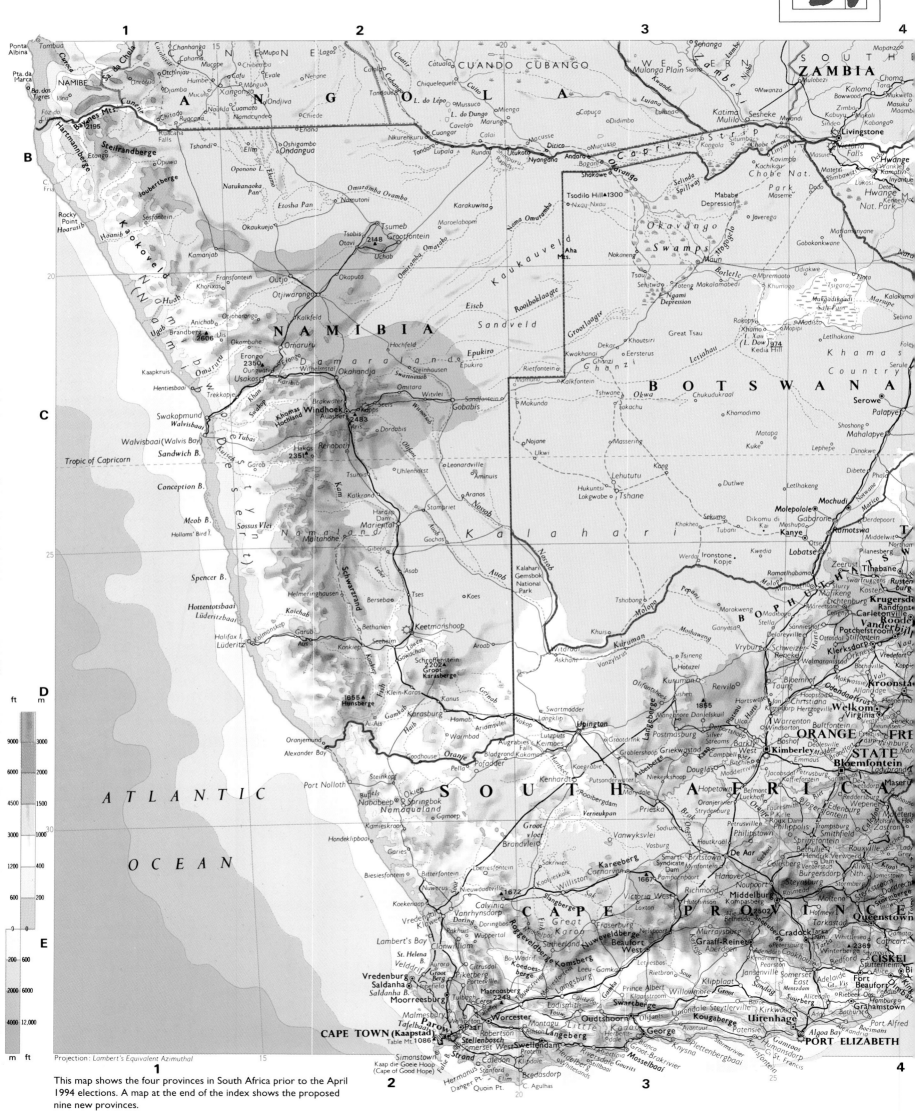

This map shows the four provinces in South Africa prior to the April 1994 elections. A map at the end of the index shows the proposed nine new provinces.

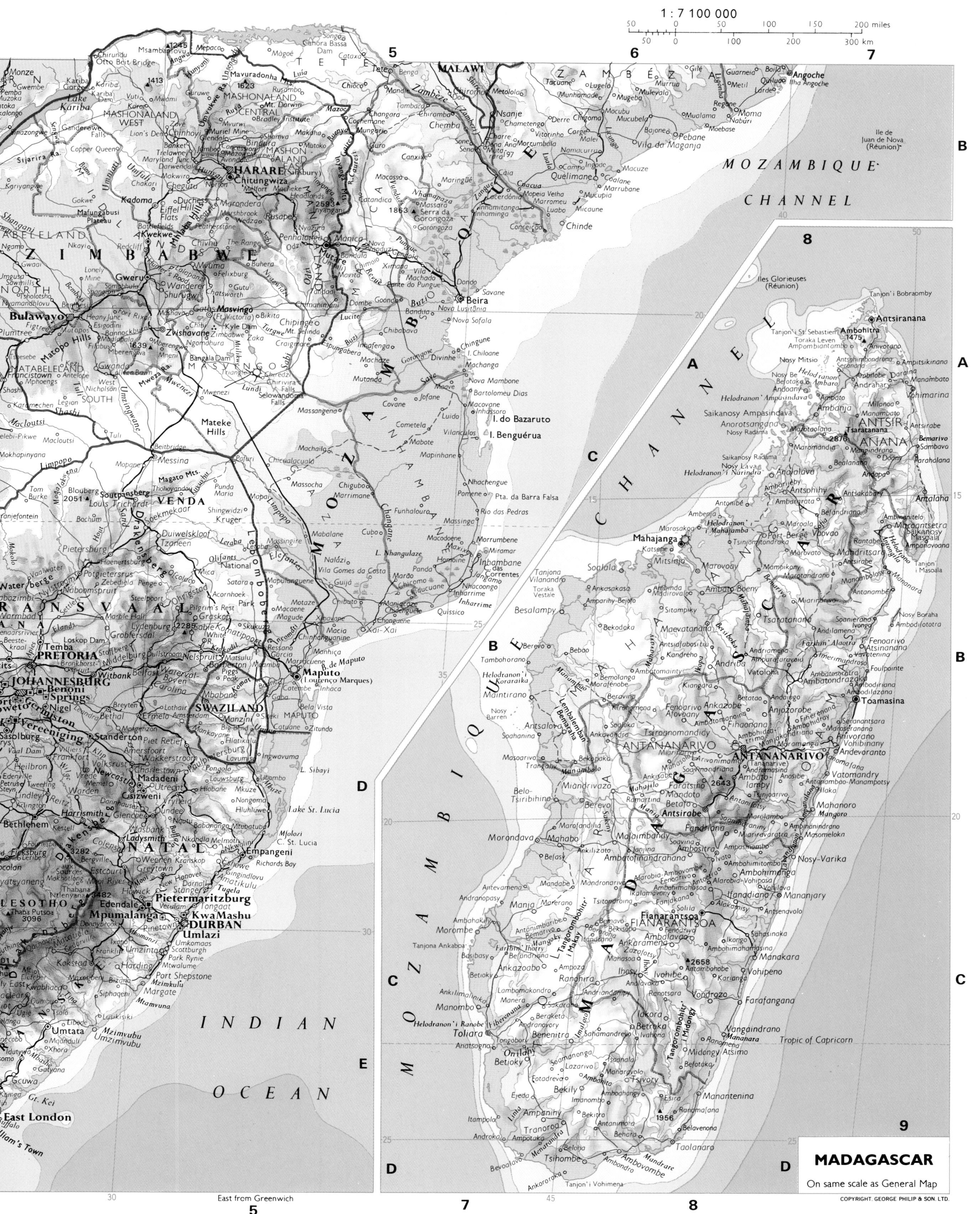

1 : 7 100 000

50   0   50   100   150   200 miles

50   0   50   100   200   300 km

5   6   7

MALAWI

ZAMBÉZIA

Ile de
Juan de Nova
(Réunion)

M O Z A M B I Q U E ·

C H A N N E L   B

40

8

Iles Glorieuses
(Réunion)

Antsiranana

I. do Bazaruto

I. Benguérua

C   **ANTSIR-
ANANA**

Mahajanga

A

15

MAHAJANGA

ANTANANARIVO

ANTANANARIVO
(Tananarive)

Antsirabe

B

Toamasina

Fianarantsoa

FIANARANTSOA

Tropic of Capricorn

C

Toliara

25

MADAGASCAR

On same scale as General Map

D

COPYRIGHT. GEORGE PHILIP & SON, LTD.

ZIMBABWE

HARARE

Bulawayo

MATABELELAND

M A S V I N G O

V E N D A

M O Z A M B I Q U E

Beira

PRETORIA

JOHANNESBURG

SWAZILAND

MAPUTO

Maputo
(Lourenço Marques)

T R A N S V A A L

N A T A L

DURBAN

KwaMashu

Umlazi

Pietermaritzburg

LESOTHO

East London

I N D I A N

O C E A N

M O Z A M B I Q U E   C H A N N E L

East from Greenwich

30   5   7   45   8

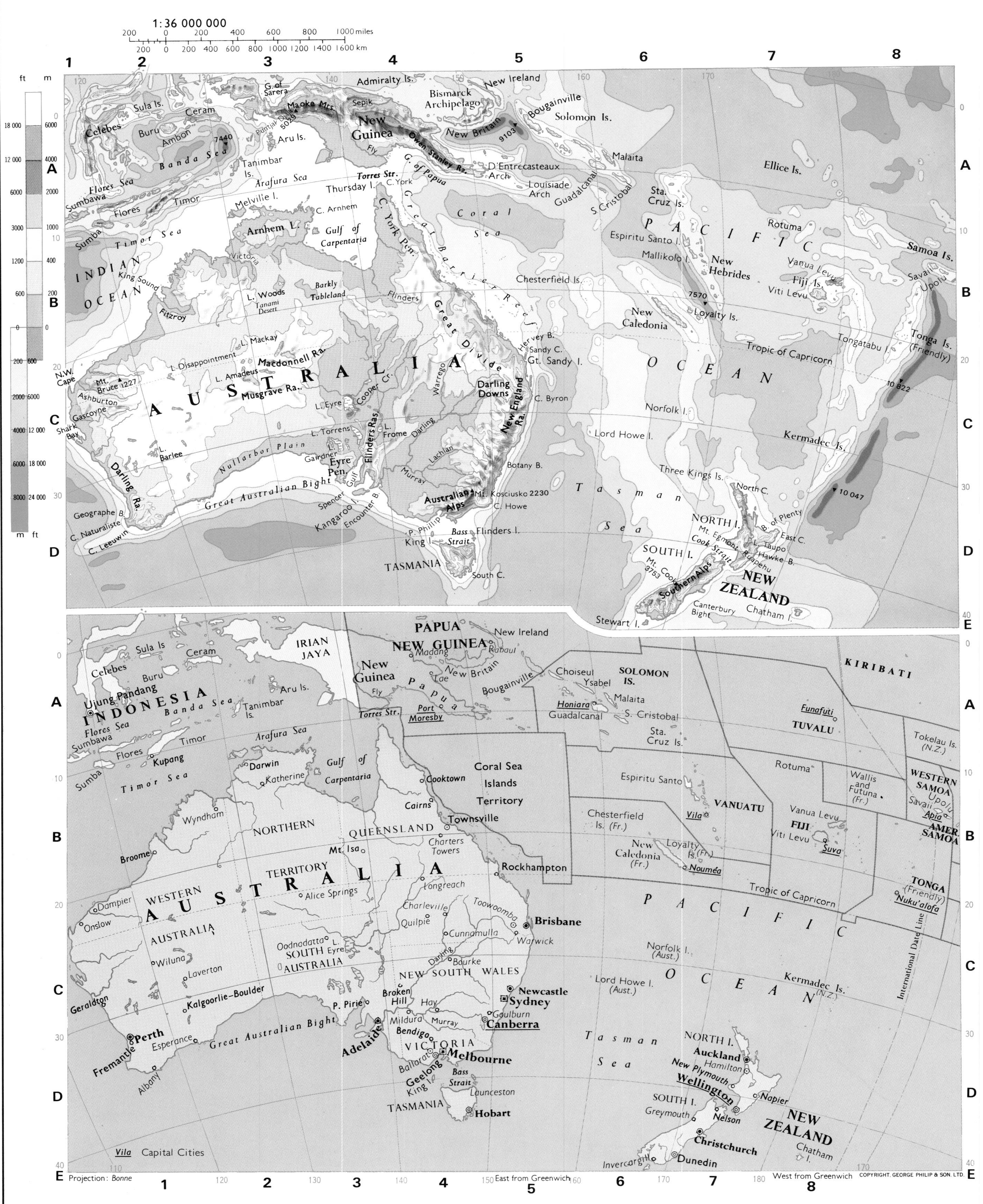
1:36 000 000
AUSTRALIA
New Guinea
New Zealand
Coral Sea
Tasman Sea
Great Australian Bight
Pacific Ocean
Indian Ocean
Timor Sea
Arafura Sea
Banda Sea
Gulf of Carpentaria
Great Barrier Reef
Great Dividing Ra.
Macdonnell Ra.
Musgrave Ra.
Nullarbor Plain
Australian Alps
Mt. Kosciusko 2230
Southern Alps
Mt. Cook 3753
Tasmania
Bass Strait
Tropic of Capricorn
INDONESIA
PAPUA NEW GUINEA
SOLOMON IS.
VANUATU
FIJI
TONGA (Friendly)
WESTERN SAMOA
AMER. SAMOA
TUVALU
KIRIBATI
Coral Sea Islands Territory
WESTERN AUSTRALIA
NORTHERN TERRITORY
QUEENSLAND
SOUTH AUSTRALIA
NEW SOUTH WALES
VICTORIA
Perth
Adelaide
Melbourne
Canberra
Sydney
Brisbane
Hobart
Darwin
Port Moresby
Honiara
Vila
Nouméa
Suva
Apia
Nuku'alofa
Funafuti
Auckland
Wellington
Christchurch
Dunedin
International Date Line
Vila Capital Cities
Projection: Bonne
East from Greenwich
West from Greenwich

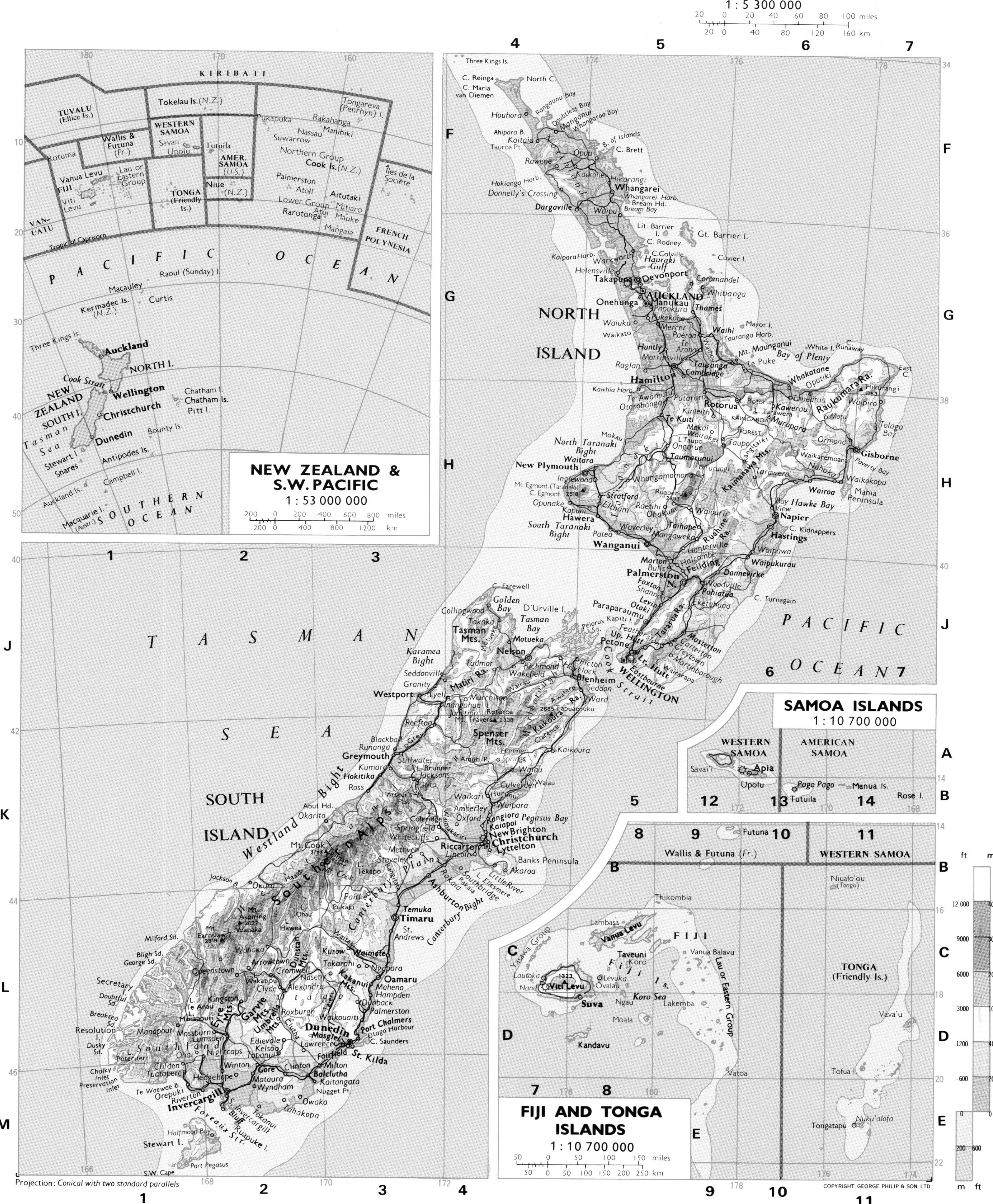

1 : 5 300 000

NEW ZEALAND & S.W. PACIFIC
1 : 53 000 000

SAMOA ISLANDS
1 : 10 700 000

FIJI AND TONGA ISLANDS
1 : 10 700 000

Projection: Conical with two standard parallels

COPYRIGHT. GEORGE PHILIP & SON LTD.

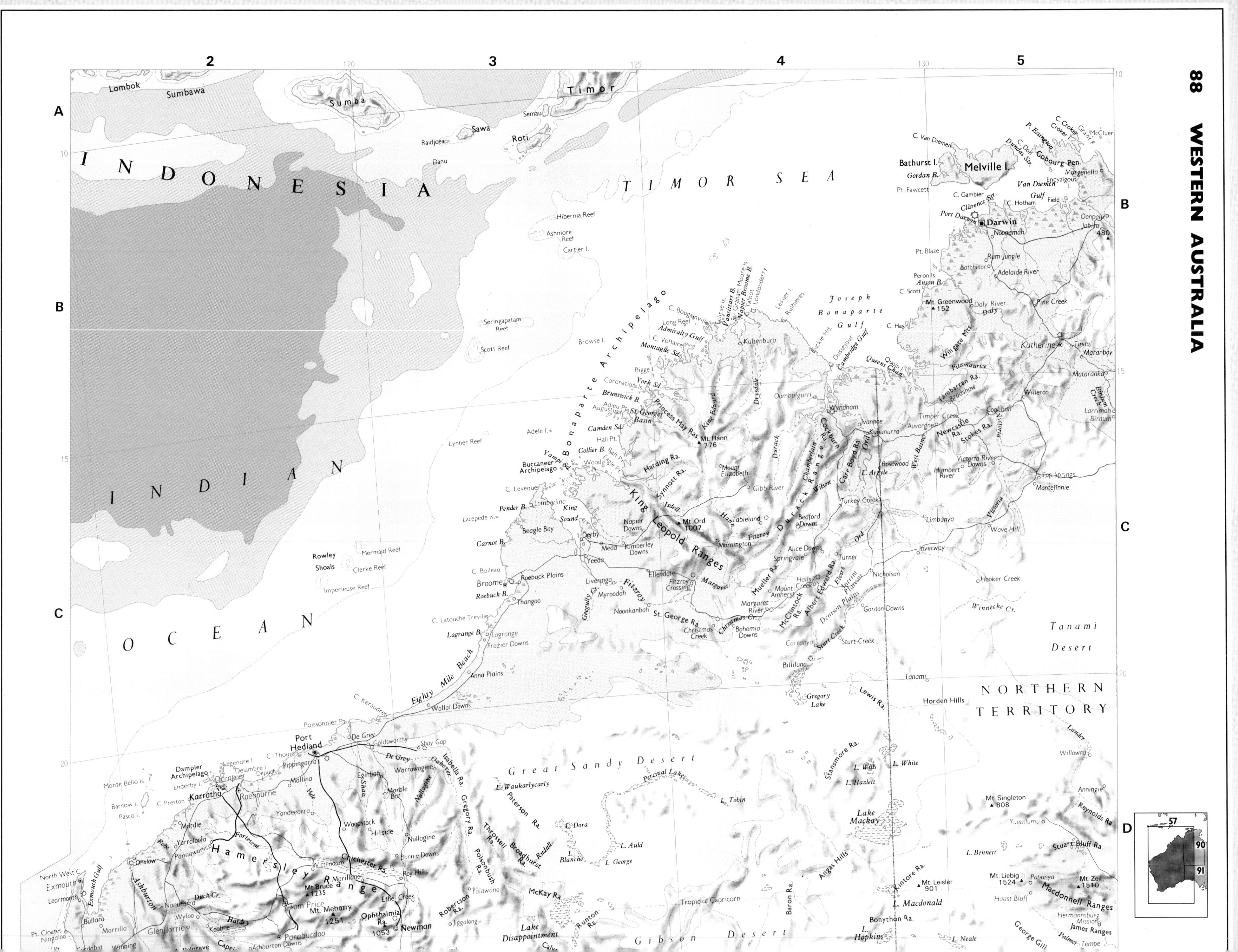

INDONESIA
TIMOR SEA
INDIAN OCEAN
NORTHERN TERRITORY
Lombok
Sumbawa
Sumba
Timor
Sawa
Roti
Semau
Melville I.
Bathurst I.
Darwin
Katherine
Joseph Bonaparte Gulf
Bonaparte Archipelago
Cambridge Gulf
Wyndham
Kununurra
King Leopold Ranges
Mt. Ord 1007
Mt. Hann 776
Fitzroy
Derby
Broome
Roebuck B.
King Sound
Buccaneer Archipelago
Eighty Mile Beach
Port Hedland
De Grey
Karratha
Roebourne
Dampier
Dampier Archipelago
Hamersley Range
Mt. Meharry 1251
Mt. Bruce 1235
Newman
Ophthalmia Ra.
Chichester Ra.
Onslow
Exmouth
Exmouth Gulf
North West C.
Great Sandy Desert
Gibson Desert
Tanami Desert
Tropic of Capricorn
Lake Mackay
L. Macdonald
Lake Disappointment
Macdonnell Ranges
Mt. Zeil 1510
Mt. Liebig 1524
Rowley Shoals
Scott Reef
Ashmore Reef
Cartier I.
Hibernia Reef
Browse I.
Adele I.
Lacepede Is.

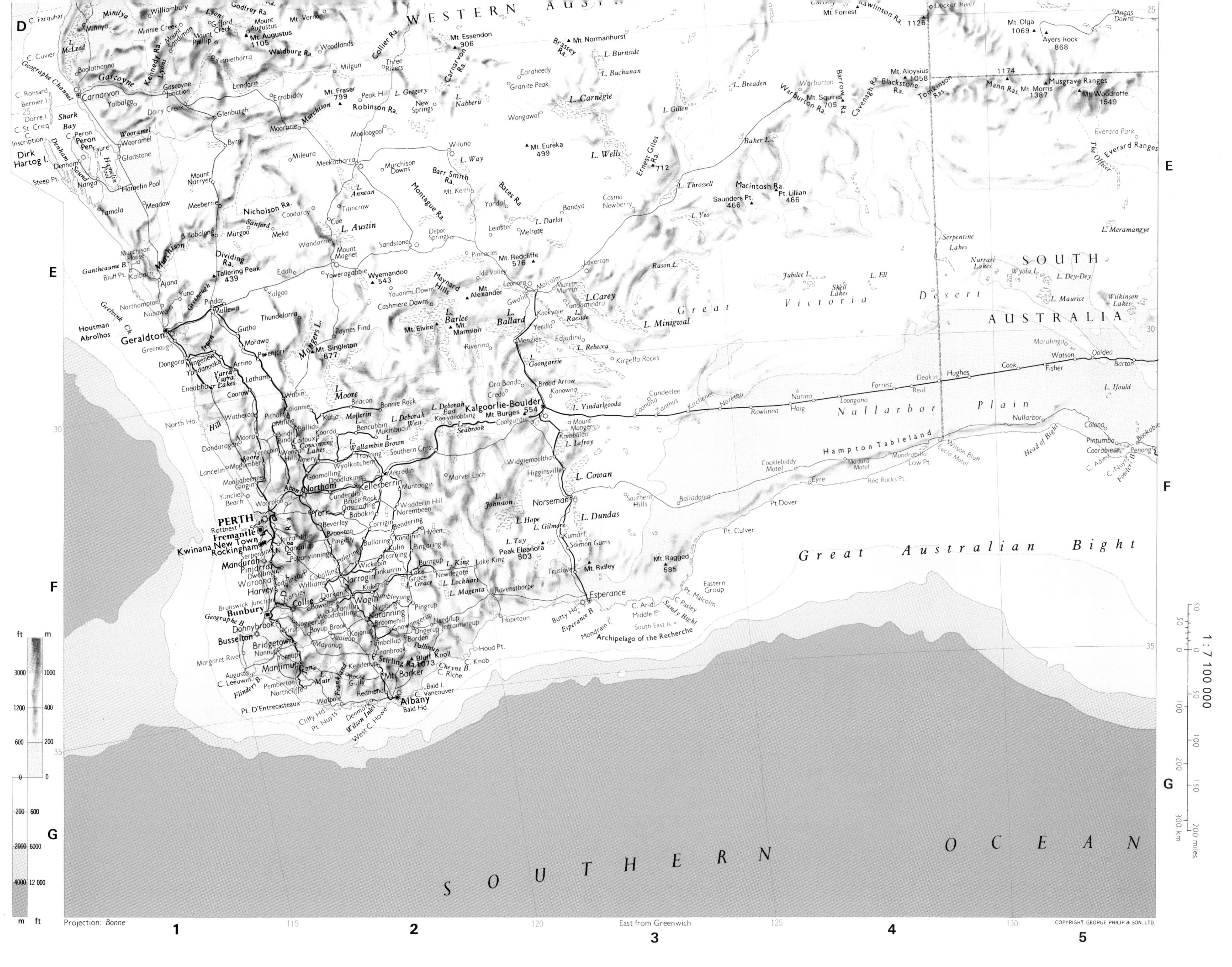

89

1 : 7 100 000

Projection: Bonne

COPYRIGHT GEORGE PHILIP & SON LTD.

CORAL SEA

Great Barrier Reef

TASMANIA
Bass Strait
King Island
Flinders Island
Furneaux Group
Kent Group
Launceston
Devonport
Burnie
Wynyard
Hobart
Queenstown
Strahan
Mt. Ossa 1617
New Norfolk
Glenorchy
Bruny I.
Storm Bay
S.E. Cape
Port Davey
Bathurst Bay
S.W. Cape
Maria I.
Freycinet Pen.
Tasman Pen.
Schouten I.

GREAT DIVIDING RANGE
Great Dividing Range
Cape York Peninsula
Gulf of Carpentaria
Arnhem Land
NORTHERN TERRITORY
QUEENSLAND
Simpson Desert
Barkly Tableland

Thursday I.
C. York
Prince of Wales I.
Endeavour Str.
Cairns
Townsville
Mackay
Rockhampton
Gladstone
Yeppoon
Curtis I.
Bowen
Ayr
Ingham
Innisfail
Mareeba
Atherton
Cooktown
Normanton
Cloncurry
Mount Isa
Hughenden
Richmond
Winton
Longreach
Charters Towers
Alice Springs
Macdonnell Ranges
Tropic of Capricorn

Gulf of Carpentaria
Groote Eylandt
Wessel Is.
Sir Edward Pellew Group
Mornington I.
Wellesley Is.
Bentinck I.
Vanderlin I.

Whitsunday I.
Cumberland Islands
Northumberland Islands
Hinchinbrook I.
Hervey
Lady Elliott I.
Bundaberg
Maryborough

Gregory Range
Selwyn Ranges
Kangaroo Mts.
Toko Range
Davenport Range
Gowan Range
Drummond Range
Expedition Range

Flinders
Mitchell
Gilbert
Norman
Leichhardt
McArthur River
Georgina
Diamantina
Thomson
Barcoo
Finke
Todd

1 : 7 100 000

50   0   50   100   150   200 miles

50   0   100   200   300 km

T A S M A N   S E A

S O U T H   A U S T R A L I A

N E W   S O U T H   W A L E S

V I C T O R I A

BRISBANE

SYDNEY

CANBERRA

ADELAIDE

MELBOURNE

Newcastle

Wollongong

Broken Hill

Port Augusta

Whyalla

Port Pirie

Port Lincoln

Bass Strait

King Island

Flinders Island

Furneaux Group

Cape Barren I.

Fraser Island

Maryborough

Darling Range

Dividing Range

Grey Range

Barrier Range

Flinders Range

Lake Eyre (North)

Lake Eyre (South)

Lake Torrens

Lake Gairdner

Lake Frome

Lake Blanche

Spencer Gulf

Kangaroo I.

Eyre Peninsula

Cooper Cr.

Darling

Murray

Murrumbidgee

Lachlan

Liverpool Plains

East from Greenwich

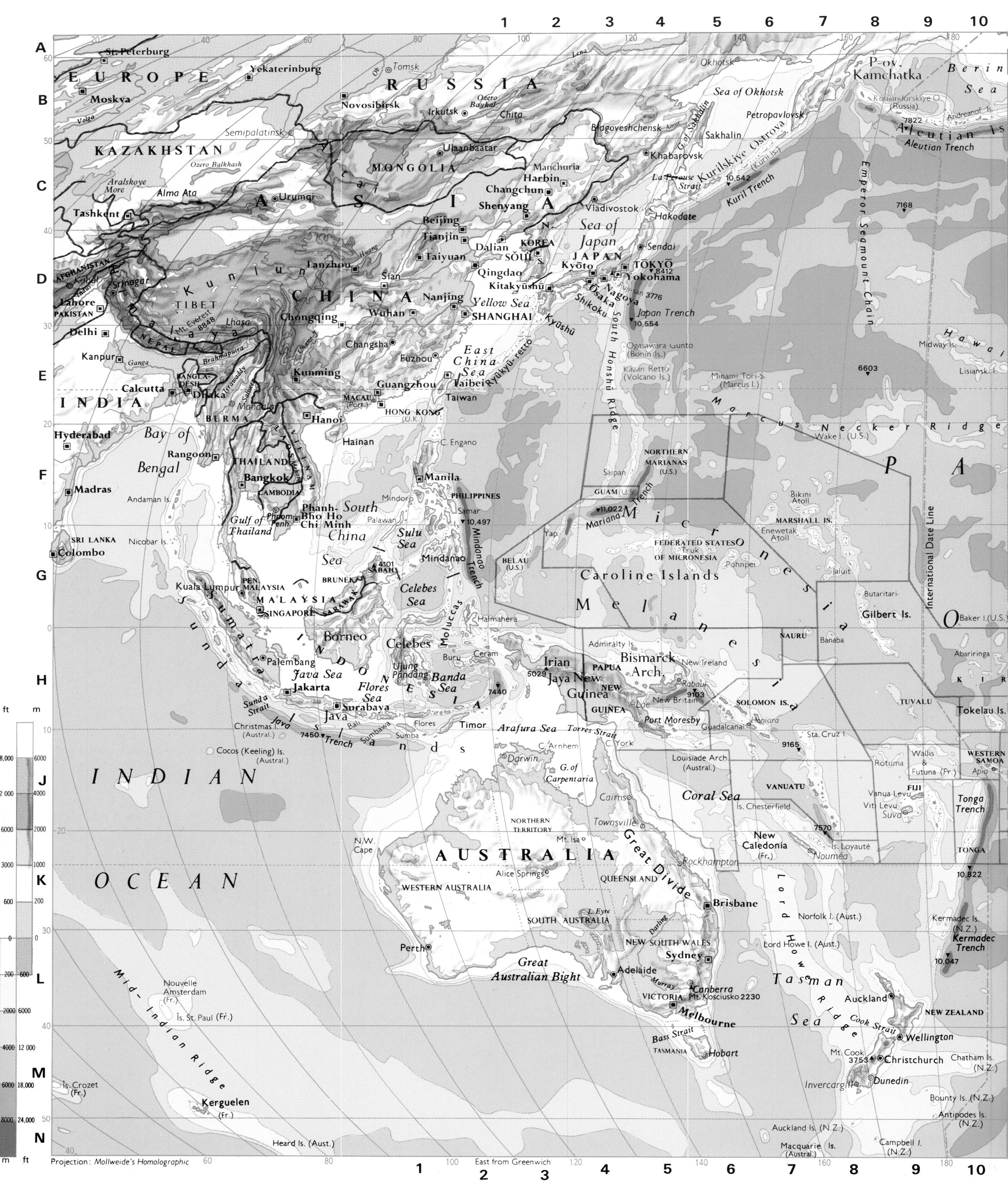

A
B
C
D
E
F
G
H
J
K
L
M
N

St. Peterburg
EUROPE
Moskva
Yekaterinburg
Volga
Tomsk
RUSSIA
Novosibirsk
KAZAKHSTAN
Irkutsk
Chita
Ozero Baykal
Lena
Okhotsk
Sea of Okhotsk
P-ov. Kamchatka
Bering Sea
Semipalatinsk
Ozero Balkhash
MONGOLIA
Ulaanbaatar
Blagoveshchensk
Amur
Sakhalin
Petropavlovsk
Komandorskiye O. (Russia)
Andreanof Is.
Aleutian Is.
Aralskoye More
Alma Ata
Urumqi
Khabarovsk
La Perouse Strait
Kurilskiye Ostrova (Kuril Is.)
7822
Aleutian Trench
Tashkent
A
S
I
A
Manchuria
Harbin
Vladivostok
Hakodate
10,542
Kuril Trench
Emperor Seamount Chain
7168
Changchun
Shenyang
Sea of Japan
AFGHANISTAN
Kabul
Kuniun
Beijing
Tianjin
Dalian
KOREA
SŎUL
JAPAN
Kyōto
TOKYO
Yokohama
8412
Sendai
Srinagar
Taiyuan
Qingdao
Ōsaka
Nagoya
Fuji 3776
Midway Is.
Hawai
Lahore
PAKISTAN
Lanzhou
Sian
CHINA
Kitakyūshū
Shikoku
Honshū
South
Japan Trench
10,554
Ogasawara Gunto (Bonin Is.)
Lisianski
Delhi
TIBET
Mt. Everest 8048
Lhasa
Nanjing
SHANGHAI
Kyūshū
Ryūkyū-retto
6603
Kanpur
Chongqing
Wuhan
Yellow Sea
Kazan Retto (Volcano Is.)
Minami-Tori-S. (Marcus I.)
Midway Is.
Ganga
Brahmaputra
NEPAL
Changsha
East China Sea
Marcus Necker Ridge
Wake I. (U.S.)
Calcutta
Kunming
Fuzhou
Taibei
Ryūkyū-retto
Ogasawara
INDIA
Mandalay
Guangzhou
MACAU (Port.)
Taiwan
NORTHERN MARIANAS (U.S.)
PACIFIC
Hyderabad
BANGLA-DESH
Dhaka
BURMA
HONG KONG (U.K.)
Hainan
C. Engano
Saipan
Bay of Bengal
Rangoon
THAILAND
Hanoi
GUAM (U.S.)
Bikini Atoll
Madras
Bangkok
CAMBODIA
Manila
11,022
Mariana Trench
MARSHALL IS.
Enewetak Atoll
Andaman Is.
Phanh- Bho Ho Chi Minh
South China Sea
Mindoro
Samar
10,497
Yap
FEDERATED STATES OF MICRONESIA
Truk
Pohnpei
Jaluit
Phnom Penh
Gulf of Thailand
Palawan
Mindanao Trench
BELAU (U.S.)
SRI LANKA
Nicobar Is.
Sulu Sea
4101
SABAH
Mindanao
Caroline Islands
Butaritari
Colombo
PEN. MALAYSIA
BRUNEI
Celebes Sea
Melanesia
Gilbert Is.
Baker I. (U.S.)
Kuala Lumpur
SARAWAK
MALAYSIA
SINGAPORE
Borneo
Celebes
Moluccas
Ceram
Halmahera
NAURU
Banaba
Abariringa
Sumatra
Palembang
INDONESIA
Buru
Admiralty Is.
Bismarck Arch.
New Ireland
Java Sea
Jakarta
Ujung Pandang
Banda Sea
5029
Irian Jaya
PAPUA NEW GUINEA
Rabaul
New Britain
SOLOMON IS.
TUVALU
Tokelau Is.
Sunda Strait
Java
7440
9103
KIR
Christmas (Austral.)
Bali
Flores Sea
Flores
Sumbawa
Sumba
Timor
NEW GUINEA
Port Moresby
Guadalcanal
Honiara
Sta. Cruz I.
Wallis & Futuna (Fr.)
WESTERN SAMOA
Apia
Cocos (Keeling) Is. (Austral.)
7450
Java Trench
Arafura Sea
Torres Strait
9165
Rotuma
INDIAN
C. Arnhem
C. York
Louisiade Arch. (Austral.)
FIJI
Vanua Levu
Darwin
G. of Carpentaria
VANUATU
Coral Sea
Viti Levu
Suva
N.W. Cape
NORTHERN TERRITORY
Cairns
7570
Is. Chesterfield
Tonga Trench
OCEAN
Townsville
Great Divide
New Caledonia (Fr.)
Noumée
Is. Loyauté
TONGA
AUSTRALIA
Mt. Isa
Rockhampton
Norfolk I. (Aust.)
10,822
WESTERN AUSTRALIA
Alice Springs
QUEENSLAND
Brisbane
Lord Howe I. (Aust.)
Kermadec Is. (N.Z.)
L. Eyre
SOUTH AUSTRALIA
Darling
NEW SOUTH WALES
Perth
Sydney
Lord Howe Ridge
Kermadec Trench
10,047
Nouvelle Amsterdam (Fr.)
Murray
Canberra
Mt. Kosciusko 2230
Adelaide
VICTORIA
Tasman Sea
Auckland
Îs. St. Paul (Fr.)
Great Australian Bight
Melbourne
Cook Strait
NEW ZEALAND
Mid-Indian Ridge
Bass Strait
Mt. Cook 3753
Christchurch
Chatham Is. (N.Z.)
Is. Crozet (Fr.)
TASMANIA
Hobart
Invercargill
Dunedin
Kerguelen (Fr.)
Bounty Is. (N.Z.)
Antipodes Is. (N.Z.)
Heard Is. (Aust.)
Auckland Is. (N.Z.)
Macquarie Is. (Austral.)
Campbell I. (N.Z.)

ft m
18,000 6000
12,000 4000
6000 2000
3000 1000
600 200
0 0
200 600
2000 6000
4000 12,000
6000 18,000
8000 24,000
m ft

Projection: Mollweide's Homolographic

East from Greenwich

1 2 3 4 5 6 7 8 9 10

1 : 48 000 000

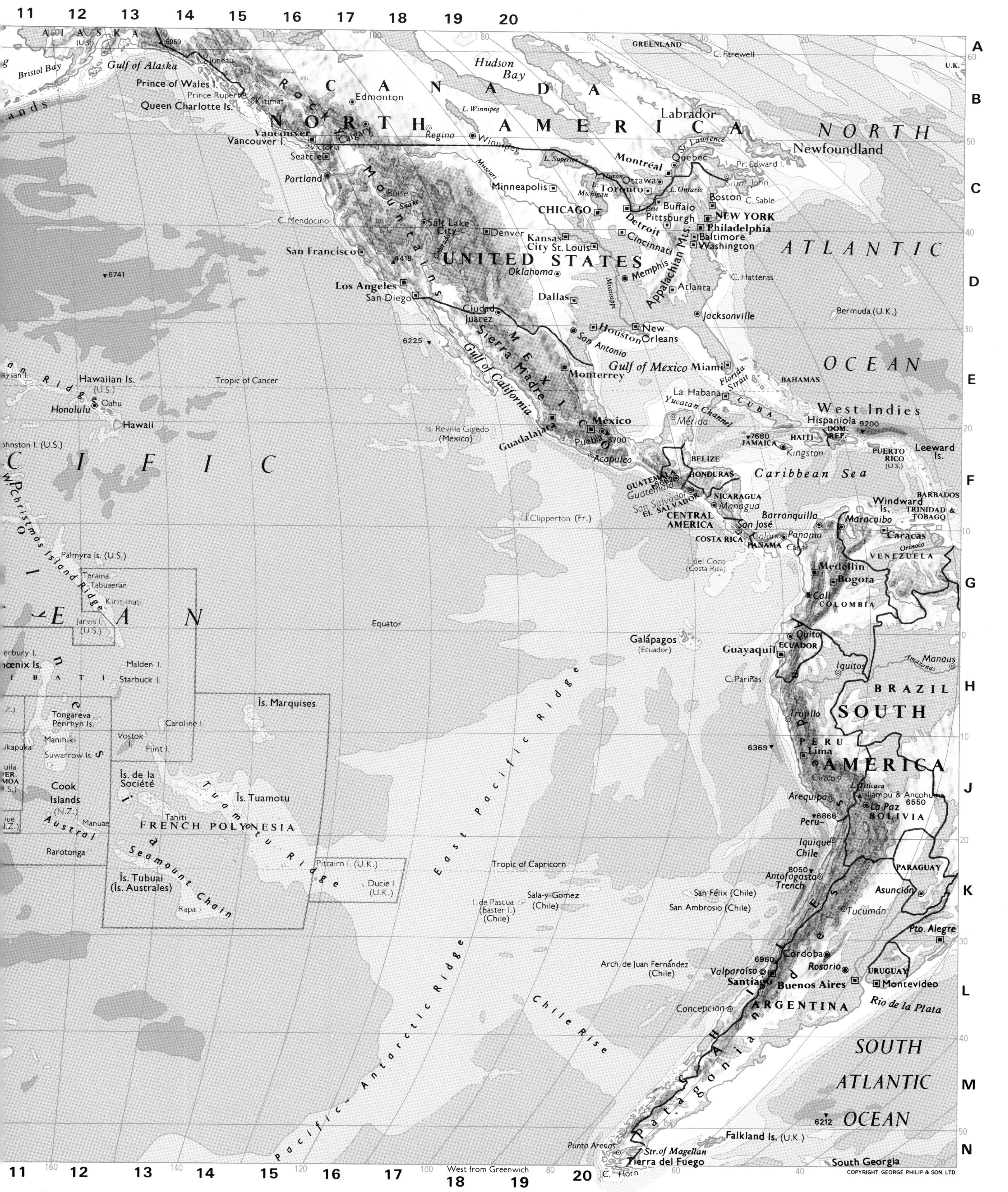

NORTH AMERICA
CANADA
UNITED STATES
MEXICO
Hudson Bay
Gulf of Alaska
Bristol Bay
ALASKA (U.S.)
Prince of Wales I.
Queen Charlotte Is.
Prince Rupert
Kitimat
Juneau
Edmonton
Calgary
Regina
Winnipeg
L. Winnipeg
Vancouver
Vancouver I.
Victoria
Seattle
Portland
Rocky Mountains
Boise
Snake
Salt Lake City
Colorado
Denver
Kansas City
St. Louis
Missouri
Minneapolis
CHICAGO
Detroit
Cincinnati
Memphis
Mississippi
Appalachian Mts.
Atlanta
Jacksonville
Dallas
Oklahoma
Houston
San Antonio
New Orleans
Miami
Florida Strait
Gulf of Mexico
Monterrey
Ciudad Juarez
Sierra Madre
Gulf of California
Guadalajara
México
Puebla
Acapulco
Mérida
Yucatan Channel
La Habana
CUBA
BAHAMAS
C. Mendocino
San Francisco
Los Angeles
San Diego
L. Superior
L. Huron
L. Michigan
L. Erie
L. Ontario
Toronto
Ottawa
Montréal
Quebec
St. Lawrence
Labrador
Newfoundland
Pr. Edward I.
Saint John
C. Sable
Boston
Buffalo
Pittsburgh
NEW YORK
Philadelphia
Baltimore
Washington
C. Hatteras
Bermuda (U.K.)
GREENLAND
C. Farewell
U.K.
ATLANTIC OCEAN
NORTH
West Indies
Hispaniola
HAITI
DOM. REP.
PUERTO RICO (U.S.)
Leeward Is.
JAMAICA
Kingston
Caribbean Sea
BELIZE
HONDURAS
GUATEMALA
Guatemala
San Salvador
EL SALVADOR
NICARAGUA
Managua
CENTRAL AMERICA
COSTA RICA
San José
PANAMA
Colón
Panama
Canal
Barranquilla
Maracaibo
Caracas
Orinoco
VENEZUELA
Windward Is.
BARBADOS
TRINIDAD & TOBAGO
Medellín
Bogota
Cali
COLOMBIA
Quito
ECUADOR
Guayaquil
Iquitos
Amazonas
Manaus
BRAZIL
SOUTH AMERICA
C. Pariñas
Trujillo
PERU
Lima
Cuzco
L. Titicaca
Illampu & Ancohuma
La Paz
BOLIVIA
Arequipa
Peru-Chile Trench
Iquique
Antofagasta
PARAGUAY
Asunción
Tucumán
Pto. Alegre
Córdoba
Rosario
Valparaíso
Santiago
Buenos Aires
URUGUAY
Montevideo
Río de la Plata
ARGENTINA
Concepcion
ANDES
Patagonia
SOUTH ATLANTIC OCEAN
Falkland Is. (U.K.)
South Georgia
Punta Arenas
Str. of Magellan
Tierra del Fuego
C. Horn
Galápagos (Ecuador)
I. del Coco (Costa Rica)
I. Clipperton (Fr.)
Is. Revilla Gigedo (Mexico)
Tropic of Cancer
Equator
Tropic of Capricorn
East Pacific Ridge
Pacific-Antarctic Ridge
Chile Rise
San Félix (Chile)
San Ambrosio (Chile)
Arch. de Juan Fernández (Chile)
I. de Pascua (Easter I.) (Chile)
Sala-y-Gomez (Chile)
Pitcairn I. (U.K.)
Ducie I (U.K.)
PACIFIC OCEAN
Hawaiian Is. (U.S.)
Oahu
Honolulu
Hawaii
Johnston I. (U.S.)
Christmas Island Ridge
Palmyra Is. (U.S.)
Teraina
Tabuaeran
Kiritimati
Jarvis I. (U.S.)
Malden I.
Starbuck I.
Phoenix Is.
KIRIBATI
Tongareva
Penrhyn Is.
Manihiki
Suwarrow Is.
Pukapuka
Caroline I.
Vostok I.
Flint I.
Is. Marquises
Is. de la Société
Is. Tuamotu
Tuamotu Ridge
Tahiti
FRENCH POLYNESIA
Cook Islands (N.Z.)
Manuae
Austral Seamount Chain
Rarotonga
Is. Tubuai (Is. Australes)
Rapa
5959
4418
6741
6225
5700
6662
7680
9200
6369
6866
6550
8050
6960
6212

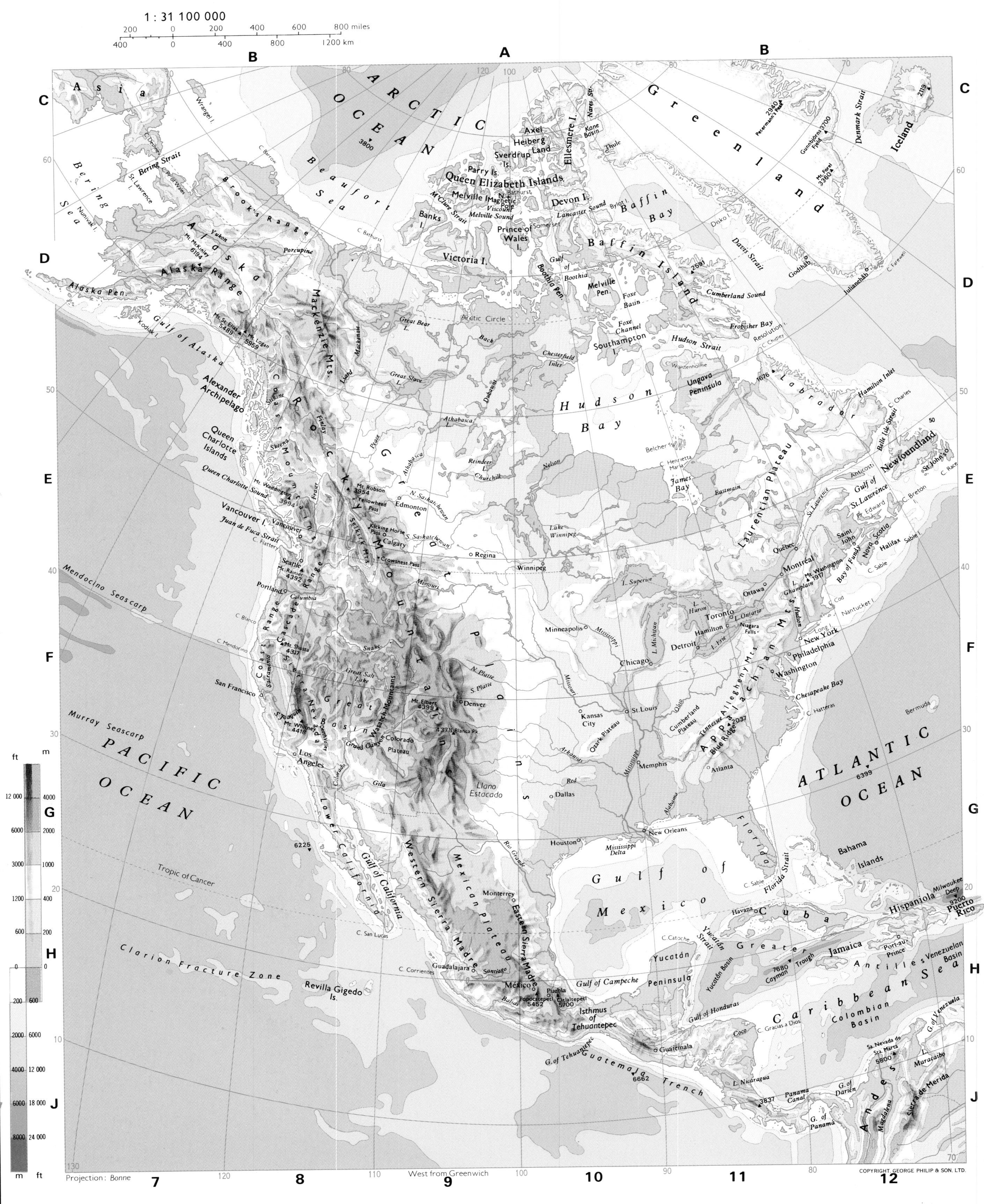

1 : 31 100 000

West from Greenwich

Projection: Bonne

COPYRIGHT. GEORGE PHILIP & SON. LTD.

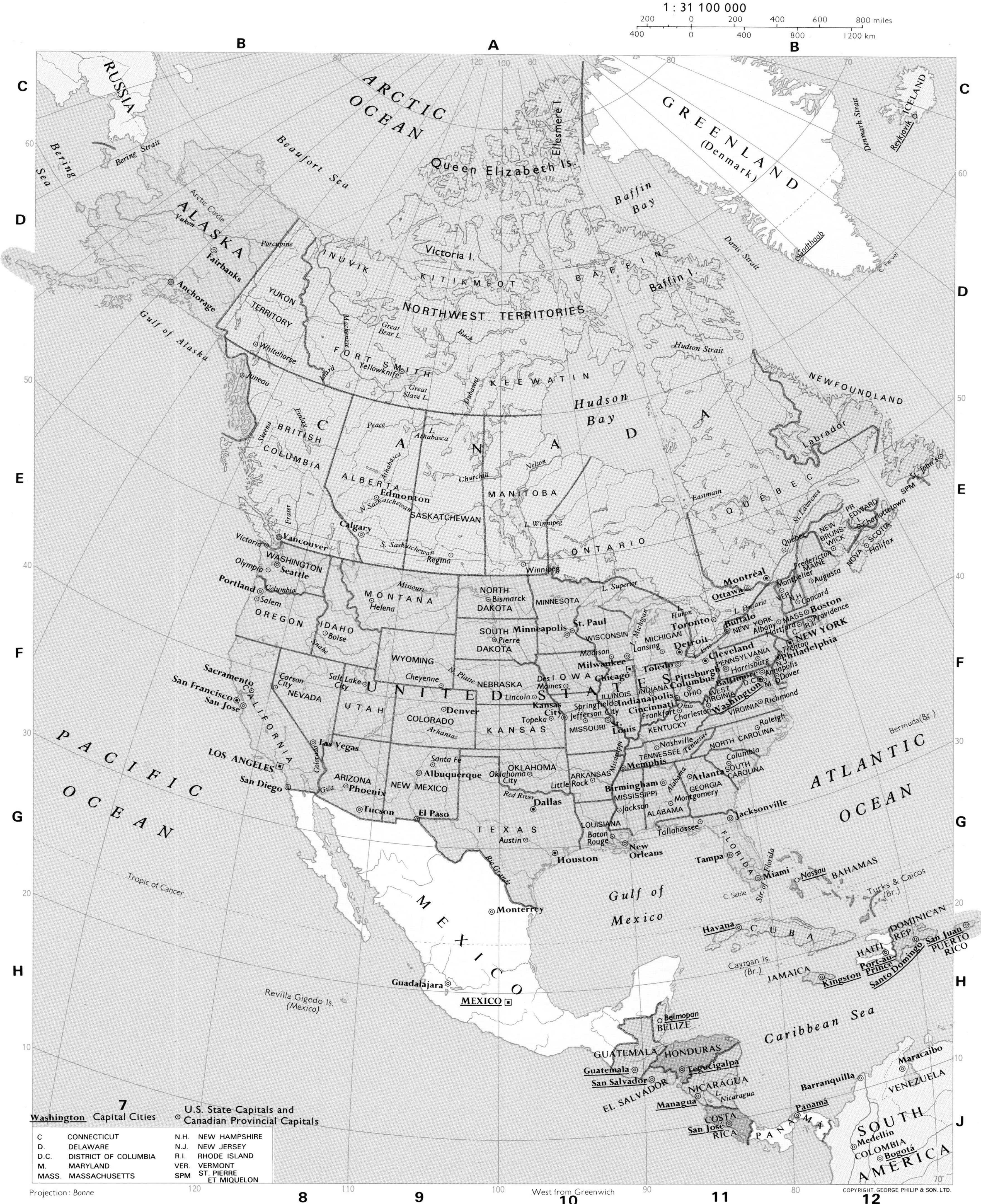

1 : 31 100 000
200 0 200 400 600 800 miles
400 0 400 800 1200 km
A
B
C
D
E
F
G
H
J
7
8
9
10
11
12
RUSSIA
ARCTIC OCEAN
Bering Sea
Bering Strait
Beaufort Sea
Queen Elizabeth Is.
Ellesmere I.
GREENLAND (Denmark)
Denmark Strait
ICELAND
Reykjavik
Baffin Bay
Davis Strait
Godthaab
C. Farvel
Arctic Circle
ALASKA
Yukon
Porcupine
Fairbanks
Anchorage
Gulf of Alaska
Juneau
Whitehorse
YUKON TERRITORY
INUVIK
KITIKMEOT
BAFFIN
Victoria I.
Baffin I.
NORTHWEST TERRITORIES
Great Bear L.
Mackenzie
Back
FORT SMITH
Yellowknife
Great Slave L.
Dubawnt
KEEWATIN
Hudson Strait
NEWFOUNDLAND
Hudson Bay
Labrador
St. John's
CANADA
BRITISH COLUMBIA
Skeena
Finlay
Peace
L. Athabasca
Athabasca
ALBERTA
Edmonton
N. Saskatchewan
SASKATCHEWAN
Churchill
Nelson
MANITOBA
Eastmain
QUEBEC
St. Lawrence
L. Winnipeg
Fraser
Calgary
S. Saskatchewan
Regina
Winnipeg
ONTARIO
Victoria
Vancouver
Québec
NEW BRUNSWICK
PR. EDWARD I.
Charlottetown
NOVA SCOTIA
Halifax
SPM
Fredericton
WASHINGTON
Olympia
Seattle
Portland
Columbia
Salem
OREGON
IDAHO
Boise
Snake
MONTANA
Missouri
Helena
NORTH DAKOTA
Bismarck
MINNESOTA
L. Superior
Montréal
Ottawa
Montpelier
MAINE
Augusta
VER.
N.H.
Concord
Boston
MASS.
Providence
R.I.
C.
Hartford
Albany
NEW YORK
Toronto
L. Ontario
Buffalo
L. Huron
L. Michigan
SOUTH DAKOTA
Pierre
Minneapolis
St. Paul
WISCONSIN
MICHIGAN
Lansing
Detroit
WYOMING
Cheyenne
N. Platte
NEBRASKA
Lincoln
Des Moines
IOWA
Madison
Milwaukee
Chicago
Toledo
Cleveland
PENNSYLVANIA
Harrisburg
Pittsburgh
Trenton
N.J.
Philadelphia
Annapolis
Baltimore
Dover
D.
D.C.
M.
Sacramento
San Francisco
San Jose
CALIFORNIA
Carson City
NEVADA
Salt Lake City
UTAH
UNITED STATES
ILLINOIS
Springfield
INDIANA
Indianapolis
OHIO
Columbus
WEST VIRGINIA
Washington
Richmond
VIRGINIA
Denver
COLORADO
Arkansas
KANSAS
Topeka
Kansas City
Jefferson City
MISSOURI
St. Louis
Cincinnati
Frankfort
Ohio
Charleston
KENTUCKY
Raleigh
NORTH CAROLINA
Nashville
TENNESSEE
Tennessee
Columbia
SOUTH CAROLINA
Memphis
Bermuda (Br.)
Las Vegas
LOS ANGELES
Colorado
San Diego
Santa Fe
Albuquerque
ARIZONA
Phoenix
Gila
NEW MEXICO
OKLAHOMA
Oklahoma City
Little Rock
ARKANSAS
Mississippi
Birmingham
MISSISSIPPI
Alabama
Atlanta
GEORGIA
Montgomery
ALABAMA
Jackson
Red River
Dallas
Tucson
El Paso
TEXAS
Austin
LOUISIANA
Baton Rouge
New Orleans
Tallahassee
Jacksonville
FLORIDA
Houston
Tampa
Miami
Str. of Florida
PACIFIC OCEAN
ATLANTIC OCEAN
Tropic of Cancer
Rio Grande
Nassau
BAHAMAS
C. Sable
Turks & Caicos (Br.)
MEXICO
Monterrey
Gulf of Mexico
Havana
CUBA
DOMINICAN REP.
San Juan
PUERTO RICO
HAITI
Port-au-Prince
Santo Domingo
Cayman Is. (Br.)
JAMAICA
Kingston
Guadalajara
Revilla Gigedo Is. (Mexico)
MEXICO
Belmopan
BELIZE
Caribbean Sea
GUATEMALA
HONDURAS
Guatemala
Tegucigalpa
San Salvador
EL SALVADOR
NICARAGUA
L. Nicaragua
Managua
Maracaibo
Barranquilla
VENEZUELA
Panamá
PANAMA
COSTA RICA
San José
SOUTH AMERICA
Medellín
COLOMBIA
Bogotá
Washington Capital Cities
U.S. State Capitals and Canadian Provincial Capitals
C. CONNECTICUT
D. DELAWARE
D.C. DISTRICT OF COLUMBIA
M. MARYLAND
MASS. MASSACHUSETTS
N.H. NEW HAMPSHIRE
N.J. NEW JERSEY
R.I. RHODE ISLAND
VER. VERMONT
SPM ST. PIERRE ET MIQUELON
Projection: Bonne
West from Greenwich
COPYRIGHT GEORGE PHILIP & SON. LTD.

102 103

PACIFIC OCEAN

ALASKA

YUKON TERRITORY

BRITISH COLUMBIA

ALBERTA

SASKATCHEWAN

MANITOBA

NORTHWEST TERRITORIES

KITIKMEOT

KEEWATIN

Victoria Island

Banks Island

Prince Albert Pen.

Somerset Island

Prince of Wales Island

Boothia Peninsula

Melville

Amundsen Gulf

Coronation Gulf

Queen Maud Gulf

Gt. Bear Lake

Gt. Slave Lake

Yellowknife

Lake Athabasca

Reindeer Lake

Edmonton

Calgary

Vancouver

Victoria

Saskatoon

Regina

Winnipeg

Lake Winnipeg

WASHINGTON

Seattle

Spokane

MONTANA

NORTH DAKOTA

SOUTH DAKOTA

WYOMING

NEBRASKA

MINNESOTA

WISCONSIN

IOWA

UNITED STATES

Minneapolis

St. Paul

Omaha

Des Moines

ALASKA
1 : 26 700 000

100   0   100   200   300 miles
100   0   200   400 km

BERING SEA

Brooks Range

Fairbanks

Anchorage

Nome

Aleutian Is.

Kodiak I.

GULF OF ALASKA

Bristol Bay

Kuskokwim Bay

Projection: Bonne

West from Greenwich

ft m
9000 3000
6000 2000
4500 1500
3000 1000
1200 400
600 200
0
200 600
2000 6000
m ft

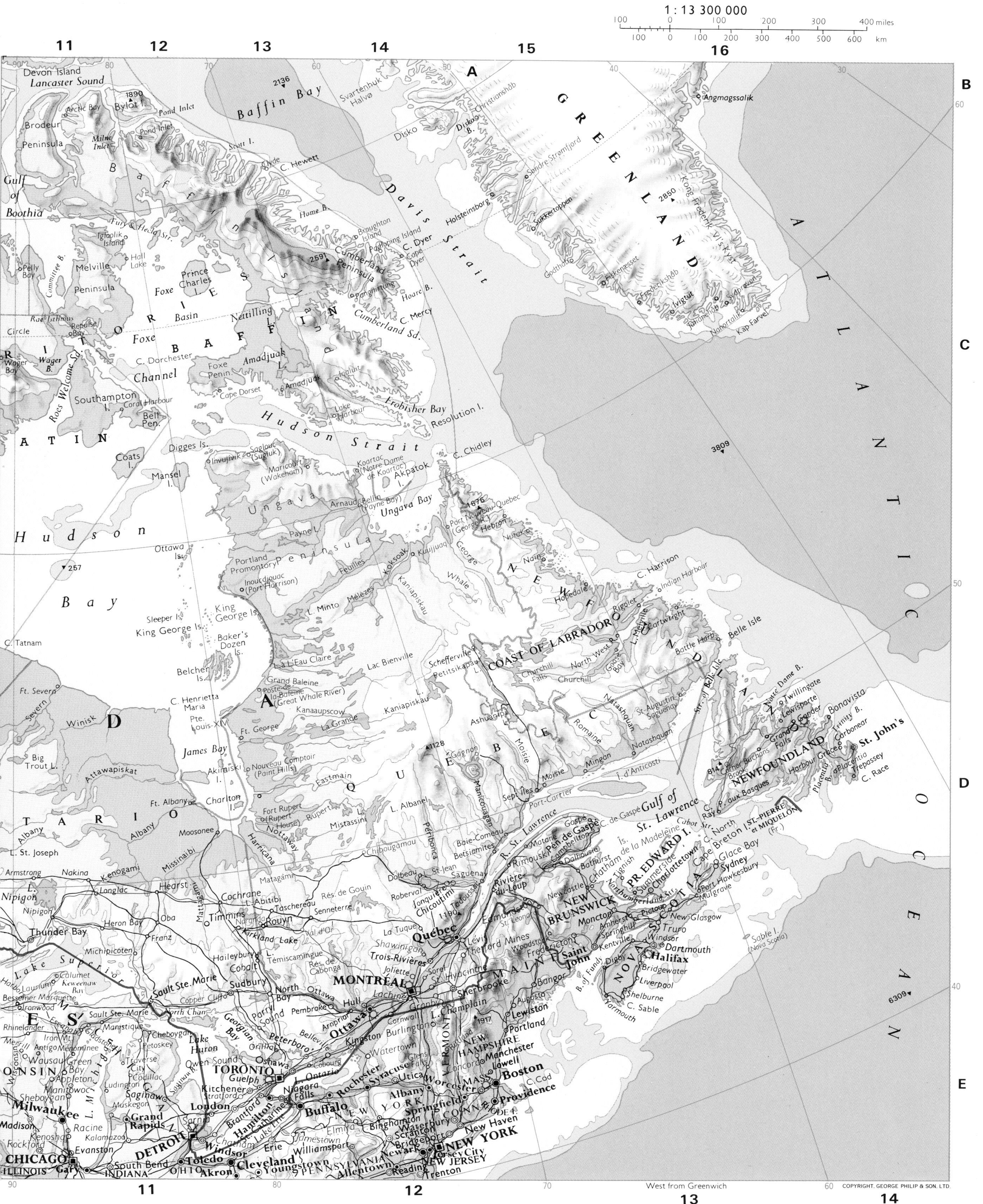

1 : 13 300 000

100   0   100   200   300   400 miles

100   0   100   200   300   400   500   600   km

11   **12**   **13**   **14**   **15**   **16**

B

Devon Island
Lancaster Sound
2136
Baffin Bay
Svartenhuk
Halvø
Christianshåb
Angmagssalik
B
60

Arctic Bay
Bylot I.
Pond Inlet
1890
Scott I.
Disko
Disko B.
Svartenhuk
Halvø
G R E E N L A N D
A T L A N T I C

Brodeur
Peninsula
Milne
Inlet
Pond Inlet
C. Hewett
Clyde
Holsteinsborg
Sukkertoppen
2850
Kong Frederik VI's Kyst

Gulf
of
Boothia
Fury & Hecla Str.
Broughton
Island
Pangnirtung
C. Dyer
Cape
Dyer
Davis Strait
Godthåb
Frederikshåb
Fiskenæsset

Igloolik
Island
Hall
Lake
2591
Cumberland
Peninsula
Frederikshåb
Julianehåb

C

Pelly
Bay
Melville
Peninsula
Prince
Charles
I.
Foxe
Basin
Nettilling
L.
Pangnirtung
Hoare B.
Kap Farvel

Rae Isthmus
Repulse
Bay
Committee B.
C. Dorchester
Foxe
Penin.
Amadjuak
L.
C. Mercy
Cumberland Sd.

Circle
Wager
Bay
Roes Welcome Sd.
Southampton
I.
Coral Harbour
B A F F I N   I S L A N D
Foxe
Channel
Cape Dorset
Amadjuak
Iqaluit
Lake
Harbour
Frobisher Bay
Resolution I.

Wager
Bay
Coats
I.
Bell
Pen.
H u d s o n   S t r a i t
C. Chidley

Digges Is.
Mansel
I.
Invujivik
Saglouc
(Sugluk)
Koartac
Notre Dame
de Koartoc
Akpatok
I.
50

Maricourt
(Wakeham)
Arnaud
(Bellin,
Payne Bay)
Port Nouveau Quebec
George R.
Hebron
3809

H u d s o n
Ottawa
Is.
Portland
Promontory
Inoucdjouac
(Port Harrison)
Payne L.
U n g a v a
Koksoak
Kuujjuaq
Ungava Bay
George
Whale
Nutak
Nain

257
Peninsula
Feuilles
Kaniapiskau
N E W

B a y
Sleeper Is.
King
George Is.
L. Minto
Melezes
Hopedale
Indian Harbour

King George Is.
Baker's
Dozen
Is.
Schefferville
Petitsikapau
C O A S T   O F   L A B R A D O R
Makkovik
Rigolet
Cartwright
Belle Isle

C. Tatnam
à l'Eau Claire
Lac Bienville
Petitsikapau
North
West
River
L. Melville
Bottle Harb.
Belle Isle

Belcher
Is.
Grand Baleine
Churchill
Falls
Churchill
Grand L.
Natashquan
Notre Dame B.
Twillingate
Bonavista

Ft. Severn
C. Henrietta
Maria
Postede-la-Baleine
(Great Whale River)
Kanaaupscow
Ashuapig
Romaine
St. Augustin
Saguenay
Str. of Belle Isle
Lewisporte
Gander
Trinity B.

Winisk
Pte.
Louis-XIV
Ft. George
La Grande
4128
Gagnon
Moisie
Mingan
Grand
Falls
St. John's

D
Big
Trout L.
James Bay
Nouveau Comptoir
(Paint Hills)
Eastmain
Q U E B E C
Moisie
Î. d'Anticosti
NEWFOUNDLAND
Placentia
Trepassey
C. Race
D

Attawapiskat
Akimiski
I.
Ft. Albany
Charlton I.
Fort Rupert
(Rupert
House)
Rupert L.
L. Albanel
Mistassini
Péribonca
Port-Cartier
Sept-Îles
Corner
Brook
Br. d'Or
Harbour
Grace
Carbonear

Albany
Moosonee
Nottaway
Harricana
Chibougamau
L. Albanel
Baie-Comeau
Betsiamites
Gulf   of
St. Lawrence
P. aux Basques
Cabot Str.

L. St. Joseph
Matagami
Res. de Gouin
Dolbeau
St. Jean
Saguenay
R. St. Lawrence
Pen. de Gaspé
Îs. de la Madeleine
Cape Breton I.
ST-PIERRE
et MIQUELON
(Fr.)

Armstrong
Nakina
Kenogami
Hearst
Cochrane
Abitibi
Taschereau
Senneterre
Roberval
Chicoutimi
Jonquière
Tadoussac
Rimouski
Matane
Gaspé
Ray
North
Glace Bay

L.
Nipigon
Langlac
Thunder Bay
Heron Bay
Oba
Timmins
Narand.da
Rouyn
Val d'Or
La Tuque
Chicoutimi
Rivière-
du-Loup
Edmunston
Bathurst
Chatham
Dalhousie
Tignish
Charlottetown
Sydney
Port Hawkesbury
Mulgrave

Nipigon
Heron Bay
Franz
Kirkland Lake
Shawinigan
Trois-Rivières
Québec
Lévis
Thetford Mines
Woodstock
Newcastle
Summerside
Northumberland Str.
Pictou
New Glasgow
Sable I.
(Nova Scotia)

Thunder Bay
Michipicoten
Haileybury
Cobalt
Témiscamingue
Res. de
Cabonga
Joliette
Sorel
St. Hyacinthe
MAIN
Fredericton
Saint
John
Amherst
Springhill
Truro
Windsor
Dartmouth

Lake   Superior
Sault Ste. Marie
Copper Cliff
Sudbury
North
Bay
Ottawa
MONTRÉAL
Lachine
Sherbrooke
Bangor
NEW
BRUNSWICK
Moncton
NOVA
SCOTIA
Halifax

40

Bessemer
Marquette
Sault Ste. Marie
North Chan.
Parry
Sound
Pembroke
Arnprior
Hull
Ottawa
Cornwall
L. Champlain
Augusta
B. of Fundy
Digby
Bridgewater
Liverpool
C. Sable
6309

Ironwood
Keweenaw
Bay
Manistique
Cheboygan
Georgian
Bay
Belleville
Kingston
Burlington
VERMONT
1917
Lewiston
Portland
Yarmouth
Shelburne

Rhinelander
Iron Mt.
L. Michigan
Petoskey
Lake
Huron
Orillia
L. Ontario
Watertown
NEW
HAMPSHIRE
Concord
Manchester
C. Cod

WISCONSIN
Antigo
Menominee
Green
Bay
Traverse
City
Owen Sound
Oshawa
TORONTO
Rochester
Syracuse
Utica
Worcester
MASS.
Boston
E

Wausau
Appleton
Manitowoc
Ludington
Saginaw
Guelph
Hamilton
Niagara
Falls
Buffalo
L. Erie
NEW
YORK
Albany
Springfield
CONN.
Providence

Milwaukee
Madison
Racine
Kenosha
Kalamazoo
London
Brantford
St. Catharines
Elmira
Binghamton
Scranton
Waterbury
New Haven
Bridgeport
New York
New Jersey

Rockford
Evanston
Grand
Rapids
DETROIT
Windsor
Chatham
Lake Erie
Erie
Williamsport
PENNSYLVANIA
Allentown
Reading
Trenton
Jersey City

CHICAGO
ILLINOIS
Gary
INDIANA
South Bend
Toledo
Cleveland
Akron
Youngstown
OHIO
Newark
NEW YORK

11   **12**   West from Greenwich   **13**   **14**

COPYRIGHT. GEORGE PHILIP & SON, LTD.

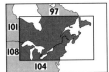

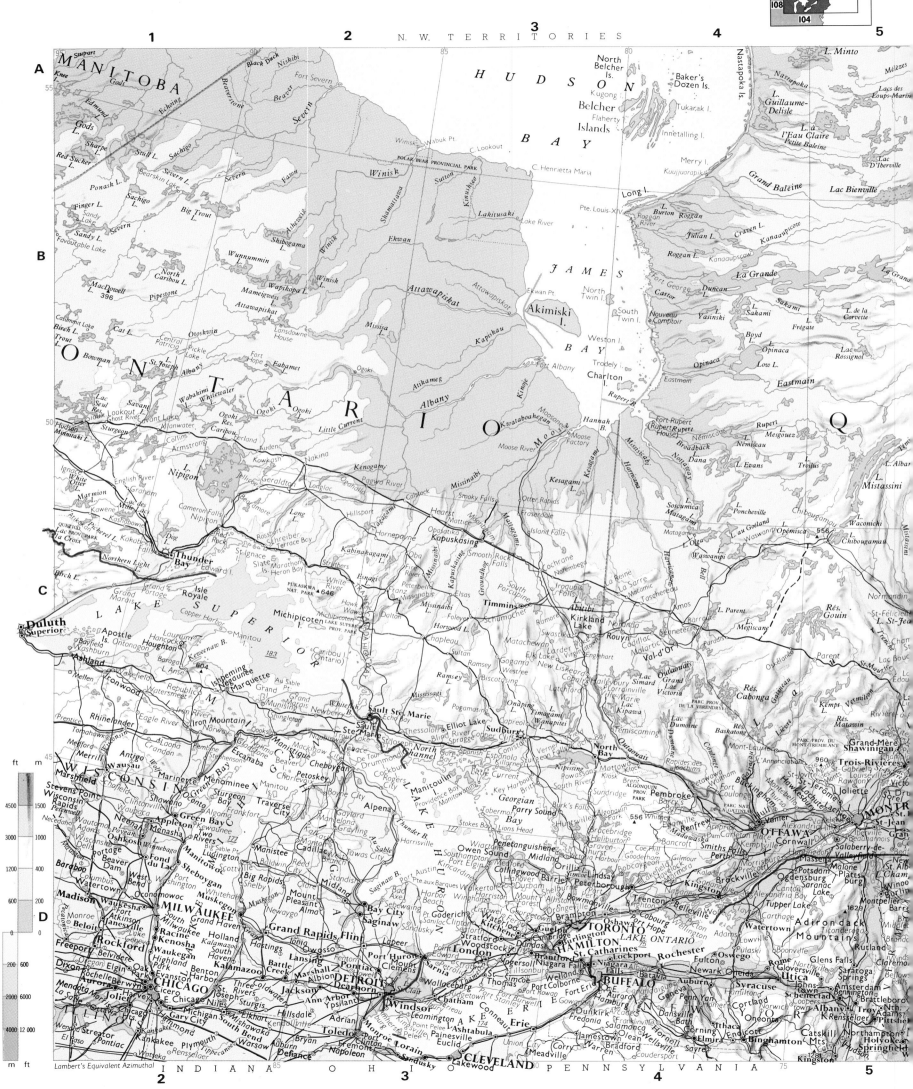

MANITOBA

N . W .   T E R R I T O R I E S

H U D S O N

North Belcher Is.
Baker's Dozen Is.
Kugong I.
Belcher Flaherty Islands
Innetalling I.
Tukarak I.

B A Y

C. Lookout
Polar Bear Provincial Park
Winisk
Sutton
C. Henrietta Maria

L. Minto
Nastapoka Is.
L. des Loups-Marins
L. Guillaume-Delisle
L. à l'Eau Claire Petite Baleine
Grand Baleine
Lac Bienville

J A M E S

Ekwan Pt.
Akimiski I.
North Twin I.
South Twin I.
Weston I.

B A Y

Charlton
Trodely I.
Eastmain

Fort George
La Grande
Duncan
Castor
Yasinski
Boyd
Opinaca
Low L.
Eastmain

O N T A R I O

Q

Moosonee
Rupert B.
Fort Rupert (Rupert House)
Nemiscau
Mistassini

L A K E   S U P E R I O R

Thunder Bay
Duluth Superior
Isle Royale

Timmins
Kirkland Lake
Rouyn
Val-d'Or

W I S C O N S I N

Sault Ste Marie
Sudbury
North Bay
Pembroke
OTTAWA
MONTREAL

MILWAUKEE
CHICAGO

Green Bay

M I C H I G A N

L A K E   H U R O N

Georgian Bay
Parry Sound
Barrie
TORONTO
HAMILTON
Peterborough
Kingston
Brockville
Cornwall

Grand Rapids Flint
DETROIT
Windsor
London

L A K E   O N T A R I O

St. Catharines
BUFFALO
Rochester
Syracuse
Utica
Albany

I N D I A N A   **O H I O**   **P E N N S Y L V A N I A**

CLEVELAND
Toledo
Erie

Adirondack Mountains

Lambert's Equivalent Azimuthal

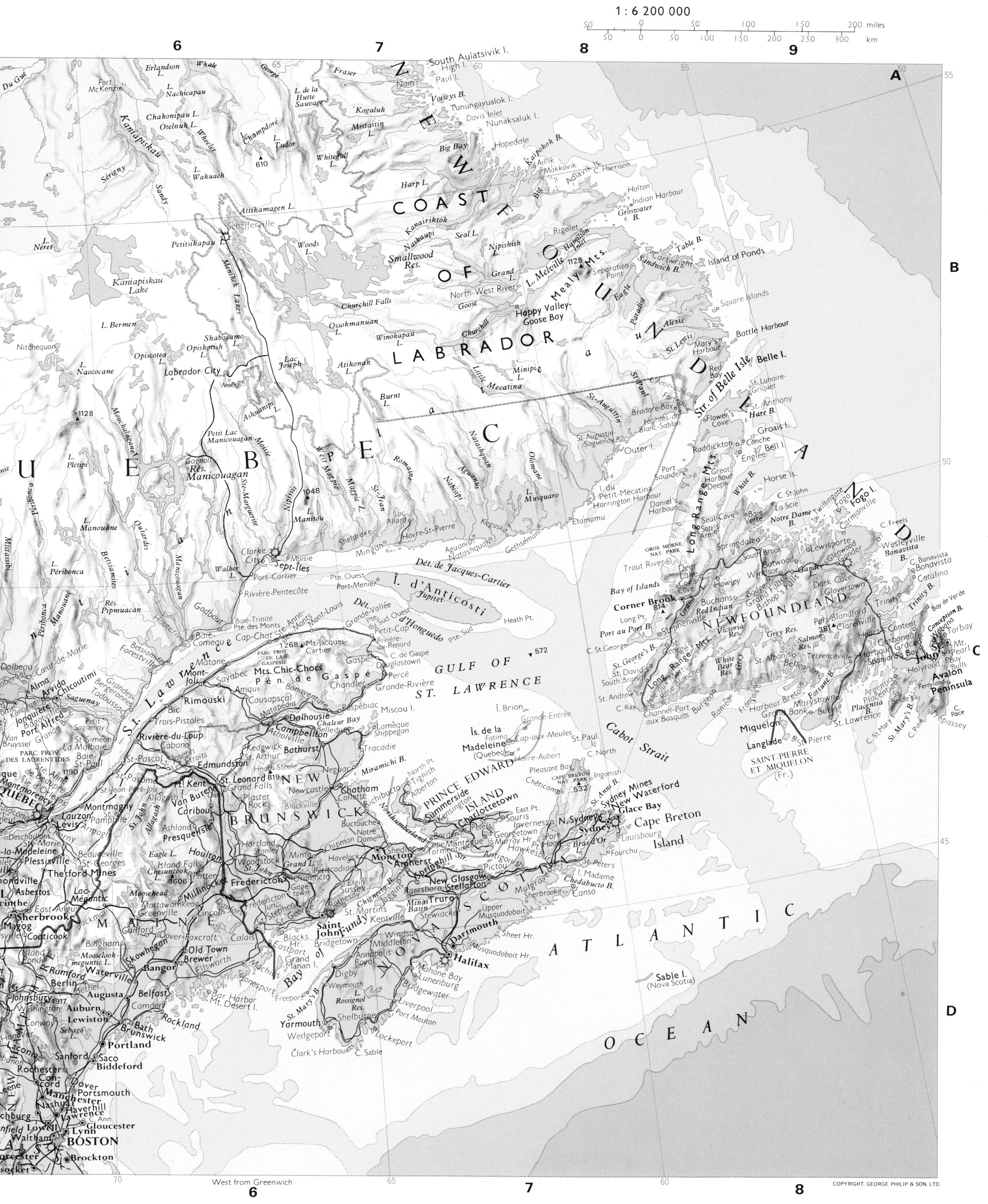
1 : 6 200 000
50 0 50 100 150 200 miles
50 0 50 100 150 200 250 300 km
6
7
8
9
A
B
C
D
QUEBEC
NEWFOUNDLAND
COAST OF LABRADOR
LABRADOR
NEWFOUNDLAND
NEW BRUNSWICK
NOVA SCOTIA
PRINCE EDWARD ISLAND
MAINE
GULF OF ST. LAWRENCE
ATLANTIC OCEAN
Cabot Strait
Str. of Belle Isle
Bay of Fundy
St. Lawrence
Î. d'Anticosti
Dét. de Jacques-Cartier
Dét. d'Honguedo
Pén. de Gaspé
Mts. Chic-Chocs
Cape Breton Island
Sable I. (Nova Scotia)
SAINT-PIERRE ET MIQUELON (Fr.)
Miquelon
Langlade
St. Pierre
Îs. de la Madeleine (Quebec)
Smallwood Res.
Mealy Mts.
L. Melville
Happy Valley-Goose Bay
North West River
Churchill Falls
Labrador City
Schefferville
Kaniapiskau Lake
Res. Manicouagan
Sept-Îles
Port-Cartier
Baie-Comeau
Havre-St-Pierre
Nain
Hopedale
Makkovik
Rigolet
Cartwright
Battle Harbour
Belle I.
Corner Brook
Stephenville
Gander
Grand Falls
Botwood
Lewisporte
Clarenville
St. John's
Avalon Peninsula
Conception B.
Trinity B.
Bonavista
Fogo I.
Long Range Mts.
Channel-Port aux Basques
C. Race
Halifax
Dartmouth
Truro
New Glasgow
Sydney
Glace Bay
New Waterford
Sydney Mines
Yarmouth
Lunenburg
Liverpool
Digby
Annapolis Royal
Kentville
Amherst
Moncton
Saint John
Fredericton
Bathurst
Campbellton
Edmundston
Chatham
Newcastle
Charlottetown
Summerside
Dalhousie
Gaspé
Percé
Chandler
Matane
Rimouski
Rivière-du-Loup
Chicoutimi
Jonquière
Alma
Saguenay
QUEBEC
Lévis
Lauzon
Montmagny
Thetford Mines
Sherbrooke
Magog
Coaticook
Lac-Mégantic
Asbestos
Bangor
Augusta
Waterville
Old Town
Brewer
Belfast
Bar Harbor
Mt. Desert I.
Bath
Brunswick
Portland
Lewiston
Auburn
Rockland
Biddeford
Saco
Sanford
Rochester
Concord
Dover
Portsmouth
Manchester
Nashua
Haverhill
Lawrence
Lowell
Lynn
Gloucester
Waltham
BOSTON
Brockton
Presque Isle
Caribou
Houlton
Millinocket
Moosehead L.
West from Greenwich
70
65
60
55
50
45
COPYRIGHT, GEORGE PHILIP & SON, LTD.

YUKON TERRITORY

NORTHWEST

GREAT SLAVE LAKE

BRITISH COLUMBIA

ALBERTA

ALASKA

ALEXANDER ARCH.

QUEEN CHARLOTTE ISLANDS

PACIFIC OCEAN

VANCOUVER ISLAND

WASHINGTON

IDAHO

Whitehorse · Carcross · Atlin · Teslin · Watson Lake · Fort Nelson · Fort Liard · Fort Simpson · Yellowknife · Fort Providence · Fort Resolution · Pine Point · Hay River · Fort Smith

Juneau · Skagway · Haines · Sitka · Petersburg · Wrangell · Ketchikan · Prince Rupert · Terrace · Kitimat · Smithers · Hazelton · Houston · Burns Lake · Vanderhoof · Prince George · Quesnel · Williams Lake · McBride · Jasper · Hinton · Edson

EDMONTON · CALGARY · Red Deer · Camrose · Wetaskiwin · Ponoka · Lacombe · Stettler · Innisfail · Didsbury · Olds · Banff · Lake Louise · Golden · Revelstoke · Kamloops · Kelowna · Vernon · Penticton · Nelson · Trail · Cranbrook · Kimberley · Fernie · Lethbridge

VANCOUVER · New Westminster · North Vancouver · Victoria · Nanaimo · Port Alberni · Hope · Chilliwack · Merritt · Princeton

SEATTLE · Bellingham · Everett · Mount Vernon · Port Angeles · Bremerton · Wenatchee · Colville

Great Slave Lake · Athabasca · Lesser Slave Lake · Williston Lake · Babine Lake · Stuart Lake · Francois L. · Ootsa L. · Quesnel L. · Shuswap L. · Okanagan L. · Kootenay L.

Rocky Mountains · Selkirk Mountains · Purcell Mts. · Cariboo Mountains · Coast Mountains · Skeena Mountains · Cassiar Mountains · St. Elias Mts.

Mackenzie · Liard · Peace · Athabasca · Fraser · Columbia · Thompson · Skeena · Stikine · Nass

Projection: Lambert's Equivalent Azimuthal

West from Greenwich

ft m — 12 000 / 4000 — 9000 / 3000 — 6000 / 2000 — 4500 / 1500 — 3000 / 1000 — 1200 / 400 — 600 / 200 — 0 / 0 — 600 / 200 — 6000 / 2000

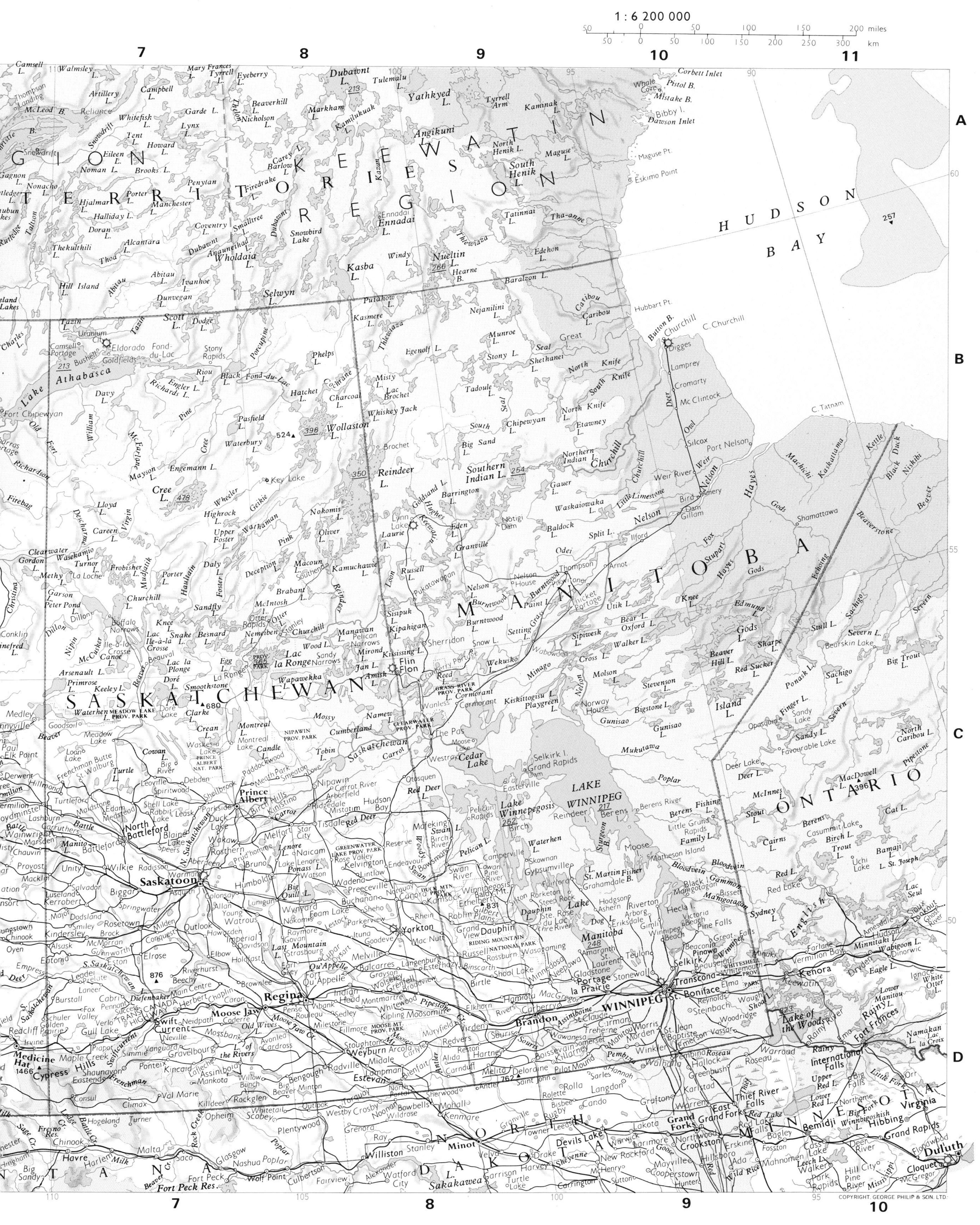
1 : 6 200 000
50 0 50 100 150 200 miles
50 0 50 100 150 200 250 300 km
7
8
9
10
11
A
B
C
D
KEEWATIN
REGION
HUDSON
BAY
SASKATCHEWAN
MANITOBA
ONTARIO
LAKE WINNIPEG
Lake Winnipegosis
Lake Athabasca
Reindeer L.
Wollaston L.
Southern Indian L.
Lake of the Woods
Saskatoon
Regina
WINNIPEG
Prince Albert
North Battleford
Moose Jaw
Swift Current
Medicine Hat
Brandon
Yorkton
Flin Flon
The Pas
Churchill
Kenora
Fort Frances
Duluth
Minot
Grand Forks
NORTH DAKOTA
MINNESOTA
Fort Peck Res.
L. Sakakawea
Devils Lake
Red Lake
Gods L.
Island L.
Cedar Lake
Lake Manitoba
Dauphin
Portage la Prairie
Selkirk
Nelson
Hayes
Churchill
Saskatchewan
110
105
100
95
90
60
55
50
7
8
9
10

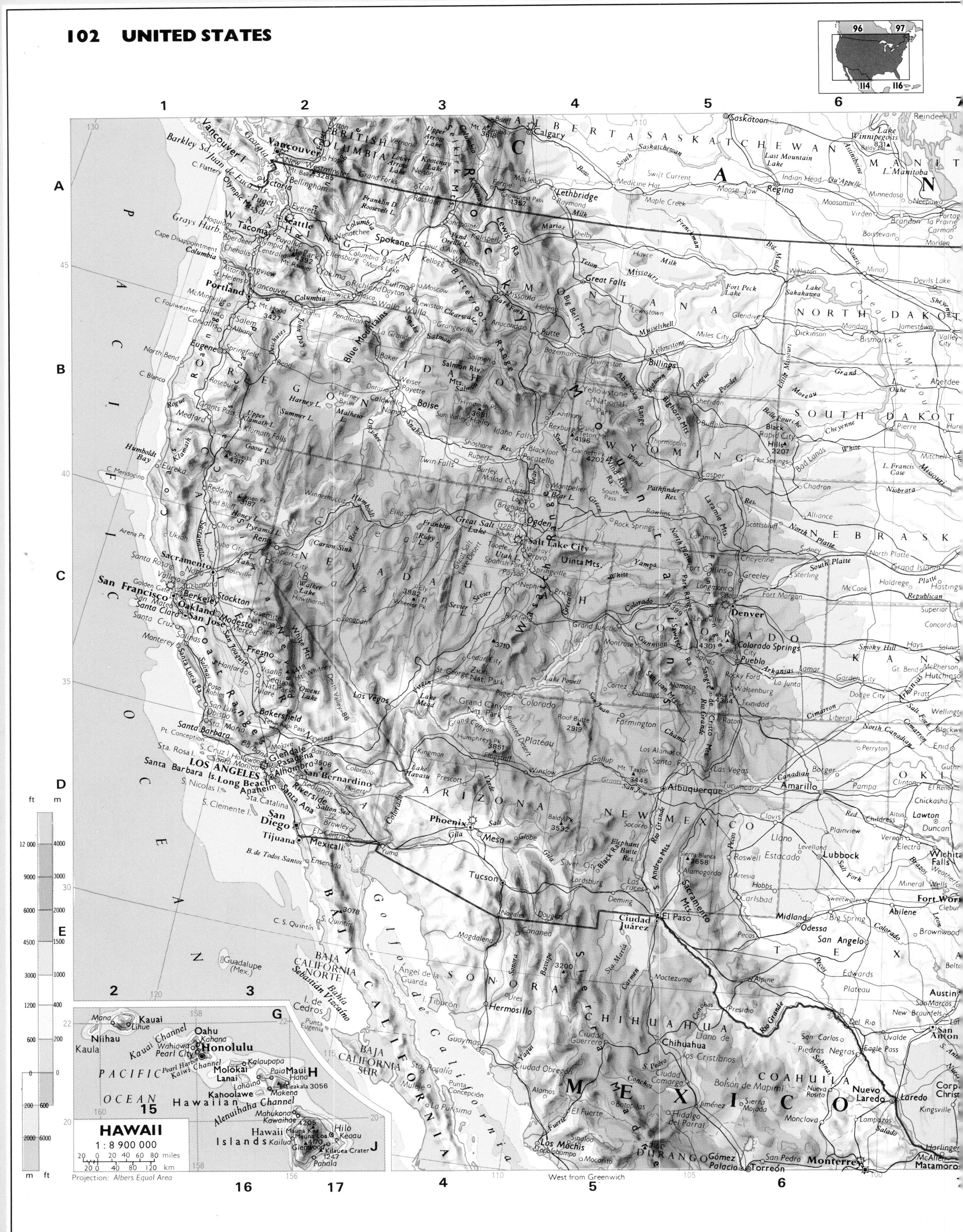

PACIFIC OCEAN
CANADA
BRITISH COLUMBIA
ALBERTA
SASKATCHEWAN
MANITOBA
WASHINGTON
OREGON
IDAHO
MONTANA
WYOMING
NEVADA
UTAH
CALIFORNIA
ARIZONA
NEW MEXICO
COLORADO
NORTH DAKOTA
SOUTH DAKOTA
NEBRASKA
KANSAS
TEXAS
MEXICO
SONORA
CHIHUAHUA
COAHUILA
DURANGO
BAJA CALIFORNIA NORTE
BAJA CALIFORNIA SUR
Golfo de California
Rocky Mts.
Sierra Nevada
Coast Ranges
Cascade Ra.
Great Salt Lake
Vancouver
Victoria
Seattle
Tacoma
Spokane
Portland
Eugene
Boise
Salt Lake City
Ogden
Reno
Sacramento
San Francisco
Oakland
San Jose
Fresno
Stockton
Bakersfield
Las Vegas
LOS ANGELES
Long Beach
San Diego
Tijuana
Mexicali
Phoenix
Tucson
Albuquerque
El Paso
Ciudad Juárez
Denver
Colorado Springs
Pueblo
Cheyenne
Casper
Billings
Great Falls
Helena
Butte
Calgary
Lethbridge
Regina
Saskatoon
Amarillo
Lubbock
Midland
Odessa
San Angelo
Abilene
Chihuahua
Hermosillo
Torreón
Monterrey
Nuevo Laredo
Laredo
HAWAII
1 : 8 900 000
Kauai
Oahu
Honolulu
Molokai
Lanai
Maui
Kahoolawe
Hawaii
Hilo
Hawaiian Islands
PACIFIC OCEAN
Projection: Albers Equal Area
West from Greenwich

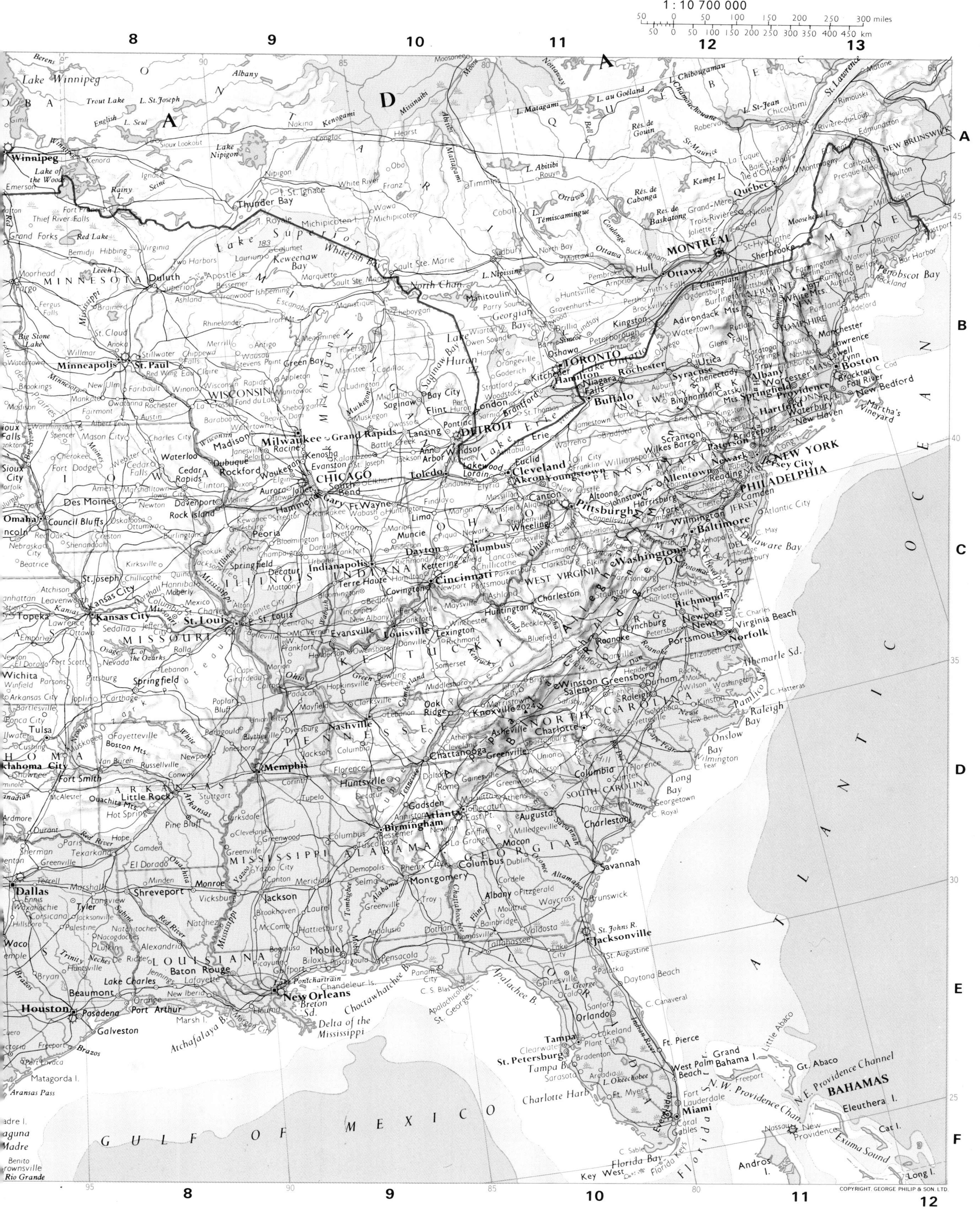
1 : 10 700 000
50 0 50 100 150 200 250 300 miles
50 0 50 100 150 200 250 300 350 400 450 km
8
9
10
11
12
13
A
B
C
D
E
F
CANADA
ONTARIO
QUEBEC
NEW BRUNSWICK
MAINE
VERMONT
NEW HAMPSHIRE
MASS.
CONN.
NEW YORK
PENNSYLVANIA
NEW JERSEY
DEL.
MARYLAND
WEST VIRGINIA
VIRGINIA
NORTH CAROLINA
SOUTH CAROLINA
GEORGIA
FLORIDA
ALABAMA
MISSISSIPPI
LOUISIANA
ARKANSAS
TENNESSEE
KENTUCKY
OHIO
INDIANA
ILLINOIS
MICHIGAN
WISCONSIN
MINNESOTA
IOWA
MISSOURI
BAHAMAS
Lake Winnipeg
Lake Superior
Lake Michigan
Lake Huron
Lake Erie
Lake Ontario
Georgian Bay
Lake of the Woods
ATLANTIC OCEAN
GULF OF MEXICO
Winnipeg
Thunder Bay
Duluth
Minneapolis
St. Paul
Milwaukee
CHICAGO
DETROIT
Toledo
Cleveland
Pittsburgh
Buffalo
TORONTO
Ottawa
MONTRÉAL
Québec
Boston
NEW YORK
PHILADELPHIA
Baltimore
Washington D.C.
Richmond
Norfolk
Indianapolis
Cincinnati
Louisville
St. Louis
Kansas City
Des Moines
Omaha
Memphis
Nashville
Atlanta
Birmingham
Charlotte
Jacksonville
New Orleans
Houston
Dallas
Tampa
Miami
Appalachian Mts.
Delta of the Mississippi
Florida Keys
Key West
Andros I.
Gt. Abaco
Grand Bahama I.
Eleuthera I.
COPYRIGHT. GEORGE PHILIP & SON, LTD.

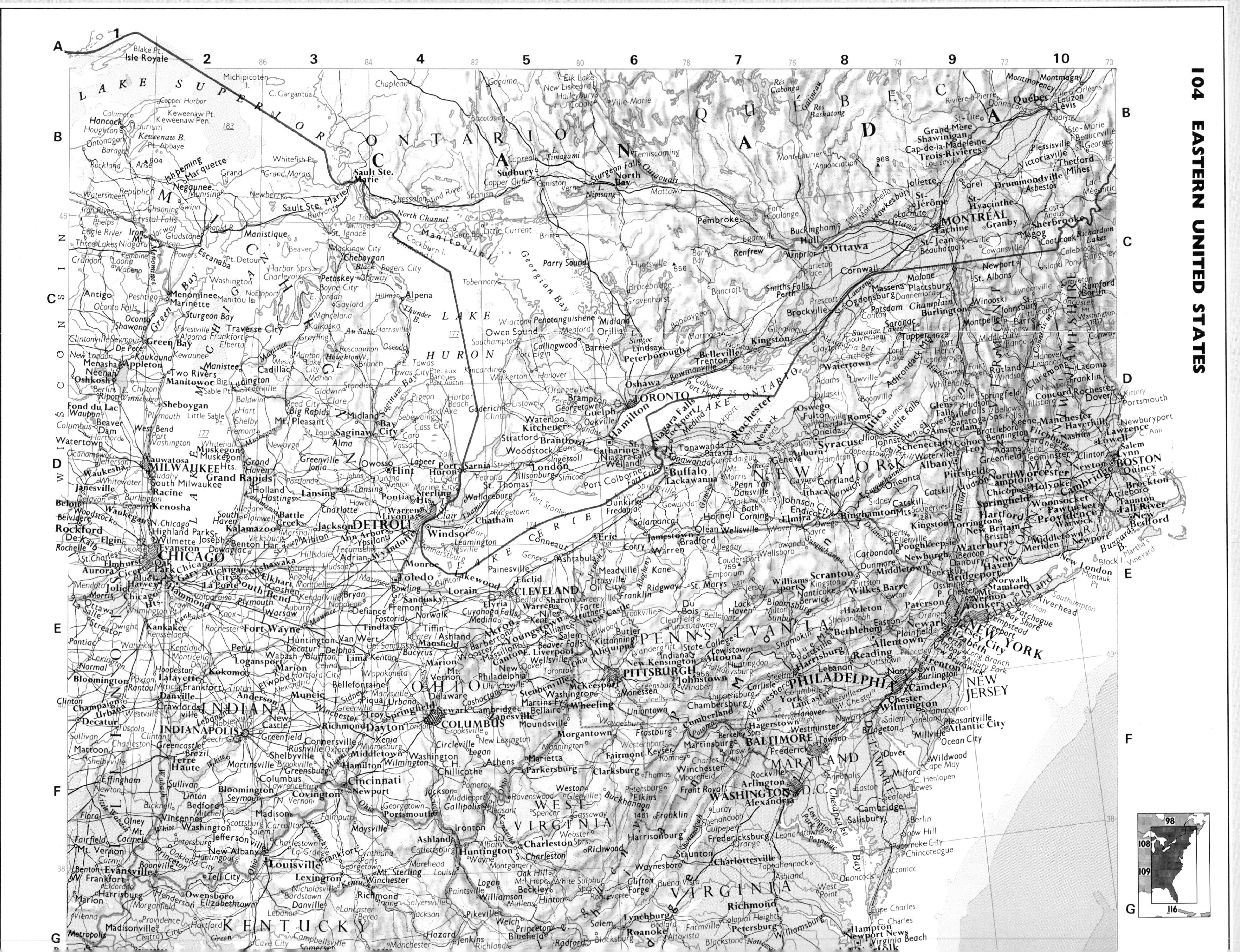
LAKE SUPERIOR
LAKE HURON
LAKE ERIE
LAKE ONTARIO
Georgian Bay
QUÉBEC
ONTARIO
CANADA
MICHIGAN
WISCONSIN
NEW YORK
PENNSYLVANIA
OHIO
INDIANA
ILLINOIS
KENTUCKY
WEST VIRGINIA
VIRGINIA
MARYLAND
NEW JERSEY
DELAWARE
VERMONT
NEW HAMPSHIRE
MASS.
MONTREAL
Ottawa
Québec
TORONTO
DETROIT
CHICAGO
MILWAUKEE
CLEVELAND
COLUMBUS
INDIANAPOLIS
PITTSBURGH
PHILADELPHIA
BALTIMORE
WASHINGTON D.C.
BOSTON
NEW YORK

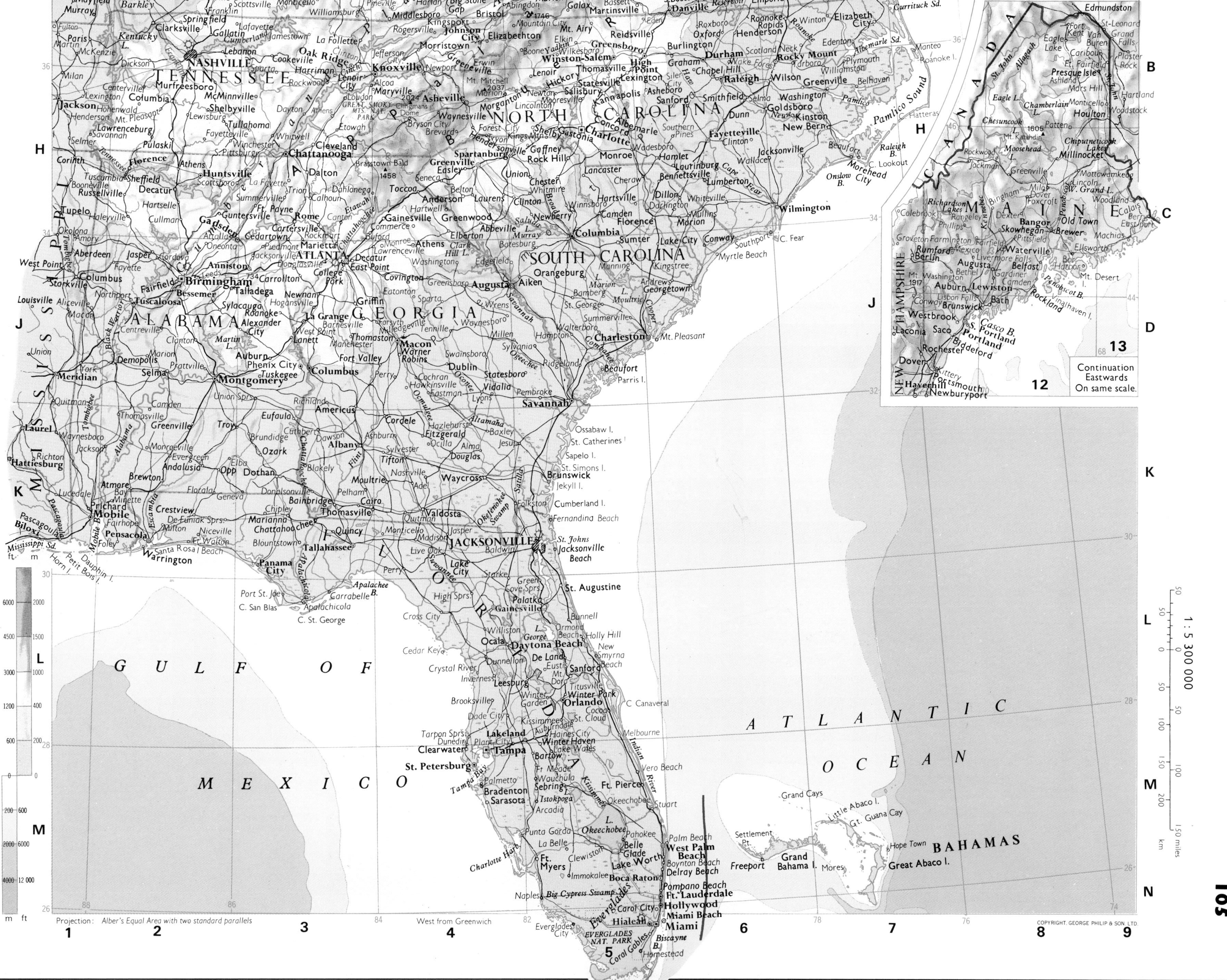

1: 5 300 000
50 0 50 100 150 miles
50 0 50 100 150 200 km
Continuation Eastwards On same scale.
ATLANTIC OCEAN
GULF OF MEXICO
BAHAMAS
NORTH CAROLINA
SOUTH CAROLINA
GEORGIA
ALABAMA
TENNESSEE
MAINE
NEW HAMPSHIRE
CANADA
ATLANTA
JACKSONVILLE
NASHVILLE
Charleston
Savannah
Columbia
Charlotte
Raleigh
Wilmington
Birmingham
Montgomery
Mobile
Tallahassee
Orlando
Tampa
St. Petersburg
Miami
Knoxville
Chattanooga
Macon
Augusta
Portland
Bangor
Grand Bahama I.
Great Abaco I.
Freeport
Projection: Alber's Equal Area with two standard parallels
West from Greenwich
COPYRIGHT. GEORGE PHILIP & SON, LTD.

98
104
104

1 2 3 4 5 6 7

A B C D E F G

Georgian Bay

Lucas Channel
Yeo I.
Fitzwilliam I.
Cove I.
Flowerpot I.
Tobermory
C. Hurd
Cabot Hd.
Dyer Bay
Bruce Peninsula
Greenough Pt.
Lion's Head
Lyal I.
C. Croker
Hope I.
Christian I.
Penetanguishene
Midland
Port Severn

North Pt.
Thunder Bay
South Pt.
Blackriver
Harrisville
Greenbush
Oscoda
Au Sable
Au Sable Pt.

LAKE HURON
208
176

Shawanaga
McKellar
Nobel
Waubamik
Emsdale
Novar
Parry Sound
Huntsville
Dwight
Rosseau
L. Joseph
L. MacTier
Utterson
L. of Bays
Dorset
Bracebridge
Gravenhurst
Minden
Gooderham
Coe Hill

C A N A D A
O N T A R I O
Algonquin Park
Whitney
Bark L.
Madawaska
L. Clear
Combermere
Maberly
Griffith
Denbigh
Westmkoon L.
Bancroft
Wilberforce
Haliburton

Killaloe Sta.
Golden L.
Barry's Bay
Eagle Lake
Kinmount
Fenelon Falls
Bobcaygeon
Buckhorn L.
Lakefield
Havelock
Stony L.
Pigeon L.
Norwood

Apsley
Millbridge
Cloyne
Bannockburn
Arden
Kaladar
Eldorado
Madoc
Marmora
Tweed
Tamworth
Marlbank
Newburgh
Napanee

Port Austin
Pte Aux Barques
Kinde
Port Hope
Parkhead
Shallow Lake
Owen Sound
Tara
Chatsworth
Collingwood
Wasaga Beach
Stayner
Creemore
Camp Borden
Alliston
Beeton

Nottawasaga Bay
Meaford
Thornbury
Clarksburg
Flesherton
Dundalk
Shelburne
Hornings Mills

L. Simcoe
Orillia
Atherley
Brechin
Beaverton
Sunderland
Cannington
Lindsay
Omemee
Bethany
Millbrook

Peterborough
Keene
Rice L.
Campbellford
Stirling
Frankford
Trent
Belleville

44
43
42
41

MICHIGAN
Deckerville
Sandusky
Carsonville
Port Sanilac
Black
Cass
Brown City
Croswell
Lexington
Kettle Pt.
Thedford
Forest
Ausable

Kincardine
Pt. Clark
Ripley
Lucknow
Dungannon
Wingham
Teeswater
Mildmay
Walkerton
Hanover
Durham
Chesley
Paisley
Sullivan

Mount Forest
Harriston
Palmerston
Arthur
Fergus
Elora
Grand
Alton
Orangeville
Bolton
Richmond Hill
Woodbridge
Malton
Brampton
Georgetown
Acton
Rockwood

Newmarket
Aurora
Stouffville
Markham
Brooklin
Whitby
Ajax
Pickering

TORONTO
Mississauga
Port Credit
Oshawa
Bowmanville
Cobourg
Port Hope
Brighton
Colborne
Wicked Pt.
Wellington
Conseon

Wright Pt.
Goderich
Blyth
Brussels
Listowel
Atwood
Monkton
Milverton
Linwood
Elmira
Waterloo
Kitchener
Guelph
Preston
Cambridge
Galt

LAKE ONTARIO
75
236

Sebringville
Stratford
St. Marys
Exeter
Crediton
Parkhill
Lucan
Woodstock
Ingersoll
Tavistock
Nith
Ayr
Paris
Brantford
Burford

Oakville
Milton
Burlington
Hamilton
Dundas
Ancaster
Caledonia
Grimsby
Beamsville
Smithville
Dunnville

Niagara-on-the-Lake
St. Catharines
Thorold
Welland
Niagara Falls
Lewiston
Youngstown
Olcott
Wilson
Newfane
Lockport
Middleport
Medina
Barker
Lyndonville
Hamlin
Holley
Albion
Bergen
Batavia
Le Roy

Irondequoit
Greece
Gates
Rochester
Brighton
Webster
Williamson
Sodus
Palmyra
Scottsville
Caledonia
Victor
Canandaigua
Avon
Geneva
Phelps

NEW YORK

London
Dorchester
Belmont
Delhi
Tillsonburg
Simcoe
Waterford
Scotland
Hagersville
Jarvis
Cayuga
Dunnville
Port Colborne

BUFFALO
Lackawanna
West Seneca
Amherst
N. Tonawanda
Fort Erie
Blasdell
Hamburg
Eden
Holland
Lancaster
Depew
E. Aurora
Attica
Warsaw
Pavilion

Chatham
Blenheim
Ridgetown
Rondeau Prov. Pk.
Pte aux Pins
Erieau
Wheatley
Leamington
Kingsville
Essex
Windsor
DETROIT
Lake St. Clair

Long Point Bay
Port Burwell
Port Rowan
Long Pt.
64

Silver Creek
Angola
N. Collins
Springville
Arcade
Bliss
Castile
Nunda
Springwater
Wayland
Dansville
Keuka L.
Dundee
Middlesex
Naples

LAKE ERIE
174

Pelee I.
Middle Bass I.
S. Bass I.
Kelleys I.
Lakeside
Pt. Pelee Nat. Pk.

Erie
Wesleyville
Presque I.
Lake City
North East
Ripley
Westfield
Brocton
Fredonia
Dunkirk

Mayville
Sinclairville
Cassadaga
Gowanda
Machias
Franklinville
Delevan
Houghton
Arkport
Hornell
Belfast

Cuba
Belmont
Alfred
Canisteo
Andover
Whitesville
Genesee
Wellsville
Westfield
Addison

CLEVELAND
Lakewood
Euclid
N. Olmsted
Cleveland Hts.
Shaker Hts.
Brook Park
Parma
Bedford
Chagrin Falls
Eastlake
Willoughby
Willowick
Mentor
Wickliffe
Chardon

Sandusky
Vermilion
Lorain
Elyria
Oberlin
Amherst
Norwalk
Bellevue
Huron
Castalia

Conneaut
Ashtabula
N. Kingsville
Geneva
Madison
Fairport Harbor
Painesville
Jefferson
Andover
Dorset
Rock Creek

Jamestown
Falconer
Lakewood
Frewsburg
Randolph
Salamanca
Little Valley
Cattaraugus
Ellicottville
Franklinville

Olean
Allegany
Portville
Bolivar
Bradford
Eldred
Port Allegany
Coudersport
Shinglehouse
Gold
Galeton
Sabinsville
Mansfield
Tioga
Knoxville

OHIO
Mansfield
Ashland
Shelby
Crestline
Galion
Bucyrus
Wooster
Orrville
Massillon
Canton
Alliance
Sebring
Salem
Columbiana
E. Liverpool

PENNSYLVANIA
Meadville
Conneaut Lake
Titusville
Pleasantville
Oil City
Franklin
Polk
Stoneboro
Mercer
Grove City
Greenville
Sharpsville
Sharon
Farrell
Hermitage

Warren
Youngstown
Niles
Girard
Campbell
Struthers
Boardman
New Castle
Lowellville
Hubbard

Kane
Mt. Jewett
Smethport
Crosby
Wilcox
Johnsonburg
Ridgway
St. Marys
Emporium
Driftwood
Renovo
Austin

Titusville
Corry
Union City
Spartansburg
Cambridge Springs
Saegertown
Tidioute
Tionesta
Marienville

Clarion
Brookville
Brockway
Falls Creek
Du Bois
Reynoldsville
Sykesville
Sandy
Punxsutawney
Big Run
Sligo
Rimersburg

Williamsport
Jersey Shore
Avis
Lock Haven
Howard
Beech Creek
Mill Hall
Flemington
Montgomery
Muncy

Akron
Barberton
Cuyahoga Falls
Stow
Kent
Ravenna
Tallmadge
Medina
Wadsworth
Brunswick
Strongsville

Warren
Newton Falls
Champion
Southington
Farmdale
Orwell
Mesopotamia
Middlefield
Chardon
Burton
Aurora
Twinsburg
Macedonia
Streetsboro

Mosquito Creek L.
Pymatuning Res.
Andover
Greenville
Jamestown
Cochranton
Rouseville
Pleasantville

Emlenton
Parker
E. Brady
Karns City
Petrolia
Chicora
Kittanning
Ford City
Apollo
Vandergrift
Leechburg
Sagamore
Arcadia
Indiana
Homer City
Clymer
Creekside
Marion Center

Clearfield
Grampian
Curwensville
Mahaffey
Big Run
Woodland
Philipsburg
Osceola Mills
Houtzdale
Madera
Snow Shoe

Lewistown
Reedsville
McClure
Burnham
Milroy
Belleville
Mifflintown
Port Royal
Thompsontown

State College
Bellefonte
Boalsburg
Pine Grove Mills
Millheim
Spring Mills
Centre Hall
Pleasant Gap

Mansfield
Louisville
E. Palestine
Lisbon
Wellsville
Calcutta
East Liverpool
Chester
New Cumberland

Butler
Saxonburg
Evans City
Zelienople
Harmony
Mars
Cranberry
Freeport
Natrona
Tarentum
New Kensington
Springdale

Dayton
Smicksburg
Plumville
Cherry Tree
Spangler
Patton
Ashville
Carrolltown
Ebensburg
Cresson
Gallitzin

Altoona
Hollidaysburg
Duncansville
Williamsburg
Tyrone
Bellwood
Roaring Spring
Martinsburg
Claysburg

Huntingdon
Petersburg
Alexandria
Mount Union
Orbisonia
Three Springs
Saltillo

MICHIGAN
Imlay City
Almont
Memphis
Richmond
New Haven
Marine City
St. Clair
Sombra
Wallaceburg
Dresden
Thamesville

Port Huron
Sarnia
Marysville
Wyoming
Watford
Strathroy
Mt. Brydges
Glencoe
Bothwell
Ridgetown

Mt. Clemens
Utica
Roseville
E. Detroit
Fraser
Tecumseh
Windsor
Comber
Tilbury
Comber

OHIO
Newark
Zanesville
Coshocton
Cambridge
New Concord
Baltimore
Buckeye Lake
Granville
Johnstown
Centerburg
Mt. Vernon
Gambier
Fredericktown
Danville
Millersburg
Loudonville

New Philadelphia
Dover
Uhrichsville
Dennison
Newcomerstown
Carrollton
Minerva
Hanoverton
Lisbon

Steubenville
Weirton
Mingo Junction
Wellsburg
Brilliant
Toronto
Wintersville
Cadiz
Jewett
Scio
Freeport

PITTSBURGH
Wilkinsburg
Penn Hills
Monroeville
McKeesport
W. Mifflin
Clairton
Jeannette
Greensburg
Latrobe
Irwin
Murrysville
Export
New Kensington
Aliquippa
Ambridge
Baden
Beaver
Rochester
Midland

Weirton
Follansbee
Wellsburg
Bethany
Wheeling
Bellaire
Martins Ferry
Bridgeport
Shadyside
Moundsville
McMechen
Benwood

W. VA.
Washington
Canonsburg
McDonald
Carnegie
Bethel Park
Monongahela
Donora
Charleroi
California
Brownsville
Belle Vernon
Monessen
Uniontown
Connellsville
Mt. Pleasant
Scottdale
Ligonier
Somerset
Windber
Johnstown

Carlisle
Newville
Shippensburg
Chambersburg
Mechanicsburg
Dillsburg
York Springs

ft m
6000 2000
4500 1500
3000 1000
1200 400
600 200
0
200 600
m ft

Projection: Bonne

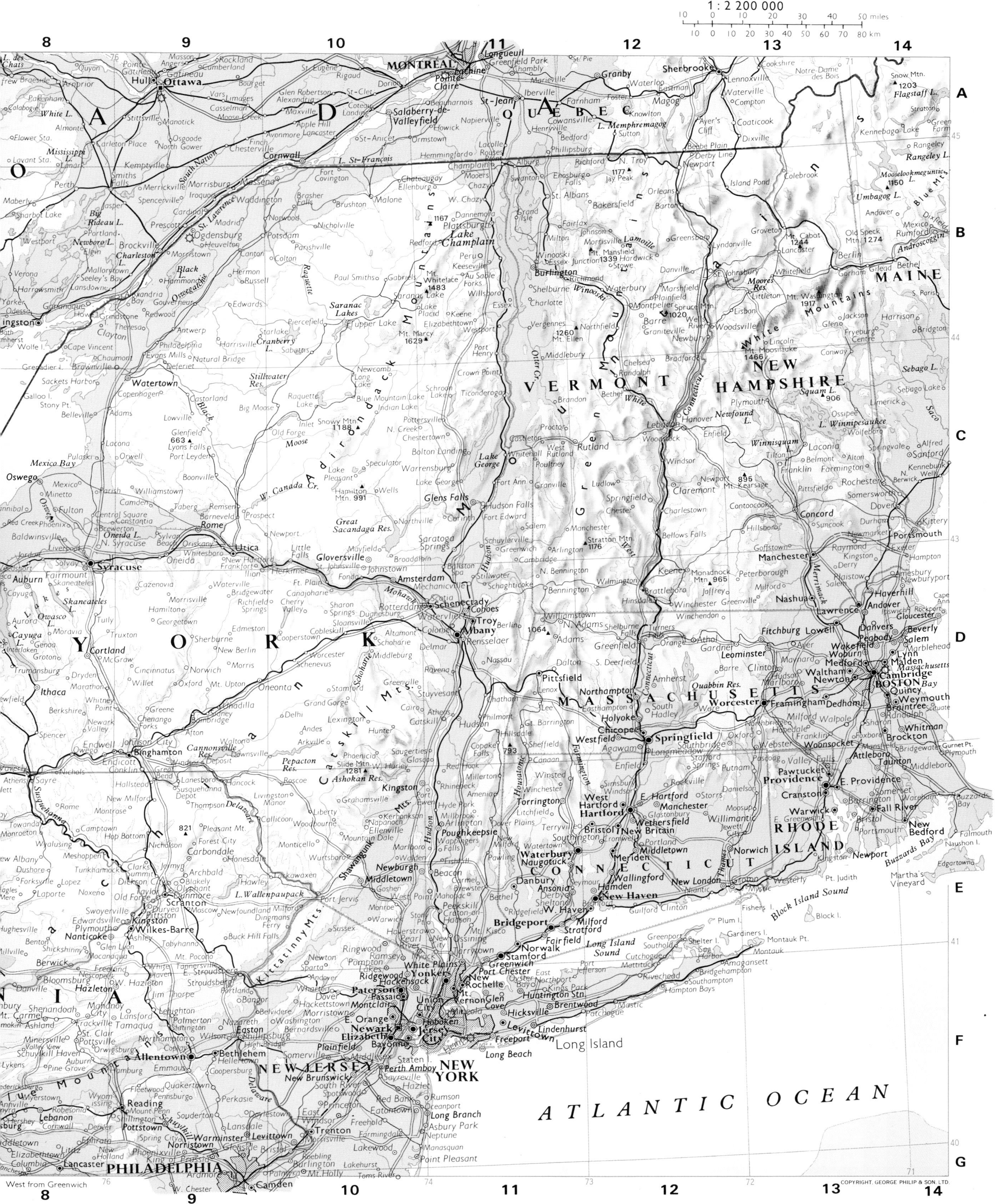
1 : 2 200 000
10 0 10 20 30 40 50 miles
10 0 10 20 30 40 50 60 70 80 km
8
9
10
11
12
13
14
A
B
C
D
E
F
G
MONTREAL
Ottawa
Hull
Sherbrooke
Granby
Cornwall
Kingston
Q U E B E C
C A N A D A
O
MAINE
NEW HAMPSHIRE
VERMONT
MASSACHUSETTS
CONNECTICUT
RHODE ISLAND
NEW JERSEY
NEW YORK
Y O R K
ATLANTIC OCEAN
Long Island
Long Island Sound
Block Island Sound
Martha's Vineyard
Adirondack Mountains
Green Mountains
White Mountains
Catskill Mts.
Kittatinny Mts.
L. Champlain
Lake George
Great Sacandaga Res.
L. Winnipesaukee
Quabbin Res.
Syracuse
Utica
Rome
Oswego
Watertown
Schenectady
Albany
Troy
Binghamton
Ithaca
Cortland
Scranton
Wilkes-Barre
Hazleton
Allentown
Bethlehem
Easton
Reading
PHILADELPHIA
Camden
Trenton
Newark
Paterson
Jersey City
Yonkers
New Rochelle
Stamford
Bridgeport
New Haven
Waterbury
Hartford
New Britain
Springfield
Holyoke
Pittsfield
Worcester
Fitchburg
Lowell
Lawrence
BOSTON
Cambridge
Quincy
Brockton
Providence
Pawtucket
Fall River
New Bedford
Newport
Concord
Manchester
Nashua
Portsmouth
Burlington
Montpelier
Rutland
Poughkeepsie
Kingston
Newburgh
Long Branch
Asbury Park
Levittown
Freeport
Long Beach
Mt. Marcy 1629
Mt. Washington 1917
West from Greenwich
COPYRIGHT, GEORGE PHILIP & SON, LTD.

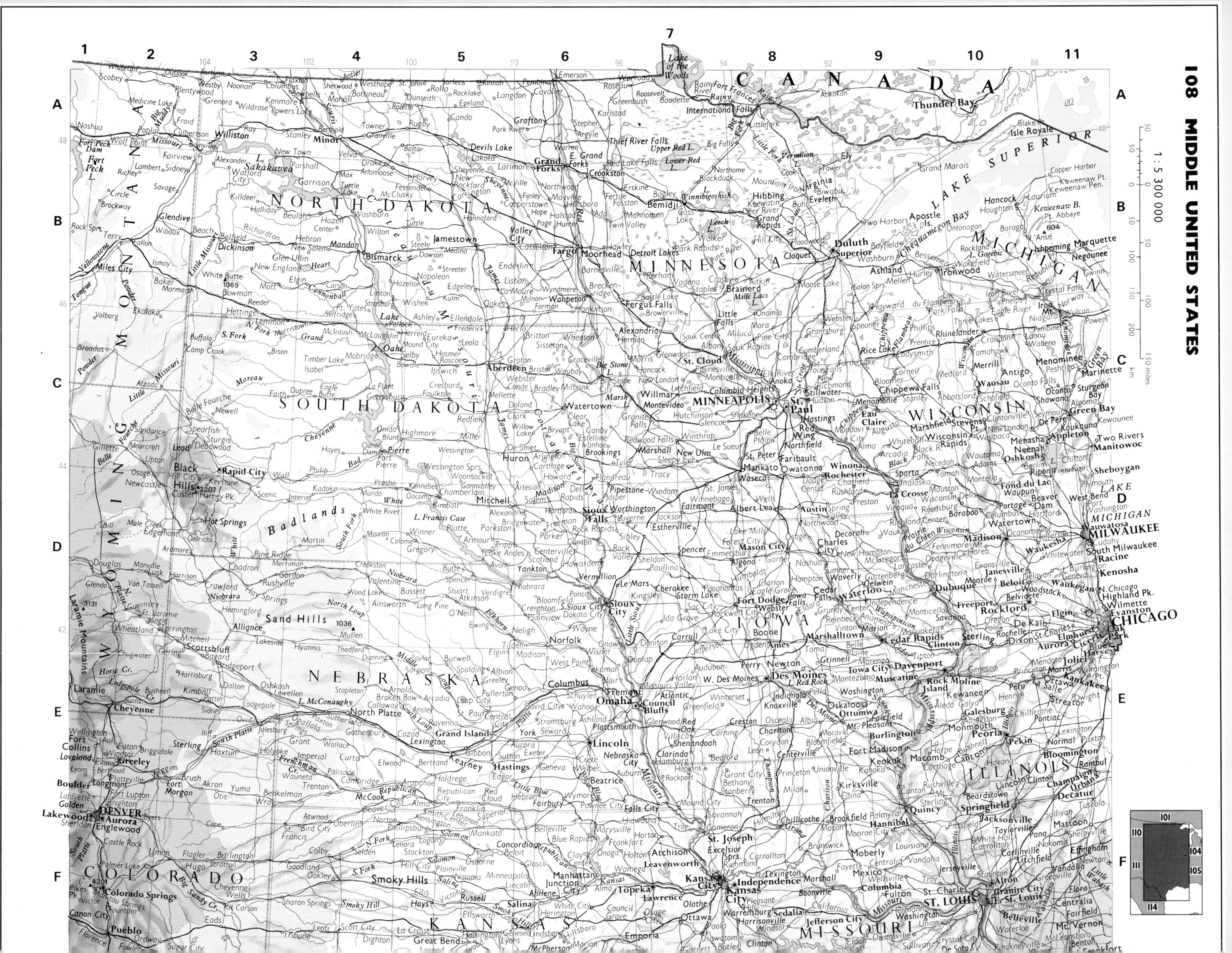
1 : 5 300 000
50 0 50 100 150 miles
50 0 50 100 150 200 km
CANADA
LAKE SUPERIOR
LAKE MICHIGAN
MONTANA
NORTH DAKOTA
SOUTH DAKOTA
MINNESOTA
WISCONSIN
MICHIGAN
IOWA
ILLINOIS
NEBRASKA
WYOMING
COLORADO
KANSAS
MISSOURI
MINNEAPOLIS
St. Paul
MILWAUKEE
CHICAGO
ST. LOUIS
DENVER
Kansas City
Omaha
Des Moines
Duluth
Madison
Lincoln
Sioux Falls
Fargo
Bismarck
Pierre
Cheyenne
Rapid City
Thunder Bay
Lake of the Woods
Black Hills
Badlands
Sand Hills
Smoky Hills
Laramie Mountains
Mississippi
Missouri

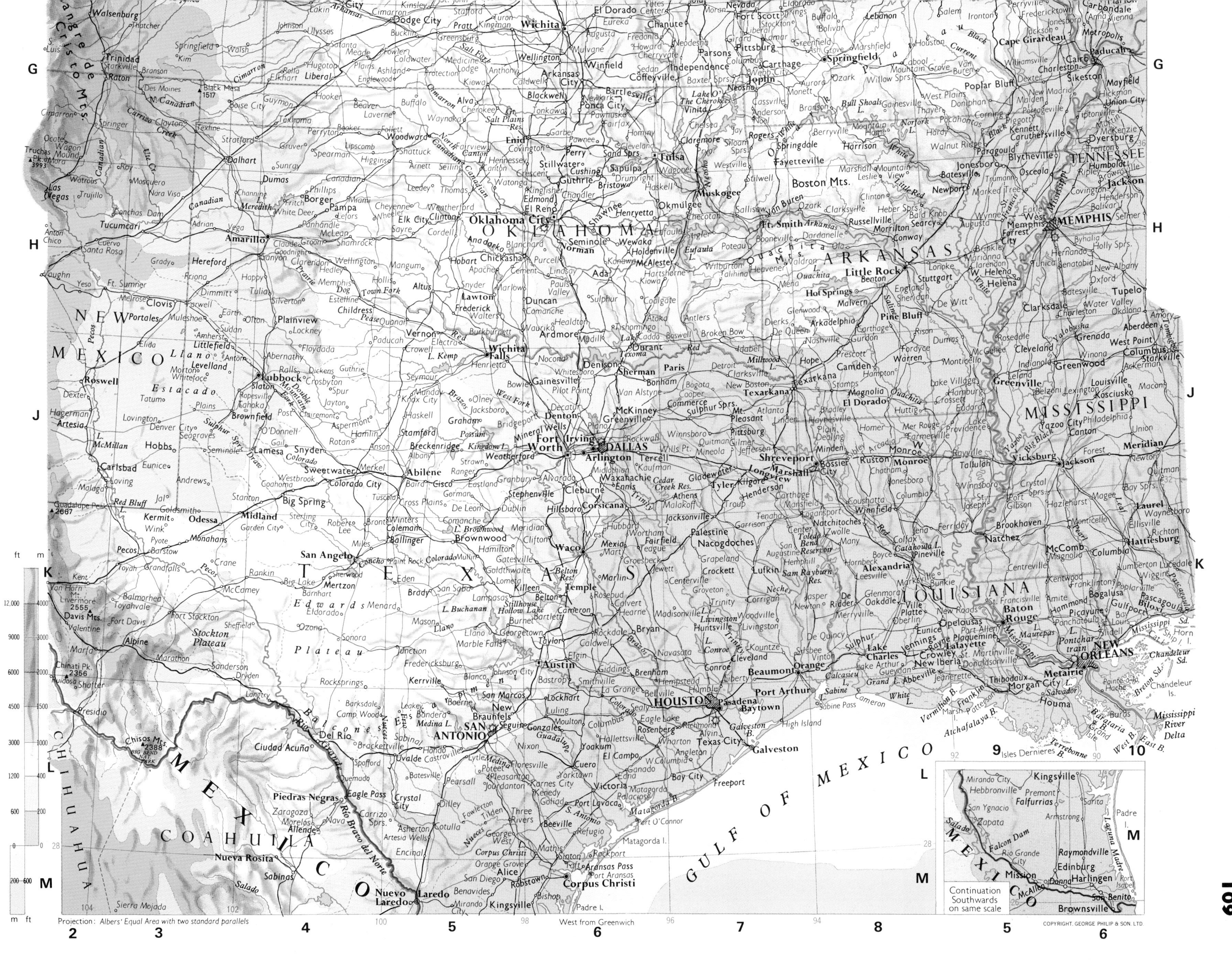

Projection: Albers' Equal Area with two standard parallels

COPYRIGHT GEORGE PHILIP & SON LTD

SASKATCHEWAN

ALBERTA

CANADA

BRITISH COLUMBIA

WASHINGTON

OREGON

IDAHO

MONTANA

WYOMING

NEVADA

UTAH

CALIFORNIA

VANCOUVER

SEATTLE

PORTLAND

Spokane

Salt Lake City

GREAT SALT LAKE

Ogden

Provo

Reno

Sacramento

Billings

Helena

Butte

Boise

Bighorn Mountains

Medicine Bow Mts.

Park Range

Front Range

Lewis Range

Bitterroot Range

Lemhi Range

Salmon River Mountains

Sawtooth Range

Wind River Range

Absaroka Range

Crazy Mts.

Little Belt Mts.

Big Belt Mts.

Clearwater Mountains

Cabinet Mts.

Blue Mountains

Wallowa Mts.

Olympic Mts.

North Cascades Nat. Park

Mt. Rainier

Mt. Baker

Mt. Adams

Mt. Hood

Mt. Jefferson

Three Sisters

Mt. Shasta

Mt. Lassen

Crater Lake Nat. Park

Klamath Mts.

Coast Ranges

Great Sandy Desert

Harney Basin

Alvord Desert

Santa Rosa Range

Independence Mts.

Ruby Mts.

Shoshone Mountains

Toiyabe Mountains

Stillwater Ra.

Diamond Mts.

Uinta Mountains

Flaming Gorge Res.

Missouri

Columbia

Snake

Yellowstone

Yellowstone Nat. Park

Great Salt Lake Desert

Juan de Fuca Strait

Milk River

Fort Peck Lake

Pend Oreille

Flathead L.

Bearpaw Mts.

1 : 5 300 000

50　　　0　　　　　50　　　　　　　　100　miles
50　　0　　50　　　100　　　150　km

COPYRIGHT GEORGE PHILIP & SON LTD

West from Greenwich

Projection: Albers' Equal Area with two standard parallels

COLORADO

NEW MEXICO

TEXAS

CHIHUAHUA

ARIZONA

SONORA

CALIFORNIA

BAJA CALIFORNIA

MEXICO

PACIFIC OCEAN

Golfo de California

LOS ANGELES

SAN DIEGO

PHOENIX

Tucson

El Paso

Ciudad Juárez

Albuquerque

Santa Fe

Las Vegas

Chihuahua Aquiles Serdán

Hermosillo

Mexicali

Tijuana

San Luis Río Colorado

Grand Canyon

Painted Desert

Sonora Desert

Gran Desierto

Desierto de Altar

Mojave Desert

Death Valley

Lake Mead

ft m

12,000 4000
9000 3000
6000 2000
4500 1500
3000 1000
1200 400
600 200
0 0
200 600
2000 6000
4000 12,000
m ft

SEATTLE–PORTLAND REGION
On same scale

CANADA

Vancouver Island

Strait of Georgia

Juan de Fuca Strait

Victoria

PACIFIC OCEAN

Olympic Mountains
OLYMPIC NATIONAL PARK

WASHINGTON

SEATTLE
Tacoma
Lakewood
Bremerton
Olympia

OREGON
PORTLAND
Vancouver
Longview
Columbia

White Mts.

Inyo Mts.
Owens

Sierra Nevada
YOSEMITE NATIONAL PARK
SEQUOIA NAT. PARK
KINGS CANYON NATIONAL PARK

Reno
Sparks
Carson City

Mono L.

CALIFORNIA

Sacramento
Stockton
Modesto
Merced
Fresno
Clovis

San Joaquin

Chico
Oroville
Yuba City
Marysville
Auburn

Napa
Santa Rosa

Vallejo
Fairfield
Vacaville
Concord
Walnut Creek
Antioch
Pittsburg
Livermore

SAN FRANCISCO
Daly City
Oakland
Berkeley
Richmond
San Rafael
San Mateo
Redwood City
Palo Alto
Mountain View
Sunnyvale
Santa Clara
SAN JOSE
Fremont
Hayward

Santa Cruz
Monterey Bay
Monterey
Seaside

Salinas

Santa Lucia Range

Diablo Range

Coast Ranges

PACIFIC OCEAN

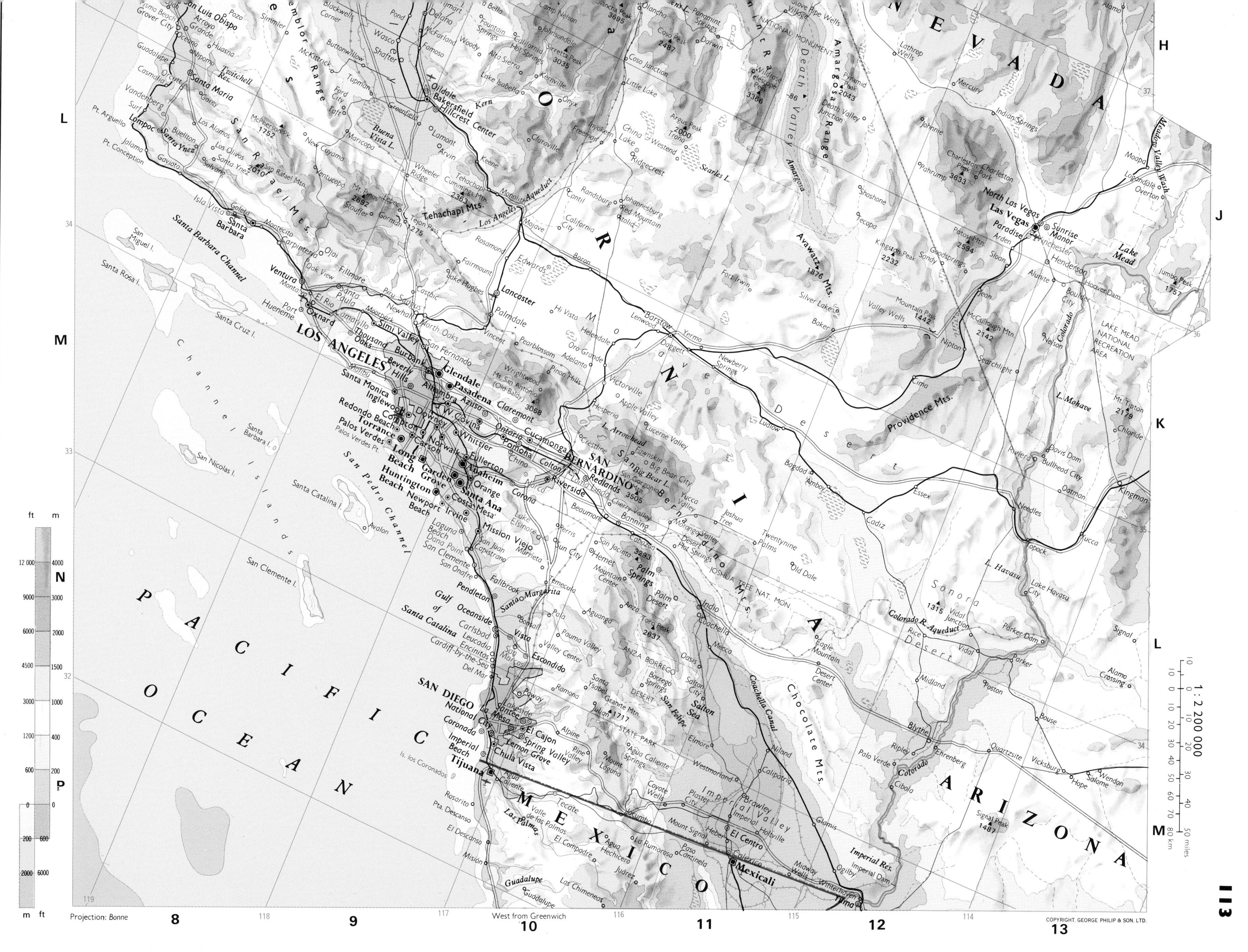

1 : 2 200 000

Projection: Bonne

COPYRIGHT. GEORGE PHILIP & SON, LTD.

West from Greenwich

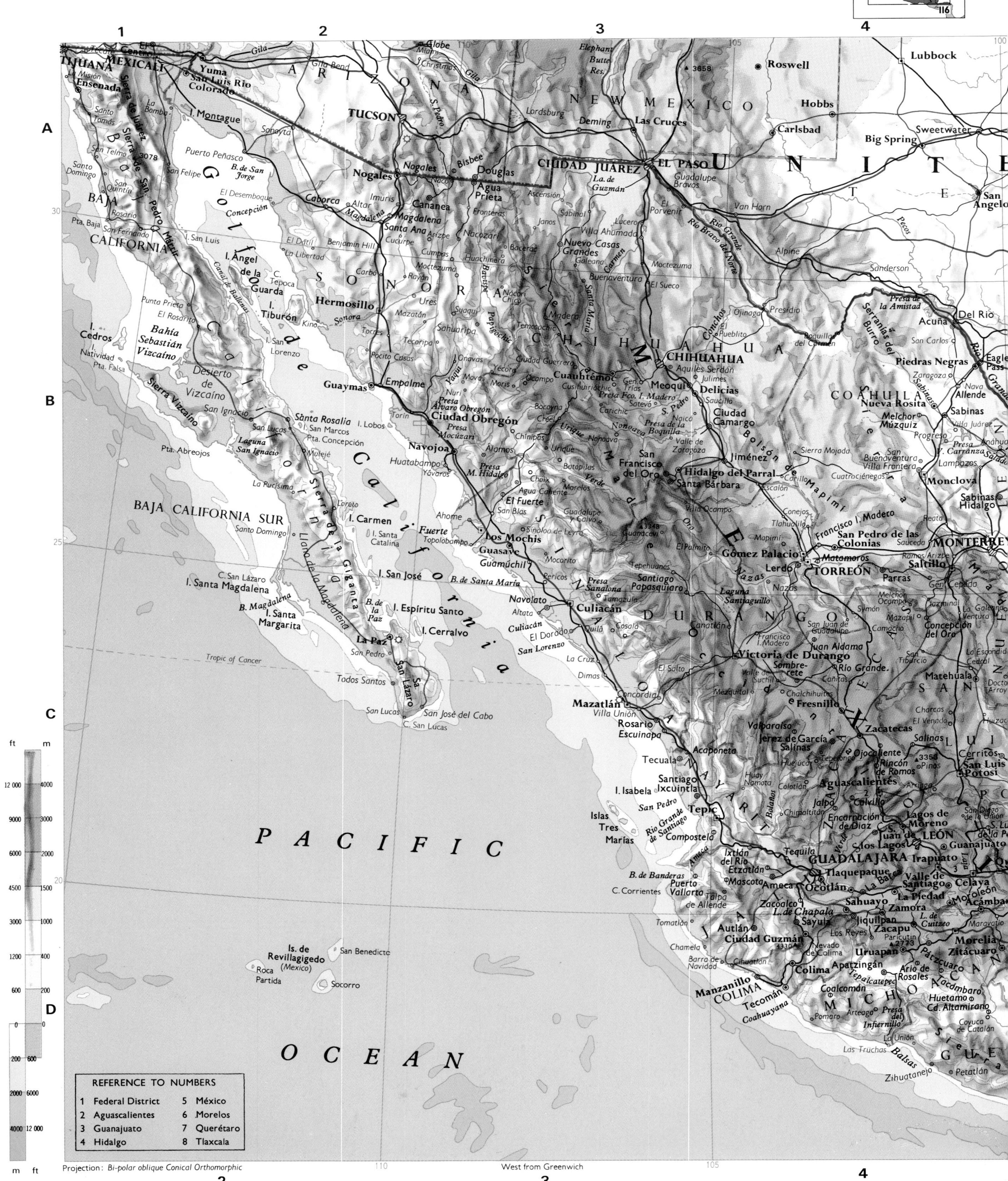

1   **2**   **3**   **4**

Lubbock

Roswell

Hobbs

Sweetwater

Carlsbad   Big Spring

San Angelo

A

TIJUANA   MEXICALI   Yuma   San Luis Río Colorado

TUCSON

ARIZONA   NEW MEXICO   UNITED

Ensenada

Nogales   Douglas   CIUDAD JUÁREZ   EL PASO

Agua Prieta

Deming   Las Cruces

BAJA CALIFORNIA

SONORA

Hermosillo

Cananea   Santa Ana   Magdalena

Del Río

Acuña

Piedras Negras   Eagle Pass

B

Guaymas

Ciudad Obregón

Navojoa

CHIHUAHUA

Cuauhtémoc   CHIHUAHUA   Delicias   Ciudad Camargo

Hidalgo del Parral   Santa Bárbara

Jiménez

San Francisco del Oro

COAHUILA

Nueva Rosita   Sabinas

Melchor Múzquiz

Monclova

Sabinas Hidalgo

Los Mochis   Guasave   Guamúchil

Gómez Palacio   Lerdo   Matamoros

San Pedro de las Colonias

MONTERREY   Saltillo

C

La Paz

BAJA CALIFORNIA SUR

Culiacán   Navolato

DURANGO

TORREÓN   Parras

Victoria de Durango

Fresnillo

Zacatecas

SAN LUIS POTOSÍ

Matehuala

Tropic of Cancer

San Lucas   San José del Cabo

Mazatlán   Rosario

Aguascalientes   Lagos de Moreno

San Luis Potosí   Cerritos

D

Tepic   GUADALAJARA   Irapuato   Guanajuato

León   Celaya

Manzanillo   COLIMA   Colima   Uruapan   Morelia   Zitácuaro

Puerto Vallarta   L. de Chapala   Zamora   Zacapu

Ciudad Guzmán

MICHOACÁN

PACIFIC OCEAN

Is. de Revillagigedo (Mexico)   San Benedicto   Roca Partida   Socorro

Zihuatanejo   Petatlán

REFERENCE TO NUMBERS

1	Federal District	5	México
2	Aguascalientes	6	Morelos
3	Guanajuato	7	Querétaro
4	Hidalgo	8	Tlaxcala

ft   m
12 000   4000
9000   3000
6000   2000
4500   1500
3000   1000
1200   400
600   200
0   0
200   600
2000   6000
4000   12 000
m   ft

Projection: Bi-polar oblique Conical Orthomorphic

West from Greenwich

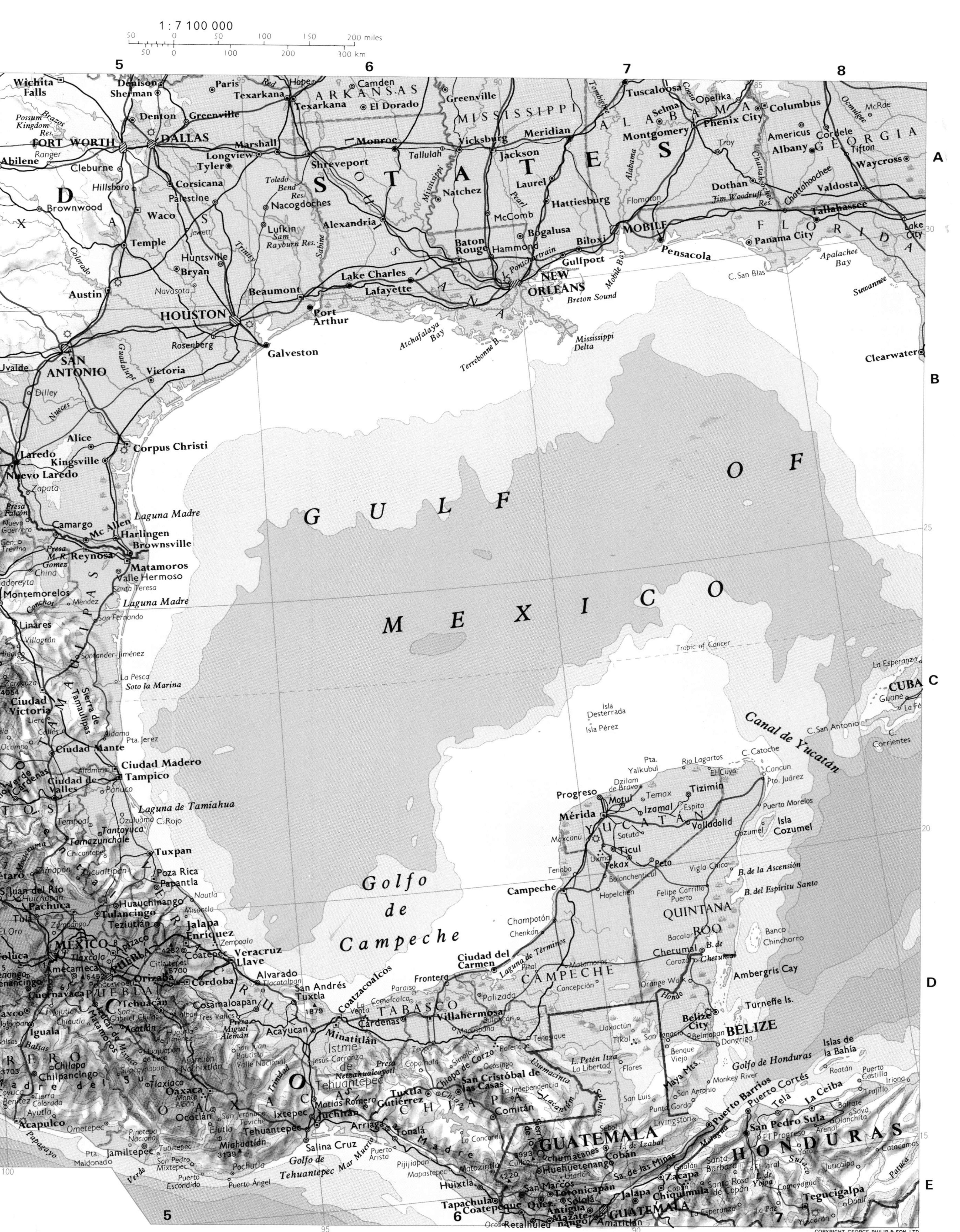

1 : 7 100 000

50   0   50   100   150   200 miles
50   0   100   200   300 km

GULF OF MEXICO

Golfo de Campeche

Tropic of Cancer

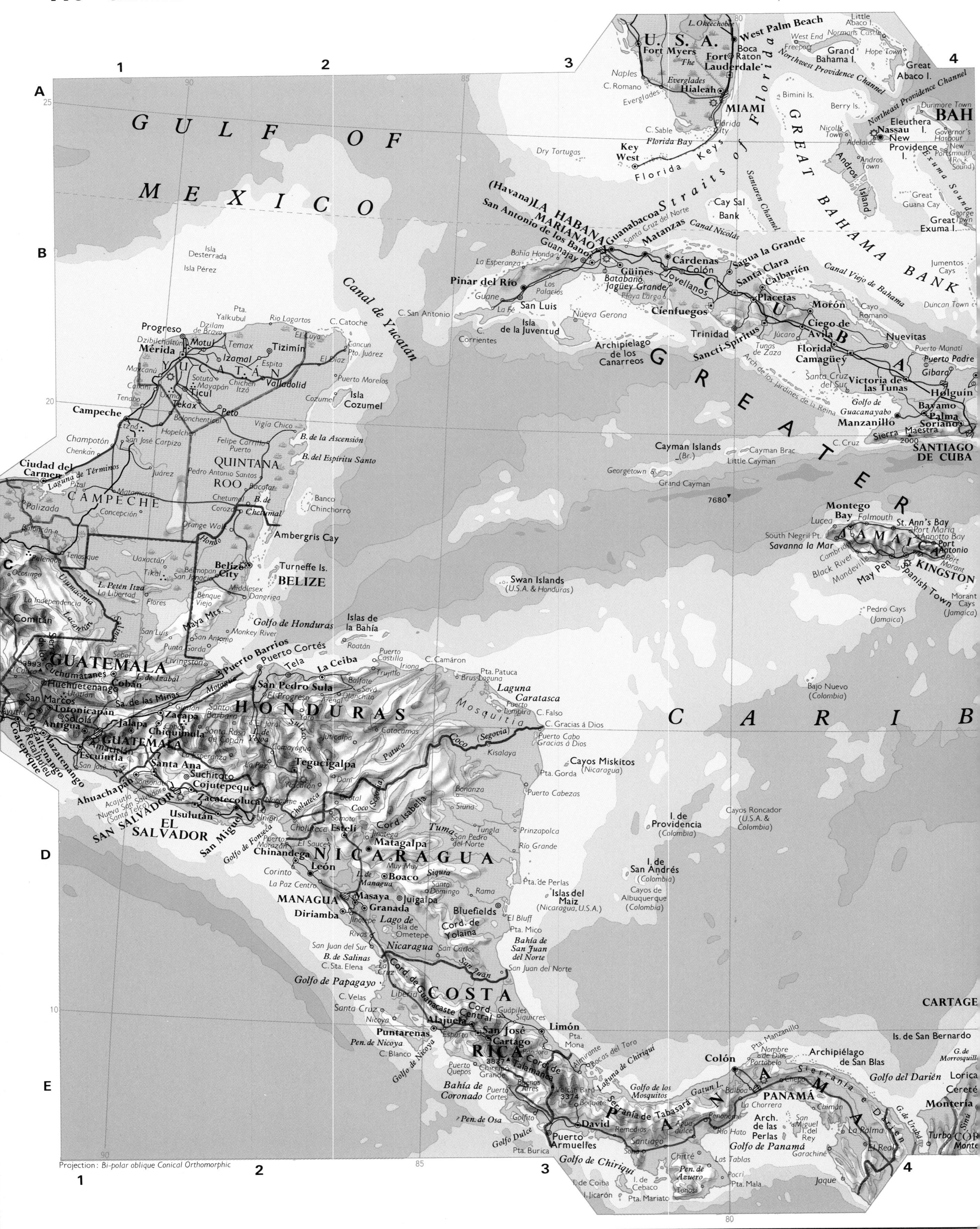

1 : 7 100 000

50   100   150   200 miles
50   100   200   300 km

5   **6**   **7**   **8**

BAMAS

A T L A N T I C

O C E A N

Tropic of Cancer

Arthur's Town
The Bight
Cat I.
San Salvador
(Watling I., Guanahani)
Conception I.
Rum Cay
Long I.
Clarence Town
Cay Verde
Crooked I. Passage
Atwood or
Samana Cay
Albert Town
Richmond
Crooked I.
Plana Cays
Snug Corner
Mira por vos Cay
Acklins I.
Mayaguana I.
Hogsty Reef
Little Inagua I.
Cay Santa Domingo
Lake Rose
Great Inagua I.
Matthew Town
Caicos Passage
Turks I. Passage
Caicos Islands (Br.)
Turks Islands (Br.)

Banes
Mayari
ntilla
Moa
Baracoa
Guantánamo
Pta. de Maisí
Paso de los Vientos
(Windward Passage)
Jean-Rabel
Cap-à-Foux
Cap-Haïtien
Port-de-Paix
Fort-Liberté
Î. de la Tortue
La Isabela
Monte Cristi
Puerto Plata
C. Frances Viejo
San Francisco de Macoris
Puerto Rico Trench
Milwaukee Deep 9200

HAITI
DOMINICAN REP.
Santiago de los Cabelleros
Cord. Central
3175
La Vega
Nagua
Sánchez
Sabana de La Mar
Bayamón
SAN JUAN
Carolina
Virgin Gorda
Anegada
Virgin Is. (Br.)
Sombrero (Anguilla)

Golfe de la Gonâve
St.-Marc
Gonaïves
Hinche
San Juan
Hato Mayor
C. Engaño
Arecibo
Aguadilla
Fajardo
St. Thomas
Tortola
Road Town
Anguilla (Br.)
St.-Martin (Guad.)
St.-Barthélemy (Fr.)

Jérémie
Dame-Marie
PORT-AU-PRINCE
San Juan
Azua de Compostela
Bani
Higuay
La Romana
B. de Yuma
I. Saona
Ponce
Carolina
Virgin Is. (U.S.A.)
Charlotte Amalie
Frederiksted
St. Croix
Christiansted
St. Maarten (Neth.)
Saba (Neth.)
St. Eustatius (Neth.)
Basseterre
Nevis
CHRISTOPHER- NEVIS
ANTIGUA & BARBUDA
St. Johns
Antigua
Barbuda

Navassa I. (U.S.A.)
Massif de la Hotte
C. C. Casse
Aquin
Les Cayes
Pointe-à-Gravois
Î.-à-Vache
2280
Enriquillo
Jacmel
L. Enriquillo
Barahona
Pedernales
I. Beata
C. Beata
SANTO DOMINGO
San Cristóbal
Isla Mona (U.S.A.)
Canal de la Mona
Mayagüez
PUERTO RICO (U.S.A.)
Guayama
Redonda
Montserrat

HISPANIOLA
ANTILLES

BEAN   SEA
Guadeloupe Passage
Ste-Rose
Moule
Désirade
GUADELOUPE
Basse-Terre
Pointe-à-Pitre
Marie-Galante (Fr.)
Grand-Bourg
I. des Saintes (Guad.)
Dominica Passage
Portsmouth
Roseau
DOMINICA

I. de Aves (Bird I.) (Venezuela)

Martinique Passage
Mt. Pelée 1397
Ste-Marie
François
Riviére-Pilote
Fort-de-France
MARTINIQUE
St. Lucia Channel (Fr.)
Castries
ST. LUCIA
Soufrière

LEEWARD ISLANDS
LESSER ANTILLES
WINDWARD ISLANDS

St. Vincent Passage
Soufrière 1234
ST. VINCENT
Kingstown
Speightstown
Bridgetown
THE BARBADOS
GRENADINES
Hillsborough
GRENADA
St. George's

LESSER ANTILLES

Pta. Gallinas
Aruba (Neth)
Curaçao
Bonaire
NETH. ANTILLES
Willemstad
Is. de Aves (Ven.)
I. Orchila (Ven.)
I. Blanquilla (Ven.)
I. Los Hermanos (Ven.)
Tobago
Scarborough

Pen. de la Guajira
Pta. Espada
C. San Román
Pen. de Paraguaná
Punto Fijo
Puerto Cumarebo
Is. Los Roques (Ven.)
I. La Tortuga (Ven.)
I. Los Testigos (Ven.)
I. Margarita
La Asunción
Porlamar
Dragon's Mouth
Port of Spain
Galera Pt.

Ríohacha
C. San Juan de Guía
Uribia
GUAJIRA
San Rafael
Punta Cardón
Golfo de Venezuela
Coro
La Vela de Coro
NUEVA ESPARTA
Pen. de Paria
Güiria
Arima
Trinidad

BARRAN-QUILLA
Santa Marta
Cienaga
MARACAIBO
La Concepción
Santa Rita
Cabimas
FALCÓN
Mene de Mauroa
Baragud
Tocuyo
Maracay
Maiquetía
La Guaira
CARACAS
DISTRITO FEDERAL
Higuerote
Puerto La Cruz
Cumaná
Carúpano
Río Caribe
Golfo de Paria
San Fernando
TRINIDAD & TOBAGO

Baranoa
Soledad
Sabanalarga
Fundación
Calamar
Plato
Zambrano
Agustín Codazzi
Valledupar
Villa del Rosario
Machiques
Ciudad Ojeda
Mene Grande
Lago de Maracaibo
La Ceiba
Puerto Cabello
San Felipe
Carora
Valencia
Villa de Cura
S. Juan de los Morros
Los Teques
MIRANDA
Ocumare del Tuy
Río Chico
Barcelona
Caicara
Maturín
MONAGAS
DELTA
AMACUR

ZULIA
CÉSAR
NORTE
Ocaña
El Banco
Magangué
Mompos
Majagual
Sincé
Sahagún
Ayapel
BOLIVAR
Caucasia
Simiti
SANTANDER
Cúcuta
TÁCHIRA
San Cristóbal
MÉRIDA
Mérida
Barinas
BARINAS
Ciudad Bolivia
San Fernando de Apure
Achaguas
Calabozo
GUÁRICO
Santa María de Ipire
El Tigre
ANZOÁTEGUI
Soledad
El Poo
Ciudad Guayana
Upata
Sierra Imataca

BARQUISIMETO
LARA
Trujillo
TRUJILLO
Valera
Betijoque
Acarigua
PORTUGUESA
Guanare
El Baúl
San Carlos
COJEDES
El Sombrero
Valle de la Pascua
El Poo
Pariaguán
Anaco
Cantaura
Unare
Manapire
Mapire
Emb. de Guri
Caicara
Guasdualito
Tumeremo
El Callao

VENEZUELA

West from Greenwich
5   **6**   **7**

ft | m
12,000 | 4000
9000 | 3000
6000 | 2000
4500
1200 | 400
600 | 200
0
200 | 600
2000 | 6000
4000 | 12,000
6000 | 18,000
8000 | 24,000
m | ft

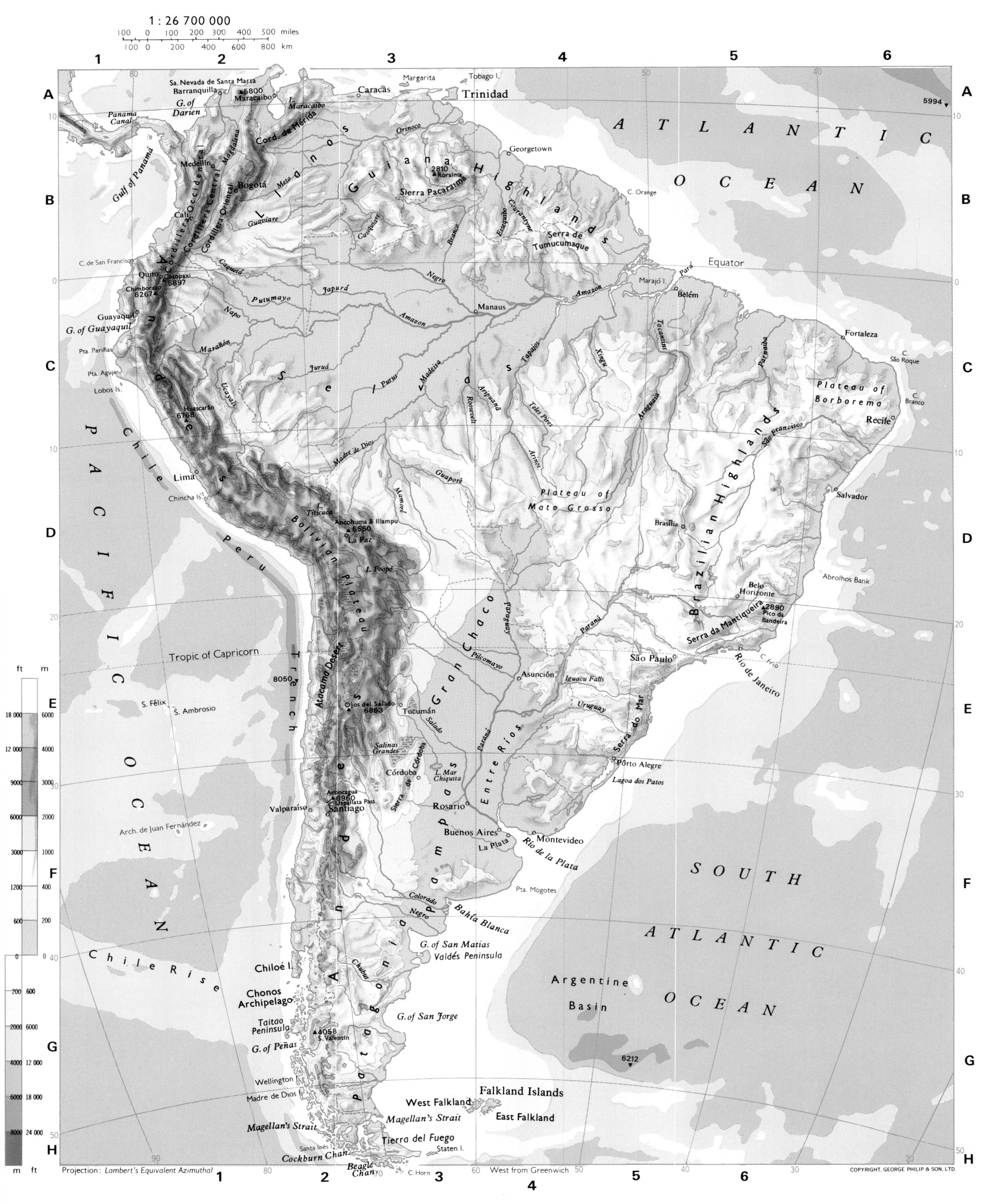

1 : 26 700 000

100 0 100 200 300 400 500 miles
100 0 200 400 600 800 km

1 **2** **3** **4** **5** **6**

Sa. Nevada de Santa Marta
Barranquilla
▲5800
Maracaibo
L. Maracaibo
Caracas
Margarita
Tobago I.
Trinidad
5994▼

A

Panama Canal
G. of Darien
Cord. de Mérida
Orinoco
Georgetown
C. Orange

B

Medellín
Bogotá
Guaviare
Cali
Cordillera Occidental
Cordillera Central
Cordillera Oriental
Magdalena
Llanos
Guiana Highlands
Sierra Pacaraima
2810 ▲ Roraima
Serra de Tumucumaque

Equator

C. de San Francisco
Quito
Cotopaxi 5897
Chimborazo 6267 ▲
Guayaquil
G. of Guayaquil
Napo
Marañón
Putumayo
Japurá
Caquetá
Negro
Amazon
Manaus
Marajó I.
Pará
Belém

C

Pta. Pariñas
Pta. Aguja
Lobos Is.
Huascarán 6768
Ucayali
Juruá
Amazon
Purús
Madeira
Roosevelt
Aripuanã
Tapajós
Xingu
Telles Pires
Tocantins
Araguaia
Parnaíba
Fortaleza
C. São Roque
C. Branco
Plateau of Borborema
Recife

PACIFIC

Chile

Peru

Trench

D

Lima
Chincha Is.
Titicaca
Ancohuma & Illampu ▲6550
La Paz
Bolivian Plateau
L. Poopó
Madre de Dios
Guaporé
Mamoré
Guaporé
Plateau of Mato Grosso
Brasília
Brazilian Highlands
São Francisco
Belo Horizonte
Abrolhos Bank
Salvador

Tropic of Capricorn

S. Félix
S. Ambrosio
8050
Atacama Desert
Ojos del Salado 6863
Tucumán
Gran Chaco
Pilcomayo
Asunción
Iguaçu Falls
São Paulo
2890 ▲ Pico da Bandeira
Serra da Mantiqueira
Rio de Janeiro
C. Frio

E

OCEAN

Arch. de Juan Fernández
Salinas Grandes
Córdoba
Sierra de Córdoba
L. Mar Chiquita
Aconcagua ▲6960
Uspallata Pass
Santiago
Valparaíso
Rosario
Paraná
Entre Ríos
Uruguay
Serra do Mar
Pôrto Alegre
Lagoa dos Patos

F

Buenos Aires
La Plata
Montevideo
Rio de la Plata
Pta. Mogotes
Colorado
Negro
Bahía Blanca
Pampas

SOUTH

ATLANTIC

G. of San Matias
Valdés Peninsula
Argentine Basin

Chile Rise

Chiloé I.
Chonos Archipelago
Taitao Peninsula
Chubut
Patagonia
G. of San Jorge
6212 ▼

OCEAN

G

G. of Peñas
▲4058 S. Valentín
Wellington
Madre de Dios

H

Magellan's Strait
Santa Inés
Cockburn Chan.
Beagle Chan.
C. Horn
Tierra del Fuego
Staten I.
West Falkland
Falkland Islands
East Falkland
Magellan's Strait

West from Greenwich

ft m
18 000 6000
12 000 4000
9000 3000
6000 2000
3000 1000
1200 400
600 200
0 0

m ft
200 600
2000 6000
4000 12 000
6000 18 000
8000 24 000

Projection: Lambert's Equivalent Azimuthal

COPYRIGHT. GEORGE PHILIP & SON. LTD.

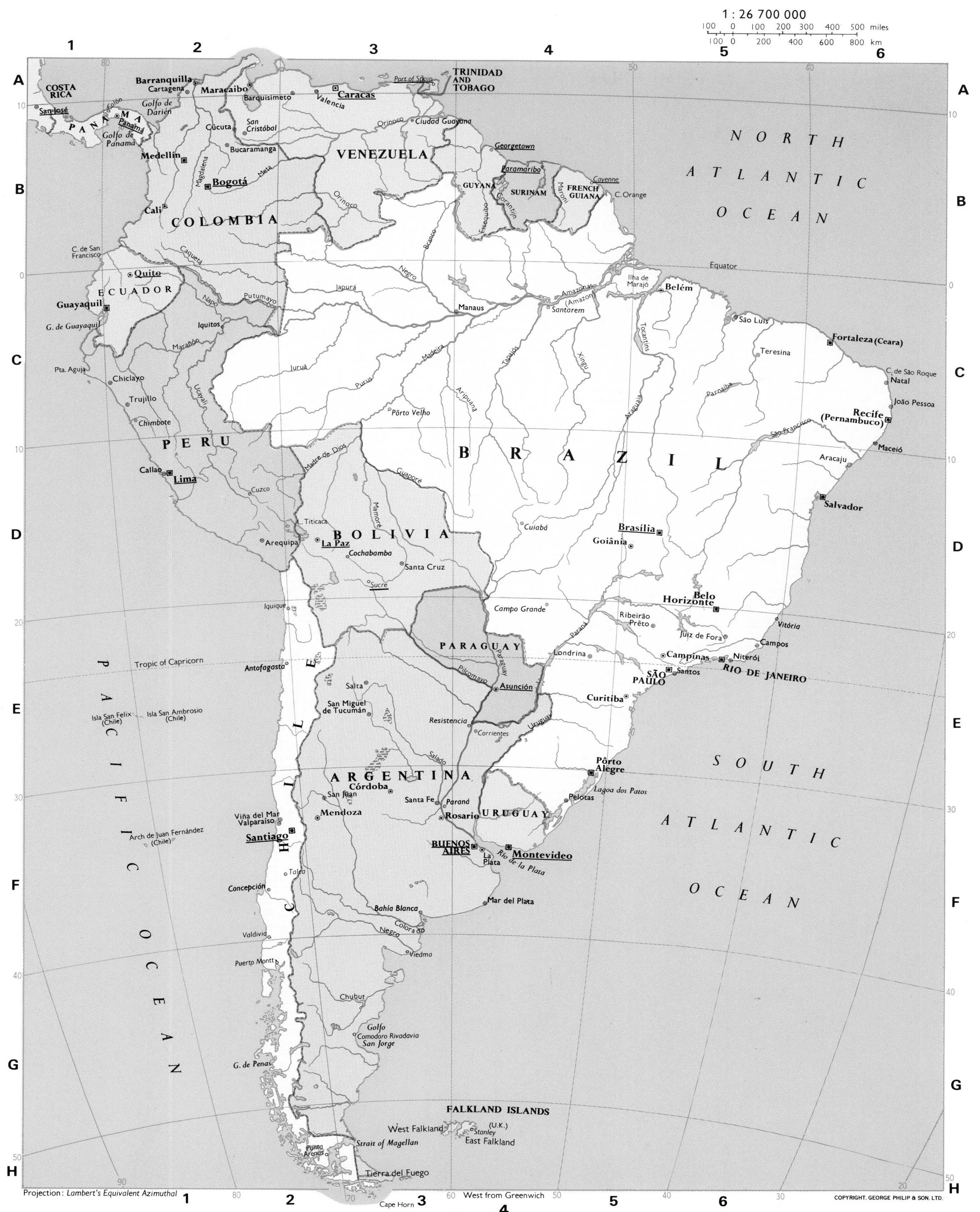

1 : 26 700 000

100 0 100 200 300 400 500 miles
100 0 200 400 600 800 km

Projection: Lambert's Equivalent Azimuthal

West from Greenwich

COSTA RICA
San José
PANAMA
Panamá
Golfo de Panamá
Golfo de Darién
Barranquilla
Cartagena
Maracaibo
Cúcuta
San Cristóbal
Barquisimeto
Valencia
Caracas
Port of Spain
TRINIDAD AND TOBAGO
Medellín
Bucaramanga
Magdalena
Bogotá
Cali
COLOMBIA
VENEZUELA
Orinoco
Ciudad Guayana
Georgetown
Paramaribo
GUYANA
SURINAM
FRENCH GUIANA
Cayenne
C. Orange
Meta
C. de San Francisco
Quito
ECUADOR
Guayaquil
G. de Guayaquil
Napo
Putumayo
Caquetá
Negro
Japurá
Amazon
(Amazon)
Manaus
Santarem
Ilha de Marajó
Belém
Equator
São Luís
Teresina
Fortaleza (Ceara)
C. de São Roque
Natal
NORTH ATLANTIC OCEAN
Pta. Aguja
Chiclayo
Trujillo
Chimbote
PERU
Iquitos
Marañón
Juruá
Ucayali
Purus
Madre de Dios
Pôrto Velho
Madeira
Aripuanã
Tapajós
Xingu
Tocantins
Araguaia
BRAZIL
Parnaiba
João Pessoa
Recife (Pernambuco)
Maceió
Callao
Lima
Cuzco
L. Titicaca
Arequipa
La Paz
Cochabamba
BOLIVIA
Sucre
Santa Cruz
Mamoré
Guaporé
São Francisco
Aracaju
Salvador
Cuiabá
Brasília
Goiânia
Belo Horizonte
Vitória
Iquique
Campo Grande
Paraná
PARAGUAY
Ribeirão Prêto
Juiz de Fora
Campos
Tropic of Capricorn
Antofagasta
Pilcomayo
Paraguay
Asunción
Londrina
Campinas
Niterói
SÃO PAULO
RIO DE JANEIRO
Santos
Isla San Félix (Chile)
Isla San Ambrosio (Chile)
Salta
San Miguel de Tucumán
Resistencia
Corrientes
Uruguay
Curitiba
Pôrto Alegre
SOUTH ATLANTIC OCEAN
CHILE
Salado
ARGENTINA
Córdoba
San Juan
Santa Fe
Paraná
Rosario
URUGUAY
Pelotas
Lagoa dos Patos
PACIFIC OCEAN
Arch de Juan Fernández (Chile)
Viña del Mar
Valparaíso
Santiago
Mendoza
BUENOS AIRES
La Plata
Montevideo
Río de la Plata
Concepción
Mar del Plata
Valdivia
Bahía Blanca
Colorado
Negro
Viedma
Puerto Montt
Chubut
Golfo Comodoro Rivadavia San Jorge
G. de Penas
FALKLAND ISLANDS
West Falkland
(U.K.)
Stanley
East Falkland
Punta Arenas
Strait of Magellan
Tierra del Fuego
Cape Horn

CARIBBEAN SEA

NETH. ANTILLES

PACIFIC OCEAN

PANAMA

COLOMBIA

ECUADOR

PERU

VENEZUELA

Projection: Lambert's Equivalent Azimuthal

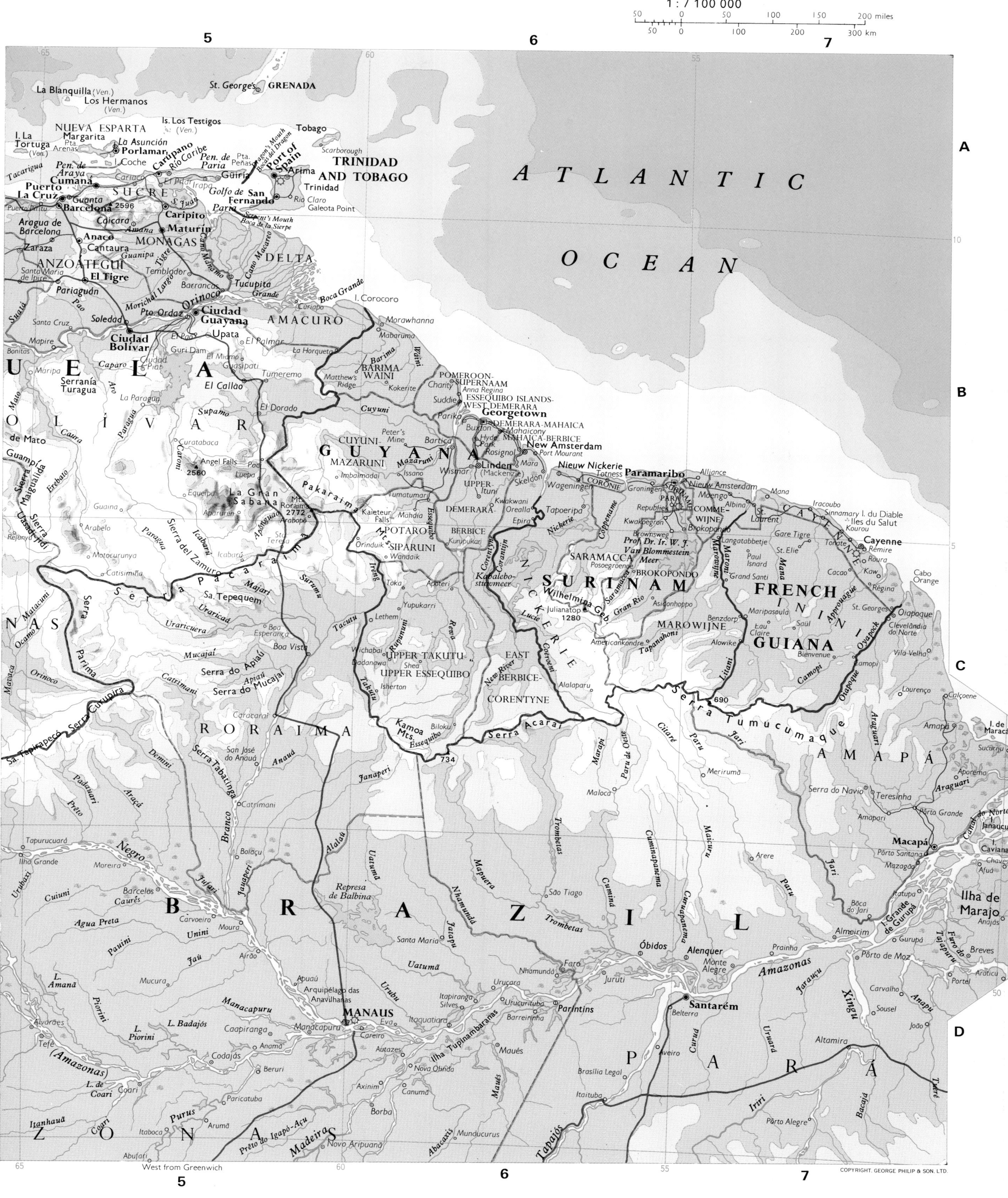

1 : 7 100 000

50   0   50   100   150   200 miles
50   0   100   200   300 km

5 **6** **7**

La Blanquilla (Ven.)
Los Hermanos (Ven.)
St. George's GRENADA
Is. Los Testigos (Ven.)
Tobago
Scarborough

NUEVA ESPARTA
Margarita
La Asunción
I. La Tortuga (Ven.)
Pta. Arenas
Porlamar
Coche
Pen. de Araya
Cumaná
Carúpano
Rio Caribe
Pen. de Paria
Pta. Peñas
Boca del Dragón
Port of Spain
Arima
TRINIDAD AND TOBAGO
Trinidad
Rio Claro
Galeota Point

A

SUCRE
2596
Güiria
Golfo de San Fernando
Paria
Serpent's Mouth
Boca de la Sierpe

Puerto La Cruz
Barcelona
Caripito
Maturín

ATLANTIC

Aragua de Barcelona
Anaco
Cantaura
MONAGAS

Zaraza
ANZOATEGUI
El Tigre
Temblador
Barrancas
Tucupita
Grande
Boca Grande
I. Corocoro

OCEAN

Santa Maria de Ipire
Pariaguán
Pariagudo
Orinoco
Morichal Largo
DELTA

Ciudad Guayana
AMACURO
Morawhanna
Mabaruma
Waini

B

Pto. Ordaz
Upata
Guri Dam
El Palmar
Barima
Kokerite
Charity
Anna Regina
POMEROON-SUPERNAAM
ESSEQUIBO ISLANDS-
WEST DEMERARA
Suddie
Parika
Georgetown

El Dorado
Cuyuni
CUYUNI
MAZARUNI
Bartica
Rosignol
DEMERARA-MAHAICA
MAHAICA-BERBICE
New Amsterdam
Port Mourant

GUYANA
Mazaruni
Issano
Wismar
Linden
(Mackenzie)
Nieuw Nickerie
Totness
Paramaribo
Alliance
Nieuw Amsterdam
Mana

2560
La Gran Sabana
Pakaraima
Mt. Roraima
2772
Kaieteur Falls
Mahdia
UPPER ITUNI
Skeldon
Wageningen
CORONIE
Groningen
COMME-WIJNE
Laurent
Iracoubo
Iles du Salut
Cayenne
Rémire

C

SURINAM
Wilhelmina Geb.
Julianatop
1280
SARAMACCA
BROKOPONDO
FRENCH
GUIANA

RORAIMA

BRAZIL

Represa de Balbina
MANAUS

Amazonas
Santarém
Óbidos
Alenquer

D

PARÁ

West from Greenwich   COPYRIGHT. GEORGE PHILIP & SON. LTD.

5 **6** **7**

ATLANTIC OCEAN

FORTALEZA (Ceará)
NATAL
RECIFE (Pernambuco)
MACEIÓ
BELÉM (Pará)
SÃO LUIS
Macapá

AMAPÁ
PARÁ
MARANHÃO
CEARÁ
RIO GRANDE DO NORTE
PARAÍBA
PERNAMBUCO
ALAGOAS
PIAUÍ
TOCANTINS
BAHIA

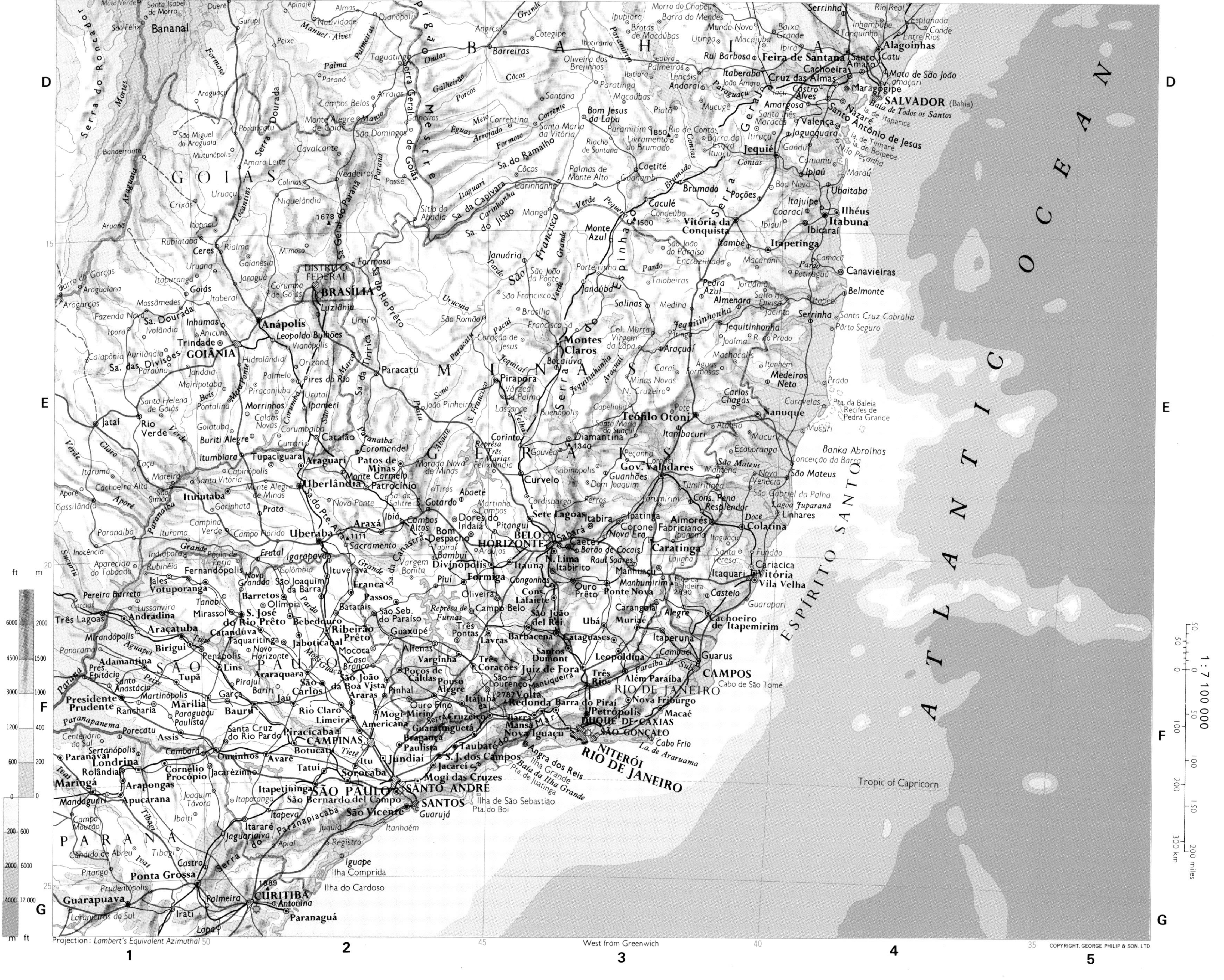

1 : 7 100 000

ATLANTIC OCEAN

Projection: Lambert's Equivalent Azimuthal 50

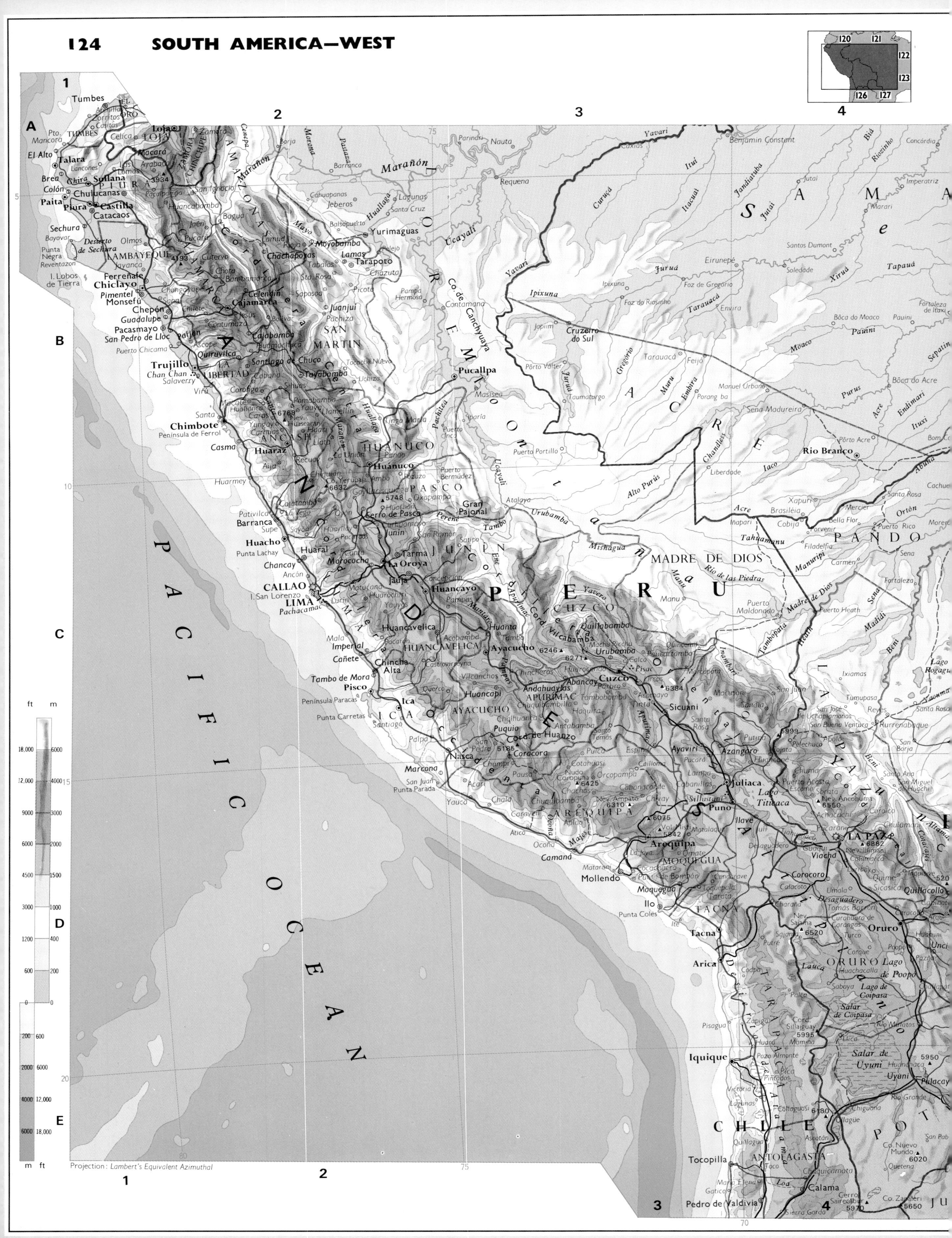

PACIFIC OCEAN
PERU
ANDES
Cordillera Central
Cordillera Occidental
Cordillera Oriental
S A M A
ACRE
PANDO
MADRE DE DIOS
CUZCO
APURIMAC
AYACUCHO
HUANCAVELICA
ICA
AREQUIPA
MOQUEGUA
TACNA
JUNIN
PASCO
HUANUCO
ANCASH
LA LIBERTAD
SAN MARTIN
CAJAMARCA
LAMBAYEQUE
PIURA
AMAZONAS
TUMBES
LOJA
EL ORO
ORURO
TARAPACA
ANTOFAGASTA
CHILE
Tumbes
Talara
Sullana
Paita
Piura
Castilla
Catacaos
Chulucanas
Sechura
Desierto de Sechura
Chiclayo
Ferreñafe
Pimentel
Monsefú
Chepén
Guadalupe
Pacasmayo
San Pedro de Lloc
Puerto Chicama
Trujillo
Chan Chan
Salaverry
Virú
Chimbote
Península de Ferrol
Casma
Huaraz
Huarmey
Pativilca
Barranca
Supe
Huacho
Punta Lachay
Chancay
Ancón
Huaral
CALLAO
I. San Lorenzo
LIMA
Pachacamac
Mala
Imperial
Cañete
Tambo de Mora
Chincha Alta
Pisco
Península Paracas
Punta Carretas
Ica
Palpa
Nasca
Marcona
San Juan
Punta Parada
Yauca
Chala
Atico
Ocoña
Camaná
Mollendo
Moquegua
Ilo
Punta Coles
Tacna
Arica
Pisagua
Iquique
Tocopilla
Pedro de Valdivia
Calama
Cajamarca
Chachapoyas
Moyobamba
Tarapoto
Yurimaguas
Juanjuí
Huánuco
Cerro de Pasco
Tarma
La Oroya
Jauja
Huancayo
Huancavelica
Ayacucho
Huanta
Andahuaylas
Abancay
Cuzco
Pisac
Urubamba
Quillabamba
Sicuani
Ayaviri
Azángaro
Juliaca
Puno
Lago Titicaca
Arequipa
Pucallpa
Requena
Nauta
Benjamin Constant
Cruzeiro do Sul
Rio Branco
Brasiléia
Cobija
Puerto Maldonado
LA PAZ
Viacha
Corocoro
Oruro
Lago Poopó
Lago de Coipasa
Salar de Coipasa
Salar de Uyuni
Uyuni
Marañón
Ucayali
Huallaga
Urubamba
Yavari
Juruá
Purus
Madre de Dios
Beni
6768
6632
5748
6246
6271
6384
5999
6425
6310
6075
5842
6550
6882
6520
5995
6180
5950
6020
5970
5650
Projection: Lambert's Equivalent Azimuthal

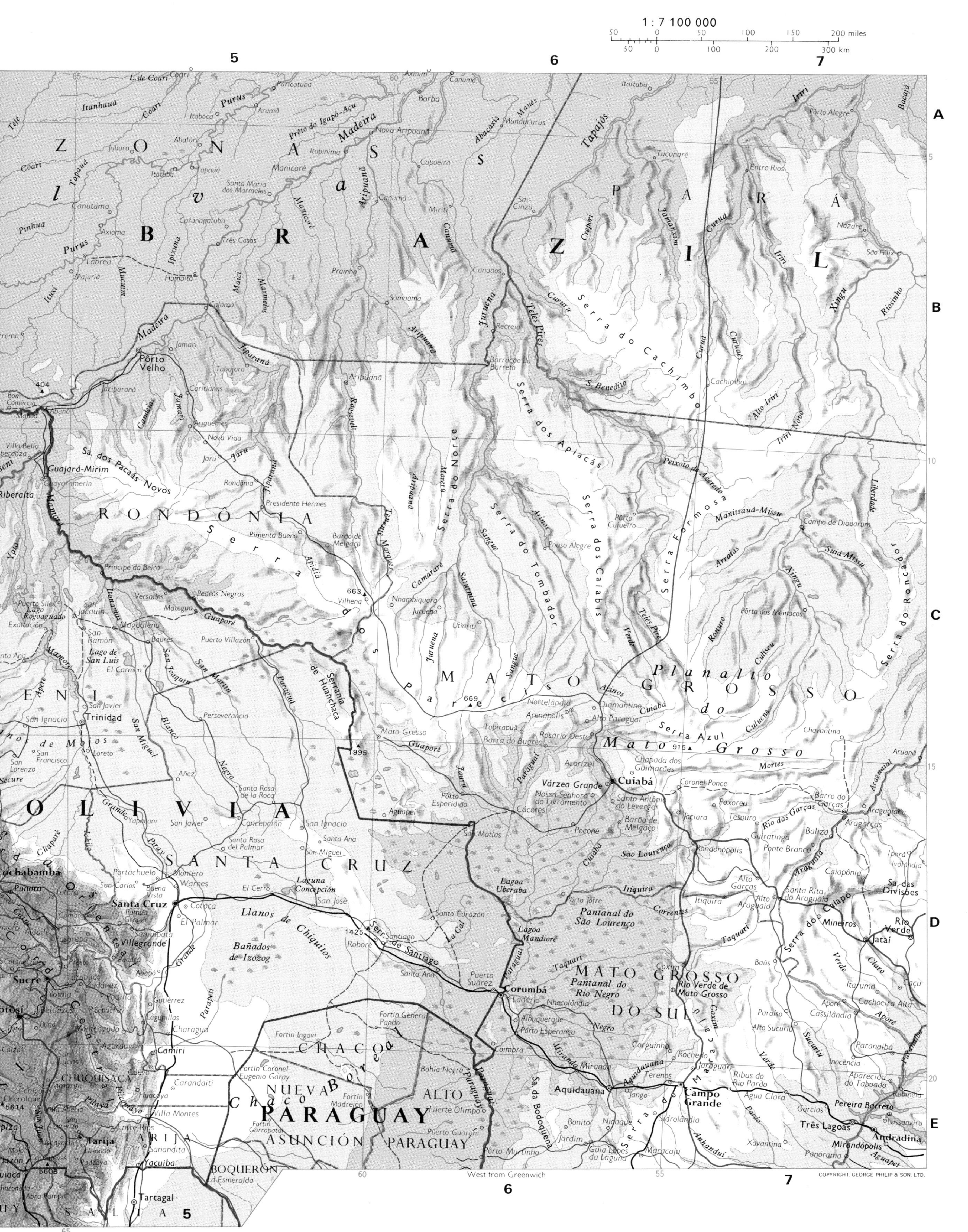

1 : 7 100 000

50   0   50   100   150   200 miles

50   0   100   200   300 km

ft	m
18 000	6000
12 000	4000
9000	3000
6000	2000
4500	1500
3000	1000
1200	400
600	200
0	0
200	600
2000	6000
4000	12 000
6000	18 000
m	ft

Projection: *Lambert's Equivalent Azimuthal*

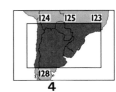

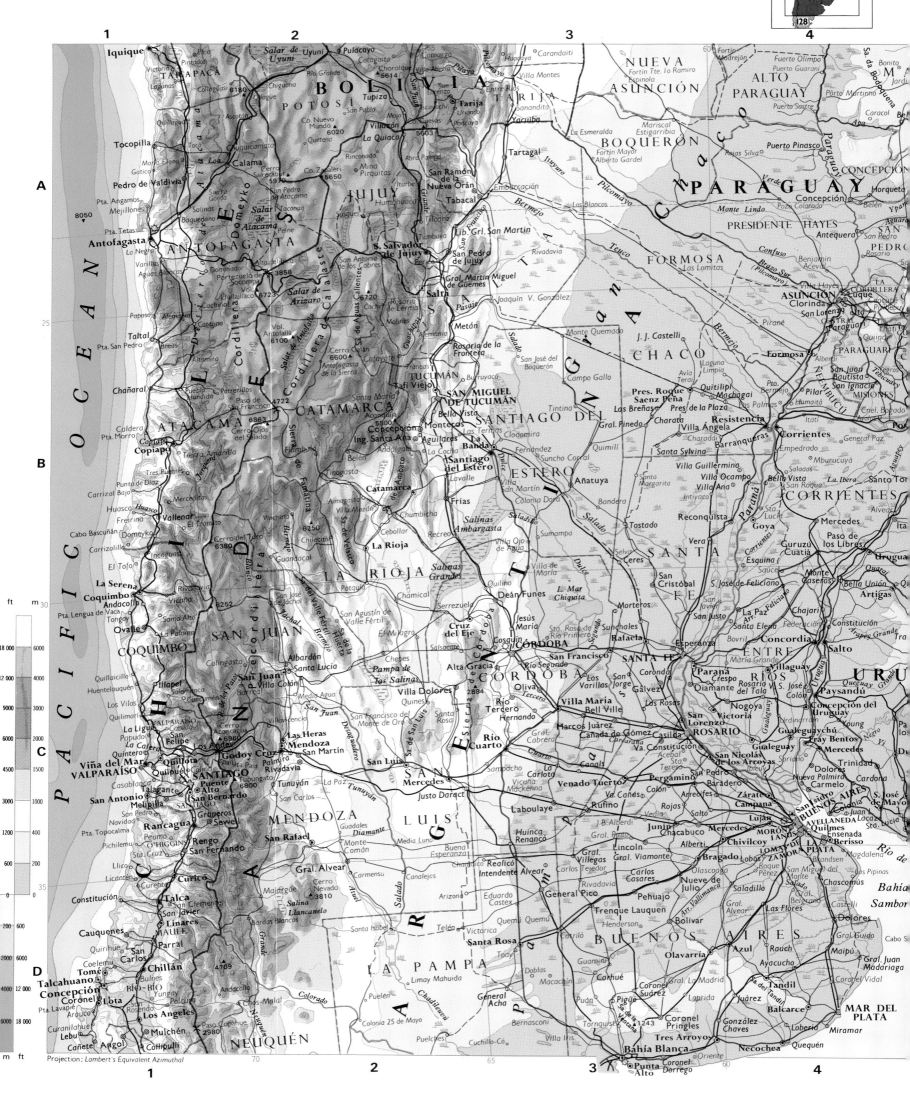

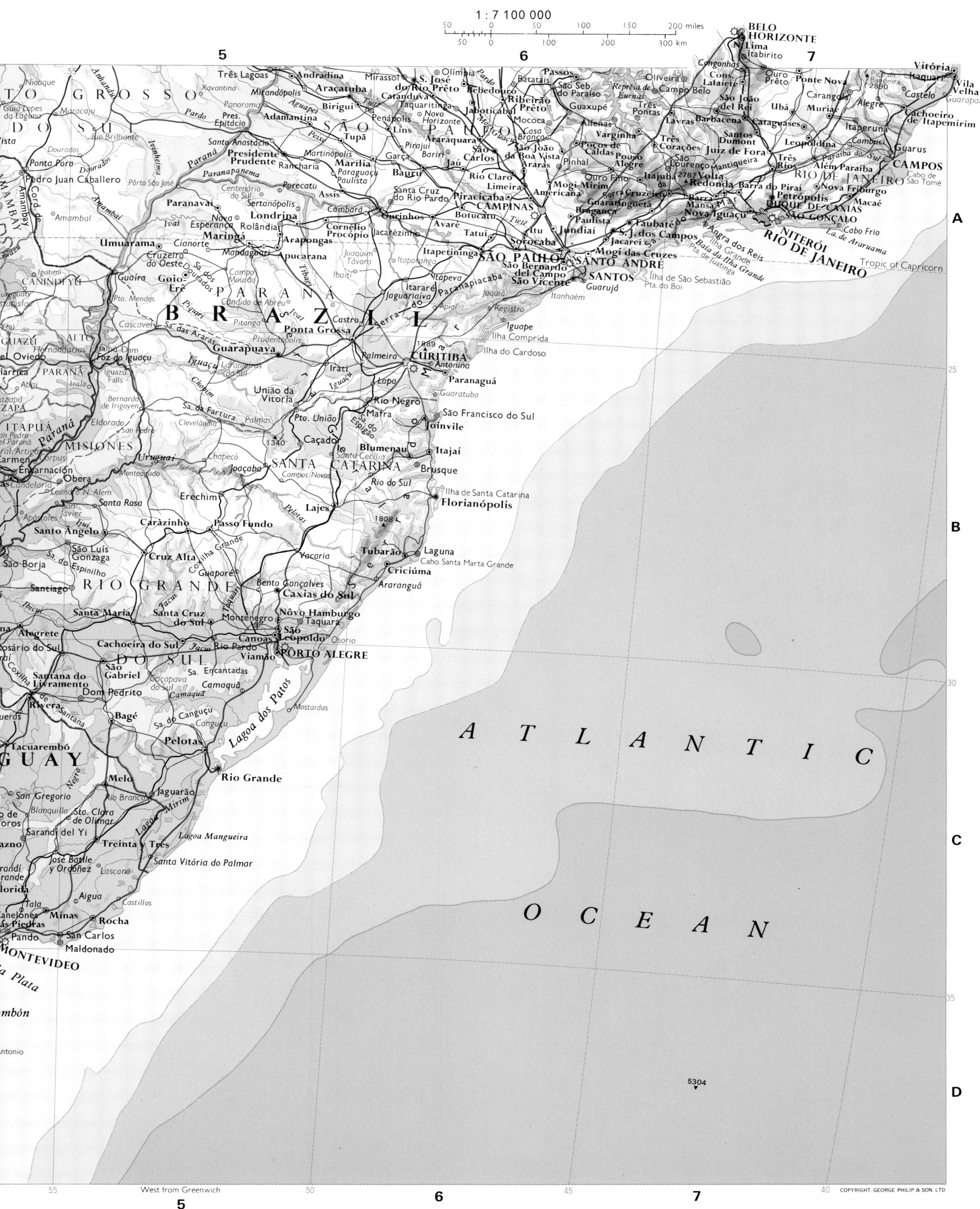

1 : 7 100 000

50 · 0 · 50 · 100 · 150 · 200 miles
50 · 0 · 100 · 200 · 300 km

5 · **6** · **7**

BELO
HORIZONTE

TO GROSSO
DO SUL

SÃO PAULO

PARANÁ

B R A Z I L

SANTA CATARINA

RIO GRANDE
DO SUL

CURITIBA

Florianópolis

PORTO ALEGRE

RIO DE JANEIRO
NITERÓI

Vitória
Vila
Velha

CAMPOS

SÃO PAULO
SANTO ANDRÉ
SANTOS

Tropic of Capricorn

A T L A N T I C

O C E A N

5304

GUAY

MONTEVIDEO

25

30

35

A

B

C

D

1 : 7 100 000

50   0   50   100   150   200 miles
50   0   100   200   300 km

126 127

Major regions / labels

LA PAMPA
BUENOS AIRES
RÍO NEGRO
ARAUCANIA
NEUQUÉN
LOS LAGOS
CHUBUT
SANTA CRUZ
MAGALLANES
TIERRA DEL FUEGO

PACIFIC OCEAN
SOUTH ATLANTIC OCEAN
SOUTHERN OCEAN

FALKLAND ISLANDS
(ISLAS MALVINAS)
West Falkland
East Falkland
King George B.
Queen Charlotte B.
Mt. Adam 700
Mt. Usborne 705
Jason Is.
Pebble I.
C. Dolphin
Weddell I.
Port
Darwin
Stanley
Falkland Sound
C. Meredith
Beauchêne I.

Selected place names

Arauco, Cañete, Angol, Mulchén, Collipulli, Victoria, Paso Copahue 2980, Colonia 25 de Mayo, Puelches, Bernasconi, Tornquist 1243, Coronel Pringles, González Chaves, Juárez, Balcarce, Loberia, Quequén
Capitán Pastene, Curacautín, Lautaro, Cherquenco 3124, Lonquimay 1824, Las Lajas, Paso Pino Hachado, Anelo, Colorado, Villa Iris, Coronel Dorrego, Necochea
I. Mocha, Temuco, Freire, Cunco, Zapala, Cutral-Có, Neuquén, Cipolletti, Fortín Uno, Bahía Blanca, Médanos, Punta Alta, Oriente
ARAUCANIA, Pitrufquén, Toltén, Loncoche, Paso Mamuíl Malal 1253, Picún Leufú, Gral. Roca, Allen, Choele Choel, Río Colorado, Mayor Buratovich, B. Blanca, I. Trinidad
Valdivia, Corral, Pta. Galera, Los Lagos, Panguipulli, Villarrica 3776, San Martín de los Andes, Junín de los Andes, El Cuy, Lamarque, Gral. Conesa, Stroeder, B. Anegada
La Unión, Osorno, Río Bueno, L. Ranco, Lago Ranco, Las Coloradas, Piedra del Águila, La Esperanza, Sa. Colorada 1314, Valcheta, San Antonio Oeste, Carmen de Patagones, Pta. Rasa
LOS LAGOS, Río Negro, Puyehue, Vol. Osorno 2660, Mte. Tronador 3554, San Carlos de Bariloche, Maquinchao, Ingeniero Jacobacci, El Cain, Salado, Viedma, Golfo San Matías
Puerto Varas, Puerto Montt, L. Llanquihue, La Ensenada, El Bolsón, Norquinco, Quetrequile, Sierra Grande, Cona Niyeu, Verde, Pta. Norte
G. de los Coronados, Moullin, Ancud, G. de Ancud, El Maitén, Gastre, Gan Gan, Telsen, Puerto Lobos, G. San José, Pen. Valdés, Puerto Pirámides, Punta Delgada
Isla de Chiloé, Castro, Achao, Chaitén 2470, L. Menéndez, Esquel, Gualjaina, G. Nuevo, Puerto Madryn
Puerto Quellón, C. Quilán, 2440, 2300, Tecka, Gaimán, Rawson, Trelew
Boca del Guafo, I. Guafo, Islas Guaitecas, Yelcho, El Burro 2075, Corcovado, Pampa de Agnia, Las Plumas, Perdido, Meseta de Montemayor, C. Raso
Archipiélago de los Chonos, Palena, Palena, L. Gral. Vintter, Río Pico, José de San Martín, Paso de Indios, Chubut
I. Guamblin, Magdalena, La Plata 2020, L. Fontana, 1245, Gran Laguna Salada, Chico, Camarones, B. Camarones, C. Dos Bahías
Coihaique, Alto Río Senguerr, L. Musters, L. Colhué Huapí, Sarmiento, B. Bustamante
C. Taitao 1372, Puerto Aisén, Mayo, Río Mayo, Facundo, Holdich, Golfo San Jorge, Comodoro Rivadavia
Peninsula de Taitao, Balmaceda, Chile Chico, L. Buenos Aires, Los Monos, Colonia Las Heras, Caleta Olivia, San Jorge
Mte. San Valentín 4058, L. Gral. Carrera, Perito Moreno, Los Antiguos, Pico Truncado, Mazarredo, C. Tres Puntas, C. Blanco
Archipiélago Guayaneco, Arenales 3437, Cochrane 2726, 1335, Fitz Roy, Jaramillo, Deseado, Puerto Deseado
C. Tres Montes, I. Javier, Co. San Lorenzo 3700, L. Pueyrredón, Lago Posadas, Pta. Medanosa
I. Campana, I. Patricio Lynch, Mellizo Sur 3050, Las Horquetas, Mt. Inés 1120, Gob. Gregores, Bahía Laura
I. Esmeralda, 2280, SANTA CRUZ, Gran Altiplanicie Central, San Julián
G. Ladrillero, L. San Martín, L. Cardiel, Chico
I. Mornington, G. Trinidad, Mte. Fitzroy 3375, L. Viedma, Tres Lagos, Cmte. Luis Piedrabuena, San Julián
I. Madre de Dios, I. Wellington, Muralón 3600, Shehuen, Santa Cruz
I. Duque de York, C. Santiago, B. Salvación, Lago Argentino, Calafate, Bahía Grande
I. Hanover, Esperanza, Puerto Coig
I. Mornington, C. Jorge, Estrecho Nelson, Puerto Natales, El Turbio, Coig, Guer Aike, Río Gallegos
Arch. Reina Adelaida, Pen. Muñoz, Almirante Montt, Seno Skyring, Gallegos, Monte Dinero, C. Vírgenes
Estrecho de Magallanes, C. Deseado, I. Riesco, Seno de Otway, Gamero, Strait of Magellan, Cerro Sombrero
I. Desolación, Punta Arenas, Pen. Brunswick, Porvenir, San Sebastián, Isla Grande de Tierra del Fuego, Río Grande
Santa Inés, B. Otway, Dawson, B. Inútil, TIERRA DEL FUEGO
Clarence, Capt. Aracena, Pen. Brecknock, 2469, Mte. Darwin, Ushuaia, L. Fagnano, Misión Fagnano, C. San Diego
I. Stewart, I. Londonderry, Gordon, Canal Beagle, Picton, I. de los Estados (Staten I.)
B. Cook, I. Hoste, I. Navarino, B. Nassau, Nueva, Lennox, Est. de Le Maire
Pen. Hardy, Islas Wollaston, Is. Hermite, Cabo de Hornos (Cape Horn)
Islas Diego Ramírez

West from Greenwich

Projection: Lambert's Equivalent Azimuthal

COPYRIGHT. GEORGE PHILIP & SON LTD

Elevation key (ft / m)

9000 / 3000
6000 / 2000
4500 / 1500
3000 / 1000
1200 / 400
0 / 200
200 / 0
2000 / 600
6000 / 2000
12,000 / 4000

INDEX

The index contains the names of all the principal places and features shown on the World Maps. Each name is followed by an additional entry in italics giving the country or region within which it is located. The alphabetical order of names composed of two or more words is governed primarily by the first word and then by the second. This is an example of the rule:

Mīr Kūh, *Iran* **65** **E8**
Mīr Shahdād, *Iran* **65** **E8**
Miraj, *India* **60** **L9**
Miram Shah, *Pakistan* **62** **C4**
Miramar, *Mozam.* **85** **C6**

Physical features composed of a proper name (Erie) and a description (Lake) are positioned alphabetically by the proper name. The description is positioned after the proper name and is usually abbreviated:

Erie, L., *N. Amer.* **106** **D3**

Where a description forms part of a settlement or administrative name however, it is always written in full and put in its true alphabetic position:

Mount Morris, *U.S.A.* **106** **D7**

Names beginning with M' and Mc are indexed as if they were spelt Mac. Names beginning St. are alphabetised under Saint, but Sankt, Sint, Sant', Santa and San are all spelt in full and are alphabetised accordingly. If the same place name occurs two or more times in the index and all are in the same country, each is followed by the name of the administrative subdivision in which it is located. The names are placed in the alphabetical order of the subdivisions. For example:

Jackson, *Ky., U.S.A.* **104** **G4**
Jackson, *Mich., U.S.A.* **104** **D3**
Jackson, *Minn., U.S.A.* **108** **D7**

The number in bold type which follows each name in the index refers to the number of the map page where that feature or place will be found. This is usually the largest scale at which the place or feature appears. The letter and figure which are in bold type immediately after the page number give the grid square on the map page, within which the feature is situated. The letter represents the latitude and the figure the longitude.

In some cases the feature itself may fall within the specified square, while the name is outside. This is usually the case only with features which are larger than a grid square. Rivers are indexed to their mouths or confluences, and carry the symbol → after their names. A solid square ■ follows the name of a country while, an open square □ refers to a first order administrative area.

ABBREVIATIONS USED IN THE INDEX

A.C.T. — Australian Capital Territory
Afghan. — Afghanistan
Ala. — Alabama
Alta. — Alberta
Amer. — America(n)
Arch. — Archipelago
Ariz. — Arizona
Ark. — Arkansas
Atl. Oc. — Atlantic Ocean
B. — Baie, Bahía, Bay, Bucht, Bugt
B.C. — British Columbia
Bangla. — Bangladesh
Barr. — Barrage
Bos.-H. — Bosnia-Herzegovina
C. — Cabo, Cap, Cape, Coast
C.A.R. — Central African Republic
C. Prov. — Cape Province
Calif. — California
Cent. — Central
Chan. — Channel
Colo. — Colorado
Conn. — Connecticut
Cord. — Cordillera
Cr. — Creek
Czech. — Czech Republic
D.C. — District of Columbia
Del. — Delaware
Dep. — Dependency
Des. — Desert
Dist. — District
Dj. — Djebel
Domin. — Dominica
Dom. Rep. — Dominican Republic
E. — East
El Salv. — El Salvador

Eq. Guin. — Equatorial Guinea
Fla. — Florida
Falk. Is. — Falkland Is.
G. — Golfe, Golfo, Gulf, Guba, Gebel
Ga. — Georgia
Gt. — Great, Greater
Guinea-Biss. — Guinea-Bissau
H.K. — Hong Kong
H.P. — Himachal Pradesh
Hants. — Hampshire
Harb. — Harbor, Harbour
Hd. — Head
Hts. — Heights
I.(s). — Île, Ilha, Insel, Isla, Island, Isle
Ill. — Illinois
Ind. — Indiana
Ind. Oc. — Indian Ocean
Ivory C. — Ivory Coast
J. — Jabal, Jebel, Jazira
Junc. — Junction
K. — Kap, Kapp
Kans. — Kansas
Kep. — Kepulauan
Ky. — Kentucky
L. — Lac, Lacul, Lago, Lagoa, Lake, Limni, Loch, Lough
La. — Louisiana
Liech. — Liechtenstein
Lux. — Luxembourg
Mad. P. — Madhya Pradesh
Madag. — Madagascar
Man. — Manitoba
Mass. — Massachusetts
Md. — Maryland

Me. — Maine
Medit. S. — Mediterranean Sea
Mich. — Michigan
Minn. — Minnesota
Miss. — Mississippi
Mo. — Missouri
Mont. — Montana
Moza. — Mozambique
Mt.(e). — Mont, Monte, Monti, Montaña, Mountain
N. — Nord, Norte, North, Northern, Nouveau
N.B. — New Brunswick
N.C. — North Carolina
N. Cal. — New Caledonia
N. Dak. — North Dakota
N.H. — New Hampshire
N.I. — North Island
N.J. — New Jersey
N. Mex. — New Mexico
N.S. — Nova Scotia
N.S.W. — New South Wales
N.W.T. — North West Territory
N.Y. — New York
N.Z. — New Zealand
Nebr. — Nebraska
Neths. — Netherlands
Nev. — Nevada
Nfld. — Newfoundland
Nic. — Nicaragua
O. — Oued, Ouadi
Occ. — Occidentale
O.F.S. — Orange Free State
Okla. — Oklahoma
Ont. — Ontario
Or. — Orientale

Oreg. — Oregon
Os. — Ostrov
Oz. — Ozero
P. — Pass, Passo, Pasul, Pulau
P.E.I. — Prince Edward Island
Pa. — Pennsylvania
Pac. Oc. — Pacific Ocean
Papua N.G. — Papua New Guinea
Pass. — Passage
Pen. — Peninsula, Péninsule
Phil. — Philippines
Pk. — Park, Peak
Plat. — Plateau
P-ov. — Poluostrov
Prov. — Province, Provincial
Pt. — Point
Pta. — Ponta, Punta
Pte. — Pointe
Qué. — Québec
Queens. — Queensland
R. — Rio, River
R.I. — Rhode Island
Ra.(s). — Range(s)
Raj. — Rajasthan
Reg. — Region
Rep. — Republic
Res. — Reserve, Reservoir
S. — San, South, Sea
Si. Arabia — Saudi Arabia
S.C. — South Carolina
S. Dak. — South Dakota
S.I. — South Island
S. Leone — Sierra Leone
Sa. — Serra, Sierra
Sask. — Saskatchewan
Scot. — Scotland

Sd. — Sound
Sev. — Severnaya
Sib. — Siberia
Sprs. — Springs
St. — Saint, Sankt, Sint
Sta. — Santa, Station
Ste. — Sainte
Sto. — Santo
Str. — Strait, Stretto
Switz. — Switzerland
Tas. — Tasmania
Tenn. — Tennessee
Tex. — Texas
Tg. — Tanjung
Trin. & Tob. — Trinidad & Tobago
U.A.E. — United Arab Emirates
U.K. — United Kingdom
U.S.A. — United States of America
Ut. P. — Uttar Pradesh
Va. — Virginia
Vdkhr. — Vodokhranilishche
Vf. — Vîrful
Vic. — Victoria
Vol. — Volcano
Vt. — Vermont
W. — Wadi, West
W. Va. — West Virginia
Wash. — Washington
Wis. — Wisconsin
Wlkp. — Wielkopolski
Wyo. — Wyoming
Yorks. — Yorkshire
Yug. — Yugoslavia

A Coruña

A

A Coruña = La Coruña, Spain 30 B2
Aachen, Germany 18 E2
Aadorf, Switz. 23 B7
Aalborg = Ålborg, Denmark 11 G3
Aalen, Germany 19 G6
A'âli en Nîl □, Sudan 77 F3
Aalsmeer, Neths. 16 D5
Aalst, Belgium 17 G4
Aalst, Neths. 17 F6
Aalten, Neths. 16 E9
Aalter, Belgium 17 F2
Aarau, Switz. 22 B6
Aarberg, Switz. 22 B4
Aardenburg, Belgium 17 F2
Aare →, Switz. 22 A6
Aargau □, Switz. 22 B6
Aarhus = Århus, Denmark 11 H4
Aarle, Neths. 17 E7
Aarschot, Belgium 17 G5
Aarsele, Belgium 17 G2
Aartrijke, Belgium 17 F2
Aarwangen, Switz. 22 B5
Aba, China 52 A3
Aba, Nigeria 79 D6
Aba, Zaïre 82 B3
Âbâ, Jazîrat, Sudan 77 E3
Abacaxis →, Brazil 121 D6
Ābādān, Iran 65 D6
Abade, Ethiopia 77 F4
Ābādeh, Iran 65 D7
Abadin, Spain 30 B3
Abadla, Algeria 75 B4
Abaeté, Brazil 123 E2
Abaeté →, Brazil 123 E2
Abaetetuba, Brazil 122 B2
Abagnar Qi, China 50 C9
Abai, Paraguay 127 B4
Abak, Nigeria 79 E6
Abakaliki, Nigeria 79 D6
Abakan, Russia 45 D10
Abalemma, Niger 79 B6
Abana, Turkey 66 C6
Abancay, Peru 124 C3
Abanilla, Spain 29 G3
Abano Terme, Italy 33 C8
Abapó, Bolivia 125 D5
Abarán, Spain 29 G3
Abariringa, Kiribati 92 H10
Abarqū, Iran 65 D7
Abashiri, Japan 48 B12
Abashiri-Wan, Japan 48 B12
Abaújszántó, Hungary 21 G11
Abay, Kazakhstan 44 E8
Abaya, L., Ethiopia 77 F4
Abaza, Russia 44 D10
Abbadia San Salvatore, Italy 33 F8
'Abbāsābād, Iran 65 C8
Abbay = Nîl el Azraq →, Sudan 77 D3
Abbaye, Pt., U.S.A. 104 B1
Abbé, L., Ethiopia 77 E5
Abbeville, France 25 B8
Abbeville, La., U.S.A. 109 K8
Abbeville, S.C., U.S.A. 105 H4
Abbiategrasso, Italy 32 C5
Abbieglassie, Australia 91 D4
Abbot Ice Shelf, Antarctica 5 D16
Abbotsford, Canada 100 D4
Abbotsford, U.S.A. 108 C9
Abbottabad, Pakistan 62 B5
Abcoude, Neths. 16 D5
Abd al Kūrī, Ind. Oc. 68 E5
Ābdar, Iran 65 D7
'Abdolābād, Iran 65 C8
Abéché, Chad 73 F9
Abejar, Spain 28 D2
Abekr, Sudan 77 E2
Abêlessa, Algeria 75 D5
Abengourou, Ivory C. 78 D4
Åbenrå, Denmark 11 J3
Abensberg, Germany 19 G7
Abeokuta, Nigeria 79 D5
Aber, Uganda 82 B3
Aberaeron, U.K. 13 E3
Aberayron = Aberaeron, U.K. 13 E3
Abercorn = Mbala, Zambia 83 D3
Abercorn, Australia 91 D5
Aberdare, U.K. 13 F4
Aberdare Ra., Kenya 82 C4
Aberdeen, Australia 91 E5
Aberdeen, Canada 101 C7
Aberdeen, S. Africa 84 E3
Aberdeen, U.K. 14 D6
Aberdeen, Ala., U.S.A. 105 J1
Aberdeen, Idaho, U.S.A. 110 E7
Aberdeen, S. Dak., U.S.A. 108 C5
Aberdeen, Wash., U.S.A. 112 D3
Aberdovey = Aberdyfi, U.K. 13 E3
Aberdyfi, U.K. 13 E3
Aberfeldy, U.K. 14 E5
Abergaria-a-Velha, Portugal 30 E2
Abergavenny, U.K. 13 F4
Abernathy, U.S.A. 109 J4
Abert, L., U.S.A. 110 E3
Aberystwyth, U.K. 13 E3
Abha, Si. Arabia 76 D5
Abhar, Iran 65 B6
Abhayapuri, India 63 F14
Abia □, Nigeria 79 D6
Abidiya, Sudan 76 D3
Abidjan, Ivory C. 78 D4
Abilene, Kans., U.S.A. 108 F6
Abilene, Tex., U.S.A. 109 J5
Abingdon, U.K. 13 F6
Abingdon, Ill., U.S.A. 108 E9
Abingdon, Va., U.S.A. 105 G5
Abington Reef, Australia 90 B4
Abitau →, Canada 101 B7
Abitau L., Canada 101 A7
Abitibi L., Canada 98 C4
Abiy Adi, Ethiopia 77 E4
Abkhaz Republic □, Georgia 43 E9
Abkit, Russia 45 C16
Abminga, Australia 91 D1
Abnûb, Egypt 76 B3
Abocho, Nigeria 79 D6
Abohar, India 62 D6
Aboisso, Ivory C. 78 D4
Abomey, Benin 79 D5
Abondance, France 27 B10
Abong-Mbang, Cameroon 80 D2
Abonnema, Nigeria 79 E6
Abony, Hungary 21 H10
Aboso, Ghana 78 D4
Abou-Deïa, Chad 73 F8
Aboyne, U.K. 14 D6
Abra Pampa, Argentina 126 A2
Abrantes, Portugal 31 F2
Abraveses, Portugal 30 E3
Abreojos, Pta., Mexico 114 B2
Abreschviller, France 25 D14
Abri, Esh Shamâliya, Sudan 76 C3
Abri, Janub Kordofân, Sudan 77 E3
Abrolhos, Banka, Brazil 123 E4
Abruzzi □, Italy 33 F10
Absaroka Range, U.S.A. 110 D9
Abū al Khaṣīb, Iraq 65 D6
Abū 'Alī, Si. Arabia 65 E6
Abū 'Alī →, Lebanon 69 A4
Abu 'Arīsh, Si. Arabia 68 D3
Abû Ballas, Egypt 76 C2
Abu Deleiq, Sudan 77 D3
Abu Dhabi = Abū Ẓāby, U.A.E. 65 E7
Abû Dis, Sudan 76 D3
Abû Dom, Sudan 77 D3
Abū Du'ān, Syria 64 B3
Abu el Gairi, W. →, Egypt 69 F2
Abû Gabra, Sudan 77 E2
Abu Ga'da, W. →, Egypt 69 F1
Abû Gubeiha, Sudan 77 E3
Abu Habl, Khawr →, Sudan 77 E3
Abū Ḥadrīyah, Si. Arabia 65 E6
Abu Hamed, Sudan 76 D3
Abu Haraz, An Nîl el Azraq, Sudan 77 E3
Abû Haraz, Esh Shamâliya, Sudan 76 D3
Abû Higar, Sudan 77 E3
Abū Kamāl, Syria 64 C4
Abū Madd, Ra's, Si. Arabia 64 E3
Abu Matariq, Sudan 77 E2
Abu Qir, Egypt 76 H7
Abu Qireiya, Egypt 76 C4
Abu Qurqâs, Egypt 76 J7
Abu Şafāt, W. →, Jordan 69 E5
Abû Simbel, Egypt 76 C3
Abū Şukhayr, Iraq 64 D5
Abu Tig, Egypt 76 B3
Abu Tiga, Sudan 77 E3
Abû Zabad, Sudan 77 E2
Abū Ẓāby, U.A.E. 65 E7
Abū Zeydābād, Iran 65 C6
Abufari, Brazil 125 B5
Abuja, Nigeria 79 D6
Abukuma-Gawa →, Japan 48 E10
Abukuma-Sammyaku, Japan 48 F10
Abunã, Brazil 125 B4
Abunã →, Brazil 125 B4
Aburo, Zaïre 82 B3
Abut Hd., N.Z. 87 K3
Abwong, Sudan 77 F3
Åby, Sweden 11 F10
Aby, Lagune, Ivory C. 78 D4
Acacías, Colombia 120 C3
Acajutla, El Salv. 116 D2
Açallândia, Brazil 122 C2
Acámbaro, Mexico 114 C4
Acaponeta, Mexico 114 C3
Acapulco, Mexico 115 D5
Acarai, Serra, Brazil 121 C6
Acaraú, Brazil 122 B3
Acari, Brazil 122 C4
Acarí, Peru 124 D3
Acarigua, Venezuela 120 B4
Acatlán, Mexico 115 D5
Acayucan, Mexico 115 D6
Accéglio, Italy 32 D3
Accomac, U.S.A. 104 G8
Accous, France 26 E3
Accra, Ghana 79 D4
Accrington, U.K. 12 D5
Acebal, Argentina 126 C3
Aceh □, Indonesia 56 D1
Acerenza, Italy 35 B8
Acerra, Italy 35 B7
Aceuchal, Spain 31 G4
Achacachi, Bolivia 124 D4
Achaguas, Venezuela 120 B4
Achalpur, India 60 J10
Achao, Chile 128 B2
Achel, Belgium 17 F6
Acheng, China 51 B14
Achenkirch, Austria 19 H7
Achensee, Austria 19 H7
Acher, India 62 H5
Achern, Germany 19 G4
Achill, Ireland 15 C2
Achill Hd., Ireland 15 C1
Achill I., Ireland 15 C1
Achill Sd., Ireland 15 C2
Achim, Germany 18 B5
Achinsk, Russia 45 D10
Achol, Sudan 77 F3
Acıgöl, Turkey 66 E3
Acireale, Italy 35 E8
Ackerman, U.S.A. 109 J10
Acklins I., Bahamas 117 B5
Acme, Canada 100 C6
Acobamba, Peru 124 C3
Acomayo, Peru 124 C3
Aconcagua □, Chile 126 C1
Aconcagua, Cerro, Argentina 126 C2
Aconquija, Mt., Argentina 126 B2
Acopiara, Brazil 122 C4
Açores, Is. dos = Azores, Atl. Oc. 2 C8
Acorizal, Brazil 125 D6
Acquapendente, Italy 33 F8
Acquasanta, Italy 33 F10
Acquaviva delle Fonti, Italy 35 B9
Acqui, Italy 32 D5
Acraman, L., Australia 91 E2
Acre = 'Akko, Israel 69 C4
Acre □, Brazil 124 B3
Acre →, Brazil 124 B4
Acri, Italy 35 C9
Acs, Hungary 21 H8
Acton, Canada 106 C4
Açu, Brazil 122 C4
Ad Dammām, Si. Arabia 65 E6
Ad Dawhah, Qatar 65 E6
Ad Dawr, Iraq 64 C4
Ad Dir'īyah, Si. Arabia 64 E5
Ad Dīwānīyah, Iraq 64 D5
Ad Dujayl, Iraq 64 C5
Ad Durūz, J., Jordan 69 C5
Ada, Ghana 79 D5
Ada, Serbia 21 K10
Ada, Minn., U.S.A. 108 B6
Ada, Okla., U.S.A. 109 H6
Adaja →, Spain 30 D6
Ådalslinden, Sweden 10 A10
Adam, Mt., Falk. Is. 128 D4
Adamantina, Brazil 123 F1
Adamaoua, Massif de l', Cameroon 79 D7
Adamawa □, Nigeria 79 D7
Adamawa Highlands = Adamaoua, Massif de l', Cameroon 79 D7
Adamello, Mt., Italy 32 B7
Adami Tulu, Ethiopia 77 F4
Adaminaby, Australia 91 F4
Adams, Mass., U.S.A. 107 D11
Adams, N.Y., U.S.A. 107 C8
Adams, Wis., U.S.A. 108 D10
Adam's Bridge, Sri Lanka 60 Q11
Adams L., Canada 100 C5
Adams Mt., U.S.A. 112 D5
Adam's Peak, Sri Lanka 60 R12
Adamuz, Spain 31 G6
Adana, Turkey 66 E6
Adana □, Turkey 66 E6
Adanero, Spain 30 E6
Adapazarı, Turkey 66 C4
Adarama, Sudan 77 D3
Adare, C., Antarctica 5 D11
Adaut, Indonesia 57 F8
Adavale, Australia 91 D3
Adda →, Italy 32 C6
Addis Ababa = Addis Abeba, Ethiopia 77 F4
Addis Abeba, Ethiopia 77 F4
Addis Alem, Ethiopia 77 F4
Addison, U.S.A. 106 D7
Addo, S. Africa 84 E4
Adebour, Niger 79 C7
Ādeh, Iran 64 B5
Adel, U.S.A. 105 K4
Adelaide, Australia 91 E2
Adelaide, Bahamas 116 A4
Adelaide, S. Africa 84 E4
Adelaide I., Antarctica 5 C17
Adelaide Pen., Canada 96 B10
Adelaide River, Australia 88 B5
Adelanto, U.S.A. 113 L9
Adelboden, Switz. 22 D5
Adele I., Australia 88 C3
Adélie, Terre, Antarctica 5 C10
Adélie Land = Adélie, Terre, Antarctica 5 C10
Ademuz, Spain 28 E3
Aden = Al 'Adan, Yemen 68 E4
Aden, G. of, Asia 68 E4
Adendorp, S. Africa 84 E3
Adh Dhayd, U.A.E. 65 E7
Adhoi, India 62 H4
Adi, Indonesia 57 E8
Adi Daro, Ethiopia 77 E4
Adi Keyih, Eritrea 77 E4
Adi Kwala, Eritrea 77 E4
Adi Ugri, Eritrea 77 E4
Adieu, C., Australia 89 F5
Adieu Pt., Australia 88 C3
Adigala, Ethiopia 77 E5
Adige →, Italy 33 C9
Adigrat, Ethiopia 77 E4
Adilabad, India 60 K11
Adin, U.S.A. 110 F3
Adin Khel, Afghan. 60 C6
Adinkerke, Belgium 17 F1
Adirondack Mts., U.S.A. 107 C10
Adıyaman, Turkey 67 E8
Adiyaman □, Turkey 67 E8
Adjim, Tunisia 75 B7
Adjohon, Benin 79 D5
Adjud, Romania 38 C10
Adjumani, Uganda 82 B3
Adlavik Is., Canada 99 B8
Adler, Russia 43 E8
Adliswil, Switz. 23 B7
Admer, Algeria 75 D6
Admer, Erg d', Algeria 75 D6
Admiralty G., Australia 88 B4
Admiralty I., U.S.A. 96 C6
Admiralty Inlet, U.S.A. 110 C2
Admiralty Is., Papua N. G. 92 H6
Ado, Nigeria 79 D5
Ado Ekiti, Nigeria 79 D6
Adok, Sudan 77 F3
Adola, Ethiopia 77 E5
Adonara, Indonesia 57 F6
Adoni, India 60 M10
Adony, Hungary 21 H8
Adour →, France 26 E2
Adra, India 63 H12
Adra, Spain 29 J1
Adrano, Italy 35 E7
Adrar, Algeria 75 C4
Adré, Chad 73 F9
Adrī, Libya 75 C7
Ádria, Italy 33 C9
Adrian, Mich., U.S.A. 104 E3
Adrian, Tex., U.S.A. 109 H3
Adriatic Sea, Europe 6 G9
Adua, Indonesia 57 E7
Adula, Switz. 23 D8
Adwa, Ethiopia 77 E4
Adzhar Republic □, Georgia 43 F10
Adzopé, Ivory C. 78 D4
Ægean Sea, Europe 39 L8
Æolian Is. = Eólie, Is., Italy 35 D7
Aerhtai Shan, Mongolia 54 B4
Ærø, Denmark 11 K4
Ærøskøbing, Denmark 11 K4
Aesch, Switz. 22 B5
'Afak, Iraq 64 C5
Afándou, Greece 37 C10
Afarag, Erg, Algeria 75 D5
Afars & Issas, Terr. of = Djibouti ■, Africa 68 E3
Affreville = Khemis Miliana, Algeria 75 A5
Afghanistan ■, Asia 60 C4
Afgoi, Somali Rep. 68 G3
Afikpo, Nigeria 79 D6
Aflou, Algeria 75 B5
Afogados da Ingàzeira, Brazil 122 C4
Afognak I., U.S.A. 96 C4
Afragola, Italy 35 B7
Afrera, Ethiopia 77 E5
Africa 70 E6
'Afrīn, Syria 64 B3
Afşin, Turkey 66 D7
Afton, U.S.A. 107 D9
Aftout, Algeria 74 C4
Afuá, Brazil 121 D7
Afula, Israel 69 C4
Afyonkarahisar, Turkey 66 D4
Afyonkarahisar □, Turkey 66 D4
Aga, Egypt 76 H7
Agadès = Agadez, Niger 79 B6
Agadez, Niger 79 B6
Agadir, Morocco 74 B3
Agaete, Canary Is. 36 F4
Agailás, Mauritania 74 D2
Agapa, Russia 45 B9
Agar, India 62 H7
Agaro, Ethiopia 77 F4
Agartala, India 61 H17
Agassiz, Canada 100 D4
Agats, Indonesia 57 F9
Agbélouvé, Togo 79 D5
Agboville, Ivory C. 78 D4
Agdam, Azerbaijan 43 G12
Agdash, Azerbaijan 43 F12
Agde, France 26 E7
Agde, C. d', France 26 E7
Agdz, Morocco 74 B3
Agdzhabedi, Azerbaijan 43 F12
Agen, France 26 D4
Agersø, Denmark 11 J5
Ageyevo, Russia 41 D10
Agger, Denmark 11 H2
Ággius, Italy 34 B2
Āgh Kand, Iran 65 B6
Aghoueyyît, Mauritania 74 D1
Aginskoye, Russia 45 D12
Agira, Italy 35 E7
Ağlasun, Turkey 66 E4
Agly →, France 26 F7
Agnibilékrou, Ivory C. 78 D4
Agnita, Romania 38 D7
Agnone, Italy 35 A7
Agofie, Ghana 79 D5
Agogna →, Italy 32 C5
Agogo, Sudan 77 F2
Agon, France 24 C5
Agön, Sweden 10 C11
Ágordo, Italy 33 B9
Agout →, France 26 E5
Agra, India 62 F7
Agramunt, Spain 28 D6
Agreda, Spain 28 D3
Ağri, Turkey 67 D10
Ağri □, Turkey 67 D10
Agri →, Italy 35 B9
Ağrı Dağı, Turkey 67 D11
Ağrı Karakose, Turkey 67 D10
Agrigento, Italy 34 E6
Agrinion, Greece 39 L4
Agrópoli, Italy 35 B7
Água Branca, Brazil 122 C3
Agua Caliente, Baja Calif. N., Mexico 113 N10
Agua Caliente, Sinaloa, Mexico 114 B3
Agua Caliente Springs, U.S.A. 113 N10
Água Clara, Brazil 125 E7
Agua Hechicero, Mexico 113 N10
Agua Preta →, Brazil 121 D5
Agua Prieta, Mexico 114 A3
Aguachica, Colombia 120 B3
Aguada Cecilio, Argentina 128 B3
Aguadas, Colombia 120 B2
Aguadilla, Puerto Rico 117 C6
Aguadulce, Panama 116 E3
Aguanga, U.S.A. 113 M10
Aguanish, Canada 99 B7
Aguanus →, Canada 99 B7
Aguapeí, Brazil 125 D6
Aguapeí →, Brazil 123 F1
Aguapey →, Argentina 126 B4
Aguaray Guazú →, Paraguay 126 A4
Aguarico →, Ecuador 120 D2
Aguas →, Spain 28 D4
Aguas Blancas, Chile 126 A2
Aguas Calientes, Sierra de, Argentina 126 B2
Águas Formosas, Brazil 123 E3
Aguascalientes, Mexico 114 C4
Aguascalientes □, Mexico 114 C4
Agudo, Spain 31 G6
Águeda, Portugal 30 E2
Agueda →, Spain 30 D4
Aguié, Niger 79 C6
Aguilafuente, Spain 30 D6
Aguilar, Spain 31 H6
Aguilar de Campóo, Spain 30 C6
Aguilares, Argentina 126 B2
Aguilas, Spain 29 H3
Agüimes, Canary Is. 36 G4
Aguja, C. de la, Colombia 120 A3
Agulaa, Ethiopia 77 E4
Agulhas, C., S. Africa 84 E3
Agulo, Canary Is. 36 F2
Agung, Indonesia 56 F5
Agur, Uganda 82 B3
Agusan →, Phil. 55 G6
Agustín Codazzi, Colombia 120 A3
Agvali, Russia 43 E12
Aha Mts., Botswana 84 B3
Ahaggar, Algeria 75 D6
Ahamansu, Ghana 79 D5
Ahar, Iran 64 B5
Ahaus, Germany 18 C3
Ahelledjem, Algeria 75 C6
Ahipara B., N.Z. 87 F4
Ahiri, India 60 K12
Ahlen, Germany 18 D3
Ahmad Wal, Pakistan 62 E1
Ahmadabad, India 62 H5
Aḥmadābād, Khorāsān, Iran 65 C9
Aḥmadābād, Khorāsān, Iran 65 C8
Aḥmadī, Iran 65 E8
Ahmadnagar, India 60 K9
Ahmadpur, Pakistan 62 E4
Ahmar, Ethiopia 77 F5
Ahmedabad = Ahmadabad, India 62 H5
Ahmednagar = Ahmadnagar, India 60 K9
Ahoada, Nigeria 79 D6
Ahome, Mexico 114 B3
Ahr →, Germany 18 E3
Ahram, Iran 65 D6
Ahrax Pt., Malta 37 D1
Ahrensbök, Germany 18 A6
Ahrweiler, Germany 18 E3
Āhū, Iran 65 C6
Ahuachapán, El Salv. 116 D2
Ahvāz, Iran 65 D6
Ahvenanmaa = Åland, Finland 9 F16
Aḥwar, Yemen 68 E4
Ahzar, Mali 79 B5
Aiari →, Brazil 120 C4
Aichach, Germany 19 G7
Aichi □, Japan 49 G8

Aidone, *Italy* 35 E7
Aiello Cálabro, *Italy* 35 C9
Aigle, *Switz.* 22 D3
Aignay-le-Duc, *France* 25 E11
Aigoual, Mt., *France* 26 D7
Aigre, *France* 26 C4
Aigua, *Uruguay* 127 C5
Aigueperse, *France* 26 B7
Aigues →, *France* 27 D8
Aigues-Mortes, *France* 27 E8
Aigues-Mortes, G. d', *France* 27 E8
Aiguilles, *France* 27 D10
Aiguillon, *France* 26 D4
Aigurande, *France* 26 B5
Aihui, *China* 54 A7
Aija, *Peru* 124 B2
Aikawa, *Japan* 48 E9
Aiken, *U.S.A.* 105 J5
Ailao Shan, *China* 52 F3
Aillant-sur-Tholon, *France* 25 E10
Aillik, *Canada* 99 A8
Ailly-sur-Noye, *France* 25 C9
Ailsa Craig, *U.K.* 14 F3
'Ailūn, *Jordan* 69 C4
Aim, *Russia* 45 D14
Aimere, *Indonesia* 57 F6
Aimogasta, *Argentina* 126 B2
Aimorés, *Brazil* 123 E3
Ain □, *France* 27 B9
Ain →, *France* 27 C9
Aïn Beïda, *Algeria* 75 A6
Aïn Ben Khellil, *Algeria* 75 B4
Aïn Ben Tili, *Mauritania* 74 C3
Aïn Beni Mathar, *Morocco* 75 B4
Aïn Benian, *Algeria* 75 A5
Ain Dalla, *Egypt* 76 B2
Ain el Mafki, *Egypt* 76 B2
Ain Girba, *Egypt* 76 B2
Aïn M'lila, *Algeria* 75 A6
Ain Qeiqab, *Egypt* 76 B1
Aïn-Sefra, *Algeria* 75 B4
Ain Sheikh Murzûk, *Egypt* 76 B2
'Ain Sudr, *Egypt* 69 F2
Ain Sukhna, *Egypt* 76 J8
Aïn Tédelès, *Algeria* 75 A5
Aïn-Témouchent, *Algeria* 75 A4
Aïn Touta, *Algeria* 75 A6
Ain Zeitûn, *Egypt* 76 B2
Aïn Zorah, *Morocco* 75 B4
Ainabo, *Somali Rep.* 68 F4
Ainaži, *Latvia* 40 C4
Aínos Óros, *Greece* 39 L3
Ainsworth, *U.S.A.* 108 D5
Aipe, *Colombia* 120 C2
Aiquile, *Bolivia* 125 D4
Aïr, *Niger* 79 B6
Air Hitam, *Malaysia* 59 M4
Airaines, *France* 25 C8
Airão, *Brazil* 121 D5
Airdrie, *U.K.* 14 F5
Aire →, *France* 25 C11
Aire →, *U.K.* 12 D7
Aire, I. del, *Spain* 36 B11
Aire-sur-la-Lys, *France* 25 B9
Aire-sur-l'Adour, *France* 26 E3
Airlie Beach, *Australia* 90 C4
Airolo, *Switz.* 23 C7
Airvault, *France* 24 F6
Aisch →, *Germany* 19 F7
Aisen □, *Chile* 128 C2
Aisne □, *France* 25 C10
Aisne →, *France* 25 C9
Aitana, Sierra de, *Spain* 29 G4
Aitkin, *U.S.A.* 108 B8
Aitolikón, *Greece* 39 L4
Aiuaba, *Brazil* 122 C3
Aiud, *Romania* 38 C6
Aix-en-Provence, *France* 27 E9
Aix-la-Chapelle = Aachen, *Germany* 18 E2
Aix-les-Bains, *France* 27 C9
Aixe-sur-Vienne, *France* 26 C5
Aiyansh, *Canada* 100 B3
Aíyina, *Greece* 39 M6
Aiyínion, *Greece* 39 J5
Aiyion, *Greece* 39 L5
Aizawl, *India* 61 H18
Aizenay, *France* 24 F5
Aizpute, *Latvia* 40 C2
Aizuwakamatsu, *Japan* 48 F9
Ajaccio, *France* 27 G12
Ajaccio, G. d', *France* 27 G12
Ajaju →, *Colombia* 120 C3
Ajalpan, *Mexico* 115 D5
Ajanta Ra., *India* 60 J9
Ajari Rep. = Adzhar Republic □, *Georgia* 43 F10
Ajax, *Canada* 106 C5
Ajdâbiyah, *Libya* 73 B9
Ajdovščina, *Slovenia* 33 C10
Ajibar, *Ethiopia* 77 E4
Ajka, *Hungary* 21 H7
'Ajmān, *U.A.E.* 65 E7
Ajmer, *India* 62 F6
Ajo, *U.S.A.* 111 K7
Ajoie, *Switz.* 22 B4
Ajok, *Sudan* 77 F2
Ajuy, *Phil.* 55 F5
Ak Dağ, *Antalya, Turkey* 66 E3
Ak Dağ, *Sivas, Turkey* 66 D7
Akaba, *Togo* 79 D5
Akabira, *Japan* 48 C11
Akabli, *Algeria* 75 C5
Akaki Beseka, *Ethiopia* 77 F4
Akala, *Sudan* 77 D4
Akamas □, *Cyprus* 37 D11
Akanthou, *Cyprus* 37 D12
Akaroa, *N.Z.* 87 K4
Akasha, *Sudan* 76 C3
Akashi, *Japan* 49 G7
Akbou, *Algeria* 75 A5
Akçaabat, *Turkey* 67 C8
Akçakoca, *Turkey* 66 C4
Akchâr, *Mauritania* 74 D2
Akdağmadeni, *Turkey* 66 D6
Akelamo, *Indonesia* 57 D7
Akershus fylke □, *Norway* 10 E5
Aketi, *Zaïre* 80 D4
Akhalkalaki, *Georgia* 43 F10
Akhaltsikhe, *Georgia* 43 F10
Akharnaí, *Greece* 39 L6
Akhelóös →, *Greece* 39 L4
Akhendria, *Greece* 39 Q8
Akhéron →, *Greece* 39 K3
Akhladhókambos, *Greece* 39 M5
Akhmîm, *Egypt* 76 B3
Akhnur, *India* 63 C6
Akhtubinsk, *Russia* 43 B12
Akhty, *Russia* 43 F12
Akhtyrka, *Ukraine* 40 F9
Aki, *Japan* 49 H6
Akimiski I., *Canada* 98 B3
Akimovka, *Ukraine* 42 C6
Akita, *Japan* 48 E10
Akita □, *Japan* 48 E10
Akjoujt, *Mauritania* 78 B2
Akka, *Morocco* 74 C3
Akkeshi, *Japan* 48 C12
'Akko, *Israel* 69 C4
Akkol, *Kazakhstan* 44 E8
Akkrum, *Neths.* 16 B7
Aklampa, *Benin* 79 D5
Aklavik, *Canada* 96 B6
Akmolinsk = Tselinograd, *Kazakhstan* 44 D8
Akmonte, *Spain* 31 H4
Aknoul, *Morocco* 75 B4
Akō, *Japan* 49 G7
Ako, *Nigeria* 79 C7
Akobo →, *Ethiopia* 77 F3
Akola, *India* 60 J10
Akonolinga, *Cameroon* 79 E7
Akordat, *Eritrea* 77 D4
Akosombo Dam, *Ghana* 79 D5
Akot, *Sudan* 77 F3
Akpatok I., *Canada* 97 B13
Akranes, *Iceland* 8 D3
Akreïjit, *Mauritania* 78 B3
Akrítas Venétiko, Ákra, *Greece* 39 N4
Akron, *Colo., U.S.A.* 108 E3
Akron, *Ohio, U.S.A.* 106 E3
Akrotiri, *Cyprus* 37 E11
Akrotíri, Ákra, *Greece* 39 J8
Akrotiri Bay, *Cyprus* 37 E12
Aksai Chih, *India* 63 B8
Aksaray, *Turkey* 66 D6
Aksarka, *Russia* 44 C7
Aksay, *Kazakhstan* 44 D6
Akşehir, *Turkey* 66 D4
Akşehir Gölü, *Turkey* 66 D4
Aksenovo Zilovskoye, *Russia* 45 D12
Akstafa, *Azerbaijan* 43 F11
Aksu, *China* 54 B3
Aksu →, *Turkey* 66 E4
Aksum, *Ethiopia* 77 E4
Aktogay, *Kazakhstan* 44 E8
Aktyubinsk, *Kazakhstan* 44 D6
Aku, *Nigeria* 79 D6
Akure, *Nigeria* 79 D6
Akureyri, *Iceland* 8 D4
Akuseki-Shima, *Japan* 49 K4
Akusha, *Russia* 43 E12
Akwa-Ibom □, *Nigeria* 79 E6
Akyab = Sittwe, *Burma* 61 J18
Akyazı, *Turkey* 66 C4
Al 'Adan, *Yemen* 68 E4
Al Aḩsā, *Si. Arabia* 65 E6
Al Ajfar, *Si. Arabia* 64 E4
Al Amādīyah, *Iraq* 64 B4
Al Amārah, *Iraq* 64 D5
Al 'Aqabah, *Jordan* 69 F4
Al Arak, *Syria* 64 C3
Al 'Aramah, *Si. Arabia* 64 E5
Al Arţāwīyah, *Si. Arabia* 64 E5
Al 'Āşimah □, *Jordan* 69 D5
Al' Assāfīyah, *Si. Arabia* 64 D3
Al 'Ayn, *Oman* 65 E7
Al 'Ayn, *Si. Arabia* 64 E3
Al A'zamīyah, *Iraq* 64 C5
Al 'Azīzīyah, *Iraq* 64 C5
Al 'Azīzīyah, *Libya* 75 B7
Al Bāb, *Syria* 64 B3
Al Bad', *Si. Arabia* 64 D2
Al Bādī, *Iraq* 64 C4
Al Baḩrah, *Kuwait* 64 D5
Al Balqā' □, *Jordan* 69 C4
Al Barkāt, *Libya* 75 D7
Al Bārūk, J., *Lebanon* 69 B4
Al Başrah, *Iraq* 64 D5
Al Baţḩā, *Iraq* 64 D5
Al Batrūn, *Lebanon* 69 A4
Al Bi'r, *Si. Arabia* 64 D3
Al Bu'ayrāt, *Libya* 73 B8
Al Burayj, *Syria* 69 A5
Al Fallūjah, *Iraq* 64 C4
Al Fāw, *Iraq* 65 D6
Al Fujayrah, *U.A.E.* 65 E8
Al Ghadaf, W. →, *Jordan* 69 D5
Al Ghammās, *Iraq* 64 D5
Al Ḩābah, *Si. Arabia* 64 E5
Al Ḩadīthah, *Iraq* 64 C4
Al Ḩadīthah, *Si. Arabia* 64 D3
Al Ḩājānah, *Syria* 69 B5
Al Ḩāmad, *Si. Arabia* 64 D3
Al Hamdānīyah, *Syria* 64 C3
Al Ḩamidīyah, *Syria* 69 A4
Al Ḩammādah al Ḩamrā', *Libya* 75 C7
Al Ḩammār, *Iraq* 64 D5
Al Ḩarīr, W. →, *Syria* 69 C4
Al Ḩasā, W. →, *Jordan* 69 D4
Al Ḩasakah, *Syria* 64 B4
Al Ḩawrah, *Yemen* 68 E4
Al Ḩaydān, W. →, *Jordan* 69 D4
Al Ḩayy, *Iraq* 64 C5
Al Ḩijāz, *Si. Arabia* 68 B2
Al Ḩillah, *Iraq* 64 C5
Al Ḩillah, *Si. Arabia* 68 C4
Al Hirmil, *Lebanon* 69 A5
Al Hoceïma, *Morocco* 74 A4
Al Ḩudaydah, *Yemen* 68 E3
Al Ḩufūf, *Si. Arabia* 65 E6
Al Ḩumaydah, *Si. Arabia* 64 D2
Al Ḩunayy, *Si. Arabia* 65 E6
Al Irq, *Libya* 73 C9
Al Īsāwīyah, *Si. Arabia* 64 D3
Al Ittihad = Madīnat ash Sha'b, *Yemen* 68 E3
Al Jafr, *Jordan* 69 E5
Al Jaghbūb, *Libya* 73 C9
Al Jahrah, *Kuwait* 64 D5
Al Jalāmīd, *Si. Arabia* 64 D3
Al Jamalīyah, *Qatar* 65 E6
Al Janūb □, *Lebanon* 69 B4
Al Jawf, *Libya* 73 D9
Al Jawf, *Si. Arabia* 64 D3
Al Jazirah, *Iraq* 64 C5
Al Jazirah, *Libya* 73 C9
Al Jithāmīyah, *Si. Arabia* 64 E4
Al Jubayl, *Si. Arabia* 65 E6
Al Jubaylah, *Si. Arabia* 64 E5
Al Jubb, *Si. Arabia* 64 E4
Al Junaynah, *Sudan* 73 F9
Al Kabā'ish, *Iraq* 64 D5
Al Karak, *Jordan* 69 D4
Al Karak □, *Jordan* 69 E5
Al Kāzim Tyah, *Iraq* 64 C5
Al Khalīl, *Jordan* 69 D4
Al Khalīl □, *Jordan* 69 D4
Al Khawr, *Qatar* 65 E6
Al Khiḑr, *Iraq* 64 D5
Al Khiyām, *Lebanon* 69 B4
Al Kiswah, *Syria* 69 B5
Al Kufrah, *Libya* 73 D9
Al Kuhayfīyah, *Si. Arabia* 64 E4
Al Kūt, *Iraq* 64 C5
Al Kuwayt, *Kuwait* 64 D5
Al Labwah, *Lebanon* 69 A5
Al Lādhiqīyah, *Syria* 64 C2
Al Līth, *Si. Arabia* 76 C5
Al Liwā', *Oman* 65 E8
Al Luḩayyah, *Yemen* 68 D3
Al Madīnah, *Iraq* 64 D5
Al Madīnah, *Si. Arabia* 64 E3
Al-Mafraq, *Jordan* 69 C5
Al Maḩmūdīyah, *Iraq* 64 C5
Al Majma'ah, *Si. Arabia* 64 E5
Al Makhruq, W. →, *Jordan* 69 D6
Al Makḩūl, *Si. Arabia* 64 E4
Al Manāmah, *Bahrain* 65 E6
Al Maqwa', *Kuwait* 64 D5
Al Marj, *Libya* 73 B9
Al Maţlā, *Kuwait* 64 D5
Al Mawjib, W. →, *Jordan* 69 D4
Al Mawşil, *Iraq* 64 B4
Al Mayādin, *Syria* 64 C4
Al Mazār, *Jordan* 69 D4
Al Midhnab, *Si. Arabia* 64 E5
Al Minā', *Lebanon* 69 A4
Al Miqdādīyah, *Iraq* 64 C5
Al Mubarraz, *Si. Arabia* 65 E6
Al Mughayrā', *U.A.E.* 65 E7
Al Muḩarraq, *Bahrain* 65 E6
Al Mukallā, *Yemen* 68 E4
Al Mukhā, *Yemen* 68 E3
Al Musayjīd, *Si. Arabia* 64 E3
Al Musayyib, *Iraq* 64 C5
Al Muwayliḩ, *Si. Arabia* 64 E2
Al Owuho = Otukpa, *Nigeria* 79 D6
Al Qā'im, *Iraq* 64 C4
Al Qalībah, *Si. Arabia* 64 D3
Al Qaryatayn, *Syria* 69 A6
Al Qaşabát, *Libya* 73 B7
Al Qaţ'ā, *Syria* 64 C4
Al Qaţīf, *Si. Arabia* 65 E6
Al Qatrānah, *Jordan* 69 D5
Al Qaţrūn, *Libya* 73 D8
Al Qayşūmah, *Si. Arabia* 64 D5
Al Quds = Jerusalem, *Israel* 69 D4
Al Quds □, *Jordan* 69 D4
Al Qunaytirah, *Syria* 69 C4
Al Qunfudhah, *Si. Arabia* 76 D5
Al Qurnah, *Iraq* 64 D5
Al Quşayr, *Iraq* 64 D5
Al Quşayr, *Syria* 69 A5
Al Qutayfah, *Syria* 69 B5
Al' Uḑaylīyah, *Si. Arabia* 65 E6
Al 'Ulā, *Si. Arabia* 64 E3
Al Uqaylah ash Sharqīgah, *Libya* 73 B8
Al Uqayr, *Si. Arabia* 65 E6
Al 'Uwaynid, *Si. Arabia* 64 E5
Al' 'Uwayqīlah, *Si. Arabia* 64 D4
Al 'Uyūn, *Si. Arabia* 64 E4
Al 'Uyūn, *Si. Arabia* 64 E3
Al Wajh, *Si. Arabia* 64 E3
Al Wakrah, *Qatar* 65 E6
Al Wannān, *Si. Arabia* 65 E6
Al Waqbah, *Si. Arabia* 64 D5
Al Wari'āh, *Si. Arabia* 64 E5
Al Wātīyah, *Libya* 75 B7
Al Wusayl, *Qatar* 65 E6
Ala, *Italy* 32 C8
Ala Dağları, *Turkey* 67 D10
Alabama □, *U.S.A.* 105 J2
Alabama →, *U.S.A.* 105 K2
Alaca, *Turkey* 66 C6
Alaçam, *Turkey* 66 C6
Alaçam Dağları, *Turkey* 66 D3
Alaejos, *Spain* 30 D5
Alaérma, *Greece* 37 C9
Alagna Valsésia, *Italy* 32 C4
Alagoa Grande, *Brazil* 122 C4
Alagoas □, *Brazil* 122 C4
Alagoinhas, *Brazil* 123 D4
Alagón, *Spain* 28 D3
Alagón →, *Spain* 31 F4
Alajero, *Canary Is.* 36 F2
Alajuela, *Costa Rica* 116 D3
Alakamisy, *Madag.* 85 C8
Alalapura, *Surinam* 121 C6
Alalaú →, *Brazil* 121 D5
Alameda, *Spain* 31 H6
Alameda, *Calif., U.S.A.* 112 H4
Alameda, *N. Mex., U.S.A.* 111 J10
Alaminos, *Phil.* 55 C3
Alamo, *U.S.A.* 113 J11
Alamo Crossing, *U.S.A.* 113 L13
Alamogordo, *U.S.A.* 111 K11
Alamos, *Mexico* 114 B3
Alamosa, *U.S.A.* 111 H11
Åland, *Finland* 9 F16
Alandroal, *Portugal* 31 G3
Ålands hav, *Sweden* 9 G15
Alandur, *India* 60 N12
Alange, Presa de, *Spain* 31 G4
Alanis, *Spain* 31 G5
Alanya, *Turkey* 66 E4
Alaotra, Farihin', *Madag.* 85 B8
Alapayevsk, *Russia* 44 D7
Alar del Rey, *Spain* 30 C6
Alaraz, *Spain* 30 E5
Alaşehir, *Turkey* 66 D3
Alaska □, *U.S.A.* 96 B5
Alaska, G. of, *Pac. Oc.* 96 C5
Alaska Highway, *Canada* 100 B3
Alaska Peninsula, *U.S.A.* 96 C4
Alaska Range, *U.S.A.* 96 B4
Alássio, *Italy* 32 D5
Alataw Shankou, *China* 54 B3
Alatri, *Italy* 34 A6
Alatyr, *Russia* 41 D15
Alatyr →, *Russia* 41 D15
Alausi, *Ecuador* 120 D2
Álava □, *Spain* 28 C2
Alava, C., *U.S.A.* 110 B1
Alaverdi, *Armenia* 43 F11
Alawoona, *Australia* 91 E3
'Alayh, *Lebanon* 69 B4
Alayor, *Spain* 36 B11
Alazan →, *Azerbaijan* 43 F12
Alba, *Italy* 32 D5
Alba de Tormes, *Spain* 30 E5
Alba Iulia, *Romania* 38 C6
Albac, *Romania* 38 C6
Albacete, *Spain* 29 G3
Albacete □, *Spain* 29 G3
Albacutya, L., *Australia* 91 F3
Ålbæk, *Denmark* 11 G4
Ålbæk Bugt, *Denmark* 11 G4
Albaida, *Spain* 29 G4
Albalate de las Nogueras, *Spain* 28 E2
Albalate del Arzobispo, *Spain* 28 D4
Albania ■, *Europe* 39 J3
Albano Laziale, *Italy* 34 A5
Albany, *Australia* 89 G2
Albany, *Ga., U.S.A.* 105 K3
Albany, *Minn., U.S.A.* 108 C7
Albany, *N.Y., U.S.A.* 107 D11
Albany, *Oreg., U.S.A.* 110 D2
Albany, *Tex., U.S.A.* 109 J5
Albany →, *Canada* 98 B3
Albardón, *Argentina* 126 C2
Albarracín, *Spain* 28 E3
Albarracín, Sierra de, *Spain* 28 E3
Albatross B., *Australia* 90 A3
Albegna →, *Italy* 33 F8
Albemarle, *U.S.A.* 105 H5
Albemarle Sd., *U.S.A.* 105 H7
Albenga, *Italy* 32 D5
Alberche →, *Spain* 30 F6
Alberdi, *Paraguay* 126 B4
Alberes, Mts., *Spain* 28 C7
Alberique, *Spain* 29 F4
Albersdorf, *Germany* 18 A5
Albert, *France* 25 B9
Albert, L. = Mobutu Sese Seko, L., *Africa* 82 B3
Albert, L., *Australia* 91 F2
Albert Canyon, *Canada* 100 C5
Albert Edward Ra., *Australia* 88 C4
Albert Lea, *U.S.A.* 108 D8
Albert Nile →, *Uganda* 82 B3
Albert Town, *Bahamas* 117 B5
Alberta □, *Canada* 100 C6
Alberti, *Argentina* 126 D3
Albertinia, *S. Africa* 84 E3
Albertkanaal →, *Belgium* 17 F4
Alberton, *Canada* 99 C7
Albertville = Kalemie, *Zaïre* 82 D2
Albertville, *France* 27 C10
Albi, *France* 26 E6
Albia, *U.S.A.* 108 E8
Albina, *Surinam* 121 B7
Albina, Ponta, *Angola* 84 B1
Albino, *Italy* 32 C6
Albion, *Idaho, U.S.A.* 110 E7
Albion, *Mich., U.S.A.* 104 D3
Albion, *Nebr., U.S.A.* 108 E5
Albion, *Pa., U.S.A.* 106 E4
Alblasserdam, *Neths.* 16 E5
Albocácer, *Spain* 28 E5
Alborán, *Medit. S.* 31 K7
Alborea, *Spain* 29 F3
Ålborg, *Denmark* 11 G3
Ålborg Bugt, *Denmark* 11 H4
Alborz, Reshteh-ye Kūhhā-ye, *Iran* 65 C7
Albox, *Spain* 29 H2
Albreda, *Canada* 100 C5
Albufeira, *Portugal* 31 H2
Albula →, *Switz.* 23 C8
Albuñol, *Spain* 29 J1
Albuquerque, *Brazil* 125 D6
Albuquerque, *U.S.A.* 111 J10
Albuquerque, Cayos de, *Caribbean* 116 D3
Alburg, *U.S.A.* 107 B11
Alburno, Mte., *Italy* 35 B8
Alburquerque, *Spain* 31 F4
Albury, *Australia* 91 F4
Alby, *Sweden* 10 B9
Alcácer do Sal, *Portugal* 31 G2
Alcaçovas, *Portugal* 31 G2
Alcalá de Chisvert, *Spain* 28 E5
Alcalá de Guadaira, *Spain* 31 H5
Alcalá de Henares, *Spain* 28 E1
Alcalá de los Gazules, *Spain* 31 J5
Alcalá la Real, *Spain* 31 H7
Alcamo, *Italy* 34 E5
Alcanadre, *Spain* 28 C2
Alcanadre →, *Spain* 28 D4
Alcanar, *Spain* 28 E5
Alcanede, *Portugal* 31 F2
Alcanena, *Portugal* 31 F2
Alcañices, *Spain* 30 D4
Alcaníz, *Spain* 28 D4
Alcântara, *Brazil* 122 B3
Alcántara, *Spain* 31 F4
Alcantara L., *Canada* 101 A7
Alcantarilla, *Spain* 29 H3
Alcaracejos, *Spain* 31 G6
Alcaraz, *Spain* 29 G2
Alcaraz, Sierra de, *Spain* 29 G2
Alcaudete, *Spain* 31 H6
Alcázar de San Juan, *Spain* 29 F1
Alchevsk = Kommunarsk, *Ukraine* 43 B8
Alcira, *Spain* 29 F4
Alcoa, *U.S.A.* 105 H4
Alcobaça, *Portugal* 31 F2
Alcobendas, *Spain* 28 E1
Alcolea del Pinar, *Spain* 28 D2
Alcora, *Spain* 28 E4
Alcorcón, *Spain* 30 E7
Alcoutim, *Portugal* 31 H3
Alcova, *U.S.A.* 110 E10
Alcoy, *Spain* 29 G4
Alcubierre, Sierra de, *Spain* 28 D4
Alcublas, *Spain* 28 F4
Alcudia, *Spain* 36 B10
Alcudia, B. de, *Spain* 36 B10
Alcudia, Sierra de la, *Spain* 31 G6
Aldabra Is., *Seychelles* 71 G8
Aldama, *Mexico* 115 C5
Aldan, *Russia* 45 D13
Aldan →, *Russia* 45 C13
Aldea, Pta. de la, *Canary Is.* 36 G4
Aldeburgh, *U.K.* 13 E9
Aldeia Nova, *Portugal* 31 H3
Alder, *U.S.A.* 110 D7
Alder Pk., *U.S.A.* 112 K5
Alderney, *Chan. Is.* 13 H5
Aldershot, *U.K.* 13 F7
Aledo, *U.S.A.* 108 E9
Alefa, *Ethiopia* 77 E4
Aleg, *Mauritania* 78 B2
Alegranza, *Canary Is.* 36 E6
Alegranza, I., *Canary Is.* 36 E6
Alegre, *Brazil* 123 F3
Alegrete, *Brazil* 127 B4
Aleisk, *Russia* 44 D9
Aleksandriya, *Ukraine* 40 F5
Aleksandriya, *Ukraine* 42 B5
Aleksandriyskaya, *Russia* 43 E12
Aleksandrov, *Russia* 41 C11
Aleksandrovac, *Serbia* 21 L11
Aleksandrovka, *Ukraine* 42 B5
Aleksandrovo, *Bulgaria* 38 F7
Aleksandrovsk-Sakhalinskiy, *Russia* 45 D15
Aleksandrovskiy Zavod, *Russia* 45 D12
Aleksandrovskoye, *Russia* 44 C8

Aleksandrów Kujawski, *Poland* 20 C8
Aleksandrów Łódźki, *Poland* 20 D9
Alekseyevka, *Russia* 41 F11
Aleksin, *Russia* 41 D10
Aleksinac, *Serbia* 21 M11
Além Paraíba, *Brazil* 123 F3
Alemania, *Argentina* 126 B2
Alemania, *Chile* 126 B2
Ålen, *Norway* 10 B5
Alençon, *France* 24 D7
Alenuihaha Channel, *U.S.A.* 102 H17
Aleppo = Ḥalab, *Syria* 64 B3
Aléria, *France* 27 F13
Alert Bay, *Canada* 100 C3
Alès, *France* 27 D8
Aleşd, *Romania* 38 B5
Alessándria, *Italy* 32 D5
Ålestrup, *Denmark* 11 H3
Ålesund, *Norway* 8 E9
Alet-les-Bains, *France* 26 F6
Aletschhorn, *Switz.* 22 D6
Aleutian Is., *Pac. Oc.* 96 C2
Aleutian Trench, *Pac. Oc.* 92 B10
Alexander, *U.S.A.* 108 B3
Alexander, Mt., *Australia* 89 E3
Alexander Arch., *U.S.A.* 100 B2
Alexander B., *S. Africa* 84 D2
Alexander Bay, *S. Africa* 84 D2
Alexander City, *U.S.A.* 105 J3
Alexander I., *Antarctica* 5 C17
Alexandra, *Australia* 91 F4
Alexandra, *N.Z.* 87 L2
Alexandra Falls, *Canada* 100 A5
Alexandretta = İskenderun, *Turkey* 66 E7
Alexandria = El Iskandarîya, *Egypt* 76 H6
Alexandria, *Australia* 90 B2
Alexandria, *B.C., Canada* 100 C4
Alexandria, *Ont., Canada* 98 C5
Alexandria, *Romania* 38 F8
Alexandria, *S. Africa* 84 E4
Alexandria, *Ind., U.S.A.* 104 E3
Alexandria, *La., U.S.A.* 109 K8
Alexandria, *Minn., U.S.A.* 108 C7
Alexandria, *S. Dak., U.S.A.* 108 D6
Alexandria, *Va., U.S.A.* 104 F7
Alexandria Bay, *U.S.A.* 107 B9
Alexandrina, L., *Australia* 91 F2
Alexandroúpolis, *Greece* 39 J8
Alexis →, *Canada* 99 B8
Alexis Creek, *Canada* 100 C4
Alfabia, *Spain* 36 B9
Alfambra, *Spain* 28 E3
Alfândega da Fé, *Portugal* 30 D4
Alfaro, *Spain* 28 C3
Alfeld, *Germany* 18 D5
Alfenas, *Brazil* 127 A6
Alfiós →, *Greece* 39 M4
Alfonsine, *Italy* 33 D9
Alford, *U.K.* 14 D6
Alfred, *Maine, U.S.A.* 107 C14
Alfred, *N.Y., U.S.A.* 106 D7
Alfreton, *U.K.* 12 D6
Alga, *Kazakhstan* 44 E6
Algaida, *Spain* 36 B9
Algar, *Spain* 31 J5
Algarinejo, *Spain* 31 H6
Algarve, *Portugal* 31 J2
Algeciras, *Spain* 31 J5
Algemesí, *Spain* 29 F4
Alger, *Algeria* 75 A5
Algeria ■, *Africa* 75 C5
Alghero, *Italy* 34 B1
Algiers = Alger, *Algeria* 75 A5
Algoa B., *S. Africa* 84 E4
Algodonales, *Spain* 31 J5
Algodor →, *Spain* 30 F7
Algoma, *U.S.A.* 104 C2
Algona, *U.S.A.* 108 D7
Algonac, *U.S.A.* 106 D2
Alhama de Almería, *Spain* 29 J2
Alhama de Aragón, *Spain* 28 D3
Alhama de Granada, *Spain* 31 J7
Alhama de Murcia, *Spain* 29 H3
Alhambra, *Spain* 29 G1
Alhambra, *U.S.A.* 113 L8
Alhaurín el Grande, *Spain* 31 J6
Alhucemas = Al Hoceïma, *Morocco* 74 A4
'Alī al Gharbī, *Iraq* 64 C5
Alī ash Sharqī, *Iraq* 64 C5
Ali Bayramly, *Azerbaijan* 43 G13
'Alī Khēl, *Afghan.* 62 C3
Ali Sahîh, *Djibouti* 77 E5
Alī Shāh, *Iran* 64 B5
Ália, *Italy* 34 E6
'Alīābād, *Khorāsān, Iran* 65 C8
Alīābād, *Kordestān, Iran* 64 C5
'Alīābād, *Yazd, Iran* 65 D7
Aliaga, *Spain* 28 E4
Aliağa, *Turkey* 66 D2
Aliákmon →, *Greece* 39 J5
Alibo, *Ethiopia* 77 F4
Alibunar, *Serbia* 21 K10
Alicante, *Spain* 29 G4
Alicante □, *Spain* 29 G4
Alice, *S. Africa* 84 E4
Alice, *U.S.A.* 109 M5
Alice →, *Queens., Australia* 90 C3
Alice →, *Queens., Australia* 90 B3
Alice, Punta dell', *Italy* 35 C10
Alice Arm, *Canada* 100 B3
Alice Downs, *Australia* 88 C4
Alice Springs, *Australia* 90 C1
Alicedale, *S. Africa* 84 E4
Aliceville, *U.S.A.* 105 J1
Alick Cr. →, *Australia* 90 C3
Alicudi, I., *Italy* 35 D7
Alida, *Canada* 101 D8
Aligarh, *Raj., India* 62 G7
Aligarh, *Ut. P., India* 62 F8
Alīgūdarz, *Iran* 65 C6
Alijó, *Portugal* 30 D3
Alimena, *Italy* 35 E7
Alimnía, *Greece* 37 C9
Alingsås, *Sweden* 11 G6
Alipur, *Pakistan* 62 E4
Alipur Duar, *India* 61 F16
Aliquippa, *U.S.A.* 106 F4
Aliste →, *Spain* 30 D5
Alitus, *Lithuania* 40 D4
Alivérion, *Greece* 39 L7
Aliwal North, *S. Africa* 84 E4
Alix, *Canada* 100 C6
Aljezur, *Portugal* 31 H2
Aljustrel, *Portugal* 31 H2
Alkamari, *Niger* 79 C7
Alken, *Belgium* 17 G6
Alkmaar, *Neths.* 16 C5
All American Canal, *U.S.A.* 111 K6
Allada, *Benin* 79 D5
Allah Dad, *Pakistan* 62 G2
Allahabad, *India* 63 G9
Allakh-Yun, *Russia* 45 C14
Allal Tazi, *Morocco* 74 B3
Allan, *Canada* 101 C7
Allanche, *France* 26 C6
Allanmyo, *Burma* 61 K19
Allanridge, *S. Africa* 84 D4
Allanwater, *Canada* 98 B1
Allaqi, Wadi →, *Egypt* 76 C3
Allariz, *Spain* 30 C3
Allassac, *France* 26 C5
Alle, *Belgium* 17 J5
Allegan, *U.S.A.* 104 D3
Allegany, *U.S.A.* 106 D6
Allegheny →, *U.S.A.* 106 F5
Allegheny Plateau, *U.S.A.* 104 G6
Allegheny Reservoir, *U.S.A.* 106 E6
Allègre, *France* 26 C7
Allen, *Argentina* 128 A3
Allen, Bog of, *Ireland* 15 C4
Allen, L., *Ireland* 15 B3
Allende, *Mexico* 114 B4
Allentown, *U.S.A.* 107 F9
Alleppey, *India* 60 Q10
Aller →, *Germany* 18 C5
Alleur, *Belgium* 17 G7
Allevard, *France* 27 C10
Alliance, *Surinam* 121 B7
Alliance, *Nebr., U.S.A.* 108 D3
Alliance, *Ohio, U.S.A.* 106 F3
Allier □, *France* 26 B6
Allier →, *France* 25 F10
Allingåbro, *Denmark* 11 H4
Alliston, *Canada* 98 D4
Alloa, *U.K.* 14 E5
Allora, *Australia* 91 D5
Allos, *France* 27 D10
Alluitsup Paa = Sydprøven, *Greenland* 4 C5
Alma, *Canada* 99 C5
Alma, *Ga., U.S.A.* 105 K4
Alma, *Kans., U.S.A.* 108 F6
Alma, *Mich., U.S.A.* 104 D3
Alma, *Nebr., U.S.A.* 108 E5
Alma, *Wis., U.S.A.* 108 C9
Alma Ata, *Kazakhstan* 44 E8
Almada, *Portugal* 31 G1
Almaden, *Australia* 90 B3
Almadén, *Spain* 31 G6
Almagro, *Spain* 31 G7
Almanor, L., *U.S.A.* 110 F3
Almansa, *Spain* 29 G3
Almanza, *Spain* 30 C5
Almanzor, Pico de, *Spain* 30 E5
Almanzora →, *Spain* 29 H3
Almas, *Brazil* 123 D2
Almaty = Alma Ata, *Kazakhstan* 44 E8
Almazán, *Spain* 28 D2
Almazora, *Spain* 28 F4
Almeirim, *Brazil* 121 D7
Almeirim, *Portugal* 31 F2
Almelo, *Neths.* 16 D9
Almenar, *Spain* 28 D2
Almenara, *Brazil* 123 E3
Almenara, *Spain* 28 F4
Almenara, Sierra de, *Spain* 29 H3
Almendralejo, *Spain* 31 G4
Almería, *Spain* 29 J2
Almería □, *Spain* 29 H2
Almería, G. de, *Spain* 29 J2
Almirante, *Panama* 116 E3
Almirante Montt, G., *Chile* 128 D2
Almirós, *Greece* 39 K5
Almiroú, Kólpos, *Greece* 37 D6
Almodôvar, *Portugal* 31 H2
Almodóvar del Campo, *Spain* 31 G6
Almogia, *Spain* 31 J6
Almonaster la Real, *Spain* 31 H4
Almont, *U.S.A.* 106 D1
Almonte, *Canada* 107 A8
Almonte →, *Spain* 31 F4
Almora, *India* 63 E8
Almoradi, *Spain* 29 G4
Almorox, *Spain* 30 E6
Almoustarat, *Mali* 79 B5
Almuñécar, *Spain* 31 J7
Alnif, *Morocco* 74 B3
Alnwick, *U.K.* 12 B6
Aloi, *Uganda* 82 B3
Alon, *Burma* 61 H19
Alor, *Indonesia* 57 F6
Alor Setar, *Malaysia* 59 J3
Alora, *Spain* 31 J6
Alosno, *Spain* 31 H3
Alougoum, *Morocco* 74 B3
Aloysius, Mt., *Australia* 89 E4
Alpaugh, *U.S.A.* 112 K7
Alpedrinha, *Portugal* 30 E3
Alpena, *U.S.A.* 104 C4
Alpercatas →, *Brazil* 122 C3
Alpes-de-Haute-Provence □, *France* 27 D10
Alpes-Maritimes □, *France* 27 E11
Alpha, *Australia* 90 C4
Alphen, *Neths.* 17 F5
Alphen aan den Rijn, *Neths.* 16 D5
Alpiarça, *Portugal* 31 F2
Alpine, *Ariz., U.S.A.* 111 K9
Alpine, *Calif., U.S.A.* 113 N10
Alpine, *Tex., U.S.A.* 109 K3
Alpnach, *Switz.* 23 C6
Alps, *Europe* 6 F7
Alpu, *Turkey* 66 D4
Alrø, *Denmark* 11 J4
Alroy Downs, *Australia* 90 B2
Alsace, *France* 25 D14
Alsask, *Canada* 101 C7
Alsásua, *Spain* 28 C2
Alsen, *Sweden* 10 A7
Alsfeld, *Germany* 18 E5
Alsten, *Norway* 8 D12
Alta, *Norway* 8 B17
Alta, Sierra, *Spain* 28 E3
Alta Gracia, *Argentina* 126 C3
Alta Lake, *Canada* 100 C4
Alta Sierra, *U.S.A.* 113 K8
Altaelva →, *Norway* 8 B17
Altafjorden, *Norway* 8 A17
Altagracia, *Venezuela* 120 A3
Altagracia de Orituco, *Venezuela* 120 B4
Altai = Aerhtai Shan, *Mongolia* 54 B4
Altamachi →, *Bolivia* 124 D4
Altamaha →, *U.S.A.* 105 K5
Altamira, *Brazil* 121 D7
Altamira, *Chile* 126 B2
Altamira, *Colombia* 120 C2
Altamira, *Mexico* 115 C5
Altamira, Cuevas de, *Spain* 30 B6
Altamont, *U.S.A.* 107 D10
Altamura, *Italy* 35 B9
Altanbulag, *Mongolia* 54 A5
Altar, *Mexico* 114 A2
Altata, *Mexico* 114 C3
Altavista, *U.S.A.* 104 G6
Altay, *China* 54 B3
Altdorf, *Switz.* 23 C7
Alte Mellum, *Germany* 18 B4
Altea, *Spain* 29 G4
Altenberg, *Germany* 18 E9
Altenbruch, *Germany* 18 B4
Altenburg, *Germany* 18 E8
Altenkirchen, *Mecklenburg-Vorpommern, Germany* 18 A9
Altenkirchen, *Rhld-Pfz., Germany* 18 E3
Altenteptow, *Germany* 18 B9
Alter do Chão, *Portugal* 31 F3
Altıntas, *Turkey* 66 D4
Altiplano, *Bolivia* 124 D4
Altkirch, *France* 25 E14
Altmühl →, *Germany* 19 G7
Alto Adige = Trentino-Alto Adige □, *Italy* 32 B8
Alto Araguaia, *Brazil* 125 D7
Alto Cuchumatanes = Cuchumatanes, Sierra de los, *Guatemala* 116 C1
Alto del Inca, *Chile* 126 A2
Alto Garças, *Brazil* 125 D7
Alto Iriri →, *Brazil* 125 B7
Alto Ligonha, *Mozam.* 83 F4
Alto Molocue, *Mozam.* 83 F4
Alto Paraguai, *Brazil* 125 C6
Alto Paraguay □, *Paraguay* 126 A4
Alto Paraná □, *Paraguay* 127 B5
Alto Parnaíba, *Brazil* 122 C2
Alto Purús →, *Peru* 124 B3
Alto Río Senguerr, *Argentina* 128 C2
Alto Santo, *Brazil* 122 C4
Alto Sucuriú, *Brazil* 125 D7
Alto Turi, *Brazil* 122 B2
Alton, *Canada* 106 C4
Alton, *U.S.A.* 108 F9
Alton Downs, *Australia* 91 D2
Altoona, *U.S.A.* 106 F6
Altopáscio, *Italy* 32 E7
Altos, *Brazil* 122 C3
Altötting, *Germany* 19 G8
Altstätten, *Switz.* 23 B9
Altūn Kūprī, *Iraq* 64 C5
Altun Shan, *China* 54 C3
Alturas, *U.S.A.* 110 F3
Altus, *U.S.A.* 109 H5
Alubijid, *Phil.* 55 G6
Alucra, *Turkey* 43 F8
Alūksne, *Latvia* 40 C5
Alùla, *Somali Rep.* 68 E5
Alunite, *U.S.A.* 113 K12
Alupka, *Ukraine* 42 D6
Alushta, *Ukraine* 42 D6
Alusi, *Indonesia* 57 F8
Alustante, *Spain* 28 E3
Al'Uzayr, *Iraq* 64 D5
Alva, *U.S.A.* 109 G5
Alvaiázere, *Portugal* 30 F2
Älvängen, *Sweden* 11 G6
Alvarado, *Mexico* 115 D5
Alvarado, *U.S.A.* 109 J6
Alvarães, *Brazil* 121 D5
Alvaro Obregón, Presa, *Mexico* 114 B3
Alvdal, *Norway* 10 B4
Alvear, *Argentina* 126 B4
Alverca, *Portugal* 31 G1
Alveringen, *Belgium* 17 F1
Alvesta, *Sweden* 9 H13
Alvie, *Australia* 91 F3
Alvin, *U.S.A.* 109 L7
Alvinston, *Canada* 106 D3
Alvito, *Portugal* 31 G3
Älvkarleby, *Sweden* 9 F14
Älvros, *Sweden* 10 B8
Älvsborgs län □, *Sweden* 11 F6
Älvsbyn, *Sweden* 8 D16
Älvsered, *Sweden* 11 G6
Alwar, *India* 62 F7
Alxa Zuoqi, *China* 50 E3
Alyaskitovyy, *Russia* 45 C15
Alyata, *Azerbaijan* 43 G13
Alyth, *U.K.* 14 E5
Alzada, *U.S.A.* 108 C2
Alzano Lombardo, *Italy* 32 C6
Alzette →, *Lux.* 17 J8
Alzey, *Germany* 19 F4
Am Dam, *Chad* 73 F9
Am-Timan, *Chad* 73 F9
Amacuro □, *Venezuela* 121 B5
Amadeus, L., *Australia* 89 D5
Amâdi, *Sudan* 77 F3
Amadi, *Zaïre* 82 B2
Amadjuak, *Canada* 97 B12
Amadjuak L., *Canada* 97 B12
Amadora, *Portugal* 31 G1
Amagasaki, *Japan* 49 G7
Amager, *Denmark* 11 J6
Amakusa-Shotō, *Japan* 49 H5
Amalfi, *Colombia* 120 B2
Amalfi, *Italy* 35 B7
Amaliás, *Greece* 39 M4
Amalner, *India* 60 J9
Amambaí, *Brazil* 127 A4
Amambaí →, *Brazil* 127 A5
Amambay □, *Paraguay* 127 A4
Amambay, Cordillera de, *S. Amer.* 127 A4
Amami-Guntō, *Japan* 49 L4
Amami-Ō-Shima, *Japan* 49 L4
Amana →, *Venezuela* 121 B5
Amaná, L., *Brazil* 121 D5
Amanda Park, *U.S.A.* 112 C3
Amándola, *Italy* 33 F10
Amangeldy, *Kazakhstan* 44 D7
Amantea, *Italy* 35 C9
Amapá, *Brazil* 121 C7
Amapá □, *Brazil* 121 C7
Amapari, *Brazil* 121 C7
Amara, *Sudan* 77 E3
Amarante, *Brazil* 122 C3
Amarante, *Portugal* 30 D2
Amarante do Maranhão, *Brazil* 122 C2
Amaranth, *Canada* 101 C9
Amareleja, *Portugal* 31 G3
Amargosa, *Brazil* 123 D4
Amargosa →, *U.S.A.* 113 J10
Amargosa Range, *U.S.A.* 113 J10
Amári, *Greece* 37 D6
Amarillo, *U.S.A.* 109 H4
Amaro, Mt., *Italy* 33 F11
Amaro Leite, *Brazil* 123 D2
Amarpur, *India* 63 G12
Amasra, *Turkey* 66 C5
Amassama, *Nigeria* 79 D6
Amasya, *Turkey* 66 C6
Amasya □, *Turkey* 66 C6
Amataurá, *Brazil* 120 D4
Amatikulu, *S. Africa* 85 D5
Amatitlán, *Guatemala* 116 D1
Amatrice, *Italy* 33 F10
Amay, *Belgium* 17 G6
Amazon = Amazonas →, *S. Amer.* 121 D7
Amazonas □, *Brazil* 125 B5
Amazonas □, *Peru* 124 B2
Amazonas □, *Venezuela* 120 C4
Amazonas →, *S. Amer.* 121 D7
Ambahakily, *Madag.* 85 C7
Ambala, *India* 62 D7
Ambalavao, *Madag.* 85 C8
Ambalindum, *Australia* 90 C2
Ambam, *Cameroon* 80 D2
Ambanja, *Madag.* 85 A8
Ambarchik, *Russia* 45 C17
Ambarijeby, *Madag.* 85 A8
Ambaro, Helodranon', *Madag.* 85 A8
Ambartsevo, *Russia* 44 D9
Ambato, *Ecuador* 120 D2
Ambato, Sierra de, *Argentina* 126 B2
Ambato Boeny, *Madag.* 85 B8
Ambatofinandrahana, *Madag.* 85 C8
Ambatolampy, *Madag.* 85 B8
Ambatondrazaka, *Madag.* 85 B8
Ambatosoratra, *Madag.* 85 B8
Ambenja, *Madag.* 85 B8
Amberg, *Germany* 19 F7
Ambergris Cay, *Belize* 115 D7
Ambérieu-en-Bugey, *France* 27 C9
Amberley, *N.Z.* 87 K4
Ambert, *France* 26 C7
Ambidédi, *Mali* 78 C2
Ambikapur, *India* 63 H10
Ambikol, *Sudan* 76 C3
Ambilobé, *Madag.* 85 A8
Ambinanindrano, *Madag.* 85 C8
Ambjörnarp, *Sweden* 11 G7
Ambleside, *U.K.* 12 C5
Amblève, *Belgium* 17 H8
Amblève →, *Belgium* 17 H7
Ambo, *Ethiopia* 77 E4
Ambo, *Peru* 124 C2
Ambodifototra, *Madag.* 85 B8
Ambodilazana, *Madag.* 85 B8
Ambohimahasoa, *Madag.* 85 C8
Ambohimanga, *Madag.* 85 C8
Ambohitra, *Madag.* 85 A8
Ambon, *Indonesia* 57 E7
Amboseli L., *Kenya* 82 C4
Ambositra, *Madag.* 85 C8
Ambovombé, *Madag.* 85 D8
Amboy, *U.S.A.* 113 L11
Amboyna I., *S. China Sea* 56 C4
Ambridge, *U.S.A.* 106 F4
Ambriz, *Angola* 80 F2
Amby, *Australia* 91 D4
Amchitka I., *U.S.A.* 96 C1
Amderma, *Russia* 44 C7
Ameca, *Mexico* 114 C4
Ameca →, *Mexico* 114 C3
Amecameca, *Mexico* 115 D5
Ameland, *Neths.* 16 B7
Amélia, *Italy* 33 F9
Amélie-les-Bains-Palalda, *France* 26 F6
Amen, *Russia* 45 C18
Amendolaro, *Italy* 35 C9
America, *Neths.* 17 F7
American Falls, *U.S.A.* 110 E7
American Falls Reservoir, *U.S.A.* 110 E7
American Highland, *Antarctica* 5 D6
American Samoa ■, *Pac. Oc.* 87 B13
Americana, *Brazil* 127 A6
Americus, *U.S.A.* 105 J3
Amersfoort, *Neths.* 16 D6
Amersfoort, *S. Africa* 85 D4
Amery, *Australia* 89 F2
Amery, *Canada* 101 B10
Amery Ice Shelf, *Antarctica* 5 C6
Ames, *U.S.A.* 108 E8
Amesbury, *U.S.A.* 107 D14
Amfíklia, *Greece* 39 L5
Amfilokhía, *Greece* 39 L4
Amga, *Russia* 45 C14
Amga →, *Russia* 45 C14
Amgu, *Russia* 45 E14
Amgun →, *Russia* 45 D14
Amherst, *Burma* 61 L20
Amherst, *Canada* 99 C7
Amherst, *Mass., U.S.A.* 107 D12
Amherst, *N.Y., U.S.A.* 106 D6
Amherst, *Ohio, U.S.A.* 106 E2
Amherst, *Tex., U.S.A.* 109 H3
Amherst I., *Canada* 107 B8
Amherstburg, *Canada* 98 D3
Amiata, Mte., *Italy* 33 F8
Amiens, *France* 25 C9
Amindaion, *Greece* 39 J4
Amīrābād, *Iran* 64 C5
Amirante Is., *Seychelles* 3 E12
Amisk L., *Canada* 101 C8
Amistad, Presa de la, *Mexico* 114 B4
Amite, *U.S.A.* 109 K9
Amizmiz, *Morocco* 74 B3
Åmli, *Norway* 11 F2
Amlwch, *U.K.* 12 D3
Amm Adam, *Sudan* 77 D4
'Ammān, *Jordan* 69 D4
Ammanford, *U.K.* 13 F3
Ammassalik = Angmagssalik, *Greenland* 4 C6
Ammerån, *Sweden* 10 A10
Ammerån →, *Sweden* 10 A10
Ammersee, *Germany* 19 G7
Ammerzoden, *Neths.* 16 E6
Amnat Charoen, *Thailand* 58 E5
Amo Jiang →, *China* 52 F3
Āmol, *Iran* 65 B7
Amorebieta, *Spain* 28 B2
Amorgós, *Greece* 39 N8
Amory, *U.S.A.* 105 J1

Amos, *Canada* 98 C4
Åmot, *Buskerud, Norway* 10 E3
Åmot, *Telemark, Norway* 10 E2
Åmotsdal, *Norway* 10 E2
Amour, Djebel, *Algeria* 75 B5
Amoy = Xiamen, *China* 53 E12
Ampang, *Malaysia* 59 L3
Ampanihy, *Madag.* 85 C7
Ampasindava, Helodranon', *Madag.* 85 A8
Ampasindava, Saikanosy, *Madag.* 85 A8
Ampato, Nevado, *Peru* 124 D3
Ampenan, *Indonesia* 56 F5
Amper, *Nigeria* 79 D6
Amper →, *Germany* 19 G7
Ampère, *Algeria* 75 A6
Ampezzo, *Italy* 33 B9
Amposta, *Spain* 28 E5
Ampotaka, *Madag.* 85 D7
Ampoza, *Madag.* 85 C7
Amqui, *Canada* 99 C6
Amravati, *India* 60 J10
Amreli, *India* 62 J4
Amrenene el Kasba, *Algeria* 75 D5
Amriswil, *Switz.* 23 A8
Amritsar, *India* 62 D6
Amroha, *India* 63 E8
Amrum, *Germany* 18 A4
Amsel, *Algeria* 75 D6
Amsterdam, *Neths.* 16 D5
Amsterdam, *U.S.A.* 107 D10
Amsterdam, I., *Ind. Oc.* 3 F13
Amstetten, *Austria* 21 G4
Amudarya →, *Uzbekistan* 44 E6
Amundsen Gulf, *Canada* 96 A7
Amundsen Sea, *Antarctica* 5 D15
Amuntai, *Indonesia* 56 E5
Amur →, *Russia* 45 D15
Amurang, *Indonesia* 57 D6
Amuri Pass, *N.Z.* 87 K4
Amurrio, *Spain* 28 B1
Amursk, *Russia* 45 D14
Amurzet, *Russia* 45 E14
Amusco, *Spain* 30 C6
Amvrakikós Kólpos, *Greece* 39 L4
Amvrosiyevka, *Ukraine* 43 C8
Amyderya = Amudarya →, *Uzbekistan* 44 E6
Amzeglouf, *Algeria* 75 C5
An Bien, *Vietnam* 59 H5
An Hoa, *Vietnam* 58 E7
An Khe, *Vietnam* 58 F7
An Nabatīyah at Tahta, *Lebanon* 69 B4
An Nabk, *Si. Arabia* 64 D3
An Nabk, *Syria* 69 A5
An Nabk Abū Qaşr, *Si. Arabia* 64 D3
An Nafūd, *Si. Arabia* 64 D4
An Najaf, *Iraq* 64 C5
An Nāşirīyah, *Iraq* 64 D5
An Nhon, *Vietnam* 58 F7
An Nîl □, *Sudan* 76 D3
An Nîl el Abyad □, *Sudan* 77 E3
An Nîl el Azraq □, *Sudan* 77 E3
An Nu'ayrīyah, *Si. Arabia* 65 E6
An Nuwayb'ī, W. →, *Si. Arabia* 69 F3
An Thoi, Dao, *Vietnam* 59 H4
An Uaimh, *Ireland* 15 C5
Anabar →, *Russia* 45 B12
'Anabtā, *Jordan* 69 C4
Anaco, *Venezuela* 121 B5
Anaconda, *U.S.A.* 110 C7
Anacortes, *U.S.A.* 112 B4
Anacuao, Mt., *Phil.* 55 C4
Anadarko, *U.S.A.* 109 H5
Anadia, *Brazil* 122 C4
Anadia, *Portugal* 30 E2
Anadolu, *Turkey* 66 D4
Anadyr, *Russia* 45 C18
Anadyr →, *Russia* 45 C18
Anadyrskiy Zaliv, *Russia* 45 C19
Anáfi, *Greece* 39 N8
Anafópoulo, *Greece* 39 N8
Anaga, Pta. de, *Canary Is.* 36 F3
Anagni, *Italy* 34 A6
'Ānah, *Iraq* 64 C4
Anaheim, *U.S.A.* 113 M9
Anahim Lake, *Canada* 100 C3
Anáhuac, *Mexico* 114 B4
Anajás, *Brazil* 122 B2
Anajatuba, *Brazil* 122 B3
Anakapalle, *India* 61 L13
Anakie, *Australia* 90 C4
Anaklia, *Georgia* 43 E9
Analalava, *Madag.* 85 A8
Análipsis, *Greece* 37 A3
Anamã, *Brazil* 121 D5
Anambar →, *Pakistan* 62 D3
Anambas, Kepulauan, *Indonesia* 56 D3
Anambas Is. = Anambas, Kepulauan, *Indonesia* 56 D3
Anambra □, *Nigeria* 79 D6
Anamoose, *U.S.A.* 108 B4
Anamosa, *U.S.A.* 108 D9
Anamur, *Turkey* 66 E5
Anamur Burnu, *Turkey* 66 E5
Anan, *Japan* 49 H7
Anand, *India* 62 H5
Anantnag, *India* 63 C6
Ananyev, *Ukraine* 42 C3
Anapa, *Russia* 42 D7
Anapodháris →, *Greece* 37 E7
Anápolis, *Brazil* 123 E2
Anapu →, *Brazil* 121 D7
Anār, *Iran* 65 D7
Anārak, *Iran* 65 C7
Anatolia = Anadolu, *Turkey* 66 D4
Anatone, *U.S.A.* 110 C5
Anatsogno, *Madag.* 85 C7
Añatuya, *Argentina* 126 B3
Anauá →, *Brazil* 121 C5
Anaunethad L., *Canada* 101 A8
Anavilhanas, Arquipélago das, *Brazil* 121 D5
Anaye, *Niger* 73 E7
Anbyŏn, *N. Korea* 51 E14
Ancash □, *Peru* 124 B2
Ancenis, *France* 24 E5
Ancho, Canal, *Chile* 128 D2
Anchor Bay, *U.S.A.* 112 G3
Anchorage, *U.S.A.* 96 B5
Anci, *China* 50 E9
Ancohuma, Nevada, *Bolivia* 124 D4
Ancón, *Peru* 124 C2
Ancona, *Italy* 33 E10
Ancud, *Chile* 128 B2
Ancud, G. de, *Chile* 128 B2
Andacollo, *Argentina* 126 D1
Andacollo, *Chile* 126 C1
Andado, *Australia* 90 D2
Andahuaylas, *Peru* 124 C3
Andalgalá, *Argentina* 126 B2
Åndalsnes, *Norway* 10 B1
Andalucía □, *Spain* 31 H6
Andalusia, *U.S.A.* 105 K2
Andalusia □ = Andalucía □, *Spain* 31 H6
Andaman Is., *Ind. Oc.* 46 H13
Andaman Sea, *Ind. Oc.* 56 B1
Andara, *Namibia* 84 B3
Andaraí, *Brazil* 123 D3
Andeer, *Switz.* 23 C8
Andelfingen, *Switz.* 23 A7
Andelot, *France* 25 D12
Andenne, *Belgium* 17 H6
Andéranboukane, *Mali* 79 B5
Anderlecht, *Belgium* 17 G4
Anderlues, *Belgium* 17 H4
Andermatt, *Switz.* 23 C7
Andernach, *Germany* 18 E3
Andernos-les-Bains, *France* 26 D2
Anderslöv, *Sweden* 11 J7
Anderson, *Calif., U.S.A.* 110 F2
Anderson, *Ind., U.S.A.* 104 E3
Anderson, *Mo., U.S.A.* 109 G7
Anderson, *S.C., U.S.A.* 105 H4
Anderson →, *Canada* 96 B7
Anderson, Mt., *S. Africa* 85 D5
Andes = Andes, Cord. de los, *S. Amer.* 124 C3
Andes, *S. Amer.* 124 C2
Andes, Cord. de los, *S. Amer.* 124 C3
Andfjorden, *Norway* 8 B14
Andhra Pradesh □, *India* 60 L11
Andijon = Andizhan, *Uzbekistan* 44 E8
Andikíthira, *Greece* 39 P6
Andīmeshk, *Iran* 65 C6
Andímilos, *Greece* 39 N7
Andípaxoi, *Greece* 39 K3
Andizhan, *Uzbekistan* 44 E8
Andoany, *Madag.* 85 A8
Andoas, *Peru* 120 D2
Andong, *S. Korea* 51 F15
Andongwei, *China* 51 G10
Andorra ■, *Europe* 28 C6
Andorra La Vella, *Andorra* 28 C6
Andover, *U.K.* 13 F6
Andover, *Mass., U.S.A.* 107 D13
Andover, *N.Y., U.S.A.* 106 D7
Andover, *Ohio, U.S.A.* 106 E4
Andradina, *Brazil* 123 F1
Andrahary, Mt., *Madag.* 85 A8
Andraitx, *Spain* 36 B9
Andramasina, *Madag.* 85 B8
Andranopasy, *Madag.* 85 C7
Andreanof Is., *U.S.A.* 96 C2
Andreapol, *Russia* 40 C8
Andrespol, *Poland* 20 D9
Andrewilla, *Australia* 91 D2
Andrews, *S.C., U.S.A.* 105 J6
Andrews, *Tex., U.S.A.* 109 J3
Ándria, *Italy* 35 A9
Andriba, *Madag.* 85 B8
Andrijevica, *Montenegro* 21 N9
Andrítsaina, *Greece* 39 M4
Androka, *Madag.* 85 C7
Andropov = Rybinsk, *Russia* 41 B11
Ándros, *Greece* 39 M7
Andros I., *Bahamas* 116 B4
Andros Town, *Bahamas* 116 B4
Andújar, *Spain* 31 G6
Andulo, *Angola* 80 G3
Anegada, B., *Argentina* 128 B4
Anegada I., *Virgin Is.* 117 C7
Anegada Passage, *W. Indies* 117 C7
Anécho, *Togo* 79 D5
Añelo, *Argentina* 128 A3
Anergane, *Morocco* 74 B3
Aneto, Pico de, *Spain* 28 C5
Añez, *Bolivia* 125 D5
Anfu, *China* 53 D10
Ang Thong, *Thailand* 58 E3
Angamos, Punta, *Chile* 126 A1
Ang'angxi, *China* 54 B7
Angara →, *Russia* 45 D10
Angarab, *Ethiopia* 77 E4
Angarsk, *Russia* 45 D11
Angas Downs, *Australia* 89 E5
Angas Hills, *Australia* 88 D4
Angaston, *Australia* 91 E2
Ånge, *Sweden* 10 B9
Ángel de la Guarda, I., *Mexico* 114 B2
Angel Falls, *Venezuela* 121 B5
Angeles, *Phil.* 55 D4
Ängelholm, *Sweden* 11 H6
Angellala, *Australia* 91 D4
Angels Camp, *U.S.A.* 111 G3
Anger →, *Ethiopia* 77 F4
Angereb →, *Ethiopia* 77 E4
Ångermanälven →, *Sweden* 10 B12
Angermünde, *Germany* 18 B10
Angers, *Canada* 107 A9
Angers, *France* 24 E6
Angerville, *France* 25 D8
Ångesån →, *Sweden* 8 C17
Anghiari, *Italy* 33 E9
Angical, *Brazil* 123 D3
Angikuni L., *Canada* 101 A9
Angkor, *Cambodia* 58 F4
Anglés, *Spain* 28 D7
Anglesey, *U.K.* 12 D3
Anglet, *France* 26 E2
Angleton, *U.S.A.* 109 L7
Angleur, *Belgium* 17 G7
Anglin →, *France* 26 B4
Anglisidhes, *Cyprus* 37 E12
Anglure, *France* 25 D10
Angmagssalik, *Greenland* 4 C6
Ango, *Zaïre* 82 B2
Angoche, *Mozam.* 83 F4
Angoche, I., *Mozam.* 83 F4
Angol, *Chile* 126 D1
Angola, *Ind., U.S.A.* 104 E3
Angola, *N.Y., U.S.A.* 106 D5
Angola ■, *Africa* 81 G3
Angoon, *U.S.A.* 100 B2
Angoulême, *France* 26 C4
Angoumois, *France* 26 C4
Angra dos Reis, *Brazil* 127 A7
Angren, *Uzbekistan* 44 E8
Angtassom, *Cambodia* 59 G5
Angu, *Zaïre* 82 B1
Anguang, *China* 51 B12
Anguilla ■, *W. Indies* 117 C7
Anguo, *China* 50 E8
Angurugu, *Australia* 90 A2
Angus, Braes of, *U.K.* 14 E5
Anhanduí →, *Brazil* 127 A5
Anhée, *Belgium* 17 H5
Anholt, *Denmark* 11 H5
Anhua, *China* 53 C8
Anhui □, *China* 53 B11
Anhwei □ = Anhui □, *China* 53 B11
Anichab, *Namibia* 84 C1
Anicuns, *Brazil* 123 E2
Ánidhros, *Greece* 39 N8
Anie, *Togo* 79 D5
Animas, *U.S.A.* 111 L9
Ånimskog, *Sweden* 11 F6
Anina, *Romania* 38 D4
Anivorano, *Madag.* 85 B8
Anjar, *India* 62 H4
Anjidiv I., *India* 60 M9
Anjou, *France* 24 E6
Anjozorobe, *Madag.* 85 B8
Anju, *N. Korea* 51 E13
Anka, *Nigeria* 79 C6
Ankaboa, Tanjona, *Madag.* 85 C7
Ankang, *China* 50 H5
Ankara, *Turkey* 66 D5
Ankara □, *Turkey* 66 D5
Ankaramena, *Madag.* 85 C8
Ankazoabo, *Madag.* 85 C7
Ankazobe, *Madag.* 85 B8
Ankisabe, *Madag.* 85 B8
Anklam, *Germany* 18 B9
Ankober, *Ethiopia* 77 F4
Ankoro, *Zaïre* 82 D2
Anlong, *China* 52 E5
Anlu, *China* 53 B9
Anmyŏn-do, *S. Korea* 51 F14
Ann, *Sweden* 10 A6
Ann, C., *U.S.A.* 107 D14
Ann Arbor, *U.S.A.* 104 D4
Anna, *Russia* 41 F12
Anna, *U.S.A.* 109 G10
Anna Plains, *Australia* 88 C3
Anna Regina, *Guyana* 121 B6
Annaba, *Algeria* 75 A6
Annaberg-Buchholz, *Germany* 18 E8
Annalee →, *Ireland* 15 B4
Annam = Trung-Phan, *Vietnam* 58 E7
Annamitique, Chaîne, *Asia* 58 D6
Annan, *U.K.* 14 G5
Annan →, *U.K.* 14 G5
Annapolis, *U.S.A.* 104 F7
Annapolis Royal, *Canada* 99 D6
Annapurna, *Nepal* 63 E10
Annean, L., *Australia* 89 E2
Anneberg, *Sweden* 11 G6
Annecy, *France* 27 C10
Annecy, L. d', *France* 27 C10
Annemasse, *France* 27 B10
Anning, *China* 52 E4
Anningie, *Australia* 88 D5
Anniston, *U.S.A.* 105 J3
Annobón, *Atl. Oc.* 71 G4
Annonay, *France* 27 C8
Annot, *France* 27 E10
Annotto Bay, *Jamaica* 116 C4
Annuello, *Australia* 91 E3
Annville, *U.S.A.* 107 F8
Annweiler, *Germany* 19 F3
Áno Viánnos, *Greece* 37 D7
Anoka, *U.S.A.* 108 C8
Anorotsangana, *Madag.* 85 A8
Anóyia, *Greece* 37 D6
Anping, *Hebei, China* 50 E8
Anping, *Liaoning, China* 51 D12
Anpu Gang, *China* 52 G7
Anqing, *China* 53 B11
Anqiu, *China* 51 F10
Anren, *China* 53 D9
Ans, *Belgium* 17 G7
Ansai, *China* 50 F5
Ansbach, *Germany* 19 F6
Anseba →, *Eritrea* 77 D4
Anserma, *Colombia* 120 B2
Anseroeul, *Belgium* 17 G3
Anshan, *China* 54 B7
Anshan, *Liaoning, China* 51 D12
Anshun, *China* 52 D5
Ansião, *Portugal* 30 F2
Ansirabe, *Madag.* 85 B8
Ansley, *U.S.A.* 108 E5
Ansó, *Spain* 28 C4
Anson, *U.S.A.* 109 J5
Anson B., *Australia* 88 B5
Ansongo, *Mali* 79 B5
Ansonia, *U.S.A.* 107 E11
Anstruther, *U.K.* 14 E6
Ansudu, *Indonesia* 57 E9
Antabamba, *Peru* 124 C3
Antakya, *Turkey* 66 E7
Antalaha, *Madag.* 85 A9
Antalya, *Turkey* 66 E4
Antalya □, *Turkey* 66 E4
Antalya Körfezi, *Turkey* 66 E4
Antananarivo, *Madag.* 85 B8
Antananarivo □, *Madag.* 85 B8
Antanimbaribe, *Madag.* 85 C7
Antarctic Pen., *Antarctica* 5 C18
Antarctica 5 E3
Antelope, *Zimbabwe* 83 G2
Antenor Navarro, *Brazil* 122 C4
Antequera, *Paraguay* 126 A4
Antequera, *Spain* 31 H6
Antero, Mt., *U.S.A.* 111 G10
Anthony, *Kans., U.S.A.* 109 G5
Anthony, *N. Mex., U.S.A.* 111 K10
Anthony Lagoon, *Australia* 90 B2
Anti Atlas, *Morocco* 74 C2
Anti-Lebanon = Ash Sharqi, Al Jabal, *Lebanon* 69 B5
Antibes, *France* 27 E11
Antibes, C. d', *France* 27 E11
Anticosti, I. d', *Canada* 99 C7
Antifer, C. d', *France* 24 C7
Antigo, *U.S.A.* 108 C10
Antigonish, *Canada* 99 C7
Antigua, *Canary Is.* 36 F5
Antigua, *Guatemala* 116 D1
Antigua, *W. Indies* 117 C7
Antigua & Barbuda ■, *W. Indies* 117 C7
Antilla, *Cuba* 116 B4
Antimony, *U.S.A.* 111 G8
Antioch, *U.S.A.* 112 G5
Antioche, Pertuis d', *France* 26 B2
Antioquia, *Colombia* 120 B2
Antioquia □, *Colombia* 120 B2
Antipodes Is., *Pac. Oc.* 92 M9
Antler, *U.S.A.* 108 A4
Antler →, *Canada* 101 D8
Antlers, *U.S.A.* 109 H7
Antofagasta, *Chile* 126 A1
Antofagasta □, *Chile* 126 A2
Antofagasta de la Sierra, *Argentina* 126 B2
Antofalla, *Argentina* 126 B2
Antofalla, Salar de, *Argentina* 126 B2
Antoing, *Belgium* 17 G2
Anton, *U.S.A.* 109 J3
Anton Chico, *U.S.A.* 111 J11
Antongila, Helodrano, *Madag.* 85 B8
Antonibé, *Madag.* 85 B8
Antonibé, Presqu'île d', *Madag.* 85 A8
Antonina, *Brazil* 127 B6
Antonito, *U.S.A.* 111 H10
Antonovo, *Kazakhstan* 43 B14
Antrain, *France* 24 D5
Antrim, *U.K.* 15 B5
Antrim □, *U.K.* 15 B5
Antrim, Mts. of, *U.K.* 15 B5
Antrim Plateau, *Australia* 88 C4
Antrodoco, *Italy* 33 F10
Antropovo, *Russia* 41 B13
Antsalova, *Madag.* 85 B7
Antsiranana, *Madag.* 85 A8
Antsohihy, *Madag.* 85 A8
Antsohimbondrona Seranana, *Madag.* 85 A8
Antu, *China* 51 C15
Antwerp = Antwerpen, *Belgium* 17 F4
Antwerp, *U.S.A.* 107 B9
Antwerpen, *Belgium* 17 F4
Antwerpen □, *Belgium* 17 F5
Anupgarh, *India* 62 E5
Anuradhapura, *Sri Lanka* 60 Q12
Anveh, *Iran* 65 E7
Anvers = Antwerpen, *Belgium* 17 F4
Anvers I., *Antarctica* 5 C17
Anxi, *Fujian, China* 53 E12
Anxi, *Gansu, China* 54 B4
Anxiang, *China* 53 C9
Anxious B., *Australia* 91 E1
Anyama, *Ivory C.* 78 D4
Anyang, *China* 50 F8
Anyi, *Jiangxi, China* 53 C10
Anyi, *Shanxi, China* 50 G6
Anyuan, *China* 53 E10
Anza, *U.S.A.* 113 M10
Anze, *China* 50 F7
Anzhero-Sudzhensk, *Russia* 44 D9
Ánzio, *Italy* 34 A5
Anzoátegui □, *Venezuela* 121 B5
Aoga-Shima, *Japan* 49 H9
Aoiz, *Spain* 28 C3
Aomori, *Japan* 48 D10
Aomori □, *Japan* 48 D10
Aonla, *India* 63 E8
Aosta, *Italy* 32 C4
Aoudéras, *Niger* 79 B6
Aouinet Torkoz, *Morocco* 74 C3
Aoukar, *Mali* 74 D4
Aouker, *Mauritania* 78 B3
Aoulef el Arab, *Algeria* 75 C5
Apa →, *S. Amer.* 126 A4
Apache, *U.S.A.* 109 H5
Apalachee B., *U.S.A.* 105 L3
Apalachicola, *U.S.A.* 105 L3
Apalachicola →, *U.S.A.* 105 L3
Apapa, *Nigeria* 79 D5
Apaporis →, *Colombia* 120 D4
Aparecida do Taboado, *Brazil* 123 F1
Aparri, *Phil.* 55 B4
Aparurén, *Venezuela* 121 B5
Apateu, *Romania* 38 C4
Apatin, *Serbia* 21 K8
Apatzingán, *Mexico* 114 D4
Apeldoorn, *Neths.* 16 D7
Apeldoornsch Kanal →, *Neths.* 16 D8
Apen, *Germany* 18 B3
Apennines = Appennini, *Italy* 32 D7
Apere →, *Bolivia* 125 C4
Apia, *W. Samoa* 87 A13
Apiacás, Serra dos, *Brazil* 125 B6
Apiaú →, *Brazil* 121 C5
Apiaú, Serra do, *Brazil* 121 C5
Apidiá →, *Brazil* 125 C5
Apinajé, *Brazil* 123 D2
Apizaco, *Mexico* 115 D5
Aplao, *Peru* 124 D3
Apo, Mt., *Phil.* 57 C7
Apodi, *Brazil* 122 C4
Apolakkiá, *Greece* 37 C9
Apolakkiá, Órmos, *Greece* 37 C9
Apolda, *Germany* 18 D7
Apollonia = Marsá Susah, *Libya* 73 B9
Apollonia, *Greece* 39 N7
Apolo, *Bolivia* 124 C4
Apónguao →, *Venezuela* 121 C5
Aporé, *Brazil* 125 D7
Aporé →, *Brazil* 123 E1
Aporema, *Brazil* 122 A1
Apostle Is., *U.S.A.* 108 B9
Apóstoles, *Argentina* 127 B4
Apostolos Andreas, C., *Cyprus* 37 D13
Apostolovo, *Ukraine* 42 C5
Apoteri, *Guyana* 121 C6
Appalachian Mts., *U.S.A.* 104 G6
Appelscha, *Neths.* 16 C8
Appennini, *Italy* 32 D7
Appennino Ligure, *Italy* 32 D5
Appenzell, *Switz.* 23 B8
Appenzell-Ausser Rhoden □, *Switz.* 23 B8
Appenzell-Inner Rhoden □, *Switz.* 23 B8
Appiano, *Italy* 33 B8
Appingedam, *Neths.* 16 B9
Apple Hill, *Canada* 107 A10
Apple Valley, *U.S.A.* 113 L9
Appleby, *U.K.* 12 C5
Appleton, *U.S.A.* 104 C1
Approuague, *Fr. Guiana* 121 C7
Approuague →, *Fr. Guiana* 121 C7
Apricena, *Italy* 35 A8
Aprigliano, *Italy* 35 C9
Aprília, *Italy* 34 A5
Apsheronsk, *Russia* 43 D8
Apt, *France* 27 E9
Apuane, Alpi, *Italy* 32 D7
Apuaú, *Brazil* 121 D5
Apucarana, *Brazil* 127 A5

Apulia = Púglia □, Italy ..	35	B9
Apure □, Venezuela	120	B4
Apure →, Venezuela	120	B4
Apurímac □, Peru	124	C3
Apurimac →, Peru	124	C3
Apuseni, Munţii, Romania	38	C5
Aqabah = Al 'Aqabah, Jordan	69	F4
'Aqabah, Khalīj al, Red Sea	64	D2
'Aqdā, Iran	65	C7
Aqîq, Sudan	76	D4
Aqîq, Khalîg, Sudan	76	D4
Aqmola = Tselinograd, Kazakhstan	44	D8
Aqrah, Iraq	64	B4
Aqtöbe = Aktyubinsk, Kazakhstan	44	D6
Aquidauana, Brazil	125	E6
Aquidauana →, Brazil ...	125	D6
Aquiles Serdán, Mexico ..	114	B3
Aquin, Haiti	117	C5
Ar Rachidiya, Morocco ..	74	B4
Ar Rafîd, Syria	69	C4
Ar Raḥḥālīyah, Iraq	64	C4
Ar Ramādī, Iraq	64	C4
Ar Ramthā, Jordan	69	C5
Ar Raqqah, Syria	64	C3
Ar Rass, Si. Arabia	64	E4
Ar Rifa'i, Si. Arabia ...	64	D5
Ar Riyāḍ, Si. Arabia ...	64	E5
Ar Ru'ays, Qatar	65	E6
Ar Rukhaymīyah, Iraq ..	64	D5
Ar Ruqayyidah, Si. Arabia	65	E6
Ar Ruṣāfah, Syria	64	C3
Ar Ruṭbah, Iraq	64	C4
Ara, India	63	G11
'Arab, Bahr el →, Sudan	77	F2
Arab, Khalîg el, Egypt ..	76	H6
'Arabābād, Iran	65	C8
Araban, Turkey	67	E7
Arabatskaya Strelka, Ukraine	42	D6
Arabba, Italy	33	B8
Arabelo, Venezuela	121	C5
Arabia, Asia	68	C4
Arabian Desert = Es Sahrâ' Esh Sharqîya, Egypt	76	B3
Arabian Gulf = Gulf, The, Asia	65	E6
Arabian Sea, Ind. Oc. ...	46	H10
Araç, Turkey	66	C5
Aracaju, Brazil	122	D4
Aracataca, Colombia	120	A3
Aracati, Brazil	122	B4
Araçatuba, Brazil	127	A5
Aracena, Spain	31	H4
Aracena, Sierra de, Spain .	31	H4
Araçuaí, Brazil	123	E3
Araçuaí →, Brazil	123	E3
'Arad, Israel	69	D4
Arad, Romania	38	C4
Arada, Chad	73	F9
Aradhippou, Cyprus	37	E12
Arafura Sea, E. Indies ..	57	F8
Aragarças, Brazil	125	D7
Aragats, Armenia	43	F11
Aragón □, Spain	28	D4
Aragón →, Spain	28	C3
Aragona, Italy	34	E6
Aragua □, Venezuela ...	120	B4
Aragua de Barcelona, Venezuela	121	B5
Araguacema, Brazil	122	C2
Araguaçu, Brazil	123	D2
Araguaia →, Brazil	122	C2
Araguaiana, Brazil	125	D7
Araguaína, Brazil	122	C2
Araguari, Brazil	123	E2
Araguari →, Brazil	121	C8
Araguatins, Brazil	122	C2
Araioses, Brazil	122	B3
Arak, Algeria	75	C5
Arāk, Iran	65	C6
Arakan Coast, Burma ...	61	K19
Arakan Yoma, Burma ...	61	K19
Arakli, Turkey	67	C9
Araks = Aras, Rūd-e →, Iran	64	B5
Aral Sea = Aralskoye More, Asia	44	E7
Aralsk, Kazakhstan	44	E7
Aralskoye More, Asia ...	44	E7
Aramac, Australia	90	C4
Arambag, India	63	H12
Aran I., Ireland	15	B3
Aran Is., Ireland	15	C2
Aranda de Duero, Spain ..	28	D1
Arandān, Iran	64	C5
Aranjuez, Spain	30	E7
Aranos, Namibia	84	C2
Aransas Pass, U.S.A. ...	109	M6
Aranzazu, Colombia	120	B3
Araouane, Mali	78	B4
Arapahoe, U.S.A.	108	E5
Arapari, Brazil	122	C2
Arapey Grande →, Uruguay	126	C4
Arapiraca, Brazil	122	C4
Arapkir, Turkey	67	D8
Arapongas, Brazil	127	A5
Ar'ar, Si. Arabia	64	D4
Araracuara, Colombia ..	120	D3
Araranguá, Brazil	127	B6
Araraquara, Brazil	123	F2
Araras, Serra das, Brazil .	127	B5
Ararat, Australia	91	F3
Ararat, Mt. = Ağrı Dağı, Turkey	67	D11
Arari, Brazil	122	B3
Araria, India	63	F12
Araripe, Chapada do, Brazil	122	C3
Araripina, Brazil	122	C3
Araruama, L. de, Brazil .	123	F3
Araruna, Brazil	122	C4
Aras, Rūd-e →, Iran ..	64	B5
Araticu, Brazil	122	B2
Arauca, Colombia	120	B3
Arauca □, Colombia	120	B3
Arauca →, Venezuela ..	120	B4
Arauco, Chile	126	D1
Arauco □, Chile	126	D1
Araújos, Brazil	123	E2
Arauquita, Colombia ...	120	B3
Araure, Venezuela	120	B4
Arawa, Ethiopia	77	F5
Araxá, Brazil	123	E2
Araya, Pen. de, Venezuela	121	A5
Arba Minch, Ethiopia ..	77	F4
Arbat, Iraq	64	C5
Arbatax, Italy	34	C2
Arbaza, Russia	45	D10
Arbedo, Switz.	23	D8
Arbīl, Iraq	64	B5
Arbois, France	25	F12
Arboletes, Colombia ...	120	B2
Arbon, Switz.	23	A8
Arbore, Ethiopia	77	F4
Arborea, Italy	34	C1
Arborfield, Canada ...	101	C8
Arborg, Canada	101	C9
Arbrå, Sweden	10	C10
Arbroath, U.K.	14	E6
Arbuckle, U.S.A.	112	F4
Arbus, Italy	34	C1
Arbuzinka, Ukraine ...	42	C4
Arc →, France	26	D2
Arcachon, France	26	D2
Arcachon, Bassin d', France	26	D2
Arcade, U.S.A.	106	D6
Arcadia, Fla., U.S.A. ..	105	M5
Arcadia, La., U.S.A. ..	109	J8
Arcadia, Nebr., U.S.A. .	108	E5
Arcadia, Pa., U.S.A. ..	106	F6
Arcadia, Wis., U.S.A. .	108	C9
Arcata, U.S.A.	110	F1
Arcévia, Italy	33	E9
Archangel = Arkhangelsk, Russia	44	C5
Archar, Bulgaria	38	F5
Archbald, U.S.A.	107	E9
Archena, Spain	29	G3
Archer →, Australia ..	90	A3
Archer B., Australia ..	90	A3
Archers Post, Kenya ..	82	B4
Archidona, Spain	31	H6
Arci, Monte, Italy	34	C1
Arcidosso, Italy	33	F8
Arcila = Asilah, Morocco	74	A3
Arcis-sur-Aube, France .	25	D11
Arckaringa, Australia .	91	D1
Arckaringa Cr. →, Australia	91	D2
Arco, Italy	32	C7
Arco, U.S.A.	110	E7
Arcola, Canada	101	D8
Arcos, Spain	28	D2
Arcos de los Frontera, Spain	31	J5
Arcos de Valdevez, Portugal	30	D2
Arcot, India	60	N11
Arcoverde, Brazil	122	C4
Arctic Bay, Canada ...	97	A11
Arctic Ocean, Arctic ...	4	B18
Arctic Red River, Canada	96	B6
Arda →, Bulgaria	39	H9
Arda →, Italy	32	D6
Ardabīl, Iran	65	B6
Ardahan, Turkey	67	C10
Ardakān = Sepīdān, Iran	65	D7
Ardales, Spain	31	J6
Ardalstangen, Norway .	10	C1
Ardatov, Russia	41	D15
Ardea, Greece	39	J5
Ardèche □, France ...	27	D8
Ardèche →, France ..	27	D8
Ardee, Ireland	15	C5
Arden, Canada	106	B8
Arden, Denmark	11	H3
Arden, Calif., U.S.A. .	112	G5
Arden, Nev., U.S.A. ..	113	J11
Ardenne, Belgium	25	C12
Ardennes = Ardenne, Belgium	25	C12
Ardennes □, France ..	25	C11
Ardentes, France	25	F8
Ardeşen, Turkey	67	C9
Ardestān, Iran	65	C7
Ardgour, U.K.	14	E3
Árdhas →, Greece ...	39	H9
Ardila →, Portugal ..	31	G3
Ardlethan, Australia .	91	E4
Ardmore, Australia ..	90	C2
Ardmore, Okla., U.S.A.	109	H6
Ardmore, Pa., U.S.A. .	107	G9
Ardmore, S. Dak., U.S.A.	108	D3
Ardnacrusha, Ireland	15	D3
Ardnamurchan, Pt. of, U.K.	14	E2
Ardooie, Belgium	17	G2
Ardore Marina, Italy	35	D9
Ardres, France	25	B8
Ardrossan, Australia ...	91	E2
Ardrossan, U.K.	14	F4
Ards □, U.K.	15	B6
Ards Pen., U.K.	15	B6
Ardud, Romania	38	B5
Ardunac, Turkey	43	F10
Åre, Sweden	10	A7
Arecibo, Puerto Rico ...	117	C6
Areia Branca, Brazil ...	122	B4
Arena, Pt., U.S.A.	112	G3
Arenales, Cerro, Chile ..	128	C2
Arenápolis, Brazil	125	C6
Arenas, Spain	30	B6
Arenas de San Pedro, Spain	30	E5
Arendal, Norway	11	F2
Arendonk, Belgium	17	F6
Arendsee, Germany	18	C7
Arenillas, Ecuador	120	D1
Arenys de Mar, Spain ..	28	D7
Arenzano, Italy	32	D5
Areópolis, Greece	39	N5
Arequipa, Peru	124	D3
Arequipa □, Peru	124	D3
Arere, Brazil	121	D7
Arero, Ethiopia	77	G4
Arès, France	26	D2
Arévalo, Spain	30	D6
Arezzo, Italy	33	E8
Arga →, Spain	28	C3
Argalastí, Greece	39	K6
Argamakmur, Indonesia .	56	E2
Argamasilla de Alba, Spain	29	F1
Arganda, Spain	28	E1
Arganil, Portugal	30	E2
Argelès-Gazost, France .	26	F3
Argelès-sur-Mer, France .	26	F7
Argens →, France ...	27	E10
Argent-sur-Sauldre, France	25	E9
Argenta, Italy	33	D8
Argentan, France ...	24	D6
Argentário, Mte., Italy .	33	F8
Argentat, France	26	C5
Argentera, Italy	32	D3
Argentera, Monte del, Italy	32	D4
Argenteuil, France ...	25	D9
Argentia, Canada ...	99	C9
Argentiera, C. dell', Italy .	34	B1
Argentière, Aiguilles d', Switz.	22	E4
Argentina ■, S. Amer. ..	128	B3
Argentina Is., Antarctica .	5	C17
Argentino, L., Argentina .	128	D2
Argenton-Château, France	24	F6
Argenton-sur-Creuse, France	26	B5
Argeş →, Romania ...	38	E9
Arghandab →, Afghan. .	62	D1
Argo, Sudan	76	D3
Argolikós Kólpos, Greece .	39	M5
Argonne, France	25	C12
Árgos, Greece	39	M5
Argostólion, Greece ..	39	L3
Arguedas, Spain	28	C3
Arguello, Pt., U.S.A. ..	113	L6
Arguineguín, Canary Is. .	36	G4
Argun →, Russia	45	D13
Argungu, Nigeria	79	C5
Argus Pk., U.S.A. ...	113	K9
Argyle, U.S.A.	108	A6
Argyle, L., Australia ..	88	C4
Arhavi, Turkey	67	C9
Århus, Denmark	11	H4
Århus Amtskommune □, Denmark	11	H4
Ariadnoye, Russia ...	48	B7
Ariamsvlei, Namibia ..	84	D2
Ariana, Tunisia	75	A7
Ariano Irpino, Italy ...	35	A8
Ariano nel Polèsine, Italy .	33	D9
Ariari →, Colombia ...	120	C3
Aribinda, Burkina Faso .	79	C4
Arica, Chile	124	D3
Arica, Colombia	120	D3
Arico, Canary Is.	36	F3
Arid, C., Australia ...	89	F3
Arida, Japan	49	G7
Ariège □, France ...	26	F5
Ariège →, France ...	26	E5
Arieş →, Romania ..	38	C6
Arīḥā, Syria	64	C3
Arīḷḷa, Ákra, Greece ..	37	A3
Arima, Trin. & Tob. ..	117	D7
Arinos →, Brazil ...	125	C6
Ario de Rosales, Mexico .	114	D4
Aripuanã, Brazil	125	B5
Aripuanã →, Brazil ..	125	B5
Ariquemes, Brazil ...	125	B5
Arisaig, U.K.	14	E3
Arîsh, W. el →, Egypt .	76	H8
Arismendi, Venezuela .	120	B4
Arissa, Ethiopia	77	E5
Aristazabal I., Canada .	100	C3
Arivaca, U.S.A.	111	L8
Arivonimamo, Madag. .	85	B8
Ariza, Spain	28	D2
Arizaro, Salar de, Argentina	126	A2
Arizona, Argentina ...	126	D2
Arizona □, U.S.A.	111	J8
Arizpe, Mexico	114	A2
Arjeplog, Sweden	8	C15
Arjona, Colombia	120	A2
Arjona, Spain	31	H6
Arjuno, Indonesia	57	G15
Arka, Russia	45	C15
Arkadak, Russia	41	F13
Arkadelphia, U.S.A. ...	109	H8
Arkaig, L., U.K.	14	E3
Arkalyk, Kazakhstan ...	44	D7
Arkansas □, U.S.A.	109	H8
Arkansas →, U.S.A. ...	109	J9
Arkansas City, U.S.A. ..	109	G6
Árkathos →, Greece ...	39	K4
Arkhángelos, Greece ...	37	C10
Arkhangelsk, Russia ...	44	C5
Arkhangelskoye, Russia .	41	F12
Arkiko, Eritrea	77	D4
Arklow, Ireland	15	D5
Arkona, Kap, Germany .	18	A9
Arkösund, Sweden	11	F10
Arkticheskiy, Mys, Russia	45	A10
Arkul, Russia	41	C17
Arlanc, France	26	C7
Arlanza →, Spain ...	30	C6
Arlanzón →, Spain ..	30	C6
Arlberg Pass, Austria ..	19	H6
Arlee, U.S.A.	110	C6
Arles, France	27	E8
Arlesheim, Switz. ...	22	B5
Arlington, S. Africa ...	85	D4
Arlington, Oreg., U.S.A. .	110	D3
Arlington, S. Dak., U.S.A.	108	C6
Arlington, Va., U.S.A. ..	104	F7
Arlington, Wash., U.S.A.	112	B4
Arlon, Belgium	17	J7
Arlöv, Sweden	11	J7
Arly, Burkina Faso ...	79	C5
Armagh, U.K.	15	B5
Armagh □, U.K.	15	B5
Armagnac, France ...	26	E4
Armançon →, France .	25	E10
Armavir, Russia	43	D9
Armenia, Colombia ...	120	C2
Armenia ■, Asia	43	F11
Armenistís, Ákra, Greece	37	C9
Armentières, France ..	25	B9
Armidale, Australia ..	91	E5
Armour, U.S.A.	108	D5
Armstrong, B.C., Canada	100	C5
Armstrong, Ont., Canada	98	B2
Armstrong, U.S.A. ..	109	M6
Armstrong →, Australia	88	C5
Arnarfjörður, Iceland .	8	D2
Arnaud →, Canada ..	97	B12
Arnauti, C., Cyprus ..	37	D11
Arnay-le-Duc, France .	25	E11
Arnedillo, Spain	28	C2
Arnedo, Spain	28	C2
Arnemuiden, Neths. ..	17	F3
Árnes, Iceland	8	C3
Árnes, Norway	10	D5
Arnett, U.S.A.	109	G5
Arnhem, Neths.	16	E7
Arnhem, C., Australia .	90	A2
Arnhem B., Australia .	90	A2
Arnhem Land, Australia	90	A1
Arno →, Italy	32	E7
Arno Bay, Australia ..	91	E2
Arnold, Calif., U.S.A. .	112	G6
Arnold, Nebr., U.S.A. .	108	E4
Arnoldstein, Austria ..	21	J3
Arnon →, France ...	25	E9
Arnot, Canada	101	B9
Arnøy, Norway	8	A16
Arnprior, Canada ...	98	C4
Arnsberg, Germany ..	18	D4
Arnstadt, Germany ..	18	E6
Aro →, Venezuela ..	121	B5
Aroab, Namibia	84	D2
Aroche, Spain	31	H4
Aroeiras, Brazil	122	C4
Arolla, Switz.	22	D4
Arolsen, Germany ..	18	D5
Aron →, France ...	26	B7
Arona, Italy	32	C5
Aroroy, Phil.	55	E5
Arosa, Switz.	23	C9
Arosa, Ria de, Spain .	30	C2
Arpajon, France ...	25	D9
Arpajon-sur-Cère, France	26	D6
Arpino, Italy	34	A6
Arque, Bolivia	124	D4
Arrabury, Australia .	91	D3
Arrah = Ara, India ..	63	G11
Arraias, Brazil ...	123	D2
Arraias →, Mato Grosso, Brazil	125	C7
Arraias →, Pará, Brazil .	122	C2
Arraiolos, Portugal ..	31	G3
Arran, U.K.	14	F3
Arrandale, Canada ..	100	C3
Arras, France	25	B9
Arrats →, France ..	26	D4
Arreau, France ...	26	F4
Arrecife, Canary Is. .	36	F6
Arrecifes, Argentina .	126	C3
Arrée, Mts. d', France .	24	D3
Arriaga, Chiapas, Mexico .	115	D6
Arriaga, San Luis Potosí, Mexico	114	C4
Arrilalah P.O., Australia .	90	C3
Arrino, Australia ...	89	E2
Arrojado →, Brazil ..	123	D3
Arromanches-les-Bains, France	24	C6
Arronches, Portugal ...	31	F3
Arros →, France	26	E3
Arrou, France	24	D8
Arrow, L., Ireland ...	15	B3
Arrow Rock Res., U.S.A.	110	E6
Arrowhead, Canada ..	100	C5
Arrowhead, L., U.S.A. .	113	L9
Arrowtown, N.Z. ...	87	L2
Arroyo de la Luz, Spain .	31	F4
Arroyo Grande, U.S.A. .	113	K6
Års, Denmark	11	H3
Ars, Iran	64	B5
Ars-en-Ré, France ..	26	B2
Ars-sur-Moselle, France .	25	C13
Arsenault L., Canada .	101	B7
Arsenev, Russia ...	48	B6
Arsi □, Ethiopia ...	77	F4
Arsiero, Italy	33	C8
Arsin, Turkey	67	C8
Arsk, Russia	41	C16
Árta, Greece	39	K4
Artá, Spain	36	B10
Arteaga, Mexico ...	114	D4
Arteche, Phil.	55	E6
Arteijo, Spain	30	B2
Artem, Russia	48	C6
Artem, Ostrov, Azerbaijan	43	F14
Artemovsk, Russia .	45	D10
Artemovsk, Ukraine .	42	B8
Artemovski, Russia .	43	C9
Artenay, France ...	25	D8
Artern, Germany ..	18	D7
Artesa de Segre, Spain .	28	D6
Artesia = Mosomane, Botswana	84	C4
Artesia, U.S.A. ...	109	J2
Artesia Wells, U.S.A. .	109	L5
Artesian, U.S.A. ...	108	C6
Arth, Switz.	23	B7
Arthez-de-Béarn, France .	26	E3
Arthington, Liberia ..	78	D2
Arthur →, Australia .	90	G3
Arthur Cr. →, Australia	90	C2
Arthur Pt., Australia .	90	C5
Arthur's Pass, N.Z. ..	87	K3
Arthur's Town, Bahamas .	117	B4
Artigas, Uruguay ...	126	C4
Artik, Armenia	43	F10
Artillery L., Canada .	101	A7
Artois, France	25	B9
Artsiz, Ukraine ...	42	C3
Artvin, Turkey ...	43	F9
Artvin □, Turkey ..	67	C9
Aru, Kepulauan, Indonesia	57	F8
Aru Is. = Aru, Kepulauan, Indonesia	57	F8
Aru Meru □, Tanzania .	82	C4
Arua, Uganda	82	B3
Aruanã, Brazil	123	D1
Aruba ■, W. Indies ..	117	D6
Arucas, Canary Is. ..	36	G4
Arudy, France	26	E3
Arumã, Brazil	121	D5
Arumpo, Australia ..	91	E3
Arun →, Nepal ...	63	F12
Arunachal Pradesh □, India	61	E19
Arusha, Tanzania ...	82	C4
Arusha □, Tanzania ..	82	C4
Arusha Chini, Tanzania .	82	C4
Aruwimi →, Zaïre ..	82	B1
Arvada, U.S.A. ...	110	D10
Arvayheer, Mongolia .	54	B5
Arve →, France ...	27	B10
Árvi, Greece	37	E7
Arvida, Canada ...	99	C5
Arvidsjaur, Sweden .	8	D15
Arvika, Sweden ...	9	G12
Arvin, U.S.A.	113	K8
Arxan, China	54	B6
Aryiráthes, Greece .	37	B3
Aryiroúpolis, Greece .	37	D6
Arys, Kazakhstan ..	44	E7
Arzachena, Italy ...	34	A2
Arzamas, Russia ...	41	D13
Arzew, Algeria ...	75	A4
Arzgir, Russia	43	D11
Arzignano, Italy ...	33	C8
As, Belgium	17	F7
Aş Şadr, U.A.E. ...	65	E7
Aş Şafā, Syria ...	69	B6
'As Saffānīyah, Si. Arabia	65	D6
As Safirah, Syria ..	64	B3
Aş Şahm, Oman ..	65	E8
As Sājir, Si. Arabia .	64	E5
As Salamīyah, Syria .	64	C3
As Salt, Jordan ...	69	C4
As Sal'w'a, Qatar ..	65	E6
As Samāwah, Iraq ..	64	D5
As Sanamayn, Syria .	69	B5
As Sukhnah, Syria .	64	C3
As Sulaymānīyah, Iraq .	64	C5
As Sulaymī, Si. Arabia .	64	E4
As Summān, Si. Arabia .	64	E5
As Suwaydā, Syria ..	69	C5
As Suwaydā □, Syria .	69	C5
As Suwayrah, Iraq ..	64	C5
Asab, Namibia	84	D2
Asaba, Nigeria	79	D6
Asafo, Ghana	78	D4
Asahi-Gawa →, Japan .	49	G6
Asahigawa, Japan ..	48	C11
Asale, L., Ethiopia ..	77	E5

Az Zībār

Asamankese, *Ghana* 79 D4
Asansol, *India* 63 H12
Åsarna, *Sweden* 10 B8
Asbe Teferi, *Ethiopia* 77 F5
Asbesberge, *S. Africa* 84 D3
Asbestos, *Canada* 99 C5
Asbury Park, *U.S.A.* 107 F10
Ascensión, *Mexico* 114 A3
Ascensión, B. de la, *Mexico* 115 D7
Ascension I., *Atl. Oc.* 2 E9
Aschaffenburg, *Germany* 19 F5
Aschendorf, *Germany* 18 B3
Aschersleben, *Germany* 18 D7
Asciano, *Italy* 33 E8
Áscoli Piceno, *Italy* 33 F10
Áscoli Satriano, *Italy* 35 A8
Ascona, *Switz.* 23 D7
Ascope, *Peru* 124 B2
Ascotán, *Chile* 126 A2
Aseb, *Eritrea* 68 E3
Asedjrad, *Algeria* 75 D5
Asela, *Ethiopia* 77 F4
Asenovgrad, *Bulgaria* 39 G7
Asfeld, *France* 25 C11
Asfûn el Matâ'na, *Egypt* 76 B3
Åsgårdstrand, *Norway* 10 E4
Asgata, *Cyprus* 37 E12
Ash Fork, *U.S.A.* 111 J7
Ash Grove, *U.S.A.* 109 G8
Ash Shamāl □, *Lebanon* 69 A5
Ash Shāmīyah, *Iraq* 64 D5
Ash Shāriqah, *U.A.E.* 65 E7
Ash Sharmah, *Si. Arabia* 64 D2
Ash Sharqāt, *Iraq* 64 C4
Ash Sharqi, Al Jabal, *Lebanon* 69 B5
Ash Shaṭrah, *Iraq* 64 D5
Ash Shawbak, *Jordan* 64 D2
Ash Shawmari, J., *Jordan* 69 E5
Ash Shaykh, J., *Lebanon* 69 B4
Ash Shināfīyah, *Iraq* 64 D5
Ash Shu'aybah, *Si. Arabia* 64 E5
Ash Shumlūl, *Si. Arabia* 64 E5
Ash Shūr'a, *Iraq* 64 C4
Ash Shurayf, *Si. Arabia* 64 E3
Ash Shuwayfāt, *Lebanon* 69 B4
Ashanti □, *Ghana* 79 D4
Ashau, *Vietnam* 58 D6
Ashburn, *U.S.A.* 105 K4
Ashburton, *N.Z.* 87 K3
Ashburton →, *Australia* 88 D1
Ashburton Downs, *Australia* 88 D2
Ashby de la Zouch, *U.K.* 12 E6
Ashcroft, *Canada* 100 C4
Ashdod, *Israel* 69 D3
Asheboro, *U.S.A.* 105 H6
Asherton, *U.S.A.* 109 L5
Asheville, *U.S.A.* 105 H4
Asheweig →, *Canada* 98 B2
Ashford, *Australia* 91 D5
Ashford, *U.K.* 13 F8
Ashford, *U.S.A.* 110 C2
Ashgabat = Ashkhabad, *Turkmenistan* 44 F6
Ashibetsu, *Japan* 48 C11
Ashikaga, *Japan* 49 F9
Ashizuri-Zaki, *Japan* 49 H6
Ashkarkot, *Afghan.* 62 C2
Ashkhabad, *Turkmenistan* 44 F6
Ashland, *Kans., U.S.A.* 109 G5
Ashland, *Ky., U.S.A.* 104 F4
Ashland, *Maine, U.S.A.* 99 C6
Ashland, *Mont., U.S.A.* 110 D10
Ashland, *Nebr., U.S.A.* 108 E6
Ashland, *Ohio, U.S.A.* 106 F2
Ashland, *Oreg., U.S.A.* 110 E2
Ashland, *Pa., U.S.A.* 107 F8
Ashland, *Va., U.S.A.* 104 G7
Ashland, *Wis., U.S.A.* 108 B9
Ashley, *N. Dak., U.S.A.* 108 B5
Ashley, *Pa., U.S.A.* 107 E9
Ashmont, *Canada* 100 C6
Ashmore Reef, *Australia* 88 B3
Ashmûn, *Egypt* 76 H7
Ashq'elon, *Israel* 69 D3
Ashtabula, *U.S.A.* 106 E4
Ashton, *S. Africa* 84 E3
Ashton, *U.S.A.* 110 D8
Ashton under Lyne, *U.K.* 12 D5
Ashuanipi, L., *Canada* 99 B6
Asia 46 E11
Asia, Kepulauan, *Indonesia* 57 D8
Āsīā Bak, *Iran* 65 C6
Asiago, *Italy* 33 C8
Asidonhoppo, *Surinam* 121 C6
Asifabad, *India* 60 K11
Asike, *Indonesia* 57 F10
Asilah, *Morocco* 74 A3
Asinara, *Italy* 34 A1
Asinara, G. dell', *Italy* 34 B1
Asino, *Russia* 44 D9
'Asīr □, *Si. Arabia* 68 D3
Asir, Ras, *Somali Rep.* 68 E5
Aşkale, *Turkey* 67 D9
Asker, *Norway* 10 E4
Askersund, *Sweden* 11 F8
Askham, *S. Africa* 84 D3
Askim, *Norway* 10 E5
Askja, *Iceland* 8 D5
Asl, *Egypt* 76 J8
Asmara = Asmera, *Eritrea* 77 D4
Asmera, *Eritrea* 77 D4
Asnæs, *Denmark* 11 J5
Asni, *Morocco* 74 B3
Ásola, *Italy* 32 C7
Asoteriba, Jebel, *Sudan* 76 C4
Asotin, *U.S.A.* 110 C5
Aspe, *Spain* 29 G4
Aspen, *U.S.A.* 111 G10
Aspendos, *Turkey* 66 E4
Aspermont, *U.S.A.* 109 J4
Aspiring, Mt., *N.Z.* 87 L2
Aspres-sur-Buëch, *France* 27 D9
Asprókavos, Ákra, *Greece* 37 B4
Aspromonte, *Italy* 35 D8
Aspur, *India* 62 H6
Asquith, *Canada* 101 C7
Assa, *Morocco* 74 C3
Assâba, *Mauritania* 78 B2
Assam □, *India* 61 F18
Assamakka, *Niger* 79 B6
Asse, *Belgium* 17 H4
Assebroek, *Belgium* 17 F2
Assekrem, *Algeria* 75 D6
Assémini, *Italy* 34 C2
Assen, *Neths.* 16 C9
Assendelft, *Neths.* 16 D5
Assenede, *Belgium* 17 F3
Assens, *Århus, Denmark* 11 H4
Assens, *Fyn, Denmark* 11 J3
Assesse, *Belgium* 17 H6
Assini, *Ivory C.* 78 D4
Assiniboia, *Canada* 101 D7
Assiniboine →, *Canada* 101 D9
Assis, *Brazil* 127 A5
Assisi, *Italy* 33 E9
Assynt, L., *U.K.* 14 C3
Astaffort, *France* 26 D4
Astara, *Azerbaijan* 67 D13
Asten, *Neths.* 17 F7
Asteroúsia, *Greece* 37 E7
Asti, *Italy* 32 D5
Astipálaia, *Greece* 39 N9
Astorga, *Spain* 30 C4
Astoria, *U.S.A.* 112 D3
Åstorp, *Sweden* 11 H6
Astrakhan, *Russia* 43 C13
Astudillo, *Spain* 30 C6
Asturias □, *Spain* 30 B5
Asunción, *Paraguay* 126 B4
Asunción Nochixtlán, *Mexico* 115 D5
Asutri, *Sudan* 77 D4
Aswa →, *Uganda* 82 B3
Aswad, Ras al, *Si. Arabia* 76 C4
Aswân, *Egypt* 76 C3
Aswân High Dam = Sadd el Aali, *Egypt* 76 C3
Asyût, *Egypt* 76 B3
Asyûti, Wadi →, *Egypt* 76 B3
Aszód, *Hungary* 21 H9
At Ṭafīlah, *Jordan* 69 E4
At Ṭā'if, *Si. Arabia* 68 C3
Aṭ Ṭirāq, *Si. Arabia* 64 E5
Atacama □, *Chile* 126 B2
Atacama, Desierto de, *Chile* 126 A2
Atacama, Salar de, *Chile* 126 A2
Ataco, *Colombia* 120 C2
Atakor, *Algeria* 75 D6
Atakpamé, *Togo* 79 D5
Atalándi, *Greece* 39 L5
Atalaya, *Peru* 124 C3
Atalaya de Femes, *Canary Is.* 36 F6
Ataléia, *Brazil* 123 E3
Atami, *Japan* 49 G9
Atapupu, *Indonesia* 57 F6
Atâr, *Mauritania* 74 D2
Atara, *Russia* 45 C13
Ataram, Erg n-, *Algeria* 75 D5
Atarfe, *Spain* 31 H7
Atascadero, *Calif., U.S.A.* 111 J3
Atascadero, *Calif., U.S.A.* 112 K6
Atasu, *Kazakhstan* 44 E8
Atauro, *Indonesia* 57 F7
Atbara, *Sudan* 76 D3
'Atbara →, *Sudan* 76 D3
Atbasar, *Kazakhstan* 44 D7
Atchafalaya B., *U.S.A.* 109 L9
Atchison, *U.S.A.* 108 F7
Atebubu, *Ghana* 79 D4
Ateca, *Spain* 28 D3
Aterno →, *Italy* 33 F10
Atesine, Alpi, *Italy* 32 B8
Atessa, *Italy* 33 F11
Ath, *Belgium* 17 G3
Athabasca, *Canada* 100 C6
Athabasca →, *Canada* 101 B6
Athabasca, L., *Canada* 101 B7
Athboy, *Ireland* 15 C5
Athenry, *Ireland* 15 C3
Athens = Athínai, *Greece* 39 M6
Athens, *Ala., U.S.A.* 105 H2
Athens, *Ga., U.S.A.* 105 J4
Athens, *N.Y., U.S.A.* 107 D11
Athens, *Ohio, U.S.A.* 104 F4
Athens, *Pa., U.S.A.* 107 E8
Athens, *Tenn., U.S.A.* 105 H3
Athens, *Tex., U.S.A.* 109 J7
Atherley, *Canada* 106 B5
Atherton, *Australia* 90 B4
Athiéme, *Benin* 79 D5
Athienou, *Cyprus* 37 D12
Athínai, *Greece* 39 M6
Athlone, *Ireland* 15 C4
Athna, *Cyprus* 37 D12
Atholl, Forest of, *U.K.* 14 E5
Atholville, *Canada* 99 C6
Áthos, *Greece* 39 J7
Athus, *Belgium* 17 J7
Athy, *Ireland* 15 D5
Ati, *Chad* 73 F8
Ati, *Sudan* 77 E2
Atiak, *Uganda* 82 B3
Atico, *Peru* 124 D3
Atienza, *Spain* 28 D2
Atikokan, *Canada* 98 C1
Atikonak L., *Canada* 99 B7
Atimonan, *Phil.* 55 E4
Atka, *Russia* 45 C16
Atkarsk, *Russia* 41 F14
Atkinson, *U.S.A.* 108 D5
Atlanta, *Ga., U.S.A.* 105 J3
Atlanta, *Tex., U.S.A.* 109 J7
Atlantic, *U.S.A.* 108 E7
Atlantic City, *U.S.A.* 104 F8
Atlantic Ocean 2 E9
Atlántico □, *Colombia* 120 A2
Atlas Mts. = Haut Atlas, *Morocco* 74 B3
Atlin, *Canada* 100 B2
Atlin, L., *Canada* 100 B2
Atmore, *U.S.A.* 105 K2
Atoka, *U.S.A.* 109 H6
Átokos, *Greece* 39 L3
Atolia, *U.S.A.* 113 K9
Atouguia, *Portugal* 31 F1
Atoyac →, *Mexico* 115 D5
Atrak →, *Iran* 65 B8
Ätran, *Sweden* 11 G6
Atrato →, *Colombia* 120 B2
Atrauli, *India* 62 E8
Atri, *Italy* 33 F10
Atsbi, *Ethiopia* 77 E4
Atsoum, Mts., *Cameroon* 79 D7
Atsuta, *Japan* 48 C10
Attalla, *U.S.A.* 105 H2
Attáviros, *Greece* 37 C9
Attawapiskat, *Canada* 98 B3
Attawapiskat →, *Canada* 98 B3
Attawapiskat, L., *Canada* 98 B2
Attendorn, *Germany* 18 D3
Attert, *Belgium* 17 J7
Attica, *U.S.A.* 104 E2
Attichy, *France* 25 C10
Attigny, *France* 25 C11
Attikamagen L., *Canada* 99 A6
Attleboro, *U.S.A.* 107 E13
Attock, *Pakistan* 62 C5
Attopeu, *Laos* 58 E6
Attur, *India* 60 P11
Atuel →, *Argentina* 126 D2
Atvacik, *Turkey* 66 D2
Åtvidaberg, *Sweden* 11 F10
Atwater, *U.S.A.* 111 H3
Atwood, *Canada* 106 C3
Atwood, *U.S.A.* 108 F4
Atyrau, *Kazakhstan* 43 C14
Au Sable →, *U.S.A.* 104 C4
Au Sable Pt., *U.S.A.* 98 C2
Aubagne, *France* 27 E9
Aubange, *Belgium* 17 J7
Aubarca, C., *Spain* 36 B7
Aube □, *France* 25 D11
Aube →, *France* 25 D10
Aubel, *Belgium* 17 G7
Aubenas, *France* 27 D8
Aubenton, *France* 25 C11
Auberry, *U.S.A.* 112 H7
Aubigny-sur-Nère, *France* 25 E9
Aubin, *France* 26 D6
Aubrac, Mts. d', *France* 26 D7
Auburn, *Ala., U.S.A.* 105 J3
Auburn, *Calif., U.S.A.* 112 G5
Auburn, *Ind., U.S.A.* 104 E3
Auburn, *N.Y., U.S.A.* 107 D8
Auburn, *Nebr., U.S.A.* 108 E7
Auburn, *Wash., U.S.A.* 112 C4
Auburn Ra., *Australia* 91 D5
Auburndale, *U.S.A.* 105 L5
Aubusson, *France* 26 C6
Auch, *France* 26 E4
Auchel, *France* 25 B9
Auchi, *Nigeria* 79 D6
Auckland, *N.Z.* 87 G5
Auckland Is., *Pac. Oc.* 92 N8
Aude □, *France* 26 E6
Aude →, *France* 26 E7
Auden, *Canada* 98 B2
Auderghem, *Belgium* 17 G4
Auderville, *France* 24 C5
Audierne, *France* 24 D2
Audincourt, *France* 25 E13
Audo, *Ethiopia* 77 F5
Audubon, *U.S.A.* 108 E7
Aue, *Germany* 18 E8
Auerbach, *Germany* 18 E8
Aueti Paraná →, *Brazil* 120 D4
Aufist, *W. Sahara* 74 C2
Augathella, *Australia* 91 D4
Augrabies Falls, *S. Africa* 84 D3
Augsburg, *Germany* 19 G6
Augusta, *Italy* 35 E8
Augusta, *Ark., U.S.A.* 109 H9
Augusta, *Ga., U.S.A.* 105 J5
Augusta, *Kans., U.S.A.* 109 G6
Augusta, *Maine, U.S.A.* 99 D6
Augusta, *Mont., U.S.A.* 110 C7
Augusta, *Wis., U.S.A.* 108 C9
Augustenborg, *Denmark* 11 K3
Augustów, *Poland* 20 B12
Augustus, Mt., *Australia* 88 D2
Augustus Downs, *Australia* 90 B2
Augustus I., *Australia* 88 C3
Aukan, *Eritrea* 77 D5
Aukum, *U.S.A.* 112 G6
Auld, L., *Australia* 88 D3
Aulla, *Italy* 32 D6
Aulnay, *France* 26 B3
Aulne →, *France* 24 D2
Aulnoye-Aymeries, *France* 25 B10
Ault, *France* 24 B8
Ault, *U.S.A.* 108 E2
Aulus-les-Bains, *France* 26 F5
Aumale, *France* 25 C8
Aumont-Aubrac, *France* 26 D7
Auna, *Nigeria* 79 C5
Aunis, *France* 26 B3
Auponhia, *Indonesia* 57 E7
Aups, *France* 27 E10
Aur, P., *Malaysia* 59 L5
Auraiya, *India* 63 F8
Aurangabad, *Bihar, India* 63 G11
Aurangabad, *Maharashtra, India* 60 K9
Auray, *France* 24 E4
Aurès, *Algeria* 75 A6
Aurich, *Germany* 18 B3
Aurilândia, *Brazil* 123 E1
Aurillac, *France* 26 D6
Auronza, *Italy* 33 B9
Aurora, *Canada* 106 C5
Aurora, *S. Africa* 84 E2
Aurora, *Colo., U.S.A.* 108 F2
Aurora, *Ill., U.S.A.* 104 E1
Aurora, *Mo., U.S.A.* 109 G8
Aurora, *Nebr., U.S.A.* 108 E6
Aurora, *Ohio, U.S.A.* 106 E3
Aursmoen, *Norway* 10 E5
Aurukun Mission, *Australia* 90 A3
Aus, *Namibia* 84 D2
Auschwitz = Oświecim, *Poland* 20 E9
Aust-Agder fylke □, *Norway* 9 G9
Austin, *Minn., U.S.A.* 108 D8
Austin, *Nev., U.S.A.* 110 G5
Austin, *Pa., U.S.A.* 106 E6
Austin, *Tex., U.S.A.* 109 K6
Austin, L., *Australia* 89 E2
Austral Downs, *Australia* 90 C2
Austral Is. = Tubuai Is., *Pac. Oc.* 93 K12
Austral Seamount Chain, *Pac. Oc.* 93 K13
Australia ■, *Oceania* 92 K5
Australian Alps, *Australia* 91 F4
Australian Capital Territory □, *Australia* 91 F4
Austria ■, *Europe* 21 H4
Austvågøy, *Norway* 8 B13
Autazes, *Brazil* 121 D6
Autelbas, *Belgium* 17 J7
Auterive, *France* 26 E5
Authie →, *France* 25 B8
Authon-du-Perche, *France* 24 D7
Autlán, *Mexico* 114 D4
Autun, *France* 25 F11
Auvelais, *Belgium* 17 H5
Auvergne, *Australia* 88 C5
Auvergne, *France* 26 C7
Auvergne, Mts. d', *France* 26 C6
Auvézére →, *France* 26 C4
Auxerre, *France* 25 E10
Auxi-le-Château, *France* 25 B9
Auxonne, *France* 25 E12
Auzances, *France* 26 B6
Auzat-sur-Allier, *France* 26 C7
Avallon, *France* 25 E10
Avalon, *U.S.A.* 113 M8
Avalon Pen., *Canada* 99 C9
Avaré, *Brazil* 127 A6
Ávas, *Greece* 39 J8
Avawatz Mts., *U.S.A.* 113 K10
Aveiro, *Brazil* 121 D6
Aveiro, *Portugal* 30 E2
Aveiro □, *Portugal* 30 E2
Āvej, *Iran* 65 C6
Avelgem, *Belgium* 17 G2
Avellaneda, *Argentina* 126 C4
Avellino, *Italy* 35 B7
Avenal, *U.S.A.* 112 K6
Avenches, *Switz.* 22 C4
Averøya, *Norway* 10 A1
Aversa, *Italy* 35 B7
Avery, *U.S.A.* 110 C6
Aves, I. de, *W. Indies* 117 C7
Aves, Is. de, *Venezuela* 117 D6
Avesnes-sur-Helpe, *France* 25 B10
Avesta, *Sweden* 9 F14
Aveyron □, *France* 26 D6
Aveyron →, *France* 26 D5
Avezzano, *Italy* 33 F10
Aviá Terai, *Argentina* 126 B3
Aviano, *Italy* 33 B9
Avigliana, *Italy* 32 C4
Avigliano, *Italy* 35 B8
Avignon, *France* 27 E8
Ávila, *Spain* 30 E6
Ávila □, *Spain* 30 E6
Ávila, Sierra de, *Spain* 30 E5
Avila Beach, *U.S.A.* 113 K6
Avilés, *Spain* 30 B5
Avisio →, *Italy* 33 B8
Aviz, *Portugal* 31 F3
Avize, *France* 25 D11
Avoca, *Ireland* 15 D5
Avoca, *U.S.A.* 106 D7
Avoca →, *Australia* 91 F3
Avola, *Canada* 100 C5
Avola, *Italy* 35 F8
Avon, *N.Y., U.S.A.* 106 D7
Avon, *S. Dak., U.S.A.* 108 D5
Avon □, *U.K.* 13 F5
Avon →, *Australia* 89 F2
Avon →, *Avon, U.K.* 13 F5
Avon →, *Hants., U.K.* 13 G6
Avon →, *Warks., U.K.* 13 F5
Avondale, *Zimbabwe* 83 F3
Avonlea, *Canada* 101 D7
Avonmore, *Canada* 107 A10
Avonmouth, *U.K.* 13 F5
Avranches, *France* 24 D5
Avre →, *France* 24 D8
Awag el Baqar, *Sudan* 77 E3
A'waj →, *Syria* 69 B5
Awaji-Shima, *Japan* 49 G7
'Awālī, *Bahrain* 65 E6
Awantipur, *India* 63 C6
Awasa, L., *Ethiopia* 77 F4
Awash, *Ethiopia* 68 F3
Awash →, *Ethiopia* 77 E5
Awaso, *Ghana* 78 D4
Awatere →, *N.Z.* 87 J5
Awbārī, *Libya* 75 C7
Awbārī □, *Libya* 75 C7
Awe, L., *U.K.* 14 E3
Aweil, *Sudan* 77 F2
Awgu, *Nigeria* 79 D6
Awjilah, *Libya* 73 C9
Ax-les-Thermes, *France* 26 F5
Axarfjörður, *Iceland* 8 C5
Axel, *Neths.* 17 F3
Axel Heiberg I., *Canada* 4 B3
Axim, *Ghana* 78 E4
Axinim, *Brazil* 121 D6
Axintele, *Romania* 38 E9
Axioma, *Brazil* 125 B5
Axiós →, *Greece* 39 J5
Axminster, *U.K.* 13 G4
Axvall, *Sweden* 11 F7
Aÿ, *France* 25 C11
Ayabaca, *Peru* 124 A2
Ayabe, *Japan* 49 G7
Ayacucho, *Argentina* 126 D4
Ayacucho, *Peru* 124 C3
Ayaguz, *Kazakhstan* 44 E9
Ayamonte, *Spain* 31 H3
Ayan, *Russia* 45 D14
Ayancık, *Turkey* 42 F6
Ayapel, *Colombia* 120 B2
Ayas, *Turkey* 42 F5
Ayaviri, *Peru* 124 C3
Aybastı, *Turkey* 66 C7
Aydın, *Turkey* 66 E2
Aydin □, *Turkey* 66 E2
Aye, *Belgium* 17 H6
Ayenngré, *Togo* 79 D5
Ayer's Cliff, *Canada* 107 A12
Ayers Rock, *Australia* 89 E5
Ayiá, *Greece* 39 K5
Ayía Aikateríni, Ákra, *Greece* 37 A3
Ayia Dhéka, *Greece* 37 D6
Ayia Gálini, *Greece* 37 D6
Ayía Marína, *Greece* 39 M9
Ayia Napa, *Cyprus* 37 E13
Ayía Paraskeví, *Greece* 39 K9
Áyia Phyla, *Cyprus* 37 E12
Ayia Rouméli, *Greece* 39 P6
Ayia Varvára, *Greece* 37 D7
Áyios Amvrósios, *Cyprus* 37 D12
Áyios Andréas, *Greece* 39 M5
Ayíos Evstrátios, *Greece* 39 K7
Áyios Ioánnis, Ákra, *Greece* 37 D7
Áyios Isidhoros, *Greece* 37 C9
Áyios Kiríkos, *Greece* 39 M9
Áyios Matthaíos, *Greece* 37 B3
Áyios Mírono, *Greece* 39 P8
Áyios Nikólaos, *Greece* 37 D7
Áyios Seryios, *Cyprus* 37 D12
Ayios Theodhoros, *Cyprus* 37 D13
Aykathonisi, *Greece* 39 M9
Aylesbury, *U.K.* 13 F7
Aylmer, *Canada* 106 D4
Aylmer, L., *Canada* 96 B8
Ayna, *Spain* 29 G2
Ayolas, *Paraguay* 126 B4
Ayom, *Sudan* 77 F2
Ayon, Ostrov, *Russia* 45 C17
Ayora, *Spain* 29 F3
Ayr, *Australia* 90 B4
Ayr, *U.K.* 14 F4
Ayr →, *U.K.* 14 F4
Ayrancı, *Turkey* 66 E5
Ayre, Pt. of, *U.K.* 12 C3
Aysha, *Ethiopia* 77 E5
Aytos, *Bulgaria* 38 G10
Ayu, Kepulauan, *Indonesia* 57 D8
Ayutla, *Guatemala* 116 D1
Ayutla, *Mexico* 115 D5
Ayvacık, *Turkey* 66 C7
Ayvalık, *Turkey* 66 D2
Aywaille, *Belgium* 17 H7
Az Zabdānī, *Syria* 69 B5
Aẓ Ẓāhirīyah, *Jordan* 69 D3
Aẓ Ẓahrān, *Si. Arabia* 65 E6
Az Zarqā, *Jordan* 69 C5
Az Zāwiyah, *Libya* 75 B7
Az Zībār, *Iraq* 64 B5

Az-Zilfī

Az-Zilfī, *Si. Arabia* 64 E5
Az Zubayr, *Iraq* 64 D5
Azambuja, *Portugal* 31 F2
Azamgarh, *India* 63 F10
Azangaro, *Peru* 124 C3
Azaouak, Vallée de l', *Mali* 79 B5
Āzār Shahr, *Iran* 64 B5
Azärbayjan = Azerbaijan ■, *Asia* 43 F12
Āzarbāyjān-e Gharbī □, *Iran* 64 B5
Āzarbāyjān-e Sharqī □, *Iran* 64 B5
Azare, *Nigeria* 79 C7
Azay-le-Rideau, *France* 24 E7
A'zāz, *Syria* 64 B3
Azazga, *Algeria* 75 A5
Azbine = Aïr, *Niger* 79 B6
Azefal, *Mauritania* 74 D2
Azeffoun, *Algeria* 75 A5
Azemmour, *Morocco* 74 B3
Azerbaijan ■, *Asia* 43 F12
Azerbaijchan = Azerbaijan ■, *Asia* 43 F12
Azezo, *Ethiopia* 77 E4
Azimganj, *India* 63 G13
Aznalcóllar, *Spain* 31 H4
Azogues, *Ecuador* 120 D2
Azores, *Atl. Oc.* 2 C8
Azov, *Russia* 43 C8
Azov, Sea of = Azovskoye More, *Europe* 42 C7
Azovskoye More, *Europe* 42 C7
Azovy, *Russia* 44 C7
Azpeitia, *Spain* 28 B2
Azrou, *Morocco* 74 B3
Aztec, *U.S.A.* 111 H10
Azúa, *Dom. Rep.* 117 C5
Azuaga, *Spain* 31 G5
Azuara, *Spain* 28 D4
Azuay □, *Ecuador* 120 D2
Azuer →, *Spain* 31 F7
Azuero, Pen. de, *Panama* 116 E3
Azul, *Argentina* 126 D4
Azul, Serra, *Brazil* 125 C7
Azurduy, *Bolivia* 125 D5
Azusa, *U.S.A.* 113 L9
Azzaba, *Algeria* 75 A6
Azzano Décimo, *Italy* 33 C9
'Azzūn, *Jordan* 69 C4

B

Ba Don, *Vietnam* 58 D6
Ba Dong, *Vietnam* 59 H6
Ba Ngoi = Cam Lam, *Vietnam* 59 G7
Ba Ria, *Vietnam* 59 G6
Ba Tri, *Vietnam* 59 G6
Ba Xian, *China* 50 E9
Baa, *Indonesia* 57 F6
Baamonde, *Spain* 30 B3
Baar, *Switz.* 23 B7
Baarle Nassau, *Belgium* 17 F5
Baarlo, *Neths.* 17 F8
Baarn, *Neths.* 16 D6
Bab el Mandeb, *Red Sea* 68 E3
Baba Burnu, *Turkey* 66 D2
Baba dag, *Azerbaijan* 43 F13
Bābā Kalū, *Iran* 65 D6
Babaçulândia, *Brazil* 122 C2
Babadag, *Romania* 38 E11
Babadayhan = Kirovsk, *Turkmenistan* 44 F7
Babaeski, *Turkey* 66 C2
Babahoyo, *Ecuador* 120 D2
Babakin, *Australia* 89 F2
Babana, *Nigeria* 79 C5
Babar, *Algeria* 75 A6
Babar, *Indonesia* 57 F7
Babar, *Pakistan* 62 D3
Babarkach, *Pakistan* 62 E2
Babayevo, *Russia* 41 B9
Babb, *U.S.A.* 110 B7
Babenhausen, *Germany* 19 F4
Babi Besar, P., *Malaysia* 59 L4
Babian Jiang →, *China* 52 F3
Babile, *Ethiopia* 77 F5
Babinda, *Australia* 90 B4
Babine, *Canada* 100 B3
Babine →, *Canada* 100 B3
Babine L., *Canada* 100 C3
Babo, *Indonesia* 57 E8
Bābol, *Iran* 65 B7
Bābol Sar, *Iran* 65 B7
Baboua, *C.A.R.* 80 C2
Babruysk = Bobruysk, *Belorussia* 40 E6
Babura, *Nigeria* 79 C6
Babusar Pass, *Pakistan* 63 B5
Babušnica, *Serbia* 21 M12
Babuyan Chan., *Phil.* 55 B4
Babuyan Is., *Phil.* 55 B4
Babylon, *Iraq* 64 C5
Bac Can, *Vietnam* 58 A5
Bac Giang, *Vietnam* 58 B6
Bac Ninh, *Vietnam* 58 B6
Bac Phan, *Vietnam* 58 B5
Bac Quang, *Vietnam* 58 A5
Bacabal, *Brazil* 122 B3
Bacajá →, *Brazil* 121 D7
Bacalar, *Mexico* 115 D7
Bacan, *Indonesia* 57 F7
Bacan, Kepulauan, *Indonesia* 57 E7
Bacan, Pulau, *Indonesia* 57 E7
Bacarra, *Phil.* 55 B4
Bacău, *Romania* 38 C9
Baccarat, *France* 25 D13
Bacerac, *Mexico* 114 A3
Băceşti, *Romania* 38 C10
Bach Long Vi, Dao, *Vietnam* 58 B6
Bachaquero, *Venezuela* 120 B3
Bacharach, *Germany* 19 E3
Bachelina, *Russia* 44 D7
Bachuma, *Ethiopia* 77 F4
Bačina, *Serbia* 21 M11
Back →, *Canada* 96 B9
Bačka Palanka, *Serbia* 21 K9
Bačka Topola, *Serbia* 21 K9
Bäckefors, *Sweden* 11 F6
Backnang, *Germany* 19 G5
Backstairs Passage, *Australia* 91 F2
Baco, Mt., *Phil.* 55 E4
Bacolod, *Phil.* 55 F5
Bacqueville-en-Caux, *France* 24 C8
Bácsalmás, *Hungary* 21 J9
Bacuag, *Phil.* 55 G6
Bacuk, *Malaysia* 59 J4
Bād, *Iran* 65 C7
Bad →, *U.S.A.* 108 C4
Bad Axe, *U.S.A.* 106 C2
Bad Bergzabern, *Germany* 19 F4
Bad Berleburg, *Germany* 18 D4
Bad Bevensen, *Germany* 18 B6
Bad Bramstedt, *Germany* 18 B5
Bad Brückenau, *Germany* 19 E5
Bad Doberan, *Germany* 18 A7
Bad Driburg, *Germany* 18 D5
Bad Ems, *Germany* 19 E3
Bad Frankenhausen, *Germany* 18 D7
Bad Freienwalde, *Germany* 18 C10
Bad Godesberg, *Germany* 18 E3
Bad Hersfeld, *Germany* 18 E5
Bad Hofgastein, *Austria* 21 H3
Bad Homburg, *Germany* 19 E4
Bad Honnef, *Germany* 18 E3
Bad Ischl, *Austria* 21 H3
Bad Kissingen, *Germany* 19 E6
Bad Königshofen, *Germany* 19 E6
Bad Kreuznach, *Germany* 19 F3
Bad Laasphe, *Germany* 18 E4
Bad Lands, *U.S.A.* 108 D3
Bad Langensalza, *Germany* 18 D6
Bad Lauterberg, *Germany* 18 D6
Bad Lippspringe, *Germany* 18 D4
Bad Mergentheim, *Germany* 19 F5
Bad Münstereifel, *Germany* 18 E2
Bad Muskau, *Germany* 18 D10
Bad Nauheim, *Germany* 19 E4
Bad Oeynhausen, *Germany* 18 C4
Bad Oldesloe, *Germany* 18 B6
Bad Orb, *Germany* 19 E5
Bad Pyrmont, *Germany* 18 D5
Bad Ragaz, *Switz.* 23 B9
Bad Reichenhall, *Germany* 19 H8
Bad Säckingen, *Germany* 19 H3
Bad Salzuflen, *Germany* 18 C4
Bad Segeberg, *Germany* 18 B6
Bad Tölz, *Germany* 19 H7
Bad Urach, *Germany* 19 G5
Bad Waldsee, *Germany* 19 H5
Bad Wildungen, *Germany* 18 D5
Bad Wimpfen, *Germany* 19 F5
Bad Windsheim, *Germany* 19 F6
Badagara, *India* 60 P9
Badagri, *Nigeria* 79 D5
Badajós, L., *Brazil* 121 D5
Badajoz, *Spain* 31 G4
Badajoz □, *Spain* 31 G4
Badalona, *Spain* 28 D7
Badalzai, *Afghan.* 62 E1
Badampahar, *India* 61 H15
Badanah, *Si. Arabia* 64 D4
Badarinath, *India* 63 D8
Badas, *Brunei* 56 D4
Badas, Kepulauan, *Indonesia* 56 D3
Baddo →, *Pakistan* 60 F4
Bade, *Indonesia* 57 F9
Baden, *Austria* 21 G6
Baden, *Switz.* 23 B6
Baden-Baden, *Germany* 19 G4
Baden-Württemberg □, *Germany* 19 G5
Badenoch, *U.K.* 14 E4
Badger, *Canada* 99 C8
Badger, *U.S.A.* 112 J7
Bādghīsāt □, *Afghan.* 60 B3
Badgom, *India* 63 B6
Badhoevedorp, *Neths.* 16 D5
Badia Polèsine, *Italy* 33 C8
Badin, *Pakistan* 62 G3
Badogo, *Mali* 78 C3
Badong, *China* 53 B8
Baduen, *Somali Rep.* 68 F4
Badulla, *Sri Lanka* 60 R12
Baena, *Spain* 31 H6
Baexem, *Neths.* 17 F7
Baeza, *Ecuador* 120 D2
Baeza, *Spain* 29 H1
Bafa Gölü, *Turkey* 66 E2
Bafang, *Cameroon* 79 D7
Bafatá, *Guinea-Biss.* 78 C2
Baffin B., *Canada* 4 B4
Baffin I., *Canada* 97 B12
Bafia, *Cameroon* 79 E7
Bafilo, *Togo* 79 D5
Bafing →, *Mali* 78 C2
Bafliyūn, *Syria* 64 B3
Baflo, *Neths.* 16 B9
Bafoulabé, *Mali* 78 C2
Bafoussam, *Cameroon* 79 D7
Bāfq, *Iran* 65 D7
Bafra, *Turkey* 42 F6
Bafra Burnu, *Turkey* 42 F6
Bāft, *Iran* 65 D8
Bafut, *Cameroon* 79 D7
Bafwasende, *Zaïre* 82 B2
Bagamoyo, *Tanzania* 82 D4
Bagamoyo □, *Tanzania* 82 D4
Bagan Datoh, *Malaysia* 59 L3
Bagan Serai, *Malaysia* 59 K3
Baganga, *Phil.* 55 H7
Bagani, *Namibia* 84 B3
Bagansiapiapi, *Indonesia* 56 D2
Bagasra, *India* 62 J4
Bagawi, *Sudan* 77 E3
Bagdad, *U.S.A.* 113 L11
Bagdarin, *Russia* 45 D12
Bagé, *Brazil* 127 C5
Bagenalstown = Muine Bheag, *Ireland* 15 D5
Baggs, *U.S.A.* 110 F10
Bagh, *Pakistan* 63 C5
Baghdād, *Iraq* 64 C5
Bagheria, *Italy* 34 D6
Baghlān, *Afghan.* 60 A6
Bagley, *U.S.A.* 108 B7
Bagnacavallo, *Italy* 33 D8
Bagnara Cálabra, *Italy* 35 D8
Bagnères-de-Bigorre, *France* 26 E4
Bagnères-de-Luchon, *France* 26 F4
Bagni di Lucca, *Italy* 32 D7
Bagno di Romagna, *Italy* 33 E8
Bagnoles-de-l'Orne, *France* 24 D6
Bagnoli di Sopra, *Italy* 33 C8
Bagnolo Mella, *Italy* 32 C7
Bagnols-sur-Cèze, *France* 27 D8
Bagnorégio, *Italy* 33 F9
Bagolino, *Italy* 32 C7
Bagotville, *Canada* 99 C5
Bagua, *Peru* 124 B2
Baguio, *Phil.* 55 C4
Bahabón de Esgueva, *Spain* 28 D1
Bahadurgarh, *India* 62 E7
Bahama, Canal Viejo de, *W. Indies* 116 B4
Bahamas ■, *N. Amer.* 117 B5
Baharampur, *India* 63 G13
Baharîya, El Wâhât al, *Egypt* 76 J6
Bahau, *Malaysia* 59 L4
Bahawalnagar, *Pakistan* 62 D5
Bahawalpur, *Pakistan* 62 E4
Bahçe, *Turkey* 66 E7
Baheri, *India* 63 E8
Bahi, *Tanzania* 82 D4
Bahi Swamp, *Tanzania* 82 D4
Bahía = Salvador, *Brazil* 123 D4
Bahía □, *Brazil* 123 D3
Bahía, Is. de la, *Honduras* 116 C2
Bahía Blanca, *Argentina* 126 D3
Bahía de Caráquez, *Ecuador* 120 D1
Bahía Honda, *Cuba* 116 B3
Bahía Laura, *Argentina* 128 C3
Bahía Negra, *Paraguay* 125 E6
Bahir Dar, *Ethiopia* 77 E4
Bahmanzād, *Iran* 65 D6
Bahmer, *Algeria* 75 C4
Bahönye, *Hungary* 21 J7
Bahr Aouk →, *C.A.R.* 80 C3
Bahr el Ahmar □, *Sudan* 76 C3
Bahr el Ghazâl □, *Sudan* 77 F2
Bahr Salamat →, *Chad* 73 G8
Bahr Yûsef →, *Egypt* 76 J7
Bahra el Burullus, *Egypt* 76 H7
Bahraich, *India* 63 F9
Bahrain ■, *Asia* 65 E6
Bahret Assad, *Syria* 64 C3
Bahror, *India* 62 F7
Bāhū Kalāt, *Iran* 65 E9
Bai, *Mali* 78 C4
Bai Bung, Mui, *Vietnam* 59 H5
Bai Duc, *Vietnam* 58 C5
Bai Thuong, *Vietnam* 58 C5
Baia Mare, *Romania* 38 B6
Baia-Sprie, *Romania* 38 B6
Baião, *Brazil* 122 B2
Baïbokoum, *Chad* 73 G8
Baicheng, *China* 51 B12
Baidoa, *Somali Rep.* 68 G3
Baie Comeau, *Canada* 99 C6
Baie-St-Paul, *Canada* 99 C5
Baie Trinité, *Canada* 99 C6
Baie Verte, *Canada* 99 C8
Baignes-Ste.-Radegonde, *France* 26 C3
Baigneux-les-Juifs, *France* 25 E11
Baihe, *China* 50 H6
Baihe, *Taiwan* 53 F13
Ba'ījī, *Iraq* 64 C4
Baikal, L. = Baykal, Oz., *Russia* 45 D11
Baile Atha Cliath = Dublin, *Ireland* 15 C5
Bailei, *Ethiopia* 77 F5
Bailén, *Spain* 31 G7
Băileşti, *Romania* 38 E6
Baileux, *Belgium* 17 H4
Bailique, Ilha, *Brazil* 122 A2
Bailleul, *France* 25 B9
Bailundo, *Angola* 81 G3
Baima, *China* 52 A3
Bain-de-Bretagne, *France* 24 E5
Bainbridge, *Ga., U.S.A.* 105 K3
Bainbridge, *N.Y., U.S.A.* 107 D9
Baing, *Indonesia* 57 F6
Bainiu, *China* 50 H7
Bainville, *U.S.A.* 108 A2
Bā'ir, *Jordan* 69 E5
Baird, *U.S.A.* 109 J5
Baird Mts., *U.S.A.* 96 B3
Bairin Youqi, *China* 51 C10
Bairin Zuoqi, *China* 51 C10
Bairnsdale, *Australia* 91 F4
Bais, *Phil.* 55 G5
Baisha, *China* 50 G7
Baïsole →, *France* 26 E4
Baissa, *Nigeria* 79 D7
Baitadi, *Nepal* 63 E9
Baixa Grande, *Brazil* 123 D3
Baiyin, *China* 50 F3
Baiyü, *China* 52 B2
Baiyu Shan, *China* 50 F4
Baiyuda, *Sudan* 76 D3
Baj Baj, *India* 63 H13
Baja, *Hungary* 21 J8
Baja, Pta., *Mexico* 114 B1
Baja California, *Mexico* 114 A1
Bajamar, *Canary Is.* 36 F3
Bajana, *India* 62 H4
Bājgīrān, *Iran* 65 B8
Bajimba, Mt., *Australia* 91 D5
Bajo Nuevo, *Caribbean* 116 C4
Bajoga, *Nigeria* 79 C7
Bajool, *Australia* 90 C5
Bakala, *C.A.R.* 73 G9
Bakar, *Croatia* 33 C11
Bakchar, *Russia* 44 D9
Bakel, *Neths.* 17 E7
Bakel, *Senegal* 78 C2
Baker, *Calif., U.S.A.* 113 K10
Baker, *Mont., U.S.A.* 108 B2
Baker, *Oreg., U.S.A.* 110 D5
Baker, Canal, *Chile* 128 C2
Baker, L., *Canada* 96 B10
Baker I., *Pac. Oc.* 92 G10
Baker L., *Australia* 89 E4
Baker Lake, *Canada* 96 B10
Baker Mt., *U.S.A.* 110 B3
Bakers Creek, *Australia* 90 C4
Baker's Dozen Is., *Canada* 98 A4
Bakersfield, *Calif., U.S.A.* 113 K7
Bakersfield, *Vt., U.S.A.* 107 B12
Bakhchisaray, *Ukraine* 42 D5
Bakhmach, *Ukraine* 40 F8
Bākhtarān, *Iran* 64 C5
Bakhtārān □, *Iran* 64 C5
Bakırdaği, *Turkey* 66 D6
Bakırköy, *Turkey* 39 H11
Bakkafjörður, *Iceland* 8 C6
Bakkagerði, *Iceland* 8 D7
Bakony →, *Hungary* 21 H7
Bakony Forest = Bakony Hegyseg, *Hungary* 21 H7
Bakony Hegyseg, *Hungary* 21 H7
Bakori, *Nigeria* 79 C6
Bakouma, *C.A.R.* 73 G9
Baku, *Azerbaijan* 43 F13
Bakutis Coast, *Antarctica* 5 D15
Baky = Baku, *Azerbaijan* 43 F13
Bala, *Canada* 106 A5
Bâlâ, *Turkey* 66 D5
Bala, L., *U.K.* 12 E4
Balabac I., *Phil.* 55 H2
Balabac Str., *E. Indies* 56 C5
Balabagh, *Afghan.* 62 B4
Balabakk, *Lebanon* 69 A5
Balabalangan, Kepulauan, *Indonesia* 56 E5
Bălăciţa, *Romania* 38 E6
Balad, *Iraq* 64 C5
Balad Rūz, *Iraq* 64 C5
Bālādeh, *Fārs, Iran* 65 D6
Baladeh, *Māzandaran, Iran* 65 B6
Balaghat, *India* 60 J12
Balaghat Ra., *India* 60 K10
Balaguer, *Spain* 28 D5
Balakhna, *Russia* 41 C13
Balaklava, *Australia* 91 E2
Balaklava, *Ukraine* 42 D5
Balakleya, *Ukraine* 42 B7
Balakovo, *Russia* 41 E15
Balancán, *Mexico* 115 D6
Balanda, *Russia* 41 F14
Balashikha, *Russia* 41 D10
Balashov, *Russia* 41 F13
Balasinor, *India* 62 H5
Balasore = Baleshwar, *India* 61 J15
Balassagyarmat, *Hungary* 21 G9
Balât, *Egypt* 76 B2
Balaton, *Hungary* 21 J7
Balayan, *Phil.* 55 E4
Balazote, *Spain* 29 G2
Balboa, *Panama* 116 E4
Balbriggan, *Ireland* 15 C5
Balcarce, *Argentina* 126 D4
Balcarres, *Canada* 101 C8
Balchik, *Bulgaria* 38 F11
Balclutha, *N.Z.* 87 M2
Bald Hd., *Australia* 89 G2
Bald I., *Australia* 89 F2
Bald Knob, *U.S.A.* 109 H9
Baldock L., *Canada* 101 B9
Baldwin, *Fla., U.S.A.* 105 K4
Baldwin, *Mich., U.S.A.* 104 D3
Baldwinsville, *U.S.A.* 107 C8
Baldy Peak, *U.S.A.* 111 K9
Bale, *Croatia* 33 C10
Bale □, *Ethiopia* 77 F5
Baleares □, *Spain* 28 F7
Baleares, Is., *Spain* 36 B10
Balearic Is. = Baleares, Is., *Spain* 36 B10
Baleia, Pta. da, *Brazil* 123 E4
Balen, *Belgium* 17 F6
Baler, *Phil.* 55 D4
Baler Bay, *Phil.* 55 D4
Balerna, *Switz.* 23 E8
Baleshwar, *India* 61 J15
Balfate, *Honduras* 116 C2
Balfe's Creek, *Australia* 90 C4
Balfour, *S. Africa* 85 D4
Bali, *Cameroon* 79 D6
Balí, *Greece* 37 D6
Bali, *Indonesia* 56 F5
Bali □, *Indonesia* 56 F5
Bali, Selat, *Indonesia* 57 H16
Baligród, *Poland* 20 F12
Balık Gölü, *Turkey* 67 D10
Balikeşir, *Turkey* 66 D2
Balikeşir □, *Turkey* 66 D2
Balikpapan, *Indonesia* 56 E5
Balimbing, *Phil.* 57 C5
Baling, *Malaysia* 59 K3
Balintang Channel, *Phil.* 55 B4
Balipara, *India* 61 F18
Baliza, *Brazil* 125 D7
Balk, *Neths.* 16 C7
Balkan Mts. = Stara Planina, *Bulgaria* 38 F6
Balkan Peninsula, *Europe* 6 G10
Balkhash, *Kazakhstan* 44 E8
Balkhash, Ozero, *Kazakhstan* 44 E8
Balla, *Bangla.* 61 G17
Ballachulish, *U.K.* 14 E3
Balladonia, *Australia* 89 F3
Ballarat, *Australia* 91 F3
Ballard, L., *Australia* 89 E3
Ballater, *U.K.* 14 D5
Ballenas, Canal de, *Mexico* 114 B2
Balleny Is., *Antarctica* 5 C11
Ballesteros, *Phil.* 55 B4
Ballia, *India* 63 G11
Ballidu, *Australia* 89 F2
Ballina, *Australia* 91 D5
Ballina, *Mayo, Ireland* 15 B2
Ballina, *Tipp., Ireland* 15 D3
Ballinasloe, *Ireland* 15 C3
Ballinger, *U.S.A.* 109 K5
Ballinrobe, *Ireland* 15 C2
Ballinskelligs B., *Ireland* 15 E1
Ballon, *France* 24 D7
Ballycastle, *U.K.* 15 A5
Ballymena, *U.K.* 15 B5
Ballymena □, *U.K.* 15 B5
Ballymoney, *U.K.* 15 A5
Ballymoney □, *U.K.* 15 A5
Ballyshannon, *Ireland* 15 B3
Balmaceda, *Chile* 128 C2
Balmazújváros, *Hungary* 21 H11
Balmhorn, *Switz.* 22 D5
Balmoral, *Australia* 91 F3
Balmoral, *U.K.* 14 D5
Balmorhea, *U.S.A.* 109 K3
Balonne →, *Australia* 91 D4
Balqash Kol = Balkhash, Ozero, *Kazakhstan* 44 E8
Balrampur, *India* 63 F10
Balranald, *Australia* 91 E3
Balş, *Romania* 38 E7
Balsapuerto, *Peru* 124 B2
Balsas, *Mexico* 115 D5
Balsas →, *Goiás, Brazil* 122 C2
Balsas →, *Maranhão, Brazil* 122 C3
Balsas →, *Mexico* 114 D4
Bålsta, *Sweden* 10 E11
Balsthal, *Switz.* 22 B5
Balston Spa, *U.S.A.* 107 D11
Balta, *Romania* 38 E5
Balta, *Russia* 43 E11
Balta, *Ukraine* 42 B3
Balta, *U.S.A.* 108 A4
Baltanás, *Spain* 30 D6
Bălţi = Beltsy, *Moldavia* 42 C3
Baltic Sea, *Europe* 9 H15
Baltîm, *Egypt* 76 H7
Baltimore, *Ireland* 15 E2
Baltimore, *U.S.A.* 104 F7
Baltit, *Pakistan* 63 A6
Baltrum, *Germany* 18 B3
Baluchistan □, *Pakistan* 60 F4
Balurghat, *India* 63 G13
Balya, *Turkey* 66 D2
Balygychan, *Russia* 45 C16
Balzar, *Ecuador* 120 D2
Bam, *Iran* 65 D8
Bama, *China* 52 E6
Bama, *Nigeria* 79 C7
Bamako, *Mali* 78 C3

Bamba, *Mali* 79 B4
Bambamarca, *Peru* 124 B2
Bambari, *C.A.R.* 73 G9
Bambaroo, *Australia* 90 B4
Bamberg, *Germany* 19 F6
Bamberg, *U.S.A.* 105 J5
Bambesi, *Ethiopia* 77 F3
Bambey, *Senegal* 78 C1
Bambili, *Zaïre* 82 B2
Bambuí, *Brazil* 123 F2
Bamenda, *Cameroon* 79 D7
Bamfield, *Canada* 100 D3
Bāmīān □, *Afghan.* 60 B5
Bamiancheng, *China* 51 C13
Bamkin, *Cameroon* 79 D7
Bampūr, *Iran* 65 E9
Ban Aranyaprathet, *Thailand* 58 F4
Ban Ban, *Laos* 58 C4
Ban Bang Hin, *Thailand* 59 H2
Ban Chiang Klang, *Thailand* 58 C3
Ban Chik, *Laos* 58 D4
Ban Choho, *Thailand* 58 E4
Ban Dan Lan Hoi, *Thailand* 58 D2
Ban Don = Surat Thani, *Thailand* 59 H2
Ban Don, *Vietnam* 58 F6
Ban Don, Ao, *Thailand* 59 H2
Ban Dong, *Thailand* 58 C3
Ban Hong, *Thailand* 58 C2
Ban Kaeng, *Thailand* 58 D3
Ban Keun, *Laos* 58 C4
Ban Khai, *Thailand* 58 F3
Ban Kheun, *Laos* 58 B3
Ban Khlong Kua, *Thailand* 59 J3
Ban Khuan Mao, *Thailand* 59 J2
Ban Khun Yuam, *Thailand* 58 C1
Ban Ko Yai Chim, *Thailand* 59 G2
Ban Kok, *Thailand* 58 D4
Ban Laem, *Thailand* 58 F2
Ban Lao Ngam, *Laos* 58 E6
Ban Le Kathe, *Thailand* 58 E2
Ban Mae Chedi, *Thailand* 58 C2
Ban Mae Laeng, *Thailand* 58 B2
Ban Mae Sariang, *Thailand* 58 C1
Ban Mê Thuôt = Buon Me Thuot, *Vietnam* 58 F7
Ban Mi, *Thailand* 58 E3
Ban Muong Mo, *Laos* 58 C4
Ban Na Mo, *Laos* 58 D5
Ban Na San, *Thailand* 59 H2
Ban Na Tong, *Laos* 58 B3
Ban Nam Bac, *Laos* 58 B4
Ban Nam Ma, *Laos* 58 A3
Ban Ngang, *Laos* 58 E6
Ban Nong Bok, *Laos* 58 D5
Ban Nong Boua, *Laos* 58 E6
Ban Nong Pling, *Thailand* 58 E3
Ban Pak Chan, *Thailand* 59 G2
Ban Phai, *Thailand* 58 D4
Ban Pong, *Thailand* 58 F2
Ban Ron Phibun, *Thailand* 59 H2
Ban Sanam Chai, *Thailand* 59 J3
Ban Sangkha, *Thailand* 58 E4
Ban Tak, *Thailand* 58 D2
Ban Tako, *Thailand* 58 E4
Ban Tha Dua, *Thailand* 58 D2
Ban Tha Li, *Thailand* 58 D3
Ban Tha Nun, *Thailand* 59 H2
Ban Thahine, *Laos* 58 E5
Ban Xien Kok, *Laos* 58 B3
Ban Yen Nhan, *Vietnam* 58 B6
Baña, Punta de la, *Spain* 28 E5
Banaba, *Kiribati* 92 H8
Bañalbufar, *Spain* 36 B9
Banalia, *Zaïre* 82 B2
Banam, *Cambodia* 59 G5
Banamba, *Mali* 78 C3
Banana, *Australia* 90 C5
Bananal, I. do, *Brazil* 123 D1
Banaras = Varanasi, *India* 63 G10
Banas →, *Gujarat, India* 62 H4
Banas →, *Mad. P., India* 63 G9
Bânâs, Ras, *Egypt* 76 C4
Banaz, *Turkey* 66 D3
Banbān, *Si. Arabia* 64 E5
Banbridge, *U.K.* 15 B5
Banbridge □, *U.K.* 15 B5
Banbury, *U.K.* 13 E6
Banchory, *U.K.* 14 D6
Bancroft, *Canada* 98 C4
Band Bonī, *Iran* 65 E8
Band Qīr, *Iran* 65 D6
Banda, *India* 63 G9
Banda, Kepulauan, *Indonesia* 57 E7
Banda Aceh, *Indonesia* 56 C1
Banda Banda, Mt., *Australia* 91 E5
Banda Elat, *Indonesia* 57 F8
Banda Is. = Banda, Kepulauan, *Indonesia* 57 E7
Banda Sea, *Indonesia* 57 F7
Bandai-San, *Japan* 48 F10
Bandama →, *Ivory C.* 78 D3
Bandān, *Iran* 65 D9
Bandanaira, *Indonesia* 57 E7
Bandanwara, *India* 62 F6
Bandar = Machilipatnam, *India* 61 L12
Bandār 'Abbās, *Iran* 65 E8
Bandar-e Anzalī, *Iran* 65 B6
Bandar-e Chārak, *Iran* 65 E7
Bandar-e Deylam, *Iran* 65 D6
Bandar-e Khomeyni, *Iran* 65 D6
Bandar-e Lengeh, *Iran* 65 E7
Bandar-e Maqām, *Iran* 65 E7
Bandar-e Ma'shur, *Iran* 65 D6
Bandar-e Nakhīlū, *Iran* 65 E7
Bandar-e Rīg, *Iran* 65 D6
Bandar-e Torkeman, *Iran* 65 B7
Bandar Maharani = Muar, *Malaysia* 59 L4
Bandar Penggaram = Batu Pahat, *Malaysia* 59 M4
Bandar Seri Begawan, *Brunei* 56 C4
Bandawe, *Malawi* 83 E3
Bande, *Belgium* 17 H6
Bande, *Spain* 30 C3
Bandeira, Pico da, *Brazil* 123 F3
Bandeirante, *Brazil* 123 D1
Bandera, *Argentina* 126 B3
Bandera, *U.S.A.* 109 L5
Banderas, B. de, *Mexico* 114 C3
Bandiagara, *Mali* 78 C4
Bandırma, *Turkey* 66 C3
Bandon, *Ireland* 15 E3
Bandon →, *Ireland* 15 E3
Bandula, *Mozam.* 83 F3
Bandundu, *Zaïre* 80 E3
Bandung, *Indonesia* 57 G12
Bandya, *Australia* 89 E3
Bāneh, *Iran* 64 C5
Bañeres, *Spain* 29 G4
Banes, *Cuba* 117 B4
Banff, *Canada* 100 C5
Banff, *U.K.* 14 D6
Banff Nat. Park, *Canada* 100 C5
Banfora, *Burkina Faso* 78 C4
Bang Fai →, *Laos* 58 D5
Bang Hieng →, *Laos* 58 D5
Bang Krathum, *Thailand* 58 D3
Bang Lamung, *Thailand* 58 F3
Bang Mun Nak, *Thailand* 58 D3
Bang Pa In, *Thailand* 58 E3
Bang Rakam, *Thailand* 58 D3
Bang Saphan, *Thailand* 59 G2
Bangala Dam, *Zimbabwe* 83 G3
Bangalore, *India* 60 N10
Bangante, *Cameroon* 79 D7
Bangaon, *India* 63 H13
Bangassou, *C.A.R.* 80 D4
Banggai, Kepulauan, *Indonesia* 57 E6
Banggi, P., *Malaysia* 56 C5
Banghāzī, *Libya* 73 B9
Bangil, *Indonesia* 57 G15
Bangjang, *Sudan* 77 E3
Bangka, P., *Sulawesi, Indonesia* 57 D7
Bangka, P., *Sumatera, Indonesia* 56 E3
Bangka, Selat, *Indonesia* 56 E3
Bangkalan, *Indonesia* 57 G15
Bangkinang, *Indonesia* 56 D2
Bangko, *Indonesia* 56 E2
Bangkok, *Thailand* 58 F3
Bangladesh ■, *Asia* 61 H17
Bangolo, *Ivory C.* 78 D3
Bangong Co, *India* 63 B8
Bangor, *Down, U.K.* 15 B6
Bangor, *Gwynedd, U.K.* 12 D3
Bangor, *Maine, U.S.A.* 99 D6
Bangor, *Pa., U.S.A.* 107 F9
Bangued, *Phil.* 55 C4
Bangui, *C.A.R.* 80 D3
Bangui, *Phil.* 55 B4
Banguru, *Zaïre* 82 B2
Bangweulu, L., *Zambia* 83 E3
Bangweulu Swamp, *Zambia* 83 E3
Bani, *Dom. Rep.* 117 C5
Bani →, *Mali* 78 C4
Bani, Djebel, *Morocco* 74 C3
Bani Bangou, *Niger* 79 B5
Banī Sa'd, *Iraq* 64 C5
Banī Walīd, *Libya* 73 B7
Bania, *Ivory C.* 78 D4
Banihal Pass, *India* 63 C6
Banīnah, *Libya* 73 B9
Bāniyās, *Syria* 64 C3
Banja Luka, *Bos.-H.* 21 L7
Banjar, *Indonesia* 57 G13
Banjarmasin, *Indonesia* 56 E4
Banjarnegara, *Indonesia* 57 G13
Banjul, *Gambia* 78 C1
Banka Banka, *Australia* 90 B1
Banket, *Zimbabwe* 83 F3
Bankilaré, *Niger* 79 C5
Bankipore, *India* 63 G11
Banks I., *B.C., Canada* 100 C3
Banks I., *N.W.T., Canada* 96 A7
Banks Pen., *N.Z.* 87 K4
Banks Str., *Australia* 90 G4
Bankura, *India* 63 H12
Bann →, *Down, U.K.* 15 B5
Bann →, *L'derry., U.K.* 15 A5
Banna, *Phil.* 55 C4
Bannalec, *France* 24 E3
Bannang Sata, *Thailand* 59 J3
Banning, *U.S.A.* 113 M10
Banningville = Bandundu, *Zaïre* 80 E3
Bannockburn, *Canada* 106 B7
Bannockburn, *U.K.* 14 E5
Bannockburn, *Zimbabwe* 83 G2
Bannu, *Pakistan* 60 C7
Bañolas, *Spain* 28 C7
Banon, *France* 27 D9
Baños de la Encina, *Spain* 31 G7
Baños de Molgas, *Spain* 30 C3
Banská Bystrica, *Slovak Rep.* 20 G9
Banská Štiavnica, *Slovak Rep.* 21 G8
Banswara, *India* 62 H6
Bantayan, *Phil.* 55 F5
Banten, *Indonesia* 57 G12
Bantry, *Ireland* 15 E2
Bantry B., *Ireland* 15 E2
Bantul, *Indonesia* 57 G14
Bantva, *India* 62 J4
Banu, *Afghan.* 60 B6
Banyak, Kepulauan, *Indonesia* 56 D1
Banyo, *Cameroon* 79 D7
Banyuls-sur-Mer, *France* 26 F7
Banyumas, *Indonesia* 57 G13
Banyuwangi, *Indonesia* 57 H16
Banzare Coast, *Antarctica* 5 C9
Banzyville = Mobayi, *Zaïre* 80 D4
Bao Ha, *Vietnam* 58 A5
Bao Lac, *Vietnam* 58 A5
Bao Loc, *Vietnam* 59 G6
Bao'an, *China* 53 F10
Baocheng, *China* 50 H4
Baode, *China* 50 E6
Baodi, *China* 51 E9
Baoding, *China* 50 E8
Baoji, *China* 50 G4
Baojing, *China* 52 C7
Baokang, *China* 53 B8
Baoshan, *Shanghai, China* 53 B13
Baoshan, *Yunnan, China* 52 E2
Baotou, *China* 50 D6
Baoying, *China* 51 H10
Bap, *India* 62 F5
Bapatla, *India* 61 M12
Bapaume, *France* 25 B9
Bāqerābād, *Iran* 65 C6
Ba'qūbah, *Iraq* 64 C5
Baquedano, *Chile* 126 A2
Bar, *Montenegro* 21 N9
Bar, *Ukraine* 42 B2
Bar Bigha, *India* 63 G11
Bar Harbor, *U.S.A.* 99 D6
Bar-le-Duc, *France* 25 D12
Bar-sur-Aube, *France* 25 D11
Bar-sur-Seine, *France* 25 D11
Barabai, *Indonesia* 56 E5
Barabinsk, *Russia* 44 D8
Baraboo, *U.S.A.* 108 D10
Baracaldo, *Spain* 28 B2
Baracoa, *Cuba* 117 B5
Baradero, *Argentina* 126 C4
Baraga, *U.S.A.* 108 B10
Barahona, *Dom. Rep.* 117 C5
Barahona, *Spain* 28 D2
Barail Range, *India* 61 G18
Baraka →, *Sudan* 76 D4
Barakhola, *India* 61 G18
Barakot, *India* 63 J11
Barakpur, *India* 63 H13
Barakula, *Australia* 91 D5
Baralaba, *Australia* 90 C4
Baralzon L., *Canada* 101 B9
Barameiya, *Sudan* 76 D4
Baramula, *India* 63 B6
Baran, *India* 62 G7
Baranavichy = Baranovichi, *Belorussia* 40 E5
Baranoa, *Colombia* 120 A3
Baranof I., *U.S.A.* 100 B1
Baranovichi, *Belorussia* 40 E5
Barão de Cocais, *Brazil* 123 E3
Barão de Grajaú, *Brazil* 122 C3
Barão de Melgaço, *Mato Grosso, Brazil* 125 D6
Barão de Melgaço, *Rondônia, Brazil* 125 C5
Baraolt, *Romania* 38 C8
Barapasi, *Indonesia* 57 E9
Barasat, *India* 63 H13
Barat Daya, Kepulauan, *Indonesia* 57 F7
Barataria B., *U.S.A.* 109 L10
Baraut, *India* 62 E7
Baraya, *Colombia* 120 C2
Barbacena, *Brazil* 123 F3
Barbacoas, *Colombia* 120 C2
Barbacoas, *Venezuela* 120 B4
Barbados ■, *W. Indies* 117 D8
Barbalha, *Brazil* 122 C4
Barban, *Croatia* 33 C11
Barbastro, *Spain* 28 C5
Barbate, *Spain* 31 J5
Barberino di Mugello, *Italy* 33 D8
Barberton, *S. Africa* 85 D5
Barberton, *U.S.A.* 106 E3
Barbezieux, *France* 26 C3
Barbosa, *Colombia* 120 B3
Barbourville, *U.S.A.* 105 G4
Barbuda, *W. Indies* 117 C7
Barcaldine, *Australia* 90 C4
Barcarrota, *Spain* 31 G4
Barcellona Pozzo di Gotto, *Italy* 35 D8
Barcelona, *Spain* 28 D7
Barcelona, *Venezuela* 121 A5
Barcelona □, *Spain* 28 D7
Barcelonette, *France* 27 D10
Barcelos, *Brazil* 121 D5
Barcoo →, *Australia* 90 D3
Barcs, *Hungary* 21 K7
Barda, *Azerbaijan* 43 F12
Barda del Medio, *Argentina* 128 A3
Bardai, *Chad* 73 D8
Bardas Blancas, *Argentina* 126 D2
Barddhaman, *India* 63 H12
Bardejov, *Slovak Rep.* 20 F11
Bardera, *Somali Rep.* 68 G3
Bardi, *Italy* 32 D6
Bardia, *Libya* 73 B9
Bardolino, *Italy* 32 C7
Bardsey I., *U.K.* 12 E3
Bardstown, *U.S.A.* 104 G3
Bareilly, *India* 63 E8
Barentin, *France* 24 C7
Barenton, *France* 24 D6
Barents Sea, *Arctic* 4 B9
Barentu, *Eritrea* 77 D4
Barfleur, *France* 24 C5
Barfleur, Pte. de, *France* 24 C5
Barga, *China* 54 C3
Barga, *Italy* 32 D7
Bargal, *Somali Rep.* 68 E5
Bargara, *Australia* 90 C5
Barge, *Italy* 32 D4
Bargnop, *Sudan* 77 F2
Bargteheide, *Germany* 18 B6
Barguzin, *Russia* 45 D11
Barh, *India* 63 G11
Barhaj, *India* 63 F10
Barhi, *India* 63 G11
Bari, *India* 62 F7
Bari, *Italy* 35 A9
Bari Doab, *Pakistan* 62 D5
Bariadi □, *Tanzania* 82 C3
Barīm, *Yemen* 68 E3
Barima →, *Guyana* 121 B5
Barinas, *Venezuela* 120 B3
Barinas □, *Venezuela* 120 B4
Baring, C., *Canada* 96 B8
Baringo, *Kenya* 82 B4
Baringo □, *Kenya* 82 B4
Baringo, L., *Kenya* 82 B4
Barinitas, *Venezuela* 120 B3
Bariri, *Brazil* 123 F2
Bârîs, *Egypt* 76 C3
Barisal, *Bangla.* 61 H17
Barisan, Bukit, *Indonesia* 56 E2
Barito →, *Indonesia* 56 E4
Barjac, *France* 27 D8
Barjols, *France* 27 E10
Barjūj, Wadi →, *Libya* 75 C7
Bark L., *Canada* 106 A7
Barka = Baraka →, *Sudan* 76 D4
Barkam, *China* 52 B4
Barker, *U.S.A.* 106 C6
Barkley Sound, *Canada* 100 D3
Barkly Downs, *Australia* 90 C2
Barkly East, *S. Africa* 84 E4
Barkly Tableland, *Australia* 90 B2
Barkly West, *S. Africa* 84 D3
Barkol, Wadi →, *Sudan* 76 D3
Barksdale, *U.S.A.* 109 L4
Barlee, L., *Australia* 89 E2
Barlee, Mt., *Australia* 89 D4
Barletta, *Italy* 35 A9
Barlinek, *Poland* 20 C5
Barlovento, *Canary Is.* 36 F2
Barlow L., *Canada* 101 A8
Barmedman, *Australia* 91 E4
Barmer, *India* 62 G4
Barmera, *Australia* 91 E3
Barmouth, *U.K.* 12 E3
Barmstedt, *Germany* 18 B5
Barnagar, *India* 62 H6
Barnard Castle, *U.K.* 12 C6
Barnato, *Australia* 91 E3
Barnaul, *Russia* 44 D9
Barnesville, *U.S.A.* 105 J3
Barnet, *U.K.* 13 F7
Barneveld, *Neths.* 16 D7
Barneveld, *U.S.A.* 107 C9
Barneville-Cartevert, *France* 24 C5
Barngo, *Australia* 90 D4
Barnhart, *U.S.A.* 109 K4
Barnsley, *U.K.* 12 D6
Barnstaple, *U.K.* 13 F3
Barnsville, *U.S.A.* 108 B6
Baro, *Nigeria* 79 D6
Baro →, *Ethiopia* 77 F3
Baroda = Vadodara, *India* 62 H5
Baroda, *India* 62 G7
Baroe, *S. Africa* 84 E3
Baron Ra., *Australia* 88 D4
Barpeta, *India* 61 F17
Barques, Pt. Aux, *U.S.A.* 104 C4
Barquinha, *Portugal* 31 F2
Barquísimeto, *Venezuela* 120 A4
Barr, *France* 25 D14
Barra, *Brazil* 122 D3
Barra, *U.K.* 14 E1
Barra, Sd. of, *U.K.* 14 D1
Barra da Estiva, *Brazil* 123 D3
Barra de Navidad, *Mexico* 114 D4
Barra do Corda, *Brazil* 122 C2
Barra do Mendes, *Brazil* 123 D3
Barra do Piraí, *Brazil* 123 F3
Barra Falsa, Pta. da, *Mozam.* 85 C6
Barra Hd., *U.K.* 14 E1
Barra Mansa, *Brazil* 123 F3
Barraba, *Australia* 91 E5
Barracão do Barreto, *Brazil* 125 B6
Barrackpur = Barakpur, *India* 63 H13
Barrafranca, *Italy* 35 E7
Barranca, *Lima, Peru* 124 C2
Barranca, *Loreto, Peru* 120 D2
Barrancabermeja, *Colombia* 120 B3
Barrancas, *Colombia* 120 A3
Barrancas, *Venezuela* 121 B5
Barrancos, *Portugal* 31 G4
Barranqueras, *Argentina* 126 B4
Barranquilla, *Colombia* 120 A3
Barras, *Brazil* 122 B3
Barras, *Colombia* 120 D3
Barraute, *Canada* 98 C4
Barre, *Mass., U.S.A.* 107 D12
Barre, *Vt., U.S.A.* 107 B12
Barre do Bugres, *Brazil* 125 C6
Barreal, *Argentina* 126 C2
Barreiras, *Brazil* 123 D3
Barreirinha, *Brazil* 121 D6
Barreirinhas, *Brazil* 122 B3
Barreiro, *Portugal* 31 G1
Barreiros, *Brazil* 122 C4
Barrême, *France* 27 E10
Barren, Nosy, *Madag.* 85 B7
Barretos, *Brazil* 123 F2
Barrhead, *Canada* 100 C6
Barrie, *Canada* 98 D4
Barrier Ra., *Australia* 91 E3
Barrière, *Canada* 100 C4
Barrington, *U.S.A.* 107 E13
Barrington L., *Canada* 101 B8
Barrington Tops, *Australia* 91 E5
Barringun, *Australia* 91 D4
Barro do Garças, *Brazil* 125 D7
Barrow, *U.S.A.* 96 A4
Barrow →, *Ireland* 15 D4
Barrow, C., *U.S.A.* 94 B4
Barrow Creek, *Australia* 90 C1
Barrow I., *Australia* 88 D2
Barrow-in-Furness, *U.K.* 12 C4
Barrow Pt., *Australia* 90 A3
Barrow Ra., *Australia* 89 E4
Barrow Str., *Canada* 4 B3
Barruecopardo, *Spain* 30 D4
Barruelo, *Spain* 30 C6
Barry, *U.K.* 13 F4
Barry's Bay, *Canada* 98 C4
Barsalogho, *Burkina Faso* 79 C4
Barsat, *Pakistan* 63 A5
Barsham, *Syria* 64 C4
Barsi, *India* 60 K9
Barsø, *Denmark* 11 J3
Barsoi, *India* 61 G15
Barstow, *Calif., U.S.A.* 113 L9
Barstow, *Tex., U.S.A.* 109 K3
Barth, *Germany* 18 A8
Barthélemy, Col, *Vietnam* 58 C5
Bartica, *Guyana* 121 B6
Bartin, *Turkey* 66 C5
Bartlesville, *U.S.A.* 109 G7
Bartlett, *Calif., U.S.A.* 112 J8
Bartlett, *Tex., U.S.A.* 109 K6
Bartlett, L., *Canada* 100 A5
Bartolomeu Dias, *Mozam.* 83 G4
Barton, *Australia* 89 F5
Barton upon Humber, *U.K.* 12 D7
Bartoszyce, *Poland* 20 A10
Bartow, *U.S.A.* 105 M5
Barú, I. de, *Colombia* 120 A2
Barú, Volcan, *Panama* 116 E3
Barumba, *Zaïre* 82 B1
Baruth, *Germany* 18 C9
Barvaux, *Belgium* 17 H6
Barvenkovo, *Ukraine* 42 B7
Barwani, *India* 62 H6
Barysaw = Borisov, *Belorussia* 40 D6
Barysh, *Russia* 41 E15
Barzān, *Iraq* 64 B5
Bas-Rhin □, *France* 25 D14
Bašaid, *Serbia* 21 K10
Bāsa'idū, *Iran* 65 E7
Basal, *Pakistan* 62 C5
Basankusa, *Zaïre* 80 D3
Basawa, *Afghan.* 62 B4
Bascharage, *Lux.* 17 J7
Bascuñán, C., *Chile* 126 B1
Basècles, *Belgium* 17 G3
Basel, *Switz.* 22 A5
Basel-Stadt □, *Switz.* 22 A5
Baselland □, *Switz.* 22 B5
Basento →, *Italy* 35 B9
Bāshī, *Iran* 65 D6
Bashi Channel, *Phil.* 54 D7
Bashkir Republic □, *Russia* 44 D6
Bashkortostan = Bashkir Republic □, *Russia* 44 D6
Basilan, *Phil.* 55 H5
Basilan Str., *Phil.* 55 H5
Basildon, *U.K.* 13 F8
Basilicata □, *Italy* 35 B9
Basim = Washim, *India* 60 J10
Basin, *U.S.A.* 110 D9
Basingstoke, *U.K.* 13 F6
Baška, *Croatia* 33 D11
Başkale, *Turkey* 67 D10
Baskatong, Rés., *Canada* 98 C4
Basle = Basel, *Switz.* 22 A5
Basoda, *India* 62 H7
Basodino, *Switz.* 23 D6
Basoka, *Zaïre* 82 B1
Basongo, *Zaïre* 80 E4
Basque, Pays, *France* 26 E2
Basque Provinces = País Vasco □, *Spain* 28 C2

Basra = Al Baṣrah, *Iraq* .. 64 D5
Bass Rock, *U.K.* 14 E6
Bass Str., *Australia* 90 F4
Bassano, *Canada* 100 C6
Bassano del Grappa, *Italy* 33 C8
Bassar, *Togo* 79 D5
Bassas da India, *Ind. Oc.* . 81 J7
Basse Santa-Su, *Gambia* .. 78 C2
Basse-Terre, *Guadeloupe* . 117 C7
Bassecourt, *Switz.* 22 B4
Bassein, *Burma* 61 L19
Basseterre,
St. Christopher-Nevis ... 117 C7
Bassett, *Nebr., U.S.A.* 108 D5
Bassett, *Va., U.S.A.* 105 G6
Bassevelde, *Belgium* 17 F3
Bassi, *India* 62 D7
Bassigny, *France* 25 E12
Bassikounou, *Mauritania* . 78 B3
Bassilly, *Belgium* 17 G3
Bassum, *Germany* 18 C4
Båstad, *Sweden* 11 H6
Bastak, *Iran* 65 E7
Baştām, *Iran* 65 B7
Bastar, *India* 61 K12
Bastelica, *France* 27 F13
Basti, *India* 63 F10
Bastia, *France* 27 F13
Bastia Umbra, *Italy* 33 E9
Bastogne, *Belgium* 17 H7
Bastrop, *U.S.A.* 109 K6
Bat Yam, *Israel* 69 C3
Bata, *Eq. Guin.* 80 D1
Bata, *Romania* 38 C5
Bataan, *Phil.* 55 D4
Batabanó, *Cuba* 116 B3
Batabanó, G. de, *Cuba* ... 116 B3
Batac, *Phil.* 55 B4
Batagoy, *Russia* 45 C14
Batak, *Bulgaria* 39 H7
Batalha, *Portugal* 31 F2
Batama, *Zaïre* 82 B2
Batamay, *Russia* 45 C13
Batan I., *Phil.* 55 A4
Batanes Is., *Phil.* 55 A4
Batang, *China* 52 B2
Batang, *Indonesia* 57 G13
Batangafo, *C.A.R.* 73 G8
Batangas, *Phil.* 55 E4
Batanta, *Indonesia* 57 E8
Batatais, *Brazil* 127 A6
Batavia, *U.S.A.* 106 D6
Bataysk, *Russia* 43 C8
Batchelor, *Australia* 88 B5
Bateman's B., *Australia* .. 91 F5
Batemans Bay, *Australia* .. 91 F5
Bates Ra., *Australia* 89 E3
Batesburg, *U.S.A.* 105 J5
Batesville, *Ark., U.S.A.* .. 109 H9
Batesville, *Miss., U.S.A.* . 109 H10
Batesville, *Tex., U.S.A.* .. 109 L5
Bath, *U.K.* 13 F5
Bath, *Maine, U.S.A.* 99 D6
Bath, *N.Y., U.S.A.* 106 D7
Batheay, *Cambodia* 59 G5
Bathgate, *U.K.* 14 F5
Bathmen, *Neths.* 16 D8
Bathurst = Banjul, *Gambia* 78 C1
Bathurst, *Australia* 91 E4
Bathurst, *Canada* 99 C6
Bathurst, *S. Africa* 84 E4
Bathurst, C., *Canada* 96 A7
Bathurst B., *Australia* 90 A3
Bathurst Harb., *Australia* . 90 G4
Bathurst I., *Australia* 88 B5
Bathurst I., *Canada* 4 B2
Bathurst Inlet, *Canada* ... 96 B9
Batie, *Burkina Faso* 78 D4
Batlow, *Australia* 91 F4
Batman, *Turkey* 67 E9
Batna, *Algeria* 75 A6
Batobato, *Phil.* 55 H7
Batoka, *Zambia* 83 F2
Baton Rouge, *U.S.A.* 109 K9
Batong, Ko, *Thailand* 59 J2
Batopilas, *Mexico* 114 B3
Batouri, *Cameroon* 80 D2
Battambang, *Cambodia* ... 58 F4
Batticaloa, *Sri Lanka* 60 R12
Battice, *Belgium* 17 G7
Battipáglia, *Italy* 35 B7
Battle, *U.K.* 13 G8
Battle →, *Canada* 101 C7
Battle Camp, *Australia* ... 90 B3
Battle Creek, *U.S.A.* 104 D3
Battle Ground, *U.S.A.* ... 112 E4
Battle Harbour, *Canada* .. 99 B8
Battle Lake, *U.S.A.* 108 B7
Battle Mountain, *U.S.A.* . 110 F5
Battlefields, *Zimbabwe* ... 83 F2
Battleford, *Canada* 101 C7
Battonya, *Hungary* 21 J11
Batu, *Ethiopia* 68 F2
Batu, Kepulauan, *Indonesia* 56 E1
Batu Caves, *Malaysia* 59 L3
Batu Gajah, *Malaysia* 59 K3
Batu Is. = Batu,
Kepulauan, Indonesia .. 56 E1
Batu Pahat, *Malaysia* 59 M4
Batuata, *Indonesia* 57 F6
Batumi, *Georgia* 43 F9
Baturaja, *Indonesia* 56 E2
Baturité, *Brazil* 122 B4
Bau, *Malaysia* 56 D4
Baubau, *Indonesia* 57 F6
Bauchi, *Nigeria* 79 C6
Bauchi □, *Nigeria* 79 C6
Baud, *France* 24 E3
Baudette, *U.S.A.* 108 A7
Baudour, *Belgium* 17 H3
Bauer, C., *Australia* 91 E1
Baugé, *France* 24 E6
Bauhinia Downs, *Australia* 90 C4
Bauma, *Switz.* 23 B7
Baume-les-Dames, *France* 25 E13
Baunatal, *Germany* 18 D5
Baunei, *Italy* 34 B2
Baures, *Bolivia* 125 C5
Bauru, *Brazil* 127 A6
Baús, *Brazil* 125 D7
Bauska, *Latvia* 40 C4
Bautzen, *Germany* 18 D10
Bavānāt, *Iran* 65 D7
Bavaria = Bayern □,
Germany 19 F7
Båven, *Sweden* 10 F10
Bavi Sadri, *India* 62 G6
Bavispe →, *Mexico* 114 B3
Bawdwin, *Burma* 61 H20
Bawean, *Indonesia* 56 F4
Bawku, *Ghana* 79 C4
Bawlake, *Burma* 61 K20
Bawolung, *China* 52 C3
Baxley, *U.S.A.* 105 K4
Baxoi, *China* 52 B1
Baxter Springs, *U.S.A.* ... 109 G7
Bay, L. de, *Phil.* 57 B6
Bay Bulls, *Canada* 99 C9
Bay City, *Mich., U.S.A.* .. 104 D4
Bay City, *Oreg., U.S.A.* .. 110 D2
Bay City, *Tex., U.S.A.* .. 109 L7
Bay de Verde, *Canada* ... 99 C9
Bay Minette, *U.S.A.* 105 K2
Bay St. Louis, *U.S.A.* 109 K10
Bay Springs, *U.S.A.* 109 K10
Bay View, *N.Z.* 87 H6
Baya, *Zaïre* 83 E2
Bayamo, *Cuba* 116 B4
Bayamón, *Puerto Rico* ... 117 C6
Bayan Har Shan, *China* .. 54 C4
Bayan Hot = Alxa Zuoqi,
China 50 E3
Bayan Obo, *China* 50 D5
Bayan-Ovoo, *Mongolia* ... 50 C4
Bayana, *India* 62 F7
Bayanaul, *Kazakhstan* 44 D8
Bayandalay, *Mongolia* 50 C2
Bayanhongor, *Mongolia* .. 54 B5
Bayard, *U.S.A.* 108 E3
Bayawan, *Phil.* 55 G5
Baybay, *Phil.* 55 F6
Bayburt, *Turkey* 67 C9
Bayerischer Wald,
Germany 19 F8
Bayern □, *Germany* 19 F7
Bayeux, *France* 24 C6
Bayfield, *Canada* 106 C3
Bayfield, *U.S.A.* 108 B9
Bayındır, *Turkey* 66 D2
Baykal, Oz., *Russia* 45 D11
Baykit, *Russia* 45 C10
Baykonur, *Kazakhstan* ... 44 E7
Baynes Mts., *Namibia* 84 B1
Bayombong, *Phil.* 55 C4
Bayon, *France* 25 D13
Bayona, *Spain* 30 C2
Bayonne, *France* 26 E2
Bayonne, *U.S.A.* 107 F10
Bayovar, *Peru* 124 B1
Bayram-Ali, *Turkmenistan* 44 F7
Bayramiç, *Turkey* 66 D2
Bayreuth, *Germany* 19 F7
Bayrischzell, *Germany* ... 19 H8
Bayrūt, *Lebanon* 69 B4
Bayt Lahm, *Jordan* 69 D4
Baytown, *U.S.A.* 109 L7
Bayzo, *Niger* 79 C5
Baza, *Spain* 29 H2
Bazar Dyuzi, *Russia* 43 F12
Bazarny Karabulak, *Russia* 41 E15
Bazarnyy Syzgan, *Russia* . 41 E15
Bazartobe, *Kazakhstan* ... 43 B14
Bazaruto, I. do, *Mozam.* . 85 C6
Bazas, *France* 26 D3
Bazhong, *China* 52 B6
Bazmān, Kūh-e, *Iran* 65 D9
Beach, *U.S.A.* 108 B3
Beach City, *U.S.A.* 106 F3
Beachport, *Australia* 91 F2
Beachy Hd., *U.K.* 13 G8
Beacon, *Australia* 89 F2
Beacon, *U.S.A.* 107 E11
Beaconia, *Canada* 101 C9
Beagle, Canal, *S. Amer.* . 128 E3
Beagle Bay, *Australia* 88 C3
Bealanana, *Madag.* 85 A8
Beamsville, *Canada* 106 C5
Bear →, *U.S.A.* 112 G5
Béar, C., *France* 26 F7
Bear I., *Ireland* 15 E2
Bear L., *B.C., Canada* ... 100 B3
Bear L., *Man., Canada* ... 101 B9
Bear L., *U.S.A.* 110 E8
Bearcreek, *U.S.A.* 110 D9
Beardmore, *Canada* 98 C2
Beardmore Glacier,
Antarctica 5 E11
Beardstown, *U.S.A.* 108 F9
Béarn, *France* 26 E3
Bearpaw Mts., *U.S.A.* 110 B9
Bearskin Lake, *Canada* ... 98 B1
Beas de Segura, *Spain* 29 G2
Beasain, *Spain* 28 B2
Beata, C., *Dom. Rep.* 117 C5
Beata, I., *Dom. Rep.* 117 C5
Beatrice, *U.S.A.* 108 E6
Beatrice, *Zimbabwe* 83 F3
Beatrice, C., *Australia* 90 A2
Beatton →, *Canada* 100 B4
Beatton River, *Canada* ... 100 B4
Beatty, *U.S.A.* 111 H5
Beaucaire, *France* 27 E8
Beauce, Plaine de la,
France 25 D8
Beauceville, *Canada* 99 C5
Beauchêne, I., *Falk. Is.* .. 128 D5
Beaudesert, *Australia* 91 D5
Beaufort, *Malaysia* 56 C5
Beaufort, *N.C., U.S.A.* 105 H7
Beaufort, *S.C., U.S.A.* 105 J5
Beaufort Sea, *Arctic* 4 B1
Beaufort West, *S. Africa* . 84 E3
Beaugency, *France* 25 E8
Beauharnois, *Canada* 98 C5
Beaujeu, *France* 27 B8
Beaulieu →, *Canada* 100 A6
Beaulieu-sur-Dordogne,
France 26 D5
Beaulieu-sur-Mer, *France* . 27 E11
Beauly, *U.K.* 14 D4
Beauly →, *U.K.* 14 D4
Beaumaris, *U.K.* 12 D3
Beaumetz-lès-Loges, *France* 25 B9
Beaumont, *Belgium* 17 H4
Beaumont, *France* 26 D4
Beaumont, *Calif., U.S.A.* . 113 M10
Beaumont, *Tex., U.S.A.* .. 109 K7
Beaumont-de-Lomagne,
France 26 E4
Beaumont-le-Roger, *France* 24 C7
Beaumont-sur-Oise, *France* 25 C9
Beaumont-sur-Sarthe,
France 24 D7
Beaune, *France* 25 E11
Beaune-la-Rolande, *France* 25 D9
Beaupréau, *France* 24 E6
Beauraing, *Belgium* 17 H5
Beauséjour, *Canada* 101 C9
Beauvais, *France* 25 C9
Beauval, *Canada* 101 B7
Beauvoir-sur-Mer, *France* . 24 F4
Beauvoir-sur-Niort, *France* 26 B3
Beaver, *Alaska, U.S.A.* .. 96 B5
Beaver, *Okla., U.S.A.* ... 109 G4
Beaver, *Pa., U.S.A.* 106 F4
Beaver, *Utah, U.S.A.* 111 G7
Beaver →, *B.C., Canada* 100 B4
Beaver →, *Ont., Canada* . 98 A2
Beaver →, *Sask., Canada* 101 B7
Beaver City, *U.S.A.* 108 E5
Beaver Dam, *U.S.A.* 108 D10
Beaver Falls, *U.S.A.* 106 F4
Beaver Hill L., *Canada* ... 101 C10
Beaver I., *U.S.A.* 104 C3
Beaverhill L., *Alta.,*
Canada 100 C6
Beaverhill L., *N.W.T.,*
Canada 101 A8
Beaverlodge, *Canada* 100 B5
Beavermouth, *Canada* 100 C5
Beaverstone →, *Canada* . 98 B2
Beaverton, *Canada* 106 B5
Beaverton, *U.S.A.* 112 E4
Beawar, *India* 62 F6
Bebedouro, *Brazil* 127 A6
Beboa, *Madag.* 85 B7
Bebra, *Germany* 18 E5
Beccles, *U.K.* 13 E9
Bečej, *Serbia* 21 K10
Becerreá, *Spain* 30 C3
Béchar, *Algeria* 75 B4
Beckley, *U.S.A.* 104 G5
Beckum, *Germany* 18 D4
Bečva →, *Czech.* 20 F7
Bédar, *Spain* 29 H3
Bédarieux, *France* 26 E7
Bédarrides, *France* 27 D8
Beddouza, Ras, *Morocco* . 74 B3
Bedele, *Ethiopia* 77 F4
Bederkesa, *Germany* 18 B4
Bedeso, *Ethiopia* 77 F5
Bedford, *Canada* 98 C5
Bedford, *S. Africa* 84 E4
Bedford, *U.K.* 13 E7
Bedford, *Ind., U.S.A.* 104 F2
Bedford, *Iowa, U.S.A.* ... 108 E7
Bedford, *Ohio, U.S.A.* ... 106 E3
Bedford, *Pa., U.S.A.* 106 F6
Bedford, *Va., U.S.A.* 104 G6
Bedford, C., *Australia* ... 90 B4
Bedford Downs, *Australia* 88 C4
Bedfordshire □, *U.K.* ... 13 E7
Będków, *Poland* 20 D9
Bednja →, *Croatia* 33 B13
Bednodemyanovsk, *Russia* 41 E13
Bedónia, *Italy* 32 D6
Bedourie, *Australia* 90 C2
Bedretto, *Switz.* 23 C7
Bedum, *Neths.* 16 B9
Będzin, *Poland* 20 E9
Beech Grove, *U.S.A.* 104 F2
Beechy, *Canada* 101 C7
Beek, *Gelderland, Neths.* . 16 E8
Beek, *Limburg, Neths.* ... 17 G7
Beek, *Noord-Brabant,*
Neths. 17 E7
Beekbergen, *Neths.* 16 D7
Beelitz, *Germany* 18 C8
Beenleigh, *Australia* 91 D5
Be'er Menuḥa, *Israel* 64 D2
Be'er Sheva', *Israel* 69 D3
Beersheba = Be'er Sheva',
Israel 69 D3
Beerta, *Neths.* 16 B10
Beerze →, *Neths.* 16 E6
Beesd, *Neths.* 16 E6
Beeskow, *Germany* 18 C10
Beeston, *U.K.* 12 E6
Beetaloo, *Australia* 90 B1
Beetsterzwaag, *Neths.* 16 B8
Beetzendorf, *Germany* ... 18 C7
Beeville, *U.S.A.* 109 L6
Befale, *Zaïre* 80 D4
Befandriana, *Madag.* 85 C7
Befotaka, *Madag.* 85 C8
Bega, *Australia* 91 F4
Bega, Canalul, *Romania* .. 38 D3
Bégard, *France* 24 D3
Bègles, *France* 26 D3
Begna →, *Norway* 10 D4
Begonte, *Spain* 30 B3
Begusarai, *India* 63 G12
Behābād, *Iran* 65 C8
Behara, *Madag.* 85 C8
Behbehān, *Iran* 65 D6
Behshahr, *Iran* 65 B7
Bei Jiang →, *China* 53 F9
Bei'an, *China* 54 B7
Beibei, *China* 54 D5
Beigang, *Taiwan* 53 F13
Beihai, *China* 52 G7
Beijing, *China* 50 E9
Beijing □, *China* 50 E9
Beilen, *Neths.* 16 C8
Beiliu, *China* 53 F8
Beilngries, *Germany* 19 F7
Beilpajah, *Australia* 91 E3
Beilul, *Eritrea* 77 E5
Beipiao, *China* 51 D11
Beira, *Mozam.* 83 F3
Beirut = Bayrūt, *Lebanon* 69 B4
Beitaolaizhao, *China* 51 B13
Beitbridge, *Zimbabwe* 83 G3
Beiuş, *Romania* 38 C5
Beizhen, *Liaoning, China* . 51 D11
Beizhen, *Shandong, China* 51 F10
Beizhengzhen, *China* 51 B12
Beja, *Portugal* 31 G3
Béja, *Tunisia* 75 A6
Beja □, *Portugal* 31 H3
Bejaia, *Algeria* 75 A6
Béjar, *Spain* 30 E5
Bejestān, *Iran* 65 C8
Bekasi, *Indonesia* 57 G12
Békés, *Hungary* 21 J11
Békéscsaba, *Hungary* 21 J11
Bekily, *Madag.* 85 C8
Bekkevoort, *Belgium* 17 G5
Bekoji, *Ethiopia* 77 F4
Bekok, *Malaysia* 59 L4
Bekwai, *Ghana* 79 D4
Bela, *India* 63 G9
Bela, *Pakistan* 62 F2
Bela Crkva, *Serbia* 21 L11
Bela Palanka, *Serbia* 21 M12
Bela Vista, *Brazil* 126 A4
Bela Vista, *Mozam.* 85 D5
Bélâbre, *France* 26 B5
Belalcázar, *Spain* 31 G5
Belarus = Belorussia ■,
Europe 40 E5
Belau ■, *Pac. Oc.* 92 G5
Belavenona, *Madag.* 85 C8
Belawan, *Indonesia* 56 D1
Belaya, *Ethiopia* 77 E4
Belaya Glina, *Russia* 43 C9
Belaya Kalitva, *Russia* ... 43 B9
Belaya Kholunitsa, *Russia* 41 B17
Belaya Tserkov, *Ukraine* . 40 G7
Belcher Is., *Canada* 97 C12
Belchite, *Spain* 28 D4
Belden, *U.S.A.* 112 E5
Belém, *Brazil* 122 B2
Belém de São Francisco,
Brazil 122 C4
Belén, *Argentina* 126 B2
Belén, *Colombia* 120 C2
Belén, *Paraguay* 126 A4
Belen, *U.S.A.* 111 J10
Bélesta, *France* 26 F5
Belet Uen, *Somali Rep.* .. 68 G4
Belev, *Russia* 41 E10
Belfair, *U.S.A.* 112 C4
Belfast, *S. Africa* 85 D5
Belfast, *U.K.* 15 B6
Belfast, *Maine, U.S.A.* ... 99 D6
Belfast, *N.Y., U.S.A.* 106 D6
Belfast □, *U.K.* 15 B6
Belfast L., *U.K.* 15 B6
Belfeld, *Neths.* 17 F8
Belfield, *U.S.A.* 108 B3
Belfort, *France* 25 E13
Belfort, Territoire de □,
France 25 E13
Belfry, *U.S.A.* 110 D9
Belgaum, *India* 60 M9
Belgioioso, *Italy* 32 C6
Belgium ■, *Europe* 17 G5
Belgorod, *Russia* 41 F10
Belgorod-Dnestrovskiy,
Ukraine 42 C4
Belgrade = Beograd,
Serbia 21 L10
Belgrade, *U.S.A.* 110 D8
Belhaven, *U.S.A.* 105 H7
Beli Drim →, *Europe* ... 21 N10
Beli Manastir, *Croatia* 21 K8
Belice →, *Italy* 34 E5
Belin-Béliet, *France* 26 D3
Belinga, *Gabon* 80 D2
Belinskiy, *Russia* 41 E13
Belinyu, *Indonesia* 56 E3
Beliton Is. = Belitung,
Indonesia 56 E3
Belitung, *Indonesia* 56 E3
Beliu, *Romania* 38 C5
Belize ■, *Cent. Amer.* 115 D7
Belize City, *Belize* 115 D7
Beljanica, *Serbia* 21 L11
Belkovskiy, Ostrov, *Russia* 45 B14
Bell →, *Canada* 98 C4
Bell Bay, *Australia* 90 G4
Bell I., *Canada* 99 B8
Bell-Irving →, *Canada* ... 100 B3
Bell Peninsula, *Canada* ... 97 B11
Bell Ville, *Argentina* 126 C3
Bella Bella, *Canada* 100 C3
Bella Coola, *Canada* 100 C3
Bella Flor, *Bolivia* 124 C4
Bella Unión, *Uruguay* 126 C4
Bella Vista, *Corrientes,*
Argentina 126 B4
Bella Vista, *Tucuman,*
Argentina 126 B2
Bellac, *France* 26 B5
Bellágio, *Italy* 32 C6
Bellaire, *U.S.A.* 106 F4
Bellary, *India* 60 M10
Bellata, *Australia* 91 D4
Belle Fourche, *U.S.A.* 108 C3
Belle Fourche →, *U.S.A.* 108 C3
Belle Glade, *U.S.A.* 105 M5
Belle-Ile, *France* 24 E3
Belle Isle, *Canada* 99 B8
Belle Isle, Str. of, *Canada* 99 B8
Belle-Isle-en-Terre, *France* 24 D3
Belle Plaine, *Iowa, U.S.A.* 108 E8
Belle Plaine, *Minn., U.S.A.* 108 C8
Belle Yella, *Liberia* 78 D3
Belledonne, Chaîne de,
France 27 C10
Belledune, *Canada* 99 C6
Bellefontaine, *U.S.A.* 104 E4
Bellefonte, *U.S.A.* 106 F7
Bellegarde, *France* 25 E9
Bellegarde-en-Marche,
France 26 C6
Bellegarde-sur-Valserine,
France 27 B9
Bellême, *France* 24 D7
Belleoram, *Canada* 99 C8
Belleville, *Canada* 98 D4
Belleville, *France* 27 B8
Belleville, *Ill., U.S.A.* 108 F10
Belleville, *Kans., U.S.A.* . 108 F6
Belleville, *N.Y., U.S.A.* .. 107 C8
Belleville-sur-Vie, *France* . 24 F5
Bellevue, *Canada* 100 D6
Bellevue, *Idaho, U.S.A.* .. 110 E6
Bellevue, *Ohio, U.S.A.* .. 106 E2
Bellevue, *Wash., U.S.A.* .. 112 C4
Belley, *France* 27 C9
Bellin, *Canada* 97 B13
Bellingen, *Australia* 91 E5
Bellingham, *U.S.A.* 112 B4
Bellingshausen Sea,
Antarctica 5 C17
Bellinzona, *Switz.* 23 D8
Bello, *Colombia* 120 B2
Bellows Falls, *U.S.A.* 107 C12
Bellpat, *Pakistan* 62 E3
Bellpuig, *Spain* 28 D6
Belluno, *Italy* 33 B9
Bellville, *U.S.A.* 109 L6
Bellwood, *U.S.A.* 106 F6
Bélmez, *Spain* 31 G5
Belmont, *Australia* 91 E5
Belmont, *Canada* 106 D3
Belmont, *S. Africa* 84 D3
Belmont, *U.S.A.* 106 D6
Belmonte, *Brazil* 123 E4
Belmonte, *Portugal* 30 E3
Belmonte, *Spain* 28 F2
Belmopan, *Belize* 115 D7
Belmullet, *Ireland* 15 B2
Belo Horizonte, *Brazil* ... 123 E3
Belo Jardim, *Brazil* 122 C4
Belo-sur-Mer, *Madag.* 85 C7
Belo-Tsiribihina, *Madag.* . 85 B7
Belogorsk, *Russia* 45 D13
Belogorsk, *Ukraine* 42 D6
Belogradchik, *Bulgaria* ... 38 F5
Beloha, *Madag.* 85 D8
Beloit, *Kans., U.S.A.* 108 F5
Beloit, *Wis., U.S.A.* 108 D10
Belokorovichi, *Ukraine* ... 40 F6
Belomorsk, *Russia* 44 C4
Belonia, *India* 61 H17
Belopolye, *Ukraine* 40 F9
Belorussia ■, *Europe* 40 E5
Belovo, *Russia* 44 D9
Beloye More, *Russia* 44 C4
Beloye Ozero, *Russia* 43 D12
Belozersk, *Russia* 41 A10
Belpasso, *Italy* 35 E7
Belsele, *Belgium* 17 F4

Belsito, *Italy* 34 E6
Beltana, *Australia* 91 E2
Belterra, *Brazil* 121 D7
Beltinci, *Slovenia* 33 B13
Belton, *S.C., U.S.A.* 105 H4
Belton, *Tex., U.S.A.* 109 K6
Belton Res., *U.S.A.* 109 K6
Beltsy, *Moldavia* 42 C3
Belturbet, *Ireland* 15 B4
Belukha, *Russia* 44 E9
Beluran, *Malaysia* 56 C5
Belvedere Maríttimo, *Italy* 35 C8
Belvès, *France* 26 D5
Belvidere, *Ill., U.S.A.* 108 D10
Belvidere, *N.J., U.S.A.* 107 F9
Belvis de la Jara, *Spain* 31 F6
Belyando →, *Australia* 90 C4
Belyy, *Russia* 40 D8
Belyy, Ostrov, *Russia* 44 B8
Belyy Yar, *Russia* 44 D9
Belzig, *Germany* 18 C8
Belzoni, *U.S.A.* 109 J9
Bemaraha, Lembalemban' i, *Madag.* 85 B7
Bemarivo, *Madag.* 85 C7
Bemarivo →, *Madag.* 85 B8
Bemavo, *Madag.* 85 C8
Bembéréke, *Benin* 79 C5
Bembesi, *Zimbabwe* 83 F2
Bembesi →, *Zimbabwe* 83 F2
Bembézar →, *Spain* 31 H5
Bemidji, *U.S.A.* 108 B7
Bemmel, *Neths.* 16 E7
Ben, *Iran* 65 C6
Ben Cruachan, *U.K.* 14 E3
Ben Dearg, *U.K.* 14 D4
Ben Gardane, *Tunisia* 75 B7
Ben Hope, *U.K.* 14 C4
Ben Lawers, *U.K.* 14 E4
Ben Lomond, *N.S.W., Australia* 91 E5
Ben Lomond, *Tas., Australia* 90 G4
Ben Lomond, *U.K.* 14 E4
Ben Luc, *Vietnam* 59 G6
Ben Macdhui, *U.K.* 14 D5
Ben Mhor, *U.K.* 14 D1
Ben More, *Central, U.K.* 14 E4
Ben More, *Strath., U.K.* 14 E2
Ben More Assynt, *U.K.* 14 C4
Ben Nevis, *U.K.* 14 E4
Ben Quang, *Vietnam* 58 D6
Ben Slimane, *Morocco* 74 B3
Ben Tre, *Vietnam* 59 G6
Ben Vorlich, *U.K.* 14 E4
Ben Wyvis, *U.K.* 14 D4
Bena, *Nigeria* 79 C6
Bena Dibele, *Zaïre* 80 E4
Benagalbón, *Spain* 31 J6
Benagerie, *Australia* 91 E3
Benahmed, *Morocco* 74 B3
Benalla, *Australia* 91 F4
Benambra, Mt., *Australia* 91 F4
Benamejí, *Spain* 31 H6
Benares = Varanasi, *India* 63 G10
Bénat, C., *France* 27 E10
Benavente, *Portugal* 31 G2
Benavente, *Spain* 30 C5
Benavides, *Spain* 30 C5
Benavides, *U.S.A.* 109 M5
Benbecula, *U.K.* 14 D1
Benbonyathe, *Australia* 91 E2
Bencubbin, *Australia* 89 F2
Bend, *U.S.A.* 110 D3
Bender Beila, *Somali Rep.* 68 F5
Bendering, *Australia* 89 F2
Bendery, *Moldavia* 42 C3
Bendigo, *Australia* 91 F3
Bendorf, *Germany* 18 E3
Benē Beraq, *Israel* 69 C3
Beneden Knijpe, *Neths.* 16 C7
Beneditinos, *Brazil* 122 C3
Benedito Leite, *Brazil* 122 C3
Bénéna, *Mali* 78 C4
Benenitra, *Madag.* 85 C8
Benešov, *Czech.* 20 F4
Bénestroff, *France* 25 D13
Benet, *France* 26 B3
Benevento, *Italy* 35 A7
Benfeld, *France* 25 D14
Benga, *Mozam.* 83 F3
Bengal, Bay of, *Ind. Oc.* 61 K16
Bengbu, *China* 51 H9
Benghazi = Banghāzī, *Libya* 73 B9
Bengkalis, *Indonesia* 56 D2
Bengkulu, *Indonesia* 56 E2
Bengkulu □, *Indonesia* 56 E2
Bengough, *Canada* 101 D7
Benguela, *Angola* 81 G2
Benguerir, *Morocco* 74 B3
Benguérua, I., *Mozam.* 85 C6
Benha, *Egypt* 76 H7
Beni, *Zaïre* 82 B2
Beni □, *Bolivia* 125 C4
Beni →, *Bolivia* 125 C4
Beni Abbès, *Algeria* 75 B4
Beni-Haoua, *Algeria* 75 A5
Beni Mazâr, *Egypt* 76 J7
Beni Mellal, *Morocco* 74 B3
Beni Ounif, *Algeria* 75 B4
Beni Saf, *Algeria* 75 A4
Beni Suef, *Egypt* 76 J7
Beniah L., *Canada* 100 A6
Benicarló, *Spain* 28 E5
Benicia, *U.S.A.* 112 G4
Benidorm, *Spain* 29 G4
Benidorm, Islote de, *Spain* 29 G4
Benin ■, *Africa* 79 D5
Benin, Bight of, *W. Afr.* 79 D5
Benin City, *Nigeria* 79 D6
Benisa, *Spain* 29 G5
Benitses, *Greece* 37 A3
Benjamin Aceval, *Paraguay* 126 A4
Benjamin Constant, *Brazil* 120 D3
Benjamin Hill, *Mexico* 114 A2
Benkelman, *U.S.A.* 108 E4
Benkovac, *Croatia* 33 D12
Benlidi, *Australia* 90 C3
Bennebroek, *Neths.* 16 D5
Bennekom, *Neths.* 16 D7
Bennett, *Canada* 100 B2
Bennett, L., *Australia* 88 D5
Bennett, Ostrov, *Russia* 45 B15
Bennettsville, *U.S.A.* 105 H6
Bennington, *U.S.A.* 107 D11
Bénodet, *France* 24 E2
Benoni, *S. Africa* 85 D4
Benoud, *Algeria* 75 B5
Benque Viejo, *Belize* 115 D7
Bensheim, *Germany* 19 F4
Benson, *U.S.A.* 111 L8
Bent, *Iran* 65 E8
Benteng, *Indonesia* 57 F6
Bentinck I., *Australia* 90 B2
Bentiu, *Sudan* 77 F2
Bento Gonçalves, *Brazil* 127 B5
Benton, *Ark., U.S.A.* 109 H8
Benton, *Calif., U.S.A.* 112 H8
Benton, *Ill., U.S.A.* 108 F10
Benton Harbor, *U.S.A.* 104 D2
Bentu Liben, *Ethiopia* 77 F4
Bentung, *Malaysia* 59 L3
Benue □, *Nigeria* 79 D6
Benue →, *Nigeria* 79 D6
Benxi, *China* 51 D12
Benzdorp, *Surinam* 121 C7
Beo, *Indonesia* 57 D7
Beograd, *Serbia* 21 L10
Beowawe, *U.S.A.* 110 F5
Bepan Jiang →, *China* 52 E6
Beppu, *Japan* 49 H5
Berati, *Albania* 39 J2
Berau, Teluk, *Indonesia* 57 E8
Berber, *Sudan* 76 D3
Berbera, *Somali Rep.* 68 E4
Berbérati, *C.A.R.* 80 D3
Berberia, C. del, *Spain* 36 C7
Berbice →, *Guyana* 121 B6
Berceto, *Italy* 32 D7
Berchtesgaden, *Germany* 19 H8
Berdichev, *Ukraine* 42 B3
Berdsk, *Russia* 44 D9
Berdyansk, *Ukraine* 42 C7
Berdychiv = Berdichev, *Ukraine* 42 B3
Berea, *U.S.A.* 104 G3
Berebere, *Indonesia* 57 D7
Bereda, *Somali Rep.* 68 E5
Berekum, *Ghana* 78 D4
Berenice, *Egypt* 76 C4
Berens →, *Canada* 101 C9
Berens I., *Canada* 101 C9
Berens River, *Canada* 101 C9
Berestechko, *Ukraine* 40 F4
Bereşti, *Romania* 38 C10
Beretău →, *Romania* 38 B4
Berettyo →, *Hungary* 21 J11
Berettyóújfalu, *Hungary* 21 H11
Berevo, *Mahajanga, Madag.* 85 B7
Berevo, *Toliara, Madag.* 85 B7
Bereza, *Belorussia* 40 E4
Berezhany, *Ukraine* 40 G4
Berezina →, *Belorussia* 40 E7
Berezna, *Ukraine* 40 F7
Berezniki, *Russia* 44 D6
Berezovka, *Ukraine* 42 C4
Berezovo, *Russia* 44 C7
Berga, *Spain* 28 C6
Bergama, *Turkey* 66 D2
Bergambacht, *Neths.* 16 E5
Bérgamo, *Italy* 32 C6
Bergantiños, *Spain* 30 B2
Bergara, *Spain* 28 B2
Bergedorf, *Germany* 18 B6
Bergeijk, *Neths.* 17 F6
Bergen, *Germany* 18 A9
Bergen, *Neths.* 16 C5
Bergen, *Norway* 9 F8
Bergen, *U.S.A.* 106 C7
Bergen-op-Zoom, *Neths.* 17 F4
Bergerac, *France* 26 D4
Bergheim, *Germany* 18 E2
Berghem, *Neths.* 16 E7
Bergisch-Gladbach, *Germany* 18 E3
Bergschenhoek, *Neths.* 16 E5
Bergsjö, *Sweden* 10 C11
Bergues, *France* 25 B9
Bergum, *Neths.* 16 B7
Bergville, *S. Africa* 85 D4
Berhala, Selat, *Indonesia* 56 E2
Berhampore = Baharampur, *India* 63 G13
Berhampur, *India* 61 K14
Berheci →, *Romania* 38 C10
Bering Sea, *Pac. Oc.* 96 C1
Bering Strait, *U.S.A.* 96 B3
Beringen, *Belgium* 17 F6
Beringen, *Switz.* 23 A7
Beringovskiy, *Russia* 45 C18
Berislav, *Ukraine* 42 C5
Berisso, *Argentina* 126 C4
Berja, *Spain* 29 J2
Berkane, *Morocco* 75 B4
Berkel →, *Neths.* 16 D8
Berkeley, *U.K.* 13 F5
Berkeley, *U.S.A.* 112 H4
Berkeley Springs, *U.S.A.* 104 F6
Berkhout, *Neths.* 16 C5
Berkner I., *Antarctica* 5 D18
Berkovitsa, *Bulgaria* 38 F6
Berkshire □, *U.K.* 13 F6
Berlaar, *Belgium* 17 F5
Berland →, *Canada* 100 C5
Berlanga, *Spain* 31 G5
Berlare, *Belgium* 17 F4
Berlenga, I., *Portugal* 31 F1
Berlin, *Germany* 18 C9
Berlin, *Md., U.S.A.* 104 F8
Berlin, *N.H., U.S.A.* 107 B13
Berlin, *Wis., U.S.A.* 104 D1
Bermeja, Sierra, *Spain* 31 J5
Bermejo →, *Formosa, Argentina* 126 B4
Bermejo →, *San Juan, Argentina* 126 C2
Bermeo, *Spain* 28 B2
Bermillo de Sayago, *Spain* 30 D4
Bermuda ■, *Atl. Oc.* 2 C6
Bern, *Switz.* 22 C4
Bern □, *Switz.* 22 C5
Bernado, *U.S.A.* 111 J10
Bernalda, *Italy* 35 B9
Bernalillo, *U.S.A.* 111 J10
Bernardo de Irigoyen, *Argentina* 127 B5
Bernardo O'Higgins □, *Chile* 126 C1
Bernasconi, *Argentina* 126 D3
Bernau, *Bayern, Germany* 19 H8
Bernau, *Brandenburg, Germany* 18 C9
Bernay, *France* 24 C7
Bernburg, *Germany* 18 D7
Berne = Bern, *Switz.* 22 C4
Berne = Bern □, *Switz.* 22 C5
Berner Alpen, *Switz.* 22 D5
Bernese Oberland = Oberland, *Switz.* 22 C5
Bernier I., *Australia* 89 D1
Bernina, Piz, *Switz.* 23 D9
Bernina, Pizzo, *Switz.* 23 D9
Bernissart, *Belgium* 17 H3
Bernkastel-Kues, *Germany* 19 F3
Beroroha, *Madag.* 85 C8
Béroubouay, *Benin* 79 C5
Beroun, *Czech.* 20 F4
Berounka →, *Czech.* 20 F4
Berovo, *Macedonia* 39 H5
Berrahal, *Algeria* 75 A6
Berre, Étang de, *France* 27 E9
Berrechid, *Morocco* 74 B3
Berri, *Australia* 91 E3
Berriane, *Algeria* 75 B5
Berrouaghia, *Algeria* 75 A5
Berry, *Australia* 91 E5
Berry, *France* 25 F8
Berry Is., *Bahamas* 116 A4
Berryessa L., *U.S.A.* 112 G4
Berryville, *U.S.A.* 109 G8
Bersenbrück, *Germany* 18 C3
Berthold, *U.S.A.* 108 A4
Berthoud, *U.S.A.* 108 E2
Bertincourt, *France* 25 B9
Bertoua, *Cameroon* 80 D2
Bertrand, *U.S.A.* 108 E5
Bertrange, *Lux.* 17 J8
Bertrix, *Belgium* 17 J6
Berufjörður, *Iceland* 8 D6
Beruri, *Brazil* 121 D5
Berwick, *U.S.A.* 107 E8
Berwick-upon-Tweed, *U.K.* 12 B5
Berwyn Mts., *U.K.* 12 E4
Berzasca, *Romania* 38 E4
Besal, *Pakistan* 63 B5
Besalampy, *Madag.* 85 B7
Besançon, *France* 25 E13
Besar, *Indonesia* 56 E5
Beshenkovichi, *Belorussia* 40 D6
Beslan, *Russia* 43 E11
Besnard L., *Canada* 101 B7
Besni, *Turkey* 67 E7
Besor, N. →, *Egypt* 69 D3
Bessarabiya, *Moldavia* 38 B11
Bessarabka, *Moldavia* 42 C3
Bessèges, *France* 27 D8
Bessemer, *Ala., U.S.A.* 105 J2
Bessemer, *Mich., U.S.A.* 108 B9
Bessin, *France* 24 C5
Bessines-sur-Gartempe, *France* 26 B5
Best, *Neths.* 17 E6
Bet She'an, *Israel* 69 C4
Bet Shemesh, *Israel* 69 D3
Bet Tadjine, Djebel, *Algeria* 74 C4
Betafo, *Madag.* 85 B8
Betancuria, *Canary Is.* 36 F5
Betanzos, *Bolivia* 125 D4
Betanzos, *Spain* 30 B2
Bétaré Oya, *Cameroon* 80 C2
Bétera, *Spain* 28 F4
Bethal, *S. Africa* 85 D4
Bethanien, *Namibia* 84 D2
Bethany, *S. Africa* 84 D4
Bethany, *U.S.A.* 108 E7
Bethel, *Alaska, U.S.A.* 96 B3
Bethel, *Vt., U.S.A.* 107 C12
Bethel Park, *U.S.A.* 106 F4
Bethlehem = Bayt Lahm, *Jordan* 69 D4
Bethlehem, *S. Africa* 85 D4
Bethlehem, *U.S.A.* 107 F9
Bethulie, *S. Africa* 84 E4
Béthune, *France* 25 B9
Béthune →, *France* 24 C8
Bethungra, *Australia* 91 E4
Betijoque, *Venezuela* 120 B3
Betim, *Brazil* 123 E3
Betioky, *Madag.* 85 C7
Beton-Bazoches, *France* 25 D10
Betong, *Thailand* 59 K3
Betoota, *Australia* 90 D3
Betroka, *Madag.* 85 C8
Betsiamites, *Canada* 99 C6
Betsiamites →, *Canada* 99 C6
Betsiboka →, *Madag.* 85 B8
Betsjoeanaland, *S. Africa* 84 D3
Bettembourg, *Lux.* 17 J8
Bettiah, *India* 63 F11
Bèttola, *Italy* 32 D6
Betul, *India* 60 J10
Betung, *Malaysia* 56 D4
Betzdorf, *Germany* 18 E3
Beuca, *Romania* 38 E7
Beuil, *France* 27 D10
Beulah, *U.S.A.* 108 B4
Beuvron →, *France* 24 E8
Beveren, *Belgium* 17 F4
Beverley, *Australia* 89 F2
Beverley, *U.K.* 12 D7
Beverlo, *Belgium* 17 F6
Beverly, *Mass., U.S.A.* 107 D14
Beverly, *Wash., U.S.A.* 110 C4
Beverly Hills, *U.S.A.* 113 L8
Beverwijk, *Neths.* 16 D5
Bex, *Switz.* 22 D4
Bey Dağları, *Turkey* 66 E4
Beyānlū, *Iran* 64 C5
Beyin, *Ghana* 78 D4
Beyla, *Guinea* 78 D3
Beynat, *France* 26 C5
Beyneu, *Kazakhstan* 44 E6
Beypazarı, *Turkey* 66 C4
Beyşehir Gölü, *Turkey* 66 E4
Beytüşşebap, *Turkey* 67 E10
Bezhetsk, *Russia* 41 C10
Bezhitsa, *Russia* 40 E9
Béziers, *France* 26 E7
Bezwada = Vijayawada, *India* 61 L12
Bhachau, *India* 60 H7
Bhadarwah, *India* 63 C6
Bhadrakh, *India* 61 J15
Bhadravati, *India* 60 N9
Bhagalpur, *India* 63 G12
Bhakkar, *Pakistan* 62 D4
Bhakra Dam, *India* 62 D7
Bhamo, *Burma* 61 G20
Bhandara, *India* 60 J11
Bhanrer Ra., *India* 62 H8
Bharat = India ■, *Asia* 60 K11
Bharatpur, *India* 62 F7
Bhatinda, *India* 62 D6
Bhatpara, *India* 63 H13
Bhaun, *Pakistan* 62 C5
Bhaunagar = Bhavnagar, *India* 62 J5
Bhavnagar, *India* 62 J5
Bhawanipatna, *India* 61 K12
Bhera, *Pakistan* 62 C5
Bhilsa = Vidisha, *India* 62 H7
Bhilwara, *India* 62 G6
Bhima →, *India* 60 L10
Bhimavaram, *India* 61 L12
Bhimbar, *Pakistan* 63 C6
Bhind, *India* 63 F8
Bhiwandi, *India* 60 K8
Bhiwani, *India* 62 E7
Bhola, *Bangla.* 61 H17
Bhopal, *India* 62 H7
Bhubaneshwar, *India* 61 J14
Bhuj, *India* 62 H3
Bhumiphol Dam = Phumiphon, Khuan, *Thailand* 58 D2
Bhusaval, *India* 60 J9
Bhutan ■, *Asia* 61 F17
Biá →, *Brazil* 120 D4
Biafra, B. of = Bonny, Bight of, *Africa* 79 E6
Biak, *Indonesia* 57 E9
Biała →, *Poland* 20 E10
Biała Podlaska, *Poland* 20 C13
Białogard, *Poland* 20 A5
Białystok, *Poland* 20 B13
Biancavilla, *Italy* 35 E7
Bīārjmand, *Iran* 65 B7
Biaro, *Indonesia* 57 D7
Biarritz, *France* 26 E2
Biasca, *Switz.* 23 D7
Biba, *Egypt* 76 J7
Bibai, *Japan* 48 C10
Bibala, *Angola* 81 G2
Bibane, Bahiret el, *Tunisia* 75 B7
Bibbiena, *Italy* 33 E8
Bibby I., *Canada* 101 A10
Biberach, *Germany* 19 G5
Biberist, *Switz.* 22 B5
Bibey →, *Spain* 30 C3
Bibiani, *Ghana* 78 D4
Biboohra, *Australia* 90 B4
Bibungwa, *Zaïre* 82 C2
Bic, *Canada* 99 C6
Bicaz, *Romania* 38 C9
Biccari, *Italy* 35 A8
Bichena, *Ethiopia* 77 E4
Bickerton I., *Australia* 90 A2
Bicknell, *Ind., U.S.A.* 104 F2
Bicknell, *Utah, U.S.A.* 111 G8
Bida, *Nigeria* 79 D6
Bidar, *India* 60 L10
Biddeford, *U.S.A.* 99 D5
Biddwara, *Ethiopia* 77 F4
Bideford, *U.K.* 13 F3
Bidon 5 = Poste Maurice Cortier, *Algeria* 75 D5
Bidor, *Malaysia* 59 K3
Bié, Planalto de, *Angola* 81 G3
Bieber, *U.S.A.* 110 F3
Biel, *Switz.* 22 B4
Bielawa, *Poland* 20 E6
Bielé Karpaty, *Europe* 20 F7
Bielefeld, *Germany* 18 C4
Bielersee, *Switz.* 22 B4
Biella, *Italy* 32 C5
Bielsk Podlaski, *Poland* 20 C13
Bielsko-Biała, *Poland* 20 F9
Bien Hoa, *Vietnam* 59 G6
Bienfait, *Canada* 101 D8
Bienne = Biel, *Switz.* 22 B4
Bienvenida, *Spain* 31 G4
Bienvenue, *Fr. Guiana* 121 C7
Bienville, L., *Canada* 98 A5
Biescas, *Spain* 28 C4
Biese →, *Germany* 18 C7
Biesiesfontein, *S. Africa* 84 E2
Bietigheim, *Germany* 19 G5
Bievre, *Belgium* 17 J6
Biferno →, *Italy* 35 A8
Big →, *Canada* 99 B8
Big B., *Canada* 99 A7
Big Bear City, *U.S.A.* 113 L10
Big Bear Lake, *U.S.A.* 113 L10
Big Beaver, *Canada* 101 D7
Big Belt Mts., *U.S.A.* 110 C8
Big Bend, *Swaziland* 85 D5
Big Bend National Park, *U.S.A.* 109 L3
Big Black →, *U.S.A.* 109 J9
Big Blue →, *U.S.A.* 108 F6
Big Cr. →, *Canada* 100 C4
Big Creek, *U.S.A.* 112 H7
Big Cypress Swamp, *U.S.A.* 105 M5
Big Falls, *U.S.A.* 108 A8
Big Fork →, *U.S.A.* 108 A8
Big Horn Mts. = Bighorn Mts., *U.S.A.* 110 D10
Big Lake, *U.S.A.* 109 K4
Big Moose, *U.S.A.* 107 C10
Big Muddy Cr. →, *U.S.A.* 108 A2
Big Pine, *U.S.A.* 111 H4
Big Piney, *U.S.A.* 110 E8
Big Quill L., *Canada* 101 C8
Big Rapids, *U.S.A.* 104 D3
Big River, *Canada* 101 C7
Big Run, *U.S.A.* 106 F6
Big Sable Pt., *U.S.A.* 104 C2
Big Sand L., *Canada* 101 B9
Big Sandy, *U.S.A.* 110 B8
Big Sandy Cr. →, *U.S.A.* 108 F3
Big Sioux →, *U.S.A.* 108 D6
Big Spring, *U.S.A.* 109 J4
Big Springs, *U.S.A.* 108 E3
Big Stone City, *U.S.A.* 108 C6
Big Stone Gap, *U.S.A.* 105 G4
Big Stone L., *U.S.A.* 108 C6
Big Sur, *U.S.A.* 112 J5
Big Timber, *U.S.A.* 110 D9
Big Trout L., *Canada* 98 B1
Biğa, *Turkey* 66 C2
Bigadiç, *Turkey* 66 D3
Biganos, *France* 26 D3
Bigfork, *U.S.A.* 110 B6
Biggar, *Canada* 101 C7
Biggar, *U.K.* 14 F5
Bigge I., *Australia* 88 B4
Biggenden, *Australia* 91 D5
Biggs, *U.S.A.* 112 F5
Bighorn, *U.S.A.* 110 C10
Bighorn →, *U.S.A.* 110 C10
Bighorn Mts., *U.S.A.* 110 D10
Bignona, *Senegal* 78 C1
Bigorre, *France* 26 E4
Bigstone L., *Canada* 101 C9
Bigwa, *Tanzania* 82 D4
Bihać, *Bos.-H.* 33 D12
Bihar, *India* 63 G11
Bihar □, *India* 63 G11
Biharamulo, *Tanzania* 82 C3
Biharamulo □, *Tanzania* 82 C3
Bihor, Munţii, *Romania* 38 C5
Bijagós, Arquipélago dos, *Guinea-Biss.* 78 C1
Bijaipur, *India* 62 F7
Bijapur, *Karnataka, India* 60 L9
Bijapur, *Mad. P., India* 61 K12
Bījār, *Iran* 64 C5
Bijeljina, *Bos.-H.* 21 L9
Bijelo Polje, *Montenegro* 21 M9
Bijie, *China* 52 D5
Bijnor, *India* 62 E8

Bikaner, *India* 62 E5
Bikapur, *India* 63 F10
Bikeqi, *China* 50 D6
Bikfayyā, *Lebanon* 69 B4
Bikin, *Russia* 45 E14
Bikin →, *Russia* 48 A7
Bikini Atoll, *Pac. Oc.* 92 F8
Bikoué, *Cameroon* 79 E7
Bila Tserkva = Belaya Tserkov, *Ukraine* 40 G7
Bilara, *India* 62 F5
Bilaspur, *Mad. P., India* 63 H10
Bilaspur, *Punjab, India* 62 D7
Bilauk Taungdan, *Thailand* 58 F2
Bilbao, *Spain* 28 B2
Bilbeis, *Egypt* 76 H7
Bilbo = Bilbao, *Spain* 28 B2
Bilbor, *Romania* 38 B8
Bíldudalur, *Iceland* 8 D2
Bileća, *Bos.-H.* 21 N8
Bilecik, *Turkey* 66 C4
Bilecik □, *Turkey* 66 C4
Biłgoraj, *Poland* 20 E12
Bilibino, *Russia* 45 C17
Bilibiza, *Mozam.* 83 E5
Bilir, *Russia* 45 C14
Biliran I., *Phil.* 55 F6
Bill, *U.S.A.* 108 D2
Billabalong, *Australia* 89 E2
Billiluna, *Australia* 88 C4
Billingham, *U.K.* 12 C6
Billings, *U.S.A.* 110 D9
Billiton Is. = Belitung, *Indonesia* 56 E3
Billom, *France* 26 C7
Bilma, *Niger* 73 E7
Bilo Gora, *Croatia* 21 K7
Biloela, *Australia* 90 C5
Biloku, *Guyana* 121 C6
Biloxi, *U.S.A.* 109 K10
Bilpa Morea Claypan, *Australia* 90 D2
Bilthoven, *Neths.* 16 D6
Biltine, *Chad* 73 F9
Bilyana, *Australia* 90 B4
Bilyarsk, *Russia* 41 D17
Bilzen, *Belgium* 17 G7
Bima, *Indonesia* 57 F5
Bimban, *Egypt* 76 C3
Bimbila, *Ghana* 79 D5
Bimbo, *C.A.R.* 80 D3
Bimini Is., *Bahamas* 116 A4
Bin Xian, *Heilongjiang, China* 51 B14
Bin Xian, *Shaanxi, China* 50 G5
Bina-Etawah, *India* 62 G8
Bināb, *Iran* 65 B6
Binalbagan, *Phil.* 55 F5
Binalong, *Australia* 91 E4
Bīnālūd, Kūh-e, *Iran* 65 B8
Binatang, *Malaysia* 56 D4
Binbee, *Australia* 90 C4
Binche, *Belgium* 17 H4
Binchuan, *China* 52 E3
Binda, *Australia* 91 D4
Bindle, *Australia* 91 D4
Bindura, *Zimbabwe* 83 F3
Bingara, *N.S.W., Australia* 91 D5
Bingara, *Queens., Australia* 91 D3
Bingen, *Germany* 19 F3
Bingerville, *Ivory C.* 78 D4
Bingham, *U.S.A.* 99 C6
Bingham Canyon, *U.S.A.* 110 F7
Binghamton, *U.S.A.* 107 D9
Bingöl, *Turkey* 67 D9
Bingöl □, *Turkey* 67 D9
Bingöl Dağları, *Turkey* 67 D9
Binh Dinh = An Nhon, *Vietnam* 58 F7
Binh Khe, *Vietnam* 58 F7
Binh Son, *Vietnam* 58 E7
Binhai, *China* 51 G10
Binisatua, *Spain* 36 B11
Binjai, *Indonesia* 56 D1
Binnaway, *Australia* 91 E4
Binongko, *Indonesia* 57 F6
Binscarth, *Canada* 101 C8
Bintan, *Indonesia* 56 D2
Bintulu, *Malaysia* 56 D4
Bintuni, *Indonesia* 57 E8
Binyang, *China* 52 F7
Binz, *Germany* 18 A9
Binzert = Bizerte, *Tunisia* 75 A6
Bío Bío □, *Chile* 126 D1
Biograd, *Croatia* 33 E12
Bioko, *Eq. Guin.* 79 E6
Biougra, *Morocco* 74 B3
Bir, *India* 60 K9
Bir, Ras, *Djibouti* 77 E5
Bîr Abu Hashim, *Egypt* 76 C3
Bîr Abu M'nqar, *Egypt* 76 B2
Bîr Abu Muḥammad, *Egypt* 69 F3
Bi'r ad Dabbāghāt, *Jordan* 69 E4
Bîr Adal Deib, *Sudan* 76 C4
Bi'r al Butayyihāt, *Jordan* 69 F4
Bi'r al Mārī, *Jordan* 69 E4
Bi'r al Qattār, *Jordan* 69 F4
Bir Aouine, *Tunisia* 75 B6
Bîr 'Asal, *Egypt* 76 B3
Bir Autrun, *Sudan* 76 D2
Bîr Beiḍa, *Egypt* 69 E3
Bîr Diqnash, *Egypt* 76 A2
Bir el Abbes, *Algeria* 74 C3
Bir el 'Abd, *Egypt* 69 D2
Bir el Ater, *Algeria* 75 B6
Bîr el Basur, *Egypt* 76 B2
Bîr el Biarât, *Egypt* 69 F3
Bîr el Duweidar, *Egypt* 69 E1
Bîr el Garârât, *Egypt* 69 D2
Bîr el Gellaz, *Egypt* 76 A2
Bîr el Heisi, *Egypt* 69 F3
Bîr el Jafir, *Egypt* 69 E1
Bîr el Mâlḥi, *Egypt* 69 E2
Bîr el Shaqqa, *Egypt* 76 A2
Bîr el Thamâda, *Egypt* 69 E2
Bîr Fuad, *Egypt* 76 A2
Bîr Gebeil Ḥişn, *Egypt* 69 E2
Bi'r Ghadīr, *Syria* 69 A6
Bîr Haimur, *Egypt* 76 C3
Bîr Ḥasana, *Egypt* 69 E2
Bi'r Jadīd, *Iraq* 64 C4
Bir Jdid, *Morocco* 74 B3
Bîr Kanayis, *Egypt* 76 C3
Bîr Kaseiba, *Egypt* 69 E2
Bîr Kerawein, *Egypt* 76 B2
Bîr Lahfân, *Egypt* 69 D2
Bir Lahrache, *Algeria* 75 B6
Bîr Madkûr, *Egypt* 69 E1
Bîr Maql, *Egypt* 76 C3
Bîr Misaha, *Egypt* 76 C2
Bir Mogrein, *Mauritania* 74 C2
Bîr Murr, *Egypt* 76 C3
Bi'r Muṭribah, *Kuwait* 64 D5
Bîr Nakheila, *Egypt* 76 C3
Bîr Qaṭia, *Egypt* 69 E1
Bîr Qatrani, *Egypt* 76 A2
Bîr Ranga, *Egypt* 76 C4
Bîr Sahara, *Egypt* 76 C2
Bîr Seiyâla, *Egypt* 76 B3
Bir Semguine, *Morocco* 74 B3
Bîr Shalatein, *Egypt* 76 C4
Bîr Shebb, *Egypt* 76 C2
Bîr Shût, *Egypt* 76 C4
Bîr Terfawi, *Egypt* 76 C2
Bîr Umm Qubûr, *Egypt* 76 C3
Bîr Ungât, *Egypt* 76 C3
Bîr Za'farâna, *Egypt* 76 J8
Bîr Zeidûn, *Egypt* 76 B3
Bira, *Indonesia* 57 E8
Bîra, *Romania* 38 B10
Biramféro, *Guinea* 78 C3
Birao, *C.A.R.* 73 F9
Birawa, *Zaïre* 82 C2
Bîrca, *Romania* 38 F6
Birch Hills, *Canada* 101 C7
Birch I., *Canada* 101 C9
Birch L., *N.W.T., Canada* 100 A5
Birch L., *Ont., Canada* 98 B1
Birch L., *U.S.A.* 98 C1
Birch Mts., *Canada* 100 B6
Birch River, *Canada* 101 C8
Birchip, *Australia* 91 F3
Bird, *Canada* 101 B10
Bird City, *U.S.A.* 108 F4
Bird I. = Aves, I. de, *W. Indies* 117 C7
Bird I., *S. Africa* 84 E2
Birdaard, *Neths.* 16 B7
Birdlip, *U.K.* 13 F5
Birdsville, *Australia* 90 D2
Birdum, *Australia* 88 C5
Birein, *Israel* 69 E3
Bireuen, *Indonesia* 56 C1
Birifo, *Gambia* 78 C2
Birigui, *Brazil* 127 A5
Birkenfeld, *Germany* 19 F3
Birkenhead, *U.K.* 12 D4
Birket Qârûn, *Egypt* 76 J7
Birkhadem, *Algeria* 75 A5
Bîrlad, *Romania* 38 C10
Birmingham, *U.K.* 13 E6
Birmingham, *U.S.A.* 105 J2
Birmitrapur, *India* 61 H14
Birni Ngaouré, *Niger* 79 C5
Birni Nkonni, *Niger* 79 C6
Birnin Gwari, *Nigeria* 79 C6
Birnin Kebbi, *Nigeria* 79 C5
Birnin Kudu, *Nigeria* 79 C6
Birobidzhan, *Russia* 45 E14
Birr, *Ireland* 15 C4
Birrie →, *Australia* 91 D4
Birs →, *Switz.* 22 B5
Birsilpur, *India* 62 E5
Birsk, *Russia* 44 D6
Birtin, *Romania* 38 C5
Birtle, *Canada* 101 C8
Birur, *India* 60 N9
Biryuchiy, *Ukraine* 42 C6
Biržai, *Lithuania* 40 C4
Bîrzava, *Romania* 38 C4
Birzebugga, *Malta* 37 D2
Bisa, *Indonesia* 57 E7
Bisáccia, *Italy* 35 A8
Bisacquino, *Italy* 34 E6
Bisalpur, *India* 63 E8
Bisbee, *U.S.A.* 111 L9
Biscarrosse et de Parentis, Étang de, *France* 26 D2
Biscay, B. of, *Atl. Oc.* 6 F5
Biscayne B., *U.S.A.* 105 N5
Biscéglie, *Italy* 35 A9
Bischofshofen, *Austria* 21 H3
Bischofswerda, *Germany* 18 D10
Bischofszell, *Switz.* 23 B8
Bischwiller, *France* 25 D14
Biscoe Bay, *Antarctica* 5 D13
Biscoe Is., *Antarctica* 5 C17
Biscostasing, *Canada* 98 C3
Biscucuy, *Venezuela* 120 B4
Biševo, *Croatia* 33 F13
Bisha, *Eritrea* 77 D4
Bishah, W. →, *Si. Arabia* 76 C5
Bishan, *China* 52 C6
Bishkek, *Kirghizia* 44 E8
Bishnupur, *India* 63 H12
Bisho, *S. Africa* 85 E4
Bishop, *Calif., U.S.A.* 111 H4
Bishop, *Tex., U.S.A.* 109 M6
Bishop Auckland, *U.K.* 12 C6
Bishop's Falls, *Canada* 99 C8
Bishop's Stortford, *U.K.* 13 F8
Bisignano, *Italy* 35 C9
Bisina, L., *Uganda* 82 B3
Biskra, *Algeria* 75 B6
Bislig, *Phil.* 57 C7
Bismarck, *U.S.A.* 108 B4
Bismarck Arch., *Papua N. G.* 92 H6
Bismark, *Germany* 18 C7
Biso, *Uganda* 82 B3
Bison, *U.S.A.* 108 C3
Bīsotūn, *Iran* 64 C5
Bispfors, *Sweden* 8 E14
Bispgården, *Sweden* 10 A10
Bissagos = Bijagós, Arquipélago dos, *Guinea-Biss.* 78 C1
Bissau, *Guinea-Biss.* 78 C1
Bissett, *Canada* 101 C9
Bissikrima, *Guinea* 78 C2
Bistcho L., *Canada* 100 B5
Bistreţu, *Romania* 38 F6
Bistrica = Ilirska-Bistrica, *Slovenia* 33 C11
Bistriţa, *Romania* 38 B7
Bistriţa →, *Romania* 38 C9
Bistriţei, Munţii, *Romania* 38 B8
Biswan, *India* 63 F9
Bitam, *Gabon* 80 D2
Bitburg, *Germany* 19 F2
Bitche, *France* 25 C14
Bithynia, *Turkey* 66 C4
Bitkine, *Chad* 73 F8
Bitlis, *Turkey* 67 D10
Bitlis □, *Turkey* 67 D10
Bitola, *Macedonia* 39 H4
Bitolj = Bitola, *Macedonia* 39 H4
Bitonto, *Italy* 35 A9
Bitter Creek, *U.S.A.* 110 F9
Bitter L. = Buheirat-Murrat-el-Kubra, *Egypt* 76 H8
Bitterfeld, *Germany* 18 D8
Bitterfontein, *S. Africa* 84 E2
Bitterroot →, *U.S.A.* 110 C6
Bitterroot Range, *U.S.A.* 110 D6
Bitterwater, *U.S.A.* 112 J6
Bitti, *Italy* 34 B2
Bittou, *Burkina Faso* 79 C4
Biu, *Nigeria* 79 C7
Bivolari, *Romania* 38 B10
Biwa-Ko, *Japan* 49 G8
Biwabik, *U.S.A.* 108 B8
Bixad, *Romania* 38 B6
Biyang, *China* 50 H7
Biysk, *Russia* 44 D9
Bizana, *S. Africa* 85 E4
Bizen, *Japan* 49 G7
Bizerte, *Tunisia* 75 A6
Bjargtangar, *Iceland* 8 D1
Bjelasica, *Montenegro* 21 N9
Bjelovar, *Croatia* 21 K6
Bjerringbro, *Denmark* 11 H3
Bjørnøya, *Arctic* 4 B8
Bjuv, *Sweden* 11 H6
Blace, *Serbia* 21 M11
Black = Da →, *Vietnam* 58 B5
Black →, *Canada* 106 B5
Black →, *Ark., U.S.A.* 109 H9
Black →, *N.Y., U.S.A.* 107 C8
Black →, *Wis., U.S.A.* 108 D9
Black Diamond, *Canada* 100 C6
Black Forest = Schwarzwald, *Germany* 19 H4
Black Hills, *U.S.A.* 108 C3
Black I., *Canada* 101 C9
Black L., *Canada* 101 B7
Black L., *U.S.A.* 104 C3
Black Mesa, *U.S.A.* 109 G3
Black Mt. = Mynydd Du, *U.K.* 13 F4
Black Mts., *U.K.* 13 F4
Black Range, *U.S.A.* 111 K10
Black River, *Jamaica* 116 C4
Black River Falls, *U.S.A.* 108 C9
Black Sea, *Europe* 42 E6
Black Volta →, *Africa* 78 D4
Black Warrior →, *U.S.A.* 105 J2
Blackall, *Australia* 90 C4
Blackball, *N.Z.* 87 K3
Blackbull, *Australia* 90 B3
Blackburn, *U.K.* 12 D5
Blackduck, *U.S.A.* 108 B7
Blackfoot, *U.S.A.* 110 E7
Blackfoot →, *U.S.A.* 110 C7
Blackfoot River Reservoir, *U.S.A.* 110 E8
Blackie, *Canada* 100 C6
Blackpool, *U.K.* 12 D4
Blackriver, *U.S.A.* 106 B1
Blacks Harbour, *Canada* 99 C6
Blacksburg, *U.S.A.* 104 G5
Blacksod B., *Ireland* 15 B2
Blackstone, *U.S.A.* 104 G6
Blackstone →, *Canada* 100 A4
Blackstone Ra., *Australia* 89 E4
Blackville, *Canada* 99 C6
Blackwater, *Australia* 90 C4
Blackwater →, *Ireland* 15 E4
Blackwater →, *U.K.* 15 B5
Blackwater Cr. →, *Australia* 91 D3
Blackwell, *U.S.A.* 109 G6
Blackwells Corner, *U.S.A.* 113 K7
Bladel, *Neths.* 17 F6
Blaenau Ffestiniog, *U.K.* 12 E4
Blagodarnoye, *Russia* 43 D10
Blagoevgrad, *Bulgaria* 39 G6
Blagoveshchensk, *Russia* 45 D13
Blain, *France* 24 E5
Blaine, *U.S.A.* 112 B4
Blaine Lake, *Canada* 101 C7
Blainville-sur-l'Eau, *France* 25 D13
Blair, *U.S.A.* 108 E6
Blair Athol, *Australia* 90 C4
Blair Atholl, *U.K.* 14 E5
Blairgowrie, *U.K.* 14 E5
Blairmore, *Canada* 100 D6
Blairsden, *U.S.A.* 112 F6
Blairsville, *U.S.A.* 106 F5
Blaj, *Romania* 38 C6
Blake Pt., *U.S.A.* 108 A10
Blakely, *U.S.A.* 105 K3
Blâmont, *France* 25 D13
Blanc, C., *Tunisia* 75 A6
Blanc, Mont, *Alps* 27 C10
Blanca, B., *Argentina* 128 A4
Blanca Peak, *U.S.A.* 111 H11
Blanchard, *U.S.A.* 109 H6
Blanche, C., *Australia* 91 E1
Blanche, L., *S. Austral., Australia* 91 D2
Blanche, L., *W. Austral., Australia* 88 D3
Blanco, *S. Africa* 84 E3
Blanco, *U.S.A.* 109 K5
Blanco →, *Argentina* 126 C2
Blanco, C., *U.S.A.* 110 E1
Blanco, C., *Costa Rica* 116 E2
Blanco, C., *Spain* 36 B9
Blanda →, *Iceland* 8 D4
Blandford Forum, *U.K.* 13 G5
Blanding, *U.S.A.* 111 H9
Blanes, *Spain* 28 D7
Blangy-sur-Bresle, *France* 25 C8
Blanice →, *Czech.* 20 F4
Blankenberge, *Belgium* 17 F2
Blankenburg, *Germany* 18 D6
Blanquefort, *France* 26 D3
Blanquillo, *Uruguay* 127 C4
Blansko, *Czech.* 20 F6
Blantyre, *Malawi* 83 F4
Blaricum, *Neths.* 16 D6
Blarney, *Ireland* 15 E3
Blato, *Croatia* 33 F13
Blatten, *Switz.* 22 D5
Blaubeuren, *Germany* 19 G5
Blåvands Huk, *Denmark* 9 J10
Blaydon, *U.K.* 12 C6
Blaye, *France* 26 C3
Blaye-les-Mines, *France* 26 D6
Blayney, *Australia* 91 E4
Blaze, Pt., *Australia* 88 B5
Bleckede, *Germany* 18 B6
Bled, *Slovenia* 33 B11
Blednaya, Gora, *Russia* 44 B7
Bléharis, *Belgium* 17 G2
Blejeşti, *Romania* 38 E8
Blekinge län □, *Sweden* 9 H13
Blenheim, *Canada* 106 D2
Blenheim, *N.Z.* 87 J4
Bléone →, *France* 27 D10
Blerick, *Neths.* 17 F8
Bletchley, *U.K.* 13 F7
Blida, *Algeria* 75 A5
Blidet Amor, *Algeria* 75 B6
Blidö, *Sweden* 10 E12
Bligh Sound, *N.Z.* 87 L1
Blind River, *Canada* 98 C3
Blinnenhorn, *Switz.* 23 D6
Blitar, *Indonesia* 57 H15
Blitta, *Togo* 79 D5
Block I., *U.S.A.* 107 E13
Block Island Sd., *U.S.A.* 107 E13
Blodgett Iceberg Tongue, *Antarctica* 5 C9
Bloemendaal, *Neths.* 16 D5
Bloemfontein, *S. Africa* 84 D4
Bloemhof, *S. Africa* 84 D4
Blois, *France* 24 E8
Blokziji, *Neths.* 16 C7
Blönduós, *Iceland* 8 D3
Bloodvein →, *Canada* 101 C9
Bloody Foreland, *Ireland* 15 A3
Bloomer, *U.S.A.* 108 C9
Bloomfield, *Australia* 90 B4
Bloomfield, *Canada* 106 C7
Bloomfield, *Iowa, U.S.A.* 108 E8
Bloomfield, *N. Mex., U.S.A.* 111 H10
Bloomfield, *Nebr., U.S.A.* 108 D6
Bloomington, *Ill., U.S.A.* 108 E10
Bloomington, *Ind., U.S.A.* 104 F2
Bloomsburg, *U.S.A.* 107 F8
Blora, *Indonesia* 57 G14
Blossburg, *U.S.A.* 106 E7
Blouberg, *S. Africa* 85 C4
Blountstown, *U.S.A.* 105 K3
Bludenz, *Austria* 19 H5
Blue Island, *U.S.A.* 104 E2
Blue Lake, *U.S.A.* 110 F2
Blue Mesa Reservoir, *U.S.A.* 111 G10
Blue Mts., *Oreg., U.S.A.* 110 D4
Blue Mts., *Pa., U.S.A.* 107 F8
Blue Mud B., *Australia* 90 A2
Blue Nile = An Nîl el Azraq □, *Sudan* 77 E3
Blue Nile = Nîl el Azraq →, *Sudan* 77 D3
Blue Rapids, *U.S.A.* 108 F6
Blue Ridge Mts., *U.S.A.* 105 G5
Blue Stack Mts., *Ireland* 15 B3
Blueberry →, *Canada* 100 B4
Bluefield, *U.S.A.* 104 G5
Bluefields, *Nic.* 116 D3
Bluff, *Australia* 90 C4
Bluff, *N.Z.* 87 M2
Bluff, *U.S.A.* 111 H9
Bluff Knoll, *Australia* 89 F2
Bluff Pt., *Australia* 89 E1
Bluffton, *U.S.A.* 104 E3
Blumenau, *Brazil* 127 B6
Blümisalphorn, *Switz.* 22 D5
Blunt, *U.S.A.* 108 C4
Bly, *U.S.A.* 110 E3
Blyth, *Canada* 106 C3
Blyth, *U.K.* 12 B6
Blyth Bridge, *U.K.* 12 E5
Blythe, *U.S.A.* 113 M12
Bø, *Norway* 10 E3
Bo, *S. Leone* 78 D2
Bo Duc, *Vietnam* 59 G6
Bo Hai, *China* 51 E10
Bo Xian, *China* 50 H8
Boa Esperança, *Brazil* 121 C5
Boa Nova, *Brazil* 123 D3
Boa Viagem, *Brazil* 122 C4
Boa Vista, *Brazil* 121 C5
Boac, *Phil.* 55 E4
Boaco, *Nic.* 116 D2
Bo'ai, *China* 50 G7
Boal, *Spain* 30 B4
Boardman, *U.S.A.* 106 E4
Boatman, *Australia* 91 D4
Bobadah, *Australia* 91 E4
Bobai, *China* 52 F7
Bobbili, *India* 61 K13
Bóbbio, *Italy* 32 D6
Bobcaygeon, *Canada* 98 D4
Böblingen, *Germany* 19 G5
Bobo-Dioulasso, *Burkina Faso* 78 C4
Boboc, *Romania* 38 D9
Bobonaza →, *Ecuador* 120 D2
Bobov Dol, *Bulgaria* 38 G5
Bóbr →, *Poland* 20 C5
Bobraomby, Tanjon' i, *Madag.* 85 A8
Bobrinets, *Ukraine* 42 B5
Bobrov, *Russia* 41 F12
Bobruysk, *Belorussia* 40 E6
Bobures, *Venezuela* 120 B3
Boca de Drago, *Venezuela* 121 A5
Bôca do Acre, *Brazil* 124 B4
Bôca do Jari, *Brazil* 121 D7
Bôca do Moaco, *Brazil* 124 B4
Boca Grande, *Venezuela* 121 B5
Boca Raton, *U.S.A.* 105 M5
Bocaiúva, *Brazil* 123 E3
Bocanda, *Ivory C.* 78 D4
Bocaranga, *C.A.R.* 73 G8
Bocas del Toro, *Panama* 116 E3
Boceguillas, *Spain* 28 D1
Bochnia, *Poland* 20 F10
Bocholt, *Belgium* 17 F7
Bocholt, *Germany* 18 D2
Bochum, *Germany* 18 D3
Bockenem, *Germany* 18 C6
Bocognano, *France* 27 F13
Boconó, *Venezuela* 120 B3
Boconó →, *Venezuela* 120 B4
Bocoyna, *Mexico* 114 B3
Bocq →, *Belgium* 17 H5
Boda, *C.A.R.* 80 D3
Bodaybo, *Russia* 45 D12
Boddington, *Australia* 89 F2
Bodega Bay, *U.S.A.* 112 G3
Bodegraven, *Neths.* 16 D5
Boden, *Sweden* 8 D16
Bodensee, *Europe* 23 A8
Bodenteich, *Germany* 18 C6
Bodhan, *India* 60 K10
Bodinga, *Nigeria* 79 C6
Bodio, *Switz.* 23 D7
Bodmin, *U.K.* 13 G3
Bodmin Moor, *U.K.* 13 G3
Bodoquena, Serra da, *Brazil* 125 E6
Bodrog →, *Hungary* 21 G11
Bodrum, *Turkey* 66 E2
Boechout, *Belgium* 17 F5
Boegoebergdam, *S. Africa* 84 D3
Boekelo, *Neths.* 16 D9
Boelenslaan, *Neths.* 16 B8
Boën, *France* 27 C8
Boende, *Zaïre* 80 E4
Boerne, *U.S.A.* 109 L5
Boertange, *Neths.* 16 B10
Boezinge, *Belgium* 17 G1
Boffa, *Guinea* 78 C2
Bogalusa, *U.S.A.* 109 K10
Bogan Gate, *Australia* 91 E4
Bogantungan, *Australia* 90 C4
Bogata, *U.S.A.* 109 J7
Bogatić, *Serbia* 21 L9

Bracciano

Boğazlıyan, *Turkey* 66 D6
Bogense, *Denmark* 11 J4
Boggabilla, *Australia* 91 D5
Boggabri, *Australia* 91 E5
Boggeragh Mts., *Ireland* 15 D3
Bognor Regis, *U.K.* 13 G7
Bogø, *Denmark* 11 K6
Bogo, *Phil.* 55 F6
Bogodukhov, *Ukraine* 42 A6
Bogong, Mt., *Australia* 91 F4
Bogor, *Indonesia* 57 G12
Bogoroditsk, *Russia* 41 E11
Bogorodsk, *Russia* 41 C13
Bogorodskoye, *Russia* 45 D15
Bogoso, *Ghana* 78 D4
Bogotá, *Colombia* 120 C3
Bogotol, *Russia* 44 D9
Bogra, *Bangla.* 61 G16
Boguchany, *Russia* 45 D10
Boguchar, *Russia* 43 B9
Bogué, *Mauritania* 78 B2
Boguslav, *Ukraine* 42 B4
Bohain-en-Vermandois, *France* 25 C10
Bohemia Downs, *Australia* 88 C4
Bohemian Forest = Böhmerwald, *Germany* 19 F8
Bohena Cr. →, *Australia* 91 E4
Bohinjska Bistrica, *Slovenia* 33 B11
Böhmerwald, *Germany* 19 F8
Bohmte, *Germany* 18 C4
Bohol, *Phil.* 55 G6
Bohol Sea, *Phil.* 57 C6
Bohotleh, *Somali Rep.* 68 F4
Boi, *Nigeria* 79 D6
Boi, Pta. de, *Brazil* 127 A6
Boiaçu, *Brazil* 121 D5
Boiano, *Italy* 35 A7
Boileau, C., *Australia* 88 C3
Boipeba, I. de, *Brazil* 123 D4
Bois →, *Brazil* 123 E1
Boischot, *Belgium* 17 F5
Boise, *U.S.A.* 110 E5
Boise City, *U.S.A.* 109 G3
Boissevain, *Canada* 101 D8
Boite →, *Italy* 33 B9
Boitzenburg, *Germany* 18 B9
Boizenburg, *Germany* 18 B6
Bojador C., *W. Sahara* 74 C2
Bojnūrd, *Iran* 65 B8
Bojonegoro, *Indonesia* 57 G14
Boju, *Nigeria* 79 D6
Boka Kotorska, *Montenegro* 21 N8
Bokala, *Ivory C.* 78 D4
Boké, *Guinea* 78 C2
Bokhara →, *Australia* 91 D4
Bokkos, *Nigeria* 79 D6
Boknafjorden, *Norway* 9 G8
Bokoro, *Chad* 73 F8
Bokote, *Zaïre* 80 E4
Boksitogorsk, *Russia* 40 B8
Bokungu, *Zaïre* 80 E4
Bol, *Chad* 73 F7
Bol, *Croatia* 33 E13
Bolama, *Guinea-Biss.* 78 C1
Bolan Pass, *Pakistan* 60 E5
Bolaños →, *Mexico* 114 C4
Bolbec, *France* 24 C7
Boldājī, *Iran* 65 D6
Boldeşti, *Romania* 38 D9
Bole, *China* 54 B3
Bole, *Ethiopia* 77 F4
Bolekhov, *Ukraine* 40 G3
Bolesławiec, *Poland* 20 D5
Bolgatanga, *Ghana* 79 C4
Bolgrad, *Ukraine* 42 D3
Boli, *Sudan* 77 F2
Bolinao, *Phil.* 55 C3
Bolinao C., *Phil.* 57 A5
Bolívar, *Argentina* 126 D3
Bolívar, *Antioquía, Colombia* 120 B2
Bolívar, *Cauca, Colombia* 120 C2
Bolívar, *Peru* 124 B2
Bolivar, *Mo., U.S.A.* 109 G8
Bolivar, *Tenn., U.S.A.* 109 H10
Bolívar □, *Colombia* 120 B3
Bolívar □, *Ecuador* 120 D2
Bolívar □, *Venezuela* 121 B5
Bolivia ■, *S. Amer.* 125 D5
Bolivian Plateau, *S. Amer.* 118 D3
Bolkhov, *Russia* 41 E10
Bollène, *France* 27 D8
Bollnäs, *Sweden* 10 C10
Bollon, *Australia* 91 D4
Bollstabruk, *Sweden* 10 A11
Bollullos, *Spain* 31 H4
Bolobo, *Zaïre* 80 E3
Bologna, *Italy* 33 D8
Bologne, *France* 25 D12
Bologoye, *Russia* 40 C9
Bolomba, *Zaïre* 80 D3
Bolonchenticul, *Mexico* 115 D7
Bolong, *Phil.* 57 C6
Boloven, Cao Nguyen, *Laos* 58 E6
Bolpur, *India* 63 H12
Bolsena, *Italy* 33 F8
Bolsena, L. di, *Italy* 33 F8
Bolshaya Glushitsa, *Russia* 41 E17
Bolshaya Martynovka, *Russia* 43 C9
Bolshaya Vradiyevka, *Ukraine* 42 C4
Bolshereche, *Russia* 44 D8
Bolshevik, Ostrov, *Russia* 45 B11
Bolshoi Kavkas, *Asia* 43 E11
Bolshoy Anyuy →, *Russia* 45 C17
Bolshoy Atlym, *Russia* 44 C7
Bolshoy Begichev, Ostrov, *Russia* 45 B12
Bolshoy Lyakhovskiy, Ostrov, *Russia* 45 B15
Bolshoy Tokmak, *Ukraine* 42 C6
Bol'shoy Tyuters, *Estonia* 40 B5
Bolsward, *Neths.* 16 B7
Boltaña, *Spain* 28 C5
Boltigen, *Switz.* 22 C4
Bolton, *Canada* 106 C5
Bolton, *U.K.* 12 D5
Bolu, *Turkey* 66 C4
Bolu □, *Turkey* 66 C4
Boluo, *China* 53 F10
Bolvadin, *Turkey* 66 D4
Bolzano, *Italy* 33 B8
Bom Comércio, *Brazil* 125 B4
Bom Conselho, *Brazil* 122 C4
Bom Despacho, *Brazil* 123 E2
Bom Jesus, *Brazil* 122 C3
Bom Jesus da Gurguéia, Serra, *Brazil* 122 C3
Bom Jesus da Lapa, *Brazil* 123 D3
Boma, *Zaïre* 80 F2
Bomaderry, *Australia* 91 E5
Bombala, *Australia* 91 F4
Bombarral, *Portugal* 31 F1
Bombay, *India* 60 K8
Bomboma, *Zaïre* 80 D3
Bombombwa, *Zaïre* 82 B2
Bomi Hills, *Liberia* 78 D2
Bomili, *Zaïre* 82 B2
Bommel, *Neths.* 16 E4
Bomokandi →, *Zaïre* 82 B2
Bomongo, *Zaïre* 80 D3
Bomu →, *C.A.R.* 80 D4
Bon, C., *Tunisia* 75 A7
Bon Sar Pa, *Vietnam* 58 F6
Bonaduz, *Switz.* 23 C8
Bonaire, *Neth. Ant.* 117 D6
Bonang, *Australia* 91 F4
Bonanza, *Nic.* 116 D3
Bonaparte Arch., *Australia* 88 B3
Boñar, *Spain* 30 C5
Bonaventure, *Canada* 99 C6
Bonavista, *Canada* 99 C9
Bonavista, C., *Canada* 99 C9
Bonawan, *Phil.* 55 G5
Bondeno, *Italy* 33 D8
Bondo, *Zaïre* 82 B1
Bondoukou, *Ivory C.* 78 D4
Bondowoso, *Indonesia* 57 G15
Bone, Teluk, *Indonesia* 57 E6
Bone Rate, *Indonesia* 57 F6
Bone Rate, Kepulauan, *Indonesia* 57 F6
Bonefro, *Italy* 35 A7
Bo'ness, *U.K.* 14 E5
Bong Son = Hoai Nhon, *Vietnam* 58 E7
Bongabong, *Phil.* 55 E4
Bongandanga, *Zaïre* 80 D4
Bongor, *Chad* 73 F8
Bongouanou, *Ivory C.* 78 D4
Bonham, *U.S.A.* 109 J6
Bonheiden, *Belgium* 17 F5
Bonifacio, *France* 27 G13
Bonifacio, Bouches de, *Medit. S.* 34 A2
Bonin Is. = Ogasawara Gunto, *Pac. Oc.* 92 E6
Bonke, *Ethiopia* 77 F4
Bonn, *Germany* 18 E3
Bonnat, *France* 26 B5
Bonne Terre, *U.S.A.* 109 G9
Bonners Ferry, *U.S.A.* 110 B5
Bonnétable, *France* 24 D7
Bonneuil-Matours, *France* 24 F7
Bonneval, *France* 24 D8
Bonneville, *France* 27 B10
Bonney, L., *Australia* 91 F3
Bonnie Downs, *Australia* 90 C3
Bonnie Rock, *Australia* 89 F2
Bonny, *Nigeria* 79 E6
Bonny →, *Nigeria* 79 E6
Bonny, Bight of, *Africa* 79 E6
Bonny-sur-Loire, *France* 25 E9
Bonnyville, *Canada* 101 C6
Bonoi, *Indonesia* 57 E9
Bonorva, *Italy* 34 B1
Bonsall, *U.S.A.* 113 M9
Bontang, *Indonesia* 56 D5
Bonthain, *Indonesia* 57 F5
Bonthe, *S. Leone* 78 D2
Bontoc, *Phil.* 55 C4
Bonyeri, *Ghana* 78 D4
Bonython Ra., *Australia* 88 D4
Bookabie, *Australia* 89 F5
Booker, *U.S.A.* 109 G4
Boolaboolka L., *Australia* 91 E3
Booligal, *Australia* 91 E3
Boom, *Belgium* 17 F4
Boonah, *Australia* 91 D5
Boone, *Iowa, U.S.A.* 108 D8
Boone, *N.C., U.S.A.* 105 G5
Booneville, *Ark., U.S.A.* 109 H8
Booneville, *Miss., U.S.A.* 105 H1
Boonville, *Calif., U.S.A.* 112 F3
Boonville, *Ind., U.S.A.* 104 F2
Boonville, *Mo., U.S.A.* 108 F8
Boonville, *N.Y., U.S.A.* 107 C9
Boorindal, *Australia* 91 E4
Boorowa, *Australia* 91 E4
Boothia, Gulf of, *Canada* 97 A11
Boothia Pen., *Canada* 96 A10
Bootle, *Cumb., U.K.* 12 C4
Bootle, *Mersey., U.K.* 12 D4
Booué, *Gabon* 80 E2
Bophuthatswana □, *S. Africa* 84 D4
Boppard, *Germany* 19 E3
Boquerón □, *Paraguay* 125 E5
Boquete, *Panama* 116 E3
Boquilla, Presa de la, *Mexico* 114 B3
Boquillas del Carmen, *Mexico* 114 B4
Bor, *Czech.* 20 F2
Bor, *Serbia* 21 L12
Bôr, *Sudan* 77 F3
Bor, *Turkey* 66 E6
Bor Mashash, *Israel* 69 D3
Boradā →, *Syria* 69 B5
Borah Peak, *U.S.A.* 110 D7
Borama, *Somali Rep.* 68 F3
Borang, *Sudan* 77 G3
Borås, *Sweden* 11 G6
Borāzjān, *Iran* 65 D6
Borba, *Brazil* 121 D6
Borba, *Portugal* 31 G3
Borborema, Planalto da, *Brazil* 122 C4
Borçka, *Turkey* 43 F9
Borculo, *Neths.* 16 D9
Bord Khūn-e Now, *Iran* 65 D6
Borda, C., *Australia* 91 F2
Bordeaux, *France* 26 D3
Borden, *Australia* 89 F2
Borden, *Canada* 99 C7
Borden I., *Canada* 4 B2
Borders □, *U.K.* 14 F6
Bordertown, *Australia* 91 F3
Borðeyri, *Iceland* 8 D3
Bordighera, *Italy* 32 E4
Bordj bou Arreridj, *Algeria* 75 A5
Bordj Bourguiba, *Tunisia* 75 B7
Bordj el Hobra, *Algeria* 75 B5
Bordj Fly Ste. Marie, *Algeria* 74 C4
Bordj-in-Eker, *Algeria* 75 D6
Bordj Menaiel, *Algeria* 75 A5
Bordj Messouda, *Algeria* 75 B6
Bordj Nili, *Algeria* 75 B5
Bordj Omar Driss, *Algeria* 75 C6
Bordj-Tarat, *Algeria* 75 C6
Bordj Zelfana, *Algeria* 75 B5
Borensberg, *Sweden* 11 F9
Borgå, *Finland* 9 F18
Borgarnes, *Iceland* 8 D3
Børgefjellet, *Norway* 8 D12
Borger, *Neths.* 16 C9
Borger, *U.S.A.* 109 H4
Borgerhout, *Belgium* 17 F4
Borghamn, *Sweden* 11 F8
Borgholm, *Sweden* 9 H14
Bórgia, *Italy* 35 D9
Borgloon, *Belgium* 17 G6
Borgo San Dalmazzo, *Italy* 32 D4
Borgo San Lorenzo, *Italy* 33 E8
Borgo Valsugano, *Italy* 33 B8
Borgomanero, *Italy* 32 C5
Borgonovo Val Tidone, *Italy* 32 C6
Borgorose, *Italy* 33 F10
Borgosésia, *Italy* 32 C5
Borgvattnet, *Sweden* 10 A9
Borikhane, *Laos* 58 C4
Borislav, *Ukraine* 40 G3
Borisoglebsk, *Russia* 41 F13
Borisoglebskiy, *Russia* 41 C13
Borisov, *Belorussia* 40 D6
Borispol, *Ukraine* 40 F7
Borja, *Peru* 120 D2
Borja, *Spain* 28 D3
Borjas Blancas, *Spain* 28 D5
Borken, *Germany* 18 D2
Borkou, *Chad* 73 E8
Borkum, *Germany* 18 B2
Borlänge, *Sweden* 9 F13
Borley, C., *Antarctica* 5 C5
Bormida →, *Italy* 32 D5
Bórmio, *Italy* 32 B7
Born, *Neths.* 17 F7
Borna, *Germany* 18 D8
Borndiep, *Neths.* 16 B7
Borne, *Neths.* 16 D9
Bornem, *Belgium* 17 F4
Borneo, *E. Indies* 56 D5
Bornholm, *Denmark* 9 J13
Borno □, *Nigeria* 79 C7
Bornos, *Spain* 31 J5
Bornu Yassa, *Nigeria* 79 C7
Borobudur, *Indonesia* 57 G14
Borodino, *Russia* 40 D9
Borogontsy, *Russia* 45 C14
Boromo, *Burkina Faso* 78 C4
Boron, *U.S.A.* 113 L9
Borongan, *Phil.* 55 F6
Bororen, *Australia* 90 C5
Borotangba Mts., *C.A.R.* 77 F1
Borovan, *Bulgaria* 38 F6
Borovichi, *Russia* 40 B8
Borovsk, *Russia* 41 D10
Borrego Springs, *U.S.A.* 113 M10
Borriol, *Spain* 28 E4
Borroloola, *Australia* 90 B2
Borşa, *Romania* 38 B7
Borssele, *Neths.* 17 F3
Bort-les-Orgues, *France* 26 C6
Borth, *U.K.* 13 E3
Borujerd, *Iran* 65 C6
Borzhomi, *Georgia* 43 F10
Borzna, *Ukraine* 40 F8
Borzya, *Russia* 45 D12
Bosa, *Italy* 34 B1
Bosanska Dubica, *Bos.-H.* 33 C13
Bosanska Gradiška, *Bos.-H.* 21 K7
Bosanska Kostajnica, *Bos.-H.* 33 C13
Bosanska Krupa, *Bos.-H.* 33 D13
Bosanski Novi, *Bos.-H.* 33 C13
Bosanski Šamac, *Bos.-H.* 21 K8
Bosansko Grahovo, *Bos.-H.* 33 D13
Bosansko Petrovac, *Bos.-H.* 33 D13
Bosaso, *Somali Rep.* 68 E4
Boscastle, *U.K.* 13 G3
Boscotrecase, *Italy* 35 B7
Bose, *China* 52 F6
Boshan, *China* 51 F9
Boshoek, *S. Africa* 84 D4
Boshof, *S. Africa* 84 D4
Boshrūyeh, *Iran* 65 C8
Bosilegrad, *Serbia* 21 N12
Boskoop, *Neths.* 16 D5
Bosna →, *Bos.-H.* 21 K8
Bosna i Hercegovina = Bosnia-Herzegovina ■, *Europe* 21 L7
Bosnia-Herzegovina ■, *Europe* 21 L7
Bosnik, *Indonesia* 57 E9
Bosobolo, *Zaïre* 80 D3
Bosporus = Karadeniz Boğazı, *Turkey* 66 C3
Bossangoa, *C.A.R.* 73 G8
Bossekop, *Norway* 8 B17
Bossembélé, *C.A.R.* 73 G8
Bossier City, *U.S.A.* 109 J8
Bosso, *Niger* 79 C7
Bostānābād, *Iran* 64 B5
Bosten Hu, *China* 54 B3
Boston, *U.K.* 12 E7
Boston, *U.S.A.* 107 D13
Boston Bar, *Canada* 100 D4
Bosut →, *Croatia* 21 K8
Boswell, *Canada* 100 D5
Boswell, *Okla., U.S.A.* 109 H7
Boswell, *Pa., U.S.A.* 106 F5
Botad, *India* 62 H4
Botan →, *Turkey* 67 E9
Botany B., *Australia* 91 E5
Botene, *Laos* 58 D3
Botevgrad, *Bulgaria* 38 G6
Bothaville, *S. Africa* 84 D4
Bothnia, G. of, *Europe* 8 E16
Bothwell, *Australia* 90 G4
Bothwell, *Canada* 106 D3
Boticas, *Portugal* 30 D3
Botletle →, *Botswana* 84 C3
Botoşani, *Romania* 38 B9
Botro, *Ivory C.* 78 D3
Botswana ■, *Africa* 84 C3
Bottineau, *U.S.A.* 108 A4
Bottrop, *Germany* 17 E9
Botucatu, *Brazil* 127 A6
Botwood, *Canada* 99 C8
Bou Alam, *Algeria* 75 B5
Bou Ali, *Algeria* 75 C4
Bou Djébéha, *Mali* 78 B4
Bou Guema, *Algeria* 75 C5
Bou Ismael, *Algeria* 75 A5
Bou Izakarn, *Morocco* 74 C3
Boû Lanouâr, *Mauritania* 74 D1
Bou Saâda, *Algeria* 75 A5
Bou Salem, *Tunisia* 75 A6
Bouaké, *Ivory C.* 78 D3
Bouar, *C.A.R.* 80 C3
Bouârfa, *Morocco* 75 B4
Bouca, *C.A.R.* 73 G8
Boucau, *France* 26 E2
Boucaut B., *Australia* 90 A1
Bouches-du-Rhône □, *France* 27 E9
Bouda, *Algeria* 75 C4
Boudenib, *Morocco* 74 B4
Boudry, *Switz.* 22 C3
Boufarik, *Algeria* 75 A5
Bougainville, C., *Australia* 88 B4
Bougainville Reef, *Australia* 90 B4
Bougaroun, C., *Algeria* 75 A6
Bougie = Bejaia, *Algeria* 75 A6
Bougouni, *Mali* 78 C3
Bouillon, *Belgium* 17 J6
Bouïra, *Algeria* 75 A5
Boulder, *Colo., U.S.A.* 108 E2
Boulder, *Mont., U.S.A.* 110 C7
Boulder City, *U.S.A.* 113 K12
Boulder Creek, *U.S.A.* 112 H4
Boulder Dam = Hoover Dam, *U.S.A.* 113 K12
Bouli, *Mauritania* 78 B2
Boulia, *Australia* 90 C2
Bouligny, *France* 25 C12
Boulogne →, *France* 24 E5
Boulogne-sur-Gesse, *France* 26 E4
Boulogne-sur-Mer, *France* 25 B8
Bouloire, *France* 24 E7
Boulsa, *Burkina Faso* 79 C4
Boultoum, *Niger* 79 C7
Boumalne, *Morocco* 74 B3
Boun Neua, *Laos* 58 B3
Boun Tai, *Laos* 58 B3
Bouna, *Ivory C.* 78 D4
Boundary Peak, *U.S.A.* 112 H8
Boundiali, *Ivory C.* 78 D3
Bountiful, *U.S.A.* 110 F8
Bounty Is., *Pac. Oc.* 92 M9
Bourbon-Lancy, *France* 26 B7
Bourbon-l'Archambault, *France* 26 B7
Bourbonnais, *France* 26 B7
Bourbonne-les-Bains, *France* 25 E12
Bourem, *Mali* 79 B4
Bourg, *France* 26 C3
Bourg-Argental, *France* 27 C8
Bourg-de-Péage, *France* 27 C9
Bourg-en-Bresse, *France* 27 B9
Bourg-St.-Andéol, *France* 27 D8
Bourg-St.-Maurice, *France* 27 C10
Bourg-St.-Pierre, *Switz.* 22 E4
Bourganeuf, *France* 26 C5
Bourges, *France* 25 E9
Bourget, *Canada* 107 A9
Bourget, L. du, *France* 27 C9
Bourgneuf, B. de, *France* 24 E4
Bourgneuf-en-Retz, *France* 24 E5
Bourgogne, *France* 25 F11
Bourgoin-Jallieu, *France* 27 C9
Bourgueil, *France* 24 E7
Bourke, *Australia* 91 E4
Bournemouth, *U.K.* 13 G6
Bourriot-Bergonce, *France* 26 D3
Bouse, *U.S.A.* 113 M13
Boussac, *France* 26 B6
Boussens, *France* 26 E4
Bousso, *Chad* 73 F8
Boussu, *Belgium* 17 H3
Boutilimit, *Mauritania* 78 B2
Bouvet I. = Bouvetøya, *Antarctica* 3 G10
Bouvetøya, *Antarctica* 3 G10
Bouznika, *Morocco* 74 B3
Bouzonville, *France* 25 C13
Bova Marina, *Italy* 35 E8
Bovalino Marina, *Italy* 35 D9
Bovec, *Slovenia* 33 B10
Bovenkarspel, *Neths.* 16 C6
Bovigny, *Belgium* 17 H7
Bovill, *U.S.A.* 110 C5
Bovino, *Italy* 35 A8
Bow Island, *Canada* 100 D6
Bowbells, *U.S.A.* 108 A3
Bowdle, *U.S.A.* 108 C5
Bowelling, *Australia* 89 F2
Bowen, *Australia* 90 C4
Bowen Mts., *Australia* 91 F4
Bowie, *Ariz., U.S.A.* 111 K9
Bowie, *Tex., U.S.A.* 109 J6
Bowkān, *Iran* 64 B5
Bowland, Forest of, *U.K.* 12 D5
Bowling Green, *Ky., U.S.A.* 104 G2
Bowling Green, *Ohio, U.S.A.* 104 E4
Bowling Green, C., *Australia* 90 B4
Bowman, *U.S.A.* 108 B3
Bowman I., *Antarctica* 5 C8
Bowmans, *Australia* 91 E2
Bowmanville, *Canada* 98 D4
Bowmore, *U.K.* 14 F2
Bowral, *Australia* 91 E5
Bowraville, *Australia* 91 E5
Bowron →, *Canada* 100 C4
Bowser L., *Canada* 100 B3
Bowsman, *Canada* 101 C8
Bowwood, *Zambia* 83 F2
Boxholm, *Sweden* 11 F9
Boxmeer, *Neths.* 17 E7
Boxtel, *Neths.* 17 E6
Boyabat, *Turkey* 42 F6
Boyaca = Casanare □, *Colombia* 120 B3
Boyce, *U.S.A.* 109 K8
Boyer →, *Canada* 100 B5
Boyle, *Ireland* 15 C3
Boyne →, *Ireland* 15 C5
Boyne City, *U.S.A.* 104 C3
Boynton Beach, *U.S.A.* 105 M5
Boyoma, Chutes, *Zaïre* 82 B2
Boyup Brook, *Australia* 89 F2
Boz Dağ, *Turkey* 66 E3
Boz Dağları, *Turkey* 66 D3
Bozburun, *Turkey* 66 E3
Bozdoğan, *Turkey* 66 E3
Bozeman, *U.S.A.* 110 D8
Bozen = Bolzano, *Italy* 33 B8
Bozkır, *Turkey* 66 E5
Bozouls, *France* 26 D6
Bozoum, *C.A.R.* 73 G8
Bozova, *Turkey* 67 E8
Bozovici, *Romania* 38 E5
Bozüyük, *Turkey* 66 D4
Bra, *Italy* 32 D4
Brabant □, *Belgium* 17 G5
Brabant L., *Canada* 101 B8
Brabrand, *Denmark* 11 H4
Brač, *Croatia* 33 E13
Bracadale, L., *U.K.* 14 D2
Bracciano, *Italy* 33 F9

Bracciano, L. di, Italy 33 F9
Bracebridge, Canada 98 C4
Brach, Libya 73 C7
Bracieux, France 25 E8
Bräcke, Sweden 10 B9
Brackettville, U.S.A. 109 L4
Brački Kanal, Croatia 33 E13
Brad, Romania 38 C5
Brádano →, Italy 35 B9
Bradenton, U.S.A. 105 M4
Bradford, Canada 106 B5
Bradford, U.K. 12 D6
Bradford, Pa., U.S.A. 106 E6
Bradford, Vt., U.S.A. 107 C12
Brădiceni, Romania 38 D6
Bradley, Ark., U.S.A. 109 J8
Bradley, Calif., U.S.A. 112 K6
Bradley, S. Dak., U.S.A. 108 C6
Bradley Institute, Zimbabwe 83 F3
Bradore Bay, Canada 99 B8
Bradshaw, Australia 88 C5
Brady, U.S.A. 109 K5
Brædstrup, Denmark 11 J3
Braemar, Australia 91 E2
Braeside, Canada 107 A8
Braga, Portugal 30 D2
Braga □, Portugal 30 D2
Bragado, Argentina 126 D3
Bragança, Brazil 122 B2
Bragança, Portugal 30 D4
Bragança □, Portugal 30 D4
Bragança Paulista, Brazil 127 A6
Brahmanbaria, Bangla. 61 H17
Brahmani →, India 61 J15
Brahmaputra →, India 63 G13
Braich-y-pwll, U.K. 12 E3
Braidwood, Australia 91 F4
Brăila, Romania 38 D10
Braine-l'Alleud, Belgium 17 G4
Braine-le-Comte, Belgium 17 G4
Brainerd, U.S.A. 108 B7
Braintree, U.K. 13 F8
Braintree, U.S.A. 107 D14
Brak →, S. Africa 84 D3
Brake, Niedersachsen, Germany 18 B4
Brake, Nordrhein-Westfalen, Germany 18 D5
Brakel, Neths. 16 E6
Brakwater, Namibia 84 C2
Brålanda, Sweden 11 F6
Bralorne, Canada 100 C4
Bramberg, Germany 19 E6
Bramminge, Denmark 11 J2
Brämön, Sweden 10 B11
Brampton, Canada 98 D4
Bramsche, Germany 18 C3
Bramwell, Australia 90 A3
Branco →, Brazil 121 D5
Branco, C., Brazil 122 C5
Brande, Denmark 11 J3
Brandenburg = Neubrandenburg, Germany 18 B9
Brandenburg, Germany 18 C8
Brandenburg □, Germany 18 C9
Brandfort, S. Africa 84 D4
Brandon, Canada 101 D9
Brandon, U.S.A. 107 C11
Brandon B., Ireland 15 D1
Brandon Mt., Ireland 15 D1
Brandsen, Argentina 126 D4
Brandval, Norway 10 D6
Brandvlei, S. Africa 84 E3
Brandýs, Czech. 20 E4
Branford, U.S.A. 107 E12
Braniewo, Poland 20 A9
Bransfield Str., Antarctica 5 C18
Branson, Colo., U.S.A. 109 G3
Branson, Mo., U.S.A. 109 G8
Brantford, Canada 98 D3
Brantôme, France 26 C4
Branxholme, Australia 91 F3
Branzi, Italy 32 B6
Bras d'Or, L., Canada 99 C7
Brasiléia, Brazil 124 C4
Brasília, Brazil 123 E2
Brasília Legal, Brazil 121 D6
Braslav, Belorussia 40 D5
Braslovče, Slovenia 33 B12
Braşov, Romania 38 D8
Brass, Nigeria 79 E6
Brass →, Nigeria 79 E6
Brassac-les-Mines, France 26 C7
Brasschaat, Belgium 17 F4
Brassey, Banjaran, Malaysia 56 D5
Brassey Ra., Australia 89 E3
Brasstown Bald, U.S.A. 105 H4
Bratislava, Slovak Rep. 21 G7
Bratsk, Russia 45 D11
Brattleboro, U.S.A. 107 D12
Braunau, Austria 21 G3
Braunschweig, Germany 18 C6
Braunton, U.K. 13 F3
Brava, Somali Rep. 68 G3
Bråviken, Sweden 10 F10
Bravo del Norte →, Mexico 114 B5
Brawley, U.S.A. 113 N11
Bray, Ireland 15 C5
Bray, Mt., Australia 90 A1
Bray, Pays de, France 25 C8
Bray-sur-Seine, France 25 D10
Brazeau →, Canada 100 C5
Brazil, U.S.A. 104 F2
Brazil ■, S. Amer. 123 D2
Brazo Sur →, S. Amer. 126 B4
Brazos →, U.S.A. 109 L7
Brazzaville, Congo 80 E3
Brčko, Bos.-H. 21 L8
Brea, Peru 124 A1
Breadalbane, Australia 90 C2
Breadalbane, U.K. 14 E4
Breaden, L., Australia 89 E4
Breaksea Sd., N.Z. 87 L1
Bream B., N.Z. 87 F5
Bream Hd., N.Z. 87 F5
Breas, Chile 126 B1
Brebes, Indonesia 57 G13
Brechin, Canada 106 B5
Brechin, U.K. 14 E6
Brecht, Belgium 17 F5
Breckenridge, Colo., U.S.A. 110 G10
Breckenridge, Minn., U.S.A. 108 B6
Breckenridge, Tex., U.S.A. 109 J5
Breckland, U.K. 13 E8
Brecknock, Pen., Chile 128 D2
Břeclav, Czech. 20 G6
Brecon, U.K. 13 F4
Brecon Beacons, U.K. 13 F4
Breda, Neths. 17 E5
Bredasdorp, S. Africa 84 E3
Bredbo, Australia 91 F4
Bredene, Belgium 17 F1
Bredstedt, Germany 18 A4
Bree, Belgium 17 F7
Breezand, Neths. 16 C5
Bregalnica →, Macedonia 39 H5
Bregenz, Austria 19 H5
Bréhal, France 24 D5
Bréhat, I. de, France 24 D4
Breiðafjörður, Iceland 8 D2
Breil-sur-Roya, France 27 E11
Breisach, Germany 19 G3
Brejinho de Nazaré, Brazil 122 D2
Brejo, Brazil 122 B3
Bremen, Germany 18 B4
Bremen □, Germany 18 B4
Bremer I., Australia 90 A2
Bremerhaven, Germany 18 B4
Bremerton, U.S.A. 112 C4
Bremervörde, Germany 18 B5
Bremsnes, Norway 10 A1
Brenes, Spain 31 H5
Brenham, U.S.A. 109 K6
Brenner Pass, Austria 19 H7
Breno, Italy 32 C7
Brent, Canada 98 C4
Brent, U.K. 13 F7
Brenta →, Italy 33 C9
Brentwood, U.K. 13 F8
Brentwood, U.S.A. 107 F11
Bréscia, Italy 32 C7
Breskens, Neths. 17 F3
Breslau = Wrocław, Poland 20 D7
Bresle →, France 24 B8
Bresles, France 25 C9
Bressanone, Italy 33 B8
Bressay, U.K. 14 A7
Bresse, France 25 F12
Bressuire, France 24 F6
Brest, Belorussia 40 E3
Brest, France 24 D2
Brest-Litovsk = Brest, Belorussia 40 E3
Bretagne, France 24 D4
Bretçu, Romania 38 C9
Breteuil, Eure, France 24 D7
Breteuil, Oise, France 25 C9
Breton, Canada 100 C6
Breton, Pertuis, France 26 B2
Breton Sd., U.S.A. 109 L10
Brett, C., N.Z. 87 F5
Bretten, Germany 19 F4
Breukelen, Neths. 16 D6
Brevard, U.S.A. 105 H4
Breves, Brazil 122 B1
Brevik, Norway 10 E3
Brewarrina, Australia 91 D4
Brewer, U.S.A. 99 D6
Brewer, Mt., U.S.A. 112 J8
Brewster, N.Y., U.S.A. 107 E11
Brewster, Wash., U.S.A. 110 B4
Brewster, Kap, Greenland 4 B6
Brewton, U.S.A. 105 K2
Breyten, S. Africa 85 D4
Breytovo, Russia 41 B10
Brezhnev = Naberezhnyye Chelny, Russia 44 D6
Brežice, Slovenia 33 C12
Brézina, Algeria 75 B5
Březnice, Czech. 20 F3
Breznik, Bulgaria 38 G5
Brezno, Slovak Rep. 20 G9
Bria, C.A.R. 73 G9
Briançon, France 27 D10
Briare, France 25 E9
Bribie I., Australia 91 D5
Bricquebec, France 24 C5
Bridgehampton, U.S.A. 107 F12
Bridgend, U.K. 13 F4
Bridgeport, Calif., U.S.A. 111 G4
Bridgeport, Conn., U.S.A. 107 E11
Bridgeport, Nebr., U.S.A. 108 E3
Bridgeport, Tex., U.S.A. 109 J6
Bridger, U.S.A. 110 D9
Bridgeton, U.S.A. 104 F8
Bridgetown, Australia 89 F2
Bridgetown, Barbados 117 D8
Bridgetown, Canada 99 D6
Bridgewater, Canada 99 D7
Bridgewater, Mass., U.S.A. 107 E14
Bridgewater, S. Dak., U.S.A. 108 D6
Bridgewater, C., Australia 91 F3
Bridgnorth, U.K. 13 E5
Bridgton, U.S.A. 107 B14
Bridgwater, U.K. 13 F4
Bridlington, U.K. 12 C7
Bridport, Australia 90 G4
Bridport, U.K. 13 G5
Brie, Plaine de la, France 25 D10
Brie-Comte-Robert, France 25 D9
Briec, France 24 D2
Brielle, Neths. 16 E4
Brienne-le-Château, France 25 D11
Brienon-sur-Armançon, France 25 E10
Brienz, Switz. 22 C6
Brienzersee, Switz. 22 C5
Brig, Switz. 22 D5
Brigg, U.K. 12 D7
Briggsdale, U.S.A. 108 E2
Brigham City, U.S.A. 110 F7
Bright, Australia 91 F4
Brighton, Australia 91 F2
Brighton, Canada 98 D4
Brighton, U.K. 13 G7
Brighton, U.S.A. 108 F2
Brignogan-Plage, France 24 D2
Brignoles, France 27 E10
Brihuega, Spain 28 E2
Brikama, Gambia 78 C1
Brilliant, Canada 100 D5
Brilliant, U.S.A. 106 F4
Brilon, Germany 18 D4
Bríndisi, Italy 35 B10
Brinje, Croatia 33 D12
Brinkley, U.S.A. 109 H9
Brinkworth, Australia 91 E2
Brinnon, U.S.A. 112 C4
Brion, I., Canada 99 C7
Brionne, France 24 C7
Brionski, Croatia 33 D10
Brioude, France 26 C7
Briouze, France 24 D6
Brisbane, Australia 91 D5
Brisbane →, Australia 91 D5
Brisighella, Italy 33 D8
Bristol, U.K. 13 F5
Bristol, Conn., U.S.A. 107 E12
Bristol, Pa., U.S.A. 107 F10
Bristol, R.I., U.S.A. 107 E13
Bristol, S. Dak., U.S.A. 108 C6
Bristol, Tenn., U.S.A. 105 G4
Bristol B., U.S.A. 96 C4
Bristol Channel, U.K. 13 F3
Bristol I., Antarctica 5 B1
Bristol L., U.S.A. 111 J5
Bristow, U.S.A. 109 H6
British Columbia □, Canada 100 C3
British Guiana = Guyana ■, S. Amer. 121 B6
British Honduras = Belize ■, Cent. Amer. 115 D7
British Isles, Europe 6 E5
Brits, S. Africa 85 D4
Britstown, S. Africa 84 E3
Britt, Canada 98 C3
Brittany = Bretagne, France 24 D4
Britton, U.S.A. 108 C6
Brive-la-Gaillarde, France 26 C5
Briviesca, Spain 28 C1
Brixton, Australia 90 C3
Brlik, Kazakhstan 44 E8
Brno, Czech. 20 F6
Bro, Sweden 10 E11
Broad →, U.S.A. 105 J5
Broad Arrow, Australia 89 F3
Broad B., U.K. 14 C2
Broad Haven, Ireland 15 B2
Broad Law, U.K. 14 F5
Broad Sd., Australia 90 C4
Broadhurst Ra., Australia 88 D3
Broads, The, U.K. 12 E9
Broadus, U.S.A. 108 C2
Broadview, Canada 101 C8
Broager, Denmark 11 K3
Broaryd, Sweden 11 G7
Brochet, Canada 101 B8
Brochet, L., Canada 101 B8
Brock, Canada 101 C7
Brocken, Germany 18 D6
Brockport, U.S.A. 106 C7
Brockton, U.S.A. 107 D13
Brockville, Canada 98 D4
Brockway, Mont., U.S.A. 108 B2
Brockway, Pa., U.S.A. 106 E6
Brocton, U.S.A. 106 D5
Brod, Macedonia 39 H4
Brodarevo, Serbia 21 M9
Brodeur Pen., Canada 97 A11
Brodick, U.K. 14 F3
Brodnica, Poland 20 B9
Brody, Ukraine 40 F4
Broechem, Belgium 17 F5
Broek, Neths. 16 D6
Broek op Langedijk, Neths. 16 C5
Brogan, U.S.A. 110 D5
Broglie, France 24 C7
Broken Bow, Nebr., U.S.A. 108 E5
Broken Bow, Okla., U.S.A. 109 H7
Broken Hill = Kabwe, Zambia 83 E2
Broken Hill, Australia 91 E3
Brokind, Sweden 11 F9
Brokopondo, Surinam 121 B7
Brokopondo □, Surinam 121 C6
Bromfield, U.K. 13 E5
Bromley, U.K. 13 F8
Brønderslev, Denmark 11 G3
Brong-Ahafo □, Ghana 78 D4
Bronkhorstspruit, S. Africa 85 D4
Bronnitsy, Russia 41 D11
Bronte, Italy 35 E7
Bronte, U.S.A. 109 K4
Bronte Park, Australia 90 G4
Brook Park, U.S.A. 106 E4
Brookfield, U.S.A. 108 F8
Brookhaven, U.S.A. 109 K9
Brookings, Oreg., U.S.A. 110 E1
Brookings, S. Dak., U.S.A. 108 C6
Brooklin, Canada 106 C6
Brookmere, Canada 100 D4
Brooks, Canada 100 C6
Brooks B., Canada 100 C3
Brooks L., Canada 101 A7
Brooks Ra., U.S.A. 96 B5
Brooksville, U.S.A. 105 L4
Brookville, U.S.A. 104 F3
Brooloo, Australia 91 D5
Broom, L., U.K. 14 D3
Broome, Australia 88 C3
Broomehill, Australia 89 F2
Broons, France 24 D4
Brora, U.K. 14 C5
Brora →, U.K. 14 C5
Brosna →, Ireland 15 C4
Broşteni, Romania 38 B8
Brotas de Macaúbas, Brazil 123 D3
Brothers, U.S.A. 110 E3
Brøttum, Norway 10 C4
Brou, France 24 D8
Brough, U.K. 12 C5
Broughton Island, Canada 97 B13
Broughty Ferry, U.K. 14 E6
Brouwershaven, Neths. 16 E3
Brouwershavensche Gat, Neths. 16 E3
Brovary, Ukraine 40 F7
Brovst, Denmark 11 G3
Browerville, U.S.A. 108 B7
Brown, Pt., Australia 91 E1
Brown Willy, U.K. 13 G3
Brownfield, U.S.A. 109 J3
Browning, U.S.A. 110 B7
Brownlee, Canada 101 C7
Brownsville, Oreg., U.S.A. 110 D2
Brownsville, Tenn., U.S.A. 109 H10
Brownsville, Tex., U.S.A. 109 N6
Brownsweg, Surinam 121 B6
Brownwood, U.S.A. 109 K5
Brownwood, L., U.S.A. 109 K5
Browse I., Australia 88 B3
Broye →, Switz. 22 C3
Brozas, Spain 31 F4
Bruas, Malaysia 59 K3
Bruay-en-Artois, France 25 B9
Bruce, Mt., Australia 88 D2
Bruce Pen., Canada 106 A3
Bruce Rock, Australia 89 F2
Bruche →, France 25 D14
Bruchsal, Germany 19 F4
Bruck an der Leitha, Austria 21 G6
Bruck an der Mur, Austria 21 H5
Brue →, U.K. 13 F5
Brugelette, Belgium 17 G3
Bruges = Brugge, Belgium 17 F2
Brugg, Switz. 22 B6
Brugge, Belgium 17 F2
Brühl, Germany 18 E2
Bruinisse, Neths. 17 E4
Brûlé, Canada 100 C5
Brûlon, France 24 E6
Brûly, Belgium 17 J5
Brumado, Brazil 123 D3
Brumado →, Brazil 123 D3
Brumath, France 25 D14
Brummen, Neths. 16 D8
Brumunddal, Norway 10 D4
Brunchilly, Australia 90 B1
Brundidge, U.S.A. 105 K3
Bruneau, U.S.A. 110 E6
Bruneau →, U.S.A. 110 E6
Brunei = Bandar Seri Begawan, Brunei 56 C4
Brunei ■, Asia 56 D4
Brunette Downs, Australia 90 B2
Brunflo, Sweden 10 A8
Brunico, Italy 33 B8
Brünig, P., Switz. 22 C6
Brunkeberg, Norway 10 E2
Brunna, Sweden 10 E11
Brunnen, Switz. 23 C7
Brunner, L., N.Z. 87 K3
Bruno, Canada 101 C7
Brunsbüttel, Germany 18 B5
Brunssum, Neths. 17 G7
Brunswick = Braunschweig, Germany 18 C6
Brunswick, Ga., U.S.A. 105 K5
Brunswick, Maine, U.S.A. 99 D6
Brunswick, Md., U.S.A. 104 F7
Brunswick, Mo., U.S.A. 108 F8
Brunswick, Ohio, U.S.A. 106 E3
Brunswick, Pen. de, Chile 128 D2
Brunswick B., Australia 88 C3
Brunswick Junction, Australia 89 F2
Bruntál, Czech. 20 F7
Bruny I., Australia 90 G4
Brus Laguna, Honduras 116 C3
Brusartsi, Bulgaria 38 F6
Brush, U.S.A. 108 E3
Brushton, U.S.A. 107 B10
Brusio, Switz. 23 D10
Brusque, Brazil 127 B6
Brussel, Belgium 17 G4
Brussels = Brussel, Belgium 17 G4
Brussels, Canada 106 C3
Brustem, Belgium 17 G6
Bruthen, Australia 91 F4
Bruxelles = Brussel, Belgium 17 G4
Bruyères, France 25 D13
Bryan, Ohio, U.S.A. 104 E3
Bryan, Tex., U.S.A. 109 K6
Bryan, Mt., Australia 91 E2
Bryanka, Ukraine 43 B8
Bryansk, Russia 40 E9
Bryanskoye, Russia 43 D12
Bryant, U.S.A. 108 C6
Bryne, Norway 9 G8
Bryson City, U.S.A. 105 H4
Brza Palanka, Serbia 21 L12
Brzava →, Serbia 21 K10
Brzeg, Poland 20 E7
Brzeg Din, Poland 20 D6
Bsharri, Lebanon 69 A5
Bū Baqarah, U.A.E. 65 E8
Bu Craa, W. Sahara 74 C2
Bū Ḥasā, U.A.E. 65 F7
Bua Yai, Thailand 58 E4
Buapinang, Indonesia 57 E6
Buayan, Phil. 57 C7
Buba, Guinea-Biss. 78 C2
Bubanza, Burundi 82 C2
Būbiyān, Kuwait 65 D6
Bucak, Turkey 66 E4
Bucaramanga, Colombia 120 B3
Bucas Grande I., Phil. 55 G6
Buccaneer Arch., Australia 88 C3
Bucchiánico, Italy 33 F11
Bucecea, Romania 38 B9
Buchach, Ukraine 40 G4
Buchan, U.K. 14 D6
Buchan Ness, U.K. 14 D7
Buchanan, Canada 101 C8
Buchanan, Liberia 78 D2
Buchanan, L., Queens., Australia 90 C4
Buchanan, L., W. Austral., Australia 89 E3
Buchanan, L., U.S.A. 109 K5
Buchanan Cr. →, Australia 90 B2
Buchans, Canada 99 C8
Bucharest = Bucureşti, Romania 38 E9
Buchholz, Germany 18 B5
Buchloe, Germany 19 G6
Buchon, Pt., U.S.A. 112 K6
Buchs, Switz. 23 B8
Bückeburg, Germany 18 C5
Buckeye, U.S.A. 111 K7
Buckhannon, U.S.A. 104 F5
Buckhaven, U.K. 14 E5
Buckie, U.K. 14 D6
Buckingham, Canada 98 C4
Buckingham, U.K. 13 F7
Buckingham B., Australia 90 A2
Buckinghamshire □, U.K. 13 F7
Buckle Hd., Australia 88 B4
Buckleboo, Australia 91 E2
Buckley, U.S.A. 110 C2
Buckley →, Australia 90 C2
Bucklin, U.S.A. 109 G5
Bucks L., U.S.A. 112 F5
Bucquoy, France 25 B9
Buctouche, Canada 99 C7
Bucureşti, Romania 38 E9
Bucyrus, U.S.A. 104 E4
Budafok, Hungary 21 H9
Budalin, Burma 61 H19
Budapest, Hungary 21 H9
Budaun, India 63 E8
Budd Coast, Antarctica 5 C8
Buddusò, Italy 34 B2
Bude, U.K. 13 G3
Budel, Neths. 17 F7
Budennovsk, Russia 43 D11
Budeşti, Romania 38 E9
Budge Budge = Baj Baj, India 63 H13
Budgewoi, Australia 91 E5
Búðareyri, Iceland 8 D6
Búðir, Iceland 8 D2
Budia, Spain 28 E2
Budjala, Zaïre 80 D3
Búdrio, Italy 33 D8
Buea, Cameroon 79 E6
Buellton, U.S.A. 113 L6
Buena Vista, Bolivia 125 D5
Buena Vista, Colo., U.S.A. 111 G10
Buena Vista, Va., U.S.A. 104 G6

Buena Vista L., *U.S.A.* 113 K7
Buenaventura, *Colombia* 120 C2
Buenaventura, *Mexico* 114 B3
Buenaventura, B. de, *Colombia* 120 C2
Buendía, Pantano de, *Spain* 28 E2
Buenópolis, *Brazil* 123 E3
Buenos Aires, *Argentina* 126 C4
Buenos Aires, *Colombia* 120 C3
Buenos Aires, *Costa Rica* 116 E3
Buenos Aires □, *Argentina* 126 D4
Buenos Aires, L., *Chile* 128 C2
Buesaco, *Colombia* 120 C2
Buffalo, *Mo., U.S.A.* 109 G8
Buffalo, *N.Y., U.S.A.* 106 D6
Buffalo, *Okla., U.S.A.* 109 G5
Buffalo, *S. Dak., U.S.A.* 108 C3
Buffalo, *Wyo., U.S.A.* 110 D10
Buffalo →, *Canada* 100 A5
Buffalo Head Hills, *Canada* 100 B5
Buffalo L., *Canada* 100 C6
Buffalo Narrows, *Canada* 101 B7
Buffels →, *S. Africa* 84 D2
Buford, *U.S.A.* 105 H4
Bug →, *Poland* 20 C11
Bug →, *Ukraine* 42 C4
Buga, *Colombia* 120 C2
Buganda, *Uganda* 82 C3
Buganga, *Uganda* 82 C3
Bugasong, *Phil.* 55 F5
Bugeat, *France* 26 C5
Bugel, Tanjung, *Indonesia* 56 F4
Buggenhout, *Belgium* 17 F4
Bugibba, *Malta* 37 D1
Bugsuk, *Phil.* 55 G2
Buguma, *Nigeria* 79 E6
Bugun Shara, *Mongolia* 54 B5
Buguruslan, *Russia* 44 D6
Buhăeşti, *Romania* 38 C10
Buheirat-Murrat-el-Kubra, *Egypt* 76 H8
Buhl, *Idaho, U.S.A.* 110 E6
Buhl, *Minn., U.S.A.* 108 B8
Buick, *U.S.A.* 109 G9
Builth Wells, *U.K.* 13 E4
Buinsk, *Russia* 41 D16
Buíque, *Brazil* 122 C4
Buir Nur, *Mongolia* 54 B6
Buis-les-Baronnies, *France* 27 D9
Buitenpost, *Neths.* 16 B8
Buitrago, *Spain* 30 E7
Bujalance, *Spain* 31 H6
Buján, *Spain* 30 C2
Bujaraloz, *Spain* 28 D4
Buje, *Croatia* 33 C10
Bujumbura, *Burundi* 82 C2
Bukachacha, *Russia* 45 D12
Bukama, *Zaïre* 83 D2
Bukavu, *Zaïre* 82 C2
Bukene, *Tanzania* 82 C3
Bukhara, *Uzbekistan* 44 F7
Bukhoro = Bukhara, *Uzbekistan* 44 F7
Bukima, *Tanzania* 82 C3
Bukit Mertajam, *Malaysia* 59 K3
Bukittinggi, *Indonesia* 56 E2
Bukoba, *Tanzania* 82 C3
Bukoba □, *Tanzania* 82 C3
Bukuru, *Nigeria* 79 D6
Bukuya, *Uganda* 82 B3
Bula, *Guinea-Biss.* 78 C1
Bula, *Indonesia* 57 E8
Bülach, *Switz.* 23 A7
Bulahdelah, *Australia* 91 E5
Bulan, *Phil.* 55 E5
Bulancak, *Turkey* 67 C8
Bulandshahr, *India* 62 E7
Bulanık, *Turkey* 67 D10
Bûlâq, *Egypt* 76 B3
Bulawayo, *Zimbabwe* 83 G2
Buldan, *Turkey* 66 D3
Bulgan, *Mongolia* 54 B5
Bulgaria ■, *Europe* 38 G8
Bulgroo, *Australia* 91 D3
Bulgunnia, *Australia* 91 E1
Bulhar, *Somali Rep.* 68 E3
Buli, Teluk, *Indonesia* 57 D7
Buliluyan, C., *Phil.* 55 G2
Bulki, *Ethiopia* 77 F4
Bulkley →, *Canada* 100 B3
Bull Shoals L., *U.S.A.* 109 G8
Bullange, *Belgium* 17 H8
Bullaque →, *Spain* 31 G6
Bullara, *Australia* 88 D1
Bullaring, *Australia* 89 F2
Bullas, *Spain* 29 G3
Bulle, *Switz.* 22 C4
Bulli, *Australia* 91 E5
Bullock Creek, *Australia* 90 B3
Bulloo →, *Australia* 91 D3
Bulloo Downs, *Queens., Australia* 91 D3
Bulloo Downs, *W. Austral., Australia* 88 D2
Bulloo L., *Australia* 91 D3
Bulls, *N.Z.* 87 J5
Bully-les-Mines, *France* 25 B9
Bulnes, *Chile* 126 D1
Bulo Burti, *Somali Rep.* 68 G4
Bulsar = Valsad, *India* 60 J8
Bultfontein, *S. Africa* 84 D4
Bulu Karakelong, *Indonesia* 57 D7
Bulukumba, *Indonesia* 57 F6
Bulun, *Russia* 45 B13
Bumba, *Zaïre* 80 D4
Bumbiri I., *Tanzania* 82 C3
Bumhpa Bum, *Burma* 61 F20
Bumi →, *Zimbabwe* 83 F2
Buna, *Kenya* 82 B4
Bunawan, *Agusan del S., Phil.* 55 G6
Bunawan, *Davao del S., Phil.* 55 H6
Bunazi, *Tanzania* 82 C3
Bunbah, Khalīj, *Libya* 73 B9
Bunbury, *Australia* 89 F2
Buncrana, *Ireland* 15 A4
Bundaberg, *Australia* 91 C5
Bünde, *Germany* 18 C4
Bundey →, *Australia* 90 C2
Bundi, *India* 62 G6
Bundooma, *Australia* 90 C1
Bundoran, *Ireland* 15 B3
Bundukia, *Sudan* 77 F3
Bung Kan, *Thailand* 58 C4
Bungatakada, *Japan* 49 H5
Bungil Cr. →, *Australia* 90 D4
Bungo-Suidō, *Japan* 49 H6
Bungoma, *Kenya* 82 B3
Bungu, *Tanzania* 82 D4
Bunia, *Zaïre* 82 B3
Bunji, *Pakistan* 63 B6
Bunkie, *U.S.A.* 109 K8
Bunnell, *U.S.A.* 105 L5
Bunnik, *Neths.* 16 D6
Buñol, *Spain* 29 F4
Bunsbeek, *Belgium* 17 G5
Bunschoten, *Neths.* 16 D6
Buntok, *Indonesia* 56 E4
Bununu, *Nigeria* 79 D6
Bununu Dass, *Nigeria* 79 C6
Bünyan, *Turkey* 66 D6
Bunyu, *Indonesia* 56 D5
Bunza, *Nigeria* 79 C5
Buol, *Indonesia* 57 D6
Buon Brieng, *Vietnam* 58 F7
Buon Me Thuot, *Vietnam* 58 F7
Buong Long, *Cambodia* 58 F6
Buorkhaya, Mys, *Russia* 45 B14
Buqayq, *Si. Arabia* 65 E6
Buqbua, *Egypt* 76 A2
Bur Acaba, *Somali Rep.* 68 G3
Bûr Fuad, *Egypt* 76 H8
Bûr Safâga, *Egypt* 76 B3
Bûr Sa'îd, *Egypt* 76 H8
Bûr Sûdân, *Sudan* 76 D4
Bûr Taufiq, *Egypt* 76 J8
Bura, *Kenya* 82 C4
Burao, *Somali Rep.* 68 F4
Burâq, *Syria* 69 B5
Buras, *U.S.A.* 109 L10
Buraydah, *Si. Arabia* 64 E5
Burbank, *U.S.A.* 113 L8
Burcher, *Australia* 91 E4
Burdekin →, *Australia* 90 B4
Burdett, *Canada* 100 D6
Burdur, *Turkey* 66 E4
Burdur □, *Turkey* 66 E4
Burdur Gölü, *Turkey* 66 E4
Burdwan = Barddhaman, *India* 63 H12
Bure, *Ethiopia* 77 E4
Bure →, *U.K.* 12 E9
Büren, *Germany* 18 D4
Buren, *Neths.* 16 E6
Bureya →, *Russia* 45 E13
Burford, *Canada* 106 C4
Burg, *Sachsen-Anhalt, Germany* 18 C7
Burg, *Schleswig-Holstein, Germany* 18 A7
Burg el Arab, *Egypt* 76 H6
Burg et Tuyur, *Sudan* 76 C2
Burg Stargard, *Germany* 18 B9
Burgas, *Bulgaria* 38 G10
Burgdorf, *Germany* 18 C5
Burgdorf, *Switz.* 22 B5
Burgeo, *Canada* 99 C8
Burgersdorp, *S. Africa* 84 E4
Burges, Mt., *Australia* 89 F3
Burghausen, *Germany* 19 G8
Búrgio, *Italy* 34 E6
Bürglen, *Switz.* 23 C7
Burglengenfeld, *Germany* 19 F8
Burgo de Osma, *Spain* 28 D1
Burgohondo, *Spain* 30 E6
Burgos, *Spain* 28 C1
Burgos □, *Spain* 28 C1
Burgstädt, *Germany* 18 E8
Burgsvik, *Sweden* 9 H15
Burguillos del Cerro, *Spain* 31 G4
Burgundy = Bourgogne, *France* 25 F11
Burhanpur, *India* 60 J10
Burhou, *U.K.* 24 C4
Buri Pen., *Eritrea* 77 D4
Burias, *Phil.* 55 E5
Burica, Pta., *Costa Rica* 116 E3
Burigi, L., *Tanzania* 82 C3
Burin, *Canada* 99 C8
Buriram, *Thailand* 58 E4
Buriti Alegre, *Brazil* 123 E2
Buriti Bravo, *Brazil* 122 C3
Buriti dos Lopes, *Brazil* 122 B3
Burj Sāfitā, *Syria* 64 C3
Burji, *Ethiopia* 77 F4
Burkburnett, *U.S.A.* 109 H5
Burke, *U.S.A.* 110 C6
Burke →, *Australia* 90 C2
Burketown, *Australia* 90 B2
Burkina Faso ■, *Africa* 78 C4
Burk's Falls, *Canada* 98 C4
Burley, *U.S.A.* 110 E7
Burlingame, *U.S.A.* 112 H4
Burlington, *Canada* 106 C5
Burlington, *Colo., U.S.A.* 108 F3
Burlington, *Iowa, U.S.A.* 108 E9
Burlington, *Kans., U.S.A.* 108 F7
Burlington, *N.C., U.S.A.* 105 G6
Burlington, *N.J., U.S.A.* 107 F10
Burlington, *Vt., U.S.A.* 107 B11
Burlington, *Wash., U.S.A.* 112 B4
Burlington, *Wis., U.S.A.* 104 D1
Burlyu-Tyube, *Kazakhstan* 44 E8
Burma ■, *Asia* 61 J20
Burnaby I., *Canada* 100 C2
Burnet, *U.S.A.* 109 K5
Burney, *U.S.A.* 110 F3
Burngup, *Australia* 89 F2
Burnham, *U.S.A.* 106 F7
Burnie, *Australia* 90 G4
Burnley, *U.K.* 12 D5
Burns, *Oreg., U.S.A.* 110 E4
Burns, *Wyo., U.S.A.* 108 E2
Burns Lake, *Canada* 100 C3
Burnside →, *Canada* 96 B9
Burnside, L., *Australia* 89 E3
Burnt River, *Canada* 106 B6
Burntwood →, *Canada* 101 B9
Burntwood L., *Canada* 101 B8
Burqān, *Kuwait* 64 D5
Burqin, *China* 54 B3
Burra, *Australia* 91 E2
Burramurra, *Australia* 90 C2
Burreli, *Albania* 39 H3
Burren Junction, *Australia* 91 E4
Burrendong Dam, *Australia* 91 E4
Burriana, *Spain* 28 F4
Burrinjuck Res., *Australia* 91 F4
Burro, Serranías del, *Mexico* 114 B4
Burruyacú, *Argentina* 126 B3
Burry Port, *U.K.* 13 F3
Bursa, *Turkey* 66 C3
Bursa □, *Turkey* 66 C3
Burseryd, *Sweden* 11 G7
Burstall, *Canada* 101 C7
Burton L., *Canada* 98 B4
Burton upon Trent, *U.K.* 12 E6
Burtundy, *Australia* 91 E3
Buru, *Indonesia* 57 E7
Burullus, Bahra el, *Egypt* 76 H7
Burûn, Râs, *Egypt* 69 D2
Burundi ■, *Africa* 82 C3
Bururi, *Burundi* 82 C2
Burutu, *Nigeria* 79 D6
Burwell, *U.S.A.* 108 E5
Bury, *U.K.* 12 D5
Bury St. Edmunds, *U.K.* 13 E8
Buryat Republic □, *Russia* 45 D11
Buryn, *Ukraine* 40 F8
Busalla, *Italy* 32 D5
Busango Swamp, *Zambia* 83 E2
Buşayrah, *Syria* 64 C4
Buşayyah, *Iraq* 64 D5
Busca, *Italy* 32 D4
Būshehr, *Iran* 65 D6
Būshehr □, *Iran* 65 D6
Bushell, *Canada* 101 B7
Bushenyi, *Uganda* 82 C3
Bushire = Būshehr, *Iran* 65 D6
Bushnell, *Ill., U.S.A.* 108 E9
Bushnell, *Nebr., U.S.A.* 108 E3
Busia □, *Kenya* 82 B3
Busie, *Ghana* 78 C4
Businga, *Zaïre* 80 D4
Buskerud fylke □, *Norway* 10 D3
Busko Zdrój, *Poland* 20 E10
Busoga □, *Uganda* 82 B3
Busovača, *Bos.-H.* 21 L7
Busra ash Shām, *Syria* 69 C5
Bussang, *France* 25 E13
Busselton, *Australia* 89 F2
Busseto, *Italy* 32 D7
Bussigny, *Switz.* 22 C3
Bussum, *Neths.* 16 D6
Bustamante, B., *Argentina* 128 C3
Busto, C., *Spain* 30 B4
Busto Arsizio, *Italy* 32 C5
Busu-Djanoa, *Zaïre* 80 D4
Busuanga, *Phil.* 55 E3
Büsum, *Germany* 18 A4
Buta, *Zaïre* 82 B1
Butare, *Rwanda* 82 C2
Butaritari, *Kiribati* 92 G9
Bute, *U.K.* 14 F3
Bute Inlet, *Canada* 100 C4
Butemba, *Uganda* 82 B3
Butembo, *Zaïre* 82 B2
Butera, *Italy* 35 E7
Bütgenbach, *Belgium* 17 H8
Butha Qi, *China* 54 B7
Butiaba, *Uganda* 82 B3
Butler, *Mo., U.S.A.* 108 F7
Butler, *Pa., U.S.A.* 106 F5
Bütschwil, *Switz.* 23 B8
Butte, *Mont., U.S.A.* 110 C7
Butte, *Nebr., U.S.A.* 108 D5
Butte Creek →, *U.S.A.* 112 F5
Butterworth = Gcuwa, *S. Africa* 85 E4
Butterworth, *Malaysia* 59 K3
Buttfield, Mt., *Australia* 89 D4
Button B., *Canada* 101 B10
Buttonwillow, *U.S.A.* 113 K7
Butty Hd., *Australia* 89 F3
Butuan, *Phil.* 55 G6
Butuku-Luba, *Eq. Guin.* 79 E6
Butung, *Indonesia* 57 E6
Buturlinovka, *Russia* 41 F12
Butzbach, *Germany* 18 E4
Bützow, *Germany* 18 B7
Buxar, *India* 63 G10
Buxton, *Guyana* 121 B6
Buxton, *S. Africa* 84 D3
Buxton, *U.K.* 12 D6
Buxy, *France* 25 F11
Buy, *Russia* 41 B12
Buyaga, *Russia* 45 D13
Buynaksk, *Russia* 43 E12
Büyük Menderes →, *Turkey* 66 E2
Büyükçekmece, *Turkey* 39 H11
Buzançais, *France* 24 F8
Buzău, *Romania* 38 D9
Buzău →, *Romania* 38 D10
Buzău, Pasul, *Romania* 38 D9
Buzen, *Japan* 49 H5
Buzet, *Croatia* 33 C10
Buzi →, *Mozam.* 83 F3
Buziaş, *Romania* 38 D4
Buzuluk, *Russia* 44 D6
Buzuluk →, *Russia* 41 F13
Buzzards Bay, *U.S.A.* 107 E14
Bwana Mkubwe, *Zaïre* 83 E2
Byala, *Bulgaria* 38 F8
Byala Slatina, *Bulgaria* 38 F6
Byandovan, Mys, *Azerbaijan* 43 G13
Bychawa, *Poland* 20 D12
Bydgoszcz, *Poland* 20 B8
Byelarus = Belorussia ■, *Europe* 40 E5
Byelorussia = Belorussia ■, *Europe* 40 E5
Byers, *U.S.A.* 108 F2
Byesville, *U.S.A.* 106 G3
Byhalia, *U.S.A.* 109 H10
Bykhov, *Belorussia* 40 E7
Bykovo, *Russia* 43 B11
Bylas, *U.S.A.* 111 K8
Bylderup, *Denmark* 11 K3
Bylot I., *Canada* 97 A12
Byrd, C., *Antarctica* 5 C17
Byro, *Australia* 89 E2
Byrock, *Australia* 91 E4
Byron Bay, *Australia* 91 D5
Byrranga, Gory, *Russia* 45 B11
Byrranga Mts. = Byrranga, Gory, *Russia* 45 B11
Byrum, *Denmark* 11 G5
Byske, *Sweden* 8 D16
Byske älv →, *Sweden* 8 D16
Bystrzyca Kłodzka, *Poland* 20 E6
Byten, *Belorussia* 40 E4
Bytom, *Poland* 20 E8
Bytów, *Poland* 20 A7
Byumba, *Rwanda* 82 C3

C

C.I.S. = Commonwealth of Independent States ■, *Eurasia* 45 D11
Ca →, *Vietnam* 58 C5
Ca Mau = Quan Long, *Vietnam* 59 H5
Ca Mau, Mui = Bai Bung, Mui, *Vietnam* 59 H5
Ca Na, *Vietnam* 59 G7
Caacupé, *Paraguay* 126 B4
Caála, *Angola* 81 G3
Caamano Sd., *Canada* 100 C3
Caapiranga, *Brazil* 121 D5
Caazapá, *Paraguay* 126 B4
Caazapá □, *Paraguay* 127 B4
Cabadbaran, *Phil.* 55 G6
Cabalian, *Phil.* 55 F6
Caballeria, C. de, *Spain* 36 A11
Cabana, *Peru* 124 B2
Cabanaconde, *Peru* 124 D3
Cabañaquinta, *Spain* 30 B5
Cabanatuan, *Phil.* 55 D4
Cabanes, *Spain* 28 E5
Cabanillas, *Peru* 124 D3
Cabano, *Canada* 99 C6
Čabar, *Croatia* 33 C11
Cabazon, *U.S.A.* 113 M10
Cabedelo, *Brazil* 122 C5
Cabeza del Buey, *Spain* 31 G5
Cabildo, *Chile* 126 C1
Cabimas, *Venezuela* 120 A3
Cabinda, *Angola* 80 F2
Cabinda □, *Angola* 80 F2
Cabinet Mts., *U.S.A.* 110 C6
Cabo Blanco, *Argentina* 128 C3
Cabo Frio, *Brazil* 123 F3
Cabo Pantoja, *Peru* 120 D2
Cabo Raso, *Argentina* 128 B3
Cabonga, Réservoir, *Canada* 98 C4
Cabool, *U.S.A.* 109 G8
Caboolture, *Australia* 91 D5
Cabora Bassa Dam = Cahora Bassa Dam, *Mozam.* 83 F3
Caborca, *Mexico* 114 A2
Cabot, Mt., *U.S.A.* 107 B13
Cabot Str., *Canada* 99 C8
Cabra, *Spain* 31 H6
Cabra del Santo Cristo, *Spain* 29 H1
Cábras, *Italy* 34 C1
Cabrera, I., *Spain* 36 B9
Cabrera, Sierra, *Spain* 30 C4
Cabri, *Canada* 101 C7
Cabriel →, *Spain* 29 F3
Cabruta, *Venezuela* 120 B4
Cabugao, *Phil.* 55 C4
Cabuyaro, *Colombia* 120 C3
Cacabelos, *Spain* 30 C4
Čačak, *Serbia* 21 M10
Cacao, *Fr. Guiana* 121 C7
Cáceres, *Brazil* 125 D6
Cáceres, *Colombia* 120 B2
Cáceres, *Spain* 31 F4
Cáceres □, *Spain* 31 F4
Cache Bay, *Canada* 98 C4
Cache Cr. →, *U.S.A.* 112 G5
Cachepo, *Portugal* 31 H3
Cachéu, *Guinea-Biss.* 78 C1
Cachi, *Argentina* 126 B2
Cachimbo, *Brazil* 125 B7
Cachimbo, Serra do, *Brazil* 125 B6
Cachoeira, *Brazil* 123 D4
Cachoeira Alta, *Brazil* 123 E1
Cachoeira de Itapemirim, *Brazil* 123 F3
Cachoeira do Sul, *Brazil* 127 C5
Cachoeiro do Arari, *Brazil* 122 B2
Cachopo, *Portugal* 31 H3
Cachuela Esperanza, *Bolivia* 125 C4
Cacólo, *Angola* 80 G3
Caconda, *Angola* 81 G3
Cacongo, *Angola* 80 F2
Caçu, *Brazil* 123 E1
Caculé, *Brazil* 123 D3
Cadarache, *France* 27 E9
Čadca, *Slovak Rep.* 20 F8
Caddo, *U.S.A.* 109 H6
Cadell Cr. →, *Australia* 90 C3
Cadenazzo, *Switz.* 23 D7
Cader Idris, *U.K.* 12 E4
Cadí, Sierra del, *Spain* 28 C6
Cadibarrawirracanna, L., *Australia* 91 D2
Cadillac, *Canada* 98 C4
Cadillac, *France* 26 D3
Cadillac, *U.S.A.* 104 C3
Cadiz, *Phil.* 55 F5
Cádiz, *Spain* 31 J4
Cadiz, *U.S.A.* 106 F4
Cádiz □, *Spain* 31 J5
Cádiz, G. de, *Spain* 31 J4
Cadney Park, *Australia* 91 D1
Cadomin, *Canada* 100 C5
Cadotte →, *Canada* 100 B5
Cadours, *France* 26 E5
Cadoux, *Australia* 89 F2
Caen, *France* 24 C6
Caernarfon, *U.K.* 12 D3
Caernarfon B., *U.K.* 12 D3
Caernarvon = Caernarfon, *U.K.* 12 D3
Caerphilly, *U.K.* 13 F4
Caesarea, *Israel* 69 C3
Caeté, *Brazil* 123 E3
Caetité, *Brazil* 123 D3
Cafayate, *Argentina* 126 B2
Cafifi, *Colombia* 120 B3
Cafu, *Angola* 84 B2
Cagayan →, *Phil.* 55 B4
Cagayan de Oro, *Phil.* 55 G6
Cagayan Is., *Phil.* 55 G4
Cagayan Sulu I., *Phil.* 55 H3
Cagli, *Italy* 33 E9
Cágliari, *Italy* 34 C2
Cágliari, G. di, *Italy* 34 C2
Cagnano Varano, *Italy* 35 A8
Cagnes-sur-Mer, *France* 27 E11
Caguán →, *Colombia* 120 D3
Caguas, *Puerto Rico* 117 C6
Caha Mts., *Ireland* 15 E2
Cahama, *Angola* 84 B1
Caher, *Ireland* 15 D4
Cahersiveen, *Ireland* 15 E1
Cahora Bassa Dam, *Mozam.* 83 F3
Cahore Pt., *Ireland* 15 D5
Cahors, *France* 26 D5
Cahuapanas, *Peru* 124 B2
Cahuinari →, *Colombia* 120 D3
Cai Bau, Dao, *Vietnam* 58 B6
Cai Nuoc, *Vietnam* 59 H5
Caia, *Mozam.* 83 F4
Caiabis, Serra dos, *Brazil* 125 C6
Caianda, *Angola* 83 E1
Caiapó, Serra do, *Brazil* 125 D7
Caiapônia, *Brazil* 125 D7
Caibarién, *Cuba* 116 B4
Caibiran, *Phil.* 55 F6
Caicara, *Bolívar, Venezuela* 120 B4
Caicara, *Monagas, Venezuela* 121 B5
Caicó, *Brazil* 122 C4
Caicos Is., *W. Indies* 117 B5
Caicos Passage, *W. Indies* 117 B5
Cailloma, *Peru* 124 D3
Caine →, *Bolivia* 125 D4
Caird Coast, *Antarctica* 5 D1
Cairn Gorm, *U.K.* 14 D5

Cairn Toul

Cairn Toul, *U.K.* 14 D5
Cairngorm Mts., *U.K.* 14 D5
Cairns, *Australia* 90 B4
Cairo = El Qâhira, *Egypt* 76 H7
Cairo, *Ga., U.S.A.* 105 K3
Cairo, *Ill., U.S.A.* 109 G10
Cairo Montenotte, *Italy* 32 D5
Caithness, Ord of, *U.K.* 14 C5
Caiundo, *Angola* 81 H3
Caiza, *Bolivia* 125 E4
Cajabamba, *Peru* 124 B2
Cajamarca, *Peru* 124 B2
Cajamarca □, *Peru* 124 B2
Cajapió, *Brazil* 122 B3
Cajarc, *France* 26 D5
Cajatambo, *Peru* 124 C2
Cajàzeiras, *Brazil* 122 C4
Čajetina, *Serbia* 21 M9
Çakirgol, *Turkey* 43 F8
Čakovec, *Croatia* 33 B13
Çal, *Turkey* 66 D3
Cala, *Spain* 31 H4
Cala →, *Spain* 31 H4
Cala Cadolar, Punta de, *Spain* 29 G6
Cala d'Or, *Spain* 36 B10
Cala Figuera, C., *Spain* 36 B9
Cala Forcat, *Spain* 36 A10
Cala Mayor, *Spain* 36 B9
Cala Mezquida, *Spain* 36 B11
Cala Millor, *Spain* 36 B10
Cala Ratjada, *Spain* 36 B10
Calabanga, *Phil.* 55 E5
Calabar, *Nigeria* 79 E6
Calabozo, *Venezuela* 120 B4
Calábria □, *Italy* 35 C9
Calaburras, Pta. de, *Spain* 31 J6
Calaceite, *Spain* 28 D5
Calacota, *Bolivia* 124 D4
Calafate, *Argentina* 128 D2
Calahorra, *Spain* 28 C3
Calais, *France* 25 B8
Calais, *U.S.A.* 99 C6
Calais, Pas de, *France* 25 B8
Calalaste, Cord. de, *Argentina* 126 B2
Calama, *Brazil* 125 B5
Calama, *Chile* 126 A2
Calamar, *Bolívar, Colombia* 120 A3
Calamar, *Vaupés, Colombia* 120 C3
Calamarca, *Bolivia* 124 D4
Calamba, *Phil.* 55 F5
Calamian Group, *Phil.* 55 F3
Calamocha, *Spain* 28 E3
Calán Porter, *Spain* 36 B11
Calañas, *Spain* 31 H4
Calanda, *Spain* 28 E4
Calang, *Indonesia* 56 D1
Calangiánus, *Italy* 34 B2
Calapan, *Phil.* 55 E4
Călăraşi, *Romania* 38 E10
Calasparra, *Spain* 29 G3
Calatafimi, *Italy* 34 E5
Calatayud, *Spain* 28 D3
Calato = Kálathos, *Greece* 39 N11
Calauag, *Phil.* 55 E5
Calavà, C., *Italy* 35 D7
Calavite, C., *Phil.* 55 E4
Calayan, *Phil.* 55 B4
Calbayog, *Phil.* 55 E6
Calbe, *Germany* 18 D7
Calca, *Peru* 124 C3
Calcasieu L., *U.S.A.* 109 L8
Calci, *Italy* 32 E7
Calcutta, *India* 63 H13
Caldaro, *Italy* 33 B8
Caldas □, *Colombia* 120 B2
Caldas da Rainha, *Portugal* 31 F1
Caldas de Reyes, *Spain* 30 C2
Caldas Novas, *Brazil* 123 E2
Calder →, *U.K.* 12 D6
Caldera, *Chile* 126 B1
Caldwell, *Idaho, U.S.A.* 110 E5
Caldwell, *Kans., U.S.A.* 109 G6
Caldwell, *Tex., U.S.A.* 109 K6
Caledon, *S. Africa* 84 E2
Caledon →, *S. Africa* 84 E4
Caledon B., *Australia* 90 A2
Caledonia, *Canada* 106 C5
Caledonia, *U.S.A.* 106 D7
Calella, *Spain* 28 D7
Calemba, *Angola* 84 B2
Calenzana, *France* 27 F12
Caleta Olivia, *Argentina* 128 C3
Calexico, *U.S.A.* 113 N11
Calf of Man, *U.K.* 12 C3
Calgary, *Canada* 100 C6
Calheta, *Madeira* 36 D2
Calhoun, *U.S.A.* 105 H3
Cali, *Colombia* 120 C2
Calicut, *India* 60 P9
Caliente, *U.S.A.* 111 H6
California, *Mo., U.S.A.* 108 F8
California, *Pa., U.S.A.* 106 F5
California □, *U.S.A.* 111 H4
California, Baja, *Mexico* 114 A1
California, Baja, T.N. □, *Mexico* 114 B2
California, Baja, T.S. □, *Mexico* 114 B2
California, G. de, *Mexico* 114 B2
California City, *U.S.A.* 113 K9
California Hot Springs, *U.S.A.* 113 K8
Călimăneşti, *Romania* 38 D7
Călimani, Munţii, *Romania* 38 B8
Călineşti, *Romania* 38 D7
Calingasta, *Argentina* 126 C2
Calipatria, *U.S.A.* 113 M11
Calistoga, *U.S.A.* 112 G4
Calitri, *Italy* 35 B8
Calitzdorp, *S. Africa* 84 E3
Callabonna, L., *Australia* 91 D3
Callac, *France* 24 D3
Callan, *Ireland* 15 D4
Callander, *U.K.* 14 E4
Callantsoog, *Neths.* 16 C5
Callao, *Peru* 124 C2
Callaway, *U.S.A.* 108 E5
Calles, *Mexico* 115 C5
Callide, *Australia* 90 C5
Calling Lake, *Canada* 100 B6
Calliope, *Australia* 90 C5
Callosa de Ensarriá, *Spain* 29 G4
Callosa de Segura, *Spain* 29 G4
Calola, *Angola* 84 B2
Calolbon, *Phil.* 55 E6
Caloocan, *Phil.* 55 D4
Calore →, *Italy* 35 A7
Caloundra, *Australia* 91 D5
Calpe, *Spain* 29 G5
Calpella, *U.S.A.* 112 F3
Calpine, *U.S.A.* 112 F6
Calstock, *Canada* 98 C3
Caltabellotta, *Italy* 34 E6
Caltagirone, *Italy* 35 E7
Caltanissetta, *Italy* 35 E7
Calulo, *Angola* 80 G2
Calumet, *U.S.A.* 104 B1
Calunda, *Angola* 81 G4
Caluso, *Italy* 32 C4
Calvados □, *France* 24 C6
Calvert, *U.S.A.* 109 K6
Calvert →, *Australia* 90 B2
Calvert Hills, *Australia* 90 B2
Calvert I., *Canada* 100 C3
Calvert Ra., *Australia* 88 D3
Calvi, *France* 27 F12
Calvillo, *Mexico* 114 C4
Calvinia, *S. Africa* 84 E2
Calw, *Germany* 19 G4
Calwa, *U.S.A.* 112 J7
Calzada Almuradiel, *Spain* 29 G1
Calzada de Calatrava, *Spain* 31 G7
Cam →, *U.K.* 13 E8
Cam Lam, *Vietnam* 59 G7
Cam Pha, *Vietnam* 58 B6
Cam Ranh, *Vietnam* 59 G7
Cam Xuyen, *Vietnam* 58 C6
Camabatela, *Angola* 80 F3
Camacã, *Brazil* 123 E4
Camaçari, *Brazil* 123 D4
Camacha, *Madeira* 36 D3
Camacho, *Mexico* 114 C4
Camacupa, *Angola* 81 G3
Camaguán, *Venezuela* 120 B4
Camagüey, *Cuba* 116 B4
Camaiore, *Italy* 32 E7
Camamu, *Brazil* 123 D4
Camaná, *Peru* 124 D3
Camanche Reservoir, *U.S.A.* 112 G6
Camaquã →, *Brazil* 127 C5
Câmara de Lobos, *Madeira* 36 D3
Camararé →, *Brazil* 125 C6
Camarat, C., *France* 27 E10
Camaret, *France* 24 D2
Camargo, *Bolivia* 125 E4
Camargue, *France* 27 E8
Camarillo, *U.S.A.* 113 L7
Camariñas, *Spain* 30 B1
Camarón, C., *Honduras* 116 C2
Camarones, *Argentina* 128 B3
Camarones, B., *Argentina* 128 B3
Camas, *U.S.A.* 112 E4
Camas Valley, *U.S.A.* 110 E2
Cambados, *Spain* 30 C2
Cambará, *Brazil* 127 A5
Cambay = Khambhat, *India* 62 H5
Cambay, G. of = Khambat, G. of, *India* 62 J5
Cambil, *Spain* 29 H1
Cambo-les-Bains, *France* 26 E2
Cambodia ■, *Asia* 58 F5
Camborne, *U.K.* 13 G2
Cambrai, *France* 25 B10
Cambria, *U.S.A.* 111 J3
Cambrian Mts., *U.K.* 13 E4
Cambridge, *Canada* 98 D3
Cambridge, *Jamaica* 116 C4
Cambridge, *N.Z.* 87 G5
Cambridge, *U.K.* 13 E8
Cambridge, *Idaho, U.S.A.* 110 D5
Cambridge, *Mass., U.S.A.* 107 D13
Cambridge, *Md., U.S.A.* 104 F7
Cambridge, *Minn., U.S.A.* 108 C8
Cambridge, *N.Y., U.S.A.* 107 C11
Cambridge, *Nebr., U.S.A.* 108 E4
Cambridge, *Ohio, U.S.A.* 106 F3
Cambridge Bay, *Canada* 96 B9
Cambridge G., *Australia* 88 B4
Cambridge Springs, *U.S.A.* 106 E4
Cambridgeshire □, *U.K.* 13 E8
Cambrils, *Spain* 28 D6
Cambuci, *Brazil* 123 F3
Cambundi-Catembo, *Angola* 80 G3
Camden, *Ala., U.S.A.* 105 K2
Camden, *Ark., U.S.A.* 109 J8
Camden, *Maine, U.S.A.* 99 D6
Camden, *N.J., U.S.A.* 107 G9
Camden, *S.C., U.S.A.* 105 H5
Camden Sd., *Australia* 88 C3
Camdenton, *U.S.A.* 109 F8
Çameli, *Turkey* 66 E3
Camembert, *France* 24 D7
Cámeri, *Italy* 32 C5
Camerino, *Italy* 33 E10
Cameron, *Ariz., U.S.A.* 111 J8
Cameron, *La., U.S.A.* 109 L8
Cameron, *Mo., U.S.A.* 108 F7
Cameron, *Tex., U.S.A.* 109 K6
Cameron Falls, *Canada* 98 C2
Cameron Highlands, *Malaysia* 59 K3
Cameron Hills, *Canada* 100 B5
Cameroon ■, *Africa* 73 G7
Camerota, *Italy* 35 B8
Cameroun →, *Cameroon* 79 E6
Cameroun, Mt., *Cameroon* 79 E6
Cametá, *Brazil* 122 B2
Camiguin □, *Phil.* 55 G6
Camiguin I., *Phil.* 55 B4
Camiling, *Phil.* 55 D4
Caminha, *Portugal* 30 D2
Camino, *U.S.A.* 112 G6
Camira Creek, *Australia* 91 D5
Camiranga, *Brazil* 122 B2
Camiri, *Bolivia* 125 E5
Camissombo, *Angola* 80 F4
Cammal, *U.S.A.* 106 E7
Camocim, *Brazil* 122 B3
Camogli, *Italy* 32 D6
Camooweal, *Australia* 90 B2
Camopi, *Fr. Guiana* 121 C7
Camopi →, *Fr. Guiana* 121 C7
Camotes Is., *Phil.* 55 F6
Camotes Sea, *Phil.* 55 F6
Camp Crook, *U.S.A.* 108 C3
Camp Nelson, *U.S.A.* 113 J8
Camp Wood, *U.S.A.* 109 L4
Campagna, *Italy* 35 B8
Campana, *Argentina* 126 C4
Campana, I., *Chile* 128 C1
Campanário, *Madeira* 36 D2
Campanario, *Spain* 31 G5
Campania □, *Italy* 35 B7
Campbell, *S. Africa* 84 D3
Campbell, *Calif., U.S.A.* 112 H5
Campbell, *Ohio, U.S.A.* 106 E4
Campbell I., *Pac. Oc.* 92 N8
Campbell L., *Canada* 101 A7
Campbell River, *Canada* 100 C3
Campbell Town, *Australia* 90 G4
Campbellford, *Canada* 106 B7
Campbellpur, *Pakistan* 62 C5
Campbellsville, *U.S.A.* 104 G3
Campbellton, *Canada* 99 C6
Campbelltown, *Australia* 91 E5
Campbeltown, *U.K.* 14 F3
Campeche, *Mexico* 115 D6
Campeche □, *Mexico* 115 D6
Campeche, B. de, *Mexico* 115 D6
Camperdown, *Australia* 91 F3
Camperville, *Canada* 101 C8
Campi Salentina, *Italy* 35 B11
Campidano, *Italy* 34 C1
Campíglia Maríttima, *Italy* 32 E7
Campillo de Altobuey, *Spain* 28 F3
Campillo de Llerena, *Spain* 31 G5
Campillos, *Spain* 31 H6
Campina Grande, *Brazil* 122 C4
Campina Verde, *Brazil* 123 E2
Campinas, *Brazil* 127 A6
Campine, *Belgium* 17 F6
Campli, *Italy* 33 F10
Campo, *Cameroon* 80 D1
Campo, *Spain* 28 C5
Campo Belo, *Brazil* 123 F2
Campo de Criptana, *Spain* 29 F1
Campo de Diauarum, *Brazil* 125 C7
Campo de Gibraltar, *Spain* 31 J5
Campo Flórido, *Brazil* 123 E2
Campo Formoso, *Brazil* 122 D3
Campo Grande, *Brazil* 125 E7
Campo Maíor, *Brazil* 122 B3
Campo Maior, *Portugal* 31 G3
Campo Mourão, *Brazil* 127 A5
Campo Tencia, *Switz.* 23 D7
Campo Túres, *Italy* 33 B8
Campoalegre, *Colombia* 120 C2
Campobasso, *Italy* 35 A7
Campobello di Licata, *Italy* 34 E6
Campobello di Mazara, *Italy* 34 E5
Campofelice, *Italy* 34 E6
Camporeale, *Italy* 34 E6
Campos, *Brazil* 123 F3
Campos Altos, *Brazil* 123 E2
Campos Belos, *Brazil* 123 D2
Campos del Puerto, *Spain* 36 B10
Campos Novos, *Brazil* 127 B5
Campos Sales, *Brazil* 122 C3
Camprodón, *Spain* 28 C7
Camptonville, *U.S.A.* 112 F5
Campuya →, *Peru* 120 D3
Camrose, *Canada* 100 C6
Camsell Portage, *Canada* 101 B7
Çan, *Turkey* 66 C2
Can Clavo, *Spain* 36 C7
Can Creu, *Spain* 36 C7
Can Gio, *Vietnam* 59 G6
Can Tho, *Vietnam* 59 G5
Canaan, *U.S.A.* 107 D11
Canada ■, *N. Amer.* 96 C10
Cañada de Gómez, *Argentina* 126 C3
Canadian, *U.S.A.* 109 H4
Canadian →, *U.S.A.* 109 H7
Canadian Shield, *Canada* 97 C10
Çanakkale, *Turkey* 39 J9
Çanakkale □, *Turkey* 66 C2
Çanakkale Boğazı, *Turkey* 66 C2
Canal Flats, *Canada* 100 C5
Canalejas, *Argentina* 126 D2
Canals, *Argentina* 126 C3
Canals, *Spain* 29 G4
Canandaigua, *U.S.A.* 106 D7
Cananea, *Mexico* 114 A2
Cañar, *Ecuador* 120 D2
Cañar □, *Ecuador* 120 D2
Canarias, Is., *Atl. Oc.* 36 F4
Canarreos, Arch. de los, *Cuba* 116 B3
Canary Is. = Canarias, Is., *Atl. Oc.* 36 F4
Canastra, Serra da, *Brazil* 123 F2
Canatlán, *Mexico* 114 C4
Canaveral, C., *U.S.A.* 105 L5
Cañaveras, *Spain* 28 E2
Canavieiras, *Brazil* 123 E4
Canbelego, *Australia* 91 E4
Canberra, *Australia* 91 F4
Canby, *Calif., U.S.A.* 110 F3
Canby, *Minn., U.S.A.* 108 C6
Canby, *Oreg., U.S.A.* 112 E4
Cancale, *France* 24 D5
Canche →, *France* 25 B8
Canchyuaya, Cordillera de, *Peru* 124 B3
Cancún, *Mexico* 115 C7
Candala, *Somali Rep.* 68 E4
Candarave, *Peru* 124 D3
Candas, *Spain* 30 B5
Candé, *France* 24 E5
Candeias →, *Brazil* 125 B5
Candela, *Italy* 35 A8
Candelaria, *Argentina* 127 B4
Candelaria, *Canary Is.* 36 F3
Candelaria, Pta. de la, *Spain* 30 B2
Candeleda, *Spain* 30 E5
Candelo, *Australia* 91 F4
Candia = Iráklion, *Greece* 37 D7
Candia, Sea of = Crete, Sea of, *Greece* 39 N8
Cândido de Abreu, *Brazil* 123 F1
Cândido Mendes, *Brazil* 122 B2
Candle L., *Canada* 101 C7
Candlemas I., *Antarctica* 5 B1
Cando, *U.S.A.* 108 A5
Candon, *Phil.* 55 C4
Canea = Khaniá, *Greece* 37 D6
Canela, *Brazil* 122 D2
Canelli, *Italy* 32 D5
Canelones, *Uruguay* 127 C4
Canet-Plage, *France* 26 F7
Cañete, *Chile* 126 D1
Cañete, *Peru* 124 C2
Cañete, *Spain* 28 E3
Cañete de las Torres, *Spain* 31 H6
Canfranc, *Spain* 28 C4
Cangas, *Spain* 30 C2
Cangas de Narcea, *Spain* 30 B4
Cangas de Onís, *Spain* 30 B5
Canguaretama, *Brazil* 122 C4
Canguçu, *Brazil* 127 C5
Cangxi, *China* 52 B5
Cangyuan, *China* 52 F2
Cangzhou, *China* 50 E9
Cani, I., *Tunisia* 75 A7
Canicattì, *Italy* 34 E6
Canicattini, *Italy* 35 E8
Canim Lake, *Canada* 100 C4
Canindé, *Brazil* 122 B4
Canindé →, *Brazil* 122 C3
Canindeyu □, *Paraguay* 127 A4
Canipaan, *Phil.* 56 C5
Canisteo, *U.S.A.* 106 D7
Canisteo →, *U.S.A.* 106 D7
Cañitas, *Mexico* 114 C4
Cañizal, *Spain* 30 D5
Canjáyar, *Spain* 29 H2
Çankırı, *Turkey* 66 C5
Çankırı □, *Turkey* 66 C5
Cankuzo, *Burundi* 82 C3
Canmore, *Canada* 100 C5
Cann River, *Australia* 91 F4
Canna, *U.K.* 14 D2
Cannanore, *India* 60 P9
Cannes, *France* 27 E11
Canning Town = Port Canning, *India* 63 H13
Cannington, *Canada* 106 B5
Cannock, *U.K.* 12 E5
Cannon Ball →, *U.S.A.* 108 B4
Cannondale Mt., *Australia* 90 D4
Caño Colorado, *Colombia* 120 C4
Canoas, *Brazil* 127 B5
Canoe L., *Canada* 101 B7
Canon City, *U.S.A.* 108 F2
Canora, *Canada* 101 C8
Canosa di Púglia, *Italy* 35 A9
Canowindra, *Australia* 91 E4
Canso, *Canada* 99 C7
Canta, *Peru* 124 C2
Cantabria □, *Spain* 30 B6
Cantabria, Sierra de, *Spain* 28 C2
Cantabrian Mts. = Cantábrica, Cordillera, *Spain* 30 C5
Cantábrica, Cordillera, *Spain* 30 C5
Cantal □, *France* 26 C6
Cantal, Plomb du, *France* 26 C6
Cantanhede, *Portugal* 30 E2
Cantaura, *Venezuela* 121 B5
Cantavieja, *Spain* 28 E4
Canterbury, *Australia* 90 D3
Canterbury, *U.K.* 13 F9
Canterbury □, *N.Z.* 87 K3
Canterbury Bight, *N.Z.* 87 L3
Canterbury Plains, *N.Z.* 87 K3
Cantil, *U.S.A.* 113 K9
Cantillana, *Spain* 31 H5
Canto do Buriti, *Brazil* 122 C3
Canton = Guangzhou, *China* 53 F9
Canton, *Ga., U.S.A.* 105 H3
Canton, *Ill., U.S.A.* 108 E9
Canton, *Miss., U.S.A.* 109 J9
Canton, *Mo., U.S.A.* 108 E9
Canton, *N.Y., U.S.A.* 107 B9
Canton, *Ohio, U.S.A.* 106 F3
Canton, *Okla., U.S.A.* 109 G5
Canton, *S. Dak., U.S.A.* 108 D6
Canton L., *U.S.A.* 109 G5
Cantù, *Italy* 32 C6
Canudos, *Brazil* 125 B6
Canumã, *Amazonas, Brazil* 121 D6
Canumã, *Amazonas, Brazil* 125 B5
Canumã →, *Brazil* 125 A6
Canutama, *Brazil* 125 B5
Canutillo, *U.S.A.* 111 L10
Canyon, *Tex., U.S.A.* 109 H4
Canyon, *Wyo., U.S.A.* 110 D8
Canyonlands National Park, *U.S.A.* 111 G9
Canyonville, *U.S.A.* 110 E2
Canzo, *Italy* 32 C6
Cao Bang, *Vietnam* 58 A6
Cao He →, *China* 51 D13
Cao Lanh, *Vietnam* 59 G5
Cao Xian, *China* 50 G8
Cáorle, *Italy* 33 C9
Cap-aux-Meules, *Canada* 99 C7
Cap-Chat, *Canada* 99 C6
Cap-de-la-Madeleine, *Canada* 98 C5
Cap-Haïtien, *Haiti* 117 C5
Cap St.-Jacques = Vung Tau, *Vietnam* 59 G6
Capa, *Vietnam* 58 A4
Capa Stilo, *Italy* 35 D9
Capáccio, *Italy* 35 B8
Capaia, *Angola* 80 F4
Capanaparo →, *Venezuela* 120 B4
Capanema, *Brazil* 122 B2
Caparo →, *Barinas, Venezuela* 120 B3
Caparo →, *Bolívar, Venezuela* 121 B5
Capatárida, *Venezuela* 120 A3
Capbreton, *France* 26 E2
Capdenac, *France* 26 D6
Cape →, *Australia* 90 C4
Cape Barren I., *Australia* 90 G4
Cape Breton Highlands Nat. Park, *Canada* 99 C7
Cape Breton I., *Canada* 99 C7
Cape Charles, *U.S.A.* 104 G8
Cape Coast, *Ghana* 79 D4
Cape Dorset, *Canada* 97 B12
Cape Dyer, *Canada* 97 B13
Cape Fear →, *U.S.A.* 105 H6
Cape Girardeau, *U.S.A.* 109 G10
Cape Jervis, *Australia* 91 F2
Cape May, *U.S.A.* 104 F8
Cape May Point, *U.S.A.* 103 C12
Cape Palmas, *Liberia* 78 E3
Cape Province □, *S. Africa* 84 E3
Cape Tormentine, *Canada* 99 C7
Cape Town, *S. Africa* 84 E2
Cape Verde Is. ■, *Atl. Oc.* 2 D8
Cape Vincent, *U.S.A.* 107 B8
Cape York Peninsula, *Australia* 90 A3
Capela, *Brazil* 122 D4
Capela de Campo, *Brazil* 122 B3
Capelinha, *Brazil* 123 E3
Capella, *Australia* 90 C4
Capendu, *France* 26 E6
Capestang, *France* 26 E7
Capim, *Brazil* 122 B2
Capim →, *Brazil* 122 B2
Capinópolis, *Brazil* 123 E2
Capinota, *Bolivia* 124 D4
Capitan, *U.S.A.* 111 K11
Capitán Aracena, I., *Chile* 128 D2
Capitán Pastene, *Chile* 128 A2
Capitola, *U.S.A.* 112 J5
Capivara, Serra da, *Brazil* 123 D3
Capizzi, *Italy* 35 E7
Čapljina, *Bos.-H.* 21 M7
Capoche →, *Mozam.* 83 F3
Capoeira, *Brazil* 125 B6
Cappadocia, *Turkey* 66 D6
Capraia, *Italy* 32 E6
Caprarola, *Italy* 33 F9
Capreol, *Canada* 98 C3

Caprera, *Italy* 34 A2
Capri, *Italy* 35 B7
Capricorn Group, *Australia* 90 C5
Capricorn Ra., *Australia* 88 D2
Caprino Veronese, *Italy* 32 C7
Caprivi Strip, *Namibia* 84 B3
Captainganj, *India* 63 F10
Captain's Flat, *Australia* 91 F4
Captieux, *France* 26 D3
Cápua, *Italy* 35 A7
Caquetá □, *Colombia* 120 C3
Caquetá →, *Colombia* 120 D4
Carabobo, *Venezuela* 120 A4
Carabobo □, *Venezuela* 120 A4
Caracal, *Romania* 38 E7
Caracaraí, *Brazil* 121 C5
Caracas, *Venezuela* 120 A4
Caracol, *Brazil* 122 C3
Caracollo, *Bolivia* 124 D4
Caradoc, *Australia* 91 E3
Caráglio, *Italy* 32 D4
Carahue, *Chile* 128 A2
Caraí, *Brazil* 123 E3
Carajás, Serra dos, *Brazil* 122 C1
Caranapatuba, *Brazil* 125 B5
Carandaiti, *Bolivia* 125 E5
Carangola, *Brazil* 123 F3
Carani, *Australia* 89 F2
Caransebeş, *Romania* 38 D5
Carantec, *France* 24 D3
Caraparaná →, *Colombia* 120 D3
Carapelle →, *Italy* 35 A8
Caras, *Peru* 124 B2
Caratasca, L., *Honduras* 116 C3
Caratinga, *Brazil* 123 E3
Caraúbas, *Brazil* 122 C4
Caravaca, *Spain* 29 G3
Caravággio, *Italy* 32 C6
Caravelas, *Brazil* 123 E4
Caraveli, *Peru* 124 D3
Caràzinho, *Brazil* 127 B5
Carballino, *Spain* 30 C2
Carballo, *Spain* 30 B2
Carberry, *Canada* 101 D9
Carbia, *Spain* 30 C2
Carbó, *Mexico* 114 B2
Carbon, *Canada* 100 C6
Carbonara, C., *Italy* 34 C2
Carbondale, *Colo., U.S.A.* 110 G10
Carbondale, *Ill., U.S.A.* 109 G10
Carbondale, *Pa., U.S.A.* 107 E9
Carbonear, *Canada* 99 C9
Carboneras, *Spain* 29 J3
Carboneras de Guadazaón, *Spain* 28 F3
Carbonia, *Italy* 34 C1
Carcabuey, *Spain* 31 H6
Carcagente, *Spain* 29 F4
Carcajou, *Canada* 100 B5
Carcar, *Phil.* 55 F5
Carcasse, C., *Haiti* 117 C5
Carcassonne, *France* 26 E6
Carche, *Spain* 29 G3
Carchi □, *Ecuador* 120 C2
Carcross, *Canada* 96 B6
Cardabia, *Australia* 88 D1
Çardak, *Turkey* 66 E3
Cardamon Hills, *India* 60 Q10
Cárdenas, *Cuba* 116 B3
Cárdenas, *San Luis Potosí, Mexico* 115 C5
Cárdenas, *Tabasco, Mexico* 115 D6
Cardenete, *Spain* 28 F3
Cardiel, L., *Argentina* 128 C2
Cardiff, *U.K.* 13 F4
Cardiff-by-the-Sea, *U.S.A.* 113 M9
Cardigan, *U.K.* 13 E3
Cardigan B., *U.K.* 13 E3
Cardinal, *Canada* 107 B9
Cardón, Punta, *Venezuela* 120 A3
Cardona, *Spain* 28 D6
Cardona, *Uruguay* 126 C4
Cardoner →, *Spain* 28 D6
Cardross, *Canada* 101 D7
Cardston, *Canada* 100 D6
Cardwell, *Australia* 90 B4
Careen L., *Canada* 101 B7
Carei, *Romania* 38 B5
Careiro, *Brazil* 121 D6
Careme, *Indonesia* 57 G13
Carentan, *France* 24 C5
Carey, *Idaho, U.S.A.* 110 E7
Carey, *Ohio, U.S.A.* 104 E4
Carey, L., *Australia* 89 E3
Carey L., *Canada* 101 A8
Careysburg, *Liberia* 78 D2
Cargèse, *France* 27 F12
Carhaix-Plouguer, *France* 24 D3
Carhuamayo, *Peru* 124 C2
Carhuas, *Peru* 124 B2
Carhué, *Argentina* 126 D3
Caria, *Turkey* 66 E3
Cariacica, *Brazil* 123 F3
Caribbean Sea, *W. Indies* 117 C5
Cariboo Mts., *Canada* 100 C4
Caribou, *U.S.A.* 99 C6
Caribou →, *Man., Canada* 101 B10
Caribou →, *N.W.T., Canada* 100 A3
Caribou I., *Canada* 98 C2
Caribou Is., *Canada* 100 A6
Caribou L., *Man., Canada* 101 B9
Caribou L., *Ont., Canada* 98 B2
Caribou Mts., *Canada* 100 B5
Carichic, *Mexico* 114 B3
Carigara, *Phil.* 55 F6
Carignan, *France* 25 C12
Carignano, *Italy* 32 D4
Carillo, *Mexico* 114 B4
Carinda, *Australia* 91 E4
Cariñena, *Spain* 28 D3
Carinhanha, *Brazil* 123 D3
Carinhanha →, *Brazil* 123 D3
Carini, *Italy* 34 D6
Carinola, *Italy* 34 A6
Caripito, *Venezuela* 121 A5
Caritianas, *Brazil* 125 B5
Carlbrod = Dimitrovgrad, *Serbia* 21 M12
Carlentini, *Italy* 35 E8
Carleton Place, *Canada* 98 C4
Carletonville, *S. Africa* 84 D4
Carlin, *U.S.A.* 110 F5
Carlingford, L., *Ireland* 15 B5
Carlinville, *U.S.A.* 108 F10
Carlisle, *U.K.* 12 C5
Carlisle, *U.S.A.* 106 F7
Carlit, Pic, *France* 26 F5
Carloforte, *Italy* 34 C1
Carlos Casares, *Argentina* 126 D3
Carlos Chagas, *Brazil* 123 E3
Carlos Tejedor, *Argentina* 126 D3
Carlow, *Ireland* 15 D5
Carlow □, *Ireland* 15 D5
Carlsbad, *Calif., U.S.A.* 113 M9
Carlsbad, *N. Mex., U.S.A.* 109 J2
Carlyle, *Canada* 101 D8
Carlyle, *U.S.A.* 108 F10
Carmacks, *Canada* 96 B6
Carmagnola, *Italy* 32 D4
Carman, *Canada* 101 D9
Carmangay, *Canada* 100 C6
Carmanville, *Canada* 99 C9
Carmarthen, *U.K.* 13 F3
Carmarthen B., *U.K.* 13 F3
Carmaux, *France* 26 D6
Carmel, *U.S.A.* 107 E11
Carmel-by-the-Sea, *U.S.A.* 111 H3
Carmel Valley, *U.S.A.* 112 J5
Carmelo, *Uruguay* 126 C4
Carmen, *Bolivia* 124 C4
Carmen, *Colombia* 120 B2
Carmen, *Paraguay* 127 B4
Carmen →, *Mexico* 114 A3
Carmen, I., *Mexico* 114 B2
Carmen de Patagones, *Argentina* 128 B4
Cármenes, *Spain* 30 C5
Carmensa, *Argentina* 126 D2
Carmi, *U.S.A.* 104 F1
Carmichael, *U.S.A.* 112 G5
Carmila, *Australia* 90 C4
Carmona, *Spain* 31 H5
Carnarvon, *Queens., Australia* 90 C4
Carnarvon, *W. Austral., Australia* 89 D1
Carnarvon, *S. Africa* 84 E3
Carnarvon Ra., *Queens., Australia* 90 D4
Carnarvon Ra., *W. Austral., Australia* 89 E3
Carnation, *U.S.A.* 112 C5
Carnaxide, *Portugal* 31 G1
Carndonagh, *Ireland* 15 A4
Carnduff, *Canada* 101 D8
Carnegie, *U.S.A.* 106 F4
Carnegie, L., *Australia* 89 E3
Carnic Alps = Karnische Alpen, *Europe* 21 J3
Carniche Alpi = Karnische Alpen, *Europe* 21 J3
Carnot, *C.A.R.* 80 D3
Carnot, C., *Australia* 91 E2
Carnot B., *Australia* 88 C3
Carnsore Pt., *Ireland* 15 D5
Caro, *U.S.A.* 104 D4
Carol City, *U.S.A.* 105 N5
Carolina, *Brazil* 122 C2
Carolina, *Puerto Rico* 117 C6
Carolina, *S. Africa* 85 D5
Caroline I., *Kiribati* 93 H12
Caroline Is., *Pac. Oc.* 92 G6
Caron, *Canada* 101 C7
Caroni →, *Venezuela* 121 B5
Caroona, *Australia* 91 E5
Carora, *Venezuela* 120 A3
Carovigno, *Italy* 35 B10
Carpathians, *Europe* 20 F11
Carpaţii Meridionali, *Romania* 38 D8
Carpenédolo, *Italy* 32 C7
Carpentaria, G. of, *Australia* 90 A2
Carpentaria Downs, *Australia* 90 B3
Carpentras, *France* 27 D9
Carpi, *Italy* 32 D7
Carpina, *Brazil* 122 C4
Carpino, *Italy* 35 A8
Carpinteria, *U.S.A.* 113 L7
Carpio, *Spain* 30 D5
Carpolac = Morea, *Australia* 91 F3
Carr Boyd Ra., *Australia* 88 C4
Carrabelle, *U.S.A.* 105 L3
Carranya, *Australia* 88 C4
Carrara, *Italy* 32 D7
Carrascal, *Phil.* 55 G6
Carrascosa del Campo, *Spain* 28 E2
Carrauntoohill, *Ireland* 15 E2
Carretas, Punta, *Peru* 124 C2
Carrick-on-Shannon, *Ireland* 15 C3
Carrick-on-Suir, *Ireland* 15 D4
Carrickfergus, *U.K.* 15 B6
Carrickfergus □, *U.K.* 15 B6
Carrickmacross, *Ireland* 15 C5
Carrieton, *Australia* 91 E2
Carrington, *U.S.A.* 108 B5
Carrión →, *Spain* 30 D6
Carrión de los Condes, *Spain* 30 C6
Carrizal Bajo, *Chile* 126 B1
Carrizalillo, *Chile* 126 B1
Carrizo Cr. →, *U.S.A.* 109 G3
Carrizo Springs, *U.S.A.* 109 L5
Carrizozo, *U.S.A.* 111 K11
Carroll, *U.S.A.* 108 D7
Carrollton, *Ga., U.S.A.* 105 J3
Carrollton, *Ill., U.S.A.* 108 F9
Carrollton, *Ky., U.S.A.* 104 F3
Carrollton, *Mo., U.S.A.* 108 F8
Carrollton, *Ohio, U.S.A.* 106 F3
Carron →, *U.K.* 14 D3
Carron, L., *U.K.* 14 D3
Carrot →, *Canada* 101 C8
Carrot River, *Canada* 101 C8
Carrouges, *France* 24 D6
Carruthers, *Canada* 101 C7
Çarşamba, *Turkey* 66 C7
Carse of Gowrie, *U.K.* 14 E5
Carsoli, *Italy* 33 F10
Carson, *Calif., U.S.A.* 113 M8
Carson, *N. Dak., U.S.A.* 108 B4
Carson →, *U.S.A.* 112 F8
Carson City, *U.S.A.* 112 F7
Carson Sink, *U.S.A.* 110 G4
Carstairs, *U.K.* 14 F5
Cartagena, *Colombia* 120 A2
Cartagena, *Spain* 29 H4
Cartago, *Colombia* 120 C2
Cartago, *Costa Rica* 116 E3
Cartaxo, *Portugal* 31 F2
Cartaya, *Spain* 31 H3
Carteret, *France* 24 C5
Cartersville, *U.S.A.* 105 H3
Carterton, *N.Z.* 87 J5
Carthage, *Ark., U.S.A.* 109 H8
Carthage, *Ill., U.S.A.* 108 E9
Carthage, *Mo., U.S.A.* 109 G7
Carthage, *S. Dak., U.S.A.* 108 C6
Carthage, *Tex., U.S.A.* 109 J7
Cartier I., *Australia* 88 B3
Cartwright, *Canada* 99 B8
Caruaru, *Brazil* 122 C4
Carúpano, *Venezuela* 121 A5
Carutapera, *Brazil* 122 B2
Caruthersville, *U.S.A.* 109 G10
Carvalho, *Brazil* 121 D7
Carvin, *France* 25 B9
Carvoeiro, *Brazil* 121 D5
Carvoeiro, C., *Portugal* 31 F1
Casa Branca, *Brazil* 123 F2
Casa Branca, *Portugal* 31 G2
Casa Grande, *U.S.A.* 111 K8
Casablanca, *Chile* 126 C1
Casablanca, *Morocco* 74 B3
Casacalenda, *Italy* 35 A7
Casal di Principe, *Italy* 35 B7
Casalbordino, *Italy* 33 F11
Casale Monferrato, *Italy* 32 C5
Casalmaggiore, *Italy* 32 D7
Casalpusterlengo, *Italy* 32 C6
Casamance →, *Senegal* 78 C1
Casamássima, *Italy* 35 B9
Casanare □, *Colombia* 120 B3
Casanare □, *Colombia* 120 B3
Casanare →, *Colombia* 120 B4
Casarano, *Italy* 35 B11
Casares, *Spain* 31 J5
Casas Grandes, *Mexico* 114 A3
Casas Ibañez, *Spain* 29 F3
Casasimarro, *Spain* 29 F2
Casatejada, *Spain* 30 F5
Casavieja, *Spain* 30 E6
Cascade, *Idaho, U.S.A.* 110 D5
Cascade, *Mont., U.S.A.* 110 C8
Cascade Locks, *U.S.A.* 112 E5
Cascade Ra., *U.S.A.* 112 D5
Cascais, *Portugal* 31 G1
Cascavel, *Brazil* 127 A5
Cáscina, *Italy* 32 E7
Caselle Torinese, *Italy* 32 C4
Caserta, *Italy* 35 A7
Cashel, *Ireland* 15 D4
Cashmere, *U.S.A.* 110 C3
Cashmere Downs, *Australia* 89 E2
Casibare →, *Colombia* 120 C3
Casiguran, *Phil.* 55 C5
Casilda, *Argentina* 126 C3
Casino, *Australia* 91 D5
Casiquiare →, *Venezuela* 120 C4
Casitas, *Peru* 124 A1
Caslan, *Canada* 100 C6
Čáslav, *Czech.* 20 F5
Casma, *Peru* 124 B2
Casmalia, *U.S.A.* 113 L6
Casola Valsenio, *Italy* 33 D8
Cásoli, *Italy* 33 F11
Caspe, *Spain* 28 D4
Casper, *U.S.A.* 110 E10
Caspian Sea, *Asia* 44 E6
Casquets, *Chan. Is.* 24 C4
Cass City, *U.S.A.* 104 D4
Cass Lake, *U.S.A.* 108 B7
Cassà de la Selva, *Spain* 28 D7
Cassano Iónio, *Italy* 35 C9
Cassel, *France* 25 B9
Casselman, *Canada* 107 A9
Casselton, *U.S.A.* 108 B6
Cassiar, *Canada* 100 B3
Cassiar Mts., *Canada* 100 B2
Cassilândia, *Brazil* 125 D7
Cassinga, *Angola* 81 H3
Cassino, *Italy* 34 A6
Cassis, *France* 27 E9
Cassville, *U.S.A.* 109 G8
Cástagneto Carducci, *Italy* 32 E7
Castaic, *U.S.A.* 113 L8
Castanhal, *Brazil* 122 B2
Casteau, *Belgium* 17 G4
Castéggio, *Italy* 32 C6
Castejón de Monegros, *Spain* 28 D4
Castel di Sangro, *Italy* 33 G11
Castel San Giovanni, *Italy* 32 C6
Castel San Pietro, *Italy* 33 D8
Castelbuono, *Italy* 35 E7
Casteldelfino, *Italy* 32 D4
Castelfiorentino, *Italy* 32 E7
Castelfranco Emília, *Italy* 32 D8
Castelfranco Véneto, *Italy* 33 C8
Casteljaloux, *France* 26 D4
Castellabate, *Italy* 35 B7
Castellammare, G. di, *Italy* 34 D5
Castellammare del Golfo, *Italy* 34 D5
Castellammare di Stábia, *Italy* 35 B7
Castellamonte, *Italy* 32 C4
Castellana Grotte, *Italy* 35 B10
Castellane, *France* 27 E10
Castellaneta, *Italy* 35 B9
Castellar de Santisteban, *Spain* 29 G1
Castelleone, *Italy* 32 C6
Castelli, *Argentina* 126 D4
Castelló de Ampurias, *Spain* 28 C8
Castellón □, *Spain* 28 E4
Castellón de la Plana, *Spain* 28 F4
Castellote, *Spain* 28 E4
Castellterçol, *Spain* 28 D7
Castelmáuro, *Italy* 35 A7
Castelnau-de-Médoc, *France* 26 C3
Castelnaudary, *France* 26 E5
Castelnovo ne' Monti, *Italy* 32 D7
Castelnuovo di Val di Cécina, *Italy* 32 E7
Castelo, *Brazil* 123 F3
Castelo Branco, *Portugal* 30 F3
Castelo Branco □, *Portugal* 30 F3
Castelo de Paiva, *Portugal* 30 D2
Castelo de Vide, *Portugal* 31 F3
Castelo do Piauí, *Brazil* 122 C3
Castelsarrasin, *France* 26 D5
Casteltérmini, *Italy* 34 E6
Castelvetrano, *Italy* 34 E5
Casterton, *Australia* 91 F3
Castets, *France* 26 E2
Castiglione del Lago, *Italy* 33 E9
Castiglione della Pescáia, *Italy* 32 F7
Castiglione della Stiviere, *Italy* 32 C7
Castiglione Fiorentino, *Italy* 33 E8
Castilblanco, *Spain* 31 F5
Castilla, *Peru* 124 B1
Castilla, Playa de, *Spain* 31 H4
Castilla La Mancha □, *Spain* 31 F7
Castilla La Nueva = Castilla La Mancha □, *Spain* 31 F7
Castilla La Vieja = Castilla y Leon □, *Spain* 30 D6
Castilla y Leon □, *Spain* 30 D6
Castillon, Barr. de, *France* 27 E10
Castillon-en-Couserans, *France* 26 F5
Castillon-la-Bataille, *France* 26 D3
Castillonès, *France* 26 D4
Castillos, *Uruguay* 127 C5
Castle Dale, *U.S.A.* 110 G8
Castle Douglas, *U.K.* 14 G5
Castle Rock, *Colo., U.S.A.* 108 F2
Castle Rock, *Wash., U.S.A.* 112 D4
Castlebar, *Ireland* 15 C2
Castleblaney, *Ireland* 15 B5
Castlegar, *Canada* 100 D5
Castlemaine, *Australia* 91 F3
Castlereagh, *Ireland* 15 C3
Castlereagh □, *U.K.* 15 B6
Castlereagh →, *Australia* 91 E4
Castlereagh B., *Australia* 90 A2
Castletown, *I. of Man* 12 C3
Castletown Bearhaven, *Ireland* 15 E2
Castlevale, *Australia* 90 C4
Castor, *Canada* 100 C6
Castres, *France* 26 E6
Castricum, *Neths.* 16 C5
Castries, *St. Lucia* 117 D7
Castril, *Spain* 29 H2
Castro, *Brazil* 127 A5
Castro, *Chile* 128 B2
Castro Alves, *Brazil* 123 D4
Castro del Río, *Spain* 31 H6
Castro Marim, *Portugal* 31 H3
Castro Urdiales, *Spain* 28 B1
Castro Verde, *Portugal* 31 H2
Castrojeriz, *Spain* 30 C6
Castropol, *Spain* 30 B3
Castroreale, *Italy* 35 D8
Castrovillari, *Italy* 35 C9
Castroville, *Calif., U.S.A.* 112 J5
Castroville, *Tex., U.S.A.* 109 L5
Castrovirreyna, *Peru* 124 C2
Castuera, *Spain* 31 G5
Casummit Lake, *Canada* 98 B1
Çat, *Turkey* 67 D9
Cat Ba, Dao, *Vietnam* 58 B6
Cat I., *Bahamas* 117 B4
Cat I., *U.S.A.* 109 K10
Cat L., *Canada* 98 B1
Catacamas, *Honduras* 116 D2
Catacáos, *Peru* 124 B1
Cataguases, *Brazil* 123 F3
Catahoula L., *U.S.A.* 109 K8
Çatak, *Turkey* 67 D10
Catalão, *Brazil* 123 E2
Çatalca, *Turkey* 66 C3
Catalina, *Canada* 99 C9
Catalonia = Cataluña □, *Spain* 28 D6
Cataluña □, *Spain* 28 D6
Çatalzeytin, *Turkey* 66 C6
Catamarca, *Argentina* 126 B2
Catamarca □, *Argentina* 126 B2
Catanauan, *Phil.* 55 E5
Catanduanes, *Phil.* 55 E6
Catanduva, *Brazil* 127 A6
Catánia, *Italy* 35 E8
Catánia, G. di, *Italy* 35 E8
Catanzaro, *Italy* 35 D9
Cataonia, *Turkey* 66 E6
Catarman, *Phil.* 55 E6
Catbalogan, *Phil.* 55 F6
Cateel, *Phil.* 55 H7
Catende, *Brazil* 122 C4
Cathcart, *S. Africa* 84 E4
Cathlamet, *U.S.A.* 112 D3
Catio, *Guinea-Biss.* 78 C1
Catisimiña, *Venezuela* 121 C5
Catita, *Brazil* 122 C3
Catlettsburg, *U.S.A.* 104 F4
Catoche, C., *Mexico* 115 C7
Catolé do Rocha, *Brazil* 122 C4
Catral, *Spain* 29 G4
Catria, Mt., *Italy* 33 E9
Catrimani, *Brazil* 121 C5
Catrimani →, *Brazil* 121 C5
Catskill, *U.S.A.* 107 D11
Catskill Mts., *U.S.A.* 107 D10
Catt, Mt., *Australia* 90 A1
Cattaraugus, *U.S.A.* 106 D6
Cattólica, *Italy* 33 E9
Cattólica Eraclea, *Italy* 34 E6
Catu, *Brazil* 123 D4
Catuala, *Angola* 84 B2
Catur, *Mozam.* 83 E4
Catwick Is., *Vietnam* 59 G7
Cauca □, *Colombia* 120 C2
Cauca →, *Colombia* 120 B3
Caucaia, *Brazil* 122 B4
Caucasia, *Colombia* 120 B2
Caucasus = Bolshoi Kavkas, *Asia* 43 E11
Caudebec-en-Caux, *France* 24 C7
Caudete, *Spain* 29 G3
Caudry, *France* 25 B10
Caulnes, *France* 24 D4
Caulónia, *Italy* 35 D9
Caúngula, *Angola* 80 F3
Cauquenes, *Chile* 126 D1
Caura →, *Venezuela* 121 B5
Caurés →, *Brazil* 121 D5
Cauresi →, *Mozam.* 83 F3
Causapscal, *Canada* 99 C6
Caussade, *France* 26 D5
Causse-Méjean, *France* 26 D7
Cauterets, *France* 26 F3
Cautín □, *Chile* 128 A2
Cauvery →, *India* 60 P11
Caux, Pays de, *France* 24 C7
Cava dei Tirreni, *Italy* 35 B7
Cávado →, *Portugal* 30 D2
Cavaillon, *France* 27 E9
Cavalaire-sur-Mer, *France* 27 E10
Cavalcante, *Brazil* 123 D2
Cavalese, *Italy* 33 B8
Cavalier, *U.S.A.* 108 A6
Cavalla = Cavally →, *Africa* 78 E3
Cavallo, I. de, *France* 27 G13
Cavally →, *Africa* 78 E3
Cavan, *Ireland* 15 C4
Cavan □, *Ireland* 15 C4
Cavárzere, *Italy* 33 C9
Cave City, *U.S.A.* 104 G3
Cavenagh Ra., *Australia* 89 E4
Cavendish, *Australia* 91 F3
Caviana, I., *Brazil* 121 C7
Cavite, *Phil.* 55 D4
Cavour, *Italy* 32 D4
Cavtat, *Croatia* 21 N8
Cavuşcu Gölü, *Turkey* 66 D4
Cawndilla L., *Australia* 91 E3
Cawnpore = Kanpur, *India* 63 F9
Caxias, *Brazil* 122 B3
Caxias do Sul, *Brazil* 127 B5
Caxine, C., *Algeria* 75 A4

Caxito, *Angola* 80 F2
Çay, *Turkey* 66 D4
Cay Sal Bank, *Bahamas* 116 B3
Cayambe, *Ecuador* 120 C2
Cayambe, *Ecuador* 120 C2
Çaycuma, *Turkey* 66 C5
Çayeli, *Turkey* 67 C9
Cayenne, *Fr. Guiana* 121 B7
Cayenne □, *Fr. Guiana* 121 C7
Cayeux-sur-Mer, *France* 25 B8
Cayiralan, *Turkey* 66 D6
Caylus, *France* 26 D5
Cayman Brac, *Cayman Is.* 116 C4
Cayman Is. ■, *W. Indies* 116 C3
Cayo Romano, *Cuba* 117 B4
Cayuga, *Canada* 106 D5
Cayuga, *U.S.A.* 107 D8
Cayuga L., *U.S.A.* 107 D8
Cazalla de la Sierra, *Spain* 31 H5
Căzăneşti, *Romania* 38 E10
Cazaux et de Sanguinet, Étang de, *France* 26 D2
Cazères, *France* 26 E5
Cazin, *Bos.-H.* 33 D12
Čazma, *Croatia* 33 C13
Čazma →, *Croatia* 33 C13
Cazombo, *Angola* 81 G4
Cazorla, *Spain* 29 H1
Cazorla, *Venezuela* 120 B4
Cazorla, Sierra de, *Spain* 29 G2
Cea →, *Spain* 30 C5
Ceanannus Mor, *Ireland* 15 C5
Ceará = Fortaleza, *Brazil* 122 B4
Ceará □, *Brazil* 122 C4
Ceará Mirim, *Brazil* 122 C4
Cebaco, I. de, *Panama* 116 E3
Cebollar, *Argentina* 126 B2
Cebollera, Sierra de, *Spain* 28 D2
Cebreros, *Spain* 30 E6
Cebu, *Phil.* 55 F5
Ceccano, *Italy* 34 A6
Cechi, *Ivory C.* 78 D4
Čechy, *Czech.* 19 F9
Cecil Plains, *Australia* 91 D5
Cécina, *Italy* 32 E7
Cécina →, *Italy* 32 E7
Ceclavin, *Spain* 30 F4
Cedar →, *U.S.A.* 108 E9
Cedar City, *U.S.A.* 111 H7
Cedar Creek Reservoir, *U.S.A.* 109 J6
Cedar Falls, *Iowa, U.S.A.* 108 D8
Cedar Falls, *Wash., U.S.A.* 112 C5
Cedar Key, *U.S.A.* 105 L4
Cedar L., *Canada* 101 C8
Cedar Rapids, *U.S.A.* 108 E9
Cedartown, *U.S.A.* 105 H3
Cedarvale, *Canada* 100 B3
Cedarville, *S. Africa* 85 E4
Cedarville, *U.S.A.* 110 F3
Cedeira, *Spain* 30 B2
Cedral, *Mexico* 114 C4
Cedrino →, *Italy* 34 B2
Cedro, *Brazil* 122 C4
Cedros, I. de, *Mexico* 114 B1
Ceduna, *Australia* 91 E1
Cefalù, *Italy* 35 D7
Cega →, *Spain* 30 D6
Cegléd, *Hungary* 21 H9
Céglie Messápico, *Italy* 35 B10
Cehegín, *Spain* 29 G3
Ceheng, *China* 52 E5
Cehu-Silvaniei, *Romania* 38 B6
Ceira →, *Portugal* 30 E2
Cekhira, *Tunisia* 75 B7
Celano, *Italy* 33 F10
Celanova, *Spain* 30 C3
Celaya, *Mexico* 114 C4
Celbridge, *Ireland* 15 C5
Celebes = Sulawesi □, *Indonesia* 57 E6
Celebes Sea = Sulawesi Sea, *Indonesia* 57 D6
Celendín, *Peru* 124 B2
Čelić, *Bos.-H.* 21 L8
Celica, *Ecuador* 120 D2
Celina, *U.S.A.* 104 E3
Celje, *Slovenia* 33 B12
Celle, *Germany* 18 C6
Celles, *Belgium* 17 G2
Celorico da Beira, *Portugal* 30 E3
Cement, *U.S.A.* 109 H5
Çemişgezek, *Turkey* 67 D8
Cenepa →, *Peru* 120 D2
Cengong, *China* 52 D7
Ceno →, *Italy* 32 D7
Centallo, *Italy* 32 D4
Centenário do Sul, *Brazil* 123 F1
Center, *N. Dak., U.S.A.* 108 B4
Center, *Tex., U.S.A.* 109 K7
Centerfield, *U.S.A.* 111 G8
Centerville, *Calif., U.S.A.* 112 J7
Centerville, *Iowa, U.S.A.* 108 E8
Centerville, *Pa., U.S.A.* 106 F5
Centerville, *S. Dak., U.S.A.* 108 D6
Centerville, *Tenn., U.S.A.* 105 H2
Centerville, *Tex., U.S.A.* 109 K7
Cento, *Italy* 33 D8
Central, *Brazil* 122 D3
Central, *U.S.A.* 111 K9
Central □, *Kenya* 82 C4
Central □, *Malawi* 83 E3
Central □, *U.K.* 14 E4
Central □, *Zambia* 83 E2
Central, Cordillera, *Bolivia* 125 D5
Central, Cordillera, *Colombia* 120 C2
Central, Cordillera, *Costa Rica* 116 D3
Central, Cordillera, *Dom. Rep.* 117 C5
Central, Cordillera, *Peru* 124 B2
Central, Cordillera, *Phil.* 55 C4
Central, Sistema, *Spain* 30 E5
Central African Rep. ■, *Africa* 73 G9
Central City, *Ky., U.S.A.* 104 G2
Central City, *Nebr., U.S.A.* 108 E5
Central I., *Kenya* 82 B4
Central Makran Range, *Pakistan* 60 F4
Central Patricia, *Canada* 98 B1
Central Russian Uplands, *Europe* 6 E13
Central Siberian Plateau, *Russia* 46 C14
Centralia, *Ill., U.S.A.* 108 F10
Centralia, *Mo., U.S.A.* 108 F8
Centralia, *Wash., U.S.A.* 112 D4
Centreville, *Ala., U.S.A.* 105 J2
Centreville, *Miss., U.S.A.* 109 K9
Centúripe, *Italy* 35 E7
Cephalonia = Kefallinía, *Greece* 39 L3
Ceprano, *Italy* 34 A6
Cepu, *Indonesia* 57 G14
Ceram = Seram, *Indonesia* 57 E7
Ceram Sea = Seram Sea, *Indonesia* 57 E7
Cerbère, *France* 26 F7
Cerbicales, Is., *France* 27 G13
Cercal, *Portugal* 31 H2
Cercemaggiore, *Italy* 35 A7
Cerdaña, *Spain* 28 C6
Cerdedo, *Spain* 30 C2
Cère →, *France* 26 D5
Cerea, *Italy* 33 C8
Ceres, *Argentina* 126 B3
Ceres, *Brazil* 123 E2
Ceres, *Italy* 32 C4
Ceres, *S. Africa* 84 E2
Ceres, *U.S.A.* 112 H6
Céret, *France* 26 F6
Cereté, *Colombia* 120 B2
Cerfontaine, *Belgium* 17 H4
Cerignola, *Italy* 35 A8
Cerigo = Kíthira, *Greece* 39 N7
Cérilly, *France* 26 B6
Cerisiers, *France* 25 D10
Cerizay, *France* 24 F6
Çerkeş, *Turkey* 66 C5
Çerkezköy, *Turkey* 66 C2
Cerknica, *Slovenia* 33 C11
Çermik, *Turkey* 67 D8
Cerna →, *Romania* 38 E7
Cernavodă, *Romania* 38 E11
Cernay, *France* 25 E14
Cernik, *Croatia* 21 K7
Cerralvo, I., *Mexico* 114 C3
Cerreto Sannita, *Italy* 35 A7
Cerritos, *Mexico* 114 C4
Cerro Sombrero, *Chile* 128 D3
Certaldo, *Italy* 32 E8
Cervaro →, *Italy* 35 A8
Cervera, *Spain* 28 D6
Cervera de Pisuerga, *Spain* 30 C6
Cervera del Río Alhama, *Spain* 28 C3
Cérvia, *Italy* 33 D9
Cervignano del Friuli, *Italy* 33 C10
Cervinara, *Italy* 35 A7
Cervione, *France* 27 F13
Cervo, *Spain* 30 B3
César □, *Colombia* 120 B3
Cesaro, *Italy* 35 E7
Cesena, *Italy* 33 D9
Cesenático, *Italy* 33 D9
Cēsis, *Latvia* 40 C4
Česká Lípa, *Czech.* 20 E4
České Budějovice, *Czech.* 20 G4
Ceskomoravská Vrchovina, *Czech.* 20 F5
Český Brod, *Czech.* 20 E4
Český Krumlov, *Czech.* 20 G4
Český Těšín, *Czech.* 20 F8
Çeşme, *Turkey* 66 D2
Cessnock, *Australia* 91 E5
Cestos →, *Liberia* 78 D3
Cétin Grad, *Croatia* 33 C12
Cetina →, *Croatia* 33 E13
Cetraro, *Italy* 35 C8
Ceuta, *Morocco* 74 A3
Ceva, *Italy* 32 D5
Cévennes, *France* 26 D7
Ceyhan, *Turkey* 66 E6
Ceyhan →, *Turkey* 66 E6
Ceylânpınar, *Turkey* 67 E9
Ceylon = Sri Lanka ■, *Asia* 60 R12
Cèze →, *France* 27 D8
Cha-am, *Thailand* 58 F2
Chaam, *Neths.* 17 E5
Chabeuil, *France* 27 D9
Chablais, *France* 27 B10
Chablis, *France* 25 E10
Chabounia, *Algeria* 75 A5
Chacabuco, *Argentina* 126 C3
Chachapoyas, *Peru* 124 B2
Chachasp, *Peru* 124 D3
Chachoengsao, *Thailand* 58 F3
Chachran, *Pakistan* 60 E7
Chachro, *Pakistan* 62 G4
Chaco □, *Argentina* 126 B3
Chaco □, *Paraguay* 126 B3
Chad ■, *Africa* 73 E8
Chad, L. = Tchad, L., *Chad* 73 F7
Chadan, *Russia* 45 D10
Chadileuvú →, *Argentina* 126 D2
Chadiza, *Zambia* 83 E3
Chadron, *U.S.A.* 108 D3
Chadyr-Lunga, *Moldavia* 42 C3
Chae Hom, *Thailand* 58 C2
Chaem →, *Thailand* 58 C2
Chaeryŏng, *N. Korea* 51 E13
Chagai Hills, *Afghan.* 60 E3
Chagda, *Russia* 45 D14
Chagny, *France* 25 F11
Chagoda, *Russia* 40 B9
Chagos Arch., *Ind. Oc.* 46 K11
Chāh Ākhvor, *Iran* 65 C8
Chāh Bahār, *Iran* 65 E9
Chāh-e-Malek, *Iran* 65 D8
Chāh Kavīr, *Iran* 65 D7
Chahar Burjak, *Afghan.* 60 D3
Chaibasa, *India* 61 H14
Chaillé-les-Marais, *France* 26 B2
Chainat, *Thailand* 58 E3
Chaitén, *Chile* 128 B2
Chaiya, *Thailand* 59 H2
Chaj Doab, *Pakistan* 62 C5
Chajari, *Argentina* 126 C4
Chake Chake, *Tanzania* 82 D4
Chakhānsūr, *Afghan.* 60 D3
Chakonipau, L., *Canada* 99 A6
Chakradharpur, *India* 63 H11
Chakwal, *Pakistan* 62 C5
Chala, *Peru* 124 D3
Chalais, *France* 26 C4
Chalchihuites, *Mexico* 114 C4
Chalcis = Khalkís, *Greece* 39 L6
Chaleur B., *Canada* 99 C6
Chalfant, *U.S.A.* 112 H8
Chalhuanca, *Peru* 124 C3
Chalindrey, *France* 25 E12
Chaling, *China* 53 D9
Chalisgaon, *India* 60 J9
Chalkar, *Kazakhstan* 43 A14
Chalkar, Ozero, *Kazakhstan* 43 A14
Chalky Inlet, *N.Z.* 87 M1
Challans, *France* 24 F5
Challapata, *Bolivia* 124 D4
Challis, *U.S.A.* 110 D6
Chalna, *India* 63 H13
Chalon-sur-Saône, *France* 25 F11
Chalonnes-sur-Loire, *France* 24 E6
Châlons-sur-Marne, *France* 25 D11
Châlus, *France* 26 C4
Chalyaphum, *Thailand* 58 E4
Cham, *Germany* 19 F8
Cham, *Switz.* 23 B6
Cham, Cu Lao, *Vietnam* 58 E7
Chama, *U.S.A.* 111 H10
Chaman, *Pakistan* 60 D5
Chamba, *India* 62 C7
Chamba, *Tanzania* 83 E4
Chambal →, *India* 63 F8
Chamberlain, *U.S.A.* 108 D5
Chamberlain →, *Australia* 88 C4
Chambers, *U.S.A.* 111 J9
Chambersburg, *U.S.A.* 104 F7
Chambéry, *France* 27 C9
Chambly, *Canada* 107 A11
Chambord, *Canada* 99 C5
Chamchamal, *Iraq* 64 C5
Chamela, *Mexico* 114 D3
Chamical, *Argentina* 126 C2
Chamkar Luong, *Cambodia* 59 G4
Chamonix-Mont-Blanc, *France* 27 C10
Champa, *India* 63 H10
Champagne, *Canada* 100 A1
Champagne, *France* 25 D11
Champagne, Plaine de, *France* 25 D11
Champagnole, *France* 25 F12
Champaign, *U.S.A.* 104 E1
Champassak, *Laos* 58 E5
Champaubert, *France* 25 D10
Champdeniers, *France* 26 B3
Champeix, *France* 26 C7
Champlain, *Canada* 104 B9
Champlain, *U.S.A.* 107 B11
Champlain, L., *U.S.A.* 107 B11
Champotón, *Mexico* 115 D6
Chamusca, *Portugal* 31 F2
Chan Chan, *Peru* 124 B2
Chana, *Thailand* 59 J3
Chañaral, *Chile* 126 B1
Chanārān, *Iran* 65 B8
Chanasma, *India* 62 H5
Chancay, *Peru* 124 C2
Chancy, *Switz.* 22 D1
Chandannagar, *India* 63 H13
Chandausi, *India* 63 E8
Chandeleur Is., *U.S.A.* 109 L10
Chandeleur Sd., *U.S.A.* 109 L10
Chandigarh, *India* 62 D7
Chandler, *Australia* 91 D1
Chandler, *Canada* 99 C7
Chandler, *Ariz., U.S.A.* 111 K8
Chandler, *Okla., U.S.A.* 109 H6
Chandless →, *Brazil* 124 B4
Chandmani, *Mongolia* 54 B4
Chandpur, *Bangla.* 61 H17
Chandpur, *India* 62 E8
Chandrapur, *India* 60 K11
Chānf, *Iran* 65 E9
Chang, *Pakistan* 62 F3
Chang, Ko, *Thailand* 59 F4
Ch'ang Chiang = Chang Jiang →, *China* 53 B13
Chang Jiang →, *China* 53 B13
Changa, *India* 63 C7
Changanacheri, *India* 60 Q10
Changane →, *Mozam.* 85 C5
Changbai, *China* 51 D15
Changbai Shan, *China* 51 C15
Changchiak'ou = Zhangjiakou, *China* 50 D8
Ch'angchou = Changzhou, *China* 53 B12
Changchun, *China* 51 C13
Changchunling, *China* 51 B13
Changde, *China* 53 C8
Changdo-ri, *N. Korea* 51 E14
Changfeng, *China* 53 A11
Changhai = Shanghai, *China* 53 B13
Changhua, *China* 53 B12
Changhŭng, *S. Korea* 51 G14
Changhŭngni, *N. Korea* 51 D15
Changjiang, *China* 54 E5
Changjin, *N. Korea* 51 D14
Changjin-chŏsuji, *N. Korea* 51 D14
Changle, *China* 53 E12
Changli, *China* 51 E10
Changling, *China* 51 B12
Changlun, *Malaysia* 59 J3
Changning, *Hunan, China* 53 D9
Changning, *Yunnan, China* 52 E2
Changping, *China* 50 D9
Changsha, *China* 53 C9
Changshan, *China* 53 C12
Changshou, *China* 52 C6
Changshu, *China* 53 B13
Changshun, *China* 52 D6
Changtai, *China* 53 E11
Changting, *China* 53 E11
Changwu, *China* 50 G4
Changxing, *China* 53 B12
Changyang, *China* 53 B8
Changyi, *China* 51 F10
Changyŏn, *N. Korea* 51 E13
Changyuan, *China* 50 G8
Changzhi, *China* 50 F7
Changzhou, *China* 53 B12
Chanhanga, *Angola* 84 B1
Chanlar, *Azerbaijan* 43 F12
Channapatna, *India* 60 N10
Channel Is., *U.K.* 13 H5
Channel Is., *U.S.A.* 113 M7
Channel-Port aux Basques, *Canada* 99 C8
Channing, *Mich., U.S.A.* 104 B1
Channing, *Tex., U.S.A.* 109 H3
Chantada, *Spain* 30 C3
Chanthaburi, *Thailand* 58 F4
Chantilly, *France* 25 C9
Chantonnay, *France* 24 F5
Chantrey Inlet, *Canada* 96 B10
Chanute, *U.S.A.* 109 G7
Chanza →, *Spain* 31 H3
Chao Hu, *China* 53 B11
Chao Phraya →, *Thailand* 58 F3
Chao Phraya Lowlands, *Thailand* 58 E3
Chao Xian, *China* 53 B11
Chao'an, *China* 53 F11
Chaocheng, *China* 50 F8
Chaoyang, *Guangdong, China* 53 F11
Chaoyang, *Liaoning, China* 51 D11
Chapada dos Guimarães, *Brazil* 125 D6
Chapala, *Mozam.* 83 F4
Chapala, L. de, *Mexico* 114 C4
Chaparé →, *Bolivia* 125 D5
Chaparral, *Colombia* 120 C2
Chapayevo, *Kazakhstan* 43 A14
Chapayevsk, *Russia* 41 E16
Chapecó, *Brazil* 127 B5
Chapel Hill, *U.S.A.* 105 H6
Chapleau, *Canada* 98 C3
Chaplin, *Canada* 101 C7
Chaplino, *Ukraine* 42 B7
Chaplygin, *Russia* 41 E12
Chapra = Chhapra, *India* 63 G11
Châr, *Mauritania* 74 D2
Chara, *Russia* 45 D12
Charadai, *Argentina* 126 B4
Charagua, *Bolivia* 125 D5
Charalá, *Colombia* 120 B3
Charambirá, Punta, *Colombia* 120 C2
Charaña, *Bolivia* 124 D4
Charapita, *Colombia* 120 D3
Charata, *Argentina* 126 B3
Charcas, *Mexico* 114 C4
Charcoal L., *Canada* 101 B8
Chard, *U.K.* 13 G5
Chardara, *Kazakhstan* 44 E7
Chardon, *U.S.A.* 106 E3
Chardzhou, *Turkmenistan* 44 F7
Charente □, *France* 26 C4
Charente →, *France* 26 C2
Charente-Maritime □, *France* 26 C3
Charentsavan, *Armenia* 43 F11
Chari →, *Chad* 73 F7
Chārīkār, *Afghan.* 60 B6
Chariton →, *U.S.A.* 108 F8
Charity, *Guyana* 121 B6
Chärjew = Chardzhou, *Turkmenistan* 44 F7
Charkhari, *India* 63 G8
Charkhi Dadri, *India* 62 E7
Charleroi, *Belgium* 17 H4
Charleroi, *U.S.A.* 106 F5
Charles, C., *U.S.A.* 104 G8
Charles City, *U.S.A.* 108 D8
Charles L., *Canada* 101 B6
Charles Town, *U.S.A.* 104 F7
Charleston, *Ill., U.S.A.* 104 F1
Charleston, *Miss., U.S.A.* 109 H9
Charleston, *Mo., U.S.A.* 109 G10
Charleston, *S.C., U.S.A.* 105 J6
Charleston, *W. Va., U.S.A.* 104 F5
Charleston Peak, *U.S.A.* 113 J11
Charlestown, *S. Africa* 85 D4
Charlestown, *U.S.A.* 104 F3
Charlesville, *Zaïre* 80 F4
Charleville = Rath Luirc, *Ireland* 15 D3
Charleville, *Australia* 91 D4
Charleville-Mézières, *France* 25 C11
Charlevoix, *U.S.A.* 104 C3
Charlieu, *France* 27 B8
Charlotte, *Mich., U.S.A.* 104 D3
Charlotte, *N.C., U.S.A.* 105 H5
Charlotte Amalie, *Virgin Is.* 117 C7
Charlotte Harbor, *U.S.A.* 105 M4
Charlottesville, *U.S.A.* 104 F6
Charlottetown, *Canada* 99 C7
Charlton, *Australia* 91 F3
Charlton, *U.S.A.* 108 E8
Charlton I., *Canada* 98 B4
Charmes, *France* 25 D13
Charny, *Canada* 99 C5
Charolles, *France* 27 B8
Chârost, *France* 25 F9
Charouine, *Algeria* 75 C4
Charre, *Mozam.* 83 F4
Charroux, *France* 26 B4
Charsadda, *Pakistan* 62 B4
Charters Towers, *Australia* 90 C4
Chartres, *France* 24 D8
Chascomús, *Argentina* 126 D4
Chasefu, *Zambia* 83 E3
Chasovnya-Uchurskaya, *Russia* 45 D14
Chasseneuil-sur-Bonnieure, *France* 26 C4
Chāt, *Iran* 65 B7
Chatal Balkan = Udvoy Balkan, *Bulgaria* 38 G9
Château-Arnoux, *France* 27 D10
Château-Chinon, *France* 25 E10
Château d'Oex, *Switz.* 22 D4
Château-du-Loir, *France* 24 E7
Château-Gontier, *France* 24 E6
Château-la-Vallière, *France* 24 E7
Château-Landon, *France* 25 D9
Château-Porcien, *France* 25 C11
Château-Renault, *France* 24 E7
Château-Salins, *France* 25 D13
Château-Thierry, *France* 25 C10
Châteaubourg, *France* 24 D5
Châteaubriant, *France* 24 E5
Châteaudun, *France* 24 D8
Châteaugiron, *France* 24 D5
Châteaulin, *France* 24 D2
Châteaumeillant, *France* 26 B6
Châteauneuf-du-Faou, *France* 24 D3
Châteauneuf-en-Thymerais, *France* 24 D8
Châteauneuf-sur-Charente, *France* 26 C3
Châteauneuf-sur-Cher, *France* 25 F9
Châteauneuf-sur-Loire, *France* 25 E9
Châteaurenard, *Bouches-du-Rhône, France* 27 E8
Châteaurenard, *Loiret, France* 25 E9
Châteauroux, *France* 25 F8
Châtel-St.-Denis, *Switz.* 22 C3
Châtelaillon-Plage, *France* 26 B2
Châtelaudren, *France* 24 D4
Chatelet, *Belgium* 17 H5
Châtelguyon, *France* 26 C7
Châtellerault, *France* 24 F7
Châtelus-Malvaleix, *France* 26 B6
Chatfield, *U.S.A.* 108 D9
Chatham, *N.B., Canada* 99 C6
Chatham, *Ont., Canada* 98 D3
Chatham, *U.K.* 13 F8
Chatham, *La., U.S.A.* 109 J8
Chatham, *N.Y., U.S.A.* 107 D11
Chatham, I., *Chile* 128 D2
Chatham Is., *Pac. Oc.* 92 M10
Chatham Str., *U.S.A.* 100 B2
Chatillon, *Italy* 32 C4
Châtillon-Coligny, *France* 25 E9
Châtillon-en-Bazois, *France* 25 E10
Châtillon-en-Diois, *France* 27 D9
Châtillon-sur-Indre, *France* 24 F8
Châtillon-sur-Loire, *France* 25 E9

Châtillon-sur-Marne, France 25 C10
Châtillon-sur-Seine, France 25 E11
Chatmohar, Bangla. 63 G13
Chatra, India 63 G11
Chatrapur, India 61 K14
Chats, L. des, Canada 107 A8
Chatsworth, Canada 106 B4
Chatsworth, Zimbabwe 83 F3
Chattahoochee →, U.S.A. 105 K3
Chattanooga, U.S.A. 105 H3
Chaturat, Thailand 58 E3
Chau Doc, Vietnam 59 G5
Chaudanne, Barr. de, France 27 E10
Chaudes-Aigues, France 26 D7
Chauffailles, France 27 B8
Chauk, Burma 61 J19
Chaukan La, Burma 61 F20
Chaulnes, France 25 C9
Chaumont, France 25 D12
Chaumont, U.S.A. 107 B8
Chaumont-en-Vexin, France 25 C8
Chaumont-sur-Loire, France 24 E8
Chaunay, France 26 B4
Chauny, France 25 C10
Chausey, Is., France 24 D5
Chaussin, France 25 F12
Chautauqua L., U.S.A. 106 D5
Chauvigny, France 24 F7
Chauvin, Canada 101 C6
Chavantina, Brazil 125 C7
Chaves, Brazil 122 B2
Chaves, Portugal 30 D3
Chavuma, Zambia 81 G4
Chawang, Thailand 59 H2
Chazelles-sur-Lyon, France 27 C8
Chazuta, Peru 124 B2
Chazy, U.S.A. 107 B11
Cheb, Czech. 20 E2
Cheboksary, Russia 41 C15
Cheboygan, U.S.A. 104 C3
Chebsara, Russia 41 B11
Chech, Erg, Africa 74 D4
Chechaouen, Morocco 74 A3
Chechen, Os., Russia 43 E12
Checheno-Ingush Republic □, Russia 43 E11
Chechon, S. Korea 51 F15
Chęciny, Poland 20 E10
Checleset B., Canada 100 C3
Checotah, U.S.A. 109 H7
Chedabucto B., Canada 99 C7
Cheduba I., Burma 61 K18
Cheepie, Australia 91 D4
Chef-Boutonne, France 26 B3
Chegdomyn, Russia 45 D14
Chegga, Mauritania 74 C3
Chegutu, Zimbabwe 83 F3
Chehalis, U.S.A. 112 D4
Cheiron, Mt., France 27 E10
Cheju Do, S. Korea 51 H14
Chekalin, Russia 41 D10
Chekiang = Zhejiang □, China 53 C13
Chel = Kuru, Bahr el →, Sudan 77 F2
Chela, Sa. da, Angola 84 B1
Chelan, U.S.A. 110 C4
Chelan, L., U.S.A. 110 C3
Cheleken, Turkmenistan 44 F6
Chelforó, Argentina 128 A3
Chéliff, O. →, Algeria 75 A5
Chelkar, Kazakhstan 44 E6
Chelkar Tengiz, Solonchak, Kazakhstan 44 E7
Chellala Dahrania, Algeria 75 B5
Chelles, France 25 D9
Chełm, Poland 20 D13
Chełmek, Poland 20 E9
Chełmno, Poland 20 B8
Chelmsford, U.K. 13 F8
Chelmsford Dam, S. Africa 85 D4
Chełmża, Poland 20 B8
Chelsea, Okla., U.S.A. 109 G7
Chelsea, Vt., U.S.A. 107 C12
Cheltenham, U.K. 13 F5
Chelva, Spain 28 F4
Chelyabinsk, Russia 44 D7
Chelyuskin, C., Russia 46 B14
Chemainus, Canada 100 D4
Chembar = Belinskiy, Russia 41 E13
Chemillé, France 24 E6
Chemnitz, Germany 18 E8
Chemult, U.S.A. 110 E3
Chen, Gora, Russia 45 C15
Chen Xian, China 53 E9
Chenab →, Pakistan 62 D4
Chenachane, O. →, Algeria 74 C4
Chenango Forks, U.S.A. 107 D9
Chencha, Ethiopia 77 F4
Chenchiang = Zhenjiang, China 53 A12
Chênée, Belgium 17 G7
Cheney, U.S.A. 110 C5
Cheng Xian, China 50 H3
Chengbu, China 53 D8
Chengcheng, China 50 G5
Chengchou = Zhengzhou, China 50 G7
Chengde, China 51 D9
Chengdong Hu, China 53 A11
Chengdu, China 52 B5
Chenggong, China 52 E4
Chenggu, China 50 H4
Chengjiang, China 52 E4
Chengkou, China 52 B7
Ch'engtu = Chengdu, China 52 B5
Chengwu, China 50 G8
Chengxi Hu, China 53 A11
Chengyang, China 51 F11
Chenjiagang, China 51 G10
Chenkán, Mexico 115 D6
Chenxi, China 53 C8
Cheo Reo, Vietnam 58 F7
Cheom Ksan, Cambodia 58 E5
Chepelare, Bulgaria 39 H7
Chepén, Peru 124 B2
Chepes, Argentina 126 C2
Chepo, Panama 116 E4
Cheptsa →, Russia 41 B17
Cheptulil, Mt., Kenya 82 B4
Chequamegon B., U.S.A. 108 B9
Cher □, France 25 E9
Cher →, France 24 E7
Cherasco, Italy 32 D4
Cheratte, Belgium 17 G7
Cheraw, U.S.A. 105 H6
Cherbourg, France 24 C5
Cherchell, Algeria 75 A5
Cherdakly, Russia 41 D16
Cherdyn, Russia 44 C6
Cheremkhovo, Russia 45 D11
Cherepanovo, Russia 44 D9
Cherepovets, Russia 41 B10
Chergui, Chott ech, Algeria 75 B5
Cherikov, Belorussia 40 E7
Cherkassy, Ukraine 42 B5
Cherkasy = Cherkassy, Ukraine 42 B5
Cherkessk, Russia 43 D10
Cherlak, Russia 44 D8
Chernaya Kholunitsa, Russia 41 B17
Cherni, Bulgaria 38 G6
Chernigov, Ukraine 40 F7
Chernihiv = Chernigov, Ukraine 40 F7
Chernivtsi = Chernovtsy, Ukraine 42 B1
Chernobyl, Ukraine 40 F7
Chernogorsk, Russia 45 D10
Chernomorskoye, Ukraine 42 D5
Chernovskoye, Russia 41 B15
Chernovtsy, Ukraine 42 B1
Chernoye, Russia 45 B9
Chernyakhovsk, Russia 40 D2
Chernyshkovskiy, Russia 43 B10
Chernyshovskiy, Russia 45 C12
Cherokee, Iowa, U.S.A. 108 D7
Cherokee, Okla., U.S.A. 109 G5
Cherokees, Lake O' The, U.S.A. 109 G7
Cherquenco, Chile 128 A2
Cherrapunji, India 61 G17
Cherry Creek, U.S.A. 110 G6
Cherry Valley, U.S.A. 113 M10
Cherryvale, U.S.A. 109 G7
Cherskiy, Russia 45 C17
Cherskogo Khrebet, Russia 45 C15
Chertkovo, Russia 43 B9
Cherven, Belorussia 40 E6
Cherven-Bryag, Bulgaria 38 F7
Chervonograd, Ukraine 40 F4
Cherwell →, U.K. 13 F6
Chesapeake, U.S.A. 104 G7
Chesapeake B., U.S.A. 104 F7
Cheshire □, U.K. 12 D5
Cheshskaya Guba, Russia 44 C5
Cheslatta L., Canada 100 C3
Chesley, Canada 106 B3
Cheste, Spain 29 F4
Chester, U.K. 12 D5
Chester, Calif., U.S.A. 110 F3
Chester, Ill., U.S.A. 109 G10
Chester, Mont., U.S.A. 110 B8
Chester, Pa., U.S.A. 104 F8
Chester, S.C., U.S.A. 105 H5
Chesterfield, U.K. 12 D6
Chesterfield, Is., N. Cal. 92 J7
Chesterfield Inlet, Canada 96 B10
Chesterton Ra., Australia 91 D4
Chesterville, Canada 107 A9
Chesuncook L., U.S.A. 99 C6
Chetaibi, Algeria 75 A6
Chéticamp, Canada 99 C7
Chetumal, B. de, Mexico 115 D7
Chetwynd, Canada 100 B4
Chevanceaux, France 26 C3
Cheviot, The, U.K. 12 B5
Cheviot Hills, U.K. 12 B5
Cheviot Ra., Australia 90 D3
Chew Bahir, Ethiopia 77 G4
Chewelah, U.S.A. 110 B5
Cheyenne, Okla., U.S.A. 109 H5
Cheyenne, Wyo., U.S.A. 108 E2
Cheyenne →, U.S.A. 108 C4
Cheyenne Wells, U.S.A. 108 F3
Cheyne B., Australia 89 F2
Chhabra, India 62 G7
Chhapra, India 63 G11
Chhata, India 62 F7
Chhatarpur, India 63 G8
Chhep, Cambodia 58 F5
Chhindwara, India 63 H8
Chhlong, Cambodia 59 F5
Chhuk, Cambodia 59 G5
Chi →, Thailand 58 E5
Chiamis, Indonesia 57 G13
Chiamussu = Jiamusi, China 54 B8
Chiang Dao, Thailand 58 C2
Chiang Kham, Thailand 58 C3
Chiang Khan, Thailand 58 D3
Chiang Khong, Thailand 58 B3
Chiang Mai, Thailand 58 C2
Chiang Saen, Thailand 58 B3
Chiange, Angola 81 H2
Chiapa →, Mexico 115 D6
Chiapa de Corzo, Mexico 115 D6
Chiapas □, Mexico 115 D6
Chiaramonte Gulfi, Italy 35 E7
Chiaravalle, Italy 33 E10
Chiaravalle Centrale, Italy 35 D9
Chiari, Italy 32 C6
Chiasso, Switz. 23 E8
Chiatura, Georgia 43 E10
Chiautla, Mexico 115 D5
Chiávari, Italy 32 D6
Chiavenna, Italy 32 B6
Chiba, Japan 49 G10
Chibabava, Mozam. 85 C5
Chibatu, Indonesia 57 G12
Chibemba, Cunene, Angola 81 H2
Chibemba, Huila, Angola 84 B2
Chibia, Angola 81 H2
Chibougamau, Canada 98 C5
Chibougamau L., Canada 98 C5
Chibuk, Nigeria 79 C7
Chic-Chocs, Mts., Canada 99 C6
Chicacole = Srikakulam, India 61 K13
Chicago, U.S.A. 104 E2
Chicago Heights, U.S.A. 104 E2
Chichagof I., U.S.A. 100 B1
Chichaoua, Morocco 74 B3
Chicheng, China 50 D8
Chichester, U.K. 13 G7
Chichibu, Japan 49 F9
Ch'ich'ihaerh = Qiqihar, China 45 E13
Chickasha, U.S.A. 109 H5
Chiclana de la Frontera, Spain 31 J4
Chiclayo, Peru 124 B2
Chico, U.S.A. 112 F5
Chico →, Chubut, Argentina 128 B3
Chico →, Santa Cruz, Argentina 128 C3
Chicomo, Mozam. 85 C5
Chicontepec, Mexico 115 C5
Chicopee, U.S.A. 107 D12
Chicoutimi, Canada 99 C5
Chicualacuala, Mozam. 85 C5
Chidambaram, India 60 P11
Chidenguele, Mozam. 85 C5
Chidley, C., Canada 97 B13
Chiede, Angola 84 B2
Chiefs Pt., Canada 106 B3
Chiem Hoa, Vietnam 58 A5
Chiemsee, Germany 19 H8
Chiengi, Zambia 83 D2
Chiengmai = Chiang Mai, Thailand 58 C2
Chienti →, Italy 33 E10
Chieri, Italy 32 D4
Chiers →, France 25 C11
Chiese →, Italy 32 C7
Chieti, Italy 33 F11
Chièvres, Belgium 17 G3
Chifeng, China 51 C10
Chigirin, Ukraine 42 B5
Chignecto B., Canada 99 C7
Chigorodó, Colombia 120 B2
Chiguana, Bolivia 126 A2
Chiha-ri, N. Korea 51 E14
Chihli, G. of = Bo Hai, China 51 E10
Chihuahua, Mexico 114 B3
Chihuahua □, Mexico 114 B3
Chiili, Kazakhstan 44 E7
Chik Bollapur, India 60 N10
Chikmagalur, India 60 N9
Chikwawa, Malawi 83 F3
Chilac, Mexico 115 D5
Chilako →, Canada 100 C4
Chilam Chavki, Pakistan 63 B6
Chilanga, Zambia 83 F2
Chilapa, Mexico 115 D5
Chilas, Pakistan 63 B6
Chilaw, Sri Lanka 60 R11
Chilcotin →, Canada 100 C4
Childers, Australia 91 D5
Childress, U.S.A. 109 H4
Chile ■, S. Amer. 128 B2
Chile Chico, Chile 128 C2
Chile Rise, Pac. Oc. 93 L18
Chilecito, Argentina 126 B2
Chilete, Peru 124 B2
Chilia, Braţul →, Romania 38 D12
Chililabombwe, Zambia 83 E2
Chilin = Jilin, China 51 C14
Chilka L., India 61 K14
Chilko →, Canada 100 C4
Chilko, L., Canada 100 C4
Chillagoe, Australia 90 B3
Chillán, Chile 126 D1
Chillicothe, Ill., U.S.A. 108 E10
Chillicothe, Mo., U.S.A. 108 F8
Chillicothe, Ohio, U.S.A. 104 F4
Chilliwack, Canada 100 D4
Chilo, India 62 F5
Chiloane, I., Mozam. 85 C5
Chiloé □, Chile 128 B2
Chiloé, I. de, Chile 128 B2
Chilpancingo, Mexico 115 D5
Chiltern Hills, U.K. 13 F7
Chilton, U.S.A. 104 C1
Chiluage, Angola 80 F4
Chilubi, Zambia 83 E2
Chilubula, Zambia 83 E3
Chilumba, Malawi 83 E3
Chilwa, L., Malawi 83 F4
Chimaltitán, Mexico 114 C4
Chimán, Panama 116 E4
Chimay, Belgium 17 H4
Chimbay, Uzbekistan 44 E6
Chimborazo, Ecuador 120 D2
Chimborazo □, Ecuador 120 D2
Chimbote, Peru 124 B2
Chimkent, Kazakhstan 44 E7
Chimoio, Mozam. 83 F3
Chimpembe, Zambia 83 D2
Chin □, Burma 61 J18
Chin Ling Shan = Qinling Shandi, China 50 H5
China, Mexico 115 B5
China ■, Asia 50 E3
China Lake, U.S.A. 113 K9
Chinacota, Colombia 120 B3
Chinan = Jinan, China 50 F9
Chinandega, Nic. 116 D2
Chinati Peak, U.S.A. 109 K2
Chincha Alta, Peru 124 C2
Chinchilla, Australia 91 D5
Chinchilla de Monte Aragón, Spain 29 G3
Chinchón, Spain 28 E1
Chinchorro, Banco, Mexico 115 D7
Chinchou = Jinzhou, China 51 D11
Chincoteague, U.S.A. 104 G8
Chinde, Mozam. 83 F4
Chindo, S. Korea 51 G14
Chindwin →, Burma 61 J19
Chineni, India 63 C6
Chinga, Mozam. 83 F4
Chingola, Zambia 83 E2
Chingole, Malawi 83 E3
Ch'ingtao = Qingdao, China 51 F11
Chinguetti, Mauritania 74 D2
Chingune, Mozam. 85 C5
Chinhae, S. Korea 51 G15
Chinhanguanine, Mozam. 85 D5
Chinhoyi, Zimbabwe 83 F3
Chiniot, Pakistan 62 D5
Chínipas, Mexico 114 B3
Chinju, S. Korea 51 G15
Chinle, U.S.A. 111 H9
Chinnampo, N. Korea 51 E13
Chino, Japan 49 G9
Chino, U.S.A. 113 L9
Chino Valley, U.S.A. 111 J7
Chinon, France 24 E7
Chinook, Canada 101 C6
Chinook, U.S.A. 110 B9
Chinsali, Zambia 83 E3
Chióggia, Italy 33 C9
Chíos = Khíos, Greece 39 L9
Chipata, Zambia 83 E3
Chipewyan L., Canada 101 B9
Chipinge, Zimbabwe 83 G3
Chipiona, Spain 31 J4
Chipley, U.S.A. 105 K3
Chipman, Canada 99 C6
Chipoka, Malawi 83 E3
Chippenham, U.K. 13 F5
Chippewa →, U.S.A. 108 C8
Chippewa Falls, U.S.A. 108 C9
Chiquián, Peru 124 C2
Chiquimula, Guatemala 116 D2
Chiquinquira, Colombia 120 B3
Chiquitos, Llanos de, Bolivia 125 D5
Chir →, Russia 43 B10
Chirala, India 60 M12
Chiramba, Mozam. 83 F3
Chirawa, India 62 E6
Chirchik, Uzbekistan 44 E7
Chirgua →, Venezuela 120 B4
Chiricahua Peak, U.S.A. 111 L9
Chiriquí, G. de, Panama 116 E3
Chiriquí, L. de, Panama 116 E3
Chirivira Falls, Zimbabwe 83 G3
Chirmiri, India 61 H13
Chiromo, Malawi 81 H7
Chirpan, Bulgaria 38 G8
Chirripó Grande, Cerro, Costa Rica 116 E3
Chisamba, Zambia 83 E2
Chisapani Garhi, Nepal 61 F14
Chisholm, Canada 100 C6
Chishtian Mandi, Pakistan 62 E5
Chishui, China 52 C5
Chishui He →, China 52 C5
Chisimba Falls, Zambia 83 E3
Chişinău = Kishinev, Moldavia 42 C3
Chisone →, Italy 32 D4
Chisos Mts., U.S.A. 109 L3
Chistopol, Russia 41 D17
Chita, Colombia 120 B3
Chita, Russia 45 D12
Chitado, Angola 81 H2
Chitembo, Angola 81 G3
Chitipa, Malawi 83 D3
Chitose, Japan 48 C10
Chitral, Pakistan 60 B7
Chitré, Panama 116 E3
Chittagong, Bangla. 61 H17
Chittagong □, Bangla. 61 G17
Chittaurgarh, India 62 G6
Chittoor, India 60 N11
Chitungwiza, Zimbabwe 83 F3
Chiusa, Italy 33 B8
Chiusi, Italy 33 E8
Chiva, Spain 29 F4
Chivacoa, Venezuela 120 A4
Chivasso, Italy 32 C4
Chivay, Peru 124 D3
Chivhu, Zimbabwe 83 F3
Chivilcoy, Argentina 126 C4
Chiwanda, Tanzania 83 E3
Chixi, China 53 G9
Chizera, Zambia 83 E1
Chkalov = Orenburg, Russia 44 D6
Chkolovsk, Russia 41 C13
Chloride, U.S.A. 113 K12
Cho Bo, Vietnam 58 B5
Cho-do, N. Korea 51 E13
Cho Phuoc Hai, Vietnam 59 G6
Choba, Kenya 82 B4
Chobe National Park, Botswana 84 B3
Chochiwŏn, S. Korea 51 F14
Chociwel, Poland 20 B5
Chocó □, Colombia 120 B2
Chocontá, Colombia 120 B3
Choctawhatchee B., U.S.A. 103 D9
Chodecz, Poland 20 C9
Chodziez, Poland 20 C6
Choele Choel, Argentina 128 A3
Choisy-le-Roi, France 25 D9
Choix, Mexico 114 B3
Chojnice, Poland 20 B7
Chojnów, Poland 20 D5
Chōkai-San, Japan 48 E10
Choke, Ethiopia 77 E4
Chokurdakh, Russia 45 B15
Cholame, U.S.A. 112 K6
Cholet, France 24 E6
Choluteca, Honduras 116 D2
Choluteca →, Honduras 116 D2
Chom Bung, Thailand 58 F2
Chom Thong, Thailand 58 C2
Choma, Zambia 83 F2
Chomen Swamp, Ethiopia 77 F4
Chomun, India 62 F6
Chomutov, Czech. 20 E3
Chon Buri, Thailand 58 F3
Chon Thanh, Vietnam 59 G6
Chonan, S. Korea 51 F14
Chone, Ecuador 120 D2
Chong Kai, Cambodia 58 F4
Chong Mek, Thailand 58 E5
Chong'an, China 53 D12
Chongde, China 53 B13
Chŏngdo, S. Korea 51 G15
Chŏngha, S. Korea 51 F15
Chongjin, N. Korea 51 D15
Chŏngju, N. Korea 51 E13
Chŏngju, S. Korea 51 F14
Chongli, China 50 D8
Chongming, China 53 B13
Chongming Dao, China 53 B13
Chongoyape, Peru 124 B2
Chongqing, Sichuan, China 52 C6
Chongqing, Sichuan, China 52 B4
Chongren, China 53 D11
Chŏngŭp, S. Korea 51 G14
Chongzuo, China 52 F6
Chŏnju, S. Korea 51 G14
Chonos, Arch. de los, Chile 128 C2
Chopim →, Brazil 127 B5
Chorbat La, India 63 B7
Chorley, U.K. 12 D5
Chornobyl = Chernobyl, Ukraine 40 F7
Chorolque, Cerro, Bolivia 126 A2
Chorregon, Australia 90 C3
Chortkov, Ukraine 40 G4
Chŏrwŏn, S. Korea 51 E14
Chorzów, Poland 20 E8
Chos-Malal, Argentina 126 D1
Chosan, N. Korea 51 D13
Choszczno, Poland 20 B5
Chota, Peru 124 B2
Choteau, U.S.A. 110 C7
Chotila, India 62 H4
Chowchilla, U.S.A. 111 H3
Choybalsan, Mongolia 54 B6
Christchurch, N.Z. 87 K4
Christchurch, U.K. 13 G6
Christian I., Canada 106 B4
Christiana, S. Africa 84 D4
Christiansfeld, Denmark 11 J3
Christiansted, Virgin Is. 117 C7
Christie B., Canada 101 A6
Christina →, Canada 101 B6
Christmas Cr. →, Australia 88 C4
Christmas Creek, Australia 88 C4
Christmas I. = Kiritimati, Kiribati 93 G12
Christmas I., Ind. Oc. 92 J2
Christopher L., Australia 89 D4
Chrudim, Czech. 20 F5
Chrzanów, Poland 20 E9
Chtimba, Malawi 83 E3

Chu, *Kazakhstan* 44 E8
Chu →, *Vietnam* 58 C5
Chu Chua, *Canada* 100 C4
Chu Lai, *Vietnam* 58 E7
Chu Xian, *China* 53 A12
Ch'uanchou = Quanzhou, *China* 53 E12
Chuankou, *China* 50 G6
Chūbu □, *Japan* 49 F8
Chubut □, *Argentina* 128 B3
Chubut →, *Argentina* 128 B3
Chuchi L., *Canada* 100 B4
Chudovo, *Russia* 40 B7
Chudskoye, Oz., *Estonia* 40 B5
Chūgoku □, *Japan* 49 G6
Chūgoku-Sanchi, *Japan* 49 G6
Chuguyev, *Ukraine* 42 B7
Chugwater, *U.S.A.* 108 E2
Chukhloma, *Russia* 41 B13
Chukotskiy Khrebet, *Russia* 45 C18
Chukotskoye More, *Russia* 45 C19
Chula Vista, *U.S.A.* 113 N9
Chulman, *Russia* 45 D13
Chulucanas, *Peru* 124 B1
Chulumani, *Bolivia* 124 D4
Chulym →, *Russia* 44 D9
Chum Phae, *Thailand* 58 D4
Chum Saeng, *Thailand* 58 E3
Chuma, *Bolivia* 124 D4
Chumar, *India* 63 C8
Chumbicha, *Argentina* 126 B2
Chumerna, *Bulgaria* 38 G8
Chumikan, *Russia* 45 D14
Chumphon, *Thailand* 59 G2
Chumpi, *Peru* 124 D3
Chumuare, *Mozam.* 83 E3
Chumunjin, *S. Korea* 51 F15
Chuna →, *Russia* 45 D10
Chun'an, *China* 53 C12
Chunchŏn, *S. Korea* 51 F14
Chunchura, *India* 63 H13
Chunga, *Zambia* 83 F2
Chunggang-ŭp, *N. Korea* 51 D14
Chunghwa, *N. Korea* 51 E13
Chungju, *S. Korea* 51 F14
Chungking = Chongqing, *China* 52 C6
Chungmu, *S. Korea* 51 G15
Chungt'iaoshan = Zhongtiao Shan, *China* 50 G6
Chunian, *Pakistan* 62 D6
Chunya, *Tanzania* 83 D3
Chunya □, *Tanzania* 82 D3
Chunyang, *China* 51 C15
Chuquibamba, *Peru* 124 D3
Chuquibambilla, *Peru* 124 C3
Chuquicamata, *Chile* 126 A2
Chuquisaca □, *Bolivia* 125 E5
Chur, *Switz.* 23 C9
Churachandpur, *India* 61 G18
Churchill, *Canada* 101 B10
Churchill →, *Man., Canada* 101 B10
Churchill →, *Nfld., Canada* 99 B7
Churchill, C., *Canada* 101 B10
Churchill Falls, *Canada* 99 B7
Churchill L., *Canada* 101 B7
Churchill Pk., *Canada* 100 B3
Churfisten, *Switz.* 23 B8
Churu, *India* 62 E6
Churwalden, *Switz.* 23 C9
Chushal, *India* 63 C8
Chusovoy, *Russia* 44 D6
Chuuronjang, *N. Korea* 51 D15
Chuvash Republic □, *Russia* 41 D15
Chuwārtah, *Iraq* 64 C5
Chuxiong, *China* 52 E3
Ci Xian, *China* 50 F8
Ciacova, *Romania* 38 D4
Cianjur, *Indonesia* 57 G12
Cibadok, *Indonesia* 57 G12
Cibatu, *Indonesia* 57 G12
Cibola, *U.S.A.* 113 M12
Cicero, *U.S.A.* 104 E2
Cícero Dantas, *Brazil* 122 D4
Cidacos →, *Spain* 28 C3
Cide, *Turkey* 42 F5
Ciechanów, *Poland* 20 C10
Ciego de Avila, *Cuba* 116 B4
Ciénaga, *Colombia* 120 A3
Ciénaga de Oro, *Colombia* 120 B2
Cienfuegos, *Cuba* 116 B3
Cieplice Śląskie Zdrój, *Poland* 20 E5
Cierp, *France* 26 F4
Cíes, Is., *Spain* 30 C2
Cieszyn, *Poland* 20 F8
Cieza, *Spain* 29 G3
Çifteler, *Turkey* 66 D4
Cifuentes, *Spain* 28 E2
Cihanbeyli, *Turkey* 66 D5
Cihuatlán, *Mexico* 114 D4
Cijara, Pantano de, *Spain* 31 F6
Cijulang, *Indonesia* 57 G13
Cikajang, *Indonesia* 57 G12
Cikampek, *Indonesia* 57 G12
Cilacap, *Indonesia* 57 G13
Çıldır, *Turkey* 43 F10
Çıldır Gölü, *Turkey* 67 C10
Cili, *China* 53 C8
Cilicia, *Turkey* 66 E5
Cilo Dağı, *Turkey* 67 E10
Cima, *U.S.A.* 113 K11
Cimahi, *Indonesia* 57 G12
Cimarron, *Kans., U.S.A.* 109 G4
Cimarron, *N. Mex., U.S.A.* 109 G2
Cimarron →, *U.S.A.* 109 G6
Cimone, Mte., *Italy* 32 D7
Cîmpina, *Romania* 38 D8
Cîmpulung, *Argeş, Romania* 38 D8
Cîmpulung, *Suceava, Romania* 38 B8
Çinar, *Turkey* 67 E9
Cinca →, *Spain* 28 D5
Cincinnati, *U.S.A.* 104 F3
Cîndeşti, *Romania* 38 D9
Çine, *Turkey* 66 E3
Ciney, *Belgium* 17 H6
Cíngoli, *Italy* 33 E10
Cinigiano, *Italy* 33 F8
Cinto, Mte., *France* 27 F12
Ciorani, *Romania* 38 E9
Čiovo, *Croatia* 33 E13
Cipó, *Brazil* 122 D4
Circeo, Monte, *Italy* 34 A6
Çirçir, *Turkey* 66 C7
Circle, *Alaska, U.S.A.* 96 B5
Circle, *Mont., U.S.A.* 108 B2
Circleville, *Ohio, U.S.A.* 104 F4
Circleville, *Utah, U.S.A.* 111 G7
Cirebon, *Indonesia* 57 G13
Cirencester, *U.K.* 13 F6
Cirey-sur-Vezouze, *France* 25 D13
Ciriè, *Italy* 32 C4
Cirium, *Cyprus* 37 E11
Cirò, *Italy* 35 C10
Ciron →, *France* 26 D3
Cisco, *U.S.A.* 109 J5
Ciskei □, *S. Africa* 85 E4
Cislău, *Romania* 38 D9
Cisneros, *Colombia* 120 B2
Cisterna di Latina, *Italy* 34 A5
Cisternino, *Italy* 35 B10
Citaré →, *Brazil* 121 C7
Citeli-Ckaro, *Georgia* 43 F12
Citlaltépetl, *Mexico* 115 D5
Citrus Heights, *U.S.A.* 112 G5
Citrusdal, *S. Africa* 84 E2
Città della Pieve, *Italy* 33 F9
Città di Castello, *Italy* 33 E9
Città Sant' Angelo, *Italy* 33 F11
Cittadella, *Italy* 33 C8
Cittaducale, *Italy* 33 F9
Cittanova, *Italy* 35 D9
Ciucaş, *Romania* 38 D8
Ciudad Altamirano, *Mexico* 114 D4
Ciudad Bolívar, *Venezuela* 121 B5
Ciudad Camargo, *Mexico* 114 B3
Ciudad Chetumal, *Mexico* 115 D7
Ciudad de Valles, *Mexico* 115 C5
Ciudad del Carmen, *Mexico* 115 D6
Ciudad Delicias = Delicias, *Mexico* 114 B3
Ciudad Guayana, *Venezuela* 121 B5
Ciudad Guerrero, *Mexico* 114 B3
Ciudad Guzmán, *Mexico* 114 D4
Ciudad Juárez, *Mexico* 114 A3
Ciudad Madero, *Mexico* 115 C5
Ciudad Mante, *Mexico* 115 C5
Ciudad Obregón, *Mexico* 114 B3
Ciudad Ojeda, *Venezuela* 120 A3
Ciudad Real, *Spain* 31 G7
Ciudad Real □, *Spain* 31 G7
Ciudad Rodrigo, *Spain* 30 E4
Ciudad Trujillo = Santo Domingo, *Dom. Rep.* 117 C6
Ciudad Victoria, *Mexico* 115 C5
Ciudadela, *Spain* 36 B10
Ciulniţa, *Romania* 38 E10
Civa Burnu, *Turkey* 66 C7
Cividale del Friuli, *Italy* 33 B10
Cívita Castellana, *Italy* 33 F9
Civitanova Marche, *Italy* 33 E10
Civitavécchia, *Italy* 33 F8
Civitella del Tronto, *Italy* 33 F10
Civray, *France* 26 B4
Çivril, *Turkey* 66 D3
Cixerri →, *Italy* 34 C1
Cizre, *Turkey* 67 E10
Clacton-on-Sea, *U.K.* 13 F9
Clain →, *France* 24 F7
Claire, L., *Canada* 100 B6
Clairemont, *U.S.A.* 109 J4
Clairton, *U.S.A.* 106 F5
Clairvaux-les-Lacs, *France* 27 B9
Clallam Bay, *U.S.A.* 112 B2
Clamecy, *France* 25 E10
Clanton, *U.S.A.* 105 J2
Clanwilliam, *S. Africa* 84 E2
Clara, *Ireland* 15 C4
Clara →, *Australia* 90 B3
Claraville, *U.S.A.* 113 K8
Clare, *Australia* 91 E2
Clare, *U.S.A.* 104 D3
Clare □, *Ireland* 15 D3
Clare →, *Ireland* 15 C2
Clare I., *Ireland* 15 C2
Claremont, *Calif., U.S.A.* 113 L9
Claremont, *N.H., U.S.A.* 107 C12
Claremont Pt., *Australia* 90 A3
Claremore, *U.S.A.* 109 G7
Claremorris, *Ireland* 15 C3
Clarence →, *Australia* 91 D5
Clarence →, *N.Z.* 87 K4
Clarence, I., *Chile* 128 D2
Clarence I., *Antarctica* 5 C18
Clarence Str., *Australia* 88 B5
Clarence Str., *U.S.A.* 100 B2
Clarence Town, *Bahamas* 117 B5
Clarendon, *Ark., U.S.A.* 109 H9
Clarendon, *Tex., U.S.A.* 109 H4
Clarenville, *Canada* 99 C9
Claresholm, *Canada* 100 C6
Clarie Coast, *Antarctica* 5 C9
Clarinda, *U.S.A.* 108 E7
Clarion, *Iowa, U.S.A.* 108 D8
Clarion, *Pa., U.S.A.* 106 E5
Clarion →, *U.S.A.* 106 E5
Clark, *U.S.A.* 108 C6
Clark, Pt., *Canada* 106 B3
Clark Fork, *U.S.A.* 110 B5
Clark Fork →, *U.S.A.* 110 B5
Clark Hill Res., *U.S.A.* 105 J4
Clarkdale, *U.S.A.* 111 J7
Clarke City, *Canada* 99 B6
Clarke I., *Australia* 90 G4
Clarke L., *Canada* 101 C7
Clarke Ra., *Australia* 90 C4
Clark's Fork →, *U.S.A.* 110 D9
Clark's Harbour, *Canada* 99 D6
Clarks Summit, *U.S.A.* 107 E9
Clarksburg, *U.S.A.* 104 F5
Clarksdale, *U.S.A.* 109 H9
Clarkston, *U.S.A.* 110 C5
Clarksville, *Ark., U.S.A.* 109 H8
Clarksville, *Tenn., U.S.A.* 105 G2
Clarksville, *Tex., U.S.A.* 109 J7
Claro →, *Brazil* 123 E1
Clatskanie, *U.S.A.* 112 D3
Claude, *U.S.A.* 109 H4
Claveria, *Phil.* 55 B4
Clay, *U.S.A.* 112 G5
Clay Center, *U.S.A.* 108 F6
Claypool, *U.S.A.* 111 K8
Claysville, *U.S.A.* 106 F4
Clayton, *Idaho, U.S.A.* 110 D6
Clayton, *N. Mex., U.S.A.* 109 G3
Cle Elum, *U.S.A.* 110 C3
Clear, C., *Ireland* 15 E2
Clear I., *Ireland* 15 E2
Clear L., *U.S.A.* 112 F4
Clear Lake, *S. Dak., U.S.A.* 108 C6
Clear Lake, *Wash., U.S.A.* 110 B2
Clear Lake Reservoir, *U.S.A.* 110 F3
Clearfield, *Pa., U.S.A.* 104 E6
Clearfield, *Utah, U.S.A.* 110 F7
Clearlake Highlands, *U.S.A.* 112 G4
Clearmont, *U.S.A.* 110 D10
Clearwater, *Canada* 100 C4
Clearwater, *U.S.A.* 105 M4
Clearwater →, *Alta., Canada* 100 C6
Clearwater →, *Alta., Canada* 101 B6
Clearwater Cr. →, *Canada* 100 A3
Clearwater Mts., *U.S.A.* 110 C6
Clearwater Prov. Park, *Canada* 101 C8
Cleburne, *U.S.A.* 109 J6
Cleethorpes, *U.K.* 12 D7
Cleeve Hill, *U.K.* 13 F6
Clelles, *France* 27 D9
Clemency, *Lux.* 17 J7
Clerke Reef, *Australia* 88 C2
Clermont, *Australia* 90 C4
Clermont, *France* 25 C9
Clermont-en-Argonne, *France* 25 C12
Clermont-Ferrand, *France* 26 C7
Clermont-l'Hérault, *France* 26 E7
Clerval, *France* 25 E13
Clervaux, *Lux.* 17 H8
Cléry-St.-André, *France* 25 E8
Cles, *Italy* 32 B8
Cleveland, *Australia* 91 D5
Cleveland, *Miss., U.S.A.* 109 J9
Cleveland, *Ohio, U.S.A.* 106 E3
Cleveland, *Okla., U.S.A.* 109 G6
Cleveland, *Tenn., U.S.A.* 105 H3
Cleveland, *Tex., U.S.A.* 109 K7
Cleveland □, *U.K.* 12 C9
Cleveland, C., *Australia* 90 B4
Cleveland Heights, *U.S.A.* 106 E3
Clevelândia, *Brazil* 127 B5
Clevelândia do Norte, *Brazil* 121 C7
Clew B., *Ireland* 15 C2
Clewiston, *U.S.A.* 105 M5
Clifden, *Ireland* 15 C1
Clifden, *N.Z.* 87 M1
Cliffdell, *U.S.A.* 112 D5
Clifton, *Australia* 91 D5
Clifton, *Ariz., U.S.A.* 111 K9
Clifton, *Tex., U.S.A.* 109 K6
Clifton Beach, *Australia* 90 B4
Clifton Forge, *U.S.A.* 104 G6
Clifton Hills, *Australia* 91 D2
Climax, *Canada* 101 D7
Clinch →, *U.S.A.* 105 H3
Clingmans Dome, *U.S.A.* 105 H4
Clint, *U.S.A.* 111 L10
Clinton, *B.C., Canada* 100 C4
Clinton, *Ont., Canada* 98 D3
Clinton, *N.Z.* 87 M2
Clinton, *Ark., U.S.A.* 109 H8
Clinton, *Ill., U.S.A.* 108 E10
Clinton, *Ind., U.S.A.* 104 F2
Clinton, *Iowa, U.S.A.* 108 E9
Clinton, *Mass., U.S.A.* 107 D13
Clinton, *Mo., U.S.A.* 108 F8
Clinton, *N.C., U.S.A.* 105 H6
Clinton, *Okla., U.S.A.* 109 H5
Clinton, *S.C., U.S.A.* 105 H5
Clinton, *Tenn., U.S.A.* 105 G3
Clinton, *Wash., U.S.A.* 112 C4
Clinton C., *Australia* 90 C5
Clinton Colden L., *Canada* 96 B9
Clintonville, *U.S.A.* 108 C10
Clipperton, I., *Pac. Oc.* 93 F17
Clisson, *France* 24 E5
Clive L., *Canada* 100 A5
Cliza, *Bolivia* 125 D4
Cloates, Pt., *Australia* 88 D1
Clocolan, *S. Africa* 85 D4
Clodomira, *Argentina* 126 B3
Clonakilty, *Ireland* 15 E3
Clonakilty B., *Ireland* 15 E3
Cloncurry, *Australia* 90 C3
Cloncurry →, *Australia* 90 B3
Clones, *Ireland* 15 B4
Clonmel, *Ireland* 15 D4
Cloppenburg, *Germany* 18 C4
Cloquet, *U.S.A.* 108 B8
Clorinda, *Argentina* 126 B4
Cloud Peak, *U.S.A.* 110 D10
Cloudcroft, *U.S.A.* 111 K11
Cloverdale, *U.S.A.* 112 G4
Clovis, *Calif., U.S.A.* 111 H4
Clovis, *N. Mex., U.S.A.* 109 H3
Cloyes-sur-le-Loir, *France* 24 E8
Cluj-Napoca, *Romania* 38 C6
Clunes, *Australia* 91 F3
Cluny, *France* 27 B8
Cluses, *France* 27 B10
Clusone, *Italy* 32 C6
Clutha →, *N.Z.* 87 M2
Clwyd □, *U.K.* 12 D4
Clwyd →, *U.K.* 12 D4
Clyde, *N.Z.* 87 L2
Clyde, *U.S.A.* 106 C8
Clyde →, *U.K.* 14 F4
Clyde, Firth of, *U.K.* 14 F4
Clyde River, *Canada* 97 A13
Clydebank, *U.K.* 14 F4
Clymer, *U.S.A.* 106 D5
Côa →, *Portugal* 30 D3
Coachella, *U.S.A.* 113 M10
Coachella Canal, *U.S.A.* 113 N12
Coahoma, *U.S.A.* 109 J4
Coahuayana →, *Mexico* 114 D4
Coahuayutla, *Mexico* 114 D4
Coahuila □, *Mexico* 114 B4
Coal →, *Canada* 100 B3
Coalane, *Mozam.* 83 F4
Coalcomán, *Mexico* 114 D4
Coaldale, *Canada* 100 D6
Coalgate, *U.S.A.* 109 H6
Coalinga, *U.S.A.* 111 H3
Coalville, *U.K.* 12 E6
Coalville, *U.S.A.* 110 F8
Coaraci, *Brazil* 123 D4
Coari, *Brazil* 121 D5
Coari →, *Brazil* 121 D5
Coari, L. de, *Brazil* 121 D5
Coast □, *Kenya* 82 C4
Coast Mts., *Canada* 100 C3
Coast Ranges, *U.S.A.* 112 E4
Coatbridge, *U.K.* 14 F4
Coatepec, *Mexico* 115 D5
Coatepeque, *Guatemala* 116 D1
Coatesville, *U.S.A.* 104 F8
Coaticook, *Canada* 99 C5
Coats I., *Canada* 97 B11
Coats Land, *Antarctica* 5 D1
Coatzacoalcos, *Mexico* 115 D6
Cobalt, *Canada* 98 C4
Cobán, *Guatemala* 116 C1
Cobar, *Australia* 91 E4
Cóbh, *Ireland* 15 E3
Cobham, *Australia* 91 E3
Cobija, *Bolivia* 124 C4
Cobleskill, *U.S.A.* 107 D10
Coboconk, *Canada* 106 B6
Cobourg, *Canada* 98 D4
Cobourg Pen., *Australia* 88 B5
Cobram, *Australia* 91 F4
Cobre, *U.S.A.* 110 F6
Cóbué, *Mozam.* 83 E3
Coburg, *Germany* 19 E6
Coca, *Spain* 30 D6
Coca →, *Ecuador* 120 D2
Cocachacra, *Peru* 124 D3
Cocal, *Brazil* 122 B3
Cocanada = Kakinada, *India* 61 L13
Cocentaina, *Spain* 29 G4
Cochabamba, *Bolivia* 125 D4
Coche, I., *Venezuela* 121 A5
Cochem, *Germany* 19 E3
Cochemane, *Mozam.* 83 F3
Cochin, *India* 60 Q10
Cochin China = Nam-Phan, *Vietnam* 59 G6
Cochise, *U.S.A.* 111 K9
Cochran, *U.S.A.* 105 J4
Cochrane, *Alta., Canada* 100 C6
Cochrane, *Ont., Canada* 98 C3
Cochrane →, *Canada* 101 B8
Cochrane, L., *Chile* 128 C2
Cockburn, *Australia* 91 E3
Cockburn, Canal, *Chile* 128 D2
Cockburn I., *Canada* 98 C3
Cockburn Ra., *Australia* 88 C4
Cocklebiddy Motel, *Australia* 89 F4
Coco →, *Cent. Amer.* 116 D3
Coco, Pta., *Colombia* 120 C2
Cocoa, *U.S.A.* 105 L5
Cocobeach, *Gabon* 80 D1
Côcos, *Brazil* 123 D3
Côcos →, *Brazil* 123 D3
Cocos, I. del, *Pac. Oc.* 93 G19
Cocos Is., *Ind. Oc.* 92 J1
Cod, C., *U.S.A.* 103 B13
Codajás, *Brazil* 121 D5
Codera, C., *Venezuela* 120 A4
Coderre, *Canada* 101 C7
Codigoro, *Italy* 33 D9
Codó, *Brazil* 122 B3
Codogno, *Italy* 32 C6
Codpa, *Chile* 124 D4
Codróipo, *Italy* 33 C10
Cody, *U.S.A.* 110 D9
Coe Hill, *Canada* 98 D4
Coelemu, *Chile* 126 D1
Coelho Neto, *Brazil* 122 B3
Coen, *Australia* 90 A3
Coeroeni →, *Surinam* 121 C6
Coesfeld, *Germany* 18 D3
Cœur d'Alene, *U.S.A.* 110 C5
Cœur d'Alene L., *U.S.A.* 110 C5
Coevorden, *Neths.* 16 C9
Cofete, *Canary Is.* 36 F5
Coffeyville, *U.S.A.* 109 G7
Coffin B., *Australia* 91 E2
Coffin Bay Peninsula, *Australia* 91 E2
Coffs Harbour, *Australia* 91 E5
Cofrentes, *Spain* 29 F3
Cogealac, *Romania* 38 E11
Coghinas →, *Italy* 34 B1
Coghinas, L. di, *Italy* 34 B2
Cognac, *France* 26 C3
Cogne, *Italy* 32 C4
Cogolludo, *Spain* 28 E1
Cohagen, *U.S.A.* 110 C10
Cohoes, *U.S.A.* 107 D11
Cohuna, *Australia* 91 F3
Coiba, I., *Panama* 116 E3
Coig →, *Argentina* 128 D3
Coihaique, *Chile* 128 C2
Coimbatore, *India* 60 P10
Coimbra, *Brazil* 125 D6
Coimbra, *Portugal* 30 E2
Coimbra □, *Portugal* 30 E2
Coín, *Spain* 31 J6
Coipasa, L. de, *Bolivia* 124 D4
Coipasa, Salar de, *Bolivia* 124 D4
Cojata, *Peru* 124 D4
Cojedes □, *Venezuela* 120 B4
Cojedes →, *Venezuela* 120 B4
Cojimies, *Ecuador* 120 C1
Cojocna, *Romania* 38 C6
Cojutepequé, *El Salv.* 116 D2
Cokeville, *U.S.A.* 110 E8
Colac, *Australia* 91 F3
Colares, *Portugal* 31 G1
Colatina, *Brazil* 123 E3
Colbeck, C., *Antarctica* 5 D13
Colbinabbin, *Australia* 91 F3
Colborne, *Canada* 106 B7
Colby, *U.S.A.* 108 F4
Colchagua □, *Chile* 126 C1
Colchester, *U.K.* 13 F8
Coldstream, *U.K.* 14 F6
Coldwater, *Canada* 106 B5
Coldwater, *U.S.A.* 109 G5
Colebrook, *Australia* 90 G4
Colebrook, *U.S.A.* 107 B13
Coleman, *Canada* 100 D6
Coleman, *U.S.A.* 109 K5
Coleman →, *Australia* 90 B3
Colenso, *S. Africa* 85 D4
Coleraine, *Australia* 91 F3
Coleraine, *U.K.* 15 A5
Coleraine □, *U.K.* 15 A5
Coleridge, L., *N.Z.* 87 K3
Colesberg, *S. Africa* 84 E4
Coleville, *U.S.A.* 112 G7
Colfax, *Calif., U.S.A.* 112 F6
Colfax, *La., U.S.A.* 109 K8
Colfax, *Wash., U.S.A.* 110 C5
Colhué Huapi, L., *Argentina* 128 C3
Cólico, *Italy* 32 B6
Coligny, *France* 27 B9
Coligny, *S. Africa* 85 D4
Colima, *Mexico* 114 D4
Colima □, *Mexico* 114 D4
Colima, Nevado de, *Mexico* 114 D4
Colina, *Chile* 126 C1
Colina do Norte, *Guinea-Biss.* 78 C2
Colinas, *Goiás, Brazil* 123 D2
Colinas, *Maranhão, Brazil* 122 C3
Coll, *U.K.* 14 E2
Collaguasi, *Chile* 126 A2
Collarada, Peña, *Spain* 28 C4
Collarenebri, *Australia* 91 D4
Collbran, *U.S.A.* 111 G10
Colle di Val d'Elsa, *Italy* 33 E8
Colle Salvetti, *Italy* 32 E7
Colle Sannita, *Italy* 35 A7
Colléchio, *Italy* 32 D7
Colleen Bawn, *Zimbabwe* 83 G2
College Park, *U.S.A.* 105 J3
Collette, *Canada* 99 C6
Collie, *Australia* 89 F2

Collier B., *Australia* 88 C3
Collier Ra., *Australia* 88 D2
Colline Metallifere, *Italy* 32 E7
Collingwood, *Canada* 98 D3
Collingwood, *N.Z.* 87 J4
Collins, *Canada* 98 B2
Collinsville, *Australia* 90 C4
Collipulli, *Chile* 126 D1
Collo, *Algeria* 75 A6
Collonges, *France* 27 B9
Collooney, *Ireland* 15 B3
Colmar, *France* 25 D14
Colmars, *France* 27 D10
Colmenar, *Spain* 31 J6
Colmenar de Oreja, *Spain* 28 E1
Colmenar Viejo, *Spain* 30 E7
Colne, *U.K.* 12 D5
Colo →, *Australia* 91 E5
Cologna Véneta, *Italy* 33 C8
Cologne = Köln, *Germany* 18 E2
Colom, I., *Spain* 36 B11
Coloma, *U.S.A.* 112 G6
Colomb-Béchar = Béchar, *Algeria* 75 B4
Colombey-les-Belles, *France* 25 D12
Colombey-les-Deux-Églises, *France* 25 D11
Colômbia, *Brazil* 123 F2
Colombia ■, *S. Amer.* 120 C3
Colombier, *Switz.* 22 C3
Colombo, *Sri Lanka* 60 R11
Colome, *U.S.A.* 108 D5
Colón, *Argentina* 126 C4
Colón, *Cuba* 116 B3
Colón, *Panama* 116 E4
Colón, *Peru* 124 A1
Colona, *Australia* 89 F5
Colonella, *Italy* 33 F10
Colonia, *Uruguay* 126 C4
Colonia de San Jordi, *Spain* 36 B9
Colonia Dora, *Argentina* 126 B3
Colonial Heights, *U.S.A.* 104 G7
Colonne, C. delle, *Italy* 35 C10
Colonsay, *Canada* 101 C7
Colonsay, *U.K.* 14 E2
Colorado □, *U.S.A.* 111 G10
Colorado →, *Argentina* 128 A4
Colorado →, *N. Amer.* 111 L6
Colorado →, *U.S.A.* 109 L7
Colorado City, *U.S.A.* 109 J4
Colorado Desert, *U.S.A.* 102 D3
Colorado Plateau, *U.S.A.* 111 H8
Colorado River Aqueduct, *U.S.A.* 113 L12
Colorado Springs, *U.S.A.* 108 F2
Colorno, *Italy* 32 D7
Colotlán, *Mexico* 114 C4
Colquechaca, *Bolivia* 125 D4
Colton, *Calif., U.S.A.* 113 L9
Colton, *N.Y., U.S.A.* 107 B10
Colton, *Wash., U.S.A.* 110 C5
Columbia, *La., U.S.A.* 109 J8
Columbia, *Miss., U.S.A.* 109 K10
Columbia, *Mo., U.S.A.* 108 F8
Columbia, *Pa., U.S.A.* 107 F8
Columbia, *S.C., U.S.A.* 105 H5
Columbia, *Tenn., U.S.A.* 105 H2
Columbia →, *U.S.A.* 110 C1
Columbia, C., *Canada* 4 A4
Columbia, District of □, *U.S.A.* 104 F7
Columbia, Mt., *Canada* 100 C5
Columbia Basin, *U.S.A.* 110 C4
Columbia Falls, *U.S.A.* 110 B6
Columbia Heights, *U.S.A.* 108 C8
Columbiana, *U.S.A.* 106 F4
Columbretes, Is., *Spain* 28 F5
Columbus, *Ga., U.S.A.* 105 J3
Columbus, *Ind., U.S.A.* 104 F3
Columbus, *Kans., U.S.A.* 109 G7
Columbus, *Miss., U.S.A.* 105 J1
Columbus, *Mont., U.S.A.* 110 D9
Columbus, *N. Dak., U.S.A.* 108 A3
Columbus, *N. Mex., U.S.A.* 111 L10
Columbus, *Nebr., U.S.A.* 108 E6
Columbus, *Ohio, U.S.A.* 104 F4
Columbus, *Tex., U.S.A.* 109 L6
Columbus, *Wis., U.S.A.* 108 D10
Colunga, *Spain* 30 B5
Colusa, *U.S.A.* 112 F4
Colville, *U.S.A.* 110 B5
Colville →, *U.S.A.* 96 A4
Colville, C., *N.Z.* 87 G5
Colwyn Bay, *U.K.* 12 D4
Coma, *Ethiopia* 77 F4
Comácchio, *Italy* 33 D9
Comalcalco, *Mexico* 115 D6
Comallo, *Argentina* 128 B2
Comanche, *Okla., U.S.A.* 109 H6
Comanche, *Tex., U.S.A.* 109 K5
Comandante Luis Piedrabuena, *Argentina* 128 C3
Comăneşti, *Romania* 38 C9
Comarapa, *Bolivia* 125 D5
Comayagua, *Honduras* 116 D2
Combahee →, *U.S.A.* 105 J5
Combeaufontaine, *France* 25 E12
Comber, *Canada* 106 D2
Comblain-au-Pont, *Belgium* 17 H7
Combles, *France* 25 B9
Combourg, *France* 24 D5
Combronde, *France* 26 C7
Comeragh Mts., *Ireland* 15 D4
Comet, *Australia* 90 C4
Comilla, *Bangla.* 61 H17
Comines, *Belgium* 17 G1
Comino, *Malta* 37 C1
Comino, C., *Italy* 34 B2
Cómiso, *Italy* 35 F7
Comitán, *Mexico* 115 D6
Commentry, *France* 26 B6
Commerce, *Ga., U.S.A.* 105 H4
Commerce, *Tex., U.S.A.* 109 J7
Commercy, *France* 25 D12
Commewijne □, *Surinam* 121 B7
Committee B., *Canada* 97 B11
Commonwealth B., *Antarctica* 5 C10
Commonwealth of Independent States ■, *Eurasia* 45 D11
Commoron Cr. →, *Australia* 91 D5
Communism Pk. = Kommunizma, Pik, *Tajikistan* 44 F8
Como, *Italy* 32 C6
Como, L. di, *Italy* 32 B6
Comodoro Rivadavia, *Argentina* 128 C3
Comorin, C., *India* 60 Q10
Comoro Is. = Comoros ■, *Ind. Oc.* 71 H8
Comoros ■, *Ind. Oc.* 71 H8
Comox, *Canada* 100 D4
Compiègne, *France* 25 C9
Comporta, *Portugal* 31 G2
Compostela, *Mexico* 114 C4
Comprida, I., *Brazil* 127 A6
Compton, *U.S.A.* 113 M8
Compton Downs, *Australia* 91 E4
Con Cuong, *Vietnam* 58 C5
Con Son, Is., *Vietnam* 59 H6
Cona Niyeu, *Argentina* 128 B3
Conakry, *Guinea* 78 D2
Conara Junction, *Australia* 90 G4
Concarneau, *France* 24 E3
Conceição, *Brazil* 122 C4
Conceição, *Mozam.* 83 F4
Conceição da Barra, *Brazil* 123 E4
Conceição do Araguaia, *Brazil* 122 C2
Conceição do Canindé, *Brazil* 122 C3
Concepción, *Argentina* 126 B2
Concepción, *Bolivia* 125 D5
Concepción, *Chile* 126 D1
Concepción, *Mexico* 115 D6
Concepción, *Paraguay* 126 A4
Concepción, *Peru* 124 C2
Concepción □, *Chile* 126 D1
Concepción →, *Mexico* 114 A2
Concepción, Est. de, *Chile* 128 D2
Concepción, L., *Bolivia* 125 D5
Concepción, Punta, *Mexico* 114 B2
Concepción del Oro, *Mexico* 114 C4
Concepción del Uruguay, *Argentina* 126 C4
Conception, Pt., *U.S.A.* 113 L6
Conception B., *Namibia* 84 C1
Conception I., *Bahamas* 117 B4
Concession, *Zimbabwe* 83 F3
Conchas Dam, *U.S.A.* 109 H2
Conche, *Canada* 99 B8
Concho, *U.S.A.* 111 J9
Concho →, *U.S.A.* 109 K5
Conchos →, *Chihuahua, Mexico* 114 B4
Conchos →, *Tamaulipas, Mexico* 115 B5
Concord, *Calif., U.S.A.* 112 H4
Concord, *N.C., U.S.A.* 105 H5
Concord, *N.H., U.S.A.* 107 C13
Concordia, *Argentina* 126 C4
Concórdia, *Brazil* 120 D4
Concordia, *Mexico* 114 C3
Concordia, *U.S.A.* 108 F6
Concots, *France* 26 D5
Concrete, *U.S.A.* 110 B3
Condamine, *Australia* 91 D5
Condat, *France* 26 C6
Conde, *Brazil* 123 D4
Conde, *U.S.A.* 108 C5
Condé-sur-l'Escaut, *France* 25 B10
Condé-sur-Noireau, *France* 24 D6
Condeúba, *Brazil* 123 D3
Condobolin, *Australia* 91 E4
Condom, *France* 26 E4
Condon, *U.S.A.* 110 D3
Condove, *Italy* 32 C4
Conegliano, *Italy* 33 C9
Conejera, I., *Spain* 36 B9
Conejos, *Mexico* 114 B4
Conflans-en-Jarnisy, *France* 25 C12
Confolens, *France* 26 B4
Confuso →, *Paraguay* 126 B4
Congjiang, *China* 52 E7
Congleton, *U.K.* 12 D5
Congo = Zaïre →, *Africa* 80 F2
Congo, *Brazil* 122 C4
Congo (Kinshasa) = Zaïre ■, *Africa* 80 E4
Congo ■, *Africa* 80 E3
Congo Basin, *Africa* 70 G6
Congonhas, *Brazil* 123 F3
Congress, *U.S.A.* 111 J7
Conil, *Spain* 31 J4
Coniston, *Canada* 98 C3
Conjeeveram = Kanchipuram, *India* 60 N11
Conjuboy, *Australia* 90 B3
Conklin, *Canada* 101 B6
Conlea, *Australia* 91 E3
Conn, L., *Ireland* 15 B2
Connacht, *Ireland* 15 C3
Conneaut, *U.S.A.* 106 E4
Connecticut □, *U.S.A.* 107 E12
Connecticut →, *U.S.A.* 107 E12
Connell, *U.S.A.* 110 C4
Connellsville, *U.S.A.* 106 F5
Connemara, *Ireland* 15 C2
Connemaugh →, *U.S.A.* 106 F5
Connerré, *France* 24 D7
Connersville, *U.S.A.* 104 F3
Connors Ra., *Australia* 90 C4
Conoble, *Australia* 91 E3
Cononaco →, *Ecuador* 120 D2
Cononbridge, *U.K.* 14 D4
Conquest, *Canada* 101 C7
Conrad, *U.S.A.* 110 B8
Conran, C., *Australia* 91 F4
Conroe, *U.S.A.* 109 K7
Conselheiro Lafaiete, *Brazil* 123 F3
Conselheiro Pena, *Brazil* 123 E3
Consort, *Canada* 101 C6
Constance = Konstanz, *Germany* 19 H5
Constance, L. = Bodensee, *Europe* 23 A8
Constanţa, *Romania* 38 E11
Constantina, *Spain* 31 H5
Constantine, *Algeria* 75 A6
Constitución, *Chile* 126 D1
Constitución, *Uruguay* 126 C4
Consuegra, *Spain* 31 F7
Consul, *Canada* 101 D7
Contact, *U.S.A.* 110 F6
Contai, *India* 63 J12
Contamana, *Peru* 124 B3
Contarina, *Italy* 33 C9
Contas →, *Brazil* 123 D4
Contes, *France* 27 E11
Conthey, *Switz.* 22 D4
Contoocook, *U.S.A.* 107 C13
Contra Costa, *Mozam.* 85 D5
Contres, *France* 24 E8
Contrexéville, *France* 25 D12
Contumaza, *Peru* 124 B2
Convención, *Colombia* 120 B3
Conversano, *Italy* 35 B10
Conway = Conwy, *U.K.* 12 D4
Conway = Conwy →, *U.K.* 12 D4
Conway, *Ark., U.S.A.* 109 H8
Conway, *N.H., U.S.A.* 107 C13
Conway, *S.C., U.S.A.* 105 J6
Conway, L., *Australia* 91 D2
Conwy, *U.K.* 12 D4
Conwy →, *U.K.* 12 D4
Coober Pedy, *Australia* 91 D1
Cooch Behar = Koch Bihar, *India* 61 F16
Coodardy, *Australia* 89 E2
Cook, *Australia* 89 F5
Cook, *U.S.A.* 108 B8
Cook, B., *Chile* 128 E2
Cook, Mt., *N.Z.* 87 K3
Cook Inlet, *U.S.A.* 96 C4
Cook Is., *Pac. Oc.* 93 J11
Cook Strait, *N.Z.* 87 J5
Cookeville, *U.S.A.* 105 G3
Cookhouse, *S. Africa* 84 E4
Cookshire, *Canada* 107 A13
Cookstown, *U.K.* 15 B5
Cookstown □, *U.K.* 15 B5
Cooksville, *Canada* 106 C5
Cooktown, *Australia* 90 B4
Coolabah, *Australia* 91 E4
Cooladdi, *Australia* 91 D4
Coolah, *Australia* 91 E4
Coolamon, *Australia* 91 E4
Coolangatta, *Australia* 91 D5
Coolgardie, *Australia* 89 F3
Coolibah, *Australia* 88 C5
Coolidge, *U.S.A.* 111 K8
Coolidge Dam, *U.S.A.* 111 K8
Cooma, *Australia* 91 F4
Coonabarabran, *Australia* 91 E4
Coonamble, *Australia* 91 E4
Coonana, *Australia* 89 F3
Coondapoor, *India* 60 N9
Coongie, *Australia* 91 D3
Coongoola, *Australia* 91 D4
Cooninie, L., *Australia* 91 D2
Cooper, *U.S.A.* 109 J7
Cooper →, *U.S.A.* 105 J6
Cooper Cr. →, *Australia* 91 D2
Cooperstown, *N. Dak., U.S.A.* 108 B5
Cooperstown, *N.Y., U.S.A.* 107 D10
Coorabie, *Australia* 89 F5
Coorabulka, *Australia* 90 C3
Coorow, *Australia* 89 E2
Cooroy, *Australia* 91 D5
Coos Bay, *U.S.A.* 110 E1
Cootamundra, *Australia* 91 E4
Cootehill, *Ireland* 15 B4
Cooyar, *Australia* 91 D5
Cooyeana, *Australia* 90 C2
Copahue Paso, *Argentina* 126 D1
Copainalá, *Mexico* 115 D6
Copán, *Honduras* 116 D2
Copatana, *Brazil* 120 D4
Cope, *U.S.A.* 108 F3
Cope, C., *Spain* 29 H3
Copenhagen = København, *Denmark* 11 J6
Copertino, *Italy* 35 B11
Copiapó, *Chile* 126 B1
Copiapó →, *Chile* 126 B1
Copley, *Australia* 91 E2
Copp L., *Canada* 100 A6
Copparo, *Italy* 33 D8
Coppename →, *Surinam* 121 B6
Copper Center, *U.S.A.* 96 B5
Copper Cliff, *Canada* 98 C3
Copper Harbor, *U.S.A.* 104 B2
Copper Queen, *Zimbabwe* 83 F2
Copperbelt □, *Zambia* 83 E2
Coppermine, *Canada* 96 B8
Coppermine →, *Canada* 96 B8
Copperopolis, *U.S.A.* 112 H6
Coquet →, *U.K.* 12 B6
Coquilhatville = Mbandaka, *Zaïre* 80 D3
Coquille, *U.S.A.* 110 E1
Coquimbo, *Chile* 126 B1
Coquimbo □, *Chile* 126 C1
Corabia, *Romania* 38 F7
Coração de Jesus, *Brazil* 123 E3
Coracora, *Peru* 124 D3
Coradi, Is., *Italy* 35 B10
Coral Gables, *U.S.A.* 105 N5
Coral Harbour, *Canada* 97 B11
Coral Sea, *Pac. Oc.* 92 J7
Corantijn →, *Surinam* 121 B6
Coraopolis, *U.S.A.* 106 F4
Corato, *Italy* 35 A9
Corbeil-Essonnes, *France* 25 D9
Corbie, *France* 25 C9
Corbières, *France* 26 F6
Corbigny, *France* 25 E10
Corbin, *U.S.A.* 104 G3
Corbion, *Belgium* 17 J6
Corbones →, *Spain* 31 H5
Corby, *U.K.* 13 E7
Corby Glen, *U.K.* 13 E7
Corcoles →, *Spain* 29 F1
Corcoran, *U.S.A.* 111 H4
Corcubión, *Spain* 30 C1
Cordele, *U.S.A.* 105 K4
Cordell, *U.S.A.* 109 H5
Cordenons, *Italy* 33 C9
Cordes, *France* 26 D5
Cordisburgo, *Brazil* 123 E3
Córdoba, *Argentina* 126 C3
Córdoba, *Mexico* 115 D5
Córdoba, *Spain* 31 H6
Córdoba □, *Argentina* 126 C3
Córdoba □, *Colombia* 120 B2
Córdoba □, *Spain* 31 G6
Córdoba, Sierra de, *Argentina* 126 C3
Cordon, *Phil.* 55 C4
Cordova, *Ala., U.S.A.* 105 J2
Cordova, *Alaska, U.S.A.* 96 B5
Corella, *Spain* 28 C3
Corella →, *Australia* 90 B3
Coremas, *Brazil* 122 C4
Corentyne →, *Guyana* 121 B6
Corfield, *Australia* 90 C3
Corfu = Kérkira, *Greece* 37 A3
Corfu, Str of, *Greece* 37 A4
Corgo, *Spain* 30 C3
Corguinho, *Brazil* 125 D7
Cori, *Italy* 34 A5
Coria, *Spain* 30 F4
Corigliano Cálabro, *Italy* 35 C9
Coringa Is., *Australia* 90 B4
Corinna, *Australia* 90 G4
Corinth = Kórinthos, *Greece* 39 M5
Corinth, *Miss., U.S.A.* 105 H1
Corinth, *N.Y., U.S.A.* 107 C11
Corinth, G. of = Korinthiakós Kólpos, *Greece* 39 L5
Corinth Canal, *Greece* 39 M6
Corinto, *Brazil* 123 E3
Corinto, *Nic.* 116 D2
Cork, *Ireland* 15 E3
Cork □, *Ireland* 15 E3
Cork Harbour, *Ireland* 15 E3
Corlay, *France* 24 D3
Corleone, *Italy* 34 E6
Corleto Perticara, *Italy* 35 B9
Çorlu, *Turkey* 39 H10
Cormack L., *Canada* 100 A4
Cormóns, *Italy* 33 C10
Cormorant, *Canada* 101 C8
Cormorant L., *Canada* 101 C8
Corn Is. = Maiz, Is. del, *Nic.* 116 D3
Cornélio Procópio, *Brazil* 127 A5
Cornell, *U.S.A.* 108 C9
Corner Brook, *Canada* 99 C8
Cornígliо, *Italy* 32 D7
Corning, *Ark., U.S.A.* 109 G9
Corning, *Calif., U.S.A.* 110 G2
Corning, *Iowa, U.S.A.* 108 E7
Corning, *N.Y., U.S.A.* 106 D7
Corno, Monte, *Italy* 33 F10
Cornwall, *Canada* 98 C5
Cornwall □, *U.K.* 13 G3
Corny Pt., *Australia* 91 E2
Coro, *Venezuela* 120 A4
Coroaci, *Brazil* 123 E3
Coroatá, *Brazil* 122 B3
Corocoro, *Bolivia* 124 D4
Corocoro, I., *Venezuela* 121 B5
Coroico, *Bolivia* 124 D4
Coromandel, *Brazil* 123 E2
Coromandel, *N.Z.* 87 G5
Coromandel Coast, *India* 60 N12
Corona, *Australia* 91 E3
Corona, *Calif., U.S.A.* 113 M9
Corona, *N. Mex., U.S.A.* 111 J11
Coronado, *U.S.A.* 113 N9
Coronado, B. de, *Costa Rica* 116 E3
Coronados, G. de los, *Chile* 128 B2
Coronados, Is. los, *U.S.A.* 113 N9
Coronation, *Canada* 100 C6
Coronation Gulf, *Canada* 96 B8
Coronation I., *Antarctica* 5 C18
Coronation I., *U.S.A.* 100 B2
Coronation Is., *Australia* 88 B3
Coronda, *Argentina* 126 C3
Coronel, *Chile* 126 D1
Coronel Bogado, *Paraguay* 126 B4
Coronel Dorrego, *Argentina* 126 D3
Coronel Fabriciano, *Brazil* 123 E3
Coronel Murta, *Brazil* 123 E3
Coronel Oviedo, *Paraguay* 126 B4
Coronel Ponce, *Brazil* 125 D6
Coronel Pringles, *Argentina* 126 D3
Coronel Suárez, *Argentina* 126 D3
Coronel Vidal, *Argentina* 126 D4
Corongo, *Peru* 124 B2
Coronie □, *Surinam* 121 B6
Coropuna, Nevado, *Peru* 124 D3
Çorovoda, *Albania* 39 J3
Corowa, *Australia* 91 F4
Corozal, *Belize* 115 D7
Corozal, *Colombia* 120 B2
Corps, *France* 27 D9
Corpus, *Argentina* 127 B4
Corpus Christi, *U.S.A.* 109 M6
Corpus Christi, L., *U.S.A.* 109 L6
Corque, *Bolivia* 124 D4
Corral, *Chile* 128 A2
Corral de Almaguer, *Spain* 28 F1
Corralejo, *Canary Is.* 36 F6
Corréggio, *Italy* 32 D7
Corrente, *Brazil* 122 D2
Corrente →, *Brazil* 123 D3
Correntes →, *Brazil* 125 D6
Correntes, C. das, *Mozam.* 85 C6
Correntina, *Brazil* 123 D3
Corrèze □, *France* 26 C5
Corrèze →, *France* 26 C5
Corrib, L., *Ireland* 15 C2
Corrientes, *Argentina* 126 B4
Corrientes □, *Argentina* 126 B4
Corrientes →, *Argentina* 126 C4
Corrientes →, *Peru* 120 D3
Corrientes, C., *Colombia* 120 B2
Corrientes, C., *Cuba* 116 B3
Corrientes, C., *Mexico* 114 C3
Corrigan, *U.S.A.* 109 K7
Corrigin, *Australia* 89 F2
Corry, *U.S.A.* 106 E5
Corse, *France* 27 F13
Corse, C., *France* 27 E13
Corse-du-Sud □, *France* 27 G13
Corsica = Corse, *France* 27 F13
Corsicana, *U.S.A.* 109 J6
Corte, *France* 27 F13
Corte do Pinto, *Portugal* 31 H3
Cortegana, *Spain* 31 H4
Cortez, *U.S.A.* 111 H9
Cortina d'Ampezzo, *Italy* 33 B9
Cortland, *U.S.A.* 107 D8
Cortona, *Italy* 33 E8
Coruche, *Portugal* 31 G2
Çoruh →, *Turkey* 67 C9
Çorum, *Turkey* 66 C6
Çorum □, *Turkey* 66 C6
Corumbá, *Brazil* 125 D6
Corumbá →, *Brazil* 123 E2
Corumbá de Goiás, *Brazil* 123 E2
Corumbaíba, *Brazil* 123 E2
Corunna = La Coruña, *Spain* 30 B2
Corvallis, *U.S.A.* 110 D2
Corvette, L. de la, *Canada* 98 B5
Corydon, *U.S.A.* 108 E8
Cosalá, *Mexico* 114 C3
Cosamaloapan, *Mexico* 115 D5
Cosenza, *Italy* 35 C9
Coshocton, *U.S.A.* 106 F3
Cosmo Newberry, *Australia* 89 E3
Cosne-sur-Loire, *France* 25 E9
Coso Junction, *U.S.A.* 113 J9
Coso Pk., *U.S.A.* 113 J9
Cospeito, *Spain* 30 B3
Cosquín, *Argentina* 126 C3
Cossato, *Italy* 32 C5
Cossé-le-Vivien, *France* 24 E6
Cosson →, *France* 24 E8
Costa Blanca, *Spain* 29 G4
Costa Brava, *Spain* 28 D8
Costa del Sol, *Spain* 31 J6
Costa Dorada, *Spain* 28 E6
Costa Mesa, *U.S.A.* 113 M9
Costa Rica ■, *Cent. Amer.* 116 D3
Costa Smeralda, *Italy* 34 A2
Costigliole d'Asti, *Italy* 32 D5
Costilla, *U.S.A.* 111 H11

Cosumnes →, *U.S.A.* 112 G5
Coswig, *Germany* 18 D8
Cotabato, *Phil.* 55 H6
Cotacajes →, *Bolivia* 124 D4
Cotagaita, *Bolivia* 126 A2
Cotahuasi, *Peru* 124 D3
Côte d'Azur, *France* 27 E11
Côte-d'Ivoire ■ = Ivory Coast ■, *Africa* 78 D3
Côte d'Or, *France* 25 E11
Côte-d'Or □, *France* 25 E11
Coteau des Prairies, *U.S.A.* 108 C6
Coteau du Missouri, *U.S.A.* 108 B4
Coteau Landing, *Canada* 107 A10
Cotegipe, *Brazil* 123 D3
Cotentin, *France* 24 C5
Côtes-d'Armor □, *France* 24 D4
Côtes de Meuse, *France* 25 C12
Côtes-du-Nord = Côtes-d'Armor □, *France* 24 D4
Cotiella, *Spain* 28 C5
Cotillo, *Canary Is.* 36 F5
Cotina →, *Bos.-H.* 21 M8
Cotoca, *Bolivia* 125 D5
Cotonou, *Benin* 79 D5
Cotopaxi, *Ecuador* 120 D2
Cotopaxi □, *Ecuador* 120 D2
Cotronei, *Italy* 35 C9
Cotswold Hills, *U.K.* 13 F5
Cottage Grove, *U.S.A.* 110 E2
Cottbus, *Germany* 18 D10
Cottingham, *U.K.* 12 C5
Cottonwood, *U.S.A.* 111 J7
Cotulla, *U.S.A.* 109 L5
Coubre, Pte. de la, *France* 26 C2
Couches, *France* 25 F11
Couço, *Portugal* 31 G2
Coudersport, *U.S.A.* 106 E6
Couedic, C. du, *Australia* 91 F2
Couëron, *France* 24 E5
Couesnon →, *France* 24 D5
Couhé, *France* 26 B4
Coulanges-sur-Yonne, *France* 25 E10
Coulee City, *U.S.A.* 110 C4
Coulman I., *Antarctica* 5 D11
Coulommiers, *France* 25 D10
Coulonge →, *Canada* 98 C4
Coulonges-sur-l'Autize, *France* 26 B3
Coulterville, *U.S.A.* 112 H6
Council, *Alaska, U.S.A.* 96 B3
Council, *Idaho, U.S.A.* 110 D5
Council Bluffs, *U.S.A.* 108 E7
Council Grove, *U.S.A.* 108 F6
Coupeville, *U.S.A.* 112 B4
Courantyne →, *S. Amer.* 121 B6
Courcelles, *Belgium* 17 H4
Courçon, *France* 26 B3
Couronne, C., *France* 27 E9
Cours-la-Ville, *France* 27 B8
Coursan, *France* 26 E7
Courseulles-sur-Mer, *France* 24 C6
Court-St.-Etienne, *Belgium* 17 G5
Courtenay, *Canada* 100 D3
Courtland, *U.S.A.* 112 G5
Courtrai = Kortrijk, *Belgium* 17 G2
Courtright, *Canada* 106 D2
Courville-sur-Eure, *France* 24 D8
Coushatta, *U.S.A.* 109 J8
Coutances, *France* 24 C5
Couterne, *France* 24 D6
Coutras, *France* 26 C3
Coutts, *Canada* 100 D6
Couvet, *Switz.* 22 C3
Couvin, *Belgium* 17 H4
Covarrubias, *Spain* 28 C1
Coveñas, *Colombia* 120 B2
Coventry, *U.K.* 13 E6
Coventry L., *Canada* 101 A7
Covilhã, *Portugal* 30 E3
Covington, *Ga., U.S.A.* 105 J4
Covington, *Ky., U.S.A.* 104 F3
Covington, *Okla., U.S.A.* 109 G6
Covington, *Tenn., U.S.A.* 109 H10
Cowal, L., *Australia* 91 E4
Cowan, *Canada* 101 C8
Cowan, L., *Australia* 89 F3
Cowan L., *Canada* 101 C7
Cowangie, *Australia* 91 F3
Cowansville, *Canada* 107 A12
Cowarie, *Australia* 91 D2
Cowcowing Lakes, *Australia* 89 F2
Cowdenbeath, *U.K.* 14 E5
Cowell, *Australia* 91 E2
Cowes, *U.K.* 13 G6
Cowlitz →, *U.S.A.* 112 D4
Cowra, *Australia* 91 E4
Coxilha Grande, *Brazil* 127 B5
Coxim, *Brazil* 125 D7
Coxim →, *Brazil* 125 D7
Cox's Bazar, *Bangla.* 61 J17
Cox's Cove, *Canada* 99 C8
Coyame, *Mexico* 114 B3
Coyote Wells, *U.S.A.* 113 N11
Coyuca de Benítez, *Mexico* 115 D4
Coyuca de Catalan, *Mexico* 114 D4
Cozad, *U.S.A.* 108 E5
Cozumel, *Mexico* 115 C7
Cozumel, I. de, *Mexico* 115 C7
Craboon, *Australia* 91 E4
Cracow = Kraków, *Poland* 20 E9
Cracow, *Australia* 91 D5
Cradock, *S. Africa* 84 E4
Craig, *Alaska, U.S.A.* 100 B2
Craig, *Colo., U.S.A.* 110 F10
Craigavon = Lurgan, *U.K.* 15 B5
Craigmore, *Zimbabwe* 83 G3
Crailsheim, *Germany* 19 F6
Craiova, *Romania* 38 E6
Cramsie, *Australia* 90 C3
Cranberry Portage, *Canada* 101 C8
Cranbrook, *Tas., Australia* 90 G4
Cranbrook, *W. Austral., Australia* 89 F2
Cranbrook, *Canada* 100 D5
Crandon, *U.S.A.* 108 C10
Crane, *Oreg., U.S.A.* 110 E4
Crane, *Tex., U.S.A.* 109 K3
Cranston, *U.S.A.* 107 E13
Craon, *France* 24 E6
Craonne, *France* 25 C10
Craponne-sur-Arzon, *France* 26 C7
Crasna, *Romania* 38 C10
Crater L., *U.S.A.* 110 E2
Crateús, *Brazil* 122 C3
Crati →, *Italy* 35 C9
Crato, *Brazil* 122 C4
Crato, *Portugal* 31 F3
Cravo Norte, *Colombia* 120 B3
Cravo Norte →, *Colombia* 120 B3
Crawford, *U.S.A.* 108 D3
Crawfordsville, *U.S.A.* 104 E2
Crawley, *U.K.* 13 F7
Crazy Mts., *U.S.A.* 110 C8
Crean L., *Canada* 101 C7
Crécy-en-Brie, *France* 25 D9
Crécy-en-Ponthieu, *France* 25 B8
Crediton, *Canada* 106 C3
Credo, *Australia* 89 F3
Cree →, *Canada* 101 B7
Cree →, *U.K.* 14 G4
Cree L., *Canada* 101 B7
Creede, *U.S.A.* 111 H10
Creel, *Mexico* 114 B3
Creighton, *U.S.A.* 108 D6
Creil, *France* 25 C9
Crema, *Italy* 32 C6
Cremona, *Italy* 32 C7
Crepori →, *Brazil* 125 B6
Crépy, *France* 25 C10
Crépy-en-Valois, *France* 25 C9
Cres, *Croatia* 33 D11
Cresbard, *U.S.A.* 108 C5
Crescent, *Okla., U.S.A.* 109 H6
Crescent, *Oreg., U.S.A.* 110 E3
Crescent City, *U.S.A.* 110 F1
Crescentino, *Italy* 32 C5
Crespino, *Italy* 33 D8
Crespo, *Argentina* 126 C3
Cressy, *Australia* 91 F3
Crest, *France* 27 D9
Cresta, Mt., *Phil.* 55 C5
Crested Butte, *U.S.A.* 111 G10
Crestline, *Calif., U.S.A.* 113 L9
Crestline, *Ohio, U.S.A.* 106 F2
Creston, *Canada* 100 D5
Creston, *Calif., U.S.A.* 112 K6
Creston, *Iowa, U.S.A.* 108 E7
Creston, *Wash., U.S.A.* 110 C4
Crestview, *Calif., U.S.A.* 112 H8
Crestview, *Fla., U.S.A.* 105 K2
Crete = Kríti, *Greece* 37 D7
Crete, *U.S.A.* 108 E6
Crete, Sea of, *Greece* 39 N8
Creus, C., *Spain* 28 C8
Creuse □, *France* 26 B6
Creuse →, *France* 26 B4
Creuzburg, *Germany* 18 D6
Crevalcore, *Italy* 33 D8
Crèvecœur-le-Grand, *France* 25 C9
Crevillente, *Spain* 29 G4
Crewe, *U.K.* 12 D5
Criciúma, *Brazil* 127 B6
Crieff, *U.K.* 14 E5
Crikvenica, *Croatia* 33 C11
Crimea = Krymskiy Poluostrov, *Ukraine* 42 D5
Crimmitschau, *Germany* 18 E8
Cristalândia, *Brazil* 122 D2
Cristino Castro, *Brazil* 122 C3
Crişul Alb →, *Romania* 38 C4
Crişul Negru →, *Romania* 38 C4
Crişul Repede →, *Romania* 38 C3
Crivitz, *Germany* 18 B7
Crixás, *Brazil* 123 D2
Crna Gora = Montenegro □, *Montenegro* 21 N9
Crni Drim →, *Macedonia* 39 H3
Črnomelj, *Slovenia* 33 C12
Croaghpatrick, *Ireland* 15 C2
Croatia ■, *Europe* 33 C13
Crocker, Banjaran, *Malaysia* 56 C5
Crockett, *U.S.A.* 109 K7
Crocodile = Krokodil →, *Mozam.* 85 D5
Crocodile Is., *Australia* 90 A1
Crocq, *France* 26 C6
Croisette, C., *France* 27 E9
Croisic, Pte. du, *France* 24 E4
Croix, L. La, *Canada* 98 C1
Croker, C., *Australia* 88 B5
Croker I., *Australia* 88 B5
Cromarty, *Canada* 101 B10
Cromarty, *U.K.* 14 D4
Cromer, *U.K.* 12 E9
Cromwell, *N.Z.* 87 L2
Cronat, *France* 25 F10
Cronulla, *Australia* 91 E5
Crooked →, *Canada* 100 C4
Crooked →, *U.S.A.* 110 D3
Crooked I., *Bahamas* 117 B5
Crooked Island Passage, *Bahamas* 117 B5
Crookston, *Minn., U.S.A.* 108 B6
Crookston, *Nebr., U.S.A.* 108 D4
Crooksville, *U.S.A.* 104 F4
Crookwell, *Australia* 91 E4
Crosby, *Minn., U.S.A.* 108 B8
Crosby, *N. Dak., U.S.A.* 101 D8
Crosby, *Pa., U.S.A.* 106 E6
Crosbyton, *U.S.A.* 109 J4
Cross →, *Nigeria* 79 E6
Cross City, *U.S.A.* 105 L4
Cross Fell, *U.K.* 12 C5
Cross L., *Canada* 101 C9
Cross Plains, *U.S.A.* 109 J5
Cross River □, *Nigeria* 79 D6
Cross Sound, *U.S.A.* 96 C6
Crossett, *U.S.A.* 109 J9
Crossfield, *Canada* 100 C6
Crosshaven, *Ireland* 15 E3
Croton-on-Hudson, *U.S.A.* 107 E11
Crotone, *Italy* 35 C10
Crow →, *Canada* 100 B4
Crow Agency, *U.S.A.* 110 D10
Crow Hd., *Ireland* 15 E1
Crowell, *U.S.A.* 109 J5
Crowley, *U.S.A.* 109 K8
Crowley, L., *U.S.A.* 112 H8
Crown Point, *U.S.A.* 104 E2
Crows Landing, *U.S.A.* 112 H5
Crows Nest, *Australia* 91 D5
Crowsnest Pass, *Canada* 100 D6
Croydon, *Australia* 90 B3
Croydon, *U.K.* 13 F7
Crozet Is., *Ind. Oc.* 3 G12
Crozon, *France* 24 D2
Cruz, C., *Cuba* 116 C4
Cruz Alta, *Brazil* 127 B5
Cruz das Almas, *Brazil* 123 D4
Cruz de Malta, *Brazil* 122 C3
Cruz del Eje, *Argentina* 126 C3
Cruzeiro, *Brazil* 123 F2
Cruzeiro do Oeste, *Brazil* 127 A5
Cruzeiro do Sul, *Brazil* 124 B3
Cry L., *Canada* 100 B3
Crystal Bay, *U.S.A.* 112 F7
Crystal Brook, *Australia* 91 E2
Crystal City, *Mo., U.S.A.* 108 F9
Crystal City, *Tex., U.S.A.* 109 L5
Crystal Falls, *U.S.A.* 104 B1
Crystal River, *U.S.A.* 105 L4
Crystal Springs, *U.S.A.* 109 K9
Csongrád, *Hungary* 21 J10
Csorna, *Hungary* 21 H7
Csurgo, *Hungary* 21 J7
Cu Lao Hon, *Vietnam* 59 G7
Cua Rao, *Vietnam* 58 C5
Cuácua →, *Mozam.* 83 F4
Cuamato, *Angola* 84 B2
Cuamba, *Mozam.* 83 E4
Cuando →, *Angola* 81 H4
Cuando Cubango □, *Angola* 84 B3
Cuangar, *Angola* 84 B2
Cuanza →, *Angola* 70 G5
Cuarto →, *Argentina* 126 C3
Cuatrociénegas, *Mexico* 114 B4
Cuauhtémoc, *Mexico* 114 B3
Cuba, *Portugal* 31 G3
Cuba, *N. Mex., U.S.A.* 111 J10
Cuba, *N.Y., U.S.A.* 106 D6
Cuba ■, *W. Indies* 116 B4
Cuballing, *Australia* 89 F2
Cubango →, *Africa* 84 B3
Çubuk, *Turkey* 66 C5
Cucamonga, *U.S.A.* 113 L9
Cuchi, *Angola* 81 G3
Cuchillo-Có, *Argentina* 128 A4
Cuchivero →, *Venezuela* 120 B4
Cuchumatanes, Sierra de los, *Guatemala* 116 C1
Cucuí, *Brazil* 120 C4
Cucurpe, *Mexico* 114 A2
Cucurrupí, *Colombia* 120 C2
Cúcuta, *Colombia* 120 B3
Cudahy, *U.S.A.* 104 D2
Cudalbi, *Romania* 38 D10
Cuddalore, *India* 60 P11
Cuddapah, *India* 60 M11
Cuddapan, L., *Australia* 90 D3
Cudgewa, *Australia* 91 F4
Cudillero, *Spain* 30 B4
Cue, *Australia* 89 E2
Cuéllar, *Spain* 30 D6
Cuenca, *Ecuador* 120 D2
Cuenca, *Spain* 28 E2
Cuenca □, *Spain* 28 F2
Cuenca, Serranía de, *Spain* 28 F3
Cuerdo del Pozo, Pantano de la, *Spain* 28 D2
Cuernavaca, *Mexico* 115 D5
Cuero, *U.S.A.* 109 L6
Cuers, *France* 27 E10
Cuervo, *U.S.A.* 109 H2
Cuesmes, *Belgium* 17 H3
Cuevas, Cerro, *Bolivia* 125 E4
Cuevas del Almanzora, *Spain* 29 H3
Cuevo, *Bolivia* 125 E5
Cuiabá, *Brazil* 125 D6
Cuiabá →, *Brazil* 125 D6
Cuilco, *Guatemala* 116 C1
Cuillin Hills, *U.K.* 14 D2
Cuillin Sd., *U.K.* 14 D2
Cuima, *Angola* 81 G3
Cuiseaux, *France* 27 B9
Cuité, *Brazil* 122 C4
Cuito →, *Angola* 84 B3
Cuitzeo, L. de, *Mexico* 114 D4
Cuiuni →, *Brazil* 121 D5
Cukai, *Malaysia* 59 K4
Culan, *France* 26 B6
Culbertson, *U.S.A.* 108 A2
Culcairn, *Australia* 91 F4
Culebra, Sierra de la, *Spain* 30 D4
Culemborg, *Neths.* 16 E6
Culgoa →, *Australia* 91 D4
Culiacán, *Mexico* 114 C3
Culiacán →, *Mexico* 114 C3
Culion, *Phil.* 55 F4
Culiseu →, *Brazil* 125 C7
Cúllar de Baza, *Spain* 29 H2
Cullarin Ra., *Australia* 91 E4
Cullen, *U.K.* 14 D6
Cullen Pt., *Australia* 90 A3
Cullera, *Spain* 29 F4
Cullman, *U.S.A.* 105 H2
Culloden Moor, *U.K.* 14 D4
Culoz, *France* 27 C9
Culpeper, *U.S.A.* 104 F7
Culuene →, *Brazil* 125 C7
Culver, Pt., *Australia* 89 F3
Culverden, *N.Z.* 87 K4
Cumaná, *Venezuela* 121 A5
Cumare, *Colombia* 120 C3
Cumari, *Brazil* 123 E2
Cumberland, *Canada* 100 D3
Cumberland, *Md., U.S.A.* 104 F6
Cumberland, *Wis., U.S.A.* 108 C8
Cumberland →, *U.S.A.* 105 G2
Cumberland I., *U.S.A.* 105 K5
Cumberland Is., *Australia* 90 C4
Cumberland L., *Canada* 101 C8
Cumberland Pen., *Canada* 97 B13
Cumberland Plateau, *U.S.A.* 105 H3
Cumberland Sd., *Canada* 97 B13
Cumborah, *Australia* 91 D4
Cumbres Mayores, *Spain* 31 G4
Cumbria □, *U.K.* 12 C5
Cumbrian Mts., *U.K.* 12 C4
Cumbum, *India* 60 M11
Cuminá →, *Brazil* 121 D6
Cuminapanema →, *Brazil* 121 D7
Cummings Mt., *U.S.A.* 113 K8
Cummins, *Australia* 91 E2
Cumnock, *Australia* 91 E4
Cumnock, *U.K.* 14 F4
Cumpas, *Mexico* 114 A3
Cumplida, Pta., *Canary Is.* 36 F2
Çumra, *Turkey* 66 E5
Cuncumén, *Chile* 126 C1
Cundeelee, *Australia* 89 F3
Cunderdin, *Australia* 89 F2
Cundinamarca □, *Colombia* 120 C3
Cunene →, *Angola* 84 B1
Cúneo, *Italy* 32 D4
Cunillera, I., *Spain* 36 C7
Cunlhat, *France* 26 C7
Cunnamulla, *Australia* 91 D4
Cuorgnè, *Italy* 32 C4
Cupar, *Canada* 101 C8
Cupar, *U.K.* 14 E5
Cupica, G. de, *Colombia* 120 B2
Ćuprija, *Serbia* 21 M11
Curaçá, *Brazil* 122 C4
Curaçao, *Neth. Ant.* 117 D6
Curacautín, *Chile* 128 A2
Curahuara de Carangas, *Bolivia* 124 D4
Curanilahue, *Chile* 126 D1
Curaray →, *Peru* 120 D3
Curatabaca, *Venezuela* 121 B5
Cure →, *France* 25 E10
Curepto, *Chile* 126 D1
Curiapo, *Venezuela* 121 B5
Curicó, *Chile* 126 C1
Curicó □, *Chile* 126 C1
Curicuriari →, *Brazil* 120 D4
Curimatá, *Brazil* 122 D3
Curiplaya, *Colombia* 120 C3
Curitiba, *Brazil* 127 B6
Currabubula, *Australia* 91 E5
Currais Novos, *Brazil* 122 C4
Curralinho, *Brazil* 122 B2
Currant, *U.S.A.* 110 G6
Curraweena, *Australia* 91 E4
Currawilla, *Australia* 90 D3
Current →, *U.S.A.* 109 G9
Currie, *Australia* 90 F3
Currie, *U.S.A.* 110 F6
Currie, Mt., *S. Africa* 85 E4
Currituck Sd., *U.S.A.* 105 G8
Curtea de Argeş, *Romania* 38 D7
Curtis, *Spain* 30 B2
Curtis, *U.S.A.* 108 E4
Curtis Group, *Australia* 90 F4
Curtis I., *Australia* 90 C5
Curuá →, *Pará, Brazil* 121 D7
Curuá →, *Pará, Brazil* 125 B7
Curuá, I., *Brazil* 122 A1
Curuaés →, *Brazil* 125 B7
Curuápanema →, *Brazil* 121 D6
Curuçá, *Brazil* 122 B2
Curuguaty, *Paraguay* 127 A4
Curup, *Indonesia* 56 E2
Curupira, Serra, *S. Amer.* 121 C5
Cururu →, *Brazil* 125 B6
Cururupu, *Brazil* 122 B3
Curuzú Cuatiá, *Argentina* 126 B4
Curvelo, *Brazil* 123 E3
Cushing, *U.S.A.* 109 H6
Cushing, Mt., *Canada* 100 B3
Cusihuiriáchic, *Mexico* 114 B3
Cusna, Monte, *Italy* 32 D7
Cusset, *France* 26 B7
Custer, *U.S.A.* 108 D3
Cut Bank, *U.S.A.* 110 B7
Cutervo, *Peru* 124 B2
Cuthbert, *U.S.A.* 105 K3
Cutler, *U.S.A.* 112 J7
Cutral-Có, *Argentina* 128 A3
Cutro, *Italy* 35 C9
Cuttaburra →, *Australia* 91 D3
Cuttack, *India* 61 J14
Cuvier, C., *Australia* 89 D1
Cuvier I., *N.Z.* 87 G5
Cuxhaven, *Germany* 18 B4
Cuyabeno, *Ecuador* 120 D2
Cuyahoga Falls, *U.S.A.* 106 E3
Cuyapo, *Phil.* 55 D4
Cuyo, *Phil.* 55 F4
Cuyo East Pass, *Phil.* 55 F4
Cuyo West Pass, *Phil.* 55 F4
Cuyuni →, *Guyana* 121 B6
Cuzco, *Bolivia* 124 E4
Cuzco, *Peru* 124 C3
Cuzco □, *Peru* 124 C3
Cwmbran, *U.K.* 13 F4
Cyangugu, *Rwanda* 82 C2
Cyclades = Kikládhes, *Greece* 39 M7
Cygnet, *Australia* 90 G4
Cynthiana, *U.S.A.* 104 F3
Cypress Hills, *Canada* 101 D7
Cyprus ■, *Asia* 37 E12
Cyrenaica, *Libya* 70 C6
Cyrene = Shaḥḥāt, *Libya* 73 B9
Czar, *Canada* 101 C6
Czarne, *Poland* 20 B6
Czech Rep. ■, *Europe* 20 F4
Czersk, *Poland* 20 B7
Częstochowa, *Poland* 20 E9

D

Da →, *Vietnam* 58 B5
Da Hinggan Ling, *China* 54 B7
Da Lat, *Vietnam* 59 G7
Da Nang, *Vietnam* 58 D7
Da Qaidam, *China* 54 C4
Da Yunhe →, *China* 51 G11
Da'an, *China* 51 B13
Daarlerveen, *Neths.* 16 D9
Dab'a, Râs el, *Egypt* 76 H6
Daba Shan, *China* 52 B7
Dabai, *Nigeria* 79 C6
Dabajuro, *Venezuela* 120 A3
Dabakala, *Ivory C.* 78 D4
Dabeiba, *Colombia* 120 B2
Dabhoi, *India* 62 H5
Dąbie, *Poland* 20 B4
Dabie Shan, *China* 53 B10
Dabo, *Indonesia* 56 E2
Dabola, *Guinea* 78 C2
Dabou, *Ivory C.* 78 D4
Daboya, *Ghana* 79 D4
Dabrowa Tarnówska, *Poland* 20 E10
Dabu, *China* 53 E11
Dabung, *Malaysia* 59 K4
Dabus →, *Ethiopia* 77 E4
Dacato →, *Ethiopia* 77 F5
Dacca = Dhaka, *Bangla.* 63 H14
Dacca = Dhaka □, *Bangla.* 63 G14
Dachau, *Germany* 19 G7
Dadanawa, *Guyana* 121 C6
Daday, *Turkey* 42 F5
Dade City, *U.S.A.* 105 L4
Dades, Oued →, *Morocco* 74 B3
Dadiya, *Nigeria* 79 D7
Dadra and Nagar Haveli □, *India* 60 J8
Dadri = Charkhi Dadri, *India* 62 E7
Dadu, *Pakistan* 62 F2
Dadu He →, *China* 52 C4
Dăeni, *Romania* 38 E11
Daet, *Phil.* 55 D5
Dafang, *China* 52 D5
Dagana, *Senegal* 78 B1
Dagash, *Sudan* 76 D3
Dagestanskiye Ogni, *Russia* 43 E13
Daggett, *U.S.A.* 113 L10
Daghestan Republic □, *Russia* 43 E12
Daghfeli, *Sudan* 76 D3
Dagö = Hiiumaa, *Estonia* 40 B3
Dagu, *China* 51 E9
Daguan, *China* 52 D4
Dagupan, *Phil.* 55 C4
Dahab, *Egypt* 76 B3

Dahlak Kebir, *Eritrea*	68	D3
Dahlenburg, *Germany*	18	B6
Dahlonega, *U.S.A.*	105	H4
Dahme, *Germany*	18	D9
Dahod, *India*	62	H6
Dahomey = Benin ■, *Africa*	79	D5
Dahong Shan, *China*	53	B9
Dahra, *Senegal*	78	B1
Dahra, Massif de, *Algeria*	75	A5
Dai Hao, *Vietnam*	58	C6
Dai-Sen, *Japan*	49	G6
Dai Shan, *China*	53	B14
Dai Xian, *China*	50	E7
Daicheng, *China*	50	E9
Daimiel, *Spain*	29	F1
Daingean, *Ireland*	15	C4
Dainkog, *China*	52	A1
Daintree, *Australia*	90	B4
Daiō-Misaki, *Japan*	49	G8
Dairût, *Egypt*	76	B3
Daisetsu-Zan, *Japan*	48	C11
Dajarra, *Australia*	90	C2
Dajia, *Taiwan*	53	E13
Dajin Chuan →, *China*	52	B3
Dak Dam, *Cambodia*	58	F6
Dak Nhe, *Vietnam*	58	E6
Dak Pek, *Vietnam*	58	E6
Dak Song, *Vietnam*	59	F6
Dak Sui, *Vietnam*	58	E6
Dakar, *Senegal*	78	C1
Dakhla, *W. Sahara*	74	D1
Dakhla, El Wâhât el-, *Egypt*	76	B2
Dakhovskaya, *Russia*	43	D9
Dakingari, *Nigeria*	79	C5
Dakor, *India*	62	H5
Dakoro, *Niger*	79	C6
Dakota City, *U.S.A.*	108	D6
Đakovica, *Serbia*	21	N10
Đakovo, *Croatia*	21	K8
Dalaba, *Guinea*	78	C2
Dalachi, *China*	50	F3
Dalai Nur, *China*	50	C9
Dālakī, *Iran*	65	D6
Dalälven, *Sweden*	9	F14
Dalaman, *Turkey*	66	E3
Dalaman →, *Turkey*	66	E3
Dalandzadgad, *Mongolia*	50	C3
Dalarö, *Sweden*	9	G15
Dālbandīn, *Pakistan*	60	E4
Dalbeattie, *U.K.*	14	G5
Dalbosjön, *Sweden*	11	F6
Dalby, *Australia*	91	D5
Dalby, *Sweden*	11	J7
Dalen, *Neths.*	16	C9
Dalen, *Norway*	10	E2
Dalfsen, *Neths.*	16	C8
Dalga, *Egypt*	76	B3
Dalgān, *Iran*	65	E8
Dalhart, *U.S.A.*	109	G3
Dalhousie, *Canada*	99	C6
Dalhousie, *India*	62	C6
Dali, Shaanxi, *China*	50	G5
Dali, Yunnan, *China*	52	E3
Dalian, *China*	51	E11
Daliang Shan, *China*	52	D4
Dalias, *Spain*	29	J2
Daling He →, *China*	51	D11
Dāliyat el Karmel, *Israel*	69	C4
Dalkeith, *U.K.*	14	F5
Dall I., *U.S.A.*	100	C2
Dallarnil, *Australia*	91	D5
Dallas, Oreg., *U.S.A.*	110	D2
Dallas, Tex., *U.S.A.*	109	J6
Dallol, *Ethiopia*	77	E5
Dalmacija = Dalmatia □, *Croatia*	21	M7
Dalmatia □, *Croatia*	21	M7
Dalmellington, *U.K.*	14	F4
Dalnegorsk, *Russia*	45	E14
Dalnerechensk, *Russia*	45	E14
Daloa, *Ivory C.*	78	D3
Dalou Shan, *China*	52	C6
Dalsjöfors, *Sweden*	11	G7
Dalskog, *Sweden*	11	F6
Daltenganj, *India*	63	G11
Dalton, *Canada*	98	C3
Dalton, Ga., *U.S.A.*	105	H3
Dalton, Mass., *U.S.A.*	107	D11
Dalton, Nebr., *U.S.A.*	108	E3
Dalton Iceberg Tongue, *Antarctica*	5	C9
Dalupiri I., *Phil.*	55	B4
Dalvík, *Iceland*	8	D4
Daly →, *Australia*	88	B5
Daly City, *U.S.A.*	112	H4
Daly L., *Canada*	101	B7
Daly Waters, *Australia*	90	B1
Dam Doi, *Vietnam*	59	H5
Dam Ha, *Vietnam*	58	B6
Daman, *India*	60	J8
Dāmaneh, *Iran*	65	C6
Damanhûr, *Egypt*	76	H7
Damanzhuang, *China*	50	E9
Damar, *Indonesia*	57	F7
Damaraland, *Namibia*	84	C2
Damascus = Dimashq, *Syria*	69	B5
Damaturu, *Nigeria*	79	C7
Damävand, *Iran*	65	C7
Damävand, Qolleh-ye, *Iran*	65	C7
Damba, *Angola*	80	F3
Dame Marie, *Haiti*	117	C5
Dāmghān, *Iran*	65	B7
Dămienesti, *Romania*	38	C10
Damietta = Dumyât, *Egypt*	76	H7
Daming, *China*	50	F8
Damīr Qābū, *Syria*	64	B4
Dammam = Ad Dammām, *Si. Arabia*	65	E6
Dammarie, *France*	24	D8
Dammartin-en-Goële, *France*	25	C9
Dammastock, *Switz.*	23	C6
Damme, *Germany*	18	C4
Damodar →, *India*	63	H12
Damoh, *India*	63	H8
Damous, *Algeria*	75	A5
Dampier, *Australia*	88	D2
Dampier, Selat, *Indonesia*	57	E8
Dampier Arch., *Australia*	88	D2
Damrei, Chuor Phnum, *Cambodia*	59	G4
Damville, *France*	24	D8
Damvillers, *France*	25	C12
Dan-Gulbi, *Nigeria*	79	C6
Dana, *Indonesia*	57	F6
Dana, L., *Canada*	98	B4
Dana, Mt., *U.S.A.*	112	H7
Danakil Depression, *Ethiopia*	77	E5
Danao, *Phil.*	55	F6
Danbury, *U.S.A.*	107	E11
Danby L., *U.S.A.*	111	J6
Dand, *Afghan.*	62	D1
Dandaragan, *Australia*	89	F2
Dandeldhura, *Nepal*	63	E9
Dandeli, *India*	60	M9
Dandenong, *Australia*	91	F4
Dandong, *China*	51	D13
Danfeng, *China*	50	H6
Danforth, *U.S.A.*	99	C6
Dangan Liedao, *China*	53	F10
Danger Is. = Pukapuka, *Cook Is.*	93	J11
Danger Pt., *S. Africa*	84	E2
Dangla, *Ethiopia*	77	E4
Dangora, *Nigeria*	79	C6
Dangrek, Phnom, *Thailand*	58	E5
Dangriga, *Belize*	115	D7
Dangshan, *China*	50	G9
Dangtu, *China*	53	B12
Dangyang, *China*	53	B8
Daniel, *U.S.A.*	110	E8
Daniel's Harbour, *Canada*	99	B8
Danielskuil, *S. Africa*	84	D3
Danielson, *U.S.A.*	107	E13
Danilov, *Russia*	41	B12
Danilovka, *Russia*	41	F14
Daning, *China*	50	F6
Danissa, *Kenya*	82	B5
Danja, *Nigeria*	79	C6
Dankalwa, *Nigeria*	79	C7
Dankama, *Nigeria*	79	C6
Dankhar Gompa, *India*	60	C11
Dankov, *Russia*	41	E11
Danleng, *China*	52	B4
Danlí, *Honduras*	116	D2
Dannemora, *Sweden*	9	F14
Dannemora, *U.S.A.*	107	B11
Dannenberg, *Germany*	18	B7
Dannevirke, *N.Z.*	87	J6
Dannhauser, *S. Africa*	85	D5
Danshui, *Taiwan*	53	E13
Dansville, *U.S.A.*	106	D7
Dantan, *India*	63	J12
Dante, *Somali Rep.*	68	E5
Danvers, *U.S.A.*	107	D14
Danville, Ill., *U.S.A.*	104	E2
Danville, Ky., *U.S.A.*	104	G3
Danville, Va., *U.S.A.*	105	G6
Danyang, *China*	53	B12
Danzhai, *China*	52	D6
Danzig = Gdańsk, *Poland*	20	A8
Dao, *Phil.*	57	B6
Dão →, *Portugal*	30	E2
Dao Xian, *China*	53	E8
Daocheng, *China*	52	C3
Daora, *W. Sahara*	74	C2
Daoud = Aïn Beïda, *Algeria*	75	A6
Daoulas, *France*	24	D2
Dapitan, *Phil.*	55	G5
Dapong, *Togo*	79	C5
Daqing Shan, *China*	50	D6
Daqu Shan, *China*	53	B14
Dar es Salaam, *Tanzania*	82	D4
Dar Mazār, *Iran*	65	D8
Dar'ā, *Syria*	69	C5
Dar'ā □, *Syria*	69	C5
Dārāb, *Iran*	65	D7
Daraj, *Libya*	75	B7
Dārān, *Iran*	65	C6
Daravica, *Serbia*	21	N10
Daraw, *Egypt*	76	C3
Dārayyā, *Syria*	69	B5
Darazo, *Nigeria*	79	C7
Darband, *Pakistan*	62	B5
Darband, Kūh-e, *Iran*	65	D8
Darbhanga, *India*	63	F11
Darby, *U.S.A.*	110	C6
Dardanelle, Ark., *U.S.A.*	109	H8
Dardanelle, Calif., *U.S.A.*	112	G7
Dardanelles = Çanakkale Boğazı, *Turkey*	66	C2
Darende, *Turkey*	66	D7
Dārestān, *Iran*	65	D8
Darfo, *Italy*	32	C7
Dârfûr, *Sudan*	70	E6
Dargai, *Pakistan*	62	B4
Dargan Ata, *Uzbekistan*	44	E7
Dargaville, *N.Z.*	87	F4
Darhan Muminggan Lianheqi, *China*	50	D6
Dari, *Sudan*	77	F3
Daxi, *Taiwan*	53	E13
Darién, G. del, *Colombia*	120	B2
Darién, Serranía del, *Colombia*	120	B2
Dariganga, *Mongolia*	50	B7
Darjeeling = Darjiling, *India*	63	F13
Darjiling, *India*	63	F13
Dark Cove, *Canada*	99	C9
Darkan, *Australia*	89	F2
Darkhazīneh, *Iran*	65	D6
Darkot Pass, *Pakistan*	63	A5
Darling →, *Australia*	91	E3
Darling Downs, *Australia*	91	D5
Darling Ra., *Australia*	89	F2
Darlington, *U.K.*	12	C6
Darlington, S.C., *U.S.A.*	105	H6
Darlington, Wis., *U.S.A.*	108	D9
Darlot, L., *Australia*	89	E3
Darłowo, *Poland*	20	A6
Darmstadt, *Germany*	19	F4
Darnah, *Libya*	73	B9
Darnall, *S. Africa*	85	D5
Darnétal, *France*	24	C8
Darney, *France*	25	D13
Darnley, C., *Antarctica*	5	C6
Darnley B., *Canada*	96	B7
Daroca, *Spain*	28	D3
Darr →, *Australia*	90	C3
Darr →, *Australia*	90	C3
Darrington, *U.S.A.*	110	B3
Darsser Ort, *Germany*	18	A8
Dart →, *U.K.*	13	G4
Dart, C., *Antarctica*	5	D14
Dartmoor, *U.K.*	13	G4
Dartmouth, *Australia*	90	C3
Dartmouth, *Canada*	99	D7
Dartmouth, *U.K.*	13	G4
Dartmouth, L., *Australia*	91	D4
Dartuch, C., *Spain*	36	B10
Darvaza, *Turkmenistan*	44	E6
Darvel, Teluk, *Malaysia*	57	D5
Darwha, *India*	60	J10
Darwin, *Australia*	88	B5
Darwin, *U.S.A.*	113	J9
Darwin, Mt., *Chile*	128	D3
Darwin River, *Australia*	88	B5
Daryoi Amu = Amudarya →, *Uzbekistan*	44	E6
Dās, *U.A.E.*	65	E7
Dashetai, *China*	50	D5
Dashkesan, *Azerbaijan*	43	F12
Dasht, *Iran*	65	B8
Dasht →, *Pakistan*	60	G2
Dasht-e Mārgow, *Afghan.*	60	D3
Dasht-i-Nawar, *Afghan.*	62	C3
Daska, *Pakistan*	62	C6
Dassa-Zoume, *Benin*	79	D5
Dasseneiland, *S. Africa*	84	E2
Datça, *Turkey*	66	E2
Datia, *India*	63	G8
Datian, *China*	53	E11
Datong, Anhui, *China*	53	B11
Datong, Shanxi, *China*	50	D7
Datu, Tanjung, *Indonesia*	56	D3
Datu Piang, *Phil.*	55	H6
Daud Khel, *Pakistan*	62	C4
Daugava →, *Latvia*	40	C4
Daugavpils, *Latvia*	40	D5
Daule, *Ecuador*	120	D2
Daule →, *Ecuador*	120	D2
Daulpur, *India*	62	F7
Daun, *Germany*	19	E2
Dauphin, *Canada*	101	C8
Dauphin, *U.S.A.*	105	K1
Dauphin L., *Canada*	101	C9
Dauphiné, *France*	27	C9
Daura, Borno, *Nigeria*	79	C7
Daura, Kaduna, *Nigeria*	79	C6
Dausa, *India*	62	F7
Davangere, *India*	60	M9
Davao, *Phil.*	55	H6
Davao, G. of, *Phil.*	55	H6
Davenport, Calif., *U.S.A.*	112	H4
Davenport, Iowa, *U.S.A.*	108	E9
Davenport, Wash., *U.S.A.*	110	C4
Davenport Downs, *Australia*	90	C3
Davenport Ra., *Australia*	90	C1
David, *Panama*	116	E3
David City, *U.S.A.*	108	E6
David Gorodok, *Belorussia*	40	E5
Davidson, *Canada*	101	C7
Davis, *U.S.A.*	112	G5
Davis Dam, *U.S.A.*	113	K12
Davis Inlet, *Canada*	99	A7
Davis Mts., *U.S.A.*	109	K2
Davis Sea, *Antarctica*	5	C7
Davis Str., *N. Amer.*	97	B14
Davos, *Switz.*	23	C9
Davy L., *Canada*	101	B7
Dawa →, *Ethiopia*	77	G5
Dawaki, Bauchi, *Nigeria*	79	D6
Dawaki, Kano, *Nigeria*	79	C6
Dawes Ra., *Australia*	90	C5
Dawson, *Canada*	96	B6
Dawson, Ga., *U.S.A.*	105	K3
Dawson, N. Dak., *U.S.A.*	108	B5
Dawson, I., *Chile*	128	D2
Dawson Creek, *Canada*	100	B4
Dawson Inlet, *Canada*	101	A10
Dawson Ra., *Australia*	90	C4
Dawu, *China*	52	B3
Dax, *France*	26	E2
Daxi, *Taiwan*	53	E13
Daxian, *China*	52	B6
Daxin, *China*	52	F6
Daxindian, *China*	51	F11
Daxinggou, *China*	51	C15
Daxue Shan, Sichuan, *China*	52	B3
Daxue Shan, Yunnan, *China*	52	F2
Dayao, *China*	52	E3
Daye, *China*	53	B10
Dayi, *China*	52	B4
Daylesford, *Australia*	91	F3
Dayong, *China*	53	C8
Dayr az Zawr, *Syria*	64	C4
Daysland, *Canada*	100	C6
Dayton, Nev., *U.S.A.*	112	F7
Dayton, Ohio, *U.S.A.*	104	F3
Dayton, Pa., *U.S.A.*	106	F5
Dayton, Tenn., *U.S.A.*	105	H3
Dayton, Wash., *U.S.A.*	110	C4
Daytona Beach, *U.S.A.*	105	L5
Dayu, *China*	53	E10
Dazhu, *China*	52	B6
Dazu, *China*	52	C5
De Aar, *S. Africa*	84	E3
De Bilt, *Neths.*	16	D6
De Funiak Springs, *U.S.A.*	105	K2
De Grey, *Australia*	88	D2
De Grey →, *Australia*	88	D2
De Kalb, *U.S.A.*	108	E10
De Koog, *Neths.*	16	B5
De Land, *U.S.A.*	105	L5
De Leon, *U.S.A.*	109	J5
De Panne, *Belgium*	17	F1
De Pere, *U.S.A.*	104	C1
De Queen, *U.S.A.*	109	H7
De Quincy, *U.S.A.*	109	K8
De Ridder, *U.S.A.*	109	K8
De Rijp, *Neths.*	16	C5
De Smet, *U.S.A.*	108	C6
De Soto, *U.S.A.*	108	F9
De Tour Village, *U.S.A.*	104	C4
De Witt, *U.S.A.*	109	H9
Dead Sea, *Asia*	69	D4
Deadwood, *U.S.A.*	108	C3
Deadwood L., *Canada*	100	B3
Deakin, *Australia*	89	F4
Deal, *U.K.*	13	F9
Deal I., *Australia*	90	F4
Dealesville, *S. Africa*	84	D4
De'an, *China*	53	C10
Dean, Forest of, *U.K.*	13	F5
Deán Funes, *Argentina*	126	C3
Dearborn, *U.S.A.*	98	D3
Dease →, *Canada*	100	B3
Dease L., *Canada*	100	B2
Dease Lake, *Canada*	100	B2
Death Valley, *U.S.A.*	113	J10
Death Valley Junction, *U.S.A.*	113	J10
Death Valley National Monument, *U.S.A.*	113	J10
Deauville, *France*	24	C7
Deba Habe, *Nigeria*	79	C7
Debaltsevo, *Ukraine*	42	B8
Debao, *China*	52	F6
Debar, *Macedonia*	39	H3
Debden, *Canada*	101	C7
Debdou, *Morocco*	75	B4
Dębica, *Poland*	20	E11
Dęblin, *Poland*	20	D11
Débo, L., *Mali*	78	B4
Debolt, *Canada*	100	B5
Deborah East, L., *Australia*	89	F2
Deborah West, L., *Australia*	89	F2
Debre Birhan, *Ethiopia*	77	F4
Debre Markos, *Ethiopia*	77	E4
Debre May, *Ethiopia*	77	E4
Debre Sina, *Ethiopia*	77	F4
Debre Tabor, *Ethiopia*	77	E4
Debre Zebit, *Ethiopia*	77	E4
Debrecen, *Hungary*	21	H11
Dečani, *Serbia*	21	N10
Decatur, Ala., *U.S.A.*	105	H2
Decatur, Ga., *U.S.A.*	105	J3
Decatur, Ill., *U.S.A.*	108	F10
Decatur, Ind., *U.S.A.*	104	E3
Decatur, Tex., *U.S.A.*	109	J6
Decazeville, *France*	26	D6
Deccan, *India*	60	M10
Deception L., *Canada*	101	B8
Dechang, *China*	52	D4
Děčín, *Czech.*	20	E4
Decize, *France*	25	F10
Deckerville, *U.S.A.*	106	C2
Decollatura, *Italy*	35	C9
Decorah, *U.S.A.*	108	D9
Dedéagach = Alexandroúpolis, *Greece*	39	J8
Dedegöl Dağları, *Turkey*	66	E4
Dedemsvaart, *Neths.*	16	C8
Dedham, *U.S.A.*	107	D13
Dedilovo, *Russia*	41	E10
Dédougou, *Burkina Faso*	78	C4
Dedza, *Malawi*	83	E3
Dee →, Clwyd, *U.K.*	12	D4
Dee →, Gramp., *U.K.*	14	D6
Deep B., *Canada*	100	A5
Deep Well, *Australia*	90	C1
Deepwater, *Australia*	91	D5
Deer →, *Canada*	101	B10
Deer Lake, Nfld., *Canada*	99	C8
Deer Lake, Ont., *Canada*	101	C10
Deer Lodge, *U.S.A.*	110	C7
Deer Park, *U.S.A.*	110	C5
Deer River, *U.S.A.*	108	B8
Deeral, *Australia*	90	B4
Deerdepoort, *S. Africa*	84	C4
Deerlijk, *Belgium*	17	G2
Deferiet, *U.S.A.*	107	B9
Defiance, *U.S.A.*	104	E3
Dêgê, *China*	52	B2
Degebe →, *Portugal*	31	G3
Degeh Bur, *Ethiopia*	68	F3
Degema, *Nigeria*	79	E6
Degersheim, *Switz.*	23	B8
Deggendorf, *Germany*	19	G8
Deh Bīd, *Iran*	65	D7
Deh-e Shīr, *Iran*	65	D7
Dehaj, *Iran*	65	D7
Dehdez, *Iran*	65	D6
Dehestān, *Iran*	65	D7
Dehgolān, *Iran*	64	C5
Dehi Titan, *Afghan.*	60	C3
Dehibat, *Tunisia*	75	B7
Dehlorān, *Iran*	64	C5
Dehnow-e Kūhestān, *Iran*	65	E8
Dehra Dun, *India*	62	D8
Dehri, *India*	63	G11
Dehua, *China*	53	E12
Dehui, *China*	51	B13
Deinze, *Belgium*	17	G3
Dej, *Romania*	38	B6
Dejiang, *China*	52	C7
Dekemhare, *Eritrea*	77	D4
Dekese, *Zaïre*	80	E4
Del Mar, *U.S.A.*	113	N9
Del Norte, *U.S.A.*	111	H10
Del Rio, *U.S.A.*	109	L4
Delai, *Sudan*	76	D4
Delano, *U.S.A.*	113	K7
Delareyville, *S. Africa*	84	D4
Delavan, *U.S.A.*	108	D10
Delaware, *U.S.A.*	104	E4
Delaware □, *U.S.A.*	104	F8
Delaware →, *U.S.A.*	107	F10
Delaware B., *U.S.A.*	103	C12
Delegate, *Australia*	91	F4
Delémont, *Switz.*	22	B4
Delft, *Neths.*	16	D4
Delfzijl, *Neths.*	16	B9
Delgado, C., *Mozam.*	83	E5
Delgerhet, *Mongolia*	50	B6
Delgo, *Sudan*	76	C3
Delhi, *Canada*	106	D4
Delhi, *India*	62	E7
Delhi, *U.S.A.*	107	D10
Delia, *Canada*	100	C6
Delice, *Turkey*	66	D6
Delice →, *Turkey*	66	D6
Delicias, *Mexico*	114	B3
Delījān, *Iran*	65	C6
Delitzsch, *Germany*	18	D8
Dell City, *U.S.A.*	111	L11
Dell Rapids, *U.S.A.*	108	D6
Delle, *France*	25	E14
Dellys, *Algeria*	75	A5
Delmar, *U.S.A.*	107	D11
Delmenhorst, *Germany*	18	B4
Delmiro Gouveia, *Brazil*	122	C4
Delnice, *Croatia*	33	C11
Delong, Ostrova, *Russia*	45	B15
Deloraine, *Australia*	90	G4
Deloraine, *Canada*	101	D8
Delphi, *U.S.A.*	104	E2
Delphos, *U.S.A.*	104	E3
Delportshoop, *S. Africa*	84	D3
Delray Beach, *U.S.A.*	105	M5
Delsbo, *Sweden*	10	C10
Delta, Colo., *U.S.A.*	111	G9
Delta, Utah, *U.S.A.*	110	G7
Delta □, *Nigeria*	79	D6
Delta Amacuro □, *Venezuela*	121	B5
Delungra, *Australia*	91	D5
Delvina, *Albania*	39	K3
Delvinákion, *Greece*	39	K3
Demanda, Sierra de la, *Spain*	28	C1
Demavand = Damāvand, *Iran*	65	C7
Demba, *Zaïre*	80	F4
Dembecha, *Ethiopia*	77	E4
Dembi, *Ethiopia*	77	F4
Dembia, *Zaïre*	82	B2
Dembidolo, *Ethiopia*	77	F3
Demer →, *Belgium*	17	G5
Demidov, *Russia*	40	D7
Deming, N. Mex., *U.S.A.*	111	K10
Deming, Wash., *U.S.A.*	112	B4
Demini →, *Brazil*	121	D5
Demirci, *Turkey*	66	D3
Demirköy, *Turkey*	66	C2
Demmin, *Germany*	18	B9
Demnate, *Morocco*	74	B3
Demonte, *Italy*	32	D4
Demopolis, *U.S.A.*	105	J2
Dempo, *Indonesia*	56	E2
Demyansk, *Russia*	40	C8
Den Burg, *Neths.*	16	B5
Den Chai, *Thailand*	58	D3
Den Dungen, *Neths.*	17	E6

Den Haag = 's-Gravenhage, Neths. 16 D4
Den Ham, Neths. 16 D8
Den Helder, Neths. 16 C5
Den Hulst, Neths. 16 C8
Den Oever, Neths. 16 C6
Denain, France 25 B10
Denair, U.S.A. 112 H6
Denau, Uzbekistan 44 F7
Denbigh, U.K. 12 D4
Dendang, Indonesia 56 E3
Dender →, Belgium 17 F4
Denderhoutem, Belgium 17 G4
Denderleeuw, Belgium 17 G4
Dendermonde, Belgium 17 F4
Deneba, Ethiopia 77 F4
Denekamp, Neths. 16 D10
Deng Xian, China 53 A9
Dengchuan, China 52 E3
Denge, Nigeria 79 C6
Dengfeng, China 50 G7
Dengi, Nigeria 79 D6
Dengkou, China 50 D4
Denham, Australia 89 E1
Denham Ra., Australia 90 C4
Denham Sd., Australia 89 E1
Denia, Spain 29 G5
Denial B., Australia 91 E1
Deniliquin, Australia 91 F3
Denison, Iowa, U.S.A. 108 D7
Denison, Tex., U.S.A. 109 J6
Denison Plains, Australia 88 C4
Denizli, Turkey 66 E3
Denizli □, Turkey 66 E3
Denman Glacier, Antarctica 5 C7
Denmark, Australia 89 F2
Denmark ■, Europe 11 J3
Denmark Str., Atl. Oc. 4 C6
Dennison, U.S.A. 106 F3
Denpasar, Indonesia 56 F5
Denton, Mont., U.S.A. 110 C9
Denton, Tex., U.S.A. 109 J6
D'Entrecasteaux, Pt., Australia 89 F2
Dents du Midi, Switz. 22 D3
Denu, Ghana 79 D5
Denver, U.S.A. 108 F2
Denver City, U.S.A. 109 J3
Deoband, India 62 E7
Deoghar, India 63 G12
Deolali, India 60 K8
Deoli = Devli, India 62 G6
Deoria, India 63 F10
Deosai Mts., Pakistan 63 B6
Deping, China 51 F9
Deposit, U.S.A. 107 D9
Depot Springs, Australia 89 E3
Deputatskiy, Russia 45 C14
Dêqên, China 52 C2
Deqing, China 53 F8
Dera Ghazi Khan, Pakistan 62 D4
Dera Ismail Khan, Pakistan 62 D4
Derbent, Russia 43 E13
Derby, Australia 88 C3
Derby, U.K. 12 E6
Derby, Conn., U.S.A. 107 E11
Derby, N.Y., U.S.A. 106 D6
Derbyshire □, U.K. 12 E6
Dereli, Turkey 67 C8
Derg →, U.K. 15 B4
Derg, L., Ireland 15 D3
Dergachi, Ukraine 42 A7
Dergaon, India 61 F19
Derik, Turkey 67 E9
Derinkuyu, Turkey 66 D6
Dernieres, Isles, U.S.A. 109 L9
Dêrong, China 52 C2
Derry = Londonderry, U.K. 15 B4
Derryveagh Mts., Ireland 15 B3
Derudub, Sudan 76 D4
Derval, France 24 E5
Dervéni, Greece 39 L5
Derwent, Canada 101 C6
Derwent →, Derby, U.K. 12 E6
Derwent →, N. Yorks., U.K. 12 D7
Derwent Water, U.K. 12 C4
Des Moines, Iowa, U.S.A. 108 E8
Des Moines, N. Mex., U.S.A. 109 G3
Des Moines →, U.S.A. 108 E9
Desaguadero →, Argentina 126 C2
Desaguadero →, Bolivia 124 D4
Descanso, Pta., Mexico 113 N9
Descartes, France 26 B4
Deschaillons, Canada 99 C5
Descharme →, Canada 101 B7
Deschutes →, U.S.A. 110 D3
Dese, Ethiopia 68 E2
Deseado, C., Chile 128 D2
Desenzano del Gardo, Italy 32 C7
Desert Center, U.S.A. 113 M11
Desert Hot Springs, U.S.A. 113 M10
Désirade, I., Guadeloupe 117 C7
Deskenatlata L., Canada 100 A6
Desna →, Ukraine 40 F7
Desnătui →, Romania 38 E6
Desolación, I., Chile 128 D2
Despeñaperros, Paso, Spain 29 G1
Despotovac, Serbia 21 L11
Dessau, Germany 18 D8
Dessel, Belgium 17 F6
Dessye = Dese, Ethiopia 68 E2
D'Estrees B., Australia 91 F2
Desuri, India 62 G5
Desvres, France 25 B8
Det Udom, Thailand 58 E5
Dete, Zimbabwe 83 F2
Detinja →, Serbia 21 M9
Detmold, Germany 18 D4
Detour, Pt., U.S.A. 104 C2
Detroit, Mich., U.S.A. 98 D3
Detroit, Tex., U.S.A. 109 J7
Detroit Lakes, U.S.A. 108 B7
Deurne, Belgium 17 F4
Deurne, Neths. 17 F7
Deutsche Bucht, Germany 18 A4
Deutschlandsberg, Austria 21 J5
Deux-Sèvres □, France 24 F6
Deva, Romania 38 D5
Devakottai, India 60 Q11
Devaprayag, India 63 D8
Dévaványa, Hungary 21 H10
Deveci Dağı, Turkey 42 F7
Deveci Dağları, Turkey 66 C6
Develi, Turkey 66 D6
Deventer, Neths. 16 D8
Deveron →, U.K. 14 D6
Devgadh Bariya, India 62 H5
Devils Den, U.S.A. 112 K7
Devils Lake, U.S.A. 108 A5
Devils Paw, Canada 100 B2
Devizes, U.K. 13 F6
Devli, India 62 G6
Devnya, Bulgaria 38 F10
Devolii →, Albania 39 J3
Devon, Canada 100 C6
Devon □, U.K. 13 G4
Devon I., Canada 4 B3
Devonport, Australia 90 G4
Devonport, N.Z. 87 G5
Devonport, U.K. 13 G3
Devrek, Turkey 66 C4
Devrekâni, Turkey 66 C5
Devrez →, Turkey 66 C6
Dewas, India 62 H7
Dewetsdorp, S. Africa 84 D4
Dewsbury, U.K. 12 D6
Dexing, China 53 C11
Dexter, Mo., U.S.A. 109 G9
Dexter, N. Mex., U.S.A. 109 J2
Dey-Dey, L., Australia 89 E5
Deyang, China 52 B5
Deyhūk, Iran 65 C8
Deyyer, Iran 65 E6
Dezadeash L., Canada 100 A1
Dezfūl, Iran 65 C6
Dezhneva, Mys, Russia 45 C19
Dezhou, China 50 F9
Dháfni, Greece 37 D7
Dhahaban, Si. Arabia 76 C4
Dhahiriya = Az Zāhirīyah, Jordan 69 D3
Dhahran = Az Zahrān, Si. Arabia 65 E6
Dhaka, Bangla. 63 H14
Dhaka □, Bangla. 63 G14
Dhali, Cyprus 37 D12
Dhamar, Yemen 68 E3
Dhamási, Greece 39 K5
Dhampur, India 63 E8
Dhamtari, India 61 J12
Dhanbad, India 63 H12
Dhangarhi, Nepal 61 E12
Dhankuta, Nepal 63 F12
Dhar, India 62 H6
Dharampur, India 62 H6
Dharamsala = Dharmsala, India 62 C7
Dharmapuri, India 60 N11
Dharmsala, India 62 C7
Dharwad, India 60 M9
Dharwar, India 60 M9
Dhaulagiri, Nepal 63 E10
Dhebar, L., India 62 G6
Dheftera, Cyprus 37 D12
Dhenkanal, India 61 J14
Dhenoúsa, Greece 39 M8
Dherinia, Cyprus 37 D12
Dheskáti, Greece 39 K4
Dhespotikó, Greece 39 N7
Dhestina, Greece 39 L5
Dhiarrizos →, Cyprus 37 E11
Dhībān, Jordan 69 D4
Dhíkti Óros, Greece 37 D7
Dhimitsána, Greece 39 M5
Dhírfis, Greece 39 L6
Dhodhekánisos, Greece 39 N10
Dholiana, Greece 39 K3
Dholka, India 62 H5
Dhoraji, India 62 J4
Dhoxáton, Greece 39 H7
Dhráhstis, Ákra, Greece 37 A3
Dhrangadhra, India 62 H4
Dhrápanon, Ákra, Greece 37 D6
Dhrol, India 62 H4
Dhuburi, India 61 F16
Dhule, India 60 J9
Dhut →, Somali Rep. 68 E5
Di Linh, Vietnam 59 G7
Di Linh, Cao Nguyen, Vietnam 59 G7
Día, Greece 37 D7
Diablo, Mt., U.S.A. 112 H5
Diablo Range, U.S.A. 112 J5
Diafarabé, Mali 78 C4
Diala, Mali 78 C3
Dialakoro, Mali 78 C3
Diallassagou, Mali 78 C4
Diamante, Argentina 126 C3
Diamante →, Argentina 126 C2
Diamantina, Brazil 123 E3
Diamantina →, Australia 91 D2
Diamantino, Brazil 125 C6
Diamond Harbour, India 63 H13
Diamond Is., Australia 90 B5
Diamond Mts., U.S.A. 110 G6
Diamond Springs, U.S.A. 112 G6
Diamondville, U.S.A. 110 F8
Dianbai, China 53 G8
Diancheng, China 53 G8
Diano Marina, Italy 32 E5
Dianópolis, Brazil 123 D2
Dianra, Ivory C. 78 D3
Diapaga, Burkina Faso 79 C5
Diapangou, Burkina Faso 79 C5
Diariguila, Guinea 78 C2
Dībā, Oman 65 E8
Dibaya, Zaïre 80 F4
Dibaya-Lubue, Zaïre 80 E3
Dibbi, Ethiopia 68 G3
Dibete, Botswana 84 C4
Dibrugarh, India 61 F19
Dickinson, U.S.A. 108 B3
Dickson, U.S.A. 105 G2
Dickson City, U.S.A. 107 E9
Dicomano, Italy 33 E8
Didam, Neths. 16 E8
Didesa, W. →, Ethiopia 77 E4
Didiéni, Mali 78 C3
Didsbury, Canada 100 C6
Didwana, India 62 F6
Die, France 27 D9
Diébougou, Burkina Faso 78 C4
Diefenbaker L., Canada 101 C7
Diego Garcia, Ind. Oc. 3 E13
Diekirch, Lux. 17 J8
Diélette, France 24 C5
Diéma, Mali 78 C3
Diémbéring, Senegal 78 C1
Diemen, Neths. 16 D5
Dien Ban, Vietnam 58 E7
Dien Bien, Vietnam 58 B4
Dien Khanh, Vietnam 59 F7
Diepenbeek, Belgium 17 G6
Diepenheim, Neths. 16 D9
Diepenveen, Neths. 16 D8
Diepholz, Germany 18 C4
Diepoldsau, Switz. 23 B9
Dieppe, France 24 C8
Dieren, Neths. 16 D8
Dierks, U.S.A. 109 H7
Diessen, Neths. 17 F6
Diessenhofen, Switz. 23 A7
Diest, Belgium 17 G6
Dietikon, Switz. 23 B6
Dieulefit, France 27 D9
Dieuze, France 25 D13
Diever, Neths. 16 C8
Differdange, Lux. 17 J7
Dig, India 62 F7
Digba, Zaïre 82 B2
Digby, Canada 99 D6
Digges, Canada 101 B10
Digges Is., Canada 97 B12
Dighinala, Bangla. 61 H18
Dighton, U.S.A. 108 F4
Digne, France 27 D10
Digoin, France 26 B7
Digor, Turkey 67 C10
Digos, Phil. 55 H6
Digranes, Iceland 8 C6
Digul →, Indonesia 57 F9
Dihang →, India 61 F19
Dīhōk, Iraq 64 B3
Dijlah, Nahr →, Asia 64 D5
Dijle →, Belgium 17 G5
Dijon, France 25 E12
Dikala, Sudan 77 G3
Dikkil, Djibouti 77 E5
Dikomu di Kai, Botswana 84 C3
Diksmuide, Belgium 17 F1
Dikson, Russia 44 B9
Dikwa, Nigeria 79 C7
Dila, Ethiopia 77 F4
Dilbeek, Belgium 17 G4
Dili, Indonesia 57 F7
Dilizhan, Armenia 43 F11
Dillenburg, Germany 18 E4
Dilley, U.S.A. 109 L5
Dilling, Sudan 77 E2
Dillingen, Germany 19 G6
Dillingham, U.S.A. 96 C4
Dillon, Canada 101 B7
Dillon, Mont., U.S.A. 110 D7
Dillon, S.C., U.S.A. 105 H6
Dillon →, Canada 101 B7
Dilolo, Zaïre 80 G4
Dilsen, Belgium 17 F7
Dilston, Australia 90 G4
Dimas, Mexico 114 C3
Dimashq, Syria 69 B5
Dimashq □, Syria 69 B5
Dimbaza, S. Africa 85 E4
Dimbokro, Ivory C. 78 D4
Dimboola, Australia 91 F3
Dîmboviţa →, Romania 38 E9
Dîmbovnic →, Romania 38 E8
Dimbulah, Australia 90 B4
Dimitrovgrad, Bulgaria 39 G8
Dimitrovgrad, Russia 41 D16
Dimitrovgrad, Serbia 21 M12
Dimitrovo = Pernik, Bulgaria 38 G6
Dimmitt, U.S.A. 109 H3
Dimo, Sudan 77 F2
Dimona, Israel 69 D4
Dimovo, Bulgaria 38 F5
Dinagat, Phil. 55 F6
Dinajpur, Bangla. 61 G16
Dinan, France 24 D4
Dīnān Āb, Iran 65 C8
Dinant, Belgium 17 H5
Dinapur, India 63 G11
Dinar, Turkey 66 D4
Dinara Planina, Croatia 33 E13
Dinard, France 24 D4
Dinaric Alps = Dinara Planina, Croatia 33 E13
Dinder, Nahr ed →, Sudan 77 E3
Dindigul, India 60 P11
Ding Xian, China 50 E8
Dingalan, Phil. 55 D4
Dingbian, China 50 F4
Dingelstädt, Germany 18 D6
Dinghai, China 53 B14
Dingle, Ireland 15 D1
Dingle B., Ireland 15 D1
Dingmans Ferry, U.S.A. 107 E10
Dingnan, China 53 E10
Dingo, Australia 90 C4
Dingolfing, Germany 19 G8
Dingtao, China 50 G8
Dinguiraye, Guinea 78 C2
Dingwall, U.K. 14 D4
Dingxi, China 50 G3
Dingxiang, China 50 E7
Dingyuan, China 53 A11
Dinh, Mui, Vietnam 59 G7
Dinh Lap, Vietnam 58 B6
Dinkel →, Neths. 16 D9
Dinokwe, Botswana 84 C4
Dinosaur National Monument, U.S.A. 110 F9
Dinslaken, Germany 17 E9
Dintel →, Neths. 17 E4
Dinteloord, Neths. 17 E4
Dinuba, U.S.A. 111 H4
Dinxperlo, Neths. 16 E9
Diósgyör, Hungary 21 G10
Diourbel, Senegal 78 C1
Diplo, Pakistan 62 G3
Dipolog, Phil. 55 G5
Dipşa, Romania 38 C7
Dir, Pakistan 60 B7
Diré, Mali 78 B4
Dire Dawa, Ethiopia 68 F3
Diriamba, Nic. 116 D2
Dirico, Angola 81 H4
Dirk Hartog I., Australia 89 E1
Dirranbandi, Australia 91 D4
Disa, India 62 G5
Disa, Sudan 77 E3
Disappointment, C., U.S.A. 110 C1
Disappointment, L., Australia 88 D3
Disaster B., Australia 91 F4
Discovery B., Australia 91 F3
Disentis, Switz. 23 C7
Dishna, Egypt 76 B3
Disina, Nigeria 79 C6
Disko, Greenland 4 C5
Disko Bugt, Greenland 4 C5
Disna →, Belorussia 40 D6
Dison, Belgium 17 G7
Disteghil Sar, Pakistan 63 A6
Distrito Federal □, Brazil 123 E2
Distrito Federal □, Venezuela 120 A4
Disûq, Egypt 76 H7
Diu, India 62 J4
Dīvāndarreh, Iran 64 C5
Dives →, France 24 C6
Dives-sur-Mer, France 24 C6
Divichi, Azerbaijan 43 F13
Divide, U.S.A. 110 D7
Dividing Ra., Australia 89 E2
Divinópolis, Brazil 123 F3
Divisões, Serra dos, Brazil 123 E1
Divnoye, Russia 43 D10
Divo, Ivory C. 78 D3
Divriği, Turkey 67 D8
Dīwāl Kol, Afghan. 62 B2
Dixie Mt., U.S.A. 112 F6
Dixon, Calif., U.S.A. 112 G5
Dixon, Ill., U.S.A. 108 E10
Dixon, Mont., U.S.A. 110 C6
Dixon, N. Mex., U.S.A. 111 H11
Dixon Entrance, U.S.A. 100 C2
Dixonville, Canada 100 B5
Diyadin, Turkey 67 D10
Diyarbakır, Turkey 67 E9
Diyarbakir □, Turkey 67 E9
Djado, Niger 73 D7
Djakarta = Jakarta, Indonesia 57 G12
Djamâa, Algeria 75 B6
Djamba, Angola 84 B1
Djambala, Congo 80 E2
Djanet, Algeria 75 D6
Djawa = Jawa, Indonesia 57 G14
Djebiniana, Tunisia 75 A7
Djelfa, Algeria 75 B5
Djema, C.A.R. 82 A2
Djendel, Algeria 75 A5
Djeneïene, Tunisia 75 B7
Djenné, Mali 78 C4
Djenoun, Garet el, Algeria 75 C6
Djerba, Tunisia 75 B7
Djerba, I. de, Tunisia 73 B7
Djerid, Chott, Tunisia 75 B6
Djibo, Burkina Faso 79 C4
Djibouti, Djibouti 68 E3
Djibouti ■, Africa 68 E3
Djolu, Zaïre 80 D4
Djougou, Benin 79 D5
Djoum, Cameroon 80 D2
Djourab, Chad 73 E8
Djugu, Zaïre 82 B3
Djúpivogur, Iceland 8 D6
Djursholm, Sweden 10 E12
Djursland, Denmark 11 H4
Dmitriev-Lgovskiy, Russia 40 E9
Dmitriya Lapteva, Proliv, Russia 45 B15
Dmitrov, Russia 41 C10
Dmitrovsk-Orlovskiy, Russia 40 E9
Dnepr →, Ukraine 42 C5
Dneprodzerzhinsk, Ukraine 42 B6
Dneprodzerzhinskoye Vdkhr., Ukraine 42 B6
Dnepropetrovsk, Ukraine 42 B6
Dneprorudnoye, Ukraine 42 C6
Dnestr →, Europe 42 C4
Dnestrovski = Belgorod, Russia 41 F10
Dnieper = Dnepr →, Ukraine 42 C5
Dniester = Dnestr →, Europe 42 C4
Dnipro = Dnepr →, Ukraine 42 C5
Dniprodzerzhynsk = Dneprodzerzhinsk, Ukraine 42 B6
Dnipropetrovsk = Dnepropetrovsk, Ukraine 42 B6
Dno, Russia 40 C6
Dnyapro = Dnepr →, Ukraine 42 C5
Doan Hung, Vietnam 58 B5
Doba, Chad 73 G8
Dobbiaco, Italy 33 B9
Dobbyn, Australia 90 B3
Döbeln, Germany 18 D9
Doberai, Jazirah, Indonesia 57 E8
Dobiegniew, Poland 20 C5
Doblas, Argentina 126 D3
Dobo, Indonesia 57 F8
Doboj, Bos.-H. 21 L8
Dobra, Dîmbovita, Romania 38 E8
Dobra, Hunedoara, Romania 38 D5
Dobreta-Turnu-Severin, Romania 38 E5
Dobrinishta, Bulgaria 39 H6
Dobrodzień, Poland 20 E8
Dobropole, Ukraine 42 B7
Dobruja, Romania 38 E11
Dobrush, Belorussia 40 E7
Dobtong, Sudan 77 F3
Doc, Mui, Vietnam 58 D6
Doce →, Brazil 123 E4
Doda, India 63 C6
Dodecanese = Dhodhekánisos, Greece 39 N10
Dodewaard, Neths. 16 E7
Dodge Center, U.S.A. 108 C8
Dodge City, U.S.A. 109 G5
Dodge L., Canada 101 B7
Dodgeville, U.S.A. 108 D9
Dodo, Sudan 77 F2
Dodola, Ethiopia 77 F4
Dodoma, Tanzania 82 D4
Dodoma □, Tanzania 82 D4
Dodsland, Canada 101 C7
Dodson, U.S.A. 110 B9
Doesburg, Neths. 16 D8
Doetinchem, Neths. 16 E8
Dog Creek, Canada 100 C4
Dog L., Man., Canada 101 C9
Dog L., Ont., Canada 98 C2
Doğanşehir, Turkey 67 D7
Dogger Bank, N. Sea 6 E6
Dogi, Afghan. 60 C3
Dogliani, Italy 32 D4
Dogondoutchi, Niger 79 C5
Dogran, Pakistan 62 D5
Doğubayazıt, Turkey 67 D11
Doguéraoua, Niger 79 C6
Doha = Ad Dawhah, Qatar 65 E6
Dohazari, Bangla. 61 H18
Doi, Indonesia 57 D7
Doi Luang, Thailand 58 C3
Doi Saket, Thailand 58 C2
Doig →, Canada 100 B4
Dois Irmãos, Sa., Brazil 122 C3
Dokka, Norway 9 F11
Dokka →, Norway 10 D4
Dokkum, Neths. 16 B7
Dokkumer Ee →, Neths. 16 B7
Dokri, Pakistan 62 F3
Dol-de-Bretagne, France 24 D5
Doland, U.S.A. 108 C5
Dolbeau, Canada 99 C5
Dole, France 25 E12
Doleib, Wadi →, Sudan 77 E3
Dolgellau, U.K. 12 E4
Dolgelley = Dolgellau, U.K. 12 E4
Dolginovo, Belorussia 40 D5

Dolianova, *Italy* 34 C2
Dolinskaya, *Ukraine* 42 B5
Dollart, *Neths.* 16 B10
Dolna Banya, *Bulgaria* 38 G6
Dolni Dŭbnik, *Bulgaria* 38 F7
Dolo, *Ethiopia* 77 G5
Dolo, *Italy* 33 C9
Dolomites = Dolomiti, *Italy* 33 B8
Dolomiti, *Italy* 33 B8
Dolores, *Argentina* 126 D4
Dolores, *Uruguay* 126 C4
Dolores, *U.S.A.* 111 H9
Dolores →, *U.S.A.* 111 G9
Dolphin, C., *Falk. Is.* 128 D5
Dolphin and Union Str., *Canada* 96 B8
Dom, *Switz.* 22 D5
Dom Joaquim, *Brazil* 123 E3
Dom Pedrito, *Brazil* 127 C5
Dom Pedro, *Brazil* 122 B3
Doma, *Nigeria* 79 D6
Domaniç, *Turkey* 66 D3
Domasi, *Malawi* 83 F4
Domat Ems, *Switz.* 23 C8
Domazlice, *Czech.* 20 F2
Dombarovskiy, *Russia* 44 D6
Dombås, *Norway* 9 E10
Dombasle-sur-Meurthe, *France* 25 D13
Dombes, *France* 27 B8
Dombóvár, *Hungary* 21 J8
Domburg, *Neths.* 17 E3
Domérat, *France* 26 B6
Domeyko, *Chile* 126 B1
Domeyko, Cordillera, *Chile* 126 A2
Domfront, *France* 24 D6
Dominador, *Chile* 126 A2
Dominica ■, *W. Indies* 117 C7
Dominica Passage, *W. Indies* 117 C7
Dominican Rep. ■, *W. Indies* 117 C5
Dömitz, *Germany* 18 B7
Domme, *France* 26 D5
Dommel →, *Neths.* 17 E6
Domo, *Ethiopia* 68 F4
Domodóssola, *Italy* 32 B5
Dompaire, *France* 25 D13
Dompierre-sur-Besbre, *France* 26 B7
Dompim, *Ghana* 78 D4
Domrémy-la-Pucelle, *France* 25 D12
Domsjö, *Sweden* 10 A12
Domville, Mt., *Australia* 91 D5
Domvraína, *Greece* 39 L5
Domžale, *Slovenia* 33 B11
Don →, *Russia* 43 C8
Don →, *Gramp., U.K.* 14 D6
Don →, *S. Yorks., U.K.* 12 D7
Don, C., *Australia* 88 B5
Don Benito, *Spain* 31 G5
Don Duong, *Vietnam* 59 G7
Don Martín, Presa de, *Mexico* 114 B4
Dona Ana = Nhamaabué, *Mozam.* 83 F4
Donaghadee, *U.K.* 15 B6
Donald, *Australia* 91 F3
Donalda, *Canada* 100 C6
Donaldsonville, *U.S.A.* 109 K9
Donalsonville, *U.S.A.* 105 K3
Donau →, *Austria* 21 G7
Donaueschingen, *Germany* 19 H4
Donauwörth, *Germany* 19 G6
Doncaster, *U.K.* 12 D6
Dondo, *Angola* 80 F2
Dondo, *Mozam.* 83 F3
Dondo, Teluk, *Indonesia* 57 D6
Dondra Head, *Sri Lanka* 60 S12
Donegal, *Ireland* 15 B3
Donegal □, *Ireland* 15 B4
Donegal B., *Ireland* 15 B3
Donets →, *Russia* 43 C9
Donetsk, *Ukraine* 42 C7
Dong Ba Thin, *Vietnam* 59 F7
Dong Dang, *Vietnam* 58 B6
Dong Giam, *Vietnam* 58 C5
Dong Ha, *Vietnam* 58 D6
Dong Hene, *Laos* 58 D5
Dong Hoi, *Vietnam* 58 D6
Dong Jiang →, *China* 53 F10
Dong Khe, *Vietnam* 58 A6
Dong Ujimqin Qi, *China* 50 B9
Dong Van, *Vietnam* 58 A5
Dong Xoai, *Vietnam* 59 G6
Donga, *Nigeria* 79 D7
Dong'an, *China* 53 D8
Dongara, *Australia* 89 E1
Dongbei, *China* 51 D13
Dongchuan, *China* 52 D4
Dongen, *Neths.* 17 E5
Donges, *France* 24 E4
Dongfang, *China* 58 C7
Dongfeng, *China* 51 C13
Donggala, *Indonesia* 57 E5
Donggan, *China* 52 F5
Donggou, *China* 51 E13
Dongguan, *China* 53 F9
Dongguang, *China* 50 F9
Donghai Dao, *China* 53 G8
Dongjingcheng, *China* 51 B15
Donglan, *China* 52 E6
Dongliu, *China* 53 B11
Dongmen, *China* 52 F6
Dongning, *China* 51 B16
Dongnyi, *China* 52 C3
Dongola, *Sudan* 76 D3
Dongou, *Congo* 80 D3
Dongping, *China* 50 G9
Dongshan, *China* 53 F11
Dongsheng, *China* 50 E6
Dongshi, *Taiwan* 53 E13
Dongtai, *China* 51 H11
Dongting Hu, *China* 53 C9
Dongxiang, *China* 53 C11
Dongxing, *China* 52 G7
Dongyang, *China* 53 C13
Dongzhi, *China* 53 B11
Donington, C., *Australia* 91 E2
Doniphan, *U.S.A.* 109 G9
Donja Stubica, *Croatia* 33 C13
Donji Dušnik, *Serbia* 21 M12
Donji Miholjac, *Croatia* 21 K8
Donji Milanovac, *Serbia* 21 L12
Donji Vakuf, *Bos.-H.* 21 L7
Dønna, *Norway* 8 C12
Donna, *U.S.A.* 109 M5
Donnaconna, *Canada* 99 C5
Donnelly's Crossing, *N.Z.* 87 F4
Donnybrook, *Australia* 89 F2
Donnybrook, *S. Africa* 85 D4
Donora, *U.S.A.* 106 F5
Donor's Hill, *Australia* 90 B3
Donostia = San Sebastián, *Spain* 28 B3
Donskoy, *Russia* 41 E11
Donsol, *Phil.* 55 E5
Donya Lendava, *Slovenia* 33 B13
Donzère, *France* 27 D8
Donzère-Mondragon, Barr. de, *France* 27 D8
Donzy, *France* 25 E10
Doon →, *U.K.* 14 F4
Doorn, *Neths.* 16 D6
Dora, L., *Australia* 88 D3
Dora Báltea →, *Italy* 32 C5
Dora Riparia →, *Italy* 32 C4
Doran L., *Canada* 101 A7
Dorchester, *U.K.* 13 G5
Dorchester, C., *Canada* 97 B12
Dordogne □, *France* 26 C4
Dordogne →, *France* 26 C3
Dordrecht, *Neths.* 16 E5
Dordrecht, *S. Africa* 84 E4
Dore →, *France* 26 C7
Dore, Mts., *France* 26 C6
Doré L., *Canada* 101 C7
Doré Lake, *Canada* 101 C7
Dores do Indaiá, *Brazil* 123 E2
Dorfen, *Germany* 19 G8
Dorgali, *Italy* 34 B2
Dori, *Burkina Faso* 79 C4
Doring →, *S. Africa* 84 E2
Doringbos, *S. Africa* 84 E2
Dorion, *Canada* 98 C5
Dormaa-Ahenkro, *Ghana* 78 D4
Dormo, Ras, *Eritrea* 77 E5
Dornach, *Switz.* 22 B5
Dornberg, *Slovenia* 33 C10
Dornbirn, *Austria* 19 H5
Dornes, *France* 25 F10
Dornoch, *U.K.* 14 D4
Dornoch Firth, *U.K.* 14 D4
Dornogovĭ □, *Mongolia* 50 B6
Doro, *Mali* 79 B4
Dorogobuzh, *Russia* 40 D8
Dorohoi, *Romania* 38 B9
Döröö Nuur, *Mongolia* 54 B4
Dorr, *Iran* 65 C6
Dorre I., *Australia* 89 E1
Dorrigo, *Australia* 91 E5
Dorris, *U.S.A.* 110 F3
Dorset, *Canada* 106 A6
Dorset, *U.S.A.* 106 E4
Dorset □, *U.K.* 13 G5
Dorsten, *Germany* 18 D2
Dortmund, *Germany* 18 D3
Dörtyol, *Turkey* 66 E7
Dorum, *Germany* 18 B4
Doruma, *Zaïre* 82 B2
Dorūneh, *Iran* 65 C8
Dos Bahías, C., *Argentina* 128 B3
Dos Hermanas, *Spain* 31 H5
Dos Palos, *U.S.A.* 112 J6
Dosso, *Niger* 79 C5
Dothan, *U.S.A.* 105 K3
Dottignies, *Belgium* 17 G2
Doty, *U.S.A.* 112 D3
Douai, *France* 25 B10
Douala, *Cameroon* 79 E6
Douarnenez, *France* 24 D2
Double Island Pt., *Australia* 91 D5
Doubrava →, *Czech.* 20 F5
Doubs □, *France* 25 E13
Doubs →, *France* 25 F12
Doubtful Sd., *N.Z.* 87 L1
Doubtless B., *N.Z.* 87 F4
Doudeville, *France* 24 C7
Doué-la-Fontaine, *France* 24 E6
Douentza, *Mali* 78 C4
Douglas, *S. Africa* 84 D3
Douglas, *U.K.* 12 C3
Douglas, *Alaska, U.S.A.* 100 B2
Douglas, *Ariz., U.S.A.* 111 L9
Douglas, *Ga., U.S.A.* 105 K4
Douglas, *Wyo., U.S.A.* 108 D2
Douglastown, *Canada* 99 C7
Douglasville, *U.S.A.* 105 J3
Douirat, *Morocco* 74 B4
Doukáton, Ákra, *Greece* 39 L3
Doulevant-le-Château, *France* 25 D11
Doullens, *France* 25 B9
Doumé, *Cameroon* 80 D2
Douna, *Mali* 78 C3
Dounan, *Taiwan* 53 F13
Dounreay, *U.K.* 14 C5
Dour, *Belgium* 17 H3
Dourada, Serra, *Brazil* 123 D2
Dourados, *Brazil* 127 A5
Dourados →, *Brazil* 127 A5
Dourdan, *France* 25 D9
Douro →, *Europe* 30 D2
Douvaine, *France* 27 B10
Douz, *Tunisia* 75 B6
Douze →, *France* 26 E3
Dove →, *U.K.* 12 E6
Dove Creek, *U.S.A.* 111 H9
Dover, *Australia* 90 G4
Dover, *U.K.* 13 F9
Dover, *Del., U.S.A.* 104 F8
Dover, *N.H., U.S.A.* 107 C14
Dover, *N.J., U.S.A.* 107 F10
Dover, *Ohio, U.S.A.* 106 F3
Dover, Pt., *Australia* 89 F4
Dover, Str. of, *Europe* 24 B8
Dover-Foxcroft, *U.S.A.* 99 C6
Dover Plains, *U.S.A.* 107 E11
Dovey = Dyfi →, *U.K.* 13 E4
Dovrefjell, *Norway* 10 B3
Dow Rūd, *Iran* 65 C6
Dowa, *Malawi* 83 E3
Dowagiac, *U.S.A.* 104 E2
Dowgha'i, *Iran* 65 B8
Dowlatābād, *Iran* 65 D8
Down □, *U.K.* 15 B6
Downey, *Calif., U.S.A.* 113 M8
Downey, *Idaho, U.S.A.* 110 E7
Downham Market, *U.K.* 13 E8
Downieville, *U.S.A.* 112 F6
Downpatrick, *U.K.* 15 B6
Downpatrick Hd., *Ireland* 15 B2
Dowsārī, *Iran* 65 D8
Doyle, *U.S.A.* 112 E6
Doylestown, *U.S.A.* 107 F9
Draa, C., *Morocco* 74 C2
Draa, Oued →, *Morocco* 74 C2
Drac →, *France* 27 C9
Drachten, *Neths.* 16 B8
Drăgăneşti, *Romania* 38 E7
Drăgăneşti-Viaşca, *Romania* 38 E8
Dragaš, *Serbia* 21 N10
Drăgăşani, *Romania* 38 E7
Dragonera, I., *Spain* 36 B9
Draguignan, *France* 27 E10
Drain, *U.S.A.* 110 E2
Drake, *Australia* 91 D5
Drake, *U.S.A.* 108 B4
Drake Passage, *S. Ocean* 5 B17
Drakensberg, *S. Africa* 85 E4
Dráma, *Greece* 39 H7
Drammen, *Norway* 10 E4
Drangajökull, *Iceland* 8 C2
Drangedal, *Norway* 10 E3
Dranov, Ostrov, *Romania* 38 E12
Dras, *India* 63 B6
Drau = Drava →, *Croatia* 21 K8
Drava →, *Croatia* 21 K8
Draveil, *France* 25 D9
Dravograd, *Slovenia* 33 B12
Drawa →, *Poland* 20 C5
Drawno, *Poland* 20 B5
Drayton Valley, *Canada* 100 C6
Dreibergen, *Neths.* 16 D6
Drenthe □, *Neths.* 16 C9
Drentsche Hoofdvaart, *Neths.* 16 C8
Drepanum, C., *Cyprus* 37 E11
Dresden, *Canada* 106 D2
Dresden, *Germany* 18 D9
Dreux, *France* 24 D8
Driel, *Neths.* 16 E7
Driffield = Great Driffield, *U.K.* 12 C7
Driftwood, *U.S.A.* 106 E6
Driggs, *U.S.A.* 110 E8
Drin i zi →, *Albania* 39 H3
Drina →, *Bos.-H.* 21 L9
Drincea →, *Romania* 38 E5
Drini →, *Albania* 38 G3
Drinjača →, *Bos.-H.* 21 L9
Drissa = Verkhnedvinsk, *Belorussia* 40 D5
Drivstua, *Norway* 10 B3
Drniš, *Croatia* 33 E13
Drøbak, *Norway* 10 E4
Drogheda, *Ireland* 15 C5
Drogichin, *Belorussia* 40 E4
Drogobych, *Ukraine* 40 G3
Drohobych = Drogobych, *Ukraine* 40 G3
Droichead Nua, *Ireland* 15 C5
Droitwich, *U.K.* 13 E5
Drôme □, *France* 27 D9
Drôme →, *France* 27 D8
Dromedary, C., *Australia* 91 F5
Dronero, *Italy* 32 D4
Dronfield, *Australia* 90 C3
Dronne →, *France* 26 C3
Dronninglund, *Denmark* 11 G4
Dronrijp, *Neths.* 16 B7
Dropt →, *France* 26 D3
Drumbo, *Canada* 106 C4
Drumheller, *Canada* 100 C6
Drummond, *U.S.A.* 110 C7
Drummond I., *U.S.A.* 98 C3
Drummond Pt., *Australia* 91 E2
Drummond Ra., *Australia* 90 C4
Drummondville, *Canada* 98 C5
Drumright, *U.S.A.* 109 H6
Drunen, *Neths.* 17 E6
Druskininkai, *Lithuania* 40 D3
Drut →, *Belorussia* 40 E7
Druten, *Neths.* 16 E7
Druya, *Latvia* 40 D5
Druzhina, *Russia* 45 C15
Drvar, *Bos.-H.* 33 D13
Drvenik, *Croatia* 33 E13
Dry Tortugas, *U.S.A.* 116 B3
Dryanovo, *Bulgaria* 38 G8
Dryden, *Canada* 101 D10
Dryden, *U.S.A.* 109 K3
Drygalski I., *Antarctica* 5 C7
Drysdale →, *Australia* 88 B4
Drysdale I., *Australia* 90 A2
Dschang, *Cameroon* 79 D7
Du Bois, *U.S.A.* 106 E6
Du Quoin, *U.S.A.* 108 G10
Duanesburg, *U.S.A.* 107 D10
Duaringa, *Australia* 90 C4
Ḍubā, *Si. Arabia* 64 E2
Dubai = Dubayy, *U.A.E.* 65 E7
Dubawnt →, *Canada* 101 A8
Dubawnt, L., *Canada* 101 A8
Dubayy, *U.A.E.* 65 E7
Dubbeldam, *Neths.* 16 E5
Dubbo, *Australia* 91 E4
Dubele, *Zaïre* 82 B2
Dübendorf, *Switz.* 23 B7
Dubica, *Croatia* 33 C13
Dublin, *Ireland* 15 C5
Dublin, *Ga., U.S.A.* 105 J4
Dublin, *Tex., U.S.A.* 109 J5
Dublin □, *Ireland* 15 C5
Dublin B., *Ireland* 15 C5
Dubna, *Russia* 41 C10
Dubna, *Russia* 41 D10
Dubno, *Ukraine* 40 F4
Dubois, *U.S.A.* 110 D7
Dubossary, *Moldavia* 42 C3
Dubossary Vdkhr., *Moldavia* 42 C3
Dubovka, *Russia* 43 B11
Dubovskoye, *Russia* 43 C10
Dubrajpur, *India* 63 H12
Dubréka, *Guinea* 78 D2
Dubrovitsa, *Ukraine* 40 F5
Dubrovnik, *Croatia* 21 N8
Dubrovskoye, *Russia* 45 D12
Dubuque, *U.S.A.* 108 D9
Duchang, *China* 53 C11
Duchesne, *U.S.A.* 110 F8
Duchess, *Australia* 90 C2
Ducie I., *Pac. Oc.* 93 K15
Duck Cr. →, *Australia* 88 D2
Duck Lake, *Canada* 101 C7
Duck Mountain Prov. Park, *Canada* 101 C8
Duckwall, Mt., *U.S.A.* 112 H6
Düdelange, *Lux.* 17 K8
Duderstadt, *Germany* 18 D6
Dudhi, *India* 61 G13
Düdingen, *Switz.* 22 C4
Dudinka, *Russia* 45 C9
Dudley, *U.K.* 13 E5
Dueñas, *Spain* 30 D6
Dueré, *Brazil* 123 D2
Duero = Douro →, *Europe* 30 D2
Duffel, *Belgium* 17 F5
Dufftown, *U.K.* 14 D5
Dufourspitz, *Switz.* 22 E5
Dugi Otok, *Croatia* 33 E12
Dugo Selo, *Croatia* 33 C13
Duifken Pt., *Australia* 90 A3
Duisburg, *Germany* 18 D2
Duitama, *Colombia* 120 B3
Duiveland, *Neths.* 17 E4
Duiwelskloof, *S. Africa* 85 C5
Dūkdamīn, *Iran* 65 C8
Duke I., *U.S.A.* 100 C2
Dukhān, *Qatar* 65 E6
Dukhovshchina, *Russia* 40 D8
Duki, *Pakistan* 60 D6
Duku, *Bauchi, Nigeria* 79 C7
Duku, *Sokoto, Nigeria* 79 C5
Dulag, *Phil.* 55 F6
Dulce →, *Argentina* 126 C3
Dulce, G., *Costa Rica* 116 E3
Dulf, *Iraq* 64 C5
Dŭlgopol, *Bulgaria* 38 F10
Dulit, Banjaran, *Malaysia* 56 D4
Duliu, *China* 50 E9
Dullewala, *Pakistan* 62 D4
Dülmen, *Germany* 18 D3
Dulovo, *Bulgaria* 38 F10
Dulq Maghār, *Syria* 64 B3
Dululu, *Australia* 90 C5
Duluth, *U.S.A.* 108 B8
Dum Dum, *India* 63 H13
Dum Duma, *India* 61 F19
Dum Hadjer, *Chad* 73 F8
Dūmā, *Lebanon* 69 A4
Dūmā, *Syria* 69 B5
Dumaguete, *Phil.* 55 G5
Dumai, *Indonesia* 56 D2
Dumaran, *Phil.* 55 F3
Dumas, *Ark., U.S.A.* 109 J9
Dumas, *Tex., U.S.A.* 109 H4
Dumbarton, *U.K.* 14 F4
Dumbleyung, *Australia* 89 F2
Dumfries, *U.K.* 14 F5
Dumfries & Galloway □, *U.K.* 14 F5
Dumka, *India* 63 G12
Dümmersee, *Germany* 18 C4
Dumoine →, *Canada* 98 C4
Dumoine L., *Canada* 98 C4
Dumraon, *India* 63 G11
Dumyât, *Egypt* 76 H7
Dumyât, Masabb, *Egypt* 76 H7
Dun Laoghaire, *Ireland* 15 C5
Dun-le-Palestel, *France* 26 B5
Dun-sur-Auron, *France* 25 F9
Duna →, *Hungary* 21 K8
Dunaföldvár, *Hungary* 21 J8
Dunaj →, *Slovak Rep.* 21 H8
Dunajec →, *Poland* 20 E10
Dunajska Streda, *Slovak Rep.* 21 H7
Dunapatai, *Hungary* 21 J9
Dunărea →, *Romania* 38 D12
Dunaújváros, *Hungary* 21 J8
Dunav →, *Serbia* 21 L11
Dunay, *Russia* 48 C6
Dunback, *N.Z.* 87 L3
Dunbar, *Australia* 90 B3
Dunbar, *U.K.* 14 E6
Dunblane, *U.K.* 14 E5
Duncan, *Canada* 100 D4
Duncan, *Ariz., U.S.A.* 111 K9
Duncan, *Okla., U.S.A.* 109 H6
Duncan, L., *Canada* 98 B4
Duncan L., *Canada* 100 A6
Duncan Town, *Bahamas* 116 B4
Duncannon, *U.S.A.* 106 F7
Dundalk, *Canada* 106 B4
Dundalk, *Ireland* 15 B5
Dundalk Bay, *Ireland* 15 C5
Dundas, *Canada* 98 D4
Dundas, L., *Australia* 89 F3
Dundas I., *Canada* 100 C2
Dundas Str., *Australia* 88 B5
Dundee, *S. Africa* 85 D5
Dundee, *U.K.* 14 E6
Dundgovĭ □, *Mongolia* 50 B4
Dundoo, *Australia* 91 D3
Dundrum, *U.K.* 15 B6
Dundrum B., *U.K.* 15 B6
Dundwara, *India* 63 F8
Dunedin, *N.Z.* 87 L3
Dunedin, *U.S.A.* 105 L4
Dunedin →, *Canada* 100 B4
Dunfermline, *U.K.* 14 E5
Dungannon, *Canada* 106 C3
Dungannon, *U.K.* 15 B5
Dungannon □, *U.K.* 15 B5
Dungarpur, *India* 62 H5
Dungarvan, *Ireland* 15 D4
Dungarvan Bay, *Ireland* 15 D4
Dungeness, *U.K.* 13 G8
Dungo, L. do, *Angola* 84 B2
Dungog, *Australia* 91 E5
Dungu, *Zaïre* 82 B2
Dungunâb, *Sudan* 76 C4
Dungunâb, Khalij, *Sudan* 76 C4
Dunhua, *China* 51 C15
Dunhuang, *China* 54 B4
Dunières, *France* 27 C8
Dunk I., *Australia* 90 B4
Dunkeld, *U.K.* 14 E5
Dunkerque, *France* 25 A9
Dunkery Beacon, *U.K.* 13 F4
Dunkirk = Dunkerque, *France* 25 A9
Dunkirk, *U.S.A.* 106 D5
Dunkuj, *Sudan* 77 E3
Dunkwa, *Central, Ghana* 78 D4
Dunkwa, *Central, Ghana* 79 D4
Dunlap, *U.S.A.* 108 E7
Dúnleary = Dun Laoghaire, *Ireland* 15 C5
Dunmanus B., *Ireland* 15 E2
Dunmara, *Australia* 90 B1
Dunmore, *U.S.A.* 107 E9
Dunmore Hd., *Ireland* 15 D1
Dunmore Town, *Bahamas* 116 A4
Dunn, *U.S.A.* 105 H6
Dunnellon, *U.S.A.* 105 L4
Dunnet Hd., *U.K.* 14 C5
Dunning, *U.S.A.* 108 E4
Dunnville, *Canada* 106 D5
Dunolly, *Australia* 91 F3
Dunoon, *U.K.* 14 F4
Dunqul, *Egypt* 76 C3
Duns, *U.K.* 14 F6
Dunseith, *U.S.A.* 108 A4
Dunsmuir, *U.S.A.* 110 F2
Dunstable, *U.K.* 13 F7
Dunstan Mts., *N.Z.* 87 L2
Dunster, *Canada* 100 C5
Dunvegan L., *Canada* 101 A7
Duolun, *China* 50 C9
Duong Dong, *Vietnam* 59 G4
Dupree, *U.S.A.* 108 C4
Dupuyer, *U.S.A.* 110 B7
Duque de Caxias, *Brazil* 123 F3
Duque de York, I., *Chile* 128 D1
Durack →, *Australia* 88 C4
Durack Ra., *Australia* 88 C4
Durağan, *Turkey* 66 C6
Durance →, *France* 27 E8

Durand, *U.S.A.* 104 D4
Durango = Victoria de Durango, *Mexico* 114 C4
Durango, *Spain* 28 B2
Durango, *U.S.A.* 111 H10
Durango □, *Mexico* 114 C4
Duranillin, *Australia* 89 F2
Durant, *U.S.A.* 109 J6
Duratón →, *Spain* 30 D6
Durazno, *Uruguay* 126 C4
Durazzo = Durrësi, *Albania* 39 H2
Durban, *France* 26 F6
Durban, *S. Africa* 85 D5
Dúrcal, *Spain* 31 J7
Düren, *Germany* 18 E2
Durg, *India* 61 J12
Durgapur, *India* 63 H12
Durham, *Canada* 98 D3
Durham, *U.K.* 12 C6
Durham, *Calif., U.S.A.* 112 F5
Durham, *N.C., U.S.A.* 105 G6
Durham □, *U.K.* 12 C6
Durham Downs, *Australia* 91 D4
Durmitor, *Montenegro* 21 M9
Durness, *U.K.* 14 C4
Durrësi, *Albania* 39 H2
Durrie, *Australia* 90 D3
Dursunbey, *Turkey* 66 D3
Durtal, *France* 24 E6
Duru, *Zaïre* 82 B2
D'Urville, Tanjung, *Indonesia* 57 E9
D'Urville I., *N.Z.* 87 J4
Duryea, *U.S.A.* 107 E9
Dusa Mareb, *Somali Rep.* 68 F4
Dûsh, *Egypt* 76 C3
Dushak, *Turkmenistan* 44 F7
Dushan, *China* 52 E6
Dushanbe, *Tajikistan* 44 F7
Dusheti, *Georgia* 43 E11
Dusky Sd., *N.Z.* 87 L1
Dussejour, C., *Australia* 88 B4
Düsseldorf, *Germany* 18 D2
Dussen, *Neths.* 16 E5
Dutch Harbor, *U.S.A.* 96 C3
Dutlwe, *Botswana* 84 C3
Dutsan Wai, *Nigeria* 79 C6
Dutton, *Canada* 106 D3
Dutton →, *Australia* 90 C3
Duved, *Sweden* 10 A6
Duvno, *Bos.-H.* 21 M7
Duyun, *China* 52 D6
Düzce, *Turkey* 66 C4
Duzdab = Zāhedān, *Iran* 65 D9
Dvina, Sev. →, *Russia* 44 C5
Dvinsk = Daugavpils, *Latvia* 40 D5
Dvor, *Croatia* 33 C13
Dwarka, *India* 62 H3
Dwellingup, *Australia* 89 F2
Dwight, *Canada* 106 A5
Dwight, *U.S.A.* 104 E1
Dyakovskoya, *Russia* 41 A12
Dyatkovo, *Russia* 40 E9
Dyatlovo, *Belorussia* 40 E4
Dyer, C., *Canada* 97 B13
Dyer Plateau, *Antarctica* 5 D17
Dyersburg, *U.S.A.* 109 G10
Dyfed □, *U.K.* 13 E3
Dyfi →, *U.K.* 13 E4
Dyje →, *Czech.* 20 G6
Dyle →, *Belgium* 17 G5
Dynevor Downs, *Australia* 91 D3
Dynów, *Poland* 20 F12
Dysart, *Canada* 101 C8
Dzamin Üüd, *Mongolia* 50 C6
Dzerzhinsk, *Belorussia* 40 E5
Dzerzhinsk, *Russia* 41 C13
Dzhalinda, *Russia* 45 D13
Dzhambeyty, *Kazakhstan* 43 A15
Dzhambul, *Kazakhstan* 44 E8
Dzhankoi, *Ukraine* 42 D6
Dzhanybek, *Kazakhstan* 43 B12
Dzhardzhan, *Russia* 45 C13
Dzhelinde, *Russia* 45 C12
Dzhetygara, *Kazakhstan* 44 D7
Dzhezkazgan, *Kazakhstan* 44 E7
Dzhikimde, *Russia* 45 D13
Dzhizak, *Uzbekistan* 44 E7
Dzhugdzur, Khrebet, *Russia* 45 D14
Dzhvari, *Georgia* 43 E10
Działdowo, *Poland* 20 B10
Działoszyn, *Poland* 20 D8
Dzierzgoń, *Poland* 20 B9
Dzierzoniów, *Poland* 20 E6
Dzilam de Bravo, *Mexico* 115 C7
Dzioua, *Algeria* 75 B6
Dzungaria = Junggar Pendi, *China* 54 B3
Dzungarian Gate = Alataw Shankou, *China* 54 B3
Dzuumod, *Mongolia* 54 B5

E

Eabamet, L., *Canada* 98 B2
Eads, *U.S.A.* 108 F3
Eagle, *U.S.A.* 110 G10
Eagle →, *Canada* 99 B8
Eagle Butte, *U.S.A.* 108 C4
Eagle Grove, *U.S.A.* 108 D8
Eagle L., *Calif., U.S.A.* 110 F3
Eagle L., *Maine, U.S.A.* 99 C6
Eagle Lake, *U.S.A.* 109 L6
Eagle Mountain, *U.S.A.* 113 M11
Eagle Nest, *U.S.A.* 111 H11
Eagle Pass, *U.S.A.* 109 L4
Eagle Pk., *U.S.A.* 112 G7
Eagle Pt., *Australia* 88 C3
Eagle River, *U.S.A.* 108 C10
Ealing, *U.K.* 13 F7
Earaheedy, *Australia* 89 E3
Earl Grey, *Canada* 101 C8
Earle, *U.S.A.* 109 H9
Earlimart, *U.S.A.* 113 K7
Earn →, *U.K.* 14 E5
Earn, L., *U.K.* 14 E4
Earnslaw, Mt., *N.Z.* 87 L2
Earth, *U.S.A.* 109 H3
Easley, *U.S.A.* 105 H4
East Angus, *Canada* 99 C5
East Aurora, *U.S.A.* 106 D6
East B., *U.S.A.* 109 L10
East Bengal, *Bangla.* 61 G17
East Beskids = Vychodné Beskydy, *Europe* 20 F11
East Brady, *U.S.A.* 106 F5
East C., *N.Z.* 87 G7
East Chicago, *U.S.A.* 104 E2
East China Sea, *Asia* 54 C7
East Coulee, *Canada* 100 C6
East Falkland, *Falk. Is.* 128 D5
East Grand Forks, *U.S.A.* 108 B6
East Greenwich, *U.S.A.* 107 E13
East Hartford, *U.S.A.* 107 E12
East Helena, *U.S.A.* 110 C8
East Indies, *Asia* 57 E6
East Jordan, *U.S.A.* 104 C3
East Lansing, *U.S.A.* 104 D3
East Liverpool, *U.S.A.* 106 F4
East London, *S. Africa* 85 E4
East Main = Eastmain, *Canada* 98 B4
East Orange, *U.S.A.* 107 F10
East Pacific Ridge, *Pac. Oc.* 93 J17
East Pakistan = Bangladesh ■, *Asia* 61 H17
East Palestine, *U.S.A.* 106 F4
East Pine, *Canada* 100 B4
East Pt., *Canada* 99 C7
East Point, *U.S.A.* 105 J3
East Providence, *U.S.A.* 107 E13
East Retford, *U.K.* 12 D7
East St. Louis, *U.S.A.* 108 F9
East Schelde → = Oosterschelde, *Neths.* 17 E4
East Siberian Sea, *Russia* 45 B17
East Stroudsburg, *U.S.A.* 107 E9
East Sussex □, *U.K.* 13 G8
East Tawas, *U.S.A.* 104 C4
East Toorale, *Australia* 91 E4
East Walker →, *U.S.A.* 112 G7
Eastbourne, *N.Z.* 87 J5
Eastbourne, *U.K.* 13 G8
Eastend, *Canada* 101 D7
Easter Dal = Österdalälven →, *Sweden* 9 F12
Easter Islands = Pascua, I. de, *Pac. Oc.* 93 K17
Eastern □, *Kenya* 82 B4
Eastern □, *Uganda* 82 B3
Eastern Cr. →, *Australia* 90 C3
Eastern Ghats, *India* 60 N11
Eastern Group = Lau Group, *Fiji* 87 C9
Eastern Group, *Australia* 89 F3
Eastern Province □, *S. Leone* 78 D2
Easterville, *Canada* 101 C9
Easthampton, *U.S.A.* 107 D12
Eastland, *U.S.A.* 109 J5
Eastleigh, *U.K.* 13 G6
Eastmain, *Canada* 98 B4
Eastmain →, *Canada* 98 B4
Eastman, *Canada* 107 A12
Eastman, *U.S.A.* 105 J4
Easton, *Md., U.S.A.* 104 F7
Easton, *Pa., U.S.A.* 107 F9
Easton, *Wash., U.S.A.* 112 C5
Eastport, *U.S.A.* 99 D6
Eastsound, *U.S.A.* 112 B4
Eaton, *U.S.A.* 108 E2
Eatonia, *Canada* 101 C7
Eatonton, *U.S.A.* 105 J4
Eatontown, *U.S.A.* 107 F10
Eatonville, *U.S.A.* 112 D4
Eau Claire, *Fr. Guiana* 121 C7
Eau Claire, *U.S.A.* 108 C9
Eauze, *France* 26 E4
Ebagoola, *Australia* 90 A3
Eban, *Nigeria* 79 D5
Ebbw Vale, *U.K.* 13 F4
Ebeggui, *Algeria* 75 C6
Ebeltoft, *Denmark* 9 H11
Ebensburg, *U.S.A.* 106 F6
Ebensee, *Austria* 21 H3
Eber Gölü, *Turkey* 66 D4
Eberbach, *Germany* 19 F4
Eberswalde, *Germany* 18 C9
Ebetsu, *Japan* 48 C10
Ebian, *China* 52 C4
Ebikon, *Switz.* 23 B6
Ebingen, *Germany* 19 G5
Ebnat-Kappel, *Switz.* 23 B8
Eboli, *Italy* 35 B8
Ebolowa, *Cameroon* 79 E7
Ebrach, *Germany* 19 F6
Ébrié, Lagune, *Ivory C.* 78 D4
Ebro →, *Spain* 28 E5
Ebro, Pantano del, *Spain* 30 B7
Ebstorf, *Germany* 18 B6
Ecaussines-d' Enghien, *Belgium* 17 G4
Eceabat, *Turkey* 66 C2
Ech Cheliff, *Algeria* 75 A5
Echallens, *Switz.* 22 C3
Echeng, *China* 53 B10
Echigo-Sammyaku, *Japan* 49 F9
Echizen-Misaki, *Japan* 49 G7
Echmiadzin, *Armenia* 43 F11
Echo Bay, *N.W.T., Canada* 96 B8
Echo Bay, *Ont., Canada* 98 C3
Echoing →, *Canada* 101 B10
Echt, *Neths.* 17 F7
Echternach, *Lux.* 17 J8
Echuca, *Australia* 91 F3
Ecija, *Spain* 31 H5
Eckernförde, *Germany* 18 A5
Eclipse Is., *Australia* 88 B4
Écommoy, *France* 24 E7
Ecoporanga, *Brazil* 123 E3
Écos, *France* 25 C8
Écouché, *France* 24 D6
Ecuador ■, *S. Amer.* 120 D2
Écueillé, *France* 24 E8
Ed, *Sweden* 11 F5
Ed Dabbura, *Sudan* 76 D3
Ed Dâmer, *Sudan* 76 D3
Ed Debba, *Sudan* 76 D3
Ed-Déffa, *Egypt* 76 A2
Ed Deim, *Sudan* 77 E2
Ed Dueim, *Sudan* 77 E3
Edah, *Australia* 89 E2
Edam, *Canada* 101 C7
Edam, *Neths.* 16 C6
Eday, *U.K.* 14 B6
Edd, *Eritrea* 68 E3
Eddrachillis B., *U.K.* 14 C3
Eddystone, *U.K.* 13 G3
Eddystone Pt., *Australia* 90 G4
Ede, *Neths.* 16 D7
Ede, *Nigeria* 79 D5
Édea, *Cameroon* 79 E7
Edegem, *Belgium* 17 F4
Edehon L., *Canada* 101 A9
Edekel, Adrar, *Algeria* 75 D6
Eden, *Australia* 91 F4
Eden, *N.C., U.S.A.* 105 G6
Eden, *N.Y., U.S.A.* 106 D6
Eden, *Tex., U.S.A.* 109 K5
Eden, *Wyo., U.S.A.* 110 E9
Eden →, *U.K.* 12 C4
Eden L., *Canada* 101 B8
Edenburg, *S. Africa* 84 D4
Edendale, *S. Africa* 85 D5
Edenderry, *Ireland* 15 C4
Edenton, *U.S.A.* 105 G7
Edenville, *S. Africa* 85 D4
Eder →, *Germany* 18 D5
Ederstausee, *Germany* 18 D4
Edgar, *U.S.A.* 108 E5
Edgartown, *U.S.A.* 107 E14
Edge Hill, *U.K.* 13 E6
Edgefield, *U.S.A.* 105 J5
Edgeley, *U.S.A.* 108 B5
Edgemont, *U.S.A.* 108 D3
Edgeøya, *Svalbard* 4 B9
Edhessa, *Greece* 39 J5
Edievale, *N.Z.* 87 L2
Edina, *Liberia* 78 D2
Edina, *U.S.A.* 108 E8
Edinburg, *U.S.A.* 109 M5
Edinburgh, *U.K.* 14 F5
Edirne, *Turkey* 39 H9
Edirne □, *Turkey* 66 C2
Edison, *U.S.A.* 112 B4
Edithburgh, *Australia* 91 F2
Edjeleh, *Algeria* 75 C6
Edjudina, *Australia* 89 E3
Edmeston, *U.S.A.* 107 D9
Edmond, *U.S.A.* 109 H6
Edmonds, *U.S.A.* 112 C4
Edmonton, *Australia* 90 B4
Edmonton, *Canada* 100 C6
Edmund L., *Canada* 101 C10
Edmundston, *Canada* 99 C6
Edna, *U.S.A.* 109 L6
Edna Bay, *U.S.A.* 100 B2
Edo □, *Nigeria* 79 D6
Edolo, *Italy* 32 B7
Edremit, *Turkey* 66 D2
Edremit Körfezi, *Turkey* 66 D2
Edsbyn, *Sweden* 10 C9
Edsele, *Sweden* 10 A10
Edson, *Canada* 100 C5
Eduardo Castex, *Argentina* 126 D3
Edward →, *Australia* 91 F3
Edward, L., *Africa* 82 C2
Edward I., *Canada* 98 C2
Edward River, *Australia* 90 A3
Edward VII Land, *Antarctica* 5 E13
Edwards, *U.S.A.* 113 L9
Edwards Plateau, *U.S.A.* 109 K4
Edwardsville, *U.S.A.* 107 E9
Edzo, *Canada* 100 A5
Eefde, *Neths.* 16 D8
Eekloo, *Belgium* 17 F3
Eelde, *Neths.* 16 B9
Eem →, *Neths.* 16 D6
Eems →, *Neths.* 16 B9
Eems Kanaal, *Neths.* 16 B9
Eenrum, *Neths.* 16 B8
Eernegem, *Belgium* 17 F2
Eerste Valthermond, *Neths.* 16 C9
Efferi, *Algeria* 75 D6
Effingham, *U.S.A.* 104 F1
Effretikon, *Switz.* 23 B7
Eforie Sud, *Romania* 38 E11
Ega →, *Spain* 28 C3
Égadi, Ísole, *Italy* 34 E5
Eganville, *Canada* 98 C4
Egeland, *U.S.A.* 108 A5
Egenolf L., *Canada* 101 B9
Eger = Cheb, *Czech.* 20 E2
Eger, *Hungary* 21 H10
Eger →, *Hungary* 21 H10
Egersund, *Norway* 9 G9
Egg L., *Canada* 101 B7
Eggenburg, *Austria* 20 G5
Eggenfelden, *Germany* 19 G8
Eggiwil, *Switz.* 22 C5
Éghezée, *Belgium* 17 G5
Eginbah, *Australia* 88 D2
Égletons, *France* 26 C6
Eglisau, *Switz.* 23 A7
Egmond-aan-Zee, *Neths.* 16 C5
Egmont, C., *N.Z.* 87 H4
Egmont, Mt., *N.Z.* 87 H5
Eğridir, *Turkey* 66 E4
Eğridir Gölü, *Turkey* 66 E4
Egtved, *Denmark* 11 J3
Éguas →, *Brazil* 123 D3
Egume, *Nigeria* 79 D6
Éguzon, *France* 26 B5
Egvekinot, *Russia* 45 C19
Egypt ■, *Africa* 76 J7
Eha Amufu, *Nigeria* 79 D6
Ehime □, *Japan* 49 H6
Ehingen, *Germany* 19 G5
Ehrenberg, *U.S.A.* 113 M12
Ehrwald, *Austria* 19 H6
Eibar, *Spain* 28 B2
Eibergen, *Neths.* 16 D9
Eichstatt, *Germany* 19 G7
Eider →, *Germany* 18 A4
Eidsvold, *Australia* 91 D5
Eidsvoll, *Norway* 9 F11
Eifel, *Germany* 19 E2
Eiffel Flats, *Zimbabwe* 83 F3
Eigg, *U.K.* 14 E2
Eighty Mile Beach, *Australia* 88 C3
Eil, *Somali Rep.* 68 F4
Eil, L., *U.K.* 14 E3
Eildon, L., *Australia* 91 F4
Eileen L., *Canada* 101 A7
Eilenburg, *Germany* 18 D8
Ein el Luweiqa, *Sudan* 77 E3
Einasleigh, *Australia* 90 B3
Einasleigh →, *Australia* 90 B3
Einbeck, *Germany* 18 D5
Eindhoven, *Neths.* 17 F6
Einsiedeln, *Switz.* 23 B7
Eire ■ = Ireland ■, *Europe* 15 D4
Eiríksjökull, *Iceland* 8 D3
Eirlandsche Gat, *Neths.* 16 B5
Eirunepé, *Brazil* 124 B4
Eisden, *Belgium* 17 G7
Eisenach, *Germany* 18 E6
Eisenberg, *Germany* 18 E7
Eisenerz, *Austria* 21 H4
Eisenhüttenstadt, *Germany* 18 C10
Eisenstadt, *Austria* 21 H6
Eiserfeld, *Germany* 18 E3
Eisfeld, *Germany* 18 E6
Eisleben, *Germany* 18 D7
Eivissa = Ibiza, *Spain* 36 C7
Ejby, *Denmark* 11 J3
Eje, Sierra del, *Spain* 30 C4
Ejea de los Caballeros, *Spain* 28 C3
Ejutla, *Mexico* 115 D5
Ekalaka, *U.S.A.* 108 C2
Ekeren, *Belgium* 17 F4
Eket, *Nigeria* 79 E6
Eketahuna, *N.Z.* 87 J5
Ekhínos, *Greece* 39 H8
Ekibastuz, *Kazakhstan* 44 D8
Ekimchan, *Russia* 45 D14
Ekoli, *Zaïre* 82 C1
Eksel, *Belgium* 17 F6
Ekwan →, *Canada* 98 B3
Ekwan Pt., *Canada* 98 B3
El Aaiún, *W. Sahara* 74 C2
El Aargub, *Mauritania* 74 D1
El Abiodh-Sidi-Cheikh, *Algeria* 75 B5
El 'Agrûd, *Egypt* 69 E3
El Aïoun, *Morocco* 75 B4
El 'Aiyat, *Egypt* 76 J7
El Alamein, *Egypt* 76 H6
El Alto, *Peru* 124 A1
El 'Aqaba, W. →, *Egypt* 69 E2
El 'Arag, *Egypt* 76 B2
El Arahal, *Spain* 31 H5
El Arenal, *Spain* 36 B9
El Aricha, *Algeria* 75 B4
El Arīhā, *Jordan* 69 D4
El Arish, *Australia* 90 B4
El 'Arîsh, *Egypt* 69 D2
El 'Arîsh, W. →, *Egypt* 69 D2
El Arrouch, *Algeria* 75 A6
El Asnam = Ech Cheliff, *Algeria* 75 A5
El Astillero, *Spain* 30 B7
El Badâri, *Egypt* 76 B3
El Bahrein, *Egypt* 76 B2
El Ballâs, *Egypt* 76 B3
El Balyana, *Egypt* 76 B3
El Banco, *Colombia* 120 B3
El Baqeir, *Sudan* 76 D3
El Barco de Ávila, *Spain* 30 E5
El Barco de Valdeorras, *Spain* 30 C4
El Bauga, *Sudan* 76 D3
El Baúl, *Venezuela* 120 B4
El Bawiti, *Egypt* 76 J6
El Bayadh, *Algeria* 75 B5
El Bierzo, *Spain* 30 C4
El Bluff, *Nic.* 116 D3
El Bolsón, *Argentina* 128 B2
El Bonillo, *Spain* 29 G2
El Brûk, W. →, *Egypt* 69 E2
El Buheirat □, *Sudan* 77 F2
El Caín, *Argentina* 128 B3
El Cajon, *U.S.A.* 113 N10
El Callao, *Venezuela* 121 B5
El Camp, *Spain* 28 D6
El Campo, *U.S.A.* 109 L6
El Carmen, *Bolivia* 125 C5
El Carmen, *Venezuela* 120 C4
El Castillo, *Spain* 31 H4
El Centro, *U.S.A.* 113 N11
El Cerro, *Bolivia* 125 D5
El Cerro, *Spain* 31 H4
El Cocuy, *Colombia* 120 B3
El Compadre, *Mexico* 113 N10
El Corcovado, *Argentina* 128 B2
El Coronil, *Spain* 31 H5
El Cuy, *Argentina* 128 A3
El Cuyo, *Mexico* 115 C7
El Dab'a, *Egypt* 76 H6
El Daheir, *Egypt* 69 D3
El Deir, *Egypt* 76 B3
El Dere, *Somali Rep.* 68 G4
El Descanso, *Mexico* 113 N10
El Desemboque, *Mexico* 114 A2
El Dilingat, *Egypt* 76 H7
El Diviso, *Colombia* 120 C2
El Djem, *Tunisia* 75 A7
El Djouf, *Mauritania* 70 D3
El Dorado, *Ark., U.S.A.* 109 J8
El Dorado, *Kans., U.S.A.* 109 G6
El Dorado, *Venezuela* 121 B5
El Eglab, *Algeria* 74 C4
El Escorial, *Spain* 30 E6
El Eulma, *Algeria* 75 A6
El Faiyûm, *Egypt* 76 J7
El Fâsher, *Sudan* 77 E2
El Fashn, *Egypt* 76 J7
El Ferrol, *Spain* 30 B2
El Fifi, *Sudan* 77 E1
El Fuerte, *Mexico* 114 B3
El Gal, *Somali Rep.* 68 E5
El Gebir, *Sudan* 77 E2
El Gedida, *Egypt* 76 B2
El Geteina, *Sudan* 77 E3
El Gezira □, *Sudan* 77 E3
El Gîza, *Egypt* 76 H7
El Goléa, *Algeria* 75 B5
El Guettar, *Algeria* 75 B5
El Hadeb, *W. Sahara* 74 C2
El Hadjira, *Algeria* 75 B6
El Hagiz, *Sudan* 77 D4
El Hajeb, *Morocco* 74 B3
El Hammam, *Egypt* 76 H6
El Hammâmi, *Mauritania* 74 D2
El Hank, *Mauritania* 74 D3
El Harrach, *Algeria* 75 A5
El Hasian, *W. Sahara* 74 C2
El Hawata, *Sudan* 77 E3
El Heiz, *Egypt* 76 B2
El 'Idisât, *Egypt* 76 B3
El Iskandarîya, *Egypt* 76 H6
El Jadida, *Morocco* 74 B3
El Jebelein, *Sudan* 77 E3
El Kab, *Sudan* 76 D3
El Kabrît, G., *Egypt* 69 F2
El Kala, *Algeria* 75 A6
El Kalâa, *Morocco* 74 B3
El Kamlin, *Sudan* 77 D3
El Kantara, *Algeria* 75 A6
El Kantara, *Tunisia* 75 B7
El Karaba, *Sudan* 76 D3
El Kef, *Tunisia* 75 A6
El Khandaq, *Sudan* 76 D3
El Khârga, *Egypt* 76 B3
El Khartûm, *Sudan* 77 D3
El Khartûm □, *Sudan* 77 D3
El Khartûm Bahrî, *Sudan* 77 D3
El Khroub, *Algeria* 75 A6
El Kseur, *Algeria* 75 A5
El Ksiba, *Morocco* 74 B3
El Kuntilla, *Egypt* 69 E3
El Laqâwa, *Sudan* 77 E2
El Laqeita, *Egypt* 76 B3
El Leiya, *Sudan* 77 D4
El Mafâza, *Sudan* 77 E3
El Mahalla el Kubra, *Egypt* 76 H7
El Mahârîq, *Egypt* 76 B3
El Mahmûdîya, *Egypt* 76 H7
El Maitén, *Argentina* 128 B2
El Maiz, *Algeria* 75 C4
El-Maks el-Bahari, *Egypt* 76 C3
El Manshâh, *Egypt* 76 B3
El Mansour, *Algeria* 75 C4
El Mansûra, *Egypt* 76 H7

El Mantico, *Venezuela* 121 B5
El Manzala, *Egypt* 76 H7
El Marâgha, *Egypt* 76 B3
El Masid, *Sudan* 77 D3
El Matariya, *Egypt* 76 H8
El Medano, *Canary Is.* 36 F3
El Meghaier, *Algeria* 75 B6
El Meraguen, *Algeria* 75 C4
El Metemma, *Sudan* 77 D3
El Miamo, *Venezuela* 121 B5
El Milagro, *Argentina* 126 C2
El Milia, *Algeria* 75 A6
El Minyâ, *Egypt* 76 J7
El Molar, *Spain* 28 E1
El Mreyye, *Mauritania* 78 B3
El Obeid, *Sudan* 77 E3
El Odaiya, *Sudan* 77 E2
El Oro, *Mexico* 115 D4
El Oro □, *Ecuador* 120 D2
El Oued, *Algeria* 75 B6
El Palmar, *Bolivia* 125 D5
El Palmar, *Venezuela* 121 B5
El Palmito, Presa, *Mexico* 114 B3
El Panadés, *Spain* 28 D6
El Pardo, *Spain* 30 E7
El Paso, *U.S.A.* 111 L10
El Paso Robles, *U.S.A.* 112 K6
El Pedernoso, *Spain* 29 F2
El Pedroso, *Spain* 31 H5
El Pobo de Dueñas, *Spain* 28 E3
El Portal, *U.S.A.* 111 H4
El Porvenir, *Mexico* 114 A3
El Prat de Llobregat, *Spain* 28 D7
El Progreso, *Honduras* 116 C2
El Provencío, *Spain* 29 F2
El Pueblito, *Mexico* 114 B3
El Pueblo, *Canary Is.* 36 F2
El Qâhira, *Egypt* 76 H7
El Qantara, *Egypt* 69 E1
El Qasr, *Egypt* 76 B2
El Quseima, *Egypt* 69 E3
El Qusîya, *Egypt* 76 B3
El Râshda, *Egypt* 76 B2
El Reno, *U.S.A.* 109 H6
El Ribero, *Spain* 30 C2
El Ridisiya, *Egypt* 76 C3
El Rio, *U.S.A.* 113 L7
El Ronquillo, *Spain* 31 H4
El Roque, Pta., *Canary Is.* 36 F4
El Rosarito, *Mexico* 114 B2
El Rubio, *Spain* 31 H5
El Saff, *Egypt* 76 J7
El Saheira, W. →, *Egypt* 69 E2
El Salto, *Mexico* 114 C3
El Salvador ■, *Cent. Amer.* 116 D2
El Sancejo, *Spain* 31 H5
El Sauce, *Nic.* 116 D2
El Shallal, *Egypt* 76 C3
El Simbillawein, *Egypt* 76 H7
El Sombrero, *Venezuela* 120 B4
El Suweis, *Egypt* 76 J8
El Tamarâni, W. →, *Egypt* 69 E3
El Thamad, *Egypt* 69 F3
El Tigre, *Venezuela* 121 B5
El Tîh, G., *Egypt* 69 F2
El Tîna, Khalîg, *Egypt* 69 D1
El Tocuyo, *Venezuela* 120 B4
El Tofo, *Chile* 126 B1
El Tránsito, *Chile* 126 B1
El Tûr, *Egypt* 76 J8
El Turbio, *Argentina* 128 D2
El Uqsur, *Egypt* 76 B3
El Vado, *Spain* 28 D1
El Vallés, *Spain* 28 D7
El Venado, *Mexico* 114 C4
El Vigía, *Venezuela* 120 B3
El Wabeira, *Egypt* 69 F2
El Wak, *Kenya* 82 B5
El Waqf, *Egypt* 76 B3
El Wâsta, *Egypt* 76 J7
El Weguet, *Ethiopia* 77 F5
El Wuz, *Sudan* 77 D3
Elafónisos, *Greece* 39 N5
Elandsvlei, *S. Africa* 84 E2
Élassa, *Greece* 39 P9
Elassón, *Greece* 39 K5
Elat, *Israel* 69 F3
Elâzığ, *Turkey* 67 D8
Elâzığ □, *Turkey* 67 D8
Elba, *Italy* 32 F7
Elba, *U.S.A.* 105 K2
Elbasani, *Albania* 39 H3
Elbe, *U.S.A.* 112 D4
Elbe →, *Europe* 18 B4
Elbe-Seiten Kanal, *Germany* 18 C6
Elbert, Mt., *U.S.A.* 111 G10
Elberta, *U.S.A.* 104 C2
Elberton, *U.S.A.* 105 H4
Elbeuf, *France* 24 C8
Elbing = Elbląg, *Poland* 20 A9
Elbistan, *Turkey* 66 D7
Elbląg, *Poland* 20 A9
Elbow, *Canada* 101 C7
Elbrus, *Asia* 43 E10
Elburg, *Neths.* 16 D7
Elburz Mts. = Alborz, Reshteh-ye Kūhhā-ye, *Iran* 65 C7
Elche, *Spain* 29 G4
Elche de la Sierra, *Spain* 29 G2
Elcho I., *Australia* 90 A2
Elda, *Spain* 29 G4
Eldon, *Mo., U.S.A.* 108 F8
Eldon, *Wash., U.S.A.* 112 C3
Eldora, *U.S.A.* 108 D8
Eldorado, *Argentina* 127 B5
Eldorado, *Canada* 101 B7
Eldorado, *Mexico* 114 C3
Eldorado, *Ill., U.S.A.* 104 G1
Eldorado, *Tex., U.S.A.* 109 K4
Eldorado Springs, *U.S.A.* 109 G8
Eldoret, *Kenya* 82 B4
Eldred, *U.S.A.* 106 E6
Elea, C., *Cyprus* 37 D13
Electra, *U.S.A.* 109 H5
Elefantes →, *Mozam.* 85 C5
Elefantes, G., *Chile* 128 C2
Elektrogorsk, *Russia* 41 D11
Elektrostal, *Russia* 41 D11
Elele, *Nigeria* 79 D6
Elephant Butte Reservoir, *U.S.A.* 111 K10
Elephant I., *Antarctica* 5 C18
Elesbão Veloso, *Brazil* 122 C3
Eleşkirt, *Turkey* 67 D10
Eleuthera, *Bahamas* 116 A4
Elgepiggen, *Norway* 10 B5
Elgeyo-Marakwet □, *Kenya* 82 B4
Elgg, *Switz.* 23 B7
Elgin, *N.B., Canada* 99 C6
Elgin, *Ont., Canada* 107 B8
Elgin, *U.K.* 14 D5
Elgin, *Ill., U.S.A.* 104 D1
Elgin, *N. Dak., U.S.A.* 108 B4
Elgin, *Nebr., U.S.A.* 108 E5
Elgin, *Nev., U.S.A.* 111 H6
Elgin, *Oreg., U.S.A.* 110 D5
Elgin, *Tex., U.S.A.* 109 K6
Elgon, Mt., *Africa* 82 B3
Eliase, *Indonesia* 57 F8
Elida, *U.S.A.* 109 J3
Elikón, *Greece* 39 L5
Elim, *S. Africa* 84 E2
Elisabethville = Lubumbashi, *Zaïre* 83 E2
Eliseu Martins, *Brazil* 122 C3
Elista, *Russia* 43 C11
Elizabeth, *Australia* 91 E2
Elizabeth, *U.S.A.* 107 F10
Elizabeth City, *U.S.A.* 105 G7
Elizabethton, *U.S.A.* 105 G4
Elizabethtown, *Ky., U.S.A.* 104 G3
Elizabethtown, *N.Y., U.S.A.* 107 B11
Elizabethtown, *Pa., U.S.A.* 107 F8
Elizondo, *Spain* 28 B3
Elk, *Poland* 20 B12
Elk City, *U.S.A.* 109 H5
Elk Creek, *U.S.A.* 112 F4
Elk Grove, *U.S.A.* 112 G5
Elk Island Nat. Park, *Canada* 100 C6
Elk Lake, *Canada* 98 C3
Elk Point, *Canada* 101 C6
Elk River, *Idaho, U.S.A.* 110 C5
Elk River, *Minn., U.S.A.* 108 C8
Elkedra, *Australia* 90 C2
Elkedra →, *Australia* 90 C2
Elkhart, *Ind., U.S.A.* 104 E3
Elkhart, *Kans., U.S.A.* 109 G4
Elkhorn, *Canada* 101 D8
Elkhorn →, *U.S.A.* 108 E6
Elkhotovo, *Russia* 43 E11
Elkhovo, *Bulgaria* 38 G9
Elkin, *U.S.A.* 105 G5
Elkins, *U.S.A.* 104 F6
Elko, *Canada* 100 D5
Elko, *U.S.A.* 110 F6
Ell, L., *Australia* 89 E4
Ellecom, *Neths.* 16 D8
Ellef Ringnes I., *Canada* 4 B2
Ellendale, *Australia* 88 C3
Ellendale, *U.S.A.* 108 B5
Ellensburg, *U.S.A.* 110 C3
Ellenville, *U.S.A.* 107 E10
Ellery, Mt., *Australia* 91 F4
Ellesmere, L., *N.Z.* 87 M4
Ellesmere I., *Canada* 4 B4
Ellesmere Port, *U.K.* 12 D5
Ellezelles, *Belgium* 17 G3
Ellice Is. = Tuvalu ■, *Pac. Oc.* 92 H9
Ellinwood, *U.S.A.* 108 F5
Elliot, *Australia* 90 B1
Elliot, *S. Africa* 85 E4
Elliot Lake, *Canada* 98 C3
Elliotdale = Xhora, *S. Africa* 85 E4
Ellis, *U.S.A.* 108 F5
Elliston, *Australia* 91 E1
Ellisville, *U.S.A.* 109 K10
Ellon, *U.K.* 14 D6
Ellore = Eluru, *India* 61 L12
Ells →, *Canada* 100 B6
Ellsworth, *U.S.A.* 108 F5
Ellsworth Land, *Antarctica* 5 D16
Ellsworth Mts., *Antarctica* 5 D16
Ellwangen, *Germany* 19 G6
Ellwood City, *U.S.A.* 106 F4
Elm, *Switz.* 23 C8
Elma, *Canada* 101 D9
Elma, *U.S.A.* 112 D3
Elmadağ, *Turkey* 66 D5
Elmalı, *Turkey* 66 E3
Elmhurst, *U.S.A.* 104 E2
Elmina, *Ghana* 79 D4
Elmira, *Canada* 106 C4
Elmira, *U.S.A.* 106 D8
Elmore, *Australia* 91 F3
Elmore, *U.S.A.* 113 M11
Elmshorn, *Germany* 18 B5
Elmvale, *Canada* 106 B5
Elne, *France* 26 F6
Elora, *Canada* 106 C4
Elorza, *Venezuela* 120 B4
Eloúnda, *Greece* 37 D7
Eloy, *U.S.A.* 111 K8
Éloyes, *France* 25 D13
Elrose, *Canada* 101 C7
Elsas, *Canada* 98 C3
Elsie, *U.S.A.* 112 E3
Elsinore = Helsingør, *Denmark* 11 H6
Elsinore, *U.S.A.* 111 G7
Elspe, *Germany* 18 D4
Elspeet, *Neths.* 16 D7
Elst, *Neths.* 16 E7
Elster →, *Germany* 18 D7
Elsterwerda, *Germany* 18 D9
Elten, *Neths.* 16 E8
Eltham, *N.Z.* 87 H5
Elton, *Russia* 43 B12
Eluanbi, *Taiwan* 53 G13
Eluru, *India* 61 L12
Elvas, *Portugal* 31 G3
Elven, *France* 24 E4
Elverum, *Norway* 10 D5
Elvire →, *Australia* 88 C4
Elvo →, *Italy* 32 C5
Elvran, *Norway* 10 A5
Elwood, *Ind., U.S.A.* 104 E3
Elwood, *Nebr., U.S.A.* 108 E5
Elx = Elche, *Spain* 29 G4
Ely, *U.K.* 13 E8
Ely, *Minn., U.S.A.* 108 B9
Ely, *Nev., U.S.A.* 110 G6
Elyria, *U.S.A.* 106 E2
Elz →, *Germany* 19 G3
Emāmrūd, *Iran* 65 B7
Emba, *Kazakhstan* 44 E6
Emba →, *Kazakhstan* 44 E6
Embarcación, *Argentina* 126 A3
Embarras Portage, *Canada* 101 B6
Embetsu, *Japan* 48 B10
Embira →, *Brazil* 124 B3
Embóna, *Greece* 37 C9
Embrach, *Switz.* 23 A7
Embrun, *France* 27 D10
Embu, *Kenya* 82 C4
Embu □, *Kenya* 82 C4
Emden, *Germany* 18 B3
Emerald, *Australia* 90 C4
Emerson, *Canada* 101 D9
Emery, *U.S.A.* 111 G8
Emet, *Turkey* 66 D3
Emi Koussi, *Chad* 73 E8
Emilia-Romagna □, *Italy* 32 D7
Emilius, Mte., *Italy* 32 C4
Eminabad, *Pakistan* 62 C6
Emirdağ, *Turkey* 66 D4
Emlenton, *U.S.A.* 106 E5
Emlichheim, *Germany* 18 C2
Emme →, *Switz.* 22 B5
Emmeloord, *Neths.* 16 C7
Emmen, *Neths.* 16 C9
Emmendingen, *Germany* 19 G3
Emmental, *Switz.* 22 C4
Emmer-Compascuum, *Neths.* 16 C10
Emmerich, *Germany* 18 D2
Emmet, *Australia* 90 C3
Emmetsburg, *U.S.A.* 108 D7
Emmett, *U.S.A.* 110 E5
Empalme, *Mexico* 114 B2
Empangeni, *S. Africa* 85 D5
Empedrado, *Argentina* 126 B4
Emperor Seamount Chain, *Pac. Oc.* 92 D9
Empoli, *Italy* 32 E7
Emporia, *Kans., U.S.A.* 108 F6
Emporia, *Va., U.S.A.* 105 G7
Emporium, *U.S.A.* 106 E6
Empress, *Canada* 101 C6
Emptinne, *Belgium* 17 H6
Empty Quarter = Rub' al Khali, *Si. Arabia* 68 D4
Ems →, *Germany* 18 B3
Emsdale, *Canada* 106 A5
Emsdetten, *Germany* 18 C3
Emu, *China* 51 C15
Emu Park, *Australia* 90 C5
'En 'Avrona, *Israel* 69 F3
En Nahud, *Sudan* 77 E2
Ena, *Japan* 49 G8
Enafors, *Sweden* 10 A6
Enambú, *Colombia* 120 C3
Enana, *Namibia* 84 B2
Enånger, *Sweden* 10 C11
Enaratoli, *Indonesia* 57 E9
Enard B., *U.K.* 14 C3
Enare = Inarijärvi, *Finland* 8 B19
Encantadas, Serra, *Brazil* 127 C5
Encanto, C., *Phil.* 57 A6
Encarnación, *Paraguay* 127 B4
Encarnación de Diaz, *Mexico* 114 C4
Enchi, *Ghana* 78 D4
Encinal, *U.S.A.* 109 L5
Encinitas, *U.S.A.* 113 M9
Encino, *U.S.A.* 111 J11
Encontrados, *Venezuela* 120 B3
Encounter B., *Australia* 91 F2
Encruzilhada, *Brazil* 123 E3
Ende, *Indonesia* 57 F6
Endeavour, *Canada* 101 C8
Endeavour Str., *Australia* 90 A3
Endelave, *Denmark* 11 J4
Enderbury I., *Kiribati* 92 H10
Enderby, *Canada* 100 C5
Enderby I., *Australia* 88 D2
Enderby Land, *Antarctica* 5 C5
Enderlin, *U.S.A.* 108 B6
Endicott, *N.Y., U.S.A.* 107 D8
Endicott, *Wash., U.S.A.* 110 C5
Endimari →, *Brazil* 124 B4
Endyalgout I., *Australia* 88 B5
Ene →, *Peru* 124 C3
Enewetak Atoll, *Pac. Oc.* 92 F8
Enez, *Turkey* 66 C2
Enfida, *Tunisia* 75 A7
Enfield, *U.K.* 13 F7
Engadin, *Switz.* 19 J6
Engaño, C., *Dom. Rep.* 117 C6
Engaño, C., *Phil.* 57 A6
Engcobo, *S. Africa* 85 E4
Engelberg, *Switz.* 23 C6
Engels = Pokrovsk, *Russia* 41 F15
Engemann L., *Canada* 101 B7
Enger, *Norway* 10 D4
Enggano, *Indonesia* 56 F2
Enghien, *Belgium* 17 G4
Engil, *Morocco* 74 B4
Engkilili, *Malaysia* 56 D4
England, *U.S.A.* 109 H9
England □, *U.K.* 7 E5
Englee, *Canada* 99 B8
Englehart, *Canada* 98 C4
Engler L., *Canada* 101 B7
Englewood, *Colo., U.S.A.* 108 F2
Englewood, *Kans., U.S.A.* 109 G5
English →, *Canada* 101 C10
English Bazar = Ingraj Bazar, *India* 63 G13
English Channel, *Europe* 13 G6
English River, *Canada* 98 C1
Enid, *U.S.A.* 109 G6
Enipévs →, *Greece* 39 K5
Enkhuizen, *Neths.* 16 C6
Enköping, *Sweden* 10 E11
Enle, *China* 52 E3
Enna, *Italy* 35 E7
Ennadai, *Canada* 101 A8
Ennadai L., *Canada* 101 A8
Ennedi, *Chad* 73 E9
Enngonia, *Australia* 91 D4
Ennis, *Ireland* 15 D3
Ennis, *Mont., U.S.A.* 110 D8
Ennis, *Tex., U.S.A.* 109 J6
Enniscorthy, *Ireland* 15 D5
Enniskillen, *U.K.* 15 B4
Ennistimon, *Ireland* 15 D2
Enns →, *Austria* 21 G4
Enontekiö, *Finland* 8 B17
Enping, *China* 53 F9
Enriquillo, L., *Dom. Rep.* 117 C5
Ens, *Neths.* 16 C7
Enschede, *Neths.* 16 D9
Ensenada, *Argentina* 126 C4
Ensenada, *Mexico* 114 A1
Enshi, *China* 52 B7
Ensiola, Pta., *Spain* 36 B9
Ensisheim, *France* 25 E14
Entebbe, *Uganda* 82 B3
Enter, *Neths.* 16 D9
Enterprise, *Canada* 100 A5
Enterprise, *Oreg., U.S.A.* 110 D5
Enterprise, *Utah, U.S.A.* 111 H7
Entlebuch, *Switz.* 22 C6
Entre Ríos, *Bolivia* 126 A3
Entre Rios, *Bahia, Brazil* 123 D4
Entre Rios, *Pará, Brazil* 125 B7
Entre Ríos □, *Argentina* 126 C4
Entrepeñas, Pantano de, *Spain* 28 E2
Enugu, *Nigeria* 79 D6
Enugu □, *Nigeria* 79 D6
Enugu Ezike, *Nigeria* 79 D6
Enumclaw, *U.S.A.* 112 C5
Envermeu, *France* 24 C8
Envigado, *Colombia* 120 B2
Envira, *Brazil* 124 B3
Enz →, *Germany* 19 F5
Enza →, *Italy* 32 D7
Eólie, Is., *Italy* 35 D7
Epanomí, *Greece* 39 J5
Epe, *Neths.* 16 D7
Epe, *Nigeria* 79 D5
Épernay, *France* 25 C10
Épernon, *France* 25 D8
Ephesus, *Turkey* 66 E2
Ephraim, *U.S.A.* 110 G8
Ephrata, *U.S.A.* 110 C4
Epila, *Spain* 28 D3
Épinac-les-Mines, *France* 25 F11
Épinal, *France* 25 D13
Epira, *Guyana* 121 B6
Episkopi, *Cyprus* 37 E11
Episkopí, *Greece* 37 D6
Episkopi Bay, *Cyprus* 37 E11
Epping, *U.K.* 13 F8
Epukiro, *Namibia* 84 C2
Equatorial Guinea ■, *Africa* 80 D1
Equeipa, *Venezuela* 121 B5
Er Rahad, *Sudan* 77 E3
Er Rif, *Morocco* 75 A4
Er Roseires, *Sudan* 77 E3
Erāwadī Myit = Irrawaddy →, *Burma* 61 M19
Erba, *Italy* 32 C6
Erba, *Sudan* 76 D4
Erbaa, *Turkey* 66 C7
Erbil = Arbīl, *Iraq* 64 B5
Erçek Gölü, *Turkey* 67 D10
Ercha, *Russia* 45 C15
Erçis, *Turkey* 67 D10
Erciyaş Dağı, *Turkey* 66 D6
Erdao Jiang →, *China* 51 C14
Erdek, *Turkey* 66 C2
Erdemli, *Turkey* 66 E6
Erdene, *Mongolia* 50 B6
Erding, *Germany* 19 G7
Erdre →, *France* 24 E5
Erebato →, *Venezuela* 121 B5
Erebus, Mt., *Antarctica* 5 D11
Erechim, *Brazil* 127 B5
Ereğli, *Konya, Turkey* 66 E6
Ereğli, *Zonguldak, Turkey* 66 C4
Erei, Monti, *Italy* 35 E7
Erembodegem, *Belgium* 17 G4
Erenhot, *China* 50 C7
Eresma →, *Spain* 30 D6
Erewadi Myitwanya, *Burma* 61 M19
Erfenisdam, *S. Africa* 84 D4
Erfoud, *Morocco* 74 B4
Erft →, *Germany* 18 D2
Erfurt, *Germany* 18 E7
Ergani, *Turkey* 67 D8
Ergeni Vozvyshennost, *Russia* 43 C11
Ērgli, *Latvia* 40 C4
Eria →, *Spain* 30 C5
Eriba, *Sudan* 77 D4
Eriboll, L., *U.K.* 14 C4
Erica, *Neths.* 16 C9
Érice, *Italy* 34 D5
Erie, *U.S.A.* 106 D4
Erie, L., *N. Amer.* 106 D3
Erie Canal, *U.S.A.* 106 C6
Erieau, *Canada* 106 D3
Erigavo, *Somali Rep.* 68 E4
Erikoúsa, *Greece* 37 A3
Eriksdale, *Canada* 101 C9
Erikslund, *Sweden* 10 B9
Erímanthos, *Greece* 39 M4
Erimo-misaki, *Japan* 48 D11
Eriswil, *Switz.* 22 B5
Erithraí, *Greece* 39 L6
Eritrea ■, *Africa* 77 E4
Erjas →, *Portugal* 31 F3
Erlangen, *Germany* 19 F7
Erldunda, *Australia* 90 D1
Erlin, *Taiwan* 53 F13
Ermelo, *Neths.* 16 D7
Ermelo, *S. Africa* 85 D4
Ermenak, *Turkey* 66 E5
Ermióni, *Greece* 39 M6
Ermones, *Greece* 37 A3
Ermoúpolis = Síros, *Greece* 39 M7
Ernakulam = Cochin, *India* 60 Q10
Erne →, *Ireland* 15 B3
Erne, Lower L., *U.K.* 15 B4
Erne, Upper L., *U.K.* 15 B4
Ernée, *France* 24 D6
Ernest Giles Ra., *Australia* 89 E3
Ernstberg, *Germany* 19 E2
Erode, *India* 60 P10
Eromanga, *Australia* 91 D3
Erongo, *Namibia* 84 C2
Erp, *Neths.* 17 E7
Erquelinnes, *Belgium* 17 H4
Erquy, *France* 24 D4
Erquy, C. d', *France* 24 D4
Err, Piz d', *Switz.* 23 C9
Errabiddy, *Australia* 89 E2
Erramala Hills, *India* 60 M11
Errer →, *Ethiopia* 77 F5
Errigal, *Ireland* 15 A3
Erris Hd., *Ireland* 15 B1
Erseka, *Albania* 39 J3
Erskine, *U.S.A.* 108 B7
Erstein, *France* 25 D14
Erstfeld, *Switz.* 23 C7
Ertil, *Russia* 41 F12
Ertis = Irtysh →, *Russia* 44 C7
Ertvelde, *Belgium* 17 F3
Eruh, *Turkey* 67 E10
Eruwa, *Nigeria* 79 D5
Ervy-le-Châtel, *France* 25 D10
Erwin, *U.S.A.* 105 G4
Eryuan, *China* 52 D2
Erzgebirge, *Germany* 18 E9
Erzin, *Russia* 45 D10
Erzincan, *Turkey* 67 D8
Erzincan □, *Turkey* 67 D8
Erzurum, *Turkey* 67 D9
Erzurum □, *Turkey* 67 D9
Es Caló, *Spain* 36 C8
Es Caná, *Spain* 36 B8
Es Sahrâ' Esh Sharqîya, *Egypt* 76 B3
Es Sînâ', *Egypt* 76 J8
Es Sûkî, *Sudan* 77 E3
Esambo, *Zaïre* 82 C1
Esan-Misaki, *Japan* 48 D10
Esashi, *Hokkaidō, Japan* 48 B11
Esashi, *Hokkaidō, Japan* 48 D10
Esbjerg, *Denmark* 11 J2
Escada, *Brazil* 122 C4
Escalante, *U.S.A.* 111 H8
Escalante →, *U.S.A.* 111 H8
Escalón, *Mexico* 114 B4
Escalona, *Spain* 30 E6
Escambia →, *U.S.A.* 105 K2

Escanaba

Escanaba, *U.S.A.* 104 **C2**
Escaut →, *Belgium* 17 **F3**
Esch-sur-Alzette, *Lux.* 17 **J7**
Eschede, *Germany* 18 **C6**
Escholzmatt, *Switz.* 22 **C5**
Eschwege, *Germany* 18 **D6**
Eschweiler, *Germany* 18 **E2**
Escoma, *Bolivia* 124 **D4**
Escondido, *U.S.A.* 113 **M9**
Escuinapa, *Mexico* 114 **C3**
Escuintla, *Guatemala* 116 **D1**
Eséka, *Cameroon* 79 **E7**
Esens, *Germany* 18 **B3**
Esera →, *Spain* 28 **C5**
Eşfahān, *Iran* 65 **C6**
Esfīdeh, *Iran* 65 **C8**
Esgueva →, *Spain* 30 **D6**
Esh Sham = Dimashq, *Syria* 69 **B5**
Esh Shamâlîya □, *Sudan* 76 **D2**
Eshan, *China* 52 **E4**
Eshowe, *S. Africa* 85 **D5**
Esiama, *Ghana* 78 **E4**
Esil = Ishim →, *Russia* 44 **D8**
Esino →, *Italy* 33 **E10**
Esk →, *Dumf. & Gall., U.K.* 14 **G5**
Esk →, *N. Yorks., U.K.* 12 **C7**
Eskifjörður, *Iceland* 8 **D7**
Eskilstuna, *Sweden* 10 **E10**
Eskimalatya, *Turkey* 67 **D8**
Eskimo Pt., *Canada* 101 **A10**
Eskişehir, *Turkey* 66 **D4**
Eskişehir □, *Turkey* 66 **D4**
Esla →, *Spain* 30 **D4**
Esla, Pantano del, *Spain* 30 **D4**
Eslāmābād-e Gharb, *Iran* 64 **C5**
Eslöv, *Sweden* 11 **J7**
Eşme, *Turkey* 66 **D3**
Esmeralda, I., *Chile* 128 **C1**
Esmeraldas, *Ecuador* 120 **C2**
Esmeraldas □, *Ecuador* 120 **C2**
Esmeraldas →, *Ecuador* 120 **C2**
Esneux, *Belgium* 17 **G7**
Espada, Pta., *Colombia* 120 **A3**
Espalion, *France* 26 **D6**
Espalmador, I., *Spain* 36 **C7**
Espanola, *Canada* 98 **C3**
Espardell, I. del, *Spain* 36 **C7**
Esparraguera, *Spain* 28 **D6**
Esparta, *Costa Rica* 116 **E3**
Espejo, *Spain* 31 **H6**
Esperança, *Brazil* 122 **C4**
Esperance, *Australia* 89 **F3**
Esperance B., *Australia* 89 **F3**
Esperantinópolis, *Brazil* 122 **B3**
Esperanza, *Santa Cruz, Argentina* 128 **D2**
Esperanza, *Santa Fe, Argentina* 126 **C3**
Esperanza, *Phil.* 55 **G6**
Espéraza, *France* 26 **F6**
Espichel, C., *Portugal* 31 **G1**
Espiel, *Spain* 31 **G5**
Espigão, Serra do, *Brazil* 127 **B5**
Espinal, *Colombia* 120 **C3**
Espinar, *Peru* 124 **C3**
Espinazo, Sierra del = Espinhaço, Serra do, *Brazil* 123 **E3**
Espinhaço, Serra do, *Brazil* 123 **E3**
Espinho, *Portugal* 30 **D2**
Espinilho, Serra do, *Brazil* 127 **B5**
Espino, *Venezuela* 120 **B4**
Espinosa de los Monteros, *Spain* 30 **B7**
Espírito Santo □, *Brazil* 123 **F3**
Espíritu Santo, B. del, *Mexico* 115 **D7**
Espíritu Santo, I., *Mexico* 114 **C2**
Espita, *Mexico* 115 **C7**
Espiye, *Turkey* 67 **C8**
Esplanada, *Brazil* 123 **D4**
Espluga de Francolí, *Spain* 28 **D6**
Espuña, Sierra, *Spain* 29 **H3**
Espungabera, *Mozam.* 85 **C5**
Esquel, *Argentina* 128 **B2**
Esquina, *Argentina* 126 **B4**
Essaouira, *Morocco* 74 **B3**
Essebie, *Zaïre* 82 **B3**
Essen, *Belgium* 17 **F4**
Essen, *Germany* 18 **D2**
Essendon, Mt., *Australia* 89 **E3**
Essequibo →, *Guyana* 121 **B6**
Essex, *Canada* 106 **D2**
Essex, *Calif., U.S.A.* 113 **L11**
Essex, *N.Y., U.S.A.* 107 **B11**
Essex □, *U.K.* 13 **F8**
Esslingen, *Germany* 19 **G5**
Essonne □, *France* 25 **D9**
Essvik, *Sweden* 10 **B11**
Estaca, Pta. del, *Spain* 30 **B3**
Estadilla, *Spain* 28 **C5**
Estados, I. de Los, *Argentina* 128 **D4**
Estagel, *France* 26 **F6**
Eşţahbānāt, *Iran* 65 **D7**
Estallenchs, *Spain* 36 **B9**
Estância, *Brazil* 122 **D4**
Estancia, *U.S.A.* 111 **J10**
Estārm, *Iran* 65 **D8**
Estarreja, *Portugal* 30 **E2**
Estats, Pic d', *Spain* 28 **C6**
Estavayer-le-Lac, *Switz.* 22 **C3**
Estcourt, *S. Africa* 85 **D4**
Este, *Italy* 33 **C8**
Esteban, *Spain* 30 **B4**
Estelí, *Nic.* 116 **D2**
Estella, *Spain* 28 **C2**
Estelline, *S. Dak., U.S.A.* 108 **C6**
Estelline, *Tex., U.S.A.* 109 **H4**
Estena →, *Spain* 31 **F6**
Estepa, *Spain* 31 **H6**
Estepona, *Spain* 31 **J5**
Esterhazy, *Canada* 101 **C8**
Esternay, *France* 25 **D10**
Esterri de Aneu, *Spain* 28 **C6**
Estevan, *Canada* 101 **D8**
Estevan Group, *Canada* 100 **C3**
Estherville, *U.S.A.* 108 **D7**
Estissac, *France* 25 **D10**
Eston, *Canada* 101 **C7**
Estonia ■, *Europe* 40 **B4**
Estoril, *Portugal* 31 **G1**
Estouk, *Mali* 79 **B5**
Estrêla, Serra da, *Portugal* 30 **E3**
Estrella, *Spain* 29 **G1**
Estremoz, *Portugal* 31 **G3**
Estrondo, Serra do, *Brazil* 122 **C2**
Esztergom, *Hungary* 21 **H8**
Et Tîdra, *Mauritania* 78 **B1**
Étables-sur-Mer, *France* 24 **D4**
Etadunna, *Australia* 91 **D2**
Etah, *India* 63 **F8**
Étain, *France* 25 **C12**
Etalle, *Belgium* 17 **J7**
Etamamu, *Canada* 99 **B8**
Étampes, *France* 25 **D9**
Étang-sur-Arroux, *France* 27 **B8**
Etanga, *Namibia* 84 **B1**
Étaples, *France* 25 **B8**
Etawah, *India* 63 **F8**
Etawah →, *U.S.A.* 105 **H3**
Etawney L., *Canada* 101 **B9**
Ete, *Nigeria* 79 **D6**
Éthe, *Belgium* 17 **J7**
Ethel, *U.S.A.* 112 **D4**
Ethel, Oued el →, *Algeria* 74 **C4**
Ethel Creek, *Australia* 88 **D3**
Ethelbert, *Canada* 101 **C8**
Ethiopia ■, *Africa* 68 **F3**
Ethiopian Highlands, *Ethiopia* 70 **E7**
Etive, L., *U.K.* 14 **E3**
Etna, *Italy* 35 **E8**
Etoile, *Zaïre* 83 **E2**
Etolin I., *U.S.A.* 100 **B2**
Etosha Pan, *Namibia* 84 **B2**
Etowah, *U.S.A.* 105 **H3**
Étrépagny, *France* 25 **C8**
Étretat, *France* 24 **C7**
Ettelbruck, *Lux.* 17 **J8**
Etten, *Neths.* 17 **E5**
Ettlingen, *Germany* 19 **G4**
Ettrick Water →, *U.K.* 14 **F6**
Etuku, *Zaïre* 82 **C2**
Etzatlán, *Mexico* 114 **C4**
Eu, *France* 24 **B8**
Euboea = Évvoia, *Greece* 39 **L7**
Eucla Motel, *Australia* 89 **F4**
Euclid, *U.S.A.* 106 **E3**
Euclides da Cunha, *Brazil* 122 **D4**
Eucumbene, L., *Australia* 91 **F4**
Eudora, *U.S.A.* 109 **J9**
Eufaula, *Ala., U.S.A.* 105 **K3**
Eufaula, *Okla., U.S.A.* 109 **H7**
Eufaula L., *U.S.A.* 109 **H7**
Eugene, *U.S.A.* 110 **E2**
Eugowra, *Australia* 91 **E4**
Eulo, *Australia* 91 **D4**
Eunice, *La., U.S.A.* 109 **K8**
Eunice, *N. Mex., U.S.A.* 109 **J3**
Eupen, *Belgium* 17 **G8**
Euphrates = Furāt, Nahr al →, *Asia* 64 **D5**
Eure □, *France* 24 **C8**
Eure →, *France* 24 **C8**
Eure-et-Loir □, *France* 24 **D8**
Eureka, *Canada* 4 **B3**
Eureka, *Calif., U.S.A.* 110 **F1**
Eureka, *Kans., U.S.A.* 109 **G6**
Eureka, *Mont., U.S.A.* 110 **B6**
Eureka, *Nev., U.S.A.* 110 **G5**
Eureka, *S. Dak., U.S.A.* 108 **C5**
Eureka, *Utah, U.S.A.* 110 **G7**
Eureka, Mt., *Australia* 89 **E3**
Euroa, *Australia* 91 **F4**
Europa, I., *Ind. Oc.* 81 **J8**
Europa, Picos de, *Spain* 30 **B6**
Europa, Pta. de, *Gib.* 31 **J5**
Europa Pt. = Europa, Pta. de, *Gib.* 31 **J5**
Europe 6 **F10**
Europoort, *Neths.* 16 **E4**
Euskirchen, *Germany* 18 **E2**
Eustis, *U.S.A.* 105 **L5**
Eutin, *Germany* 18 **A6**
Eutsuk L., *Canada* 100 **C3**
Eva, *Brazil* 121 **D6**
Eva Downs, *Australia* 90 **B1**
Evale, *Angola* 84 **B2**
Evans, *U.S.A.* 108 **E2**
Evans Head, *Australia* 91 **D5**
Evans L., *Canada* 98 **B4**
Evans Mills, *U.S.A.* 107 **B9**
Evanston, *Ill., U.S.A.* 104 **D2**
Evanston, *Wyo., U.S.A.* 110 **F8**
Evansville, *Ind., U.S.A.* 104 **F2**
Evansville, *Wis., U.S.A.* 108 **D10**
Évaux-les-Bains, *France* 26 **B6**
Evaz, *Iran* 65 **E7**
Eveleth, *U.S.A.* 108 **B8**
Evensk, *Russia* 45 **C16**
Evenstad, *Norway* 10 **C5**
Everard, L., *Australia* 91 **E1**
Everard Park, *Australia* 89 **E5**
Everard Ras., *Australia* 89 **E5**
Evere, *Belgium* 17 **G4**
Everest, Mt., *Nepal* 63 **E12**
Everett, *Pa., U.S.A.* 106 **F6**
Everett, *Wash., U.S.A.* 112 **C4**
Evergem, *Belgium* 17 **F3**
Everglades, The, *U.S.A.* 105 **N5**
Everglades City, *U.S.A.* 105 **N5**
Everglades National Park, *U.S.A.* 105 **N5**
Evergreen, *U.S.A.* 105 **K2**
Everson, *U.S.A.* 110 **B2**
Evesham, *U.K.* 13 **E6**
Évian-les-Bains, *France* 27 **B10**
Evinayong, *Eq. Guin.* 80 **D2**
Évinos →, *Greece* 39 **L4**
Évisa, *France* 27 **F12**
Évora, *Portugal* 31 **G3**
Évora □, *Portugal* 31 **G3**
Evowghlī, *Iran* 64 **B5**
Évreux, *France* 24 **C8**
Évron, *France* 24 **D6**
Evrótas →, *Greece* 39 **N5**
Évvoia, *Greece* 39 **L7**
Évvoia □, *Greece* 39 **L6**
Ewe, L., *U.K.* 14 **D3**
Ewing, *U.S.A.* 108 **D5**
Ewo, *Congo* 80 **E2**
Exaltación, *Bolivia* 125 **C4**
Excelsior Springs, *U.S.A.* 108 **F7**
Excideuil, *France* 26 **C5**
Exe →, *U.K.* 13 **G4**
Exeter, *Canada* 106 **C3**
Exeter, *U.K.* 13 **G4**
Exeter, *Calif., U.S.A.* 111 **H4**
Exeter, *N.H., U.S.A.* 107 **D14**
Exeter, *Nebr., U.S.A.* 108 **E6**
Exloo, *Neths.* 16 **C9**
Exmes, *France* 24 **D7**
Exmoor, *U.K.* 13 **F4**
Exmouth, *Australia* 88 **D1**
Exmouth, *U.K.* 13 **G4**
Exmouth G., *Australia* 88 **D1**
Expedition Ra., *Australia* 90 **C4**
Extremadura □, *Spain* 31 **F4**
Exuma Sound, *Bahamas* 116 **B4**
Eyasi, L., *Tanzania* 82 **C4**
Eyeberry L., *Canada* 101 **A8**
Eyemouth, *U.K.* 14 **F6**
Eygurande, *France* 26 **C6**
Eyjafjörður, *Iceland* 8 **C4**
Eymet, *France* 26 **D4**
Eymoutiers, *France* 26 **C5**
Eynesil, *Turkey* 67 **C8**
Eyrarbakki, *Iceland* 8 **E3**
Eyre, *Australia* 89 **F4**
Eyre (North), L., *Australia* 91 **D2**
Eyre (South), L., *Australia* 91 **D2**
Eyre Cr. →, *Australia* 91 **D2**
Eyre Mts., *N.Z.* 87 **L2**
Eyre Pen., *Australia* 91 **E2**
Eyvānkī, *Iran* 65 **C6**
Ez Zeidab, *Sudan* 76 **D3**
Ezcaray, *Spain* 28 **C2**
Ezine, *Turkey* 66 **D2**
Ezmul, *Mauritania* 74 **D1**
Ezouza →, *Cyprus* 37 **E11**

F

Fabens, *U.S.A.* 111 **L10**
Fåborg, *Denmark* 11 **J4**
Fabriano, *Italy* 33 **E9**
Făcăeni, *Romania* 38 **E10**
Facatativá, *Colombia* 120 **C3**
Fachi, *Niger* 72 **E7**
Facture, *France* 26 **D3**
Fada, *Chad* 73 **E9**
Fada-n-Gourma, *Burkina Faso* 79 **C5**
Faddeyevskiy, Ostrov, *Russia* 45 **B15**
Fadghāmī, *Syria* 64 **C4**
Fadlab, *Sudan* 76 **D3**
Faenza, *Italy* 33 **D8**
Fafa, *Mali* 79 **B5**
Fafe, *Portugal* 30 **D2**
Fagam, *Nigeria* 79 **C7**
Făgăras, *Romania* 38 **D7**
Făgăras, Munţii, *Romania* 38 **D7**
Fågelsjö, *Sweden* 10 **C8**
Fagernes, *Norway* 9 **F10**
Fagersta, *Sweden* 9 **F13**
Făget, *Romania* 38 **D5**
Fagnano, L., *Argentina* 128 **D3**
Fagnano Castello, *Italy* 35 **C9**
Fagnières, *France* 25 **D11**
Fahlīān, *Iran* 65 **D6**
Fahraj, *Kermān, Iran* 65 **D8**
Fahraj, *Yazd, Iran* 65 **D7**
Faial, *Madeira* 36 **D3**
Faido, *Switz.* 23 **D7**
Fair Hd., *U.K.* 15 **A5**
Fair Oaks, *U.S.A.* 112 **G5**
Fairbank, *U.S.A.* 111 **L8**
Fairbanks, *U.S.A.* 96 **B5**
Fairbury, *U.S.A.* 108 **E6**
Fairfax, *U.S.A.* 109 **G6**
Fairfield, *Ala., U.S.A.* 105 **J2**
Fairfield, *Calif., U.S.A.* 112 **G4**
Fairfield, *Conn., U.S.A.* 107 **E11**
Fairfield, *Idaho, U.S.A.* 110 **E6**
Fairfield, *Ill., U.S.A.* 104 **F1**
Fairfield, *Iowa, U.S.A.* 108 **E9**
Fairfield, *Mont., U.S.A.* 110 **C8**
Fairfield, *Tex., U.S.A.* 109 **K7**
Fairford, *Canada* 101 **C9**
Fairhope, *U.S.A.* 105 **K2**
Fairlie, *N.Z.* 87 **L3**
Fairmead, *U.S.A.* 112 **H6**
Fairmont, *Minn., U.S.A.* 108 **D7**
Fairmont, *W. Va., U.S.A.* 104 **F5**
Fairmount, *U.S.A.* 113 **L8**
Fairplay, *U.S.A.* 111 **G11**
Fairport, *U.S.A.* 106 **C7**
Fairport Harbor, *U.S.A.* 106 **E3**
Fairview, *Australia* 90 **B3**
Fairview, *Canada* 100 **B5**
Fairview, *Mont., U.S.A.* 108 **B2**
Fairview, *Okla., U.S.A.* 109 **G5**
Fairview, *Utah, U.S.A.* 110 **G8**
Fairweather, Mt., *U.S.A.* 96 **C6**
Faisalabad, *Pakistan* 62 **D5**
Faith, *U.S.A.* 108 **C3**
Faizabad, *India* 63 **F10**
Fajardo, *Puerto Rico* 117 **C6**
Fakfak, *Indonesia* 57 **E8**
Fakobli, *Ivory C.* 78 **D3**
Fakse, *Denmark* 11 **J6**
Fakse B., *Denmark* 11 **J6**
Fakse Ladeplads, *Denmark* 11 **J6**
Faku, *China* 51 **C12**
Falaise, *France* 24 **D6**
Falaise, Mui, *Vietnam* 58 **C5**
Falam, *Burma* 61 **H18**
Falces, *Spain* 28 **C3**
Fălciu, *Romania* 38 **C11**
Falcón □, *Venezuela* 120 **A4**
Falcón, C., *Spain* 36 **C7**
Falcon, C., *Algeria* 75 **A4**
Falcon Dam, *U.S.A.* 109 **M5**
Falconara Marittima, *Italy* 33 **E10**
Falconer, *U.S.A.* 106 **D5**
Faléa, *Mali* 78 **C2**
Falenki, *Russia* 41 **B17**
Faleshty, *Moldavia* 42 **C2**
Falfurrias, *U.S.A.* 109 **M5**
Falher, *Canada* 100 **B5**
Falirakí, *Greece* 37 **C10**
Falkenberg, *Germany* 18 **D9**
Falkenberg, *Sweden* 11 **H6**
Falkensee, *Germany* 18 **C9**
Falkenstein, *Germany* 18 **E8**
Falkirk, *U.K.* 14 **F5**
Falkland, East, I., *Falk. Is.* 128 **D5**
Falkland, West, I., *Falk. Is.* 128 **D4**
Falkland Is. ■, *Atl. Oc.* 128 **D5**
Falkland Is. Dependency □, *Atl. Oc.* 5 **B1**
Falkland Sd., *Falk. Is.* 128 **D5**
Falköping, *Sweden* 11 **F7**
Fall River, *U.S.A.* 107 **E13**
Fall River Mills, *U.S.A.* 110 **F3**
Fallbrook, *U.S.A.* 111 **K5**
Fallbrook, *Calif., U.S.A.* 113 **M9**
Fallon, *Mont., U.S.A.* 108 **B2**
Fallon, *Nev., U.S.A.* 110 **G4**
Falls City, *Nebr., U.S.A.* 108 **E7**
Falls City, *Oreg., U.S.A.* 110 **D2**
Falls Creek, *U.S.A.* 106 **E6**
Falmouth, *Jamaica* 116 **C4**
Falmouth, *U.K.* 13 **G2**
Falmouth, *U.S.A.* 104 **F3**
False B., *S. Africa* 84 **E2**
Falset, *Spain* 28 **D5**
Falso, C., *Honduras* 116 **C3**
Falster, *Denmark* 11 **K5**
Falsterbo, *Sweden* 11 **J6**
Fălticeni, *Romania* 38 **B9**
Falun, *Sweden* 9 **F13**
Famagusta, *Cyprus* 37 **D12**
Famagusta Bay, *Cyprus* 37 **D13**
Famatina, Sierra de, *Argentina* 126 **B2**
Family L., *Canada* 101 **C9**
Famoso, *U.S.A.* 113 **K7**
Fan Xian, *China* 50 **G8**
Fana, *Mali* 78 **C3**
Fandriana, *Madag.* 85 **C8**
Fang, *Thailand* 58 **C2**
Fang Xian, *China* 53 **A8**
Fangchang, *China* 53 **B12**
Fangcheng, *Guangxi Zhuangzu, China* 52 **G7**
Fangcheng, *Henan, China* 50 **H7**
Fangliao, *Taiwan* 53 **F13**
Fangshan, *China* 50 **E6**
Fangzi, *China* 51 **F10**
Fani i Madh →, *Albania* 39 **H3**
Fanjiatun, *China* 51 **C13**
Fannich, L., *U.K.* 14 **D4**
Fannūj, *Iran* 65 **E8**
Fanny Bay, *Canada* 100 **D4**
Fanø, *Denmark* 11 **J2**
Fano, *Italy* 33 **E10**
Fanshaw, *U.S.A.* 100 **B2**
Fanshi, *China* 50 **E7**
Fao = Al Fāw, *Iraq* 65 **D6**
Faqirwali, *Pakistan* 62 **E5**
Fara in Sabina, *Italy* 33 **F9**
Faradje, *Zaïre* 82 **B2**
Farafangana, *Madag.* 85 **C8**
Farâfra, El Wâhât el-, *Egypt* 76 **B2**
Farāh, *Afghan.* 60 **C3**
Farāh □, *Afghan.* 60 **C3**
Farahalana, *Madag.* 85 **A9**
Faraid, Gebel, *Egypt* 76 **C4**
Faramana, *Burkina Faso* 78 **C4**
Faranah, *Guinea* 78 **C2**
Farasān, Jazā'ir, *Si. Arabia* 68 **D3**
Farasan Is. = Farasān, Jazā'ir, *Si. Arabia* 68 **D3**
Faratsiho, *Madag.* 85 **B8**
Fardes →, *Spain* 29 **H1**
Fareham, *U.K.* 13 **G6**
Farewell, C., *N.Z.* 87 **J4**
Farewell C. = Farvel, Kap, *Greenland* 4 **D5**
Farghona = Fergana, *Uzbekistan* 44 **E8**
Fargo, *U.S.A.* 108 **B6**
Fari'a →, *Jordan* 69 **C4**
Faribault, *U.S.A.* 108 **C8**
Faridkot, *India* 62 **D6**
Faridpur, *Bangla.* 63 **H13**
Färila, *Sweden* 10 **C9**
Farim, *Guinea-Biss.* 78 **C1**
Farīmān, *Iran* 65 **C8**
Farina, *Australia* 91 **E2**
Farinha →, *Brazil* 122 **C2**
Fariones, Pta., *Canary Is.* 36 **E6**
Fâriskûr, *Egypt* 76 **H7**
Farmerville, *U.S.A.* 109 **J8**
Farmington, *Calif., U.S.A.* 112 **H6**
Farmington, *N.H., U.S.A.* 107 **C13**
Farmington, *N. Mex., U.S.A.* 111 **H9**
Farmington, *Utah, U.S.A.* 110 **F8**
Farmington →, *U.S.A.* 107 **E12**
Farmville, *U.S.A.* 104 **G6**
Farnborough, *U.K.* 13 **F7**
Farne Is., *U.K.* 12 **B6**
Farnham, *Canada* 107 **A12**
Faro, *Brazil* 121 **D6**
Faro, *Portugal* 31 **H3**
Fårö, *Sweden* 9 **H15**
Faro □, *Portugal* 31 **H2**
Faroe Is. = Føroyar, *Atl. Oc.* 7 **C4**
Farquhar, C., *Australia* 89 **D1**
Farrars Cr. →, *Australia* 90 **D3**
Farrāshband, *Iran* 65 **D7**
Farrell, *U.S.A.* 106 **E4**
Farrell Flat, *Australia* 91 **E2**
Farrokhī, *Iran* 65 **C8**
Farruch, C., *Spain* 36 **B10**
Farrukhabad-cum-Fatehgarh, *India* 63 **F8**
Fārs □, *Iran* 65 **D7**
Fársala, *Greece* 39 **K5**
Farsø, *Denmark* 11 **H3**
Farsund, *Norway* 9 **G9**
Fartak, Râs, *Si. Arabia* 64 **D2**
Fartura, Serra da, *Brazil* 127 **B5**
Faru, *Nigeria* 79 **C6**
Fārūj, *Iran* 65 **B8**
Farum, *Denmark* 11 **J6**
Farvel, Kap, *Greenland* 4 **D5**
Farwell, *U.S.A.* 109 **H3**
Fasā, *Iran* 65 **D7**
Fasano, *Italy* 35 **B10**
Fashoda, *Sudan* 77 **F3**
Fastnet Rock, *Ireland* 15 **E2**
Fastov, *Ukraine* 40 **F6**
Fatagar, Tanjung, *Indonesia* 57 **E8**
Fatehgarh, *India* 63 **F8**
Fatehpur, *Raj., India* 62 **F6**
Fatehpur, *Ut. P., India* 63 **G9**
Fatesh, *Russia* 41 **E9**
Fatick, *Senegal* 78 **C1**
Fatima, *Canada* 99 **C7**
Fátima, *Portugal* 31 **F2**
Fatoya, *Guinea* 78 **C3**
Faucille, Col de la, *France* 27 **B10**
Faulkton, *U.S.A.* 108 **C5**
Faulquemont, *France* 25 **C13**
Fauquembergues, *France* 25 **B9**
Faure I., *Australia* 89 **E1**
Făurei, *Romania* 38 **D10**
Fauresmith, *S. Africa* 84 **D4**
Fauske, *Norway* 8 **C13**
Fauvillers, *Belgium* 17 **J7**
Favara, *Italy* 34 **E6**
Favaritx, C., *Spain* 36 **A11**
Favignana, *Italy* 34 **E5**
Favignana, I., *Italy* 34 **E5**
Favourable Lake, *Canada* 98 **B1**
Fawn →, *Canada* 98 **A2**
Fawnskin, *U.S.A.* 113 **L10**
Faxaflói, *Iceland* 8 **D2**
Faya-Largeau, *Chad* 73 **E8**
Fayd, *Si. Arabia* 64 **E4**
Fayence, *France* 27 **E10**
Fayette, *Ala., U.S.A.* 105 **J2**
Fayette, *Mo., U.S.A.* 108 **F8**
Fayetteville, *Ark., U.S.A.* 109 **G7**
Fayetteville, *N.C., U.S.A.* 105 **H6**
Fayetteville, *Tenn., U.S.A.* 105 **H2**
Fayón, *Spain* 28 **D5**
Fazenda Nova, *Brazil* 123 **E1**
Fazilka, *India* 62 **D6**
Fazilpur, *Pakistan* 62 **E4**
Fdérik, *Mauritania* 74 **D2**
Feale →, *Ireland* 15 **D2**

Fear, C., U.S.A. 105 J7
Feather →, U.S.A. 110 G3
Feather Falls, U.S.A. 112 F5
Featherston, N.Z. 87 J5
Featherstone, Zimbabwe 83 F3
Fécamp, France 24 C7
Fedala = Mohammedia, Morocco 74 B3
Federación, Argentina 126 C4
Fedeshkūh, Iran 65 D7
Fedjadj, Chott el, Tunisia 75 B6
Fehmarn, Germany 18 A7
Fehmarn Bælt, Denmark 18 A7
Fei Xian, China 51 G9
Feijó, Brazil 124 B3
Feilding, N.Z. 87 J5
Feira de Santana, Brazil 123 D4
Feixiang, China 50 F8
Fejø, Denmark 11 K5
Feke, Turkey 66 E6
Felanitx, Spain 36 B10
Feldberg, Baden-W., Germany 19 H3
Feldberg, Mecklenburg-Vorpommern, Germany 18 B9
Feldkirch, Austria 19 H5
Felipe Carrillo Puerto, Mexico 115 D7
Felixlândia, Brazil 123 E3
Felixstowe, U.K. 13 F9
Felletin, France 26 C6
Felton, U.K. 12 B6
Felton, U.S.A. 112 H4
Feltre, Italy 33 B8
Femø, Denmark 11 K5
Femunden, Norway 10 B5
Fen He →, China 50 G6
Fenelon Falls, Canada 106 B6
Feneroa, Ethiopia 77 E4
Feng Xian, Jiangsu, China 50 G9
Feng Xian, Shaanxi, China 50 H4
Fengári, Greece 39 J8
Fengcheng, Jiangxi, China 53 C10
Fengcheng, Liaoning, China 51 D13
Fengdu, China 52 C6
Fengfeng, China 50 F8
Fenggang, China 52 D6
Fenghua, China 53 C13
Fenghuang, China 52 D7
Fenghuangzui, China 52 A7
Fengjie, China 52 B7
Fengkai, China 53 F8
Fengle, China 53 B9
Fengning, China 50 D9
Fengqing, China 52 E2
Fengqiu, China 50 G8
Fengrun, China 51 E10
Fengshan, Guangxi Zhuangzu, China 52 E7
Fengshan, Guangxi Zhuangzu, China 52 E6
Fengtai, Anhui, China 53 A11
Fengtai, Beijing, China 50 E9
Fengxian, China 53 B13
Fengxiang, China 50 G4
Fengxin, China 53 C10
Fengyang, China 51 H9
Fengyi, China 52 E3
Fengzhen, China 50 D7
Fenit, Ireland 15 D2
Fennimore, U.S.A. 108 D9
Feno, C. de, France 27 G12
Fenoarivo Afovoany, Madag. 85 B8
Fenoarivo Atsinanana, Madag. 85 B8
Fens, The, U.K. 12 E8
Fenton, U.S.A. 104 D4
Fenxi, China 50 F6
Fenyang, China 54 C6
Fenyang, Shanxi, China 50 F6
Fenyi, China 53 D10
Feodosiya, Ukraine 42 D6
Fer, C. de, Algeria 75 A6
Ferdows, Iran 65 C8
Fère-Champenoise, France 25 D10
Fère-en-Tardenois, France 25 C10
Ferentino, Italy 34 A6
Ferfer, Somali Rep. 68 F4
Fergana, Uzbekistan 44 E8
Fergus, Canada 98 D3
Fergus Falls, U.S.A. 108 B6
Fériana, Tunisia 75 B6
Feričanci, Croatia 21 K8
Ferkane, Algeria 75 B6
Ferkéssédougou, Ivory C. 78 D3
Ferlach, Austria 21 J4
Ferland, Canada 98 B2
Ferlo, Vallée du, Senegal 78 B2
Fermanagh □, U.K. 15 B4
Fermo, Italy 33 E10
Fermoselle, Spain 30 D4
Fermoy, Ireland 15 D3
Fernán Nuñéz, Spain 31 H6
Fernández, Argentina 126 B3
Fernandina Beach, U.S.A. 105 K5
Fernando de Noronha, Brazil 122 B5
Fernando Póo = Bioko, Eq. Guin. 79 E6
Fernandópolis, Brazil 123 F1
Ferndale, Calif., U.S.A. 110 F1
Ferndale, Wash., U.S.A. 112 B4
Fernie, Canada 100 D5
Fernlees, Australia 90 C4
Fernley, U.S.A. 110 G4
Ferozepore = Firozpur, India 62 D6
Férrai, Greece 39 J9
Ferrandina, Italy 35 B9
Ferrara, Italy 33 D8
Ferrato, C., Italy 34 C2
Ferreira do Alentejo, Portugal 31 G2
Ferreñafe, Peru 124 B2
Ferrerías, Spain 36 B11
Ferret, C., France 26 D2
Ferrette, France 25 E14
Ferriday, U.S.A. 109 K9
Ferrières, France 25 D9
Ferriete, Italy 32 D6
Ferrol = El Ferrol, Spain 30 B2
Ferrol, Pen. de, Peru 124 B2
Ferron, U.S.A. 111 G8
Ferros, Brazil 123 E3
Ferryland, Canada 99 C9
Fertile, U.S.A. 108 B6
Fertília, Italy 34 B1
Fès, Morocco 74 B4
Feschaux, Belgium 17 H5
Feshi, Zaïre 80 F3
Fessenden, U.S.A. 108 B5
Feteşti, Romania 38 E10
Fethiye, Turkey 66 E3
Fetlar, U.K. 14 A8
Feuerthalen, Switz. 23 A7
Feuilles →, Canada 97 C12
Feurs, France 27 C8
Fezzan, Libya 70 D5
Ffestiniog, U.K. 12 E4
Fiambalá, Argentina 126 B2
Fianarantsoa, Madag. 85 C8
Fianarantsoa □, Madag. 85 B8
Fianga, Cameroon 73 G8
Fichtelgebirge, Germany 19 E7
Ficksburg, S. Africa 85 D4
Fidenza, Italy 32 D7
Fiditi, Nigeria 79 D5
Field, Canada 98 C3
Field →, Australia 90 C2
Field I., Australia 88 B5
Fieri, Albania 39 J2
Fiesch, Switz. 22 D6
Fife □, U.K. 14 E5
Fife Ness, U.K. 14 E6
Fifth Cataract, Sudan 76 D3
Figeac, France 26 D6
Figline Valdarno, Italy 33 E8
Figtree, Zimbabwe 83 G2
Figueira Castelo Rodrigo, Portugal 30 E4
Figueira da Foz, Portugal 30 E2
Figueiró dos Vinhos, Portugal 30 F2
Figueras, Spain 28 C7
Figuig, Morocco 75 B4
Fihaonana, Madag. 85 B8
Fiherenana, Madag. 85 B8
Fiherenana →, Madag. 85 C7
Fiji ■, Pac. Oc. 87 C8
Fika, Nigeria 79 C7
Filabres, Sierra de los, Spain 29 H2
Filadelfia, Bolivia 124 C4
Filadélfia, Brazil 122 C2
Filadélfia, Italy 35 D9
Filer, U.S.A. 110 E6
Filey, U.K. 12 C7
Filfla, Malta 37 D1
Filiaşi, Romania 38 E6
Filiátes, Greece 39 K3
Filiatrá, Greece 39 M4
Filicudi, Italy 35 D7
Filiourí →, Greece 39 H8
Filipstad, Sweden 9 G13
Filisur, Switz. 23 C9
Fillmore, Canada 101 D8
Fillmore, Calif., U.S.A. 113 L8
Fillmore, Utah, U.S.A. 111 G7
Filottrano, Italy 33 E10
Filyos, Turkey 42 F5
Finale Lígure, Italy 32 D5
Finale nell' Emília, Italy 33 D8
Fiñana, Spain 29 H2
Finch, Canada 107 A9
Findhorn →, U.K. 14 D5
Findlay, U.S.A. 104 E4
Finger L., Canada 101 C10
Fingõe, Mozam. 83 E3
Finike, Turkey 66 E4
Finistère □, France 24 D2
Finisterre, Spain 30 C1
Finisterre, C., Spain 30 C1
Finke, Australia 90 D1
Finke →, Australia 91 D2
Finland ■, Europe 9 E19
Finland, G. of, Europe 9 G19
Finlay →, Canada 100 B3
Finley, Australia 91 F4
Finley, U.S.A. 108 B6
Finn →, Ireland 15 B4
Finnigan, Mt., Australia 90 B4
Finniss, C., Australia 91 E1
Finnmark fylke □, Norway 8 B18
Finsteraarhorn, Switz. 22 C6
Finsterwalde, Germany 18 D9
Finsterwolde, Neths. 16 B10
Fiora →, Italy 33 F8
Fiorenzuola d'Arda, Italy 32 D6
Fīq, Syria 69 C4
Firat = Furāt, Nahr al →, Asia 64 D5
Fire River, Canada 98 C3
Firebag →, Canada 101 B6
Firebaugh, U.S.A. 112 J6
Firedrake L., Canada 101 A8
Firenze, Italy 33 E8
Firk →, Iraq 64 D5
Firmi, France 26 D6
Firminy, France 27 C8
Firozabad, India 63 F8
Firozpur, India 62 D6
Fīrūzābād, Iran 65 D7
Fīrūzkūh, Iran 65 C7
Firvale, Canada 100 C3
Fish →, Namibia 84 D2
Fish →, S. Africa 84 E3
Fisher, Australia 89 F5
Fisher B., Canada 101 C9
Fishguard, U.K. 13 F3
Fishing L., Canada 101 C9
Fismes, France 25 C10
Fitchburg, U.S.A. 107 D13
Fitero, Spain 28 C3
Fitri, L., Chad 73 F8
Fitz Roy, Argentina 128 C3
Fitzgerald, Canada 100 B6
Fitzgerald, U.S.A. 105 K4
Fitzmaurice →, Australia 88 B5
Fitzroy →, Queens., Australia 90 C5
Fitzroy →, W. Austral., Australia 88 C3
Fitzroy Crossing, Australia 88 C4
Fitzwilliam I., Canada 106 A3
Fiume = Rijeka, Croatia 33 C11
Fiumefreddo Brúzio, Italy 35 C9
Five Points, U.S.A. 112 J6
Fivizzano, Italy 32 D7
Fizi, Zaïre 82 C2
Fjellerup, Denmark 11 H4
Fjerritslev, Denmark 11 G3
Fkih ben Salah, Morocco 74 B3
Flå, Norway 10 A4
Flagler, U.S.A. 108 F3
Flagstaff, U.S.A. 111 J8
Flaherty I., Canada 98 A4
Flåm, Norway 9 F9
Flambeau →, U.S.A. 108 C9
Flamborough Hd., U.K. 12 C7
Flaming Gorge Dam, U.S.A. 110 F9
Flaming Gorge Reservoir, U.S.A. 110 F9
Flamingo, Teluk, Indonesia 57 F9
Flanders = West-Vlaanderen □, Belgium 17 G2
Flandre Occidentale = West-Vlaanderen □, Belgium 17 G2
Flandre Orientale = Oost-Vlaanderen □, Belgium 17 F3
Flandreau, U.S.A. 108 C6
Flanigan, U.S.A. 112 E7
Flannan Is., U.K. 14 C1
Flåsjön, Sweden 8 D13
Flat →, Canada 100 A3
Flat River, U.S.A. 109 G9
Flatey, Barðastrandarsýsla, Iceland 8 C5
Flatey, Suður-þingeyjarsýsla, Iceland 8 D2
Flathead L., U.S.A. 110 C6
Flattery, C., U.S.A. 112 B2
Flattery, C., Australia 90 A4
Flavy-le-Martel, France 25 C10
Flawil, Switz. 23 B8
Flaxton, U.S.A. 108 A3
Fleetwood, U.K. 12 D4
Flekkefjord, Norway 9 G9
Flémalle, Belgium 17 G6
Flemington, U.S.A. 106 E7
Flensborg Fjord, Germany 11 K3
Flensburg, Germany 18 A5
Flers, France 24 D6
Flesherton, Canada 106 B4
Flesko, Tanjung, Indonesia 57 D6
Fleurance, France 26 E4
Fleurier, Switz. 22 C3
Fleurus, Belgium 17 H5
Flevoland □, Neths. 16 C7
Flims, Switz. 23 C8
Flin Flon, Canada 101 C8
Flinders →, Australia 90 B3
Flinders B., Australia 89 F2
Flinders Group, Australia 90 A3
Flinders I., Australia 90 F4
Flinders Ras., Australia 91 E2
Flinders Reefs, Australia 90 B4
Flint, U.K. 12 D4
Flint, U.S.A. 104 D4
Flint →, U.S.A. 105 K3
Flint I., Kiribati 93 J12
Flinton, Australia 91 D4
Flix, Spain 28 D5
Flixecourt, France 25 B9
Flobecq, Belgium 17 G3
Flodden, U.K. 12 B5
Floodwood, U.S.A. 108 B8
Flora, Norway 10 A5
Flora, U.S.A. 104 F1
Florac, France 26 D7
Florala, U.S.A. 105 K2
Florânia, Brazil 122 C4
Floreffe, Belgium 17 H5
Florence = Firenze, Italy 33 E8
Florence, Ala., U.S.A. 105 H2
Florence, Ariz., U.S.A. 111 K8
Florence, Colo., U.S.A. 108 F2
Florence, Oreg., U.S.A. 110 E1
Florence, S.C., U.S.A. 105 H6
Florence, L., Australia 91 D2
Florennes, Belgium 17 H5
Florensac, France 26 E7
Florenville, Belgium 17 J6
Flores, Brazil 122 C4
Flores, Guatemala 116 C2
Flores, Indonesia 57 F6
Flores I., Canada 100 D3
Flores Sea, Indonesia 57 F6
Floresta, Brazil 122 C4
Floresville, U.S.A. 109 L5
Floriano, Brazil 122 C3
Florianópolis, Brazil 127 B6
Florida, Cuba 116 B4
Florida, Uruguay 127 C4
Florida □, U.S.A. 105 L5
Florida, Straits of, U.S.A. 116 B3
Florida B., U.S.A. 116 A3
Florida Keys, U.S.A. 103 F10
Florídia, Italy 35 E8
Floridsdorf, Austria 21 G6
Flórina, Greece 39 J4
Florø, Norway 9 F8
Flower Station, Canada 107 A8
Flower's Cove, Canada 99 B8
Floydada, U.S.A. 109 J4
Fluk, Indonesia 57 E7
Flumen →, Spain 28 D4
Flumendosa →, Italy 34 C2
Fluminimaggiore, Italy 34 C1
Flushing = Vlissingen, Neths. 17 F3
Fluviá →, Spain 28 C8
Flying Fish, C., Antarctica 5 D15
Foam Lake, Canada 101 C8
Foča, Bos.-H. 21 M8
Foça, Turkey 66 D2
Focşani, Romania 38 D10
Fogang, China 53 F9
Foggaret el Arab, Algeria 75 C5
Foggaret ez Zoua, Algeria 75 C5
Fóggia, Italy 35 A8
Foggo, Nigeria 79 C6
Foglia →, Italy 33 E9
Fogo, Canada 99 C9
Fogo I., Canada 99 C9
Fohnsdorf, Austria 21 H4
Föhr, Germany 18 A4
Foia, Portugal 31 H2
Foix, France 26 F5
Fokino, Russia 40 E9
Folda, Nord-Trøndelag, Norway 8 D11
Folda, Nordland, Norway 8 C13
Foleyet, Canada 98 C3
Folgefonn, Norway 9 F9
Foligno, Italy 33 F9
Folkestone, U.K. 13 F9
Folkston, U.S.A. 105 K5
Follett, U.S.A. 109 G4
Follónica, Italy 32 F7
Follónica, G. di, Italy 32 F7
Folsom Res., U.S.A. 112 G5
Fond-du-Lac, Canada 101 B7
Fond du Lac, U.S.A. 108 D10
Fond-du-Lac →, Canada 101 B7
Fonda, U.S.A. 107 D10
Fondi, Italy 34 A6
Fonfría, Spain 30 D4
Fongen, Norway 10 A5
Fonni, Italy 34 B2
Fonsagrada, Spain 30 B3
Fonseca, G. de, Cent. Amer. 116 D2
Fontaine-Française, France 25 E12
Fontainebleau, France 25 D9
Fontana, L., Argentina 128 B2
Fontas →, Canada 100 B4
Fonte Boa, Brazil 120 D4
Fontem, Cameroon 79 D6
Fontenay-le-Comte, France 26 B3
Fontur, Iceland 8 C6
Fonyód, Hungary 21 J7
Foochow = Fuzhou, China 53 D12
Foping, China 50 H4
Foppiano, Italy 32 B5
Forbach, France 25 C13
Forbes, Australia 91 E4
Forbesganj, India 63 F12
Forcados, Nigeria 79 D6
Forcados →, Nigeria 79 D6
Forcall →, Spain 28 E4
Forcalquier, France 27 E9
Forchheim, Germany 19 F7
Forclaz, Col de la, Switz. 22 D4
Ford City, Calif., U.S.A. 113 K7
Ford City, Pa., U.S.A. 106 F5
Ford's Bridge, Australia 91 D4
Fordyce, U.S.A. 109 J8
Forécariah, Guinea 78 D2
Forel, Mt., Greenland 4 C6
Foremost, Canada 100 D6
Forenza, Italy 35 B8
Forest, Belgium 17 G4
Forest, Canada 106 C3
Forest, U.S.A. 109 J10
Forest City, Iowa, U.S.A. 108 D8
Forest City, N.C., U.S.A. 105 H5
Forest City, Pa., U.S.A. 107 E9
Forest Grove, U.S.A. 112 E3
Forestburg, Canada 100 C6
Foresthill, U.S.A. 112 F6
Forestier Pen., Australia 90 G4
Forestville, Canada 99 C6
Forestville, Calif., U.S.A. 112 G4
Forestville, Wis., U.S.A. 104 C2
Forez, Mts. du, France 26 C7
Forfar, U.K. 14 E6
Forges-les-Eaux, France 25 C8
Forks, U.S.A. 112 C2
Forlì, Italy 33 D9
Forman, U.S.A. 108 B6
Formazza, Italy 32 B5
Formby Pt., U.K. 12 D4
Formentera, Spain 36 C7
Formentor, C. de, Spain 36 B10
Fórmia, Italy 34 A6
Formiga, Brazil 123 F2
Formigine, Italy 32 D7
Formiguères, France 26 F6
Formosa = Taiwan ■, Asia 53 F13
Formosa, Argentina 126 B4
Formosa, Brazil 123 E2
Formosa □, Argentina 126 B3
Formosa, Serra, Brazil 125 C6
Formosa Bay, Kenya 82 C5
Formosa Strait, Asia 53 E12
Formoso →, Brazil 123 D2
Fornells, Spain 36 A11
Fornos de Algodres, Portugal 30 E3
Fornovo di Taro, Italy 32 D7
Føroyar, Atl. Oc. 7 C4
Forres, U.K. 14 D5
Forrest, Vic., Australia 91 F3
Forrest, W. Austral., Australia 89 F4
Forrest, Mt., Australia 89 D4
Forrest City, U.S.A. 109 H9
Forrières, Belgium 17 H6
Forsa, Sweden 10 C10
Forsayth, Australia 90 B3
Forsmo, Sweden 10 A11
Forst, Germany 18 D10
Forster, Australia 91 E5
Forsyth, Ga., U.S.A. 105 J4
Forsyth, Mont., U.S.A. 110 C10
Fort Albany, Canada 98 B3
Fort Apache, U.S.A. 111 K9
Fort Assiniboine, Canada 100 C6
Fort Augustus, U.K. 14 D4
Fort Beaufort, S. Africa 84 E4
Fort Benton, U.S.A. 110 C8
Fort Bragg, U.S.A. 110 G2
Fort Bridger, U.S.A. 110 F8
Fort Chipewyan, Canada 101 B6
Fort Collins, U.S.A. 108 E2
Fort-Coulonge, Canada 98 C4
Fort Davis, U.S.A. 109 K3
Fort-de-France, Martinique 117 D7
Fort de Possel = Possel, C.A.R. 80 C3
Fort Defiance, U.S.A. 111 J9
Fort Dodge, U.S.A. 108 D7
Fort Edward, U.S.A. 107 C11
Fort Frances, Canada 101 D10
Fort Franklin, Canada 96 B7
Fort Garland, U.S.A. 111 H11
Fort George, Canada 98 B4
Fort Good-Hope, Canada 96 B7
Fort Hancock, U.S.A. 111 L11
Fort Hertz = Putao, Burma 61 F20
Fort Hope, Canada 98 B2
Fort Irwin, U.S.A. 113 K10
Fort Jameson = Chipata, Zambia 83 E3
Fort Kent, U.S.A. 99 C6
Fort Klamath, U.S.A. 110 E3
Fort Lallemand, Algeria 75 B6
Fort-Lamy = Ndjamena, Chad 73 F7
Fort Laramie, U.S.A. 108 D2
Fort Lauderdale, U.S.A. 105 M5
Fort Liard, Canada 100 A4
Fort Liberté, Haiti 117 C5
Fort Lupton, U.S.A. 108 E2
Fort Mackay, Canada 100 B6
Fort McKenzie, Canada 99 A6
Fort Macleod, Canada 100 D6
Fort MacMahon, Algeria 75 C5
Fort McMurray, Canada 100 B6
Fort McPherson, Canada 96 B6
Fort Madison, U.S.A. 108 E9
Fort Meade, U.S.A. 105 M5
Fort Miribel, Algeria 75 C5
Fort Morgan, U.S.A. 108 E3
Fort Myers, U.S.A. 105 M5
Fort Nelson, Canada 100 B4
Fort Nelson →, Canada 100 B4
Fort Norman, Canada 96 B7
Fort Payne, U.S.A. 105 H3
Fort Peck, U.S.A. 110 B10
Fort Peck Dam, U.S.A. 110 C10
Fort Peck L., U.S.A. 110 C10
Fort Pierce, U.S.A. 105 M5
Fort Pierre, U.S.A. 108 C4
Fort Pierre Bordes = Ti-n-Zaouatène, Algeria 75 E5
Fort Plain, U.S.A. 107 D10

Fort Portal, *Uganda* 82 B3
Fort Providence, *Canada* 100 A5
Fort Qu'Appelle, *Canada* 101 C8
Fort Resolution, *Canada* 100 A6
Fort Rixon, *Zimbabwe* 83 G2
Fort Rosebery = Mansa, *Zambia* 83 E2
Fort Ross, *U.S.A.* 112 G3
Fort Rupert, *Canada* 98 B4
Fort Saint, *Tunisia* 75 B6
Fort St. James, *Canada* 100 C4
Fort St. John, *Canada* 100 B4
Fort Sandeman, *Pakistan* 62 D3
Fort Saskatchewan, *Canada* 100 C6
Fort Scott, *U.S.A.* 109 G7
Fort Severn, *Canada* 98 A2
Fort Shevchenko, *Kazakhstan* 43 E14
Fort-Sibut, *C.A.R.* 73 G8
Fort Simpson, *Canada* 100 A4
Fort Smith, *Canada* 100 B6
Fort Smith, *U.S.A.* 109 H7
Fort Stanton, *U.S.A.* 111 K11
Fort Stockton, *U.S.A.* 109 K3
Fort Sumner, *U.S.A.* 109 H2
Fort Trinquet = Bir Mogrein, *Mauritania* 74 C2
Fort Valley, *U.S.A.* 105 J4
Fort Vermilion, *Canada* 100 B5
Fort Walton Beach, *U.S.A.* 105 K2
Fort Wayne, *U.S.A.* 104 E3
Fort William, *U.K.* 14 E3
Fort Worth, *U.S.A.* 109 J6
Fort Yates, *U.S.A.* 108 B4
Fort Yukon, *U.S.A.* 96 B5
Fortaleza, *Bolivia* 124 C4
Fortaleza, *Brazil* 122 B4
Forteau, *Canada* 99 B8
Forth →, *U.K.* 14 E5
Forth, Firth of, *U.K.* 14 E6
Forthassa Rharbia, *Algeria* 75 B4
Fortín Coronel Eugenio Garay, *Paraguay* 125 E5
Fortín Garrapatal, *Paraguay* 125 E5
Fortín General Pando, *Paraguay* 125 D6
Fortín Madrejón, *Paraguay* 125 E6
Fortín Uno, *Argentina* 128 A3
Fortore →, *Italy* 33 G12
Fortrose, *U.K.* 14 D4
Fortuna, *Spain* 29 G3
Fortuna, *Calif., U.S.A.* 110 F1
Fortuna, *N. Dak., U.S.A.* 108 A3
Fortune B., *Canada* 99 C8
Fos-sur-Mer, *France* 27 E8
Foshan, *China* 53 F9
Fossacesia, *Italy* 33 F11
Fossano, *Italy* 32 D4
Fosses-la-Ville, *Belgium* 17 H5
Fossil, *U.S.A.* 110 D3
Fossilbrook, *Australia* 90 B3
Fossombrone, *Italy* 33 E9
Fosston, *U.S.A.* 108 B7
Foster, *Canada* 107 A12
Foster →, *Canada* 101 B7
Fosters Ra., *Australia* 90 C1
Fostoria, *U.S.A.* 104 E4
Fougamou, *Gabon* 80 E2
Fougères, *France* 24 D5
Foul Pt., *Sri Lanka* 60 Q12
Foula, *U.K.* 14 A6
Foulness I., *U.K.* 13 F8
Foulpointe, *Madag.* 85 B8
Foum Assaka, *Morocco* 74 C2
Foum Zguid, *Morocco* 74 B3
Foumban, *Cameroon* 79 D7
Foundiougne, *Senegal* 78 C1
Fountain, *Colo., U.S.A.* 108 F2
Fountain, *Utah, U.S.A.* 110 G8
Fountain Springs, *U.S.A.* 113 K8
Fourchambault, *France* 25 E10
Fourchu, *Canada* 99 C7
Fouriesburg, *S. Africa* 84 D4
Fourmies, *France* 25 B11
Foúrnoi, *Greece* 39 M9
Fours, *France* 25 F10
Fouta Djalon, *Guinea* 78 C2
Foux, Cap-à-, *Haiti* 117 C5
Foveaux Str., *N.Z.* 87 M2
Fowey, *U.K.* 13 G3
Fowler, *Calif., U.S.A.* 111 H4
Fowler, *Colo., U.S.A.* 108 F2
Fowler, *Kans., U.S.A.* 109 G4
Fowlers B., *Australia* 89 F5
Fowlerton, *U.S.A.* 109 L5
Fox →, *Canada* 101 B10
Fox Valley, *Canada* 101 C7
Foxe Basin, *Canada* 97 B12
Foxe Chan., *Canada* 97 B11
Foxe Pen., *Canada* 97 B12
Foxhol, *Neths.* 16 B9
Foxpark, *U.S.A.* 110 F10
Foxton, *N.Z.* 87 J5
Foyle, Lough, *U.K.* 15 A4
Foynes, *Ireland* 15 D2
Foz, *Spain* 30 B3
Fôz do Cunene, *Angola* 84 B1
Foz do Gregório, *Brazil* 124 B3
Foz do Iguaçu, *Brazil* 127 B5
Foz do Riosinho, *Brazil* 124 B3
Frackville, *U.S.A.* 107 F8
Fraga, *Spain* 28 D5
Fraire, *Belgium* 17 H5
Frameries, *Belgium* 17 H3
Framingham, *U.S.A.* 107 D13
Franca, *Brazil* 123 F2
Francavilla al Mare, *Italy* 33 F11
Francavilla Fontana, *Italy* 35 B10
France ■, *Europe* 7 F6
Frances, *Australia* 91 F3
Frances →, *Canada* 100 A3
Frances L., *Canada* 100 A3
Francés Viejo, C., *Dom. Rep.* 117 C6
Franceville, *Gabon* 80 E2
Franche-Comté, *France* 25 F12
Franches Montagnes, *Switz.* 22 B4
Francisco de Orellana, *Ecuador* 120 D2
Francisco I. Madero, *Coahuila, Mexico* 114 B4
Francisco I. Madero, *Durango, Mexico* 114 C4
Francisco Sá, *Brazil* 123 E3
Francistown, *Botswana* 85 C4
Francofonte, *Italy* 35 E7
François, *Canada* 99 C8
François L., *Canada* 100 C3
Francorchamps, *Belgium* 17 H7
Franeker, *Neths.* 16 B7
Frankado, *Djibouti* 77 E5
Frankenberg, *Germany* 18 D4
Frankenthal, *Germany* 19 F4
Frankenwald, *Germany* 19 E7
Frankfort, *S. Africa* 85 D4
Frankfort, *Ind., U.S.A.* 104 E2
Frankfort, *Kans., U.S.A.* 108 F6
Frankfort, *Ky., U.S.A.* 104 F3
Frankfort, *Mich., U.S.A.* 104 C2
Frankfurt am Main, *Germany* 19 E4
Frankfurt an der Oder, *Germany* 18 C10
Fränkische Alb, *Germany* 19 F7
Fränkische Rezal →, *Germany* 19 F7
Fränkische Saale →, *Germany* 19 E5
Fränkische Schweiz, *Germany* 19 F7
Frankland →, *Australia* 89 G2
Franklin, *Ky., U.S.A.* 105 G2
Franklin, *La., U.S.A.* 109 L9
Franklin, *Mass., U.S.A.* 107 D13
Franklin, *N.H., U.S.A.* 107 C13
Franklin, *Nebr., U.S.A.* 108 E5
Franklin, *Pa., U.S.A.* 106 E5
Franklin, *Tenn., U.S.A.* 105 H2
Franklin, *Va., U.S.A.* 105 G7
Franklin, *W. Va., U.S.A.* 104 F6
Franklin B., *Canada* 96 B7
Franklin D. Roosevelt L., *U.S.A.* 110 B4
Franklin I., *Antarctica* 5 D11
Franklin L., *U.S.A.* 110 F6
Franklin Mts., *Canada* 96 B7
Franklin Str., *Canada* 96 A10
Franklinton, *U.S.A.* 109 K9
Franklinville, *U.S.A.* 106 D6
Franks Pk., *U.S.A.* 110 E9
Frankston, *Australia* 91 F4
Fränsta, *Sweden* 10 B10
Frantsa Iosifa, Zemlya, *Russia* 44 A6
Franz, *Canada* 98 C3
Franz Josef Land = Frantsa Iosifa, Zemlya, *Russia* 44 A6
Franzburg, *Germany* 18 A8
Frascati, *Italy* 34 A5
Fraser →, *B.C., Canada* 100 D4
Fraser →, *Nfld., Canada* 99 A7
Fraser, Mt., *Australia* 89 E2
Fraser I., *Australia* 91 D5
Fraser Lake, *Canada* 100 C4
Fraserburg, *S. Africa* 84 E3
Fraserburgh, *U.K.* 14 D6
Fraserdale, *Canada* 98 C3
Frasne, *France* 25 F13
Frauenfeld, *Switz.* 23 A7
Fray Bentos, *Uruguay* 126 C4
Frazier Downs, *Australia* 88 C3
Frechilla, *Spain* 30 C6
Fredericia, *Denmark* 11 J3
Frederick, *Md., U.S.A.* 104 F7
Frederick, *Okla., U.S.A.* 109 H5
Frederick, *S. Dak., U.S.A.* 108 C5
Frederick Sd., *U.S.A.* 100 B2
Fredericksburg, *Tex., U.S.A.* 109 K5
Fredericksburg, *Va., U.S.A.* 104 F7
Fredericktown, *U.S.A.* 109 G9
Frederico I. Madero, Presa, *Mexico* 114 B3
Fredericton, *Canada* 99 C6
Fredericton Junc., *Canada* 99 C6
Frederikshåb, *Greenland* 4 C5
Frederikshavn, *Denmark* 11 G4
Frederikssund, *Denmark* 11 J6
Frederiksted, *Virgin Is.* 117 C7
Fredonia, *Ariz., U.S.A.* 111 H7
Fredonia, *Kans., U.S.A.* 109 G7
Fredonia, *N.Y., U.S.A.* 106 D5
Fredrikstad, *Norway* 10 E4
Freehold, *U.S.A.* 107 F10
Freel Peak, *U.S.A.* 112 G7
Freeland, *U.S.A.* 107 E9
Freels, C., *Canada* 99 C9
Freeman, *Calif., U.S.A.* 113 K9
Freeman, *S. Dak., U.S.A.* 108 D6
Freeport, *Bahamas* 116 A4
Freeport, *Canada* 99 D6
Freeport, *Ill., U.S.A.* 108 D10
Freeport, *N.Y., U.S.A.* 107 F11
Freeport, *Tex., U.S.A.* 109 L7
Freetown, *S. Leone* 78 D2
Frégate, L., *Canada* 98 B5
Fregenal de la Sierra, *Spain* 31 G4
Fregene, *Italy* 34 A5
Fréhel, C., *France* 24 D4
Freiberg, *Germany* 18 E9
Freibourg = Fribourg, *Switz.* 22 C4
Freiburg, *Baden-W., Germany* 19 H3
Freiburg, *Niedersachsen, Germany* 18 B5
Freiburger Alpen, *Switz.* 22 C4
Freire, *Chile* 128 A2
Freirina, *Chile* 126 B1
Freising, *Germany* 19 G7
Freistadt, *Austria* 20 G4
Freital, *Germany* 18 E9
Fréjus, *France* 27 E10
Fremantle, *Australia* 89 F2
Fremont, *Calif., U.S.A.* 111 H2
Fremont, *Mich., U.S.A.* 104 D3
Fremont, *Nebr., U.S.A.* 108 E6
Fremont, *Ohio, U.S.A.* 104 E4
Fremont →, *U.S.A.* 111 G8
Fremont L., *U.S.A.* 110 E9
French Camp, *U.S.A.* 112 H5
French Creek →, *U.S.A.* 106 E5
French Guiana ■, *S. Amer.* 121 C7
French Pass, *N.Z.* 87 J4
French Polynesia ■, *Pac. Oc.* 93 J13
French Terr. of Afars & Issas = Djibouti ■, *Africa* 68 E3
Frenchglen, *U.S.A.* 110 E4
Frenchman Butte, *Canada* 101 C7
Frenchman Cr. →, *Mont., U.S.A.* 110 B10
Frenchman Cr. →, *Nebr., U.S.A.* 108 E4
Frenda, *Algeria* 75 A5
Fresco →, *Brazil* 125 B7
Freshfield, C., *Antarctica* 5 C10
Fresnay-sur-Sarthe, *France* 24 D7
Fresnillo, *Mexico* 114 C4
Fresno, *U.S.A.* 111 H4
Fresno Alhandiga, *Spain* 30 E5
Fresno Reservoir, *U.S.A.* 110 B9
Freudenstadt, *Germany* 19 G4
Freux, *Belgium* 17 J6
Frévent, *France* 25 B9
Frew →, *Australia* 90 C2
Frewena, *Australia* 90 B2
Freycinet Pen., *Australia* 90 G4
Freyming-Merlebach, *France* 25 C13
Freyung, *Germany* 19 G9
Fria, *Guinea* 78 C2
Fria, C., *Namibia* 84 B1
Friant, *U.S.A.* 112 J7
Frías, *Argentina* 126 B2
Fribourg, *Switz.* 22 C4
Fribourg □, *Switz.* 22 C4
Frick, *Switz.* 22 A6
Friday Harbor, *U.S.A.* 112 B3
Friedberg, *Bayern, Germany* 19 G6
Friedberg, *Hessen, Germany* 19 E4
Friedland, *Germany* 18 B9
Friedrichshafen, *Germany* 19 H5
Friedrichskoog, *Germany* 18 A4
Friedrichstadt, *Germany* 18 A5
Friendly Is. = Tonga ■, *Pac. Oc.* 87 D11
Friesack, *Germany* 18 C8
Friesche Wad, *Neths.* 16 B7
Friesland □, *Neths.* 16 B7
Friesoythe, *Germany* 18 B3
Frillesås, *Sweden* 11 G6
Frio →, *U.S.A.* 109 L5
Friona, *U.S.A.* 109 H3
Frisian Is., *Europe* 18 B2
Fristad, *Sweden* 11 G7
Fritch, *U.S.A.* 109 H4
Fritsla, *Sweden* 11 G6
Fritzlar, *Germany* 18 D5
Friuli-Venezia Giulia □, *Italy* 33 B10
Frobisher B., *Canada* 97 B13
Frobisher Bay = Iqaluit, *Canada* 97 B13
Frobisher L., *Canada* 101 B7
Frohavet, *Norway* 8 E10
Froid, *U.S.A.* 108 A2
Froid-Chapelle, *Belgium* 17 H4
Frolovo, *Russia* 43 B10
Fromberg, *U.S.A.* 110 D9
Frome, *U.K.* 13 F5
Frome, L., *Australia* 91 E2
Frome Downs, *Australia* 91 E2
Frómista, *Spain* 30 C6
Front Range, *U.S.A.* 110 G11
Front Royal, *U.S.A.* 104 F6
Fronteira, *Portugal* 31 F3
Fronteiras, *Brazil* 122 C3
Frontera, *Canary Is.* 36 G2
Frontera, *Mexico* 115 D6
Frontignan, *France* 26 E7
Frosinone, *Italy* 34 A6
Frosolone, *Italy* 35 A7
Frostburg, *U.S.A.* 104 F6
Frostisen, *Norway* 8 B14
Frouard, *France* 25 D13
Frøya, *Norway* 8 E10
Fruges, *France* 25 B9
Frumoasa, *Romania* 38 C8
Frunze = Bishkek, *Kirghizia* 44 E8
Frutal, *Brazil* 123 F2
Frutigen, *Switz.* 22 C5
Frýdek-Místek, *Czech.* 20 F8
Frýdlant, *Czech.* 20 E5
Fu Jiang →, *China* 52 C6
Fu Xian, *Liaoning, China* 51 E11
Fu Xian, *Shaanxi, China* 50 F5
Fu'an, *China* 53 D12
Fubian, *China* 52 B4
Fucécchio, *Italy* 32 E7
Fucheng, *China* 50 F9
Fuchou = Fuzhou, *China* 53 D12
Fuchū, *Japan* 49 G6
Fuchuan, *China* 53 E8
Fuchun Jiang →, *China* 53 B13
Fúcino, Conca del, *Italy* 33 F10
Fuding, *China* 53 D13
Fuencaliente, *Canary Is.* 36 F2
Fuencaliente, *Spain* 31 G6
Fuencaliente, Pta., *Canary Is.* 36 F2
Fuengirola, *Spain* 31 J6
Fuente Alamo, *Albacete, Spain* 29 G3
Fuente Álamo, *Murcia, Spain* 29 H3
Fuente de Cantos, *Spain* 31 G4
Fuente del Maestre, *Spain* 31 G4
Fuente el Fresno, *Spain* 31 F7
Fuente Ovejuna, *Spain* 31 G5
Fuentes de Andalucía, *Spain* 31 H5
Fuentes de Ebro, *Spain* 28 D4
Fuentes de León, *Spain* 31 G4
Fuentes de Oñoro, *Spain* 30 E4
Fuentesaúco, *Spain* 30 D5
Fuerte →, *Mexico* 114 B3
Fuerte Olimpo, *Paraguay* 126 A4
Fuerteventura, *Canary Is.* 36 F6
Fufeng, *China* 50 G4
Fuga I., *Phil.* 55 B4
Fugløysund, *Norway* 8 A16
Fugong, *China* 52 D2
Fugou, *China* 50 G8
Fugu, *China* 50 E6
Fuhai, *China* 54 B3
Fuḥaymī, *Iraq* 64 C4
Fuji, *Japan* 49 G9
Fuji-San, *Japan* 49 G9
Fuji-yoshida, *Japan* 49 G9
Fujian □, *China* 53 E12
Fujinomiya, *Japan* 49 G9
Fujisawa, *Japan* 49 G9
Fukien = Fujian □, *China* 53 E12
Fukuchiyama, *Japan* 49 G7
Fukue-Shima, *Japan* 49 H4
Fukui, *Japan* 49 F8
Fukui □, *Japan* 49 G8
Fukuoka, *Japan* 49 H5
Fukuoka □, *Japan* 49 H5
Fukushima, *Japan* 48 F10
Fukushima □, *Japan* 48 F10
Fukuyama, *Japan* 49 G6
Fulda, *Germany* 18 E5
Fulda →, *Germany* 18 D5
Fuling, *China* 52 C6
Fullerton, *Calif., U.S.A.* 113 M9
Fullerton, *Nebr., U.S.A.* 108 E5
Fulongquan, *China* 51 B13
Fulton, *Mo., U.S.A.* 108 F9
Fulton, *N.Y., U.S.A.* 107 C8
Fulton, *Tenn., U.S.A.* 105 G1
Fuluälven →, *Sweden* 10 C7
Fulufjället, *Sweden* 10 C6
Fumay, *France* 25 C11
Fumel, *France* 26 D4
Fumin, *China* 52 E4
Funabashi, *Japan* 49 G10
Funchal, *Madeira* 36 D3
Fundación, *Colombia* 120 A3
Fundão, *Brazil* 123 E3
Fundão, *Portugal* 30 E3
Fundy, B. of, *Canada* 99 D6
Funing, *Hebei, China* 51 E10
Funing, *Jiangsu, China* 51 H10
Funing, *Yunnan, China* 52 F5
Funiu Shan, *China* 50 H7
Funsi, *Ghana* 78 C4
Funtua, *Nigeria* 79 C6
Fuping, *Hebei, China* 50 E8
Fuping, *Shaanxi, China* 50 G5
Fuqing, *China* 53 E12
Fuquan, *China* 52 D6
Fur, *Denmark* 11 H3
Furano, *Japan* 48 C11
Furāt, Nahr al →, *Asia* 64 D5
Fūrg, *Iran* 65 D7
Furkapass, *Switz.* 23 C7
Furmanov, *Russia* 41 C12
Furmanovo, *Kazakhstan* 43 B13
Furnás, *Spain* 36 B8
Furnas, Represa de, *Brazil* 123 F2
Furneaux Group, *Australia* 90 G4
Furness, *U.K.* 12 C4
Furqlus, *Syria* 69 A6
Fürstenau, *Germany* 18 C3
Fürstenberg, *Germany* 18 B9
Fürstenfeld, *Austria* 21 H6
Fürstenfeldbruck, *Germany* 19 G7
Fürstenwalde, *Germany* 18 C10
Fürth, *Germany* 19 F6
Furth im Wald, *Germany* 19 F8
Furtwangen, *Germany* 19 G4
Furukawa, *Japan* 48 E10
Furusund, *Sweden* 10 E12
Fury and Hecla Str., *Canada* 97 B11
Fusagasuga, *Colombia* 120 C3
Fuscaldo, *Italy* 35 C9
Fushan, *Shandong, China* 51 F11
Fushan, *Shanxi, China* 50 G6
Fushun, *Liaoning, China* 51 D12
Fushun, *Sichuan, China* 52 C5
Fusio, *Switz.* 23 D7
Fusong, *China* 51 C14
Füssen, *Germany* 19 H6
Fusui, *China* 52 F6
Futrono, *Chile* 128 B2
Futuna, *Wall. & F. Is.* 87 B8
Fuwa, *Egypt* 76 H7
Fuxin, *China* 51 C11
Fuyang, *Anhui, China* 50 H8
Fuyang, *Zhejiang, China* 53 B12
Fuyang He →, *China* 50 E9
Fuying Dao, *China* 53 D13
Fuyu, *China* 51 B13
Fuyuan, *Heilongjiang, China* 54 B8
Fuyuan, *Yunnan, China* 52 E5
Fuzhou, *China* 53 D12
Fylde, *U.K.* 12 D5
Fyn, *Denmark* 11 J4
Fyne, L., *U.K.* 14 F3
Fyns Amtskommune □, *Denmark* 11 J4
Fyresvatn, *Norway* 10 E2

G

Gaanda, *Nigeria* 79 C7
Gabarin, *Nigeria* 79 C7
Gabas →, *France* 26 E3
Gabela, *Angola* 80 G2
Gabès, *Tunisia* 75 B7
Gabès, G. de, *Tunisia* 75 B7
Gabgaba, W. →, *Egypt* 76 C3
Gabon ■, *Africa* 80 E2
Gaborone, *Botswana* 84 C4
Gabriels, *U.S.A.* 107 B10
Gābrīk, *Iran* 65 E8
Gabrovo, *Bulgaria* 38 G8
Gacé, *France* 24 D7
Gāch Sār, *Iran* 65 B6
Gachsārān, *Iran* 65 D6
Gacko, *Bos.-H.* 21 M8
Gadag, *India* 60 M9
Gadamai, *Sudan* 77 D4
Gadap, *Pakistan* 62 G2
Gadarwara, *India* 63 H8
Gadebusch, *Germany* 18 B7
Gadein, *Sudan* 77 F2
Gadhada, *India* 62 J4
Gadmen, *Switz.* 23 C6
Gádor, Sierra de, *Spain* 29 J2
Gadsden, *Ala., U.S.A.* 105 H2
Gadsden, *Ariz., U.S.A.* 111 K6
Gadwal, *India* 60 L10
Gadyach, *Ukraine* 40 F9
Găeşti, *Romania* 38 E8
Gaeta, *Italy* 34 A6
Gaeta, G. di, *Italy* 34 A6
Gaffney, *U.S.A.* 105 H5
Gafsa, *Tunisia* 75 B6
Gagarin = Gzhatsk, *Russia* 40 D9
Gagetown, *Canada* 99 C6
Gagino, *Russia* 41 D14
Gagliano del Capo, *Italy* 35 C11
Gagnoa, *Ivory C.* 78 D3
Gagnon, *Canada* 99 B6
Gagnon, L., *Canada* 101 A6
Gagra, *Georgia* 43 E9
Gahini, *Rwanda* 82 C3
Gahmar, *India* 63 G10
Gai Xian, *China* 51 D12
Gaïdhouronísi, *Greece* 37 E7
Gail, *U.S.A.* 109 J4
Gail →, *Austria* 21 J3
Gaillac, *France* 26 E5
Gaillon, *France* 24 C8
Gaimán, *Argentina* 128 B3
Gaines, *U.S.A.* 106 E7
Gainesville, *Fla., U.S.A.* 105 L4
Gainesville, *Ga., U.S.A.* 105 H4
Gainesville, *Mo., U.S.A.* 109 G8
Gainesville, *Tex., U.S.A.* 109 J6
Gainsborough, *U.K.* 12 D7
Gairdner, L., *Australia* 91 E2
Gairloch, L., *U.K.* 14 D3
Gais, *Switz.* 23 B8
Gakuch, *Pakistan* 63 A5
Galán, Cerro, *Argentina* 126 B2
Galana →, *Kenya* 82 C5
Galangue, *Angola* 81 G3
Galápagos, *Pac. Oc.* 93 H18
Galashiels, *U.K.* 14 F6
Galaţi, *Romania* 38 D11

Galatia, Turkey 66 D5
Galatina, Italy 35 B11
Galátone, Italy 35 B11
Galax, U.S.A. 105 G5
Galaxídhion, Greece 39 L5
Galbraith, Australia 90 B3
Galcaio, Somali Rep. 68 F4
Galdhøpiggen, Norway 10 C2
Galeana, Mexico 114 C4
Galela, Indonesia 57 D7
Galera, Spain 29 H2
Galera, Pta., Chile 128 A2
Galera Point, Trin. & Tob. 117 D7
Galesburg, U.S.A. 108 E9
Galeton, U.S.A. 106 E7
Galheirão →, Brazil 123 D2
Galheiros, Brazil 123 D2
Gali, Georgia 43 E9
Galich, Russia 41 B13
Galiche, Bulgaria 38 F6
Galicia □, Spain 30 C3
Galilee = Hagalil, Israel 69 C4
Galilee, L., Australia 90 C4
Galilee, Sea of = Yam Kinneret, Israel 69 C4
Galinoporni, Cyprus 37 D13
Galion, U.S.A. 106 F2
Galite, Is. de la, Tunisia 75 A6
Galiuro Mts., U.S.A. 111 K8
Gallabat, Sudan 77 E4
Gallardon, France 25 D8
Gallarte, Italy 32 C5
Gallatin, U.S.A. 105 G2
Galle, Sri Lanka 60 R12
Gállego →, Spain 28 D4
Gallegos →, Argentina 128 D3
Galley Hd., Ireland 15 E3
Galliate, Italy 32 C5
Gallinas, Pta., Colombia 120 A3
Gallipoli = Gelibolu, Turkey 39 J9
Gallípoli, Italy 35 B11
Gallipolis, U.S.A. 104 F4
Gällivare, Sweden 8 C16
Gallo, C., Italy 34 D6
Gallocanta, L. de, Spain 28 E3
Galloway, U.K. 14 G4
Galloway, Mull of, U.K. 14 G4
Gallup, U.S.A. 111 J9
Gallur, Spain 28 D3
Galong, Australia 91 E4
Galoya, Sri Lanka 60 Q12
Galt, U.S.A. 112 G5
Galtström, Sweden 10 B11
Galtür, Austria 19 J6
Galty Mts., Ireland 15 D3
Galtymore, Ireland 15 D3
Galva, U.S.A. 108 E9
Galvarino, Chile 128 A2
Galve de Sorbe, Spain 28 D1
Galveston, U.S.A. 109 L7
Galveston B., U.S.A. 109 L7
Gálvez, Argentina 126 C3
Gálvez, Spain 31 F6
Galway, Ireland 15 C2
Galway □, Ireland 15 C2
Galway B., Ireland 15 C2
Gam →, Vietnam 58 B5
Gamagori, Japan 49 G8
Gamari, L., Ethiopia 77 E5
Gamawa, Nigeria 79 C7
Gamay, Phil. 55 E6
Gambaga, Ghana 79 C4
Gambat, Pakistan 62 F3
Gambela, Ethiopia 77 F3
Gambia ■, W. Afr. 78 C1
Gambia →, W. Afr. 78 C1
Gambier, C., Australia 88 B5
Gambier Is., Australia 91 F2
Gamboli, Pakistan 62 E3
Gamboma, Congo 80 E3
Gamerco, U.S.A. 111 J9
Gamlakarleby = Kokkola, Finland 8 E17
Gammon →, Canada 101 C9
Gammouda, Tunisia 75 A6
Gamu-Gofa □, Ethiopia 77 F4
Gan, France 26 E3
Gan Gan, Argentina 128 B3
Gan Goriama, Mts., Cameroon 79 D7
Gan Jiang →, China 53 C10
Ganado, Ariz., U.S.A. 111 J9
Ganado, Tex., U.S.A. 109 L6
Gananoque, Canada 98 D4
Ganaveh, Iran 65 D6
Gäncä = Gyandzha, Azerbaijan 43 F12
Gand = Gent, Belgium 17 F3
Ganda, Angola 81 G2
Gandak →, India 63 G11
Gandava, Pakistan 62 E2
Gander, Canada 99 C9
Gander L., Canada 99 C9
Ganderowe Falls, Zimbabwe 83 F2
Gandesa, Spain 28 D5
Gandhi Sagar, India 62 G6
Gandi, Nigeria 79 C6
Gandía, Spain 29 G4
Gandino, Italy 32 C6
Gando, Pta., Canary Is. 36 G4
Gandole, Nigeria 79 D7
Gandu, Brazil 123 D4
Ganedidalem = Gani, Indonesia 57 E7
Ganetti, Sudan 76 D3
Ganga →, India 63 H14
Ganga, Mouths of the, India 63 J13
Ganganagar, India 62 E5
Gangapur, India 62 F7
Gangara, Niger 79 C6
Gangaw, Burma 61 H19
Gangdisê Shan, China 61 D12
Ganges = Ganga →, India 63 H14
Ganges, France 26 E7
Gangoh, India 62 E7
Gangtok, India 61 F16
Gangu, China 50 G3
Gangyao, China 51 B14
Gani, Indonesia 57 E7
Ganj, India 63 F8
Gannat, France 26 B7
Gannett Peak, U.S.A. 110 E9
Gannvalley, U.S.A. 108 C5
Ganquan, China 50 F5
Gänserdorf, Austria 21 G6
Ganshui, China 52 C6
Gansu □, China 50 G3
Ganta, Liberia 78 D3
Gantheaume, C., Australia 91 F2
Gantheaume B., Australia 89 E1
Gantsevichi, Belorussia 40 E5
Ganyem, Indonesia 57 E10
Ganyu, China 51 G10
Ganyushkino, Kazakhstan 43 C13
Ganzhou, China 53 E10
Gao, Mali 79 B5
Gao Xian, China 52 C5
Gao'an, China 53 C10
Gaohe, China 53 F9
Gaohebu, China 53 B11
Gaokeng, China 53 D9
Gaolan Dao, China 53 G9
Gaoligong Shan, China 52 E2
Gaomi, China 51 F10
Gaoping, China 50 G7
Gaotang, China 50 F9
Gaoua, Burkina Faso 78 C4
Gaoual, Guinea 78 C2
Gaoxiong, Taiwan 53 F13
Gaoyang, China 50 E8
Gaoyou, China 53 A12
Gaoyou Hu, China 51 H10
Gaoyuan, China 51 F9
Gaozhou, China 53 G8
Gap, France 27 D10
Gapan, Phil. 55 D4
Gar, China 54 C2
Garabogazkol Aylagy = Kara Bogaz Gol, Zaliv, Turkmenistan 44 E6
Garachico, Canary Is. 36 F3
Garachiné, Panama 116 E4
Garafia, Canary Is. 36 F2
Garajonay, Canary Is. 36 F2
Garanhuns, Brazil 122 C4
Garawe, Liberia 78 E3
Garba Tula, Kenya 82 B4
Garber, U.S.A. 109 G6
Garberville, U.S.A. 110 F2
Garça, Brazil 123 F2
Garças →, Mato Grosso, Brazil 125 D7
Garças →, Pernambuco, Brazil 122 C4
Garcias, Brazil 125 E7
Gard, Somali Rep. 68 F4
Gard □, France 27 D8
Gard →, France 27 E8
Garda, L. di, Italy 32 C7
Gardanne, France 27 E9
Garde L., Canada 101 A7
Gardelegen, Germany 18 C7
Garden City, Kans., U.S.A. 109 G4
Garden City, Tex., U.S.A. 109 K4
Garden Grove, U.S.A. 113 M9
Gardēz, Afghan. 62 C3
Gardiner, U.S.A. 110 D8
Gardiners I., U.S.A. 107 E12
Gardner, U.S.A. 107 D13
Gardner Canal, Canada 100 C3
Gardnerville, U.S.A. 112 G7
Gare Tigre, Fr. Guiana 121 C7
Garéssio, Italy 32 D5
Garey, U.S.A. 113 L6
Garfield, U.S.A. 110 C5
Gargan, Mt., France 26 C5
Gargano, Mte., Italy 35 A8
Gargouna, Mali 79 B5
Garhshankar, India 62 D7
Garibaldi Prov. Park, Canada 100 D4
Garies, S. Africa 84 E2
Garigliano →, Italy 34 A6
Garissa, Kenya 82 C4
Garissa □, Kenya 82 C5
Garkida, Nigeria 79 C7
Garko, Nigeria 79 C6
Garland, U.S.A. 110 F7
Garlasco, Italy 32 C5
Garm, Tajikistan 44 F8
Garmāb, Iran 65 C8
Garmisch-Partenkirchen, Germany 19 H7
Garmsār, Iran 65 C7
Garner, U.S.A. 108 D8
Garnett, U.S.A. 108 F7
Garo Hills, India 63 G14
Garoe, Somali Rep. 68 F4
Garonne →, France 26 C3
Garonne, Canal Latéral à la →, France 26 D4
Garoua, Cameroon 79 D7
Garrel, Germany 18 C3
Garrigue, France 26 E7
Garrison, Mont., U.S.A. 110 C7
Garrison, N. Dak., U.S.A. 108 B4
Garrison, Tex., U.S.A. 109 K7
Garrison Res. = Sakakawea, L., U.S.A. 108 B3
Garrovillas, Spain 31 F4
Garrucha, Spain 29 H3
Garry →, U.K. 14 E5
Garry, L., Canada 96 B9
Garsen, Kenya 82 C5
Garson L., Canada 101 B6
Gartempe →, France 26 B4
Gartz, Germany 18 B10
Garu, Ghana 79 C4
Garub, Namibia 84 D2
Garut, Indonesia 57 G12
Garvão, Portugal 31 H2
Garvie Mts., N.Z. 87 L2
Garwa = Garoua, Cameroon 79 D7
Garwa, India 63 G10
Garwolin, Poland 20 D11
Gary, U.S.A. 104 E2
Garz, Germany 18 A9
Garzê, China 52 B3
Garzón, Colombia 120 C2
Gas-San, Japan 48 E10
Gasan Kuli, Turkmenistan 44 F6
Gascogne, France 26 E4
Gascogne, G. de, Europe 28 B2
Gascony = Gascogne, France 26 E4
Gascoyne →, Australia 89 D1
Gascoyne Junc. T.O., Australia 89 E2
Gascueña, Spain 28 E2
Gash, Wadi →, Ethiopia 77 D4
Gashaka, Nigeria 79 D7
Gasherbrum, Pakistan 63 B7
Gashua, Nigeria 79 C7
Gaspé, Canada 99 C7
Gaspé, C. de, Canada 99 C7
Gaspé, Pén. de, Canada 99 C6
Gaspésie, Parc Prov. de la, Canada 99 C6
Gassaway, U.S.A. 104 F5
Gasselte, Neths. 16 C9
Gasselternijveen, Neths. 16 C9
Gássino Torinese, Italy 32 C4
Gassol, Nigeria 79 D7
Gasteiz = Vitoria, Spain 28 C2
Gastonia, U.S.A. 105 H5
Gastoúni, Greece 39 M4
Gastoúri, Greece 39 K2
Gastre, Argentina 128 B3
Gata, C., Cyprus 37 E12
Gata, C. de, Spain 29 J2
Gata, Sierra de, Spain 30 E4
Gataga →, Canada 100 B3
Gătaia, Romania 38 D4
Gatchina, Russia 40 B7
Gates, U.S.A. 106 C7
Gateshead, U.K. 12 C6
Gatesville, U.S.A. 109 K6
Gaths, Zimbabwe 83 G3
Gatico, Chile 126 A1
Gâtinais, France 25 D9
Gâtine, Hauteurs de, France 26 B3
Gatineau →, Canada 98 C4
Gatineau, Parc de la, Canada 98 C4
Gattaran, Phil. 55 B4
Gattinara, Italy 32 C5
Gatun, L., Panama 116 E4
Gatyana, S. Africa 85 E4
Gau, Fiji 87 D8
Gaucín, Spain 31 J5
Gauer L., Canada 101 B9
Gauhati, India 63 F14
Gauja →, Latvia 40 C4
Gaula →, Norway 8 E11
Gaurain-Ramecroix, Belgium 17 G3
Gausta, Norway 10 E2
Gāv Koshī, Iran 65 D8
Gavá, Spain 28 D6
Gāvakān, Iran 65 D7
Gavarnie, France 26 F3
Gavāter, Iran 65 E9
Gāvbandī, Iran 65 E7
Gavdhopoúla, Greece 37 E6
Gávdhos, Greece 37 E6
Gavere, Belgium 17 G3
Gavião, Portugal 31 F3
Gaviota, U.S.A. 113 L6
Gävleborgs län □, Sweden 10 C10
Gavorrano, Italy 32 F7
Gavray, France 24 D5
Gavrilov Yam, Russia 41 C11
Gawachab, Namibia 84 D2
Gawilgarh Hills, India 60 J10
Gawler, Australia 91 E2
Gaxun Nur, China 54 B5
Gaya, India 63 G11
Gaya, Niger 79 C5
Gaya, Nigeria 79 C6
Gaylord, U.S.A. 104 C3
Gayndah, Australia 91 D5
Gaysin, Ukraine 42 B3
Gayvoron, Ukraine 42 B3
Gaza, Egypt 69 D3
Gaza □, Mozam. 85 C5
Gaza Strip, Egypt 69 D3
Gazaoua, Niger 79 C6
Gāzbor, Iran 65 D8
Gazi, Zaïre 82 B1
Gaziantep, Turkey 66 E7
Gaziantep □, Turkey 66 E7
Gazipaşa, Turkey 66 E5
Gazli, Uzbekistan 44 E7
Gbarnga, Liberia 78 D3
Gbekebo, Nigeria 79 D5
Gboko, Nigeria 79 D6
Gbongan, Nigeria 79 D5
Gcuwa, S. Africa 85 E4
Gdańsk, Poland 20 A8
Gdańska, Zatoka, Poland 20 A9
Gdov, Russia 40 B5
Gdynia, Poland 20 A8
Gebe, Indonesia 57 D7
Gebeit Mine, Sudan 76 C4
Gebel Mûsa, Egypt 76 J8
Gebze, Turkey 66 C3
Gecha, Ethiopia 77 F4
Gedaref, Sudan 77 E4
Gede, Tanjung, Indonesia 56 F3
Gedinne, Belgium 17 J5
Gediz, Turkey 66 D3
Gediz →, Turkey 66 D2
Gedo, Ethiopia 77 F4
Gèdre, France 26 F4
Gedser, Denmark 11 K5
Gedser Odde, Denmark 11 K5
Geegully Cr. →, Australia 88 C3
Geel, Belgium 17 F5
Geelong, Australia 91 F3
Geelvink Chan., Australia 89 E1
Geer →, Belgium 17 G7
Geesthacht, Germany 18 B6
Geffen, Neths. 16 E6
Geidam, Nigeria 79 C7
Geikie →, Canada 101 B8
Geili, Sudan 77 D3
Geilo, Norway 10 D2
Geisingen, Germany 19 H4
Geislingen, Germany 19 G5
Geita, Tanzania 82 C3
Geita □, Tanzania 82 C3
Gejiu, China 52 F4
Gel →, Sudan 77 F2
Gel River, Sudan 77 F2
Gela, Italy 35 E7
Gela, G. di, Italy 35 F7
Geladi, Ethiopia 68 F4
Gelderland □, Neths. 16 D8
Geldermalsen, Neths. 16 E6
Geldern, Germany 18 D2
Geldrop, Neths. 17 F7
Geleen, Neths. 17 G7
Gelehun, S. Leone 78 D2
Gelendost, Turkey 66 D4
Gelendzhik, Russia 42 D8
Gelibolu, Turkey 39 J9
Gelidonya Burnu, Turkey 66 E4
Gelnhausen, Germany 19 E5
Gelsenkirchen, Germany 18 D3
Gelting, Germany 18 A5
Gemas, Malaysia 59 L4
Gembloux, Belgium 17 G5
Gemena, Zaïre 80 D3
Gemerek, Turkey 66 D7
Gemert, Neths. 17 E7
Gemlik, Turkey 66 C3
Gemona del Friuli, Italy 33 B10
Gemsa, Egypt 76 B3
Gemünden, Germany 19 E5
Genale, Ethiopia 77 F4
Genappe, Belgium 17 G4
Genç, Turkey 67 D9
Gençay, France 26 B4
Gendringen, Neths. 16 E8
Gendt, Neths. 16 E7
Geneina, Gebel, Egypt 76 J8
Genemuiden, Neths. 16 C8
General Acha, Argentina 126 D3
General Alvear, Buenos Aires, Argentina 126 D3
General Alvear, Mendoza, Argentina 126 D2
General Artigas, Paraguay 126 B4
General Belgrano, Argentina 126 D4
General Cabrera, Argentina 126 C3
General Carrera, L., Chile 128 C2
General Cepeda, Mexico 114 B4
General Conesa, Argentina 128 B4
General Guido, Argentina 126 D4
General Juan Madariaga, Argentina 126 D4
General La Madrid, Argentina 126 D3
General Lorenzo Vintter, Argentina 128 B4
General MacArthur, Phil. 55 F6
General Martin Miguel de Güemes, Argentina 126 A3
General Paz, Argentina 126 B4
General Pico, Argentina 126 D3
General Pinedo, Argentina 126 B3
General Pinto, Argentina 126 C3
General Sampaio, Brazil 122 B4
General Santos, Phil. 55 H6
General Toshevo, Bulgaria 38 F11
General Trevino, Mexico 115 B5
General Trías, Mexico 114 B3
General Viamonte, Argentina 126 D3
General Villegas, Argentina 126 D3
General Vintter, L., Argentina 128 B2
Generoso, Mte., Switz. 23 E8
Genesee, Idaho, U.S.A. 110 C5
Genesee, Pa., U.S.A. 106 E7
Genesee →, U.S.A. 106 C7
Geneseo, Ill., U.S.A. 108 E9
Geneseo, Kans., U.S.A. 108 F5
Geneseo, N.Y., U.S.A. 106 D7
Geneva = Genève, Switz. 22 D2
Geneva, Ala., U.S.A. 105 K3
Geneva, N.Y., U.S.A. 106 D7
Geneva, Nebr., U.S.A. 108 E6
Geneva, Ohio, U.S.A. 106 E4
Geneva, L. = Léman, Lac, Switz. 22 D3
Geneva, L., U.S.A. 104 D1
Genève, Switz. 22 D2
Genève □, Switz. 22 D2
Gengenbach, Germany 19 G4
Gengma, China 52 F2
Genichesk, Ukraine 42 C6
Genil →, Spain 31 H5
Génissiat, Barr. de, France 27 B9
Genk, Belgium 17 G7
Genlis, France 25 E12
Gennargentu, Mti. del, Italy 34 C2
Gennep, Neths. 17 E7
Gennes, France 24 E6
Genoa = Génova, Italy 32 D5
Genoa, Australia 91 F4
Genoa, N.Y., U.S.A. 107 D8
Genoa, Nebr., U.S.A. 108 E6
Genoa, Nev., U.S.A. 112 F7
Genoa →, Argentina 128 B2
Génova, Italy 32 D5
Génova, G. di, Italy 32 E6
Gent, Belgium 17 F3
Gentbrugge, Belgium 17 F3
Genthin, Germany 18 C8
Gentio do Ouro, Brazil 122 D3
Geographe B., Australia 89 F2
Geographe Chan., Australia 89 D1
Geokchay, Azerbaijan 43 F12
Georga, Zemlya, Russia 44 A5
George, S. Africa 84 E3
George →, Canada 99 A6
George, L., N.S.W., Australia 91 F4
George, L., S. Austral., Australia 91 F3
George, L., W. Austral., Australia 88 D3
George, L., Uganda 82 B3
George, L., Fla., U.S.A. 105 L5
George, L., N.Y., U.S.A. 107 C11
George Gill Ra., Australia 88 D5
George River = Port Nouveau-Québec, Canada 97 C13
George Sound, N.Z. 87 L1
George Town, Bahamas 116 B4
George Town, Malaysia 59 K3
George V Land, Antarctica 5 C10
George VI Sound, Antarctica 5 D17
George West, U.S.A. 109 L5
Georgetown, Australia 90 B3
Georgetown, Ont., Canada 98 D4
Georgetown, P.E.I., Canada 99 C7
Georgetown, Cayman Is. 116 C3
Georgetown, Gambia 78 C2
Georgetown, Guyana 121 B6
Georgetown, Calif., U.S.A. 112 G6
Georgetown, Colo., U.S.A. 110 G11
Georgetown, Ky., U.S.A. 104 F3
Georgetown, S.C., U.S.A. 105 J6
Georgetown, Tex., U.S.A. 109 K6
Georgia □, U.S.A. 105 J4
Georgia ■, Asia 43 E10
Georgia, Str. of, Canada 100 D4
Georgian B., Canada 98 C3
Georgievsk, Russia 43 D10
Georgina →, Australia 90 C2
Georgina Downs, Australia 90 C2
Georgiu-Dezh = Liski, Russia 41 F11
Gera, Germany 18 E8
Geraardsbergen, Belgium 17 G3
Geral, Serra, Bahia, Brazil 123 D3
Geral, Serra, Goiás, Brazil 122 D2
Geral, Serra, Sta. Catarina, Brazil 127 B6
Geral de Goiás, Serra, Brazil 123 D2
Geral do Paraná Serra, Brazil 123 E2
Geraldine, U.S.A. 110 C8
Geraldton, Australia 89 E1
Geraldton, Canada 98 C2
Gérardmer, France 25 D13
Gercüş, Turkey 67 E9
Gerede, Turkey 42 F5
Gereshk, Afghan. 60 D4
Gérgal, Spain 29 H2
Gerik, Malaysia 59 K3
Gering, U.S.A. 108 E3
Gerlach, U.S.A. 110 F4

Gerlachovka

Gerlachovka, *Slovak Rep.* 20 F10
Gerlogubi, *Ethiopia* 68 F4
Germansen Landing, *Canada* 100 B4
Germany ■, *Europe* 18 E6
Germersheim, *Germany* 19 F4
Germiston, *S. Africa* 85 D4
Gernsheim, *Germany* 19 F4
Gero, *Japan* 49 G8
Gerolstein, *Germany* 19 E2
Gerolzhofen, *Germany* 19 F6
Gerona, *Spain* 28 D7
Gerona □, *Spain* 28 C7
Gérouville, *Belgium* 17 J6
Gerrard, *Canada* 100 C5
Gers □, *France* 26 E4
Gers →, *France* 26 D4
Gersfeld, *Germany* 18 E5
Gerze, *Turkey* 66 C6
Geseke, *Germany* 18 D4
Geser, *Indonesia* 57 E8
Gesso →, *Italy* 32 D4
Gestro, Wabi →, *Ethiopia* 77 G5
Gesves, *Belgium* 17 H6
Getafe, *Spain* 30 E7
Gethsémani, *Canada* 99 B7
Gettysburg, *Pa., U.S.A.* 104 F7
Gettysburg, *S. Dak., U.S.A.* 108 C5
Getz Ice Shelf, *Antarctica* 5 D14
Geul →, *Neths.* 17 G7
Gevaş, *Turkey* 67 D10
Gévaudan, *France* 26 D7
Gevgelija, *Macedonia* 39 H5
Gévora →, *Spain* 31 G4
Gex, *France* 27 B10
Geyser, *U.S.A.* 110 C8
Geyserville, *U.S.A.* 112 G4
Geysir, *Iceland* 8 D3
Geyve, *Turkey* 66 C4
Ghâbat el Arab = Wang Kai, *Sudan* 77 F2
Ghaghara →, *India* 63 G11
Ghalla, Wadi el →, *Sudan* 77 E2
Ghallamane, *Mauritania* 74 D3
Ghana ■, *W. Afr.* 79 D4
Ghansor, *India* 63 H9
Ghanzi, *Botswana* 84 C3
Ghanzi □, *Botswana* 84 C3
Gharb el Istiwa'iya □, *Sudan* 77 F2
Gharbîya, Es Sahrâ el, *Egypt* 76 B2
Ghard Abû Muharik, *Egypt* 76 B2
Ghardaïa, *Algeria* 75 B5
Ghârib, G., *Egypt* 76 J8
Ghârib, Râs, *Egypt* 76 J8
Gharyān, *Libya* 75 B7
Gharyān □, *Libya* 75 B7
Ghat, *Libya* 75 D7
Ghatal, *India* 63 H12
Ghatampur, *India* 63 F9
Ghaṭṭī, *Si. Arabia* 64 D3
Ghawdex = Gozo, *Malta* 37 C1
Ghazal, Bahr el →, *Chad* 73 F8
Ghazâl, Bahr el →, *Sudan* 77 F3
Ghazaouet, *Algeria* 75 A4
Ghaziabad, *India* 62 E7
Ghazipur, *India* 63 G10
Ghaznī, *Afghan.* 62 C3
Ghaznī □, *Afghan.* 60 C6
Ghedi, *Italy* 32 C7
Ghèlinsor, *Somali Rep.* 68 F4
Ghent = Gent, *Belgium* 17 F3
Gheorghe Gheorghiu-Dej, *Romania* 38 C9
Gheorgheni, *Romania* 38 C8
Ghergani, *Romania* 38 E8
Gherla, *Romania* 38 B6
Ghilarza, *Italy* 34 B1
Ghisonaccia, *France* 27 F13
Ghisoni, *France* 27 F13
Ghizao, *Afghan.* 62 C1
Ghizar →, *Pakistan* 63 A5
Ghogha, *India* 62 J5
Ghot Ogrein, *Egypt* 76 A2
Ghotaru, *India* 62 F4
Ghotki, *Pakistan* 62 E3
Ghowr □, *Afghan.* 60 C4
Ghudaf, W. al →, *Iraq* 64 C4
Ghudāmis, *Libya* 75 B6
Ghughri, *India* 63 H9
Ghugus, *India* 60 K11
Ghulam Mohammad Barrage, *Pakistan* 62 G3
Ghūrīān, *Afghan.* 60 B2
Gia Dinh, *Vietnam* 59 G6
Gia Lai = Pleiku, *Vietnam* 58 F7
Gia Nghia, *Vietnam* 59 G6
Gia Ngoc, *Vietnam* 58 E7
Gia Vuc, *Vietnam* 58 E7
Gian, *Phil.* 57 C7
Giannutri, *Italy* 32 F8
Giant Forest, *U.S.A.* 112 J8
Giant Mts. = Krkonoše, *Czech.* 20 E5
Giants Causeway, *U.K.* 15 A5
Giarabub = Al Jaghbūb, *Libya* 73 C9
Giarre, *Italy* 35 E8
Giaveno, *Italy* 32 C4
Gibara, *Cuba* 116 B4
Gibb River, *Australia* 88 C4
Gibbon, *U.S.A.* 108 E5
Gibe →, *Ethiopia* 77 F4
Gibellina, *Italy* 34 E6
Gibraléon, *Spain* 31 H4
Gibraltar ■, *Europe* 31 J5
Gibraltar, Str. of, *Medit. S.* 31 K5
Gibson Desert, *Australia* 88 D4
Gibsons, *Canada* 100 D4
Gibsonville, *U.S.A.* 112 F6
Giddings, *U.S.A.* 109 K6
Gidole, *Ethiopia* 77 F4
Gien, *France* 25 E9
Giessen, *Germany* 18 E4
Gieten, *Neths.* 16 B9
Gīfān, *Iran* 65 B8
Gifatin, Geziret, *Egypt* 76 B3
Gifford Creek, *Australia* 88 D2
Gifhorn, *Germany* 18 C6
Gifu, *Japan* 49 G8
Gifu □, *Japan* 49 G8
Gigant, *Russia* 43 C9
Giganta, Sa. de la, *Mexico* 114 B2
Gigen, *Bulgaria* 38 F7
Gigha, *U.K.* 14 F3
Giglio, *Italy* 32 F7
Gignac, *France* 26 E7
Gigüela →, *Spain* 29 F1
Gijón, *Spain* 30 B5
Gil I., *Canada* 100 C3
Gila →, *U.S.A.* 111 K6
Gila Bend, *U.S.A.* 111 K7
Gila Bend Mts., *U.S.A.* 111 K7
Gīlān □, *Iran* 65 B6
Gilbert →, *Australia* 90 B3
Gilbert Is., *Kiribati* 92 G9
Gilbert Plains, *Canada* 101 C8
Gilbert River, *Australia* 90 B3
Gilberton, *Australia* 90 B3
Gilbués, *Brazil* 122 C2
Gilf el Kebîr, Hadabat el, *Egypt* 76 C2
Gilford I., *Canada* 100 C3
Gilgandra, *Australia* 91 E4
Gilgil, *Kenya* 82 C4
Gilgit, *India* 63 B6
Gilgit →, *Pakistan* 63 B6
Giljeva Planina, *Serbia* 21 M10
Gillam, *Canada* 101 B10
Gilleleje, *Denmark* 11 H6
Gillen, L., *Australia* 89 E3
Gilles, L., *Australia* 91 E2
Gillette, *U.S.A.* 108 C2
Gilliat, *Australia* 90 C3
Gillingham, *U.K.* 13 F8
Gilly, *Belgium* 17 H4
Gilmer, *U.S.A.* 109 J7
Gilmore, *Australia* 91 F4
Gilmore, L., *Australia* 89 F3
Gilmour, *Canada* 98 D4
Gilo →, *Ethiopia* 77 F3
Gilort →, *Romania* 38 E6
Gilroy, *U.S.A.* 111 H3
Gilze, *Neths.* 17 E5
Gimbi, *Ethiopia* 77 F4
Gimigliano, *Italy* 35 D9
Gimli, *Canada* 101 C9
Gimone →, *France* 26 E5
Gimont, *France* 26 E4
Gin Gin, *Australia* 91 D5
Ginâh, *Egypt* 76 B3
Gindie, *Australia* 90 C4
Gingin, *Australia* 89 F2
Gîngiova, *Romania* 38 F6
Ginir, *Ethiopia* 68 F3
Ginosa, *Italy* 35 B9
Ginzo de Limia, *Spain* 30 C3
Giohar, *Somali Rep.* 68 G4
Gióia, G. di, *Italy* 35 D8
Gióia del Colle, *Italy* 35 B9
Gióia Táuro, *Italy* 35 D8
Gioiosa Iónica, *Italy* 35 D9
Gióna, Óros, *Greece* 39 L5
Giovi, Passo dei, *Italy* 32 D5
Giovinazzo, *Italy* 35 A9
Gir Hills, *India* 62 J4
Girab, *India* 62 F4
Girâfi, W. →, *Egypt* 69 F3
Giraltovce, *Slovak Rep.* 20 F11
Girard, *Kans., U.S.A.* 109 G7
Girard, *Ohio, U.S.A.* 106 E4
Girard, *Pa., U.S.A.* 106 D4
Girardot, *Colombia* 120 C3
Girdle Ness, *U.K.* 14 D6
Giresun, *Turkey* 67 C8
Giresun □, *Turkey* 67 C8
Girga, *Egypt* 76 B3
Giridih, *India* 63 G12
Girifalco, *Italy* 35 D9
Girilambone, *Australia* 91 E4
Giro, *Nigeria* 79 C5
Giromagny, *France* 25 E13
Girona = Gerona, *Spain* 28 D7
Gironde □, *France* 26 D3
Gironde →, *France* 26 C2
Gironella, *Spain* 28 C6
Giru, *Australia* 90 B4
Girvan, *U.K.* 14 F4
Gisborne, *N.Z.* 87 H7
Gisenyi, *Rwanda* 82 C2
Gisors, *France* 25 C8
Gistel, *Belgium* 17 F1
Giswil, *Switz.* 22 C6
Gitega, *Burundi* 82 C2
Gits, *Belgium* 17 F2
Giuba →, *Somali Rep.* 68 G3
Giubiasco, *Switz.* 23 D8
Giugliano in Campania, *Italy* 35 B7
Giulianova, *Italy* 33 F10
Giurgeni, *Romania* 38 E10
Giurgiu, *Romania* 38 F8
Give, *Denmark* 11 J3
Givet, *France* 25 B11
Givors, *France* 27 C8
Givry, *Belgium* 17 H4
Givry, *France* 25 F11
Giyon, *Ethiopia* 77 F4
Giza = El Gîza, *Egypt* 76 H7
Gizhiga, *Russia* 45 C17
Gizhiginskaya Guba, *Russia* 45 C16
Giżycko, *Poland* 20 A11
Gizzeria, *Italy* 35 D9
Gjegjan, *Albania* 39 H3
Gjerstad, *Norway* 10 F3
Gjirokastra, *Albania* 39 J3
Gjoa Haven, *Canada* 96 B10
Gjøl, *Denmark* 11 G3
Gjøvik, *Norway* 10 D4
Glace Bay, *Canada* 99 C8
Glacier Bay, *U.S.A.* 100 B1
Glacier Nat. Park, *Canada* 100 C5
Glacier Park, *U.S.A.* 110 B7
Glacier Peak, *U.S.A.* 110 B3
Gladewater, *U.S.A.* 109 J7
Gladstone, *Queens., Australia* 90 C5
Gladstone, *S. Austral., Australia* 91 E2
Gladstone, *W. Austral., Australia* 89 E1
Gladstone, *Canada* 101 C9
Gladstone, *U.S.A.* 104 C2
Gladwin, *U.S.A.* 104 D3
Gladys L., *Canada* 100 B2
Gláma, *Iceland* 8 D2
Glåma →, *Norway* 10 E4
Glamis, *U.S.A.* 113 N11
Glamoč, *Bos.-H.* 33 D13
Glan, *Sweden* 11 F10
Glanerbrug, *Neths.* 16 D9
Glarner Alpen, *Switz.* 23 C8
Glärnisch, *Switz.* 23 C7
Glarus, *Switz.* 23 B8
Glarus □, *Switz.* 23 C8
Glasco, *Kans., U.S.A.* 108 F6
Glasco, *N.Y., U.S.A.* 107 D11
Glasgow, *U.K.* 14 F4
Glasgow, *Ky., U.S.A.* 104 G3
Glasgow, *Mont., U.S.A.* 110 B10
Glastonbury, *U.K.* 13 F5
Glastonbury, *U.S.A.* 107 E12
Glatt →, *Switz.* 23 B7
Glattfelden, *Switz.* 23 A7
Glauchau, *Germany* 18 E8
Glazov, *Russia* 41 B18
Gleiwitz = Gliwice, *Poland* 20 E8
Glen, *U.S.A.* 107 B13
Glen Affric, *U.K.* 14 D4
Glen Canyon Dam, *U.S.A.* 111 H8
Glen Canyon National Recreation Area, *U.S.A.* 111 H8
Glen Coe, *U.K.* 14 E4
Glen Cove, *U.S.A.* 107 F11
Glen Garry, *U.K.* 14 D3
Glen Innes, *Australia* 91 D5
Glen Lyon, *U.S.A.* 107 E8
Glen Mor, *U.K.* 14 D4
Glen Moriston, *U.K.* 14 D4
Glen Orchy, *U.K.* 14 E4
Glen Spean, *U.K.* 14 E4
Glen Ullin, *U.S.A.* 108 B4
Glénan, Is. de, *France* 24 E2
Glenburgh, *Australia* 89 E2
Glencoe, *Canada* 106 D3
Glencoe, *S. Africa* 85 D5
Glencoe, *U.S.A.* 108 C7
Glendale, *Ariz., U.S.A.* 111 K7
Glendale, *Calif., U.S.A.* 113 L8
Glendale, *Oreg., U.S.A.* 110 E2
Glendale, *Zimbabwe* 83 F3
Glendive, *U.S.A.* 108 B2
Glendo, *U.S.A.* 108 D2
Glenelg, *Australia* 91 E2
Glenelg →, *Australia* 91 F3
Glenflorrie, *Australia* 88 D2
Glengarriff, *Ireland* 15 E2
Glengyle, *Australia* 90 C2
Glenmora, *U.S.A.* 109 K8
Glenmorgan, *Australia* 91 D4
Glenn, *U.S.A.* 112 F4
Glenns Ferry, *U.S.A.* 110 E6
Glenorchy, *Australia* 90 G4
Glenore, *Australia* 90 B3
Glenormiston, *Australia* 90 C2
Glenreagh, *Australia* 91 E5
Glenrock, *U.S.A.* 110 E11
Glenrothes, *U.K.* 14 E5
Glens Falls, *U.S.A.* 107 C11
Glenties, *Ireland* 15 B3
Glenville, *U.S.A.* 104 F5
Glenwood, *Alta., Canada* 100 D6
Glenwood, *Nfld., Canada* 99 C9
Glenwood, *Ark., U.S.A.* 109 H8
Glenwood, *Hawaii, U.S.A.* 102 J17
Glenwood, *Iowa, U.S.A.* 108 E7
Glenwood, *Minn., U.S.A.* 108 C7
Glenwood, *Wash., U.S.A.* 112 D5
Glenwood Springs, *U.S.A.* 110 G10
Gletsch, *Switz.* 23 C6
Glina, *Croatia* 33 C13
Glittertind, *Norway* 10 C2
Gliwice, *Poland* 20 E8
Globe, *U.S.A.* 111 K8
Glödnitz, *Austria* 21 J4
Głogów, *Poland* 20 D6
Glorieuses, Is., *Ind. Oc.* 85 A8
Glossop, *U.K.* 12 D6
Gloucester, *Australia* 91 E5
Gloucester, *U.K.* 13 F5
Gloucester, *U.S.A.* 107 D14
Gloucester I., *Australia* 90 B4
Gloucestershire □, *U.K.* 13 F5
Gloversville, *U.S.A.* 107 C10
Glovertown, *Canada* 99 C9
Głowno, *Poland* 20 D9
Głubczyce, *Poland* 20 E7
Glubokiy, *Russia* 43 B9
Glubokoye, *Belorussia* 40 D5
Głuchołazy, *Poland* 20 E7
Glücksburg, *Germany* 18 A5
Glückstadt, *Germany* 18 B5
Glukhov, *Ukraine* 40 F8
Glussk, *Belorussia* 40 E6
Glyngøre, *Denmark* 11 H2
Gmünd, *Kärnten, Austria* 21 J3
Gmünd, *Niederösterreich, Austria* 20 G5
Gnarp, *Sweden* 10 B11
Gnesta, *Sweden* 10 E11
Gniew, *Poland* 20 B8
Gniezno, *Poland* 20 C7
Gnoien, *Germany* 18 B8
Gnowangerup, *Australia* 89 F2
Go Cong, *Vietnam* 59 G6
Gō-no-ura, *Japan* 49 H4
Go Quao, *Vietnam* 59 H5
Goa, *India* 60 M8
Goa □, *India* 60 M8
Goalen Hd., *Australia* 91 F5
Goalpara, *India* 61 F17
Goalundo Ghat, *Bangla.* 63 H13
Goaso, *Ghana* 78 D4
Goat Fell, *U.K.* 14 F3
Goba, *Ethiopia* 68 F2
Goba, *Mozam.* 85 D5
Gobabis, *Namibia* 84 C2
Gobernador Gregores, *Argentina* 128 C2
Gobi, *Asia* 50 C5
Gobō, *Japan* 49 H7
Gobo, *Sudan* 77 F3
Goch, *Germany* 18 D2
Gochas, *Namibia* 84 C2
Godavari →, *India* 61 L13
Godavari Point, *India* 61 L13
Godbout, *Canada* 99 C6
Godda, *India* 63 G12
Godegård, *Sweden* 11 F9
Goderich, *Canada* 98 D3
Goderville, *France* 24 C7
Godhavn, *Greenland* 4 C5
Godhra, *India* 62 H5
Gödöllö, *Hungary* 21 H9
Godoy Cruz, *Argentina* 126 C2
Gods →, *Canada* 101 B10
Gods L., *Canada* 101 C10
Godthåb, *Greenland* 97 B14
Godwin Austen = K2, Mt., *Pakistan* 63 B7
Goeie Hoop, Kaap die = Good Hope, C. of, *S. Africa* 84 E2
Goéland, L. au, *Canada* 98 C4
Goeree, *Neths.* 16 E4
Goes, *Neths.* 17 F3
Gogama, *Canada* 98 C3
Gogango, *Australia* 90 C5
Gogebic, L., *U.S.A.* 108 B10
Gogra = Ghaghara →, *India* 63 G11
Gogriâl, *Sudan* 77 F2
Goiana, *Brazil* 122 C5
Goianésia, *Brazil* 123 E2
Goiânia, *Brazil* 123 E2
Goiás, *Brazil* 123 E1
Goiás □, *Brazil* 122 D2
Goiatuba, *Brazil* 123 E2
Goio-Ere, *Brazil* 127 A5
Goirle, *Neths.* 17 E6
Góis, *Portugal* 30 E2
Gojam □, *Ethiopia* 77 E4
Gojeb, Wabi →, *Ethiopia* 77 F4
Gojō, *Japan* 49 G7
Gojra, *Pakistan* 62 D5
Gokarannath, *India* 63 F9
Gökçeada, *Turkey* 39 J8
Gökırmak →, *Turkey* 66 C6
Göksu →, *Turkey* 66 E6
Göksun, *Turkey* 66 D7
Gokteik, *Burma* 61 H20
Gokurt, *Pakistan* 62 E2
Gola, *India* 63 E9
Golakganj, *India* 63 F13
Golan Heights = Hagolan, *Syria* 69 B4
Golāshkerd, *Iran* 65 E8
Golaya Pristen, *Ukraine* 42 C5
Gölbaşı, *Adiyaman, Turkey* 67 E7
Gölbaşı, *Ankara, Turkey* 66 D5
Golchikha, *Russia* 4 B12
Golconda, *U.S.A.* 110 F5
Gölcük, *Kocaeli, Turkey* 66 C3
Gölcük, *Niğde, Turkey* 66 D6
Gold Beach, *U.S.A.* 110 E1
Gold Coast, *Australia* 91 D5
Gold Coast, *W. Afr.* 70 F3
Gold Hill, *U.S.A.* 110 E2
Goldach, *Switz.* 23 B8
Goldau, *Switz.* 23 B7
Goldberg, *Germany* 18 B8
Golden, *Canada* 100 C5
Golden, *U.S.A.* 108 F2
Golden B., *N.Z.* 87 J4
Golden Gate, *U.S.A.* 110 H2
Golden Hinde, *Canada* 100 D3
Golden Lake, *Canada* 106 A7
Golden Prairie, *Canada* 101 C7
Golden Vale, *Ireland* 15 D3
Goldendale, *U.S.A.* 110 D3
Goldfield, *U.S.A.* 111 H5
Goldfields, *Canada* 101 B7
Goldsand L., *Canada* 101 B8
Goldsboro, *U.S.A.* 105 H7
Goldsmith, *U.S.A.* 109 K3
Goldsworthy, *Australia* 88 D2
Goldthwaite, *U.S.A.* 109 K5
Golegã, *Portugal* 31 F2
Goleniów, *Poland* 20 B4
Golestānak, *Iran* 65 D7
Goleta, *U.S.A.* 113 L7
Golfito, *Costa Rica* 116 E3
Golfo Aranci, *Italy* 34 B2
Gölgeli Dağları, *Turkey* 66 E3
Goliad, *U.S.A.* 109 L6
Golija, *Serbia* 21 M10
Gölköy, *Turkey* 67 C7
Golo →, *France* 27 F13
Golovanevsk, *Ukraine* 42 B4
Golpāyegān, *Iran* 65 C6
Gölpazarı, *Turkey* 66 C4
Golra, *Pakistan* 62 C5
Golspie, *U.K.* 14 D5
Golyama Kamchiya →, *Bulgaria* 38 F10
Goma, *Rwanda* 82 C2
Goma, *Zaïre* 82 C2
Gomati →, *India* 63 G10
Gombari, *Zaïre* 82 B2
Gombe, *Nigeria* 79 C7
Gombe →, *Tanzania* 82 C3
Gombi, *Nigeria* 79 C7
Gomel, *Belorussia* 40 E7
Gomera, *Canary Is.* 36 F2
Gómez Palacio, *Mexico* 114 B4
Gomīshān, *Iran* 65 B7
Gommern, *Germany* 18 C7
Gomogomo, *Indonesia* 57 F8
Gomoh, *India* 61 H15
Gompa = Ganta, *Liberia* 78 D3
Goms, *Switz.* 22 D6
Gonābād, *Iran* 65 C8
Gonaïves, *Haiti* 117 C5
Gonâve, G. de la, *Haiti* 117 C5
Gonâve, I. de la, *Haiti* 117 C5
Gonbab-e Kāvūs, *Iran* 65 B7
Gonda, *India* 63 F9
Gondal, *India* 62 J4
Gonder, *Ethiopia* 77 E4
Gonder □, *Ethiopia* 77 E4
Gondia, *India* 60 J12
Gondola, *Mozam.* 83 F3
Gondomar, *Portugal* 30 D2
Gondomar, *Spain* 30 C2
Gondrecourt-le-Château, *France* 25 D12
Gönen, *Turkey* 66 C2
Gong Xian, *China* 52 C5
Gong'an, *China* 53 B9
Gongcheng, *China* 53 E8
Gongga Shan, *China* 52 C3
Gongguan, *China* 52 G7
Gonghe, *China* 54 C5
Gongola →, *Nigeria* 79 D7
Gongolgon, *Australia* 91 E4
Gongshan, *China* 52 D2
Gongtan, *China* 52 C7
Goniadz, *Poland* 20 B12
Goniri, *Nigeria* 79 C7
Gonjo, *China* 52 B2
Gonnesa, *Italy* 34 C1
Gónnos, *Greece* 39 K5
Gonnosfanadiga, *Italy* 34 C1
Gonzaga, *Phil.* 55 B5
Gonzales, *Calif., U.S.A.* 111 H3
Gonzales, *Tex., U.S.A.* 109 L6
González Chaves, *Argentina* 126 D3
Good Hope, C. of, *S. Africa* 84 E2
Gooderham, *Canada* 98 D4
Goodeve, *Canada* 101 C8
Gooding, *U.S.A.* 110 E6
Goodland, *U.S.A.* 108 F4
Goodnight, *U.S.A.* 109 H4
Goodooga, *Australia* 91 D4
Goodsoil, *Canada* 101 C7
Goodsprings, *U.S.A.* 111 J6
Goole, *U.K.* 12 D7
Goolgowi, *Australia* 91 E4
Goomalling, *Australia* 89 F2
Goombalie, *Australia* 91 D4
Goonda, *Mozam.* 83 F3
Goondiwindi, *Australia* 91 D5
Goongarrie, L., *Australia* 89 F3
Goonyella, *Australia* 90 C4
Goor, *Neths.* 16 D9
Gooray, *Australia* 91 D5
Goose →, *Canada* 99 B7
Goose L., *U.S.A.* 110 F3
Gop, *India* 60 H6
Gopalganj, *India* 63 F11
Goppenstein, *Switz.* 22 D5
Göppingen, *Germany* 19 G5

Gresham

Gor, *Spain* 29 H2
Góra, *Poland* 20 D6
Gorakhpur, *India* 63 F10
Gorbatov, *Russia* 41 C13
Gorbea, Peña, *Spain* 28 B2
Gorda, *U.S.A.* 112 K5
Gorda, Pta., *Nic.* 116 D3
Gorda, Pta., *Canary Is.* 36 F2
Gordan B., *Australia* 88 B5
Gordon, *U.S.A.* 108 D3
Gordon →, *Australia* 90 G4
Gordon, I., *Chile* 128 D3
Gordon Downs, *Australia* 88 C4
Gordon L., *Alta., Canada* 101 B6
Gordon L., *N.W.T., Canada* 100 A6
Gordonia, *S. Africa* 84 D3
Gordonvale, *Australia* 90 B4
Gore, *Australia* 91 D5
Goré, *Chad* 73 G8
Gore, *Ethiopia* 77 F4
Gore, *N.Z.* 87 M2
Gore Bay, *Canada* 98 C3
Görele, *Turkey* 67 C8
Gorey, *Ireland* 15 D5
Gorg, *Iran* 65 D8
Gorgān, *Iran* 65 B7
Gorgona, *Italy* 32 E6
Gorgora, *Ethiopia* 77 E4
Gorham, *U.S.A.* 107 B13
Gori, *Georgia* 43 E11
Gorinchem, *Neths.* 16 E5
Gorinhatã, *Brazil* 123 E2
Goritsy, *Russia* 41 C10
Gorízia, *Italy* 33 C10
Gorki = Nizhniy Novgorod, *Russia* 41 C14
Gorki, *Belorussia* 40 D7
Gorkiy = Nizhniy Novgorod, *Russia* 41 C14
Gorkovskoye Vdkhr., *Russia* 41 C13
Gørlev, *Denmark* 11 J5
Gorlice, *Poland* 20 F11
Görlitz, *Germany* 18 D10
Gorlovka, *Ukraine* 42 B8
Gorman, *Calif., U.S.A.* 113 L8
Gorman, *Tex., U.S.A.* 109 J5
Gorna Dzhumayo = Blagoevgrad, *Bulgaria* 39 G6
Gorna Oryakhovitsa, *Bulgaria* 38 F8
Gornja Radgona, *Slovenia* 33 B13
Gornja Tuzla, *Bos.-H.* 21 L8
Gornji Grad, *Slovenia* 33 B11
Gornji Milanovac, *Serbia* 21 M10
Gornji Vakuf, *Bos.-H.* 21 M7
Gorno-Altaysk, *Russia* 44 D9
Gorno Slinkino, *Russia* 44 C8
Gornyi, *Russia* 48 B6
Gornyy, *Russia* 41 F16
Gorodenka, *Ukraine* 42 B1
Gorodets, *Russia* 41 C13
Gorodishche, *Russia* 41 E14
Gorodishche, *Ukraine* 42 B4
Gorodnitsa, *Ukraine* 40 F5
Gorodnya, *Ukraine* 40 F7
Gorodok, *Belorussia* 40 D7
Gorodok, *Ukraine* 40 G3
Gorokhov, *Ukraine* 40 F4
Gorokhovets, *Russia* 41 C13
Gorom Gorom, *Burkina Faso* 79 C4
Goromonzi, *Zimbabwe* 83 F3
Gorongose →, *Mozam.* 85 C5
Gorongoza, *Mozam.* 83 F3
Gorongoza, Sa. da, *Mozam.* 83 F3
Gorontalo, *Indonesia* 57 D6
Goronyo, *Nigeria* 79 C6
Gorredijk, *Neths.* 16 C8
Gorron, *France* 24 D6
Gorssel, *Neths.* 16 D8
Gort, *Ireland* 15 C3
Gortis, *Greece* 37 D6
Gorzkowice, *Poland* 20 D9
Gorzów Śląski, *Poland* 20 D8
Gorzów Wielkopolski, *Poland* 20 C5
Göschenen, *Switz.* 23 C7
Gosford, *Australia* 91 E5
Goshen, *Calif., U.S.A.* 112 J7
Goshen, *Ind., U.S.A.* 104 E3
Goshen, *N.Y., U.S.A.* 107 E10
Goshogawara, *Japan* 48 D10
Goslar, *Germany* 18 D6
Gospič, *Croatia* 33 D12
Gosport, *U.K.* 13 G6
Gossau, *Switz.* 23 B8
Gosse →, *Australia* 90 B1
Gostivar, *Macedonia* 39 H3
Gostyń, *Poland* 20 D7
Gostynin, *Poland* 20 C9
Göta älv →, *Sweden* 11 G5
Göta kanal, *Sweden* 9 G12
Göteborg, *Sweden* 11 G5
Göteborgs och Bohus län □, *Sweden* 9 G11
Götene, *Sweden* 11 F7
Gotha, *Germany* 18 E6
Gothenburg, *U.S.A.* 108 E4
Gotland, *Sweden* 9 H15
Gotse Delchev, *Bulgaria* 39 H6
Gotska Sandön, *Sweden* 9 G15
Gōtsu, *Japan* 49 G6
Göttingen, *Germany* 18 D5
Gottwald = Zmiyev, *Ukraine* 42 B7
Gottwaldov = Zlin, *Czech.* 20 F7
Goubangzi, *China* 51 D11
Gouda, *Neths.* 16 D5
Goúdhoura, Ákra, *Greece* 37 E8
Goudiry, *Senegal* 78 C2
Gough I., *Atl. Oc.* 2 G9
Gouin, Rés., *Canada* 98 C5
Gouitafla, *Ivory C.* 78 D3
Goulburn, *Australia* 91 E4
Goulburn Is., *Australia* 90 A1
Goulia, *Ivory C.* 78 C3
Goulimine, *Morocco* 74 C3
Goulmina, *Morocco* 74 B4
Gounou-Gaya, *Chad* 73 G8
Goúra, *Greece* 39 M5
Gouraya, *Algeria* 75 A5
Gourdon, *France* 26 D5
Gouré, *Niger* 79 C7
Gouri, *Chad* 73 E8
Gourits →, *S. Africa* 84 E3
Gourma Rharous, *Mali* 79 B4
Goúrnais, *Greece* 37 D7
Gournay-en-Bray, *France* 25 C8
Gourock Ra., *Australia* 91 F4
Goursi, *Burkina Faso* 78 C4
Gouvêa, *Brazil* 123 E3
Gouverneur, *U.S.A.* 107 B9
Gouviá, *Greece* 37 A3
Gouzon, *France* 26 B6
Govan, *Canada* 101 C8
Governador Valadares, *Brazil* 123 E3
Governor's Harbour, *Bahamas* 116 A4
Gowan Ra., *Australia* 90 C4
Gowanda, *U.S.A.* 106 D6
Gowd-e Zirreh, *Afghan.* 60 E3
Gower, *U.K.* 13 F3
Gowna, L., *Ireland* 15 C4
Goya, *Argentina* 126 B4
Goyder Lagoon, *Australia* 91 D2
Goyllarisquisga, *Peru* 124 C2
Göynük, *Turkey* 66 C4
Goz Beïda, *Chad* 73 F9
Goz Regeb, *Sudan* 77 D4
Gozo, *Malta* 37 C1
Graaff-Reinet, *S. Africa* 84 E3
Grabow, *Germany* 18 B7
Grabs, *Switz.* 23 B8
Gračac, *Croatia* 33 D12
Gračanica, *Bos.-H.* 21 L8
Graçay, *France* 25 E8
Grace, *U.S.A.* 110 E8
Graceville, *U.S.A.* 108 C6
Gracias a Dios, C., *Honduras* 116 C3
Graciosa, I., *Canary Is.* 36 E6
Gradaús, *Brazil* 122 C1
Gradaús, Serra dos, *Brazil* 122 C1
Gradets, *Bulgaria* 38 G9
Grado, *Italy* 33 C10
Grado, *Spain* 30 B4
Gradule, *Australia* 91 D4
Grady, *U.S.A.* 109 H3
Graeca, Lacul, *Romania* 38 E9
Graénalon, L., *Iceland* 8 D5
Grafenau, *Germany* 19 G9
Gräfenberg, *Germany* 19 F7
Grafton, *Australia* 91 D5
Grafton, *U.S.A.* 108 A6
Gragnano, *Italy* 35 B7
Graham, *Canada* 98 C1
Graham, *N.C., U.S.A.* 105 G6
Graham, *Tex., U.S.A.* 109 J5
Graham →, *Canada* 100 B4
Graham, Mt., *U.S.A.* 111 K9
Graham Bell, Os., *Russia* 44 A7
Graham I., *Canada* 100 C2
Graham Land, *Antarctica* 5 C17
Grahamdale, *Canada* 101 C9
Grahamstown, *S. Africa* 84 E4
Graïba, *Tunisia* 75 B7
Graide, *Belgium* 17 J6
Graie, Alpi, *Europe* 32 C4
Grain Coast, *W. Afr.* 70 F2
Grajaú, *Brazil* 122 C2
Grajaú →, *Brazil* 122 B3
Grajewo, *Poland* 20 B12
Gramada, *Bulgaria* 38 F5
Gramat, *France* 26 D5
Grammichele, *Italy* 35 E7
Grampian □, *U.K.* 14 D6
Grampian Highlands = Grampian Mts., *U.K.* 14 E5
Grampian Mts., *U.K.* 14 E5
Gran →, *Surinam* 121 C6
Gran Altiplanicie Central, *Argentina* 128 C3
Gran Canaria, *Canary Is.* 36 F4
Gran Chaco, *S. Amer.* 126 B3
Gran Paradiso, *Italy* 32 C4
Gran Sasso d'Italia, *Italy* 33 F10
Granada, *Nic.* 116 D2
Granada, *Spain* 29 H1
Granada, *U.S.A.* 109 F3
Granada □, *Spain* 31 H7
Granadilla de Abona, *Canary Is.* 36 F3
Granard, *Ireland* 15 C4
Granbury, *U.S.A.* 109 J6
Granby, *Canada* 98 C5
Grand →, *Mo., U.S.A.* 108 F8
Grand →, *S. Dak., U.S.A.* 108 C4
Grand Bahama, *Bahamas* 116 A4
Grand Bank, *Canada* 99 C8
Grand Bassam, *Ivory C.* 78 D4
Grand Béréby, *Ivory C.* 78 E3
Grand-Bourg, *Guadeloupe* 117 C7
Grand Canal = Yun Ho →, *China* 51 E9
Grand Canyon, *U.S.A.* 111 H7
Grand Canyon National Park, *U.S.A.* 111 H7
Grand Cayman, *Cayman Is.* 116 C3
Grand Cess, *Liberia* 78 E3
Grand Coulee, *U.S.A.* 110 C4
Grand Coulee Dam, *U.S.A.* 110 C4
Grand Erg Occidental, *Algeria* 75 B5
Grand Erg Oriental, *Algeria* 75 C6
Grand Falls, *Canada* 99 C8
Grand Forks, *Canada* 100 D5
Grand Forks, *U.S.A.* 108 B6
Grand-Fougeray, *France* 24 E5
Grand Haven, *U.S.A.* 104 D2
Grand I., *U.S.A.* 104 B2
Grand Island, *U.S.A.* 108 E5
Grand Isle, *U.S.A.* 109 L10
Grand Junction, *U.S.A.* 111 G9
Grand L., *U.S.A.* 109 L8
Grand Lac Victoria, *Canada* 98 C4
Grand Lahou, *Ivory C.* 78 D3
Grand L., *N.B., Canada* 99 C6
Grand L., *Nfld., Canada* 99 C8
Grand L., *Nfld., Canada* 99 B7
Grand Lake, *U.S.A.* 110 F11
Grand-Leez, *Belgium* 17 G5
Grand-Lieu, L. de, *France* 24 E5
Grand Manan I., *Canada* 99 D6
Grand Marais, *Canada* 108 B9
Grand Marais, *U.S.A.* 104 B3
Grand-Mère, *Canada* 98 C5
Grand Popo, *Benin* 79 D5
Grand Portage, *U.S.A.* 98 C2
Grand Rapids, *Canada* 101 C9
Grand Rapids, *Mich., U.S.A.* 104 D2
Grand Rapids, *Minn., U.S.A.* 108 B8
Grand St-Bernard, Col du, *Switz.* 22 E4
Grand Santi, *Fr. Guiana* 121 C7
Grand Teton, *U.S.A.* 110 E8
Grand Valley, *U.S.A.* 110 G9
Grand View, *Canada* 101 C8
Grandas de Salime, *Spain* 30 B4
Grande →, *Jujuy, Argentina* 126 A2
Grande →, *Mendoza, Argentina* 126 D2
Grande →, *Bolivia* 125 D5
Grande →, *Bahia, Brazil* 122 D3
Grande →, *Minas Gerais, Brazil* 123 F1
Grande →, *Spain* 29 F4
Grande →, *Venezuela* 121 B5
Grande, B., *Argentina* 128 D3
Grande, I., *Brazil* 123 F3
Grande, Rio →, *U.S.A.* 109 N6
Grande, Serra, *Goiás, Brazil* 122 D2
Grande, Serra, *Piauí, Brazil* 122 C2
Grande Baie, *Canada* 99 C5
Grande Baleine, R. de la →, *Canada* 98 A4
Grande Cache, *Canada* 100 C5
Grande de Santiago →, *Mexico* 114 C3
Grande Dixence, Barr. de la, *Switz.* 22 D4
Grande-Entrée, *Canada* 99 C7
Grande Prairie, *Canada* 100 B5
Grande-Rivière, *Canada* 99 C7
Grande Sauldre →, *France* 25 E9
Grande-Vallée, *Canada* 99 C6
Grandes-Bergeronnes, *Canada* 99 C6
Grandfalls, *U.S.A.* 109 K3
Grandoe Mines, *Canada* 100 B3
Grândola, *Portugal* 31 G2
Grandpré, *France* 25 C11
Grandson, *Switz.* 22 C3
Grandview, *U.S.A.* 110 C4
Grandvilliers, *France* 25 C8
Graneros, *Chile* 126 C1
Grangemouth, *U.K.* 14 E5
Granger, *Wash., U.S.A.* 110 C3
Granger, *Wyo., U.S.A.* 110 F9
Grangeville, *U.S.A.* 110 D5
Granite City, *U.S.A.* 108 F9
Granite Falls, *U.S.A.* 108 C7
Granite Mt., *U.S.A.* 113 M10
Granite Peak, *Australia* 89 E3
Granite Peak, *U.S.A.* 110 D9
Granity, *N.Z.* 87 J3
Granja, *Brazil* 122 B3
Granja de Moreruela, *Spain* 30 D5
Granja de Torrehermosa, *Spain* 31 G5
Granollers, *Spain* 28 D7
Gransee, *Germany* 18 B9
Grant, *U.S.A.* 108 E4
Grant, Mt., *U.S.A.* 110 G4
Grant City, *U.S.A.* 108 E7
Grant I., *Australia* 88 B5
Grant Range, *U.S.A.* 111 G6
Grantham, *U.K.* 12 E7
Grantown-on-Spey, *U.K.* 14 D5
Grants, *U.S.A.* 111 J10
Grants Pass, *U.S.A.* 110 E2
Grantsburg, *U.S.A.* 108 C8
Grantsville, *U.S.A.* 110 F7
Granville, *France* 24 D5
Granville, *N. Dak., U.S.A.* 108 A4
Granville, *N.Y., U.S.A.* 104 D9
Granville L., *Canada* 101 B8
Grao de Gandía, *Spain* 29 F4
Grapeland, *U.S.A.* 109 K7
Gras, L. de, *Canada* 96 B8
Graskop, *S. Africa* 85 C5
Grass →, *Canada* 101 B9
Grass Range, *U.S.A.* 110 C9
Grass River Prov. Park, *Canada* 101 C8
Grass Valley, *Calif., U.S.A.* 112 F6
Grass Valley, *Oreg., U.S.A.* 110 D3
Grassano, *Italy* 35 B9
Grasse, *France* 27 E10
Grassmere, *Australia* 91 E3
Graubünden □, *Switz.* 23 C9
Graulhet, *France* 26 E5
Graus, *Spain* 28 C5
Gravatá, *Brazil* 122 C4
Grave, *Neths.* 16 E7
Grave, Pte. de, *France* 26 C2
's-Graveland, *Neths.* 16 D6
Gravelbourg, *Canada* 101 D7
Gravelines, *France* 25 B9
's-Gravendeel, *Neths.* 16 E5
's-Gravenhage, *Neths.* 16 D4
Gravenhurst, *Canada* 106 B5
's-Gravenpolder, *Neths.* 17 F3
's-Gravensande, *Neths.* 16 D4
Gravesend, *Australia* 91 D5
Gravesend, *U.K.* 13 F8
Gravina di Púglia, *Italy* 35 B9
Gravois, Pointe-à-, *Haiti* 117 C5
Gravone →, *France* 27 G12
Gray, *France* 25 E12
Grayling, *U.S.A.* 104 C3
Grayling →, *Canada* 100 B3
Grays Harbor, *U.S.A.* 110 C1
Grays L., *U.S.A.* 110 E8
Grays River, *U.S.A.* 112 D3
Grayson, *Canada* 101 C8
Graz, *Austria* 21 H5
Grazalema, *Spain* 31 J5
Greasy L., *Canada* 100 A4
Great Abaco I., *Bahamas* 116 A4
Great Artesian Basin, *Australia* 90 C3
Great Australian Bight, *Australia* 89 F5
Great Bahama Bank, *Bahamas* 116 B4
Great Barrier I., *N.Z.* 87 G5
Great Barrier Reef, *Australia* 90 B4
Great Barrington, *U.S.A.* 107 D11
Great Basin, *U.S.A.* 110 G5
Great Bear →, *Canada* 96 B7
Great Bear L., *Canada* 96 B7
Great Belt = Store Bælt, *Denmark* 11 J5
Great Bend, *Kans., U.S.A.* 108 F5
Great Bend, *Pa., U.S.A.* 107 E9
Great Blasket I., *Ireland* 15 D1
Great Britain, *Europe* 6 E5
Great Central, *Canada* 100 D3
Great Dividing Ra., *Australia* 90 C4
Great Driffield, *U.K.* 12 C7
Great Exuma I., *Bahamas* 116 B4
Great Falls, *Canada* 101 C9
Great Falls, *U.S.A.* 110 C8
Great Fish = Groot Vis →, *S. Africa* 84 E4
Great Guana Cay, *Bahamas* 116 B4
Great Harbour Deep, *Canada* 99 B8
Great Inagua I., *Bahamas* 117 B5
Great Indian Desert = Thar Desert, *India* 62 F4
Great I., *Canada* 101 B9
Great Karoo, *S. Africa* 84 E3
Great Lake, *Australia* 90 G4
Great Ormes Head, *U.K.* 12 D4
Great Ouse →, *U.K.* 12 E8
Great Palm I., *Australia* 90 B4
Great Plains, *N. Amer.* 102 A6
Great Ruaha →, *Tanzania* 82 D4
Great Saint Bernard P. = Grand St-Bernard, Col du, *Switz.* 22 E4
Great Salt L., *U.S.A.* 110 F7
Great Salt Lake Desert, *U.S.A.* 110 F7
Great Salt Plains L., *U.S.A.* 109 G5
Great Sandy Desert, *Australia* 88 D3
Great Sangi = Sangihe, P., *Indonesia* 57 D7
Great Scarcies →, *S. Leone* 78 D2
Great Slave L., *Canada* 100 A5
Great Smoky Mts. Nat. Pk., *U.S.A.* 105 H4
Great Stour = Stour →, *U.K.* 13 F9
Great Victoria Desert, *Australia* 89 E4
Great Wall, *China* 50 E5
Great Whernside, *U.K.* 12 C6
Great Yarmouth, *U.K.* 12 E9
Greater Antilles, *W. Indies* 117 C5
Greater London □, *U.K.* 13 F7
Greater Manchester □, *U.K.* 12 D5
Greater Sunda Is., *Indonesia* 56 F4
Grebbestad, *Sweden* 11 F5
Grebenka, *Ukraine* 40 F8
Greco, C., *Cyprus* 37 E13
Greco, Mte., *Italy* 34 A6
Gredos, Sierra de, *Spain* 30 E5
Greece, *U.S.A.* 106 C7
Greece ■, *Europe* 39 K6
Greeley, *Colo., U.S.A.* 108 E2
Greeley, *Nebr., U.S.A.* 108 E5
Green →, *Ky., U.S.A.* 104 G2
Green →, *Utah, U.S.A.* 111 G9
Green B., *U.S.A.* 104 C2
Green Bay, *U.S.A.* 104 C2
Green C., *Australia* 91 F5
Green Cove Springs, *U.S.A.* 105 L5
Green River, *U.S.A.* 111 G8
Greenbank, *U.S.A.* 112 B4
Greenbush, *Mich., U.S.A.* 106 B1
Greenbush, *Minn., U.S.A.* 108 A6
Greencastle, *U.S.A.* 104 F2
Greene, *U.S.A.* 107 D9
Greenfield, *Calif., U.S.A.* 112 J5
Greenfield, *Calif., U.S.A.* 113 K8
Greenfield, *Ind., U.S.A.* 104 F3
Greenfield, *Iowa, U.S.A.* 108 E7
Greenfield, *Mass., U.S.A.* 107 D12
Greenfield, *Mo., U.S.A.* 109 G8
Greenfield Park, *Canada* 107 A11
Greenland ■, *N. Amer.* 4 C5
Greenland Sea, *Arctic* 4 B7
Greenock, *U.K.* 14 F4
Greenore, *Ireland* 15 B5
Greenore Pt., *Ireland* 15 D5
Greenough →, *Australia* 89 E1
Greenport, *U.S.A.* 107 E12
Greensboro, *Ga., U.S.A.* 105 J4
Greensboro, *N.C., U.S.A.* 105 G6
Greensburg, *Ind., U.S.A.* 104 F3
Greensburg, *Kans., U.S.A.* 109 G5
Greensburg, *Pa., U.S.A.* 106 F5
Greenville, *Liberia* 78 D3
Greenville, *Ala., U.S.A.* 105 K2
Greenville, *Calif., U.S.A.* 112 E6
Greenville, *Ill., U.S.A.* 108 F10
Greenville, *Maine, U.S.A.* 99 C6
Greenville, *Mich., U.S.A.* 104 D3
Greenville, *Miss., U.S.A.* 109 J9
Greenville, *N.C., U.S.A.* 105 H7
Greenville, *Ohio, U.S.A.* 104 E3
Greenville, *Pa., U.S.A.* 106 E4
Greenville, *S.C., U.S.A.* 105 H4
Greenville, *Tenn., U.S.A.* 105 G4
Greenville, *Tex., U.S.A.* 109 J6
Greenwater Lake Prov. Park, *Canada* 101 C8
Greenwich, *U.K.* 13 F8
Greenwich, *Conn., U.S.A.* 107 E11
Greenwich, *N.Y., U.S.A.* 107 C11
Greenwich, *Ohio, U.S.A.* 106 E2
Greenwood, *Canada* 100 D5
Greenwood, *Miss., U.S.A.* 109 J9
Greenwood, *S.C., U.S.A.* 105 H4
Greenwood, Mt., *Australia* 88 B5
Gregório →, *Brazil* 124 B3
Gregory, *U.S.A.* 108 D5
Gregory →, *Australia* 90 B2
Gregory, L., *S. Austral., Australia* 91 D2
Gregory, L., *W. Austral., Australia* 89 E2
Gregory Downs, *Australia* 90 B2
Gregory L., *Australia* 88 D4
Gregory Ra., *Queens., Australia* 90 B3
Gregory Ra., *W. Austral., Australia* 88 D3
Greiffenberg, *Germany* 18 B9
Greifswald, *Germany* 18 A9
Greifswalder Bodden, *Germany* 18 A9
Grein, *Austria* 21 G4
Greiz, *Germany* 18 E8
Gremikha, *Russia* 44 C4
Grenå, *Denmark* 11 H4
Grenada, *U.S.A.* 109 J10
Grenada ■, *W. Indies* 117 D7
Grenade, *France* 26 E5
Grenadines, *W. Indies* 117 D7
Grenchen, *Switz.* 22 B4
Grenen, *Denmark* 11 G4
Grenfell, *Australia* 91 E4
Grenfell, *Canada* 101 C8
Grenoble, *France* 27 C9
Grenora, *U.S.A.* 108 A3
Grenville, C., *Australia* 90 A3
Grenville Chan., *Canada* 100 C3
Gréoux-les-Bains, *France* 27 E9
Gresham, *U.S.A.* 112 E4

Gresik, *Indonesia* 57 G15
Grëssoney St. Jean, *Italy* 32 C4
Gretna Green, *U.K.* 14 F5
Grevelingen Krammer, *Neths.* 16 E4
Greven, *Germany* 18 C3
Grevená, *Greece* 39 J4
Grevenbroich, *Germany* 18 D2
Grevenmacher, *Lux.* 17 J8
Grevesmühlen, *Germany* 18 B7
Grevie, *Sweden* 11 H6
Grey →, *N.Z.* 87 K3
Grey, C., *Australia* 90 A2
Grey Ra., *Australia* 91 D3
Grey Res., *Canada* 99 C8
Greybull, *U.S.A.* 110 D9
Greymouth, *N.Z.* 87 K3
Greytown, *N.Z.* 87 J5
Greytown, *S. Africa* 85 D5
Gribanovskiy, *Russia* 41 F12
Gribbell I., *Canada* 100 C3
Gridley, *U.S.A.* 112 F5
Griekwastad, *S. Africa* 84 D3
Griffin, *U.S.A.* 105 J3
Griffith, *Australia* 91 E4
Grijpskerk, *Neths.* 16 B8
Grillby, *Sweden* 10 E11
Grimari, *C.A.R.* 73 G9
Grimaylov, *Ukraine* 40 G5
Grimbergen, *Belgium* 17 G4
Grimes, *U.S.A.* 112 F5
Grimma, *Germany* 18 D8
Grimmen, *Germany* 18 A9
Grimsby, *Canada* 106 C5
Grimsby, *U.K.* 12 D7
Grimselpass, *Switz.* 23 C6
Grímsey, *Iceland* 8 C5
Grimshaw, *Canada* 100 B5
Grimstad, *Norway* 11 F2
Grindelwald, *Switz.* 22 C6
Grindsted, *Denmark* 11 J2
Grindu, *Romania* 38 E9
Grinnell, *U.S.A.* 108 E8
Griñón, *Spain* 30 E7
Grintavec, *Slovenia* 33 B11
Grip, *Norway* 10 A1
Gris-Nez, C., *France* 25 B8
Grisolles, *France* 26 E5
Grisons = Graubünden □, *Switz.* 23 C9
Grivegnée, *Belgium* 17 G7
Grmeč Planina, *Bos.-H.* 33 D13
Groais I., *Canada* 99 B8
Groblersdal, *S. Africa* 85 D4
Grobming, *Austria* 21 H3
Grodno, *Belorussia* 40 E3
Grodzisk Mázowiecki, *Poland* 20 C10
Grodzisk Wielkopolski, *Poland* 20 C6
Grodzyanka, *Belorussia* 40 E6
Groenlo, *Neths.* 16 D9
Groesbeck, *U.S.A.* 109 K6
Groesbeek, *Neths.* 16 E7
Groix, *France* 24 E3
Groix, I. de, *France* 24 E3
Grójec, *Poland* 20 D10
Grolloo, *Neths.* 16 C9
Gronau, *Niedersachsen, Germany* 18 C5
Gronau, *Nordrhein-Westfalen, Germany* 18 C3
Grong, *Norway* 8 D12
Groningen, *Neths.* 16 B9
Groningen, *Surinam* 121 B6
Groningen □, *Neths.* 16 B9
Groninger Wad, *Neths.* 16 B9
Gronsveld, *Neths.* 17 G7
Groom, *U.S.A.* 109 H4
Groot →, *S. Africa* 84 E3
Groot Berg →, *S. Africa* 84 E2
Groot-Brakrivier, *S. Africa* 84 E3
Groot-Kei →, *S. Africa* 85 E4
Groot Vis →, *S. Africa* 84 E4
Groote Eylandt, *Australia* 90 A2
Grootebroek, *Neths.* 16 C6
Grootfontein, *Namibia* 84 B2
Grootlaagte →, *Africa* 84 C3
Grootvloer, *S. Africa* 84 E3
Gros C., *Canada* 100 A6
Grosa, Pta., *Spain* 36 B8
Grósio, *Italy* 32 B7
Grosne →, *France* 27 B8
Gross Glockner, *Austria* 21 H2
Grossenbrode, *Germany* 18 A7
Grossenhain, *Germany* 18 D9
Grosseto, *Italy* 32 F8
Groswater B., *Canada* 99 B8
Grote Gette →, *Neths.* 17 G6
Grote Nete →, *Belgium* 17 F5
Groton, *Conn., U.S.A.* 107 E12
Groton, *S. Dak., U.S.A.* 108 C5
Grottáglie, *Italy* 35 B10
Grottaminarda, *Italy* 35 A8
Grottammare, *Italy* 33 F10
Grouard Mission, *Canada* 100 B5
Grouin, Pte. du, *France* 24 D5
Groundhog →, *Canada* 98 C3
Grouse Creek, *U.S.A.* 110 F7
Grouw, *Neths.* 16 B7
Grove City, *U.S.A.* 106 E4
Groveland, *U.S.A.* 112 H6
Grover City, *U.S.A.* 113 K6
Groveton, *N.H., U.S.A.* 107 B13
Groveton, *Tex., U.S.A.* 109 K7
Grožnjan, *Croatia* 33 C10
Groznyy, *Russia* 43 E11
Grubbenvorst, *Neths.* 17 F8
Grudziądz, *Poland* 20 B8
Gruissan, *France* 26 E7
Grumo Áppula, *Italy* 35 A9
Grünberg, *Germany* 18 E4
Grundy Center, *U.S.A.* 108 D8
Gruver, *U.S.A.* 109 G4
Gruyères, *Switz.* 22 C4
Gryazi, *Russia* 41 E11
Gryazovets, *Russia* 41 B12
Gstaad, *Switz.* 22 D4
Gua, *India* 61 H14
Gua Musang, *Malaysia* 59 K3
Guacanayabo, G. de, *Cuba* 116 B4
Guacara, *Venezuela* 120 A4
Guachípas →, *Argentina* 126 B2
Guachiría →, *Colombia* 120 B3
Guadajoz →, *Spain* 31 H6
Guadalajara, *Mexico* 114 C4
Guadalajara, *Spain* 28 E1
Guadalajara □, *Spain* 28 E2
Guadalcanal, *Solomon Is.* 92 H8
Guadalcanal, *Spain* 31 G5
Guadalén →, *Spain* 31 G7
Guadales, *Argentina* 126 C2
Guadalete →, *Spain* 31 J4
Guadalhorce →, *Spain* 31 J6
Guadalimar →, *Spain* 29 G1
Guadalmena →, *Spain* 29 G2
Guadalmez →, *Spain* 31 G5
Guadalope →, *Spain* 28 D4
Guadalquivir →, *Spain* 31 J4
Guadalupe = Guadeloupe ■, *W. Indies* 117 C7
Guadalupe, *Brazil* 122 C3
Guadalupe, *Mexico* 113 N10
Guadalupe, *Spain* 31 F5
Guadalupe, *U.S.A.* 113 L6
Guadalupe →, *Mexico* 113 N10
Guadalupe →, *U.S.A.* 109 L6
Guadalupe, Sierra de, *Spain* 31 F5
Guadalupe Bravos, *Mexico* 114 A3
Guadalupe Peak, *U.S.A.* 111 L11
Guadalupe y Calvo, *Mexico* 114 B3
Guadarrama, Sierra de, *Spain* 30 E6
Guadeloupe ■, *W. Indies* 117 C7
Guadeloupe Passage, *W. Indies* 117 C7
Guadiamar →, *Spain* 31 J4
Guadiana →, *Portugal* 31 H3
Guadiana Menor →, *Spain* 29 H1
Guadiaro →, *Spain* 31 J5
Guadiato →, *Spain* 31 H5
Guadiela →, *Spain* 28 E2
Guadix, *Spain* 29 H1
Guafo, Boca del, *Chile* 128 B2
Guafo, I., *Chile* 128 B2
Guainía □, *Colombia* 120 C4
Guainía →, *Colombia* 120 C4
Guaíra, *Brazil* 127 A5
Guaitecas, Is., *Chile* 128 B2
Guajará-Mirim, *Brazil* 125 C4
Guajira □, *Colombia* 120 A3
Guajira, Pen. de la, *Colombia* 120 A3
Gualaceo, *Ecuador* 120 D2
Gualán, *Guatemala* 116 C2
Gualdo Tadino, *Italy* 33 E9
Gualeguay, *Argentina* 126 C4
Gualeguaychú, *Argentina* 126 C4
Gualicho, Salina, *Argentina* 128 B3
Gualjaina, *Argentina* 128 B2
Guam ■, *Pac. Oc.* 92 F6
Guamá, *Brazil* 122 B2
Guamá →, *Brazil* 122 B2
Guamblin, I., *Chile* 128 B1
Guaminí, *Argentina* 126 D3
Guamote, *Ecuador* 120 D2
Guampí, Sierra de, *Venezuela* 121 B4
Guamúchil, *Mexico* 114 B3
Guan Xian, *China* 52 B4
Guanabacoa, *Cuba* 116 B3
Guanacaste, Cordillera del, *Costa Rica* 116 D2
Guanaceví, *Mexico* 114 B3
Guanahani = San Salvador, *Bahamas* 117 B5
Guanajay, *Cuba* 116 B3
Guanajuato, *Mexico* 114 C4
Guanajuato □, *Mexico* 114 C4
Guanambi, *Brazil* 123 D3
Guanare, *Venezuela* 120 B4
Guanare →, *Venezuela* 120 B4
Guandacol, *Argentina* 126 B2
Guane, *Cuba* 116 B3
Guang'an, *China* 52 B6
Guangchang, *China* 53 D11
Guangde, *China* 53 B12
Guangdong □, *China* 53 F9
Guangfeng, *China* 53 C12
Guanghan, *China* 52 B5
Guanghua, *China* 53 A8
Guangji, *China* 53 C10
Guangling, *China* 50 E8
Guangning, *China* 53 F9
Guangrao, *China* 51 F10
Guangshun, *China* 52 D6
Guangwu, *China* 50 F3
Guangxi Zhuangzu Zizhiqu □, *China* 52 E7
Guangyuan, *China* 52 A5
Guangze, *China* 53 D11
Guangzhou, *China* 53 F9
Guanhães, *Brazil* 123 E3
Guanipa →, *Venezuela* 121 B5
Guanling, *China* 52 E5
Guannan, *China* 51 G10
Guanta, *Venezuela* 121 A5
Guantánamo, *Cuba* 117 B4
Guantao, *China* 50 F8
Guanyang, *China* 53 E8
Guanyun, *China* 51 G10
Guapí, *Colombia* 120 C2
Guápiles, *Costa Rica* 116 D3
Guaporé →, *Brazil* 125 C4
Guaqui, *Bolivia* 124 D4
Guara, Sierra de, *Spain* 28 C4
Guarabira, *Brazil* 122 C4
Guaranda, *Ecuador* 120 D2
Guarapari, *Brazil* 123 F3
Guarapuava, *Brazil* 123 G1
Guaratinguetá, *Brazil* 127 A6
Guaratuba, *Brazil* 127 B6
Guarda, *Portugal* 30 E3
Guarda □, *Portugal* 30 E3
Guardafui, C. = Asir, Ras, *Somali Rep.* 68 E5
Guardamar del Segura, *Spain* 29 G4
Guardavalle, *Italy* 35 D9
Guardiagrele, *Italy* 33 F11
Guardo, *Spain* 30 C6
Guareña, *Spain* 31 G4
Guareña →, *Spain* 30 D5
Guaria □, *Paraguay* 126 B4
Guárico □, *Venezuela* 120 B4
Guarrojo →, *Colombia* 120 C3
Guarujá, *Brazil* 127 A6
Guarus, *Brazil* 123 F3
Guasave, *Mexico* 114 B3
Guascama, Pta., *Colombia* 120 C2
Guasdualito, *Venezuela* 120 B3
Guasipati, *Venezuela* 121 B5
Guastalla, *Italy* 32 D7
Guatemala, *Guatemala* 116 D1
Guatemala ■, *Cent. Amer.* 116 C1
Guatire, *Venezuela* 120 A4
Guaviare □, *Colombia* 120 C3
Guaviare →, *Colombia* 120 C4
Guaxupé, *Brazil* 127 A6
Guayabero →, *Colombia* 120 C3
Guayama, *Puerto Rico* 117 C6
Guayaneco, Arch., *Chile* 128 C1
Guayaquil, *Ecuador* 120 D2
Guayaquil, G. de, *Ecuador* 120 D1
Guayaramerín, *Bolivia* 125 C4
Guayas →, *Ecuador* 120 D2
Guaymas, *Mexico* 114 B2
Guazhou, *China* 53 A12
Guba, *Zaïre* 83 E2
Gûbâl, Madîq, *Egypt* 76 B3
Gubat, *Phil.* 55 E6
Gúbbio, *Italy* 33 E9
Gubio, *Nigeria* 79 C7
Gubkin, *Russia* 41 F10
Gudata, *Georgia* 43 E9
Gudbrandsdalen, *Norway* 9 F10
Guddu Barrage, *Pakistan* 60 E6
Gudenå, *Denmark* 11 H3
Gudermes, *Russia* 43 E12
Gudivada, *India* 61 L12
Gudur, *India* 60 M11
Guebwiller, *France* 25 E14
Guecho, *Spain* 28 B2
Guékédou, *Guinea* 78 D2
Guelma, *Algeria* 75 A6
Guelph, *Canada* 98 D3
Guelt es Stel, *Algeria* 75 A5
Guelttara, *Algeria* 75 C4
Guemar, *Algeria* 75 B6
Guéméné-Penfao, *France* 24 E5
Guéméné-sur-Scorff, *France* 24 D3
Guéné, *Benin* 79 C5
Güepi, *Peru* 120 D2
Guer, *France* 24 E4
Güer Aike, *Argentina* 128 D3
Guérande, *France* 24 E4
Guercif, *Morocco* 75 B4
Guéréda, *Chad* 73 F9
Guéret, *France* 26 B5
Guérigny, *France* 25 E10
Guerneville, *U.S.A.* 112 G4
Guernica, *Spain* 28 B2
Guernsey, *U.K.* 13 H5
Guernsey, *U.S.A.* 108 D2
Guerrara, *Oasis, Algeria* 75 B5
Guerrara, *Saoura, Algeria* 75 C4
Guerrero □, *Mexico* 115 D5
Guerzim, *Algeria* 75 C4
Gueugnon, *France* 27 B8
Gueydan, *U.S.A.* 109 K8
Gūgher, *Iran* 65 D8
Guglionesi, *Italy* 35 A7
Gui Jiang →, *China* 53 F8
Gui Xian, *China* 52 F7
Guia, *Canary Is.* 36 F4
Guia de Isora, *Canary Is.* 36 F3
Guia Lopes da Laguna, *Brazil* 127 A4
Guichi, *China* 53 B11
Guider, *Cameroon* 79 D7
Guidimouni, *Niger* 79 C6
Guiding, *China* 52 D6
Guidong, *China* 53 D9
Guiglo, *Ivory C.* 78 D3
Guijá, *Mozam.* 85 C5
Guijo de Coria, *Spain* 30 E4
Guildford, *U.K.* 13 F7
Guilford, *U.S.A.* 99 C6
Guilin, *China* 53 E8
Guillaumes, *France* 27 D10
Guillestre, *France* 27 D10
Guilvinec, *France* 24 E2
Güimar, *Canary Is.* 36 F3
Guimarães, *Brazil* 122 B3
Guimarães, *Portugal* 30 D2
Guimaras, *Phil.* 55 F5
Guinda, *U.S.A.* 112 G4
Guinea ■, *W. Afr.* 78 C2
Guinea, Gulf of, *Atl. Oc.* 70 F3
Guinea-Bissau ■, *Africa* 78 C2
Güines, *Cuba* 116 B3
Guingamp, *France* 24 D3
Guipavas, *France* 24 D2
Guiping, *China* 53 F8
Guipúzcoa □, *Spain* 28 B2
Guir, O. →, *Algeria* 75 B4
Guiratinga, *Brazil* 125 D7
Güiria, *Venezuela* 121 A5
Guiscard, *France* 25 C10
Guise, *France* 25 C10
Guitiriz, *Spain* 30 B3
Guiuan, *Phil.* 55 F6
Guixi, *China* 53 C11
Guiyang, *Guizhou, China* 52 D6
Guiyang, *Hunan, China* 53 E9
Guizhou □, *China* 52 D6
Gujan-Mestras, *France* 26 D2
Gujarat □, *India* 62 H4
Gujiang, *China* 53 D10
Gujranwala, *Pakistan* 62 C6
Gujrat, *Pakistan* 62 C6
Gukovo, *Russia* 43 B8
Gulbarga, *India* 60 L10
Gulbene, *Latvia* 40 C5
Gulf, The, *Asia* 65 E6
Gulfport, *U.S.A.* 109 K10
Gulgong, *Australia* 91 E4
Gulin, *China* 52 C5
Gulistan, *Pakistan* 62 D2
Gull Lake, *Canada* 101 C7
Gullegem, *Belgium* 17 G2
Güllük, *Turkey* 66 E2
Gulma, *Nigeria* 79 C5
Gulmarg, *India* 63 B6
Gülnar, *Turkey* 66 E5
Gulpen, *Neths.* 17 G7
Gülşehir, *Turkey* 66 D6
Gulshad, *Kazakhstan* 44 E8
Gulsvik, *Norway* 10 D3
Gulu, *Uganda* 82 B3
Gulwe, *Tanzania* 82 D4
Gulyaypole, *Ukraine* 42 C7
Gum Lake, *Australia* 91 E3
Gumal →, *Pakistan* 62 D4
Gumbaz, *Pakistan* 62 D3
Gumel, *Nigeria* 79 C6
Gumiel de Hizán, *Spain* 28 D1
Gumlu, *Australia* 90 B4
Gumma □, *Japan* 49 F9
Gummersbach, *Germany* 18 D3
Gummi, *Nigeria* 79 C6
Gümüşhaciköy, *Turkey* 42 F6
Gümüşhane, *Turkey* 67 C8
Gümüşhane □, *Turkey* 67 C8
Gumzai, *Indonesia* 57 F8
Guna, *Ethiopia* 77 E4
Guna, *India* 62 G7
Gundagai, *Australia* 91 F4
Gundelfingen, *Germany* 19 G6
Gundih, *Indonesia* 57 G14
Guneydogu Toroslar, *Turkey* 67 D9
Gungu, *Zaïre* 80 F3
Gunisao →, *Canada* 101 C9
Gunisao L., *Canada* 101 C9
Gunnbjørn Fjeld, *Greenland* 4 C6
Gunnedah, *Australia* 91 E5
Gunningbar Cr. →, *Australia* 91 E4
Gunnison, *Colo., U.S.A.* 111 G10
Gunnison, *Utah, U.S.A.* 110 G8
Gunnison →, *U.S.A.* 111 G9
Gunpowder, *Australia* 90 B2
Guntakal, *India* 60 M10
Guntersville, *U.S.A.* 105 H2
Guntong, *Malaysia* 59 K3
Guntur, *India* 61 L12
Gunungapi, *Indonesia* 57 F7
Gunungsitoli, *Indonesia* 56 D1
Günz →, *Germany* 19 G6
Gunza, *Angola* 80 G2
Günzburg, *Germany* 19 G6
Gunzenhausen, *Germany* 19 F6
Guo He →, *China* 51 H9
Guoyang, *China* 50 H9
Gupis, *Pakistan* 63 A5
Gura Humorului, *Romania* 38 B8
Gurag, *Ethiopia* 77 F4
Gurdaspur, *India* 62 C6
Gurdon, *U.S.A.* 109 J8
Gurdzhaani, *Georgia* 43 F11
Gurgaon, *India* 62 E7
Gürgentepe, *Turkey* 67 C8
Gurguéia →, *Brazil* 122 C3
Gurha, *India* 62 G4
Guri, Embalse de, *Venezuela* 121 B5
Gurk →, *Austria* 21 J4
Gurkha, *Nepal* 63 E11
Gurley, *Australia* 91 D4
Gurué, *Mozam.* 83 F4
Gurun, *Malaysia* 59 K3
Gürün, *Turkey* 66 D7
Gurupá, *Brazil* 121 D7
Gurupá, I. Grande de, *Brazil* 121 D7
Gurupi, *Brazil* 123 D2
Gurupi →, *Brazil* 122 B2
Gurupi, Serra do, *Brazil* 122 C2
Guryev = Atyrau, *Kazakhstan* 43 C14
Gus-Khrustalnyy, *Russia* 41 D12
Gusau, *Nigeria* 79 C6
Gusev, *Russia* 40 D3
Gushan, *China* 51 E12
Gushi, *China* 53 A10
Gushiago, *Ghana* 79 D4
Gusinje, *Montenegro* 21 N9
Gusinoozersk, *Russia* 45 D11
Gúspini, *Italy* 34 C1
Gustanj, *Slovenia* 33 B11
Gustine, *U.S.A.* 111 H3
Güstrow, *Germany* 18 B8
Gusum, *Sweden* 11 F10
Guta = Kalárovo, *Slovak Rep.* 21 H7
Gütersloh, *Germany* 18 D4
Gutha, *Australia* 89 E2
Guthalongra, *Australia* 90 B4
Guthrie, *U.S.A.* 109 H6
Gutian, *China* 53 D12
Gutiérrez, *Bolivia* 125 D5
Guttannen, *Switz.* 23 C6
Guttenberg, *U.S.A.* 108 D9
Guyana ■, *S. Amer.* 121 B6
Guyane française ■ = French Guiana ■, *S. Amer.* 121 C7
Guyang, *China* 50 D6
Guyenne, *France* 26 D4
Guymon, *U.S.A.* 109 G4
Guyra, *Australia* 91 E5
Guyuan, *Hebei, China* 50 D8
Guyuan, *Ningxia Huizu, China* 50 F4
Guzhang, *China* 52 C7
Guzhen, *China* 51 H9
Guzmán, L. de, *Mexico* 114 A3
Gwa, *Burma* 61 L19
Gwaai, *Zimbabwe* 83 F2
Gwabegar, *Australia* 91 E4
Gwadabawa, *Nigeria* 79 C6
Gwādar, *Pakistan* 60 G3
Gwagwada, *Nigeria* 79 C6
Gwalia, *Australia* 89 E3
Gwalior, *India* 62 F8
Gwanda, *Zimbabwe* 83 G2
Gwandu, *Nigeria* 79 C5
Gwane, *Zaïre* 82 B2
Gwaram, *Nigeria* 79 C7
Gwarzo, *Nigeria* 79 C6
Gweebarra B., *Ireland* 15 B3
Gweedore, *Ireland* 15 A3
Gwent □, *U.K.* 13 F5
Gweru, *Zimbabwe* 83 F2
Gwi, *Nigeria* 79 D6
Gwinn, *U.S.A.* 104 B2
Gwio Kura, *Nigeria* 79 C7
Gwol, *Ghana* 78 C4
Gwoza, *Nigeria* 79 C7
Gwydir →, *Australia* 91 D4
Gwynedd □, *U.K.* 12 E4
Gyandzha, *Azerbaijan* 43 F12
Gyaring Hu, *China* 54 C4
Gydanskiy P-ov., *Russia* 44 C8
Gympie, *Australia* 91 D5
Gyoma, *Hungary* 21 J10
Gyöngyös, *Hungary* 21 H9
Györ, *Hungary* 21 H7
Gypsum Pt., *Canada* 100 A6
Gypsumville, *Canada* 101 C9
Gyula, *Hungary* 21 J11
Gyumri = Kumayri, *Armenia* 43 F10
Gzhatsk, *Russia* 40 D9

H

Ha 'Arava →, *Israel* 69 E4
Ha Coi, *Vietnam* 58 B6
Ha Dong, *Vietnam* 58 B5
Ha Giang, *Vietnam* 58 A5
Ha Tien, *Vietnam* 59 G5
Ha Tinh, *Vietnam* 58 C5
Ha Trung, *Vietnam* 58 C5
Haacht, *Belgium* 17 G5
Haag, *Germany* 19 G8
Haaksbergen, *Neths.* 16 D9
Haaltert, *Belgium* 17 G4
Haamstede, *Neths.* 17 E3
Haapamäki, *Finland* 8 E18
Haapsalu, *Estonia* 40 B3
Haarlem, *Neths.* 16 D5
Haast →, *N.Z.* 87 K2
Haast Bluff, *Australia* 88 D5
Haastrecht, *Neths.* 16 E5
Hab Nadi Chauki, *Pakistan* 62 G2
Habaswein, *Kenya* 82 B4
Habay, *Canada* 100 B5
Habay-la-Neuve, *Belgium* 17 J7

Hauterive

Habbānīyah, *Iraq* 64 C4
Haboro, *Japan* 48 B10
Haccourt, *Belgium* 17 G7
Hachenburg, *Germany* 18 E3
Hachijō-Jima, *Japan* 49 H9
Hachinohe, *Japan* 48 D10
Hachiōji, *Japan* 49 G9
Hachŏn, *N. Korea* 51 D15
Hachy, *Belgium* 17 J7
Hacıbektaş, *Turkey* 66 D6
Hacılar, *Turkey* 66 D6
Hackensack, *U.S.A.* 107 F10
Haçli Gölü, *Turkey* 67 D10
Hadali, *Pakistan* 62 C5
Hadarba, Ras, *Sudan* 76 C4
Hadarom □, *Israel* 69 E3
Haddington, *U.K.* 14 F6
Hadejia, *Nigeria* 79 C7
Hadejia →, *Nigeria* 79 C7
Haden, *Australia* 91 D5
Ḩadera, *Israel* 69 C3
Ḩadera, N. →, *Israel* 69 C3
Haderslev, *Denmark* 11 J3
Hadhramaut = Ḩaḑramawt, *Yemen* 68 D4
Hadım, *Turkey* 66 E5
Hadjeb El Aïoun, *Tunisia* 75 A6
Hadong, *S. Korea* 51 G14
Ḩaḑramawt, *Yemen* 68 D4
Ḩadrānīyah, *Iraq* 64 C4
Hadrian's Wall, *U.K.* 12 C5
Hadsten, *Denmark* 11 H4
Hadsund, *Denmark* 11 H4
Haeju, *N. Korea* 51 E13
Haenam, *S. Korea* 51 G14
Haerhpin = Harbin, *China* 51 B14
Hafar al Bāţin, *Si. Arabia* 64 D5
Hafik, *Turkey* 66 D7
Ḩafīrat al 'Aydā, *Si. Arabia* 64 E3
Hafizabad, *Pakistan* 62 C5
Haflong, *India* 61 G18
Hafnarfjörður, *Iceland* 8 D3
Hafun, Ras, *Somali Rep.* 68 E5
Hagalil, *Israel* 69 C4
Hagen, *Germany* 18 D3
Hagenow, *Germany* 18 B7
Hagerman, *U.S.A.* 109 J2
Hagerstown, *U.S.A.* 104 F7
Hagetmau, *France* 26 E3
Hagfors, *Sweden* 9 F12
Häggenås, *Sweden* 10 A8
Hagi, *Iceland* 8 D2
Hagi, *Japan* 49 G5
Hagolan, *Syria* 69 B4
Hagondange-Briey, *France* 25 C13
Hags Hd., *Ireland* 15 D2
Hague, C. de la, *France* 24 C5
Hague, The = 's-Gravenhage, *Neths.* 16 D4
Haguenau, *France* 25 D14
Hai □, *Tanzania* 82 C4
Hai Duong, *Vietnam* 58 B6
Hai'an, *Guangdong, China* 53 G8
Hai'an, *Jiangsu, China* 53 A13
Haicheng, *Fujian, China* 53 E11
Haicheng, *Liaoning, China* 51 D12
Haidar Khel, *Afghan.* 62 C3
Haifa = Ḩefa, *Israel* 69 C3
Haifeng, *China* 53 F10
Haig, *Australia* 89 F4
Haiger, *Germany* 18 E4
Haikang, *China* 53 G8
Haikou, *China* 54 D6
Ḩā'il, *Si. Arabia* 64 E4
Hailar, *China* 54 B6
Hailey, *U.S.A.* 110 E6
Haileybury, *Canada* 98 C4
Hailin, *China* 51 B15
Hailing Dao, *China* 53 G8
Hailong, *China* 51 C13
Hailun, *China* 54 B7
Hailuoto, *Finland* 8 D18
Haimen, *Guangdong, China* 53 F11
Haimen, *Jiangsu, China* 53 B13
Haimen, *Zhejiang, China* 53 C13
Hainan □, *China* 54 E5
Hainaut □, *Belgium* 17 H4
Haines, *U.S.A.* 110 D5
Haines City, *U.S.A.* 105 L5
Haines Junction, *Canada* 100 A1
Haining, *China* 53 B13
Haiphong, *Vietnam* 54 D5
Haiti ■, *W. Indies* 117 C5
Haiya Junction, *Sudan* 76 D4
Haiyan, *China* 53 B13
Haiyang, *China* 51 F11
Haiyuan, *Guangxi Zhuangzu, China* 52 F6
Haiyuan, *Ningxia Huizu, China* 50 F3
Haizhou, *China* 51 G10
Haizhou Wan, *China* 51 G10
Haja, *Indonesia* 57 E7
Hajar Bangar, *Sudan* 73 F9
Hajdúböszörmény, *Hungary* 21 H11
Hajdúszoboszló, *Hungary* 21 H11
Hajipur, *India* 63 G11
Ḩājjī Muḩsin, *Iraq* 64 C5
Ḩājjīābād, *Eşfahan, Iran* 65 C7
Ḩājjīābād, *Hormozgān, Iran* 65 D7
Hakansson, Mts., *Zaïre* 83 D2
Håkantorp, *Sweden* 11 F6
Hakkâri, *Turkey* 67 E10
Hakkâri □, *Turkey* 67 E10
Hakkâri Dağları, *Turkey* 67 E10
Hakken-Zan, *Japan* 49 G7
Hakodate, *Japan* 48 D10
Haku-San, *Japan* 49 F8
Hakui, *Japan* 49 F8
Hala, *Pakistan* 60 G6
Ḩalab, *Syria* 64 B3
Ḩalabjah, *Iraq* 64 C5
Halaib, *Sudan* 76 C4
Halanzy, *Belgium* 17 J7
Hālat' Ammār, *Si. Arabia* 64 D3
Halbā, *Lebanon* 69 A5
Halberstadt, *Germany* 18 D7
Halcombe, *N.Z.* 87 J5
Halcon, Mt., *Phil.* 57 B6
Halden, *Norway* 10 E5
Haldensleben, *Germany* 18 C7
Haldia, *India* 61 H16
Haldwani, *India* 63 E8
Hale →, *Australia* 90 C2
Haleakala Crater, *U.S.A.* 102 H16
Halen, *Belgium* 17 G6
Haleyville, *U.S.A.* 105 H2
Half Assini, *Ghana* 78 D4
Halfway →, *Canada* 100 B4
Haliburton, *Canada* 98 C4
Halifax, *Australia* 90 B4
Halifax, *Canada* 99 D7
Halifax, *U.K.* 12 D6
Halifax B., *Australia* 90 B4
Halifax I., *Namibia* 84 D2
Halīl →, *Iran* 65 E8
Hall, *Austria* 19 H7
Hall Beach, *Canada* 97 B11
Hall Pt., *Australia* 88 C3
Hallands län □, *Sweden* 11 H6
Hallands Väderö, *Sweden* 11 H6
Hallandsås, *Sweden* 11 H7
Halle, *Belgium* 17 G4
Halle, *Nordrhein-Westfalen, Germany* 18 C4
Halle, *Sachsen-Anhalt, Germany* 18 D7
Hällefors, *Sweden* 9 G13
Hallein, *Austria* 21 H3
Hällekis, *Sweden* 11 F7
Hallett, *Australia* 91 E2
Hallettsville, *U.S.A.* 109 L6
Hällevadsholm, *Sweden* 11 F5
Halliday, *U.S.A.* 108 B3
Halliday L., *Canada* 101 A7
Hallim, *S. Korea* 51 H14
Hallingdal →, *Norway* 9 F10
Hällnäs, *Sweden* 8 D15
Hallock, *U.S.A.* 101 D9
Halls Creek, *Australia* 88 C4
Hallstahammar, *Sweden* 10 E10
Hallstead, *U.S.A.* 107 E9
Halmahera, *Indonesia* 57 D7
Halmeu, *Romania* 38 B6
Halmstad, *Sweden* 11 H6
Halq el Oued, *Tunisia* 75 A7
Hals, *Denmark* 11 H4
Halsafjorden, *Norway* 10 A2
Hälsingborg = Helsingborg, *Sweden* 11 H6
Halstad, *U.S.A.* 108 B6
Haltdalen, *Norway* 10 B5
Haltern, *Germany* 18 D3
Halul, *Qatar* 65 E7
Ḩalvān, *Iran* 65 C8
Ham, *France* 25 C10
Ham Tan, *Vietnam* 59 G6
Ham Yen, *Vietnam* 58 A5
Hamab, *Namibia* 84 D2
Hamad, *Sudan* 77 D3
Hamada, *Japan* 49 G6
Hamadān, *Iran* 65 C6
Hamadān □, *Iran* 65 C6
Hamadia, *Algeria* 75 A5
Hamāh, *Syria* 64 C3
Hamamatsu, *Japan* 49 G8
Hamar, *Norway* 10 D5
Hamarøy, *Norway* 8 B13
Hamâta, Gebel, *Egypt* 76 C3
Hambantota, *Sri Lanka* 60 R12
Hamber Prov. Park, *Canada* 100 C5
Hamburg, *Germany* 18 B5
Hamburg, *Ark., U.S.A.* 109 J9
Hamburg, *Iowa, U.S.A.* 108 E7
Hamburg, *N.Y., U.S.A.* 106 D6
Hamburg, *Pa., U.S.A.* 107 F9
Hamburg □, *Germany* 18 B6
Ḩamḑ, W. al →, *Si. Arabia* 64 E3
Hamden, *U.S.A.* 107 E12
Hame □ = Hämeen lääni □, *Finland* 9 F18
Hämeen lääni □, *Finland* 9 F18
Hämeenlinna, *Finland* 9 F18
Hamélé, *Ghana* 78 C4
Hamelin Pool, *Australia* 89 E1
Hameln, *Germany* 18 C5
Hamer Koke, *Ethiopia* 77 F4
Hamerkaz □, *Israel* 69 C3
Hamersley Ra., *Australia* 88 D2
Hamhung, *N. Korea* 51 E14
Hami, *China* 54 B4
Hamilton, *Australia* 91 F3
Hamilton, *Canada* 98 D4
Hamilton, *N.Z.* 87 G5
Hamilton, *U.K.* 14 F4
Hamilton, *Mo., U.S.A.* 108 F8
Hamilton, *Mont., U.S.A.* 110 C6
Hamilton, *N.Y., U.S.A.* 107 D9
Hamilton, *Ohio, U.S.A.* 104 F3
Hamilton, *Tex., U.S.A.* 109 K5
Hamilton →, *Australia* 90 C2
Hamilton City, *U.S.A.* 112 F4
Hamilton Hotel, *Australia* 90 C3
Hamilton Inlet, *Canada* 99 B8
Hamiota, *Canada* 101 C8
Hamlet, *U.S.A.* 105 H6
Hamley Bridge, *Australia* 91 E2
Hamlin = Hameln, *Germany* 18 C5
Hamlin, *N.Y., U.S.A.* 106 C7
Hamlin, *Tex., U.S.A.* 109 J4
Hamm, *Germany* 18 D3
Hammam Bouhadjar, *Algeria* 75 A4
Hammamet, *Tunisia* 75 A7
Hammamet, G. de, *Tunisia* 75 A7
Hammarstrand, *Sweden* 10 A10
Hamme, *Belgium* 17 F4
Hamme-Mille, *Belgium* 17 G5
Hammel, *Denmark* 11 H3
Hammelburg, *Germany* 19 E5
Hammerfest, *Norway* 8 A17
Hammond, *Ind., U.S.A.* 104 E2
Hammond, *La., U.S.A.* 109 K9
Hammonton, *U.S.A.* 104 F8
Hamoir, *Belgium* 17 H7
Hamont, *Belgium* 17 F7
Hamoyet, Jebel, *Sudan* 76 D4
Hampden, *N.Z.* 87 L3
Hampshire □, *U.K.* 13 F6
Hampshire Downs, *U.K.* 13 F6
Hampton, *Ark., U.S.A.* 109 J8
Hampton, *Iowa, U.S.A.* 108 D8
Hampton, *N.H., U.S.A.* 107 D14
Hampton, *S.C., U.S.A.* 105 J5
Hampton, *Va., U.S.A.* 104 G7
Hampton Tableland, *Australia* 89 F4
Hamrat esh Sheykh, *Sudan* 77 E2
Hamur, *Turkey* 67 D10
Hamyang, *S. Korea* 51 G14
Han Jiang →, *China* 53 F11
Han Shui →, *China* 53 B10
Hana, *U.S.A.* 102 H17
Hanak, *Si. Arabia* 64 E3
Hanamaki, *Japan* 48 E10
Hanang, *Tanzania* 82 C4
Hanau, *Germany* 19 E4
Hanbogd, *Mongolia* 50 C4
Hancheng, *China* 50 G6
Hanchuan, *China* 53 B9
Hancock, *Mich., U.S.A.* 108 B10
Hancock, *Minn., U.S.A.* 108 C7
Hancock, *N.Y., U.S.A.* 107 E9
Handa, *Japan* 49 G8
Handa, *Somali Rep.* 68 E5
Handan, *China* 50 F8
Handen, *Sweden* 10 E12
Handeni, *Tanzania* 82 D4
Handeni □, *Tanzania* 82 D4
Handub, *Sudan* 76 D4
Handwara, *India* 63 B6
Handzame, *Belgium* 17 F2
Hanegev, *Israel* 69 E3
Haney, *Canada* 100 D4
Hanford, *U.S.A.* 111 H4
Hang Chat, *Thailand* 58 C2
Hang Dong, *Thailand* 58 C2
Hangang →, *S. Korea* 51 F14
Hangayn Nuruu, *Mongolia* 54 B4
Hangchou = Hangzhou, *China* 53 B13
Hanggin Houqi, *China* 50 D4
Hanggin Qi, *China* 50 E5
Hangö, *Finland* 9 G17
Hangu, *China* 51 E9
Hangzhou, *China* 53 B13
Hangzhou Wan, *China* 53 B13
Hanhongor, *Mongolia* 50 C3
Ḩanīdh, *Si. Arabia* 65 E6
Ḩanīsh, *Yemen* 68 E3
Hanjiang, *China* 53 E12
Hankinson, *U.S.A.* 108 B6
Hanko = Hangö, *Finland* 9 G17
Hanko, *Finland* 9 G17
Hankou, *China* 53 B10
Hanksville, *U.S.A.* 111 G8
Hanle, *India* 63 C8
Hanmer Springs, *N.Z.* 87 K4
Hann →, *Australia* 88 C4
Hann, Mt., *Australia* 88 C4
Hanna, *Canada* 100 C6
Hannaford, *U.S.A.* 108 B5
Hannah, *U.S.A.* 108 A5
Hannah B., *Canada* 98 B4
Hannibal, *U.S.A.* 108 F9
Hannik, *Sudan* 76 D3
Hannover, *Germany* 18 C5
Hannut, *Belgium* 17 G6
Hanoi, *Vietnam* 54 D5
Hanover = Hannover, *Germany* 18 C5
Hanover, *Canada* 106 B3
Hanover, *S. Africa* 84 E3
Hanover, *N.H., U.S.A.* 107 C12
Hanover, *Ohio, U.S.A.* 106 F2
Hanover, *Pa., U.S.A.* 104 F7
Hanover, I., *Chile* 128 D2
Hanshou, *China* 53 C8
Hansi, *India* 62 E6
Hanson, L., *Australia* 91 E2
Hanyang, *China* 53 B10
Hanyin, *China* 52 A7
Hanyuan, *China* 52 C4
Hanzhong, *China* 50 H4
Hanzhuang, *China* 51 G9
Haora, *India* 63 H13
Haoxue, *China* 53 B9
Haparanda, *Sweden* 8 D18
Hapert, *Neths.* 17 F6
Happy, *U.S.A.* 109 H4
Happy Camp, *U.S.A.* 110 F2
Happy Valley-Goose Bay, *Canada* 99 B7
Hapsu, *N. Korea* 51 D15
Hapur, *India* 62 E7
Ḩaql, *Si. Arabia* 69 F3
Haquira, *Peru* 124 C3
Har, *Indonesia* 57 F8
Har-Ayrag, *Mongolia* 50 B5
Har Hu, *China* 54 C4
Har Us Nuur, *Mongolia* 54 B4
Har Yehuda, *Israel* 69 D3
Ḩaraḑ, *Si. Arabia* 68 C4
Haranomachi, *Japan* 48 F10
Harardera, *Somali Rep.* 68 G4
Harare, *Zimbabwe* 83 F3
Harat, *Eritrea* 77 D4
Harazé, *Chad* 73 F8
Harbin, *China* 51 B14
Harbiye, *Turkey* 66 E7
Harboør, *Denmark* 11 H2
Harbor Beach, *U.S.A.* 104 D4
Harbor Springs, *U.S.A.* 104 C3
Harbour Breton, *Canada* 99 C8
Harbour Grace, *Canada* 99 C9
Harburg, *Germany* 18 B5
Hårby, *Denmark* 11 J4
Harda, *India* 62 H7
Hardangerfjorden, *Norway* 9 F8
Hardap Dam, *Namibia* 84 C2
Hardegarijp, *Neths.* 16 B7
Hardenberg, *Neths.* 16 C9
Harderwijk, *Neths.* 16 D7
Hardey →, *Australia* 88 D2
Hardin, *U.S.A.* 110 D10
Harding, *S. Africa* 85 E4
Harding Ra., *Australia* 88 C3
Hardisty, *Canada* 100 C6
Hardman, *U.S.A.* 110 D4
Hardoi, *India* 63 F9
Hardwar = Haridwar, *India* 62 E8
Hardwick, *U.S.A.* 107 B12
Hardy, *U.S.A.* 109 G9
Hardy, Pen., *Chile* 128 E3
Hare B., *Canada* 99 B8
Harelbeke, *Belgium* 17 G2
Haren, *Germany* 18 C3
Haren, *Neths.* 16 B9
Harer, *Ethiopia* 68 F3
Harerge □, *Ethiopia* 77 F5
Hareto, *Ethiopia* 77 F4
Harfleur, *France* 24 C7
Hargeisa, *Somali Rep.* 68 F3
Hargshamn, *Sweden* 9 F15
Hari →, *Indonesia* 56 E2
Haria, *Canary Is.* 36 E6
Haricha, Hamada el, *Mali* 74 D4
Haridwar, *India* 62 E8
Haringhata →, *Bangla.* 61 J16
Haringvliet, *Neths.* 16 E4
Harīrūd →, *Asia* 60 A2
Harlan, *Iowa, U.S.A.* 108 E7
Harlan, *Ky., U.S.A.* 105 G4
Harlech, *U.K.* 12 E3
Harlem, *U.S.A.* 110 B9
Harlingen, *Neths.* 16 B6
Harlingen, *U.S.A.* 109 M6
Harlowton, *U.S.A.* 110 C9
Harmånger, *Sweden* 10 C11
Harmil, *Eritrea* 77 D5
Harney Basin, *U.S.A.* 110 E4
Harney L., *U.S.A.* 110 E4
Harney Peak, *U.S.A.* 108 D3
Härnön, *Sweden* 10 B12
Härnösand, *Sweden* 10 B11
Haro, *Spain* 28 C2
Harp L., *Canada* 99 A7
Harper, *Liberia* 78 E3
Harplinge, *Sweden* 11 H6
Harrand, *Pakistan* 62 E4
Harriman, *U.S.A.* 105 H3
Harrington Harbour, *Canada* 99 B8
Harris, *U.K.* 14 D2
Harris, Sd. of, *U.K.* 14 D1
Harris L., *Australia* 91 E2
Harrisburg, *Ill., U.S.A.* 109 G10
Harrisburg, *Nebr., U.S.A.* 108 E3
Harrisburg, *Oreg., U.S.A.* 110 D2
Harrisburg, *Pa., U.S.A.* 106 F8
Harrismith, *S. Africa* 85 D4
Harrison, *Ark., U.S.A.* 109 G8
Harrison, *Idaho, U.S.A.* 110 C5
Harrison, *Nebr., U.S.A.* 108 D3
Harrison, C., *Canada* 99 B8
Harrison Bay, *U.S.A.* 96 A4
Harrison L., *Canada* 100 D4
Harrisonburg, *U.S.A.* 104 F6
Harrisonville, *U.S.A.* 108 F7
Harriston, *Canada* 98 D3
Harrisville, *U.S.A.* 106 B1
Harrogate, *U.K.* 12 D6
Harrow, *U.K.* 13 F7
Harsefeld, *Germany* 18 B5
Harsīn, *Iran* 64 C5
Harskamp, *Neths.* 16 D7
Harstad, *Norway* 8 B14
Hart, *U.S.A.* 104 D2
Hart, L., *Australia* 91 E2
Hartbees →, *S. Africa* 84 D3
Hartberg, *Austria* 21 H5
Hartford, *Conn., U.S.A.* 107 E12
Hartford, *Ky., U.S.A.* 104 G2
Hartford, *S. Dak., U.S.A.* 108 D6
Hartford, *Wis., U.S.A.* 108 D10
Hartford City, *U.S.A.* 104 E3
Hartland, *Canada* 99 C6
Hartland Pt., *U.K.* 13 F3
Hartlepool, *U.K.* 12 C6
Hartley Bay, *Canada* 100 C3
Hartmannberge, *Namibia* 84 B1
Hartney, *Canada* 101 D8
Harts →, *S. Africa* 84 D3
Hartselle, *U.S.A.* 105 H2
Hartshorne, *U.S.A.* 109 H7
Hartsville, *U.S.A.* 105 H5
Hartwell, *U.S.A.* 105 H4
Harunabad, *Pakistan* 62 E5
Harvand, *Iran* 65 D7
Harvey, *Australia* 89 F2
Harvey, *Ill., U.S.A.* 104 E2
Harvey, *N. Dak., U.S.A.* 108 B5
Harwich, *U.K.* 13 F9
Haryana □, *India* 62 E7
Harz, *Germany* 18 D6
Harzé, *Belgium* 17 H7
Harzgerode, *Germany* 18 D7
Hasaheisa, *Sudan* 77 E3
Hasan Kīādeh, *Iran* 65 B6
Ḩasanābād, *Iran* 65 C7
Hasanpur, *India* 62 E8
Haselünne, *Germany* 18 C3
Hashimoto, *Japan* 49 G7
Hashtjerd, *Iran* 65 C6
Håsjö, *Sweden* 10 A10
Haskell, *Okla., U.S.A.* 109 H7
Haskell, *Tex., U.S.A.* 109 J5
Haslach, *Germany* 19 G4
Haslev, *Denmark* 11 J5
Hasparren, *France* 26 E2
Hassa, *Turkey* 66 E7
Hasselt, *Belgium* 17 G6
Hasselt, *Neths.* 16 C8
Hassene, Adrar, *Algeria* 75 D5
Hassfurt, *Germany* 19 E6
Hassi Berrekrem, *Algeria* 75 B6
Hassi bou Khelala, *Algeria* 75 B4
Hassi Daoula, *Algeria* 75 B6
Hassi Djafou, *Algeria* 75 B5
Hassi el Abiod, *Algeria* 75 B5
Hassi el Biod, *Algeria* 75 C6
Hassi el Gassi, *Algeria* 75 B6
Hassi el Hadjar, *Algeria* 75 B5
Hassi er Rmel, *Algeria* 75 B5
Hassi Imoulaye, *Algeria* 75 C6
Hassi Inifel, *Algeria* 75 C5
Hassi Messaoud, *Algeria* 75 B6
Hassi Rhénami, *Algeria* 75 B6
Hassi Tartrat, *Algeria* 75 B6
Hassi Zerzour, *Morocco* 74 B4
Hastière-Lavaux, *Belgium* 17 H5
Hastings, *N.Z.* 87 H6
Hastings, *U.K.* 13 G8
Hastings, *Mich., U.S.A.* 104 D3
Hastings, *Minn., U.S.A.* 108 C8
Hastings, *Nebr., U.S.A.* 108 E5
Hastings Ra., *Australia* 91 E5
Hat Yai, *Thailand* 59 J3
Hatanbulag, *Mongolia* 50 C5
Hatay = Antalya, *Turkey* 66 E4
Hatay □, *Turkey* 66 E7
Hatch, *U.S.A.* 111 K10
Hatches Creek, *Australia* 90 C2
Hatchet L., *Canada* 101 B8
Haţeg, *Romania* 38 D5
Haţeg, Mţii., *Romania* 38 D6
Hatert, *Neths.* 16 E7
Hateruma-Shima, *Japan* 49 M1
Hatfield P.O., *Australia* 91 E3
Hatgal, *Mongolia* 54 A5
Hathras, *India* 62 F8
Hatia, *Bangla.* 61 H17
Hato de Corozal, *Colombia* 120 B3
Hato Mayor, *Dom. Rep.* 117 C6
Hattah, *Australia* 91 E3
Hattem, *Neths.* 16 D8
Hatteras, C., *U.S.A.* 105 H8
Hattiesburg, *U.S.A.* 109 K10
Hatvan, *Hungary* 21 H9
Hau Bon = Cheo Reo, *Vietnam* 58 F7
Hau Duc, *Vietnam* 58 E7
Haug, *Norway* 10 D4
Haugastøl, *Norway* 10 D1
Haugesund, *Norway* 9 G8
Haulerwijk, *Neths.* 16 B8
Haultain →, *Canada* 101 B7
Hauraki G., *N.Z.* 87 G5
Haut Atlas, *Morocco* 74 B3
Haut-Rhin □, *France* 25 E14
Haut Zaïre □, *Zaïre* 82 B2
Haute-Corse □, *France* 27 F13
Haute-Garonne □, *France* 26 E5
Haute-Loire □, *France* 26 C7
Haute-Marne □, *France* 25 D12
Haute-Saône □, *France* 25 E13
Haute-Savoie □, *France* 27 C10
Haute-Vienne □, *France* 26 C5
Hauterive, *Canada* 99 C6

Hautes-Alpes □, *France* 27 D10
Hautes Fagnes = Hohe Venn, *Belgium* 17 H8
Hautes Fagnes, *Belgium* 17 G8
Hautes-Pyrénées □, *France* 26 F4
Hauteville-Lompnès, *France* 27 C9
Hautmont, *France* 25 B10
Hautrage, *Belgium* 17 H3
Hauts-de-Seine □, *France* 25 D9
Hauts Plateaux, *Algeria* 75 B4
Hauzenberg, *Germany* 19 G9
Havana = La Habana, *Cuba* 116 B3
Havana, *U.S.A.* 108 E9
Havant, *U.K.* 13 G7
Havasu, L., *U.S.A.* 113 L12
Havel →, *Germany* 18 C8
Havelange, *Belgium* 17 H6
Havelian, *Pakistan* 62 B5
Havelock, *N.B., Canada* 99 C6
Havelock, *Ont., Canada* 98 D4
Havelock, *N.Z.* 87 J4
Havelte, *Neths.* 16 C8
Haverfordwest, *U.K.* 13 F3
Haverhill, *U.S.A.* 107 D13
Havering, *U.K.* 13 F8
Haverstraw, *U.S.A.* 107 E11
Håverud, *Sweden* 11 F6
Havlíčkův Brod, *Czech.* 20 F5
Havneby, *Denmark* 11 J2
Havre, *U.S.A.* 110 B9
Havre-Aubert, *Canada* 99 C7
Havre-St.-Pierre, *Canada* 99 B7
Havza, *Turkey* 66 C6
Haw →, *U.S.A.* 105 H6
Hawaii □, *U.S.A.* 102 H16
Hawaii I., *Pac. Oc.* 102 J17
Hawaiian Is., *Pac. Oc.* 102 H17
Hawaiian Ridge, *Pac. Oc.* 93 E11
Hawarden, *Canada* 101 C7
Hawarden, *U.S.A.* 108 D6
Hawea, L., *N.Z.* 87 L2
Hawera, *N.Z.* 87 H5
Hawick, *U.K.* 14 F6
Hawk Junction, *Canada* 98 C3
Hawke B., *N.Z.* 87 H6
Hawker, *Australia* 91 E2
Hawkesbury, *Canada* 98 C5
Hawkesbury I., *Canada* 100 C3
Hawkesbury Pt., *Australia* 90 A1
Hawkinsville, *U.S.A.* 105 J4
Hawkwood, *Australia* 91 D5
Hawley, *U.S.A.* 108 B6
Hawrān, *Syria* 69 C5
Hawsh Mūssá, *Lebanon* 69 B4
Hawthorne, *U.S.A.* 110 G4
Hawzen, *Ethiopia* 77 E4
Haxtun, *U.S.A.* 108 E3
Hay, *Australia* 91 E3
Hay →, *Australia* 90 C2
Hay →, *Canada* 100 A5
Hay, C., *Australia* 88 B4
Hay L., *Canada* 100 B5
Hay Lakes, *Canada* 100 C6
Hay-on-Wye, *U.K.* 13 E4
Hay River, *Canada* 100 A5
Hay Springs, *U.S.A.* 108 D3
Hayachine-San, *Japan* 48 E10
Hayange, *France* 25 C13
Hayden, *Ariz., U.S.A.* 111 K8
Hayden, *Colo., U.S.A.* 110 F10
Haydon, *Australia* 90 B3
Hayes, *U.S.A.* 108 C4
Hayes →, *Canada* 101 B10
Haymana, *Turkey* 66 D5
Haynesville, *U.S.A.* 109 J8
Hayrabolu, *Turkey* 66 C2
Hays, *Canada* 100 C6
Hays, *U.S.A.* 108 F5
Hayward, *Calif., U.S.A.* 112 H4
Hayward, *Wis., U.S.A.* 108 B9
Haywards Heath, *U.K.* 13 F7
Hazafon □, *Israel* 69 C4
Hazar Gölü, *Turkey* 67 D8
Hazarām, Kūh-e, *Iran* 65 D8
Hazard, *U.S.A.* 104 G4
Hazaribag, *India* 63 H11
Hazaribag Road, *India* 63 G11
Hazebrouck, *France* 25 B9
Hazelton, *Canada* 100 B3
Hazelton, *U.S.A.* 108 B4
Hazen, *N. Dak., U.S.A.* 108 B4
Hazen, *Nev., U.S.A.* 110 G4
Hazerswoude, *Neths.* 16 D5
Hazlehurst, *Ga., U.S.A.* 105 K4
Hazlehurst, *Miss., U.S.A.* 109 K9
Hazleton, *U.S.A.* 107 F9
Hazlett, L., *Australia* 88 D4
Hazor, *Israel* 69 B4
He Xian, *Anhui, China* 53 B12
He Xian, *Guangxi Zhuangzu, China* 53 E8
Head of Bight, *Australia* 89 F5
Headlands, *Zimbabwe* 83 F3
Healdsburg, *U.S.A.* 112 G4
Healdton, *U.S.A.* 109 H6
Healesville, *Australia* 91 F4
Heanor, *U.K.* 12 D6
Heard I., *Ind. Oc.* 3 G13
Hearne, *U.S.A.* 109 K6
Hearne B., *Canada* 101 A9
Hearne L., *Canada* 100 A6
Hearst, *Canada* 98 C3
Heart →, *U.S.A.* 108 B4
Heart's Content, *Canada* 99 C9
Heath →, *Bolivia* 124 C4
Heath Pt., *Canada* 99 C7
Heath Steele, *Canada* 99 C6
Heavener, *U.S.A.* 109 H7
Hebbronville, *U.S.A.* 109 M5
Hebei □, *China* 50 E9
Hebel, *Australia* 91 D4
Heber, *U.S.A.* 113 N11
Heber Springs, *U.S.A.* 109 H9
Hebert, *Canada* 101 C7
Hebgen L., *U.S.A.* 110 D8
Hebi, *China* 50 G8
Hebrides, *U.K.* 14 D1
Hebron = Al Khalīl, *Jordan* 69 D4
Hebron, *Canada* 97 C13
Hebron, *N. Dak., U.S.A.* 108 B3
Hebron, *Nebr., U.S.A.* 108 E6
Hecate Str., *Canada* 100 C2
Hechi, *China* 52 E7
Hechingen, *Germany* 19 G4
Hechtel, *Belgium* 17 F6
Hechuan, *China* 52 B6
Hecla, *U.S.A.* 108 C5
Hecla I., *Canada* 101 C9
Heddal, *Norway* 10 E3
Hédé, *France* 24 D5
Hede, *Sweden* 10 B7
Hedemora, *Sweden* 9 F13
Hedley, *U.S.A.* 109 H4
Hedmark fylke □, *Norway* 10 C5
Hedrum, *Norway* 10 E4
Heeg, *Neths.* 16 C7
Heegermeer, *Neths.* 16 C7
Heemskerk, *Neths.* 16 C5
Heemstede, *Neths.* 16 D5
Heer, *Neths.* 17 G7
Heerde, *Neths.* 16 D8
's Heerenburg, *Neths.* 16 E8
Heerenveen, *Neths.* 16 C7
Heerhugowaard, *Neths.* 16 C5
Heerlen, *Neths.* 17 G7
Heers, *Belgium* 17 G6
Heesch, *Neths.* 16 E7
Heestert, *Belgium* 17 G2
Heeze, *Neths.* 17 F7
Ḥefa, *Israel* 69 C3
Ḥefa □, *Israel* 69 C4
Hefei, *China* 53 B11
Hegang, *China* 54 B8
Hegyalja, *Hungary* 21 G11
Heichengzhen, *China* 50 F4
Heide, *Germany* 18 A5
Heidelberg, *Germany* 19 F4
Heidelberg, *C. Prov., S. Africa* 84 E3
Heidelberg, *Trans., S. Africa* 85 D4
Heidenheim, *Germany* 19 G6
Heijing, *China* 52 E3
Heilbron, *S. Africa* 85 D4
Heilbronn, *Germany* 19 F5
Heiligenblut, *Austria* 21 H2
Heiligenhafen, *Germany* 18 A6
Heiligenstadt, *Germany* 18 D6
Heilongjiang □, *China* 51 B14
Heilunkiang = Heilongjiang □, *China* 51 B14
Heino, *Neths.* 16 D8
Heinola, *Finland* 9 F19
Heinsch, *Belgium* 17 J7
Heinze Is., *Burma* 61 M20
Heishan, *China* 51 D12
Heishui, *Liaoning, China* 51 C10
Heishui, *Sichuan, China* 52 A4
Heist, *Belgium* 17 F2
Heist-op-den-Berg, *Belgium* 17 F5
Hejaz = Al Ḥijāz, *Si. Arabia* 68 B2
Hejian, *China* 50 E9
Hejiang, *China* 52 C5
Hejin, *China* 50 G6
Hekelgem, *Belgium* 17 G4
Hekımhan, *Turkey* 67 D7
Hekla, *Iceland* 8 E4
Hekou, *Gansu, China* 50 F2
Hekou, *Guangdong, China* 53 F9
Hekou, *Yunnan, China* 54 D5
Helagsfjället, *Sweden* 10 B6
Helan Shan, *China* 50 E3
Helchteren, *Belgium* 17 F6
Helden, *Neths.* 17 F7
Helechosa, *Spain* 31 F6
Helena, *Ark., U.S.A.* 109 H9
Helena, *Mont., U.S.A.* 110 C7
Helendale, *U.S.A.* 113 L9
Helensburgh, *U.K.* 14 E4
Helensville, *N.Z.* 87 G5
Helgeroa, *Norway* 10 F3
Helgoland, *Germany* 18 A3
Heligoland = Helgoland, *Germany* 18 A3
Heligoland B. = Deutsche Bucht, *Germany* 18 A4
Heliopolis, *Egypt* 76 H7
Hellebæk, *Denmark* 11 H6
Hellendoorn, *Neths.* 16 D8
Hellevoetsluis, *Neths.* 16 E4
Hellín, *Spain* 29 G3
Helmand □, *Afghan.* 60 D4
Helmand →, *Afghan.* 60 D2
Helme →, *Germany* 18 D7
Helmond, *Neths.* 17 F7
Helmsdale, *U.K.* 14 C5
Helmstedt, *Germany* 18 C7
Helnæs, *Denmark* 11 J4
Helong, *China* 51 C15
Helper, *U.S.A.* 110 G8
Helsingborg, *Sweden* 11 H6
Helsinge, *Denmark* 11 H6
Helsingfors, *Finland* 9 F18
Helsingør, *Denmark* 11 H6
Helsinki, *Finland* 9 F18
Helston, *U.K.* 13 G2
Helvellyn, *U.K.* 12 C4
Helvoirt, *Neths.* 17 E6
Helwân, *Egypt* 76 J7
Hemet, *U.S.A.* 113 M10
Hemingford, *U.S.A.* 108 D3
Hemphill, *U.S.A.* 109 K8
Hempstead, *U.S.A.* 109 K6
Hemse, *Sweden* 9 H15
Hemsö, *Sweden* 10 B12
Henan □, *China* 50 G8
Henares →, *Spain* 28 E1
Henashi-Misaki, *Japan* 48 D9
Hendaye, *France* 26 E2
Hendek, *Turkey* 66 C4
Henderson, *Argentina* 126 D3
Henderson, *Ky., U.S.A.* 104 G2
Henderson, *N.C., U.S.A.* 105 G6
Henderson, *Nev., U.S.A.* 113 J12
Henderson, *Tenn., U.S.A.* 105 H1
Henderson, *Tex., U.S.A.* 109 J7
Hendersonville, *U.S.A.* 105 H4
Hendījān, *Iran* 65 D6
Hendon, *Australia* 91 D5
Heng Xian, *China* 52 F7
Hengcheng, *China* 50 E4
Hengdaohezi, *China* 51 B15
Hengelo, *Gelderland, Neths.* 16 D8
Hengelo, *Overijssel, Neths.* 16 D9
Hengfeng, *China* 53 C10
Hengshan, *Hunan, China* 53 D9
Hengshan, *Shaanxi, China* 50 F5
Hengshui, *China* 50 F8
Hengyang, *Hunan, China* 53 D9
Hengyang, *Hunan, China* 53 D9
Hénin-Beaumont, *France* 25 B9
Henlopen, C., *U.S.A.* 104 F8
Hennan, *Sweden* 10 B9
Hennebont, *France* 24 E3
Hennenman, *S. Africa* 84 D4
Hennessey, *U.S.A.* 109 G6
Hennigsdorf, *Germany* 18 C9
Henrichemont, *France* 25 E9
Henrietta, *U.S.A.* 109 J5
Henrietta, Ostrov, *Russia* 45 B16
Henrietta Maria C., *Canada* 98 A3
Henry, *U.S.A.* 108 E10
Henryetta, *U.S.A.* 109 H6
Hensall, *Canada* 106 C3
Hentiyn Nuruu, *Mongolia* 54 B5
Henty, *Australia* 91 F4
Henzada, *Burma* 61 L19
Heping, *China* 53 E10
Heppner, *U.S.A.* 110 D4
Hepu, *China* 52 G7
Hepworth, *Canada* 106 B3
Heqing, *China* 52 D3
Hequ, *China* 50 E6
Héraðsflói, *Iceland* 8 D6
Héraðsvötn →, *Iceland* 8 D4
Herald Cays, *Australia* 90 B4
Herāt, *Afghan.* 60 B3
Herāt □, *Afghan.* 60 B3
Hérault □, *France* 26 E7
Hérault →, *France* 26 E7
Herbault, *France* 24 E8
Herbert →, *Australia* 90 B4
Herbert Downs, *Australia* 90 C2
Herberton, *Australia* 90 B4
Herbignac, *France* 24 E4
Herborn, *Germany* 18 E4
Herby, *Poland* 20 E8
Herceg-novi, *Montenegro* 21 N8
Herðubreið, *Iceland* 8 D5
Hereford, *U.K.* 13 E5
Hereford, *U.S.A.* 109 H3
Hereford and Worcester □, *U.K.* 13 E5
Herefoss, *Norway* 11 F2
Herent, *Belgium* 17 G5
Herentals, *Belgium* 17 F5
Herenthout, *Belgium* 17 F5
Herfølge, *Denmark* 11 J6
Herford, *Germany* 18 C4
Héricourt, *France* 25 E13
Herington, *U.S.A.* 108 F6
Herisau, *Switz.* 23 B8
Hérisson, *France* 26 B6
Herjehogna, *Norway* 9 F12
Herk →, *Belgium* 17 G6
Herkenbosch, *Neths.* 17 F8
Herkimer, *U.S.A.* 107 D10
Herlong, *U.S.A.* 112 E6
Herm, *Chan. Is.* 24 C4
Hermagor-Pressegger See, *Austria* 21 J3
Herman, *U.S.A.* 108 C6
Hermann, *U.S.A.* 108 F9
Hermannsburg, *Germany* 18 C6
Hermannsburg Mission, *Australia* 88 D5
Hermanus, *S. Africa* 84 E2
Herment, *France* 26 C6
Hermidale, *Australia* 91 E4
Hermiston, *U.S.A.* 110 D4
Hermitage, *N.Z.* 87 K3
Hermite, I., *Chile* 128 E3
Hermon, Mt. = Ash Shaykh, J., *Lebanon* 69 B4
Hermosillo, *Mexico* 114 B2
Hernád →, *Hungary* 21 H11
Hernandarias, *Paraguay* 127 B5
Hernandez, *U.S.A.* 112 J6
Hernando, *Argentina* 126 C3
Hernando, *U.S.A.* 109 H10
Herne, *Belgium* 17 G4
Herne, *Germany* 17 E10
Herne Bay, *U.K.* 13 F9
Herning, *Denmark* 11 H2
Heroica = Caborca, *Mexico* 114 A2
Heroica Nogales = Nogales, *Mexico* 114 A2
Heron Bay, *Canada* 98 C2
Herradura, Pta. de la, *Canary Is.* 36 F5
Herreid, *U.S.A.* 108 C4
Herrera, *Spain* 31 H6
Herrera de Alcántar, *Spain* 31 F3
Herrera de Pisuerga, *Spain* 30 C6
Herrera del Duque, *Spain* 31 F5
Herrick, *Australia* 90 G4
Herrin, *U.S.A.* 109 G10
Herrljunga, *Sweden* 11 F7
Hersbruck, *Germany* 19 F7
Herseaux, *Belgium* 17 G2
Herselt, *Belgium* 17 F5
Hersonissos, *Greece* 37 D7
Herstal, *Belgium* 17 G7
Hertford, *U.K.* 13 F7
Hertfordshire □, *U.K.* 13 F7
's-Hertogenbosch, *Neths.* 17 E6
Hertzogville, *S. Africa* 84 D4
Hervás, *Spain* 30 E5
Herve, *Belgium* 17 G7
Herwijnen, *Neths.* 16 E6
Herzberg, *Brandenburg, Germany* 18 D9
Herzberg, *Niedersachsen, Germany* 18 D6
Herzele, *Belgium* 17 G3
Herzliyya, *Israel* 69 C3
Herzogenbuchsee, *Switz.* 22 B5
Ḥeṣār, *Fārs, Iran* 65 D6
Ḥeṣār, *Markazī, Iran* 65 C6
Hesdin, *France* 25 B9
Hesel, *Germany* 18 B3
Heshui, *China* 50 G5
Heshun, *China* 50 F7
Hesperange, *Lux.* 17 J8
Hesperia, *U.S.A.* 113 L9
Hesse = Hessen □, *Germany* 18 E5
Hessen □, *Germany* 18 E5
Hetch Hetchy Aqueduct, *U.S.A.* 112 H5
Hettinger, *U.S.A.* 108 C3
Hettstedt, *Germany* 18 D7
Heugem, *Neths.* 17 G7
Heule, *Belgium* 17 G2
Heusden, *Belgium* 17 F6
Heusden, *Neths.* 16 E6
Hève, C. de la, *France* 24 C7
Heverlee, *Belgium* 17 G5
Hewett, C., *Canada* 97 A13
Hexham, *U.K.* 12 C5
Hexi, *Yunnan, China* 52 E4
Hexi, *Zhejiang, China* 53 D12
Hexigten Qi, *China* 51 C9
Hexrivier, *S. Africa* 84 E2
Ḥeydarābād, *Iran* 65 D7
Heyfield, *Australia* 91 F4
Heysham, *U.K.* 12 C5
Heythuysen, *Neths.* 17 F7
Heyuan, *China* 53 F10
Heywood, *Australia* 91 F3
Heze, *China* 50 G8
Hezhang, *China* 52 D5
Hi Vista, *U.S.A.* 113 L9
Hialeah, *U.S.A.* 105 N5
Hiawatha, *Kans., U.S.A.* 108 F7
Hiawatha, *Utah, U.S.A.* 110 G8
Hibbing, *U.S.A.* 108 B8
Hibbs B., *Australia* 90 G4
Hibernia Reef, *Australia* 88 B3
Hickory, *U.S.A.* 105 H5
Hicks, Pt., *Australia* 91 F4
Hicksville, *U.S.A.* 107 F11
Hida, *Romania* 38 B6
Hida-Gawa →, *Japan* 49 G8
Hida-Sammyaku, *Japan* 49 F8
Hidaka-Sammyaku, *Japan* 48 C11
Hidalgo, *Mexico* 115 C5
Hidalgo □, *Mexico* 115 C5
Hidalgo, Presa M., *Mexico* 114 B3
Hidalgo, Pta. del, *Canary Is.* 36 F3
Hidalgo del Parral, *Mexico* 114 B3
Hiddensee, *Germany* 18 A9
Hidrolândia, *Brazil* 123 E2
Hieflau, *Austria* 21 H4
Hiendelaencina, *Spain* 28 D1
Hierapolis, *Turkey* 66 E3
Hierro, *Canary Is.* 36 G1
Higashiajima-San, *Japan* 48 F10
Higashiōsaka, *Japan* 49 G7
Higgins, *U.S.A.* 109 G4
Higgins Corner, *U.S.A.* 112 F5
Higginsville, *Australia* 89 F3
High Atlas = Haut Atlas, *Morocco* 74 B3
High I., *Canada* 99 A7
High Island, *U.S.A.* 109 L7
High Level, *Canada* 100 B5
High Point, *U.S.A.* 105 H6
High Prairie, *Canada* 100 B5
High River, *Canada* 100 C6
High Springs, *U.S.A.* 105 L4
High Tatra = Tatry, *Slovak Rep.* 20 F9
High Wycombe, *U.K.* 13 F7
Highbury, *Australia* 90 B3
Highland □, *U.K.* 14 D4
Highland Park, *U.S.A.* 104 D2
Highmore, *U.S.A.* 108 C5
Highrock L., *Canada* 101 B7
Higüay, *Dom. Rep.* 117 C6
Hihya, *Egypt* 76 H7
Hiiumaa, *Estonia* 40 B3
Híjar, *Spain* 28 D4
Ḥijāz □, *Si. Arabia* 68 C2
Hijken, *Neths.* 16 C8
Hijo = Tagum, *Phil.* 55 H6
Hikari, *Japan* 49 H5
Hiko, *U.S.A.* 111 H6
Hikone, *Japan* 49 G8
Hikurangi, *N.Z.* 87 F5
Hikurangi, Mt., *N.Z.* 87 H6
Hildburghhausen, *Germany* 19 E6
Hildesheim, *Germany* 18 C5
Hill →, *Australia* 89 F2
Hill City, *Idaho, U.S.A.* 110 E6
Hill City, *Kans., U.S.A.* 108 F5
Hill City, *Minn., U.S.A.* 108 B8
Hill City, *S. Dak., U.S.A.* 108 D3
Hill Island L., *Canada* 101 A7
Hillared, *Sweden* 11 G7
Hillcrest Center, *U.S.A.* 113 K8
Hillegom, *Neths.* 16 D5
Hillerød, *Denmark* 11 J6
Hillingdon, *U.K.* 13 F7
Hillman, *U.S.A.* 104 C4
Hillmond, *Canada* 101 C7
Hillsboro, *Kans., U.S.A.* 108 F6
Hillsboro, *N. Dak., U.S.A.* 108 B6
Hillsboro, *N.H., U.S.A.* 107 C13
Hillsboro, *N. Mex., U.S.A.* 111 K10
Hillsboro, *Oreg., U.S.A.* 112 E4
Hillsboro, *Tex., U.S.A.* 109 J6
Hillsborough, *Grenada* 117 D7
Hillsdale, *Mich., U.S.A.* 104 E3
Hillsdale, *N.Y., U.S.A.* 107 D11
Hillside, *Australia* 88 D2
Hillsport, *Canada* 98 C2
Hillston, *Australia* 91 E4
Hilo, *U.S.A.* 102 J17
Hilton, *U.S.A.* 106 C7
Hilvan, *Turkey* 67 E8
Hilvarenbeek, *Neths.* 17 F6
Hilversum, *Neths.* 16 D6
Himachal Pradesh □, *India* 62 D7
Himalaya, *Asia* 63 E11
Himamaylan, *Phil.* 55 F5
Himara, *Albania* 39 J2
Himatnagar, *India* 60 H8
Himeji, *Japan* 49 G7
Himi, *Japan* 49 F8
Himmerland, *Denmark* 11 H3
Ḥimṣ, *Syria* 69 A5
Ḥimṣ □, *Syria* 69 A5
Hinche, *Haiti* 117 C5
Hinchinbrook I., *Australia* 90 B4
Hinckley, *U.K.* 13 E6
Hinckley, *U.S.A.* 110 G7
Hindås, *Sweden* 11 G6
Hindaun, *India* 62 F7
Hindmarsh, L., *Australia* 91 F3
Hindsholm, *Denmark* 11 J4
Hindu Bagh, *Pakistan* 62 D2
Hindu Kush, *Asia* 60 B7
Hindubagh, *Pakistan* 60 D5
Hindupur, *India* 60 N10
Hines Creek, *Canada* 100 B5
Hinganghat, *India* 60 J11
Hingeon, *Belgium* 17 G5
Hingham, *U.S.A.* 110 B8
Hingoli, *India* 60 K10
Hinigaran, *Phil.* 55 F5
Hinis, *Turkey* 67 D9
Hinna = Imi, *Ethiopia* 68 F3
Hinna, *Nigeria* 79 C7
Hinojosa del Duque, *Spain* 31 G5
Hinsdale, *U.S.A.* 110 B10
Hinterrhein →, *Switz.* 23 C8
Hinton, *Canada* 100 C5
Hinton, *U.S.A.* 104 G5
Hinwil, *Switz.* 23 B7
Hınzır Burnu, *Turkey* 66 E6
Hippolytushoef, *Neths.* 16 C5
Hirado, *Japan* 49 H4
Hirakud Dam, *India* 61 J13
Hiratsuka, *Japan* 49 G9
Hirfanlı Baraji, *Turkey* 66 D5
Hirhafok, *Algeria* 75 D6
Hîrlău, *Romania* 38 B9
Hiroo, *Japan* 48 C11
Hirosaki, *Japan* 48 D10
Hiroshima, *Japan* 49 G6
Hiroshima □, *Japan* 49 G6
Hirsholmene, *Denmark* 11 G4
Hirson, *France* 25 C11
Hîrşova, *Romania* 38 E10
Hirtshals, *Denmark* 11 G3
Hisar, *India* 62 E6

Hisb →, *Iraq* 64 D5
Ḥismá, *Si. Arabia* 64 D3
Hispaniola, *W. Indies* 117 C5
Hīt, *Iraq* 64 C4
Hita, *Japan* 49 H5
Hitachi, *Japan* 49 F10
Hitchin, *U.K.* 13 F7
Hitoyoshi, *Japan* 49 H5
Hitra, *Norway* 8 E10
Hitzacker, *Germany* 18 B7
Ḥiyyon, N. →, *Israel* 69 E4
Hjalmar L., *Canada* 101 A7
Hjälmare kanal, *Sweden* 10 E9
Hjälmaren, *Sweden* 10 E9
Hjartdal, *Norway* 10 E2
Hjerkinn, *Norway* 10 B3
Hjørring, *Denmark* 11 G3
Hjortkvarn, *Sweden* 11 F9
Hlinsko, *Czech.* 20 F5
Hluhluwe, *S. Africa* 85 D5
Ho, *Ghana* 79 D5
Ho Chi Minh City = Phanh Bho Ho Chi Minh, *Vietnam* 59 G6
Ho Thuong, *Vietnam* 58 C5
Hoa Binh, *Vietnam* 58 B5
Hoa Da, *Vietnam* 59 G7
Hoa Hiep, *Vietnam* 59 G5
Hoai Nhon, *Vietnam* 58 E7
Hoare B., *Canada* 97 B13
Hobart, *Australia* 90 G4
Hobart, *U.S.A.* 109 H5
Hobbs, *U.S.A.* 109 J3
Hobbs Coast, *Antarctica* 5 D14
Hobo, *Colombia* 120 C2
Hoboken, *Belgium* 17 F4
Hoboken, *U.S.A.* 107 F10
Hobro, *Denmark* 11 H3
Hobscheid, *Lux.* 17 J7
Hoburgen, *Sweden* 9 H15
Hochdorf, *Switz.* 23 B6
Hochschwab, *Austria* 21 H5
Höchstadt, *Germany* 19 F6
Hockenheim, *Germany* 19 F4
Hodaka-Dake, *Japan* 49 F8
Hodgson, *Canada* 101 C9
Hódmezövásárhely, *Hungary* 21 J10
Hodna, Chott el, *Algeria* 75 A5
Hodna, Monts du, *Algeria* 75 A5
Hodonín, *Czech.* 20 G7
Hoeamdong, *N. Korea* 51 C16
Hœdic, I. de, *France* 24 E4
Hoegaarden, *Belgium* 17 G5
Hoek van Holland, *Neths.* 16 E4
Hoeksche Waard, *Neths.* 16 E4
Hoenderloo, *Neths.* 16 D7
Hoengsŏng, *S. Korea* 51 F14
Hoensbroek, *Neths.* 17 G7
Hoeryong, *N. Korea* 51 C15
Hoeselt, *Belgium* 17 G6
Hoeven, *Neths.* 17 E5
Hoeyang, *N. Korea* 51 E14
Hof, *Germany* 19 E7
Hof, *Iceland* 8 D6
Höfðakaupstaður, *Iceland* 8 D3
Hofgeismar, *Germany* 18 D5
Hofmeyr, *S. Africa* 84 E4
Hofsjökull, *Iceland* 8 D4
Hofsós, *Iceland* 8 D4
Hōfu, *Japan* 49 G5
Hogan Group, *Australia* 90 F4
Hogansville, *U.S.A.* 105 J3
Hogeland, *U.S.A.* 110 B9
Hoggar = Ahaggar, *Algeria* 75 D6
Högsäter, *Sweden* 11 F6
Hogsty Reef, *Bahamas* 117 B5
Hoh →, *U.S.A.* 112 C2
Hoh Xil Shan, *China* 54 C3
Hohe Rhön, *Germany* 19 E5
Hohe Tauern, *Austria* 21 H2
Hohe Venn, *Belgium* 17 H8
Hohenau, *Austria* 20 G6
Hohenems, *Austria* 19 H5
Hohenstein-Ernstthal, *Germany* 18 E8
Hohenwald, *U.S.A.* 105 H2
Hohenwestedt, *Germany* 18 A5
Hohhot, *China* 50 D6
Hóhlakas, *Greece* 37 D9
Hohoe, *Ghana* 79 D5
Hoi An, *Vietnam* 58 E7
Hoi Xuan, *Vietnam* 58 B5
Hoisington, *U.S.A.* 108 F5
Højer, *Denmark* 11 K2
Hōjō, *Japan* 49 H6
Hökerum, *Sweden* 11 G7
Hokianga Harbour, *N.Z.* 87 F4
Hokitika, *N.Z.* 87 K3
Hokkaidō □, *Japan* 48 C11
Hokksund, *Norway* 10 E3
Hol-Hol, *Djibouti* 77 E5
Holbæk, *Denmark* 11 J5
Holbrook, *Australia* 91 F4
Holbrook, *U.S.A.* 111 J8
Holden, *Canada* 100 C6
Holden, *U.S.A.* 110 G7
Holdenville, *U.S.A.* 109 H6
Holderness, *U.K.* 12 D7
Holdfast, *Canada* 101 C7
Holdich, *Argentina* 128 C3
Holdrege, *U.S.A.* 108 E5
Holguín, *Cuba* 116 B4
Hollabrunn, *Austria* 20 G6
Hollams Bird I., *Namibia* 84 C1
Holland, *U.S.A.* 104 D2
Hollandia = Jayapura, *Indonesia* 57 E10
Hollandsch Diep, *Neths.* 17 E5
Hollandsch IJssel →, *Neths.* 16 E5
Hollfeld, *Germany* 19 F7
Hollidaysburg, *U.S.A.* 106 F6
Hollis, *U.S.A.* 109 H5
Hollister, *Calif., U.S.A.* 111 H3
Hollister, *Idaho, U.S.A.* 110 E6
Hollum, *Neths.* 16 B7
Holly, *U.S.A.* 108 F3
Holly Hill, *U.S.A.* 105 L5
Holly Springs, *U.S.A.* 109 H10
Hollywood, *Calif., U.S.A.* 111 J4
Hollywood, *Fla., U.S.A.* 105 N5
Holm, *Sweden* 10 B10
Holman Island, *Canada* 96 A8
Hólmavík, *Iceland* 8 D3
Holmes Reefs, *Australia* 90 B4
Holmestrand, *Norway* 10 E4
Holmsbu, *Norway* 10 E4
Holmsjön, *Sweden* 10 B9
Holmsland Klit, *Denmark* 11 J2
Holmsund, *Sweden* 8 E16
Holroyd →, *Australia* 90 A3
Holstebro, *Denmark* 11 H2
Holsworthy, *U.K.* 13 G3
Holt, *Iceland* 8 E4
Holte, *Denmark* 11 J6
Holten, *Neths.* 16 D8
Holton, *Canada* 99 B8
Holton, *U.S.A.* 108 F7
Holtville, *U.S.A.* 113 N11
Holwerd, *Neths.* 16 B7
Holy Cross, *U.S.A.* 96 B4
Holy I., *Gwynedd, U.K.* 12 D3
Holy I., *Northumb., U.K.* 12 B6
Holyhead, *U.K.* 12 D3
Holyoke, *Colo., U.S.A.* 108 E3
Holyoke, *Mass., U.S.A.* 107 D12
Holyrood, *Canada* 99 C9
Holzkirchen, *Germany* 19 H7
Holzminden, *Germany* 18 D5
Homa Bay, *Kenya* 82 C3
Homa Bay □, *Kenya* 82 C3
Homalin, *Burma* 61 G19
Homand, *Iran* 65 C8
Homberg, *Germany* 18 D5
Hombori, *Mali* 79 B4
Homburg, *Germany* 19 F3
Home B., *Canada* 97 B13
Home Hill, *Australia* 90 B4
Homedale, *U.S.A.* 110 E5
Homer, *Alaska, U.S.A.* 96 C4
Homer, *La., U.S.A.* 109 J8
Homestead, *Australia* 90 C4
Homestead, *Fla., U.S.A.* 105 N5
Homestead, *Oreg., U.S.A.* 110 D5
Homewood, *U.S.A.* 112 F6
Hominy, *U.S.A.* 109 G6
Homoine, *Mozam.* 85 C6
Homoljske Planina, *Serbia* 21 L11
Homorod, *Romania* 38 C8
Homs = Ḥimş, *Syria* 69 A5
Homyel = Gomel, *Belorussia* 40 E7
Hon Chong, *Vietnam* 59 G5
Hon Me, *Vietnam* 58 C5
Hon Quan, *Vietnam* 59 G6
Honan = Henan □, *China* 50 G8
Honbetsu, *Japan* 48 C11
Honcut, *U.S.A.* 112 F5
Honda, *Colombia* 120 B3
Honda Bay, *Phil.* 55 G3
Hondeklipbaai, *S. Africa* 84 E2
Hondo, *Japan* 49 H5
Hondo, *U.S.A.* 109 L5
Hondo →, *Belize* 115 D7
Honduras ■, *Cent. Amer.* 116 D2
Honduras, G. de, *Caribbean* 116 C2
Hønefoss, *Norway* 9 F11
Honesdale, *U.S.A.* 107 E9
Honey L., *U.S.A.* 112 E6
Honfleur, *France* 24 C7
Hong Gai, *Vietnam* 58 B6
Hong He →, *China* 50 H8
Hong Kong ■, *Asia* 53 F10
Hong'an, *China* 53 B10
Hongchŏn, *S. Korea* 51 F14
Honghai Wan, *China* 53 F10
Honghu, *China* 53 C9
Hongjiang, *China* 52 D7
Hongliu He →, *China* 50 F5
Hongor, *Mongolia* 50 B7
Hongsa, *Laos* 58 C3
Hongshui He →, *China* 52 F7
Hongsŏng, *S. Korea* 51 F14
Hongtong, *China* 50 F6
Honguedo, Détroit d', *Canada* 99 C7
Hongwon, *N. Korea* 51 E14
Hongya, *China* 52 C4
Hongyuan, *China* 52 A4
Hongze Hu, *China* 51 H10
Honiara, *Solomon Is.* 92 H7
Honiton, *U.K.* 13 G4
Honjō, *Japan* 48 E10
Honkorâb, Ras, *Egypt* 76 C4
Honolulu, *U.S.A.* 102 H16
Honshū, *Japan* 49 G9
Hontoria del Pinar, *Spain* 28 D1
Hood, Mt., *U.S.A.* 110 D3
Hood, Pt., *Australia* 89 F2
Hood River, *U.S.A.* 110 D3
Hoodsport, *U.S.A.* 112 C3
Hooge, *Germany* 18 A4
Hoogerheide, *Neths.* 17 F4
Hoogeveen, *Neths.* 16 C8
Hoogeveensche Vaart, *Neths.* 16 C8
Hoogezand, *Neths.* 16 B9
Hooghly → = Hughli →, *India* 63 J13
Hooghly-Chinsura = Chunchura, *India* 63 H13
Hoogkerk, *Neths.* 16 B9
Hooglede, *Belgium* 17 G2
Hoogstraten, *Belgium* 17 F5
Hoogvliet, *Neths.* 16 E4
Hook Hd., *Ireland* 15 D5
Hook I., *Australia* 90 C4
Hook of Holland = Hoek van Holland, *Neths.* 16 E4
Hooker, *U.S.A.* 109 G4
Hooker Creek, *Australia* 88 C5
Hoopeston, *U.S.A.* 104 E2
Hoopstad, *S. Africa* 84 D4
Hoorn, *Neths.* 16 C6
Hoover Dam, *U.S.A.* 113 K12
Hooversville, *U.S.A.* 106 F6
Hop Bottom, *U.S.A.* 107 E9
Hopa, *Turkey* 43 F9
Hope, *Canada* 100 D4
Hope, *Ariz., U.S.A.* 113 M13
Hope, *Ark., U.S.A.* 109 J8
Hope, *N. Dak., U.S.A.* 108 B6
Hope, L., *Australia* 91 D2
Hope, Pt., *U.S.A.* 96 B3
Hope Town, *Bahamas* 116 A4
Hopedale, *Canada* 99 A7
Hopefield, *S. Africa* 84 E2
Hopei = Hebei □, *China* 50 E9
Hopelchén, *Mexico* 115 D7
Hopetoun, *Vic., Australia* 91 F3
Hopetoun, *W. Austral., Australia* 89 F3
Hopetown, *S. Africa* 84 D3
Hopkins, *U.S.A.* 108 E7
Hopkins, L., *Australia* 88 D4
Hopkinsville, *U.S.A.* 105 G2
Hopland, *U.S.A.* 112 G3
Hoptrup, *Denmark* 11 J3
Hoquiam, *U.S.A.* 112 D3
Horasan, *Turkey* 67 C10
Horcajo de Santiago, *Spain* 28 F1
Hordaland fylke □, *Norway* 9 F9
Horden Hills, *Australia* 88 D5
Horezu, *Romania* 38 D6
Horgen, *Switz.* 23 B7
Horinger, *China* 50 D6
Horlick Mts., *Antarctica* 5 E15
Horlivka = Gorlovka, *Ukraine* 42 B8
Hormoz, *Iran* 65 E7
Hormoz, Jaz. ye, *Iran* 65 E8
Hormuz Str. of, *The Gulf* 65 E8
Horn, *Ísafjarðarsýsla, Iceland* 8 C2
Horn, *Suður-Múlasýsla, Iceland* 8 D7
Horn, *Neths.* 17 F7
Horn →, *Canada* 100 A5
Horn, Cape = Hornos, C. de, *Chile* 128 E3
Horn Head, *Ireland* 15 A3
Horn I., *Australia* 90 A3
Horn I., *U.S.A.* 105 K1
Horn Mts., *Canada* 100 A5
Hornachuelos, *Spain* 31 H5
Hornavan, *Sweden* 8 C14
Hornbæk, *Denmark* 11 H6
Hornbeck, *U.S.A.* 109 K8
Hornbrook, *U.S.A.* 110 F2
Hornburg, *Germany* 18 C6
Horncastle, *U.K.* 12 D7
Hornell, *U.S.A.* 106 D7
Hornell L., *Canada* 100 A5
Hornepayne, *Canada* 98 C3
Hornitos, *U.S.A.* 112 H6
Hornos, C. de, *Chile* 128 E3
Hornoy, *France* 25 C8
Hornsby, *Australia* 91 E5
Hornsea, *U.K.* 12 D7
Hornslandet, *Sweden* 10 C11
Hornslet, *Denmark* 11 H4
Hornu, *Belgium* 17 H3
Hörnum, *Germany* 18 A4
Horobetsu, *Japan* 48 C10
Horqin Youyi Qianqi, *China* 51 A12
Horqueta, *Paraguay* 126 A4
Horred, *Sweden* 11 G6
Horse Creek, *U.S.A.* 108 E3
Horse Is., *Canada* 99 B8
Horsefly L., *Canada* 100 C4
Horsens, *Denmark* 11 J3
Horsens Fjord, *Denmark* 11 J4
Horsham, *Australia* 91 F3
Horsham, *U.K.* 13 F7
Horst, *Neths.* 17 F8
Horten, *Norway* 10 E4
Hortobágy →, *Hungary* 21 H11
Horton, *U.S.A.* 108 F7
Horton →, *Canada* 96 B7
Horw, *Switz.* 23 B6
Horwood, L., *Canada* 98 C3
Hosaina, *Ethiopia* 77 F4
Hose, Gunung-Gunung, *Malaysia* 56 D4
Ḥoseynābād, *Khuzestān, Iran* 65 C6
Ḥoseynābād, *Kordestān, Iran* 64 C5
Hoshangabad, *India* 62 H7
Hoshiarpur, *India* 62 D6
Hosingen, *Lux.* 17 H8
Hosmer, *U.S.A.* 108 C5
Hospental, *Switz.* 23 C7
Hospet, *India* 60 M10
Hospitalet de Llobregat, *Spain* 28 D7
Hoste, I., *Chile* 128 E3
Hostens, *France* 26 D3
Hot, *Thailand* 58 C2
Hot Creek Range, *U.S.A.* 110 G5
Hot Springs, *Ark., U.S.A.* 109 H8
Hot Springs, *S. Dak., U.S.A.* 108 D3
Hotagen, *Sweden* 8 E13
Hotan, *China* 54 C2
Hotazel, *S. Africa* 84 D3
Hotchkiss, *U.S.A.* 111 G10
Hotham, C., *Australia* 88 B5
Hoting, *Sweden* 8 D14
Hotte, Massif de la, *Haiti* 117 C5
Hottentotsbaai, *Namibia* 84 D1
Hotton, *Belgium* 17 H6
Houat, I. de, *France* 24 E4
Houck, *U.S.A.* 111 J9
Houdan, *France* 25 D8
Houdeng-Goegnies, *Belgium* 17 H4
Houei Sai, *Laos* 58 B3
Houffalize, *Belgium* 17 H7
Houghton, *U.S.A.* 108 B10
Houghton L., *U.S.A.* 104 C3
Houghton-le-Spring, *U.K.* 12 C6
Houhora Heads, *N.Z.* 87 F4
Houille →, *Belgium* 17 H5
Houlton, *U.S.A.* 99 C6
Houma, *U.S.A.* 109 L9
Houndé, *Burkina Faso* 78 C4
Hourtin, *France* 26 C2
Hourtin-Carcans, Étang d', *France* 26 C2
Houston, *Canada* 100 C3
Houston, *Mo., U.S.A.* 109 G9
Houston, *Tex., U.S.A.* 109 L7
Houten, *Neths.* 16 D6
Houthalen, *Belgium* 17 F6
Houthem, *Belgium* 17 G1
Houthulst, *Belgium* 17 G2
Houtman Abrolhos, *Australia* 89 E1
Houyet, *Belgium* 17 H6
Hov, *Denmark* 11 J4
Hova, *Sweden* 11 F8
Høvåg, *Norway* 11 F2
Hovd, *Mongolia* 54 B4
Hove, *U.K.* 13 G7
Hoveyzeh, *Iran* 65 D6
Hövsgöl, *Mongolia* 50 C5
Hövsgöl Nuur, *Mongolia* 54 A5
Howakil, *Eritrea* 77 D5
Howar, Wadi →, *Sudan* 77 D2
Howard, *Australia* 91 D5
Howard, *Kans., U.S.A.* 109 G6
Howard, *Pa., U.S.A.* 106 E7
Howard, *S. Dak., U.S.A.* 108 C6
Howard I., *Australia* 90 A2
Howard L., *Canada* 101 A7
Howe, *U.S.A.* 110 E7
Howe, C., *Australia* 91 F5
Howell, *U.S.A.* 104 D4
Howick, *Canada* 107 A11
Howick, *S. Africa* 85 D5
Howick Group, *Australia* 90 A4
Howitt, L., *Australia* 91 D2
Howley, *Canada* 99 C8
Howrah = Haora, *India* 63 H13
Howth Hd., *Ireland* 15 C5
Höxter, *Germany* 18 D5
Hoy, *U.K.* 14 C5
Hoya, *Germany* 18 C5
Høyanger, *Norway* 9 F9
Hoyerswerda, *Germany* 18 D10
Hoyos, *Spain* 30 E4
Hpungan Pass, *Burma* 61 F20
Hradec Králové, *Czech.* 20 E5
Hranice, *Czech.* 20 F7
Hrodna = Grodno, *Belorussia* 40 E3
Hron →, *Slovak Rep.* 21 H8
Hrubieszów, *Poland* 20 E13
Hrvatska = Croatia ■, *Europe* 33 C13
Hsenwi, *Burma* 61 H20
Hsiamen = Xiamen, *China* 53 E12
Hsian = Xi'an, *China* 50 G5
Hsinhailien = Lianyungang, *China* 51 G10
Hsisha Chuntao, *Pac. Oc.* 56 A4
Hsüchou = Xuzhou, *China* 51 G9
Hu Xian, *China* 50 G5
Hua Hin, *Thailand* 58 F2
Hua Xian, *Henan, China* 50 G8
Hua Xian, *Shaanxi, China* 50 G5
Hua'an, *China* 53 E11
Huacaya, *Bolivia* 125 E5
Huacheng, *China* 53 E10
Huachinera, *Mexico* 114 A3
Huacho, *Peru* 124 C2
Huachón, *Peru* 124 C2
Huade, *China* 50 D7
Huadian, *China* 51 C14
Huai He →, *China* 53 A12
Huai Yot, *Thailand* 59 J2
Huai'an, *Hebei, China* 50 D8
Huai'an, *Jiangsu, China* 51 H10
Huaide, *China* 51 C13
Huaidezhen, *China* 51 C13
Huaihua, *China* 52 D7
Huaiji, *China* 53 F9
Huainan, *China* 53 A11
Huaining, *China* 53 B11
Huairen, *China* 50 E7
Huairou, *China* 50 D9
Huaiyang, *China* 50 H8
Huaiyuan, *Anhui, China* 51 H9
Huaiyuan, *Guangxi Zhuangzu, China* 52 E7
Huajianzi, *China* 51 D13
Huajuapan de Leon, *Mexico* 115 D5
Hualapai Peak, *U.S.A.* 111 J7
Hualian, *Taiwan* 53 F13
Huallaga →, *Peru* 124 B2
Huallanca, *Peru* 124 B2
Huamachuco, *Peru* 124 B2
Huambo, *Angola* 81 G3
Huan Jiang →, *China* 50 G5
Huan Xian, *China* 50 F4
Huancabamba, *Peru* 124 B2
Huancane, *Peru* 124 D4
Huancapi, *Peru* 124 C3
Huancavelica, *Peru* 124 C2
Huancavelica □, *Peru* 124 C3
Huancayo, *Peru* 124 C2
Huanchaca, *Bolivia* 124 E4
Huanchaca, Serranía de, *Bolivia* 125 C5
Huang Hai = Yellow Sea, *China* 51 G12
Huang He →, *China* 51 F10
Huang Xian, *China* 51 F11
Huangchuan, *China* 53 A10
Huanggang, *China* 53 B10
Huangling, *China* 50 G5
Huangliu, *China* 54 E5
Huanglong, *China* 50 G5
Huanglongtan, *China* 53 A8
Huangmei, *China* 53 B10
Huangpi, *China* 53 B10
Huangping, *China* 52 D6
Huangshi, *China* 53 B10
Huangsongdian, *China* 51 C14
Huangyan, *China* 53 C13
Huangyangsi, *China* 53 D8
Huaning, *China* 52 E4
Huanjiang, *China* 52 E7
Huanta, *Peru* 124 C3
Huantai, *China* 51 F9
Huánuco, *Peru* 124 B2
Huánuco □, *Peru* 124 B2
Huanuni, *Bolivia* 124 D4
Huanzo, Cordillera de, *Peru* 124 C3
Huaping, *China* 52 D3
Huaral, *Peru* 124 C2
Huaraz, *Peru* 124 B2
Huari, *Peru* 124 B2
Huarmey, *Peru* 124 C2
Huarochiri, *Peru* 124 C2
Huarocondo, *Peru* 124 C3
Huarong, *China* 53 C9
Huascarán, *Peru* 124 B2
Huascarán, Nevado, *Peru* 124 B2
Huasco, *Chile* 126 B1
Huasco →, *Chile* 126 B1
Huasna, *U.S.A.* 113 K6
Huatabampo, *Mexico* 114 B3
Huauchinango, *Mexico* 115 C5
Huautla de Jiménez, *Mexico* 115 D5
Huaxi, *China* 52 D6
Huay Namota, *Mexico* 114 C4
Huayin, *China* 50 G6
Huayllay, *Peru* 124 C2
Huayuan, *China* 52 C7
Huazhou, *China* 53 G8
Hubbard, *U.S.A.* 109 K6
Hubbart Pt., *Canada* 101 B10
Hubei □, *China* 53 B9
Hubli-Dharwad = Dharwad, *India* 60 M9
Huchang, *N. Korea* 51 D14
Hückelhoven, *Germany* 18 D2
Huddersfield, *U.K.* 12 D6
Hudi, *Sudan* 76 D3
Hudiksvall, *Sweden* 10 C11
Hudson, *Canada* 101 C10
Hudson, *Mass., U.S.A.* 107 D13
Hudson, *Mich., U.S.A.* 104 E3
Hudson, *N.Y., U.S.A.* 107 D11
Hudson, *Wis., U.S.A.* 108 C8
Hudson, *Wyo., U.S.A.* 110 E9
Hudson →, *U.S.A.* 107 F10
Hudson Bay, *N.W.T., Canada* 97 C11
Hudson Bay, *Sask., Canada* 101 C8
Hudson Falls, *U.S.A.* 107 C11
Hudson Mts., *Antarctica* 5 D16
Hudson Str., *Canada* 97 B13
Hudson's Hope, *Canada* 100 B4
Hue, *Vietnam* 58 D6
Huebra →, *Spain* 30 D4

Huechucuicui, Pta.

Huechucuicui, Pta., *Chile* 128 B2
Huedin, *Romania* 38 C6
Huehuetenango, *Guatemala* 116 C1
Huejúcar, *Mexico* 114 C4
Huelgoat, *France* 24 D3
Huelma, *Spain* 29 H1
Huelva, *Spain* 31 H4
Huelva □, *Spain* 31 H4
Huelva →, *Spain* 31 H5
Huentelauquén, *Chile* 126 C1
Huércal Overa, *Spain* 29 H3
Huerta, Sa. de la, *Argentina* 126 C2
Huertas, C. de las, *Spain* 29 G4
Huerva →, *Spain* 28 D4
Huesca, *Spain* 28 C4
Huesca □, *Spain* 28 C5
Huéscar, *Spain* 29 H2
Huetamo, *Mexico* 114 D4
Huete, *Spain* 28 E2
Hugh →, *Australia* 90 D1
Hughenden, *Australia* 90 C3
Hughes, *Australia* 89 F4
Hughli →, *India* 63 J13
Hugo, *U.S.A.* 108 F3
Hugoton, *U.S.A.* 109 G4
Hui Xian, *Gansu, China* 50 H4
Hui Xian, *Henan, China* 50 G7
Hui'an, *China* 53 E12
Hui'anbu, *China* 50 F4
Huichang, *China* 53 E10
Huichapán, *Mexico* 115 C5
Huidong, *China* 52 D4
Huifa He →, *China* 51 C14
Huila □, *Colombia* 120 C2
Huila, Nevado del, *Colombia* 120 C2
Huilai, *China* 53 F11
Huili, *China* 52 D4
Huimin, *China* 51 F9
Huinan, *China* 51 C14
Huinca Renancó, *Argentina* 126 C3
Huining, *China* 50 G3
Huinong, *China* 50 E4
Huise, *Belgium* 17 G3
Huishui, *China* 52 D6
Huisne →, *France* 24 E7
Huissen, *Neths.* 16 E7
Huiting, *China* 50 G9
Huitong, *China* 52 D7
Huixtla, *Mexico* 115 D6
Huize, *China* 52 D4
Huizen, *Neths.* 16 D6
Huizhou, *China* 53 F10
Hukawng Valley, *Burma* 61 F20
Hukou, *China* 53 C11
Hukuntsi, *Botswana* 84 C3
Hula, *Ethiopia* 77 F4
Hulan, *China* 54 B7
Ḥulayfā', *Si. Arabia* 64 E4
Huld, *Mongolia* 50 B3
Hulin He →, *China* 51 B12
Hull = Kingston upon Hull, *U.K.* 12 D7
Hull, *Canada* 98 C4
Hull →, *U.K.* 12 D7
Hulst, *Neths.* 17 F4
Hulun Nur, *China* 54 B6
Humahuaca, *Argentina* 126 A2
Humaitá, *Brazil* 125 B5
Humaitá, *Paraguay* 126 B4
Humansdorp, *S. Africa* 84 E3
Humbe, *Angola* 84 B1
Humber →, *U.K.* 12 D7
Humberside □, *U.K.* 12 D7
Humbert River, *Australia* 88 C5
Humble, *U.S.A.* 109 L8
Humboldt, *Canada* 101 C7
Humboldt, *Iowa, U.S.A.* 108 D7
Humboldt, *Tenn., U.S.A.* 109 H10
Humboldt →, *U.S.A.* 110 F4
Humboldt Gletscher, *Greenland* 4 B4
Hume, *U.S.A.* 112 J8
Hume, L., *Australia* 91 F4
Humenné, *Slovak Rep.* 20 G11
Humphreys, Mt., *U.S.A.* 112 H8
Humphreys Peak, *U.S.A.* 111 J8
Humpolec, *Czech.* 20 F5
Humptulips, *U.S.A.* 112 C3
Hūn, *Libya* 73 C8
Hun Jiang →, *China* 51 D13
Húnaflói, *Iceland* 8 D3
Hunan □, *China* 53 D9
Hunchun, *China* 51 C16
Hundested, *Denmark* 11 J5
Hundred Mile House, *Canada* 100 C4
Hunedoara, *Romania* 38 D5
Hünfeld, *Germany* 18 E5
Hung Yen, *Vietnam* 58 B6
Hungary ■, *Europe* 21 H9
Hungary, Plain of, *Europe* 6 F9
Hungerford, *Australia* 91 D3
Hŭngnam, *N. Korea* 51 E14
Huni Valley, *Ghana* 78 D4
Hunsberge, *Namibia* 84 D2
Hunsrück, *Germany* 19 F3
Hunstanton, *U.K.* 12 E8
Hunte →, *Germany* 18 C4
Hunter, *N. Dak., U.S.A.* 108 B6
Hunter, *N.Y., U.S.A.* 107 D10
Hunter I., *Australia* 90 G3
Hunter I., *Canada* 100 C3
Hunter Ra., *Australia* 91 E5
Hunters Road, *Zimbabwe* 83 F2
Hunterville, *N.Z.* 87 H5
Huntingburg, *U.S.A.* 104 F2
Huntingdon, *Canada* 98 C5
Huntingdon, *U.K.* 13 E7
Huntingdon, *U.S.A.* 106 F6
Huntington, *Ind., U.S.A.* 104 E3
Huntington, *N.Y., U.S.A.* 107 F11
Huntington, *Oreg., U.S.A.* 110 D5
Huntington, *Utah, U.S.A.* 110 G8
Huntington, *W. Va., U.S.A.* 104 F4
Huntington Beach, *U.S.A.* 113 M8
Huntington Park, *U.S.A.* 111 K4
Huntly, *N.Z.* 87 G5
Huntly, *U.K.* 14 D6
Huntsville, *Canada* 98 C4
Huntsville, *Ala., U.S.A.* 105 H2
Huntsville, *Tex., U.S.A.* 109 K7
Hunyani →, *Zimbabwe* 83 F3
Hunyuan, *China* 50 E7
Hunza →, *India* 63 B6
Huo Xian, *China* 50 F6
Huong Hoa, *Vietnam* 58 D6
Huong Khe, *Vietnam* 58 C5
Huonville, *Australia* 90 G4
Huoqiu, *China* 53 A11
Huoshan, *Anhui, China* 53 A12
Huoshan, *Anhui, China* 53 B11
Huoshao Dao, *Taiwan* 53 F13
Hupeh = Hubei □, *China* 53 B9
Ḥūr, *Iran* 65 D8
Hure Qi, *China* 51 C11
Hurezani, *Romania* 38 E6
Hurghada, *Egypt* 76 B3
Hurley, *N. Mex., U.S.A.* 111 K9
Hurley, *Wis., U.S.A.* 108 B9
Huron, *Calif., U.S.A.* 112 J6
Huron, *Ohio, U.S.A.* 106 E2
Huron, *S. Dak., U.S.A.* 108 C5
Huron, L., *U.S.A.* 106 B2
Hurricane, *U.S.A.* 111 H7
Hurso, *Ethiopia* 77 F5
Hurum, *Norway* 10 C2
Hurunui →, *N.Z.* 87 K4
Hurup, *Denmark* 11 H2
Húsavík, *Iceland* 8 C5
Huşi, *Romania* 38 C11
Huskvarna, *Sweden* 9 H13
Hussar, *Canada* 100 C6
Husum, *Germany* 18 A5
Husum, *Sweden* 10 A13
Hutchinson, *Kans., U.S.A.* 109 F6
Hutchinson, *Minn., U.S.A.* 108 C7
Huttig, *U.S.A.* 109 J8
Hutton, Mt., *Australia* 91 D4
Huttwil, *Switz.* 22 B5
Huwun, *Ethiopia* 77 G5
Huy, *Belgium* 17 G6
Hvammur, *Iceland* 8 D3
Hvar, *Croatia* 33 E13
Hvarski Kanal, *Croatia* 33 E13
Hvítá, *Iceland* 8 D3
Hvítá →, *Iceland* 8 D3
Hvítárvatn, *Iceland* 8 D4
Hwachon-chosuji, *S. Korea* 51 E14
Hwang Ho = Huang He →, *China* 51 F10
Hwange, *Zimbabwe* 83 F2
Hwange Nat. Park, *Zimbabwe* 84 B4
Hyannis, *U.S.A.* 108 E4
Hyargas Nuur, *Mongolia* 54 B4
Hybo, *Sweden* 10 C10
Hyde Park, *Guyana* 121 B6
Hyden, *Australia* 89 F2
Hyderabad, *India* 60 L11
Hyderabad, *Pakistan* 62 G3
Hyères, *France* 27 E10
Hyères, Is. d', *France* 27 F10
Hyesan, *N. Korea* 51 D15
Hyland →, *Canada* 100 B3
Hyltebruk, *Sweden* 11 H7
Hymia, *India* 63 C8
Hyndman Peak, *U.S.A.* 110 E6
Hyōgo □, *Japan* 49 G7
Hyrum, *U.S.A.* 110 F8
Hysham, *U.S.A.* 110 C10
Hythe, *U.K.* 13 F9
Hyūga, *Japan* 49 H5
Hyvinge = Hyvinkää, *Finland* 9 F18
Hyvinkää, *Finland* 9 F18

I

I-n-Échaï, *Mali* 74 D4
I-n-Gall, *Niger* 79 B6
Iabès, Erg, *Algeria* 75 C4
Iaco →, *Brazil* 124 B4
Iaçu, *Brazil* 123 D3
Iakora, *Madag.* 85 C8
Iaşi, *Romania* 38 B10
Iauaretê, *Colombia* 120 C4
Iba, *Phil.* 55 D3
Ibadan, *Nigeria* 79 D5
Ibagué, *Colombia* 120 C2
Ibaiti, *Brazil* 123 F1
Iballja, *Albania* 38 G3
Ibăneşti, *Romania* 38 C7
Ibar →, *Serbia* 21 M10
Ibaraki □, *Japan* 49 F10
Ibarra, *Ecuador* 120 C2
Ibba, *Sudan* 77 G2
Ibba, Bahr el →, *Sudan* 77 F2
Ibbenbüren, *Germany* 18 C3
Ibembo, *Zaïre* 82 B1
Ibera, L., *Argentina* 126 B4
Iberian Peninsula, *Europe* 6 G5
Iberico, Sistema, *Spain* 28 E2
Iberville, *Canada* 98 C5
Iberville, Lac d', *Canada* 98 A5
Ibi, *Nigeria* 79 D6
Ibiá, *Brazil* 123 E2
Ibicaraí, *Brazil* 123 D4
Ibicuí, *Brazil* 123 D4
Ibicuy, *Argentina* 126 C4
Ibioapaba, Sa. da, *Brazil* 122 B3
Ibipetuba, *Brazil* 122 D3
Ibitiara, *Brazil* 123 D3
Ibiza, *Spain* 36 C7
Íblei, Monti, *Italy* 35 E7
Ibo, *Mozam.* 83 E5
Ibonma, *Indonesia* 57 E8
Ibotirama, *Brazil* 123 D3
Ibrāhīm →, *Lebanon* 69 A4
Ibshawâi, *Egypt* 76 J7
Ibu, *Indonesia* 57 D7
Iburg, *Germany* 18 C4
Ibusuki, *Japan* 49 J5
Icá, *Peru* 124 C2
Ica □, *Peru* 124 C2
Içá →, *Brazil* 124 A4
Icabarú, *Venezuela* 121 C5
Icabarú →, *Venezuela* 121 C5
Içana, *Brazil* 120 C4
Içana →, *Brazil* 120 C4
Icatu, *Brazil* 122 B3
Içel = Mersin, *Turkey* 66 E6
Içel □, *Turkey* 66 E6
Iceland ■, *Europe* 8 D4
Icha, *Russia* 45 D16
Ich'ang = Yichang, *China* 53 B8
Ichchapuram, *India* 61 K14
Ichihara, *Japan* 49 G10
Ichikawa, *Japan* 49 G9
Ichilo →, *Bolivia* 125 D5
Ichinohe, *Japan* 48 D10
Ichinomiya, *Japan* 49 G8
Ichinoseki, *Japan* 48 E10
Ichnya, *Ukraine* 40 F8
Ichŏn, *S. Korea* 51 F14
Icht, *Morocco* 74 C3
Ichtegem, *Belgium* 17 F2
Icó, *Brazil* 122 C4
Icod, *Canary Is.* 36 F3
Icoraci, *Brazil* 122 B2
Icy Str., *U.S.A.* 100 B1
Ida Grove, *U.S.A.* 108 D7
Ida Valley, *Australia* 89 E3
Idabel, *U.S.A.* 109 J7
Idaga Hamus, *Ethiopia* 77 E4
Idah, *Nigeria* 79 D6
Idaho □, *U.S.A.* 110 D6
Idaho City, *U.S.A.* 110 E6
Idaho Falls, *U.S.A.* 110 E7
Idaho Springs, *U.S.A.* 110 G11
Idanha-a-Nova, *Portugal* 30 F3
Idar-Oberstein, *Germany* 19 F3
Idd el Ghanam, *Sudan* 73 F9
Iddan, *Somali Rep.* 68 F4
Idehan, *Libya* 75 C7
Idehan Marzūq, *Libya* 73 D7
Idelès, *Algeria* 75 D6
Idfû, *Egypt* 76 C3
Ídhi Óros, *Greece* 37 D6
Ídhra, *Greece* 39 M6
Idi, *Indonesia* 56 C1
Idiofa, *Zaïre* 80 E3
Idku, Bahra el, *Egypt* 76 H7
Idlib, *Syria* 64 C3
Idria, *U.S.A.* 112 J6
Idrija, *Slovenia* 33 B11
Idritsa, *Russia* 40 C6
Idstein, *Germany* 19 E4
Idutywa, *S. Africa* 85 E4
Ieper, *Belgium* 17 G1
Ierápetra, *Greece* 37 E7
Ierissós, *Greece* 39 J6
Ierzu, *Italy* 34 C2
Iesi, *Italy* 33 E10
Ifach, Punta, *Spain* 29 G5
'Ifāl, W. al →, *Si. Arabia* 64 D2
Ifanadiana, *Madag.* 85 C8
Ife, *Nigeria* 79 D5
Iférouâne, *Niger* 79 B6
Iffley, *Australia* 90 B3
Ifni, *Morocco* 74 C2
Ifon, *Nigeria* 79 D6
Iforas, Adrar des, *Mali* 79 B5
Ifould, L., *Australia* 89 F5
Ifrane, *Morocco* 74 B3
Iganga, *Uganda* 82 B3
Igara Paraná →, *Colombia* 120 D3
Igarapava, *Brazil* 123 F2
Igarapé Açu, *Brazil* 122 B2
Igarapé-Mirim, *Brazil* 122 B2
Igarka, *Russia* 44 C9
Igatimi, *Paraguay* 127 A4
Igbetti, *Nigeria* 79 D5
Igbo-Ora, *Nigeria* 79 D5
Igboho, *Nigeria* 79 D5
Iğdır, *Turkey* 67 D11
Iggesund, *Sweden* 10 C11
Ighil Izane, *Algeria* 75 A5
Iglésias, *Italy* 34 C1
Igli, *Algeria* 75 B4
Igloolik, *Canada* 97 B11
Igma, Gebel el, *Egypt* 76 J8
Ignace, *Canada* 98 C1
İğneada Burnu, *Turkey* 66 C3
Igoshevo, *Russia* 41 B13
Iguaçu →, *Brazil* 127 B5
Iguaçu, Cat. del, *Brazil* 127 B5
Iguaçu Falls = Iguaçu, Cat. del, *Brazil* 127 B5
Iguala, *Mexico* 115 D5
Igualada, *Spain* 28 D6
Iguape, *Brazil* 123 F2
Iguassu = Iguaçu →, *Brazil* 127 B5
Iguatu, *Brazil* 122 C4
Iguéla, *Gabon* 80 E1
Igunga □, *Tanzania* 82 C3
Iheya-Shima, *Japan* 49 L3
Ihiala, *Nigeria* 79 D6
Ihosy, *Madag.* 85 C8
Ihotry, L., *Madag.* 85 C7
Ii, *Finland* 8 D18
Ii-Shima, *Japan* 49 L3
Iida, *Japan* 49 G8
Iijoki →, *Finland* 8 D18
Iisalmi, *Finland* 8 E19
Iiyama, *Japan* 49 F9
Iizuka, *Japan* 49 H5
Ijâfene, *Mauritania* 74 D3
Ijebu-Igbo, *Nigeria* 79 D5
Ijebu-Ode, *Nigeria* 79 D5
IJmuiden, *Neths.* 16 D5
IJssel →, *Neths.* 16 C7
IJsselmeer, *Neths.* 16 C6
IJsselmuiden, *Neths.* 16 C7
IJsselstein, *Neths.* 16 D6
Ijuí →, *Brazil* 127 B4
IJzendijke, *Neths.* 17 F3
IJzer →, *Belgium* 17 F1
Ikale, *Nigeria* 79 D6
Ikare, *Nigeria* 79 D6
Ikaría, *Greece* 39 M9
Ikast, *Denmark* 11 H3
Ikeda, *Japan* 49 G6
Ikeja, *Nigeria* 79 D5
Ikela, *Zaïre* 80 E4
Ikerre-Ekiti, *Nigeria* 79 D6
Ikhtiman, *Bulgaria* 38 G6
Iki, *Japan* 49 H4
Ikimba L., *Tanzania* 82 C3
Ikire, *Nigeria* 79 D5
İkizdere, *Turkey* 67 C9
Ikom, *Nigeria* 79 D6
Ikopa →, *Madag.* 85 B8
Ikot Ekpene, *Nigeria* 79 D6
Ikungu, *Tanzania* 82 C3
Ikurun, *Nigeria* 79 D5
Ila, *Nigeria* 79 D5
Ilagan, *Phil.* 55 C4
Īlām, *Iran* 64 C5
Ilam, *Nepal* 63 F12
Ilanskiy, *Russia* 45 D10
Ilanz, *Switz.* 23 C8
Ilaro, *Nigeria* 79 D5
Iława, *Poland* 20 B9
Ilbilbie, *Australia* 90 C4
Ile-à-la-Crosse, *Canada* 101 B7
Ile-à-la-Crosse, Lac, *Canada* 101 B7
Île-de-France, *France* 25 D9
Ilebo, *Zaïre* 80 E4
Ileje □, *Tanzania* 83 D3
Ilek, *Russia* 44 D6
Ilek →, *Russia* 44 D6
Ilero, *Nigeria* 79 D5
Ilesha, *Kwara, Nigeria* 79 D5
Ilesha, *Oyo, Nigeria* 79 D5
Ilford, *Canada* 101 B9
Ilfracombe, *Australia* 90 C3
Ilfracombe, *U.K.* 13 F3
Ilgaz, *Turkey* 66 C5
Ilgaz Dağları, *Turkey* 66 C5
Ilgın, *Turkey* 66 D4
Ilha Grande, *Brazil* 121 D4
Ilha Grande, B. da, *Brazil* 123 F3
Ílhavo, *Portugal* 30 E2
Ilhéus, *Brazil* 123 D4
Ili →, *Kazakhstan* 44 E8
Iliç, *Turkey* 67 D8
Ilich, *Kazakhstan* 44 E7
Iliff, *U.S.A.* 108 E3
Iligan, *Phil.* 55 G6
Iligan Bay, *Phil.* 55 G6
Ilíkí, L., *Greece* 39 L6
Ilin I., *Phil.* 55 E4
Iliodhrómia, *Greece* 39 K6
Ilion, *U.S.A.* 107 D9
Ilirska-Bistrica, *Slovenia* 33 C11
Ilkeston, *U.K.* 12 E6
Illampu = Ancohuma, Nevada, *Bolivia* 124 D4
Illana B., *Phil.* 55 H5
Illapel, *Chile* 126 C1
Ille-et-Vilaine □, *France* 24 D5
Ille-sur-Têt, *France* 26 F6
Iller →, *Germany* 19 G5
Illescas, *Spain* 30 E7
Illetas, *Spain* 36 B9
Illiers-Combray, *France* 24 D8
Illimani, *Bolivia* 124 D4
Illinois □, *U.S.A.* 103 C9
Illinois →, *U.S.A.* 103 C8
Illium = Troy, *Turkey* 66 D2
Illizi, *Algeria* 75 C6
Illora, *Spain* 31 H7
Ilm →, *Germany* 18 D7
Ilmen, Oz., *Russia* 40 B7
Ilmenau, *Germany* 18 E6
Ilo, *Peru* 124 D3
Ilobu, *Nigeria* 79 D5
Iloilo, *Phil.* 55 F5
Ilora, *Nigeria* 79 D5
Ilorin, *Nigeria* 79 D5
Iloulya, *Russia* 43 B11
Ilovatka, *Russia* 41 F14
Ilovlya →, *Russia* 43 B10
Ilubabor □, *Ethiopia* 77 F3
Ilūkste, *Latvia* 40 D5
Ilva Mică, *Romania* 38 B7
Ilwaco, *U.S.A.* 112 D2
Ilwaki, *Indonesia* 57 F7
Ilyichevsk, *Ukraine* 42 C4
Imabari, *Japan* 49 G6
Imaloto →, *Madag.* 85 C8
İmamoğlu, *Turkey* 66 E6
Imandra, Oz., *Russia* 44 C4
Imari, *Japan* 49 H4
Imasa, *Sudan* 76 D4
Imbâbah, *Egypt* 76 H7
Imbabura □, *Ecuador* 120 C2
Imbaimadai, *Guyana* 121 B5
Imbler, *U.S.A.* 110 D5
Imdahane, *Morocco* 74 B3
imeni 26 Bakinskikh Komissarov, *Azerbaijan* 67 D13
Imeni Poliny Osipenko, *Russia* 45 D14
Imeri, Serra, *Brazil* 120 C4
Imerimandroso, *Madag.* 85 B8
Imesan, *Mauritania* 74 D1
Imi, *Ethiopia* 68 F3
Imishly, *Azerbaijan* 43 G13
Imitek, *Morocco* 74 C3
Imlay, *U.S.A.* 110 F4
Imlay City, *U.S.A.* 106 C1
Immenstadt, *Germany* 19 H6
Immingham, *U.K.* 12 D7
Immokalee, *U.S.A.* 105 M5
Imo □, *Nigeria* 79 D6
Imola, *Italy* 33 D8
Imotski, *Croatia* 21 M7
Imperatriz, *Amazonas, Brazil* 124 B4
Imperatriz, *Maranhão, Brazil* 122 C2
Impéria, *Italy* 32 E5
Imperial, *Canada* 101 C7
Imperial, *Peru* 124 C2
Imperial, *Calif., U.S.A.* 113 N11
Imperial, *Nebr., U.S.A.* 108 E4
Imperial Beach, *U.S.A.* 113 N9
Imperial Dam, *U.S.A.* 113 N12
Imperial Reservoir, *U.S.A.* 113 N12
Imperial Valley, *U.S.A.* 113 N11
Imperieuse Reef, *Australia* 88 C2
Impfondo, *Congo* 80 D3
Imphal, *India* 61 G18
Imphy, *France* 26 B7
İmralı, *Turkey* 66 C3
Imranlı, *Turkey* 67 D8
İmroz = Gökçeada, *Turkey* 39 J8
Imst, *Austria* 19 H6
Imuruan B., *Phil.* 57 B5
In Belbel, *Algeria* 75 C5
In Delimane, *Mali* 79 B5
In Rhar, *Algeria* 75 C5
In Salah, *Algeria* 75 C5
In Tallak, *Mali* 79 B5
Ina, *Japan* 49 G8
Inajá, *Brazil* 122 C4
Inangahua Junction, *N.Z.* 87 J3
Inanwatan, *Indonesia* 57 E8
Iñapari, *Peru* 124 C4
Inari, *Finland* 8 B19
Inarijärvi, *Finland* 8 B19
Inawashiro-Ko, *Japan* 48 F10
Inca, *Spain* 36 B9
Incaguasi, *Chile* 126 B1
İnce-Burnu, *Turkey* 42 E6
İncekum Burnu, *Turkey* 66 E5
Inchon, *S. Korea* 51 F14
Incio, *Spain* 30 C3
İncirliova, *Turkey* 66 E2
Incomáti →, *Mozam.* 85 D5
Inda Silase, *Ethiopia* 77 E4
Indalsälven →, *Sweden* 10 B11
Indaw, *Burma* 61 G20
Indbir, *Ethiopia* 77 F4
Independence, *Calif., U.S.A.* 111 H4
Independence, *Iowa, U.S.A.* 108 D9
Independence, *Kans., U.S.A.* 109 G7
Independence, *Mo., U.S.A.* 108 F7
Independence, *Oreg., U.S.A.* 110 D2
Independence Fjord, *Greenland* 4 A6
Independence Mts., *U.S.A.* 110 F5
Independência, *Brazil* 122 C3
Independenţa, *Romania* 38 D10
Inderborskiy, *Kazakhstan* 43 B14
Index, *U.S.A.* 112 C5
India ■, *Asia* 60 K11
Indian →, *U.S.A.* 105 M5
Indian Cabins, *Canada* 100 B5
Indian Harbour, *Canada* 99 B8
Indian Head, *Canada* 101 C8
Indian Ocean 46 K11

Indian Springs, *U.S.A.* 113 J11
Indiana, *U.S.A.* 106 F5
Indiana □, *U.S.A.* 104 E3
Indianapolis, *U.S.A.* 104 F2
Indianola, *Iowa, U.S.A.* 108 E8
Indianola, *Miss., U.S.A.* 109 J9
Indiapora, *Brazil* 123 E1
Indiga, *Russia* 44 C5
Indigirka →, *Russia* 45 B15
Inđija, *Serbia* 21 K10
Indio, *U.S.A.* 113 M10
Indonesia ■, *Asia* 56 F5
Indore, *India* 62 H6
Indramayu, *Indonesia* 57 G13
Indravati →, *India* 61 K12
Indre □, *France* 25 F8
Indre →, *France* 24 E7
Indre-et-Loire □, *France* 24 E7
Indus →, *Pakistan* 62 G2
Indus, Mouth of the, *Pakistan* 62 H2
İnebolu, *Turkey* 66 C5
İnegöl, *Turkey* 66 C3
Inés, Mt., *Argentina* 128 C3
Ineu, *Romania* 38 C4
Inezgane, *Morocco* 74 B3
Infantes, *Spain* 29 G1
Infiernillo, Presa del, *Mexico* 114 D4
Infiesto, *Spain* 30 B5
Ingapirca, *Ecuador* 120 D2
Ingelmunster, *Belgium* 17 G2
Ingende, *Zaïre* 80 E3
Ingeniero Jacobacci, *Argentina* 128 B3
Ingenio, *Canary Is.* 36 G4
Ingenio Santa Ana, *Argentina* 126 B2
Ingersoll, *Canada* 106 C4
Ingham, *Australia* 90 B4
Ingleborough, *U.K.* 12 C5
Inglewood, *Queens., Australia* 91 D5
Inglewood, *Vic., Australia* 91 F3
Inglewood, *N.Z.* 87 H5
Inglewood, *U.S.A.* 113 M8
Ingólfshöfði, *Iceland* 8 E5
Ingolstadt, *Germany* 19 G7
Ingomar, *U.S.A.* 110 C10
Ingonish, *Canada* 99 C7
Ingore, *Guinea-Biss.* 78 C1
Ingraj Bazar, *India* 63 G13
Ingrid Christensen Coast, *Antarctica* 5 C6
Ingul →, *Ukraine* 42 C5
Ingulec, *Ukraine* 42 C5
Ingulets →, *Ukraine* 42 C5
Inguri →, *Georgia* 43 E9
Ingwavuma, *S. Africa* 85 D5
Inhaca, I., *Mozam.* 85 D5
Inhafenga, *Mozam.* 85 C5
Inhambane, *Mozam.* 85 C6
Inhambane □, *Mozam.* 85 C5
Inhambupe, *Brazil* 123 D4
Inhaminga, *Mozam.* 83 F4
Inharrime, *Mozam.* 85 C6
Inharrime →, *Mozam.* 85 C6
Inhuma, *Brazil* 122 C3
Inhumas, *Brazil* 123 E2
Iniesta, *Spain* 29 F3
Ining = Yining, *China* 44 E9
Inini □, *Fr. Guiana* 121 C7
Inírida →, *Colombia* 120 C4
Inishbofin, *Ireland* 15 C1
Inishmore, *Ireland* 15 C2
Inishowen, *Ireland* 15 A4
Injune, *Australia* 91 D4
Inklin, *Canada* 100 B2
Inklin →, *Canada* 100 B2
Inkom, *U.S.A.* 110 E7
Inle L., *Burma* 61 J20
Inn →, *Austria* 19 G9
Innamincka, *Australia* 91 D3
Inner Hebrides, *U.K.* 14 D2
Inner Mongolia = Nei Monggol Zizhiqu □, *China* 50 C6
Inner Sound, *U.K.* 14 D3
Innerkip, *Canada* 106 C4
Innerkirchen, *Switz.* 22 C6
Innerste →, *Germany* 18 C5
Innetalling I., *Canada* 98 A4
Innisfail, *Australia* 90 B4
Innisfail, *Canada* 100 C6
In'no-shima, *Japan* 49 G6
Innsbruck, *Austria* 19 H7
Inny →, *Ireland* 15 C4
Inocência, *Brazil* 123 E1
Inongo, *Zaïre* 80 E3
Inoucdjouac, *Canada* 97 C12
Inowrocław, *Poland* 20 C8
Inpundong, *N. Korea* 51 D14
Inquisivi, *Bolivia* 124 D4
Ins, *Switz.* 22 B4
Inscription, C., *Australia* 89 E1
Insein, *Burma* 61 L20
Însurăţei, *Romania* 38 E10
Intendente Alvear, *Argentina* 126 D3
Interior, *U.S.A.* 108 D4
Interlaken, *Switz.* 25 F14
International Falls, *U.S.A.* 108 A8
Intiyaco, *Argentina* 126 B3
Intragna, *Switz.* 23 D7
Intutu, *Peru* 120 D3
Inútil, B., *Chile* 128 D2
Inuvik, *Canada* 96 B6
Inveraray, *U.K.* 14 E3
Inverbervie, *U.K.* 14 E6
Invercargill, *N.Z.* 87 M2
Inverell, *Australia* 91 D5
Invergordon, *U.K.* 14 D4
Invermere, *Canada* 100 C5
Inverness, *Canada* 99 C7
Inverness, *U.K.* 14 D4
Inverness, *U.S.A.* 105 L4
Inverurie, *U.K.* 14 D6
Inverway, *Australia* 88 C4
Investigator Group, *Australia* 91 E1
Investigator Str., *Australia* 91 F2
Inya, *Russia* 44 D9
Inyanga, *Zimbabwe* 83 F3
Inyangani, *Zimbabwe* 83 F3
Inyantue, *Zimbabwe* 83 F2
Inyo Mts., *U.S.A.* 111 H5
Inyokern, *U.S.A.* 113 K9
Inza, *Russia* 41 E15
Inzhavino, *Russia* 41 E13
Iō-Jima, *Japan* 49 J5
Ioánnina, *Greece* 39 K3
Iola, *U.S.A.* 109 G7
Ion Corvin, *Romania* 38 E10
Iona, *U.K.* 14 E2
Ione, *Calif., U.S.A.* 112 G6
Ione, *Wash., U.S.A.* 110 B5
Ionia, *U.S.A.* 104 D3
Ionian Is. = Iónioi Nísoi, *Greece* 39 L3
Ionian Sea, *Europe* 6 H9
Iónioi Nísoi, *Greece* 39 L3
Iori →, *Azerbaijan* 43 F12
Íos, *Greece* 39 N8
Iowa □, *U.S.A.* 108 D8
Iowa City, *U.S.A.* 108 E9
Iowa Falls, *U.S.A.* 108 D8
Ipala, *Tanzania* 82 C3
Ipameri, *Brazil* 123 E2
Iparía, *Peru* 124 B3
Ipáti, *Greece* 39 L5
Ipatinga, *Brazil* 123 E3
Ipatovo, *Russia* 43 D10
Ipel →, *Europe* 21 G9
Ipiales, *Colombia* 120 C2
Ipiaú, *Brazil* 123 D4
Ipin = Yibin, *China* 52 C5
Ipirá, *Brazil* 123 D4
Ipiranga, *Brazil* 120 D4
Ipixuna, *Brazil* 124 B3
Ipixuna →, *Amazonas, Brazil* 124 B3
Ipixuna →, *Amazonas, Brazil* 125 B5
Ipoh, *Malaysia* 59 K3
Iporá, *Brazil* 123 D1
Ippy, *C.A.R.* 73 G9
İpsala, *Turkey* 66 C2
Ipsárion Óros, *Greece* 39 J7
Ipswich, *Australia* 91 D5
Ipswich, *U.K.* 13 E9
Ipswich, *Mass., U.S.A.* 107 D14
Ipswich, *S. Dak., U.S.A.* 108 C5
Ipu, *Brazil* 122 B3
Ipueiras, *Brazil* 122 B3
Ipupiara, *Brazil* 123 D3
Iput →, *Belorussia* 40 E7
Iqaluit, *Canada* 97 B13
Iquique, *Chile* 124 E3
Iquitos, *Peru* 120 D3
Irabu-Jima, *Japan* 49 M2
Iracoubo, *Fr. Guiana* 121 B7
Īrafshān, *Iran* 65 E9
Irahuan, *Phil.* 55 G3
Iráklia, *Greece* 39 N8
Iráklion, *Greece* 37 D7
Iráklion □, *Greece* 37 D7
Irala, *Paraguay* 127 B5
Iramba □, *Tanzania* 82 C3
Iran ■, *Asia* 65 C7
Iran, Gunung-Gunung, *Malaysia* 56 D4
Iran Ra. = Iran, Gunung-Gunung, *Malaysia* 56 D4
Īrānshahr, *Iran* 65 E9
Irapa, *Venezuela* 121 A5
Irapuato, *Mexico* 114 C4
Iraq ■, *Asia* 64 C5
Irarrar, O. →, *Mali* 75 D5
Irati, *Brazil* 127 B5
Irbid, *Jordan* 69 C4
Irbid □, *Jordan* 69 C5
Irebu, *Zaïre* 80 E3
Irecê, *Brazil* 122 D3
Iregua →, *Spain* 28 C7
Ireland ■, *Europe* 15 D4
Ireland's Eye, *Ireland* 15 C5
Irele, *Nigeria* 79 D6
Ireng →, *Brazil* 121 C6
Iret, *Russia* 45 C16
Irgiz, Bolshaya →, *Russia* 41 E16
Irhârharene, *Algeria* 75 C6
Irharrhar, O. →, *Algeria* 75 C6
Irherm, *Morocco* 74 B3
Irhil Mgoun, *Morocco* 74 B3
Irhyangdong, *N. Korea* 51 D15
Iri, *S. Korea* 51 G14
Irian Jaya □, *Indonesia* 57 E9
Irié, *Guinea* 78 D3
Iriga, *Phil.* 55 E5
Iringa, *Tanzania* 82 D4
Iringa □, *Tanzania* 82 D4
Iriomote-Jima, *Japan* 49 M1
Iriona, *Honduras* 116 C2
Iriri →, *Brazil* 121 D7
Iriri Novo →, *Brazil* 125 B7
Irish Republic ■, *Europe* 15 D4
Irish Sea, *Europe* 12 D3
Irkineyeva, *Russia* 45 D10
Irkutsk, *Russia* 45 D11
Irma, *Canada* 101 C6
Irō-Zaki, *Japan* 49 G9
Iroise, Mer d', *France* 24 D2
Iron Baron, *Australia* 91 E2
Iron Gate = Portile de Fier, *Europe* 38 E5
Iron Knob, *Australia* 91 E2
Iron Mountain, *U.S.A.* 104 C1
Iron Ra., *Australia* 90 A3
Iron River, *U.S.A.* 108 B10
Ironbridge, *U.K.* 13 E5
Irondequoit, *U.S.A.* 106 C7
Ironstone Kopje, *Botswana* 84 D3
Ironton, *Mo., U.S.A.* 109 G9
Ironton, *Ohio, U.S.A.* 104 F4
Ironwood, *U.S.A.* 108 B9
Iroquois Falls, *Canada* 98 C3
Irosin, *Phil.* 55 E6
Irpen, *Ukraine* 40 F7
Irrara Cr. →, *Australia* 91 D4
Irrawaddy □, *Burma* 61 L19
Irrawaddy →, *Burma* 61 M19
Irsina, *Italy* 35 B9
Irtysh →, *Russia* 44 C7
Irumu, *Zaïre* 82 B2
Irún, *Spain* 28 B3
Irunea = Pamplona, *Spain* 28 C3
Irurzun, *Spain* 28 C3
Irvine, *Canada* 101 D6
Irvine, *U.K.* 14 F4
Irvine, *Calif., U.S.A.* 113 M9
Irvine, *Ky., U.S.A.* 104 G4
Irvinestown, *U.K.* 15 B4
Irving, *U.S.A.* 109 J6
Irvona, *U.S.A.* 106 F6
Irwin →, *Australia* 89 E1
Irymple, *Australia* 91 E3
Is-sur-Tille, *France* 25 E12
Isa, *Nigeria* 79 C6
Isaac →, *Australia* 90 C4
Isabel, *U.S.A.* 108 C4
Isabela, I., *Mexico* 114 C3
Isabella, *Phil.* 55 H5
Isabella, Cord., *Nic.* 116 D2
Isabella Ra., *Australia* 88 D3
Ísafjarðardjúp, *Iceland* 8 C2
Ísafjörður, *Iceland* 8 C2
Isagarh, *India* 62 G7
Isahaya, *Japan* 49 H5
Isaka, *Tanzania* 82 C3
Isana = Içana →, *Brazil* 120 C4
Isangi, *Zaïre* 80 D4
Isar →, *Germany* 19 G8
Isarco →, *Italy* 33 B8
Ísari, *Greece* 39 M5
Isbergues, *France* 25 B9
Iscayachi, *Bolivia* 125 E4
Ischia, *Italy* 34 B6
Iscuandé, *Colombia* 120 C2
Isdell →, *Australia* 88 C3
Ise, *Japan* 49 G8
Ise-Wan, *Japan* 49 G8
Isefjord, *Denmark* 11 J5
Iseltwald, *Switz.* 22 C5
Isenthal, *Switz.* 23 C7
Iseo, *Italy* 32 C7
Iseo, L. d', *Italy* 32 C7
Iseramagazi, *Tanzania* 82 C3
Isère □, *France* 27 C9
Isère →, *France* 27 D8
Iserlohn, *Germany* 18 D3
Isérnia, *Italy* 35 A7
Iseyin, *Nigeria* 79 D5
Isherton, *Guyana* 121 C6
Ishigaki-Shima, *Japan* 49 M2
Ishikari-Gawa →, *Japan* 48 C10
Ishikari-Sammyaku, *Japan* 48 C11
Ishikari-Wan, *Japan* 48 C10
Ishikawa □, *Japan* 49 F8
Ishim, *Russia* 44 D7
Ishim →, *Russia* 44 D8
Ishinomaki, *Japan* 48 E10
Ishioka, *Japan* 49 F10
Ishkuman, *Pakistan* 63 A5
Ishpeming, *U.S.A.* 104 B2
Isigny-sur-Mer, *France* 24 C5
Isil Kul, *Russia* 44 D8
Isiolo, *Kenya* 82 B4
Isiolo □, *Kenya* 82 B4
Isipingo Beach, *S. Africa* 85 E5
Isiro, *Zaïre* 82 B2
Isisford, *Australia* 90 C3
İskederun, *Turkey* 66 E7
İskenderun, *Turkey* 66 E7
İskenderun Körfezi, *Turkey* 66 E6
İskilip, *Turkey* 42 F6
Iskŭr →, *Bulgaria* 38 F7
Iskut →, *Canada* 100 B2
Isla →, *U.K.* 14 E5
Isla Cristina, *Spain* 31 H3
Isla Vista, *U.S.A.* 113 L7
İslâhiye, *Turkey* 66 E7
Islamabad, *Pakistan* 62 C5
Islamkot, *Pakistan* 62 G4
Island →, *Canada* 100 A4
Island Falls, *Canada* 98 C3
Island Falls, *U.S.A.* 99 C6
Island L., *Canada* 101 C10
Island Lagoon, *Australia* 91 E2
Island Pond, *U.S.A.* 107 B13
Islands, B. of, *Canada* 99 C8
Islay, *U.K.* 14 F2
Isle →, *France* 26 D3
Isle aux Morts, *Canada* 99 C8
Isle of Wight □, *U.K.* 13 G6
Isle Royale, *U.S.A.* 108 A10
Isleta, *U.S.A.* 111 J10
Isleton, *U.S.A.* 112 G5
Ismail, *Ukraine* 42 D3
Ismâ'ilîya, *Egypt* 76 H8
Ismaning, *Germany* 19 G7
Ismay, *U.S.A.* 108 B2
Isna, *Egypt* 76 B3
Isogstalo, *India* 63 B8
Isola del Gran Sasso d'Italia, *Italy* 33 F10
Ísola del Liri, *Italy* 34 A6
Ísola della Scala, *Italy* 32 C8
Ísola di Capo Rizzuto, *Italy* 35 D10
İsparta, *Turkey* 66 E4
İsparta □, *Turkey* 66 E4
Isperikh, *Bulgaria* 38 F9
Ispica, *Italy* 35 F7
İspir, *Turkey* 43 F9
Israel ■, *Asia* 69 D3
Issano, *Guyana* 121 B6
Issia, *Ivory C.* 78 D3
Issoire, *France* 26 C7
Issoudun, *France* 25 F8
Issyk-Kul, Ozero, *Kirghizia* 44 E8
Ist, *Croatia* 33 D11
Istaihah, *U.A.E.* 65 F7
İstanbul, *Turkey* 66 C3
İstanbul □, *Turkey* 66 C3
Istmina, *Colombia* 120 B2
Istok, *Serbia* 21 N10
Istokpoga, L., *U.S.A.* 105 M5
Istra, *Croatia* 33 C11
Istra, *Russia* 41 D10
İstranca Dağları, *Turkey* 39 H10
Istres, *France* 27 E8
Istria = Istra, *Croatia* 33 C11
Itá, *Paraguay* 126 B4
Itabaiana, *Paraíba, Brazil* 122 C4
Itabaiana, *Sergipe, Brazil* 122 D4
Itabaianinha, *Brazil* 122 D4
Itaberaba, *Brazil* 123 D3
Itaberaí, *Brazil* 123 E2
Itabira, *Brazil* 123 E3
Itabirito, *Brazil* 123 F3
Itaboca, *Brazil* 121 D5
Itabuna, *Brazil* 123 D4
Itacajá, *Brazil* 122 C2
Itacaunas →, *Brazil* 122 C2
Itacoatiara, *Brazil* 121 D6
Itacuaí →, *Brazil* 124 A3
Itaguaçu, *Brazil* 123 E3
Itaguari →, *Brazil* 123 D3
Itaguatins, *Brazil* 122 C2
Itaim →, *Brazil* 122 C3
Itainópolis, *Brazil* 122 C3
Itaipu Dam, *Brazil* 127 B5
Itaituba, *Brazil* 121 D6
Itajaí, *Brazil* 127 B6
Itajubá, *Brazil* 123 F2
Itajuípe, *Brazil* 123 D4
Itaka, *Tanzania* 83 D3
Italy ■, *Europe* 7 G8
Itamataré, *Brazil* 122 B2
Itambacuri, *Brazil* 123 E3
Itambé, *Brazil* 123 E3
Itampolo, *Madag.* 85 C7
Itanhauã →, *Brazil* 121 D5
Itanhém, *Brazil* 123 E3
Itapaci, *Brazil* 123 D2
Itapagé, *Brazil* 122 B4
Itaparica, I. de, *Brazil* 123 D4
Itapebi, *Brazil* 123 E4
Itapecuru-Mirim, *Brazil* 122 B3
Itaperuna, *Brazil* 123 F3
Itapetinga, *Brazil* 123 E3
Itapetininga, *Brazil* 127 A6
Itapeva, *Brazil* 127 A6
Itapicuru →, *Bahia, Brazil* 122 D4
Itapicuru →, *Maranhão, Brazil* 122 B3
Itapinima, *Brazil* 125 B5
Itapipoca, *Brazil* 122 B4
Itapiranga, *Brazil* 121 D6
Itapiúna, *Brazil* 122 B4
Itaporanga, *Brazil* 122 C4
Itapuá □, *Paraguay* 127 B4
Itapuranga, *Brazil* 123 E2
Itaquari, *Brazil* 123 F3
Itaquatiara, *Brazil* 121 D6
Itaquí, *Brazil* 126 B4
Itararé, *Brazil* 127 A6
Itarsi, *India* 62 H7
Itarumã, *Brazil* 123 E1
Itatí, *Argentina* 126 B4
Itatira, *Brazil* 122 B4
Itatuba, *Brazil* 125 B5
Itatupa, *Brazil* 121 D7
Itaueira, *Brazil* 122 C3
Itaueira →, *Brazil* 122 C3
Itaúna, *Brazil* 123 F3
Itbayat, *Phil.* 55 A4
Itchen →, *U.K.* 13 G6
Ite, *Peru* 124 D3
Itezhi Tezhi, L., *Zambia* 83 F2
Ithaca = Itháki, *Greece* 39 L3
Ithaca, *U.S.A.* 107 D8
Itháki, *Greece* 39 L3
Itinga, *Brazil* 123 E3
Itiquira, *Brazil* 125 D7
Itiquira →, *Brazil* 125 D6
Itiruçu, *Brazil* 123 D3
Itiúba, *Brazil* 122 D4
Ito, *Japan* 49 G9
Itoigawa, *Japan* 49 F8
Iton →, *France* 24 C8
Itonamas →, *Bolivia* 125 C5
Itsa, *Egypt* 76 J7
Íttiri, *Italy* 34 B1
Ittoqqortoormiit = Scoresbysund, *Greenland* 4 B6
Itu, *Brazil* 127 A6
Itu, *Nigeria* 79 D6
Ituaçu, *Brazil* 123 D3
Ituango, *Colombia* 120 B2
Ituiutaba, *Brazil* 123 E2
Itumbiara, *Brazil* 123 E2
Ituna, *Canada* 101 C8
Itunge Port, *Tanzania* 83 D3
Ituni, *Guyana* 121 B6
Itupiranga, *Brazil* 122 C2
Iturama, *Brazil* 123 E1
Iturbe, *Argentina* 126 A2
Ituri →, *Zaïre* 82 B2
Iturup, Ostrov, *Russia* 45 E15
Ituverava, *Brazil* 123 F2
Ituxi →, *Brazil* 125 B5
Ituyuro →, *Argentina* 126 A3
Itzehoe, *Germany* 18 B5
Ivaí →, *Brazil* 127 A5
Ivalo, *Finland* 8 B19
Ivalojoki →, *Finland* 8 B19
Ivangorod, *Russia* 40 B6
Ivanhoe, *N.S.W., Australia* 91 E3
Ivanhoe, *W. Austral., Australia* 88 C4
Ivanhoe, *U.S.A.* 112 J7
Ivanhoe L., *Canada* 101 A7
Ivanić Grad, *Croatia* 33 C13
Ivanjica, *Serbia* 21 M10
Ivanjšcice, *Croatia* 33 B13
Ivankoyskoye Vdkhr., *Russia* 41 C10
Ivano-Frankivsk = Ivano-Frankovsk, *Ukraine* 40 G4
Ivano-Frankovsk, *Ukraine* 40 G4
Ivanovo, *Belorussia* 40 E4
Ivanovo, *Russia* 41 C12
Ivato, *Madag.* 85 C8
Ivaylovgrad, *Bulgaria* 39 H9
Ivinheima →, *Brazil* 127 A5
Iviza = Ibiza, *Spain* 36 C7
Ivohibe, *Madag.* 85 C8
Ivolândia, *Brazil* 123 E1
Ivory Coast ■, *Africa* 78 D3
Ivrea, *Italy* 32 C4
Ivugivik, *Canada* 97 B12
Iwahig, *Phil.* 56 C5
Iwaizumi, *Japan* 48 E10
Iwaki, *Japan* 49 F10
Iwakuni, *Japan* 49 G6
Iwamizawa, *Japan* 48 C10
Iwanai, *Japan* 48 C10
Iwata, *Japan* 49 G8
Iwate □, *Japan* 48 E10
Iwate-San, *Japan* 48 E10
Iwo, *Nigeria* 79 D5
Ixiamas, *Bolivia* 124 C4
Ixopo, *S. Africa* 85 E5
Ixtepec, *Mexico* 115 D5
Ixtlán del Río, *Mexico* 114 C4
Iyo, *Japan* 49 H6
Izabal, L. de, *Guatemala* 116 C2
Izamal, *Mexico* 115 C7
Izberbash, *Russia* 43 E12
Izegem, *Belgium* 17 G2
Izena-Shima, *Japan* 49 L3
Izhevsk, *Russia* 44 D6
Izmayil = Ismail, *Ukraine* 42 D3
İzmir, *Turkey* 66 D2
İzmir □, *Turkey* 66 D2
İzmit, *Turkey* 66 C3
Iznajar, *Spain* 31 H6
Iznalloz, *Spain* 29 H1
İznik Gölü, *Turkey* 66 C3
Izobil'nyy, *Russia* 43 D9
Izola, *Slovenia* 33 C10
Izozog, Bañados de, *Bolivia* 125 D5
Izra, *Syria* 69 C5
Iztochni Rodopi, *Bulgaria* 39 H8
Izu-Shotō, *Japan* 49 G10
Izumi-sano, *Japan* 49 G7
Izumo, *Japan* 49 G6
Izyaslav, *Ukraine* 40 F5
Izyum, *Ukraine* 42 B7

J

J.F. Rodrigues, *Brazil* 122 B1
Jaba, *Ethiopia* 77 F4
Jabal el Awlîya, *Sudan* 77 D3
Jabal Lubnān, *Lebanon* 69 B4
Jabalón →, *Spain* 31 G6
Jabalpur, *India* 63 H8
Jabbūl, *Syria* 64 B3
Jablah, *Syria* 64 C3
Jablanac, *Croatia* 33 D11
Jablonec, *Czech.* 20 E5

Jabłonowo, Poland 20 B9
Jaboatão, Brazil 122 C4
Jaboticabal, Brazil 127 A6
Jaburu, Brazil 125 B5
Jaca, Spain 28 C4
Jacaré, Brazil 122 D3
Jacareí, Brazil 127 A6
Jacarèzinho, Brazil 127 A6
Jaciara, Brazil 125 D7
Jacinto, Brazil 123 E3
Jaciparaná, Brazil 125 B5
Jackman, U.S.A. 99 C5
Jacksboro, U.S.A. 109 J5
Jackson, Australia 91 D4
Jackson, Ala., U.S.A. 105 K2
Jackson, Calif., U.S.A. 112 G6
Jackson, Ky., U.S.A. 104 G4
Jackson, Mich., U.S.A. 104 D3
Jackson, Minn., U.S.A. 108 D7
Jackson, Miss., U.S.A. 109 J9
Jackson, Mo., U.S.A. 109 G10
Jackson, Ohio, U.S.A. 104 F4
Jackson, Tenn., U.S.A. 105 H1
Jackson, Wyo., U.S.A. 110 E8
Jackson B., N.Z. 87 K2
Jackson L., U.S.A. 110 E8
Jacksons, N.Z. 87 K3
Jacksonville, Ala., U.S.A. 105 J3
Jacksonville, Calif., U.S.A. 112 H6
Jacksonville, Fla., U.S.A. 105 K5
Jacksonville, Ill., U.S.A. 108 F9
Jacksonville, N.C., U.S.A. 105 H7
Jacksonville, Oreg., U.S.A. 110 E2
Jacksonville, Tex., U.S.A. 109 K7
Jacksonville Beach, U.S.A. 105 K5
Jacmel, Haiti 117 C5
Jacob Lake, U.S.A. 111 H7
Jacobabad, Pakistan 62 E3
Jacobina, Brazil 122 D3
Jacques-Cartier, Mt., Canada 99 C6
Jacqueville, Ivory C. 78 D4
Jacuí →, Brazil 127 C5
Jacumba, U.S.A. 113 N10
Jacundá →, Brazil 122 B1
Jade, Germany 18 B4
Jadebusen, Germany 18 B4
Jadoigne, Belgium 17 G5
Jadotville = Likasi, Zaïre 83 E2
Jadraque, Spain 28 E2
Jādū, Libya 75 B7
Jaén, Peru 124 B2
Jaén, Spain 31 H7
Jaén □, Spain 31 H7
Jafène, Africa 74 D3
Jaffa = Tel Aviv-Yafo, Israel 69 C3
Jaffa, C., Australia 91 F2
Jaffna, Sri Lanka 60 Q12
Jagadhri, India 62 D7
Jagadishpur, India 63 G11
Jagdalpur, India 61 K12
Jagersfontein, S. Africa 84 D4
Jagraon, India 60 D9
Jagst →, Germany 19 F5
Jagtial, India 60 K11
Jaguaquara, Brazil 123 D3
Jaguariaíva, Brazil 127 A6
Jaguaribe, Brazil 122 C4
Jaguaribe →, Brazil 122 B4
Jaguaruana, Brazil 122 B4
Jagüey Grande, Cuba 116 B3
Jahangirabad, India 62 E8
Jahrom, Iran 65 D7
Jaicós, Brazil 122 C3
Jailolo, Indonesia 57 D7
Jailolo, Selat, Indonesia 57 D7
Jaipur, India 62 F6
Jājarm, Iran 65 B8
Jajce, Bos.-H. 21 L7
Jakarta, Indonesia 57 G12
Jakobstad, Finland 8 E17
Jakupica, Macedonia 39 H4
Jal, U.S.A. 109 J3
Jalalabad, Afghan. 62 B4
Jalalabad, India 63 F8
Jalalpur Jattan, Pakistan 62 C6
Jalama, U.S.A. 113 L6
Jalapa, Guatemala 116 D2
Jalapa Enríquez, Mexico 115 D5
Jalaun, India 63 F8
Jales, Brazil 123 F1
Jaleswar, Nepal 63 F11
Jalgaon, Maharashtra, India 60 J10
Jalgaon, Maharashtra, India 60 J9
Jalhay, Belgium 17 G7
Jalībah, Iraq 64 D5
Jalingo, Nigeria 79 D7
Jalisco □, Mexico 114 C4
Jalkot, Pakistan 63 B5
Jallas →, Spain 30 C1
Jalna, India 60 K9
Jalón →, Spain 28 D3
Jalpa, Mexico 114 C4
Jalpaiguri, India 61 F16
Jaluit I., Pac. Oc. 92 G8
Jalūlā, Iraq 64 C5
Jamaari, Nigeria 79 C6
Jamaica ■, W. Indies 116 C4
Jamalpur, Bangla. 61 G16
Jamalpur, India 63 G12
Jamalpurganj, India 63 H13
Jamanxim →, Brazil 125 A6
Jamari, Brazil 125 B5
Jamari →, Brazil 125 B5

Jambe, Indonesia 57 E8
Jambes, Belgium 17 H5
Jambi, Indonesia 56 E2
Jambi □, Indonesia 56 E2
Jambusar, India 62 H5
James →, U.S.A. 108 D6
James B., Canada 97 C11
James Ras., Australia 88 D5
James Ross I., Antarctica 5 C18
Jamestown, Australia 91 E2
Jamestown, S. Africa 84 E4
Jamestown, Ky., U.S.A. 104 G3
Jamestown, N. Dak., U.S.A. 108 B5
Jamestown, N.Y., U.S.A. 106 D5
Jamestown, Pa., U.S.A. 106 E4
Jamestown, Tenn., U.S.A. 105 G3
Jamīlābād, Iran 65 C6
Jamiltepec, Mexico 115 D5
Jamkhandi, India 60 L9
Jammerbugt, Denmark 11 G3
Jammu, India 62 C6
Jammu & Kashmir □, India 63 B7
Jamnagar, India 62 H4
Jamoigne, Belgium 17 J6
Jampur, Pakistan 62 E4
Jamrud, Pakistan 62 C4
Jamshedpur, India 63 H12
Jamtara, India 63 H12
Jämtlands län □, Sweden 10 B7
Jan Kempdorp, S. Africa 84 D3
Jan L., Canada 101 C8
Jan Mayen, Arctic 4 B7
Janaúba, Brazil 123 E3
Janaucu, I., Brazil 122 A1
Jand, Pakistan 62 C5
Janda, L. de la, Spain 31 J5
Jandaia, Brazil 123 E1
Jandaq, Iran 65 C7
Jandia, Canary Is. 36 F5
Jandia, Pta. de, Canary Is. 36 F5
Jandiatuba →, Brazil 120 D4
Jandola, Pakistan 62 C4
Jandowae, Australia 91 D5
Jandrain-Jandrenouilles, Belgium 17 G5
Jándula →, Spain 31 G6
Janesville, U.S.A. 108 D10
Janga, Ghana 79 C4
Jango, Brazil 125 E6
Janīn, Jordan 69 C4
Janjina, Croatia 21 N7
Janos, Mexico 114 A3
Jánosháza, Hungary 21 H7
Janów Podlaski, Poland 20 C13
Januária, Brazil 123 E3
Janub Dârfûr □, Sudan 77 E2
Janub Kordofân □, Sudan 77 E3
Janubio, Canary Is. 36 F6
Janville, France 25 D8
Janzé, France 24 E5
Jaora, India 62 H6
Japan ■, Asia 49 G8
Japan, Sea of, Asia 48 E7
Japan Trench, Pac. Oc. 92 D6
Japen = Yapen, Indonesia 57 E9
Japurá →, Brazil 120 D4
Jaque, Panama 120 B2
Jarābulus, Syria 64 B3
Jaraguá, Brazil 123 E2
Jaraguari, Brazil 125 E7
Jaraicejo, Spain 31 F5
Jaraíz, Spain 30 E5
Jarama →, Spain 28 E1
Jaramillo, Argentina 128 C3
Jarandilla, Spain 30 E5
Jaranwala, Pakistan 62 D5
Jarash, Jordan 69 C4
Jarauçu →, Brazil 121 D7
Jardim, Brazil 126 A4
Jardín, Spain 29 G2
Jardines de la Reina, Is., Cuba 116 B4
Jargalang, China 51 C12
Jargalant = Hovd, Mongolia 54 B4
Jargeau, France 25 E9
Jari →, Brazil 121 D7
Jarīr, W. al →, Si. Arabia 64 E4
Jarmen, Germany 18 B9
Jarnac, France 26 C3
Jarny, France 25 C12
Jarocin, Poland 20 D7
Jarosław, Poland 20 E12
Järpås, Sweden 11 F6
Järpen, Sweden 10 A7
Jarrahdale, Australia 89 F2
Jarres, Plaine des, Laos 58 C4
Jarso, Ethiopia 77 F4
Jartai, China 50 E3
Jaru, Brazil 125 C5
Jaru →, Brazil 125 C5
Jarud Qi, China 51 B11
Jarvis, Canada 106 D4
Jarvis I., Pac. Oc. 93 H12
Jarwa, India 63 F10
Jaša Tomić, Serbia 21 K10
Jāsimīyah, Iraq 64 C5
Jasin, Malaysia 59 L4
Jäsk, Iran 65 E8
Jasło, Poland 20 F11
Jason, Is., Falk. Is. 128 D4
Jasper, Alta., Canada 100 C5
Jasper, Ont., Canada 107 B9
Jasper, Ala., U.S.A. 105 J2

Jasper, Fla., U.S.A. 105 K4
Jasper, Minn., U.S.A. 108 D6
Jasper, Tex., U.S.A. 109 K8
Jasper Nat. Park, Canada 100 C5
Jassy = Iași, Romania 38 B10
Jastrebarsko, Croatia 33 C12
Jastrzębie Zdrój, Poland 20 F8
Jászárokszállás, Hungary 21 H10
Jászberény, Hungary 21 H10
Jászladány, Hungary 21 H10
Jataí, Brazil 123 E1
Jatapu →, Brazil 121 D6
Jati, Pakistan 62 G3
Jatibarang, Indonesia 57 G13
Jatinegara, Indonesia 57 G12
Játiva, Spain 29 G4
Jatobal, Brazil 122 B2
Jaú, Brazil 127 A6
Jaú →, Brazil 121 D5
Jauaperí →, Brazil 121 D5
Jauche, Belgium 17 G5
Jauja, Peru 124 C2
Jaunjelgava, Latvia 40 C4
Jaunpur, India 63 G10
Jauru →, Brazil 125 D6
Java = Jawa, Indonesia 57 G14
Java Sea, Indonesia 56 E3
Java Trench, Ind. Oc. 92 H2
Jávea, Spain 29 G5
Javhlant = Ulyasutay, Mongolia 54 B4
Javier, I., Chile 128 C2
Javron, France 24 D6
Jawa, Indonesia 57 G14
Jawor, Poland 20 D6
Jaworzno, Poland 20 E9
Jay, U.S.A. 109 G7
Jaya, Puncak, Indonesia 57 E9
Jayanca, Peru 124 B2
Jayanti, India 61 F16
Jayapura, Indonesia 57 E10
Jayawijaya, Pegunungan, Indonesia 57 E9
Jaynagar, India 61 F15
Jayrūd, Syria 64 C3
Jayton, U.S.A. 109 J4
Jazīreh-ye Shīf, Iran 65 D6
Jazminal, Mexico 114 C4
Jazzīn, Lebanon 69 B4
Jean, U.S.A. 113 K11
Jean Marie River, Canada 100 A4
Jean Rabel, Haiti 117 C5
Jeanerette, U.S.A. 109 L9
Jeanette, Ostrov, Russia 45 B16
Jeannette, U.S.A. 106 F5
Jebba, Morocco 74 A4
Jebba, Nigeria 79 D5
Jebel, Bahr el →, Sudan 77 F3
Jebel Qerri, Sudan 77 D3
Jeberos, Peru 124 B2
Jedburgh, U.K. 14 F6
Jedda = Jiddah, Si. Arabia 68 C2
Jędrzejów, Poland 20 E10
Jedway, Canada 100 C2
Jeetzel →, Germany 18 B7
Jefferson, Iowa, U.S.A. 108 D7
Jefferson, Ohio, U.S.A. 106 E4
Jefferson, Tex., U.S.A. 109 J7
Jefferson, Wis., U.S.A. 108 D10
Jefferson, Mt., Nev., U.S.A. 110 G5
Jefferson, Mt., Oreg., U.S.A. 110 D3
Jefferson City, Mo., U.S.A. 108 F8
Jefferson City, Tenn., U.S.A. 105 G4
Jeffersonville, U.S.A. 104 F3
Jega, Nigeria 79 C5
Jēkabpils, Latvia 40 C4
Jelenia Góra, Poland 20 E5
Jelgava, Latvia 9 H20
Jelli, Sudan 77 F3
Jellicoe, Canada 98 C2
Jemaja, Indonesia 56 D3
Jemaluang, Malaysia 59 L4
Jemappes, Belgium 17 H3
Jember, Indonesia 57 H15
Jembongan, Malaysia 56 C5
Jemeppe, Belgium 17 G7
Jemnice, Czech. 20 F5
Jena, Germany 18 E7
Jena, U.S.A. 109 K8
Jendouba, Tunisia 75 A6
Jenkins, U.S.A. 104 G4
Jenner, U.S.A. 112 G3
Jennings, U.S.A. 109 K8
Jennings →, Canada 100 B2
Jeparit, Australia 91 F3
Jequié, Brazil 123 D3
Jequitaí →, Brazil 123 E3
Jequitinhonha, Brazil 123 E3
Jequitinhonha →, Brazil 123 E4
Jerada, Morocco 74 B4
Jerantut, Malaysia 59 L4
Jérémie, Haiti 117 C5
Jeremoabo, Brazil 122 D4
Jerez, Punta, Mexico 115 C5
Jerez de García Salinas, Mexico 114 C4
Jerez de la Frontera, Spain 31 J4
Jerez de los Caballeros, Spain 31 G4
Jericho = Arīḥā, Syria 64 C3
Jericho = El Arīḥā, Jordan 69 D4
Jericho, Australia 90 C4

Jerichow, Germany 18 C8
Jerilderie, Australia 91 F4
Jermyn, U.S.A. 107 E9
Jerome, U.S.A. 111 J8
Jersey, Chan. Is. 13 H5
Jersey City, U.S.A. 107 F10
Jersey Shore, U.S.A. 106 E7
Jerseyville, U.S.A. 108 F9
Jerusalem, Israel 69 D4
Jervis B., Australia 91 F5
Jesenice, Slovenia 33 B11
Jesenké, Slovak Rep. 21 G10
Jesselton = Kota Kinabalu, Malaysia 56 C5
Jessnitz, Germany 18 D8
Jessore, Bangla. 61 H16
Jesup, U.S.A. 105 K5
Jesús, Peru 124 B2
Jesús Carranza, Mexico 115 D5
Jesús María, Argentina 126 C3
Jetmore, U.S.A. 109 F5
Jetpur, India 62 J4
Jette, Belgium 17 G4
Jevnaker, Norway 10 D4
Jewett, Ohio, U.S.A. 106 F3
Jewett, Tex., U.S.A. 109 K6
Jewett City, U.S.A. 107 E13
Jeyḥūnābād, Iran 65 C6
Jeypore, India 61 K13
Jhajjar, India 62 E7
Jhal Jhao, Pakistan 60 F4
Jhalawar, India 62 G7
Jhang Maghiana, Pakistan 62 D5
Jhansi, India 63 G8
Jharia, India 63 H12
Jharsaguda, India 61 J14
Jhelum, Pakistan 62 C5
Jhelum →, Pakistan 62 D5
Jhunjhunu, India 62 E6
Ji Xian, Hebei, China 50 F8
Ji Xian, Henan, China 50 G8
Ji Xian, Shanxi, China 50 F6
Jia Xian, Henan, China 50 H7
Jia Xian, Shaanxi, China 50 E6
Jiading, China 53 B13
Jiahe, China 53 E9
Jiali, Taiwan 53 F13
Jialing Jiang →, China 52 C6
Jiamusi, China 54 B8
Ji'an, Jiangxi, China 53 D10
Ji'an, Jilin, China 51 D14
Jianchang, China 51 D11
Jianchangying, China 51 D10
Jianchuan, China 52 D2
Jiande, China 53 C12
Jiangbei, China 52 C6
Jiangcheng, China 52 F3
Jiangdi, China 52 D4
Jiange, China 52 A5
Jiangjin, China 52 C6
Jiangkou, China 52 D7
Jiangle, China 53 D11
Jiangling, China 53 B9
Jiangmen, China 53 F9
Jiangshan, China 53 C12
Jiangsu □, China 51 H10
Jiangxi □, China 53 D10
Jiangyin, China 53 B13
Jiangyong, China 53 E8
Jiangyou, China 52 B5
Jianhe, China 52 D7
Jianli, China 53 C9
Jianning, China 53 D11
Jian'ou, China 53 D12
Jianshi, China 52 B7
Jianshui, China 52 F4
Jianyang, Fujian, China 53 D12
Jianyang, Sichuan, China 52 B5
Jiao Xian, China 51 F11
Jiaohe, Hebei, China 50 E9
Jiaohe, Jilin, China 51 C14
Jiaoling, China 53 E11
Jiaozhou Wan, China 51 F11
Jiaozuo, China 50 G7
Jiashan, China 53 A11
Jiawang, China 51 G9
Jiaxiang, China 50 G9
Jiaxing, China 53 B13
Jiayi, Taiwan 53 F13
Jiayu, China 53 C9
Jibão, Serra do, Brazil 123 D3
Jibiya, Nigeria 79 C6
Jibou, Romania 38 B6
Jibuti = Djibouti ■, Africa 68 E3
Jicarón, I., Panama 116 E3
Jičín, Czech. 20 E5
Jiddah, Si. Arabia 68 C2
Jido, India 61 E19
Jieshou, China 50 H8
Jiexiu, China 50 F6
Jieyang, China 53 F11
Jigawa □, Nigeria 79 C6
Jiggalong, Australia 88 D3
Jihlava, Czech. 20 F5
Jihlava →, Czech. 20 G6
Jijel, Algeria 75 A6
Jijiga, Ethiopia 68 F3
Jijona, Spain 29 G4
Jikamshi, Nigeria 79 C6
Jilin, China 51 C14
Jilin □, China 51 C13
Jiloca →, Spain 28 D3
Jilong, Taiwan 53 E13
Jima, Ethiopia 77 F4
Jimbolia, Romania 38 D3

Jimena de la Frontera, Spain 31 J5
Jiménez, Mexico 114 B4
Jimo, China 51 F11
Jin Jiang →, China 53 C10
Jin Xian, Hebei, China 50 E8
Jin Xian, Liaoning, China 51 E11
Jinan, China 50 F9
Jincheng, China 50 G7
Jinchuan, China 52 B4
Jind, India 62 E7
Jindabyne, Australia 91 F4
Jindřichův Hradec, Czech. 20 F5
Jing He →, China 50 G5
Jing Shan, China 53 B8
Jing Xian, Anhui, China 53 B12
Jing Xian, Hunan, China 52 D7
Jing'an, China 53 C10
Jingbian, China 50 F5
Jingchuan, China 50 G4
Jingde, China 53 B12
Jingdezhen, China 53 C11
Jingdong, China 52 E3
Jinggu, China 52 F3
Jinghai, China 50 E9
Jinghong, China 52 F3
Jingjiang, China 53 A13
Jingle, China 50 E6
Jingmen, China 53 B9
Jingning, China 50 G3
Jingpo Hu, China 51 C15
Jingshan, China 53 B9
Jingtai, China 50 F3
Jingxi, China 52 F6
Jingxing, China 50 E8
Jingyang, China 50 G5
Jingyu, China 51 C14
Jingyuan, China 50 F3
Jingziguan, China 50 H6
Jinhua, China 53 C12
Jining, Nei Mongol Zizhiqu, China 50 D7
Jining, Shandong, China 50 G9
Jinja, Uganda 82 B3
Jinjang, Malaysia 59 L3
Jinji, China 50 F4
Jinjiang, Fujian, China 53 E12
Jinjiang, Yunnan, China 52 D3
Jinjie, China 52 F6
Jinjini, Ghana 78 D4
Jinkou, China 53 B10
Jinmen Dao, China 53 E12
Jinnah Barrage, Pakistan 60 C7
Jinning, China 52 E4
Jinotega, Nic. 116 D2
Jinotepe, Nic. 116 D2
Jinping, Guizhou, China 52 D7
Jinping, Yunnan, China 52 F4
Jinsha, China 52 D6
Jinsha Jiang →, China 52 C5
Jinshan, China 53 B13
Jinshi, China 53 C8
Jintan, China 53 B12
Jinxi, Jiangxi, China 53 D11
Jinxi, Liaoning, China 51 D11
Jinxian, China 53 C11
Jinxiang, China 50 G9
Jinyun, China 53 C13
Jinzhai, China 53 B10
Jinzhou, China 51 D11
Jiparaná →, Brazil 125 B5
Jipijapa, Ecuador 120 D1
Jiquilpan, Mexico 114 D4
Jishan, China 50 G6
Jishou, China 52 C7
Jishui, China 53 D10
Jisr ash Shughūr, Syria 64 C3
Jitarning, Australia 89 F2
Jitra, Malaysia 59 J3
Jiu →, Romania 38 F6
Jiudengkou, China 50 E4
Jiujiang, Guangdong, China 53 F9
Jiujiang, Jiangxi, China 53 C10
Jiuling Shan, China 53 C10
Jiulong, China 52 C3
Jiuquan, China 54 C4
Jiutai, China 51 B13
Jiuxiangcheng, China 50 H8
Jiuxincheng, China 50 E8
Jiuyuhang, China 53 B12
Jixi, Anhui, China 53 B12
Jixi, Heilongjiang, China 51 B16
Jiyang, China 51 F9
Jīzān, Si. Arabia 68 D3
Jize, China 50 F8
Jizera →, Czech. 20 E4
Jizō-Zaki, Japan 49 G6
Joaçaba, Brazil 127 B5
Joaíma, Brazil 123 E3
João, Brazil 122 B1
João Amaro, Brazil 123 D3
João Câmara, Brazil 122 C4
João Pessoa, Brazil 122 C5
João Pinheiro, Brazil 123 E2
Joaquim Távora, Brazil 123 F2
Joaquín V. González, Argentina 126 B3
Jobourg, Nez de, France 24 C5
Jódar, Spain 29 H1
Jodhpur, India 62 F5
Jœuf, France 25 C13
Jofane, Mozam. 85 C5
Joggins, Canada 99 C7
Jogjakarta = Yogyakarta, Indonesia 57 G14

Johannesburg, *S. Africa* 85 D4
Johannesburg, *U.S.A.* 113 K9
John Day, *U.S.A.* 110 D4
John Day →, *U.S.A.* 110 D3
John H. Kerr Reservoir, *U.S.A.* 105 G6
John o' Groats, *U.K.* 14 C5
Johnnie, *U.S.A.* 113 J10
John's Ra., *Australia* 90 C1
Johnson, *U.S.A.* 109 G4
Johnson City, *N.Y., U.S.A.* 107 D9
Johnson City, *Tenn., U.S.A.* 105 G4
Johnson City, *Tex., U.S.A.* 109 K5
Johnsonburg, *U.S.A.* 106 E6
Johnsondale, *U.S.A.* 113 K8
Johnson's Crossing, *Canada* 100 A2
Johnston, L., *Australia* 89 F3
Johnston Falls = Mambilima Falls, *Zambia* 83 E2
Johnston I., *Pac. Oc.* 93 F11
Johnstone Str., *Canada* 100 C3
Johnstown, *N.Y., U.S.A.* 107 C10
Johnstown, *Pa., U.S.A.* 106 F6
Johor Baharu, *Malaysia* 59 M4
Joigny, *France* 25 E10
Joinvile, *Brazil* 127 B6
Joinville, *France* 25 D12
Joinville I., *Antarctica* 5 C18
Jojutla, *Mexico* 115 D5
Jokkmokk, *Sweden* 8 C15
Jökulsá á Bru →, *Iceland* 8 D6
Jökulsá á Fjöllum →, *Iceland* 8 C5
Jolfā, *Āzarbājān-e Sharqī, Iran* 64 B5
Jolfā, *Eşfahan, Iran* 65 C6
Joliet, *U.S.A.* 104 E1
Joliette, *Canada* 98 C5
Jolo, *Phil.* 55 J4
Jolon, *U.S.A.* 112 K5
Jomalig, *Phil.* 55 D5
Jombang, *Indonesia* 57 G15
Jomda, *China* 52 B2
Jome, *Indonesia* 57 E7
Jomfruland, *Norway* 11 F3
Jönåker, *Sweden* 11 F10
Jonava, *Lithuania* 40 D4
Jones Sound, *Canada* 4 B3
Jonesboro, *Ark., U.S.A.* 109 H9
Jonesboro, *Ill., U.S.A.* 109 G10
Jonesboro, *La., U.S.A.* 109 J8
Jonesport, *U.S.A.* 99 D6
Jonglei, *Sudan* 77 F3
Jonglei □, *Sudan* 77 F3
Joniškis, *Lithuania* 40 C3
Jönköping, *Sweden* 9 H13
Jönköpings län □, *Sweden* 9 H13
Jonquière, *Canada* 99 C5
Jonsberg, *Sweden* 11 F10
Jonsered, *Sweden* 11 G6
Jonzac, *France* 26 C3
Joplin, *U.S.A.* 109 G7
Jordan, *U.S.A.* 110 C10
Jordan ■, *Asia* 69 E5
Jordan →, *Asia* 69 D4
Jordan Valley, *U.S.A.* 110 E5
Jordânia, *Brazil* 123 E3
Jorge, C., *Chile* 128 D1
Jorhat, *India* 61 F19
Jörn, *Sweden* 8 D16
Jorong, *Indonesia* 56 E4
Jorquera →, *Chile* 126 B2
Jos, *Nigeria* 79 D6
José Batlle y Ordóñez, *Uruguay* 127 C4
José de San Martín, *Argentina* 128 B2
Joseph, *U.S.A.* 110 D5
Joseph, L., *Nfld., Canada* 99 B6
Joseph, L., *Ont., Canada* 106 A5
Joseph Bonaparte G., *Australia* 88 B4
Joseph City, *U.S.A.* 111 J8
Joshua Tree, *U.S.A.* 113 L10
Joshua Tree National Monument, *U.S.A.* 113 M10
Josselin, *France* 24 E4
Jostedal, *Norway* 9 F9
Jotunheimen, *Norway* 10 C2
Jourdanton, *U.S.A.* 109 L5
Joure, *Neths.* 16 C7
Joussard, *Canada* 100 B5
Jovellanos, *Cuba* 116 B3
Joyeuse, *France* 27 D8
Józefów, *Poland* 20 C11
Ju Xian, *China* 51 F10
Juan Aldama, *Mexico* 114 C4
Juan Bautista Alberdi, *Argentina* 126 C3
Juan de Fuca Str., *Canada* 112 B2
Juan de Nova, *Ind. Oc.* 85 B7
Juan Fernández, Arch. de, *Pac. Oc.* 93 L20
Juan José Castelli, *Argentina* 126 B3
Juan L. Lacaze, *Uruguay* 126 C4
Juanjuí, *Peru* 124 B2
Juárez, *Argentina* 126 D4
Juárez, *Mexico* 113 N11
Juárez, Sierra de, *Mexico* 114 A1
Juatinga, Ponta de, *Brazil* 123 F3
Juàzeiro, *Brazil* 122 C3
Juàzeiro do Norte, *Brazil* 122 C4
Jubayl, *Lebanon* 69 A4
Jubbah, *Si. Arabia* 64 D4
Jubbulpore = Jabalpur, *India* 63 H8
Jübek, *Germany* 18 A5
Jubga, *Russia* 43 D8
Jubilee L., *Australia* 89 E4
Juby, C., *Morocco* 72 C2
Júcar →, *Spain* 29 F4
Júcaro, *Cuba* 116 B4
Juchitán, *Mexico* 115 D5
Judaea = Har Yehuda, *Israel* 69 D3
Judenburg, *Austria* 21 H4
Judith →, *U.S.A.* 110 C9
Judith, Pt., *U.S.A.* 107 E13
Judith Gap, *U.S.A.* 110 C9
Jufari →, *Brazil* 121 D5
Jugoslavia = Yugoslavia ■, *Europe* 21 M10
Juigalpa, *Nic.* 116 D2
Juillac, *France* 26 C5
Juist, *Germany* 18 B2
Juiz de Fora, *Brazil* 123 F3
Jujuy □, *Argentina* 126 A2
Julesburg, *U.S.A.* 108 E3
Juli, *Peru* 124 D4
Julia Cr. →, *Australia* 90 C3
Julia Creek, *Australia* 90 C3
Juliaca, *Peru* 124 D3
Julian, *U.S.A.* 113 M10
Julian Alps = Julijske Alpe, *Slovenia* 33 B11
Julianakanaal, *Neths.* 17 F7
Julianatop, *Surinam* 121 C6
Julianehåb, *Greenland* 4 C5
Jülich, *Germany* 18 E2
Julierpass, *Switz.* 23 D9
Julijske Alpe, *Slovenia* 33 B11
Julimes, *Mexico* 114 B3
Jullundur, *India* 62 D6
Julu, *China* 50 F8
Jumbo, *Zimbabwe* 83 F3
Jumbo Pk., *U.S.A.* 113 J12
Jumentos Cays, *Bahamas* 117 B4
Jumet, *Belgium* 17 H4
Jumilla, *Spain* 29 G3
Jumla, *Nepal* 63 E10
Jumna = Yamuna →, *India* 63 G9
Junagadh, *India* 62 J4
Junction, *Tex., U.S.A.* 109 K5
Junction, *Utah, U.S.A.* 111 G7
Junction B., *Australia* 90 A1
Junction City, *Kans., U.S.A.* 108 F6
Junction City, *Oreg., U.S.A.* 110 D2
Junction Pt., *Australia* 90 A1
Jundah, *Australia* 90 C3
Jundiaí, *Brazil* 127 A6
Juneau, *U.S.A.* 96 C6
Junee, *Australia* 91 E4
Jungfrau, *Switz.* 22 C5
Junggar Pendi, *China* 54 B3
Junglinster, *Lux.* 17 J8
Jungshahi, *Pakistan* 62 G2
Juniata →, *U.S.A.* 106 F7
Junín, *Argentina* 126 C3
Junín, *Peru* 124 C2
Junín □, *Peru* 124 C3
Junín de los Andes, *Argentina* 128 A2
Jūniyah, *Lebanon* 69 B4
Juntura, *U.S.A.* 110 E4
Juparanã, L., *Brazil* 123 E3
Jupiter →, *Canada* 99 C7
Juquiá, *Brazil* 123 F2
Jur, Nahr el →, *Sudan* 77 F2
Jura = Jura, Mts. du, *Europe* 27 B10
Jura = Schwäbische Alb, *Germany* 19 G5
Jura, *Europe* 25 F13
Jura, *U.K.* 14 F3
Jura □, *France* 25 F12
Jura, Mts. du, *Europe* 27 B10
Jura, Sd. of, *U.K.* 14 F3
Jura Suisse, *Switz.* 22 B3
Jurado, *Colombia* 120 B2
Jurilovca, *Romania* 38 E11
Jurong, *China* 53 B12
Juruá →, *Brazil* 120 D4
Juruena, *Brazil* 125 C6
Juruena →, *Brazil* 125 B6
Juruti, *Brazil* 121 D6
Jussey, *France* 25 E12
Justo Daract, *Argentina* 126 C2
Jutaí, *Brazil* 124 B4
Jutaí →, *Brazil* 120 D4
Jüterbog, *Germany* 18 D9
Juticalpa, *Honduras* 116 D2
Jutland = Jylland, *Denmark* 11 H3
Jutphaas, *Neths.* 16 D6
Juventud, I. de la, *Cuba* 116 B3
Juvigny-sous-Andaine, *France* 24 D6
Juvisy-sur-Orge, *France* 25 D9
Juwain, *Afghan.* 60 D2
Jūy Zar, *Iran* 64 C5
Juye, *China* 50 G9
Juzennecourt, *France* 25 D11
Jylland, *Denmark* 11 H3
Jyväskylä, *Finland* 8 E18

K

K2, Mt., *Pakistan* 63 B7
Kaap Plateau, *S. Africa* 84 D3
Kaapkruis, *Namibia* 84 C1
Kaapstad = Cape Town, *S. Africa* 84 E2
Kaatsheuvel, *Neths.* 17 E6
Kabaena, *Indonesia* 57 F6
Kabala, *S. Leone* 78 D2
Kabale, *Uganda* 82 C3
Kabalo, *Zaïre* 82 D2
Kabambare, *Zaïre* 82 C2
Kabango, *Zaïre* 83 D2
Kabanjahe, *Indonesia* 56 D1
Kabankalan, *Phil.* 55 G5
Kabara, *Mali* 78 B4
Kabardinka, *Russia* 42 D7
Kabardino-Balkar Republic □, *Russia* 43 E10
Kabare, *Indonesia* 57 E8
Kabarega Falls, *Uganda* 82 B3
Kabasalan, *Phil.* 55 H5
Kabba, *Nigeria* 79 D6
Kabin Buri, *Thailand* 58 F3
Kabinakagami L., *Canada* 98 C3
Kabīr, Zab al →, *Iraq* 64 C4
Kabkabīyah, *Sudan* 73 F9
Kabna, *Sudan* 76 D3
Kabompo, *Zambia* 83 E1
Kabompo →, *Zambia* 81 G4
Kabondo, *Zaïre* 83 D2
Kabongo, *Zaïre* 82 D2
Kabou, *Togo* 79 D5
Kaboudia, Rass, *Tunisia* 75 A7
Kabra, *Australia* 90 C5
Kabūd Gonbad, *Iran* 65 B8
Kabugao, *Phil.* 55 B4
Kābul, *Afghan.* 62 B3
Kābul □, *Afghan.* 60 B6
Kabul →, *Pakistan* 62 C5
Kabunga, *Zaïre* 82 C2
Kaburuang, *Indonesia* 57 D7
Kabushiya, *Sudan* 77 D3
Kabwe, *Zambia* 83 E2
Kačanik, *Serbia* 21 N11
Kachanovo, *Russia* 40 C5
Kachchh, Gulf of, *India* 62 H3
Kachchh, Rann of, *India* 62 G4
Kachebera, *Zambia* 83 E3
Kachin □, *Burma* 61 F20
Kachira, L., *Uganda* 82 C3
Kachiry, *Kazakhstan* 44 D8
Kachisi, *Ethiopia* 77 F4
Kachot, *Cambodia* 59 G4
Kackar, *Turkey* 43 F9
Kadan Kyun, *Burma* 56 B1
Kadanai →, *Afghan.* 62 D1
Kadarkút, *Hungary* 21 J7
Kade, *Ghana* 79 D4
Kadi, *India* 62 H5
Kadina, *Australia* 91 E2
Kadınhanı, *Turkey* 66 D5
Kadirli, *Turkey* 66 E7
Kadiyevka, *Ukraine* 43 B8
Kadoka, *U.S.A.* 108 D4
Kadom, *Russia* 41 D13
Kadoma, *Zimbabwe* 83 F2
Kâdugli, *Sudan* 77 E2
Kaduna, *Nigeria* 79 C6
Kaduna □, *Nigeria* 79 C6
Kaédi, *Mauritania* 78 B2
Kaelé, *Cameroon* 79 C7
Kaeng Khoï, *Thailand* 58 E3
Kaesŏng, *N. Korea* 51 F14
Kāf, *Si. Arabia* 64 D3
Kafakumba, *Zaïre* 80 F4
Kafan, *Armenia* 67 D12
Kafanchan, *Nigeria* 79 D6
Kafareti, *Nigeria* 79 C7
Kaffrine, *Senegal* 78 C1
Kafia Kingi, *Sudan* 73 G9
Kafinda, *Zambia* 83 E3
Kafirévs, Ákra, *Greece* 39 L7
Kafr el Dauwâr, *Egypt* 76 H7
Kafr el Sheikh, *Egypt* 76 H7
Kafue, *Zambia* 83 F2
Kafue →, *Zambia* 81 H5
Kafue Flats, *Zambia* 83 F2
Kafue Nat. Park, *Zambia* 83 F2
Kafulwe, *Zambia* 83 D2
Kaga, *Afghan.* 62 B4
Kaga Bandoro, *C.A.R.* 73 G8
Kagan, *Uzbekistan* 44 F7
Kagawa □, *Japan* 49 G6
Kagera □, *Tanzania* 82 C3
Kagera →, *Uganda* 82 C3
Kağizman, *Turkey* 67 C10
Kagoshima, *Japan* 49 J5
Kagoshima □, *Japan* 49 J5
Kagul, *Moldavia* 42 D3
Kahak, *Iran* 65 B6
Kahama, *Tanzania* 82 C3
Kahama □, *Tanzania* 82 C3
Kahang, *Malaysia* 59 L4
Kahayan →, *Indonesia* 56 E4
Kahe, *Tanzania* 82 C4
Kahemba, *Zaïre* 80 F3
Kahil, Djebel bou, *Algeria* 75 B5
Kahniah →, *Canada* 100 B4
Kahnūj, *Iran* 65 E8
Kahoka, *U.S.A.* 108 E9
Kahoolawe, *U.S.A.* 102 H16
Kahramanmaraş, *Turkey* 66 E7
Kahramanmaraş □, *Turkey* 66 E7
Kâhta, *Turkey* 67 E8
Kahuta, *Pakistan* 62 C5
Kai, Kepulauan, *Indonesia* 57 F8
Kai Besar, *Indonesia* 57 F8
Kai Is. = Kai, Kepulauan, *Indonesia* 57 F8
Kai-Ketil, *Indonesia* 57 F8
Kai Xian, *China* 52 B7
Kaiama, *Nigeria* 79 D5
Kaiapoi, *N.Z.* 87 K4
Kaieteur Falls, *Guyana* 121 B6
Kaifeng, *China* 50 G8
Kaihua, *China* 53 C12
Kaikohe, *N.Z.* 87 F4
Kaikoura, *N.Z.* 87 K4
Kaikoura Ra., *N.Z.* 87 J4
Kailahun, *S. Leone* 78 D2
Kaili, *China* 52 D6
Kailu, *China* 51 C11
Kailua Kona, *U.S.A.* 102 J17
Kaimana, *Indonesia* 57 E8
Kaimanawa Mts., *N.Z.* 87 H5
Kaimganj, *India* 63 F8
Kaimur Hills, *India* 63 G9
Kaingaroa Forest, *N.Z.* 87 H6
Kainji Res., *Nigeria* 79 C5
Kaipara Harbour, *N.Z.* 87 G5
Kaiping, *China* 53 F9
Kaipokok B., *Canada* 99 B8
Kairana, *India* 62 E7
Kaironi, *Indonesia* 57 E8
Kairouan, *Tunisia* 75 A7
Kaiserslautern, *Germany* 19 F3
Kaitaia, *N.Z.* 87 F4
Kaitangata, *N.Z.* 87 M2
Kaithal, *India* 62 E7
Kaitu →, *Pakistan* 62 C4
Kaiwi Channel, *U.S.A.* 102 H16
Kaiyang, *China* 52 D6
Kaiyuan, *Liaoning, China* 51 C13
Kaiyuan, *Yunnan, China* 52 F4
Kajaani, *Finland* 8 D19
Kajabbi, *Australia* 90 B3
Kajana = Kajaani, *Finland* 8 D19
Kajang, *Malaysia* 59 L3
Kajiado, *Kenya* 82 C4
Kajiado □, *Kenya* 82 C4
Kajo Kaji, *Sudan* 77 G3
Kaka, *Sudan* 77 E3
Kakabeka Falls, *Canada* 98 C2
Kakamas, *S. Africa* 84 D3
Kakamega, *Kenya* 82 B3
Kakamega □, *Kenya* 82 B3
Kakanj, *Bos.-H.* 21 L8
Kakanui Mts., *N.Z.* 87 L3
Kake, *Japan* 49 G6
Kakegawa, *Japan* 49 G9
Kakeroma-Jima, *Japan* 49 K4
Kakhib, *Russia* 43 E12
Kakhovka, *Ukraine* 42 C5
Kakhovskoye Vdkhr., *Ukraine* 42 C6
Kakinada, *India* 61 L13
Kakisa →, *Canada* 100 A5
Kakisa L., *Canada* 100 A5
Kakogawa, *Japan* 49 G7
Kakwa →, *Canada* 100 C5
Kāl Güsheh, *Iran* 65 D8
Kal Safīd, *Iran* 64 C5
Kala, *Nigeria* 79 C7
Kalaa-Kebira, *Tunisia* 75 A7
Kalabagh, *Pakistan* 62 C4
Kalabahi, *Indonesia* 57 F6
Kalabáka, *Greece* 39 K4
Kalabo, *Zambia* 81 G4
Kalach, *Russia* 41 F12
Kalach na Donu, *Russia* 43 B10
Kaladan →, *Burma* 61 J18
Kaladar, *Canada* 106 B7
Kalahari, *Africa* 84 C3
Kalahari Gemsbok Nat. Park, *S. Africa* 84 D3
Kalāk, *Iran* 65 E8
Kalakamati, *Botswana* 85 C4
Kalakan, *Russia* 45 D12
Kalakh, *Syria* 64 C3
K'alak'unlun Shank'ou, *Pakistan* 63 B7
Kalam, *Pakistan* 63 B5
Kalama, *U.S.A.* 112 E4
Kalama, *Zaïre* 82 C2
Kalamariá, *Greece* 39 J5
Kalamata, *Greece* 39 M5
Kalamazoo, *U.S.A.* 104 D3
Kalamazoo →, *U.S.A.* 104 D2
Kalambo Falls, *Tanzania* 83 D3
Kálamos, *Greece* 39 L3
Kalannie, *Australia* 89 F2
Kalāntarī, *Iran* 65 C7
Kalao, *Indonesia* 57 F6
Kalaotoa, *Indonesia* 57 F6
Kälarne, *Sweden* 10 B10
Kalárovo, *Slovak Rep.* 21 H7
Kalasin, *Thailand* 58 D4
Kalat, *Pakistan* 60 E5
Kalāteh, *Iran* 65 B7
Kalāteh-ye-Ganj, *Iran* 65 E8
Kálathos, *Greece* 39 N11
Kalaus →, *Russia* 43 D11
Kalávrita, *Greece* 39 L5
Kalbarri, *Australia* 89 E1
Kale, *Turkey* 66 E3
Kalecik, *Turkey* 42 F5
Kalegauk Kyun, *Burma* 61 M20
Kalehe, *Zaïre* 82 C2
Kalema, *Tanzania* 82 C3
Kalemie, *Zaïre* 82 D2
Kalety, *Poland* 20 E8
Kalewa, *Burma* 61 H19
Kálfafellsstaður, *Iceland* 8 D6
Kalgan = Zhangjiakou, *China* 50 D8
Kalgoorlie-Boulder, *Australia* 89 F3
Kaliakra, Nos, *Bulgaria* 38 F11
Kalianda, *Indonesia* 56 F3
Kalibo, *Phil.* 55 F5
Kaliganj, *Bangla.* 63 H13
Kalima, *Zaïre* 82 C2
Kalimantan, *Indonesia* 56 E4
Kalimantan Barat □, *Indonesia* 56 E4
Kalimantan Selatan □, *Indonesia* 56 E5
Kalimantan Tengah □, *Indonesia* 56 E4
Kalimantan Timur □, *Indonesia* 56 D5
Kálimnos, *Greece* 39 N10
Kalimpong, *India* 63 F13
Kalinin = Tver, *Russia* 41 C9
Kaliningrad, *Russia* 40 D2
Kalinkavichy = Kalinkovichi, *Belorussia* 40 E6
Kalinkovichi, *Belorussia* 40 E6
Kalinovik, *Bos.-H.* 21 M8
Kalipetrovo, *Bulgaria* 38 E10
Kaliro, *Uganda* 82 B3
Kalispell, *U.S.A.* 110 B6
Kalisz, *Poland* 20 D8
Kaliua, *Tanzania* 82 D3
Kalix →, *Sweden* 8 D17
Kalka, *India* 62 D7
Kalkan, *Turkey* 66 E3
Kalkaska, *U.S.A.* 104 C3
Kalkfeld, *Namibia* 84 C2
Kalkfontein, *Botswana* 84 C3
Kalkrand, *Namibia* 84 C2
Kållandsö, *Sweden* 11 F7
Kallithéa, *Greece* 39 M6
Kallonís, Kólpos, *Greece* 39 K9
Kallsjön, *Sweden* 8 E12
Kalmalo, *Nigeria* 79 C6
Kalmar, *Sweden* 9 H14
Kalmthout, *Belgium* 17 F4
Kalmyk Republic □, *Russia* 43 C12
Kalmykovo, *Kazakhstan* 43 B14
Kalna, *India* 63 H13
Kalocsa, *Hungary* 21 J9
Kalokhorio, *Cyprus* 37 E12
Kaloko, *Zaïre* 82 D2
Kalol, *Gujarat, India* 62 H5
Kalol, *Gujarat, India* 62 H5
Kalolímnos, *Greece* 39 M10
Kalomo, *Zambia* 83 F2
Kalpi, *India* 63 F8
Kaltbrunn, *Switz.* 23 B8
Kaltungo, *Nigeria* 79 D7
Kalu, *Pakistan* 62 G2
Kaluga, *Russia* 41 D10
Kalulushi, *Zambia* 83 E2
Kalundborg, *Denmark* 11 J5
Kalush, *Ukraine* 40 G4
Kałuszyn, *Poland* 20 C11
Kalutara, *Sri Lanka* 60 R11
Kalyazin, *Russia* 41 C10
Kama, *Zaïre* 82 C2
Kama →, *Russia* 44 D6
Kamachumu, *Tanzania* 82 C3
Kamaishi, *Japan* 48 E10
Kamalia, *Pakistan* 62 D5
Kamapanda, *Zambia* 83 E1
Kamaran, *Yemen* 68 D3
Kamativi, *Zimbabwe* 83 F2
Kamba, *Nigeria* 79 C5
Kambalda, *Australia* 89 F3
Kambar, *Pakistan* 62 F3
Kambia, *S. Leone* 78 D2
Kambolé, *Zambia* 83 D3
Kambos, *Cyprus* 37 D11
Kambove, *Zaïre* 83 E2
Kamchatka, P-ov., *Russia* 45 D16
Kamchatka Pen. = Kamchatka, P-ov., *Russia* 45 D16
Kamen, *Russia* 44 D9
Kamen Kashirskiy, *Ukraine* 40 F4
Kamen-Rybolov, *Russia* 48 B6
Kamenets-Podolskiy, *Ukraine* 42 B2
Kamenjak, Rt., *Croatia* 33 D10
Kamenka, *Russia* 41 E14
Kamenka, *Russia* 41 F11
Kamenka, *Ukraine* 42 B5
Kamenka Bugskaya, *Ukraine* 40 F4
Kamenka Dneprovskaya, *Ukraine* 42 C6
Kamenolomini, *Russia* 43 C9
Kamensk-Shakhtinskiy, *Russia* 43 B9
Kamensk Uralskiy, *Russia* 44 D7
Kamenskiy, *Russia* 41 F14
Kamenskiy, *Russia* 43 B9
Kamenskoye, *Russia* 45 C17
Kamenyak, *Bulgaria* 38 F9
Kamenz, *Germany* 18 D10
Kameoka, *Japan* 49 G7
Kamiah, *U.S.A.* 110 C5
Kamień Pomorski, *Poland* 20 B4

Kamieskroon, *S. Africa* 84 E2
Kamilukuak, L., *Canada* 101 A8
Kamina, *Zaïre* 83 D1
Kaminak L., *Canada* 101 A9
Kaminoyama, *Japan* 48 E10
Kamiros, *Greece* 37 C9
Kamituga, *Zaïre* 82 C2
Kamloops, *Canada* 100 C4
Kamnik, *Slovenia* 33 B11
Kamo, *Armenia* 43 F11
Kamo, *Japan* 48 F9
Kamoa Mts., *Guyana* 121 C6
Kamoke, *Pakistan* 62 C6
Kamp →, *Austria* 21 G5
Kampala, *Uganda* 82 B3
Kampar, *Malaysia* 59 K3
Kampar →, *Indonesia* 56 D2
Kampen, *Neths.* 16 C7
Kamperland, *Neths.* 17 E3
Kamphaeng Phet, *Thailand* 58 D2
Kampolombo, L., *Zambia* 83 E2
Kampong To, *Thailand* 59 J3
Kampot, *Cambodia* 59 G5
Kampti, *Burkina Faso* 78 C4
Kampuchea = Cambodia ■, *Asia* 58 F5
Kampung →, *Indonesia* 57 F9
Kampung Air Putih, *Malaysia* 59 K4
Kampung Jerangau, *Malaysia* 59 K4
Kampung Raja, *Malaysia* 59 K4
Kampungbaru = Tolitoli, *Indonesia* 57 D6
Kamrau, Teluk, *Indonesia* 57 E8
Kamsack, *Canada* 101 C8
Kamskoye Ustye, *Russia* 41 D16
Kamuchawie L., *Canada* 101 B8
Kamui-Misaki, *Japan* 48 C10
Kamyanets-Podilskyy = Kamenets-Podolskiy, *Ukraine* 42 B2
Kāmyārān, *Iran* 64 C5
Kamyshin, *Russia* 41 F14
Kamyzyak, *Russia* 43 C13
Kanaaupscow, *Canada* 98 B4
Kanab, *U.S.A.* 111 H7
Kanab →, *U.S.A.* 111 H7
Kanagi, *Japan* 48 D10
Kanairiktok →, *Canada* 99 A7
Kanália, *Greece* 39 K5
Kananga, *Zaïre* 80 F4
Kanarraville, *U.S.A.* 111 H7
Kanash, *Russia* 41 D15
Kanaskat, *U.S.A.* 112 C5
Kanawha →, *U.S.A.* 104 F4
Kanazawa, *Japan* 49 F8
Kanchanaburi, *Thailand* 58 E2
Kanchenjunga, *Nepal* 63 F13
Kanchipuram, *India* 60 N11
Kanda Kanda, *Zaïre* 80 F4
Kandahar = Qandahār, *Afghan.* 60 D4
Kandalaksha, *Russia* 44 C4
Kandalu, *Afghan.* 60 E3
Kandangan, *Indonesia* 56 E5
Kandanos, *Greece* 37 D5
Kander →, *Switz.* 22 C5
Kandersteg, *Switz.* 22 D5
Kandhíla, *Greece* 39 M5
Kandhkot, *Pakistan* 62 E3
Kandhla, *India* 62 E7
Kandi, *Benin* 79 C5
Kandi, *India* 63 H13
Kandıra, *Turkey* 66 C4
Kandla, *India* 62 H4
Kandos, *Australia* 91 E4
Kandy, *Sri Lanka* 60 R12
Kane, *U.S.A.* 106 E6
Kane Basin, *Greenland* 4 B4
Kanevskaya, *Russia* 43 C8
Kanfanar, *Croatia* 33 C10
Kangaba, *Mali* 78 C3
Kangal, *Turkey* 66 D7
Kangān, *Fārs, Iran* 65 E7
Kangān, *Hormozgān, Iran* 65 E8
Kangar, *Malaysia* 59 J3
Kangaroo I., *Australia* 91 F2
Kangavar, *Iran* 65 C6
Kangding, *China* 52 B3
Kăngdong, *N. Korea* 51 E14
Kangean, Kepulauan, *Indonesia* 56 F5
Kangean Is. = Kangean, Kepulauan, *Indonesia* 56 F5
Kanggye, *N. Korea* 51 D14
Kanggyŏng, *S. Korea* 51 F14
Kanghwa, *S. Korea* 51 F14
Kangnŭng, *S. Korea* 51 F15
Kango, *Gabon* 80 D2
Kangping, *China* 51 C12
Kangto, *India* 61 F18
Kani, *Ivory C.* 78 D3
Kaniama, *Zaïre* 82 D1
Kaniapiskau →, *Canada* 99 A6
Kaniapiskau L., *Canada* 99 B6
Kanin, P-ov., *Russia* 44 C5
Kanin Nos, Mys, *Russia* 44 C5
Kanin Pen. = Kanin, P-ov., *Russia* 44 C5
Kaniva, *Australia* 91 F3
Kanjiža, *Serbia* 21 J10
Kanjut Sar, *Pakistan* 63 A6
Kankakee, *U.S.A.* 104 E2
Kankakee →, *U.S.A.* 104 E1
Kankan, *Guinea* 78 C3
Kanker, *India* 61 J12
Kankunskiy, *Russia* 45 D13
Kannapolis, *U.S.A.* 105 H5
Kannauj, *India* 63 F8
Kannod, *India* 60 H10
Kano, *Nigeria* 79 C6
Kano □, *Nigeria* 79 C6
Kan'onji, *Japan* 49 G6
Kanoroba, *Ivory C.* 78 D3
Kanowit, *Malaysia* 56 D4
Kanowna, *Australia* 89 F3
Kanoya, *Japan* 49 J5
Kanpetlet, *Burma* 61 J18
Kanpur, *India* 63 F9
Kansas □, *U.S.A.* 108 F6
Kansas →, *U.S.A.* 108 F7
Kansas City, *Kans., U.S.A.* 108 F7
Kansas City, *Mo., U.S.A.* 108 F7
Kansenia, *Zaïre* 83 E2
Kansk, *Russia* 45 D10
Kansŏng, *S. Korea* 51 E15
Kansu = Gansu □, *China* 50 G3
Kantang, *Thailand* 59 J2
Kantché, *Niger* 79 C6
Kanté, *Togo* 79 D5
Kantemirovka, *Russia* 43 B8
Kantharalak, *Thailand* 58 E5
Kantō □, *Japan* 49 F9
Kantō-Sanchi, *Japan* 49 G9
Kanturk, *Ireland* 15 D3
Kanuma, *Japan* 49 F9
Kanus, *Namibia* 84 D2
Kanye, *Botswana* 84 C4
Kanzenze, *Zaïre* 83 E2
Kanzi, Ras, *Tanzania* 82 D4
Kaohsiung = Gaoxiong, *Taiwan* 53 F13
Kaokoveld, *Namibia* 84 B1
Kaolack, *Senegal* 78 C1
Kaoshan, *China* 51 B13
Kapadvanj, *India* 62 H5
Kapanga, *Zaïre* 80 F4
Kapchagai, *Kazakhstan* 44 E8
Kapellen, *Belgium* 17 F4
Kapéllo, Ákra, *Greece* 39 N6
Kapema, *Zaïre* 83 E2
Kapfenberg, *Austria* 21 H5
Kapiri Mposhi, *Zambia* 83 E2
Kapiskau →, *Canada* 98 B3
Kapit, *Malaysia* 56 D4
Kapiti I., *N.Z.* 87 J5
Kaplice, *Czech.* 20 G4
Kapoe, *Thailand* 59 H2
Kapoeta, *Sudan* 77 G3
Kapos →, *Hungary* 21 J8
Kaposvár, *Hungary* 21 J7
Kapowsin, *U.S.A.* 112 D4
Kappeln, *Germany* 18 A5
Kapps, *Namibia* 84 C2
Kaprije, *Croatia* 33 E12
Kaprijke, *Belgium* 17 F3
Kapsan, *N. Korea* 51 D15
Kapsukas = Mariyampol, *Lithuania* 40 D3
Kapuas →, *Indonesia* 56 E3
Kapuas Hulu, Pegunungan, *Malaysia* 56 D4
Kapuas Hulu Ra. = Kapuas Hulu, Pegunungan, *Malaysia* 56 D4
Kapulo, *Zaïre* 83 D2
Kapunda, *Australia* 91 E2
Kapuni, *N.Z.* 87 H5
Kapurthala, *India* 62 D6
Kapuskasing, *Canada* 98 C3
Kapuskasing →, *Canada* 98 C3
Kapustin Yar, *Russia* 43 B11
Kaputar, *Australia* 91 E5
Kaputir, *Kenya* 82 B4
Kapuvár, *Hungary* 21 H7
Kara, *Russia* 44 C7
Kara Bogaz Gol, Zaliv, *Turkmenistan* 44 E6
Kara Kalpak Republic □, *Uzbekistan* 44 E6
Kara Kum = Karakum, Peski, *Turkmenistan* 44 F6
Kara Sea, *Russia* 44 B7
Karabük, *Turkey* 42 F5
Karaburun, *Turkey* 66 D2
Karaburuni, *Albania* 39 J2
Karabutak, *Kazakhstan* 44 E7
Karacabey, *Turkey* 66 C3
Karacasu, *Turkey* 66 E3
Karachala, *Azerbaijan* 43 G13
Karachayevsk, *Russia* 43 E9
Karachev, *Russia* 40 E9
Karachi, *Pakistan* 62 G2
Karad, *India* 60 L9
Karadeniz Boğazı, *Turkey* 66 C3
Karaga, *Ghana* 79 D4
Karaganda, *Kazakhstan* 44 E8
Karagayly, *Kazakhstan* 44 E8
Karaginskiy, Ostrov, *Russia* 45 D17
Karagüney Dağları, *Turkey* 66 C6
Karagwe □, *Tanzania* 82 C3
Karaikal, *India* 60 P11
Karaikkudi, *India* 60 P11
Karaisali, *Turkey* 66 E6
Karaj, *Iran* 65 C6
Karak, *Malaysia* 59 L4
Karakas, *Kazakhstan* 44 E9
Karakitang, *Indonesia* 57 D7
Karaklis, *Armenia* 43 F11
Karakoçan, *Turkey* 67 D9
Karakoram Pass, *Pakistan* 63 B7
Karakoram Ra., *Pakistan* 63 B7
Karakum, Peski, *Turkmenistan* 44 F6
Karakurt, *Turkey* 67 C10
Karalon, *Russia* 45 D12
Karaman, *Turkey* 66 E5
Karamay, *China* 54 B3
Karambu, *Indonesia* 56 E5
Karamea Bight, *N.Z.* 87 J3
Karamoja □, *Uganda* 82 B3
Karamsad, *India* 62 H5
Karand, *Iran* 64 C5
Karanganyar, *Indonesia* 57 G13
Karapınar, *Turkey* 66 E5
Karasburg, *Namibia* 84 D2
Karasino, *Russia* 44 C9
Karasjok, *Norway* 8 B18
Karasu, *Turkey* 66 C4
Karasu →, *Turkey* 67 D8
Karasuk, *Russia* 44 D8
Karasuyama, *Japan* 49 F10
Karataş Burnu, *Turkey* 66 E6
Karatau, *Kazakhstan* 44 E8
Karatau, Khrebet, *Kazakhstan* 44 E7
Karatepe, *Turkey* 66 E7
Karauli, *India* 62 F7
Karavostasi, *Cyprus* 37 D11
Karawang, *Indonesia* 57 G12
Karawanken, *Europe* 21 J4
Karayazı, *Turkey* 67 D10
Karazhal, *Kazakhstan* 44 E8
Karbalā, *Iraq* 64 C5
Kårböle, *Sweden* 10 C9
Karcag, *Hungary* 21 H10
Karcha →, *Pakistan* 63 B7
Karda, *Russia* 45 D11
Kardhámila, *Greece* 39 L9
Kardhítsa, *Greece* 39 K4
Kärdla, *Estonia* 40 B3
Kareeberge, *S. Africa* 84 E3
Kareima, *Sudan* 76 D3
Karelian Republic □, *Russia* 44 C4
Kārevāndar, *Iran* 65 E9
Kargasok, *Russia* 44 D9
Kargat, *Russia* 44 D9
Kargı, *Turkey* 42 F6
Kargil, *India* 63 B7
Karguéri, *Niger* 79 C7
Karia ba Mohammed, *Morocco* 74 B3
Karīān, *Iran* 65 E8
Kariba, *Zimbabwe* 83 F2
Kariba, L., *Zimbabwe* 83 F2
Kariba Dam, *Zimbabwe* 83 F2
Kariba Gorge, *Zambia* 83 F2
Karibib, *Namibia* 84 C2
Karimata, Kepulauan, *Indonesia* 56 E3
Karimata, Selat, *Indonesia* 56 E3
Karimata Is. = Karimata, Kepulauan, *Indonesia* 56 E3
Karimnagar, *India* 60 K11
Karimunjawa, Kepulauan, *Indonesia* 56 F4
Karin, *Somali Rep.* 68 E4
Karīt, *Iran* 65 C8
Kariya, *Japan* 49 G8
Karkaralinsk, *Kazakhstan* 44 E8
Karkinitskiy Zaliv, *Ukraine* 42 D5
Karkur Tohl, *Egypt* 76 C2
Karl Libknekht, *Russia* 40 F9
Karl-Marx-Stadt = Chemnitz, *Germany* 18 E8
Karla, L. = Voiviïs Límni, *Greece* 39 K5
Karlobag, *Croatia* 33 D12
Karlovac, *Croatia* 33 C12
Karlovka, *Ukraine* 42 B6
Karlovy Vary, *Czech.* 20 E2
Karlsbad = Karlovy Vary, *Czech.* 20 E2
Karlsborg, *Sweden* 11 F8
Karlshamn, *Sweden* 9 H13
Karlskoga, *Sweden* 9 G13
Karlskrona, *Sweden* 9 H13
Karlsruhe, *Germany* 19 F4
Karlstad, *Sweden* 9 G12
Karlstad, *U.S.A.* 108 A6
Karlstadt, *Germany* 19 F5
Karnal, *India* 62 E7
Karnali →, *Nepal* 63 E9
Karnaphuli Res., *Bangla.* 61 H18
Karnataka □, *India* 60 N10
Karnes City, *U.S.A.* 109 L6
Karnische Alpen, *Europe* 21 J3
Karo, *Mali* 78 C4
Karoi, *Zimbabwe* 83 F2
Karonga, *Malawi* 83 D3
Karoonda, *Australia* 91 F2
Karora, *Sudan* 76 D4
Káros, *Greece* 39 N8
Karousádhes, *Greece* 39 K2
Karpasia □, *Cyprus* 37 D13
Kárpathos, *Greece* 39 P10
Kárpathos, Stenón, *Greece* 39 P10
Karrebæk, *Denmark* 11 J5
Kars, *Turkey* 43 F10
Kars □, *Turkey* 67 C10
Karsakpay, *Kazakhstan* 44 E7
Karsha, *Kazakhstan* 43 B14
Karshi, *Uzbekistan* 44 F7
Karsiyang, *India* 63 F13
Karst, *Croatia* 33 C11
Karsun, *Russia* 41 D15
Kartaly, *Russia* 44 D7
Kartapur, *India* 62 D6
Karthaus, *U.S.A.* 106 E6
Kartuzy, *Poland* 20 A8
Karufa, *Indonesia* 57 E8
Karumba, *Australia* 90 B3
Karumo, *Tanzania* 82 C3
Karumwa, *Tanzania* 82 C3
Karungu, *Kenya* 82 C3
Karup, *Denmark* 11 H3
Karviná, *Czech.* 20 F8
Karwar, *India* 60 M9
Karwi, *India* 63 G9
Kaş, *Turkey* 66 E3
Kasache, *Malawi* 83 E3
Kasai →, *Zaïre* 80 E3
Kasai Oriental □, *Zaïre* 82 C1
Kasaji, *Zaïre* 83 E1
Kasama, *Zambia* 83 E3
Kasan-dong, *N. Korea* 51 D14
Kasane, *Namibia* 84 B3
Kasanga, *Tanzania* 83 D3
Kasangulu, *Zaïre* 80 E3
Kasaragod, *India* 60 N9
Kasba L., *Canada* 101 A8
Kasba Tadla, *Morocco* 74 B3
Kāseh Garān, *Iran* 64 C5
Kasempa, *Zambia* 83 E2
Kasenga, *Zaïre* 83 E2
Kasese, *Uganda* 82 B3
Kasewa, *Zambia* 83 E2
Kasganj, *India* 63 F8
Kashabowie, *Canada* 98 C1
Kāshān, *Iran* 65 C6
Kashi, *China* 54 C2
Kashimbo, *Zaïre* 83 E2
Kashin, *Russia* 41 C10
Kashipur, *India* 63 E8
Kashira, *Russia* 41 D11
Kashiwazaki, *Japan* 49 F9
Kashk-e Kohneh, *Afghan.* 60 B3
Kāshmar, *Iran* 65 C8
Kashmir, *Asia* 63 C7
Kashmor, *Pakistan* 62 E3
Kashpirovka, *Russia* 41 E16
Kashun Noerh = Gaxun Nur, *China* 54 B5
Kasimov, *Russia* 41 D12
Kasinge, *Zaïre* 82 D2
Kasiruta, *Indonesia* 57 E7
Kaskaskia →, *U.S.A.* 108 G10
Kaskattama →, *Canada* 101 B10
Kaskinen, *Finland* 8 E16
Kaskö, *Finland* 8 E16
Kaslo, *Canada* 100 D5
Kasmere L., *Canada* 101 B8
Kasongo, *Zaïre* 82 C2
Kasongo Lunda, *Zaïre* 80 F3
Kásos, *Greece* 39 P9
Kásos, Stenón, *Greece* 39 P9
Kaspi, *Georgia* 43 F11
Kaspiysk, *Russia* 43 E12
Kaspiyskiy, *Russia* 43 D12
Kassab ed Doleib, *Sudan* 77 E3
Kassaba, *Egypt* 76 C2
Kassala, *Sudan* 77 D4
Kassalâ □, *Sudan* 77 D4
Kassel, *Germany* 18 D5
Kassinger, *Sudan* 76 D3
Kassiópi, *Greece* 37 A3
Kassue, *Indonesia* 57 F9
Kastamonu, *Turkey* 66 C5
Kastamonu □, *Turkey* 66 C5
Kastav, *Croatia* 33 C11
Kastélli, *Greece* 37 D5
Kastéllion, *Greece* 37 D7
Kastellou, Ákra, *Greece* 39 P10
Kasterlee, *Belgium* 17 F5
Kastóri, *Greece* 39 M5
Kastoría, *Greece* 39 J4
Kastornoye, *Russia* 41 F11
Kástron, *Greece* 39 K8
Kasulu, *Tanzania* 82 C3
Kasulu □, *Tanzania* 82 C3
Kasumi, *Japan* 49 G7
Kasumkent, *Azerbaijan* 43 F13
Kasungu, *Malawi* 83 E3
Kasur, *Pakistan* 62 D6
Kata, *Russia* 45 D11
Kataba, *Zambia* 83 F2
Katako Kombe, *Zaïre* 82 C1
Katákolon, *Greece* 39 M4
Katale, *Tanzania* 82 C3
Katamatite, *Australia* 91 F4
Katanda, *Kivu, Zaïre* 82 C2
Katanda, *Shaba, Zaïre* 82 D1
Katangi, *India* 60 J11
Katangli, *Russia* 45 D15
Katavi Swamp, *Tanzania* 82 D3
Kateríni, *Greece* 39 J5
Katha, *Burma* 61 G20
Katherîna, Gebel, *Egypt* 76 J8
Katherine, *Australia* 88 B5
Kathiawar, *India* 62 H4
Kathikas, *Cyprus* 37 E11
Kati, *Mali* 78 C3
Katihar, *India* 63 G12
Katima Mulilo, *Zambia* 84 B3
Katimbira, *Malawi* 83 E3
Katingan = Mendawai →, *Indonesia* 56 E4
Katiola, *Ivory C.* 78 D3
Katmandu, *Nepal* 63 F11
Kato Akhaïa, *Greece* 39 L4
Káto Arkhánai, *Greece* 37 D7
Káto Khorió, *Greece* 37 D7
Kato Pyrgos, *Cyprus* 37 D11
Káto Stavros, *Greece* 39 J6
Katompe, *Zaïre* 82 D2
Katonga →, *Uganda* 82 B3
Katoomba, *Australia* 91 E5
Katowice, *Poland* 20 E9
Katrine, L., *U.K.* 14 E4
Katrineholm, *Sweden* 10 E10
Katsepe, *Madag.* 85 B8
Katsina, *Nigeria* 79 C6
Katsina □, *Nigeria* 79 C6
Katsina Ala →, *Nigeria* 79 D6
Katsumoto, *Japan* 49 H4
Katsuura, *Japan* 49 G10
Katsuyama, *Japan* 49 F8
Kattaviá, *Greece* 37 D9
Kattegatt, *Denmark* 11 H5
Katumba, *Zaïre* 82 D2
Katungu, *Kenya* 82 C5
Katwa, *India* 63 H13
Katwijk-aan-Zee, *Neths.* 16 D4
Kauai, *U.S.A.* 102 H15
Kauai Channel, *U.S.A.* 102 H15
Kaub, *Germany* 19 E3
Kaufbeuren, *Germany* 19 H6
Kaufman, *U.S.A.* 109 J6
Kaukauna, *U.S.A.* 104 C1
Kaukauveld, *Namibia* 84 C3
Kaukonen, *Finland* 8 C18
Kauliranta, *Finland* 8 C17
Kaunas, *Lithuania* 40 D3
Kaura Namoda, *Nigeria* 79 C6
Kautokeino, *Norway* 8 B17
Kavacha, *Russia* 45 C17
Kavadarci, *Macedonia* 39 H5
Kavaja, *Albania* 39 H2
Kavak, *Turkey* 66 C7
Kavalerovo, *Russia* 48 B7
Kavali, *India* 60 M12
Kavála, *Greece* 39 J7
Kavār, *Iran* 65 D7
Kavarna, *Bulgaria* 38 F11
Kavos, *Greece* 37 B4
Kaw, *Fr. Guiana* 121 C7
Kawa, *Sudan* 77 E3
Kawagama L., *Canada* 106 A6
Kawagoe, *Japan* 49 G9
Kawaguchi, *Japan* 49 G9
Kawaihae, *U.S.A.* 102 H17
Kawambwa, *Zambia* 83 D2
Kawanoe, *Japan* 49 G6
Kawardha, *India* 63 J9
Kawasaki, *Japan* 49 G9
Kawene, *Canada* 98 C1
Kawerau, *N.Z.* 87 H6
Kawhia Harbour, *N.Z.* 87 H5
Kawio, Kepulauan, *Indonesia* 57 D7
Kawnro, *Burma* 61 H21
Kawthoolei = Kawthule □, *Burma* 61 L20
Kawthule □, *Burma* 61 L20
Kaya, *Burkina Faso* 79 C4
Kayah □, *Burma* 61 K20
Kayan →, *Indonesia* 56 D5
Kaycee, *U.S.A.* 110 E10
Kayeli, *Indonesia* 57 E7
Kayenta, *U.S.A.* 111 H8
Kayes, *Mali* 78 C2
Kayima, *S. Leone* 78 D2
Kayl, *Lux.* 17 K8
Kayoa, *Indonesia* 57 D7
Kayomba, *Zambia* 83 E1
Kayoro, *Ghana* 79 C4
Kayrunnera, *Australia* 91 E3
Kaysatskoye, *Russia* 43 B12
Kayseri, *Turkey* 66 D6
Kayseri □, *Turkey* 66 D6
Kaysville, *U.S.A.* 110 F8
Kayuagung, *Indonesia* 56 E2
Kazachinskoye, *Russia* 45 D11
Kazachye, *Russia* 45 B14
Kazakhstan ■, *Asia* 44 E7
Kazan, *Russia* 41 D16
Kazan-Rettō, *Pac. Oc.* 92 E6
Kazanlŭk, *Bulgaria* 38 G8
Kazanskaya, *Russia* 43 B9
Kazatin, *Ukraine* 42 B3
Kazbek, *Georgia* 43 E11
Kāzerūn, *Iran* 65 D6
Kazi Magomed, *Azerbaijan* 43 F13
Kazincbarcika, *Hungary* 21 G10
Kaztalovka, *Kazakhstan* 43 B13
Kazumba, *Zaïre* 80 F4
Kazuno, *Japan* 48 D10
Kazym →, *Russia* 44 C7
Kcynia, *Poland* 20 C7
Ké-Macina, *Mali* 78 C3
Kéa, *Greece* 39 M7
Keams Canyon, *U.S.A.* 111 J8
Kearney, *U.S.A.* 108 E5
Keban, *Turkey* 67 D8
Keban Baraji, *Turkey* 67 D8
Kebbje □, *Nigeria* 79 C6
Kébi, *Ivory C.* 78 D3
Kebili, *Tunisia* 75 B6
Kebnekaise, *Sweden* 8 C15
Kebri Dehar, *Ethiopia* 68 F3
Kebumen, *Indonesia* 57 G13
Kecel, *Hungary* 21 J9
Kechika →, *Canada* 100 B3

Kecskemét, *Hungary* 21 J9
Kedada, *Ethiopia* 77 F4
Kedgwick, *Canada* 99 C6
Kédhros Óros, *Greece* 37 D6
Kedia Hill, *Botswana* 84 C3
Kediniai, *Lithuania* 40 D4
Kediri, *Indonesia* 57 G15
Kédougou, *Senegal* 78 C2
Kedzierzyn, *Poland* 20 E8
Keeler, *U.S.A.* 112 J9
Keeley L., *Canada* 101 C7
Keeling Is. = Cocos Is., *Ind. Oc.* 92 J1
Keene, *Calif., U.S.A.* 113 K8
Keene, *N.H., U.S.A.* 107 D12
Keeper Hill, *Ireland* 15 D3
Keer-Weer, C., *Australia* 90 A3
Keerbergen, *Belgium* 17 F5
Keeseville, *U.S.A.* 107 B11
Keeten Mastgat, *Neths.* 17 E4
Keetmanshoop, *Namibia* 84 D2
Keewatin, *U.S.A.* 108 B8
Keewatin □, *Canada* 101 A9
Keewatin →, *Canada* 101 B8
Kefa □, *Ethiopia* 77 F4
Kefallinía, *Greece* 39 L3
Kefamenanu, *Indonesia* 57 F6
Keffi, *Nigeria* 79 D6
Kefken, *Turkey* 66 C4
Keflavík, *Iceland* 8 D2
Keg River, *Canada* 100 B5
Kegaska, *Canada* 99 B7
Kehl, *Germany* 19 G3
Keighley, *U.K.* 12 D6
Keimoes, *S. Africa* 84 D3
Keita, *Niger* 79 C6
Keith, *Australia* 91 F3
Keith, *U.K.* 14 D6
Keith Arm, *Canada* 96 B7
Kejser Franz Joseph Fjord = Kong Franz Joseph Fd., *Greenland* 4 B6
Kekri, *India* 62 G6
Kël, *Russia* 45 C13
Kelamet, *Eritrea* 77 D4
Kelan, *China* 50 E6
Kelang, *Malaysia* 59 L3
Kelantan →, *Malaysia* 59 J4
Kelheim, *Germany* 19 G7
Kelibia, *Tunisia* 75 A7
Kelkit, *Turkey* 67 C8
Kelkit →, *Turkey* 66 C7
Kellé, *Congo* 80 E2
Keller, *U.S.A.* 110 B4
Kellerberrin, *Australia* 89 F2
Kellett, C., *Canada* 4 B1
Kelleys I., *U.S.A.* 106 E2
Kellogg, *U.S.A.* 110 C5
Kelloselkä, *Finland* 8 C20
Kells = Ceanannus Mor, *Ireland* 15 C5
Kélo, *Chad* 73 G8
Kelokedhara, *Cyprus* 37 E11
Kelowna, *Canada* 100 D5
Kelsey Bay, *Canada* 100 C3
Kelseyville, *U.S.A.* 112 G4
Kelso, *N.Z.* 87 L2
Kelso, *U.K.* 14 F6
Kelso, *U.S.A.* 112 D4
Keluang, *Malaysia* 59 L4
Kelvington, *Canada* 101 C8
Kem, *Russia* 44 C4
Kem-Kem, *Morocco* 74 B4
Kema, *Indonesia* 57 D7
Kemah, *Turkey* 67 D8
Kemaliye, *Turkey* 67 D8
Kemano, *Canada* 100 C3
Kemasik, *Malaysia* 59 K4
Kembolcha, *Ethiopia* 77 E4
Kemer, *Turkey* 66 E4
Kemerovo, *Russia* 44 D9
Kemi, *Finland* 8 D18
Kemi älv = Kemijoki →, *Finland* 8 D18
Kemijärvi, *Finland* 8 C19
Kemijoki →, *Finland* 8 D18
Kemmel, *Belgium* 17 G1
Kemmerer, *U.S.A.* 110 F8
Kemmuna = Comino, *Malta* 37 C1
Kemp, L., *U.S.A.* 109 J5
Kemp Land, *Antarctica* 5 C5
Kempsey, *Australia* 91 E5
Kempt, L., *Canada* 98 C5
Kempten, *Germany* 19 H6
Kemptville, *Canada* 98 C4
Kenadsa, *Algeria* 75 B4
Kendal, *Indonesia* 56 F4
Kendal, *U.K.* 12 C5
Kendall, *Australia* 91 E5
Kendall →, *Australia* 90 A3
Kendallville, *U.S.A.* 104 E3
Kendari, *Indonesia* 57 E6
Kendawangan, *Indonesia* 56 E4
Kende, *Nigeria* 79 C5
Kendenup, *Australia* 89 F2
Kendrapara, *India* 61 J15
Kendrew, *S. Africa* 84 E3
Kendrick, *U.S.A.* 110 C5
Kene Thao, *Laos* 58 D3
Kenedy, *U.S.A.* 109 L6
Kenema, *S. Leone* 78 D2
Keng Kok, *Laos* 58 D5
Keng Tawng, *Burma* 61 J21
Keng Tung, *Burma* 61 J21
Kenge, *Zaïre* 80 E3
Kengeja, *Tanzania* 82 D4
Kenhardt, *S. Africa* 84 D3
Kenitra, *Morocco* 74 B3
Kenli, *China* 51 F10
Kenmare, *Ireland* 15 E2
Kenmare, *U.S.A.* 108 A3
Kenmare →, *Ireland* 15 E2
Kennebec, *U.S.A.* 108 D5
Kennedy, *Zimbabwe* 83 F2
Kennedy Ra., *Australia* 89 D2
Kennedy Taungdeik, *Burma* 61 H18
Kennet →, *U.K.* 13 F7
Kenneth Ra., *Australia* 88 D2
Kennett, *U.S.A.* 109 G9
Kennewick, *U.S.A.* 110 C4
Kénogami, *Canada* 99 C5
Kenogami →, *Canada* 98 B3
Kenora, *Canada* 101 D10
Kenosha, *U.S.A.* 104 D2
Kensington, *Canada* 99 C7
Kensington, *U.S.A.* 108 F5
Kensington Downs, *Australia* 90 C3
Kent, *Ohio, U.S.A.* 106 E3
Kent, *Oreg., U.S.A.* 110 D3
Kent, *Tex., U.S.A.* 109 K2
Kent, *Wash., U.S.A.* 112 C4
Kent □, *U.K.* 13 F8
Kent Group, *Australia* 90 F4
Kent Pen., *Canada* 96 B9
Kentau, *Kazakhstan* 44 E7
Kentland, *U.S.A.* 104 E2
Kenton, *U.S.A.* 104 E4
Kentucky □, *U.S.A.* 104 G3
Kentucky →, *U.S.A.* 104 F3
Kentucky L., *U.S.A.* 105 G2
Kentville, *Canada* 99 C7
Kentwood, *La., U.S.A.* 109 K9
Kentwood, *La., U.S.A.* 109 K9
Kenya ■, *Africa* 82 B4
Kenya, Mt., *Kenya* 82 C4
Keo Neua, Deo, *Vietnam* 58 C5
Keokuk, *U.S.A.* 108 E9
Kep, *Cambodia* 59 G5
Kep, *Vietnam* 58 B6
Kepi, *Indonesia* 57 F9
Kępno, *Poland* 20 D7
Kepsut, *Turkey* 66 D3
Kerala □, *India* 60 P10
Kerama-Rettō, *Japan* 49 L3
Keran, *Pakistan* 63 B5
Kerang, *Australia* 91 F3
Keraudren, C., *Australia* 88 C2
Kerch, *Ukraine* 42 D7
Kerchenskiy Proliv, *Black Sea* 42 D7
Kerchoual, *Mali* 79 B5
Kerempe Burnu, *Turkey* 66 B5
Keren, *Eritrea* 77 D4
Kerewan, *Gambia* 78 C1
Kerguelen, *Ind. Oc.* 3 G13
Keri Kera, *Sudan* 77 E3
Kericho, *Kenya* 82 C4
Kericho □, *Kenya* 82 C4
Kerinci, *Indonesia* 56 E2
Kerkdriel, *Neths.* 16 E6
Kerkenna, Is., *Tunisia* 75 B7
Kerki, *Turkmenistan* 44 F7
Kérkira, *Greece* 37 A3
Kerkrade, *Neths.* 17 G8
Kerma, *Sudan* 76 D3
Kermadec Is., *Pac. Oc.* 92 K10
Kermadec Trench, *Pac. Oc.* 92 L10
Kermān, *Iran* 65 D8
Kerman, *U.S.A.* 112 J6
Kermān □, *Iran* 65 D8
Kermānshāh = Bākhtarān, *Iran* 64 C5
Kerme Körfezi, *Turkey* 66 E2
Kermit, *U.S.A.* 109 K3
Kern →, *U.S.A.* 113 K7
Kerns, *Switz.* 23 C6
Kernville, *U.S.A.* 113 K8
Keroh, *Malaysia* 59 K3
Kerrobert, *Canada* 101 C7
Kerrville, *U.S.A.* 109 K5
Kerry □, *Ireland* 15 D2
Kerry Hd., *Ireland* 15 D2
Kersa, *Ethiopia* 77 F5
Kerteminde, *Denmark* 11 J4
Kertosono, *Indonesia* 57 G15
Kerulen →, *Asia* 54 B6
Kerzaz, *Algeria* 75 C4
Kerzers, *Switz.* 22 C4
Kesagami →, *Canada* 98 B4
Kesagami L., *Canada* 98 B3
Keşan, *Turkey* 66 C2
Kesch, Piz, *Switz.* 23 C9
Kesennuma, *Japan* 48 E10
Keshit, *Iran* 65 D8
Keşiş Dağ, *Turkey* 67 D8
Keski-Suomen lääni □, *Finland* 8 E18
Keskin, *Turkey* 66 D5
Kessel, *Belgium* 17 F5
Kessel, *Neths.* 17 F8
Kessel-Lo, *Belgium* 17 G5
Kestell, *S. Africa* 85 D4
Kestenga, *Russia* 44 C4
Kesteren, *Neths.* 16 E7
Keswick, *U.K.* 12 C4
Keszthely, *Hungary* 21 J7
Ket →, *Russia* 44 D9
Keta, *Ghana* 79 D5
Ketapang, *Indonesia* 56 E4
Ketchikan, *U.S.A.* 96 C6
Ketchum, *U.S.A.* 110 E6
Kete Krachi, *Ghana* 79 D4
Ketef, Khalîg Umm el, *Egypt* 76 C4
Ketelmeer, *Neths.* 16 C7
Keti Bandar, *Pakistan* 62 G2
Ketri, *India* 62 E6
Kętrzyn, *Poland* 20 A11
Kettering, *U.K.* 13 E7
Kettle →, *Canada* 101 B11
Kettle Falls, *U.S.A.* 110 B4
Kettleman City, *U.S.A.* 112 J7
Kevin, *U.S.A.* 110 B8
Kewanee, *U.S.A.* 108 E10
Kewaunee, *U.S.A.* 104 C2
Keweenaw B., *U.S.A.* 104 B1
Keweenaw Pen., *U.S.A.* 104 B2
Keweenaw Pt., *U.S.A.* 104 B2
Key Harbour, *Canada* 98 C3
Key West, *U.S.A.* 103 F10
Keyser, *U.S.A.* 104 F6
Keystone, *U.S.A.* 108 D3
Kezhma, *Russia* 45 D11
Kežmarok, *Slovak Rep.* 20 F10
Khabarovo, *Russia* 44 C7
Khabarovsk, *Russia* 45 E14
Khabr, *Iran* 65 D8
Khābūr →, *Syria* 64 C4
Khachmas, *Azerbaijan* 43 F13
Khachrod, *India* 62 H6
Khadari, W. el →, *Sudan* 77 E2
Khadro, *Pakistan* 62 F3
Khadyzhensk, *Russia* 43 D8
Khadzhilyangar, *India* 63 B8
Khagaria, *India* 63 G12
Khaipur, *Bahawalpur, Pakistan* 62 E5
Khaipur, *Hyderabad, Pakistan* 62 F3
Khair, *India* 62 F7
Khairabad, *India* 63 F9
Khairagarh, *India* 63 J9
Khairpur, *Pakistan* 60 F6
Khakhea, *Botswana* 84 C3
Khalafābād, *Iran* 65 D6
Khalfallah, *Algeria* 75 B5
Khalilabad, *India* 63 F10
Khalīlī, *Iran* 65 E7
Khalkhāl, *Iran* 65 B6
Khálki, *Greece* 39 K5
Khalkís, *Greece* 39 L6
Khalmer-Sede = Tazovskiy, *Russia* 44 C8
Khalmer Yu, *Russia* 44 C7
Khalturin, *Russia* 41 B16
Khalūf, *Oman* 68 C6
Kham Keut, *Laos* 58 C5
Khamas Country, *Botswana* 84 C4
Khambat, G. of, *India* 62 J5
Khambhaliya, *India* 62 H3
Khambhat, *India* 62 H5
Khamilonísion, *Greece* 39 P9
Khamīr, *Iran* 65 E7
Khamir, *Yemen* 68 D3
Khamsa, *Egypt* 69 E1
Khān Abū Shāmat, *Syria* 69 B5
Khān Azād, *Iraq* 64 C5
Khān Mujiddah, *Iraq* 64 C4
Khān Shaykhūn, *Syria* 64 C3
Khān Yūnis, *Egypt* 69 D3
Khānaqīn, *Iraq* 64 C5
Khānbāghī, *Iran* 65 B7
Khandrá, *Greece* 39 P9
Khandwa, *India* 60 J10
Khandyga, *Russia* 45 C14
Khāneh, *Iran* 64 B5
Khanewal, *Pakistan* 62 D4
Khanh Duong, *Vietnam* 58 F7
Khaniá, *Greece* 37 D6
Khaniá □, *Greece* 37 D6
Khaníon, Kólpos, *Greece* 37 D5
Khanka, Ozero, *Asia* 45 E14
Khankendy, *Azerbaijan* 67 D12
Khanna, *India* 62 D7
Khanpur, *Pakistan* 62 E4
Khanty-Mansiysk, *Russia* 44 C7
Khapalu, *Pakistan* 63 B7
Khapcheranga, *Russia* 45 E12
Kharagpur, *India* 63 H12
Khárakas, *Greece* 37 D7
Kharan Kalat, *Pakistan* 60 E4
Kharānaq, *Iran* 65 C7
Kharda, *India* 60 K9
Khardung La, *India* 63 B7
Khârga, El Wâhât el, *Egypt* 76 B3
Khargon, *India* 60 J9
Kharit, Wadi el →, *Egypt* 76 C3
Khārk, Jazireh, *Iran* 65 D6
Kharkiv = Kharkov, *Ukraine* 42 B7
Kharkov, *Ukraine* 42 B7
Kharmanli, *Bulgaria* 39 H8
Kharovsk, *Russia* 41 B12
Khartoum = El Khartûm, *Sudan* 77 D3
Khasan, *Russia* 48 C5
Khasavyurt, *Russia* 43 E12
Khāsh, *Iran* 60 E2
Khashm el Girba, *Sudan* 77 E4
Khashuri, *Georgia* 43 F10
Khaskovo, *Bulgaria* 39 H8
Khatanga, *Russia* 45 B11
Khatanga →, *Russia* 45 B11
Khatauli, *India* 62 E7
Khātūnābād, *Iran* 65 C6
Khatyrka, *Russia* 45 C18
Khaybar, Harrat, *Si. Arabia* 64 E4
Khāzimiyah, *Iraq* 64 C4
Khazzân Jabal el Awliyâ, *Sudan* 77 D3
Khe Bo, *Vietnam* 58 C5
Khe Long, *Vietnam* 58 B5
Khed Brahma, *India* 60 G8
Khekra, *India* 62 E7
Khemarak Phouminville, *Cambodia* 59 G4
Khemelnik, *Ukraine* 42 B2
Khemis Miliana, *Algeria* 75 A5
Khemissèt, *Morocco* 74 B3
Khemmarat, *Thailand* 58 D5
Khenāmān, *Iran* 65 D8
Khenchela, *Algeria* 75 A6
Khenifra, *Morocco* 74 B3
Kherrata, *Algeria* 75 A6
Kherson, *Ukraine* 42 C5
Khersónisos Akrotíri, *Greece* 37 D6
Kheta →, *Russia* 45 B11
Khilok, *Russia* 45 D12
Khimki, *Russia* 41 D10
Khíos, *Greece* 39 L9
Khirbat Qanāfār, *Lebanon* 69 B4
Khiuma = Hiiumaa, *Estonia* 40 B3
Khiva, *Uzbekistan* 44 E7
Khīyāv, *Iran* 64 B5
Khlong Khlung, *Thailand* 58 D2
Khmelnitskiy, *Ukraine* 40 G5
Khmelnytskyy = Khmelnitskiy, *Ukraine* 40 G5
Khmer Rep. = Cambodia ■, *Asia* 58 F5
Khoai, Hon, *Vietnam* 59 H5
Khodzent, *Tajikistan* 44 E7
Khojak P., *Afghan.* 60 D5
Khok Kloi, *Thailand* 59 H2
Khok Pho, *Thailand* 59 J3
Khokholskiy, *Russia* 41 F11
Kholm, *Russia* 40 C7
Kholmsk, *Russia* 45 E15
Khomas Hochland, *Namibia* 84 C2
Khomayn, *Iran* 65 C6
Khon Kaen, *Thailand* 58 D4
Khong, *Laos* 58 E5
Khong Sedone, *Laos* 58 E5
Khonu, *Russia* 45 C15
Khoper →, *Russia* 41 G13
Khor el 'Atash, *Sudan* 77 E3
Khóra, *Greece* 39 M4
Khóra Sfakíon, *Greece* 37 D6
Khorāsān □, *Iran* 65 C8
Khorat = Nakhon Ratchasima, *Thailand* 58 E4
Khorat, Cao Nguyen, *Thailand* 58 E4
Khorb el Ethel, *Algeria* 74 C3
Khorixas, *Namibia* 84 C1
Khorog, *Tajikistan* 44 F8
Khorol, *Ukraine* 42 B5
Khorramābād, *Khorāsān, Iran* 65 C8
Khorramābād, *Lorestān, Iran* 65 C6
Khorrāmshahr, *Iran* 65 D6
Khosravī, *Iran* 65 D6
Khosrowābād, *Khuzestān, Iran* 65 D6
Khosrowābād, *Kordestān, Iran* 64 C5
Khosūyeh, *Iran* 65 D7
Khotin, *Ukraine* 42 B2
Khouribga, *Morocco* 74 B3
Khowai, *Bangla.* 61 G17
Khoyniki, *Belorussia* 40 F6
Khrami →, *Azerbaijan* 43 F11
Khrenovoye, *Russia* 41 F12
Khristianá, *Greece* 39 N8
Khrysokhou B., *Cyprus* 37 D11
Khu Khan, *Thailand* 58 E5
Khuff, *Si. Arabia* 64 E5
Khūgīānī, *Afghan.* 62 D1
Khulna, *Bangla.* 61 H16
Khulna □, *Bangla.* 61 H16
Khulo, *Georgia* 43 F10
Khumago, *Botswana* 84 C3
Khūnsorkh, *Iran* 65 E8
Khunzakh, *Russia* 43 E12
Khūr, *Iran* 65 C8
Khurai, *India* 62 G8
Khurayş, *Si. Arabia* 65 E6
Khūrīyā Mūrīyā, Jazā 'ir, *Oman* 68 D6
Khurja, *India* 62 E7
Khūsf, *Iran* 65 C8
Khush, *Afghan.* 60 C3
Khushab, *Pakistan* 62 C5
Khuzdar, *Pakistan* 62 F2
Khūzestān □, *Iran* 65 D6
Khvājeh, *Iran* 64 B5
Khvalynsk, *Russia* 41 E16
Khvānsār, *Iran* 65 D7
Khvatovka, *Russia* 41 E15
Khvor, *Iran* 65 C7
Khvorgū, *Iran* 65 E8
Khvormūj, *Iran* 65 D6
Khvoy, *Iran* 64 B5
Khvoynaya, *Russia* 40 B9
Khyber Pass, *Afghan.* 62 B4
Kiabukwa, *Zaïre* 83 D1
Kiama, *Australia* 91 E5
Kiamba, *Phil.* 55 H6
Kiambi, *Zaïre* 82 D2
Kiambu, *Kenya* 82 C4
Kiangsi = Jiangxi □, *China* 53 D10
Kiangsu = Jiangsu □, *China* 51 H10
Kibæk, *Denmark* 11 H2
Kibanga Port, *Uganda* 82 B3
Kibangou, *Congo* 80 E2
Kibara, *Tanzania* 82 C3
Kibare, Mts., *Zaïre* 82 D2
Kibombo, *Zaïre* 82 C2
Kibondo, *Tanzania* 82 C3
Kibondo □, *Tanzania* 82 C3
Kibumbu, *Burundi* 82 C2
Kibungu, *Rwanda* 82 C3
Kibuye, *Burundi* 82 C2
Kibuye, *Rwanda* 82 C2
Kibwesa, *Tanzania* 82 D2
Kibwezi, *Kenya* 82 C4
Kichiga, *Russia* 45 D17
Kicking Horse Pass, *Canada* 100 C5
Kidal, *Mali* 79 B5
Kidderminster, *U.K.* 13 E5
Kidete, *Tanzania* 82 D4
Kidira, *Senegal* 78 C2
Kidnappers, C., *N.Z.* 87 H6
Kidston, *Australia* 90 B3
Kidugallo, *Tanzania* 82 D4
Kiel, *Germany* 18 A6
Kiel Kanal = Nord-Ostsee Kanal, *Germany* 18 A5
Kielce, *Poland* 20 E10
Kieldrecht, *Belgium* 17 F4
Kieler Bucht, *Germany* 18 A6
Kien Binh, *Vietnam* 59 H5
Kien Tan, *Vietnam* 59 G5
Kienge, *Zaïre* 83 E2
Kiessé, *Niger* 79 C5
Kiev = Kiyev, *Ukraine* 40 F7
Kiffa, *Mauritania* 78 B2
Kifisiá, *Greece* 39 L6
Kifissós →, *Greece* 39 L6
Kifrī, *Iraq* 64 C5
Kigali, *Rwanda* 82 C3
Kigarama, *Tanzania* 82 C3
Kigoma □, *Tanzania* 82 D2
Kigoma-Ujiji, *Tanzania* 82 C2
Kigomasha, Ras, *Tanzania* 82 C4
Kihee, *Australia* 91 D3
Kii-Sanchi, *Japan* 49 G7
Kii-Suidō, *Japan* 49 H7
Kikaiga-Shima, *Japan* 49 K4
Kikinda, *Serbia* 21 K10
Kikládhes, *Greece* 39 M7
Kikwit, *Zaïre* 80 E3
Kílalki, *Greece* 39 N10
Kilauea Crater, *U.S.A.* 102 J17
Kilchberg, *Switz.* 23 B7
Kilcoy, *Australia* 91 D5
Kildare, *Ireland* 15 C5
Kildare □, *Ireland* 15 C5
Kilgore, *U.S.A.* 109 J7
Kilifi, *Kenya* 82 C4
Kilifi □, *Kenya* 82 C4
Kilimanjaro, *Tanzania* 82 C4
Kilimanjaro □, *Tanzania* 82 C4
Kilindini, *Kenya* 82 C4
Kilis, *Turkey* 66 E7
Kiliya, *Ukraine* 42 D3
Kilju, *N. Korea* 51 D15
Kilkee, *Ireland* 15 D2
Kilkenny, *Ireland* 15 D4
Kilkenny □, *Ireland* 15 D4
Kilkieran B., *Ireland* 15 C2
Kilkís, *Greece* 39 J5
Killala, *Ireland* 15 B2
Killala B., *Ireland* 15 B2
Killaloe, *Ireland* 15 D3
Killaloe Sta., *Canada* 106 A7
Killam, *Canada* 100 C6
Killarney, *Australia* 91 D5
Killarney, *Canada* 98 C3
Killarney, *Ireland* 15 D2
Killarney, Lakes of, *Ireland* 15 E2
Killary Harbour, *Ireland* 15 C2
Killdeer, *Canada* 101 D7
Killdeer, *U.S.A.* 108 B3
Killeen, *U.S.A.* 109 K6
Killiecrankie, Pass of, *U.K.* 14 E5
Killin, *U.K.* 14 E4
Killíni, *Ilía, Greece* 39 M4
Killíni, *Korinthía, Greece* 39 M5
Killybegs, *Ireland* 15 B3
Kilmarnock, *U.K.* 14 F4
Kilmez, *Russia* 41 C17
Kilmez →, *Russia* 41 C17
Kilmore, *Australia* 91 F3
Kilondo, *Tanzania* 83 D3
Kilosa, *Tanzania* 82 D4
Kilosa □, *Tanzania* 82 D4
Kilrush, *Ireland* 15 D2
Kilwa □, *Tanzania* 83 D4
Kilwa Kisiwani, *Tanzania* 83 D4
Kilwa Kivinje, *Tanzania* 83 D4
Kilwa Masoko, *Tanzania* 83 D4
Kim, *U.S.A.* 109 G3
Kimaam, *Indonesia* 57 F9
Kimamba, *Tanzania* 82 D4

Kimba, *Australia* 91 E2
Kimball, *Nebr., U.S.A.* 108 E3
Kimball, *S. Dak., U.S.A.* 108 D5
Kimberley, *Canada* 100 D5
Kimberley, *S. Africa* 84 D3
Kimberley Downs, *Australia* 88 C3
Kimberly, *U.S.A.* 110 E6
Kimchaek, *N. Korea* 51 D15
Kimchŏn, *S. Korea* 51 F15
Kími, *Greece* 39 L7
Kimje, *S. Korea* 51 G14
Kímolos, *Greece* 39 N7
Kimovsk, *Russia* 41 D11
Kimparana, *Mali* 78 C4
Kimry, *Russia* 41 C10
Kimsquit, *Canada* 100 C3
Kimstad, *Sweden* 11 F9
Kinabalu, Gunong, *Malaysia* 56 C5
Kínaros, *Greece* 39 N9
Kinaskan L., *Canada* 100 B2
Kinbasket L., *Canada* 100 C5
Kincaid, *Canada* 101 D7
Kincardine, *Canada* 98 D3
Kinda, *Zaïre* 83 D2
Kinder Scout, *U.K.* 12 D6
Kindersley, *Canada* 101 C7
Kindia, *Guinea* 78 C2
Kindu, *Zaïre* 82 C2
Kinel, *Russia* 41 E17
Kineshma, *Russia* 41 C13
Kinesi, *Tanzania* 82 C3
King, L., *Australia* 89 F2
King, Mt., *Australia* 90 D4
King City, *U.S.A.* 111 H3
King Cr. →, *Australia* 90 C2
King Edward →, *Australia* 88 B4
King Frederick VI Land = Kong Frederik VI.s Kyst, *Greenland* 4 C5
King George B., *Falk. Is.* 128 D4
King George I., *Antarctica* 5 C18
King George Is., *Canada* 97 C11
King I. = Kadan Kyun, *Burma* 56 B1
King I., *Australia* 90 F3
King I., *Canada* 100 C3
King Leopold Ras., *Australia* 88 C4
King Sd., *Australia* 88 C3
King William I., *Canada* 96 B10
King William's Town, *S. Africa* 84 E4
Kingaroy, *Australia* 91 D5
Kingfisher, *U.S.A.* 109 H6
Kingirbān, *Iraq* 64 C5
Kingisepp = Kuressaare, *Estonia* 40 B3
Kingisepp, *Russia* 40 B6
Kingman, *Ariz., U.S.A.* 113 K12
Kingman, *Kans., U.S.A.* 109 G5
Kingoonya, *Australia* 91 E2
Kings →, *U.S.A.* 111 H4
Kings Canyon National Park, *U.S.A.* 111 H4
King's Lynn, *U.K.* 12 E8
Kings Mountain, *U.S.A.* 105 H5
King's Peak, *U.S.A.* 110 F8
Kingsbridge, *U.K.* 13 G4
Kingsburg, *U.S.A.* 111 H4
Kingscote, *Australia* 91 F2
Kingscourt, *Ireland* 15 C5
Kingsley, *U.S.A.* 108 D7
Kingsport, *U.S.A.* 105 G4
Kingston, *Canada* 98 D4
Kingston, *Jamaica* 116 C4
Kingston, *N.Z.* 87 L2
Kingston, *N.Y., U.S.A.* 107 E10
Kingston, *Pa., U.S.A.* 107 E9
Kingston, *R.I., U.S.A.* 107 E13
Kingston Pk., *U.S.A.* 113 K11
Kingston South East, *Australia* 91 F2
Kingston upon Hull, *U.K.* 12 D7
Kingston-upon-Thames, *U.K.* 13 F7
Kingstown, *St. Vincent* 117 D7
Kingstree, *U.S.A.* 105 J6
Kingsville, *Canada* 98 D3
Kingsville, *U.S.A.* 109 M6
Kingussie, *U.K.* 14 D4
Kinistino, *Canada* 101 C7
Kinkala, *Congo* 80 E2
Kinki □, *Japan* 49 H8
Kinleith, *N.Z.* 87 H5
Kinmount, *Canada* 106 B6
Kinna, *Sweden* 11 G6
Kinnaird, *Canada* 100 D5
Kinnairds Hd., *U.K.* 14 D7
Kinnared, *Sweden* 11 G7
Kinnarodden, *Norway* 6 A11
Kino, *Mexico* 114 B2
Kinoje →, *Canada* 98 B3
Kinomoto, *Japan* 49 G8
Kinoni, *Uganda* 82 C3
Kinrooi, *Belgium* 17 F7
Kinross, *U.K.* 14 E5
Kinsale, *Ireland* 15 E3
Kinsale, Old Hd. of, *Ireland* 15 E3
Kinsha = Chang Jiang →, *China* 53 B13
Kinshasa, *Zaïre* 80 E3
Kinsley, *U.S.A.* 109 G5
Kinston, *U.S.A.* 105 H7
Kintampo, *Ghana* 79 D4
Kintap, *Indonesia* 56 E5
Kintore Ra., *Australia* 88 D4
Kintyre, *U.K.* 14 F3
Kintyre, Mull of, *U.K.* 14 F3
Kinushseo →, *Canada* 98 A3
Kinuso, *Canada* 100 B5
Kinyangiri, *Tanzania* 82 C3
Kinzig →, *Germany* 19 G3
Kinzua, *U.S.A.* 106 E6
Kinzua Dam, *U.S.A.* 106 E5
Kiosk, *Canada* 98 C4
Kiowa, *Kans., U.S.A.* 109 G5
Kiowa, *Okla., U.S.A.* 109 H7
Kipahigan L., *Canada* 101 B8
Kipanga, *Tanzania* 82 D4
Kiparissía, *Greece* 39 M4
Kiparissiakós Kólpos, *Greece* 39 M4
Kipembawe, *Tanzania* 82 D3
Kipengere Ra., *Tanzania* 83 D3
Kipili, *Tanzania* 82 D3
Kipini, *Kenya* 82 C5
Kipling, *Canada* 101 C8
Kippure, *Ireland* 15 C5
Kipushi, *Zaïre* 83 E2
Kiratpur, *India* 62 E8
Kirchberg, *Switz.* 22 B5
Kirchhain, *Germany* 18 E4
Kirchheim, *Germany* 19 G5
Kirchheim-Bolanden, *Germany* 19 F4
Kirensk, *Russia* 45 D11
Kirgella Rocks, *Australia* 89 F3
Kirghizia ■, *Asia* 44 E8
Kirghizstan = Kirghizia ■, *Asia* 44 E8
Kirgizia = Kirghizia ■, *Asia* 44 E8
Kiri, *Zaïre* 80 E3
Kiribati ■, *Pac. Oc.* 92 H10
Kırıkhan, *Turkey* 66 E7
Kırıkkale, *Turkey* 66 D5
Kirillov, *Russia* 41 B11
Kirin = Jilin, *China* 51 C14
Kirin = Jilin □, *China* 51 C13
Kirishi, *Russia* 40 B7
Kiritimati, *Kiribati* 93 G12
Kirka, *Turkey* 66 D4
Kirkcaldy, *U.K.* 14 E5
Kirkcudbright, *U.K.* 14 G4
Kirkee, *India* 60 K8
Kirkenær, *Norway* 10 D6
Kirkenes, *Norway* 8 B21
Kirkintilloch, *U.K.* 14 F4
Kirkjubæjarklaustur, *Iceland* 8 E4
Kirkland, *U.S.A.* 111 J7
Kirkland Lake, *Canada* 98 C3
Kırklareli, *Turkey* 39 H10
Kırklareli □, *Turkey* 66 C2
Kirksville, *U.S.A.* 108 E8
Kirkūk, *Iraq* 64 C5
Kirkwall, *U.K.* 14 C6
Kirkwood, *S. Africa* 84 E4
Kirn, *Germany* 19 F3
Kirov = Vyatka, *Russia* 41 B16
Kirov, *Russia* 40 D9
Kirovabad = Gyandzha, *Azerbaijan* 43 F12
Kirovakan = Karaklis, *Armenia* 43 F11
Kirovo-Chepetsk, *Russia* 41 B17
Kirovograd, *Ukraine* 42 B5
Kirovohrad = Kirovograd, *Ukraine* 42 B5
Kirovsk, *Russia* 44 C4
Kirovsk, *Turkmenistan* 44 F7
Kirovsk, *Ukraine* 43 B8
Kirovski, *Russia* 43 D13
Kirovskiy, *Russia* 45 D16
Kirovskiy, *Russia* 48 B6
Kirriemuir, *U.K.* 14 E6
Kirsanov, *Russia* 41 E13
Kırşehir, *Turkey* 66 D6
Kırşehir □, *Turkey* 66 D6
Kirstonia, *S. Africa* 84 D3
Kirtachi, *Niger* 79 C5
Kirthar Range, *Pakistan* 62 F2
Kiruna, *Sweden* 8 C16
Kirundu, *Zaïre* 82 C2
Kirup, *Australia* 89 F2
Kirya, *Russia* 41 D15
Kiryū, *Japan* 49 F9
Kisaga, *Tanzania* 82 C3
Kisalaya, *Nic.* 116 D3
Kisámou, Kólpos, *Greece* 37 D5
Kisanga, *Zaïre* 82 B2
Kisangani, *Zaïre* 82 B2
Kisar, *Indonesia* 57 F7
Kisaran, *Indonesia* 56 D1
Kisarawe, *Tanzania* 82 D4
Kisarawe □, *Tanzania* 82 D4
Kisarazu, *Japan* 49 G9
Kisbér, *Hungary* 21 H8
Kiselevsk, *Russia* 44 D9
Kishanganga →, *Pakistan* 63 B5
Kishanganj, *India* 63 F13
Kishangarh, *India* 62 F4
Kishi, *Nigeria* 79 D5
Kishinev, *Moldavia* 42 C3
Kishiwada, *Japan* 49 G7
Kishtwar, *India* 63 C6
Kisii, *Kenya* 82 C3
Kisii □, *Kenya* 82 C3
Kisiju, *Tanzania* 82 D4
Kısır Dağ, *Turkey* 43 F10
Kisizi, *Uganda* 82 C2
Kiska I., *U.S.A.* 96 C1
Kiskatinaw →, *Canada* 100 B4
Kiskittogisu L., *Canada* 101 C9
Kiskörös, *Hungary* 21 J9
Kiskundorozsma, *Hungary* 21 J10
Kiskunfélegyháza, *Hungary* 21 J9
Kiskunhalas, *Hungary* 21 J9
Kiskunmajsa, *Hungary* 21 J9
Kislovodsk, *Russia* 43 E10
Kiso-Gawa →, *Japan* 49 G8
Kiso-Sammyaku, *Japan* 49 G8
Kisofukushima, *Japan* 49 G8
Kisoro, *Uganda* 82 C2
Kispest, *Hungary* 21 H9
Kissidougou, *Guinea* 78 D2
Kissimmee, *U.S.A.* 105 L5
Kissimmee →, *U.S.A.* 105 M5
Kississing L., *Canada* 101 B8
Kissónerga, *Cyprus* 37 E11
Kistanje, *Croatia* 33 E12
Kisújszállás, *Hungary* 21 H10
Kisumu, *Kenya* 82 C3
Kisvárda, *Hungary* 21 G12
Kiswani, *Tanzania* 82 C4
Kiswere, *Tanzania* 83 D4
Kit Carson, *U.S.A.* 108 F3
Kita, *Mali* 78 C3
Kitab, *Uzbekistan* 44 F7
Kitaibaraki, *Japan* 49 F10
Kitakami, *Japan* 48 E10
Kitakami-Gawa →, *Japan* 48 E10
Kitakami-Sammyaku, *Japan* 48 E10
Kitakata, *Japan* 48 F9
Kitakyūshū, *Japan* 49 H5
Kitale, *Kenya* 82 B4
Kitami, *Japan* 48 C11
Kitami-Sammyaku, *Japan* 48 B11
Kitangiri, L., *Tanzania* 82 C3
Kitaya, *Tanzania* 83 E5
Kitchener, *Australia* 89 F3
Kitchener, *Canada* 98 D3
Kitega = Gitega, *Burundi* 82 C2
Kitengo, *Zaïre* 82 D1
Kiteto □, *Tanzania* 82 C4
Kitgum, *Uganda* 82 B3
Kíthira, *Greece* 39 N7
Kíthnos, *Greece* 39 M7
Kiti, *Cyprus* 37 E12
Kiti, C., *Cyprus* 37 E12
Kitikmeot □, *Canada* 96 A9
Kitimat, *Canada* 100 C3
Kitinen →, *Finland* 8 C19
Kitiyab, *Sudan* 77 D3
Kítros, *Greece* 39 J5
Kitsuki, *Japan* 49 H5
Kittakittaooloo, L., *Australia* 91 D2
Kittanning, *U.S.A.* 106 F5
Kittatinny Mts., *U.S.A.* 107 E10
Kittery, *U.S.A.* 105 D10
Kitui, *Kenya* 82 C4
Kitui □, *Kenya* 82 C4
Kitwe, *Zambia* 83 E2
Kitzbühel, *Austria* 19 H8
Kitzingen, *Germany* 19 F6
Kivalo, *Finland* 8 C19
Kivarli, *India* 62 G5
Kividhes, *Cyprus* 37 E11
Kivu □, *Zaïre* 82 C2
Kivu, L., *Zaïre* 82 C2
Kiyev, *Ukraine* 40 F7
Kiyevskoye Vdkhr., *Ukraine* 40 F7
Kiziguru, *Rwanda* 82 C3
Kızıl Irmak →, *Turkey* 42 F6
Kizil Jilga, *India* 63 B8
Kizil Yurt, *Russia* 43 E12
Kızılcahamam, *Turkey* 42 F5
Kızılhisar, *Turkey* 66 E3
Kızılırmak, *Turkey* 66 C5
Kızıltepe, *Turkey* 67 E9
Kizimkazi, *Tanzania* 82 D4
Kizlyar, *Russia* 43 E12
Kizyl-Arvat, *Turkmenistan* 44 F6
Kjellerup, *Denmark* 11 H3
Kladanj, *Bos.-H.* 21 L8
Kladno, *Czech.* 20 E4
Kladovo, *Serbia* 21 L12
Klaeng, *Thailand* 58 F3
Klagenfurt, *Austria* 21 J4
Klagshamn, *Sweden* 11 J6
Klagstorp, *Sweden* 11 J7
Klaipéda, *Lithuania* 40 D2
Klamath →, *U.S.A.* 110 F1
Klamath Falls, *U.S.A.* 110 E3
Klamath Mts., *U.S.A.* 110 F2
Klanjec, *Croatia* 33 B12
Klappan →, *Canada* 100 B3
Klarälven →, *Sweden* 9 G12
Klaten, *Indonesia* 57 G14
Klatovy, *Czech.* 20 F3
Klawer, *S. Africa* 84 E2
Klawock, *U.S.A.* 100 B2
Klazienaveen, *Neths.* 16 C10
Kleczew, *Poland* 20 C8
Kleena Kleene, *Canada* 100 C4
Klein, *U.S.A.* 110 C9
Klein-Karas, *Namibia* 84 D2
Kleine Gette →, *Belgium* 17 G6
Kleine Nete →, *Belgium* 17 F5
Klekovača, *Bos.-H.* 33 D13
Klenovec, *Macedonia* 39 H3
Klenovec, *Slovak Rep.* 20 G9
Klerksdorp, *S. Africa* 84 D4
Kletnya, *Russia* 40 E8
Kletsk, *Belorussia* 40 E5
Kletskiy, *Russia* 43 B10
Kleve, *Germany* 18 D2
Klickitat, *U.S.A.* 110 D3
Klickitat →, *U.S.A.* 112 E5
Klidhes, *Cyprus* 37 D13
Klimovichi, *Belorussia* 40 E8
Klin, *Russia* 41 C10
Klinaklini →, *Canada* 100 C3
Klintsey, *Russia* 40 E8
Klipdale, *S. Africa* 84 E2
Klipplaat, *S. Africa* 84 E3
Klitmøller, *Denmark* 11 G2
Kljajićevo, *Serbia* 21 K9
Ključ, *Bos.-H.* 33 D13
Kłobuck, *Poland* 20 E8
Kłodzko, *Poland* 20 E6
Kloetinge, *Neths.* 17 F3
Klondike, *Canada* 96 B6
Kloosterzande, *Neths.* 17 F4
Klosterneuburg, *Austria* 21 G6
Klosters, *Switz.* 23 C9
Kloten, *Switz.* 23 B7
Klötze, *Germany* 18 C7
Klouto, *Togo* 79 D5
Kluane L., *Canada* 96 B6
Kluczbork, *Poland* 20 E8
Klundert, *Neths.* 17 E5
Klyuchevskaya, Gora, *Russia* 45 D17
Knaresborough, *U.K.* 12 C6
Knee L., *Man., Canada* 101 B10
Knee L., *Sask., Canada* 101 B7
Kneïss, Is., *Tunisia* 75 B7
Knesselare, *Belgium* 17 F2
Knezha, *Bulgaria* 38 F7
Knić, *Serbia* 21 M10
Knight Inlet, *Canada* 100 C3
Knighton, *U.K.* 13 E4
Knights Ferry, *U.S.A.* 112 H6
Knights Landing, *U.S.A.* 112 G5
Knin, *Croatia* 33 D13
Knittelfeld, *Austria* 21 H4
Knjaževac, *Serbia* 21 M12
Knob, C., *Australia* 89 F2
Knockmealdown Mts., *Ireland* 15 D4
Knokke, *Belgium* 17 F2
Knossós, *Greece* 37 D7
Knox, *U.S.A.* 104 E2
Knox, C., *Canada* 100 C2
Knox City, *U.S.A.* 109 J5
Knox Coast, *Antarctica* 5 C8
Knoxville, *Iowa, U.S.A.* 108 E8
Knoxville, *Tenn., U.S.A.* 105 H4
Knutshø, *Norway* 10 B3
Knysna, *S. Africa* 84 E3
Knyszyn, *Poland* 20 B12
Ko Kha, *Thailand* 58 C2
Ko Tao, *Thailand* 59 G2
Koartac, *Canada* 97 B13
Koba, *Aru, Indonesia* 57 F8
Koba, *Bangka, Indonesia* 56 E3
Kobarid, *Slovenia* 33 B10
Kobayashi, *Japan* 49 J5
Kobdo = Hovd, *Mongolia* 54 B4
Kōbe, *Japan* 49 G7
Kobelyaki, *Ukraine* 42 B6
København, *Denmark* 11 J6
Kōbi-Sho, *Japan* 49 M1
Koblenz, *Germany* 19 E3
Koblenz, *Switz.* 22 A6
Kobo, *Ethiopia* 77 E4
Kobrin, *Belorussia* 40 E4
Kobroor, Kepulauan, *Indonesia* 57 F8
Kobuleti, *Georgia* 43 F9
Kobyłka, *Poland* 20 C11
Kobylkino, *Russia* 41 D13
Kobylnik, *Belorussia* 40 D5
Kocaeli = İzmit, *Turkey* 66 C3
Kocaeli □, *Turkey* 66 C3
Kočani, *Macedonia* 39 H5
Koceljevo, *Serbia* 21 L9
Kočevje, *Slovenia* 33 C11
Koch Bihar, *India* 61 F16
Kochang, *S. Korea* 51 G14
Kochas, *India* 63 G10
Kocher →, *Germany* 19 F5
Kocheya, *Russia* 45 D13
Kōchi, *Japan* 49 H6
Kōchi □, *Japan* 49 H6
Kochiu = Gejiu, *China* 52 F4
Kodiak, *U.S.A.* 96 C4
Kodiak I., *U.S.A.* 96 C4
Kodinar, *India* 62 J4
Kodori →, *Georgia* 43 E9
Koekelare, *Belgium* 17 F1
Koersel, *Belgium* 17 F6
Koes, *Namibia* 84 D2
Koffiefontein, *S. Africa* 84 D4
Kofiau, *Indonesia* 57 E7
Koforidua, *Ghana* 79 D4
Kōfu, *Japan* 49 G9
Koga, *Japan* 49 F9
Kogaluk →, *Canada* 99 A7
Kogan, *Australia* 91 D5
Kogi □, *Nigeria* 79 D6
Kogin Baba, *Nigeria* 79 D7
Koh-i-Bābā, *Afghan.* 60 B5
Koh-i-Khurd, *Afghan.* 62 C1
Kohat, *Pakistan* 62 C4
Kohima, *India* 61 G19
Kohkīlūyeh va Būyer Aḥmadi □, *Iran* 65 D6
Kohler Ra., *Antarctica* 5 D15
Kohtla-Järve, *Estonia* 40 B5
Koin-dong, *N. Korea* 51 D14
Kojŏ, *N. Korea* 51 E14
Kojonup, *Australia* 89 F2
Kojūr, *Iran* 65 B6
Koka, *Sudan* 76 C3
Kokand, *Uzbekistan* 44 E8
Kokanee Glacier Prov. Park, *Canada* 100 D5
Kokas, *Indonesia* 57 E8
Kokchetav, *Kazakhstan* 44 D7
Kokemäenjoki, *Finland* 9 F16
Kokerite, *Guyana* 121 B6
Kokhma, *Russia* 41 C12
Kokkola, *Finland* 8 E17
Koko, *Nigeria* 79 C5
Koko Kyunzu, *Burma* 61 M18
Kokolopozo, *Ivory C.* 78 D3
Kokomo, *U.S.A.* 104 E2
Kokonau, *Indonesia* 57 E9
Kokoro, *Niger* 79 C5
Koksan, *N. Korea* 51 E14
Koksoak →, *Canada* 97 C13
Kokstad, *S. Africa* 85 E4
Kokubu, *Japan* 49 J5
Kokuora, *Russia* 45 B15
Kola, *Indonesia* 57 F8
Kola, *Russia* 44 C4
Kola Pen. = Kolskiy Poluostrov, *Russia* 44 C4
Kolahoi, *India* 63 B6
Kolahun, *Liberia* 78 D2
Kolaka, *Indonesia* 57 E6
Kolar, *India* 60 N11
Kolar Gold Fields, *India* 60 N11
Kolari, *Finland* 8 C17
Kolayat, *India* 60 F8
Kolby Kås, *Denmark* 11 J4
Kolchugino = Leninsk-Kuznetskiy, *Russia* 44 D9
Kolchugino, *Russia* 41 C11
Kolda, *Senegal* 78 C2
Kolding, *Denmark* 11 J3
Kole, *Zaïre* 80 E4
Koléa, *Algeria* 75 A5
Kolepom = Yos Sudarso, Pulau, *Indonesia* 57 F9
Kolguyev, Ostrov, *Russia* 44 C5
Kolham, *Neths.* 16 B9
Kolhapur, *India* 60 L9
Kolia, *Ivory C.* 78 D3
Kolín, *Czech.* 20 E5
Kolind, *Denmark* 11 H4
Kölleda, *Germany* 18 D7
Kollum, *Neths.* 16 B8
Kolmanskop, *Namibia* 84 D2
Köln, *Germany* 18 E2
Koło, *Poland* 20 C8
Kołobrzeg, *Poland* 20 A5
Kologriv, *Russia* 41 B14
Kolokani, *Mali* 78 C3
Kolomna, *Russia* 41 D11
Kolomyya, *Ukraine* 42 B1
Kolondiéba, *Mali* 78 C3
Kolonodale, *Indonesia* 57 E6
Kolosib, *India* 61 G18
Kolpashevo, *Russia* 44 D9
Kolpino, *Russia* 40 B7
Kolpny, *Russia* 41 E10
Kolskiy Poluostrov, *Russia* 44 C4
Kolubara →, *Serbia* 21 L10
Koluszki, *Poland* 20 D9
Kolwezi, *Zaïre* 83 E2
Kolyberovo, *Russia* 41 D11
Kolyma →, *Russia* 45 C17
Kolymskoye, Okhotsko, *Russia* 45 C16
Kôm Ombo, *Egypt* 76 C3
Komandorskiye Is. = Komandorskiye Ostrova, *Russia* 45 D17
Komandorskiye Ostrova, *Russia* 45 D17
Komárno, *Slovak Rep.* 21 H8
Komárom, *Hungary* 21 H8
Komarovo, *Russia* 40 B8
Komatipoort, *S. Africa* 85 D5
Komatou Yialou, *Cyprus* 37 D13
Komatsu, *Japan* 49 F8
Komatsujima, *Japan* 49 H7
Kombissiri, *Burkina Faso* 79 C4
Kombori, *Burkina Faso* 78 C4
Komen, *Slovenia* 33 C10
Komenda, *Ghana* 79 D4
Komi Republic □, *Russia* 44 C6
Komiža, *Croatia* 33 E13
Komló, *Hungary* 21 J8
Kommunarsk, *Ukraine* 43 B8
Kommunizma, Pik, *Tajikistan* 44 F8
Komodo, *Indonesia* 57 F5
Komoé, *Ivory C.* 78 D4
Komono, *Congo* 80 E2
Komoran, Pulau, *Indonesia* 57 F9
Komoro, *Japan* 49 F9
Komotini, *Greece* 39 H8
Kompasberg, *S. Africa* 84 E3
Kompong Bang, *Cambodia* 59 F5
Kompong Cham, *Cambodia* 59 F5
Kompong Chhnang, *Cambodia* 59 F5

Kompong Chikreng, *Cambodia* 58 F5
Kompong Kleang, *Cambodia* 58 F5
Kompong Luong, *Cambodia* 59 G5
Kompong Pranak, *Cambodia* 58 F5
Kompong Som, *Cambodia* 59 G4
Kompong Som, Chhung, *Cambodia* 59 G4
Kompong Speu, *Cambodia* 59 G5
Kompong Sralao, *Cambodia* 58 E5
Kompong Thom, *Cambodia* 58 F5
Kompong Trabeck, *Cambodia* 58 F5
Kompong Trabeck, *Cambodia* 59 G5
Kompong Trach, *Cambodia* 59 G5
Kompong Tralach, *Cambodia* 59 G5
Komrat, *Moldavia* 42 C3
Komsberg, *S. Africa* 84 E3
Komsomolets, Ostrov, *Russia* 45 A10
Komsomolsk, *Russia* 41 C12
Komsomolsk, *Russia* 45 D14
Komsomolskiy, *Russia* 41 E16
Konakovo, *Russia* 41 C10
Konarhá □, *Afghan.* 60 B7
Konārī, *Iran* 65 D6
Konawa, *U.S.A.* 109 H6
Konch, *India* 63 G8
Kondakovo, *Russia* 45 C16
Konde, *Tanzania* 82 C4
Kondinin, *Australia* 89 F2
Kondoa, *Tanzania* 82 C4
Kondoa □, *Tanzania* 82 D4
Kondókali, *Greece* 37 A3
Kondratyevo, *Russia* 45 D10
Konduga, *Nigeria* 79 C7
Kong, *Ivory C.* 78 D4
Kong →, *Cambodia* 58 F5
Kong, Koh, *Cambodia* 59 G4
Kong Christian IX.s Land, *Greenland* 4 C6
Kong Christian X.s Land, *Greenland* 4 B6
Kong Franz Joseph Fd., *Greenland* 4 B6
Kong Frederik IX.s Land, *Greenland* 4 C5
Kong Frederik VI.s Kyst, *Greenland* 4 C5
Kong Frederik VIII.s Land, *Greenland* 4 B6
Kong Oscar Fjord, *Greenland* 4 B6
Kongeå →, *Denmark* 11 J3
Kongju, *S. Korea* 51 F14
Konglu, *Burma* 61 F20
Kongolo, *Kasai Or., Zaïre* 82 D1
Kongolo, *Shaba, Zaïre* 82 D2
Kongor, *Sudan* 77 F3
Kongoussi, *Burkina Faso* 79 C4
Kongsberg, *Norway* 10 E3
Kongsvinger, *Norway* 10 D6
Kongwa, *Tanzania* 82 D4
Koni, *Zaïre* 83 E2
Koni, Mts., *Zaïre* 83 E2
Königsberg = Kaliningrad, *Russia* 40 D2
Königslutter, *Germany* 18 C6
Königswusterhausen, *Germany* 18 C9
Konin, *Poland* 20 C8
Kónitsa, *Greece* 39 J3
Köniz, *Switz.* 22 C4
Konjice, *Slovenia* 33 B12
Konkiep, *Namibia* 84 D2
Konkouré →, *Guinea* 78 D2
Könnern, *Germany* 18 D7
Kono, *S. Leone* 78 D2
Konolfingen, *Switz.* 22 C5
Konongo, *Ghana* 79 D4
Konosha, *Russia* 44 C5
Kōnosu, *Japan* 49 F9
Konotop, *Ukraine* 40 F8
Konqi He →, *China* 54 B4
Końskie, *Poland* 20 D10
Konstantinovka, *Ukraine* 42 B7
Konstantinovski, *Russia* 43 C9
Konstanz, *Germany* 19 H5
Kont, *Iran* 65 E9
Kontagora, *Nigeria* 79 C6
Kontich, *Belgium* 17 F4
Kontum, *Vietnam* 58 E7
Kontum, Plateau du, *Vietnam* 58 E7
Konya, *Turkey* 66 E5
Konya □, *Turkey* 66 E5
Konya Ovasi, *Turkey* 66 D5
Konz, *Germany* 19 F2
Konza, *Kenya* 82 C4
Kookynie, *Australia* 89 E3
Kooline, *Australia* 88 D2
Kooloonong, *Australia* 91 E3
Koolyanobbing, *Australia* 89 F2
Koondrook, *Australia* 91 F3
Koonibba, *Australia* 91 E1
Koorawatha, *Australia* 91 E4
Koorda, *Australia* 89 F2
Kooskia, *U.S.A.* 110 C6
Kootenai →, *Canada* 110 B5
Kootenay L., *Canada* 100 D5
Kootenay Nat. Park, *Canada* 100 C5
Kootjieskolk, *S. Africa* 84 E3
Kopanovka, *Russia* 43 C12
Kopaonik, *Serbia* 21 M11
Kópavogur, *Iceland* 8 D3
Koper, *Slovenia* 33 C10
Kopervik, *Norway* 9 G8
Kopeysk, *Russia* 44 D7
Kopi, *Australia* 91 E2
Köping, *Sweden* 10 E10
Kopiste, *Croatia* 33 F13
Köpmanholmen, *Sweden* 10 A12
Koppang, *Norway* 10 C5
Kopparberg, *Sweden* 9 G13
Kopparbergs län □, *Sweden* 9 F13
Kopperå, *Norway* 10 A5
Koppies, *S. Africa* 85 D4
Koprivnica, *Croatia* 33 B13
Kopychintsy, *Ukraine* 40 G4
Kopys, *Belorussia* 40 D7
Korab, *Macedonia* 39 H3
Korakiána, *Greece* 37 A3
Korba, *India* 63 H10
Korbach, *Germany* 18 D4
Korbu, G., *Malaysia* 59 K3
Korça, *Albania* 39 J3
Korce = Korça, *Albania* 39 J3
Korčula, *Croatia* 33 F14
Korčulanski Kanal, *Croatia* 33 E13
Kord Kūy, *Iran* 65 B7
Kord Sheykh, *Iran* 65 D7
Kordestān □, *Iran* 64 C5
Korea, North ■, *Asia* 51 E14
Korea, South ■, *Asia* 51 F15
Korea Bay, *Korea* 51 E13
Korea Strait, *Asia* 51 G15
Korenevo, *Russia* 40 F9
Korenovsk, *Russia* 43 D8
Korets, *Ukraine* 40 F5
Korgan, *Turkey* 67 C7
Korgus, *Sudan* 76 D3
Korhogo, *Ivory C.* 78 D3
Koribundu, *S. Leone* 78 D2
Korim, *Indonesia* 57 E9
Korinthiakós Kólpos, *Greece* 39 L5
Kórinthos, *Greece* 39 M5
Korioumé, *Mali* 78 B4
Koríssa, Límni, *Greece* 37 B3
Kōriyama, *Japan* 48 F10
Korkuteli, *Turkey* 66 E4
Kormakiti, C., *Cyprus* 37 D11
Körmend, *Hungary* 21 H6
Kornat, *Croatia* 33 E12
Korneshty, *Moldavia* 42 C3
Kornsjø, *Norway* 10 F5
Kornstad, *Norway* 10 B1
Koro, *Fiji* 87 C8
Koro, *Ivory C.* 78 D3
Koro, *Mali* 78 C4
Koro Sea, *Fiji* 87 C9
Korocha, *Russia* 41 F10
Köroğlu Dağları, *Turkey* 66 C4
Korogwe, *Tanzania* 82 D4
Korogwe □, *Tanzania* 82 D4
Koroit, *Australia* 91 F3
Koronadal, *Phil.* 55 H6
Koronowo, *Poland* 20 B7
Koror, *Pac. Oc.* 57 C8
Körös →, *Hungary* 21 J10
Korosten, *Ukraine* 40 F6
Korotoyak, *Russia* 41 F11
Korraraika, Helodranon' i, *Madag.* 85 B7
Korsakov, *Russia* 45 E15
Korshunovo, *Russia* 45 D12
Korsør, *Denmark* 9 J11
Korsun Shevchenkovskiy, *Ukraine* 42 B4
Korsze, *Poland* 20 A11
Kortemark, *Belgium* 17 F2
Kortessem, *Belgium* 17 G6
Korti, *Sudan* 76 D3
Kortrijk, *Belgium* 17 G2
Korwai, *India* 62 G8
Koryakskiy Khrebet, *Russia* 45 C18
Koryŏng, *S. Korea* 51 G15
Kos, *Greece* 39 N10
Kosa, *Ethiopia* 77 F4
Kosaya Gora, *Russia* 41 D10
Kościan, *Poland* 20 C6
Kościerzyna, *Poland* 20 A7
Kosciusko, *U.S.A.* 109 J10
Kosciusko, Mt., *Australia* 91 F4
Kosciusko I., *U.S.A.* 100 B2
Kösély →, *Hungary* 21 H11
Kosha, *Sudan* 76 C3
Köshetau = Kokchetav, *Kazakhstan* 44 D7
K'oshih = Kashi, *China* 54 C2
Koshiki-Rettō, *Japan* 49 J4
Kosi, *India* 62 F7
Kosi-meer, *S. Africa* 85 D5
Košice, *Slovak Rep.* 20 G11
Kosjerić, *Serbia* 21 M9
Koskhinoú, *Greece* 37 C10
Kosŏng, *N. Korea* 51 E15
Kosovska-Mitrovica, *Serbia* 21 N10
Kostajnica, *Croatia* 33 C13
Kostanjevica, *Slovenia* 33 C12
Kostelec, *Czech.* 20 E6
Koster, *S. Africa* 84 D4
Kôstî, *Sudan* 77 E3
Kostopol, *Ukraine* 40 F5
Kostroma, *Russia* 41 C12
Kostromskoye Vdkhr., *Russia* 41 C12
Kostyantynivka = Konstantinovka, *Ukraine* 42 B7
Kostyukovichi, *Belorussia* 40 E8
Koszalin, *Poland* 20 A6
Köszeg, *Hungary* 21 H6
Kot Addu, *Pakistan* 62 D4
Kot Moman, *Pakistan* 62 C5
Kota, *India* 62 G6
Kota Baharu, *Malaysia* 59 J4
Kota Belud, *Malaysia* 56 C5
Kota Kinabalu, *Malaysia* 56 C5
Kota Tinggi, *Malaysia* 59 M4
Kotaagung, *Indonesia* 56 F2
Kotabaru, *Indonesia* 56 E5
Kotabumi, *Indonesia* 56 E2
Kotagede, *Indonesia* 57 G14
Kotamobagu, *Indonesia* 57 D6
Kotaneelee →, *Canada* 100 A4
Kotawaringin, *Indonesia* 56 E4
Kotcho L., *Canada* 100 B4
Kotelnich, *Russia* 41 B16
Kotelnikovo, *Russia* 43 C10
Kotelnyy, Ostrov, *Russia* 45 B14
Köthen, *Germany* 18 D7
Kothi, *India* 63 G9
Kotiro, *Pakistan* 62 F2
Kotka, *Finland* 9 F19
Kotlas, *Russia* 44 C5
Kotli, *Pakistan* 62 C5
Kotmul, *Pakistan* 63 B6
Kotonkoro, *Nigeria* 79 C6
Kotor, *Montenegro* 21 N8
Kotoriba, *Croatia* 33 B13
Kotovo, *Russia* 41 F14
Kotovsk, *Ukraine* 42 C3
Kotputli, *India* 62 F7
Kotri, *Pakistan* 62 G3
Kótronas, *Greece* 39 N5
Kottayam, *India* 60 Q10
Kotturu, *India* 60 M10
Kotuy →, *Russia* 45 B11
Kotzebue, *U.S.A.* 96 B3
Kouango, *C.A.R.* 80 C4
Koudekerke, *Neths.* 17 F3
Koudougou, *Burkina Faso* 78 C4
Koufonísi, *Greece* 37 E8
Kougaberge, *S. Africa* 84 E3
Kouibli, *Ivory C.* 78 D3
Kouilou →, *Congo* 80 E2
Kouki, *C.A.R.* 80 C3
Koula Moutou, *Gabon* 80 E2
Koulen, *Cambodia* 58 F5
Koulikoro, *Mali* 78 C3
Kouloúra, *Greece* 37 A3
Koúm-bournoú, Ákra, *Greece* 37 C10
Koumala, *Australia* 90 C4
Koumankou, *Mali* 78 C3
Koumbia, *Burkina Faso* 78 C4
Koumbia, *Guinea* 78 C2
Koumboum, *Guinea* 78 C2
Koumpenntoum, *Senegal* 78 C2
Koumra, *Chad* 73 G8
Koundara, *Guinea* 78 C2
Kounradskiy, *Kazakhstan* 44 E8
Kountze, *U.S.A.* 109 K7
Koupéla, *Burkina Faso* 79 C4
Kouris →, *Cyprus* 37 E11
Kourou, *Fr. Guiana* 121 B7
Kouroussa, *Guinea* 78 C3
Koussané, *Mali* 78 C2
Kousseri, *Cameroon* 73 F7
Koutiala, *Mali* 78 C3
Kouto, *Ivory C.* 78 D3
Kouvé, *Togo* 79 D5
Kovačica, *Serbia* 21 K10
Kovel, *Ukraine* 40 F4
Kovin, *Serbia* 21 L10
Kovrov, *Russia* 41 C12
Kowanyama, *Australia* 90 B3
Kowkash, *Canada* 98 B2
Kowloon, *H.K.* 53 F10
Kowŏn, *N. Korea* 51 E14
Koyabuti, *Indonesia* 57 E10
Köyceğiz, *Turkey* 66 E3
Koyuk, *U.S.A.* 96 B3
Koyukuk →, *U.S.A.* 96 B4
Koyulhisar, *Turkey* 42 F7
Koza, *Japan* 49 L3
Kozan, *Turkey* 66 E6
Kozáni, *Greece* 39 J4
Kozara, *Bos.-H.* 33 D14
Kozarac, *Bos.-H.* 33 D13
Kozelsk, *Russia* 40 D9
Kozhikode = Calicut, *India* 60 P9
Kozje, *Slovenia* 33 B12
Kozlovets, *Bulgaria* 38 F8
Kozlu, *Turkey* 66 C4
Kozluk, *Turkey* 67 D9
Koźmin, *Poland* 20 D7
Kozmodemyansk, *Russia* 41 C15
Kpabia, *Ghana* 79 D4
Kpalimé, *Togo* 79 D5
Kpandae, *Ghana* 79 D4
Kpessi, *Togo* 79 D5
Kra, Isthmus of = Kra, Kho Khot, *Thailand* 59 G2
Kra, Kho Khot, *Thailand* 59 G2
Kra Buri, *Thailand* 59 G2
Krabbendijke, *Neths.* 17 F4
Krabi, *Thailand* 59 H2
Kragan, *Indonesia* 57 G14
Kragerø, *Norway* 10 F3
Kragujevac, *Serbia* 21 L10
Krajina, *Bos.-H.* 33 D13
Krakatau = Rakata, Pulau, *Indonesia* 56 F3
Krakor, *Cambodia* 58 F5
Kraków, *Poland* 20 E9
Kraksaan, *Indonesia* 57 G15
Kråkstad, *Norway* 10 E4
Kralanh, *Cambodia* 58 F4
Králiky, *Czech.* 20 E6
Kraljevo, *Serbia* 21 M10
Kralovice, *Czech.* 20 F3
Kralupy, *Czech.* 20 E4
Kramatorsk, *Ukraine* 42 B7
Kramfors, *Sweden* 10 B11
Kramis, C., *Algeria* 75 A5
Krångede, *Sweden* 10 A10
Kranj, *Slovenia* 33 B11
Kranjska Gora, *Slovenia* 33 B10
Krankskop, *S. Africa* 85 D5
Krapina, *Croatia* 33 B12
Krapina →, *Croatia* 33 C12
Krapivna, *Russia* 41 E10
Krapkowice, *Poland* 20 E7
Kraskino, *Russia* 45 E14
Kraslice, *Czech.* 20 E2
Krasnaya Gorbatka, *Russia* 41 D12
Krasnaya Polyana, *Russia* 43 E9
Kraśnik, *Poland* 20 E12
Kraśnik Fabryczny, *Poland* 20 E12
Krasnoarmeisk, *Ukraine* 42 B7
Krasnoarmeysk, *Russia* 41 F14
Krasnoarmeysk, *Russia* 43 B11
Krasnodar, *Russia* 43 D8
Krasnodon, *Ukraine* 43 B8
Krasnodonetskaya, *Russia* 43 B9
Krasnogorskiy, *Russia* 41 C16
Krasnograd, *Ukraine* 42 B6
Krasnogvardeyskoye, *Russia* 43 D9
Krasnogvardyesk, *Ukraine* 42 D6
Krasnokutsk, *Ukraine* 40 F9
Krasnoperekopsk, *Ukraine* 42 D5
Krasnorechenskiy, *Russia* 48 B7
Krasnoselkupsk, *Russia* 44 C9
Krasnoslobodsk, *Russia* 41 D13
Krasnoslobodsk, *Russia* 43 B11
Krasnoturinsk, *Russia* 44 D7
Krasnoufimsk, *Russia* 44 D6
Krasnouralsk, *Russia* 44 D7
Krasnovodsk, *Turkmenistan* 44 E6
Krasnoyarsk, *Russia* 45 D10
Krasnoye = Krasnyy, *Russia* 40 D7
Krasnoye, *Russia* 41 B15
Krasnoye, *Russia* 43 C11
Krasnozavodsk, *Russia* 41 C11
Krasny Liman, *Ukraine* 42 B7
Krasny Sulin, *Russia* 43 C9
Krasnystaw, *Poland* 20 E13
Krasnyy, *Russia* 40 D7
Krasnyy Kholm, *Russia* 41 B10
Krasnyy Kut, *Russia* 41 F15
Krasnyy Luch, *Ukraine* 43 B8
Krasnyy Profintern, *Russia* 41 C12
Krasnyy Yar, *Russia* 41 E17
Krasnyy Yar, *Russia* 41 F14
Krasnyy Yar, *Russia* 43 C13
Krasnyye Baki, *Russia* 41 C14
Krasnyyoskolskoye Vdkhr., *Ukraine* 42 B7
Kraszna →, *Hungary* 21 G12
Kratie, *Cambodia* 58 F6
Krau, *Indonesia* 57 E10
Kravanh, Chuor Phnum, *Cambodia* 59 G4
Krefeld, *Germany* 18 D2
Krémaston, Límni, *Greece* 39 L4
Kremenchug, *Ukraine* 42 B5
Kremenchugskoye Vdkhr., *Ukraine* 42 B5
Kremenchuk = Kremenchug, *Ukraine* 42 B5
Kremenets, *Ukraine* 42 A1
Kremennaya, *Ukraine* 42 B8
Kremges = Svetlovodsk, *Ukraine* 40 G8
Kremikovtsi, *Bulgaria* 38 G6
Kremmen, *Germany* 18 C9
Kremmling, *U.S.A.* 110 F10
Krems, *Austria* 21 G5
Kremsmünster, *Austria* 21 G4
Kretinga, *Lithuania* 40 D2
Krettamia, *Algeria* 74 C4
Krettsy, *Russia* 40 B8
Kreuzberg, *Germany* 19 E5
Kreuzlingen, *Switz.* 23 A8
Kribi, *Cameroon* 79 E6
Krichem, *Bulgaria* 38 G7
Krichev, *Belorussia* 40 E7
Krim, *Slovenia* 33 C11
Krimpen, *Neths.* 16 E5
Kriós, Ákra, *Greece* 37 D5
Krishna →, *India* 61 M12
Krishnanagar, *India* 63 H13
Kristiansand, *Norway* 9 G10
Kristianstad, *Sweden* 9 H13
Kristianstads län □, *Sweden* 9 H13
Kristiansund, *Norway* 10 A1
Kristiinankaupunki, *Finland* 8 E16
Kristinehamn, *Sweden* 9 G13
Kristinestad, *Finland* 8 E16
Kríti, *Greece* 37 D7
Kritsá, *Greece* 37 D7
Kriva →, *Macedonia* 38 G4
Kriva Palanka, *Macedonia* 38 G5
Krivaja →, *Bos.-H.* 21 L8
Krivoy Rog, *Ukraine* 42 C5
Križevci, *Croatia* 33 B13
Krk, *Croatia* 33 C11
Krka →, *Slovenia* 33 C12
Krkonoše, *Czech.* 20 E5
Krnov, *Czech.* 20 E7
Krobia, *Poland* 20 D6
Krokeaí, *Greece* 39 N5
Krokodil →, *Mozam.* 85 D5
Krokom, *Sweden* 10 A8
Krolevets, *Ukraine* 40 F8
Kroměříz, *Czech.* 20 F7
Krommenie, *Neths.* 16 D5
Kromy, *Russia* 40 E9
Kronach, *Germany* 19 E7
Kronobergs län □, *Sweden* 9 H13
Kronprins Olav Kyst, *Antarctica* 5 C5
Kronshtadt, *Russia* 40 A6
Kroonstad, *S. Africa* 84 D4
Kröpelin, *Germany* 18 A7
Kropotkin, *Russia* 43 D9
Kropotkin, *Russia* 45 D12
Kropp, *Germany* 18 A5
Krościenko, *Poland* 20 F10
Krosno, *Poland* 20 F11
Krosno Odrzańskie, *Poland* 20 C5
Krotoszyn, *Poland* 20 D7
Kroussón, *Greece* 37 D6
Krško, *Slovenia* 33 C12
Kruger Nat. Park, *S. Africa* 85 C5
Krugersdorp, *S. Africa* 85 D4
Kruiningen, *Neths.* 17 F4
Kruisfontein, *S. Africa* 84 E3
Kruishoutem, *Belgium* 17 G3
Kruisland, *Neths.* 17 E4
Kruja, *Albania* 39 H2
Krulevshchina, *Belorussia* 40 D5
Kruma, *Albania* 38 G3
Krumbach, *Germany* 19 G6
Krung Thep = Bangkok, *Thailand* 58 F3
Krupanj, *Serbia* 21 L9
Krupinica →, *Slovak Rep.* 21 G8
Kruševac, *Serbia* 21 M11
Kruzof I., *U.S.A.* 100 B1
Krychaw = Krichev, *Belorussia* 40 E7
Krymsk Abinsk, *Russia* 42 D8
Krymskiy Poluostrov, *Ukraine* 42 D5
Krynica Morska, *Poland* 20 A9
Krynki, *Poland* 20 B13
Kryvyy Rih = Krivoy Rog, *Ukraine* 42 C5
Krzywiń, *Poland* 20 D6
Krzyz, *Poland* 20 C6
Ksabi, *Morocco* 74 B4
Ksar Chellala, *Algeria* 75 A5
Ksar el Boukhari, *Algeria* 75 A5
Ksar el Kebir, *Morocco* 74 B3
Ksar es Souk = Ar Rachidiya, *Morocco* 74 B4
Ksar Rhilane, *Tunisia* 75 B6
Ksour, Mts. des, *Algeria* 75 B4
Kstovo, *Russia* 41 C14
Kuala, *Indonesia* 56 D3
Kuala Berang, *Malaysia* 59 K4
Kuala Dungun, *Malaysia* 59 K4
Kuala Kangsar, *Malaysia* 59 K3
Kuala Kelawang, *Malaysia* 59 L4
Kuala Kerai, *Malaysia* 59 K4
Kuala Kubu Baharu, *Malaysia* 59 L3
Kuala Lipis, *Malaysia* 59 K4
Kuala Lumpur, *Malaysia* 59 L3
Kuala Nerang, *Malaysia* 59 J3
Kuala Pilah, *Malaysia* 59 L4
Kuala Rompin, *Malaysia* 59 L4
Kuala Selangor, *Malaysia* 59 L3
Kuala Terengganu, *Malaysia* 59 K4
Kualajelai, *Indonesia* 56 E4
Kualakapuas, *Indonesia* 56 E4
Kualakurun, *Indonesia* 56 E4
Kualapembuang, *Indonesia* 56 E4
Kualasimpang, *Indonesia* 56 D1
Kuancheng, *China* 51 D10
Kuandang, *Indonesia* 57 D6
Kuandian, *China* 51 D13
Kuangchou = Guangzhou, *China* 53 F9
Kuantan, *Malaysia* 59 L4
Kuba, *Azerbaijan* 43 F13
Kuban →, *Russia* 42 D7
Kubenskoye, Oz., *Russia* 41 B11
Kuberle, *Russia* 43 C10
Kubokawa, *Japan* 49 H6
Kubrat, *Bulgaria* 38 F9
Kučevo, *Serbia* 21 L11
Kucha Gompa, *India* 63 B7
Kuchaman, *India* 62 F6
Kuchino-eruba-Jima, *Japan* 49 J5
Kuchino-Shima, *Japan* 49 K4
Kuchinotsu, *Japan* 49 H5
Kucing, *Malaysia* 56 D4
Kuçove = Qytet Stalin, *Albania* 39 J2
Kud →, *Pakistan* 62 F2
Kuda, *India* 60 H7
Kudat, *Malaysia* 56 C5

Kudus, *Indonesia* 57 G14
Kudymkar, *Russia* 44 D6
Kueiyang = Guiyang, *China* 52 D6
Kufstein, *Austria* 19 H8
Kugong I., *Canada* 98 A4
Kūh-e Dīnār, *Iran* 65 D6
Kūh-e-Hazārām, *Iran* 65 D8
Kūhak, *Iran* 60 F3
Kūhbonān, *Iran* 65 D8
Kūhestak, *Iran* 65 E8
Kūhīn, *Iran* 65 C6
Kūhīrī, *Iran* 65 E9
Kuhnsdorf, *Austria* 21 J4
Kūhpāyeh, *Eṣfahan, Iran* 65 C7
Kūhpāyeh, *Kermān, Iran* 65 D8
Kui Buri, *Thailand* 59 F2
Kuinre, *Neths.* 16 C7
Kuito, *Angola* 81 G3
Kujang, *N. Korea* 51 E14
Kuji, *Japan* 48 D10
Kujū-San, *Japan* 49 H5
Kukawa, *Nigeria* 79 C7
Kukerin, *Australia* 89 F2
Kukmor, *Russia* 41 C17
Kukup, *Malaysia* 59 M4
Kukvidze, *Russia* 41 F13
Kula, *Serbia* 21 K9
Kulai, *Malaysia* 59 M4
Kulal, Mt., *Kenya* 82 B4
Kulaly, Os., *Kazakhstan* 43 D14
Kulasekarappattinam, *India* 60 Q11
Kuldiga, *Latvia* 40 C2
Kuldja = Yining, *China* 44 E9
Kuldu, *Sudan* 77 E2
Kulebaki, *Russia* 41 D13
Kulen Vakuf, *Bos.-H.* 33 D13
Kulgam, *India* 63 C6
Kuli, *Russia* 43 E12
Kulim, *Malaysia* 59 K3
Kulin, *Australia* 89 F2
Kulja, *Australia* 89 F2
Kulm, *U.S.A.* 108 B5
Kulmbach, *Germany* 19 E7
Kulp, *Turkey* 67 D9
Kulsary, *Kazakhstan* 44 E6
Kultay, *Kazakhstan* 43 D14
Kulti, *India* 63 H12
Kulu, *Turkey* 66 D5
Kulumbura, *Australia* 88 B4
Kulunda, *Russia* 44 D8
Kulungar, *Afghan.* 62 C3
Kūlvand, *Iran* 65 D7
Kulwin, *Australia* 91 F3
Kulyab, *Tajikistan* 44 F7
Kum Tekei, *Kazakhstan* 44 E8
Kuma →, *Russia* 43 D12
Kumaganum, *Nigeria* 79 C7
Kumagaya, *Japan* 49 F9
Kumai, *Indonesia* 56 E4
Kumamba, Kepulauan, *Indonesia* 57 E9
Kumamoto, *Japan* 49 H5
Kumamoto □, *Japan* 49 H5
Kumanovo, *Macedonia* 38 G4
Kumara, *N.Z.* 87 K3
Kumarl, *Australia* 89 F3
Kumasi, *Ghana* 78 D4
Kumayri, *Armenia* 43 F10
Kumba, *Cameroon* 79 E6
Kumbakonam, *India* 60 P11
Kumbarilla, *Australia* 91 D5
Kumbo, *Cameroon* 79 D7
Kŭmchŏn, *N. Korea* 51 E14
Kumdok, *India* 63 C8
Kume-Shima, *Japan* 49 L3
Kumeny, *Russia* 41 B16
Kŭmhwa, *S. Korea* 51 E14
Kumi, *Uganda* 82 B3
Kumla, *Sweden* 9 G13
Kumluca, *Turkey* 66 E4
Kummerower See, *Germany* 18 B8
Kumo, *Nigeria* 79 C7
Kumon Bum, *Burma* 61 F20
Kumtorkala, *Russia* 43 E12
Kumylzhenskaya, *Russia* 43 B10
Kunama, *Australia* 91 F4
Kunashir, Ostrov, *Russia* 45 E15
Kunda, *Estonia* 40 B5
Kundla, *India* 62 J4
Kungala, *Australia* 91 D5
Kungälv, *Sweden* 11 G5
Kunghit I., *Canada* 100 C2
Kungrad, *Uzbekistan* 44 E6
Kungsbacka, *Sweden* 11 G6
Kungur, *Russia* 44 D6
Kungurri, *Australia* 90 C4
Kunhar →, *Pakistan* 63 B5
Kunhegyes, *Hungary* 21 H10
Kuningan, *Indonesia* 57 G13
Kunlong, *Burma* 61 H21
Kunlun Shan, *Asia* 54 C3
Kunming, *China* 52 E4
Kunrade, *Neths.* 17 G7
Kunsan, *S. Korea* 51 G14
Kunshan, *China* 53 B13
Kununurra, *Australia* 88 C4
Kunwarara, *Australia* 90 C5
Kunya-Urgench, *Turkmenistan* 44 E6
Künzelsau, *Germany* 19 F5
Kuopio, *Finland* 8 E19
Kuopion lääni □, *Finland* 8 E19
Kupa →, *Croatia* 33 C13
Kupang, *Indonesia* 57 F6
Kupres, *Bos.-H.* 21 L7
Kupyansk, *Ukraine* 42 B7
Kupyansk-Uzlovoi, *Ukraine* 42 B7
Kuqa, *China* 54 B3
Kuranda, *Australia* 90 B4
Kurashiki, *Japan* 49 G6
Kurayoshi, *Japan* 49 G6
Kurdistan, *Asia* 67 E10
Kŭrdzhali, *Bulgaria* 39 H8
Kure, *Japan* 49 G6
Küre, *Turkey* 66 C5
Küre Dağları, *Turkey* 66 C6
Kuressaare, *Estonia* 40 B3
Kurgaldzhino, *Kazakhstan* 44 D8
Kurgan, *Russia* 44 D7
Kurganinsk, *Russia* 43 D9
Kurgannaya = Kurganinsk, *Russia* 43 D9
Kuria Maria Is. = Khūrīyā Mūrīyā, Jazā 'ir, *Oman* 68 D6
Kuridala, *Australia* 90 C3
Kurigram, *Bangla.* 61 G16
Kuril Is. = Kurilskiye Ostrova, *Russia* 45 E15
Kuril Trench, *Pac. Oc.* 92 C7
Kurilsk, *Russia* 45 E15
Kurilskiye Ostrova, *Russia* 45 E15
Kuringen, *Belgium* 17 G6
Kurino, *Japan* 49 J5
Kurkur, *Egypt* 76 C3
Kurlovskiy, *Russia* 41 D12
Kurmuk, *Sudan* 77 E3
Kurnool, *India* 60 M10
Kuro-Shima, *Kagoshima, Japan* 49 J4
Kuro-Shima, *Okinawa, Japan* 49 M2
Kurovskoye, *Russia* 41 D11
Kurow, *N.Z.* 87 L3
Kurrajong, *Australia* 91 E5
Kurram →, *Pakistan* 62 C4
Kurri Kurri, *Australia* 91 E5
Kursavka, *Russia* 43 D10
Kuršėnai, *Lithuania* 40 C3
Kursk, *Russia* 41 F10
Kuršumlija, *Serbia* 21 M11
Kurşunlu, *Turkey* 66 C5
Kurtalan, *Turkey* 67 E9
Kuru, Bahr el →, *Sudan* 77 F2
Kurucaşile, *Turkey* 66 C5
Kuruktag, *China* 54 B3
Kuruman, *S. Africa* 84 D3
Kuruman →, *S. Africa* 84 D3
Kurume, *Japan* 49 H5
Kurunegala, *Sri Lanka* 60 R12
Kurupukari, *Guyana* 121 C6
Kurya, *Russia* 45 C11
Kus Gölü, *Turkey* 66 C2
Kuşadası, *Turkey* 66 E2
Kusatsu, *Japan* 49 F9
Kusawa L., *Canada* 100 A1
Kusel, *Germany* 19 F3
Kushchevskaya, *Russia* 43 C8
Kushikino, *Japan* 49 J5
Kushima, *Japan* 49 J5
Kushimoto, *Japan* 49 H7
Kushiro, *Japan* 48 C12
Kushiro →, *Japan* 48 C12
Kūshk, *Iran* 65 D8
Kushka, *Turkmenistan* 44 F7
Kūshkī, *Īlām, Iran* 64 C5
Kūshkī, *Khorāsān, Iran* 65 B8
Kūshkū, *Iran* 65 E7
Kushol, *India* 63 C7
Kushtia, *Bangla.* 61 H16
Kushum →, *Kazakhstan* 43 B14
Kuskokwim →, *U.S.A.* 96 B3
Kuskokwim B., *U.S.A.* 96 C3
Küsnacht, *Switz.* 23 B7
Kussharo-Ko, *Japan* 48 C12
Küssnacht, *Switz.* 23 B6
Kustanay, *Kazakhstan* 44 D7
Kut, Ko, *Thailand* 59 G4
Kütahya, *Turkey* 66 D4
Kütahya □, *Turkey* 66 D3
Kutaisi, *Georgia* 43 E10
Kutaraja = Banda Aceh, *Indonesia* 56 C1
Kutch, Gulf of = Kachchh, Gulf of, *India* 62 H3
Kutch, Rann of = Kachchh, Rann of, *India* 62 G4
Kutina, *Croatia* 33 C13
Kutiyana, *India* 62 J4
Kutkashen, *Azerbaijan* 43 F12
Kutná Hora, *Czech.* 20 F5
Kutno, *Poland* 20 C9
Kuttabul, *Australia* 90 C4
Kutu, *Zaïre* 80 E3
Kutum, *Sudan* 77 E1
Kuujjuaq, *Canada* 97 C13
Kuŭp-tong, *N. Korea* 51 D14
Kuurne, *Belgium* 17 G2
Kuvshinovo, *Russia* 40 C9
Kuwait = Al Kuwayt, *Kuwait* 64 D5
Kuwait ■, *Asia* 64 D5
Kuwana, *Japan* 49 G8
Kuybyshev = Samara, *Russia* 41 E17
Kuybyshev, *Russia* 44 D8
Kuybyshevo, *Ukraine* 42 C7
Kuybyshevskoye Vdkhr., *Russia* 41 D16
Kuye He →, *China* 50 E6
Kūyeh, *Iran* 64 B5
Kūysanjaq, *Iraq* 64 B5
Kuyumba, *Russia* 45 C10
Kuzey Anadolu Dağları, *Turkey* 66 C6
Kuznetsk, *Russia* 41 E15
Kvænangen, *Norway* 8 A16
Kvam, *Norway* 10 C3
Kvareli, *Georgia* 43 F11
Kvarner, *Croatia* 33 D11
Kvarnerič, *Croatia* 33 D11
Kviteseid, *Norway* 10 E2
Kwabhaca, *S. Africa* 85 E4
Kwadacha →, *Canada* 100 B3
Kwakhanai, *Botswana* 84 C3
Kwakoegron, *Surinam* 121 B6
Kwale, *Kenya* 82 C4
Kwale, *Nigeria* 79 D6
Kwale □, *Kenya* 82 C4
KwaMashu, *S. Africa* 85 D5
Kwamouth, *Zaïre* 80 E3
Kwando →, *Africa* 84 B3
Kwangdaeri, *N. Korea* 51 D14
Kwangju, *S. Korea* 51 G14
Kwangsi-Chuang = Guangxi Zhuangzu Zizhiqu □, *China* 52 E7
Kwangtung = Guangdong □, *China* 53 F9
Kwara □, *Nigeria* 79 D5
Kwataboahegan →, *Canada* 98 B3
Kwatisore, *Indonesia* 57 E8
Kweichow = Guizhou □, *China* 52 D6
Kwekwe, *Zimbabwe* 83 F2
Kwimba □, *Tanzania* 82 C3
Kwinana New Town, *Australia* 89 F2
Kwoka, *Indonesia* 57 E8
Kyabé, *Chad* 73 G8
Kyabra Cr. →, *Australia* 91 D3
Kyabram, *Australia* 91 F4
Kyaikto, *Burma* 58 D1
Kyakhta, *Russia* 45 D11
Kyancutta, *Australia* 91 E2
Kyangin, *Burma* 61 K19
Kyaukpadaung, *Burma* 61 J19
Kyaukpyu, *Burma* 61 K18
Kyaukse, *Burma* 61 J20
Kyburz, *U.S.A.* 112 G6
Kycen, *Russia* 45 D11
Kyenjojo, *Uganda* 82 B3
Kyle Dam, *Zimbabwe* 83 G3
Kyle of Lochalsh, *U.K.* 14 D3
Kyll →, *Germany* 19 F2
Kyllburg, *Germany* 19 E2
Kyneton, *Australia* 91 F3
Kynuna, *Australia* 90 C3
Kyō-ga-Saki, *Japan* 49 G7
Kyoga, L., *Uganda* 82 B3
Kyogle, *Australia* 91 D5
Kyongju, *S. Korea* 51 G15
Kyongpyaw, *Burma* 61 L19
Kyŏngsŏng, *N. Korea* 51 D15
Kyōto, *Japan* 49 G7
Kyōto □, *Japan* 49 G7
Kyparissovouno, *Cyprus* 37 D12
Kyperounda, *Cyprus* 37 E11
Kyrenia, *Cyprus* 37 D12
Kyrgystan = Kirghizia ■, *Asia* 44 E8
Kyritz, *Germany* 18 C8
Kystatyam, *Russia* 45 C13
Kytal Ktakh, *Russia* 45 C13
Kythréa, *Cyprus* 37 D12
Kyulyunken, *Russia* 45 C14
Kyunhla, *Burma* 61 H19
Kyuquot, *Canada* 100 C3
Kyurdamir, *Azerbaijan* 43 F13
Kyūshū, *Japan* 49 H5
Kyūshū □, *Japan* 49 H5
Kyūshū-Sanchi, *Japan* 49 H5
Kyustendil, *Bulgaria* 38 G5
Kyusyur, *Russia* 45 B13
Kywong, *Australia* 91 E4
Kyyiv = Kiyev, *Ukraine* 40 F7
Kyzyl, *Russia* 45 D10
Kyzyl-Kiya, *Kirghizia* 44 E8
Kyzylkum, Peski, *Uzbekistan* 44 E7
Kzyl-Orda, *Kazakhstan* 44 E7

L

La Albuera, *Spain* 31 G4
La Alcarria, *Spain* 28 E2
La Algaba, *Spain* 31 H4
La Almarcha, *Spain* 28 F2
La Almunia de Doña Godina, *Spain* 28 D3
La Asunción, *Venezuela* 121 A5
La Banda, *Argentina* 126 B3
La Bañeza, *Spain* 30 C5
La Barca, *Mexico* 114 C4
La Barge, *U.S.A.* 110 E8
La Bassée, *France* 25 B9
La Bastide-Puylaurent, *France* 26 D7
La Baule, *France* 24 E4
La Belle, *U.S.A.* 105 M5
La Biche →, *Canada* 100 B4
La Bisbal, *Spain* 28 D8
La Blanquilla, *Venezuela* 121 A5
La Bomba, *Mexico* 114 A1
La Bresse, *France* 25 D13
La Bureba, *Spain* 28 C1
La Cal →, *Bolivia* 125 D6
La Calera, *Chile* 126 C1
La Campiña, *Spain* 31 H6
La Canal, *Spain* 36 C7
La Cañiza, *Spain* 30 C2
La Capelle, *France* 25 C10
La Carlota, *Argentina* 126 C3
La Carlota, *Phil.* 55 F5
La Carolina, *Spain* 31 G7
La Cavalerie, *France* 26 D7
La Ceiba, *Honduras* 116 C2
La Chaise-Dieu, *France* 26 C7
La Chaize-le-Vicomte, *France* 24 F5
La Chapelle d'Angillon, *France* 25 E9
La Chapelle-Glain, *France* 24 E5
La Charité-sur-Loire, *France* 25 E10
La Chartre-sur-le-Loir, *France* 24 E7
La Châtaigneraie, *France* 26 B3
La Châtre, *France* 26 B5
La Chaux de Fonds, *Switz.* 22 B3
La Chorrera, *Colombia* 120 D3
La Ciotat, *France* 27 E9
La Clayette, *France* 27 B8
La Cocha, *Argentina* 126 B2
La Concepción = Ri-Aba, *Eq. Guin.* 79 E6
La Concepción, *Venezuela* 120 A3
La Concordia, *Mexico* 115 D6
La Conner, *U.S.A.* 110 B2
La Coruña, *Spain* 30 B2
La Coruña □, *Spain* 30 B2
La Côte, *Switz.* 22 D2
La Côte-St.-André, *France* 27 C9
La Courtine-le-Trucq, *France* 26 C6
La Crau, *France* 27 E8
La Crete, *Canada* 100 B5
La Crosse, *Kans., U.S.A.* 108 F5
La Crosse, *Wis., U.S.A.* 108 D9
La Cruz, *Costa Rica* 116 D2
La Cruz, *Mexico* 114 C3
La Dorada, *Colombia* 120 B3
La Ensenada, *Chile* 128 B2
La Escondida, *Mexico* 114 C5
La Esmeralda, *Paraguay* 126 A3
La Esperanza, *Argentina* 128 B3
La Esperanza, *Cuba* 116 B3
La Esperanza, *Honduras* 116 D2
La Estrada, *Spain* 30 C2
La Fayette, *U.S.A.* 105 H3
La Fé, *Cuba* 116 B3
La Fère, *France* 25 C10
La Ferté-Bernard, *France* 24 D7
La Ferté-Macé, *France* 24 D6
La Ferté-St.-Aubin, *France* 25 E8
La Ferté-sous-Jouarre, *France* 25 D10
La Ferté-Vidame, *France* 24 D7
La Flèche, *France* 24 E6
La Follette, *U.S.A.* 105 G3
La Fregeneda, *Spain* 30 E4
La Fría, *Venezuela* 120 B3
La Fuente de San Esteban, *Spain* 30 E4
La Gineta, *Spain* 29 F2
La Gloria, *Colombia* 120 B3
La Gran Sabana, *Venezuela* 121 B5
La Grand-Combe, *France* 27 D8
La Grande, *U.S.A.* 110 D4
La Grande-Motte, *France* 27 E8
La Grange, *Calif., U.S.A.* 112 H6
La Grange, *Ga., U.S.A.* 105 J3
La Grange, *Ky., U.S.A.* 104 F3
La Grange, *Tex., U.S.A.* 109 L6
La Grita, *Venezuela* 120 B3
La Guaira, *Venezuela* 120 A4
La Guardia, *Spain* 30 D2
La Gudiña, *Spain* 30 C3
La Güera, *Mauritania* 74 D1
La Guerche-de-Bretagne, *France* 24 E5
La Guerche-sur-l'Aubois, *France* 25 F9
La Habana, *Cuba* 116 B3
La Harpe, *U.S.A.* 108 E9
La Haye-du-Puits, *France* 24 C5
La Horqueta, *Venezuela* 121 B5
La Horra, *Spain* 30 D7
La Independencia, *Mexico* 115 D6
La Isabela, *Dom. Rep.* 117 C5
La Jara, *U.S.A.* 111 H11
La Joya, *Peru* 124 D3
La Junquera, *Spain* 28 C7
La Junta, *U.S.A.* 109 F3
La Laguna, *Canary Is.* 36 F3
La Libertad, *Guatemala* 116 C1
La Libertad, *Mexico* 114 B2
La Libertad □, *Peru* 124 B2
La Ligua, *Chile* 126 C1
La Línea de la Concepción, *Spain* 31 J5
La Loche, *Canada* 101 B7
La Londe-les-Maures, *France* 27 E10
La Lora, *Spain* 30 C7
La Loupe, *France* 24 D8
La Louvière, *Belgium* 17 H4
La Machine, *France* 25 F10
La Maddalena, *Italy* 34 A2
La Malbaie, *Canada* 99 C5
La Mancha, *Spain* 29 F2
La Mariña, *Spain* 30 B3
La Mesa, *Calif., U.S.A.* 113 N9
La Mesa, *N. Mex., U.S.A.* 111 K10
La Misión, *Mexico* 114 A1
La Mothe-Achard, *France* 24 F5
La Motte, *France* 27 D10
La Motte-Chalançon, *France* 27 D9
La Moure, *U.S.A.* 108 B5
La Muela, *Spain* 28 D3
La Mure, *France* 27 D9
La Negra, *Chile* 126 A1
La Neuveville, *Switz.* 22 B4
La Oliva, *Canary Is.* 36 F6
La Oraya, *Peru* 124 C2
La Orotava, *Canary Is.* 36 F3
La Pacaudière, *France* 26 B7
La Palma, *Canary Is.* 36 F2
La Palma, *Panama* 116 E4
La Palma, *Spain* 31 H4
La Paloma, *Chile* 126 C1
La Pampa □, *Argentina* 126 D2
La Paragua, *Venezuela* 121 B5
La Paz, *Entre Ríos, Argentina* 126 C4
La Paz, *San Luis, Argentina* 126 C2
La Paz, *Bolivia* 124 D4
La Paz, *Honduras* 116 D2
La Paz, *Mexico* 114 C2
La Paz, *Phil.* 55 D4
La Paz □, *Bolivia* 124 D4
La Paz Centro, *Nic.* 116 D2
La Pedrera, *Colombia* 120 D4
La Perouse Str., *Asia* 48 B11
La Pesca, *Mexico* 115 C5
La Piedad, *Mexico* 114 C4
La Pine, *U.S.A.* 110 E3
La Plant, *U.S.A.* 108 C4
La Plata, *Argentina* 126 D4
La Plata, *Colombia* 120 C2
La Plata, L., *Argentina* 128 B2
La Pobla de Lillet, *Spain* 28 C6
La Pola de Gordón, *Spain* 30 C5
La Porte, *U.S.A.* 104 E2
La Puebla, *Spain* 28 F8
La Puebla de Cazalla, *Spain* 31 H5
La Puebla de los Infantes, *Spain* 31 H5
La Puebla de Montalbán, *Spain* 30 F6
La Puerta, *Spain* 29 G2
La Punt, *Switz.* 23 C9
La Purísima, *Mexico* 114 B2
La Push, *U.S.A.* 112 C2
La Quiaca, *Argentina* 126 A2
La Rambla, *Spain* 31 H6
La Reine, *Canada* 98 C4
La Réole, *France* 26 D3
La Restinga, *Canary Is.* 36 G2
La Rioja, *Argentina* 126 B2
La Rioja □, *Argentina* 126 B2
La Rioja □, *Spain* 28 C2
La Robla, *Spain* 30 C5
La Roche, *Switz.* 22 C4
La Roche-Bernard, *France* 24 E4
La Roche-Canillac, *France* 26 C5
La Roche-en-Ardenne, *Belgium* 17 H7
La Roche-sur-Yon, *France* 24 F5
La Rochefoucauld, *France* 26 C4
La Rochelle, *France* 26 B2
La Roda, *Albacete, Spain* 29 F2
La Roda, *Sevilla, Spain* 31 H6
La Romana, *Dom. Rep.* 117 C6
La Ronge, *Canada* 101 B7
La Rumorosa, *Mexico* 113 N10
La Sabina, *Spain* 36 C7
La Sagra, *Spain* 29 H2
La Salle, *U.S.A.* 108 E10
La Sanabria, *Spain* 30 C4
La Santa, *Canary Is.* 36 E6
La Sarraz, *Switz.* 22 C3
La Sarre, *Canada* 98 C4
La Scie, *Canada* 99 C8
La Selva, *Spain* 28 D7
La Selva Beach, *U.S.A.* 112 J5
La Serena, *Chile* 126 B1
La Serena, *Spain* 31 G5
La Seyne, *France* 27 E9
La Sila, *Italy* 35 C9
La Solana, *Spain* 29 G1
La Souterraine, *France* 26 B5
La Spézia, *Italy* 32 D6
La Suze-sur-Sarthe, *France* 24 E7
La Tagua, *Colombia* 120 C3
La Teste, *France* 26 D2
La Tortuga, *Venezuela* 117 D6
La Tour-du-Pin, *France* 27 C9
La Tranche-sur-Mer, *France* 24 F5
La Tremblade, *France* 26 C2
La Tuque, *Canada* 98 C5
La Unión, *Chile* 128 B2
La Unión, *Colombia* 120 C2
La Unión, *El Salv.* 116 D2
La Unión, *Mexico* 114 D4
La Unión, *Peru* 124 B2

La Unión, *Spain* 29 H4
La Urbana, *Venezuela* 120 B4
La Vecilla, *Spain* 30 C5
La Vega, *Dom. Rep.* 117 C5
La Vega, *Peru* 124 C2
La Vela, *Venezuela* 120 A4
La Veleta, *Spain* 31 H7
La Venta, *Mexico* 115 D6
La Ventura, *Mexico* 114 C4
La Venturosa, *Colombia* 120 B4
La Victoria, *Venezuela* 120 A4
La Voulte-sur-Rhône, *France* 27 D8
La Zarza, *Spain* 31 H4
Laaber →, *Germany* 19 G8
Laage, *Germany* 18 B8
Laba →, *Russia* 43 D8
Labason, *Phil.* 55 G5
Labastide-Murat, *France* 26 D5
Labastide-Rouairoux, *France* 26 E6
Labbézenga, *Mali* 79 B5
Labe = Elbe →, *Europe* 18 B4
Labé, *Guinea* 78 C2
Laberec →, *Slovak Rep.* 20 G11
Laberge, L., *Canada* 100 A1
Labin, *Croatia* 33 C11
Labinsk, *Russia* 43 D9
Labis, *Malaysia* 59 L4
Labo, *Phil.* 55 D5
Laboe, *Germany* 18 A6
Labouheyre, *France* 26 D3
Laboulaye, *Argentina* 126 C3
Labra, Peña, *Spain* 30 B6
Labrador, Coast of □, *Canada* 99 B7
Labrador City, *Canada* 99 B6
Lábrea, *Brazil* 125 B5
Labrède, *France* 26 D3
Labuan, Pulau, *Malaysia* 56 C5
Labuha, *Indonesia* 57 E7
Labuhan, *Indonesia* 57 G11
Labuhanbajo, *Indonesia* 57 F6
Labuissière, *Belgium* 17 H4
Labuk, Telok, *Malaysia* 56 C5
Labyrinth, L., *Australia* 91 E2
Labytnangi, *Russia* 44 C7
Lac Allard, *Canada* 99 B7
Lac Bouchette, *Canada* 99 C5
Lac du Flambeau, *U.S.A.* 108 B10
Lac Édouard, *Canada* 98 C5
Lac La Biche, *Canada* 100 C6
Lac la Martre, *Canada* 96 B8
Lac-Mégantic, *Canada* 99 C5
Lac Seul, Res., *Canada* 98 B1
Lac Thien, *Vietnam* 58 F7
Lacanau, *France* 26 D2
Lacanau, Étang de, *France* 26 D2
Lacantúm →, *Mexico* 115 D6
Lacara →, *Spain* 31 G4
Lacaune, *France* 26 E6
Lacaune, Mts. de, *France* 26 E6
Laccadive Is. = Lakshadweep Is., *Ind. Oc.* 46 J11
Lacepede B., *Australia* 91 F2
Lacepede Is., *Australia* 88 C3
Lacerdónia, *Mozam.* 83 F4
Lacey, *U.S.A.* 112 C4
Lachay, Pta., *Peru* 124 C2
Lachen, *Switz.* 23 B7
Lachhmangarh, *India* 62 F6
Lachi, *Pakistan* 62 C4
Lachine, *Canada* 98 C5
Lachlan →, *Australia* 91 E3
Lachute, *Canada* 98 C5
Lackawanna, *U.S.A.* 106 D6
Lacolle, *Canada* 107 A11
Lacombe, *Canada* 100 C6
Lacona, *U.S.A.* 107 C8
Láconi, *Italy* 34 C2
Laconia, *U.S.A.* 107 C13
Lacq, *France* 26 E3
Lacrosse, *U.S.A.* 110 C5
Ladakh Ra., *India* 63 B8
Ladário, *Brazil* 125 D6
Ládhon →, *Greece* 39 M4
Lâdik, *Turkey* 42 F6
Ladismith, *S. Africa* 84 E3
Lādīz, *Iran* 65 D9
Ladnun, *India* 62 F6
Ladoga, L. = Ladozhskoye Ozero, *Russia* 44 C4
Ladon, *France* 25 D9
Ladozhskoye Ozero, *Russia* 44 C4
Ladrillero, G., *Chile* 128 C1
Lady Grey, *S. Africa* 84 E4
Ladybrand, *S. Africa* 84 D4
Ladysmith, *Canada* 100 D4
Ladysmith, *S. Africa* 85 D4
Ladysmith, *U.S.A.* 108 C9
Lae, *Papua N. G.* 92 H6
Laem Ngop, *Thailand* 59 F4
Laem Pho, *Thailand* 59 J3
Læsø, *Denmark* 11 G4
Læsø Rende, *Denmark* 11 G4
Lafayette, *Colo., U.S.A.* 108 F2
Lafayette, *Ind., U.S.A.* 104 E2
Lafayette, *La., U.S.A.* 109 K9
Lafayette, *Tenn., U.S.A.* 105 G3
Laferte →, *Canada* 100 A5
Lafia, *Nigeria* 79 D6
Lafiagi, *Nigeria* 79 D6
Lafleche, *Canada* 101 D7
Lafon, *Sudan* 77 F3
Laforsen, *Sweden* 10 C9
Lagan →, *Sweden* 11 H7
Lagan →, *U.K.* 15 B6
Lagarfljót →, *Iceland* 8 D6
Lagarto, *Brazil* 122 D4
Lage, *Germany* 18 D4
Lage, *Spain* 30 B2
Lage-Mierde, *Neths.* 17 F6
Lågen →, *Norway* 9 F11
Lägerdorf, *Germany* 18 B5
Laghouat, *Algeria* 75 B5
Lagnieu, *France* 27 C9
Lagny, *France* 25 D9
Lago, *Italy* 35 C9
Lago Posadas, *Argentina* 128 C2
Lago Ranco, *Chile* 128 B2
Lagôa, *Portugal* 31 H2
Lagoaça, *Portugal* 30 D4
Lagodekhi, *Georgia* 43 F12
Lagónegro, *Italy* 35 B8
Lagonoy Gulf, *Phil.* 55 E5
Lagos, *Nigeria* 79 D5
Lagos, *Portugal* 31 H2
Lagos de Moreno, *Mexico* 114 C4
Lagrange, *Australia* 88 C3
Lagrange B., *Australia* 88 C3
Laguardia, *Spain* 28 C2
Laguépie, *France* 26 D5
Laguna, *Brazil* 127 B6
Laguna, *U.S.A.* 111 J10
Laguna Beach, *U.S.A.* 113 M9
Laguna de la Janda, *Spain* 31 J5
Laguna Limpia, *Argentina* 126 B4
Laguna Madre, *U.S.A.* 115 B5
Lagunas, *Chile* 126 A2
Lagunas, *Peru* 124 B2
Lagunillas, *Bolivia* 125 D5
Lahad Datu, *Malaysia* 57 C5
Lahan Sai, *Thailand* 58 E4
Lahanam, *Laos* 58 D5
Laharpur, *India* 63 F9
Lahat, *Indonesia* 56 E2
Lahewa, *Indonesia* 56 D1
Lahiang Lahiang, *Phil.* 55 H4
Lahijan, *Iran* 65 B6
Lahn →, *Germany* 19 E3
Laholm, *Sweden* 11 H7
Laholmsbukten, *Sweden* 11 H6
Lahontan Reservoir, *U.S.A.* 110 G4
Lahore, *Pakistan* 62 D6
Lahr, *Germany* 19 G3
Lahti, *Finland* 9 F18
Lahtis = Lahti, *Finland* 9 F18
Laï, *Chad* 73 G8
Lai Chau, *Vietnam* 58 A4
Lai'an, *China* 53 A12
Laibin, *China* 52 F7
Laidley, *Australia* 91 D5
Laifeng, *China* 52 C7
L'Aigle, *France* 24 D7
Laignes, *France* 25 E11
L'Aiguillon-sur-Mer, *France* 26 B2
Laikipia □, *Kenya* 82 B4
Laingsburg, *S. Africa* 84 E3
Lairg, *U.K.* 14 C4
Laishui, *China* 50 E8
Laiwu, *China* 51 F9
Laixi, *China* 51 F11
Laiyang, *China* 51 F11
Laiyuan, *China* 50 E8
Laizhou Wan, *China* 51 F10
Laja →, *Mexico* 114 C4
Lajere, *Nigeria* 79 C7
Lajes, *Rio Grande do N., Brazil* 122 C4
Lajes, *Sta. Catarina, Brazil* 127 B5
Lajinha, *Brazil* 123 F3
Lajkovac, *Serbia* 21 L10
Lajosmizse, *Hungary* 21 H9
Lak Sao, *Laos* 58 C5
Lakaband, *Pakistan* 62 D3
Lakar, *Indonesia* 57 F7
Lake Alpine, *U.S.A.* 112 G7
Lake Andes, *U.S.A.* 108 D5
Lake Anse, *U.S.A.* 104 B1
Lake Arthur, *U.S.A.* 109 K8
Lake Cargelligo, *Australia* 91 E4
Lake Charles, *U.S.A.* 109 K8
Lake City, *Colo., U.S.A.* 111 G10
Lake City, *Fla., U.S.A.* 105 K4
Lake City, *Iowa, U.S.A.* 108 D7
Lake City, *Mich., U.S.A.* 104 C3
Lake City, *Minn., U.S.A.* 108 C8
Lake City, *Pa., U.S.A.* 106 D4
Lake City, *S.C., U.S.A.* 105 J6
Lake George, *U.S.A.* 107 C11
Lake Grace, *Australia* 89 F2
Lake Harbour, *Canada* 97 B13
Lake Havasu City, *U.S.A.* 113 L12
Lake Hughes, *U.S.A.* 113 L8
Lake Isabella, *U.S.A.* 113 K8
Lake King, *Australia* 89 F2
Lake Lenore, *Canada* 101 C8
Lake Louise, *Canada* 100 C5
Lake Mead National Recreation Area, *U.S.A.* 113 K12
Lake Mills, *U.S.A.* 108 D8
Lake Nash, *Australia* 90 C2
Lake Providence, *U.S.A.* 109 J9
Lake River, *Canada* 98 B3
Lake Superior Prov. Park, *Canada* 98 C3
Lake Village, *U.S.A.* 109 J9
Lake Wales, *U.S.A.* 105 M5
Lake Worth, *U.S.A.* 105 M5
Lakefield, *Canada* 98 D4
Lakeland, *Australia* 90 B3
Lakeland, *U.S.A.* 105 L5
Lakemba, *Fiji* 87 D9
Lakeport, *U.S.A.* 112 F4
Lakes Entrance, *Australia* 91 F4
Lakeside, *Ariz., U.S.A.* 111 J9
Lakeside, *Calif., U.S.A.* 113 N10
Lakeside, *Nebr., U.S.A.* 108 D3
Lakeview, *U.S.A.* 110 E3
Lakewood, *Colo., U.S.A.* 108 F2
Lakewood, *N.J., U.S.A.* 107 F10
Lakewood, *Ohio, U.S.A.* 106 E3
Lakewood Center, *U.S.A.* 112 C4
Lakhaniá, *Greece* 37 D9
Lakhonpheng, *Laos* 58 E5
Lakhpat, *India* 62 H3
Laki, *Iceland* 8 D4
Lakin, *U.S.A.* 109 G4
Lakitusaki →, *Canada* 98 B3
Lákkoi, *Greece* 37 D5
Lakonikós Kólpos, *Greece* 39 N5
Lakota, *Ivory C.* 78 D3
Lakota, *U.S.A.* 108 A5
Laksefjorden, *Norway* 8 A19
Lakselv, *Norway* 8 A18
Lakshadweep Is., *Ind. Oc.* 46 J11
Lakshmikantapur, *India* 63 H13
Lala Ghat, *India* 61 G18
Lala Musa, *Pakistan* 62 C5
Lalago, *Tanzania* 82 C3
Lalapanzi, *Zimbabwe* 83 F3
Lalganj, *India* 63 G11
Lalibela, *Ethiopia* 77 E4
Lalin, *China* 51 B14
Lalín, *Spain* 30 C2
Lalin He →, *China* 51 B13
Lalinde, *France* 26 D4
Lalitapur = Patan, *Nepal* 61 F14
Lalitpur, *India* 63 G8
Lam, *Vietnam* 58 B6
Lam Pao Res., *Thailand* 58 D4
Lama Kara, *Togo* 79 D5
Lamaing, *Burma* 61 M20
Lamar, *Colo., U.S.A.* 108 F3
Lamar, *Mo., U.S.A.* 109 G7
Lamarque, *Argentina* 128 A3
Lamas, *Peru* 124 B2
Lamastre, *France* 27 D8
Lamballe, *France* 24 D4
Lambaréné, *Gabon* 80 E2
Lambasa, *Fiji* 87 C8
Lambay I., *Ireland* 15 C5
Lambayeque □, *Peru* 124 B2
Lambert, *U.S.A.* 108 B2
Lambert Glacier, *Antarctica* 5 D6
Lamberts Bay, *S. Africa* 84 E2
Lambesc, *France* 27 E9
Lámbia, *Greece* 39 M4
Lambro →, *Italy* 32 C6
Lame, *Nigeria* 79 C6
Lame Deer, *U.S.A.* 110 D10
Lamego, *Portugal* 30 D3
Lamèque, *Canada* 99 C7
Lameroo, *Australia* 91 F3
Lamesa, *U.S.A.* 109 J4
Lamía, *Greece* 39 L5
Lamitan, *Phil.* 55 H5
Lammermuir Hills, *U.K.* 14 F6
Lamon Bay, *Phil.* 55 D5
Lamont, *Canada* 100 C6
Lamont, *U.S.A.* 113 K8
Lampa, *Peru* 124 D3
Lampang, *Thailand* 58 C2
Lampasas, *U.S.A.* 109 K5
Lampaul, *France* 24 D1
Lampazos de Naranjo, *Mexico* 114 B4
Lampeter, *U.K.* 13 E3
Lampione, *Medit. S.* 75 A7
Lampman, *Canada* 101 D8
Lamprey, *Canada* 101 B10
Lampung □, *Indonesia* 56 F2
Lamu, *Kenya* 82 C5
Lamu □, *Kenya* 82 C5
Lamud, *Peru* 124 B2
Lamy, *U.S.A.* 111 J11
Lan Xian, *China* 50 E6
Lan Yu, *Taiwan* 53 F13
Lanai I., *U.S.A.* 102 H16
Lanak La, *India* 63 B8
Lanaken, *Belgium* 17 G7
Lanak'o Shank'ou = Lanak La, *India* 63 B8
Lanao, L., *Phil.* 55 H6
Lanark, *Canada* 107 A8
Lanark, *U.K.* 14 F5
Lancang, *China* 52 F2
Lancang Jiang →, *China* 52 G3
Lancashire □, *U.K.* 12 D5
Lancaster, *Canada* 107 A10
Lancaster, *U.K.* 12 C5
Lancaster, *Calif., U.S.A.* 113 L8
Lancaster, *Ky., U.S.A.* 104 G3
Lancaster, *N.H., U.S.A.* 107 B13
Lancaster, *N.Y., U.S.A.* 106 D6
Lancaster, *Pa., U.S.A.* 107 F8
Lancaster, *S.C., U.S.A.* 105 H5
Lancaster, *Wis., U.S.A.* 108 D9
Lancaster Sd., *Canada* 97 A11
Lancer, *Canada* 101 C7
Lanchow = Lanzhou, *China* 50 F2
Lanciano, *Italy* 33 F11
Lanco, *Chile* 128 A2
Lancones, *Peru* 124 A1
Lancun, *China* 51 F11
Łańcut, *Poland* 20 E12
Lancy, *Switz.* 22 D2
Landau, *Bayern, Germany* 19 G8
Landau, *Rhld-Pfz., Germany* 19 F4
Landeck, *Austria* 19 H6
Landen, *Belgium* 17 G6
Lander, *U.S.A.* 110 E9
Lander →, *Australia* 88 D5
Landerneau, *France* 24 D2
Landeryd, *Sweden* 11 G7
Landes, *France* 26 D3
Landes □, *France* 26 E3
Landete, *Spain* 28 F3
Landi Kotal, *Pakistan* 62 B4
Landivisiau, *France* 24 D2
Landor, *Australia* 89 E2
Landquart, *Switz.* 23 C9
Landquart →, *Switz.* 23 C9
Landrecies, *France* 25 B10
Land's End, *U.K.* 13 G2
Landsberg, *Germany* 19 G6
Landsborough Cr. →, *Australia* 90 C3
Landshut, *Germany* 19 G8
Landskrona, *Sweden* 11 J6
Landstuhl, *Germany* 19 F3
Landvetter, *Sweden* 11 G6
Laneffe, *Belgium* 17 H5
Lanesboro, *U.S.A.* 107 E9
Lanett, *U.S.A.* 105 J3
Lang Bay, *Canada* 100 D4
Lang Qua, *Vietnam* 58 A5
Lang Shan, *China* 50 D4
Lang Son, *Vietnam* 58 B6
Lang Suan, *Thailand* 59 H2
La'nga Co, *China* 61 D12
Lángadhás, *Greece* 39 J6
Langádhia, *Greece* 39 M5
Långan →, *Sweden* 10 A8
Langar, *Iran* 65 C9
Langara I., *Canada* 100 C2
Langatabbetje, *Surinam* 121 C7
Langdai, *China* 52 D5
Langdon, *U.S.A.* 108 A5
Langdorp, *Belgium* 17 G5
Langeac, *France* 26 C7
Langeais, *France* 24 E7
Langeb Baraka →, *Sudan* 76 D4
Langeberg, *S. Africa* 84 E3
Langeberge, *S. Africa* 84 D3
Langeland, *Denmark* 11 K4
Langemark, *Belgium* 17 G1
Langen, *Germany* 19 F4
Langenburg, *Canada* 101 C8
Langeness, *Germany* 18 A4
Langenthal, *Switz.* 22 B5
Langeoog, *Germany* 18 B3
Langeskov, *Denmark* 11 J4
Langesund, *Norway* 10 F3
Länghem, *Sweden* 11 G7
Langhirano, *Italy* 32 D7
Langholm, *U.K.* 14 F6
Langhus, *Norway* 10 E4
Langjökull, *Iceland* 8 D3
Langkawi, P., *Malaysia* 59 J2
Langklip, *S. Africa* 84 D3
Langkon, *Malaysia* 56 C5
Langlade, *St- P. & M.* 99 C8
Langlois, *U.S.A.* 110 E1
Langnau, *Switz.* 22 C5
Langogne, *France* 26 D7
Langon, *France* 26 D3
Langøya, *Norway* 8 B13
Langres, *France* 25 E12
Langres, Plateau de, *France* 25 E12
Langsa, *Indonesia* 56 D1
Långsele, *Sweden* 10 A11
Langtry, *U.S.A.* 109 L4
Langu, *Thailand* 59 J2
Languedoc, *France* 26 E7
Langwies, *Switz.* 23 C9
Langxi, *China* 53 B12
Langxiangzhen, *China* 50 E9
Langzhong, *China* 52 B5
Lanigan, *Canada* 101 C7
Lankao, *China* 50 G8
Lannemezan, *France* 26 E4
Lannilis, *France* 24 D2
Lannion, *France* 24 D3
L'Annonciation, *Canada* 98 C5
Lanouaille, *France* 26 C5
Lanping, *China* 52 D2
Lansdale, *U.S.A.* 107 F9
Lansdowne, *Australia* 91 E5
Lansdowne, *Canada* 107 B8
Lansdowne House, *Canada* 98 B2
L'Anse, *U.S.A.* 98 C2
L'Anse au Loup, *Canada* 99 B8
Lansford, *U.S.A.* 107 F9
Lanshan, *China* 53 E9
Lansing, *U.S.A.* 104 D3
Lanslebourg-Mont-Cenis, *France* 27 C10
Lanta Yai, Ko, *Thailand* 59 J2
Lantian, *China* 50 G5
Lanus, *Argentina* 126 C4
Lanusei, *Italy* 34 C2
Lanuza, *Phil.* 55 G7
Lanxi, *China* 53 C12
Lanzarote, *Canary Is.* 36 E6
Lanzhou, *China* 50 F2
Lanzo Torinese, *Italy* 32 C4
Lao →, *Italy* 35 C8
Lao Bao, *Laos* 58 D6
Lao Cai, *Vietnam* 58 A4
Laoag, *Phil.* 55 B4
Laoang, *Phil.* 55 E6
Laoha He →, *China* 51 C11
Laois □, *Ireland* 15 D4
Laon, *France* 25 C10
Laona, *U.S.A.* 104 C1
Laos ■, *Asia* 58 D5
Lapa, *Brazil* 127 B6
Lapalisse, *France* 26 B7
Laparan, *Phil.* 57 C6
Lapeer, *U.S.A.* 104 D4
Lapi □ = Lapin lääni □, *Finland* 8 C19
Lapin lääni □, *Finland* 8 C19
Lapithos, *Cyprus* 37 D12
Lapland = Lappland, *Europe* 8 B18
Laporte, *U.S.A.* 107 E8
Lapovo, *Serbia* 21 L11
Lappland, *Europe* 8 B18
Laprida, *Argentina* 126 D3
Laptev Sea, *Russia* 45 B13
Lăpuşul →, *Romania* 38 B6
L'Aquila, *Italy* 33 F10
Lār, *Āzarbājān-e Sharqī, Iran* 64 B5
Lār, *Fārs, Iran* 65 E7
Lara □, *Venezuela* 120 A4
Larabanga, *Ghana* 78 D4
Laracha, *Spain* 30 B2
Larache, *Morocco* 74 A3
Laragne-Montéglin, *France* 27 D9
Laramie, *U.S.A.* 108 E2
Laramie Mts., *U.S.A.* 108 E2
Laranjeiras, *Brazil* 122 D4
Laranjeiras do Sul, *Brazil* 127 B5
Larantuka, *Indonesia* 57 F6
Larap, *Phil.* 55 D5
Larat, *Indonesia* 57 F8
L'Arbresle, *France* 27 C8
Larde, *Mozam.* 83 F4
Larder Lake, *Canada* 98 C4
Lardhos, Ákra, *Greece* 37 C10
Lardhos, Órmos, *Greece* 37 C10
Laredo, *Spain* 28 B1
Laredo, *U.S.A.* 109 M5
Laredo Sd., *Canada* 100 C3
Laren, *Neths.* 16 D6
Largentière, *France* 27 D8
L'Argentière-la-Bessée, *France* 27 D10
Largs, *U.K.* 14 F4
Lari, *Italy* 32 E7
Lariang, *Indonesia* 57 E5
Larimore, *U.S.A.* 108 B6
Lārīn, *Iran* 65 C7
Larino, *Italy* 35 A7
Lárisa, *Greece* 39 K5
Larkana, *Pakistan* 62 F3
Larnaca, *Cyprus* 37 E12
Larnaca Bay, *Cyprus* 37 E12
Larne, *U.K.* 15 B6
Larned, *U.S.A.* 108 F5
Larochette, *Belgium* 17 J8
Laroquebrou, *France* 26 D6
Larrimah, *Australia* 88 C5
Larsen Ice Shelf, *Antarctica* 5 C17
Larvik, *Norway* 10 E4
Laryak, *Russia* 44 C8
Larzac, Causse du, *France* 26 E7
Las Alpujarras, *Spain* 29 J1
Las Animas, *U.S.A.* 108 F3
Las Anod, *Somali Rep.* 68 F4
Las Blancos, *Spain* 29 H4
Las Brenãs, *Argentina* 126 B3
Las Cabezas de San Juan, *Spain* 31 J5
Las Chimeneas, *Mexico* 113 N10
Las Coloradas, *Argentina* 128 A2
Las Cruces, *U.S.A.* 111 K10
Las Flores, *Argentina* 126 D4
Las Heras, *Argentina* 126 C2
Las Horquetas, *Argentina* 128 C2
Las Khoreh, *Somali Rep.* 68 E4
Las Lajas, *Argentina* 128 A2
Las Lomas, *Peru* 124 A1
Las Lomitas, *Argentina* 126 A3
Las Marismas, *Spain* 31 H4
Las Mercedes, *Venezuela* 120 B4
Las Navas de la Concepción, *Spain* 31 H5
Las Navas de Tolosa, *Spain* 31 G7
Las Navas del Marqués, *Spain* 30 E6
Las Palmas, *Argentina* 126 B4
Las Palmas, *Canary Is.* 36 F4
Las Palmas →, *Mexico* 113 N10
Las Piedras, *Uruguay* 127 C4
Las Pipinas, *Argentina* 126 D4
Las Plumas, *Argentina* 128 B3
Las Rosas, *Argentina* 126 C3
Las Tablas, *Panama* 116 E3
Las Termas, *Argentina* 126 B3
Las Truchas, *Mexico* 114 D4
Las Varillas, *Argentina* 126 C3
Las Vegas, *N. Mex., U.S.A.* 111 J11
Las Vegas, *Nev., U.S.A.* 113 J11
Lascano, *Uruguay* 127 C5
Lashburn, *Canada* 101 C7
Lashio, *Burma* 61 H20

Lashkar, *India* 62 F8
Łasin, *Poland* 20 B9
Lasíthi, *Greece* 37 D7
Lasíthi □, *Greece* 37 D7
Laško, *Slovenia* 33 B12
Lassance, *Brazil* 123 E3
Lassay, *France* 24 D6
Lassen Pk., *U.S.A.* 110 F3
Last Mountain L., *Canada* 101 C7
Lastchance Cr. →, *U.S.A.* 112 E5
Lastoursville, *Gabon* 80 E2
Lastovo, *Croatia* 33 F13
Lastovski Kanal, *Croatia* 33 F13
Lat Yao, *Thailand* 58 E2
Latacunga, *Ecuador* 120 D2
Latakia = Al Lādhiqīyah, *Syria* 64 C2
Latchford, *Canada* 98 C4
Laterza, *Italy* 35 B9
Latham, *Australia* 89 E2
Lathen, *Germany* 18 C3
Lathrop Wells, *U.S.A.* 113 J10
Latiano, *Italy* 35 B10
Latina, *Italy* 34 A5
Latisana, *Italy* 33 C10
Latium = Lazio □, *Italy* 33 F9
Laton, *U.S.A.* 112 J7
Latorica →, *Slovak Rep.* 21 G11
Latouche Treville, C., *Australia* 88 C3
Latrobe, *Australia* 90 G4
Latrobe, *U.S.A.* 106 F5
Latrónico, *Italy* 35 B9
Latvia ■, *Europe* 40 C3
Lau Group, *Fiji* 87 C9
Lauca →, *Bolivia* 124 D4
Lauchhammer, *Germany* 18 D9
Lauenburg, *Germany* 18 B6
Läufelfingen, *Switz.* 22 B5
Laufen, *Switz.* 22 B5
Lauffen, *Germany* 19 F5
Laugarbakki, *Iceland* 8 D3
Laujar, *Spain* 29 J2
Launceston, *Australia* 90 G4
Launceston, *U.K.* 13 G3
Laune →, *Ireland* 15 D2
Laupheim, *Germany* 19 G5
Laura, *Australia* 90 B3
Laureana di Borrello, *Italy* 35 D9
Laurel, *Miss., U.S.A.* 109 K10
Laurel, *Mont., U.S.A.* 110 D9
Laurencekirk, *U.K.* 14 E6
Laurens, *U.S.A.* 105 H4
Laurentian Plateau, *Canada* 99 B6
Laurentides, Parc Prov. des, *Canada* 99 C5
Lauria, *Italy* 35 B8
Laurie L., *Canada* 101 B8
Laurinburg, *U.S.A.* 105 H6
Laurium, *U.S.A.* 104 B1
Lausanne, *Switz.* 22 C3
Laut, *Indonesia* 56 D3
Laut Ketil, Kepulauan, *Indonesia* 56 E5
Lautaro, *Chile* 128 A2
Lauterbach, *Germany* 18 E5
Lauterbrunnen, *Switz.* 22 C5
Lauterecken, *Germany* 19 F3
Lautoka, *Fiji* 87 C7
Lauwe, *Belgium* 17 G2
Lauwers, *Neths.* 16 A8
Lauwers Zee, *Neths.* 16 B8
Lauzon, *Canada* 99 C5
Lava Hot Springs, *U.S.A.* 110 E7
Lavadores, *Spain* 30 C2
Lavagna, *Italy* 32 D6
Laval, *France* 24 D6
Lavalle, *Argentina* 126 B2
Lávara, *Greece* 39 H9
Lavardac, *France* 26 D4
Lavaur, *France* 26 E5
Lavaux, *Switz.* 22 D3
Lavelanet, *France* 26 F5
Lavello, *Italy* 35 A8
Laverne, *U.S.A.* 109 G5
Laverton, *Australia* 89 E3
Lavos, *Portugal* 30 E2
Lavras, *Brazil* 123 F3
Lavre, *Portugal* 31 G2
Lavrentiya, *Russia* 45 C19
Lávrion, *Greece* 39 M7
Lávris, *Greece* 37 D6
Lavumisa, *Swaziland* 85 D5
Lawas, *Malaysia* 56 D5
Lawele, *Indonesia* 57 F6
Lawn Hill, *Australia* 90 B2
Lawng Pit, *Burma* 61 G20
Lawqar, *Si. Arabia* 64 D4
Lawra, *Ghana* 78 C4
Lawrence, *N.Z.* 87 L2
Lawrence, *Kans., U.S.A.* 108 F7
Lawrence, *Mass., U.S.A.* 107 D13
Lawrenceburg, *Ind., U.S.A.* 104 F3
Lawrenceburg, *Tenn., U.S.A.* 105 H2
Lawrenceville, *U.S.A.* 105 J4
Laws, *U.S.A.* 112 H8
Lawton, *U.S.A.* 109 H5
Lawu, *Indonesia* 57 G14
Laxford, L., *U.K.* 14 C3
Laylān, *Iraq* 64 C5
Layon →, *France* 24 E6
Laysan I., *Pac. Oc.* 93 E11
Laytonville, *U.S.A.* 110 G2
Lazio □, *Italy* 33 F9
Lazo, *Russia* 48 C6
Le Barcarès, *France* 26 F7
Le Beausset, *France* 27 E9
Le Blanc, *France* 26 B5
Le Bleymard, *France* 26 D7
Le Bourgneuf-la-Fôret, *France* 24 D6
Le Bouscat, *France* 26 D3
Le Brassus, *Switz.* 22 C2
Le Bugue, *France* 26 D4
Le Canourgue, *France* 26 D7
Le Cateau, *France* 25 B10
Le Chambon-Feugerolles, *France* 27 C8
Le Château-d'Oléron, *France* 26 C2
Le Châtelard, *Switz.* 22 D3
Le Châtelet, *France* 26 B6
Le Châtelet-en-Brie, *France* 25 D9
Le Chesne, *France* 25 C11
Le Cheylard, *France* 27 D8
Le Conquet, *France* 24 D2
Le Creusot, *France* 25 F11
Le Croisic, *France* 24 E4
Le Donjon, *France* 26 B7
Le Dorat, *France* 26 B5
Le François, *Martinique* 117 D7
Le Grand-Lucé, *France* 24 E7
Le Grand-Pressigny, *France* 24 F7
Le Havre, *France* 24 C7
Le Lavandou, *France* 27 E10
Le Lion-d'Angers, *France* 24 E6
Le Locle, *Switz.* 22 B3
Le Louroux-Béconnais, *France* 24 E6
Le Luc, *France* 27 E10
Le Madonie, *Italy* 34 E6
Le Maire, Est. de, *Argentina* 128 D4
Le Mans, *France* 24 E7
Le Marinel, *Zaïre* 83 E2
Le Mars, *U.S.A.* 108 D6
Le Mêle-sur-Sarthe, *France* 24 D7
Le Merlerault, *France* 24 D7
Le Monastier-sur-Gazeille, *France* 26 D7
Le Monêtier-les-Bains, *France* 27 D10
Le Mont d'Or, *France* 25 F13
Le Mont-Dore, *France* 26 C6
Le Mont-St.-Michel, *France* 24 D5
Le Moule, *Guadeloupe* 117 C7
Le Muy, *France* 27 E10
Le Palais, *France* 24 E3
Le Perthus, *France* 26 F6
Le Pont, *Switz.* 22 C2
Le Pouldu, *France* 24 E3
Le Puy, *France* 26 C7
Le Quesnoy, *France* 25 B10
Le Roy, *U.S.A.* 109 F7
Le Sentier, *Switz.* 22 C2
Le Sueur, *U.S.A.* 108 C8
Le Teil, *France* 27 D8
Le Teilleul, *France* 24 D6
Le Theil, *France* 24 D7
Le Thillot, *France* 25 E13
Le Thuy, *Vietnam* 58 D6
Le Touquet-Paris-Plage, *France* 25 B8
Le Tréport, *France* 24 B8
Le Val-d'Ajol, *France* 25 E13
Le Verdon-sur-Mer, *France* 26 C2
Le Vigan, *France* 26 E7
Lea →, *U.K.* 13 F7
Leach, *Cambodia* 59 F4
Lead, *U.S.A.* 108 C3
Leader, *Canada* 101 C7
Leadhills, *U.K.* 14 F5
Leadville, *U.S.A.* 111 G10
Leaf →, *U.S.A.* 109 K10
Leakey, *U.S.A.* 109 L5
Leamington, *Canada* 98 D3
Leamington, *U.S.A.* 110 G7
Leamington Spa = Royal Leamington Spa, *U.K.* 13 E6
Le'an, *China* 53 D10
Leandro Norte Alem, *Argentina* 127 B4
Learmonth, *Australia* 88 D1
Leask, *Canada* 101 C7
Leavenworth, *Kans., U.S.A.* 108 F7
Leavenworth, *Wash., U.S.A.* 110 C3
Łeba, *Poland* 20 A7
Lebak, *Phil.* 55 H6
Lebam, *U.S.A.* 112 D3
Lebanon, *Ind., U.S.A.* 104 E2
Lebanon, *Kans., U.S.A.* 108 F5
Lebanon, *Ky., U.S.A.* 104 G3
Lebanon, *Mo., U.S.A.* 109 G8
Lebanon, *Oreg., U.S.A.* 110 D2
Lebanon, *Pa., U.S.A.* 107 F8
Lebanon, *Tenn., U.S.A.* 105 G2
Lebanon ■, *Asia* 69 B4
Lebbeke, *Belgium* 17 G4
Lebec, *U.S.A.* 113 L8
Lebedin, *Ukraine* 40 F9
Lebedyan, *Russia* 41 E11
Lebomboberge, *S. Africa* 85 C5
Lębork, *Poland* 20 A7
Lebrija, *Spain* 31 J4
Lebu, *Chile* 126 D1
Lecce, *Italy* 35 B11
Lecco, *Italy* 32 C6
Lecco, L. di, *Italy* 32 C6
Lécera, *Spain* 28 D4
Lech, *Austria* 19 H6
Lech →, *Germany* 19 G6
Lechang, *China* 53 E9
Lechtaler Alpen, *Austria* 19 H6
Lectoure, *France* 26 E4
Łęczyca, *Poland* 20 C9
Ledbury, *U.K.* 13 E5
Lede, *Belgium* 17 G3
Ledeberg, *Belgium* 17 F3
Ledesma, *Spain* 30 D5
Ledong, *China* 58 C7
Leduc, *Canada* 100 C6
Ledyczek, *Poland* 20 B6
Lee, *U.S.A.* 107 D11
Lee →, *Ireland* 15 E3
Lee Vining, *U.S.A.* 112 H7
Leech L., *U.S.A.* 108 B7
Leedey, *U.S.A.* 109 H5
Leeds, *U.K.* 12 D6
Leeds, *U.S.A.* 105 J2
Leek, *Neths.* 16 B8
Leek, *U.K.* 12 D5
Leende, *Neths.* 17 F7
Leer, *Germany* 18 B3
Leerdam, *Neths.* 16 E6
Leersum, *Neths.* 16 E6
Leesburg, *U.S.A.* 105 L5
Leesville, *U.S.A.* 109 K8
Leeton, *Australia* 91 E4
Leetonia, *U.S.A.* 106 F4
Leeu Gamka, *S. Africa* 84 E3
Leeuwarden, *Neths.* 16 B7
Leeuwin, C., *Australia* 89 F2
Leeward Is., *Atl. Oc.* 117 C7
Lefka, *Cyprus* 37 D11
Lefkoniko, *Cyprus* 37 D12
Lefors, *U.S.A.* 109 H4
Lefroy, L., *Australia* 89 F3
Legal, *Canada* 100 C6
Leganés, *Spain* 30 E7
Legazpi, *Phil.* 55 E5
Legendre I., *Australia* 88 D2
Leghorn = Livorno, *Italy* 32 E7
Legionowo, *Poland* 20 C10
Léglise, *Belgium* 17 J7
Legnago, *Italy* 33 C8
Legnano, *Italy* 32 C5
Legnica, *Poland* 20 D6
Legrad, *Croatia* 33 B13
Legume, *Australia* 91 D5
Leh, *India* 63 B7
Lehi, *U.S.A.* 110 F8
Lehighton, *U.S.A.* 107 F9
Lehrte, *Germany* 18 C5
Lehututu, *Botswana* 84 C3
Lei Shui →, *China* 53 D9
Leiah, *Pakistan* 62 D4
Leibnitz, *Austria* 21 J5
Leibo, *China* 52 C4
Leicester, *U.K.* 13 E6
Leicestershire □, *U.K.* 13 E6
Leichhardt →, *Australia* 90 B2
Leichhardt Ra., *Australia* 90 C4
Leiden, *Neths.* 16 D5
Leiderdorp, *Neths.* 16 D5
Leidschendam, *Neths.* 16 D4
Leie →, *Belgium* 25 A10
Leignon, *Belgium* 17 H6
Leine →, *Germany* 18 C5
Leinster, *Australia* 89 E3
Leinster □, *Ireland* 15 C4
Leinster, Mt., *Ireland* 15 D5
Leipzig, *Germany* 18 D8
Leiria, *Portugal* 31 F2
Leiria □, *Portugal* 31 F2
Leisler, Mt., *Australia* 88 D4
Leith, *U.K.* 14 F5
Leith Hill, *U.K.* 13 F7
Leitha →, *Europe* 21 H7
Leitrim, *Ireland* 15 B3
Leitrim □, *Ireland* 15 B3
Leiyang, *China* 53 D9
Leiza, *Spain* 28 B3
Leizhou Bandao, *China* 54 D6
Leizhou Wan, *China* 53 G8
Lek →, *Neths.* 16 E5
Leke, *Belgium* 17 F1
Lekkerkerk, *Neths.* 16 E5
Leksula, *Indonesia* 57 E7
Leland, *U.S.A.* 109 J9
Leland Lakes, *Canada* 101 A6
Leleque, *Argentina* 128 B2
Lelystad, *Neths.* 16 D6
Lema, *Nigeria* 79 C5
Léman, Lac, *Switz.* 22 D3
Lemelerveld, *Neths.* 16 D8
Lemera, *Zaïre* 82 C2
Lemery, *Phil.* 55 E4
Lemgo, *Germany* 18 C4
Lemhi Ra., *U.S.A.* 110 D7
Lemmer, *Neths.* 16 C7
Lemmon, *U.S.A.* 108 C3
Lemon Grove, *U.S.A.* 113 N9
Lemoore, *U.S.A.* 111 H4
Lempdes, *France* 26 C7
Lemsid, *W. Sahara* 74 C2
Lemvig, *Denmark* 11 H2
Lena →, *Russia* 45 B13
Lenclоître, *France* 24 F7
Lençóis, *Brazil* 123 D3
Léndas, *Greece* 37 E6
Lendeh, *Iran* 65 D6
Lendelede, *Belgium* 17 G2
Lendinara, *Italy* 33 C8
Lengerich, *Germany* 18 C3
Lenggong, *Malaysia* 59 K3
Lenggries, *Germany* 19 H7
Lengua de Vaca, Pta., *Chile* 126 C1
Lenin, *Russia* 43 B9
Leninabad = Khodzent, *Tajikistan* 44 E7
Leninakan = Kumayri, *Armenia* 43 F10
Leningrad = Sankt-Peterburg, *Russia* 40 B7
Lenino, *Ukraine* 42 D6
Leninogorsk = Ridder, *Kazakhstan* 44 D9
Leninsk, *Russia* 43 B11
Leninsk, *Russia* 43 C10
Leninsk-Kuznetskiy, *Russia* 44 D9
Leninskaya Sloboda, *Russia* 41 C14
Leninskoye, *Russia* 41 B15
Leninskoye, *Russia* 45 E14
Lenk, *Switz.* 22 D4
Lenkoran, *Azerbaijan* 67 D13
Lenmalu, *Indonesia* 57 E8
Lenne →, *Germany* 18 D3
Lennox, I., *Chile* 128 E3
Lennoxville, *Canada* 107 A13
Leno, *Italy* 32 C7
Lenoir, *U.S.A.* 105 H5
Lenoir City, *U.S.A.* 105 H3
Lenora, *U.S.A.* 108 F4
Lenore L., *Canada* 101 C8
Lenox, *U.S.A.* 107 D11
Lens, *Belgium* 17 G3
Lens, *France* 25 B9
Lens St. Remy, *Belgium* 17 G6
Lensk, *Russia* 45 C12
Lenskoye, *Ukraine* 42 D6
Lent, *Neths.* 16 E7
Lentini, *Italy* 35 E8
Lentvaric, *Lithuania* 40 D4
Lenwood, *U.S.A.* 113 L9
Lenzburg, *Switz.* 22 B6
Lenzen, *Germany* 18 B7
Lenzerheide, *Switz.* 23 C9
Léo, *Burkina Faso* 78 C4
Leoben, *Austria* 21 H5
Leola, *U.S.A.* 108 C5
Leominster, *U.K.* 13 E5
Leominster, *U.S.A.* 107 D13
Léon, *France* 26 E2
León, *Mexico* 114 C4
León, *Nic.* 116 D2
León, *Spain* 30 C5
Leon, *U.S.A.* 108 E8
León □, *Spain* 30 C5
León, Montañas de, *Spain* 30 C4
Leonardtown, *U.S.A.* 104 F7
Leone, Mte., *Switz.* 22 D6
Leonforte, *Italy* 35 E7
Leongatha, *Australia* 91 F4
Leonídhion, *Greece* 39 M5
Leonora, *Australia* 89 E3
Léopold II, Lac = Mai-Ndombe, L., *Zaïre* 80 E3
Leopoldina, *Brazil* 123 F3
Leopoldo Bulhões, *Brazil* 123 E2
Leopoldsburg, *Belgium* 17 F6
Léopoldville = Kinshasa, *Zaïre* 80 E3
Leoti, *U.S.A.* 108 F4
Leoville, *Canada* 101 C7
Lépa, L. do, *Angola* 84 B2
Lepe, *Spain* 31 H3
Lepel, *Belorussia* 40 D6
Lepikha, *Russia* 45 C13
Leping, *China* 53 C11
Lepontine, Alpi, *Italy* 23 D6
Lequeitio, *Spain* 28 B2
Lercara Friddi, *Italy* 34 E6
Lerdo, *Mexico* 114 B4
Léré, *Chad* 73 G7
Lere, *Nigeria* 79 D6
Leribe, *Lesotho* 85 D4
Lérici, *Italy* 32 D6
Lérida, *Spain* 28 D5
Lérida □, *Spain* 28 C6
Lérins, Is. de, *France* 27 E11
Lerma, *Spain* 30 C7
Léros, *Greece* 39 M9
Lérouville, *France* 25 D12
Lerwick, *U.K.* 14 A7
Les Abrets, *France* 27 C9
Les Andelys, *France* 24 C8
Les Arcs, *France* 27 E10
Les Baux-de-Provence, *France* 27 E8
Les Bois, *Switz.* 22 B3
Les Cayes, *Haiti* 117 C5
Les Diablerets, *Switz.* 22 D4
Les Échelles, *France* 27 C9
Les Essarts, *France* 24 F5
Les Étroits, *Canada* 99 C6
Les Eyzies-de-Tayac-Sireuil, *France* 26 D5
Les Herbiers, *France* 24 F5
Les Minquiers, *Chan. Is.* 24 D4
Les Ponts-de-Cé, *France* 24 E6
Les Riceys, *France* 25 E11
Les Sables-d'Olonne, *France* 26 B2
Les Vans, *France* 27 D8
Les Verrières, *Switz.* 22 C2
Lesbos = Lésvos, *Greece* 39 K9
Leshan, *China* 52 C4
Lésina, L. di, *Italy* 33 G12
Lesja, *Norway* 10 B2
Lesjaverk, *Norway* 10 B2
Leskov I., *Antarctica* 5 B1
Leskovac, *Serbia* 21 M11
Leslie, *U.S.A.* 109 H8
Lesneven, *France* 24 D2
Lešnica, *Serbia* 21 L9
Lesnoye, *Russia* 40 B9
Lesopilnoye, *Russia* 48 A7
Lesotho ■, *Africa* 85 D4
Lesozavodsk, *Russia* 45 E14
Lesparre-Médoc, *France* 26 C3
Lessay, *France* 24 C5
Lesse →, *Belgium* 17 H5
Lesser Antilles, *W. Indies* 117 C7
Lesser Slave L., *Canada* 100 B5
Lesser Sunda Is., *Indonesia* 57 F6
Lessines, *Belgium* 17 G3
Lester, *U.S.A.* 112 C5
Lestock, *Canada* 101 C8
Lesuer I., *Australia* 88 B4
Lésvos, *Greece* 39 K9
Leszno, *Poland* 20 D6
Letchworth, *U.K.* 13 F7
Letea, Ostrov, *Romania* 38 D12
Lethbridge, *Canada* 100 D6
Lethem, *Guyana* 121 C6
Leti, Kepulauan, *Indonesia* 57 F7
Leti Is. = Leti, Kepulauan, *Indonesia* 57 F7
Letiahau →, *Botswana* 84 C3
Leticia, *Colombia* 120 D4
Leting, *China* 51 E10
Letjiesbos, *S. Africa* 84 E3
Letlhakeng, *Botswana* 84 C3
Letpadan, *Burma* 61 L19
Letpan, *Burma* 61 K19
Letterkenny, *Ireland* 15 B4
Leu, *Romania* 38 E7
Leucadia, *U.S.A.* 113 M9
Leucate, *France* 26 F7
Leucate, Étang de, *France* 26 F7
Leuk, *Switz.* 22 D5
Leukerbad, *Switz.* 22 D5
Leupegem, *Belgium* 17 G3
Leuser, G., *Indonesia* 56 D1
Leutkirch, *Germany* 19 H6
Leuven, *Belgium* 17 G5
Leuze, *Hainaut, Belgium* 17 G3
Leuze, *Namur, Belgium* 17 G5
Lev Tolstoy, *Russia* 41 E11
Levádhia, *Greece* 39 L5
Levan, *U.S.A.* 110 G8
Levanger, *Norway* 8 E11
Levant, I. du, *France* 27 E10
Lévanto, *Italy* 32 D6
Levanzo, *Italy* 34 E5
Levelland, *U.S.A.* 109 J3
Leven, *U.K.* 14 E6
Leven, L., *U.K.* 14 E5
Leven, Toraka, *Madag.* 85 A8
Levens, *France* 27 E11
Leveque C., *Australia* 88 C3
Leverano, *Italy* 35 B10
Leverkusen, *Germany* 18 D2
Levet, *France* 25 F9
Levice, *Slovak Rep.* 21 G8
Levico, *Italy* 33 C8
Levie, *France* 27 G13
Levier, *France* 25 F13
Levin, *N.Z.* 87 J5
Lévis, *Canada* 99 C5
Levis, L., *Canada* 100 A5
Levítha, *Greece* 39 M9
Levittown, *N.Y., U.S.A.* 107 F11
Levittown, *Pa., U.S.A.* 107 F10
Lévka Óri, *Greece* 37 D6
Levkás, *Greece* 39 L3
Levkímmi, *Greece* 37 B4
Levkímmi, Ákra, *Greece* 37 B4
Levkôsia = Nicosia, *Cyprus* 37 D12
Levoča, *Slovak Rep.* 20 F10
Levroux, *France* 25 F8
Levski, *Bulgaria* 38 F8
Levskigrad, *Bulgaria* 38 G7
Lewellen, *U.S.A.* 108 E3
Lewes, *U.K.* 13 G8
Lewes, *U.S.A.* 104 F8
Lewis, *U.K.* 14 C2
Lewis →, *U.S.A.* 112 E4
Lewis, Butt of, *U.K.* 14 C2
Lewis Ra., *Australia* 88 D4
Lewis Range, *U.S.A.* 110 C7
Lewisburg, *Pa., U.S.A.* 106 F8
Lewisburg, *Tenn., U.S.A.* 105 H2
Lewisporte, *Canada* 99 C8
Lewiston, *Idaho, U.S.A.* 110 C5
Lewiston, *Maine, U.S.A.* 105 C11
Lewistown, *Mont., U.S.A.* 110 C9
Lewistown, *Pa., U.S.A.* 106 F7
Lexington, *Ill., U.S.A.* 108 E10
Lexington, *Ky., U.S.A.* 104 F3
Lexington, *Miss., U.S.A.* 109 J9
Lexington, *Mo., U.S.A.* 108 F8
Lexington, *N.C., U.S.A.* 105 H5
Lexington, *Nebr., U.S.A.* 108 E5
Lexington, *Ohio, U.S.A.* 106 F2
Lexington, *Oreg., U.S.A.* 110 D4
Lexington, *Tenn., U.S.A.* 105 H1
Lexington Park, *U.S.A.* 104 F7
Leye, *China* 52 E6
Leyre →, *France* 26 D2

Leysin, *Switz.* 22 D4
Leyte, *Phil.* 55 F6
Leyte Gulf, *Phil.* 55 F6
Lezay, *France* 26 B4
Lezha, *Albania* 39 H2
Lezhi, *China* 52 B5
Lézignan-Corbières, *France* 26 E6
Lezoux, *France* 26 C7
Lgov, *Russia* 40 F9
Lhasa, *China* 54 D4
Lhazê, *China* 54 D3
Lhokkruet, *Indonesia* 56 D1
Lhokseumawe, *Indonesia* 56 C1
Lhuntsi Dzong, *India* 61 F17
Li, *Thailand* 58 D2
Li Shui →, *China* 53 C9
Li Xian, *Gansu, China* 50 G3
Li Xian, *Hebei, China* 50 E8
Li Xian, *Hunan, China* 53 C8
Li Xian, *Sichuan, China* 52 B4
Liádhoi, *Greece* 39 N9
Lian Xian, *China* 53 E9
Liancheng, *China* 53 E11
Lianga, *Phil.* 55 G7
Liangcheng, *Nei Mongol Zizhiqu, China* 50 D7
Liangcheng, *Shandong, China* 51 G10
Liangdang, *China* 50 H4
Lianghekou, *China* 52 C7
Liangping, *China* 52 B6
Lianhua, *China* 53 D9
Lianjiang, *Fujian, China* 53 D12
Lianjiang, *Guangdong, China* 53 G8
Lianping, *China* 53 E10
Lianshan, *China* 53 E9
Lianshanguan, *China* 51 D12
Lianshui, *China* 51 H10
Lianyuan, *China* 53 D8
Lianyungang, *China* 51 G10
Liao He →, *China* 51 D11
Liaocheng, *China* 50 F8
Liaodong Bandao, *China* 51 E12
Liaodong Wan, *China* 51 D11
Liaoning □, *China* 54 B7
Liaoning □, *Liaoning, China* 51 D12
Liaoyang, *China* 51 D12
Liaoyuan, *China* 51 C13
Liaozhong, *China* 51 D12
Liapádhes, *Greece* 39 K2
Liard →, *Canada* 100 A4
Liari, *Pakistan* 62 G2
Líbano, *Colombia* 120 C2
Libau = Liepāja, *Latvia* 40 C2
Libby, *U.S.A.* 110 B6
Libenge, *Zaïre* 80 D3
Liberal, *Kans., U.S.A.* 109 G4
Liberal, *Mo., U.S.A.* 109 G7
Liberdade, *Brazil* 124 C3
Liberdade →, *Brazil* 125 B7
Liberec, *Czech.* 20 E5
Liberia, *Costa Rica* 116 D2
Liberia ■, *W. Afr.* 78 D3
Libertad, *Venezuela* 120 B4
Liberty, *Mo., U.S.A.* 108 F7
Liberty, *Tex., U.S.A.* 109 K7
Libin, *Belgium* 17 J6
Lîbîya, Sahrâ', *Africa* 73 C9
Libo, *China* 52 E6
Libobo, Tanjung, *Indonesia* 57 E7
Libode, *S. Africa* 85 E4
Libonda, *Zambia* 81 G4
Libourne, *France* 26 D3
Libramont, *Belgium* 17 J6
Libreville, *Gabon* 80 D1
Libya ■, *N. Afr.* 73 C8
Libyan Desert = Lîbîya, Sahrâ', *Africa* 73 C9
Libyan Plateau = Ed-Déffa, *Egypt* 76 A2
Licantén, *Chile* 126 D1
Licata, *Italy* 34 E6
Lice, *Turkey* 67 D9
Licheng, *China* 50 F7
Lichfield, *U.K.* 12 E6
Lichinga, *Mozam.* 83 E4
Lichtaart, *Belgium* 17 F5
Lichtenburg, *S. Africa* 84 D4
Lichtenfels, *Germany* 19 E7
Lichtenvoorde, *Neths.* 16 E9
Lichtervelde, *Belgium* 17 F2
Lichuan, *Hubei, China* 52 B7
Lichuan, *Jiangxi, China* 53 D11
Licosa, Punta, *Italy* 35 B7
Lida, *Belorussia* 40 E4
Lida, *U.S.A.* 111 H5
Lidingö, *Sweden* 10 E12
Lidköping, *Sweden* 11 F7
Lido, *Italy* 33 C9
Lido, *Niger* 79 C5
Lido di Roma = Óstia, Lido di, *Italy* 34 A5
Lidzbark Warminski, *Poland* 20 A10
Liebenwalde, *Germany* 18 C9
Lieberose, *Germany* 18 D10
Liebig, Mt., *Australia* 88 D5
Liechtenstein ■, *Europe* 23 B9
Liederkerke, *Belgium* 17 G4
Liège, *Belgium* 17 G7
Liège □, *Belgium* 17 G7
Liegnitz = Legnica, *Poland* 20 D6
Liempde, *Neths.* 17 E6
Lienart, *Zaïre* 82 B2
Lienyünchiangshih = Lianyungang, *China* 51 G10
Lienz, *Austria* 21 J2
Liepāja, *Latvia* 40 C2
Lier, *Belgium* 17 F5
Lierneux, *Belgium* 17 H7
Lieshout, *Neths.* 17 E7
Liestal, *Switz.* 22 B5
Liévin, *France* 25 B9
Lièvre →, *Canada* 98 C4
Liezen, *Austria* 21 H4
Liffey →, *Ireland* 15 C5
Lifford, *Ireland* 15 B4
Liffré, *France* 24 D5
Lifjell, *Norway* 10 E2
Lifudzin, *Russia* 48 B7
Ligao, *Phil.* 55 E5
Lightning Ridge, *Australia* 91 D4
Lignano, *Italy* 33 C10
Ligny-en-Barrois, *France* 25 D12
Ligny-le-Châtel, *France* 25 E10
Ligoúrion, *Greece* 39 M6
Ligueil, *France* 24 E7
Liguria □, *Italy* 32 D6
Ligurian Sea, *Italy* 32 E5
Lihou Reefs and Cays, *Australia* 90 B5
Lihue, *U.S.A.* 102 H15
Lijiang, *China* 52 D3
Likasi, *Zaïre* 83 E2
Likati, *Zaïre* 80 D4
Likhoslavl, *Russia* 40 C9
Likhovski, *Russia* 43 B9
Likoma I., *Malawi* 83 E3
Likumburu, *Tanzania* 83 D4
L'Île-Bouchard, *France* 24 E7
L'Ile-Rousse, *France* 27 F12
Liling, *China* 53 D9
Lille, *Belgium* 17 F5
Lille, *France* 25 B10
Lille Bælt, *Denmark* 11 J3
Lillebonne, *France* 24 C7
Lillehammer, *Norway* 10 C4
Lillers, *France* 25 B9
Lillesand, *Norway* 11 F2
Lilleshall, *U.K.* 13 E5
Lillestrøm, *Norway* 10 E5
Lillian Point, Mt., *Australia* 89 E4
Lillo, *Spain* 28 F1
Lillooet →, *Canada* 100 D4
Lilongwe, *Malawi* 83 E3
Liloy, *Phil.* 57 C6
Lim →, *Bos.-H.* 21 M9
Lima, *Indonesia* 57 E7
Lima, *Peru* 124 C2
Lima, *Mont., U.S.A.* 110 D7
Lima, *Ohio, U.S.A.* 104 E3
Lima □, *Peru* 124 C2
Lima →, *Portugal* 30 D2
Limages, *Canada* 107 A9
Liman, *Russia* 43 D12
Limassol, *Cyprus* 37 E12
Limavady, *U.K.* 15 A5
Limavady □, *U.K.* 15 B5
Limay →, *Argentina* 128 A3
Limay Mahuida, *Argentina* 126 D2
Limbang, *Brunei* 56 D5
Limbara, Monti, *Italy* 34 B2
Limbdi, *India* 62 H4
Limbe, *Cameroon* 79 E6
Limbourg, *Belgium* 17 G7
Limbri, *Australia* 91 E5
Limbunya, *Australia* 88 C4
Limburg, *Germany* 19 E4
Limburg □, *Belgium* 17 F6
Limburg □, *Neths.* 17 F7
Limeira, *Brazil* 127 A6
Limerick, *Ireland* 15 D3
Limerick □, *Ireland* 15 D3
Limestone, *U.S.A.* 106 D6
Limestone →, *Canada* 101 B10
Limfjorden, *Denmark* 11 H3
Limia = Lima →, *Portugal* 30 D2
Limmared, *Sweden* 11 G7
Limmat →, *Switz.* 23 B6
Limmen, *Neths.* 16 C5
Limmen Bight, *Australia* 90 A2
Limmen Bight →, *Australia* 90 B2
Límni, *Greece* 39 L6
Límnos, *Greece* 39 K8
Limoeiro, *Brazil* 122 C4
Limoeiro do Norte, *Brazil* 122 C4
Limoges, *France* 26 C5
Limón, *Costa Rica* 116 D3
Limon, *U.S.A.* 108 F3
Limone Piemonte, *Italy* 32 D4
Limousin, *France* 26 C5
Limousin, Plateaux du, *France* 26 C5
Limoux, *France* 26 E6
Limpopo →, *Africa* 85 D5
Limuru, *Kenya* 82 C4
Lin Xian, *China* 50 F6
Lin'an, *China* 53 B12
Linapacan I., *Phil.* 55 F3
Linapacan Str., *Phil.* 55 F3
Linares, *Chile* 126 D1
Linares, *Colombia* 120 C2
Linares, *Mexico* 115 C5
Linares, *Spain* 29 G1
Linares □, *Chile* 126 D1
Línas Mte., *Italy* 34 C1
Lincang, *China* 52 F3
Lincheng, *China* 50 F8
Linchuan, *China* 53 D11
Lincoln, *Argentina* 126 C3
Lincoln, *N.Z.* 87 K4
Lincoln, *U.K.* 12 D7
Lincoln, *Calif., U.S.A.* 112 G5
Lincoln, *Ill., U.S.A.* 108 E10
Lincoln, *Kans., U.S.A.* 108 F5
Lincoln, *Maine, U.S.A.* 99 C6
Lincoln, *N.H., U.S.A.* 107 B13
Lincoln, *N. Mex., U.S.A.* 111 K11
Lincoln, *Nebr., U.S.A.* 108 E6
Lincoln Hav = Lincoln Sea, *Arctic* 4 A5
Lincoln Sea, *Arctic* 4 A5
Lincoln Wolds, *U.K.* 12 D7
Lincolnshire □, *U.K.* 12 D7
Lincolnton, *U.S.A.* 105 H5
L'Incudine, *France* 27 G13
Lind, *U.S.A.* 110 C4
Linda, *U.S.A.* 112 F5
Lindau, *Germany* 19 H5
Linde →, *Neths.* 16 C7
Linden, *Guyana* 121 B6
Linden, *Calif., U.S.A.* 112 G5
Linden, *Tex., U.S.A.* 109 J7
Lindenheuvel, *Neths.* 17 G7
Lindenhurst, *U.S.A.* 107 F11
Linderöd, *Sweden* 11 J7
Linderödsåsen, *Sweden* 11 J7
Lindesnes, *Norway* 6 D7
Líndhos, *Greece* 37 C10
Lindi, *Tanzania* 83 D4
Lindi □, *Tanzania* 83 D4
Lindi →, *Zaïre* 82 B2
Lindoso, *Portugal* 30 D2
Lindow, *Germany* 18 C8
Lindsay, *Canada* 98 D4
Lindsay, *Calif., U.S.A.* 111 H4
Lindsay, *Okla., U.S.A.* 109 H6
Lindsborg, *U.S.A.* 108 F6
Linfen, *China* 50 F6
Ling Xian, *Hunan, China* 53 D9
Ling Xian, *Shandong, China* 50 F9
Lingao, *China* 58 C7
Lingayen, *Phil.* 57 A6
Lingayen G., *Phil.* 55 C4
Lingbi, *China* 51 H9
Lingchuan, *Guangxi Zhuangzu, China* 53 E8
Lingchuan, *Shanxi, China* 50 G7
Lingen, *Germany* 18 C3
Lingga, *Indonesia* 56 E2
Lingga, Kepulauan, *Indonesia* 56 E2
Lingga Arch. = Lingga, Kepulauan, *Indonesia* 56 E2
Lingle, *U.S.A.* 108 D2
Lingling, *China* 53 D8
Lingqiu, *China* 50 E8
Lingshan, *China* 52 F7
Lingshi, *China* 50 F6
Lingshou, *China* 50 E8
Lingshui, *China* 58 C8
Lingtai, *China* 50 G4
Linguéré, *Senegal* 78 B1
Lingwu, *China* 50 E4
Lingyuan, *China* 51 D10
Lingyun, *China* 52 E6
Linh Cam, *Vietnam* 58 C5
Linhai, *China* 53 C13
Linhares, *Brazil* 123 E3
Linhe, *China* 50 D4
Linjiang, *China* 51 D14
Linköping, *Sweden* 11 F9
Linkou, *China* 51 B16
Linli, *China* 53 C8
Linlithgow, *U.K.* 14 F5
Linnhe, L., *U.K.* 14 E3
Linosa, I., *Medit. S.* 75 A7
Linqi, *China* 50 G7
Linqing, *China* 50 F8
Linqu, *China* 51 F10
Linru, *China* 50 G7
Lins, *Brazil* 127 A6
Linshui, *China* 52 B6
Lintao, *China* 50 G2
Linth →, *Switz.* 19 H5
Linthal, *Switz.* 23 C8
Lintlaw, *Canada* 101 C8
Linton, *Canada* 99 C5
Linton, *Ind., U.S.A.* 104 F2
Linton, *N. Dak., U.S.A.* 108 B4
Lintong, *China* 50 G5
Linville, *Australia* 91 D5
Linwood, *Canada* 106 C4
Linwu, *China* 53 E9
Linxi, *China* 51 C10
Linxia, *China* 54 C5
Linxiang, *China* 53 C9
Linyanti →, *Africa* 84 B4
Linyi, *China* 51 G10
Linz, *Austria* 21 G4
Linz, *Germany* 18 E3
Linzhenzhen, *China* 50 F5
Linzi, *China* 51 F10
Lion, G. du, *France* 27 E8
Lionárisso, *Cyprus* 37 D13
Lioni, *Italy* 35 B8
Lions, G. of = Lion, G. du, *France* 27 E8
Lion's Den, *Zimbabwe* 83 F3
Lion's Head, *Canada* 98 D3
Liozno, *Belorussia* 40 D7
Lipa, *Phil.* 55 E4
Lipali, *Mozam.* 83 F4
Lípari, *Italy* 35 D7
Lípari, Is., *Italy* 35 D7
Lipetsk, *Russia* 41 E11
Liping, *China* 52 D7
Lipkany, *Moldavia* 42 B2
Lipljan, *Serbia* 21 N11
Lipno, *Poland* 20 C9
Lipova, *Romania* 38 C4
Lipovcy Manzovka, *Russia* 48 B6
Lipovets, *Ukraine* 42 B3
Lippe →, *Germany* 18 D2
Lippstadt, *Germany* 18 D4
Lipscomb, *U.S.A.* 109 G4
Lipsko, *Poland* 20 D11
Lipsói, *Greece* 39 M9
Liptovsky Svaty Milkulaš, *Slovak Rep.* 20 F9
Liptrap C., *Australia* 91 F4
Lipu, *China* 53 E8
Lira, *Uganda* 82 B3
Liri →, *Italy* 34 A6
Liria, *Spain* 28 F4
Lisala, *Zaïre* 80 D4
Lisboa, *Portugal* 31 G1
Lisboa □, *Portugal* 31 G1
Lisbon = Lisboa, *Portugal* 31 G1
Lisbon, *N. Dak., U.S.A.* 108 B6
Lisbon, *N.H., U.S.A.* 107 B13
Lisbon, *Ohio, U.S.A.* 106 F4
Lisburn, *U.K.* 15 B5
Lisburne, C., *U.S.A.* 96 B3
Liscannor, B., *Ireland* 15 D2
Liscia →, *Italy* 34 A2
Lishe Jiang →, *China* 52 E3
Lishi, *China* 50 F6
Lishu, *China* 51 C13
Lishui, *Jiangsu, China* 53 B12
Lishui, *Zhejiang, China* 53 C12
Lisianski I., *Pac. Oc.* 92 E10
Lisichansk, *Ukraine* 42 B8
Lisieux, *France* 24 C7
Liski, *Russia* 41 F11
L'Isle-Adam, *France* 25 C9
L'Isle-Jourdain, *Gers, France* 26 E5
L'Isle-Jourdain, *Vienne, France* 26 B4
L'Isle-sur-le-Doubs, *France* 25 E13
Lisle-sur-Tarn, *France* 26 E5
Lismore, *Australia* 91 D5
Lismore, *Ireland* 15 D4
Lisse, *Neths.* 16 D5
List, *Germany* 18 A4
Lista, *Norway* 9 G9
Lista, *Sweden* 9 G14
Lister, Mt., *Antarctica* 5 D11
Liston, *Australia* 91 D5
Listowel, *Canada* 98 D3
Listowel, *Ireland* 15 D2
Lit-et-Mixe, *France* 26 D2
Litang, *Guangxi Zhuangzu, China* 52 F7
Litang, *Sichuan, China* 52 B3
Litang, *Malaysia* 57 C5
Litang Qu →, *China* 52 C3
Litani →, *Lebanon* 69 B4
Litchfield, *Calif., U.S.A.* 112 E6
Litchfield, *Conn., U.S.A.* 107 E11
Litchfield, *Ill., U.S.A.* 108 F10
Litchfield, *Minn., U.S.A.* 108 C7
Lithgow, *Australia* 91 E5
Líthinon, Ákra, *Greece* 37 E6
Lithuania ■, *Europe* 40 D3
Litija, *Slovenia* 33 B11
Litókhoron, *Greece* 39 J5
Litoměřice, *Czech.* 20 E4
Little Abaco I., *Bahamas* 116 A4
Little Barrier I., *N.Z.* 87 G5
Little Belt Mts., *U.S.A.* 110 C8
Little Blue →, *U.S.A.* 108 F6
Little Bushman Land, *S. Africa* 84 D2
Little Cadotte →, *Canada* 100 B5
Little Cayman, I., *Cayman Is.* 116 C3
Little Churchill →, *Canada* 101 B9
Little Colorado →, *U.S.A.* 111 H8
Little Current, *Canada* 98 C3
Little Current →, *Canada* 98 B3
Little Falls, *Minn., U.S.A.* 108 C7
Little Falls, *N.Y., U.S.A.* 107 C10
Little Fork →, *U.S.A.* 108 A8
Little Grand Rapids, *Canada* 101 C9
Little Humboldt →, *U.S.A.* 110 F5
Little Inagua I., *Bahamas* 117 B5
Little Karoo, *S. Africa* 84 E3
Little Lake, *U.S.A.* 113 K9
Little Laut Is. = Laut Ketil, Kepulauan, *Indonesia* 56 E5
Little Minch, *U.K.* 14 D2
Little Missouri →, *U.S.A.* 108 B3
Little Namaqualand, *S. Africa* 84 D2
Little Ouse →, *U.K.* 13 E8
Little Rann, *India* 62 H4
Little Red →, *U.S.A.* 109 H9
Little River, *N.Z.* 87 K4
Little Rock, *U.S.A.* 109 H8
Little Ruaha →, *Tanzania* 82 D4
Little Sable Pt., *U.S.A.* 104 D2
Little Sioux →, *U.S.A.* 108 E6
Little Smoky →, *Canada* 100 C5
Little Snake →, *U.S.A.* 110 F9
Little Valley, *U.S.A.* 106 D6
Little Wabash →, *U.S.A.* 104 G1
Littlefield, *U.S.A.* 109 J3
Littlefork, *U.S.A.* 108 A8
Littlehampton, *U.K.* 13 G7
Littleton, *U.S.A.* 107 B13
Liu He →, *China* 51 D11
Liu Jiang →, *China* 52 F7
Liuba, *China* 50 H4
Liucheng, *China* 52 E7
Liugou, *China* 51 D10
Liuhe, *China* 51 C13
Liuheng Dao, *China* 53 C14
Liukang Tenggaja, *Indonesia* 57 F5
Liuli, *Tanzania* 83 E3
Liuwa Plain, *Zambia* 81 G4
Liuyang, *China* 53 C9
Liuzhou, *China* 52 E7
Liuzhuang, *China* 51 H11
Livadherón, *Greece* 39 J4
Livadhia, *Cyprus* 37 E12
Livarot, *France* 24 D7
Live Oak, *Calif., U.S.A.* 112 F5
Live Oak, *Fla., U.S.A.* 105 K4
Liveras, *Cyprus* 37 D11
Liveringa, *Australia* 88 C3
Livermore, *U.S.A.* 112 H5
Livermore, Mt., *U.S.A.* 109 K2
Liverpool, *Australia* 91 E5
Liverpool, *Canada* 99 D7
Liverpool, *U.K.* 12 D5
Liverpool Plains, *Australia* 91 E5
Liverpool Ra., *Australia* 91 E5
Livingston, *Guatemala* 116 C2
Livingston, *Calif., U.S.A.* 112 H6
Livingston, *Mont., U.S.A.* 110 D8
Livingston, *Tex., U.S.A.* 109 K7
Livingstone, *Zambia* 83 F2
Livingstone Mts., *Tanzania* 83 D3
Livingstonia, *Malawi* 83 E3
Livny, *Russia* 41 E10
Livonia, *U.S.A.* 104 D4
Livorno, *Italy* 32 E7
Livramento, *Brazil* 127 C4
Livramento do Brumado, *Brazil* 123 D3
Livron-sur-Drôme, *France* 27 D8
Liwale, *Tanzania* 83 D4
Liwale □, *Tanzania* 83 D4
Lixi, *China* 52 D3
Liyang, *China* 53 B12
Lizard I., *Australia* 90 A4
Lizard Pt., *U.K.* 13 H2
Lizarda, *Brazil* 122 C2
Lizzano, *Italy* 35 B10
Ljubija, *Bos.-H.* 33 D13
Ljubljana, *Slovenia* 33 B11
Ljubno, *Slovenia* 33 B11
Ljubuški, *Bos.-H.* 21 M7
Ljung, *Sweden* 11 F7
Ljungan →, *Sweden* 10 B11
Ljungaverk, *Sweden* 10 B10
Ljungby, *Sweden* 9 H12
Ljusdal, *Sweden* 10 C10
Ljusnan = Ljungan →, *Sweden* 10 B11
Ljusnan →, *Sweden* 9 F14
Ljusne, *Sweden* 9 F14
Ljutomer, *Slovenia* 33 B13
Llagostera, *Spain* 28 D7
Llamellín, *Peru* 124 B2
Llancanelo, Salina, *Argentina* 126 D2
Llandeilo, *U.K.* 13 F3
Llandovery, *U.K.* 13 F4
Llandrindod Wells, *U.K.* 13 E4
Llandudno, *U.K.* 12 D4
Llanelli, *U.K.* 13 F3
Llanes, *Spain* 30 B6
Llangollen, *U.K.* 12 E4
Llanidloes, *U.K.* 13 E4
Llano, *U.S.A.* 109 K5
Llano →, *U.S.A.* 109 K5
Llano Estacado, *U.S.A.* 109 J3
Llanos, *S. Amer.* 118 B2
Llanquihue □, *Chile* 128 B2
Llanquihue, L., *Chile* 128 B1
Llebetx, C., *Spain* 36 B9
Lleida = Lérida, *Spain* 28 D5
Llentrisca, C., *Spain* 36 C7
Llera, *Mexico* 115 C5
Llerena, *Spain* 31 G4
Llica, *Bolivia* 124 D4
Llico, *Chile* 126 C1
Llobregat →, *Spain* 28 D7
Lloret de Mar, *Spain* 28 D7
Lloyd B., *Australia* 90 A3
Lloyd L., *Canada* 101 B7
Lloydminster, *Canada* 101 C6
Lluchmayor, *Spain* 36 B9
Llullaillaco, Volcán, *S. Amer.* 126 A2
Lo, *Belgium* 17 G1
Lo →, *Vietnam* 58 B5
Loa, *U.S.A.* 111 G8
Loa →, *Chile* 126 A1
Loano, *Italy* 32 D5
Lobatse, *Botswana* 84 D4
Löbau, *Germany* 18 D10

Lobbes, *Belgium* 17 H4
Lobenstein, *Germany* 18 E7
Lobería, *Argentina* 126 D4
Lobito, *Angola* 81 G2
Lobón, Canal de, *Spain* 31 G4
Lobos, *Argentina* 126 D4
Lobos, I., *Mexico* 114 B2
Lobos, Is., *Peru* 118 C1
Lobos, I. de, *Canary Is.* 36 F6
Lobos de Tierra, I., *Peru* 124 B1
Loc Binh, *Vietnam* 58 B6
Loc Ninh, *Vietnam* 59 G6
Locarno, *Switz.* 23 D7
Lochaber, *U.K.* 14 E4
Lochcarron, *U.K.* 14 D3
Lochem, *Neths.* 16 D8
Loches, *France* 24 E8
Lochgelly, *U.K.* 14 E5
Lochgilphead, *U.K.* 14 E3
Lochinver, *U.K.* 14 C3
Lochnagar, *Australia* 90 C4
Lochnagar, *U.K.* 14 E5
Łochów, *Poland* 20 C11
Lochy →, *U.K.* 14 E3
Lock, *Australia* 91 E2
Lock Haven, *U.S.A.* 106 E7
Lockeford, *U.S.A.* 112 G5
Lockeport, *Canada* 99 D6
Lockerbie, *U.K.* 14 F5
Lockhart, *U.S.A.* 109 L6
Lockhart, L., *Australia* 89 F2
Lockney, *U.S.A.* 109 H4
Lockport, *U.S.A.* 106 C6
Locminé, *France* 24 E4
Locri, *Italy* 35 D9
Locronan, *France* 24 D2
Loctudy, *France* 24 E2
Lod, *Israel* 69 D3
Lodève, *France* 26 E7
Lodge Grass, *U.S.A.* 110 D10
Lodgepole, *U.S.A.* 108 E3
Lodgepole Cr. →, *U.S.A.* 108 E2
Lodhran, *Pakistan* 62 E4
Lodi, *Italy* 32 C6
Lodi, *U.S.A.* 112 G5
Lodja, *Zaïre* 82 C1
Lodosa, *Spain* 28 C2
Lödöse, *Sweden* 11 F6
Lodwar, *Kenya* 82 B4
Łódź, *Poland* 20 D9
Loei, *Thailand* 58 D3
Loenen, *Neths.* 16 D8
Loengo, *Zaïre* 82 C2
Loeriesfontein, *S. Africa* 84 E2
Lofoten, *Norway* 8 B13
Lofsdalen, *Sweden* 10 B7
Lofsen →, *Sweden* 10 B7
Logan, *Kans., U.S.A.* 108 F5
Logan, *Ohio, U.S.A.* 104 F4
Logan, *Utah, U.S.A.* 110 F8
Logan, *W. Va., U.S.A.* 104 G5
Logan, Mt., *Canada* 96 B5
Logan Pass, *U.S.A.* 100 D6
Logandale, *U.S.A.* 113 J12
Logansport, *Ind., U.S.A.* 104 E2
Logansport, *La., U.S.A.* 109 K8
Logo, *Sudan* 77 F3
Logone →, *Chad* 73 F8
Logroño, *Spain* 28 C2
Logrosán, *Spain* 31 F5
Løgstør, *Denmark* 11 H3
Lohardaga, *India* 63 H11
Lohr, *Germany* 19 F5
Loi-kaw, *Burma* 61 K20
Loimaa, *Finland* 9 F17
Loir →, *France* 24 E6
Loir-et-Cher □, *France* 24 E8
Loire □, *France* 27 C8
Loire →, *France* 24 E4
Loire-Atlantique □, *France* 24 E5
Loiret □, *France* 25 E9
Loitz, *Germany* 18 B9
Loja, *Ecuador* 124 A2
Loja, *Spain* 31 H6
Loja □, *Ecuador* 120 D2
Loji, *Indonesia* 57 E7
Loka, *Sudan* 77 G3
Lokandu, *Zaïre* 82 C2
Løken, *Norway* 10 E5
Lokeren, *Belgium* 17 F3
Lokhvitsa, *Ukraine* 40 F8
Lokichokio, *Kenya* 82 B3
Lokitaung, *Kenya* 82 B4
Lokka, *Finland* 8 C19
Løkken, *Denmark* 11 G3
Løkken Verk, *Norway* 10 A3
Loknya, *Russia* 40 C7
Lokoja, *Nigeria* 79 D6
Lokolama, *Zaïre* 80 E3
Lol →, *Sudan* 77 F2
Lola, *Guinea* 78 D3
Lola, Mt., *U.S.A.* 112 F6
Lolibai, Gebel, *Sudan* 77 G3
Lolimi, *Sudan* 77 G3
Loliondo, *Tanzania* 82 C4
Lolland, *Denmark* 11 K5
Lollar, *Germany* 18 E4
Lolo, *U.S.A.* 110 C6
Lolodorf, *Cameroon* 79 E7
Lom, *Bulgaria* 38 F6
Lom →, *Bulgaria* 38 F6
Lom Kao, *Thailand* 58 D3
Lom Sak, *Thailand* 58 D3
Loma, *U.S.A.* 110 C8
Loma Linda, *U.S.A.* 113 L9
Lomami →, *Zaïre* 82 B1
Lomas de Zamóra, *Argentina* 126 C4
Lombadina, *Australia* 88 C3
Lombardia □, *Italy* 32 C6
Lombardy = Lombardia □, *Italy* 32 C6
Lombez, *France* 26 E4
Lomblen, *Indonesia* 57 F6
Lombok, *Indonesia* 56 F5
Lomé, *Togo* 79 D5
Lomela, *Zaïre* 80 E4
Lomela →, *Zaïre* 80 E4
Lomello, *Italy* 32 C5
Lometa, *U.S.A.* 109 K5
Lomié, *Cameroon* 80 D2
Lomma, *Sweden* 11 J7
Lomme →, *Belgium* 17 H6
Lommel, *Belgium* 17 F6
Lomond, *Canada* 100 C6
Lomond, L., *U.K.* 14 E4
Lomonosov, *Russia* 40 B6
Lomphat, *Cambodia* 58 F6
Lompobatang, *Indonesia* 57 F5
Lompoc, *U.S.A.* 113 L6
Lomsegga, *Norway* 10 C2
Łomza, *Poland* 20 B12
Loncoche, *Chile* 128 A2
Loncopuè, *Argentina* 128 A2
Londa, *India* 60 M9
Londerzeel, *Belgium* 17 G4
Londiani, *Kenya* 82 C4
Londinières, *France* 24 C8
London, *Canada* 98 D3
London, *U.K.* 13 F7
London, *Ky., U.S.A.* 104 G3
London, *Ohio, U.S.A.* 104 F4
London, Greater □, *U.K.* 13 F7
Londonderry, *U.K.* 15 B4
Londonderry □, *U.K.* 15 B4
Londonderry, C., *Australia* 88 B4
Londonderry, I., *Chile* 128 E2
Londrina, *Brazil* 127 A5
Lone Pine, *U.S.A.* 111 H4
Long Beach, *Calif., U.S.A.* 113 M8
Long Beach, *N.Y., U.S.A.* 107 F11
Long Beach, *Wash., U.S.A.* 112 D2
Long Branch, *U.S.A.* 107 F11
Long Creek, *U.S.A.* 110 D4
Long Eaton, *U.K.* 12 E6
Long I., *Australia* 90 C4
Long I., *Bahamas* 117 B4
Long I., *U.S.A.* 107 F11
Long Island Sd., *U.S.A.* 107 E12
Long L., *Canada* 98 C2
Long Lake, *U.S.A.* 107 C10
Long Pine, *U.S.A.* 108 D5
Long Pt., *Nfld., Canada* 99 C8
Long Pt., *Ont., Canada* 106 D4
Long Point B., *Canada* 106 D4
Long Range Mts., *Canada* 99 C8
Long Reef, *Australia* 88 B4
Long Str. = Longa, Proliv, *Russia* 4 C16
Long Thanh, *Vietnam* 59 G6
Long Xian, *China* 50 G4
Long Xuyen, *Vietnam* 59 G5
Longá, *Greece* 39 N4
Longa, Proliv, *Russia* 4 C16
Long'an, *China* 52 F6
Longarone, *Italy* 33 B9
Longchang, *China* 52 C5
Longchi, *China* 52 C4
Longchuan, *Guangdong, China* 53 E10
Longchuan, *Yunnan, China* 52 E1
Longde, *China* 50 G4
Longeau, *France* 25 E12
Longford, *Australia* 90 G4
Longford, *Ireland* 15 C4
Longford □, *Ireland* 15 C4
Longguan, *China* 50 D8
Longhua, *China* 51 D9
Longhui, *China* 53 D8
Longido, *Tanzania* 82 C4
Longiram, *Indonesia* 56 E5
Longkou, *Jiangxi, China* 53 D10
Longkou, *Shandong, China* 51 F11
Longlac, *Canada* 98 C2
Longli, *China* 52 D6
Longlier, *Belgium* 17 J6
Longlin, *China* 52 E5
Longling, *China* 52 E2
Longmen, *China* 53 F10
Longming, *China* 52 F6
Longmont, *U.S.A.* 108 E2
Longnan, *China* 53 E10
Longnawan, *Indonesia* 56 D4
Longobucco, *Italy* 35 C9
Longquan, *China* 53 C12
Longreach, *Australia* 90 C3
Longshan, *China* 52 C7
Longsheng, *China* 53 E8
Longton, *Australia* 90 C4
Longtown, *U.K.* 13 F5
Longué-Jumelles, *France* 24 E6
Longueau, *France* 25 C9
Longueuil, *Canada* 107 A11
Longuyon, *France* 25 C12
Longview, *Canada* 100 C6
Longview, *Tex., U.S.A.* 109 J7
Longview, *Wash., U.S.A.* 112 D4
Longvilly, *Belgium* 17 H7
Longwy, *France* 25 C12
Longxi, *China* 50 G3
Longyou, *China* 53 C12
Longzhou, *China* 52 F6
Lonigo, *Italy* 33 C8
Löningen, *Germany* 18 C3
Lonja →, *Croatia* 33 C13
Lonoke, *U.S.A.* 109 H9
Lonquimay, *Chile* 128 A2
Lons-le-Saunier, *France* 25 F12
Lønstrup, *Denmark* 11 G3
Lookout, C., *U.S.A.* 105 H7
Lookout, C., *Canada* 98 A3
Loolmalasin, *Tanzania* 82 C4
Loon →, *Alta., Canada* 100 B5
Loon →, *Man., Canada* 101 B8
Loon Lake, *Canada* 101 C7
Loon-op-Zand, *Neths.* 17 E6
Loongana, *Australia* 89 F4
Loop Hd., *Ireland* 15 D2
Loosduinen, *Neths.* 16 D4
Lop Buri, *Thailand* 58 E3
Lop Nor = Lop Nur, *China* 54 B4
Lop Nur, *China* 54 B4
Lopare, *Bos.-H.* 21 L8
Lopatin, *Russia* 43 E12
Lopatina, G., *Russia* 45 D15
Lopaye, *Sudan* 77 F3
Lopera, *Spain* 31 H6
Lopez, *Phil.* 55 E5
Lopez, C., *Gabon* 80 E1
Loppersum, *Neths.* 16 B9
Lopphavet, *Norway* 8 A16
Lora →, *Afghan.* 60 D4
Lora, Hamun-i-, *Pakistan* 60 E4
Lora Cr. →, *Australia* 91 D2
Lora del Río, *Spain* 31 H5
Lorain, *U.S.A.* 106 E2
Loralai, *Pakistan* 62 D3
Lorca, *Spain* 29 H3
Lord Howe I., *Pac. Oc.* 92 L7
Lord Howe Ridge, *Pac. Oc.* 92 L8
Lordsburg, *U.S.A.* 111 K9
Loreto, *Bolivia* 125 D5
Loreto, *Brazil* 122 C2
Loreto, *Italy* 33 E10
Loreto, *Mexico* 114 B2
Loreto □, *Peru* 120 D3
Loreto Aprutina, *Italy* 33 F10
Lorgues, *France* 27 E10
Lorica, *Colombia* 120 B2
Lorient, *France* 24 E3
Lorn, *U.K.* 14 E3
Lorn, Firth of, *U.K.* 14 E3
Lorne, *Australia* 91 F3
Lorovouno, *Cyprus* 37 D11
Lörrach, *Germany* 19 H3
Lorraine, *France* 25 D12
Lorrainville, *Canada* 98 C4
Los, Îles de, *Guinea* 78 D2
Los Alamos, *Calif., U.S.A.* 113 L6
Los Alamos, *N. Mex., U.S.A.* 111 J10
Los Altos, *U.S.A.* 112 H4
Los Andes, *Chile* 126 C1
Los Angeles, *Chile* 126 D1
Los Angeles, *U.S.A.* 113 L8
Los Angeles Aqueduct, *U.S.A.* 113 K9
Los Antiguos, *Argentina* 128 C2
Los Banos, *U.S.A.* 111 H3
Los Barrios, *Spain* 31 J5
Los Blancos, *Argentina* 126 A3
Los Cristianos, *Canary Is.* 36 F3
Los Gatos, *U.S.A.* 112 H5
Los Hermanos, *Venezuela* 117 D7
Los Islotes, *Canary Is.* 36 E6
Los Lagos, *Chile* 128 A2
Los Llanos de Aridane, *Canary Is.* 36 F2
Los Lomas, *Peru* 124 A1
Los Lunas, *U.S.A.* 111 J10
Los Menucos, *Argentina* 128 B3
Los Mochis, *Mexico* 114 B3
Los Monegros, *Spain* 28 D4
Los Monos, *Argentina* 128 C3
Los Olivos, *U.S.A.* 113 L6
Los Palacios, *Cuba* 116 B3
Los Palacios y Villafranca, *Spain* 31 H5
Los Reyes, *Mexico* 114 D4
Los Ríos □, *Ecuador* 120 D2
Los Roques, *Venezuela* 120 A4
Los Santos de Maimona, *Spain* 31 G4
Los Teques, *Venezuela* 120 A4
Los Testigos, *Venezuela* 121 A5
Los Vilos, *Chile* 126 C1
Los Yébenes, *Spain* 31 F7
Losada →, *Colombia* 120 C3
Loshkalakh, *Russia* 45 C15
Lošinj, *Croatia* 33 D11
Losser, *Neths.* 16 D10
Lossiemouth, *U.K.* 14 D5
Lot □, *France* 26 D5
Lot →, *France* 26 D4
Lot-et-Garonne □, *France* 26 D4
Lota, *Chile* 126 D1
Løten, *Norway* 10 D5
Loţfābād, *Iran* 65 B8
Lothair, *S. Africa* 85 D5
Lothian □, *U.K.* 14 F5
Lothiers, *France* 25 F8
Lötschbergtunnel, *Switz.* 22 D5
Lottefors, *Sweden* 10 C10
Lotzwil, *Switz.* 22 B5
Loubomo, *Congo* 80 E2
Loudéac, *France* 24 D4
Loudi, *China* 53 D8
Loudon, *U.S.A.* 105 H3
Loudonville, *U.S.A.* 106 F2
Loudun, *France* 24 E7
Loué, *France* 24 E6
Loue →, *France* 25 E12
Louga, *Senegal* 78 B1
Loughborough, *U.K.* 12 E6
Loughrea, *Ireland* 15 C3
Loughros More B., *Ireland* 15 B3
Louhans, *France* 27 B9
Louis Trichardt, *S. Africa* 85 C4
Louis XIV, Pte., *Canada* 98 B4
Louisa, *U.S.A.* 104 F4
Louisbourg, *Canada* 99 C8
Louise I., *Canada* 100 C2
Louiseville, *Canada* 98 C5
Louisiade Arch., *Papua N. G.* 92 J7
Louisiana, *U.S.A.* 108 F9
Louisiana □, *U.S.A.* 109 K9
Louisville, *Ky., U.S.A.* 104 F3
Louisville, *Miss., U.S.A.* 109 J10
Loulay, *France* 26 B3
Loulé, *Portugal* 31 H2
Louny, *Czech.* 20 E3
Loup City, *U.S.A.* 108 E5
Lourdes, *France* 26 E3
Lourdes-du-Blanc-Sablon, *Canada* 99 B8
Lourenço, *Brazil* 121 C7
Lourenço-Marques = Maputo, *Mozam.* 85 D5
Loures, *Portugal* 31 G1
Lourinhã, *Portugal* 31 F1
Lousã, *Portugal* 30 E2
Louth, *Australia* 91 E4
Louth, *Ireland* 15 C5
Louth, *U.K.* 12 D7
Louth □, *Ireland* 15 C5
Louvain = Leuven, *Belgium* 17 G5
Louveigné, *Belgium* 17 G7
Louviers, *France* 24 C8
Louwsburg, *S. Africa* 85 D5
Lovat →, *Russia* 40 B7
Love, *Canada* 101 C8
Lovech, *Bulgaria* 38 F7
Loveland, *U.S.A.* 108 E2
Lovell, *U.S.A.* 110 D9
Lovelock, *U.S.A.* 110 F4
Lóvere, *Italy* 32 C7
Loviisa = Lovisa, *Finland* 9 F19
Loving, *U.S.A.* 109 J2
Lovington, *U.S.A.* 109 J3
Lovios, *Spain* 30 D2
Lovisa, *Finland* 9 F19
Lovran, *Croatia* 33 C11
Low Pt., *Australia* 89 F4
Low Tatra = Nízké Tatry, *Slovak Rep.* 20 G9
Lowa, *Zaïre* 82 C2
Lowa →, *Zaïre* 82 C2
Lowell, *U.S.A.* 107 D13
Lower Arrow L., *Canada* 100 D5
Lower California = Baja California, *Mexico* 114 A1
Lower California = California, Baja, *Mexico* 114 A1
Lower Hutt, *N.Z.* 87 J5
Lower L., *U.S.A.* 110 F3
Lower Lake, *U.S.A.* 112 G4
Lower Post, *Canada* 100 B3
Lower Red L., *U.S.A.* 108 B7
Lower Saxony = Niedersachsen □, *Germany* 18 C5
Lower Tunguska = Tunguska, Nizhnyaya →, *Russia* 45 C9
Lowestoft, *U.K.* 13 E9
Łowicz, *Poland* 20 C9
Lowville, *U.S.A.* 107 C9
Loxton, *Australia* 91 E3
Loxton, *S. Africa* 84 E3
Loyalton, *U.S.A.* 112 F6
Loyalty Is. = Loyauté, Is., *N. Cal.* 92 K8
Loyang = Luoyang, *China* 50 G7
Loyauté, Is., *N. Cal.* 92 K8
Loyev, *Belorussia* 40 F7
Loyoro, *Uganda* 82 B3
Lož, *Slovenia* 33 C11
Lozère □, *France* 26 D7
Loznica, *Serbia* 21 L9
Lozovaya, *Ukraine* 42 B7
Luachimo, *Angola* 80 F4
Luacono, *Angola* 80 G4
Lualaba →, *Zaïre* 82 B5
Luampa, *Zambia* 83 F1
Lu'an, *China* 53 B11
Luan Chau, *Vietnam* 58 B4
Luan He →, *China* 51 E10
Luan Xian, *China* 51 E10
Luancheng, *Guangxi Zhuangzu, China* 52 F7
Luancheng, *Hebei, China* 50 F8
Luanda, *Angola* 80 F2
Luang Prabang, *Laos* 58 C4
Luang Thale, *Thailand* 59 J3
Luangwa, *Zambia* 83 F3
Luangwa →, *Zambia* 83 E3
Luangwa Valley, *Zambia* 83 E3
Luanne, *China* 51 D9
Luanping, *China* 51 D9
Luanshya, *Zambia* 83 E2
Luapula □, *Zambia* 83 E2
Luapula →, *Africa* 83 D2
Luarca, *Spain* 30 B4
Luashi, *Zaïre* 83 E1
Luau, *Angola* 80 G4
Lubalo, *Angola* 80 F3
Lubań, *Poland* 20 D5
Lubana, Ozero, *Latvia* 40 C5
Lubang, *Phil.* 55 E4
Lubang Is., *Phil.* 57 B6
Lubartów, *Poland* 20 D12
Lubawa, *Poland* 20 B9
Lubbeek, *Belgium* 17 G5
Lübben, *Germany* 18 D9
Lübbenau, *Germany* 18 D9
Lubbock, *U.S.A.* 109 J4
Lübeck, *Germany* 18 B6
Lübecker Bucht, *Germany* 18 A7
Lubefu, *Zaïre* 82 C1
Lubefu →, *Zaïre* 82 C1
Lubero = Luofu, *Zaïre* 82 C2
Lubicon L., *Canada* 100 B5
Lublin, *Poland* 20 D12
Lubliniec, *Poland* 20 E8
Lubnān, J., *Lebanon* 69 B4
Lubny, *Ukraine* 40 F8
Lubon, *Poland* 20 C6
Lubongola, *Zaïre* 82 C2
Lubsko, *Poland* 20 D4
Lübtheen, *Germany* 18 B7
Lubuagan, *Phil.* 55 C4
Lubudi →, *Zaïre* 83 D2
Lubuk Antu, *Malaysia* 56 D4
Lubuklinggau, *Indonesia* 56 E2
Lubuksikaping, *Indonesia* 56 D2
Lubumbashi, *Zaïre* 83 E2
Lubunda, *Zaïre* 82 D2
Lubungu, *Zambia* 83 E2
Lubutu, *Zaïre* 82 C2
Luc An Chau, *Vietnam* 58 A5
Luc-en-Diois, *France* 27 D9
Lucan, *Canada* 106 C3
Lucban, *Phil.* 55 D4
Lucca, *Italy* 32 E7
Luce Bay, *U.K.* 14 G4
Lucea, *Jamaica* 116 C4
Lucedale, *U.S.A.* 105 K1
Lucena, *Phil.* 55 E4
Lucena, *Spain* 31 H6
Lucena del Cid, *Spain* 28 E4
Lučenec, *Slovak Rep.* 21 G9
Lucens, *Switz.* 22 C3
Lucera, *Italy* 35 A8
Lucerne = Luzern, *Switz.* 23 B6
Lucerne, *U.S.A.* 112 F4
Lucerne Valley, *U.S.A.* 113 L10
Lucero, *Mexico* 114 A3
Luchena →, *Spain* 29 H3
Lucheng, *China* 50 F7
Lucheringo →, *Mozam.* 83 E4
Lüchow, *Germany* 18 C7
Luchuan, *China* 53 F8
Lucie →, *Surinam* 121 C6
Lucira, *Angola* 81 G2
Luckau, *Germany* 18 D9
Luckenwalde, *Germany* 18 C9
Lucknow, *India* 63 F9
Luçon, *France* 26 B2
Lüda = Dalian, *China* 51 E11
Luda Kamchiya →, *Bulgaria* 38 F10
Ludbreg, *Croatia* 33 B13
Lüdenscheid, *Germany* 18 D3
Lüderitz, *Namibia* 84 D2
Ludewe □, *Tanzania* 83 D3
Ludhiana, *India* 62 D6
Ludian, *China* 52 D4
Luding Qiao, *China* 52 C4
Lüdinghausen, *Germany* 18 D3
Ludington, *U.S.A.* 104 D2
Ludlow, *U.K.* 13 E5
Ludlow, *Calif., U.S.A.* 113 L10
Ludlow, *Vt., U.S.A.* 107 C12
Ludus, *Romania* 38 C7
Ludvika, *Sweden* 9 F13
Ludwigsburg, *Germany* 19 G5
Ludwigshafen, *Germany* 19 F4
Ludwigslust, *Germany* 18 B7
Ludza, *Latvia* 40 C5
Luebo, *Zaïre* 80 F4
Lueki, *Zaïre* 82 C2
Luena, *Zaïre* 83 D2
Luena, *Zambia* 83 E3
Luepa, *Venezuela* 121 B5
Lüeyang, *China* 50 H4
Lufeng, *Guangdong, China* 53 F10
Lufeng, *Yunnan, China* 52 E4
Lufira →, *Zaïre* 83 D2
Lufkin, *U.S.A.* 109 K7
Lufupa, *Zaïre* 83 E1
Luga, *Russia* 40 B6
Luga →, *Russia* 40 B6
Lugang, *Taiwan* 53 E13
Lugano, *Switz.* 23 D7
Lugano, L. di, *Switz.* 23 E8
Lugansk, *Ukraine* 43 B8
Lugard's Falls, *Kenya* 82 C4
Lugela, *Mozam.* 83 F4
Lugenda →, *Mozam.* 83 E4
Lugh Ganana, *Somali Rep.* 68 G3
Lugnaquilla, *Ireland* 15 D5

Lugnvik, *Sweden* 10 B11
Lugo, *Italy* 33 D8
Lugo, *Spain* 30 B3
Lugo □, *Spain* 30 C3
Lugoj, *Romania* 38 D4
Lugones, *Spain* 30 B5
Lugovoye, *Kazakhstan* 44 E8
Luhansk = Lugansk, *Ukraine* 43 B8
Luhe, *China* 53 A12
Luhe -►, *Germany* 18 B6
Luhuo, *China* 52 B3
Luiana, *Angola* 84 B3
Luino, *Italy* 32 C5
Luís Correia, *Brazil* 122 B3
Luís Gonçalves, *Brazil* 122 C1
Luitpold Coast, *Antarctica* 5 D1
Luiza, *Zaïre* 80 F4
Luizi, *Zaïre* 82 D2
Luján, *Argentina* 126 C4
Lujiang, *China* 53 B11
Lukanga Swamp, *Zambia* 83 E2
Lukenie -►, *Zaïre* 80 E3
Lukhisaral, *India* 63 G12
Lŭki, *Bulgaria* 39 H7
Lukolela, *Equateur, Zaïre* 80 E3
Lukolela, *Kasai Or., Zaïre* 82 D1
Lukosi, *Zimbabwe* 83 F2
Lukovit, *Bulgaria* 38 F7
Łuków, *Poland* 20 D12
Lukoyanov, *Russia* 41 D14
Lule älv -►, *Sweden* 8 D17
Luleå, *Sweden* 8 D17
Lüleburgaz, *Turkey* 39 H10
Luliang, *China* 52 E4
Luling, *U.S.A.* 109 L6
Lulong, *China* 51 E10
Lulonga -►, *Zaïre* 80 D3
Lulua -►, *Zaïre* 80 E4
Luluabourg = Kananga, *Zaïre* 80 F4
Lumai, *Angola* 81 G4
Lumajang, *Indonesia* 57 H15
Lumbala N'guimbo, *Angola* 81 G4
Lumberton, *Miss., U.S.A.* 109 K10
Lumberton, *N.C., U.S.A.* 105 H6
Lumberton, *N. Mex., U.S.A.* 111 H10
Lumbres, *France* 25 B9
Lumbwa, *Kenya* 82 C4
Lummen, *Belgium* 17 G6
Lumsden, *N.Z.* 87 L2
Lumut, *Malaysia* 59 K3
Lumut, Tg., *Indonesia* 56 E3
Luna, *Phil.* 55 C4
Lunan, *China* 52 E4
Lunavada, *India* 62 H5
Lunca, *Romania* 38 B8
Lund, *Sweden* 11 J7
Lund, *U.S.A.* 110 G6
Lundazi, *Zambia* 83 E3
Lunde, *Norway* 10 E3
Lunderskov, *Denmark* 11 J3
Lundi -►, *Zimbabwe* 83 G3
Lundu, *Malaysia* 56 D3
Lundy, *U.K.* 13 F3
Lune -►, *U.K.* 12 C5
Lüneburg, *Germany* 18 B6
Lüneburg Heath = Lüneburger Heide, *Germany* 18 C6
Lüneburger Heide, *Germany* 18 C6
Lunel, *France* 27 E8
Lünen, *Germany* 18 D3
Lunenburg, *Canada* 99 D7
Lunéville, *France* 25 D13
Lunga -►, *Zambia* 83 E2
Lungern, *Switz.* 22 C6
Lungi Airport, *S. Leone* 78 D2
Lunglei, *India* 61 H18
Luni, *India* 62 F5
Luni -►, *India* 62 G4
Luninets, *Belorussia* 40 E5
Luning, *U.S.A.* 110 G4
Lunino, *Russia* 41 E14
Luninyets = Luninets, *Belorussia* 40 E5
Lunner, *Norway* 10 D4
Lunsemfwa -►, *Zambia* 83 E3
Lunsemfwa Falls, *Zambia* 83 E2
Lunteren, *Neths.* 16 D7
Luo He -►, *China* 50 G6
Luocheng, *China* 52 E7
Luochuan, *China* 50 G5
Luoci, *China* 52 E4
Luodian, *China* 52 E6
Luoding, *China* 53 F8
Luodong, *Taiwan* 53 E13
Luofu, *Zaïre* 82 C2
Luohe, *China* 50 H8
Luojiang, *China* 52 B5
Luonan, *China* 50 G6
Luoning, *China* 50 G6
Luoshan, *China* 53 A10
Luotian, *China* 53 B10
Luoyang, *China* 50 G7
Luoyuan, *China* 53 D12
Luozi, *Zaïre* 80 E2
Luozigou, *China* 51 C16
Lupeni, *Romania* 38 D6
Lupilichi, *Mozam.* 83 E4
Lupoing, *China* 52 E5
Luquan, *China* 52 E4
Luque, *Paraguay* 126 B4
Luque, *Spain* 31 H6
Luray, *U.S.A.* 104 F6
Lure, *France* 25 E13
Luremo, *Angola* 80 F3
Lurgan, *U.K.* 15 B5
Luribay, *Bolivia* 124 D4
Lurin, *Peru* 124 C2
Lusaka, *Zambia* 83 F2
Lusambo, *Zaïre* 82 C1
Lusangaye, *Zaïre* 82 C2
Luseland, *Canada* 101 C7
Lushan, *Henan, China* 50 H7
Lushan, *Sichuan, China* 52 B4
Lushi, *China* 50 G6
Lushnja, *Albania* 39 J2
Lushoto, *Tanzania* 82 C4
Lushoto □, *Tanzania* 82 C4
Lushui, *China* 52 E2
Lüshun, *China* 51 E11
Lusignan, *France* 26 B4
Lusigny-sur-Barse, *France* 25 D11
Lusk, *U.S.A.* 108 D2
Lussac-les-Châteaux, *France* 26 B4
Lussanvira, *Brazil* 123 F1
Luta = Dalian, *China* 51 E11
Luton, *U.K.* 13 F7
Lutong, *Malaysia* 56 D4
Lutry, *Switz.* 22 C3
Lutsk, *Ukraine* 40 F4
Lützow Holmbukta, *Antarctica* 5 C4
Lutzputs, *S. Africa* 84 D3
Luverne, *U.S.A.* 108 D6
Luvua, *Zaïre* 83 D2
Luvua -►, *Zaïre* 82 D2
Luwegu -►, *Tanzania* 83 D4
Luwuk, *Indonesia* 57 E6
Luxembourg, *Lux.* 17 J8
Luxembourg □, *Belgium* 17 J7
Luxembourg ■, *Europe* 17 J8
Luxeuil-les-Bains, *France* 25 E13
Luxi, *Hunan, China* 53 C8
Luxi, *Yunnan, China* 52 E4
Luxi, *Yunnan, China* 52 E2
Luxor = El Uqsur, *Egypt* 76 B3
Luy -►, *France* 26 E2
Luy-de-Béarn -►, *France* 26 E3
Luy-de-France -►, *France* 26 E3
Luyi, *China* 50 H8
Luyksgestel, *Neths.* 17 F6
Luz-St.-Sauveur, *France* 26 F4
Luzern, *Switz.* 23 B6
Luzern □, *Switz.* 22 B5
Luzhai, *China* 52 E7
Luzhou, *China* 52 C5
Luziânia, *Brazil* 123 E2
Luzilândia, *Brazil* 122 B3
Luzon, *Phil.* 55 D4
Luzy, *France* 25 F10
Luzzi, *Italy* 35 C9
Lviv = Lvov, *Ukraine* 40 G4
Lvov, *Ukraine* 40 G4
Lyakhovichi, *Belorussia* 40 E5
Lyakhovskiye, Ostrova, *Russia* 45 B15
Lyaki, *Azerbaijan* 43 F12
Lyallpur = Faisalabad, *Pakistan* 62 D5
Lycaonia, *Turkey* 66 D5
Lychen, *Germany* 18 B9
Lycia, *Turkey* 66 E3
Lycksele, *Sweden* 8 D15
Lydda = Lod, *Israel* 69 D3
Lydenburg, *S. Africa* 85 D5
Lydia, *Turkey* 66 D3
Lyell, *N.Z.* 87 J4
Lyell I., *Canada* 100 C2
Lygnern, *Sweden* 11 G6
Lyman, *U.S.A.* 110 F8
Lyme Regis, *U.K.* 13 G5
Lymington, *U.K.* 13 G6
Lynchburg, *U.S.A.* 104 G6
Lynd -►, *Australia* 90 B3
Lynd Ra., *Australia* 91 D4
Lynden, *Canada* 106 C4
Lynden, *U.S.A.* 112 B4
Lyndhurst, *Queens., Australia* 90 B3
Lyndhurst, *S. Austral., Australia* 91 E2
Lyndon -►, *Australia* 89 D1
Lyndonville, *N.Y., U.S.A.* 106 C6
Lyndonville, *Vt., U.S.A.* 107 B12
Lyngdal, *Norway* 10 E3
Lynher Reef, *Australia* 88 C3
Lynn, *U.S.A.* 107 D14
Lynn Canal, *U.S.A.* 100 B1
Lynn Lake, *Canada* 101 B8
Lynnwood, *U.S.A.* 112 C4
Lynton, *U.K.* 13 F4
Lyntupy, *Belorussia* 40 D5
Lynx L., *Canada* 101 A7
Lyø, *Denmark* 11 J4
Lyon, *France* 27 C8
Lyonnais, *France* 27 C8
Lyons = Lyon, *France* 27 C8
Lyons, *Colo., U.S.A.* 108 E2
Lyons, *Ga., U.S.A.* 105 J4
Lyons, *Kans., U.S.A.* 108 F5
Lyons, *N.Y., U.S.A.* 106 C8
Lyrestad, *Sweden* 11 F8
Lys = Leie -►, *Belgium* 25 A10
Lysekil, *Sweden* 11 F5
Lyskovo, *Russia* 41 D14
Lyss, *Switz.* 22 B4
Lytle, *U.S.A.* 109 L5
Lyttelton, *N.Z.* 87 K4
Lytton, *Canada* 100 C4
Lyuban, *Russia* 40 B7
Lyubcha, *Belorussia* 40 E5
Lyubertsy, *Russia* 41 D10
Lyubim, *Russia* 41 B12
Lyuboml, *Ukraine* 40 F4
Lyubotin, *Ukraine* 42 B6
Lyubytino, *Russia* 40 B8
Lyudinovo, *Russia* 40 E9

M

Ma -►, *Vietnam* 58 C5
Ma'adaba, *Jordan* 69 E4
Maamba, *Zambia* 84 B4
Ma'ān, *Jordan* 69 E4
Ma'ān □, *Jordan* 69 F5
Ma'anshan, *China* 53 B12
Maarheeze, *Neths.* 17 F7
Maarianhamina, *Finland* 9 F15
Maarn, *Neths.* 16 D6
Ma'arrat an Nu'mān, *Syria* 64 C3
Maarssen, *Neths.* 16 D6
Maartensdijk, *Neths.* 16 D6
Maas -►, *Neths.* 16 E5
Maasbracht, *Belgium* 17 F7
Maasbree, *Neths.* 17 F8
Maasdam, *Neths.* 16 E5
Maasdijk, *Neths.* 16 E4
Maaseik, *Belgium* 17 F7
Maasland, *Neths.* 16 E4
Maasniel, *Neths.* 17 F8
Maassluis, *Neths.* 16 E4
Maastricht, *Neths.* 17 G7
Maave, *Mozam.* 85 C5
Mabaruma, *Guyana* 121 B6
Mabel L., *Canada* 100 C5
Mabenge, *Zaïre* 82 B1
Mabian, *China* 52 C4
Mablethorpe, *U.K.* 12 D8
Maboma, *Zaïre* 82 B2
Mabrouk, *Mali* 79 B4
Mabton, *U.S.A.* 110 C3
Mac Bac, *Vietnam* 59 H6
Macachín, *Argentina* 126 D3
Macaé, *Brazil* 123 F3
Macaíba, *Brazil* 122 C4
Macajuba, *Brazil* 123 D3
McAlester, *U.S.A.* 109 H7
McAllen, *U.S.A.* 109 M5
Macamic, *Canada* 98 C4
Macao = Macau ■, *China* 53 F9
Macão, *Portugal* 31 F3
Macapá, *Brazil* 121 C7
Macará, *Ecuador* 120 D2
Macarani, *Brazil* 123 E3
Macarena, Serranía de la, *Colombia* 120 C3
McArthur -►, *Australia* 90 B2
McArthur, Port, *Australia* 90 B2
McArthur River, *Australia* 90 B2
Macas, *Ecuador* 120 D2
Macate, *Peru* 124 B2
Macau, *Brazil* 122 C4
Macau ■, *China* 53 F9
Macaúbas, *Brazil* 123 D3
Macaya -►, *Colombia* 120 C3
McBride, *Canada* 100 C4
McCall, *U.S.A.* 110 D5
McCamey, *U.S.A.* 109 K3
McCammon, *U.S.A.* 110 E7
McCauley I., *Canada* 100 C2
McCleary, *U.S.A.* 112 C3
Macclesfield, *U.K.* 12 D5
McClintock, *Canada* 101 B10
McClintock Ra., *Australia* 88 C4
McCloud, *U.S.A.* 110 F2
McCluer I., *Australia* 88 B5
McClure, *U.S.A.* 106 F7
McClure, L., *U.S.A.* 112 H6
M'Clure Str., *Canada* 4 B2
McClusky, *U.S.A.* 108 B4
McComb, *U.S.A.* 109 K9
McConaughy, L., *U.S.A.* 108 E4
McCook, *U.S.A.* 108 E4
McCullough Mt., *U.S.A.* 113 K11
McCusker -►, *Canada* 101 B7
McDame, *Canada* 100 B3
McDermitt, *U.S.A.* 110 F5
Macdonald, L., *Australia* 88 D4
McDonald Is., *Ind. Oc.* 3 G13
Macdonnell Ras., *Australia* 88 D5
McDouall Peak, *Australia* 91 D1
Macdougall L., *Canada* 96 B10
MacDowell L., *Canada* 98 B1
Macduff, *U.K.* 14 D6
Maceda, *Spain* 30 C3
Macedonia ■, *Europe* 39 H4
Maceió, *Brazil* 122 C4
Maceira, *Portugal* 31 F2
Macenta, *Guinea* 78 D3
Macerata, *Italy* 33 E10
McFarland, *U.S.A.* 113 K7
McFarlane -►, *Canada* 101 B7
Macfarlane, L., *Australia* 91 E2
McGehee, *U.S.A.* 109 J9
McGill, *U.S.A.* 110 G6
Macgillycuddy's Reeks, *Ireland* 15 D2
MacGregor, *Canada* 101 D9
McGregor, *U.S.A.* 108 D9
McGregor -►, *Canada* 100 B4
McGregor Ra., *Australia* 91 D3
Mach, *Pakistan* 60 E5
Māch Kowr, *Iran* 65 E9
Machacalis, *Brazil* 123 E3
Machado = Jiparaná -►, *Brazil* 125 B5
Machagai, *Argentina* 126 B3
Machakos, *Kenya* 82 C4
Machakos □, *Kenya* 82 C4
Machala, *Ecuador* 120 D2
Machanga, *Mozam.* 85 C6
Machattie, L., *Australia* 90 C2
Machava, *Mozam.* 85 D5
Machece, *Mozam.* 83 F4
Machecoul, *France* 24 F5
Machelen, *Belgium* 17 G4
Macheng, *China* 53 B10
Machevna, *Russia* 45 C18
Machezo, *Spain* 31 F6
Machias, *U.S.A.* 99 D6
Machichaco, C., *Spain* 28 B2
Machichi -►, *Canada* 101 B10
Machico, *Madeira* 36 D3
Machilipatnam, *India* 61 L12
Machiques, *Venezuela* 120 A3
Machupicchu, *Peru* 124 C3
Machynlleth, *U.K.* 13 E4
McIlwraith Ra., *Australia* 90 A3
Măcin, *Romania* 38 D11
Macina, *Mali* 78 C4
McIntosh, *U.S.A.* 108 C4
McIntosh L., *Canada* 101 B8
Macintosh Ra., *Australia* 89 E4
Macintyre -►, *Australia* 91 D5
Macizo Galaico, *Spain* 30 C3
Mackay, *Australia* 90 C4
Mackay, *U.S.A.* 110 E7
MacKay -►, *Canada* 100 B6
Mackay, L., *Australia* 88 D4
McKay Ra., *Australia* 88 D3
McKeesport, *U.S.A.* 106 F5
McKenna, *U.S.A.* 112 D4
Mackenzie, *Canada* 100 B4
Mackenzie, *Guyana* 121 B6
McKenzie, *U.S.A.* 105 G1
Mackenzie -►, *Australia* 90 C4
Mackenzie -►, *Canada* 96 B6
McKenzie -►, *U.S.A.* 110 D2
Mackenzie Bay, *Canada* 4 B1
Mackenzie City = Linden, *Guyana* 121 B6
Mackenzie Highway, *Canada* 100 B5
Mackenzie Mts., *Canada* 96 B6
Mackinaw City, *U.S.A.* 104 C3
McKinlay, *Australia* 90 C3
McKinlay -►, *Australia* 90 C3
McKinley, Mt., *U.S.A.* 96 B4
McKinley Sea, *Arctic* 4 A7
McKinney, *U.S.A.* 109 J6
Mackinnon Road, *Kenya* 82 C4
Macksville, *Australia* 91 E5
McLaughlin, *U.S.A.* 108 C4
Maclean, *Australia* 91 D5
McLean, *U.S.A.* 109 H4
McLeansboro, *U.S.A.* 108 F10
Maclear, *S. Africa* 85 E4
Macleay -►, *Australia* 91 E5
McLennan, *Canada* 100 B5
MacLeod, B., *Canada* 101 A7
McLeod, L., *Australia* 89 D1
MacLeod Lake, *Canada* 100 C4
M'Clintock Chan., *Canada* 96 A9
McLoughlin, Mt., *U.S.A.* 110 E2
McLure, *Canada* 100 C4
McMechen, *U.S.A.* 106 G4
McMillan, L., *U.S.A.* 109 J2
McMinnville, *Oreg., U.S.A.* 110 D2
McMinnville, *Tenn., U.S.A.* 105 H3
McMorran, *Canada* 101 C7
McMurdo Sd., *Antarctica* 5 D11
McMurray = Fort McMurray, *Canada* 100 B6
McMurray, *U.S.A.* 112 B4
McNary, *U.S.A.* 111 J9
MacNutt, *Canada* 101 C8
Macodoene, *Mozam.* 85 C6
Macomb, *U.S.A.* 108 E9
Macomer, *Italy* 34 B1
Mâcon, *France* 27 B8
Macon, *Ga., U.S.A.* 105 J4
Macon, *Miss., U.S.A.* 105 J1
Macon, *Mo., U.S.A.* 108 F8
Macondo, *Angola* 81 G4
Macossa, *Mozam.* 83 F3
Macoun L., *Canada* 101 B8
Macovane, *Mozam.* 85 C6
McPherson, *U.S.A.* 108 F6
McPherson Pk., *U.S.A.* 113 L7
McPherson Ra., *Australia* 91 D5
Macquarie Harbour, *Australia* 90 G4
Macquarie Is., *Pac. Oc.* 92 N7
MacRobertson Land, *Antarctica* 5 D6
Macroom, *Ireland* 15 E3
Macroy, *Australia* 88 D2
MacTier, *Canada* 106 A5
Macubela, *Mozam.* 83 F4
Macugnaga, *Italy* 32 C4
Macuiza, *Mozam.* 83 F3
Macujer, *Colombia* 120 C3
Macusani, *Peru* 124 C3
Macuse, *Mozam.* 83 F4
Macuspana, *Mexico* 115 D6
Macusse, *Angola* 84 B3
McVille, *U.S.A.* 108 B5
Madadeni, *S. Africa* 85 D5
Madagali, *Nigeria* 79 C7
Madagascar ■, *Africa* 85 C8
Madā'in Sālih, *Si. Arabia* 64 E3
Madama, *Niger* 73 D7
Madame I., *Canada* 99 C7
Madaoua, *Niger* 79 C6
Madara, *Nigeria* 79 C7
Madaripur, *Bangla.* 61 H17
Madauk, *Burma* 61 L20
Madawaska, *Canada* 106 A7
Madawaska -►, *Canada* 98 C4
Madaya, *Burma* 61 H20
Madbar, *Sudan* 77 F3
Maddaloni, *Italy* 35 A7
Made, *Neths.* 17 E5
Madeira, *Atl. Oc.* 36 D3
Madeira -►, *Brazil* 121 D6
Madeleine, Is. de la, *Canada* 99 C7
Maden, *Turkey* 67 D8
Madera, *U.S.A.* 111 H3
Madha, *India* 60 L9
Madhubani, *India* 63 F12
Madhya Pradesh □, *India* 62 J7
Madian, *China* 53 A11
Madidi -►, *Bolivia* 124 C4
Madikeri, *India* 60 N9
Madill, *U.S.A.* 109 H6
Madimba, *Zaïre* 80 E3
Ma'din, *Syria* 64 C3
Madīnat ash Sha'b, *Yemen* 68 E3
Madingou, *Congo* 80 E2
Madirovalo, *Madag.* 85 B8
Madison, *Calif., U.S.A.* 112 G5
Madison, *Fla., U.S.A.* 105 K4
Madison, *Ind., U.S.A.* 104 F3
Madison, *Nebr., U.S.A.* 108 E6
Madison, *Ohio, U.S.A.* 106 E3
Madison, *S. Dak., U.S.A.* 108 D6
Madison, *Wis., U.S.A.* 108 D10
Madison -►, *U.S.A.* 110 D8
Madisonville, *Ky., U.S.A.* 104 G2
Madisonville, *Tex., U.S.A.* 109 K7
Madista, *Botswana* 84 C4
Madiun, *Indonesia* 57 G14
Madley, *U.K.* 13 E5
Madol, *Sudan* 77 F2
Madon -►, *France* 25 D13
Madona, *Latvia* 40 C5
Madras = Tamil Nadu □, *India* 60 P10
Madras, *India* 60 N12
Madras, *U.S.A.* 110 D3
Madre, L., *Mexico* 115 B5
Madre, Laguna, *U.S.A.* 109 M6
Madre, Sierra, *Phil.* 55 C5
Madre de Dios □, *Peru* 124 C3
Madre de Dios -►, *Bolivia* 124 C4
Madre de Dios, I., *Chile* 128 D1
Madre del Sur, Sierra, *Mexico* 115 D5
Madre Occidental, Sierra, *Mexico* 114 B3
Madre Oriental, Sierra, *Mexico* 114 C4
Madri, *India* 62 G5
Madrid, *Spain* 30 E7
Madrid □, *Spain* 30 E7
Madridejos, *Spain* 31 F7
Madrigal de las Altas Torres, *Spain* 30 D6
Madrona, Sierra, *Spain* 31 G6
Madroñera, *Spain* 31 F5
Madu, *Sudan* 77 E2
Madura, Selat, *Indonesia* 57 G15
Madura Motel, *Australia* 89 F4
Madurai, *India* 60 Q11
Madurantakam, *India* 60 N11
Madzhalis, *Russia* 43 E12
Mae Chan, *Thailand* 58 B2
Mae Hong Son, *Thailand* 58 C2
Mae Khlong -►, *Thailand* 58 F3
Mae Phrik, *Thailand* 58 D2
Mae Ramat, *Thailand* 58 D2
Mae Rim, *Thailand* 58 C2
Mae Sot, *Thailand* 58 D2
Mae Suai, *Thailand* 58 C2
Mae Tha, *Thailand* 58 C2
Maebashi, *Japan* 49 F9
Maella, *Spain* 28 D5
Măeruş, *Romania* 38 D8
Maesteg, *U.K.* 13 F4
Maestra, Sierra, *Cuba* 116 B4
Maestrazgo, Mts. del, *Spain* 28 E4
Maevatanana, *Madag.* 85 B8
Mafeking = Mafikeng, *S. Africa* 84 D4
Mafeking, *Canada* 101 C8
Maféré, *Ivory C.* 78 D4
Mafeteng, *Lesotho* 84 D4
Maffe, *Belgium* 17 H6
Maffra, *Australia* 91 F4
Mafia I., *Tanzania* 82 D4
Mafikeng, *S. Africa* 84 D4
Mafra, *Brazil* 127 B6
Mafra, *Portugal* 31 G1
Mafungabusi Plateau, *Zimbabwe* 83 F2

Magadan, Russia 45 D16
Magadi, Kenya 82 C4
Magadi, L., Kenya 82 C4
Magaliesburg, S. Africa .. 85 D4
Magallanes □, Chile 128 D2
Magallanes, Estrecho de, Chile 128 D2
Magangué, Colombia 120 B3
Magaria, Niger 79 C6
Magburaka, S. Leone 78 D2
Magdalen Is. = Madeleine, Is. de la, Canada 99 C7
Magdalena, Argentina 126 D4
Magdalena, Bolivia 125 C5
Magdalena, Malaysia 56 D5
Magdalena, Mexico 114 A2
Magdalena, U.S.A. 111 J10
Magdalena □, Colombia .. 120 A3
Magdalena →, Colombia .. 120 A3
Magdalena →, Mexico ... 114 A2
Magdalena, B., Mexico ... 114 C2
Magdalena, I., Chile 128 B2
Magdalena, Llano de la, Mexico 114 C2
Magdeburg, Germany 18 C7
Magdelaine Cays, Australia 90 B5
Magdub, Sudan 77 E2
Magee, U.S.A. 109 K10
Magee, I., U.K. 15 B6
Magelang, Indonesia 57 G14
Magellan's Str. = Magallanes, Estrecho de, Chile 128 D2
Magenta, Italy 32 C5
Magenta, L., Australia 89 F2
Maggia, Switz. 23 D7
Maggia →, Switz. 23 D7
Maggiorasca, Mte., Italy .. 32 D6
Maggiore, L., Italy 32 C5
Maghama, Mauritania 78 B2
Magherafelt, U.K. 15 B5
Maghnia, Algeria 75 B4
Magione, Italy 33 E9
Magliano in Toscana, Italy 33 F8
Máglie, Italy 35 B11
Magnac-Laval, France 26 B5
Magnetic Pole (North) = North Magnetic Pole, Canada 4 B2
Magnetic Pole (South) = South Magnetic Pole, Antarctica 5 C9
Magnitogorsk, Russia 44 D6
Magnolia, Ark., U.S.A. .. 109 J8
Magnolia, Miss., U.S.A. .. 109 K9
Magnor, Norway 10 E6
Magny-en-Vexin, France .. 25 C8
Magog, Canada 99 C5
Magoro, Uganda 82 B3
Magosa = Famagusta, Cyprus 37 D12
Magouládhes, Greece 37 A3
Magoye, Zambia 83 F2
Magpie L., Canada 99 B7
Magrath, Canada 100 D6
Magro →, Spain 29 F4
Magrur, Wadi →, Sudan . 77 D2
Magu □, Tanzania 82 C3
Maguan, China 52 F5
Maguarinho, C., Brazil .. 122 B2
Maguse L., Canada 101 A9
Maguse Pt., Canada 101 A10
Magwe, Burma 61 J19
Maha Sarakham, Thailand 58 D4
Mahābād, Iran 64 B5
Mahabharat Lekh, Nepal . 63 E9
Mahabo, Madag. 85 C7
Mahadeo Hills, India 62 H8
Mahagi, Zaïre 82 B3
Mahaicony, Guyana 121 B6
Mahajamba →, Madag. .. 85 B8
Mahajamba, Helodranon' i, Madag. 85 B8
Mahajan, India 62 E5
Mahajanga, Madag. 85 B8
Mahajanga □, Madag. 85 B8
Mahajilo →, Madag. 85 B8
Mahakam →, Indonesia .. 56 E5
Mahalapye, Botswana 84 C4
Maḥallāt, Iran 65 C6
Mahān, Iran 65 D8
Mahanadi →, India 61 J15
Mahanoro, Madag. 85 B8
Mahanoy City, U.S.A. 107 F8
Maharashtra □, India 60 J9
Maharès, Tunisia 75 B7
Mahari Mts., Tanzania .. 82 D2
Mahasham, W. →, Egypt 69 E3
Mahasolo, Madag. 85 B8
Mahattat ash Shīdīyah, Jordan 69 F4
Mahattat 'Unayzah, Jordan 69 E4
Mahaxay, Laos 58 D5
Mahbes, W. Sahara 74 C3
Mahbubnagar, India 60 L10
Maḥḏah, Oman 65 E7
Mahdia, Guyana 121 B6
Mahdia, Tunisia 75 A7
Mahe, India 63 C8
Mahenge, Tanzania 83 D4
Maheno, N.Z. 87 L3
Mahesana, India 62 H5
Mahia Pen., N.Z. 87 H6
Mahilyow = Mogilev, Belorussia 40 E7

Mahirija, Morocco 75 B4
Mahmiya, Sudan 77 D3
Mahmud Kot, Pakistan .. 62 D4
Mahmudia, Romania 38 D12
Mahnomen, U.S.A. 108 B7
Mahoba, India 63 G8
Mahón, Spain 36 B11
Mahone Bay, Canada 99 D7
Mahuta, Nigeria 79 C5
Mai-Ndombe, L., Zaïre .. 80 E3
Mai-Sai, Thailand 58 B2
Maicao, Colombia 120 A3
Maîche, France 25 E13
Maici →, Brazil 125 B5
Maicurú →, Brazil 121 D7
Máida, Italy 35 D9
Maidan Khula, Afghan. .. 62 C3
Maidenhead, U.K. 13 F7
Maidi, Yemen 77 D5
Maidstone, Canada 101 C7
Maidstone, U.K. 13 F8
Maiduguri, Nigeria 79 C7
Maignelay, France 25 C9
Maigo, Phil. 55 G5
Maigualida, Sierra, Venezuela 121 B4
Maigudo, Ethiopia 77 F4
Maijdi, Bangla. 61 H17
Maikala Ra., India 61 J12
Mailly-le-Camp, France .. 25 D11
Mailsi, Pakistan 62 E5
Main →, Germany 19 F4
Main →, U.K. 15 B5
Main Centre, Canada 101 C7
Mainburg, Germany 19 G7
Maine, France 24 E6
Maine □, U.S.A. 99 C6
Maine →, Ireland 15 D2
Maine-et-Loire □, France . 24 E6
Maïne-Soroa, Niger 79 C7
Maingkwan, Burma 61 F20
Mainit, L., Phil. 55 G6
Mainland, Orkney, U.K. .. 14 C5
Mainland, Shet., U.K. .. 14 A7
Mainpuri, India 63 F8
Maintenon, France 25 D8
Maintirano, Madag. 85 B7
Mainvault, Belgium 17 G3
Mainz, Germany 19 F4
Maipú, Argentina 126 D4
Maiquetía, Venezuela .. 120 A4
Maira →, Italy 32 D4
Mairabari, India 61 F18
Mairipotaba, Brazil 123 E2
Maisí, Cuba 117 B5
Maisi, Pta. de, Cuba 117 B5
Maisse, France 25 D9
Maissin, Belgium 17 J6
Maitland, N.S.W., Australia 91 E5
Maitland, S. Austral., Australia 91 E2
Maitland →, Canada 106 C3
Maiyema, Nigeria 79 C5
Maiyuan, China 53 E11
Maiz, Is. del, Nic. 116 D3
Maizuru, Japan 49 G7
Majagual, Colombia 120 B3
Majalengka, Indonesia .. 57 G13
Majari →, Brazil 121 C5
Majene, Indonesia 57 E5
Majes →, Peru 124 D3
Maji, Ethiopia 77 F4
Majiang, China 52 D6
Major, Canada 101 C7
Majorca = Mallorca, Spain 36 B10
Majuriã, Brazil 125 B5
Maka, Senegal 78 C2
Makak, Cameroon 79 E7
Makale, Indonesia 57 E5
Makamba, Burundi 82 C2
Makari, Cameroon 80 B2
Makarikari = Makgadikgadi Salt Pans, Botswana 84 C4
Makarovo, Russia 45 D11
Makarska, Croatia 21 M7
Makaryev, Russia 41 C13
Makasar = Ujung Pandang, Indonesia 57 F5
Makasar, Selat, Indonesia . 57 E5
Makasar, Str. of = Makasar, Selat, Indonesia 57 E5
Makat, Kazakhstan 44 E6
Makedonija = Macedonia ■, Europe .. 39 H4
Makena, U.S.A. 102 H16
Makeni, S. Leone 78 D2
Makeyevka, Ukraine 42 B7
Makgadikgadi Salt Pans, Botswana 84 C4
Makhachkala, Russia 43 E12
Makhambet, Kazakhstan . 43 C14
Makharadze = Ozurgety, Georgia 43 F10
Makhmūr, Iraq 64 C4
Makian, Indonesia 57 D7
Makindu, Kenya 82 C4
Makinsk, Kazakhstan 44 D8
Makiyivka = Makeyevka, Ukraine 42 B7
Makkah, Si. Arabia 68 C2
Makkovik, Canada 99 A8
Makkum, Neths. 16 B6
Makó, Hungary 21 J10
Makokou, Gabon 80 D2

Makongo, Zaïre 82 B2
Makoro, Zaïre 82 B2
Makoua, Congo 80 E3
Makrá, Greece 39 N8
Makrai, India 60 H10
Makran Coast Range, Pakistan 60 G8
Makrana, India 62 F6
Makriyialos, Greece 37 D7
Maksimkin Yar, Russia .. 44 D9
Maktar, Tunisia 75 A6
Mākū, Iran 64 B5
Makumbi, Zaïre 80 F4
Makunda, Botswana 84 C3
Makurazaki, Japan 49 J5
Makurdi, Nigeria 79 D6
Makūyeh, Iran 65 D7
Makwassie, S. Africa 84 D4
Mal B., Ireland 15 D2
Mal i Nemërçkës, Albania 39 J3
Mal i Tomorit, Albania .. 39 J3
Mala, Peru 124 C2
Mala, Pta., Panama 116 E3
Mala Kapela, Croatia 33 D12
Malabang, Phil. 55 H6
Malabar Coast, India 60 P9
Malabo = Rey Malabo, Eq. Guin. 79 E6
Malabon, Phil. 55 D4
Malacca, Str. of, Indonesia 59 L3
Malacky, Slovak Rep. .. 21 G7
Malad City, U.S.A. 110 E7
Maladzyechna = Molodechno, Belorussia 40 D5
Málaga, Colombia 120 B3
Málaga, Spain 31 J6
Málaga, U.S.A. 109 J2
Málaga □, Spain 31 J6
Malagarasi, Tanzania 82 D3
Malagarasi →, Tanzania . 82 D2
Malagón, Spain 31 F7
Malagón →, Spain 31 H3
Malaimbandy, Madag. .. 85 C8
Malakâl, Sudan 77 F3
Malakand, Pakistan 62 B4
Malakoff, U.S.A. 109 J7
Malamyzh, Russia 45 E14
Malang, Indonesia 57 G15
Malanje, Angola 80 F3
Mälaren, Sweden 10 E11
Malargüe, Argentina 126 D2
Malartic, Canada 98 C4
Malaryta, Belorussia 40 C4
Malatya, Turkey 67 D8
Malatya □, Turkey 67 D8
Malawi ■, Africa 83 E3
Malawi, L., Africa 83 E3
Malay Pen., Asia 59 J3
Malaya Belozërka, Ukraine 42 C6
Malaya Vishera, Russia .. 40 B8
Malaya Viska, Ukraine .. 42 B4
Malaybalay, Phil. 55 G6
Malayer, Iran 65 C6
Malaysia ■, Asia 56 D4
Malazgirt, Turkey 67 D10
Malbon, Australia 90 C3
Malbooma, Australia 91 E1
Malbork, Poland 20 A9
Malcésine, Italy 32 C7
Malchin, Germany 18 B8
Malchow, Germany 18 B8
Malcolm, Australia 89 E3
Malcolm, Pt., Australia .. 89 F3
Maldegem, Belgium 17 F2
Malden, Mass., U.S.A. .. 107 D13
Malden, Mo., U.S.A. .. 109 G10
Malden I., Kiribati 93 H12
Maldives ■, Ind. Oc. .. 47 J11
Maldonado, Uruguay .. 127 C5
Maldonado, Punta, Mexico 115 D5
Malé, Italy 32 B7
Maléa, Ákra, Greece 39 N6
Malebo, Pool, Africa 70 G5
Malegaon, India 60 J9
Malei, Mozam. 83 F4
Malek Kandī, Iran 64 B5
Malela, Zaïre 82 C2
Malema, Mozam. 83 E4
Máleme, Greece 37 D5
Malerkotla, India 62 D6
Máles, Greece 37 D7
Malesherbes, France 25 D9
Malestroit, France 24 E4
Malfa, Italy 35 D7
Malgobek, Russia 43 E11
Malgomaj, Sweden 8 D14
Malgrat, Spain 28 D7
Malha, Sudan 77 D2
Malheur →, U.S.A. 110 D5
Malheur L., U.S.A. 110 E4
Mali, Guinea 78 C2
Mali ■, Africa 78 B4
Mali →, Burma 61 G20
Mali Kanal, Serbia 21 K9
Malibu, U.S.A. 113 L8
Malik, Indonesia 57 E6
Malili, Indonesia 57 E6
Malimba, Mts., Zaïre .. 82 D2
Malin, Ukraine 40 F6
Malin Hd., Ireland 15 A4
Malindi, Kenya 82 C5
Malines = Mechelen, Belgium 17 F4
Maling, Indonesia 57 D6
Malinyi, Tanzania 83 D4
Malipo, China 52 F5

Maliqi, Albania 39 J3
Malita, Phil. 57 C7
Malkara, Turkey 66 C2
Małkinia Górna, Poland . 20 C12
Malko Tŭrnovo, Bulgaria . 39 H10
Mallacoota, Australia 91 F4
Mallacoota Inlet, Australia 91 F4
Mallaig, U.K. 14 E3
Mallawan, India 63 F9
Mallawi, Egypt 76 B3
Malleco □, Chile 128 A2
Mallemort, France 27 E9
Málles Venosta, Italy 32 B7
Mállia, Greece 37 D7
Mallión, Kólpos, Greece .. 37 D7
Mallorca, Spain 36 B10
Mallorytown, Canada 107 B9
Mallow, Ireland 15 D3
Malmberget, Sweden 8 C16
Malmédy, Belgium 17 H8
Malmesbury, S. Africa .. 84 E2
Malmö, Sweden 11 J6
Malmöhus län □, Sweden . 11 J7
Malmslätt, Sweden 11 F9
Malmyzh, Russia 41 C17
Maloarkhangelsk, Russia . 41 E10
Maloca, Brazil 121 C6
Maloja, Switz. 23 D9
Maloja, P., Switz. 23 D9
Malolos, Phil. 57 B6
Malombe L., Malawi 83 E4
Malone, U.S.A. 107 B10
Malong, China 52 E4
Malorita, Belorussia 40 F4
Maloyaroslovets, Russia . 41 D10
Malpartida, Spain 31 F4
Malpaso, Canary Is. 36 G1
Malpica, Spain 30 B2
Malta, Brazil 122 C4
Malta, Idaho, U.S.A. .. 110 E7
Malta, Mont., U.S.A. .. 110 B10
Malta ■, Europe 37 D1
Malta Channel, Medit. S. . 34 F6
Maltahöhe, Namibia 84 C2
Malters, Switz. 22 B6
Malton, Canada 106 C5
Malton, U.K. 12 C7
Maluku, Indonesia 57 E7
Maluku □, Indonesia 57 E7
Maluku Sea, Indonesia .. 57 E6
Malumfashi, Nigeria 79 C6
Malvan, India 60 L8
Malvern, U.S.A. 109 H8
Malvern Hills, U.K. 13 E5
Malvik, Norway 10 A4
Malvinas, Is. = Falkland Is. ■, Atl. Oc. 128 D5
Malya, Tanzania 82 C3
Malyy Lyakhovskiy, Ostrov, Russia 45 B15
Mama, Russia 45 D12
Mamadysh, Russia 41 D17
Mamanguape, Brazil 122 C4
Mamasa, Indonesia 57 E5
Mambasa, Zaïre 82 B2
Mamberamo →, Indonesia 57 E9
Mambilima Falls, Zambia . 83 E2
Mambirima, Zaïre 83 E2
Mambo, Tanzania 82 C4
Mambrui, Kenya 82 C5
Mamburao, Phil. 55 E4
Mameigwess L., Canada . 98 B2
Mamer, Lux. 17 J8
Mamers, France 24 D7
Mamfe, Cameroon 79 D6
Mamiña, Chile 124 E4
Mámmola, Italy 35 D9
Mammoth, U.S.A. 111 K8
Mamoré →, Bolivia 125 C4
Mamou, Guinea 78 C2
Mampató, Guinea-Biss. .. 78 C2
Mampong, Ghana 79 D4
Mamuil Malal, Paso, S. Amer. 128 A2
Mamuju, Indonesia 57 E5
Man, Ivory C. 78 D3
Man, I. of, U.K. 12 C3
Man Na, Burma 61 H20
Mana, Fr. Guiana 121 B7
Mana →, Fr. Guiana .. 121 B7
Mána →, Norway 10 E2
Manaar, G. of = Mannar, G. of, Asia 60 Q11
Manabí □, Ecuador 120 D1
Manacacías →, Colombia 120 C3
Manacapuru, Brazil 121 D5
Manacapuru →, Brazil .. 121 D5
Manacor, Spain 36 B10
Manado, Indonesia 57 D6
Manage, Belgium 17 G4
Managua, Nic. 116 D2
Managua, L., Nic. 116 D2
Manakara, Madag. 85 C8
Manama = Al Manāmah, Bahrain 65 E6
Manambao →, Madag. .. 85 B7
Manambato, Madag. 85 A8
Manambolo →, Madag. .. 85 B7
Manambolosy, Madag. .. 85 B8
Manananara →, Madag. . 85 C8
Mananara, Madag. 85 B8
Mananjary, Madag. 85 C8
Manantenina, Madag. .. 85 C8
Manaos = Manaus, Brazil 121 D6
Manapire →, Venezuela .. 120 B4

Manapouri, N.Z. 87 L1
Manapouri, L., N.Z. 87 L1
Manas, China 54 B3
Manas →, India 61 F17
Manaslu, Nepal 63 E11
Manasquan, U.S.A. 107 F10
Manassa, U.S.A. 111 H11
Manaung, Burma 61 K18
Manaus, Brazil 121 D6
Manavgat, Turkey 66 E4
Manawan L., Canada 101 B8
Manay, Phil. 55 H7
Manbij, Syria 64 B3
Mancelona, U.S.A. 104 C3
Mancha Real, Spain 31 H7
Manche □, France 24 C5
Manchester, U.K. 12 D5
Manchester, Calif., U.S.A. 112 G3
Manchester, Conn., U.S.A. 107 E12
Manchester, Ga., U.S.A. . 105 J3
Manchester, Iowa, U.S.A. 108 D9
Manchester, Ky., U.S.A. . 104 G4
Manchester, N.H., U.S.A. 107 D13
Manchester, N.Y., U.S.A. 106 D7
Manchester, Vt., U.S.A. . 107 C11
Manchester L., Canada .. 101 A7
Manchuria = Dongbei, China 51 D13
Manciano, Italy 33 F8
Mancifa, Ethiopia 77 F5
Mancora, Pta., Peru 124 A1
Mand →, Iran 65 D7
Manda, Chunya, Tanzania 82 D3
Manda, Ludewe, Tanzania 83 E3
Mandabé, Madag. 85 C7
Mandaguari, Brazil 127 A5
Mandah, Mongolia 50 B5
Mandal, Norway 9 G9
Mandalay, Burma 61 J20
Mandale = Mandalay, Burma 61 J20
Mandalgovi, Mongolia .. 50 B4
Mandalī, Iraq 64 C5
Mandan, U.S.A. 108 B4
Mandaon, Phil. 55 E5
Mandar, Teluk, Indonesia 57 E5
Mandas, Italy 34 C2
Mandasor = Mandsaur, India 62 G6
Mandaue, Phil. 55 F5
Mandelieu-la-Napoule, France 27 E10
Mandera, Kenya 82 B5
Mandera □, Kenya 82 B5
Manderfeld, Belgium 17 H8
Mandi, India 62 D7
Mandimba, Mozam. 83 E4
Mandioli, Indonesia 57 E7
Mandioré, L., S. Amer. . 125 D6
Mandla, India 63 H9
Mandø, Denmark 11 J2
Mandoto, Madag. 85 B8
Mandoúdhion, Greece .. 39 L6
Mandra, Pakistan 62 C5
Mandrare →, Madag. 85 D8
Mandritsara, Madag. 85 B8
Mandsaur, India 62 G6
Mandurah, Australia 89 F2
Mandúria, Italy 35 B10
Mandvi, India 62 H3
Mandya, India 60 N10
Mandzai, Pakistan 62 D2
Mané, Burkina Faso 79 C4
Maneh, Iran 65 B8
Manengouba, Mts., Cameroon 79 D6
Maneroo, Australia 90 C3
Maneroo Cr. →, Australia 90 C3
Manfalût, Egypt 76 B3
Manfred, Australia 91 E3
Manfredónia, Italy 35 A8
Manfredónia, G. di, Italy . 35 A9
Manga, Brazil 123 D3
Manga, Burkina Faso 79 C4
Manga, Niger 79 C7
Mangabeiras, Chapada das, Brazil 122 D2
Mangalia, Romania 38 F11
Mangalore, India 60 N9
Manganeses, Spain 30 D5
Mangawaka, N.Z. 87 H5
Manggar, Indonesia 56 E3
Manggawitu, Indonesia . 57 E8
Mangkalihat, Tanjung, Indonesia 57 D5
Mangla Dam, Pakistan .. 63 C5
Manglares, C., Colombia . 120 C2
Manglaur, India 62 E7
Mangnai, China 54 C4
Mango, Togo 79 C5
Mangoche, Malawi 83 E4
Mangoky →, Madag. 85 C7
Mangole, Indonesia 57 E7
Mangombe, Zaïre 82 C2
Mangonui, N.Z. 87 F4
Mangualde, Portugal 30 E3
Mangueigne, Chad 73 F9
Mangueira, L. da, Brazil . 127 C5
Manguéni, Hamada, Niger 75 D7
Mangum, U.S.A. 109 H5
Mangyshlak Poluostrov, Kazakhstan 43 D15
Mangyshlakskiy Zaliv, Kazakhstan 43 D14
Manhattan, U.S.A. 108 F6

Manhiça, Mozam. 85 D5
Manhuaçu, Brazil 123 F3
Manhumirim, Brazil 123 F3
Maní, Colombia 120 C3
Mania →, Madag. 85 B8
Maniago, Italy 33 B9
Manica, Mozam. 85 B5
Manica e Sofala □, Mozam. 85 B5
Manicaland □, Zimbabwe 83 F3
Manicoré, Brazil 125 B5
Manicoré →, Brazil 125 B5
Manicouagan →, Canada 99 C6
Manīfah, Si. Arabia 65 E6
Manifold, Australia 90 C5
Manifold, C., Australia 90 C5
Maniganggo, China 52 B2
Manigotagan, Canada 101 C9
Manihiki, Cook Is. 93 J11
Manika, Plateau de la, Zaïre 83 E2
Manila, Phil. 55 D4
Manila, U.S.A. 110 F9
Manila B., Phil. 55 D4
Manilla, Australia 91 E5
Manimpé, Mali 78 C3
Maningrida, Australia 90 A1
Manipur □, India 61 G18
Manipur →, Burma 61 H19
Manisa, Turkey 66 D2
Manisa □, Turkey 66 D2
Manistee, U.S.A. 104 C2
Manistee →, U.S.A. 104 C2
Manistique, U.S.A. 104 C2
Manito L., Canada 101 C7
Manitoba □, Canada 101 B9
Manitoba, L., Canada 101 C9
Manitou, Canada 101 D9
Manitou I., U.S.A. 98 C2
Manitou Is., U.S.A. 104 C2
Manitou L., Canada 99 B6
Manitou Springs, U.S.A. 108 F2
Manitoulin I., Canada 98 C3
Manitowaning, Canada 98 C3
Manitowoc, U.S.A. 104 C2
Manitsauá-Missu →, Brazil 125 C7
Manizales, Colombia 120 B2
Manja, Madag. 85 C7
Manjacaze, Mozam. 85 C5
Manjakandriana, Madag. 85 B8
Manjhand, Pakistan 62 G3
Manjil, Iran 65 B6
Manjimup, Australia 89 F2
Manjra →, India 60 K10
Mankato, Kans., U.S.A. 108 F5
Mankato, Minn., U.S.A. 108 C8
Mankayane, Swaziland 85 D5
Mankono, Ivory C. 78 D3
Mankota, Canada 101 D7
Manlay, Mongolia 50 B4
Manlleu, Spain 28 C7
Manly, Australia 91 E5
Manmad, India 60 J9
Mann Ras., Australia 89 E5
Manna, Indonesia 56 E2
Mannahill, Australia 91 E3
Mannar, Sri Lanka 60 Q11
Mannar, G. of, Asia 60 Q11
Mannar I., Sri Lanka 60 Q11
Männedorf, Switz. 23 B7
Mannheim, Germany 19 F4
Manning, Canada 100 B5
Manning, Oreg., U.S.A. 112 E3
Manning, S.C., U.S.A. 105 J5
Manning Prov. Park, Canada 100 D4
Mannington, U.S.A. 104 F5
Mannu →, Italy 34 C2
Mannu, C., Italy 34 B1
Mannum, Australia 91 E2
Mano, S. Leone 78 D2
Manoa, Bolivia 125 B4
Manokwari, Indonesia 57 E8
Manombo, Madag. 85 C7
Manono, Zaïre 82 D2
Manosque, France 27 E9
Manouane, L., Canada 99 B5
Manpojin, N. Korea 51 D14
Manresa, Spain 28 D6
Mansa, Gujarat, India 62 H5
Mansa, Punjab, India 62 E6
Mansa, Zambia 83 E2
Mansehra, Pakistan 62 B5
Mansel I., Canada 97 B11
Mansfield, Australia 91 F4
Mansfield, U.K. 12 D6
Mansfield, La., U.S.A. 109 J8
Mansfield, Mass., U.S.A. 107 D13
Mansfield, Ohio, U.S.A. 106 F2
Mansfield, Pa., U.S.A. 106 E7
Mansfield, Wash., U.S.A. 110 C4
Mansidão, Brazil 122 D3
Mansilla de las Mulas, Spain 30 C5
Mansle, France 26 C4
Manso →, Brazil 123 D2
Mansoa, Guinea-Biss. 78 C1
Manson Creek, Canada 100 B4
Mansoura, Algeria 75 A5
Manta, Ecuador 120 D1
Manta, B. de, Ecuador 120 D1
Mantalingajan, Mt., Phil. 55 G2
Mantare, Tanzania 82 C3
Manteca, U.S.A. 111 H3
Mantecal, Venezuela 120 B4
Mantena, Brazil 123 E3
Manteo, U.S.A. 105 H8
Mantes-la-Jolie, France 25 D8
Manthani, India 60 K11
Manthelan, France 24 E7
Manti, U.S.A. 110 G8
Mantiqueira, Serra da, Brazil 123 F3
Manton, U.S.A. 104 C3
Mantorp, Sweden 11 F9
Mántova, Italy 32 C7
Mänttä, Finland 8 E18
Mantua = Mántova, Italy 32 C7
Manturovo, Russia 41 B14
Manu, Peru 124 C3
Manu →, Peru 124 C3
Manua Is., Amer. Samoa 87 B14
Manuae, Cook Is. 93 J12
Manuel Alves →, Brazil 123 D2
Manuel Alves Grande →, Brazil 122 C2
Manuel Urbano, Brazil 124 B4
Manui, Indonesia 57 E6
Manuripi →, Bolivia 124 C4
Manville, U.S.A. 108 D2
Many, U.S.A. 109 K8
Manyara, L., Tanzania 82 C4
Manych →, Russia 43 C8
Manych-Gudilo, Oz., Russia 43 C10
Manyonga →, Tanzania 82 C3
Manyoni, Tanzania 82 D3
Manyoni □, Tanzania 82 D3
Manzai, Pakistan 62 C4
Manzala, Bahra el, Egypt 76 H7
Manzanares, Spain 29 F1
Manzaneda, Cabeza de, Spain 30 C3
Manzanillo, Cuba 116 B4
Manzanillo, Mexico 114 D4
Manzanillo, Pta., Panama 116 E4
Manzano Mts., U.S.A. 111 J10
Manzarīyeh, Iran 65 C6
Manzhouli, China 54 B6
Manzini, Swaziland 85 D5
Mao, Chad 73 F8
Maoke, Pegunungan, Indonesia 57 E9
Maolin, China 51 C12
Maoming, China 53 G8
Maowen, China 52 B4
Maoxing, China 51 B13
Mapam Yumco, China 54 C3
Mapastepec, Mexico 115 D6
Mapia, Kepulauan, Indonesia 57 D8
Mapimí, Mexico 114 B4
Mapimí, Bolsón de, Mexico 114 B4
Maping, China 53 B9
Mapinga, Tanzania 82 D4
Mapinhane, Mozam. 85 C6
Mapire, Venezuela 121 B5
Maple Creek, Canada 101 D7
Maple Valley, U.S.A. 112 C4
Mapleton, U.S.A. 110 D2
Mapuera →, Brazil 121 D6
Maputo, Mozam. 85 D5
Maputo, B. de, Mozam. 85 D5
Maqiaohe, China 51 B16
Maqnā, Si. Arabia 64 D2
Maqteïr, Mauritania 74 D2
Maquela do Zombo, Angola 80 F3
Maquinchao, Argentina 128 B3
Maquoketa, U.S.A. 108 D9
Mar, Serra do, Brazil 127 B6
Mar Chiquita, L., Argentina 126 C3
Mar del Plata, Argentina 126 D4
Mar Menor, L., Spain 29 H4
Mara, Guyana 121 B6
Mara, Tanzania 82 C3
Mara □, Tanzania 82 C3
Maraā, Brazil 120 D4
Marabá, Brazil 122 C2
Maracá, I. de, Brazil 121 C7
Maracaibo, Venezuela 120 A3
Maracaibo, L. de, Venezuela 120 B3
Maracaju, Brazil 127 A4
Maracajú, Serra de, Brazil 125 E6
Maracanã, Brazil 122 B2
Maracás, Brazil 123 D3
Maracay, Venezuela 120 A4
Marādah, Libya 73 C8
Maradi, Niger 79 C6
Maradun, Nigeria 79 C6
Marāgheh, Iran 64 B5
Maragogipe, Brazil 123 D4
Marāh, Si. Arabia 64 E5
Marajó, B. de, Brazil 122 B2
Marajó, I. de, Brazil 122 B2
Marākand, Iran 64 B5
Maralal, Kenya 82 B4
Maralinga, Australia 89 F5
Marama, Australia 91 F3
Marampa, S. Leone 78 D2
Maran, Malaysia 59 L4
Marana, U.S.A. 111 K8
Maranboy, Australia 88 B5
Maranchón, Spain 28 D2
Marand, Iran 64 B5
Marang, Malaysia 59 K4
Maranguape, Brazil 122 B4
Maranhão = São Luís, Brazil 122 B3
Maranhão □, Brazil 122 B2
Marano, L. di, Italy 33 C10
Maranoa →, Australia 91 D4
Marañón →, Peru 124 A3
Marão, Mozam. 85 C5
Marapi →, Brazil 121 C6
Marari, Brazil 124 B4
Maraş = Kahramanmaraş, Turkey 66 E7
Mărăşeşti, Romania 38 D10
Maratea, Italy 35 C8
Marateca, Portugal 31 G2
Marathasa □, Cyprus 37 E11
Marathókambos, Greece 39 M9
Marathon, Australia 90 C3
Marathon, Canada 98 C2
Marathón, Greece 39 L6
Marathon, N.Y., U.S.A. 107 D8
Marathon, Tex., U.S.A. 109 K3
Marathóvouno, Cyprus 37 D12
Maratua, Indonesia 57 D5
Maraú, Brazil 123 D4
Maravatío, Mexico 114 D4
Marawi City, Phil. 55 G6
Marāwih, U.A.E. 65 E7
Marbella, Spain 31 J6
Marble Bar, Australia 88 D2
Marble Falls, U.S.A. 109 K5
Marblehead, U.S.A. 107 D14
Marburg, Germany 18 E4
Marby, Sweden 10 A8
Marcal →, Hungary 21 H7
Marcapata, Peru 124 C3
Marcaria, Italy 32 C7
March, U.K. 13 E8
Marchand = Rommani, Morocco 74 B3
Marche, France 26 B5
Marche □, Italy 33 E10
Marche-en-Famenne, Belgium 17 H6
Marchena, Spain 31 H5
Marches = Marche □, Italy 33 E10
Marciana Marina, Italy 32 F7
Marcianise, Italy 35 A7
Marcigny, France 27 B8
Marcillat-en-Combraille, France 26 B6
Marcinelle, Belgium 17 H4
Marck, France 25 B8
Marckolsheim, France 25 D14
Marcona, Peru 124 D2
Marcos Juárez, Argentina 126 C3
Marcus I. = Minami-Tori-Shima, Pac. Oc. 92 E7
Marcus Necker Ridge, Pac. Oc. 92 F9
Marcy, Mt., U.S.A. 107 B11
Mardan, Pakistan 62 B5
Mardie, Australia 88 D2
Mardin, Turkey 67 E9
Marechal Deodoro, Brazil 122 C4
Maree L., U.K. 14 D3
Mareeba, Australia 90 B4
Marek = Stanke Dimitrov, Bulgaria 38 G6
Marek, Indonesia 57 E6
Maremma, Italy 32 F8
Maréna, Mali 78 C3
Marenberg, Slovenia 33 B12
Marengo, U.S.A. 108 E8
Marennes, France 26 C2
Marenyi, Kenya 82 C4
Marerano, Madag. 85 C7
Maréttimo, Italy 34 E5
Mareuil-sur-Lay, France 26 B2
Marfa, U.S.A. 109 K2
Marfa Pt., Malta 37 D1
Marganets, Ukraine 42 C6
Margaret →, Australia 88 C4
Margaret Bay, Canada 100 C3
Margaret L., Canada 100 B5
Margaret River, Australia 88 C4
Margarita, I. de, Venezuela 121 A5
Margarítion, Greece 39 K3
Margaritovo, Russia 48 C7
Margate, S. Africa 85 E5
Margate, U.K. 13 F9
Margelan, Uzbekistan 44 E8
Margeride, Mts. de la, France 26 D7
Margherita di Savola, Italy 35 A9
Margosatubig, Phil. 55 H5
Marguerite, Canada 100 C4
Marhoum, Algeria 75 B4
Mari Republic □, Russia 41 C16
María Elena, Chile 126 A2
María Grande, Argentina 126 C4
Maria I., N. Terr., Australia 90 A2
Maria I., Tas., Australia 90 G4
Maria van Diemen, C., N.Z. 87 F4
Mariager, Denmark 11 H4
Mariager Fjord, Denmark 11 H4
Mariakani, Kenya 82 C4
Marian L., Canada 100 A5
Mariana Trench, Pac. Oc. 92 F6
Marianao, Cuba 116 B3
Marianna, Ark., U.S.A. 109 H9
Marianna, Fla., U.S.A. 105 K3
Mariánské Lázně, Czech. 20 F2
Marias →, U.S.A. 110 C8
Mariato, Punta, Panama 116 E3
Mariazell, Austria 21 H5
Ma'rib, Yemen 68 D4
Maribo, Denmark 11 K5
Maribor, Slovenia 33 B12
Marico →, Africa 84 C4
Maricopa, Ariz., U.S.A. 111 K7
Maricopa, Calif., U.S.A. 113 K7
Maricourt, Canada 97 C12
Marīdī, Sudan 77 G2
Maridi, Wadi →, Sudan 77 F2
Marié →, Brazil 120 D4
Marie Byrd Land, Antarctica 5 D14
Marie-Galante, Guadeloupe 117 C7
Mariecourt, Canada 97 B12
Mariefred, Sweden 10 E11
Mariehamn, Finland 9 F15
Marienbad = Mariánské Lázně, Czech. 20 F2
Marienberg, Germany 18 E9
Marienberg, Neths. 16 D9
Marienbourg, Belgium 17 H5
Mariental, Namibia 84 C2
Marienville, U.S.A. 106 E5
Mariestad, Sweden 11 F7
Marietta, Ga., U.S.A. 105 J3
Marietta, Ohio, U.S.A. 104 F5
Marieville, Canada 107 A11
Marignane, France 27 E9
Marihatag, Phil. 55 G7
Mariinsk, Russia 44 D9
Mariinskiy Posad, Russia 41 C15
Marília, Brazil 127 A5
Marillana, Australia 88 D2
Marín, Spain 30 C2
Marina, U.S.A. 112 J5
Marina di Cirò, Italy 35 C10
Marina Plains, Australia 90 A3
Marinduque, Phil. 55 E5
Marine City, U.S.A. 104 D4
Marineo, Italy 34 E6
Marinette, U.S.A. 104 C2
Maringá, Brazil 127 A5
Marinha Grande, Portugal 31 F2
Marion, Ala., U.S.A. 105 J2
Marion, Ill., U.S.A. 109 G10
Marion, Ind., U.S.A. 104 E3
Marion, Iowa, U.S.A. 108 D9
Marion, Kans., U.S.A. 108 F6
Marion, Mich., U.S.A. 104 C3
Marion, N.C., U.S.A. 105 H4
Marion, Ohio, U.S.A. 104 E4
Marion, S.C., U.S.A. 105 H6
Marion, Va., U.S.A. 105 G5
Marion, L., U.S.A. 105 J5
Maripa, Venezuela 121 B4
Maripasoula, Fr. Guiana 121 C7
Mariposa, U.S.A. 111 H4
Mariscal Estigarribia, Paraguay 126 A3
Maritime Alps = Maritimes, Alpes, Europe 27 D11
Maritimes, Alpes, Europe 27 D11
Maritsa, Greece 37 C10
Mariupol, Ukraine 42 C7
Marīvān, Iran 64 C5
Mariyampol, Lithuania 40 D3
Markam, China 52 C2
Markazī □, Iran 65 C6
Markdale, Canada 106 B4
Marke, Belgium 17 G2
Marked Tree, U.S.A. 109 H9
Markelsdorfer Huk, Germany 18 A6
Marken, Neths. 16 D6
Markermeer, Neths. 16 C6
Market Drayton, U.K. 12 E5
Market Harborough, U.K. 13 E7
Markham, Canada 106 C5
Markham, Mt., Antarctica 5 E11
Markham L., Canada 101 A8
Marki, Poland 20 C11
Markleeville, U.S.A. 112 G7
Markoupoulon, Greece 39 M6
Markovo, Russia 45 C17
Markoye, Burkina Faso 79 C5
Marks, Russia 41 F15
Marksville, U.S.A. 109 K8
Markt Schwaben, Germany 19 G7
Marktredwitz, Germany 19 E8
Marla, Australia 91 D1
Marlboro, U.S.A. 107 D13
Marlborough, Australia 90 C4
Marlborough Downs, U.K. 13 F6
Marle, France 25 C10
Marlin, U.S.A. 109 K6
Marlow, Germany 18 A8
Marlow, U.S.A. 109 H6
Marly-le-Grand, Switz. 22 C4
Marmagao, India 60 M8
Marmande, France 26 D4
Marmara, Turkey 42 F2
Marmara, Sea of = Marmara Denizi, Turkey 66 C3
Marmara Denizi, Turkey 66 C3
Marmara Gölü, Turkey 66 D3
Marmaris, Turkey 66 E3
Marmarth, U.S.A. 108 B3
Marmelos →, Brazil 125 B5
Marmion, Mt., Australia 89 E2
Marmion L., Canada 98 C1
Marmolada, Mte., Italy 33 B8
Marmolejo, Spain 31 G6
Marmora, Canada 98 D4
Marnay, France 25 E12
Marne, Germany 18 B5
Marne □, France 25 D11
Marne →, France 25 D9
Marneuli, Georgia 43 F11
Maroa, Venezuela 120 C4
Maroala, Madag. 85 B8
Maroantsetra, Madag. 85 B8
Maromandia, Madag. 85 A8
Marondera, Zimbabwe 83 F3
Maroni →, Fr. Guiana 121 B7
Maronne →, France 26 C5
Maroochydore, Australia 91 D5
Maroona, Australia 91 F3
Maros →, Hungary 21 J10
Marosakoa, Madag. 85 B8
Marostica, Italy 33 C8
Maroua, Cameroon 79 C7
Marovoay, Madag. 85 B8
Marowijne □, Surinam 121 C7
Marowijne →, Surinam 121 B7
Marquard, S. Africa 84 D4
Marqueira, Portugal 31 G1
Marquesas Is. = Marquises, Is., Pac. Oc. 93 H14
Marquette, U.S.A. 104 B2
Marquise, France 25 B8
Marquises, Is., Pac. Oc. 93 H14
Marra, Gebel, Sudan 77 F2
Marracuene, Mozam. 85 D5
Marradi, Italy 33 D8
Marrakech, Morocco 74 B3
Marrawah, Australia 90 G3
Marrecas, Serra das, Brazil 122 C3
Marree, Australia 91 D2
Marrilla, Australia 88 D1
Marrimane, Mozam. 85 C5
Marromeu, Mozam. 85 B6
Marroquí, Punta, Spain 31 K5
Marrowie Cr. →, Australia 91 E4
Marrubane, Mozam. 83 F4
Marrum, Neths. 16 B7
Marrupa, Mozam. 83 E4
Marsá Matrûh, Egypt 76 A2
Marsá Susah, Libya 73 B9
Marsabit, Kenya 82 B4
Marsabit □, Kenya 82 B4
Marsala, Italy 34 E5
Marsalforn, Malta 37 C1
Marsberg, Germany 18 D4
Marsciano, Italy 33 F9
Marsden, Australia 91 E4
Marsdiep, Neths. 16 C5
Marseillan, France 26 E7
Marseille, France 27 E9
Marseilles = Marseille, France 27 E9
Marsh I., U.S.A. 109 L9
Marsh L., U.S.A. 108 C6
Marshall, Liberia 78 D2
Marshall, Ark., U.S.A. 109 H8
Marshall, Mich., U.S.A. 104 D3
Marshall, Minn., U.S.A. 108 C7
Marshall, Mo., U.S.A. 108 F8
Marshall, Tex., U.S.A. 109 J7
Marshall →, Australia 90 C2
Marshall Is. ■, Pac. Oc. 92 G9
Marshalltown, U.S.A. 108 D8
Marshfield, Mo., U.S.A. 109 G8
Marshfield, Wis., U.S.A. 108 C9
Marshūn, Iran 65 B6
Mársico Nuovo, Italy 35 B8
Märsta, Sweden 10 E11
Marstal, Denmark 11 K4
Marstrand, Sweden 11 G5
Mart, U.S.A. 109 K6
Marta →, Italy 33 F8
Martaban, Burma 61 L20
Martaban, G. of, Burma 61 L20
Martano, Italy 35 B11
Martapura, Kalimantan, Indonesia 56 E4
Martapura, Sumatera, Indonesia 56 E2
Marte, Nigeria 79 C7
Martel, France 26 D5
Martelange, Belgium 17 J7
Martés, Sierra, Spain 29 F4
Martha's Vineyard, U.S.A. 107 E14
Martigné-Ferchaud, France 24 E5
Martigny, Switz. 22 D4
Martigues, France 27 E9
Martil, Morocco 74 A3
Martin, Slovak Rep. 20 F8
Martin, S. Dak., U.S.A. 108 D4
Martin, Tenn., U.S.A. 109 G10
Martín →, Spain 28 D4
Martin L., U.S.A. 105 J3
Martina, Switz. 23 C10
Martina Franca, Italy 35 B10
Martinborough, N.Z. 87 J5
Martinez, U.S.A. 112 G4
Martinho Campos, Brazil 123 E2
Martinique ■, W. Indies 117 D7
Martinique Passage, W. Indies 117 C7
Martínon, Greece 39 L6
Martinópolis, Brazil 127 A5
Martins Ferry, U.S.A. 106 F4
Martinsburg, Pa., U.S.A. 106 F6
Martinsburg, W. Va., U.S.A. 104 F7
Martinsville, Ind., U.S.A. 104 F2
Martinsville, Va., U.S.A. 105 G6
Marton, N.Z. 87 J5
Martorell, Spain 28 D6
Martos, Spain 31 H7

Martuni, *Armenia* 43 F11
Maru, *Nigeria* 79 C6
Marudi, *Malaysia* 56 D4
Ma'ruf, *Afghan.* 60 D5
Marugame, *Japan* 49 G6
Marúggio, *Italy* 35 B10
Maruim, *Brazil* 122 D4
Marulan, *Australia* 91 E5
Marum, *Neths.* 16 B8
Marunga, *Angola* 84 B3
Marungu, Mts., *Zaïre* 82 D2
Marvast, *Iran* 65 D7
Marvejols, *France* 26 D7
Marwar, *India* 62 G5
Mary, *Turkmenistan* 44 F7
Mary Frances L., *Canada* 101 A7
Mary Kathleen, *Australia* 90 C2
Maryborough = Port Laoise, *Ireland* 15 C4
Maryborough, *Queens., Australia* 91 D5
Maryborough, *Vic., Australia* 91 F3
Maryfield, *Canada* 101 D8
Maryland □, *U.S.A.* 104 F7
Maryland Junction, *Zimbabwe* 83 F3
Maryport, *U.K.* 12 C4
Mary's Harbour, *Canada* 99 B8
Marystown, *Canada* 99 C8
Marysvale, *U.S.A.* 111 G7
Marysville, *Canada* 100 D5
Marysville, *Calif., U.S.A.* 112 F5
Marysville, *Kans., U.S.A.* 108 F6
Marysville, *Mich., U.S.A.* 106 D2
Marysville, *Ohio, U.S.A.* 104 E4
Marysville, *Wash., U.S.A.* 112 B4
Maryvale, *Australia* 91 D5
Maryville, *U.S.A.* 105 H4
Marzo, Punta, *Colombia* 120 B2
Marzūq, *Libya* 73 C7
Masahunga, *Tanzania* 82 C3
Masai, *Malaysia* 59 M4
Masai Steppe, *Tanzania* 82 C4
Masaka, *Uganda* 82 C3
Masalembo, Kepulauan, *Indonesia* 56 F4
Masalima, Kepulauan, *Indonesia* 56 F5
Masamba, *Indonesia* 57 E6
Masan, *S. Korea* 51 G15
Masanasa, *Spain* 29 F4
Masasi, *Tanzania* 83 E4
Masasi □, *Tanzania* 83 E4
Masaya, *Nic.* 116 D2
Masba, *Nigeria* 79 C7
Masbate, *Phil.* 55 E5
Mascara, *Algeria* 75 A5
Mascota, *Mexico* 114 C4
Masela, *Indonesia* 57 F7
Maseru, *Lesotho* 84 D4
Mashaba, *Zimbabwe* 83 G3
Mashābih, *Si. Arabia* 64 E3
Mashan, *China* 52 F7
Masherbrum, *Pakistan* 63 B7
Mashhad, *Iran* 65 B8
Mashi, *Nigeria* 79 C6
Mashīz, *Iran* 65 D8
Mashkel, Hamun-i-, *Pakistan* 60 E3
Mashki Chāh, *Pakistan* 60 E3
Mashonaland Central □, *Zimbabwe* 85 B5
Mashonaland East □, *Zimbabwe* 85 B5
Mashonaland West □, *Zimbabwe* 85 B4
Mashtaga, *Azerbaijan* 43 F13
Masi, *Norway* 8 B17
Masi Manimba, *Zaïre* 80 E3
Masindi, *Uganda* 82 B3
Masindi Port, *Uganda* 82 B3
Masisea, *Peru* 124 B3
Masisi, *Zaïre* 82 C2
Masjed Soleyman, *Iran* 65 D6
Mask, L., *Ireland* 15 C2
Maslinica, *Croatia* 33 E13
Masnou, *Spain* 28 D7
Masoala, Tanjon' i, *Madag.* 85 B9
Masoarivo, *Madag.* 85 B7
Masohi, *Indonesia* 57 E7
Masomeloka, *Madag.* 85 C8
Mason, *Nev., U.S.A.* 112 G7
Mason, *Tex., U.S.A.* 109 K5
Mason City, *U.S.A.* 108 D8
Maspalomas, *Canary Is.* 36 G4
Maspalomas, Pta., *Canary Is.* 36 G4
Masqat, *Oman* 68 C6
Massa, *Italy* 32 D7
Massa, O. →, *Morocco* 74 B3
Massa Maríttima, *Italy* 32 F7
Massachusetts □, *U.S.A.* 107 D12
Massachusetts B., *U.S.A.* 107 D14
Massafra, *Italy* 35 B10
Massaguet, *Chad* 73 F8
Massakory, *Chad* 73 F8
Massanella, *Spain* 36 B9
Massangena, *Mozam.* 85 C5
Massapê, *Brazil* 122 B3
Massarosa, *Italy* 32 E7
Massat, *France* 26 F5
Massawa = Mitsiwa, *Eritrea* 77 D4
Massena, *U.S.A.* 107 B10
Massénya, *Chad* 73 F8

Masset, *Canada* 100 C2
Massiac, *France* 26 C7
Massif Central, *France* 26 D7
Massillon, *U.S.A.* 106 F3
Massinga, *Mozam.* 85 C6
Masson, *Canada* 107 A9
Masson I., *Antarctica* 5 C7
Mastanli = Momchilgrad, *Bulgaria* 39 H8
Masterton, *N.Z.* 87 J5
Mástikho, Ákra, *Greece* 39 L9
Mastuj, *Pakistan* 63 A5
Mastung, *Pakistan* 60 E5
Mastūrah, *Si. Arabia* 76 C4
Masuda, *Japan* 49 G5
Masvingo, *Zimbabwe* 83 G3
Masvingo □, *Zimbabwe* 83 G3
Maswa □, *Tanzania* 82 C3
Maşyāf, *Syria* 64 C3
Mata de São João, *Brazil* 123 D4
Matabeleland North □, *Zimbabwe* 83 F2
Matabeleland South □, *Zimbabwe* 83 G2
Mataboor, *Indonesia* 57 E9
Matachel →, *Spain* 31 G4
Matachewan, *Canada* 98 C3
Matacuni →, *Venezuela* 121 C4
Matad, *Mongolia* 54 B6
Matadi, *Zaïre* 80 F2
Matagalpa, *Nic.* 116 D2
Matagami, *Canada* 98 C4
Matagami, L., *Canada* 98 C4
Matagorda, *U.S.A.* 109 L7
Matagorda B., *U.S.A.* 109 L6
Matagorda I., *U.S.A.* 109 L6
Matak, P., *Indonesia* 59 L6
Matakana, *Australia* 91 E4
Mátala, *Greece* 37 E6
Matalaque, *Peru* 124 D3
Matam, *Senegal* 78 B2
Matameye, *Niger* 79 C6
Matamoros, *Campeche, Mexico* 115 D6
Matamoros, *Coahuila, Mexico* 114 B4
Matamoros, *Puebla, Mexico* 115 D5
Matamoros, *Tamaulipas, Mexico* 115 B5
Ma'ţan as Sarra, *Libya* 73 D9
Matandu →, *Tanzania* 83 D3
Matane, *Canada* 99 C6
Matang, *China* 52 F5
Matankari, *Niger* 79 C5
Matanzas, *Cuba* 116 B3
Matapan, C. = Taínaron, Ákra, *Greece* 39 N5
Matapédia, *Canada* 99 C6
Matara, *Sri Lanka* 60 S12
Mataram, *Indonesia* 56 F5
Matarani, *Peru* 124 D3
Mataranka, *Australia* 88 B5
Matarma, Râs, *Egypt* 69 E1
Mataró, *Spain* 28 D7
Matarraña →, *Spain* 28 D5
Matatiele, *S. Africa* 85 E4
Mataura, *N.Z.* 87 M2
Mategua, *Bolivia* 125 C5
Matehuala, *Mexico* 114 C4
Mateira, *Brazil* 123 E1
Mateke Hills, *Zimbabwe* 83 G3
Matélica, *Italy* 33 E10
Matera, *Italy* 35 B9
Mátészalka, *Hungary* 21 H12
Matetsi, *Zimbabwe* 83 F2
Mateur, *Tunisia* 75 A6
Matfors, *Sweden* 10 B11
Matha, *France* 26 C3
Matheson Island, *Canada* 101 C9
Mathis, *U.S.A.* 109 L6
Mathura, *India* 62 F7
Mati, *Phil.* 55 H7
Mati →, *Albania* 39 H2
Matías Romero, *Mexico* 115 D5
Matibane, *Mozam.* 83 E5
Matima, *Botswana* 84 C3
Matiri Ra., *N.Z.* 87 J4
Matlock, *U.K.* 12 D6
Matmata, *Tunisia* 75 B6
Matna, *Sudan* 77 E4
Mato →, *Venezuela* 121 B4
Mato, Serrania de, *Venezuela* 120 B4
Mato Grosso □, *Brazil* 125 C6
Mato Grosso, Planalto do, *Brazil* 125 C7
Mato Grosso do Sul □, *Brazil* 125 D7
Matochkin Shar, *Russia* 44 B6
Matopo Hills, *Zimbabwe* 83 G2
Matopos, *Zimbabwe* 83 G2
Matosinhos, *Portugal* 30 D2
Matour, *France* 27 B8
Matsena, *Nigeria* 79 C7
Matsesta, *Russia* 43 E8
Matsue, *Japan* 49 G6
Matsumae, *Japan* 48 D10
Matsumoto, *Japan* 49 F9
Matsusaka, *Japan* 49 G8
Matsuura, *Japan* 49 H4
Matsuyama, *Japan* 49 H6
Mattagami →, *Canada* 98 B3
Mattancheri, *India* 60 Q10
Mattawa, *Canada* 98 C4
Mattawamkeag, *U.S.A.* 99 C6
Matterhorn, *Switz.* 22 E5

Matthew Town, *Bahamas* 117 B5
Matthew's Ridge, *Guyana* 121 B5
Mattice, *Canada* 98 C3
Mattituck, *U.S.A.* 107 F12
Mattmar, *Sweden* 10 A7
Matuba, *Mozam.* 85 C5
Matucana, *Peru* 124 C2
Matun, *Afghan.* 62 C3
Maturín, *Venezuela* 121 B5
Matveyev Kurgan, *Russia* 43 C8
Mau, *India* 63 G10
Mau Escarpment, *Kenya* 82 C4
Mau Ranipur, *India* 63 G8
Maubeuge, *France* 25 B10
Maubourguet, *France* 26 E4
Maud, Pt., *Australia* 88 D1
Maude, *Australia* 91 E3
Maudin Sun, *Burma* 61 M19
Maués, *Brazil* 121 D6
Mauganj, *India* 61 G12
Maui, *U.S.A.* 102 H16
Maulamyaing = Moulmein, *Burma* 61 L20
Maule □, *Chile* 126 D1
Mauléon-Licharre, *France* 26 E3
Maullín, *Chile* 128 B2
Maumee, *U.S.A.* 104 E4
Maumee →, *U.S.A.* 104 E4
Maumere, *Indonesia* 57 F6
Maun, *Botswana* 84 B3
Mauna Kea, *U.S.A.* 102 J17
Mauna Loa, *U.S.A.* 102 J17
Maungmagan Kyunzu, *Burma* 61 M20
Maupin, *U.S.A.* 110 D3
Maure-de-Bretagne, *France* 24 E5
Maurepas, L., *U.S.A.* 109 K9
Maures, *France* 27 E10
Mauriac, *France* 26 C6
Maurice, L., *Australia* 89 E5
Mauritania ■, *Africa* 74 D3
Mauritius ■, *Ind. Oc.* 71 J9
Mauron, *France* 24 D4
Maurs, *France* 26 D6
Mauston, *U.S.A.* 108 D9
Mauterndorf, *Austria* 21 H3
Mauvezin, *France* 26 E4
Mauzé-sur-le-Mignon, *France* 26 B3
Mavaca →, *Venezuela* 121 C4
Mavinga, *Angola* 81 H4
Mavli, *India* 62 G5
Mavrova, *Albania* 39 J2
Mavuradonha Mts., *Zimbabwe* 83 F3
Mawa, *Zaïre* 82 B2
Mawana, *India* 62 E7
Mawand, *Pakistan* 62 E3
Mawk Mai, *Burma* 61 J20
Mawlaik, *Burma* 61 H19
Mawquq, *Si. Arabia* 64 E4
Mawson Coast, *Antarctica* 5 C6
Max, *U.S.A.* 108 B4
Maxcanú, *Mexico* 115 C6
Maxesibeni, *S. Africa* 85 E4
Maxhamish L., *Canada* 100 B4
Maxixe, *Mozam.* 85 C6
Maxville, *Canada* 107 A10
Maxwell, *U.S.A.* 112 F4
Maxwelton, *Australia* 90 C3
May Downs, *Australia* 90 C4
May Pen, *Jamaica* 116 C4
Maya, *Spain* 28 B3
Maya →, *Russia* 45 D14
Maya Mts., *Belize* 115 D7
Mayaguana, *Bahamas* 117 B5
Mayagüez, *Puerto Rico* 117 C6
Mayahi, *Niger* 79 C6
Mayals, *Spain* 28 D5
Mayāmey, *Iran* 65 B7
Mayang, *China* 52 D7
Mayari, *Cuba* 117 B4
Maybell, *U.S.A.* 110 F9
Maychew, *Ethiopia* 77 E4
Maydān, *Iraq* 64 C5
Maydena, *Australia* 90 G4
Mayen, *Germany* 19 E3
Mayenne, *France* 24 D6
Mayenne □, *France* 24 D6
Mayenne →, *France* 24 E6
Mayer, *U.S.A.* 111 J7
Mayerthorpe, *Canada* 100 C5
Mayfield, *U.S.A.* 105 G1
Mayhill, *U.S.A.* 111 K11
Maykop, *Russia* 43 D9
Maymyo, *Burma* 58 A1
Maynard, *U.S.A.* 112 C4
Maynard Hills, *Australia* 89 E2
Mayne →, *Australia* 90 C3
Maynooth, *Ireland* 15 C5
Mayo, *Canada* 96 B6
Mayo □, *Ireland* 15 C2
Mayo →, *Argentina* 128 C3
Mayo →, *Peru* 124 B2
Mayo L., *Canada* 96 B6
Mayon Volcano, *Phil.* 55 E5
Mayor I., *N.Z.* 87 G6
Mayorga, *Spain* 30 C5
Mayraira Pt., *Phil.* 55 B4
Maysville, *U.S.A.* 104 F4
Mayu, *Indonesia* 57 D7
Mayville, *N. Dak., U.S.A.* 108 B6
Mayville, *N.Y., U.S.A.* 106 D5
Mayya, *Russia* 45 C14

Mazabuka, *Zambia* 83 F2
Mazagán = El Jadida, *Morocco* 74 B3
Mazagão, *Brazil* 121 D7
Mazamet, *France* 26 E6
Mazán, *Peru* 120 D3
Māzandarān □, *Iran* 65 B7
Mazapil, *Mexico* 114 C4
Mazar, O. →, *Algeria* 75 B5
Mazara del Vallo, *Italy* 34 E5
Mazarredo, *Argentina* 128 C3
Mazarrón, *Spain* 29 H3
Mazarrón, G. de, *Spain* 29 H3
Mazaruni →, *Guyana* 121 B6
Mazatán, *Mexico* 114 B2
Mazatenango, *Guatemala* 116 D1
Mazatlán, *Mexico* 114 C3
Mažeikiai, *Lithuania* 40 C3
Māzhān, *Iran* 65 C8
Mazīnān, *Iran* 65 B8
Mazoe, *Mozam.* 83 F3
Mazoe →, *Mozam.* 83 F3
Mazowe, *Zimbabwe* 83 F3
Mazrûb, *Sudan* 77 E2
Mazu Dao, *China* 53 D12
Mazurian Lakes = Mazurski, Pojezierze, *Poland* 20 B10
Mazurski, Pojezierze, *Poland* 20 B10
Mazzarino, *Italy* 35 E7
Mbaba, *Senegal* 78 C1
Mbabane, *Swaziland* 85 D5
Mbagne, *Mauritania* 78 B2
M'bahiakro, *Ivory C.* 78 D4
Mbaïki, *C.A.R.* 80 D3
Mbala, *Zambia* 83 D3
Mbale, *Uganda* 82 B3
Mbalmayo, *Cameroon* 79 E7
Mbamba Bay, *Tanzania* 83 E3
Mbandaka, *Zaïre* 80 D3
Mbanga, *Cameroon* 79 E6
Mbanza Congo, *Angola* 80 F2
Mbanza Ngungu, *Zaïre* 80 F2
Mbarara, *Uganda* 82 C3
Mbashe →, *S. Africa* 85 E4
Mbatto, *Ivory C.* 78 D4
Mbenkuru →, *Tanzania* 83 D4
Mberengwa, *Zimbabwe* 83 G2
Mberengwa, Mt., *Zimbabwe* 83 G2
Mberubu, *Nigeria* 79 D6
Mbesuma, *Zambia* 83 D3
Mbeya, *Tanzania* 83 D3
Mbeya □, *Tanzania* 82 D3
Mbinga, *Tanzania* 83 E4
Mbinga □, *Tanzania* 83 E3
Mbini □, *Eq. Guin.* 80 D2
Mboki, *C.A.R.* 77 F2
Mboro, *Senegal* 78 B1
Mboune, *Senegal* 78 C2
Mbour, *Senegal* 78 C1
Mbout, *Mauritania* 78 B2
Mbozi □, *Tanzania* 83 D3
Mbuji-Mayi, *Zaïre* 82 D1
Mbulu, *Tanzania* 82 C4
Mbulu □, *Tanzania* 82 C4
Mburucuyá, *Argentina* 126 B4
Mcherrah, *Algeria* 74 C4
Mchinja, *Tanzania* 83 D4
Mchinji, *Malawi* 83 E3
Mdennah, *Mauritania* 74 D3
Mead, L., *U.S.A.* 113 J12
Meade, *U.S.A.* 109 G4
Meadow, *Australia* 89 E1
Meadow Lake, *Canada* 101 C7
Meadow Lake Prov. Park, *Canada* 101 C7
Meadow Valley Wash →, *U.S.A.* 113 J12
Meadville, *U.S.A.* 106 E4
Meaford, *Canada* 98 D3
Mealhada, *Portugal* 30 E2
Mealy Mts., *Canada* 99 B8
Meander River, *Canada* 100 B5
Meares, C., *U.S.A.* 110 D2
Mearim →, *Brazil* 122 B3
Meath □, *Ireland* 15 C5
Meath Park, *Canada* 101 C7
Meaulne, *France* 26 B6
Meaux, *France* 25 D9
Mebechi-Gawa →, *Japan* 48 D10
Mecanhelas, *Mozam.* 83 F4
Mecaya →, *Colombia* 120 C2
Mecca = Makkah, *Si. Arabia* 68 C2
Mecca, *U.S.A.* 113 M10
Mechanicsburg, *U.S.A.* 106 F8
Mechanicville, *U.S.A.* 107 D11
Mechara, *Ethiopia* 77 F5
Mechelen, *Antwerpen, Belgium* 17 F4
Mechelen, *Limburg, Belgium* 17 G7
Mecheria, *Algeria* 75 B4
Mechernich, *Germany* 18 E2
Mechetinskaya, *Russia* 43 C9
Mechra Benâbbou, *Morocco* 74 B3
Mecitözü, *Turkey* 42 F6
Mecklenburg-Vorpommern □, *Germany* 18 B8
Mecklenburger Bucht, *Germany* 18 A7

Meconta, *Mozam.* 83 E4
Meda, *Australia* 88 C3
Meda, *Portugal* 30 E3
Medan, *Indonesia* 56 D1
Médanos, *Argentina* 128 A4
Medanosa, Pta., *Argentina* 128 C3
Médéa, *Algeria* 75 A5
Medeiros Neto, *Brazil* 123 E3
Medel, Pic, *Switz.* 23 C7
Medellín, *Colombia* 120 B2
Medemblik, *Neths.* 16 C6
Médenine, *Tunisia* 75 B7
Mederdra, *Mauritania* 78 B1
Medford, *Mass., U.S.A.* 107 D13
Medford, *Oreg., U.S.A.* 110 E2
Medford, *Wis., U.S.A.* 108 C9
Medgidia, *Romania* 38 E11
Medi, *Sudan* 77 F3
Media Agua, *Argentina* 126 C2
Media Luna, *Argentina* 126 C2
Mediaş, *Romania* 38 C7
Medical Lake, *U.S.A.* 110 C5
Medicina, *Italy* 33 D8
Medicine Bow, *U.S.A.* 110 F10
Medicine Bow Pk., *U.S.A.* 110 F10
Medicine Bow Ra., *U.S.A.* 110 F10
Medicine Hat, *Canada* 101 D6
Medicine Lake, *U.S.A.* 108 A2
Medicine Lodge, *U.S.A.* 109 G5
Medina = Al Madīnah, *Si. Arabia* 64 E3
Medina, *Brazil* 123 E3
Medina, *Colombia* 120 C3
Medina, *N. Dak., U.S.A.* 108 B5
Medina, *N.Y., U.S.A.* 106 C6
Medina, *Ohio, U.S.A.* 106 E3
Medina →, *U.S.A.* 109 L5
Medina de Ríoseco, *Spain* 30 D5
Medina del Campo, *Spain* 30 D6
Medina L., *U.S.A.* 109 L5
Medina-Sidonia, *Spain* 31 J5
Medinaceli, *Spain* 28 D2
Medinipur, *India* 63 H12
Mediterranean Sea, *Europe* 70 C5
Medjerda, O. →, *Tunisia* 75 A7
Medley, *Canada* 101 C6
Médoc, *France* 26 C3
Medstead, *Canada* 101 C7
Medulin, *Croatia* 33 D10
Medveda, *Serbia* 21 N11
Medveditsa →, *Russia* 41 G13
Medveditsa →, *Russia* 41 C10
Medvedok, *Russia* 41 C17
Medvezhi, Ostrava, *Russia* 45 B17
Medvezhyegorsk, *Russia* 44 C4
Medway →, *U.K.* 13 F8
Medyn, *Russia* 41 D9
Medzilaborce, *Slovak Rep.* 20 F11
Meeberrie, *Australia* 89 E2
Meekatharra, *Australia* 89 E2
Meeker, *U.S.A.* 110 F10
Meer, *Belgium* 17 F5
Meerane, *Germany* 18 E8
Meerbeke, *Belgium* 17 G4
Meerhout, *Belgium* 17 F6
Meerle, *Belgium* 17 F5
Meersburg, *Germany* 19 H5
Meerssen, *Neths.* 17 G7
Meerut, *India* 62 E7
Meeteetse, *U.S.A.* 110 D9
Meeuwen, *Belgium* 17 F7
Mega, *Ethiopia* 77 G4
Megálo Petalí, *Greece* 39 M7
Megalópolis, *Greece* 39 M5
Meganísi, *Greece* 39 L3
Mégara, *Greece* 39 M6
Megarine, *Algeria* 75 B6
Mégève, *France* 27 C10
Meghalaya □, *India* 61 G17
Meghezez, *Ethiopia* 77 F4
Mégiscane, L., *Canada* 98 C4
Mehadia, *Romania* 38 E5
Mehaigne →, *Belgium* 17 G6
Mehaïguene, O. →, *Algeria* 75 B5
Meheisa, *Sudan* 76 D3
Mehndawal, *India* 63 F10
Mehr Jān, *Iran* 65 C7
Mehrābād, *Iran* 64 B5
Mehrān, *Iran* 64 C5
Mehrīz, *Iran* 65 D7
Mehun-sur-Yèvre, *France* 25 E9
Mei Jiang →, *China* 53 E11
Mei Xian, *Guangdong, China* 53 E11
Mei Xian, *Shaanxi, China* 50 G4
Meia Ponte →, *Brazil* 123 E2
Meicheng, *China* 53 C12
Meichengzhen, *China* 53 C8
Meichuan, *China* 53 B10
Meiganga, *Cameroon* 80 C2
Meijel, *Neths.* 17 F7
Meiktila, *Burma* 61 J19
Meilen, *Switz.* 23 B7
Meiningen, *Germany* 18 E6
Meio →, *Brazil* 123 D3
Meira, Sierra de, *Spain* 30 B3
Meiringen, *Switz.* 22 C6
Meishan, *China* 52 B4
Meissen, *Germany* 18 D9
Meissner, *Germany* 18 D5
Meitan, *China* 52 D6
Mejillones, *Chile* 126 A1
Meka, *Australia* 89 E2
Mékambo, *Gabon* 80 D2

Mekdela, *Ethiopia* 77 E4
Mekele, *Ethiopia* 77 E4
Mekhtar, *Pakistan* 60 D6
Meknès, *Morocco* 74 B3
Meko, *Nigeria* 79 D5
Mekong →, *Asia* 59 H6
Mekongga, *Indonesia* 57 E6
Melagiri Hills, *India* 60 N10
Melah, Sebkhet el, *Algeria* 75 C4
Melaka, *Malaysia* 59 L4
Melalap, *Malaysia* 56 C5
Mélambes, *Greece* 37 D6
Melanesia, *Pac. Oc.* 92 H7
Melbourne, *Australia* 91 F3
Melbourne, *U.S.A.* 105 L5
Melchor Múzquiz, *Mexico* 114 B4
Melchor Ocampo, *Mexico* 114 C4
Méldola, *Italy* 33 D9
Meldorf, *Germany* 18 A5
Melegnano, *Italy* 32 C6
Melenci, *Serbia* 21 K10
Melenki, *Russia* 41 D12
Mélèzes →, *Canada* 97 C12
Melfi, *Chad* 73 F8
Melfi, *Italy* 35 B8
Melfort, *Canada* 101 C8
Melfort, *Zimbabwe* 83 F3
Melgaço, *Madeira* 30 C2
Melgar de Fernamental, *Spain* 30 C6
Melhus, *Norway* 10 A4
Melick, *Neths.* 17 F8
Melide, *Switz.* 23 E7
Meligalá, *Greece* 39 M4
Melilla, *Morocco* 75 A4
Melipilla, *Chile* 126 C1
Mélissa, Ákra, *Greece* 37 D6
Melita, *Canada* 101 D8
Mélito di Porto Salvo, *Italy* 35 E8
Melitopol, *Ukraine* 42 C6
Melk, *Austria* 21 G5
Mellansel, *Sweden* 8 E15
Melle, *Belgium* 17 G3
Melle, *France* 26 B3
Melle, *Germany* 18 C4
Mellégue, O. →, *Tunisia* 75 A6
Mellen, *U.S.A.* 108 B9
Mellerud, *Sweden* 11 F6
Mellette, *U.S.A.* 108 C5
Mellid, *Spain* 30 C2
Mellieha, *Malta* 37 D1
Mellit, *Sudan* 77 E2
Mellizo Sur, Cerro, *Chile* 128 C2
Mellrichstadt, *Germany* 19 E6
Melnik, *Bulgaria* 39 H6
Mělník, *Czech.* 20 E4
Melo, *Uruguay* 127 C5
Melolo, *Indonesia* 57 F6
Melouprey, *Cambodia* 58 F5
Melovoye, *Ukraine* 43 B9
Melrhir, Chott, *Algeria* 75 B6
Melrose, *N.S.W., Australia* 91 E4
Melrose, *W. Austral., Australia* 89 E3
Melrose, *U.K.* 14 F6
Melrose, *U.S.A.* 109 H3
Mels, *Switz.* 23 B8
Melsele, *Belgium* 17 F4
Melstone, *U.S.A.* 110 C10
Melsungen, *Germany* 18 D5
Melton Mowbray, *U.K.* 12 E7
Melun, *France* 25 D9
Melut, *Sudan* 77 E3
Melville, *Canada* 101 C8
Melville, C., *Australia* 90 A3
Melville, L., *Canada* 99 B8
Melville B., *Australia* 90 A2
Melville I., *Australia* 88 B5
Melville I., *Canada* 4 B2
Melville Pen., *Canada* 97 B11
Melvin →, *Canada* 100 B5
Memaliaj, *Albania* 39 J2
Memba, *Mozam.* 83 E5
Memboro, *Indonesia* 57 F5
Membrilla, *Spain* 29 G1
Memel = Klaipéda, *Lithuania* 40 D2
Memel, *S. Africa* 85 D4
Memmingen, *Germany* 19 H6
Mempawah, *Indonesia* 56 D3
Memphis, *Tenn., U.S.A.* 109 H10
Memphis, *Tex., U.S.A.* 109 H4
Mena, *U.S.A.* 109 H7
Mena →, *Ethiopia* 77 F5
Menai Strait, *U.K.* 12 D3
Ménaka, *Mali* 79 B5
Menaldum, *Neths.* 16 B7
Menan = Chao Phraya →, *Thailand* 58 F3
Menarandra →, *Madag.* 85 D7
Menard, *U.S.A.* 109 K5
Menasha, *U.S.A.* 104 C1
Menate, *Indonesia* 56 E4
Mendawai →, *Indonesia* 56 E4
Mende, *France* 26 D7
Mendebo, *Ethiopia* 77 F4
Mendez, *Mexico* 115 B5
Mendhar, *India* 63 C6
Mendi, *Ethiopia* 77 F4
Mendip Hills, *U.K.* 13 F5
Mendocino, *U.S.A.* 110 G2
Mendocino, C., *U.S.A.* 110 F1
Mendota, *Calif., U.S.A.* 111 H3
Mendota, *Ill., U.S.A.* 108 E10
Mendoza, *Argentina* 126 C2
Mendoza □, *Argentina* 126 C2
Mendrisio, *Switz.* 23 E7
Mene Grande, *Venezuela* 120 B3
Menemen, *Turkey* 66 D2
Menen, *Belgium* 17 G2
Menéndez, L., *Argentina* 128 B2
Menfi, *Italy* 34 E5
Mengcheng, *China* 53 A11
Mengdingjie, *China* 52 F2
Mengeš, *Slovenia* 33 B11
Menggala, *Indonesia* 56 E3
Menghai, *China* 52 G3
Mengíbar, *Spain* 31 H7
Mengjin, *China* 50 G7
Mengla, *China* 52 G3
Menglian, *China* 52 F2
Mengoub, *Algeria* 74 C3
Mengshan, *China* 53 E8
Mengyin, *China* 51 G9
Mengzhe, *China* 52 F3
Mengzi, *China* 52 F4
Menihek L., *Canada* 99 B6
Menin = Menen, *Belgium* 17 G2
Menindee, *Australia* 91 E3
Menindee L., *Australia* 91 E3
Meningie, *Australia* 91 F2
Menlo Park, *U.S.A.* 112 H4
Menominee, *U.S.A.* 104 C2
Menominee →, *U.S.A.* 104 C2
Menomonie, *U.S.A.* 108 C9
Menongue, *Angola* 81 G3
Menorca, *Spain* 36 B11
Mentakab, *Malaysia* 59 L4
Mentawai, Kepulauan, *Indonesia* 56 E1
Menton, *France* 27 E11
Mentor, *U.S.A.* 106 E3
Mentz Dam, *S. Africa* 84 E4
Menzel-Bourguiba, *Tunisia* 75 A6
Menzel Chaker, *Tunisia* 75 B7
Menzel-Temime, *Tunisia* 75 A7
Menzies, *Australia* 89 E3
Me'ona, *Israel* 69 B4
Meoqui, *Mexico* 114 B3
Mepaco, *Mozam.* 83 F3
Meppel, *Neths.* 16 C8
Meppen, *Germany* 18 C3
Mequinenza, *Spain* 28 D5
Mer Rouge, *U.S.A.* 109 J9
Merabéllou, Kólpos, *Greece* 37 D7
Meramangye, L., *Australia* 89 E5
Meran = Merano, *Italy* 33 B8
Merano, *Italy* 33 B8
Merate, *Italy* 32 C6
Merauke, *Indonesia* 57 F10
Merbabu, *Indonesia* 57 G14
Merbein, *Australia* 91 E3
Merca, *Somali Rep.* 68 G3
Mercadal, *Spain* 36 B11
Mercato Saraceno, *Italy* 33 E9
Merced, *U.S.A.* 111 H3
Merced Pk., *U.S.A.* 112 H7
Mercedes, *Buenos Aires, Argentina* 126 C4
Mercedes, *Corrientes, Argentina* 126 B4
Mercedes, *San Luis, Argentina* 126 C2
Mercedes, *Uruguay* 126 C4
Merceditas, *Chile* 126 B1
Mercer, *N.Z.* 87 G5
Mercer, *U.S.A.* 106 E4
Merchtem, *Belgium* 17 G4
Mercier, *Bolivia* 124 C4
Mercury, *U.S.A.* 113 J11
Mercy C., *Canada* 97 B13
Merdrignac, *France* 24 D4
Mere, *Belgium* 17 G3
Meredith, C., *Falk. Is.* 128 D4
Meredith, L., *U.S.A.* 109 H4
Merelbeke, *Belgium* 17 G3
Méréville, *France* 25 D9
Merga = Nukheila, *Sudan* 76 D2
Mergenevsky, *Kazakhstan* 43 B14
Mergui Arch. = Myeik Kyunzu, *Burma* 59 G1
Mérida, *Mexico* 115 C7
Mérida, *Spain* 31 G4
Mérida, *Venezuela* 120 B3
Mérida □, *Venezuela* 120 B3
Mérida, Cord. de, *Venezuela* 118 B2
Meriden, *U.S.A.* 107 E12
Meridian, *Calif., U.S.A.* 112 F5
Meridian, *Idaho, U.S.A.* 110 E5
Meridian, *Miss., U.S.A.* 105 J1
Meridian, *Tex., U.S.A.* 109 K6
Mering, *Germany* 19 G7
Meriruma, *Brazil* 121 C7
Merkel, *U.S.A.* 109 J4
Merksem, *Belgium* 17 F4
Merksplas, *Belgium* 17 F5
Mermaid Reef, *Australia* 88 C2
Mern, *Denmark* 11 J6
Merowe, *Sudan* 76 D3
Merredin, *Australia* 89 F2
Merrick, *U.K.* 14 F4
Merrickville, *Canada* 107 B9
Merrill, *Oreg., U.S.A.* 110 E3
Merrill, *Wis., U.S.A.* 108 C10
Merriman, *U.S.A.* 108 D4
Merritt, *Canada* 100 C4
Merriwa, *Australia* 91 E5
Merriwagga, *Australia* 91 E4
Merry I., *Canada* 98 A4
Merrygoen, *Australia* 91 E4
Merryville, *U.S.A.* 109 K8
Mersa Fatma, *Eritrea* 68 E3
Mersch, *Lux.* 17 J8
Merseburg, *Germany* 18 D7
Mersey →, *U.K.* 12 D5
Merseyside □, *U.K.* 12 D5
Mersin, *Turkey* 66 E6
Mersing, *Malaysia* 59 L4
Merta, *India* 62 F6
Mertert, *Lux.* 17 J8
Merthyr Tydfil, *U.K.* 13 F4
Mértola, *Portugal* 31 H3
Mertzig, *Lux.* 17 J8
Mertzon, *U.S.A.* 109 K4
Méru, *France* 25 C9
Meru, *Kenya* 82 B4
Meru, *Tanzania* 82 C4
Meru □, *Kenya* 82 B4
Merville, *France* 25 B9
Méry-sur-Seine, *France* 25 D10
Merzifon, *Turkey* 42 F6
Merzig, *Germany* 19 F2
Merzouga, Erg Tin, *Algeria* 75 D7
Mesa, *U.S.A.* 111 K8
Mesach Mellet, *Libya* 75 D7
Mesagne, *Italy* 35 B10
Mesanagrós, *Greece* 37 C9
Mesaoría □, *Cyprus* 37 D12
Mesarás, Kólpos, *Greece* 37 D6
Meschede, *Germany* 18 D4
Mesfinto, *Ethiopia* 77 E4
Mesgouez, L., *Canada* 98 B4
Meshchovsk, *Russia* 40 D9
Meshed = Mashhad, *Iran* 65 B8
Meshoppen, *U.S.A.* 107 E8
Meshra er Req, *Sudan* 77 F2
Mesick, *U.S.A.* 104 C3
Mesilinka →, *Canada* 100 B4
Mesilla, *U.S.A.* 111 K10
Meslay-du-Maine, *France* 24 E6
Mesocco, *Switz.* 23 D8
Mesolóngion, *Greece* 39 L4
Mesopotamia = Al Jazirah, *Iraq* 64 C5
Mesoraca, *Italy* 35 C9
Mesquite, *U.S.A.* 111 H6
Mess Cr. →, *Canada* 100 B2
Messac, *France* 24 E5
Messad, *Algeria* 75 B5
Messalo →, *Mozam.* 83 E4
Méssaména, *Cameroon* 79 E7
Messancy, *Belgium* 17 J7
Messier, Canal, *Chile* 128 C2
Messina, *Italy* 35 D8
Messina, *S. Africa* 85 C5
Messina, Str. di, *Italy* 35 D8
Messíni, *Greece* 39 M5
Messiniakós Kólpos, *Greece* 39 N5
Messkirch, *Germany* 19 H5
Messonghi, *Greece* 37 B3
Mesta →, *Bulgaria* 39 H7
Mestanza, *Spain* 31 G6
Mestre, *Italy* 33 C9
Mestre, Espigão, *Brazil* 123 D2
Městys Zelezná Ruda, *Czech.* 20 F3
Meta □, *Colombia* 120 C3
Meta →, *S. Amer.* 120 B4
Metairie, *U.S.A.* 109 L9
Metaline Falls, *U.S.A.* 110 B5
Metán, *Argentina* 126 B3
Metangula, *Mozam.* 83 E3
Metauro →, *Italy* 33 E10
Metema, *Ethiopia* 77 E4
Metengobalame, *Mozam.* 83 E3
Méthana, *Greece* 39 M6
Methven, *N.Z.* 87 K3
Methy L., *Canada* 101 B7
Metil, *Mozam.* 83 F4
Metlakatla, *U.S.A.* 100 B2
Metlaoui, *Tunisia* 75 B6
Metlika, *Slovenia* 33 C12
Metropolis, *U.S.A.* 109 G10
Mettet, *Belgium* 17 H5
Mettur Dam, *India* 60 P10
Metz, *France* 25 C13
Meulaboh, *Indonesia* 56 D1
Meulan, *France* 25 C8
Meung-sur-Loire, *France* 25 E8
Meureudu, *Indonesia* 56 C1
Meurthe →, *France* 25 D13
Meurthe-et-Moselle □, *France* 25 D13
Meuse □, *France* 25 C12
Meuse →, *Europe* 17 G7
Meuselwitz, *Germany* 18 D8
Mexborough, *U.K.* 12 D6
Mexia, *U.S.A.* 109 K6
Mexiana, I., *Brazil* 122 A2
Mexicali, *Mexico* 114 A1
México, *Mexico* 115 D5
Mexico, *Maine, U.S.A.* 107 B14
Mexico, *Mo., U.S.A.* 108 F9
México □, *Mexico* 114 D5
Mexico ■, *Cent. Amer.* 114 C4
Mexico, G. of, *Cent. Amer.* 115 C7
Meyenburg, *Germany* 18 B8
Meymac, *France* 26 C6
Meymaneh, *Afghan.* 60 B4
Meyrargues, *France* 27 E9
Meyrueis, *France* 26 D7
Meyssac, *France* 26 C5
Mezdra, *Bulgaria* 38 F6
Mèze, *France* 26 E7
Mezen, *Russia* 44 C5
Mezen →, *Russia* 44 C5
Mézenc, Mt., *France* 27 D8
Mezha →, *Russia* 40 D7
Mézidon, *France* 24 C6
Mézilhac, *France* 27 D8
Mézin, *France* 26 D4
Mezöberény, *Hungary* 21 J11
Mezökövácsháza, *Hungary* 21 J10
Mezökövesd, *Hungary* 21 H10
Mézos, *France* 26 D2
Mezötúr, *Hungary* 21 J10
Mezquital, *Mexico* 114 C4
Mezzolombardo, *Italy* 32 B8
Mgeta, *Tanzania* 83 D4
Mglin, *Russia* 40 E8
Mhlaba Hills, *Zimbabwe* 83 F3
Mhow, *India* 62 H6
Miahuatlán, *Mexico* 115 D5
Miajadas, *Spain* 31 F5
Miallo, *Australia* 90 B4
Miami, *Ariz., U.S.A.* 111 K8
Miami, *Fla., U.S.A.* 105 N5
Miami, *Tex., U.S.A.* 109 H4
Miami →, *U.S.A.* 104 F3
Miami Beach, *U.S.A.* 105 N5
Miamisburg, *U.S.A.* 104 F3
Mian Xian, *China* 50 H4
Mianchi, *China* 50 G6
Mīāndowāb, *Iran* 64 B5
Miandrivazo, *Madag.* 85 B8
Mīāneh, *Iran* 64 B5
Mianning, *China* 52 C4
Mianwali, *Pakistan* 62 C4
Mianyang, *Hubei, China* 53 B9
Mianyang, *Sichuan, China* 52 B5
Mianzhu, *China* 52 B5
Miaoli, *Taiwan* 53 E13
Miarinarivo, *Madag.* 85 B8
Miass, *Russia* 44 D7
Miastko, *Poland* 20 A6
Michelstadt, *Germany* 19 F5
Michigan □, *U.S.A.* 104 C3
Michigan, L., *U.S.A.* 104 C2
Michigan City, *U.S.A.* 104 E2
Michikamau L., *Canada* 99 B7
Michipicoten, *Canada* 98 C3
Michipicoten I., *Canada* 98 C2
Michoacan □, *Mexico* 114 D4
Michurin, *Bulgaria* 38 G10
Michurinsk, *Russia* 41 E12
Miclere, *Australia* 90 C4
Mico, Pta. , *Nic.* 116 D3
Micronesia, Federated States of ■, *Pac. Oc.* 92 G7
Mid Glamorgan □, *U.K.* 13 F4
Midai, P., *Indonesia* 59 L6
Midale, *Canada* 101 D8
Middagsfjället, *Sweden* 10 A6
Middelbeers, *Neths.* 17 F6
Middelburg, *Neths.* 17 F3
Middelburg, *C. Prov., S. Africa* 84 E3
Middelburg, *Trans., S. Africa* 85 D4
Middelfart, *Denmark* 11 J3
Middelharnis, *Neths.* 16 E4
Middelkerke, *Belgium* 17 F1
Middelrode, *Neths.* 17 E6
Middelwit, *S. Africa* 84 C4
Middle Alkali L., *U.S.A.* 110 F3
Middle Fork Feather →, *U.S.A.* 112 F5
Middle I., *Australia* 89 F3
Middle Loup →, *U.S.A.* 108 E5
Middleboro, *U.S.A.* 107 E14
Middleburg, *N.Y., U.S.A.* 107 D10
Middleburg, *Pa., U.S.A.* 106 F7
Middlebury, *U.S.A.* 107 B11
Middleport, *U.S.A.* 104 F4
Middlesboro, *Ky., U.S.A.* 103 C10
Middlesboro, *Ky., U.S.A.* 105 G4
Middlesbrough, *U.K.* 12 C6
Middlesex, *Belize* 116 C2
Middlesex, *U.S.A.* 107 F10
Middleton, *Australia* 90 C3
Middleton, *Canada* 99 D6
Middletown, *Calif., U.S.A.* 112 G4
Middletown, *Conn., U.S.A.* 107 E12
Middletown, *N.Y., U.S.A.* 107 E10
Middletown, *Ohio, U.S.A.* 104 F3
Middletown, *Pa., U.S.A.* 107 F8
Midelt, *Morocco* 74 B4
Midi, Canal du →, *France* 26 E5
Midi d'Ossau, Pic du, *France* 26 F3
Midland, *Canada* 98 D4
Midland, *Calif., U.S.A.* 113 M12
Midland, *Mich., U.S.A.* 104 D3
Midland, *Pa., U.S.A.* 106 F4
Midland, *Tex., U.S.A.* 109 K3
Midlands □, *Zimbabwe* 83 F2
Midleton, *Ireland* 15 E3
Midlothian, *U.S.A.* 109 J6
Midongy, Tangorombohitr' i, *Madag.* 85 C8
Midongy Atsimo, *Madag.* 85 C8
Midou →, *France* 26 E3
Midouze →, *France* 26 E3
Midsayap, *Phil.* 55 H6
Midu, *China* 52 E3
Midway Is., *Pac. Oc.* 92 E10
Midway Wells, *U.S.A.* 113 N11
Midwest, *U.S.A.* 103 B9
Midwest, *Wyo., U.S.A.* 110 E10
Midwolda, *Neths.* 16 B9
Midyat, *Turkey* 67 E9
Mie □, *Japan* 49 G8
Miechów, *Poland* 20 E10
Międzychód, *Poland* 20 C5
Międzyrzec Podlaski, *Poland* 20 D12
Międzyrzecz, *Poland* 20 C5
Miélan, *France* 26 E4
Mielec, *Poland* 20 E11
Mienga, *Angola* 84 B2
Miercurea Ciuc, *Romania* 38 C8
Mieres, *Spain* 30 B5
Mierlo, *Neths.* 17 F7
Mieso, *Ethiopia* 77 F5
Mifflintown, *U.S.A.* 106 F7
Mifraz Ḥefa, *Israel* 69 C4
Migdāl, *Israel* 69 C4
Migennes, *France* 25 E10
Migliarino, *Italy* 33 D8
Miguel Alemán, Presa, *Mexico* 115 D5
Miguel Alves, *Brazil* 122 B3
Miguel Calmon, *Brazil* 122 D3
Mihaliççık, *Turkey* 66 D4
Mihara, *Japan* 49 G6
Mijares →, *Spain* 28 F4
Mijas, *Spain* 31 J6
Mikese, *Tanzania* 82 D4
Mikha-Tskhakaya = Senaki, *Georgia* 43 E10
Mikhailovka, *Ukraine* 42 C6
Mikhaylovgrad, *Bulgaria* 38 F6
Mikhaylovka, *Azerbaijan* 43 F13
Mikhaylovka, *Russia* 41 D11
Mikhaylovka, *Russia* 41 F13
Mikhnevo, *Russia* 41 D10
Mikínai, *Greece* 39 M5
Mikkeli, *Finland* 9 F19
Mikkeli □ = Mikkelin lääni □, *Finland* 8 F20
Mikkelin lääni □, *Finland* 8 F20
Mikkwa →, *Canada* 100 B6
Mikniya, *Sudan* 77 D3
Mikołajki, *Poland* 20 B11
Míkonos, *Greece* 39 M8
Mikrón Dhérion, *Greece* 39 H9
Mikulov, *Czech.* 20 G6
Mikumi, *Tanzania* 82 D4
Milaca, *U.S.A.* 108 C8
Milagro, *Ecuador* 120 D2
Milagros, *Phil.* 55 E5
Milan = Milano, *Italy* 32 C6
Milan, *Mo., U.S.A.* 108 E8
Milan, *Tenn., U.S.A.* 105 H1
Milang, *Australia* 91 E2
Milange, *Mozam.* 83 F4
Milano, *Italy* 32 C6
Milâs, *Turkey* 66 E2
Mílatos, *Greece* 37 D7
Milazzo, *Italy* 35 D8
Milbank, *U.S.A.* 108 C6
Milden, *Canada* 101 C7
Mildmay, *Canada* 106 B3
Mildura, *Australia* 91 E3
Mile, *China* 52 E4
Miléai, *Greece* 39 K6
Mileh Tharthār, *Iraq* 64 C4
Miles, *Australia* 91 D5
Miles, *U.S.A.* 109 K4
Miles City, *U.S.A.* 108 B2
Milestone, *Canada* 101 D8
Mileto, *Italy* 35 D9
Miletto, Mte., *Italy* 35 A7
Miletus, *Turkey* 66 E2
Mileura, *Australia* 89 E2
Milford, *Calif., U.S.A.* 112 E6
Milford, *Conn., U.S.A.* 107 E11
Milford, *Del., U.S.A.* 104 F8
Milford, *Mass., U.S.A.* 107 D13
Milford, *Pa., U.S.A.* 107 E10
Milford, *Utah, U.S.A.* 111 G7
Milford Haven, *U.K.* 13 F2
Milford Sd., *N.Z.* 87 L1
Milgun, *Australia* 89 D2
Milḥ, Baḥr al, *Iraq* 64 C4
Miliana, *Aïn Salah, Algeria* 75 C5
Miliana, *Médéa, Algeria* 75 A5
Miling, *Australia* 89 F2
Militello in Val di Catánia, *Italy* 35 E7
Milk →, *U.S.A.* 110 B10
Milk, Wadi el →, *Sudan* 76 D3
Milk River, *Canada* 100 D6
Mill, *Neths.* 17 E7
Mill City, *U.S.A.* 110 D2
Mill I., *Antarctica* 5 C8
Mill Valley, *U.S.A.* 112 H4
Millau, *France* 26 D7
Millbridge, *Canada* 106 B7
Millbrook, *Canada* 106 B6
Mille Lacs, L. des, *Canada* 98 C1
Mille Lacs L., *U.S.A.* 108 B8
Milledgeville, *U.S.A.* 105 J4
Millen, *U.S.A.* 105 J5
Miller, *U.S.A.* 108 C5
Millerovo, *Russia* 43 B9
Millersburg, *Ohio, U.S.A.* 106 F3
Millersburg, *Pa., U.S.A.* 106 F8
Millerton, *U.S.A.* 107 E11
Millerton L., *U.S.A.* 112 J7
Millevaches, Plateau de, *France* 26 C6
Millicent, *Australia* 91 F3
Millingen, *Neths.* 16 E8

Millinocket, *U.S.A.* 99 C6
Millmerran, *Australia* 91 D5
Mills L., *Canada* 100 A5
Millsboro, *U.S.A.* 106 G4
Milltown Malbay, *Ireland* 15 D2
Millville, *U.S.A.* 104 F8
Millwood L., *U.S.A.* 109 J8
Milly-la-Forêt, *France* 25 D9
Milna, *Croatia* 33 E13
Milne →, *Australia* 90 C2
Milne Inlet, *Canada* 97 A11
Milnor, *U.S.A.* 108 B6
Milo, *Canada* 100 C6
Mílos, *Greece* 39 N7
Miloševo, *Serbia* 21 K10
Milparinka P.O., *Australia* 91 D3
Miltenberg, *Germany* 19 F5
Milton, *Canada* 106 C5
Milton, *N.Z.* 87 M2
Milton, *U.K.* 14 D4
Milton, *Calif., U.S.A.* 112 G6
Milton, *Fla., U.S.A.* 105 K2
Milton, *Pa., U.S.A.* 106 F8
Milton-Freewater, *U.S.A.* 110 D4
Milton Keynes, *U.K.* 13 E7
Miltou, *Chad* 73 F8
Milverton, *Canada* 106 C4
Milwaukee, *U.S.A.* 104 D2
Milwaukee Deep, *Atl. Oc.* 117 C6
Milwaukie, *U.S.A.* 112 E4
Mim, *Ghana* 78 D4
Mimizan, *France* 26 D2
Mimoso, *Brazil* 123 E2
Min Chiang →, *China* 53 E12
Min Jiang →, *China* 52 C5
Min Xian, *China* 50 G3
Mina, *U.S.A.* 111 G4
Mina Pirquitas, *Argentina* 126 A2
Mīnā Su'ud, *Si. Arabia* 65 D6
Mīnā'al Aḥmadī, *Kuwait* 65 D6
Mīnāb, *Iran* 65 E8
Minago →, *Canada* 101 C9
Minaki, *Canada* 101 D10
Minamata, *Japan* 49 H5
Minami-Tori-Shima, *Pac. Oc.* 92 E7
Minas, *Uruguay* 127 C4
Minas, Sierra de las, *Guatemala* 116 C2
Minas Basin, *Canada* 99 C7
Minas de Rio Tinto, *Spain* 31 H4
Minas de San Quintín, *Spain* 31 G6
Minas Gerais □, *Brazil* 123 E2
Minas Novas, *Brazil* 123 E3
Minatitlán, *Mexico* 115 D6
Minbu, *Burma* 61 J19
Mincio →, *Italy* 32 C7
Mindanao, *Phil.* 55 H6
Mindanao Sea = Bohol Sea, *Phil.* 57 C6
Mindanao Trench, *Pac. Oc.* 55 F7
Mindel →, *Germany* 19 G6
Mindelheim, *Germany* 19 G6
Minden, *Canada* 106 B6
Minden, *Germany* 18 C4
Minden, *La., U.S.A.* 109 J8
Minden, *Nev., U.S.A.* 112 G7
Mindiptana, *Indonesia* 57 F10
Mindoro, *Phil.* 55 E4
Mindoro Str., *Phil.* 55 E4
Mindouli, *Congo* 80 E2
Mine, *Japan* 49 G5
Minehead, *U.K.* 13 F4
Mineiros, *Brazil* 125 D7
Mineola, *U.S.A.* 109 J7
Mineral King, *U.S.A.* 112 J8
Mineral Wells, *U.S.A.* 109 J5
Mineralnyye Vody, *Russia* 43 D10
Minersville, *Pa., U.S.A.* 107 F8
Minersville, *Utah, U.S.A.* 111 G7
Minerva, *U.S.A.* 106 F3
Minervino Murge, *Italy* 35 A9
Minetto, *U.S.A.* 107 C8
Mingan, *Canada* 99 B7
Mingechaur, *Azerbaijan* 43 F12
Mingechaurskoye Vdkhr., *Azerbaijan* 43 F12
Mingela, *Australia* 90 B4
Mingenew, *Australia* 89 E2
Mingera Cr. →, *Australia* 90 C2
Minggang, *China* 53 A10
Mingin, *Burma* 61 H19
Minglanilla, *Spain* 28 F3
Minglun, *China* 52 E7
Mingorria, *Spain* 30 E6
Mingt'iehkaitafan = Mintaka Pass, *Pakistan* 63 A6
Mingxi, *China* 53 D11
Mingyuegue, *China* 51 C15
Minhou, *China* 53 E12
Minićevo, *Serbia* 21 M12
Minidoka, *U.S.A.* 110 E7
Minigwal, L., *Australia* 89 E3
Minilya, *Australia* 89 D1
Minilya →, *Australia* 89 D1
Minipi, L., *Canada* 99 B7
Mink L., *Canada* 100 A5
Minna, *Nigeria* 79 D6
Minneapolis, *Kans., U.S.A.* 108 F6
Minneapolis, *Minn., U.S.A.* 108 C8
Minnedosa, *Canada* 101 C9
Minnesota □, *U.S.A.* 108 B7
Minnesund, *Norway* 10 D5
Minnie Creek, *Australia* 89 D2
Minnipa, *Australia* 91 E2
Minnitaki L., *Canada* 98 C1
Mino, *Japan* 49 G8
Miño →, *Spain* 30 D2
Minorca = Menorca, *Spain* 36 B11
Minore, *Australia* 91 E4
Minot, *U.S.A.* 108 A4
Minqin, *China* 50 E2
Minqing, *China* 53 D12
Minsen, *Germany* 18 B3
Minsk, *Belorussia* 40 E5
Mińsk Mazowiecki, *Poland* 20 C11
Mintaka Pass, *Pakistan* 63 A6
Minto, *U.S.A.* 96 B5
Minton, *Canada* 101 D8
Minturn, *U.S.A.* 110 G10
Minturno, *Italy* 34 A6
Minûf, *Egypt* 76 H7
Minusinsk, *Russia* 45 D10
Minutang, *India* 61 E20
Minvoul, *Gabon* 80 D2
Minya el Qamh, *Egypt* 76 H7
Mionica, *Serbia* 21 L10
Mir, *Niger* 79 C7
Mir-Bashir, *Azerbaijan* 43 F12
Mīr Kūh, *Iran* 65 E8
Mīr Shahdād, *Iran* 65 E8
Mira, *Italy* 33 C9
Mira, *Portugal* 30 E2
Mira →, *Colombia* 120 C2
Mira →, *Portugal* 31 H2
Mira por vos Cay, *Bahamas* 117 B5
Mirabella Eclano, *Italy* 35 A7
Miracema do Norte, *Brazil* 122 C2
Mirador, *Brazil* 122 C3
Miraflores, *Colombia* 120 C3
Miraj, *India* 60 L9
Miram Shah, *Pakistan* 62 C4
Miramar, *Argentina* 126 D4
Miramar, *Mozam.* 85 C6
Miramas, *France* 27 E8
Mirambeau, *France* 26 C3
Miramichi B., *Canada* 99 C7
Miramont-de-Guyenne, *France* 26 D4
Miranda, *Brazil* 125 E6
Miranda □, *Venezuela* 120 A4
Miranda →, *Brazil* 125 D6
Miranda de Ebro, *Spain* 28 C2
Miranda do Corvo, *Spain* 30 E2
Miranda do Douro, *Portugal* 30 D4
Mirande, *France* 26 E4
Mirandela, *Portugal* 30 D3
Mirando City, *U.S.A.* 109 M5
Mirandola, *Italy* 32 D8
Mirandópolis, *Brazil* 127 A5
Mirango, *Malawi* 83 E3
Mirani, *Australia* 90 C4
Mirano, *Italy* 33 C9
Mirassol, *Brazil* 127 A6
Mirbāṭ, *Oman* 68 D5
Mirear, *Egypt* 76 C4
Mirebeau, *Côte-d'Or, France* 25 E12
Mirebeau, *Vienne, France* 24 F7
Mirecourt, *France* 25 D13
Mirgorod, *Ukraine* 40 G8
Miri, *Malaysia* 56 D4
Miriam Vale, *Australia* 90 C5
Mirim, L., *S. Amer.* 127 C5
Mirimire, *Venezuela* 120 A4
Miriti, *Brazil* 125 B6
Mirnyy, *Russia* 45 C12
Mirond L., *Canada* 101 B8
Mirpur, *Pakistan* 63 C5
Mirpur Bibiwari, *Pakistan* 62 E2
Mirpur Khas, *Pakistan* 62 G3
Mirpur Sakro, *Pakistan* 62 G2
Mirria, *Niger* 79 C6
Mirror, *Canada* 100 C6
Mirşani, *Romania* 38 E6
Miryang, *S. Korea* 51 G15
Mirzaani, *Georgia* 43 F12
Mirzapur, *India* 63 G10
Mirzapur-cum-Vindhyachal = Mirzapur, *India* 63 G10
Misantla, *Mexico* 115 D5
Misawa, *Japan* 48 D10
Miscou I., *Canada* 99 C7
Mish'āb, Ra'as al, *Si. Arabia* 65 D6
Mishagua →, *Peru* 124 C3
Mishan, *China* 54 B8
Mishawaka, *U.S.A.* 104 E2
Mishbih, Gebel, *Egypt* 76 C3
Mishima, *Japan* 49 G9
Misilmeri, *Italy* 34 D6
Misión, *Mexico* 113 N10
Misión Fagnano, *Argentina* 128 D3
Misiones □, *Argentina* 127 B5
Misiones □, *Paraguay* 126 B4
Miskah, *Si. Arabia* 64 E4
Miskitos, Cayos, *Nic.* 116 D3
Miskolc, *Hungary* 21 G10
Misoke, *Zaïre* 82 C2
Misool, *Indonesia* 57 E8
Misrātah, *Libya* 73 B8
Missanabie, *Canada* 98 C3
Missão Velha, *Brazil* 122 C4
Missinaibi →, *Canada* 98 B3
Missinaibi L., *Canada* 98 C3
Mission, *S. Dak., U.S.A.* 108 D4
Mission, *Tex., U.S.A.* 109 M5
Mission City, *Canada* 100 D4
Mission Viejo, *U.S.A.* 113 M9
Missisa L., *Canada* 98 B2
Missisagi →, *Canada* 98 C3
Mississippi □, *U.S.A.* 109 J10
Mississippi →, *U.S.A.* 109 L10
Mississippi L., *Canada* 107 A8
Mississippi River Delta, *U.S.A.* 109 L9
Mississippi Sd., *U.S.A.* 109 K10
Missoula, *U.S.A.* 110 C6
Missour, *Morocco* 74 B4
Missouri □, *U.S.A.* 108 F8
Missouri →, *U.S.A.* 108 F9
Missouri Valley, *U.S.A.* 108 E7
Mist, *U.S.A.* 112 E3
Mistake B., *Canada* 101 A10
Mistassini →, *Canada* 99 C5
Mistassini L., *Canada* 98 B5
Mistastin L., *Canada* 99 A7
Mistatim, *Canada* 101 C8
Mistelbach, *Austria* 20 G6
Misterbianco, *Italy* 35 E8
Mistretta, *Italy* 35 E7
Misty L., *Canada* 101 B8
Misurata = Misrātah, *Libya* 73 B8
Mît Ghamr, *Egypt* 76 H7
Mitatib, *Sudan* 77 D4
Mitchell, *Australia* 91 D4
Mitchell, *Canada* 106 C3
Mitchell, *Ind., U.S.A.* 104 F2
Mitchell, *Nebr., U.S.A.* 108 E3
Mitchell, *Oreg., U.S.A.* 110 D3
Mitchell, *S. Dak., U.S.A.* 108 D5
Mitchell →, *Australia* 90 B3
Mitchell, Mt., *U.S.A.* 105 H4
Mitchell Ras., *Australia* 90 A2
Mitchelstown, *Ireland* 15 D3
Mitha Tiwana, *Pakistan* 62 C5
Mitilíni, *Greece* 39 K9
Mito, *Japan* 49 F10
Mitsinjo, *Madag.* 85 B8
Mitsiwa, *Eritrea* 77 D4
Mitsiwa Channel, *Eritrea* 77 D5
Mitsukaidō, *Japan* 49 F9
Mittagong, *Australia* 91 E5
Mittelland, *Switz.* 22 C4
Mittelland Kanal, *Germany* 18 C3
Mittenwalde, *Germany* 18 C9
Mitterteich, *Germany* 19 F8
Mittweida, *Germany* 18 E8
Mitú, *Colombia* 120 C3
Mituas, *Colombia* 120 C4
Mitumba, *Tanzania* 82 D3
Mitumba, Chaîne des, *Zaïre* 82 D2
Mitumba Mts. = Mitumba, Chaîne des, *Zaïre* 82 D2
Mitwaba, *Zaïre* 83 D2
Mityana, *Uganda* 82 B3
Mitzic, *Gabon* 80 D2
Mixteco →, *Mexico* 115 D5
Miyagi □, *Japan* 48 E10
Miyâh, W. el →, *Egypt* 76 B3
Miyah, W. el →, *Syria* 64 C3
Miyake-Jima, *Japan* 49 G9
Miyako, *Japan* 48 E10
Miyako-Jima, *Japan* 49 M2
Miyako-Rettō, *Japan* 49 M2
Miyakonojō, *Japan* 49 J5
Miyanoura-Dake, *Japan* 49 J5
Miyazaki, *Japan* 49 J5
Miyazaki □, *Japan* 49 H5
Miyazu, *Japan* 49 G7
Miyet, Bahr el = Dead Sea, *Asia* 69 D4
Miyi, *China* 52 D4
Miyoshi, *Japan* 49 G6
Miyun, *China* 50 D9
Miyun Shuiku, *China* 51 D9
Mizamis = Ozamiz, *Phil.* 55 G5
Mizdah, *Libya* 75 B7
Mizen Hd., *Cork, Ireland* 15 E2
Mizen Hd., *Wick., Ireland* 15 D5
Mizhi, *China* 50 F6
Mizil, *Romania* 38 E9
Mizoram □, *India* 61 H18
Mizpe Ramon, *Israel* 69 E3
Mizusawa, *Japan* 48 E10
Mjöbäck, *Sweden* 11 G6
Mjölby, *Sweden* 11 F9
Mjörn, *Sweden* 11 G6
Mjøsa, *Norway* 10 D5
Mkata, *Tanzania* 82 D4
Mkokotoni, *Tanzania* 82 D4
Mkomazi, *Tanzania* 82 C4
Mkomazi →, *S. Africa* 85 E5
Mkulwe, *Tanzania* 83 D3
Mkumbi, Ras, *Tanzania* 82 D4
Mkushi, *Zambia* 83 E2
Mkushi River, *Zambia* 83 E2
Mkuze, *S. Africa* 85 D5
Mkuze →, *S. Africa* 85 D5
Mladá Boleslav, *Czech.* 20 E4
Mladenovac, *Serbia* 21 L10
Mlala Hills, *Tanzania* 82 D3
Mlange, *Malawi* 83 F4
Mlava →, *Serbia* 21 L11
Mława, *Poland* 20 B10
Mlinište, *Bos.-H.* 33 D13
Mljet, *Croatia* 21 N7
Młynąry, *Poland* 20 A9
Mmabatho, *S. Africa* 84 D4
Mme, *Cameroon* 79 D7
Mo i Rana, *Norway* 8 C13
Moa, *Indonesia* 57 F7
Moa →, *S. Leone* 78 D2
Moab, *U.S.A.* 111 G9
Moabi, *Gabon* 80 E2
Moaco →, *Brazil* 124 B4
Moala, *Fiji* 87 D8
Moalie Park, *Australia* 91 D3
Moaña, *Spain* 30 C2
Moba, *Zaïre* 82 D2
Mobārakābād, *Iran* 65 D7
Mobārakīyeh, *Iran* 65 C6
Mobaye, *C.A.R.* 80 D4
Mobayi, *Zaïre* 80 D4
Moberly, *U.S.A.* 108 F8
Moberly →, *Canada* 100 B4
Mobile, *U.S.A.* 105 K1
Mobile B., *U.S.A.* 105 K2
Mobridge, *U.S.A.* 108 C4
Mobutu Sese Seko, L., *Africa* 82 B3
Moc Chau, *Vietnam* 58 B5
Moc Hoa, *Vietnam* 59 G5
Mocabe Kasari, *Zaïre* 83 D2
Mocajuba, *Brazil* 122 B2
Moçambique, *Mozam.* 83 F5
Moçâmedes = Namibe, *Angola* 81 H2
Mocapra →, *Venezuela* 120 B4
Mocha, I., *Chile* 128 A2
Mochudi, *Botswana* 84 C4
Mocimboa da Praia, *Mozam.* 83 E5
Moclips, *U.S.A.* 112 C2
Mocoa, *Colombia* 120 C2
Mococa, *Brazil* 127 A6
Mocorito, *Mexico* 114 B3
Moctezuma, *Mexico* 114 B3
Moctezuma →, *Mexico* 115 C5
Mocuba, *Mozam.* 83 F4
Mocúzari, Presa, *Mexico* 114 B3
Modane, *France* 27 C10
Modasa, *India* 62 H5
Modave, *Belgium* 17 H6
Modder →, *S. Africa* 84 D3
Modderrivier, *S. Africa* 84 D3
Módena, *Italy* 32 D7
Modena, *U.S.A.* 111 H7
Modesto, *U.S.A.* 111 H3
Módica, *Italy* 35 F7
Modigliana, *Italy* 33 D8
Modo, *Sudan* 77 F3
Modra, *Slovak Rep.* 21 G7
Moe, *Australia* 91 F4
Moebase, *Mozam.* 83 F4
Moëlan-sur-Mer, *France* 24 E3
Moengo, *Surinam* 121 B7
Moergestel, *Neths.* 17 E6
Moers, *Germany* 17 F9
Moësa →, *Switz.* 23 D8
Moffat, *U.K.* 14 F5
Moga, *India* 62 D6
Mogadishu = Muqdisho, *Somali Rep.* 68 G4
Mogador = Essaouira, *Morocco* 74 B3
Mogadouro, *Portugal* 30 D4
Mogalakwena →, *S. Africa* 85 C4
Mogami →, *Japan* 48 E10
Mogán, *Canary Is.* 36 G4
Mogaung, *Burma* 61 G20
Møgeltønder, *Denmark* 11 K2
Mogente, *Spain* 29 G4
Mogho, *Ethiopia* 77 G5
Mogi das Cruzes, *Brazil* 127 A6
Mogi-Guaçu →, *Brazil* 127 A6
Mogi-Mirim, *Brazil* 127 A6
Mogielnica, *Poland* 20 D10
Mogilev, *Belorussia* 40 E7
Mogilev-Podolskiy, *Moldavia* 42 B2
Mogilno, *Poland* 20 C7
Mogincual, *Mozam.* 83 F5
Mogliano Véneto, *Italy* 33 C9
Mogocha, *Russia* 45 D12
Mogoi, *Indonesia* 57 E8
Mogok, *Burma* 61 H20
Moguer, *Spain* 31 H4
Mogumber, *Australia* 89 F2
Mohács, *Hungary* 21 K8
Mohales Hoek, *Lesotho* 84 E4
Mohall, *U.S.A.* 108 A4
Moḥammadābād, *Iran* 65 B8
Mohammadia, *Algeria* 75 A5
Mohammedia, *Morocco* 74 B3
Mohave, L., *U.S.A.* 113 K12
Mohawk →, *U.S.A.* 107 D11
Möhne →, *Germany* 18 D3
Moholm, *Sweden* 11 F8
Mohoro, *Tanzania* 82 D4
Moia, *Sudan* 77 F2
Moidart, L., *U.K.* 14 E3
Moineşti, *Romania* 38 C9
Mointy, *Kazakhstan* 44 E8
Moirans, *France* 27 C9
Moirans-en-Montagne, *France* 27 B9
Moíres, *Greece* 37 D6
Moisaküla, *Estonia* 40 B4
Moisie, *Canada* 99 B6
Moisie →, *Canada* 99 B6
Moissac, *France* 26 D5
Moïssala, *Chad* 73 G8
Moita, *Portugal* 31 G2
Mojácar, *Spain* 29 H3
Mojados, *Spain* 30 D6
Mojave, *U.S.A.* 113 K8
Mojave Desert, *U.S.A.* 113 L10
Mojiang, *China* 52 F3
Mojo, *Bolivia* 126 A2
Mojo, *Ethiopia* 77 F4
Mojokerto, *Indonesia* 57 G15
Mojos, Llanos de, *Bolivia* 125 D5
Moju →, *Brazil* 122 B2
Mokai, *N.Z.* 87 H5
Mokambo, *Zaïre* 83 E2
Mokameh, *India* 63 G11
Mokelumne →, *U.S.A.* 112 G5
Mokelumne Hill, *U.S.A.* 112 G6
Mokhós, *Greece* 37 D7
Mokhotlong, *Lesotho* 85 D4
Moknine, *Tunisia* 75 A7
Mokokchung, *India* 61 F19
Mokra Gora, *Serbia* 21 N10
Mokronog, *Slovenia* 33 C12
Moksha →, *Russia* 41 D12
Mokshan, *Russia* 41 E14
Mol, *Belgium* 17 F6
Mola, C. de la, *Spain* 28 F9
Mola di Bari, *Italy* 35 A10
Moláoi, *Greece* 39 N5
Molat, *Croatia* 33 D11
Molchanovo, *Russia* 44 D9
Mold, *U.K.* 12 D4
Moldavia = Moldova, *Romania* 38 C10
Moldavia ■, *Europe* 42 C3
Molde, *Norway* 8 E9
Moldova, *Romania* 38 C10
Moldova ■ = Moldavia ■, *Europe* 42 C3
Moldova Nouă, *Romania* 38 E4
Moldoveanu, *Romania* 38 D7
Molepolole, *Botswana* 84 C4
Moléson, *Switz.* 22 C4
Molfetta, *Italy* 35 A9
Molina de Aragón, *Spain* 28 E3
Moline, *U.S.A.* 108 E9
Molinella, *Italy* 33 D8
Molinos, *Argentina* 126 B2
Moliro, *Zaïre* 82 D3
Molise □, *Italy* 33 G11
Moliterno, *Italy* 35 B8
Mollahat, *Bangla.* 63 H13
Mölle, *Sweden* 11 H6
Molledo, *Spain* 30 B6
Mollendo, *Peru* 124 D3
Mollerin, L., *Australia* 89 F2
Mollerusa, *Spain* 28 D5
Mollina, *Spain* 31 H6
Mölln, *Germany* 18 B6
Mölltorp, *Sweden* 11 F8
Mölndal, *Sweden* 11 G6
Molochansk, *Ukraine* 42 C6
Molochnaya →, *Ukraine* 42 C6
Molodechno, *Belorussia* 40 D5
Molokai, *U.S.A.* 102 H16
Moloma →, *Russia* 41 B16
Molong, *Australia* 91 E4
Molopo →, *Africa* 84 D3
Mólos, *Greece* 39 L5
Molotov = Perm, *Russia* 44 D6
Moloundou, *Cameroon* 80 D3
Molsheim, *France* 25 D14
Molson L., *Canada* 101 C9
Molteno, *S. Africa* 84 E4
Molu, *Indonesia* 57 F8
Molucca Sea = Maluku Sea, *Indonesia* 57 E6
Moluccas = Maluku, *Indonesia* 57 E7
Moma, *Mozam.* 83 F4
Moma, *Zaïre* 82 C1
Mombaça, *Brazil* 122 C4
Mombasa, *Kenya* 82 C4
Mombetsu, *Japan* 48 B11
Mombuey, *Spain* 30 C4
Momchilgrad, *Bulgaria* 39 H8
Momi, *Zaïre* 82 C2
Momignies, *Belgium* 17 H4
Mompós, *Colombia* 120 B3
Møn, *Denmark* 11 K6
Mon →, *Burma* 61 J19
Mona, Canal de la, *W. Indies* 117 C6
Mona, Isla, *Puerto Rico* 117 C6
Mona, Pta., *Costa Rica* 116 E3
Mona, Pta., *Spain* 31 J7
Monach Is., *U.K.* 14 D1
Monaco ■, *Europe* 27 E11
Monadhliath Mts., *U.K.* 14 D4
Monagas □, *Venezuela* 121 B5
Monaghan, *Ireland* 15 B5
Monaghan □, *Ireland* 15 B5
Monahans, *U.S.A.* 109 K3
Monapo, *Mozam.* 83 E5
Monarch Mt., *Canada* 100 C3
Monastir = Bitola, *Macedonia* 39 H4
Monastir, *Tunisia* 75 A7
Monastyriska, *Ukraine* 40 G4
Moncada, *Phil.* 55 D4
Moncada, *Spain* 28 F4
Moncalieri, *Italy* 32 D4
Moncalvo, *Italy* 32 C5
Monção, *Portugal* 30 C2
Moncarapacho, *Portugal* 31 H3
Moncayo, Sierra del, *Spain* 28 D3
Mönchengladbach, *Germany* 18 D2
Monchique, *Portugal* 31 H2

Monclova, *Mexico* 114 B4
Moncontour, *France* 24 D4
Moncoutant, *France* 26 B3
Moncton, *Canada* 99 C7
Mondego →, *Portugal* 30 E2
Mondego, C., *Portugal* 30 E2
Mondeodo, *Indonesia* 57 E6
Mondolfo, *Italy* 33 E10
Mondoñedo, *Spain* 30 B3
Mondoví, *Italy* 32 D4
Mondovi, *U.S.A.* 108 C9
Mondragon, *France* 27 D8
Mondragon, *Phil.* 55 E6
Mondragone, *Italy* 34 A6
Mondrain I., *Australia* 89 F3
Monduli □, *Tanzania* 82 C4
Monemvasía, *Greece* 39 N6
Monessen, *U.S.A.* 106 F5
Monesterio, *Spain* 31 G4
Monestier-de-Clermont, *France* 27 D9
Monett, *U.S.A.* 109 G8
Monfalcone, *Italy* 33 C10
Monflanquin, *France* 26 D4
Monforte, *Portugal* 31 F3
Monforte de Lemos, *Spain* 30 C3
Mong Hsu, *Burma* 61 J21
Mong Kung, *Burma* 61 J20
Mong Nai, *Burma* 61 J20
Mong Pawk, *Burma* 61 H21
Mong Ton, *Burma* 61 J21
Mong Wa, *Burma* 61 J22
Mong Yai, *Burma* 61 H21
Mongalla, *Sudan* 77 F3
Mongers, L., *Australia* 89 E2
Monghyr = Munger, *India* 63 G12
Mongo, *Chad* 73 F8
Mongolia ■, *Asia* 45 E10
Mongonu, *Nigeria* 79 C7
Mongororo, *Chad* 73 F9
Mongu, *Zambia* 81 H4
Môngua, *Angola* 84 B2
Monistrol-d'Allier, *France* 26 D7
Monistrol-sur-Loire, *France* 27 C8
Monkey Bay, *Malawi* 83 E4
Monkey River, *Belize* 115 D7
Monkira, *Australia* 90 C3
Monkoto, *Zaïre* 80 E4
Monmouth, *U.K.* 13 F5
Monmouth, *U.S.A.* 108 E9
Mono L., *U.S.A.* 111 H4
Monolith, *U.S.A.* 113 K8
Monólithos, *Greece* 37 C9
Monongahela, *U.S.A.* 106 F5
Monópoli, *Italy* 35 B10
Monor, *Hungary* 21 H9
Monóvar, *Spain* 29 G4
Monqoumba, *C.A.R.* 80 D3
Monreal del Campo, *Spain* 28 E3
Monreale, *Italy* 34 D6
Monroe, *Ga., U.S.A.* 105 J4
Monroe, *La., U.S.A.* 109 J8
Monroe, *Mich., U.S.A.* 104 E4
Monroe, *N.C., U.S.A.* 105 H5
Monroe, *N.Y., U.S.A.* 107 E10
Monroe, *Utah, U.S.A.* 111 G7
Monroe, *Wash., U.S.A.* 112 C5
Monroe, *Wis., U.S.A.* 108 D10
Monroe City, *U.S.A.* 108 F9
Monroeville, *Ala., U.S.A.* 105 K2
Monroeville, *Pa., U.S.A.* 106 F5
Monrovia, *Liberia* 78 D2
Monrovia, *U.S.A.* 111 J4
Mons, *Belgium* 17 H3
Monsaraz, *Portugal* 31 G3
Monse, *Indonesia* 57 E6
Monsefú, *Peru* 124 B2
Monségur, *France* 26 D4
Monsélice, *Italy* 33 C8
Monster, *Neths.* 16 D4
Mont Cenis, Col du, *France* 27 C10
Mont-de-Marsan, *France* 26 E3
Mont-Joli, *Canada* 99 C6
Mont-Laurier, *Canada* 98 C4
Mont-St.-Michel, Le = Le Mont-St.-Michel, *France* 24 D5
Mont-sous-Vaudrey, *France* 25 F12
Mont-sur-Marchienne, *Belgium* 17 H4
Mont Tremblant Prov. Park, *Canada* 98 C5
Montabaur, *Germany* 18 E3
Montagnac, *France* 26 E7
Montagnana, *Italy* 33 C8
Montagu, *S. Africa* 84 E3
Montagu I., *Antarctica* 5 B1
Montague, *Canada* 99 C7
Montague, *U.S.A.* 110 F2
Montague, I., *Mexico* 114 A2
Montague Ra., *Australia* 89 E2
Montague Sd., *Australia* 88 B4
Montaigu, *France* 24 F5
Montalbán, *Spain* 28 E4
Montalbano di Elicona, *Italy* 35 D8
Montalbano Iónico, *Italy* 35 B9
Montalbo, *Spain* 28 F2
Montalcino, *Italy* 33 E8
Montalegre, *Portugal* 30 D3
Montalto di Castro, *Italy* 33 F8
Montalto Uffugo, *Italy* 35 C9
Montalvo, *U.S.A.* 113 L7
Montamarta, *Spain* 30 D5
Montaña, *Peru* 124 B3
Montana, *Switz.* 22 D4
Montana □, *U.S.A.* 110 C9
Montaña Clara, I., *Canary Is.* 36 E6
Montánchez, *Spain* 31 F4
Montañita, *Colombia* 120 C2
Montargis, *France* 25 E9
Montauban, *France* 26 D5
Montauk, *U.S.A.* 107 E13
Montauk Pt., *U.S.A.* 107 E13
Montbard, *France* 25 E11
Montbéliard, *France* 25 E13
Montblanch, *Spain* 28 D6
Montbrison, *France* 27 C8
Montcalm, Pic de, *France* 26 F5
Montceau-les-Mines, *France* 25 F11
Montchanin, *France* 27 B8
Montclair, *U.S.A.* 107 F10
Montcornet, *France* 25 C11
Montcuq, *France* 26 D5
Montdidier, *France* 25 C9
Monte Albán, *Mexico* 115 D5
Monte Alegre, *Brazil* 121 D7
Monte Alegre de Goiás, *Brazil* 123 D2
Monte Alegre de Minas, *Brazil* 123 E2
Monte Azul, *Brazil* 123 E3
Monte Bello Is., *Australia* 88 D2
Monte-Carlo, *Monaco* 27 E11
Monte Carmelo, *Brazil* 123 E2
Monte Caseros, *Argentina* 126 C4
Monte Comán, *Argentina* 126 C2
Monte Cristi, *Dom. Rep.* 117 C5
Monte Dinero, *Argentina* 128 D3
Monte Lindo →, *Paraguay* 126 A4
Monte Quemado, *Argentina* 126 B3
Monte Redondo, *Portugal* 30 F2
Monte Rio, *U.S.A.* 112 G4
Monte San Giovanni, *Italy* 34 A6
Monte San Savino, *Italy* 33 E8
Monte Sant' Ángelo, *Italy* 35 A8
Monte Santu, C. di, *Italy* 34 B2
Monte Vista, *U.S.A.* 111 H10
Monteagudo, *Argentina* 127 B5
Monteagudo, *Bolivia* 125 D5
Montealegre, *Spain* 29 G3
Montebello, *Canada* 98 C5
Montebelluna, *Italy* 33 C9
Montebourg, *France* 24 C5
Montecastrilli, *Italy* 33 F9
Montecatini Terme, *Italy* 32 E7
Montecito, *U.S.A.* 113 L7
Montecristi, *Ecuador* 120 D1
Montecristo, *Italy* 32 F7
Montefalco, *Italy* 33 F9
Montefiascone, *Italy* 33 F9
Montefrío, *Spain* 31 H6
Montegnée, *Belgium* 17 G7
Montego Bay, *Jamaica* 116 C4
Montegranaro, *Italy* 33 E10
Monteiro, *Brazil* 122 C4
Montejicar, *Spain* 29 H1
Montejinnie, *Australia* 88 C5
Montelíbano, *Colombia* 120 B2
Montélimar, *France* 27 D8
Montella, *Italy* 35 B8
Montellano, *Spain* 31 J5
Montello, *U.S.A.* 108 D10
Montelupo Fiorentino, *Italy* 32 E8
Montemor-o-Novo, *Portugal* 31 G2
Montemor-o-Velho, *Portugal* 30 E2
Montemorelos, *Mexico* 115 B5
Montendre, *France* 26 C3
Montenegro, *Brazil* 127 B5
Montenegro □, *Montenegro* 21 N9
Montenero di Bisaccia, *Italy* 33 G11
Montepuez, *Mozam.* 83 E4
Montepuez →, *Mozam.* 83 E5
Montepulciano, *Italy* 33 E8
Montereale, *Italy* 33 F10
Montereau-Fault-Yonne, *France* 25 D9
Monterey, *U.S.A.* 111 H3
Monterey B., *U.S.A.* 112 J5
Montería, *Colombia* 120 B2
Montero, *Bolivia* 125 D5
Monteros, *Argentina* 126 B2
Monterotondo, *Italy* 33 F9
Monterrey, *Mexico* 114 B4
Montes Altos, *Brazil* 122 C2
Montes Claros, *Brazil* 123 E3
Montesano, *U.S.A.* 112 D3
Montesárchio, *Italy* 35 A7
Montescaglioso, *Italy* 35 B9
Montesilvano, *Italy* 33 F11
Montevarchi, *Italy* 33 E8
Montevideo, *Uruguay* 127 C4
Montevideo, *U.S.A.* 108 C7
Montezuma, *U.S.A.* 108 E8
Montfaucon, *France* 25 C12
Montfaucon-en-Velay, *France* 27 C8
Montfort, *France* 24 D5
Montfort, *Neths.* 17 F7
Montfort-l'Amaury, *France* 25 D8
Montgenèvre, *France* 27 D10
Montgomery = Sahiwal, *Pakistan* 62 D5
Montgomery, *U.K.* 13 E4
Montgomery, *Ala., U.S.A.* 105 J2
Montgomery, *W. Va., U.S.A.* 104 F5
Montguyon, *France* 26 C3
Monthey, *Switz.* 22 D3
Monticelli d'Ongina, *Italy* 32 C6
Monticello, *Ark., U.S.A.* 109 J9
Monticello, *Fla., U.S.A.* 105 K4
Monticello, *Ind., U.S.A.* 104 E2
Monticello, *Iowa, U.S.A.* 108 D9
Monticello, *Ky., U.S.A.* 105 G3
Monticello, *Minn., U.S.A.* 108 C8
Monticello, *Miss., U.S.A.* 109 K9
Monticello, *N.Y., U.S.A.* 107 E10
Monticello, *Utah, U.S.A.* 111 H9
Montichiari, *Italy* 32 C7
Montier-en-Der, *France* 25 D11
Montignac, *France* 26 C5
Montignies-sur-Sambre, *Belgium* 17 H4
Montigny, *France* 25 C13
Montigny-sur-Aube, *France* 25 E11
Montijo, *Spain* 31 G4
Montijo, Presa de, *Spain* 31 G4
Montilla, *Spain* 31 H6
Montlhéry, *France* 25 D9
Montluçon, *France* 26 B6
Montmagny, *Canada* 99 C5
Montmarault, *France* 26 B6
Montmartre, *Canada* 101 C8
Montmédy, *France* 25 C12
Montmélian, *France* 27 C10
Montmirail, *France* 25 D10
Montmoreau-St.-Cybard, *France* 26 C4
Montmorency, *Canada* 99 C5
Montmorillon, *France* 26 B4
Montmort, *France* 25 D10
Monto, *Australia* 90 C5
Montoir-sur-le-Loir, *France* 24 E7
Montório al Vomano, *Italy* 33 F10
Montoro, *Spain* 31 G6
Montour Falls, *U.S.A.* 106 D8
Montpelier, *Idaho, U.S.A.* 110 E8
Montpelier, *Ohio, U.S.A.* 104 E3
Montpelier, *Vt., U.S.A.* 107 B12
Montpellier, *France* 26 E7
Montpezat-de-Quercy, *France* 26 D5
Montpon-Ménestérol, *France* 26 D4
Montréal, *Canada* 98 C5
Montréal, *France* 26 E6
Montreal L., *Canada* 101 C7
Montreal Lake, *Canada* 101 C7
Montredon-Labessonnié, *France* 26 E6
Montréjeau, *France* 26 E4
Montrésor, *France* 24 E8
Montreuil, *France* 25 B8
Montreuil-Bellay, *France* 24 E6
Montreux, *Switz.* 22 D3
Montrevault, *France* 24 E5
Montrevel-en-Bresse, *France* 27 B9
Montrichard, *France* 24 E8
Montrose, *U.K.* 14 E6
Montrose, *Colo., U.S.A.* 111 G10
Montrose, *Pa., U.S.A.* 107 E9
Monts, Pte. des, *Canada* 99 C6
Monts-sur-Guesnes, *France* 24 F7
Montsalvy, *France* 26 D6
Montsant, Sierra de, *Spain* 28 D5
Montsauche, *France* 25 E11
Montsech, Sierra del, *Spain* 28 C5
Montseny, *Spain* 28 D2
Montserrat, *Spain* 28 D6
Montserrat ■, *W. Indies* 117 C7
Montuenga, *Spain* 30 D6
Montuiri, *Spain* 36 B9
Monveda, *Zaïre* 80 D4
Monywa, *Burma* 61 H19
Monza, *Italy* 32 C6
Monze, *Zambia* 83 F2
Monze, C., *Pakistan* 62 G2
Monzón, *Spain* 28 D5
Mooi River, *S. Africa* 85 D4
Mook, *Neths.* 16 E7
Moolawatana, *Australia* 91 D2
Mooliabeenee, *Australia* 89 F2
Mooloogool, *Australia* 89 E2
Moomin Cr. →, *Australia* 91 D4
Moonah →, *Australia* 90 C2
Moonbeam, *Canada* 98 C3
Moonda, L., *Australia* 90 D3
Moonie, *Australia* 91 D5
Moonie →, *Australia* 91 D4
Moonta, *Australia* 91 E2
Moora, *Australia* 89 F2
Mooraberree, *Australia* 90 D3
Moorarie, *Australia* 89 E2
Moorcroft, *U.S.A.* 108 C2
Moore →, *Australia* 89 F2
Moore, L., *Australia* 89 E2
Moore Reefs, *Australia* 90 B4
Moorefield, *U.S.A.* 104 F6
Moores Res., *U.S.A.* 107 B13
Mooresville, *U.S.A.* 105 H5
Moorfoot Hills, *U.K.* 14 F5
Moorhead, *U.S.A.* 108 B6
Mooroopna, *Australia* 91 F4
Moorpark, *U.S.A.* 113 L8
Moorreesburg, *S. Africa* 84 E2
Moorslede, *Belgium* 17 G2
Moosburg, *Germany* 19 G7
Moose →, *Canada* 98 B3
Moose Factory, *Canada* 98 B3
Moose I., *Canada* 101 C9
Moose Jaw, *Canada* 101 C7
Moose Jaw →, *Canada* 101 C7
Moose Lake, *Canada* 101 C8
Moose Lake, *U.S.A.* 108 B8
Moose Mountain Cr. →, *Canada* 101 D8
Moose Mountain Prov. Park, *Canada* 101 D8
Moose River, *Canada* 98 B3
Moosehead L., *U.S.A.* 99 C6
Moosomin, *Canada* 101 C8
Moosonee, *Canada* 98 B3
Moosup, *U.S.A.* 107 E13
Mopeia Velha, *Mozam.* 83 F4
Mopipi, *Botswana* 84 C3
Mopoi, *C.A.R.* 82 A2
Mopti, *Mali* 78 C4
Moqatta, *Sudan* 77 E4
Moquegua, *Peru* 124 D3
Moquegua □, *Peru* 124 D3
Mór, *Hungary* 21 H8
Móra, *Portugal* 31 G2
Mora, *Sweden* 9 F13
Mora, *Minn., U.S.A.* 108 C8
Mora, *N. Mex., U.S.A.* 111 J11
Mora de Ebro, *Spain* 28 D5
Mora de Rubielos, *Spain* 28 E4
Mora la Nueva, *Spain* 28 D5
Morača →, *Montenegro* 21 N9
Morada Nova, *Brazil* 122 C4
Morada Nova de Minas, *Brazil* 123 E2
Moradabad, *India* 63 E8
Morafenobe, *Madag.* 85 B7
Morąg, *Poland* 20 B9
Moral de Calatrava, *Spain* 29 G1
Moraleja, *Spain* 30 E4
Morales, *Colombia* 120 C2
Moramanga, *Madag.* 85 B8
Moran, *Kans., U.S.A.* 109 G7
Moran, *Wyo., U.S.A.* 110 E8
Moranbah, *Australia* 90 C4
Morano Cálabro, *Italy* 35 C9
Morant Cays, *Jamaica* 116 C4
Morant Pt., *Jamaica* 116 C4
Morar, L., *U.K.* 14 E3
Moratalla, *Spain* 29 G3
Moratuwa, *Sri Lanka* 60 R11
Morava →, *Europe* 20 G6
Moravia, *U.S.A.* 108 E8
Moravian Hts. = Ceskomoravská Vrchovina, *Czech.* 20 F5
Moravica →, *Serbia* 21 M10
Moravice →, *Czech.* 20 F7
Moraviţa, *Romania* 21 K11
Moravská Třebová, *Czech.* 20 F6
Morawa, *Australia* 89 E2
Morawhanna, *Guyana* 121 B6
Moray Firth, *U.K.* 14 D5
Morbach, *Germany* 19 F3
Morbegno, *Italy* 32 B6
Morbi, *India* 62 H4
Morbihan □, *France* 24 E4
Morcenx, *France* 26 D3
Mordelles, *France* 24 D5
Morden, *Canada* 101 D9
Mordovian Republic □, *Russia* 41 D14
Mordovo, *Russia* 41 E12
Mordvinia = Mordovian Republic □, *Russia* 41 D14
Møre og Romsdal fylke □, *Norway* 10 B2
Morea, *Australia* 91 F3
Morea, *Greece* 6 H10
Moreau →, *U.S.A.* 108 C4
Morecambe, *U.K.* 12 C5
Morecambe B., *U.K.* 12 C5
Moree, *Australia* 91 D4
Morehead, *U.S.A.* 104 F4
Morehead City, *U.S.A.* 105 H7
Morelia, *Mexico* 114 D4
Morella, *Australia* 90 C3
Morella, *Spain* 28 E4
Morelos, *Mexico* 114 B3
Morelos □, *Mexico* 115 D5
Morena, Sierra, *Spain* 31 G7
Morenci, *U.S.A.* 111 K9
Moreni, *Romania* 38 E8
Morero, *Bolivia* 125 C4
Moreru →, *Brazil* 125 C6
Moresby I., *Canada* 100 C2
Morestel, *France* 27 C9
Moret-sur-Loing, *France* 25 D9
Moreton, *Australia* 90 A3
Moreton I., *Australia* 91 D5
Moreuil, *France* 25 C9
Morey, *Spain* 36 B10
Morez, *France* 27 B10
Morgan, *Australia* 91 E2
Morgan, *U.S.A.* 110 F8
Morgan City, *U.S.A.* 109 L9
Morgan Hill, *U.S.A.* 112 H5
Morganfield, *U.S.A.* 104 G2
Morganton, *U.S.A.* 105 H5
Morgantown, *U.S.A.* 104 F6
Morgat, *France* 24 D2
Morgenzon, *S. Africa* 85 D4
Morges, *Switz.* 22 C2
Morghak, *Iran* 65 D8
Morhange, *France* 25 D13
Mori, *Italy* 32 C7
Morialmée, *Belgium* 17 H5
Morice L., *Canada* 100 C3
Morichal, *Colombia* 120 C3
Morichal Largo →, *Venezuela* 121 B5
Moriki, *Nigeria* 79 C6
Morinville, *Canada* 100 C6
Morioka, *Japan* 48 E10
Moris, *Mexico* 114 B3
Morlaàs, *France* 26 E3
Morlaix, *France* 24 D3
Morlanwelz, *Belgium* 17 H4
Mormanno, *Italy* 35 C8
Mormant, *France* 25 D9
Mornington, *Vic., Australia* 91 F4
Mornington, *W. Austral., Australia* 88 C4
Mornington, I., *Chile* 128 C1
Mornington I., *Australia* 90 B2
Mórnos →, *Greece* 39 L4
Moro, *Sudan* 77 E3
Moro G., *Phil.* 55 H5
Morocco ■, *N. Afr.* 74 B3
Morococha, *Peru* 124 C2
Morogoro, *Tanzania* 82 D4
Morogoro □, *Tanzania* 82 D4
Moroleón, *Mexico* 114 C4
Morombe, *Madag.* 85 C7
Moron, *Argentina* 126 C4
Morón, *Cuba* 116 B4
Mörön →, *Mongolia* 54 B6
Morón de Almazán, *Spain* 28 D2
Morón de la Frontera, *Spain* 31 H5
Morona →, *Peru* 120 D2
Morona-Santiago □, *Ecuador* 120 D2
Morondava, *Madag.* 85 C7
Morondo, *Ivory C.* 78 D3
Morongo Valley, *U.S.A.* 113 L10
Moronou, *Ivory C.* 78 D4
Morotai, *Indonesia* 57 D7
Moroto, *Uganda* 82 B3
Moroto Summit, *Kenya* 82 B3
Morozovsk, *Russia* 43 B9
Morpeth, *U.K.* 12 B6
Morphou, *Cyprus* 37 D11
Morphou Bay, *Cyprus* 37 D11
Morrilton, *U.S.A.* 109 H8
Morrinhos, *Ceara, Brazil* 122 B3
Morrinhos, *Minas Gerais, Brazil* 123 E2
Morrinsville, *N.Z.* 87 G5
Morris, *Canada* 101 D9
Morris, *Ill., U.S.A.* 104 E1
Morris, *Minn., U.S.A.* 108 C7
Morris, Mt., *Australia* 89 E5
Morrisburg, *Canada* 98 D4
Morrison, *U.S.A.* 108 E10
Morristown, *Ariz., U.S.A.* 111 K7
Morristown, *N.J., U.S.A.* 107 F10
Morristown, *S. Dak., U.S.A.* 108 C4
Morristown, *Tenn., U.S.A.* 105 G4
Morro, Pta., *Chile* 126 B1
Morro Bay, *U.S.A.* 111 J3
Morro del Jable, *Canary Is.* 36 F5
Morro do Chapéu, *Brazil* 123 D3
Morro Jable, Pta. de, *Canary Is.* 36 F5
Morros, *Brazil* 122 B3
Morrosquillo, G. de, *Colombia* 116 E4
Morrumbene, *Mozam.* 85 C6
Mors, *Denmark* 11 H2
Morshansk, *Russia* 41 E12
Mörsil, *Sweden* 10 A7
Mortagne →, *France* 25 D13
Mortagne-au-Perche, *France* 24 D7
Mortagne-sur-Gironde, *France* 26 C3
Mortagne-sur-Sèvre, *France* 24 F6
Mortain, *France* 24 D6
Mortara, *Italy* 32 C5
Morteau, *France* 25 E13
Morteros, *Argentina* 126 C3
Mortes, R. das →, *Brazil* 123 D1
Mortlake, *Australia* 91 F3
Morton, *Tex., U.S.A.* 109 J3
Morton, *Wash., U.S.A.* 112 D4
Mortsel, *Belgium* 17 F4
Morundah, *Australia* 91 E4
Moruya, *Australia* 91 F5
Morvan, *France* 25 E11
Morven, *Australia* 91 D4
Morvern, *U.K.* 14 E3
Morwell, *Australia* 91 F4
Mosalsk, *Russia* 40 D9
Mosbach, *Germany* 19 F5
Mošćenice, *Croatia* 33 C11
Mosciano Sant' Ángelo, *Italy* 33 F10
Moscos Is., *Burma* 58 E1
Moscow = Moskva, *Russia* 41 D10
Moscow, *U.S.A.* 110 C5
Mosel →, *Europe* 19 E3
Moselle = Mosel →, *Europe* 19 E3
Moselle □, *France* 25 D13
Moses Lake, *U.S.A.* 110 C4
Mosgiel, *N.Z.* 87 L3
Moshi, *Tanzania* 82 C4
Moshi □, *Tanzania* 82 C4
Moshupa, *Botswana* 84 C4
Mosjøen, *Norway* 8 D12
Moskenesøya, *Norway* 8 C12

Moskenstraumen, Norway 8 C12
Moskva, Russia 41 D10
Moskva →, Russia 41 D11
Moslavačka Gora, Croatia 33 C13
Mosomane, Botswana 84 C4
Mosonmagyaróvár, Hungary 21 H7
Mospino, Ukraine 42 C7
Mosquera, Colombia 120 C2
Mosquero, U.S.A. 109 H3
Mosqueruela, Spain 28 E4
Mosquitia, Honduras 116 C3
Mosquitos, G. de los, Panama 116 E3
Moss, Norway 10 E4
Moss Vale, Australia 91 E5
Mossaka, Congo 80 E3
Mossâmedes, Brazil 123 E1
Mossbank, Canada 101 D7
Mossburn, N.Z. 87 L2
Mosselbaai, S. Africa 84 E3
Mossendjo, Congo 80 E2
Mosses, Col des, Switz. 22 D4
Mossgiel, Australia 91 E3
Mossman, Australia 90 B4
Mossoró, Brazil 122 C4
Mossuril, Mozam. 83 E5
Mossy →, Canada 101 C8
Most, Czech. 20 E3
Mosta, Malta 37 D1
Moşţafāābād, Iran 65 C7
Mostaganem, Algeria 75 A5
Mostar, Bos.-H. 21 M7
Mostardas, Brazil 127 C5
Mostefa, Rass, Tunisia 75 A7
Mostiska, Ukraine 40 G3
Móstoles, Spain 30 E7
Mosty, Belorussia 40 E4
Mosul = Al Mawşil, Iraq 64 B4
Mosulpo, S. Korea 51 H14
Mota del Cuervo, Spain 28 F2
Mota del Marqués, Spain 30 D5
Motagua →, Guatemala 116 C2
Motala, Sweden 11 F9
Motherwell, U.K. 14 F5
Motihari, India 63 F11
Motilla del Palancar, Spain 28 F3
Motnik, Slovenia 33 B11
Motocurunya, Venezuela 121 C5
Motovun, Croatia 33 C10
Motozintla de Mendoza, Mexico 115 D6
Motril, Spain 29 J1
Motru →, Romania 38 E6
Mott, U.S.A. 108 B3
Móttola, Italy 35 B10
Motueka, N.Z. 87 J4
Motueka →, N.Z. 87 J4
Motul, Mexico 115 C7
Mouanda, Gabon 80 E2
Mouchalagane →, Canada 99 B6
Mouding, China 52 E3
Moudjeria, Mauritania 78 B2
Moudon, Switz. 22 C3
Mouila, Gabon 80 E2
Moulamein, Australia 91 F3
Moulianá, Greece 37 D7
Moulins, France 26 B7
Moulmein, Burma 61 L20
Moulouya, O. →, Morocco 75 A4
Moulton, U.S.A. 109 L6
Moultrie, U.S.A. 105 K4
Moultrie, L., U.S.A. 105 J5
Mound City, Mo., U.S.A. 108 E7
Mound City, S. Dak., U.S.A. 108 C4
Moúnda, Ákra, Greece 39 L3
Moundou, Chad 73 G8
Moundsville, U.S.A. 106 G4
Moung, Cambodia 58 F4
Mount Airy, U.S.A. 105 G5
Mount Albert, Canada 106 B5
Mount Amherst, Australia 88 C4
Mount Angel, U.S.A. 110 D2
Mount Augustus, Australia 88 D2
Mount Barker, S. Austral., Australia 91 F2
Mount Barker, W. Austral., Australia 89 F2
Mount Carmel, U.S.A. 104 F2
Mount Clemens, U.S.A. 98 D3
Mount Coolon, Australia 90 C4
Mount Darwin, Zimbabwe 83 F3
Mount Desert I., U.S.A. 99 D6
Mount Dora, U.S.A. 105 L5
Mount Douglas, Australia 90 C4
Mount Eba, Australia 91 E2
Mount Edgecumbe, U.S.A. 100 B1
Mount Elizabeth, Australia 88 C4
Mount Fletcher, S. Africa 85 E4
Mount Forest, Canada 98 D3
Mount Gambier, Australia 91 F3
Mount Garnet, Australia 90 B4
Mount Hope, N.S.W., Australia 91 E4
Mount Hope, S. Austral., Australia 91 E2
Mount Hope, U.S.A. 104 G5
Mount Horeb, U.S.A. 108 D10
Mount Howitt, Australia 91 D3
Mount Isa, Australia 90 C2
Mount Keith, Australia 89 E3
Mount Laguna, U.S.A. 113 N10
Mount Larcom, Australia 90 C5
Mount Lofty Ra., Australia 91 E2
Mount McKinley National Park, U.S.A. 96 B5
Mount Magnet, Australia 89 E2
Mount Margaret, Australia 91 D3
Mount Maunganui, N.Z. 87 G6
Mount Molloy, Australia 90 B4
Mount Monger, Australia 89 F3
Mount Morgan, Australia 90 C5
Mount Morris, U.S.A. 106 D7
Mount Mulligan, Australia 90 B3
Mount Narryer, Australia 89 E2
Mount Olympus = Uludağ, Turkey 66 C3
Mount Oxide Mine, Australia 90 B2
Mount Pearl, Canada 99 C9
Mount Perry, Australia 91 D5
Mount Phillips, Australia 88 D2
Mount Pleasant, Iowa, U.S.A. 108 E9
Mount Pleasant, Mich., U.S.A. 104 D3
Mount Pleasant, Pa., U.S.A. 106 F5
Mount Pleasant, S.C., U.S.A. 105 J6
Mount Pleasant, Tenn., U.S.A. 105 H2
Mount Pleasant, Tex., U.S.A. 109 J7
Mount Pleasant, Utah, U.S.A. 110 G8
Mount Pocono, U.S.A. 107 E9
Mount Rainier National Park, U.S.A. 112 D5
Mount Revelstoke Nat. Park, Canada 100 C5
Mount Robson Prov. Park, Canada 100 C5
Mount Sandiman, Australia 89 D2
Mount Shasta, U.S.A. 110 F2
Mount Signal, U.S.A. 113 N11
Mount Sterling, Ill., U.S.A. 108 F9
Mount Sterling, Ky., U.S.A. 104 F4
Mount Surprise, Australia 90 B3
Mount Union, U.S.A. 106 F7
Mount Vernon, Australia 88 D2
Mount Vernon, Ind., U.S.A. 108 F10
Mount Vernon, N.Y., U.S.A. 107 F11
Mount Vernon, Ohio, U.S.A. 106 F2
Mount Vernon, Wash., U.S.A. 112 B4
Mountain Center, U.S.A. 113 M10
Mountain City, Nev., U.S.A. 110 F6
Mountain City, Tenn., U.S.A. 105 G5
Mountain Grove, U.S.A. 109 G8
Mountain Home, Ark., U.S.A. 109 G8
Mountain Home, Idaho, U.S.A. 110 E6
Mountain Iron, U.S.A. 108 B8
Mountain Park, Canada 100 C5
Mountain Pass, U.S.A. 113 K11
Mountain View, Ark., U.S.A. 109 H8
Mountain View, Calif., U.S.A. 111 H2
Mountainair, U.S.A. 111 J10
Mountmellick, Ireland 15 C4
Moura, Australia 90 C4
Moura, Brazil 121 D5
Moura, Portugal 31 G3
Mourão, Portugal 31 G3
Mourdi, Dépression du, Chad 73 E9
Mourdiah, Mali 78 C3
Mourenx-Ville-Nouvelle, France 26 E3
Mouri, Ghana 79 D4
Mourilyan, Australia 90 B4
Mourmelon-le-Grand, France 25 C11
Mourne →, U.K. 15 B4
Mourne Mts., U.K. 15 B5
Mournies, Greece 37 D6
Mouscron, Belgium 17 G2
Moussoro, Chad 73 F8
Mouthe, France 25 F13
Moutier, Switz. 22 B4
Moûtiers, France 27 C10
Moutohara, N.Z. 87 H6
Moutong, Indonesia 57 D6
Mouy, France 25 C9
Mouzáki, Greece 39 K4
Movas, Mexico 114 B3
Moville, Ireland 15 A4
Moxhe, Belgium 17 G6
Moxotó →, Brazil 122 C4
Moy →, Ireland 15 B3
Moyale, Kenya 68 G2
Moyamba, S. Leone 78 D2
Moyen Atlas, Morocco 74 B3
Moyle □, U.K. 15 A5
Moyo, Indonesia 56 F5
Moyobamba, Peru 124 B2
Moyyero →, Russia 45 C11
Mozambique = Moçambique, Mozam. 83 F5
Mozambique ■, Africa 83 F4
Mozambique Chan., Africa 85 B7
Mozdok, Russia 43 E11
Mozdūrān, Iran 65 B9
Mozhaysk, Russia 41 D10
Mozhga, Russia 41 C18
Mozhnābād, Iran 65 C9
Mozirje, Slovenia 33 B11
Mozyr, Belorussia 40 E6
Mpanda, Tanzania 82 D3
Mpanda □, Tanzania 82 D3
Mpésoba, Mali 78 C3
Mpika, Zambia 83 E3
Mpulungu, Zambia 83 D3
Mpumalanga, S. Africa 85 D5
Mpwapwa, Tanzania 82 D4
Mpwapwa □, Tanzania 82 D4
Mrągowo, Poland 20 B11
Mramor, Serbia 21 M11
Mrimina, Morocco 74 C3
Mrkonjić Grad, Bos.-H. 21 L7
Mrkopalj, Croatia 33 C11
Msab, Oued en →, Algeria 75 B6
Msaken, Tunisia 75 A7
Msambansovu, Zimbabwe 83 F3
M'sila, Algeria 75 A5
Msoro, Zambia 83 E3
Msta →, Russia 40 B7
Mstislavl, Belorussia 40 E7
Mtama, Tanzania 83 E4
Mtilikwe →, Zimbabwe 83 G3
Mtsensk, Russia 41 E10
Mtskheta, Georgia 43 F11
Mtubatuba, S. Africa 85 D5
Mtwara-Mikindani, Tanzania 83 E5
Mu Gia, Deo, Vietnam 58 D5
Mu Us Shamo, China 50 E5
Muaná, Brazil 122 B2
Muang Chiang Rai, Thailand 58 C2
Muang Lamphun, Thailand 58 C2
Muang Pak Beng, Laos 58 C3
Muar, Malaysia 59 L4
Muarabungo, Indonesia 56 E2
Muaraenim, Indonesia 56 E2
Muarajuloi, Indonesia 56 E4
Muarakaman, Indonesia 56 E5
Muaratebo, Indonesia 56 E2
Muaratembesi, Indonesia 56 E2
Muaratewe, Indonesia 56 E4
Mubarakpur, India 63 F10
Mubarraz = Al Mubarraz, Si. Arabia 65 E6
Mubende, Uganda 82 B3
Mubi, Nigeria 79 C7
Mubur, P., Indonesia 59 L6
Mucajaí →, Brazil 121 C5
Mucajaí, Serra do, Brazil 121 C5
Muchachos, Roque de los, Canary Is. 36 F2
Mücheln, Germany 18 D7
Muchinga Mts., Zambia 83 E3
Muchkapskiy, Russia 41 F13
Muck, U.K. 14 E2
Muckadilla, Australia 91 D4
Muco →, Colombia 120 C3
Muconda, Angola 80 G4
Mucuim →, Brazil 125 B5
Mucur, Turkey 66 D6
Mucura, Brazil 121 D5
Mucuri, Brazil 123 E4
Mucurici, Brazil 123 E3
Mucusso, Angola 84 B3
Muda, Canary Is. 36 F6
Mudan Jiang →, China 51 A15
Mudanjiang, China 51 B15
Mudanya, Turkey 42 F3
Muddy Cr. →, U.S.A. 111 H8
Mudgee, Australia 91 E4
Mudjatik →, Canada 101 B7
Mudurnu, Turkey 66 C4
Muecate, Mozam. 83 E4
Muêda, Mozam. 83 E4
Mueller Ra., Australia 88 C4
Muende, Mozam. 83 E3
Muerto, Mar, Mexico 115 D6
Muertos, Punta de los, Spain 29 J3
Mufindi □, Tanzania 83 D4
Mufu Shan, China 53 C10
Mufulira, Zambia 83 E2
Mufumbiro Range, Africa 82 C2
Mugardos, Spain 30 B2
Muge, Portugal 31 F2
Muge →, Portugal 31 F2
Múggia, Italy 33 C10
Mughayrā', Si. Arabia 64 D3
Mugi, Japan 49 H7
Mugia, Spain 30 B1
Mugila, Mts., Zaïre 82 D2
Muğla, Turkey 66 E3
Muğla □, Turkey 66 E3
Müglizh, Bulgaria 38 G8
Mugu, Nepal 63 E10
Muhammad, Râs, Egypt 76 B3
Muhammad Qol, Sudan 76 C4
Muhammadabad, India 63 F10
Muhesi →, Tanzania 82 D4
Muheza □, Tanzania 82 C4
Mühldorf, Germany 19 G8
Mühlhausen, Germany 18 D6
Mühlig Hofmann fjella, Antarctica 5 D3
Muhutwe, Tanzania 82 C3
Muiden, Neths. 16 D6
Muikamachi, Japan 49 F9
Muine Bheag, Ireland 15 D5
Muiños, Spain 30 D3
Muir, L., Australia 89 F2
Mukachevo, Ukraine 40 G3
Mukah, Malaysia 56 D4
Mukawwa, Geziret, Egypt 76 C4
Mukdahan, Thailand 58 D5
Mukden = Shenyang, China 51 D12
Mukhtolovo, Russia 41 D13
Mukhtuya = Lensk, Russia 45 C12
Mukinbudin, Australia 89 F2
Mukishi, Zaïre 83 D1
Mukomuko, Indonesia 56 E2
Mukomwenze, Zaïre 82 D2
Muktsar, India 62 D6
Mukur, Afghan. 62 C2
Mukutawa →, Canada 101 C9
Mukwela, Zambia 83 F2
Mula, Spain 29 G3
Mulange, Zaïre 82 C2
Mulchén, Chile 126 D1
Mulde →, Germany 18 D8
Mule Creek, U.S.A. 108 D2
Muleba, Tanzania 82 C3
Muleba □, Tanzania 82 C3
Mulegns, Switz. 23 C9
Muleshoe, U.S.A. 109 H3
Mulgathing, Australia 91 E1
Mulgrave, Canada 99 C7
Mulhacén, Spain 29 H1
Mülheim, Germany 18 D2
Mulhouse, France 25 E14
Muli, China 52 D3
Muling, China 51 B16
Mull, U.K. 14 E3
Mullaittvu, Sri Lanka 60 Q12
Mullen, U.S.A. 108 D4
Mullengudgery, Australia 91 E4
Mullens, U.S.A. 104 G5
Muller, Pegunungan, Indonesia 56 D4
Mullet Pen., Ireland 15 B1
Mullewa, Australia 89 E2
Müllheim, Germany 19 H3
Mulligan →, Australia 90 C2
Mullin, U.S.A. 109 K5
Mullingar, Ireland 15 C4
Mullins, U.S.A. 105 H6
Mullumbimby, Australia 91 D5
Mulobezi, Zambia 83 F2
Multan, Pakistan 62 D4
Multrå, Sweden 10 A11
Mulumbe, Mts., Zaïre 83 D2
Mulungushi Dam, Zambia 83 E2
Mulvane, U.S.A. 109 G6
Mulwad, Sudan 76 D3
Mulwala, Australia 91 F4
Mumbwa, Zambia 83 E2
Mumra, Russia 43 D12
Mun →, Thailand 58 E5
Muna, Indonesia 57 F6
Munamagi, Estonia 40 C5
Münchberg, Germany 19 E7
Müncheberg, Germany 18 C10
München, Germany 19 G7
Munchen-Gladbach = Mönchengladbach, Germany 18 D2
Muncho Lake, Canada 100 B3
Munchŏn, N. Korea 51 E14
Münchwilen, Switz. 23 B7
Muncie, U.S.A. 104 E3
Muncoonie, L., Australia 90 D2
Mundala, Indonesia 57 E10
Mundare, Canada 100 C6
Munday, U.S.A. 109 J5
Münden, Germany 18 D5
Mundiwindi, Australia 88 D3
Mundo →, Spain 29 G2
Mundo Novo, Brazil 123 D3
Mundra, India 62 H3
Mundrabilla, Australia 89 F4
Munducurus, Brazil 121 D6
Munera, Spain 29 F2
Mungallala, Australia 91 D4
Mungallala Cr. →, Australia 91 D4
Mungana, Australia 90 B3
Mungaoli, India 62 G8
Mungari, Mozam. 83 F3
Mungbere, Zaïre 82 B2
Munger, India 63 G12
Mungindi, Australia 91 D4
Munhango, Angola 81 G3
Munich = München, Germany 19 G7
Munising, U.S.A. 104 B2
Munka-Ljungby, Sweden 11 H6
Munkedal, Sweden 11 F5
Munku-Sardyk, Russia 45 D11
Münnerstadt, Germany 19 E6
Muñoz Gamero, Pen., Chile 128 D2
Munroe L., Canada 101 B9
Munsan, S. Korea 51 F14
Münsingen, Switz. 22 C5
Munster, France 25 D14
Munster, Niedersachsen, Germany 18 C6
Münster, Nordrhein-Westfalen, Germany 18 D3
Münster, Switz. 23 D6
Munster □, Ireland 15 D3
Muntadgin, Australia 89 F2
Muntele Mare, Romania 38 C6
Muntok, Indonesia 56 E3
Munyak, Uzbekistan 44 E6
Munyama, Zambia 83 F2
Muong Beng, Laos 58 B3
Muong Boum, Vietnam 58 A4
Muong Et, Laos 58 B5
Muong Hai, Laos 58 B3
Muong Hiem, Laos 58 B4
Muong Houn, Laos 58 B3
Muong Hung, Vietnam 58 B4
Muong Kau, Laos 58 E5
Muong Khao, Laos 58 C4
Muong Khoua, Laos 58 B4
Muong Liep, Laos 58 C3
Muong May, Laos 58 E6
Muong Ngeun, Laos 58 B3
Muong Ngoi, Laos 58 B4
Muong Nhie, Vietnam 58 A4
Muong Nong, Laos 58 D6
Muong Ou Tay, Laos 58 A3
Muong Oua, Laos 58 C3
Muong Peun, Laos 58 B4
Muong Phalane, Laos 58 D5
Muong Phieng, Laos 58 C3
Muong Phine, Laos 58 D6
Muong Sai, Laos 58 B3
Muong Saiapoun, Laos 58 C3
Muong Sen, Vietnam 58 C5
Muong Sing, Laos 58 B3
Muong Son, Laos 58 B4
Muong Soui, Laos 58 C4
Muong Va, Laos 58 B4
Muong Xia, Vietnam 58 B5
Muonio, Finland 8 C17
Muotathal, Switz. 23 C7
Mupa, Angola 81 H3
Muping, China 51 F11
Muqaddam, Wadi →, Sudan 76 D3
Muqdisho, Somali Rep. 68 G4
Mur-de-Bretagne, France 24 D4
Mura →, Slovenia 33 B13
Muradiye, Turkey 67 D10
Murakami, Japan 48 E9
Murallón, Cuerro, Chile 128 C2
Muralto, Switz. 23 D7
Muranda, Rwanda 82 C2
Murang'a, Kenya 82 C4
Murashi, Russia 41 B16
Murat, France 26 C6
Murat →, Turkey 67 D8
Muratlı, Turkey 66 C2
Muravera, Italy 34 C2
Murayama, Japan 48 E10
Murban, U.A.E. 65 F7
Murça, Portugal 30 D3
Murchison →, Australia 89 E1
Murchison, Mt., Antarctica 5 D11
Murchison Falls = Kabarega Falls, Uganda 82 B3
Murchison House, Australia 89 E1
Murchison Ra., Australia 90 C1
Murchison Rapids, Malawi 83 F3
Murcia, Spain 29 G3
Murcia □, Spain 29 H3
Murdo, U.S.A. 108 D4
Murdoch Pt., Australia 90 A3
Mureş →, Romania 38 C3
Mureşul = Mureş →, Romania 38 C3
Muret, France 26 E5
Murfatlar, Romania 38 E11
Murfreesboro, U.S.A. 105 H2
Murg, Switz. 23 B8
Murg →, Germany 19 G4
Murgab, Tajikistan 44 F8
Murgenthal, Switz. 22 B5
Murgon, Australia 91 D5
Murgoo, Australia 89 E2
Muri, Switz. 23 B6
Muria, Indonesia 57 G14
Muriaé, Brazil 123 F3
Murias de Paredes, Spain 30 C4
Murici, Brazil 122 C4
Muriel Mine, Zimbabwe 83 F3
Müritz See, Germany 18 B8
Murka, Kenya 82 C4
Murmansk, Russia 44 C4
Murmerwoude, Neths. 16 B8
Murnau, Germany 19 H7
Muro, France 27 F12
Muro, Spain 36 B10
Muro, C. de, France 27 G12
Muro Lucano, Italy 35 B8
Murom, Russia 41 D13
Muroran, Japan 48 C10
Muros, Spain 30 C1
Muros y de Noya, Ría de, Spain 30 C2
Muroto, Japan 49 H7
Muroto-Misaki, Japan 49 H7
Murphy, U.S.A. 110 E5
Murphys, U.S.A. 112 G6
Murphysboro, U.S.A. 109 G10
Murrat, Sudan 76 D2
Murray, Ky., U.S.A. 105 G1
Murray, Utah, U.S.A. 110 F8
Murray →, Australia 91 F2
Murray →, Canada 100 B4
Murray, L., U.S.A. 105 H5
Murray Bridge, Australia 91 F2
Murray Downs, Australia 90 C1

Murray Harbour, *Canada* 99 C7
Murraysburg, *S. Africa* 84 E3
Murree, *Pakistan* 62 C5
Murrieta, *U.S.A.* 113 M9
Murrin Murrin, *Australia* 89 E3
Murrumbidgee →, *Australia* 91 E3
Murrumburrah, *Australia* 91 E4
Murrurundi, *Australia* 91 E5
Mursala, *Indonesia* 56 D1
Murshid, *Sudan* 76 C3
Murshidabad, *India* 63 G13
Murska Sobota, *Slovenia* 33 B13
Murten, *Switz.* 22 C4
Murtensee, *Switz.* 22 C4
Murtle L., *Canada* 100 C5
Murtoa, *Australia* 91 F3
Murtosa, *Portugal* 30 E2
Muru →, *Brazil* 124 B3
Murungu, *Tanzania* 82 C3
Murwara, *India* 63 H9
Murwillumbah, *Australia* 91 D5
Mürz →, *Austria* 21 H5
Mürzzuschlag, *Austria* 21 H5
Muş, *Turkey* 67 D9
Muş □, *Turkey* 67 D9
Mûsa, G., *Egypt* 76 J8
Musa Khel, *Pakistan* 62 D3
Mūsā Qal'eh, *Afghan.* 60 C4
Musaffargarh, *Pakistan* 60 D7
Musala, *Bulgaria* 38 G6
Musan, *N. Korea* 51 C15
Musangu, *Zaïre* 83 E1
Musasa, *Tanzania* 82 C3
Musay'īd, *Qatar* 65 E6
Muscat = Masqat, *Oman* 68 C6
Muscat & Oman = Oman ■, *Asia* 68 C6
Muscatine, *U.S.A.* 108 E9
Musel, *Spain* 30 B5
Musgrave, *Australia* 90 A3
Musgrave Ras., *Australia* 89 E5
Mushie, *Zaïre* 80 E3
Mushin, *Nigeria* 79 D5
Musi →, *Indonesia* 56 E2
Muskeg →, *Canada* 100 A4
Muskegon, *U.S.A.* 104 D2
Muskegon →, *U.S.A.* 104 D2
Muskegon Heights, *U.S.A.* 104 D2
Muskogee, *U.S.A.* 109 H7
Muskwa →, *Canada* 100 B4
Muslīmiyah, *Syria* 64 B3
Musmar, *Sudan* 76 D4
Musofu, *Zambia* 83 E2
Musoma, *Tanzania* 82 C3
Musoma □, *Tanzania* 82 C3
Musquaro, L., *Canada* 99 B7
Musquodoboit Harbour, *Canada* 99 D7
Musselburgh, *U.K.* 14 F5
Musselkanaal, *Neths.* 16 C10
Musselshell →, *U.S.A.* 110 C10
Mussidan, *France* 26 C4
Mussomeli, *Italy* 34 E6
Musson, *Belgium* 17 J7
Mussoorie, *India* 62 D8
Mussuco, *Angola* 84 B2
Mustafakemalpaşa, *Turkey* 66 C3
Mustang, *Nepal* 63 E10
Musters, L., *Argentina* 128 C3
Musudan, *N. Korea* 51 D15
Muswellbrook, *Australia* 91 E5
Mût, *Egypt* 76 B2
Mut, *Turkey* 66 E5
Mutanda, *Mozam.* 85 C5
Mutanda, *Zambia* 83 E2
Mutaray, *Russia* 45 C11
Mutare, *Zimbabwe* 83 F3
Muting, *Indonesia* 57 F10
Mutshatsha, *Zaïre* 83 E1
Mutsu, *Japan* 48 D10
Mutsu-Wan, *Japan* 48 D10
Muttaburra, *Australia* 90 C3
Mutuáli, *Mozam.* 83 E4
Mutunópolis, *Brazil* 123 D2
Muweilih, *Egypt* 69 E3
Muxima, *Angola* 80 F2
Muy Muy, *Nic.* 116 D2
Muya, *Russia* 45 D12
Muyinga, *Burundi* 82 C3
Muzaffarabad, *Pakistan* 63 B5
Muzaffargarh, *Pakistan* 62 D4
Muzaffarnagar, *India* 62 E7
Muzaffarpur, *India* 63 F11
Muzhi, *Russia* 44 C7
Muzillac, *France* 24 E4
Muzon, C., *U.S.A.* 100 C2
Muztag, *China* 54 C3
Mvôlô, *Sudan* 77 F2
Mvuma, *Zimbabwe* 83 F3
Mvurwi, *Zimbabwe* 83 F3
Mwadui, *Tanzania* 82 C3
Mwambo, *Tanzania* 83 E5
Mwandi, *Zambia* 83 F1
Mwanza, *Tanzania* 82 C3
Mwanza, *Zaïre* 82 D2
Mwanza, *Zambia* 83 F1
Mwanza □, *Tanzania* 82 C3
Mwaya, *Tanzania* 83 D3
Mweelrea, *Ireland* 15 C2
Mweka, *Zaïre* 80 E4
Mwenezi, *Zimbabwe* 83 G3
Mwenezi →, *Mozam.* 83 G3
Mwenga, *Zaïre* 82 C2
Mweru, L., *Zambia* 83 D2
Mweza Range, *Zimbabwe* 83 G3
Mwilambwe, *Zaïre* 82 D5
Mwimbi, *Tanzania* 83 D3
Mwinilunga, *Zambia* 83 E1
My Tho, *Vietnam* 59 G6
Mya, O. →, *Algeria* 75 B5
Myajlar, *India* 62 F4
Myanaung, *Burma* 61 K19
Myanmar = Burma ■, *Asia* 61 J20
Myaungmya, *Burma* 61 L19
Mycenae = Mikínai, *Greece* 39 M5
Myeik Kyunzu, *Burma* 59 G1
Myerstown, *U.S.A.* 107 F8
Myingyan, *Burma* 61 J19
Myitkyina, *Burma* 61 G20
Myjava, *Slovak Rep.* 20 G7
Mykolayiv = Nikolayev, *Ukraine* 42 C4
Mymensingh, *Bangla.* 61 G17
Mynydd Du, *U.K.* 13 F4
Mýrdalsjökull, *Iceland* 8 E4
Myroodah, *Australia* 88 C3
Myrtle Beach, *U.S.A.* 105 J6
Myrtle Creek, *U.S.A.* 110 E2
Myrtle Point, *U.S.A.* 110 E1
Myrtou, *Cyprus* 37 D12
Mysen, *Norway* 10 E5
Mysia, *Turkey* 66 D2
Myslenice, *Poland* 20 F9
Myślibórz, *Poland* 20 C4
Mysłowice, *Poland* 20 E9
Mysore = Karnataka □, *India* 60 N10
Mysore, *India* 60 N10
Mystic, *U.S.A.* 107 E13
Myszków, *Poland* 20 E9
Mythen, *Switz.* 23 B7
Mytishchi, *Russia* 41 D10
Myton, *U.S.A.* 110 F8
Mývatn, *Iceland* 8 D5
Mzimba, *Malawi* 83 E3
Mzimkulu →, *S. Africa* 85 E5
Mzimvubu →, *S. Africa* 85 E4
Mzuzu, *Malawi* 83 E3

N

N' Dioum, *Senegal* 78 B2
Na Noi, *Thailand* 58 C3
Na Phao, *Laos* 58 D5
Na Sam, *Vietnam* 58 A6
Na San, *Vietnam* 58 B5
Naab →, *Germany* 19 F8
Naaldwijk, *Neths.* 16 E4
Na'am, *Sudan* 77 F2
Naantali, *Finland* 9 F17
Naarden, *Neths.* 16 D6
Naas, *Ireland* 15 C5
Nababiep, *S. Africa* 84 D2
Nabadwip = Navadwip, *India* 63 H13
Nabari, *Japan* 49 G8
Nabawa, *Australia* 89 E1
Nabberu, L., *Australia* 89 E3
Nabburg, *Germany* 19 F8
Naberezhnyye Chelny, *Russia* 44 D6
Nabeul, *Tunisia* 75 A7
Nabha, *India* 62 D7
Nabīd, *Iran* 65 D8
Nabire, *Indonesia* 57 E9
Nabisar, *Pakistan* 62 G3
Nabisipi →, *Canada* 99 B7
Nabiswera, *Uganda* 82 B3
Nablus = Nābulus, *Jordan* 69 C4
Naboomspruit, *S. Africa* 85 C4
Nabua, *Phil.* 55 E5
Nābulus, *Jordan* 69 C4
Nābulus □, *Jordan* 69 C4
Nacala, *Mozam.* 83 E5
Nacala-Velha, *Mozam.* 83 E5
Nacaome, *Honduras* 116 D2
Nacaroa, *Mozam.* 83 E4
Naches, *U.S.A.* 110 C3
Naches →, *U.S.A.* 112 D6
Nachingwea, *Tanzania* 83 E4
Nachingwea □, *Tanzania* 83 E4
Nachna, *India* 62 F4
Náchod, *Czech.* 20 E6
Nacimiento Reservoir, *U.S.A.* 112 K6
Nacka, *Sweden* 10 E12
Nackara, *Australia* 91 E2
Naco, *Mexico* 114 A3
Naco, *U.S.A.* 111 L9
Nacogdoches, *U.S.A.* 109 K7
Nácori Chico, *Mexico* 114 B3
Nacozari, *Mexico* 114 A3
Nadi, *Sudan* 76 D3
Nadiad, *India* 62 H5
Nădlac, *Romania* 38 C3
Nador, *Morocco* 75 A4
Nadur, *Malta* 37 C1
Nadūshan, *Iran* 65 C7
Nadvornaya, *Ukraine* 42 B1
Nadym, *Russia* 44 C8
Nadym →, *Russia* 44 C8
Næstved, *Denmark* 11 J5
Nafada, *Nigeria* 79 C7
Näfels, *Switz.* 23 B8
Naftshahr, *Iran* 64 C5
Nafud Desert = An Nafūd, *Si. Arabia* 64 D4
Nafūsah, Jabal, *Libya* 75 B7
Nag Hammâdi, *Egypt* 76 B3
Naga, *Phil.* 55 E5
Naga, Kreb en, *Africa* 74 D3
Nagagami →, *Canada* 98 C3
Nagahama, *Japan* 49 G8
Nagai, *Japan* 48 E10
Nagaland □, *India* 61 F19
Nagano, *Japan* 49 F9
Nagano □, *Japan* 49 F9
Nagaoka, *Japan* 49 F9
Nagappattinam, *India* 60 P11
Nagar Parkar, *Pakistan* 62 G4
Nagasaki, *Japan* 49 H4
Nagasaki □, *Japan* 49 H4
Nagato, *Japan* 49 G5
Nagaur, *India* 62 F5
Nagercoil, *India* 60 Q10
Nagina, *India* 63 E8
Nagīneh, *Iran* 65 C8
Nagir, *Pakistan* 63 A6
Nagold, *Germany* 19 G4
Nagold →, *Germany* 19 G4
Nagoorin, *Australia* 90 C5
Nagornyy, *Russia* 45 D13
Nagorsk, *Russia* 41 B17
Nagoya, *Japan* 49 G8
Nagpur, *India* 60 J11
Nagua, *Dom. Rep.* 117 C6
Nagykanizsa, *Hungary* 21 J7
Nagykörös, *Hungary* 21 H9
Nagyléta, *Hungary* 21 H11
Naha, *Japan* 49 L3
Nahanni Butte, *Canada* 100 A4
Nahanni Nat. Park, *Canada* 100 A3
Nahariyya, *Israel* 64 C2
Nahāvand, *Iran* 65 C6
Nahe →, *Germany* 19 F3
Nahîya, Wadi →, *Egypt* 76 J7
Nahlin, *Canada* 100 B2
Nahuel Huapi, L., *Argentina* 128 B2
Naicá, *Mexico* 114 B3
Naicam, *Canada* 101 C8
Nā'ifah, *Si. Arabia* 68 D5
Naila, *Germany* 19 E7
Nain, *Canada* 99 A7
Nā'īn, *Iran* 65 C7
Naini Tal, *India* 63 E8
Nainpur, *India* 60 H12
Naintré, *France* 24 F7
Naipu, *Romania* 38 E8
Naira, *Indonesia* 57 E7
Nairn, *U.K.* 14 D5
Nairobi, *Kenya* 82 C4
Naivasha, *Kenya* 82 C4
Naivasha, L., *Kenya* 82 C4
Najac, *France* 26 D5
Najafābād, *Iran* 65 C6
Nájera, *Spain* 28 C2
Najerilla →, *Spain* 28 C2
Najibabad, *India* 62 E8
Najin, *N. Korea* 51 C16
Najmah, *Si. Arabia* 65 E6
Naju, *S. Korea* 51 G14
Nakadōri-Shima, *Japan* 49 H4
Nakalagba, *Zaïre* 82 B2
Nakaminato, *Japan* 49 F10
Nakamura, *Japan* 49 H6
Nakano, *Japan* 49 F9
Nakano-Shima, *Japan* 49 K4
Nakashibetsu, *Japan* 48 C12
Nakfa, *Eritrea* 77 D4
Nakhichevan, *Azerbaijan* 67 D11
Nakhichevan Republic □, *Azerbaijan* 44 F5
Nakhl, *Egypt* 69 F2
Nakhl-e Taqī, *Iran* 65 E7
Nakhodka, *Russia* 45 E14
Nakhon Nayok, *Thailand* 58 E3
Nakhon Pathom, *Thailand* 58 F3
Nakhon Phanom, *Thailand* 58 D5
Nakhon Ratchasima, *Thailand* 58 E4
Nakhon Sawan, *Thailand* 58 E3
Nakhon Si Thammarat, *Thailand* 59 H3
Nakhon Thai, *Thailand* 58 D3
Nakina, *B.C., Canada* 100 B2
Nakina, *Ont., Canada* 98 B2
Nakło nad Notecią, *Poland* 20 B7
Nakodar, *India* 62 D6
Nakskov, *Denmark* 11 K5
Näkten, *Sweden* 10 B8
Naktong →, *S. Korea* 51 G15
Nakuru, *Kenya* 82 C4
Nakuru □, *Kenya* 82 C4
Nakuru, L., *Kenya* 82 C4
Nakusp, *Canada* 100 C5
Nal →, *Pakistan* 62 G1
Nalchik, *Russia* 43 E10
Nälden, *Sweden* 10 A8
Näldsjön, *Sweden* 10 A8
Nalerigu, *Ghana* 79 C4
Nalgonda, *India* 60 L11
Nalhati, *India* 63 G12
Nalinnes, *Belgium* 17 H4
Nallamalai Hills, *India* 60 M11
Nallıhan, *Turkey* 66 C4
Nalón →, *Spain* 30 B4
Nālūt, *Libya* 75 B7
Nam Can, *Vietnam* 59 H5
Nam Co, *China* 54 C4
Nam Dinh, *Vietnam* 58 B6
Nam Du, Hon, *Vietnam* 59 H5
Nam Ngum Dam, *Laos* 58 C4
Nam-Phan, *Vietnam* 59 G6
Nam Phong, *Thailand* 58 D4
Nam Tha, *Laos* 58 B3
Nam Tok, *Thailand* 58 E2
Namacunde, *Angola* 84 B2
Namacurra, *Mozam.* 85 B6
Namak, Daryācheh-ye, *Iran* 65 C7
Namak, Kavir-e, *Iran* 65 C8
Namaland, *Namibia* 84 C2
Namangan, *Uzbekistan* 44 E8
Namapa, *Mozam.* 83 E4
Namaqualand, *S. Africa* 84 D2
Namasagali, *Uganda* 82 B3
Namber, *Indonesia* 57 E8
Nambour, *Australia* 91 D5
Nambucca Heads, *Australia* 91 E5
Namche Bazar, *Nepal* 63 F12
Namchonjŏm, *N. Korea* 51 E14
Namêche, *Belgium* 17 H6
Namecunda, *Mozam.* 83 E4
Nameh, *Indonesia* 56 D5
Nameponda, *Mozam.* 83 F4
Nametil, *Mozam.* 83 F4
Namew L., *Canada* 101 C8
Namib Desert = Namibwoestyn, *Namibia* 84 C2
Namibe, *Angola* 81 H2
Namibe □, *Angola* 84 B1
Namibia ■, *Africa* 84 C2
Namibwoestyn, *Namibia* 84 C2
Namlea, *Indonesia* 57 E7
Namoi →, *Australia* 91 E4
Namous, O. en →, *Algeria* 75 B4
Nampa, *U.S.A.* 110 E5
Nampō-Shotō, *Japan* 49 J10
Nampula, *Mozam.* 83 F4
Namrole, *Indonesia* 57 E7
Namse Shankou, *China* 61 E13
Namsen →, *Norway* 8 D11
Namsos, *Norway* 8 D11
Namtay, *Russia* 45 C13
Namtu, *Burma* 61 H20
Namtumbo, *Tanzania* 83 E4
Namu, *Canada* 100 C3
Namur, *Belgium* 17 H5
Namur □, *Belgium* 17 H6
Namutoni, *Namibia* 84 B2
Namwala, *Zambia* 83 F2
Namwŏn, *S. Korea* 51 G14
Namysłów, *Poland* 20 D7
Nan, *Thailand* 58 C3
Nan →, *Thailand* 58 E3
Nan Xian, *China* 53 C9
Nanaimo, *Canada* 100 D4
Nanam, *N. Korea* 51 D15
Nanan, *China* 53 E12
Nanango, *Australia* 91 D5
Nan'ao, *China* 53 F11
Nanao, *Japan* 49 F8
Nanbu, *China* 52 B6
Nanchang, *China* 53 C10
Nancheng, *China* 53 D11
Nanching = Nanjing, *China* 53 A12
Nanchong, *China* 52 B6
Nanchuan, *China* 52 C6
Nancy, *France* 25 D13
Nanda Devi, *India* 63 D8
Nandan, *China* 52 E6
Nandan, *Japan* 49 G7
Nanded, *India* 60 K10
Nandewar Ra., *Australia* 91 E5
Nandi, *Fiji* 87 C7
Nandi □, *Kenya* 82 B4
Nandurbar, *India* 60 J9
Nandyal, *India* 60 M11
Nanfeng, *Guangdong, China* 53 F8
Nanfeng, *Jiangxi, China* 53 D11
Nanga, *Australia* 89 E1
Nanga-Eboko, *Cameroon* 79 E7
Nanga Parbat, *Pakistan* 63 B6
Nangade, *Mozam.* 83 E4
Nangapinoh, *Indonesia* 56 E4
Nangarhár □, *Afghan.* 60 B7
Nangatayap, *Indonesia* 56 E4
Nangeya Mts., *Uganda* 82 B3
Nangis, *France* 25 D10
Nangong, *China* 50 F8
Nanhua, *China* 52 E3
Nanhuang, *China* 51 F11
Nanhui, *China* 53 B13
Nanjeko, *Zambia* 83 F1
Nanji Shan, *China* 53 D13
Nanjian, *China* 52 E3
Nanjiang, *China* 52 A6
Nanjing, *Fujian, China* 53 E11
Nanjing, *Jiangsu, China* 53 A12
Nanjirinji, *Tanzania* 83 D4
Nankana Sahib, *Pakistan* 62 D5
Nankang, *China* 53 E10
Nanking = Nanjing, *China* 53 A12
Nankoku, *Japan* 49 H6
Nanling, *China* 53 B12
Nanning, *China* 52 F7
Nannup, *Australia* 89 F2
Nanpan Jiang →, *China* 52 E6
Nanpara, *India* 63 F9
Nanpi, *China* 50 E9
Nanping, *Fujian, China* 53 D12
Nanping, *Henan, China* 53 C9
Nanri Dao, *China* 53 E12
Nanripe, *Mozam.* 83 E4
Nansei-Shotō = Ryūkyū-rettō, *Japan* 49 M2
Nansen Sd., *Canada* 4 A3
Nansio, *Tanzania* 82 C3
Nant, *France* 26 D7
Nantes, *France* 24 E5
Nanteuil-le-Haudouin, *France* 25 C9
Nantiat, *France* 26 B5
Nanticoke, *U.S.A.* 107 E8
Nanton, *Canada* 100 C6
Nantong, *China* 53 A13
Nantua, *France* 27 B9
Nantucket I., *U.S.A.* 94 E12
Nanuque, *Brazil* 123 E3
Nanutarra, *Australia* 88 D2
Nanxiong, *China* 53 E10
Nanyang, *China* 50 H7
Nanyi Hu, *China* 53 B12
Nanyuan, *China* 50 E9
Nanyuki, *Kenya* 82 B4
Nanzhang, *China* 53 B8
Náo, C. de la, *Spain* 29 G5
Naococane L., *Canada* 99 B5
Naoetsu, *Japan* 49 F9
Náousa, *Greece* 39 J5
Naozhou Dao, *China* 53 G8
Napa, *U.S.A.* 112 G4
Napa →, *U.S.A.* 112 G4
Napanee, *Canada* 98 D4
Napanoch, *U.S.A.* 107 E10
Nape, *Laos* 58 C5
Nape Pass = Keo Neua, Deo, *Vietnam* 58 C5
Napf, *Switz.* 22 B5
Napier, *N.Z.* 87 H6
Napier Broome B., *Australia* 88 B4
Napier Downs, *Australia* 88 C3
Napier Pen., *Australia* 90 A2
Naples = Nápoli, *Italy* 35 B7
Naples, *U.S.A.* 105 M5
Napo, *China* 52 F5
Napo □, *Ecuador* 120 D2
Napo →, *Peru* 120 D3
Napoleon, *N. Dak., U.S.A.* 108 B5
Napoleon, *Ohio, U.S.A.* 104 E3
Nápoli, *Italy* 35 B7
Nápoli, G. di, *Italy* 35 B7
Napopo, *Zaïre* 82 B2
Nappa Merrie, *Australia* 91 D3
Naqâda, *Egypt* 76 B3
Naqqāsh, *Iran* 65 C6
Nara, *Japan* 49 G7
Nara, *Mali* 78 B3
Nara □, *Japan* 49 G8
Nara Canal, *Pakistan* 62 G3
Nara Visa, *U.S.A.* 109 H3
Naracoorte, *Australia* 91 F3
Naradhan, *Australia* 91 E4
Narasapur, *India* 61 L12
Narathiwat, *Thailand* 59 J3
Narayanganj, *Bangla.* 61 H17
Narayanpet, *India* 60 L10
Narbonne, *France* 26 E7
Narcea →, *Spain* 30 B4
Nardīn, *Iran* 65 B7
Nardò, *Italy* 35 B11
Narembeen, *Australia* 89 F2
Nares Str., *Arctic* 94 B13
Naretha, *Australia* 89 F3
Narew →, *Poland* 20 C10
Nari →, *Pakistan* 62 E2
Narin, *Afghan.* 60 A6
Narindra, Helodranon' i, *Madag.* 85 A8
Narino □, *Colombia* 120 C2
Narita, *Japan* 49 G10
Narmada →, *India* 62 J5
Narman, *Turkey* 67 C9
Narnaul, *India* 62 E7
Narni, *Italy* 33 F9
Naro, *Ghana* 78 C4
Naro, *Italy* 34 E6
Naro Fominsk, *Russia* 41 D10
Narodnaya, *Russia* 6 B17
Narok, *Kenya* 82 C4
Narok □, *Kenya* 82 C4
Narón, *Spain* 30 B2
Narooma, *Australia* 91 F5
Narowal, *Pakistan* 62 C6
Narrabri, *Australia* 91 E4
Narran →, *Australia* 91 D4
Narrandera, *Australia* 91 E4
Narraway →, *Canada* 100 B5
Narrogin, *Australia* 89 F2
Narromine, *Australia* 91 E4
Narsimhapur, *India* 63 H8
Nartkala, *Russia* 43 E10
Naruto, *Japan* 49 G7
Narva, *Estonia* 40 B6
Narva →, *Russia* 40 B6
Narvik, *Norway* 8 B14
Narvskoye Vdkhr., *Russia* 40 B6
Narwana, *India* 62 E7
Naryan-Mar, *Russia* 44 C6
Naryilco, *Australia* 91 D3
Narym, *Russia* 44 D9
Narymskoye, *Kazakhstan* 44 E9
Naryn, *Kirghizia* 44 E8
Nasa, *Norway* 8 C13
Nasarawa, *Nigeria* 79 D6
Năsăud, *Romania* 38 B7
Naseby, *N.Z.* 87 L3
Naselle, *U.S.A.* 112 D3
Naser, Buheirat en, *Egypt* 76 C3
Nashua, *Iowa, U.S.A.* 108 D8

Nashua, *Mont., U.S.A.* ... 110 **B10**
Nashua, *N.H., U.S.A.* 107 **D13**
Nashville, *Ark., U.S.A.* .. 109 **J8**
Nashville, *Ga., U.S.A.* ... 105 **K4**
Nashville, *Tenn., U.S.A.* . 105 **G2**
Našice, *Croatia* 21 **K8**
Nasielsk, *Poland* 20 **C10**
Nasik, *India* 60 **K8**
Nasipit, *Phil.* 55 **G6**
Nasirabad, *India* 62 **F6**
Naskaupi →, *Canada* 99 **B7**
Naso, *Italy* 35 **D7**
Naṣriān-e Pā'īn, *Iran* 64 **C5**
Nass →, *Canada* 100 **B3**
Nassau, *Bahamas* 116 **A4**
Nassau, *U.S.A.* 107 **D11**
Nassau, B., *Chile* 128 **E3**
Nasser, L. = Naser, Buheirat en, *Egypt* 76 **C3**
Nasser City = Kôm Ombo, *Egypt* 76 **C3**
Nassian, *Ivory C.* 78 **D4**
Nässjö, *Sweden* 9 **H13**
Nasugbu, *Phil.* 55 **D4**
Näsviken, *Sweden* 10 **C10**
Nat Kyizin, *Burma* 61 **M20**
Nata, *Botswana* 84 **C4**
Natagaima, *Colombia* 120 **C2**
Natal, *Brazil* 122 **C4**
Natal, *Canada* 100 **D6**
Natal, *Indonesia* 56 **D1**
Natal □, *S. Africa* 85 **D5**
Natalinci, *Serbia* 21 **L10**
Naṭanz, *Iran* 65 **C6**
Natashquan, *Canada* 99 **B7**
Natashquan →, *Canada* .. 99 **B7**
Natchez, *U.S.A.* 109 **K9**
Natchitoches, *U.S.A.* 109 **K8**
Naters, *Switz.* 22 **D5**
Nathalia, *Australia* 91 **F4**
Nathdwara, *India* 62 **G5**
Nati, Pta., *Spain* 36 **A10**
Natimuk, *Australia* 91 **F3**
Nation →, *Canada* 100 **B4**
National City, *U.S.A.* 113 **N9**
Natitingou, *Benin* 79 **C5**
Natividad, I., *Mexico* 114 **B1**
Natoma, *U.S.A.* 108 **F5**
Natron, L., *Tanzania* 82 **C4**
Natrona Heights, *U.S.A.* . 106 **F5**
Natrûn, W. el →, *Egypt* . 76 **H7**
Natuna Besar, Kepulauan, *Indonesia* 59 **L7**
Natuna Is. = Natuna Besar, Kepulauan, *Indonesia* 59 **L7**
Natuna Selatan, Kepulauan, *Indonesia* .. 59 **L7**
Natural Bridge, *U.S.A.* ... 107 **B9**
Naturaliste, C., *Australia* . 90 **G4**
Nau Qala, *Afghan.* 62 **B3**
Naubinway, *U.S.A.* 98 **C2**
Naucelle, *France* 26 **D6**
Nauders, *Austria* 19 **J6**
Nauen, *Germany* 18 **C8**
Naugatuck, *U.S.A.* 107 **E11**
Naujoji Vilnia, *Lithuania* . 40 **D4**
Naumburg, *Germany* 18 **D7**
Nā'ūr at Tunayb, *Jordan* . 69 **D4**
Nauru ■, *Pac. Oc.* 92 **H8**
Naushahra = Nowshera, *Pakistan* 60 **B8**
Nauta, *Peru* 120 **D3**
Nautanwa, *India* 61 **F13**
Nautla, *Mexico* 115 **C5**
Nava, *Mexico* 114 **B4**
Nava del Rey, *Spain* 30 **D5**
Navacerrada, Puerto de, *Spain* 30 **E7**
Navadwip, *India* 63 **H13**
Navahermosa, *Spain* 31 **F6**
Navajo Reservoir, *U.S.A.* . 111 **H10**
Navalcarnero, *Spain* 30 **E6**
Navalmoral de la Mata, *Spain* 30 **F5**
Navalvillar de Pela, *Spain* . 31 **F5**
Navan = An Uaimh, *Ireland* 15 **C5**
Navarino, I., *Chile* 128 **E3**
Navarra □, *Spain* 28 **C3**
Navarre, *U.S.A.* 106 **F3**
Navarrenx, *France* 26 **E3**
Navarro →, *U.S.A.* 112 **F3**
Navasota, *U.S.A.* 109 **K6**
Navassa, *W. Indies* 117 **C4**
Nave, *Italy* 32 **C7**
Naver →, *U.K.* 14 **C4**
Navia, *Spain* 30 **B4**
Navia →, *Spain* 30 **B4**
Navia de Suarna, *Spain* ... 30 **C4**
Navidad, *Chile* 126 **C1**
Navlya, *Russia* 40 **E9**
Navoi, *Uzbekistan* 44 **E7**
Navojoa, *Mexico* 114 **B3**
Navolato, *Mexico* 114 **C3**
Návpaktos, *Greece* 39 **L4**
Návplion, *Greece* 39 **M5**
Navrongo, *Ghana* 79 **C4**
Navsari, *India* 60 **J8**
Nawa Kot, *Pakistan* 62 **E4**
Nawabganj, *Ut. P., India* . 63 **F9**
Nawabganj, *Ut. P., India* . 63 **E8**
Nawabshah, *Pakistan* 62 **F3**
Nawada, *India* 63 **G11**
Nawakot, *Nepal* 63 **F11**
Nawalgarh, *India* 62 **F6**
Nawanshahr, *India* 63 **C6**
Nawi, *Sudan* 76 **D3**
Náxos, *Greece* 39 **M8**
Nay, *France* 26 **E3**
Nāy Band, *Iran* 65 **E7**
Naya →, *Colombia* 120 **C2**
Nayakhan, *Russia* 45 **C16**
Nayarit □, *Mexico* 114 **C4**
Nayé, *Senegal* 78 **C2**
Nayong, *China* 52 **D5**
Nayoro, *Japan* 48 **B11**
Nayyāl, W. →, *Si. Arabia* 64 **D3**
Nazaré, *Bahia, Brazil* 123 **D4**
Nazaré, *Goiás, Brazil* 122 **C2**
Nazaré, *Pará, Brazil* 125 **B7**
Nazaré, *Portugal* 31 **F1**
Nazareth = Nazerat, *Israel* 69 **C4**
Nazas, *Mexico* 114 **B4**
Nazas →, *Mexico* 114 **B4**
Naze, The, *U.K.* 13 **F9**
Nazerat, *Israel* 69 **C4**
Nāzīk, *Iran* 64 **B5**
Nazik Gölü, *Turkey* 67 **D10**
Nazilli, *Turkey* 66 **E3**
Nazir Hat, *Bangla.* 61 **H17**
Nazko, *Canada* 100 **C4**
Nazko →, *Canada* 100 **C4**
Nazret, *Ethiopia* 77 **F4**
Nchanga, *Zambia* 83 **E2**
Ncheu, *Malawi* 83 **E3**
Ndala, *Tanzania* 82 **C3**
Ndalatando, *Angola* 80 **F2**
Ndali, *Benin* 79 **D5**
Ndareda, *Tanzania* 82 **C4**
Ndélé, *C.A.R.* 73 **G9**
Ndendé, *Gabon* 80 **E2**
Ndjamena, *Chad* 73 **F7**
Ndjolé, *Gabon* 80 **E2**
Ndola, *Zambia* 83 **E2**
Ndoto Mts., *Kenya* 82 **B4**
Nduguti, *Tanzania* 82 **C3**
Nea →, *Norway* 10 **A5**
Néa Flippiás, *Greece* 39 **K3**
Neagh, Lough, *U.K.* 15 **B5**
Neah Bay, *U.S.A.* 112 **B2**
Neale, L., *Australia* 88 **D5**
Neápolis, *Kozan, Greece* . 39 **J4**
Neápolis, *Kríti, Greece* ... 37 **D7**
Neápolis, *Lakonía, Greece* 39 **N6**
Near Is., *U.S.A.* 96 **C1**
Neath, *U.K.* 13 **F4**
Nebbou, *Burkina Faso* ... 79 **C4**
Nebine Cr. →, *Australia* . 91 **D4**
Nebit Dag, *Turkmenistan* . 44 **F6**
Nebolchy, *Russia* 40 **B8**
Nebraska □, *U.S.A.* 108 **E5**
Nebraska City, *U.S.A.* ... 108 **E7**
Nébrodi, Monti, *Italy* 35 **E7**
Necedah, *U.S.A.* 108 **C9**
Nechako →, *Canada* 100 **C4**
Neches →, *U.S.A.* 109 **L8**
Neckar →, *Germany* 19 **F4**
Necochea, *Argentina* 126 **D4**
Nedelišće, *Croatia* 33 **B13**
Neder Rijn →, *Neths.* ... 16 **E8**
Nederbrakel, *Belgium* 17 **G3**
Nederweert, *Neths.* 17 **F7**
Nédha →, *Greece* 39 **M4**
Nedroma, *Algeria* 75 **A4**
Neede, *Neths.* 16 **D9**
Needles, *U.S.A.* 113 **L12**
Needles, The, *U.K.* 13 **G6**
Ñeembucú □, *Paraguay* .. 126 **B4**
Neemuch = Nimach, *India* 62 **G6**
Neenah, *U.S.A.* 104 **C1**
Neepawa, *Canada* 101 **C9**
Neer, *Neths.* 17 **F7**
Neerpelt, *Belgium* 17 **F6**
Neft-chala = imeni 26 Bakinskikh Komissarov, *Azerbaijan* 67 **D13**
Nefta, *Tunisia* 75 **B6**
Neftah Sidi Boubekeur, *Algeria* 75 **A5**
Neftegorsk, *Russia* 43 **D8**
Neftekumsk, *Russia* 43 **D11**
Neftenbach, *Switz.* 23 **A7**
Negapatam = Nagappattinam, *India* 60 **P11**
Negaunee, *U.S.A.* 104 **B2**
Negele, *Ethiopia* 68 **F2**
Negev Desert = Hanegev, *Israel* 69 **E3**
Negombo, *Sri Lanka* 60 **R11**
Negotin, *Serbia* 21 **L12**
Negra, Peña, *Spain* 30 **C4**
Negra, Pta., *Mauritania* .. 74 **D1**
Negra, Pta., *Peru* 124 **B1**
Negra Pt., *Phil.* 57 **A6**
Negrais, C. = Maudin Sun, *Burma* 61 **M19**
Negreira, *Spain* 30 **C2**
Négrine, *Algeria* 75 **B6**
Negro →, *Argentina* 128 **B4**
Negro →, *Bolivia* 125 **C5**
Negro →, *Brazil* 121 **D6**
Negro →, *Uruguay* 127 **C4**
Negros, *Phil.* 55 **G5**
Nehalem →, *U.S.A.* 112 **E3**
Nehāvand, *Iran* 65 **C6**
Nehbandān, *Iran* 65 **D9**
Neheim, *Germany* 18 **D3**
Nehoiaşu, *Romania* 38 **D9**
Nei Monggol Zizhiqu □, *China* 50 **C6**
Neidpath, *Canada* 101 **C7**
Neihart, *U.S.A.* 110 **C8**
Neijiang, *China* 52 **C5**
Neilton, *U.S.A.* 110 **C2**
Neiqiu, *China* 50 **F8**
Neira de Jusá, *Spain* 30 **C3**
Neiva, *Colombia* 120 **C2**
Neixiang, *China* 50 **H6**
Nejanilini L., *Canada* 101 **B9**
Nejo, *Ethiopia* 77 **F4**
Nekā, *Iran* 65 **B7**
Nekemte, *Ethiopia* 77 **F4**
Nêkheb, *Egypt* 76 **B3**
Neksø, *Denmark* 9 **J13**
Nelas, *Portugal* 30 **E3**
Nelia, *Australia* 90 **C3**
Nelidovo, *Russia* 40 **C8**
Neligh, *U.S.A.* 108 **D5**
Nelkan, *Russia* 45 **D14**
Nellore, *India* 60 **M11**
Nelma, *Russia* 45 **E14**
Nelson, *Canada* 100 **D5**
Nelson, *N.Z.* 87 **J4**
Nelson, *U.K.* 12 **D5**
Nelson, *U.S.A.* 111 **J7**
Nelson →, *Canada* 101 **C9**
Nelson, C., *Australia* 91 **F3**
Nelson, Estrecho, *Chile* .. 128 **D2**
Nelson Forks, *Canada* 100 **B4**
Nelson House, *Canada* ... 101 **B9**
Nelson L., *Canada* 101 **B8**
Nelspoort, *S. Africa* 84 **E3**
Nelspruit, *S. Africa* 85 **D5**
Néma, *Mauritania* 78 **B3**
Neman →, *Lithuania* 40 **D2**
Nemeiben L., *Canada* 101 **B7**
Nemira, *Romania* 38 **C9**
Nemours, *France* 25 **D9**
Nemunas = Neman →, *Lithuania* 40 **D2**
Nemuro, *Japan* 48 **C12**
Nemuro-Kaikyō, *Japan* ... 48 **C12**
Nemuy, *Russia* 45 **D14**
Nen Jiang →, *China* 51 **B13**
Nenagh, *Ireland* 15 **D3**
Nenana, *U.S.A.* 96 **B5**
Nenasi, *Malaysia* 59 **L4**
Nene →, *U.K.* 12 **E8**
Nenjiang, *China* 54 **B7**
Neno, *Malawi* 83 **F3**
Nenusa, Kepulauan, *Indonesia* 57 **D7**
Neodesha, *U.S.A.* 109 **G7**
Neópolis, *Brazil* 122 **D4**
Neosho, *U.S.A.* 109 **G7**
Neosho →, *U.S.A.* 109 **H7**
Nepal ■, *Asia* 63 **F11**
Nepalganj, *Nepal* 63 **E9**
Nephi, *U.S.A.* 110 **G8**
Nephin, *Ireland* 15 **B2**
Neptune, *U.S.A.* 107 **F10**
Néra →, *Romania* 38 **E4**
Nérac, *France* 26 **D4**
Nerchinsk, *Russia* 45 **D12**
Nerchinskiy Zavod, *Russia* 45 **D12**
Nereju, *Romania* 38 **D9**
Nerekhta, *Russia* 41 **C12**
Néret L., *Canada* 99 **B5**
Neringa, *Lithuania* 40 **D2**
Nerja, *Spain* 31 **J7**
Nerl →, *Russia* 41 **C12**
Nerpio, *Spain* 29 **G2**
Nerva, *Spain* 31 **H4**
Nes, *Iceland* 8 **D5**
Nes, *Neths.* 16 **B7**
Nesbyen, *Norway* 10 **D3**
Nesebūr, *Bulgaria* 38 **G10**
Neskaupstaður, *Iceland* ... 8 **D7**
Nesland, *Norway* 10 **E1**
Neslandsvatn, *Norway* 10 **F3**
Nesle, *France* 25 **C9**
Nesodden, *Norway* 10 **E4**
Nesque →, *France* 27 **E8**
Ness, L., *U.K.* 14 **D4**
Nesslau, *Switz.* 23 **B8**
Néstos →, *Greece* 39 **H7**
Nesttun, *Norway* 9 **F8**
Nesvizh, *Belorussia* 40 **E5**
Netanya, *Israel* 69 **C3**
Nète →, *Belgium* 17 **F4**
Netherdale, *Australia* 90 **C4**
Netherlands ■, *Europe* ... 16 **E6**
Netherlands Antilles ■, *W. Indies* 120 **A4**
Neto →, *Italy* 35 **C10**
Nettancourt, *France* 25 **D11**
Nettilling L., *Canada* 97 **B12**
Nettuno, *Italy* 34 **A5**
Netzahualcoyotl, Presa, *Mexico* 115 **D6**
Neu-Isenburg, *Germany* .. 19 **E4**
Neu-Ulm, *Germany* 19 **G6**
Neubrandenburg, *Germany* 18 **B9**
Neubukow, *Germany* 18 **A7**
Neuburg, *Germany* 19 **G7**
Neuchâtel, *Switz.* 22 **C3**
Neuchâtel □, *Switz.* 22 **C3**
Neuchâtel, Lac de, *Switz.* . 22 **C3**
Neudau, *Austria* 21 **H6**
Neuenegg, *Switz.* 22 **C4**
Neuenhaus, *Germany* 18 **C2**
Neuf-Brisach, *France* 25 **D14**
Neufahrn, *Germany* 19 **G8**
Neufchâteau, *Belgium* 17 **J6**
Neufchâteau, *France* 25 **D12**
Neufchâtel-en-Bray, *France* 24 **C8**
Neufchâtel-sur-Aisne, *France* 25 **C11**
Neuhaus, *Germany* 18 **B6**
Neuhausen, *Switz.* 23 **A7**
Neuillé-Pont-Pierre, *France* 24 **E7**
Neuilly-St.-Front, *France* . 25 **C10**
Neukalen, *Germany* 18 **B8**
Neumarkt, *Germany* 19 **F7**
Neumarkt-Sankt Veit, *Germany* 19 **G8**
Neumünster, *Germany* ... 18 **A5**
Neung-sur-Beuvron, *France* 25 **E8**
Neunkirchen, *Austria* 21 **H6**
Neunkirchen, *Germany* ... 19 **F3**
Neuquén, *Argentina* 128 **A3**
Neuquén □, *Argentina* ... 126 **D2**
Neuquén →, *Argentina* .. 128 **A3**
Neuruppin, *Germany* 18 **C8**
Neuse →, *U.S.A.* 105 **H7**
Neusiedler See, *Austria* ... 21 **H6**
Neuss, *Germany* 17 **F9**
Neussargues-Moissac, *France* 26 **C7**
Neustadt, *Baden-W., Germany* 19 **H4**
Neustadt, *Bayern, Germany* 19 **F8**
Neustadt, *Bayern, Germany* 19 **G7**
Neustadt, *Bayern, Germany* 19 **F6**
Neustadt, *Bayern, Germany* 19 **E7**
Neustadt, *Brandenburg, Germany* 18 **C8**
Neustadt, *Hessen, Germany* 18 **E5**
Neustadt, *Niedersachsen, Germany* 18 **C5**
Neustadt, *Rhld-Pfz., Germany* 19 **F4**
Neustadt, *Schleswig-Holstein, Germany* 18 **A6**
Neustadt, *Thüringen, Germany* 18 **E7**
Neustrelitz, *Germany* 18 **B9**
Neuvic, *France* 26 **C6**
Neuville, *Belgium* 17 **H5**
Neuville-aux-Bois, *France* . 25 **D9**
Neuville-de-Poitou, *France* 26 **B4**
Neuville-sur-Saône, *France* 27 **C8**
Neuvy-le-Roi, *France* 24 **E7**
Neuvy-St.-Sépulchre, *France* 26 **B5**
Neuvy-sur-Barangeon, *France* 25 **E9**
Neuwerk, *Germany* 18 **B4**
Neuwied, *Germany* 18 **E3**
Neva →, *Russia* 6 **D12**
Nevada, *U.S.A.* 109 **G7**
Nevada □, *U.S.A.* 110 **G5**
Nevada, Sierra, *Spain* 29 **H1**
Nevada, Sierra, *U.S.A.* ... 110 **G3**
Nevada City, *U.S.A.* 112 **F6**
Nevado, Cerro, *Argentina* 126 **D2**
Nevanka, *Russia* 45 **D10**
Nevel, *Russia* 40 **D6**
Nevele, *Belgium* 17 **F3**
Nevers, *France* 25 **F10**
Nevertire, *Australia* 91 **E4**
Neville, *Canada* 101 **D7**
Nevinnomyssk, *Russia* ... 43 **D9**
Nevis, *W. Indies* 117 **C7**
Nevrokop = Gotse Delchev, *Bulgaria* 39 **H6**
Nevşehir, *Turkey* 66 **D6**
Nevşehir □, *Turkey* 66 **D6**
New →, *Guyana* 121 **C6**
New Albany, *Ind., U.S.A.* 104 **F3**
New Albany, *Miss., U.S.A.* 109 **H10**
New Albany, *Pa., U.S.A.* . 107 **E8**
New Amsterdam, *Guyana* 121 **B6**
New Angledool, *Australia* 91 **D4**
New Bedford, *U.S.A.* 107 **E14**
New Bern, *U.S.A.* 105 **H7**
New Bethlehem, *U.S.A.* .. 106 **E5**
New Bloomfield, *U.S.A.* .. 106 **F7**
New Boston, *U.S.A.* 109 **J7**
New Braunfels, *U.S.A.* ... 109 **L5**
New Brighton, *N.Z.* 87 **K4**
New Brighton, *U.S.A.* ... 106 **F4**
New Britain, *Papua N. G.* 92 **H7**
New Britain, *U.S.A.* 107 **E12**
New Brunswick, *U.S.A.* .. 107 **F10**
New Brunswick □, *Canada* 99 **C6**
New Bussa, *Nigeria* 79 **D5**
New Caledonia, *Pac. Oc.* . 92 **K8**
New Castile = Castilla La Mancha □, *Spain* 31 **F7**
New Castle, *Ind., U.S.A.* . 104 **F3**
New Castle, *Pa., U.S.A.* .. 106 **E4**
New City, *U.S.A.* 107 **E11**
New Cumberland, *U.S.A.* 106 **F4**
New Cuyama, *U.S.A.* 113 **L7**
New Delhi, *India* 62 **E7**
New Denver, *Canada* 100 **D5**
New Don Pedro Reservoir, *U.S.A.* 112 **H6**
New England, *U.S.A.* 108 **B3**
New England Ra., *Australia* 91 **E5**
New Forest, *U.K.* 13 **G6**
New Glasgow, *Canada* ... 99 **C7**
New Guinea, *Oceania* 92 **H5**
New Hamburg, *Canada* ... 106 **C4**
New Hampshire □, *U.S.A.* 107 **C13**
New Hampton, *U.S.A.* ... 108 **D8**
New Hanover, *S. Africa* .. 85 **D5**
New Haven, *Conn., U.S.A.* 107 **E12**
New Haven, *Mich., U.S.A.* 106 **D2**
New Hazelton, *Canada* ... 100 **B3**
New Hebrides = Vanuatu ■, *Pac. Oc.* ... 92 **J8**
New Iberia, *U.S.A.* 109 **K9**
New Ireland, *Papua N. G.* 92 **H7**
New Jersey □, *U.S.A.* 107 **F10**
New Kensington, *U.S.A.* . 106 **F5**
New Lexington, *U.S.A.* .. 104 **F4**
New Liskeard, *Canada* ... 98 **C4**
New London, *Conn., U.S.A.* 107 **E12**
New London, *Minn., U.S.A.* 108 **C7**
New London, *Ohio, U.S.A.* 106 **E2**
New London, *Wis., U.S.A.* 108 **C10**
New Madrid, *U.S.A.* 109 **G10**
New Meadows, *U.S.A.* ... 110 **D5**
New Melones L., *U.S.A.* . 112 **H6**
New Mexico □, *U.S.A.* ... 111 **J10**
New Milford, *Conn., U.S.A.* 107 **E11**
New Milford, *Pa., U.S.A.* 107 **E9**
New Norcia, *Australia* 89 **F2**
New Norfolk, *Australia* ... 90 **G4**
New Orleans, *U.S.A.* 109 **K9**
New Philadelphia, *U.S.A.* 106 **F3**
New Plymouth, *N.Z.* 87 **H5**
New Plymouth, *U.S.A.* ... 110 **E5**
New Providence, *Bahamas* 116 **A4**
New Radnor, *U.K.* 13 **E4**
New Richmond, *U.S.A.* .. 108 **C8**
New Roads, *U.S.A.* 109 **K9**
New Rochelle, *U.S.A.* ... 107 **F11**
New Rockford, *U.S.A.* ... 108 **B5**
New Ross, *Ireland* 15 **D5**
New Salem, *U.S.A.* 108 **B4**
New Scone, *U.K.* 14 **E5**
New Siberian Is. = Novaya Sibir, Ostrov, *Russia* ... 45 **B16**
New Siberian Is. = Novosibirskiye Ostrova, *Russia* 45 **B15**
New Smyrna Beach, *U.S.A.* 105 **L5**
New South Wales □, *Australia* 91 **E4**
New Springs, *Australia* ... 89 **E3**
New Town, *U.S.A.* 108 **A3**
New Ulm, *U.S.A.* 108 **C7**
New Waterford, *Canada* .. 99 **C7**
New Westminster, *Canada* 100 **D4**
New York □, *U.S.A.* 107 **D9**
New York City, *U.S.A.* .. 107 **F11**
New Zealand ■, *Oceania* . 87 **J5**
Newala, *Tanzania* 83 **E4**
Newala □, *Tanzania* 83 **E4**
Newark, *Del., U.S.A.* 104 **F8**
Newark, *N.J., U.S.A.* 107 **F10**
Newark, *N.Y., U.S.A.* ... 106 **C7**
Newark, *Ohio, U.S.A.* ... 106 **F2**
Newark-on-Trent, *U.K.* .. 12 **D7**
Newaygo, *U.S.A.* 104 **D3**
Newberg, *U.S.A.* 110 **D2**
Newberry, *Mich., U.S.A.* . 104 **B3**
Newberry, *S.C., U.S.A.* .. 105 **H5**
Newberry Springs, *U.S.A.* 113 **L10**
Newbrook, *Canada* 100 **C6**
Newburgh, *U.S.A.* 107 **E10**
Newbury, *U.K.* 13 **F6**
Newbury, *U.S.A.* 107 **B12**
Newburyport, *U.S.A.* ... 107 **D14**
Newcastle, *Australia* 91 **E5**
Newcastle, *Canada* 99 **C6**
Newcastle, *S. Africa* 85 **D4**
Newcastle, *U.K.* 15 **B6**
Newcastle, *Calif., U.S.A.* . 112 **G5**
Newcastle, *Wyo., U.S.A.* . 108 **D2**
Newcastle Emlyn, *U.K.* .. 13 **E3**
Newcastle Ra., *Australia* .. 88 **C5**
Newcastle-under-Lyme, *U.K.* 12 **D5**
Newcastle-upon-Tyne, *U.K.* 12 **C6**
Newcastle Waters, *Australia* 90 **B1**
Newdegate, *Australia* 89 **F2**
Newell, *U.S.A.* 108 **C3**
Newfoundland □, *Canada* 99 **B8**
Newhalem, *U.S.A.* 100 **D4**
Newhall, *U.S.A.* 113 **L8**
Newham, *U.K.* 13 **F8**
Newhaven, *U.K.* 13 **G8**
Newkirk, *U.S.A.* 109 **G6**
Newman, *Australia* 88 **D2**
Newman, *U.S.A.* 112 **H5**
Newmarket, *Canada* 106 **B5**
Newmarket, *Ireland* 15 **D3**
Newmarket, *U.K.* 13 **E8**
Newmarket, *U.S.A.* 107 **C14**
Newnan, *U.S.A.* 105 **J3**
Newport, *Gwent, U.K.* ... 13 **F5**
Newport, *I. of W., U.K.* .. 13 **G6**
Newport, *Shrops., U.K.* .. 13 **E5**
Newport, *Ark., U.S.A.* ... 109 **H9**
Newport, *Ky., U.S.A.* ... 104 **F3**
Newport, *N.H., U.S.A.* ... 107 **C12**
Newport, *Oreg., U.S.A.* .. 110 **D1**
Newport, *Pa., U.S.A.* 106 **F7**
Newport, *R.I., U.S.A.* ... 107 **E13**
Newport, *Tenn., U.S.A.* .. 105 **H4**
Newport, *Vt., U.S.A.* 107 **B12**
Newport, *Wash., U.S.A.* .. 110 **B5**
Newport Beach, *U.S.A.* .. 113 **M9**
Newport News, *U.S.A.* ... 104 **G7**
Newquay, *U.K.* 13 **G2**
Newry, *U.K.* 15 **B5**

Newry & Mourne □, *U.K.* 15 B5
Newton, *Iowa, U.S.A.* 108 E8
Newton, *Mass., U.S.A.* 107 D13
Newton, *Miss., U.S.A.* 109 J10
Newton, *N.C., U.S.A.* 105 H5
Newton, *N.J., U.S.A.* 107 E10
Newton, *Tex., U.S.A.* 109 K8
Newton Abbot, *U.K.* 13 G4
Newton Boyd, *Australia* 91 D5
Newton Stewart, *U.K.* 14 G4
Newtonmore, *U.K.* 14 D4
Newtown, *U.K.* 13 E4
Newtownabbey □, *U.K.* 15 B6
Newtownards, *U.K.* 15 B6
Newville, *U.S.A.* 106 F7
Nexon, *France* 26 C5
Neya, *Russia* 41 B13
Neyrīz, *Iran* 65 D7
Neyshābūr, *Iran* 65 B8
Nezhin, *Ukraine* 40 F7
Nezperce, *U.S.A.* 110 C5
Ngabang, *Indonesia* 56 D3
Ngabordamlu, Tanjung, *Indonesia* 57 F8
Ngambé, *Cameroon* 79 D7
Ngami Depression, *Botswana* 84 C3
Ngamo, *Zimbabwe* 83 F2
Nganglong Kangri, *China* 61 C12
Nganjuk, *Indonesia* 57 G14
Ngao, *Thailand* 58 C2
Ngaoundéré, *Cameroon* 80 C2
Ngapara, *N.Z.* 87 L3
Ngara, *Tanzania* 82 C3
Ngara □, *Tanzania* 82 C3
Ngawi, *Indonesia* 57 G14
Nghia Lo, *Vietnam* 58 B5
Ngoma, *Malawi* 83 E3
Ngomahura, *Zimbabwe* 83 G3
Ngomba, *Tanzania* 83 D3
Ngop, *Sudan* 77 F3
Ngoring Hu, *China* 54 C4
Ngorkou, *Mali* 78 B4
Ngorongoro, *Tanzania* 82 C4
Ngozi, *Burundi* 82 C2
Ngudu, *Tanzania* 82 C3
Nguigmi, *Niger* 73 F7
Ngukurr, *Australia* 90 A1
Ngunga, *Tanzania* 82 C3
Nguru, *Nigeria* 79 C7
Nguru Mts., *Tanzania* 82 D4
Nguyen Binh, *Vietnam* 58 A5
Nha Trang, *Vietnam* 59 F7
Nhacoongo, *Mozam.* 85 C6
Nhamaabué, *Mozam.* 83 F4
Nhambiquara, *Brazil* 125 C6
Nhamundá, *Brazil* 121 D6
Nhamundá →, *Brazil* 121 D6
Nhangutazi, L., *Mozam.* 85 C5
Nhecolândia, *Brazil* 125 D6
Nhill, *Australia* 91 F3
Nho Quan, *Vietnam* 58 B5
Nhulunbuy, *Australia* 90 A2
Nia-nia, *Zaïre* 82 B2
Niafounké, *Mali* 78 B4
Niagara, *U.S.A.* 104 C1
Niagara Falls, *Canada* 98 D4
Niagara Falls, *U.S.A.* 106 C6
Niagara-on-the-Lake, *Canada* 106 C5
Niah, *Malaysia* 56 D4
Niamey, *Niger* 79 C5
Nianforando, *Guinea* 78 D2
Nianfors, *Sweden* 10 C10
Niangara, *Zaïre* 82 B2
Nias, *Indonesia* 56 D1
Niassa □, *Mozam.* 83 E4
Nibbiano, *Italy* 32 D6
Nibe, *Denmark* 11 H3
Nicaragua ■, *Cent. Amer.* 116 D2
Nicaragua, L. de, *Nic.* 116 D2
Nicastro, *Italy* 35 D9
Nice, *France* 27 E11
Niceville, *U.S.A.* 105 K2
Nichinan, *Japan* 49 J5
Nicholás, Canal, *W. Indies* 116 B3
Nicholasville, *U.S.A.* 104 G3
Nichols, *U.S.A.* 107 D8
Nicholson, *Australia* 88 C4
Nicholson, *U.S.A.* 107 E9
Nicholson →, *Australia* 90 B2
Nicholson Ra., *Australia* 89 E2
Nickerie □, *Surinam* 121 C6
Nickerie →, *Surinam* 121 B6
Nicobar Is., *Ind. Oc.* 46 J13
Nicoclí, *Colombia* 120 B2
Nicola, *Canada* 100 C4
Nicolet, *Canada* 98 C5
Nicolls Town, *Bahamas* 116 A4
Nicosia, *Cyprus* 37 D12
Nicosia, *Italy* 35 E7
Nicótera, *Italy* 35 D8
Nicoya, *Costa Rica* 116 D2
Nicoya, G. de, *Costa Rica* 116 E3
Nicoya, Pen. de, *Costa Rica* 116 E2
Nidau, *Switz.* 22 B4
Nidd →, *U.K.* 12 C6
Nidda, *Germany* 18 E5
Nidda →, *Germany* 19 E4
Nidwalden □, *Switz.* 23 C6
Nidzica, *Poland* 20 B10
Niebüll, *Germany* 18 A4
Nied →, *Germany* 25 C13
Niederaula, *Germany* 18 E5
Niederbipp, *Switz.* 22 B5
Niederbronn-les-Bains, *France* 25 D14
Niedere Tauern, *Austria* 21 H4
Niedersachsen □, *Germany* 18 C5
Niekerkshoop, *S. Africa* 84 D3
Niel, *Belgium* 17 F4
Niellé, *Ivory C.* 78 C3
Niemba, *Zaïre* 82 D2
Niemen = Neman →, *Lithuania* 40 D2
Nienburg, *Germany* 18 C5
Niers →, *Germany* 18 D2
Niesen, *Switz.* 22 C5
Niesky, *Germany* 18 D10
Nieu Bethesda, *S. Africa* 84 E3
Nieuw-Amsterdam, *Neths.* 16 C9
Nieuw Amsterdam, *Surinam* 121 B6
Nieuw Beijerland, *Neths.* 16 E4
Nieuw-Dordrecht, *Neths.* 16 C9
Nieuw Loosdrecht, *Neths.* 16 D6
Nieuw Nickerie, *Surinam* 121 B6
Nieuw-Schoonebeek, *Neths.* 16 C10
Nieuw-Vennep, *Neths.* 16 D5
Nieuw-Vossemeer, *Neths.* 17 E4
Nieuwe-Niedorp, *Neths.* 16 C5
Nieuwe-Pekela, *Neths.* 16 B9
Nieuwe-Schans, *Neths.* 16 B10
Nieuwendijk, *Neths.* 16 E5
Nieuwerkerken, *Belgium* 17 G6
Nieuwkoop, *Neths.* 16 D5
Nieuwleusen, *Neths.* 16 C8
Nieuwnamen, *Neths.* 17 F4
Nieuwolda, *Neths.* 16 B9
Nieuwoudtville, *S. Africa* 84 E2
Nieuwpoort, *Belgium* 17 F1
Nieuwveen, *Neths.* 16 D5
Nieves, *Spain* 30 C2
Nieves, Pico de las, *Canary Is.* 36 G4
Nièvre □, *France* 25 E10
Niğde, *Turkey* 66 E6
Niğde □, *Turkey* 66 E6
Nigel, *S. Africa* 85 D4
Niger □, *Nigeria* 79 C6
Niger ■, *W. Afr.* 79 B6
Niger →, *W. Afr.* 79 D6
Nigeria ■, *W. Afr.* 79 D6
Nightcaps, *N.Z.* 87 L2
Nigríta, *Greece* 39 J6
Nihtaur, *India* 63 E8
Nii-Jima, *Japan* 49 G9
Niigata, *Japan* 48 F9
Niigata □, *Japan* 49 F9
Niihama, *Japan* 49 H6
Niihau, *U.S.A.* 102 H14
Niimi, *Japan* 49 G6
Niitsu, *Japan* 48 F9
Nijar, *Spain* 29 J2
Nijil, *Jordan* 69 E4
Nijkerk, *Neths.* 16 D7
Nijlen, *Belgium* 17 F5
Nijmegen, *Neths.* 16 E7
Nijverdal, *Neths.* 16 D8
Nīk Pey, *Iran* 65 B6
Nike, *Nigeria* 79 D6
Nikel, *Russia* 8 B21
Nikiniki, *Indonesia* 57 F6
Nikki, *Benin* 79 D5
Nikkō, *Japan* 49 F9
Nikolayev, *Ukraine* 42 C4
Nikolayevsk, *Russia* 41 G14
Nikolayevsk-na-Amur, *Russia* 45 D15
Nikolsk, *Russia* 41 B14
Nikolskoye, *Russia* 45 D17
Nikopol, *Bulgaria* 38 F7
Nikopol, *Ukraine* 42 C6
Niksar, *Turkey* 42 F7
Nīkshahr, *Iran* 65 E9
Nikšić, *Montenegro* 21 N8
Nîl, Nahr en →, *Africa* 76 H7
Nîl el Abyad →, *Sudan* 77 D3
Nîl el Azraq →, *Sudan* 77 D3
Niland, *U.S.A.* 113 M11
Nile = Nîl, Nahr en →, *Africa* 76 H7
Nile □, *Uganda* 82 B3
Nile Delta, *Egypt* 76 H7
Niles, *U.S.A.* 106 E4
Nilo Peçanha, *Brazil* 123 D4
Nimach, *India* 62 G6
Nimbahera, *India* 62 G6
Nîmes, *France* 27 E8
Nimfaíon, Ákra-, *Greece* 39 J7
Nimmitabel, *Australia* 91 F4
Nimneryskiy, *Russia* 45 D13
Nimule, *Sudan* 77 G3
Nin, *Croatia* 33 D12
Nīnawá, *Iraq* 64 B4
Nindigully, *Australia* 91 D4
Ninemile, *U.S.A.* 100 B2
Nineveh = Nīnawá, *Iraq* 64 B4
Ning Xian, *China* 50 G4
Ningaloo, *Australia* 88 D1
Ning'an, *China* 51 B15
Ningbo, *China* 53 C13
Ningcheng, *China* 51 D10
Ningde, *China* 53 D12
Ningdu, *China* 53 D10
Ninggang, *China* 53 D9
Ningguo, *China* 53 B12
Ninghai, *China* 53 C13
Ninghua, *China* 53 D11
Ningjin, *China* 50 F8
Ningjing Shan, *China* 52 B2
Ninglang, *China* 52 D3
Ningling, *China* 50 G8
Ningming, *China* 52 F6
Ningnan, *China* 52 D4
Ningpo = Ningbo, *China* 53 C13
Ningqiang, *China* 50 H4
Ningshan, *China* 50 H5
Ningsia Hui A.R. = Ningxia Huizu Zizhiqu □, *China* 50 E3
Ningwu, *China* 50 E7
Ningxia Huizu Zizhiqu □, *China* 50 E3
Ningxiang, *China* 53 C9
Ningyang, *China* 50 G9
Ningyuan, *China* 53 E8
Ninh Binh, *Vietnam* 58 B5
Ninh Giang, *Vietnam* 58 B6
Ninh Hoa, *Vietnam* 58 F7
Ninh Ma, *Vietnam* 58 F7
Ninove, *Belgium* 17 G4
Nioaque, *Brazil* 127 A4
Niobrara, *U.S.A.* 108 D6
Niobrara →, *U.S.A.* 108 D6
Niono, *Mali* 78 C3
Nioro du Rip, *Senegal* 78 C1
Nioro du Sahel, *Mali* 78 B3
Niort, *France* 26 B3
Nipawin, *Canada* 101 C8
Nipawin Prov. Park, *Canada* 101 C8
Nipigon, *Canada* 98 C2
Nipigon, L., *Canada* 98 C2
Nipin →, *Canada* 101 B7
Nipishish L., *Canada* 99 B7
Nipissing L., *Canada* 98 C4
Nipomo, *U.S.A.* 113 K6
Nipton, *U.S.A.* 113 K11
Niquelândia, *Brazil* 123 D2
Nīr, *Iran* 64 B5
Nirasaki, *Japan* 49 G9
Nirmal, *India* 60 K11
Nirmali, *India* 63 F12
Niš, *Serbia* 21 M11
Nisa, *Portugal* 31 F3
Nişāb, *Yemen* 68 E4
Nišava →, *Serbia* 21 M11
Niscemi, *Italy* 35 E7
Nishinomiya, *Japan* 49 G7
Nishin'omote, *Japan* 49 J5
Nishiwaki, *Japan* 49 G7
Nísíros, *Greece* 39 N10
Niskibi →, *Canada* 98 A2
Nispen, *Neths.* 17 F4
Nisqually →, *U.S.A.* 112 C4
Nissáki, *Greece* 37 A3
Nissan →, *Sweden* 11 H6
Nissedal, *Norway* 10 E2
Nisser, *Norway* 10 E2
Nissum Fjord, *Denmark* 11 H2
Nistelrode, *Neths.* 17 E7
Nisutlin →, *Canada* 100 A2
Nitchequon, *Canada* 99 B5
Niterói, *Brazil* 123 F3
Nith →, *U.K.* 14 F5
Nitra, *Slovak Rep.* 21 G8
Nittedal, *Norway* 10 D4
Nittendau, *Germany* 19 F8
Niuafo'ou, *Tonga* 87 B11
Niue, *Cook Is.* 93 J11
Niulan Jiang →, *China* 52 D4
Niut, *Indonesia* 56 D4
Niutou Shan, *China* 53 C13
Niuzhuang, *China* 51 D12
Nivelles, *Belgium* 17 G4
Nivernais, *France* 25 E10
Nixon, *U.S.A.* 109 L6
Nizamabad, *India* 60 K11
Nizamghat, *India* 61 E19
Nizhne Kolymsk, *Russia* 45 C17
Nizhne-Vartovsk, *Russia* 44 C8
Nizhneangarsk, *Russia* 45 D11
Nizhnegorskiy, *Ukraine* 42 D6
Nizhnekamsk, *Russia* 41 D17
Nizhneudinsk, *Russia* 45 D10
Nizhneyansk, *Russia* 45 B14
Nizhniy Lomov, *Russia* 41 E13
Nizhniy Novgorod, *Russia* 41 C14
Nizhniy Tagil, *Russia* 44 D6
Nizip, *Turkey* 67 E7
Nizké Tatry, *Slovak Rep.* 20 G9
Nizza Monferrato, *Italy* 32 D5
Njakwa, *Malawi* 83 E3
Njanji, *Zambia* 83 E3
Njinjo, *Tanzania* 83 D4
Njombe, *Tanzania* 83 D3
Njombe □, *Tanzania* 83 D3
Njombe →, *Tanzania* 82 D4
Nkambe, *Cameroon* 79 D7
Nkana, *Zambia* 83 E2
Nkawkaw, *Ghana* 79 D4
Nkayi, *Zimbabwe* 83 F2
Nkhata Bay, *Malawi* 80 G6
Nkhota Kota, *Malawi* 83 E3
Nkongsamba, *Cameroon* 79 E6
Nkurenkuru, *Namibia* 84 B2
Nkwanta, *Ghana* 78 D4
Nmai →, *Burma* 61 G20
Noakhali = Maijdi, *Bangla.* 61 H17
Noatak, *U.S.A.* 96 B3
Nobel, *Canada* 106 A4
Nobeoka, *Japan* 49 H5
Noblejas, *Spain* 28 F1
Noblesville, *U.S.A.* 104 E3
Noce →, *Italy* 32 B8
Nocera Inferiore, *Italy* 35 B7
Nocera Terinese, *Italy* 35 C9
Nocera Umbra, *Italy* 33 E9
Noci, *Italy* 35 B10
Nockatunga, *Australia* 91 D3
Nocona, *U.S.A.* 109 J6
Noda, *Japan* 49 G9
Noel, *U.S.A.* 109 G7
Nogales, *Mexico* 114 A2
Nogales, *U.S.A.* 111 L8
Nōgata, *Japan* 49 H5
Nogent-en-Bassigny, *France* 25 D12
Nogent-le-Rotrou, *France* 24 D7
Nogent-sur-Seine, *France* 25 D10
Noggerup, *Australia* 89 F2
Noginsk, *Russia* 41 D11
Noginsk, *Sib., Russia* 45 C10
Nogoa →, *Australia* 90 C4
Nogoyá, *Argentina* 126 C4
Nogueira de Ramuin, *Spain* 30 C3
Noguera Pallaresa →, *Spain* 28 D5
Noguera Ribagorzana →, *Spain* 28 D5
Nohar, *India* 62 E6
Noire, Mt., *France* 24 D3
Noirétable, *France* 26 C7
Noirmoutier, I. de, *France* 24 F4
Noirmoutier-en-l'Île, *France* 24 F4
Nojane, *Botswana* 84 C3
Nojima-Zaki, *Japan* 49 G9
Nok Kundi, *Pakistan* 60 E3
Nokaneng, *Botswana* 84 B3
Nokhtuysk, *Russia* 45 C12
Nokomis, *Canada* 101 C8
Nokomis L., *Canada* 101 B8
Nol, *Sweden* 11 G6
Nola, *C.A.R.* 80 D3
Nola, *Italy* 35 B7
Nolay, *France* 25 F11
Noli, C. di, *Italy* 32 D5
Nolinsk, *Russia* 41 C16
Noma Omuramba →, *Namibia* 84 B3
Noman L., *Canada* 101 A7
Nombre de Dios, *Panama* 116 E4
Nome, *U.S.A.* 96 B3
Nomo-Zaki, *Japan* 49 H4
Nonacho L., *Canada* 101 A7
Nonancourt, *France* 24 D8
Nonant-le-Pin, *France* 24 D7
Nonda, *Australia* 90 C3
Nong Chang, *Thailand* 58 E2
Nong Het, *Laos* 58 C4
Nong Khai, *Thailand* 58 D4
Nong'an, *China* 51 B13
Nongoma, *S. Africa* 85 D5
Nonoava, *Mexico* 114 B3
Nonthaburi, *Thailand* 58 F3
Nontron, *France* 26 C4
Nonza, *France* 27 F13
Noonamah, *Australia* 88 B5
Noonan, *U.S.A.* 108 A3
Noondoo, *Australia* 91 D4
Noonkanbah, *Australia* 88 C3
Noord-Bergum, *Neths.* 16 B8
Noord Brabant □, *Neths.* 17 E6
Noord Holland □, *Neths.* 16 D5
Noordbeveland, *Neths.* 17 E3
Noordeloos, *Neths.* 16 E5
Noordhollandsch Kanaal, *Neths.* 16 C5
Noordhorn, *Neths.* 16 B8
Noordoostpolder, *Neths.* 16 C7
Noordwijk aan Zee, *Neths.* 16 D4
Noordwijk-Binnen, *Neths.* 16 D4
Noordwijkerhout, *Neths.* 16 D5
Noordzee Kanaal, *Neths.* 16 D5
Noorwolde, *Neths.* 16 C8
Nootka, *Canada* 100 D3
Nootka I., *Canada* 100 D3
Nóqui, *Angola* 80 F2
Nora, *Eritrea* 77 D5
Noranda, *Canada* 98 C4
Nórcia, *Italy* 33 F10
Norco, *U.S.A.* 113 M9
Nord □, *France* 25 B10
Nord-Ostsee Kanal, *Germany* 18 A5
Nord-Trøndelag fylke □, *Norway* 8 D12
Nordagutu, *Norway* 10 E3
Nordaustlandet, *Svalbard* 4 B9
Nordborg, *Denmark* 11 J3
Nordby, *Århus, Denmark* 11 J4
Nordby, *Ribe, Denmark* 11 J2
Norddeich, *Germany* 18 B3
Nordegg, *Canada* 100 C5
Norden, *Germany* 18 B3
Nordenham, *Germany* 18 B4
Norderhov, *Norway* 10 D4
Norderney, *Germany* 18 B3
Nordfriesische Inseln, *Germany* 18 A4
Nordhausen, *Germany* 18 D6
Nordhorn, *Germany* 18 C3
Nordjyllands Amtskommune □, *Denmark* 11 H4
Nordkapp, *Norway* 8 A18
Nordkapp, *Svalbard* 4 A9
Nordkinn = Kinnarodden, *Norway* 6 A11
Nordland fylke □, *Norway* 8 D12
Nördlingen, *Germany* 19 G6
Nordrhein-Westfalen □, *Germany* 18 D3
Nordstrand, *Germany* 18 A4
Nordvik, *Russia* 45 B12
Nore, *Norway* 10 D3
Norefjell, *Norway* 10 D3
Norembega, *Canada* 98 C3
Noresund, *Norway* 10 D3
Norfolk, *Nebr., U.S.A.* 108 D6
Norfolk, *Va., U.S.A.* 104 G7
Norfolk □, *U.K.* 12 E9
Norfolk Broads, *U.K.* 12 E9
Norfolk I., *Pac. Oc.* 92 K8
Norfork Res., *U.S.A.* 109 G8
Norg, *Neths.* 16 B8
Norilsk, *Russia* 45 C9
Norley, *Australia* 91 D3
Norma, Mt., *Australia* 90 C3
Normal, *U.S.A.* 108 E10
Norman, *U.S.A.* 109 H6
Norman →, *Australia* 90 B3
Norman Wells, *Canada* 96 B7
Normanby →, *Australia* 90 A3
Normandie, *France* 24 D7
Normandie, Collines de, *France* 24 D6
Normandin, *Canada* 98 C5
Normandy = Normandie, *France* 24 D7
Normanhurst, Mt., *Australia* 89 E3
Normanton, *Australia* 90 B3
Norquay, *Canada* 101 C8
Norquinco, *Argentina* 128 B2
Norrbotten □, *Sweden* 8 C17
Norrby, *Sweden* 8 D15
Nørre Åby, *Denmark* 11 J3
Nørre Nebel, *Denmark* 11 J2
Nørresundby, *Denmark* 11 G3
Norris, *U.S.A.* 110 D8
Norristown, *U.S.A.* 107 F9
Norrköping, *Sweden* 11 F10
Norrland, *Sweden* 8 E13
Norrtälje, *Sweden* 10 E12
Norseman, *Australia* 89 F3
Norsholm, *Sweden* 11 F9
Norsk, *Russia* 45 D14
Norte, Pta., *Argentina* 128 B4
Norte, Pta. del, *Canary Is.* 36 G2
Norte de Santander □, *Colombia* 120 B3
Nortelândia, *Brazil* 125 C6
North Adams, *U.S.A.* 107 D11
North America 94 F10
North Battleford, *Canada* 101 C7
North Bay, *Canada* 98 C4
North Belcher Is., *Canada* 98 A4
North Bend, *Canada* 100 D4
North Bend, *Oreg., U.S.A.* 110 E1
North Bend, *Pa., U.S.A.* 106 E7
North Bend, *Wash., U.S.A.* 112 C5
North Berwick, *U.K.* 14 E6
North Berwick, *U.S.A.* 107 C14
North Buganda □, *Uganda* 82 B3
North Canadian →, *U.S.A.* 109 H7
North Cape = Nordkapp, *Norway* 8 A18
North Cape = Nordkapp, *Svalbard* 4 A9
North C., *Canada* 99 C7
North C., *N.Z.* 87 F4
North Caribou L., *Canada* 98 B1
North Carolina □, *U.S.A.* 105 H5
North Channel, *Canada* 98 C3
North Channel, *U.K.* 14 G3
North Chicago, *U.S.A.* 104 D2
North Dakota □, *U.S.A.* 108 B5
North Dandalup, *Australia* 89 F2
North Down □, *U.K.* 15 B6
North Downs, *U.K.* 13 F8
North East, *U.S.A.* 106 D5
North East Frontier Agency = Arunachal Pradesh □, *India* 61 E19
North East Providence Chan., *W. Indies* 116 A4
North Eastern □, *Kenya* 82 B5
North Esk →, *U.K.* 14 E6
North European Plain, *Europe* 6 D11
North Foreland, *U.K.* 13 F9
North Fork, *U.S.A.* 112 H7
North Fork American →, *U.S.A.* 112 G5
North Fork Feather →, *U.S.A.* 112 F5
North Frisian Is. = Nordfriesische Inseln, *Germany* 18 A4
North Henik L., *Canada* 101 A9
North Highlands, *U.S.A.* 112 G5
North Horr, *Kenya* 82 B4
North I., *Kenya* 82 B4
North I., *N.Z.* 87 H5
North Kingsville, *U.S.A.* 106 E4
North Knife →, *Canada* 101 B10
North Koel →, *India* 63 G10
North Korea ■, *Asia* 51 E14
North Lakhimpur, *India* 61 F19
North Las Vegas, *U.S.A.* 113 J11
North Loup →, *U.S.A.* 108 E5
North Magnetic Pole, *Canada* 4 B2

North Minch

North Minch, *U.K.* 14 C3
North Nahanni →, *Canada* 100 A4
North Olmsted, *U.S.A.* 106 E3
North Ossetian Republic □, *Russia* 43 E11
North Pagai, I. = Pagai Utara, *Indonesia* 56 E2
North Palisade, *U.S.A.* 111 H4
North Platte, *U.S.A.* 108 E4
North Platte →, *U.S.A.* 108 E4
North Pt., *Canada* 99 C7
North Pole, *Arctic* 4 A
North Portal, *Canada* 101 D8
North Powder, *U.S.A.* 110 D5
North Rhine Westphalia □ = Nordrhein-Westfalen □, *Germany* 18 D3
North Ronaldsay, *U.K.* 14 B6
North Saskatchewan →, *Canada* 101 C7
North Sea, *Europe* 6 D6
North Sporades = Voríai Sporádhes, *Greece* 39 K6
North Sydney, *Canada* 99 C7
North Taranaki Bight, *N.Z.* 87 H5
North Thompson →, *Canada* 100 C4
North Tonawanda, *U.S.A.* 106 C6
North Troy, *U.S.A.* 107 B12
North Truchas Pk., *U.S.A.* 111 J11
North Twin I., *Canada* 98 B3
North Tyne →, *U.K.* 12 C5
North Uist, *U.K.* 14 D1
North Vancouver, *Canada* 100 D4
North Vernon, *U.S.A.* 104 F3
North Wabasca L., *Canada* 100 B6
North Walsham, *U.K.* 12 E9
North West C., *Australia* 88 D1
North West Christmas I. Ridge, *Pac. Oc.* 93 G11
North West Frontier □, *Pakistan* 62 C4
North West Highlands, *U.K.* 14 D3
North West Providence Channel, *W. Indies* 116 A4
North West River, *Canada* 99 B7
North West Territories □, *Canada* 96 B9
North Western □, *Zambia* 83 E2
North York Moors, *U.K.* 12 C7
North Yorkshire □, *U.K.* 12 C6
Northallerton, *U.K.* 12 C6
Northam, *S. Africa* 84 C4
Northampton, *Australia* 89 E1
Northampton, *U.K.* 13 E7
Northampton, *Mass., U.S.A.* 107 D12
Northampton, *Pa., U.S.A.* 107 F9
Northampton Downs, *Australia* 90 C4
Northamptonshire □, *U.K.* 13 E7
Northbridge, *U.S.A.* 107 D13
Northcliffe, *Australia* 89 F2
Northeim, *Germany* 18 D6
Northern □, *Malawi* 83 E3
Northern □, *Uganda* 82 B3
Northern □, *Zambia* 83 E3
Northern Circars, *India* 61 L13
Northern Indian L., *Canada* 101 B9
Northern Ireland □, *U.K.* 15 B5
Northern Light, L., *Canada* 98 C1
Northern Marianas ■, *Pac. Oc.* 92 F6
Northern Province □, *S. Leone* 78 D2
Northern Territory □, *Australia* 88 D5
Northfield, *U.S.A.* 108 C8
Northland □, *N.Z.* 87 F4
Northome, *U.S.A.* 108 B7
Northport, *Ala., U.S.A.* 105 J2
Northport, *Mich., U.S.A.* 104 C3
Northport, *Wash., U.S.A.* 110 B5
Northumberland □, *U.K.* 12 B5
Northumberland, C., *Australia* 91 F3
Northumberland Is., *Australia* 90 C4
Northumberland Str., *Canada* 99 C7
Northwich, *U.K.* 12 D5
Northwood, *Iowa, U.S.A.* 108 D8
Northwood, *N. Dak., U.S.A.* 108 B6
Norton, *U.S.A.* 108 F5
Norton, *Zimbabwe* 83 F3
Norton Sd., *U.S.A.* 96 B3
Nortorf, *Germany* 18 A5
Norwalk, *Calif., U.S.A.* 113 M8
Norwalk, *Conn., U.S.A.* 107 E11
Norwalk, *Ohio, U.S.A.* 106 E2
Norway, *U.S.A.* 104 C2
Norway ■, *Europe* 8 E11
Norway House, *Canada* 101 C9
Norwegian Sea, *Atl. Oc.* 4 C8
Norwich, *Canada* 106 D4
Norwich, *U.K.* 12 E9
Norwich, *Conn., U.S.A.* 107 E12
Norwich, *N.Y., U.S.A.* 107 D9
Norwood, *Canada* 106 B7
Noshiro, *Japan* 48 D10
Nosok, *Russia* 44 B9
Nosovka, *Ukraine* 40 F7
Noss Hd., *U.K.* 14 C5
Nossa Senhora da Glória, *Brazil* 122 D4
Nossa Senhora das Dores, *Brazil* 122 D4
Nossa Senhora do Livramento, *Brazil* 125 D6
Nossebro, *Sweden* 11 F6
Nossob →, *S. Africa* 84 D3
Nosy Bé, *Madag.* 81 G9
Nosy Boraha, *Madag.* 85 B8
Nosy Mitsio, *Madag.* 81 G9
Nosy Varika, *Madag.* 85 C8
Noteć →, *Poland* 20 C5
Notigi Dam, *Canada* 101 B9
Notikewin →, *Canada* 100 B5
Notios Evvoïkos Kólpos, *Greece* 39 L7
Noto, *Italy* 35 F8
Noto, G. di, *Italy* 35 F8
Notodden, *Norway* 10 E3
Notre-Dame, *Canada* 99 C7
Notre Dame B., *Canada* 99 C8
Notre Dame de Koartac = Koartac, *Canada* 97 B13
Notre Dame d'Ivugivic = Ivugivik, *Canada* 97 B12
Notsé, *Togo* 79 D5
Nottaway →, *Canada* 98 B4
Nøtterøy, *Norway* 10 E4
Nottingham, *U.K.* 12 E6
Nottinghamshire □, *U.K.* 12 D7
Nottoway →, *U.S.A.* 104 G7
Notwane →, *Botswana* 84 C4
Nouâdhibou, *Mauritania* 74 D1
Nouâdhibou, Ras, *Mauritania* 74 D1
Nouakchott, *Mauritania* 78 B1
Nouméa, *N. Cal.* 92 K8
Noupoort, *S. Africa* 84 E3
Nouveau Comptoir, *Canada* 98 B4
Nouvelle-Calédonie = New Caledonia, *Pac. Oc.* 92 K8
Nouzonville, *France* 25 C11
Nová Baňa, *Slovak Rep.* 21 G8
Nová Bystřice, *Czech.* 20 F5
Nova Casa Nova, *Brazil* 122 C3
Nova Cruz, *Brazil* 122 C4
Nova Era, *Brazil* 123 E3
Nova Esperança, *Brazil* 127 A5
Nova Friburgo, *Brazil* 123 F3
Nova Gaia = Cambundi-Catembo, *Angola* 80 G3
Nova Gradiška, *Croatia* 21 K7
Nova Granada, *Brazil* 123 F2
Nova Iguaçu, *Brazil* 123 F3
Nova Iorque, *Brazil* 122 C3
Nova Lamego, *Guinea-Biss.* 78 C2
Nova Lima, *Brazil* 127 A7
Nova Lisboa = Huambo, *Angola* 81 G3
Nova Lusitânia, *Mozam.* 83 F3
Nova Mambone, *Mozam.* 85 C6
Nova Mesto, *Slovenia* 33 C12
Nova Ponte, *Brazil* 123 E2
Nova Scotia □, *Canada* 99 C7
Nova Sofala, *Mozam.* 85 C5
Nova Venécia, *Brazil* 123 E3
Nova Vida, *Brazil* 125 C5
Nova Zagora, *Bulgaria* 38 G8
Novaleksandrovskaya, *Russia* 43 D9
Novannenskiy, *Russia* 41 F13
Novara, *Italy* 32 C5
Novato, *U.S.A.* 112 G4
Novaya Kakhovka, *Ukraine* 42 C5
Novaya Lyalya, *Russia* 44 D7
Novaya Sibir, Ostrov, *Russia* 45 B16
Novaya Zemlya, *Russia* 44 B6
Novelda, *Spain* 29 G4
Novellara, *Italy* 32 D7
Noventa Vicentina, *Italy* 33 C8
Novgorod, *Russia* 40 B7
Novgorod-Severskiy, *Ukraine* 40 E8
Novi Bečej, *Serbia* 21 K10
Novi Grad, *Croatia* 33 C10
Novi Krichim, *Bulgaria* 38 G7
Novi Lígure, *Italy* 32 D5
Novi Pazar, *Bulgaria* 38 F10
Novi Pazar, *Serbia* 21 M10
Novi Sad, *Serbia* 21 K9
Novi Vinodolski, *Croatia* 33 C11
Novigrad, *Croatia* 33 D12
Noville, *Belgium* 17 H7
Novo Acôrdo, *Brazil* 122 D2
Novo Aripuanã, *Brazil* 121 E5
Nôvo Cruzeiro, *Brazil* 123 E3
Nôvo Hamburgo, *Brazil* 127 B5
Novo Horizonte, *Brazil* 123 F2
Novo Remanso, *Brazil* 122 C3
Novo-Zavidovskiy, *Russia* 41 C10
Novoakrainka, *Ukraine* 42 B4
Novoataysk, *Russia* 44 D9
Novoazovsk, *Ukraine* 42 C8
Novobelitsa, *Belorussia* 40 E7
Novobogatinskoye, *Kazakhstan* 43 C14
Novocherkassk, *Russia* 43 C9
Novodevichye, *Russia* 41 E16
Novograd-Volynskiy, *Ukraine* 40 F5
Novogrudok, *Belorussia* 40 E4
Novokachalinsk, *Russia* 48 B6
Novokayakent, *Russia* 43 E12
Novokazalinsk, *Kazakhstan* 44 E7
Novokhopersk, *Russia* 41 F12
Novokuybyshevsk, *Russia* 41 E16
Novokuznetsk, *Russia* 44 D9
Novomirgorod, *Ukraine* 42 B4
Novomoskovsk, *Russia* 41 D11
Novomoskovsk, *Ukraine* 42 B6
Novopolotsk, *Belorussia* 40 D6
Novorossiysk, *Russia* 42 D7
Novorybnoye, *Russia* 45 B11
Novorzhev, *Russia* 40 C6
Novoselitsa, *Ukraine* 42 B2
Novoshakhtinsk, *Russia* 43 C8
Novosibirsk, *Russia* 44 D9
Novosibirskiye Ostrova, *Russia* 45 B15
Novosil, *Russia* 41 E10
Novosokolniki, *Russia* 40 C7
Novotroitsk, *Russia* 44 D6
Novotulskiy, *Russia* 41 D10
Novouzensk, *Russia* 41 F16
Novovolynsk, *Ukraine* 40 F4
Novovyatsk, *Russia* 41 B16
Novozybkov, *Russia* 40 E8
Novska, *Croatia* 21 K6
Novvy Port, *Russia* 44 C8
Novy Bug, *Ukraine* 42 C5
Nový Bydzov, *Czech.* 20 E5
Novy Dwór Mazowiecki, *Poland* 20 C10
Novyy Afon, *Georgia* 43 E9
Novyy Oskol, *Russia* 41 F10
Now Shahr, *Iran* 65 B6
Nowa Deba, *Poland* 20 E11
Nowa Ruda, *Poland* 20 E6
Nowa Sól, *Poland* 20 D5
Nowbarān, *Iran* 65 C6
Nowe, *Poland* 20 B8
Nowghāb, *Iran* 65 C8
Nowgong, *India* 61 F18
Nowogard, *Poland* 20 B5
Nowogród, *Poland* 20 B11
Nowra, *Australia* 91 E5
Nowshera, *Pakistan* 60 B8
Nowy Korczyn, *Poland* 20 E10
Nowy Sącz, *Poland* 20 F10
Noxen, *U.S.A.* 107 E8
Noxon, *U.S.A.* 110 C6
Noya, *Spain* 30 C2
Noyant, *France* 24 E7
Noyers, *France* 25 E10
Noyes I., *U.S.A.* 100 B2
Noyon, *France* 25 C9
Noyon, *Mongolia* 50 C2
Nozay, *France* 24 E5
Nsa, O. en →, *Algeria* 75 B6
Nsanje, *Malawi* 83 F4
Nsawam, *Ghana* 79 D4
Nsomba, *Zambia* 83 E2
Nsukka, *Nigeria* 79 D6
Nu Jiang →, *China* 52 C1
Nu Shan, *China* 52 D2
Nuba Mts. = Nubah, Jibalan, *Sudan* 77 E3
Nubah, Jibalan, *Sudan* 77 E3
Nubian Desert = Nûbîya, Es Sahrâ En, *Sudan* 76 C3
Nûbîya, Es Sahrâ En, *Sudan* 76 C3
Ñuble □, *Chile* 126 D1
Nuboai, *Indonesia* 57 E9
Nubra →, *India* 63 B7
Nueces →, *U.S.A.* 109 M6
Nueltin L., *Canada* 101 A9
Nuenen, *Neths.* 17 F7
Nueva, I., *Chile* 128 E3
Nueva Antioquia, *Colombia* 120 B4
Nueva Asunción □, *Paraguay* 126 A3
Nueva Esparta □, *Venezuela* 121 A5
Nueva Gerona, *Cuba* 116 B3
Nueva Imperial, *Chile* 128 A2
Nueva Palmira, *Uruguay* 126 C4
Nueva Rosita, *Mexico* 114 B4
Nueva San Salvador, *El Salv.* 116 D2
Nuéve de Julio, *Argentina* 126 D3
Nuevitas, *Cuba* 116 B4
Nuevo, G., *Argentina* 128 B4
Nuevo Guerrero, *Mexico* 115 B5
Nuevo Laredo, *Mexico* 115 B5
Nuevo León □, *Mexico* 114 C4
Nuevo Mundo, Cerro, *Bolivia* 124 E4
Nuevo Rocafuerte, *Ecuador* 120 D2
Nugget Pt., *N.Z.* 87 M2
Nugrus, Gebel, *Egypt* 76 C3
Nuhaka, *N.Z.* 87 H6
Nuits-St.-Georges, *France* 25 E11
Nukey Bluff, *Australia* 91 E2
Nukheila, *Sudan* 76 D2
Nuku'alofa, *Tonga* 87 E11
Nukus, *Uzbekistan* 44 E6
Nuland, *Neths.* 16 E6
Nulato, *U.S.A.* 96 B4
Nules, *Spain* 28 F4
Nullagine →, *Australia* 88 D3
Nullarbor, *Australia* 89 F5
Nullarbor Plain, *Australia* 89 F4
Numalla, L., *Australia* 91 D3
Numan, *Nigeria* 79 D7
Numansdorp, *Neths.* 16 E4
Numata, *Japan* 49 F9
Numatinna →, *Sudan* 77 F2
Numazu, *Japan* 49 G9
Numbulwar, *Australia* 90 A2
Numfoor, *Indonesia* 57 E8
Numurkah, *Australia* 91 F4
Nunaksaluk I., *Canada* 99 A7
Nuneaton, *U.K.* 13 E6
Nungo, *Mozam.* 83 E4
Nungwe, *Tanzania* 82 C3
Nunivak I., *U.S.A.* 96 B3
Nunkun, *India* 63 C7
Nunspeet, *Neths.* 16 D7
Nuoro, *Italy* 34 B2
Nuquí, *Colombia* 120 B2
Nūrābād, *Iran* 65 E8
Nure →, *Italy* 32 C6
Nuremburg = Nürnberg, *Germany* 19 F7
Nuri, *Mexico* 114 B3
Nurina, *Australia* 89 F4
Nuriootpa, *Australia* 91 E2
Nurlat, *Russia* 41 D17
Nürnberg, *Germany* 19 F7
Nurran, L. = Terewah, L., *Australia* 91 D4
Nurrari Lakes, *Australia* 89 E5
Nurri, *Italy* 34 C2
Nusa Barung, *Indonesia* 57 H15
Nusa Kambangan, *Indonesia* 57 G13
Nusa Tenggara Barat □, *Indonesia* 56 F5
Nusa Tenggara Timur □, *Indonesia* 57 F6
Nushki, *Pakistan* 62 E2
Nutak, *Canada* 97 C13
Nuth, *Neths.* 17 G7
Nutwood Downs, *Australia* 90 B1
Nuuk = Godthåb, *Greenland* 97 B14
Nuwakot, *Nepal* 63 E10
Nuweiba', *Egypt* 76 B3
Nuweveldberge, *S. Africa* 84 E3
Nuyts, C., *Australia* 89 F5
Nuyts Arch., *Australia* 91 E1
Nxau-Nxau, *Botswana* 84 B3
Nyaake, *Liberia* 78 E3
Nyack, *U.S.A.* 107 E11
Nyadal, *Sweden* 10 B11
Nyah West, *Australia* 91 F3
Nyahanga, *Tanzania* 82 C3
Nyahua, *Tanzania* 82 D3
Nyahururu, *Kenya* 82 B4
Nyainqentanglha Shan, *China* 54 C4
Nyakanazi, *Tanzania* 82 C3
Nyakrom, *Ghana* 79 D4
Nyâlâ, *Sudan* 77 E1
Nyamandhlovu, *Zimbabwe* 83 F2
Nyambiti, *Tanzania* 82 C3
Nyamwaga, *Tanzania* 82 C3
Nyandekwa, *Tanzania* 82 C3
Nyanding →, *Sudan* 77 F3
Nyangana, *Namibia* 84 B3
Nyanguge, *Tanzania* 82 C3
Nyankpala, *Ghana* 79 D4
Nyanza, *Burundi* 82 C2
Nyanza, *Rwanda* 82 C2
Nyanza □, *Kenya* 82 C3
Nyarling →, *Canada* 100 A6
Nyasa, L. = Malawi, L., *Africa* 83 E3
Nyazura, *Zimbabwe* 83 F3
Nyazwidzi →, *Zimbabwe* 83 F3
Nyborg, *Denmark* 11 J4
Nybro, *Sweden* 9 H13
Nyda, *Russia* 44 C8
Nyeri, *Kenya* 82 C4
Nyerol, *Sudan* 77 F3
Nyhem, *Sweden* 10 B9
Nyiel, *Sudan* 77 F3
Nyinahin, *Ghana* 78 D4
Nyírbátor, *Hungary* 21 H12
Nyíregyháza, *Hungary* 21 H11
Nykarleby, *Finland* 8 E17
Nykøbing, *Sjælland, Denmark* 11 J5
Nykøbing, *Storstrøm, Denmark* 11 K5
Nykøbing, *Viborg, Denmark* 11 H2
Nyköping, *Sweden* 11 F11
Nykvarn, *Sweden* 10 E11
Nyland, *Sweden* 10 A11
Nylstroom, *S. Africa* 85 C4
Nymagee, *Australia* 91 E4
Nymburk, *Czech.* 20 E5
Nynäshamn, *Sweden* 10 F11
Nyngan, *Australia* 91 E4
Nyon, *Switz.* 22 D2
Nyong →, *Cameroon* 79 E6
Nyons, *France* 27 D9
Nyord, *Denmark* 11 J6
Nyou, *Burkina Faso* 79 C4
Nysa, *Poland* 20 E7
Nysa →, *Europe* 18 C10
Nyssa, *U.S.A.* 110 E5
Nysted, *Denmark* 11 K5
Nyunzu, *Zaïre* 82 D2
Nyurba, *Russia* 45 C12
Nzega, *Tanzania* 82 C3
Nzega □, *Tanzania* 82 C3
N'Zérékoré, *Guinea* 78 D3
Nzeto, *Angola* 80 F2
Nzilo, Chutes de, *Zaïre* 83 E2
Nzubuka, *Tanzania* 82 C3

O

Ō-Shima, *Nagasaki, Japan* 49 G4
Ō-Shima, *Shizuoka, Japan* 49 G9
Oacoma, *U.S.A.* 108 D5
Oahe, L., *U.S.A.* 108 C4
Oahe Dam, *U.S.A.* 108 C4
Oahu, *U.S.A.* 102 H16
Oak Creek, *U.S.A.* 110 F10
Oak Harbor, *U.S.A.* 112 B4
Oak Hill, *U.S.A.* 104 G5
Oak Park, *U.S.A.* 104 E2
Oak Ridge, *U.S.A.* 105 G3
Oak View, *U.S.A.* 113 L7
Oakan-Dake, *Japan* 48 C12
Oakbank, *Australia* 91 E3
Oakdale, *Calif., U.S.A.* 111 H3
Oakdale, *La., U.S.A.* 109 K8
Oakengates, *U.K.* 12 E5
Oakes, *U.S.A.* 108 B5
Oakesdale, *U.S.A.* 110 C5
Oakey, *Australia* 91 D5
Oakham, *U.K.* 12 E7
Oakhurst, *U.S.A.* 112 H7
Oakland, *Calif., U.S.A.* 111 H2
Oakland, *Oreg., U.S.A.* 110 E2
Oakland City, *U.S.A.* 104 F2
Oakley, *Idaho, U.S.A.* 110 E7
Oakley, *Kans., U.S.A.* 108 F4
Oakover →, *Australia* 88 D3
Oakridge, *U.S.A.* 110 E2
Oakville, *U.S.A.* 112 D3
Oamaru, *N.Z.* 87 L3
Oasis, *Calif., U.S.A.* 113 M10
Oasis, *Nev., U.S.A.* 112 H9
Oates Land, *Antarctica* 5 C11
Oatman, *U.S.A.* 113 K12
Oaxaca, *Mexico* 115 D5
Oaxaca □, *Mexico* 115 D5
Ob →, *Russia* 44 C7
Oba, *Canada* 98 C3
Obala, *Cameroon* 79 E7
Obama, *Japan* 49 G7
Oban, *U.K.* 14 E3
Obbia, *Somali Rep.* 68 F4
Obdam, *Neths.* 16 C5
Obed, *Canada* 100 C5
Ober-Aagau, *Switz.* 22 B5
Obera, *Argentina* 127 B4
Oberalppass, *Switz.* 23 C7
Oberalpstock, *Switz.* 23 C7
Oberammergau, *Germany* 19 H7
Oberdrauburg, *Austria* 21 J2
Oberengadin, *Switz.* 23 C9
Oberentfelden, *Switz.* 22 B6
Oberhausen, *Germany* 18 D2
Oberkirch, *Germany* 19 G4
Oberland, *Switz.* 22 C5
Oberlin, *Kans., U.S.A.* 108 F4
Oberlin, *La., U.S.A.* 109 K8
Oberlin, *Ohio, U.S.A.* 106 E2
Obernai, *France* 25 D14
Oberndorf, *Germany* 19 G4
Oberon, *Australia* 91 E4
Oberpfälzer Wald, *Germany* 19 F8
Obersiggenthal, *Switz.* 23 B6
Oberstdorf, *Germany* 19 H6
Oberwil, *Switz.* 22 A5
Obi, Kepulauan, *Indonesia* 57 E7
Obi Is. = Obi, Kepulauan, *Indonesia* 57 E7
Obiaruku, *Nigeria* 79 D6
Óbidos, *Brazil* 121 D6
Óbidos, *Portugal* 31 F1
Obihiro, *Japan* 48 C11
Obilatu, *Indonesia* 57 E7
Obilnoye, *Russia* 43 C11
Obing, *Germany* 19 H8
Öbisfelde, *Germany* 18 C6
Objat, *France* 26 C5
Obluchye, *Russia* 45 E14
Obninsk, *Russia* 41 D10
Obo, *C.A.R.* 82 A2
Obo, *Ethiopia* 77 G4
Oboa, Mt., *Uganda* 82 B3
Obock, *Djibouti* 77 E5
Oborniki, *Poland* 20 C6
Oboyan, *Russia* 41 F10
Obozerskaya, *Russia* 44 C5
Obrovac, *Croatia* 33 D12
Obruk, *Turkey* 66 D5
Observatory Inlet, *Canada* 100 B3
Obshchi Syrt, *Kazakhstan* 6 E16
Obskaya Guba, *Russia* 44 C8
Obuasi, *Ghana* 79 D4
Obubra, *Nigeria* 79 D6
Obwalden □, *Switz.* 22 C6
Obzor, *Bulgaria* 38 G10
Ocala, *U.S.A.* 105 L4
Ocamo →, *Venezuela* 121 C4
Ocampo, *Mexico* 114 B3
Ocaña, *Colombia* 120 B3
Ocaña, *Spain* 28 F1
Ocanomowoc, *U.S.A.* 108 D10
Ocate, *U.S.A.* 109 G2
Occidental, Cordillera, *Colombia* 120 C3
Occidental, Cordillera, *Peru* 124 C3
Ocean City, *N.J., U.S.A.* 104 F8
Ocean City, *Wash., U.S.A.* 112 C2
Ocean I. = Banaba, *Kiribati* 92 H8

Oranje Vrystaat

Ocean Park, U.S.A. 112 D2
Oceano, U.S.A. 113 K6
Oceanport, U.S.A. 107 F10
Oceanside, U.S.A. 113 M9
Ochagavia, Spain 28 C3
Ochamchire, Georgia 43 E9
Ochamps, Belgium 17 J6
Ochil Hills, U.K. 14 E5
Ochre River, Canada 101 C9
Ochsenfurt, Germany 19 F6
Ochsenhausen, Germany 19 G5
Ocilla, U.S.A. 105 K4
Ocmulgee →, U.S.A. 105 K4
Ocna Sibiului, Romania 38 D7
Ocoña, Peru 124 D3
Ocoña →, Peru 124 D3
Oconee →, U.S.A. 105 K4
Oconto, U.S.A. 104 C2
Oconto Falls, U.S.A. 104 C1
Ocosingo, Mexico 115 D6
Ocotal, Nic. 116 D2
Ocotlán, Mexico 114 C4
Ocquier, Belgium 17 H6
Ocreza →, Portugal 31 F3
Octave, U.S.A. 111 J7
Octeville, France 24 C5
Ocumare del Tuy, Venezuela 120 A4
Ocuri, Bolivia 125 D4
Oda, Ghana 79 D4
Ōda, Japan 49 G6
Oda, J., Sudan 76 C4
Ódáðahraun, Iceland 8 D5
Ödåkra, Sweden 11 H6
Odate, Japan 48 D10
Odawara, Japan 49 G9
Odda, Norway 9 F9
Odder, Denmark 11 J4
Oddur, Somali Rep. 68 G3
Ödeborg, Sweden 11 F5
Odei →, Canada 101 B9
Odemira, Portugal 31 H2
Ödemiş, Turkey 66 D3
Odendaalsrus, S. Africa 84 D4
Odense, Denmark 11 J4
Odenwald, Germany 19 F5
Oder →, Germany 18 B10
Oderzo, Italy 33 C9
Odesa = Odessa, Ukraine 42 C4
Odessa, Canada 107 B8
Odessa, Ukraine 42 C4
Odessa, Tex., U.S.A. 109 K3
Odessa, Wash., U.S.A. 110 C4
Odiakwe, Botswana 84 C4
Odiel →, Spain 31 H4
Odienné, Ivory C. 78 D3
Odintsovo, Russia 41 D10
Odiongan, Phil. 55 E4
Odobeşti, Romania 38 D10
O'Donnell, U.S.A. 109 J4
Odoorn, Neths. 16 C9
Odorheiu Secuiesc, Romania 38 C8
Odoyevo, Russia 41 E10
Odra →, Poland 20 B4
Odra →, Spain 30 C6
Odžaci, Serbia 21 K9
Odzi, Zimbabwe 85 B5
Oedelem, Belgium 17 F2
Oegstgeest, Neths. 16 D4
Oeiras, Brazil 122 C3
Oeiras, Portugal 31 G1
Oelrichs, U.S.A. 108 D3
Oelsnitz, Germany 18 E8
Oelwein, U.S.A. 108 D9
Oenpelli, Australia 88 B5
Of, Turkey 67 C9
Ofanto →, Italy 35 A9
Offa, Nigeria 79 D5
Offaly □, Ireland 15 C4
Offenbach, Germany 19 E4
Offenburg, Germany 19 G3
Offerdal, Sweden 10 A8
Offida, Italy 33 F10
Offranville, France 24 C8
Ofidhousa, Greece 39 N9
Ofotfjorden, Norway 8 B14
Ōfunato, Japan 48 E10
Oga, Japan 48 E9
Oga-Hantō, Japan 48 E9
Ogahalla, Canada 98 B2
Ōgaki, Japan 49 G8
Ogallala, U.S.A. 108 E4
Ogasawara Gunto, Pac. Oc. 92 E6
Ogbomosho, Nigeria 79 D5
Ogden, Iowa, U.S.A. 108 D8
Ogden, Utah, U.S.A. 110 F7
Ogdensburg, U.S.A. 107 B9
Ogeechee →, U.S.A. 105 K5
Ogilby, U.S.A. 113 N12
Oglio →, Italy 32 C7
Ogmore, Australia 90 C4
Ognon →, France 25 E12
Ogoja, Nigeria 79 D6
Ogoki →, Canada 98 B2
Ogoki L., Canada 98 B2
Ogoki Res., Canada 98 B2
Ogooué →, Gabon 80 E1
Ogosta →, Bulgaria 38 F6
Ogowe = Ogooué →, Gabon 80 E1
Ogr = Sharafa, Sudan 77 E2
Ogrein, Sudan 76 D3
Ogulin, Croatia 33 C12
Ogun □, Nigeria 79 D5
Oguta, Nigeria 79 D6
Ogwashi-Uku, Nigeria 79 D6
Ogwe, Nigeria 79 E6
Ohai, N.Z. 87 L2
Ohakune, N.Z. 87 H5
Ohanet, Algeria 75 C6
Ohata, Japan 48 D10
Ohau, L., N.Z. 87 L2
Ohey, Belgium 17 H6
Ohio □, U.S.A. 104 E3
Ohio →, U.S.A. 104 G1
Ohre →, Czech. 20 E4
Ohre →, Germany 18 C7
Ohrid, Macedonia 39 H3
Ohridsko, Jezero, Macedonia 39 H3
Ohrigstad, S. Africa 85 C5
Öhringen, Germany 19 F5
Oiapoque →, Brazil 121 C7
Oikou, China 51 E9
Oil City, U.S.A. 106 E5
Oildale, U.S.A. 113 K7
Oirschot, Neths. 17 E6
Oise □, France 25 C9
Oise →, France 25 D9
Oisterwijk, Neths. 17 E6
Ōita, Japan 49 H5
Ōita □, Japan 49 H5
Oiticica, Brazil 122 C3
Ojai, U.S.A. 113 L7
Ojinaga, Mexico 114 B4
Ojiya, Japan 49 F9
Ojos del Salado, Cerro, Argentina 126 B2
Oka →, Russia 41 C13
Okaba, Indonesia 57 F9
Okahandja, Namibia 84 C2
Okahukura, N.Z. 87 H5
Okanagan L., Canada 100 C5
Okandja, Gabon 80 E2
Okanogan, U.S.A. 110 B4
Okanogan →, U.S.A. 110 B4
Okaputa, Namibia 84 C2
Okara, Pakistan 62 D5
Okarito, N.Z. 87 K3
Okaukuejo, Namibia 84 B2
Okavango Swamps, Botswana 84 B3
Okaya, Japan 49 F9
Okayama, Japan 49 G6
Okayama □, Japan 49 G6
Okazaki, Japan 49 G8
Oke-Iho, Nigeria 79 D5
Okeechobee, U.S.A. 105 M5
Okeechobee, L., U.S.A. 105 M5
Okefenokee Swamp, U.S.A. 105 K4
Okehampton, U.K. 13 G3
Okene, Nigeria 79 D6
Oker →, Germany 18 C6
Okha, Russia 45 D15
Ókhi Óros, Greece 39 L7
Okhotsk, Russia 45 D15
Okhotsk, Sea of, Asia 45 D15
Okhotskiy Perevoz, Russia 45 C14
Okhotsko Kolymskoye, Russia 45 C16
Oki-Shotō, Japan 49 F6
Okiep, S. Africa 84 D2
Okigwi, Nigeria 79 D6
Okija, Nigeria 79 D6
Okinawa □, Japan 49 L3
Okinawa-Guntō, Japan 49 L3
Okinawa-Jima, Japan 49 L4
Okino-erabu-Shima, Japan 49 L4
Okitipupa, Nigeria 79 D5
Oklahoma □, U.S.A. 109 H6
Oklahoma City, U.S.A. 109 H6
Okmulgee, U.S.A. 109 H7
Oknitsa, Ukraine 42 B2
Okolo, Uganda 82 B3
Okolona, U.S.A. 109 H10
Okrika, Nigeria 79 E6
Oktabrsk, Kazakhstan 44 E6
Oktyabrsk, Russia 41 E16
Oktyabrskiy, Belorussia 40 E6
Oktyabrskoy Revolyutsii, Os., Russia 45 B10
Oktyabrskoye = Zhovtnevoye, Ukraine 42 C5
Oktyabrskoye, Russia 44 C7
Okulovka, Russia 40 B8
Okuru, N.Z. 87 K2
Okushiri-Tō, Japan 48 C9
Okuta, Nigeria 79 D5
Okwa →, Botswana 84 C3
Ola, U.S.A. 109 H8
Ólafsfjörður, Iceland 8 C4
Ólafsvík, Iceland 8 D2
Olancha, U.S.A. 113 J8
Olancha Pk., U.S.A. 113 J8
Olanchito, Honduras 116 C2
Öland, Sweden 9 H14
Olargues, France 26 E6
Olary, Australia 91 E3
Olascoaga, Argentina 126 D3
Olathe, U.S.A. 108 F7
Olavarría, Argentina 126 D3
Oława, Poland 20 E7
Ólbia, Italy 34 B2
Ólbia, G. di, Italy 34 B2
Old Bahama Chan. = Bahama, Canal Viejo de, W. Indies 116 B4
Old Baldy Pk. = San Antonio, Mt., U.S.A. 113 L9
Old Castile = Castilla y Leon □, Spain 30 D6
Old Castle, Ireland 15 C4
Old Cork, Australia 90 C3
Old Crow, Canada 96 B6
Old Dale, U.S.A. 113 L11
Old Dongola, Sudan 76 D3
Old Fletton, U.K. 13 E7
Old Forge, N.Y., U.S.A. 107 C10
Old Forge, Pa., U.S.A. 107 E9
Old Fort →, Canada 101 B6
Old Shinyanga, Tanzania 82 C3
Old Speck Mt., U.S.A. 107 B14
Old Town, U.S.A. 99 D6
Old Wives L., Canada 101 C7
Oldbury, U.K. 13 F5
Oldeani, Tanzania 82 C4
Oldenburg, Niedersachsen, Germany 18 B4
Oldenburg, Schleswig-Holstein, Germany 18 A6
Oldenzaal, Neths. 16 D9
Oldham, U.K. 12 D5
Oldman →, Canada 100 D6
Olds, Canada 100 C6
Olean, U.S.A. 106 D6
Oléggio, Italy 32 C5
Oleiros, Portugal 30 F3
Olekma →, Russia 45 C13
Olekminsk, Russia 45 C13
Olema, U.S.A. 112 G4
Olen, Belgium 17 F5
Olenek, Russia 45 C12
Olenek →, Russia 45 B13
Olenino, Russia 40 C8
Oléron, I. d', France 26 C2
Oleśnica, Poland 20 D7
Olesno, Poland 20 E8
Olevsk, Ukraine 40 F5
Olga, Russia 45 E14
Olga, L., Canada 98 C4
Olga, Mt., Australia 89 E5
Ølgod, Denmark 11 J2
Olhão, Portugal 31 H3
Olib, Croatia 33 D11
Oliena, Italy 34 B2
Oliete, Spain 28 D4
Olifants →, Africa 85 C5
Olifantshoek, S. Africa 84 D3
Ólimbos, Greece 39 P10
Ólimbos, Óros, Greece 39 J5
Olímpia, Brazil 127 A6
Olinda, Brazil 122 C5
Olindiná, Brazil 122 D4
Olite, Spain 28 C3
Oliva, Argentina 126 C3
Oliva, Spain 29 G4
Oliva, Punta del, Spain 30 B5
Oliva de la Frontera, Spain 31 G4
Olivares, Spain 28 F2
Olivehurst, U.S.A. 112 F5
Oliveira, Brazil 123 F3
Oliveira de Azemeis, Portugal 30 E2
Oliveira dos Brejinhos, Brazil 123 D3
Olivenza, Spain 31 G3
Oliver, Canada 100 D5
Oliver L., Canada 101 B8
Olivone, Switz. 23 C7
Olkhovka, Russia 43 B11
Olkusz, Poland 20 E9
Ollagüe, Chile 126 A2
Olloy, Belgium 17 H5
Olmedo, Spain 30 D6
Olmos, Peru 124 B2
Olney, Ill., U.S.A. 104 F1
Olney, Tex., U.S.A. 109 J5
Oloma, Cameroon 79 E7
Olomane →, Canada 99 B7
Olomouc, Czech. 20 F7
Olongapo, Phil. 55 D4
Oloron, Gave d' →, France 26 E2
Oloron-Ste.-Marie, France 26 E3
Olot, Spain 28 C7
Olovo, Bos.-H. 21 L8
Olovyannaya, Russia 45 D12
Oloy →, Russia 45 C16
Olpe, Germany 18 D3
Olshanka, Ukraine 42 B4
Olshany, Ukraine 42 A6
Olst, Neths. 16 D8
Olsztyn, Poland 20 B10
Olt →, Romania 38 F7
Olten, Switz. 22 B5
Olteniţa, Romania 38 E9
Olton, U.S.A. 109 H3
Oltu, Turkey 67 C9
Olur, Turkey 67 C10
Olutanga, Phil. 55 H5
Olvega, Spain 28 D3
Olvera, Spain 31 J5
Olymbos, Cyprus 37 D12
Olympia, Greece 39 M4
Olympia, U.S.A. 112 D4
Olympic Mts., U.S.A. 112 C3
Olympic Nat. Park, U.S.A. 112 C3
Olympus, Cyprus 37 E11
Olympus, Mt. = Ólimbos, Óros, Greece 39 J5
Olympus, Mt., U.S.A. 112 C3
Olyphant, U.S.A. 107 E9
Om →, Russia 44 D8
Om Hajer, Eritrea 77 E4
Om Koi, Thailand 58 D2
Ōma, Japan 48 D10
Ōmachi, Japan 49 F8
Omae-Zaki, Japan 49 G9
Ōmagari, Japan 48 E10
Omagh, U.K. 15 B4
Omagh □, U.K. 15 B4
Omaha, U.S.A. 108 E7
Omak, U.S.A. 110 B4
Omalos, Greece 37 D5
Oman ■, Asia 68 C6
Oman, G. of, Asia 65 E8
Omaruru, Namibia 84 C2
Omaruru →, Namibia 84 C1
Omate, Peru 124 D3
Ombai, Selat, Indonesia 57 F6
Omboué, Gabon 80 E1
Ombrone →, Italy 32 F8
Omdurmân, Sudan 77 D3
Omegna, Italy 32 C5
Omeonga, Zaïre 82 C1
Ometepe, I. de, Nic. 116 D2
Ometepec, Mexico 115 D5
Ominato, Japan 48 D10
Omineca →, Canada 100 B4
Omiš, Croatia 33 E13
Omišalj, Croatia 33 C11
Omitara, Namibia 84 C2
Ōmiya, Japan 49 G9
Omme Å →, Denmark 11 J2
Ommen, Neths. 16 C8
Ömnögovĭ □, Mongolia 50 C3
Omo →, Ethiopia 77 F4
Omodhos, Cyprus 37 E11
Omolon →, Russia 45 C16
Omono-Gawa →, Japan 48 E10
Omsk, Russia 44 D8
Omsukchan, Russia 45 C16
Ōmu, Japan 48 B11
Omul, Vf., Romania 38 D8
Ōmura, Japan 49 H4
Omuramba Omatako →, Namibia 81 H4
Omurtag, Bulgaria 38 F9
Ōmuta, Japan 49 H5
Omutninsk, Russia 41 B18
On, Belgium 17 H6
Oña, Spain 28 C1
Onaga, U.S.A. 108 F6
Onalaska, U.S.A. 108 D9
Onamia, U.S.A. 108 B8
Onancock, U.S.A. 104 G8
Onang, Indonesia 57 E5
Onaping L., Canada 98 C3
Oñate, Spain 28 B2
Onavas, Mexico 114 B3
Onawa, U.S.A. 108 D6
Onaway, U.S.A. 104 C3
Oncócua, Angola 84 B1
Onda, Spain 28 F4
Ondaejin, N. Korea 51 D15
Ondangua, Namibia 84 B2
Ondárroa, Spain 28 B2
Ondas →, Brazil 123 D3
Ondava →, Slovak Rep. 20 G11
Onderdijk, Neths. 16 C6
Ondjiva, Angola 84 B2
Ondo, Nigeria 79 D5
Ondo □, Nigeria 79 D6
Öndörhaan, Mongolia 54 B6
Öndörshil, Mongolia 50 B5
Öndverðarnes, Iceland 8 D1
Onega, Russia 44 C4
Onega →, Russia 6 C13
Onega, G. of = Onezhskaya Guba, Russia 44 C4
Onega, L. = Onezhskoye Ozero, Russia 44 C4
Onehunga, N.Z. 87 G5
Oneida, U.S.A. 107 C9
Oneida L., U.S.A. 107 C9
O'Neill, U.S.A. 108 D5
Onekotan, Ostrov, Russia 45 E16
Onema, Zaïre 82 C1
Oneonta, Ala., U.S.A. 105 J2
Oneonta, N.Y., U.S.A. 107 D9
Onezhskaya Guba, Russia 44 C4
Onezhskoye Ozero, Russia 44 C4
Ongarue, N.Z. 87 H5
Ongerup, Australia 89 F2
Ongjin, N. Korea 51 F13
Ongkharak, Thailand 58 E3
Ongniud Qi, China 51 C10
Ongoka, Zaïre 82 C2
Ongole, India 60 M12
Ongon, Mongolia 50 B7
Onguren, Russia 45 D11
Onhaye, Belgium 17 H5
Oni, Georgia 43 E10
Onida, U.S.A. 108 C4
Onilahy →, Madag. 85 C7
Onitsha, Nigeria 79 D6
Onoda, Japan 49 G5
Onpyŏng-ni, S. Korea 51 H14
Ons, Is. d', Spain 30 C2
Onsala, Sweden 11 G6
Onslow, Australia 88 D2
Onslow B., U.S.A. 105 H7
Onstwedde, Neths. 16 B10
Ontake-San, Japan 49 G8
Ontaneda, Spain 30 B7
Ontario, Calif., U.S.A. 113 L9
Ontario, Oreg., U.S.A. 110 D5
Ontario □, Canada 98 B2
Ontario, L., U.S.A. 98 D4
Onteniente, Spain 29 G4
Ontonagon, U.S.A. 108 B10
Ontur, Spain 29 G3
Onyx, U.S.A. 113 K8
Oodnadatta, Australia 91 D2
Ooldea, Australia 89 F5
Ooltgensplaat, Neths. 17 E4
Oombulgurri, Australia 88 C4
Oona River, Canada 100 C2
Oordegem, Belgium 17 G3
Oorindi, Australia 90 C3
Oost-Vlaanderen □, Belgium 17 F3
Oost-Vlieland, Neths. 16 B6
Oostakker, Belgium 17 F3
Oostburg, Neths. 17 F3
Oostduinkerke, Belgium 17 F1
Oostelijk-Flevoland, Neths. 16 C7
Oostende, Belgium 17 F1
Oosterbeek, Neths. 16 E7
Oosterdijk, Neths. 16 C6
Oosterend, Friesland, Neths. 16 B6
Oosterend, Noord-Holland, Neths. 16 B5
Oosterhout, Noord-Brabant, Neths. 17 E7
Oosterhout, Noord-Brabant, Neths. 17 E5
Oosterschelde, Neths. 17 E4
Oosterwolde, Neths. 16 B8
Oosterzele, Belgium 17 G3
Oostkamp, Belgium 17 F2
Oostmalle, Belgium 17 F5
Oostrozebekke, Belgium 17 G2
Oostvleteven, Belgium 17 G1
Oostvoorne, Neths. 16 E4
Oostzaan, Neths. 16 D5
Ootacamund, India 60 P10
Ootmarsum, Neths. 16 D9
Ootsa L., Canada 100 C3
Opala, Russia 45 D16
Opala, Zaïre 82 C1
Opanake, Sri Lanka 60 R12
Opasatika, Canada 98 C3
Opasquia, Canada 101 C10
Opatija, Croatia 33 C11
Opava, Czech. 20 F7
Opeinde, Neths. 16 B8
Opelousas, U.S.A. 109 K8
Opémisca, L., Canada 98 C5
Opglabbeek, Belgium 17 F7
Opheim, U.S.A. 110 B10
Ophthalmia Ra., Australia 88 D2
Opi, Nigeria 79 D6
Opinaca →, Canada 98 B4
Opinaca L., Canada 98 B4
Opiskotish, L., Canada 99 B6
Oploo, Neths. 17 E7
Opmeer, Neths. 16 C5
Opobo, Nigeria 79 E6
Opochka, Russia 40 C6
Opoczno, Poland 20 D10
Opol, Phil. 55 G6
Opole, Poland 20 E7
Oporto = Porto, Portugal 30 D2
Opotiki, N.Z. 87 H6
Opp, U.S.A. 105 K2
Oppenheim, Germany 19 F4
Opperdoes, Neths. 16 C6
Óppido Mamertina, Italy 35 D8
Oppland fylke □, Norway 10 C3
Oppstad, Norway 10 D5
Oprtalj, Croatia 33 C10
Opua, N.Z. 87 F5
Opunake, N.Z. 87 H4
Opuzen, Croatia 21 M7
Ora, Cyprus 37 E12
Ora, Italy 33 B8
Ora Banda, Australia 89 F3
Oracle, U.S.A. 111 K8
Oradea, Romania 38 B4
Öræfajökull, Iceland 8 D5
Orahovac, Serbia 21 N10
Orai, India 63 G8
Oraison, France 27 E9
Oral = Ural →, Kazakhstan 43 C14
Oral = Uralsk, Kazakhstan 44 D6
Oran, Algeria 75 A4
Oran, Argentina 126 A3
Orange = Oranje →, S. Africa 84 D2
Orange, Australia 91 E4
Orange, France 27 D8
Orange, Calif., U.S.A. 113 M9
Orange, Mass., U.S.A. 107 D12
Orange, Tex., U.S.A. 109 K8
Orange, Va., U.S.A. 104 F6
Orange, C., Brazil 121 C7
Orange Cove, U.S.A. 112 J7
Orange Free State □, S. Africa 84 D4
Orange Grove, U.S.A. 109 M6
Orange Walk, Belize 115 D7
Orangeburg, U.S.A. 105 J5
Orangeville, Canada 98 D3
Orani, Phil. 55 D4
Oranienburg, Germany 18 C9
Oranje →, S. Africa 84 D2
Oranje Vrystaat = Orange Free State □, S. Africa 84 D4

Oranjemund, *Namibia* 84 D2
Oranjerivier, *S. Africa* 84 D3
Oras, *Phil.* 55 E6
Orăştie, *Romania* 38 D6
Oraşul Stalin = Braşov, *Romania* 38 D8
Orava →, *Slovak Rep.* 20 F9
Oravita, *Romania* 38 D4
Orb →, *France* 26 E7
Orba →, *Italy* 32 D5
Ørbæk, *Denmark* 11 J4
Orbe, *Switz.* 22 C3
Orbec, *France* 24 C7
Orbetello, *Italy* 33 F8
Órbigo →, *Spain* 30 C5
Orbost, *Australia* 91 F4
Orce, *Spain* 29 H2
Orce →, *Spain* 29 H2
Orchies, *France* 25 B10
Orchila, I., *Venezuela* 120 A4
Orco →, *Italy* 32 C4
Orcopampa, *Peru* 124 D3
Orcutt, *U.S.A.* 113 L6
Ord →, *Australia* 88 C4
Ord, Mt., *Australia* 88 C4
Ordenes, *Spain* 30 B2
Orderville, *U.S.A.* 111 H7
Ording, *Germany* 18 A4
Ordos = Mu Us Shamo, *China* 50 E5
Ordu, *Turkey* 67 C7
Ordu □, *Turkey* 67 C7
Orduña, *Álava, Spain* 28 C7
Orduña, *Granada, Spain* 29 H1
Ordway, *U.S.A.* 108 F3
Ordzhonikidze = Vladikavkaz, *Russia* 43 E11
Ordzhonikidze, *Ukraine* 42 C6
Ore, *Zaïre* 82 B2
Ore Mts. = Erzgebirge, *Germany* 18 E9
Orealla, *Guyana* 121 B6
Orebić, *Croatia* 21 M7
Örebro, *Sweden* 9 G13
Örebro län □, *Sweden* 9 G13
Oregon, *U.S.A.* 108 D10
Oregon □, *U.S.A.* 110 E3
Oregon City, *U.S.A.* 112 E4
Orekhov, *Ukraine* 42 C6
Orekhovo-Zuyevo, *Russia* 41 D11
Orel, *Russia* 41 E10
Orel →, *Ukraine* 42 B6
Orellana, Canal de, *Spain* 31 F5
Orellana, Pantano de, *Spain* 31 F5
Orellana la Vieja, *Spain* 31 F5
Orem, *U.S.A.* 110 F8
Ören, *Turkey* 66 E2
Orenburg, *Russia* 44 D6
Orense, *Spain* 30 C3
Orense □, *Spain* 30 C3
Orepuki, *N.Z.* 87 M1
Orestiás, *Greece* 39 H9
Øresund, *Europe* 11 J6
Orford Ness, *U.K.* 13 E9
Organà, *Spain* 28 C6
Organos, Pta. de los, *Canary Is.* 36 F2
Orgaz, *Spain* 31 F7
Orgeyev, *Moldavia* 42 C3
Orgon, *France* 27 E9
Orhaneli, *Turkey* 66 D3
Orhangazi, *Turkey* 66 C3
Orhon Gol →, *Mongolia* 54 A5
Ória, *Italy* 35 B10
Orient, *Australia* 91 D3
Oriental, Cordillera, *Bolivia* 125 D4
Oriental, Cordillera, *Colombia* 120 B3
Oriente, *Argentina* 126 D3
Origny-Ste.-Benoîte, *France* 25 C10
Orihuela, *Spain* 29 G4
Orihuela del Tremedal, *Spain* 28 E3
Oriku, *Albania* 39 J2
Orinduik, *Guyana* 121 C5
Orinoco →, *Venezuela* 121 B5
Orissa □, *India* 61 K14
Oristano, *Italy* 34 C1
Oristano, G. di, *Italy* 34 C1
Orituco →, *Venezuela* 120 B4
Orizaba, *Mexico* 115 D5
Orizona, *Brazil* 123 E2
Orjen, *Bos.-H.* 21 N8
Orjiva, *Spain* 29 J1
Orkanger, *Norway* 10 A3
Örkelljunga, *Sweden* 11 H7
Örkény, *Hungary* 21 H9
Orkla →, *Norway* 10 A3
Orkney, *S. Africa* 84 D4
Orkney □, *U.K.* 14 C6
Orkney Is., *U.K.* 14 C6
Orland, *U.S.A.* 112 F4
Orlando, *U.S.A.* 105 L5
Orlando, C. d', *Italy* 35 D7
Orléanais, *France* 25 E9
Orléans, *France* 25 E8
Orleans, *U.S.A.* 107 B12
Orléans, I. d', *Canada* 99 C5
Orlice →, *Czech.* 20 E6
Orlov, *Slovak Rep.* 20 F10
Orlov Gay, *Russia* 41 F16
Ormara, *Pakistan* 60 G4
Ormea, *Italy* 32 D4
Ormília, *Greece* 39 J6
Ormoc, *Phil.* 55 F6
Ormond, *N.Z.* 87 H6
Ormond Beach, *U.S.A.* 105 L5
Ormož, *Slovenia* 33 B13
Ormstown, *Canada* 107 A11
Ornans, *France* 25 E13
Orne □, *France* 24 D7
Orne →, *France* 24 C6
Ørnhøj, *Denmark* 11 H2
Ornö, *Sweden* 10 E12
Örnsköldsvik, *Sweden* 10 A12
Oro, *N. Korea* 51 D14
Oro →, *Mexico* 114 B3
Oro Grande, *U.S.A.* 113 L9
Orobie, Alpi, *Italy* 32 B6
Orocué, *Colombia* 120 C3
Orodo, *Nigeria* 79 D6
Orogrande, *U.S.A.* 111 K10
Orol, *Spain* 30 B3
Oromocto, *Canada* 99 C6
Oron, *Nigeria* 79 E6
Oron, *Switz.* 22 C3
Orono, *Canada* 106 C6
Oropesa, *Spain* 30 F5
Oroquieta, *Phil.* 55 G5
Orós, *Brazil* 122 C4
Orosei, G. di, *Italy* 34 B2
Orosháza, *Hungary* 21 J10
Orotukan, *Russia* 45 C16
Oroville, *Calif., U.S.A.* 112 F5
Oroville, *Wash., U.S.A.* 110 B4
Oroville, L., *U.S.A.* 112 F5
Orroroo, *Australia* 91 E2
Orrville, *U.S.A.* 106 F3
Orsara di Púglia, *Italy* 35 A8
Orsha, *Belorussia* 40 D7
Orsières, *Switz.* 22 D4
Orsk, *Russia* 44 D6
Ørslev, *Denmark* 11 J5
Orsogna, *Italy* 33 F11
Orşova, *Romania* 38 E5
Ørsted, *Denmark* 11 H4
Orta, L. d', *Italy* 32 C5
Orta Nova, *Italy* 35 A8
Ortaca, *Turkey* 66 E3
Ortaköy, *Çorum, Turkey* 66 C6
Ortaköy, *Niğde, Turkey* 66 D6
Orte, *Italy* 33 F9
Ortegal, C., *Spain* 30 B3
Orteguaza →, *Colombia* 120 C2
Orthez, *France* 26 E3
Ortho, *Belgium* 17 H7
Ortigueira, *Spain* 30 B3
Orting, *U.S.A.* 112 C4
Ortles, *Italy* 32 B7
Ortón →, *Bolivia* 124 C4
Ortona, *Italy* 33 F11
Orūmīyeh, *Iran* 64 B5
Orūmīyeh, Daryācheh-ye, *Iran* 64 B5
Orune, *Italy* 34 B2
Oruro, *Bolivia* 124 D4
Oruro□, *Bolivia* 124 D4
Orust, *Sweden* 11 F5
Oruzgān □, *Afghan.* 60 C5
Orvault, *France* 24 E5
Orvieto, *Italy* 33 F9
Orwell, *U.S.A.* 106 E4
Orwell →, *U.K.* 13 E9
Oryakhovo, *Bulgaria* 38 F6
Orzinuovi, *Italy* 32 C6
Orzysz, *Poland* 20 B11
Osa, Pen. de, *Costa Rica* 116 E3
Osage, *Iowa, U.S.A.* 108 D8
Osage, *Wyo., U.S.A.* 108 D2
Osage →, *U.S.A.* 108 F9
Osage City, *U.S.A.* 108 F7
Ōsaka, *Japan* 49 G7
Osan, *S. Korea* 51 F14
Osawatomie, *U.S.A.* 108 F7
Osborne, *U.S.A.* 108 F5
Osceola, *Ark., U.S.A.* 109 H10
Osceola, *Iowa, U.S.A.* 108 E8
Oschatz, *Germany* 18 D9
Oschersleben, *Germany* 18 C7
Óschiri, *Italy* 34 B2
Oscoda, *U.S.A.* 106 B1
Ösel = Saaremaa, *Estonia* 40 B3
Osëry, *Russia* 41 D11
Osh, *Kirghizia* 44 E8
Oshawa, *Canada* 98 D4
Oshkosh, *Nebr., U.S.A.* 108 E3
Oshkosh, *Wis., U.S.A.* 108 C10
Oshmyany, *Belorussia* 40 D4
Oshnovīyeh, *Iran* 64 B5
Oshogbo, *Nigeria* 79 D5
Oshtorīnān, *Iran* 65 C6
Oshwe, *Zaïre* 80 E3
Osijek, *Croatia* 21 K8
Ósilo, *Italy* 34 B1
Osimo, *Italy* 33 E10
Osintorf, *Belorussia* 40 D7
Osipenko = Berdyansk, *Ukraine* 42 C7
Osipovichi, *Belorussia* 40 E6
Osizweni, *S. Africa* 85 D5
Oskaloosa, *U.S.A.* 108 E8
Oskarshamn, *Sweden* 9 H14
Oskélanéo, *Canada* 98 C4
Öskemen = Ust-Kamenogorsk, *Kazakhstan* 44 E9
Oskol →, *Ukraine* 41 G10
Oslo, *Norway* 10 E4
Oslob, *Phil.* 55 G5
Oslofjorden, *Norway* 10 E4
Osmanabad, *India* 60 K10
Osmancık, *Turkey* 42 F6
Osmaniye, *Turkey* 66 E7
Ösmo, *Sweden* 10 F11
Osnabrück, *Germany* 18 C4
Osor, *Italy* 33 D11
Osorio, *Brazil* 127 B5
Osorno, *Chile* 128 B2
Osorno, *Spain* 30 C6
Osorno □, *Chile* 128 B2
Osorno, Vol., *Chile* 128 B2
Osoyoos, *Canada* 100 D5
Ospika →, *Canada* 100 B4
Osprey Reef, *Australia* 90 A4
Oss, *Neths.* 16 E7
Ossa, Mt., *Australia* 90 G4
Óssa, Oros, *Greece* 39 K5
Ossa de Montiel, *Spain* 29 G2
Ossabaw I., *U.S.A.* 105 K5
Osse →, *France* 26 D4
Ossendrecht, *Neths.* 17 F4
Ossining, *U.S.A.* 107 E11
Ossipee, *U.S.A.* 107 C13
Ossokmanuan L., *Canada* 99 B7
Ossora, *Russia* 45 D17
Ostashkov, *Russia* 40 C8
Oste →, *Germany* 18 B5
Ostend = Oostende, *Belgium* 17 F1
Oster, *Ukraine* 40 F7
Osterburg, *Germany* 18 C7
Osterburken, *Germany* 19 F5
Österdalälven →, *Sweden* 9 F12
Östergötlands län □, *Sweden* 11 F9
Osterholz-Scharmbeck, *Germany* 18 B4
Østerild, *Denmark* 11 G2
Ostermundigen, *Switz.* 22 C4
Östersund, *Sweden* 10 A8
Østfold fylke □, *Norway* 10 E5
Ostfriesische Inseln, *Germany* 18 B3
Ostfriesland, *Germany* 18 B3
Óstia, Lido di, *Italy* 34 A5
Ostiglía, *Italy* 33 C8
Ostra, *Italy* 33 E10
Ostrava, *Czech.* 20 F8
Ostróda, *Poland* 20 B9
Ostrog, *Ukraine* 40 F5
Ostrogozhsk, *Russia* 41 F11
Ostrogróg Sźamotuły, *Poland* 20 C6
Ostrołęka, *Poland* 20 B11
Ostrov, *Bulgaria* 38 F7
Ostrov, *Romania* 38 E10
Ostrov, *Russia* 40 C6
Ostrów Mazowiecka, *Poland* 20 C11
Ostrów Wielkopolski, *Poland* 20 D7
Ostrowiec-Świętokrzyski, *Poland* 20 E11
Ostrzeszów, *Poland* 20 D7
Ostseebad-Kühlungsborn, *Germany* 18 A7
Osttirol □, *Austria* 19 J8
Ostuni, *Italy* 35 B10
Osum →, *Bulgaria* 38 F7
Osumi →, *Albania* 39 J3
Ōsumi-Kaikyō, *Japan* 49 J5
Ōsumi-Shotō, *Japan* 49 J5
Osun □, *Nigeria* 79 D5
Osuna, *Spain* 31 H5
Oswego, *U.S.A.* 107 C8
Oswestry, *U.K.* 12 E4
Oświecim, *Poland* 20 E9
Otago □, *N.Z.* 87 L2
Otago Harbour, *N.Z.* 87 L3
Ōtake, *Japan* 49 G6
Otaki, *N.Z.* 87 J5
Otaru, *Japan* 48 C10
Otaru-Wan = Ishikari-Wan, *Japan* 48 C10
Otava →, *Czech.* 20 F4
Otavalo, *Ecuador* 120 C2
Otavi, *Namibia* 84 B2
Otchinjau, *Angola* 84 B1
Otelec, *Romania* 38 D3
Otero de Rey, *Spain* 30 B3
Othello, *U.S.A.* 110 C4
Othonoí, *Greece* 39 K2
Óthris, Óros, *Greece* 39 K5
Otira Gorge, *N.Z.* 87 K3
Otis, *U.S.A.* 108 E3
Otjiwarongo, *Namibia* 84 C2
Otočac, *Croatia* 33 D12
Otoineppu, *Japan* 48 B11
Otorohanga, *N.Z.* 87 H5
Otoskwin →, *Canada* 98 B2
Otosquen, *Canada* 101 C8
Otranto, *Italy* 35 B11
Otranto, C. d', *Italy* 35 B11
Otranto, Str. of, *Italy* 35 B11
Otse, *S. Africa* 84 D4
Ōtsu, *Japan* 49 G7
Ōtsuki, *Japan* 49 G9
Otta, *Norway* 10 C3
Ottawa = Outaouais →, *Canada* 98 C5
Ottawa, *Canada* 98 C4
Ottawa, *Ill., U.S.A.* 108 E10
Ottawa, *Kans., U.S.A.* 108 F7
Ottawa Is., *Canada* 97 C11
Ottélé, *Cameroon* 79 E7
Otter L., *Canada* 101 B8
Otter Rapids, *Ont., Canada* 98 B3
Otter Rapids, *Sask., Canada* 101 B8
Otterndorf, *Germany* 18 B4
Otterup, *Denmark* 11 J4
Otterville, *Canada* 106 D4
Ottignies, *Belgium* 17 G5
Otto Beit Bridge, *Zimbabwe* 83 F2
Ottosdal, *S. Africa* 84 D4
Ottoshoop, *S. Africa* 84 D4
Ottsjön, *Sweden* 10 A7
Ottumwa, *U.S.A.* 108 E8
Otu, *Nigeria* 79 D5
Otukpa, *Nigeria* 79 D6
Oturkpo, *Nigeria* 79 D6
Otway, B., *Chile* 128 D2
Otway, C., *Australia* 91 F3
Otwock, *Poland* 20 C11
Ötz, *Austria* 19 H6
Ötz →, *Austria* 19 H6
Ötztaler Alpen, *Austria* 19 J7
Ou →, *Laos* 58 B4
Ou Neua, *Laos* 58 A3
Ou-Sammyaku, *Japan* 48 E10
Ouachita →, *U.S.A.* 109 K9
Ouachita, L., *U.S.A.* 109 H8
Ouachita Mts., *U.S.A.* 109 H7
Ouadâne, *Mauritania* 74 D2
Ouadda, *C.A.R.* 73 G9
Ouagadougou, *Burkina Faso* 79 C4
Ouahigouya, *Burkina Faso* 78 C4
Ouahila, *Algeria* 74 C3
Ouahran = Oran, *Algeria* 75 A4
Oualâta, *Mauritania* 78 B3
Ouallene, *Algeria* 75 D5
Ouanda Djallé, *C.A.R.* 73 G9
Ouango, *C.A.R.* 80 D4
Ouarâne, *Mauritania* 74 D2
Ouargla, *Algeria* 75 B6
Ouarkziz, Djebel, *Algeria* 74 C3
Ouarzazate, *Morocco* 74 B3
Ouatagouna, *Mali* 79 B5
Oubangi →, *Zaïre* 80 E3
Oubarakai, O. →, *Algeria* 75 C6
Ouche →, *France* 25 E12
Oud-Beijerland, *Neths.* 16 E4
Oud-Gastel, *Neths.* 17 E4
Oud Turnhout, *Belgium* 17 F6
Ouddorp, *Neths.* 16 E3
Oude-Pekela, *Neths.* 16 B10
Oude Rijn →, *Neths.* 16 D4
Oudega, *Neths.* 16 B8
Oudenaarde, *Belgium* 17 G3
Oudenbosch, *Neths.* 17 E5
Oudenburg, *Belgium* 17 F2
Ouderkerk, *Utrecht, Neths.* 16 D5
Ouderkerk, *Zuid-Holland, Neths.* 16 E5
Oudeschild, *Neths.* 16 B5
Oudewater, *Neths.* 16 D5
Oudkarspel, *Neths.* 16 C5
Oudon, *France* 24 E5
Oudtshoorn, *S. Africa* 84 E3
Oued Zem, *Morocco* 74 B3
Ouellé, *Ivory C.* 78 D4
Ouenza, *Algeria* 75 A6
Ouessa, *Burkina Faso* 78 C4
Ouessant, I. d', *France* 24 D1
Ouesso, *Congo* 80 D3
Ouest, Pte., *Canada* 99 C7
Ouezzane, *Morocco* 74 B3
Ouffet, *Belgium* 17 H6
Ouidah, *Benin* 79 D5
Ouistreham, *France* 24 C6
Oujda, *Morocco* 75 B4
Oujeft, *Mauritania* 74 D2
Ould Yenjé, *Mauritania* 78 B2
Ouled Djellal, *Algeria* 75 B6
Ouled Naïl, Mts. des, *Algeria* 75 B5
Oulmès, *Morocco* 74 B3
Oulu, *Finland* 8 D18
Oulu □ = Oulun lääni □, *Finland* 8 D19
Oulujärvi, *Finland* 8 D19
Oulujoki →, *Finland* 8 D18
Oulun lääni □, *Finland* 8 D19
Oulx, *Italy* 32 C3
Oum Chalouba, *Chad* 73 E9
Oum-el-Bouaghi, *Algeria* 75 A6
Oum el Ksi, *Algeria* 74 C3
Oum-er-Rbia, O. →, *Morocco* 74 B3
Oumè, *Ivory C.* 78 D3
Ounane, Dj., *Algeria* 75 C6
Ounguati, *Namibia* 84 C2
Ounianga-Kébir, *Chad* 73 E9
Ounianga Sérir, *Chad* 73 E9
Our →, *Lux.* 17 J8
Ouray, *U.S.A.* 111 G10
Ourcq →, *France* 25 C10
Oureg, Oued el →, *Algeria* 75 B5
Ourém, *Brazil* 122 B2
Ourense = Orense, *Spain* 30 C3
Ouricuri, *Brazil* 122 C3
Ourinhos, *Brazil* 127 A6
Ourique, *Portugal* 31 H2
Ouro Fino, *Brazil* 127 A6
Ouro Prêto, *Brazil* 123 F3
Ouro Sogui, *Senegal* 78 B2
Oursi, *Burkina Faso* 79 C4
Ourthe →, *Belgium* 17 H7
Ouse, *Australia* 90 G4
Ouse →, *E. Susx., U.K.* 13 G8
Ouse →, *N. Yorks., U.K.* 12 C8
Oust, *France* 26 F5
Oust →, *France* 24 E4
Outaouais →, *Canada* 98 C5
Outardes →, *Canada* 99 C6
Outat Oulad el Haj, *Morocco* 75 B4
Outer Hebrides, *U.K.* 14 D1
Outer I., *Canada* 99 B8
Outes, *Spain* 30 C2
Outjo, *Namibia* 84 C2
Outlook, *Canada* 101 C7
Outlook, *U.S.A.* 108 A2
Outreau, *France* 25 B8
Ouvèze →, *France* 27 E8
Ouyen, *Australia* 91 F3
Ouzouer-le-Marché, *France* 25 E8
Ovada, *Italy* 32 D5
Ovalau, *Fiji* 87 C8
Ovalle, *Chile* 126 C1
Ovar, *Portugal* 30 E2
Ovejas, *Colombia* 120 B2
Overdinkel, *Neths.* 16 D10
Overflakkee, *Neths.* 16 E4
Overijse, *Belgium* 17 G5
Overijssel □, *Neths.* 16 D9
Overijsselsch Kanaal →, *Neths.* 16 C8
Overpelt, *Belgium* 17 F6
Overton, *U.S.A.* 113 J12
Övertorneå, *Sweden* 8 C17
Ovid, *U.S.A.* 108 E3
Ovidiopol, *Ukraine* 42 C4
Oviedo, *Spain* 30 B5
Oviedo □, *Spain* 30 B5
Oviken, *Sweden* 10 A8
Oviksfjällen, *Sweden* 10 B7
Övör Hangay □, *Mongolia* 50 B2
Ovoro, *Nigeria* 79 D6
Ovruch, *Ukraine* 40 F6
Owaka, *N.Z.* 87 M2
Owase, *Japan* 49 G8
Owatonna, *U.S.A.* 108 C8
Owbeh, *Afghan.* 60 B3
Owego, *U.S.A.* 107 D8
Owen Falls, *Uganda* 82 B3
Owen Sound, *Canada* 98 D3
Owendo, *Gabon* 80 D1
Owens →, *U.S.A.* 112 J9
Owens L., *U.S.A.* 113 J9
Owensboro, *U.S.A.* 104 G2
Owensville, *U.S.A.* 108 F9
Owerri, *Nigeria* 79 D6
Owl →, *Canada* 101 B10
Owo, *Nigeria* 79 D6
Owosso, *U.S.A.* 104 D3
Owyhee, *U.S.A.* 110 F5
Owyhee →, *U.S.A.* 110 E5
Owyhee, L., *U.S.A.* 110 E5
Ox Mts., *Ireland* 15 B3
Oxapampa, *Peru* 124 C2
Oxelösund, *Sweden* 11 F11
Oxford, *N.Z.* 87 K4
Oxford, *U.K.* 13 F6
Oxford, *Miss., U.S.A.* 109 H10
Oxford, *N.C., U.S.A.* 105 G6
Oxford, *Ohio, U.S.A.* 104 F3
Oxford L., *Canada* 101 C9
Oxfordshire □, *U.K.* 13 F6
Oxley, *Australia* 91 E3
Oxnard, *U.S.A.* 113 L7
Oxus = Amudarya →, *Uzbekistan* 44 E6
Oya, *Malaysia* 56 D4
Oyama, *Japan* 49 F9
Oyapock →, *Fr. Guiana* 121 C7
Oyem, *Gabon* 80 D2
Oyen, *Canada* 101 C6
Øyeren, *Norway* 10 E5
Oykel →, *U.K.* 14 D4
Oymyakon, *Russia* 45 C15
Oyo, *Nigeria* 79 D5
Oyo □, *Nigeria* 79 D5
Oyón, *Peru* 124 C2
Oyonnax, *France* 27 B9
Oyster Bay, *U.S.A.* 107 F11
Ōyūbari, *Japan* 48 C11
Özalp, *Turkey* 67 D10
Ozamiz, *Phil.* 55 G5
Ozark, *Ala., U.S.A.* 105 K3
Ozark, *Ark., U.S.A.* 109 H8
Ozark, *Mo., U.S.A.* 109 G8
Ozark Plateau, *U.S.A.* 109 G9
Ozarks, L. of the, *U.S.A.* 108 F8
Ózd, *Hungary* 21 G10
Ozette L., *U.S.A.* 112 B2
Ozieri, *Italy* 34 B2
Ozona, *U.S.A.* 109 K4
Ozorków, *Poland* 20 D9
Ozuluama, *Mexico* 115 C5
Ozurgety, *Georgia* 43 F10

P

P.K. le Roux Dam, *S. Africa* 84 E3
Pa, *Burkina Faso* 78 C4
Pa-an, *Burma* 61 L20
Pa Mong Dam, *Thailand* 58 D4
Paal, *Belgium* 17 F6

Paamiut = Frederikshåb, Greenland 4 C5
Paar →, Germany 19 G6
Paarl, S. Africa 84 E2
Paatsi →, Russia 8 B20
Paauilo, U.S.A. 102 H17
Pab Hills, Pakistan 62 F2
Pabianice, Poland 20 D9
Pabna, Bangla. 61 G16
Pabo, Uganda 82 B3
Pacaás Novos, Serra dos, Brazil 125 C5
Pacaipampa, Peru 124 B2
Pacaja →, Brazil 122 B1
Pacajus, Brazil 122 B4
Pacaraima, Sierra, Venezuela 121 C5
Pacarán, Peru 124 C2
Pacaraos, Peru 124 C2
Pacasmayo, Peru 124 B2
Paceco, Italy 34 E5
Pachacamac, Peru 124 C2
Pachhar, India 62 G7
Pachino, Italy 35 F8
Pachitea →, Peru 124 B3
Pachiza, Peru 124 B2
Pacho, Colombia 120 B3
Pachpadra, India 60 G8
Pachuca, Mexico 115 C5
Pacific, Canada 100 C3
Pacific-Antarctic Ridge, Pac. Oc. 93 M16
Pacific Grove, U.S.A. 111 H3
Pacific Ocean, Pac. Oc. 93 G14
Pacifica, U.S.A. 112 H4
Pacitan, Indonesia 57 H14
Packwood, U.S.A. 112 D5
Pacuí →, Brazil 123 E2
Padaido, Kepulauan, Indonesia 57 E9
Padang, Indonesia 56 E2
Padangpanjang, Indonesia 56 E2
Padangsidempuan, Indonesia 56 D1
Padauari →, Brazil 121 D5
Padborg, Denmark 11 K3
Padcaya, Bolivia 125 E5
Paddockwood, Canada 101 C7
Paderborn, Germany 18 D4
Padilla, Bolivia 125 D5
Padloping Island, Canada 97 B13
Pádova, Italy 33 C8
Padra, India 62 H5
Padrauna, India 63 F10
Padre I., U.S.A. 109 M6
Padro, Mte., France 27 F12
Padrón, Spain 30 C2
Padstow, U.K. 13 G3
Padua = Pádova, Italy 33 C8
Paducah, Ky., U.S.A. 104 G1
Paducah, Tex., U.S.A. 109 H4
Padul, Spain 31 H7
Padula, Italy 35 B8
Paengnyong-do, S. Korea 51 F13
Paeroa, N.Z. 87 G5
Paesana, Italy 32 D4
Pafúri, Mozam. 85 C5
Pag, Croatia 33 D11
Paga, Ghana 79 C4
Pagadian, Phil. 55 H5
Pagai Selatan, P., Indonesia 56 E2
Pagai Utara, Indonesia 56 E2
Pagalu = Annobón, Atl. Oc. 71 G4
Pagastikós Kólpos, Greece 39 K6
Pagatan, Indonesia 56 E5
Page, Ariz., U.S.A. 111 H8
Page, N. Dak., U.S.A. 108 B6
Paglieta, Italy 33 F11
Pagny-sur-Moselle, France 25 D13
Pago Pago, Amer. Samoa 87 B13
Pagosa Springs, U.S.A. 111 H10
Pagwa River, Canada 98 B2
Pahala, U.S.A. 102 J17
Pahang →, Malaysia 59 L4
Pahiatua, N.Z. 87 J5
Pahokee, U.S.A. 105 M5
Pahrump, U.S.A. 113 J11
Pahute Mesa, U.S.A. 112 H10
Pai, Thailand 58 C2
Paia, U.S.A. 102 H16
Paicines, U.S.A. 112 J5
Paide, Estonia 40 B4
Paignton, U.K. 13 G4
Paiján, Peru 124 B2
Päijänne, Finland 9 F18
Paimbœuf, France 24 E4
Paimpol, France 24 D3
Painan, Indonesia 56 E2
Painesville, U.S.A. 106 E3
Paint Hills = Nouveau Comptoir, Canada 98 B4
Paint L., Canada 101 B9
Paint Rock, U.S.A. 109 K5
Painted Desert, U.S.A. 111 J8
Paintsville, U.S.A. 104 G4
País Vasco □, Spain 28 C2
Paisley, Canada 106 B3
Paisley, U.K. 14 F4
Paisley, U.S.A. 110 E3
Paita, Peru 124 B1
Paiva →, Portugal 30 D2
Paizhou, China 53 B9
Pajares, Spain 30 B5
Pajares, Puerto de, Spain 30 C5
Pak Lay, Laos 58 C3
Pak Phanang, Thailand 59 H3
Pak Sane, Laos 58 C4
Pak Song, Laos 58 E6
Pak Suong, Laos 58 C4
Pakaraima Mts., Guyana 121 B5
Pákhnes, Greece 37 D6
Pakistan ■, Asia 62 E3
Pakistan, East = Bangladesh ■, Asia 61 H17
Pakkading, Laos 58 C4
Pakokku, Burma 61 J19
Pakpattan, Pakistan 62 D5
Pakrac, Croatia 21 K7
Paks, Hungary 21 J8
Pakse, Laos 58 E5
Paktīā □, Afghan. 60 C6
Pakwach, Uganda 82 B3
Pala, Chad 73 G8
Pala, U.S.A. 113 M9
Pala, Zaïre 82 D2
Palabek, Uganda 82 B3
Palacios, U.S.A. 109 L6
Palafrugell, Spain 28 D8
Palagiano, Italy 35 B10
Palagonía, Italy 35 E7
Palagruža, Croatia 33 F13
Palaiókastron, Greece 37 D8
Palaiokhóra, Greece 37 D5
Palam, India 60 K10
Palamás, Greece 39 K5
Palamós, Spain 28 D8
Palampur, India 62 C7
Palana, Australia 90 F4
Palana, Russia 45 D16
Palanan, Phil. 55 C5
Palanan Pt., Phil. 55 C5
Palandri, Pakistan 63 C5
Palangkaraya, Indonesia 56 E4
Palani Hills, India 60 P10
Palanpur, India 62 G5
Palapye, Botswana 84 C4
Palas, Pakistan 63 B5
Palatka, Russia 45 C16
Palatka, U.S.A. 105 L5
Palau = Belau ■, Pac. Oc. 92 G5
Palawan, Phil. 55 G3
Palayankottai, India 60 Q10
Palazzo, Pte., France 27 F12
Palazzo San Gervásio, Italy 35 B8
Palazzolo Acreide, Italy 35 E7
Palca, Chile 124 D4
Paldiski, Estonia 40 B4
Paleleh, Indonesia 57 D6
Palembang, Indonesia 56 E2
Palena →, Chile 128 B2
Palena, L., Chile 128 B2
Palencia, Spain 30 C6
Palencia □, Spain 30 C6
Paleokastrítsa, Greece 37 A3
Paleometokho, Cyprus 37 D12
Palermo, Colombia 120 C2
Palermo, Italy 34 D6
Palermo, U.S.A. 110 G3
Palestine, Asia 69 D4
Palestine, U.S.A. 109 K7
Palestrina, Italy 34 A5
Paletwa, Burma 61 J18
Palghat, India 60 P10
Palgrave, Mt., Australia 88 D2
Pali, India 62 G5
Palinuro, C., Italy 35 B8
Palisade, U.S.A. 108 E4
Paliseul, Belgium 17 J6
Palitana, India 62 J4
Palizada, Mexico 115 D6
Palizzi, Italy 35 E8
Palk Bay, Asia 60 Q11
Palk Strait, Asia 60 Q11
Palkānah, Iraq 64 C5
Palla Road = Dinokwe, Botswana 84 C4
Pallanza = Verbánia, Italy 32 C5
Pallasovka, Russia 41 F15
Pallisa, Uganda 82 B3
Pallu, India 62 E6
Palm Beach, U.S.A. 105 M6
Palm Desert, U.S.A. 113 M10
Palm Is., Australia 90 B4
Palm Springs, U.S.A. 113 M10
Palma, Mozam. 83 E5
Palma →, Brazil 123 D2
Palma, B. de, Spain 36 B9
Palma de Mallorca, Spain 36 B9
Palma del Río, Spain 31 H5
Palma di Montechiaro, Italy 34 E6
Palma Soriano, Cuba 116 B4
Palmanova, Italy 33 C10
Palmares, Brazil 122 C4
Palmarito, Venezuela 120 B3
Palmarola, Italy 34 B5
Palmas, Brazil 127 B5
Palmas, C., Liberia 78 E3
Pálmas, G. di, Italy 34 C1
Palmas de Monte Alto, Brazil 123 D3
Palmdale, U.S.A. 113 L8
Palmeira, Brazil 123 G2
Palmeira dos Índios, Brazil 122 C4
Palmeirais, Brazil 122 C3
Palmeiras →, Brazil 123 D2
Palmeirinhas, Pta. das, Angola 80 F2
Palmela, Portugal 31 G2
Palmelo, Brazil 123 E2
Palmer, U.S.A. 96 B5
Palmer →, Australia 90 B3
Palmer Arch., Antarctica 5 C17
Palmer Lake, U.S.A. 108 F2
Palmer Land, Antarctica 5 D18
Palmerston, Canada 106 C4
Palmerston, N.Z. 87 L3
Palmerston North, N.Z. 87 J5
Palmerton, U.S.A. 107 F9
Palmetto, U.S.A. 105 M4
Palmi, Italy 35 D8
Palmira, Argentina 126 C2
Palmira, Colombia 120 C2
Palmyra = Tudmur, Syria 64 C3
Palmyra, Mo., U.S.A. 108 F9
Palmyra, N.Y., U.S.A. 106 C7
Palmyra Is., Pac. Oc. 93 G11
Palo Alto, U.S.A. 111 H2
Palo del Colle, Italy 35 A9
Palo Verde, U.S.A. 113 M12
Palombara Sabina, Italy 33 F9
Palompon, Phil. 55 F6
Palopo, Indonesia 57 E6
Palos, C. de, Spain 29 H4
Palos Verdes, U.S.A. 113 M8
Palos Verdes, Pt., U.S.A. 113 M8
Palouse, U.S.A. 110 C5
Palpa, Peru 124 C2
Palparara, Australia 90 C3
Pålsboda, Sweden 10 E9
Palu, Indonesia 57 E5
Paluan, Phil. 57 B6
Palwal, India 62 E7
Pama, Burkina Faso 79 C5
Pamanukan, Indonesia 57 G12
Pamekasan, Indonesia 57 G15
Pamiers, France 26 E5
Pamirs, Tajikistan 44 F8
Pamlico →, U.S.A. 105 H7
Pamlico Sd., U.S.A. 105 H8
Pampa, U.S.A. 109 H4
Pampa de Agma, Argentina 128 B3
Pampa de las Salinas, Argentina 126 C2
Pampa Grande, Bolivia 125 D5
Pampa Hermosa, Peru 124 B2
Pampanua, Indonesia 57 E6
Pamparato, Italy 32 D4
Pampas, Argentina 126 D3
Pampas, Peru 124 C3
Pampas →, Peru 124 C3
Pamphylia, Turkey 66 E4
Pamplona, Colombia 120 B3
Pamplona, Spain 28 C3
Pampoenpoort, S. Africa 84 E3
Pamukkale, Turkey 66 E3
Pan Xian, China 52 E5
Pana, U.S.A. 108 F10
Panabo, Phil. 55 H6
Panaca, U.S.A. 111 H6
Panagyurishte, Bulgaria 38 G7
Panaitan, Indonesia 57 G11
Panaji, India 60 M8
Panamá, Panama 116 E4
Panama ■, Cent. Amer. 116 E4
Panamá, G. de, Panama 116 E4
Panama Canal, Panama 116 E4
Panama City, U.S.A. 105 K3
Panamint Range, U.S.A. 113 J9
Panamint Springs, U.S.A. 113 J9
Panão, Peru 124 B2
Panaon I., Phil. 55 F6
Panare, Thailand 59 J3
Panarea, Italy 35 D8
Panaro →, Italy 32 D8
Panarukan, Indonesia 57 G15
Panay, Phil. 55 F5
Panay, G., Phil. 57 B6
Pancake Range, U.S.A. 111 G6
Pančevo, Serbia 21 L10
Pancorbo, Paso, Spain 28 C1
Pandan, Antique, Phil. 55 F5
Pandan, Catanduanes, Phil. 55 D6
Pandegelang, Indonesia 57 G12
Pandharpur, India 60 L9
Pandilla, Spain 28 D1
Pando, Uruguay 127 C4
Pando □, Bolivia 124 C4
Pando, L. = Hope, L., Australia 91 D2
Pandokrátor, Greece 37 A3
Pandora, Costa Rica 116 E3
Panevėžys, Lithuania 40 D4
Panfilov, Kazakhstan 44 E8
Panfilovo, Russia 41 F13
Pang-Long, Burma 61 H21
Pang-Yang, Burma 61 H21
Panga, Zaïre 82 B2
Pangalanes, Canal des, Madag. 85 C8
Pangani, Tanzania 82 D4
Pangani □, Tanzania 82 D4
Pangani →, Tanzania 82 D4
Pangfou = Bengbu, China 51 H9
Pangil, Zaïre 82 C2
Pangkah, Tanjung, Indonesia 57 G15
Pangkajene, Indonesia 57 E5
Pangkalanbrandan, Indonesia 56 D1
Pangkalanbuun, Indonesia 56 E4
Pangkalansusu, Indonesia 56 D1
Pangkalpinang, Indonesia 56 E3
Pangkoh, Indonesia 56 E4
Pangnirtung, Canada 97 B13
Pangrango, Indonesia 57 G12
Panguipulli, Chile 128 A2
Panguitch, U.S.A. 111 H7
Pangutaran Group, Phil. 55 H4
Panhandle, U.S.A. 109 H4
Pani Mines, India 62 H5
Pania-Mutombo, Zaïre 82 D1
Panipat, India 62 E7
Panjal Range, India 62 C7
Panjgur, Pakistan 60 F4
Panjim = Panaji, India 60 M8
Panjinad Barrage, Pakistan 60 E7
Panjwai, Afghan. 62 D1
Pankshin, Nigeria 79 D6
Panmunjŏm, N. Korea 51 F14
Panna, India 63 G9
Panna Hills, India 63 G9
Pano Lefkara, Cyprus 37 E12
Pano Panayia, Cyprus 37 E11
Panorama, Brazil 127 A5
Pánormon, Greece 37 D6
Panshan, China 51 D12
Panshi, China 51 C14
Pantar, Indonesia 57 F6
Pante Macassar, Indonesia 57 F6
Pantelleria, Italy 34 F5
Pantón, Spain 30 C3
Pánuco, Mexico 115 C5
Panyam, Nigeria 79 D6
Panyu, China 53 F9
Pao →, Anzoátegui, Venezuela 121 B5
Pao →, Apure, Venezuela 120 B4
Páola, Italy 35 C9
Paola, Malta 37 D2
Paola, U.S.A. 108 F7
Paonia, U.S.A. 111 G10
Paoting = Baoding, China 50 E8
Paot'ou = Baotou, China 50 D6
Paoua, C.A.R. 73 G8
Pápa, Hungary 21 H7
Papagayo →, Mexico 115 D5
Papagayo, G. de, Costa Rica 116 D2
Papakura, N.Z. 87 G5
Papantla, Mexico 115 C5
Papar, Malaysia 56 C5
Pápas, Ákra, Greece 39 L4
Papenburg, Germany 18 B3
Paphlagonia, Turkey 66 C5
Paphos, Cyprus 37 E11
Papien Chiang = Da →, Vietnam 58 B5
Papigochic →, Mexico 114 B3
Paposo, Chile 126 B1
Papoutsa, Cyprus 37 E12
Papua New Guinea ■, Oceania 92 H6
Papuča, Croatia 33 D12
Papudo, Chile 126 C1
Papuk, Croatia 21 K7
Papun, Burma 61 K20
Papunya, Australia 88 D5
Pará = Belém, Brazil 122 B2
Pará □, Brazil 125 A7
Pará □, Surinam 121 B6
Parábita, Italy 35 B11
Paraburdoo, Australia 88 D2
Paracale, Phil. 55 D5
Paracas, Pen., Peru 124 C2
Paracatu, Brazil 123 E2
Paracatu →, Brazil 123 E2
Paracel Is. = Hsisha Chuntao, Pac. Oc. 56 A4
Parachilna, Australia 91 E2
Parachinar, Pakistan 62 C4
Paraćin, Serbia 21 M11
Paracuru, Brazil 122 B4
Parada, Punta, Peru 124 D2
Paradas, Spain 31 H5
Paradela, Spain 30 C3
Paradhísi, Greece 37 C10
Paradip, India 61 J15
Paradise, Calif., U.S.A. 112 F5
Paradise, Mont., U.S.A. 110 C6
Paradise, Nev., U.S.A. 113 J11
Paradise →, Canada 99 B8
Paradise Valley, U.S.A. 110 F5
Parado, Indonesia 57 F5
Paragould, U.S.A. 109 G9
Paraguá →, Bolivia 125 C5
Paragua →, Venezuela 121 B5
Paraguaçu →, Brazil 123 D4
Paraguaçu Paulista, Brazil 127 A5
Paraguaipoa, Venezuela 120 A3
Paraguaná, Pen. de, Venezuela 120 A3
Paraguarí, Paraguay 126 B4
Paraguarí □, Paraguay 126 B4
Paraguay ■, S. Amer. 126 A4
Paraguay →, Paraguay 126 B4
Paraíba = João Pessoa, Brazil 122 C5
Paraíba □, Brazil 122 C4
Paraíba do Sul →, Brazil 123 F3
Parainen, Finland 9 F17
Paraiso, Mexico 115 D6
Parak, Iran 65 E7
Parakhino Paddubye, Russia 40 B8
Parakou, Benin 79 D5
Paralimni, Cyprus 37 D12
Paramaribo, Surinam 121 B6
Parambu, Brazil 122 C3
Paramillo, Nudo del, Colombia 120 B2
Paramirim, Brazil 123 D3
Paramirim →, Brazil 123 D3
Paramithiá, Greece 39 K3
Paramushir, Ostrov, Russia 45 D16
Paran →, Israel 69 E4
Paraná, Argentina 126 C3
Paranã, Brazil 123 D2
Paraná □, Brazil 127 A5
Paraná →, Argentina 126 C4
Paranaguá, Brazil 127 B6
Paranaíba →, Brazil 123 F1
Paranapanema →, Brazil 127 A5
Paranapiacaba, Serra do, Brazil 127 A6
Paranavaí, Brazil 127 A5
Parang, Jolo, Phil. 55 J4
Parang, Mindanao, Phil. 57 C6
Parangaba, Brazil 122 B4
Parapóla, Greece 39 N6
Paraspóri, Ákra, Greece 39 P10
Paratinga, Brazil 123 D3
Paratoo, Australia 91 E2
Parattah, Australia 90 G4
Paraúna, Brazil 123 E1
Paray-le-Monial, France 27 B8
Parbati →, India 62 G7
Parbhani, India 60 K10
Parchim, Germany 18 B7
Parczew, Poland 20 D12
Pardes Hanna, Israel 69 C3
Pardilla, Spain 30 D7
Pardo →, Bahia, Brazil 123 E4
Pardo →, Mato Grosso, Brazil 127 A5
Pardo →, Minas Gerais, Brazil 123 E3
Pardo →, São Paulo, Brazil 123 F2
Pardubice, Czech. 20 E5
Pare, Indonesia 57 G15
Pare □, Tanzania 82 C4
Pare Mts., Tanzania 82 C4
Parecis, Serra dos, Brazil 125 C6
Paredes de Nava, Spain 30 C6
Pareh, Iran 64 B5
Parelhas, Brazil 122 C4
Paren, Russia 45 C17
Parent, Canada 98 C5
Parent, L., Canada 98 C4
Parentis-en-Born, France 26 D2
Parepare, Indonesia 57 E5
Parfino, Russia 40 C7
Pargo, Pta. do, Madeira 36 D2
Paria, G. de, Venezuela 121 A5
Paria, Pen. de, Venezuela 121 A5
Pariaguán, Venezuela 121 B5
Pariaman, Indonesia 56 E2
Paricatuba, Brazil 121 D5
Paricutín, Cerro, Mexico 114 D4
Parigi, Java, Indonesia 57 G13
Parigi, Sulawesi, Indonesia 57 E6
Parika, Guyana 121 B6
Parima, Serra, Brazil 121 C5
Parinari, Peru 124 A3
Parîng, Romania 38 D6
Parintins, Brazil 121 D6
Pariparit Kyun, Burma 61 M18
Paris, Canada 98 D3
Paris, France 25 D9
Paris, Idaho, U.S.A. 110 E8
Paris, Ky., U.S.A. 104 F3
Paris, Tenn., U.S.A. 105 G1
Paris, Tex., U.S.A. 109 J7
Paris, Ville de □, France 25 D9
Parish, U.S.A. 107 C8
Pariti, Indonesia 57 F6
Park, U.S.A. 112 B4
Park City, U.S.A. 110 F8
Park Falls, U.S.A. 108 C9
Park Range, U.S.A. 110 G10
Park Rapids, U.S.A. 108 B7
Park River, U.S.A. 108 A6
Park Rynie, S. Africa 85 E5
Parkā Bandar, Iran 65 E8
Parker, Ariz., U.S.A. 113 L12
Parker, S. Dak., U.S.A. 108 D6
Parker Dam, U.S.A. 113 L12
Parkersburg, U.S.A. 104 F5
Parkerview, Canada 101 C8
Parkes, Australia 91 E4
Parkfield, U.S.A. 112 K6
Parkland, U.S.A. 112 C4
Parkside, Canada 101 C7
Parkston, U.S.A. 108 D5
Parksville, Canada 100 D4
Parma, Italy 32 D7
Parma, Idaho, U.S.A. 110 E5
Parma, Ohio, U.S.A. 106 E3
Parma →, Italy 32 D7
Parnaguá, Brazil 122 D3
Parnaíba, Piauí, Brazil 122 B3
Parnaíba, São Paulo, Brazil 125 D7
Parnaíba →, Brazil 122 B3
Parnamirim, Brazil 122 C4
Parnarama, Brazil 122 C3
Parnassós, Greece 39 L5
Párnis, Greece 39 L6
Párnon Óros, Greece 39 M5
Pärnu, Estonia 40 B4
Paroo →, Australia 91 E3
Páros, Greece 39 M8
Parowan, U.S.A. 111 H7
Parpaillon, France 27 D10
Parral, Chile 126 D1
Parramatta, Australia 91 E5

Parras, *Mexico* 114 B4
Parrett →, *U.K.* 13 F5
Parris I., *U.S.A.* 105 J5
Parrsboro, *Canada* 99 C7
Parry Is., *Canada* 4 B2
Parry Sound, *Canada* 98 C3
Parsberg, *Germany* 19 F7
Parshall, *U.S.A.* 108 B3
Parsnip →, *Canada* 100 B4
Parsons, *U.S.A.* 109 G7
Parsons Ra., *Australia* 90 A2
Partanna, *Italy* 34 E5
Parthenay, *France* 24 F6
Partinico, *Italy* 34 D6
Paru →, *Brazil* 121 D7
Parú →, *Venezuela* 120 C4
Paru de Oeste →, *Brazil* 121 C6
Parucito →, *Venezuela* 120 B4
Paruro, *Peru* 124 C3
Parvān □, *Afghan.* 60 B6
Parvatipuram, *India* 61 K13
Parys, *S. Africa* 84 D4
Pas-de-Calais □, *France* 25 B9
Pasadena, *Calif., U.S.A.* 113 L8
Pasadena, *Tex., U.S.A.* 109 L7
Pasaje, *Ecuador* 120 D2
Pasaje →, *Argentina* 126 B3
Pasay, *Phil.* 55 D4
Pascagoula, *U.S.A.* 109 K10
Pascagoula →, *U.S.A.* 109 K10
Paşcani, *Romania* 38 B9
Pasco, *U.S.A.* 110 C4
Pasco □, *Peru* 124 C2
Pasco, Cerro de, *Peru* 124 C2
Pascua, I. de, *Pac. Oc.* 93 K17
Pasewalk, *Germany* 18 B10
Pasfield L., *Canada* 101 B7
Pasha →, *Russia* 40 B8
Pashiwari, *Pakistan* 63 B6
Pashmakli = Smolyan, *Bulgaria* 39 H7
Pasinler, *Turkey* 67 D9
Pasirian, *Indonesia* 57 H15
Paskūh, *Iran* 65 E9
Pasley, C., *Australia* 89 F3
Pašman, *Croatia* 33 E12
Pasni, *Pakistan* 60 G3
Paso Cantinela, *Mexico* 113 N11
Paso de Indios, *Argentina* 128 B3
Paso de los Libres, *Argentina* 126 B4
Paso de los Toros, *Uruguay* 126 C4
Paso Flores, *Argentina* 128 B2
Paso Robles, *U.S.A.* 111 J3
Pasorapa, *Bolivia* 125 D5
Paspébiac, *Canada* 99 C6
Pasrur, *Pakistan* 62 C6
Passage West, *Ireland* 15 E3
Passaic, *U.S.A.* 107 F10
Passau, *Germany* 19 G9
Passendale, *Belgium* 17 G2
Passero, C., *Italy* 35 F8
Passo Fundo, *Brazil* 127 B5
Passos, *Brazil* 123 F2
Passow, *Germany* 18 B10
Passwang, *Switz.* 22 B5
Passy, *France* 27 C10
Pastaza □, *Ecuador* 120 D2
Pastaza →, *Peru* 120 D2
Pastęk, *Poland* 20 A9
Pasto, *Colombia* 120 C2
Pastos Bons, *Brazil* 122 C3
Pastrana, *Spain* 28 E2
Pasuruan, *Indonesia* 57 G15
Patagonia, *Argentina* 128 C2
Patagonia, *U.S.A.* 111 L8
Patambar, *Iran* 65 D9
Patan, *India* 60 H8
Patan, *Maharashtra, India* 62 H5
Patan, *Nepal* 61 F14
Patani, *Indonesia* 57 D7
Pataudi, *India* 62 E7
Patay, *France* 25 D8
Patchewollock, *Australia* 91 F3
Patchogue, *U.S.A.* 107 F11
Patea, *N.Z.* 87 H5
Pategi, *Nigeria* 79 D6
Patensie, *S. Africa* 84 E3
Paternò, *Italy* 35 E7
Pateros, *U.S.A.* 110 B4
Paterson, *U.S.A.* 107 F10
Paterson Ra., *Australia* 88 D3
Paterswolde, *Neths.* 16 B9
Pathankot, *India* 62 C6
Pathfinder Reservoir, *U.S.A.* 110 E10
Pathiu, *Thailand* 59 G2
Pathum Thani, *Thailand* 58 E3
Pati, *Indonesia* 57 G14
Patía, *Colombia* 120 C2
Patía →, *Colombia* 120 C2
Patiala, *India* 62 D7
Patine Kouka, *Senegal* 78 C2
Pativilca, *Peru* 124 C2
Patkai Bum, *India* 61 F19
Pátmos, *Greece* 39 M9
Patna, *India* 63 G11
Patnos, *Turkey* 67 D10
Patonga, *Uganda* 82 B3
Patos, *Brazil* 122 C4
Patos, L. dos, *Brazil* 127 C5
Patos de Minas, *Brazil* 123 E2
Patquía, *Argentina* 126 C2
Pátrai, *Greece* 39 L4
Pátraikós Kólpos, *Greece* 39 L4
Patricio Lynch, I., *Chile* 128 C1
Patrocínio, *Brazil* 123 E2
Patta, *Kenya* 82 C5
Pattada, *Italy* 34 B2
Pattani, *Thailand* 59 J3
Patten, *U.S.A.* 99 C6
Patterson, *Calif., U.S.A.* 111 H3
Patterson, *La., U.S.A.* 109 L9
Patterson, Mt., *U.S.A.* 112 G7
Patti, *India* 62 D6
Patti, *Italy* 35 D7
Pattoki, *Pakistan* 62 D5
Patton, *U.S.A.* 106 F6
Patu, *Brazil* 122 C4
Patuakhali, *Bangla.* 61 H17
Patuca →, *Honduras* 116 C3
Patuca, Punta, *Honduras* 116 C3
Pâturages, *Belgium* 17 H3
Pátzcuaro, *Mexico* 114 D4
Pau, *France* 26 E3
Pau, Gave de →, *France* 26 E2
Pau d' Arco, *Brazil* 122 C2
Pau dos Ferros, *Brazil* 122 C4
Paucartambo, *Peru* 124 C3
Pauillac, *France* 26 C3
Pauini, *Brazil* 124 B4
Pauini →, *Brazil* 121 D5
Pauk, *Burma* 61 J19
Paul I., *Canada* 99 A7
Paul Isnard, *Fr. Guiana* 121 C7
Paulhan, *France* 26 E7
Paulis = Isiro, *Zaïre* 82 B2
Paulista, *Brazil* 122 C5
Paulistana, *Brazil* 122 C3
Paullina, *U.S.A.* 108 D7
Paulo Afonso, *Brazil* 122 C4
Paulo de Faria, *Brazil* 123 F2
Paulpietersburg, *S. Africa* 85 D5
Pauls Valley, *U.S.A.* 109 H6
Pauma Valley, *U.S.A.* 113 M10
Pausa, *Peru* 124 D3
Pauto →, *Colombia* 120 B3
Pāveh, *Iran* 64 C5
Pavelets, *Russia* 41 E11
Pavia, *Italy* 32 C6
Pavlikeni, *Bulgaria* 38 F8
Pavlodar, *Kazakhstan* 44 D8
Pavlograd, *Ukraine* 42 B6
Pavlovo, *Russia* 41 D13
Pavlovo, *Russia* 45 C12
Pavlovsk, *Russia* 41 F12
Pavlovskaya, *Russia* 43 C8
Pavlovskiy-Posad, *Russia* 41 D11
Pavullo nel Frignano, *Italy* 32 D7
Pawhuska, *U.S.A.* 109 G6
Pawling, *U.S.A.* 107 E11
Pawnee, *U.S.A.* 109 G6
Pawnee City, *U.S.A.* 108 E6
Pawtucket, *U.S.A.* 107 E13
Paximádhia, *Greece* 37 D6
Paxoí, *Greece* 39 K3
Paxton, *Ill., U.S.A.* 104 E1
Paxton, *Nebr., U.S.A.* 108 E4
Payakumbuh, *Indonesia* 56 E2
Payerne, *Switz.* 22 C3
Payette, *U.S.A.* 110 D5
Paymogo, *Spain* 31 H3
Payne Bay = Bellin, *Canada* 97 B13
Payne L., *Canada* 97 C12
Paynes Find, *Australia* 89 E2
Paynesville, *Liberia* 78 D2
Paynesville, *U.S.A.* 108 C7
Paysandú, *Uruguay* 126 C4
Payson, *Ariz., U.S.A.* 111 J8
Payson, *Utah, U.S.A.* 110 F8
Paz →, *Guatemala* 116 D1
Paz, B. la, *Mexico* 114 C2
Pāzanān, *Iran* 65 D6
Pazar, *Turkey* 67 C9
Pazarcık, *Turkey* 66 E7
Pazardzhik, *Bulgaria* 38 G7
Pazin, *Croatia* 33 C10
Pazña, *Bolivia* 124 D4
Pčinja →, *Macedonia* 39 H4
Pe Ell, *U.S.A.* 112 D3
Peabody, *U.S.A.* 107 D14
Peace →, *Canada* 100 B6
Peace Point, *Canada* 100 B6
Peace River, *Canada* 100 B5
Peach Springs, *U.S.A.* 111 J7
Peak, The = Kinder Scout, *U.K.* 12 D6
Peak Downs, *Australia* 90 C4
Peak Downs Mine, *Australia* 90 C4
Peak Hill, *N.S.W., Australia* 91 E4
Peak Hill, *W. Austral., Australia* 89 E2
Peak Ra., *Australia* 90 C4
Peake, *Australia* 91 F2
Peake Cr. →, *Australia* 91 D2
Peale, Mt., *U.S.A.* 111 G9
Pearblossom, *U.S.A.* 113 L9
Pearl →, *U.S.A.* 109 K10
Pearl City, *U.S.A.* 102 H16
Pearsall, *U.S.A.* 109 L5
Pearse I., *Canada* 100 C2
Peary Land, *Greenland* 4 A6
Pease →, *U.S.A.* 109 H5
Pebane, *Mozam.* 83 F4
Pebas, *Peru* 120 D3
Pebble, I., *Falk. Is.* 128 D5
Pebble Beach, *U.S.A.* 112 J5
Peč, *Serbia* 21 N10
Peçanha, *Brazil* 123 E3
Péccioli, *Italy* 32 E7
Pechea, *Romania* 38 D10
Pechenezhin, *Ukraine* 42 B1
Pechenga, *Russia* 44 C4
Pechiguera, Pta., *Canary Is.* 36 F6
Pechnezhskoye Vdkhr., *Ukraine* 42 A7
Pechora →, *Russia* 44 C6
Pechorskaya Guba, *Russia* 44 C6
Pecica, *Romania* 38 C4
Pečka, *Serbia* 21 L9
Pécora, C., *Italy* 34 C1
Pečory, *Russia* 40 C5
Pecos, *U.S.A.* 109 K3
Pecos →, *U.S.A.* 109 L3
Pécs, *Hungary* 21 J8
Pedder, L., *Australia* 90 G4
Peddie, *S. Africa* 85 E4
Pédernales, *Dom. Rep.* 117 C5
Pedieos →, *Cyprus* 37 D12
Pedirka, *Australia* 91 D2
Pedra Azul, *Brazil* 123 E3
Pedra Grande, Recifes de, *Brazil* 123 E4
Pedras Negras, *Brazil* 125 C5
Pedreiras, *Brazil* 122 B3
Pedro Afonso, *Brazil* 122 C2
Pedro Cays, *Jamaica* 116 C4
Pedro Chico, *Colombia* 120 C3
Pedro de Valdivia, *Chile* 126 A2
Pedro Juan Caballero, *Paraguay* 127 A4
Pedro Muñoz, *Spain* 29 F2
Pedrógão Grande, *Portugal* 30 F2
Peebinga, *Australia* 91 E3
Peebles, *U.K.* 14 F5
Peekskill, *U.S.A.* 107 E11
Peel, *U.K.* 12 C3
Peel →, *Australia* 91 E5
Peel →, *Canada* 96 B6
Peene →, *Germany* 18 A9
Peera Peera Poolanna L., *Australia* 91 D2
Peers, *Canada* 100 C5
Pegasus Bay, *N.Z.* 87 K4
Pegnitz, *Germany* 19 F7
Pegnitz →, *Germany* 19 F6
Pego, *Spain* 29 G4
Pegu, *Burma* 61 L20
Pegu Yoma, *Burma* 61 K19
Pehuajó, *Argentina* 126 D3
Pei Xian, *China* 50 G9
Peine, *Chile* 126 A2
Peine, *Germany* 18 C6
Peip'ing = Beijing, *China* 50 E9
Peissenberg, *Germany* 19 H7
Peitz, *Germany* 18 D10
Peixe, *Brazil* 123 D2
Peixe →, *Brazil* 123 F1
Peixoto de Azeredo →, *Brazil* 125 C6
Peize, *Neths.* 16 B8
Pek →, *Serbia* 21 L11
Pekalongan, *Indonesia* 57 G13
Pekan, *Malaysia* 59 L4
Pekanbaru, *Indonesia* 56 D2
Pekin, *U.S.A.* 108 E10
Peking = Beijing, *China* 50 E9
Pelabuhan Kelang, *Malaysia* 59 L3
Pelabuhan Ratu, Teluk, *Indonesia* 57 G12
Pelabuhanratu, *Indonesia* 57 G12
Pélagos, *Greece* 39 K7
Pelaihari, *Indonesia* 56 E4
Pelat, Mt., *France* 27 D10
Peleaga, *Romania* 38 D5
Pelechuco, *Bolivia* 124 C4
Pelée, Mt., *Martinique* 117 D7
Pelee, Pt., *Canada* 98 D3
Pelee I., *Canada* 98 D3
Pelejo, *Peru* 124 B2
Pelekech, *Kenya* 82 B4
Peleng, *Indonesia* 57 E6
Pelham, *U.S.A.* 105 K3
Pelhřimov, *Czech.* 20 F5
Pelican L., *Canada* 101 C8
Pelican Narrows, *Canada* 101 B8
Pelican Rapids, *Canada* 101 C8
Pelkosenniemi, *Finland* 8 C19
Pella, *S. Africa* 84 D2
Pella, *U.S.A.* 108 E8
Péllaro, *Italy* 35 D8
Pellworm, *Germany* 18 A4
Pelly →, *Canada* 96 B6
Pelly Bay, *Canada* 97 B11
Pelly L., *Canada* 96 B9
Peloponnese = Pelopónnisos □, *Greece* 39 M5
Pelopónnisos □, *Greece* 39 M5
Peloritani, Monti, *Italy* 35 D8
Peloro, C., *Italy* 35 D8
Pelorus Sd., *N.Z.* 87 J4
Pelotas, *Brazil* 127 C5
Pelvoux, Massif de, *France* 27 D10
Pemalang, *Indonesia* 57 G13
Pematangsiantar, *Indonesia* 56 D1
Pemba, *Mozam.* 83 E5
Pemba, *Zambia* 83 F2
Pemba Channel, *Tanzania* 82 D4
Pemba I., *Tanzania* 82 D4
Pemberton, *Australia* 89 F2
Pemberton, *Canada* 100 C4
Pembina, *N. Dak., U.S.A.* 101 D9
Pembina, *N. Dak., U.S.A.* 108 A6
Pembina →, *U.S.A.* 101 D9
Pembine, *U.S.A.* 104 C2
Pembroke, *Canada* 98 C4
Pembroke, *U.K.* 13 F3
Pembroke, *U.S.A.* 105 J5
Pen-y-Ghent, *U.K.* 12 C5
Peña, Sierra de la, *Spain* 28 C4
Peña de Francia, Sierra de, *Spain* 30 E4
Penafiel, *Portugal* 30 D2
Peñafiel, *Spain* 30 D6
Peñaflor, *Spain* 31 H5
Peñalara, Pico, *Spain* 30 E7
Penalva, *Brazil* 122 B2
Penamacôr, *Portugal* 30 E3
Penang = Pinang, *Malaysia* 59 K3
Penápolis, *Brazil* 127 A6
Peñaranda de Bracamonte, *Spain* 30 E5
Peñarroya-Pueblonuevo, *Spain* 31 G5
Peñas, C. de, *Spain* 30 B5
Penas, G. de, *Chile* 128 C2
Peñas, Pta., *Venezuela* 121 A5
Peñas de San Pedro, *Spain* 29 G2
Peñas del Chache, *Canary Is.* 36 E6
Peñausende, *Spain* 30 D5
Pench'i = Benxi, *China* 51 D12
Pend Oreille →, *U.S.A.* 110 B5
Pend Oreille L., *U.S.A.* 110 C5
Pendembu, *S. Leone* 78 D2
Pendências, *Brazil* 122 C4
Pender B., *Australia* 88 C3
Pendleton, *Calif., U.S.A.* 113 M9
Pendleton, *Oreg., U.S.A.* 110 D4
Penedo, *Brazil* 122 D4
Penetanguishene, *Canada* 98 D4
Peng Xian, *China* 52 B4
Pengalengan, *Indonesia* 57 G12
Penge, *Kasai Or., Zaïre* 82 D1
Penge, *Kivu, Zaïre* 82 C2
Penglai, *China* 51 F11
Pengshui, *China* 52 C7
Penguin, *Australia* 90 G4
Pengxi, *China* 52 B5
Pengze, *China* 53 C11
Penhalonga, *Zimbabwe* 83 F3
Peniche, *Portugal* 31 F1
Penicuik, *U.K.* 14 F5
Penida, *Indonesia* 56 F5
Peninsular Malaysia □, *Malaysia* 59 L4
Peñíscola, *Spain* 28 E5
Penitente, Serra dos, *Brazil* 122 C2
Penmarch, *France* 24 E2
Penmarch, Pte. de, *France* 24 E2
Penn Hills, *U.S.A.* 106 F5
Penn Yan, *U.S.A.* 106 D7
Pennabilli, *Italy* 33 E9
Pennant, *Canada* 101 C7
Penne, *Italy* 33 F10
Penner →, *India* 60 M12
Pennine, Alpi, *Alps* 32 B4
Pennines, *U.K.* 12 C5
Pennington, *U.S.A.* 112 F5
Pennino, Mte., *Italy* 33 E9
Pennsylvania □, *U.S.A.* 104 E6
Penny, *Canada* 100 C4
Peno, *Russia* 40 C8
Penola, *Australia* 91 F3
Penong, *Australia* 89 F5
Penonomé, *Panama* 116 E3
Penrith, *Australia* 91 E5
Penrith, *U.K.* 12 C5
Pensacola, *U.S.A.* 105 K2
Pensacola Mts., *Antarctica* 5 E1
Pense, *Canada* 101 C8
Penshurst, *Australia* 91 F3
Pentecoste, *Brazil* 122 B4
Penticton, *Canada* 100 D5
Pentland, *Australia* 90 C4
Pentland Firth, *U.K.* 14 C5
Pentland Hills, *U.K.* 14 F5
Penylan L., *Canada* 101 A7
Penza, *Russia* 41 E14
Penzance, *U.K.* 13 G2
Penzberg, *Germany* 19 H7
Penzhino, *Russia* 45 C17
Penzhinskaya Guba, *Russia* 45 C17
Penzlin, *Germany* 18 B9
Peoria, *Ariz., U.S.A.* 111 K7
Peoria, *Ill., U.S.A.* 108 E10
Pepingen, *Belgium* 17 G4
Pepinster, *Belgium* 17 G7
Pera Hd., *Australia* 90 A3
Perabumilih, *Indonesia* 56 E2
Perakhóra, *Greece* 39 L5
Perales de Alfambra, *Spain* 28 E3
Perales del Puerto, *Spain* 30 E4
Peralta, *Spain* 28 C3
Pérama, *Kérkira, Greece* 37 A3
Pérama, *Kríti, Greece* 37 D6
Percé, *Canada* 99 C7
Perche, *France* 24 D8
Perche, Collines du, *France* 24 D7
Percival Lakes, *Australia* 88 D4
Percy, *France* 24 D5
Percy Is., *Australia* 90 C5
Perdido →, *Argentina* 128 B3
Perdido, Mte., *Spain* 26 F4
Perdu, Mt. = Perdido, Mte., *Spain* 26 F4
Pereira, *Colombia* 120 C2
Pereira Barreto, *Brazil* 123 F1
Perekerten, *Australia* 91 E3
Perené →, *Peru* 124 C3
Perenjori, *Australia* 89 E2
Pereslavl-Zalesskiy, *Russia* 41 C11
Pereyaslav Khmelnitskiy, *Ukraine* 40 F7
Pérez, I., *Mexico* 115 C7
Pergamino, *Argentina* 126 C3
Pérgine Valsugano, *Italy* 33 B8
Pérgola, *Italy* 33 E9
Perham, *U.S.A.* 108 B7
Perhentian, Kepulauan, *Malaysia* 59 K4
Periam, *Romania* 38 C3
Péribonca →, *Canada* 99 C5
Péribonca, L., *Canada* 99 B5
Perico, *Argentina* 126 A2
Pericos, *Mexico* 114 B3
Périers, *France* 24 C5
Périgord, *France* 26 D4
Périgueux, *France* 26 C4
Perijá, Sierra de, *Colombia* 120 B3
Peristéra, *Greece* 39 K6
Peristerona →, *Cyprus* 37 D12
Perito Moreno, *Argentina* 128 C2
Peritoró, *Brazil* 122 B3
Perković, *Croatia* 33 E13
Perlas, Arch. de las, *Panama* 116 E4
Perlas, Punta de, *Nic.* 116 D3
Perleberg, *Germany* 18 B7
Perlevka, *Russia* 41 F11
Perm, *Russia* 44 D6
Pernambuco = Recife, *Brazil* 122 C5
Pernambuco □, *Brazil* 122 C4
Pernatty Lagoon, *Australia* 91 E2
Pernik, *Bulgaria* 38 G6
Peron, C., *Australia* 89 E1
Peron Is., *Australia* 88 B5
Peron Pen., *Australia* 89 E1
Péronne, *France* 25 C9
Péronnes, *Belgium* 17 H4
Perosa Argentina, *Italy* 32 D4
Perow, *Canada* 100 C3
Perpendicular Pt., *Australia* 91 E5
Perpignan, *France* 26 F6
Perris, *U.S.A.* 113 M9
Perros-Guirec, *France* 24 D3
Perry, *Fla., U.S.A.* 105 K4
Perry, *Ga., U.S.A.* 105 J4
Perry, *Iowa, U.S.A.* 108 E7
Perry, *Maine, U.S.A.* 105 C12
Perry, *Okla., U.S.A.* 109 G6
Perryton, *U.S.A.* 109 G4
Perryville, *U.S.A.* 109 G10
Perşembe, *Turkey* 67 C7
Perseverancia, *Bolivia* 125 C5
Persia = Iran ■, *Asia* 65 C7
Persian Gulf = Gulf, The, *Asia* 65 E6
Perstorp, *Sweden* 11 H7
Pertek, *Turkey* 67 D8
Perth, *Australia* 89 F2
Perth, *Canada* 98 D4
Perth, *U.K.* 14 E5
Perth Amboy, *U.S.A.* 107 F10
Pertuis, *France* 27 E9
Peru, *Ill., U.S.A.* 108 E10
Peru, *Ind., U.S.A.* 104 E2
Peru ■, *S. Amer.* 120 D2
Peru-Chile Trench, *Pac. Oc.* 93 K20
Perúgia, *Italy* 33 E9
Perušić, *Croatia* 33 D12
Péruwelz, *Belgium* 17 G3
Pervomaysk, *Russia* 41 D13
Pervomaysk, *Ukraine* 42 B4
Pervouralsk, *Russia* 44 D6
Perwez, *Belgium* 17 G5
Pes, Pta. del, *Spain* 36 C7
Pésaro, *Italy* 33 E9
Pescara, *Italy* 33 F11
Pescara →, *Italy* 33 F11
Peschanokopskoye, *Russia* 43 C9
Péscia, *Italy* 32 E7
Pescina, *Italy* 33 G10
Peseux, *Switz.* 22 C3
Peshawar, *Pakistan* 62 B4
Peshtigo, *U.S.A.* 104 C2
Peski, *Russia* 41 F13
Peskovka, *Russia* 41 B18
Pêso da Régua, *Portugal* 30 D3
Pesqueira, *Brazil* 122 C4
Pessac, *France* 26 D3
Pessoux, *Belgium* 17 H6
Pestovo, *Russia* 40 B9
Pestravka, *Russia* 41 E16
Petah Tiqwa, *Israel* 69 C3
Petaling Jaya, *Malaysia* 59 L3
Petaloudhes, *Greece* 37 C10
Petaluma, *U.S.A.* 112 G4
Petange, *Lux.* 17 J7
Petatlán, *Mexico* 114 D4
Petauke, *Zambia* 83 E3
Petawawa, *Canada* 98 C4
Petegem, *Belgium* 17 G3
Petén Itzá, L., *Guatemala* 116 C2
Peter I.s Øy, *Antarctica* 5 C16
Peter Pond L., *Canada* 101 B7
Peterbell, *Canada* 98 C3
Peterborough, *Australia* 91 E2
Peterborough, *Canada* 97 D12

Peterborough, U.K. 13 E7
Peterborough, U.S.A. 107 D13
Peterhead, U.K. 14 D7
Petermann Bjerg, Greenland 94 B17
Peter's Mine, Guyana 121 B6
Petersburg, Alaska, U.S.A. 100 B2
Petersburg, Ind., U.S.A. 104 F2
Petersburg, Va., U.S.A. 104 G7
Petersburg, W. Va., U.S.A. 104 F6
Petford, Australia 90 B3
Petília Policastro, Italy 35 C9
Petit Bois I., U.S.A. 105 K1
Petit-Cap, Canada 99 C7
Petit Goâve, Haiti 117 C5
Petit Lac Manicouagan, Canada 99 B6
Petit Saint Bernard, Col du, Italy 32 C3
Petitcodiac, Canada 99 C6
Petite Baleine →, Canada 98 A4
Petite Saguenay, Canada 99 C5
Petitsikapau, L., Canada 99 B6
Petlad, India 62 H5
Peto, Mexico 115 C7
Petone, N.Z. 87 J5
Petoskey, U.S.A. 104 C3
Petra, Jordan 69 E4
Petra, Spain 36 B10
Petra, Ostrova, Russia 4 B13
Petra Velikogo, Zaliv, Russia 48 C5
Petralia, Italy 35 E7
Petrel, Spain 29 G4
Petreto-Bicchisano, France 27 G12
Petrich, Bulgaria 39 H6
Petrijanec, Croatia 33 B13
Petrikov, Belorussia 40 E6
Petrinja, Croatia 33 C13
Petrograd = Sankt-Peterburg, Russia 40 B7
Petrolândia, Brazil 122 C4
Petrolia, Canada 98 D3
Petrolina, Brazil 122 C3
Petropavlovsk, Kazakhstan 44 D7
Petropavlovsk-Kamchatskiy, Russia 45 D16
Petropavlovskiy = Akhtubinsk, Russia 43 B12
Petrópolis, Brazil 123 F3
Petroşeni, Romania 38 D6
Petrova Gora, Croatia 33 C12
Petrovac, Montenegro 21 N8
Petrovsk, Russia 41 E14
Petrovsk-Zabaykalskiy, Russia 45 D11
Petrovskoye = Svetlograd, Russia 43 D10
Petrozavodsk, Russia 44 C4
Petrus Steyn, S. Africa 85 D4
Petrusburg, S. Africa 84 D4
Petukhovka, Belorussia 40 E7
Peumo, Chile 126 C1
Peureulak, Indonesia 56 D1
Pevek, Russia 45 C18
Peveragno, Italy 32 D4
Peyrehorade, France 26 E2
Peyruis, France 27 D9
Pézenas, France 26 E7
Pfaffenhofen, Germany 19 G7
Pfäffikon, Switz. 23 B7
Pfarrkirchen, Germany 19 G8
Pfeffenhausen, Germany 19 G7
Pforzheim, Germany 19 G4
Pfullendorf, Germany 19 H5
Pfungstadt, Germany 19 F4
Phagwara, India 60 D9
Phaistós, Greece 37 D6
Phala, Botswana 84 C4
Phalera = Phulera, India 62 F6
Phalodi, India 62 F5
Phalsbourg, France 25 D14
Phan, Thailand 58 C2
Phan Rang, Vietnam 59 G7
Phan Ri = Hoa Da, Vietnam 59 G7
Phan Thiet, Vietnam 59 G7
Phanat Nikhom, Thailand 58 F3
Phangan, Ko, Thailand 59 H3
Phangnga, Thailand 59 H2
Phanh Bho Ho Chi Minh, Vietnam 59 G6
Phanom Sarakham, Thailand 58 F3
Pharenda, India 63 F10
Phatthalung, Thailand 59 J3
Phayao, Thailand 58 C2
Phelps, N.Y., U.S.A. 106 D7
Phelps, Wis., U.S.A. 108 B10
Phelps L., Canada 101 B8
Phenix City, U.S.A. 105 J3
Phet Buri, Thailand 58 F2
Phetchabun, Thailand 58 D3
Phetchabun, Thiu Khao, Thailand 58 E3
Phetchaburi = Phet Buri, Thailand 58 F2
Phi Phi, Ko, Thailand 59 J2
Phiafay, Laos 58 E6
Phibun Mangsahan, Thailand 58 E5
Phichai, Thailand 58 D3
Phichit, Thailand 58 D3
Philadelphia, Miss., U.S.A. 109 J10
Philadelphia, N.Y., U.S.A. 107 B9
Philadelphia, Pa., U.S.A. 107 F9
Philip, U.S.A. 108 C4
Philippeville, Belgium 17 H5
Philippi L., Australia 90 C2
Philippines ■, Asia 55 F5
Philippolis, S. Africa 84 E4
Philippopolis = Plovdiv, Bulgaria 38 G7
Philipsburg, Mont., U.S.A. 110 C7
Philipsburg, Pa., U.S.A. 106 F6
Philipstown, S. Africa 84 E3
Phillip I., Australia 91 F4
Phillips, Tex., U.S.A. 109 H4
Phillips, Wis., U.S.A. 108 C9
Phillipsburg, Kans., U.S.A. 108 F5
Phillipsburg, N.J., U.S.A. 107 F9
Phillott, Australia 91 D4
Philmont, U.S.A. 107 D11
Philomath, U.S.A. 110 D2
Phimai, Thailand 58 E4
Phitsanulok, Thailand 58 D3
Phnom Dangrek, Thailand 58 E5
Phnom Penh, Cambodia 59 G5
Phoenix, Ariz., U.S.A. 111 K7
Phoenix, N.Y., U.S.A. 107 C8
Phoenix Is., Kiribati 92 H10
Phoenixville, U.S.A. 107 F9
Phon, Thailand 58 E4
Phon Tiou, Laos 58 D5
Phong →, Thailand 58 D4
Phong Saly, Laos 58 B4
Phong Tho, Vietnam 58 A4
Phonhong, Laos 58 C4
Phonum, Thailand 59 H2
Phosphate Hill, Australia 90 C2
Photharam, Thailand 58 F2
Phra Chedi Sam Ong, Thailand 58 E2
Phra Nakhon Si Ayutthaya, Thailand 58 E3
Phra Thong, Ko, Thailand 59 H2
Phrae, Thailand 58 C3
Phrom Phiram, Thailand 58 D3
Phrygia, Turkey 66 D3
Phu Dien, Vietnam 58 C5
Phu Loi, Laos 58 B4
Phu Ly, Vietnam 58 B5
Phu Tho, Vietnam 58 B5
Phuc Yen, Vietnam 58 B5
Phuket, Thailand 59 J2
Phuket, Ko, Thailand 59 J2
Phulera, India 62 F6
Phumiphon, Khuan, Thailand 58 D2
Phun Phin, Thailand 59 H2
Piacá, Brazil 122 C2
Piacenza, Italy 32 C6
Piaçubaçu, Brazil 122 D4
Piádena, Italy 32 C7
Pialba, Australia 91 D5
Pian Cr. →, Australia 91 E4
Piana, France 27 F12
Pianella, Italy 33 F11
Pianoro, Italy 33 D8
Pianosa, Puglia, Italy 33 F12
Pianosa, Toscana, Italy 32 F7
Piapot, Canada 101 D7
Piare →, Italy 33 C9
Pias, Portugal 31 G3
Piaseczno, Poland 20 C11
Piatã, Brazil 123 D3
Piatra, Romania 38 F8
Piatra Neamţ, Romania 38 C9
Piauí □, Brazil 122 C3
Piaui →, Brazil 122 C3
Piave →, Italy 33 C9
Piazza Ármerina, Italy 35 E7
Pibor →, Sudan 77 F3
Pibor Post, Sudan 77 F3
Pica, Chile 124 E4
Picardie, France 25 C9
Picardie, Plaine de, France 25 C9
Picardy = Picardie, France 25 C9
Picayune, U.S.A. 109 K10
Picerno, Italy 35 B8
Pichilemu, Chile 126 C1
Pichincha, □, Ecuador 120 D2
Pickerel L., Canada 98 C1
Pickle Lake, Canada 98 B1
Pico Truncado, Argentina 128 C3
Picos, Brazil 122 C3
Picos Ancares, Sierra de, Spain 30 C4
Picota, Peru 124 B2
Picquigny, France 25 C9
Picton, Australia 91 E5
Picton, Canada 98 D4
Picton, N.Z. 87 J5
Picton, I., Chile 128 E3
Pictou, Canada 99 C7
Picture Butte, Canada 100 D6
Picuí, Brazil 122 C4
Picún Leufú, Argentina 128 A3
Pidurutalagala, Sri Lanka 60 R12
Piedecuesta, Colombia 120 B3
Piedicavallo, Italy 32 C4
Piedmont = Piemonte □, Italy 32 D4
Piedmont, U.S.A. 105 J3
Piedmont Plateau, U.S.A. 105 J5
Piedmonte d'Alife, Italy 35 A7
Piedra →, Spain 28 D3
Piedra del Anguila, Argentina 128 B2
Piedra Lais, Venezuela 120 C4
Piedrabuena, Spain 31 F6
Piedrahita, Spain 30 E5
Piedras, R. de las →, Peru 124 C4
Piedras Negras, Mexico 114 B4
Piemonte □, Italy 32 D4
Pierce, U.S.A. 110 C6
Piercefield, U.S.A. 107 B10
Pierre, U.S.A. 108 C4
Pierre Bénite, Barrage de la, France 27 C8
Pierre-de-Bresse, France 27 B9
Pierrefeu-du-Var, France 27 E10
Pierrefonds, France 25 C9
Pierrefontaine-les-Varans, France 25 E13
Pierrefort, France 26 D6
Pierrelatte, France 27 D8
Pieštany, Slovak Rep. 20 G7
Piesting →, Austria 21 G6
Piet Retief, S. Africa 85 D5
Pietarsaari = Jakobstad, Finland 8 E17
Pietermaritzburg, S. Africa 85 D5
Pietersburg, S. Africa 85 C4
Pietraperzia, Italy 35 E7
Pietrasanta, Italy 32 E7
Pietrosu, Romania 38 B8
Pietrosul, Romania 38 B7
Pieve di Cadore, Italy 33 B9
Pieve di Teco, Italy 32 D4
Pievepélago, Italy 32 D7
Pigádhia, Greece 39 P10
Pigeon, U.S.A. 104 D4
Piggott, U.S.A. 109 G9
Pigna, Italy 32 E4
Pigüe, Argentina 126 D3
Pihani, India 63 F9
Pijnacker, Neths. 16 D4
Pikalevo, Russia 40 B9
Pikes Peak, U.S.A. 108 F2
Piketberg, S. Africa 84 E2
Pikeville, U.S.A. 104 G4
Pikou, China 51 E12
Pikwitonei, Canada 101 B9
Piła, Poland 20 B6
Pila, Spain 29 G3
Pilani, India 62 E6
Pilar, Brazil 122 C4
Pilar, Paraguay 126 B4
Pilas Group, Phil. 57 C6
Pilaya →, Bolivia 125 E5
Pilcomayo →, Paraguay 126 B4
Pilibhit, India 63 E8
Pilica →, Poland 20 D11
Pilkhawa, India 62 E7
Pillaro, Ecuador 120 D2
Pílos, Greece 39 N4
Pilot Mound, Canada 101 D9
Pilot Point, U.S.A. 109 J6
Pilot Rock, U.S.A. 110 D4
Pilsen = Plzeň, Czech. 20 F3
Pilštanj, Slovenia 33 B12
Pima, U.S.A. 111 K9
Pimba, Australia 91 E2
Pimenta Bueno, Brazil 125 C5
Pimentel, Peru 124 B2
Pina, Spain 28 D4
Pinamalayan, Phil. 55 E4
Pinang, Malaysia 59 K3
Pinar, C. del, Spain 36 B10
Pinar del Río, Cuba 116 B3
Pinarbaşi, Turkey 66 D7
Pinchang, China 52 B6
Pincher Creek, Canada 100 D6
Pinchi L., Canada 100 C4
Pinckneyville, U.S.A. 108 F10
Pîncota, Romania 38 C4
Pind Dadan Khan, Pakistan 62 C5
Pindar, Australia 89 E2
Pindaré →, Brazil 122 B3
Pindaré Mirim, Brazil 122 B2
Pindi Gheb, Pakistan 62 C5
Pindiga, Nigeria 79 D7
Pindobal, Brazil 122 B2
Pindos Óros, Greece 39 K4
Pindus Mts. = Pindos Óros, Greece 39 K4
Pine, U.S.A. 111 J8
Pine →, Canada 101 B7
Pine, C., Canada 99 C9
Pine Bluff, U.S.A. 109 H8
Pine City, U.S.A. 108 C8
Pine Falls, Canada 101 C9
Pine Flat L., U.S.A. 112 J7
Pine Pass, Canada 100 B4
Pine Point, Canada 100 A6
Pine Ridge, U.S.A. 108 D3
Pine River, Canada 101 C8
Pine River, U.S.A. 108 B7
Pine Valley, U.S.A. 113 N10
Pinecrest, U.S.A. 112 G6
Pinedale, U.S.A. 112 J7
Pinega →, Russia 44 C5
Pinehill, Australia 90 C4
Pinerolo, Italy 32 D4
Pineto, Italy 33 F11
Pinetop, U.S.A. 111 J9
Pinetown, S. Africa 85 D5
Pinetree, U.S.A. 110 E11
Pineville, Ky., U.S.A. 105 G4
Pineville, La., U.S.A. 109 K8
Piney, France 25 D11
Ping →, Thailand 58 E3
Pingaring, Australia 89 F2
Pingba, China 52 D6
Pingchuan, China 52 D3
Pingding, China 50 F7
Pingdingshan, China 50 H7
Pingdong, Taiwan 53 F13
Pingdu, China 51 F10
Pingelly, Australia 89 F2
Pingguo, China 52 F6
Pinghe, China 53 E11
Pinghu, China 53 B13
Pingjiang, China 53 C9
Pingle, China 53 E8
Pingli, China 52 A7
Pingliang, China 50 G4
Pinglu, China 50 E7
Pingluo, China 50 E4
Pingnan, Fujian, China 53 D12
Pingnan, Guangxi Zhuangzu, China 53 F8
Pingquan, China 51 D10
Pingrup, Australia 89 F2
Pingtan, China 53 E12
Pingtang, China 52 E6
Pingwu, China 50 H3
Pingxiang, Guangxi Zhuangzu, China 52 F6
Pingxiang, Jiangxi, China 53 D9
Pingyao, China 50 F7
Pingyi, China 51 G9
Pingyin, China 50 F9
Pingyuan, Guangdong, China 53 E10
Pingyuan, Shandong, China 50 F9
Pingyuanjie, China 52 F4
Pinhal, Brazil 127 A6
Pinheiro, Brazil 122 B2
Pinhel, Portugal 30 E3
Pinhuá →, Brazil 125 B4
Pini, Indonesia 56 D1
Piniós →, Ilía, Greece 39 M4
Piniós →, Trikkala, Greece 39 K5
Pinjarra, Australia 89 F2
Pink →, Canada 101 B8
Pinnacles, Australia 89 E3
Pinnacles, U.S.A. 112 J5
Pinnaroo, Australia 91 F3
Pinneberg, Germany 18 B5
Pino Hachado, Paso, S. Amer. 128 A2
Pinon Hills, U.S.A. 113 L9
Pinos, Mexico 114 C4
Pinos, Mt., U.S.A. 113 L7
Pinos Pt., U.S.A. 111 H3
Pinos Puente, Spain 31 H7
Pinotepa Nacional, Mexico 115 D5
Pinrang, Indonesia 57 E5
Pinsk, Belorussia 40 E5
Pintados, Chile 124 E4
Pintumba, Australia 89 F5
Pinyang, China 53 D13
Pinyug, Russia 44 C5
Pinzolo, Italy 32 B7
Pio XII, Brazil 122 B2
Pioche, U.S.A. 111 H6
Piombino, Italy 32 F7
Piombino, Canale di, Italy 32 F7
Pioner, Os., Russia 45 B10
Pionki, Poland 20 D11
Piorini →, Brazil 121 D5
Piorini, L., Brazil 121 D5
Piotrków Trybunalski, Poland 20 D9
Piove di Sacco, Italy 33 C9
Pīp, Iran 65 E9
Pipar, India 62 F5
Piparia, India 62 H8
Pipestone, U.S.A. 108 D6
Pipestone →, Canada 98 B2
Pipestone Cr. →, Canada 101 D8
Pipmuacan, Rés., Canada 99 C5
Pippingarra, Australia 88 D2
Pipriac, France 24 E5
Piqua, U.S.A. 104 E3
Piquet Carneiro, Brazil 122 C4
Piquiri →, Brazil 127 A5
Pīr Sohrāb, Iran 65 E9
Piracanjuba, Brazil 123 E2
Piracicaba, Brazil 127 A6
Piracuruca, Brazil 122 B3
Piræus = Piraiévs, Greece 39 M6
Piraiévs, Greece 39 M6
Piráino, Italy 35 D7
Pirajuí, Brazil 127 A6
Piran, Slovenia 33 C10
Piranė, Argentina 126 B4
Piranhas, Brazil 122 C4
Pirano = Piran, Slovenia 33 C10
Pirapemas, Brazil 122 B3
Pirapora, Brazil 123 E3
Piray →, Bolivia 125 D5
Pires do Rio, Brazil 123 E2
Pírgos, Ilía, Greece 39 M4
Pírgos, Messinia, Greece 39 N5
Pirgovo, Bulgaria 38 F8
Piriac-sur-Mer, France 24 E4
Piribebuy, Paraguay 126 B4
Pirin Planina, Bulgaria 39 H6
Pirineos, Spain 28 C6
Piripiri, Brazil 122 B3
Piritu, Venezuela 120 B4
Pirmasens, Germany 19 F3
Pirna, Germany 18 E9
Pirot, Serbia 21 M12
Piru, Indonesia 57 E7
Piru, U.S.A. 113 L8
Piryatin, Ukraine 40 F8
Pisa, Italy 32 E7
Pisac, Peru 124 C3
Pisagua, Chile 124 D3
Pisarovina, Croatia 33 C12
Pisciotta, Italy 35 B8
Pisco, Peru 124 C2
Písek, Czech. 20 F4
Pishan, China 54 C2
Pishin Lora →, Pakistan 62 E1
Pisidia, Turkey 66 E4
Pising, Indonesia 57 F6
Pismo Beach, U.S.A. 113 K6
Pissos, France 26 D3
Pissouri, Cyprus 37 E11
Pisticci, Italy 35 B9
Pistóia, Italy 32 E7
Pistol B., Canada 101 A10
Pisuerga →, Spain 30 D6
Pisz, Poland 20 B11
Pitalito, Colombia 120 C2
Pitanga, Brazil 123 F1
Pitangui, Brazil 123 E3
Pitarpunga, L., Australia 91 E3
Pitcairn I., Pac. Oc. 93 K14
Pite älv →, Sweden 8 D16
Piteå, Sweden 8 D16
Piterka, Russia 41 F15
Piteşti, Romania 38 E7
Pithapuram, India 61 L13
Pithara, Australia 89 F2
Píthion, Greece 39 H9
Pithiviers, France 25 D9
Pitigliano, Italy 33 F8
Pitlochry, U.K. 14 E5
Pitrufquén, Chile 128 A2
Pitsilia □, Cyprus 37 E12
Pitt I., Canada 100 C3
Pittem, Belgium 17 F2
Pittsburg, Kans., U.S.A. 109 G7
Pittsburg, Tex., U.S.A. 109 J7
Pittsburgh, U.S.A. 106 F5
Pittsfield, Ill., U.S.A. 108 F9
Pittsfield, Mass., U.S.A. 107 D11
Pittsfield, N.H., U.S.A. 107 C13
Pittston, U.S.A. 107 E9
Pittsworth, Australia 91 D5
Pituri →, Australia 90 C2
Piuí, Brazil 123 F2
Pium, Brazil 122 D2
Piura, Peru 124 B1
Piura □, Peru 124 A2
Pivijay, Colombia 120 A3
Pixley, U.S.A. 112 K7
Piyai, Greece 39 K4
Pizarro, Colombia 120 C2
Pizol, Switz. 23 C8
Pizzo, Italy 35 D9
Placentia, Canada 99 C9
Placentia B., Canada 99 C9
Placer, Phil. 55 F5
Placerville, U.S.A. 112 G6
Placetas, Cuba 116 B4
Plaffeien, Switz. 22 C4
Plain Dealing, U.S.A. 109 J8
Plainfield, U.S.A. 107 F10
Plains, Kans., U.S.A. 109 G4
Plains, Mont., U.S.A. 110 C6
Plains, Tex., U.S.A. 109 J3
Plainview, Nebr., U.S.A. 108 D6
Plainview, Tex., U.S.A. 109 H4
Plainville, U.S.A. 108 F5
Plainwell, U.S.A. 104 D3
Plaisance, France 26 E4
Pláka, Greece 39 J8
Pláka, Ákra, Greece 37 D8
Plakhino, Russia 44 C9
Plana Cays, Bahamas 117 B5
Planada, U.S.A. 112 H6
Plancoët, France 24 D4
Plandište, Serbia 21 K11
Planeta Rica, Colombia 120 B2
Planina, Slovenia 33 B12
Planina, Slovenia 33 C11
Plankinton, U.S.A. 108 D5
Plano, U.S.A. 109 J6
Plant City, U.S.A. 105 L4
Plaquemine, U.S.A. 109 K9
Plasencia, Spain 30 E4
Plaški, Croatia 33 C12
Plaster City, U.S.A. 113 N11
Plaster Rock, Canada 99 C6
Plastun, Russia 48 B8
Plata, Río de la, S. Amer. 126 C4
Platani →, Italy 34 E6
Plátanos, Greece 37 D5
Plateau □, Nigeria 79 D6
Plateau du Coteau du Missouri, U.S.A. 108 B4
Plato, Colombia 120 B3
Platta, Piz, Switz. 23 D9
Platte, U.S.A. 108 D5
Platte →, U.S.A. 108 F7
Platteville, U.S.A. 108 E2
Plattling, Germany 19 G8
Plattsburgh, U.S.A. 107 B11
Plattsmouth, U.S.A. 108 E7
Plau, Germany 18 B8
Plauen, Germany 18 E8
Plavinas, Latvia 40 C4
Plavnica, Montenegro 21 N9
Plavsk, Russia 41 E10
Playa Blanca, Canary Is. 36 F6
Playa Blanca Sur, Canary Is. 36 F6

Playa de las Americas

Playa de las Americas, *Canary Is.* 36 F3
Playa de Mogán, *Canary Is.* 36 G4
Playa del Inglés, *Canary Is.* 36 G4
Playa Esmerelda, *Canary Is.* 36 F5
Playgreen L., *Canada* 101 C9
Pleasant Bay, *Canada* 99 C7
Pleasant Hill, *Calif., U.S.A.* 112 H4
Pleasant Hill, *Mo., U.S.A.* 108 F7
Pleasanton, *U.S.A.* 109 L5
Pleasantville, *U.S.A.* 104 F8
Pléaux, *France* 26 C6
Pleiku, *Vietnam* 58 F7
Plélan-le-Grand, *France* 24 D4
Plémet-la-Pierre, *France* 24 D4
Pléneuf-Val-André, *France* 24 D4
Plenița, *Romania* 38 E6
Plenty →, *Australia* 90 C2
Plenty, B. of, *N.Z.* 87 G6
Plentywood, *U.S.A.* 108 A2
Plessisville, *Canada* 99 C5
Plestin-les-Grèves, *France* 24 D3
Pleszew, *Poland* 20 D7
Pleternica, *Croatia* 21 K7
Pletipi L., *Canada* 99 B5
Pleven, *Bulgaria* 38 F7
Plevlja, *Montenegro* 21 M9
Płock, *Poland* 20 C9
Plöcken Passo, *Italy* 33 B9
Ploegsteert, *Belgium* 17 G1
Ploemeur, *France* 24 E3
Ploërmel, *France* 24 E4
Ploiești, *Romania* 38 E9
Plombières-les-Bains, *France* 25 E13
Plomin, *Croatia* 33 C11
Plön, *Germany* 18 A6
Plöner See, *Germany* 18 A6
Plonge, Lac la, *Canada* 101 B7
Płońsk, *Poland* 20 C10
Płoty, *Poland* 20 B5
Plouaret, *France* 24 D3
Plouay, *France* 24 E3
Ploudalmézeau, *France* 24 D2
Plougasnou, *France* 24 D3
Plouha, *France* 24 D4
Plouhinec, *France* 24 E2
Plovdiv, *Bulgaria* 38 G7
Plum, *U.S.A.* 106 F5
Plum I., *U.S.A.* 107 E12
Plumas, *U.S.A.* 112 F7
Plummer, *U.S.A.* 110 C5
Plumtree, *Zimbabwe* 83 G2
Plunge, *Lithuania* 40 D2
Pluvigner, *France* 24 E3
Plymouth, *U.K.* 13 G3
Plymouth, *Calif., U.S.A.* 112 G6
Plymouth, *Ind., U.S.A.* 104 E2
Plymouth, *Mass., U.S.A.* 107 E14
Plymouth, *N.C., U.S.A.* 105 H7
Plymouth, *N.H., U.S.A.* 107 C13
Plymouth, *Pa., U.S.A.* 107 E9
Plymouth, *Wis., U.S.A.* 104 D2
Plynlimon = Pumlumon Fawr, *U.K.* 13 E4
Plyussa, *Russia* 40 B6
Plyussa →, *Russia* 40 B6
Plzeň, *Czech.* 20 F3
Pniewy, *Poland* 20 C6
Pô, *Burkina Faso* 79 C4
Po →, *Italy* 33 D9
Po, Foci del, *Italy* 33 D9
Po Hai = Bo Hai, *China* 51 E10
Pobé, *Benin* 79 D5
Pobeda, *Russia* 45 C15
Pobedino, *Russia* 45 E15
Pobedy Pik, *Kirghizia* 44 E8
Pobiedziska, *Poland* 20 C7
Pobla de Segur, *Spain* 28 C5
Pobladura de Valle, *Spain* 30 C5
Pocahontas, *Ark., U.S.A.* 109 G9
Pocahontas, *Iowa, U.S.A.* 108 D7
Pocatello, *U.S.A.* 110 E7
Pochep, *Russia* 40 E8
Pochinki, *Russia* 41 D14
Pochinok, *Russia* 40 D8
Pochutla, *Mexico* 115 D5
Poci, *Venezuela* 121 B5
Poconhos, *Brazil* 122 C4
Pocito Casas, *Mexico* 114 B2
Poções, *Brazil* 123 D3
Pocomoke City, *U.S.A.* 104 F8
Poconé, *Brazil* 125 D6
Poços de Caldas, *Brazil* 127 A6
Poddebice, *Poland* 20 D8
Poděbrady, *Czech.* 20 E5
Podensac, *France* 26 D3
Podgorica, *Montenegro* 21 N9
Podkamennaya Tunguska →, *Russia* 45 C10
Podlapac, *Croatia* 33 D12
Podolsk, *Russia* 41 D10
Podor, *Senegal* 78 B1
Podravska Slatina, *Croatia* 21 K7
Podujevo, *Serbia* 21 N11
Poel, *Germany* 18 B7
Pofadder, *S. Africa* 84 D2
Pogamasing, *Canada* 98 C3
Poggiardo, *Italy* 35 B11
Poggibonsi, *Italy* 33 E8
Pogoanele, *Romania* 38 E9
Pogradeci, *Albania* 39 J3
Pogranitšnyi, *Russia* 48 B5
Poh, *Indonesia* 57 E6
Pohang, *S. Korea* 51 F15
Pohnpei, *Pac. Oc.* 92 G7
Pohorelá, *Slovak Rep.* 20 G10
Pohorje, *Slovenia* 33 B12
Poiana Mare, *Romania* 38 F6
Poinsett, C., *Antarctica* 5 C8
Point Edward, *Canada* 98 D3
Point Pedro, *Sri Lanka* 60 Q12
Point Pleasant, *N.J., U.S.A.* 107 F10
Point Pleasant, *W. Va., U.S.A.* 104 F4
Pointe-à-la Hache, *U.S.A.* 109 L10
Pointe-à-Pitre, *Guadeloupe* 117 C7
Pointe Noire, *Congo* 80 E2
Poirino, *Italy* 32 D4
Poisonbush Ra., *Australia* 88 D3
Poissy, *France* 25 D9
Poitiers, *France* 24 F7
Poitou, *France* 26 B3
Poitou, Seuil du, *France* 26 B4
Poix de Picardie, *France* 25 C8
Poix-Terron, *France* 25 C11
Pojoaque Valley, *U.S.A.* 111 J11
Pokaran, *India* 60 F7
Pokataroo, *Australia* 91 D4
Poko, *Sudan* 77 F3
Poko, *Zaïre* 82 B2
Pokrov, *Russia* 41 D11
Pokrovsk, *Russia* 41 F15
Pokrovsk, *Russia* 45 C13
Pol, *Spain* 30 B3
Pola = Pula, *Croatia* 33 D10
Pola de Allande, *Spain* 30 B4
Pola de Lena, *Spain* 30 B5
Pola de Siero, *Spain* 30 B5
Pola de Somiedo, *Spain* 30 B4
Polacca, *U.S.A.* 111 J8
Polan, *Iran* 65 E9
Poland ■, *Europe* 20 C9
Polanów, *Poland* 20 A6
Polatsk = Polotsk, *Belorussia* 40 D6
Polcura, *Chile* 126 D1
Polden Hills, *U.K.* 13 F5
Polessk, *Russia* 40 D2
Polesye, *Belorussia* 40 E6
Polewali, *Indonesia* 57 E5
Polgar, *Hungary* 21 H11
Pŏlgyo-ri, *S. Korea* 51 G14
Poli, *Cameroon* 80 C2
Políaigos, *Greece* 39 N7
Policastro, G. di, *Italy* 35 C8
Police, *Poland* 20 B4
Polignano a Mare, *Italy* 35 B10
Poligny, *France* 25 F12
Políkhnitas, *Greece* 39 K9
Polillo Is., *Phil.* 55 D4
Polillo Strait, *Phil.* 55 D4
Polis, *Cyprus* 37 D11
Polístena, *Italy* 35 D9
Políyiros, *Greece* 39 J6
Polk, *U.S.A.* 106 E5
Polla, *Italy* 35 B8
Pollachi, *India* 60 P10
Pollensa, *Spain* 36 B10
Pollensa, B. de, *Spain* 36 B10
Póllica, *Italy* 35 B8
Pollino, Mte., *Italy* 35 C9
Pollock, *U.S.A.* 108 C4
Polna, *Russia* 40 B6
Polnovat, *Russia* 44 C7
Polo, *U.S.A.* 108 E10
Pologi, *Ukraine* 42 C7
Polonnoye, *Ukraine* 40 F5
Polotsk, *Belorussia* 40 D6
Polson, *U.S.A.* 110 C6
Poltava, *Ukraine* 42 B6
Polunochnoye, *Russia* 44 C7
Polynesia, *Pac. Oc.* 93 H11
Polynésie française □ = French Polynesia ■, *Pac. Oc.* 93 J13
Pomarance, *Italy* 32 E7
Pomarico, *Italy* 35 B9
Pomaro, *Mexico* 114 D4
Pombal, *Brazil* 122 C4
Pombal, *Portugal* 30 F2
Pómbia, *Greece* 37 D6
Pomeroy, *Ohio, U.S.A.* 104 F4
Pomeroy, *Wash., U.S.A.* 110 C5
Pomona, *U.S.A.* 113 L9
Pomorie, *Bulgaria* 38 G10
Pomos, *Cyprus* 37 D11
Pomos, C., *Cyprus* 37 D11
Pomoshnaya, *Ukraine* 42 B4
Pompano Beach, *U.S.A.* 105 M5
Pompei, *Italy* 35 B7
Pompey, *France* 25 D13
Pompeys Pillar, *U.S.A.* 110 D10
Ponape = Pohnpei, *Pac. Oc.* 92 G7
Ponask, L., *Canada* 98 B1
Ponass L., *Canada* 101 C8
Ponca, *U.S.A.* 108 D6
Ponca City, *U.S.A.* 109 G6
Ponce, *Puerto Rico* 117 C6
Ponchatoula, *U.S.A.* 109 K9
Poncheville, L., *Canada* 98 B4
Poncin, *France* 27 B9
Pond, *U.S.A.* 113 K7
Pond Inlet, *Canada* 97 A12
Pondicherry, *India* 60 P11
Pondrôme, *Belgium* 17 H6
Ponds, I. of, *Canada* 99 B8
Ponferrada, *Spain* 30 C4
Pongo, Wadi →, *Sudan* 77 F2
Poniatowa, *Poland* 20 D12
Ponikva, *Slovenia* 33 B12
Ponnani, *India* 60 P9
Ponnyadaung, *Burma* 61 J19
Ponoi →, *Russia* 44 C5
Ponoka, *Canada* 100 C6
Ponorogo, *Indonesia* 57 G14
Pons, *France* 26 C3
Pons, *Spain* 28 D6
Ponsul →, *Portugal* 31 F3
Pont-à-Celles, *Belgium* 17 G4
Pont-à-Mousson, *France* 25 D13
Pont-Audemer, *France* 24 C7
Pont-Aven, *France* 24 E3
Pont Canavese, *Italy* 32 C4
Pont-de-Roide, *France* 25 E13
Pont-de-Salars, *France* 26 D6
Pont-de-Vaux, *France* 25 F11
Pont-de-Veyle, *France* 27 B8
Pont-l'Abbé, *France* 24 E2
Pont-l'Évêque, *France* 24 C7
Pont-St.-Esprit, *France* 27 D8
Pont-sur-Yonne, *France* 25 D10
Ponta de Pedras, *Brazil* 122 B2
Ponta do Sol, *Madeira* 36 D2
Ponta Grossa, *Brazil* 127 B5
Ponta Pora, *Brazil* 127 A4
Pontacq, *France* 26 E3
Pontailler-sur-Saône, *France* 25 E12
Pontal →, *Brazil* 122 C3
Pontalina, *Brazil* 123 E2
Pontarlier, *France* 25 F13
Pontassieve, *Italy* 33 E8
Pontaubault, *France* 24 D5
Pontaumur, *France* 26 C6
Pontcharra, *France* 27 C10
Pontchartrain L., *U.S.A.* 109 K9
Pontchâteau, *France* 24 E4
Ponte Alta, Serra do, *Brazil* 123 E2
Ponte Alta do Norte, *Brazil* 122 D2
Ponte Branca, *Brazil* 125 D7
Ponte da Barca, *Portugal* 30 D2
Ponte de Sor, *Portugal* 31 F3
Ponte dell 'Olio, *Italy* 32 D6
Ponte di Legno, *Italy* 32 B7
Ponte do Lima, *Portugal* 30 D2
Ponte do Pungué, *Mozam.* 83 F3
Ponte-Leccia, *France* 27 F13
Ponte nell' Alpi, *Italy* 33 B9
Ponte Nova, *Brazil* 123 F3
Ponte San Martino, *Italy* 32 C4
Ponte San Pietro, *Italy* 32 C6
Pontebba, *Italy* 33 B10
Pontecorvo, *Italy* 34 A6
Pontedera, *Italy* 32 E7
Pontefract, *U.K.* 12 D6
Ponteix, *Canada* 101 D7
Pontelandolfo, *Italy* 35 A7
Pontevedra, *Spain* 30 C2
Pontevedra □, *Spain* 30 C2
Pontevedra, R. de →, *Spain* 30 C2
Pontevico, *Italy* 32 C7
Pontiac, *Ill., U.S.A.* 108 E10
Pontiac, *Mich., U.S.A.* 104 D4
Pontian Kecil, *Malaysia* 59 M4
Pontianak, *Indonesia* 56 E3
Pontic Mts. = Kuzey Anadolu Dağları, *Turkey* 66 C6
Pontine Is. = Ponziane, Isole, *Italy* 34 B5
Pontine Mts. = Kuzey Anadolu Dağları, *Turkey* 66 C6
Pontínia, *Italy* 34 A6
Pontivy, *France* 24 D4
Pontoise, *France* 25 C9
Ponton →, *Canada* 100 B5
Pontorson, *France* 24 D5
Pontrémoli, *Italy* 32 D6
Pontresina, *Switz.* 23 D9
Pontrieux, *France* 24 D3
Pontypool, *Canada* 106 B6
Pontypool, *U.K.* 13 F4
Pontypridd, *U.K.* 13 F4
Ponza, *Italy* 34 B5
Ponziane, Isole, *Italy* 34 B5
Poochera, *Australia* 91 E1
Poole, *U.K.* 13 G6
Pooley I., *Canada* 100 C3
Poona = Pune, *India* 60 K8
Pooncarie, *Australia* 91 E3
Poopelloe L., *Australia* 91 E3
Poopó, *Bolivia* 124 D4
Poopó, L. de, *Bolivia* 124 D4
Popanyinning, *Australia* 89 F2
Popayán, *Colombia* 120 C2
Poperinge, *Belgium* 17 G1
Popigay, *Russia* 45 B12
Popilta, L., *Australia* 91 E3
Popio L., *Australia* 91 E3
Poplar, *U.S.A.* 108 A2
Poplar →, *Man., Canada* 101 C9
Poplar →, *N.W.T., Canada* 100 A4
Poplar Bluff, *U.S.A.* 109 G9
Poplarville, *U.S.A.* 109 K10
Popocatepetl, *Mexico* 115 D5
Popokabaka, *Zaïre* 80 F3
Pópoli, *Italy* 33 F10
Popovača, *Croatia* 33 C13
Popovo, *Bulgaria* 38 F9
Poppel, *Belgium* 17 F6
Poprád, *Slovak Rep.* 20 F10
Poprád →, *Slovak Rep.* 20 F10
Porali →, *Pakistan* 62 G2
Porangaba, *Brazil* 124 B3
Porangatu, *Brazil* 123 D2
Porbandar, *India* 62 J3
Porce →, *Colombia* 120 B3
Porcher I., *Canada* 100 C2
Porco, *Bolivia* 125 D4
Porcos →, *Brazil* 123 D2
Porcuna, *Spain* 31 H6
Porcupine →, *Canada* 101 B8
Porcupine →, *U.S.A.* 96 B5
Pordenone, *Italy* 33 C9
Poreč, *Croatia* 33 C10
Porecatu, *Brazil* 123 F1
Poretskoye, *Russia* 41 D15
Pori, *Finland* 9 F16
Porjus, *Sweden* 8 C15
Porkhov, *Russia* 40 C6
Porkkala, *Finland* 9 G18
Porlamar, *Venezuela* 121 A5
Porlezza, *Italy* 32 B6
Porma →, *Spain* 30 C5
Pornic, *France* 24 E4
Poronaysk, *Russia* 45 E15
Póros, *Greece* 39 M6
Poroshiri-Dake, *Japan* 48 C11
Poroto Mts., *Tanzania* 83 D3
Porpoise B., *Antarctica* 5 C9
Porquerolles, I. de, *France* 27 F10
Porrentruy, *Switz.* 22 B4
Porreras, *Spain* 36 B10
Porretta, Passo di, *Italy* 32 D7
Porsangen, *Norway* 8 A18
Porsgrunn, *Norway* 10 E3
Port Adelaide, *Australia* 91 E2
Port Alberni, *Canada* 100 D4
Port Alfred, *Canada* 99 C5
Port Alfred, *S. Africa* 84 E4
Port Alice, *Canada* 100 C3
Port Allegany, *U.S.A.* 106 E6
Port Allen, *U.S.A.* 109 K9
Port Alma, *Australia* 90 C5
Port Angeles, *U.S.A.* 112 B3
Port Antonio, *Jamaica* 116 C4
Port Aransas, *U.S.A.* 109 M6
Port Arthur = Lüshun, *China* 51 E11
Port Arthur, *Australia* 90 G4
Port Arthur, *U.S.A.* 109 L8
Port au Port B., *Canada* 99 C8
Port-au-Prince, *Haiti* 117 C5
Port Augusta, *Australia* 91 E2
Port Augusta West, *Australia* 91 E2
Port Austin, *U.S.A.* 98 D3
Port Bell, *Uganda* 82 B3
Port Bergé Vaovao, *Madag.* 85 B8
Port Blandford, *Canada* 99 C9
Port Bou, *Spain* 28 C8
Port Bouët, *Ivory C.* 78 D4
Port Bradshaw, *Australia* 90 A2
Port Broughton, *Australia* 91 E2
Port Burwell, *Canada* 98 D3
Port Canning, *India* 63 H13
Port-Cartier, *Canada* 99 B6
Port Chalmers, *N.Z.* 87 L3
Port Chester, *U.S.A.* 107 F11
Port Clements, *Canada* 100 C2
Port Clinton, *U.S.A.* 104 E4
Port Colborne, *Canada* 98 D4
Port Coquitlam, *Canada* 100 D4
Port Credit, *Canada* 106 C5
Port Curtis, *Australia* 90 C5
Port Dalhousie, *Canada* 106 C5
Port Darwin, *Australia* 88 B5
Port Darwin, *Falk. Is.* 128 D5
Port Davey, *Australia* 90 G4
Port-de-Bouc, *France* 27 E8
Port-de-Paix, *Haiti* 117 C5
Port Dickson, *Malaysia* 59 L3
Port Douglas, *Australia* 90 B4
Port Dover, *Canada* 106 D4
Port Edward, *Canada* 100 C2
Port Elgin, *Canada* 98 D3
Port Elizabeth, *S. Africa* 84 E4
Port Ellen, *U.K.* 14 F2
Port-en-Bessin, *France* 24 C6
Port Erin, *I. of Man* 12 C3
Port Essington, *Australia* 88 B5
Port Etienne = Nouâdhibou, *Mauritania* 74 D1
Port Fairy, *Australia* 91 F3
Port Fouâd = Bûr Fuad, *Egypt* 76 H8
Port Gamble, *U.S.A.* 112 C4
Port-Gentil, *Gabon* 80 E1
Port Gibson, *U.S.A.* 109 K9
Port Glasgow, *U.K.* 14 F4
Port Harcourt, *Nigeria* 79 E6
Port Hardy, *Canada* 100 C3
Port Harrison = Inoucdjouac, *Canada* 97 C12
Port Hawkesbury, *Canada* 99 C7
Port Hedland, *Australia* 88 D2
Port Henry, *U.S.A.* 107 B11
Port Hood, *Canada* 99 C7
Port Hope, *Canada* 98 D4
Port Hueneme, *U.S.A.* 113 L7
Port Huron, *U.S.A.* 104 D4
Port Isabel, *U.S.A.* 109 M6
Port Jefferson, *U.S.A.* 107 F11
Port Jervis, *U.S.A.* 107 E10
Port-Joinville, *France* 24 F4
Port Katon, *Russia* 43 C8
Port Kelang = Pelabuhan Kelang, *Malaysia* 59 L3
Port Kembla, *Australia* 91 E5
Port Kenny, *Australia* 91 E1
Port-la-Nouvelle, *France* 26 E7
Port Laoise, *Ireland* 15 C4
Port Lavaca, *U.S.A.* 109 L6
Port-Leucate, *France* 26 F7
Port Lincoln, *Australia* 91 E2
Port Loko, *S. Leone* 78 D2
Port Louis, *France* 24 E3
Port Lyautey = Kenitra, *Morocco* 74 B3
Port MacDonnell, *Australia* 91 F3
Port Macquarie, *Australia* 91 E5
Port Maria, *Jamaica* 116 C4
Port Mellon, *Canada* 100 D4
Port-Menier, *Canada* 99 C7
Port Morant, *Jamaica* 116 C4
Port Moresby, *Papua N. G.* 92 H6
Port Mourant, *Guyana* 121 B6
Port Mouton, *Canada* 99 D7
Port Musgrave, *Australia* 90 A3
Port-Navalo, *France* 24 E4
Port Nelson, *Canada* 101 B10
Port Nolloth, *S. Africa* 84 D2
Port Nouveau-Québec, *Canada* 97 C13
Port O'Connor, *U.S.A.* 109 L6
Port of Spain, *Trin. & Tob.* 117 D7
Port Orchard, *U.S.A.* 112 C4
Port Orford, *U.S.A.* 110 E1
Port Pegasus, *N.Z.* 87 M1
Port Perry, *Canada* 98 D4
Port Phillip B., *Australia* 91 F3
Port Pirie, *Australia* 91 E2
Port Radium = Echo Bay, *Canada* 96 B8
Port Renfrew, *Canada* 100 D4
Port Roper, *Australia* 90 A2
Port Rowan, *Canada* 98 D3
Port Safaga = Bûr Safâga, *Egypt* 76 B3
Port Said = Bûr Sa'îd, *Egypt* 76 H8
Port St. Joe, *U.S.A.* 105 L3
Port St. Johns, *S. Africa* 85 E4
Port-St.-Louis-du-Rhône, *France* 27 E8
Port San Vicente, *Phil.* 55 B5
Port Sanilac, *U.S.A.* 98 D3
Port Saunders, *Canada* 99 B8
Port Severn, *Canada* 106 B5
Port Shepstone, *S. Africa* 85 E5
Port Simpson, *Canada* 100 C2
Port Stanley = Stanley, *Falk. Is.* 128 D5
Port Stanley, *Canada* 98 D3
Port Sudan = Bûr Sûdân, *Sudan* 76 D4
Port-sur-Saône, *France* 25 E13
Port Talbot, *U.K.* 13 F4
Port Taufiq = Bûr Taufiq, *Egypt* 76 J8
Port Townsend, *U.S.A.* 112 B4
Port-Vendres, *France* 26 F7
Port Wakefield, *Australia* 91 E2
Port Washington, *U.S.A.* 104 D2
Port Weld, *Malaysia* 59 K3
Portachuelo, *Bolivia* 125 D5
Portadown, *U.K.* 15 B5
Portage, *U.S.A.* 108 D10
Portage La Prairie, *Canada* 101 D9
Portageville, *U.S.A.* 109 G10
Portalegre, *Portugal* 31 F3
Portalegre □, *Portugal* 31 F3
Portales, *U.S.A.* 109 H3
Portarlington, *Ireland* 15 C4
Porteirinha, *Brazil* 123 E3
Portel, *Brazil* 122 B1
Portel, *Portugal* 31 G3
Porter L., *N.W.T., Canada* 101 A7
Porter L., *Sask., Canada* 101 B7
Porterville, *S. Africa* 84 E2
Porterville, *U.S.A.* 111 H4
Porthcawl, *U.K.* 13 F4
Porthill, *U.S.A.* 110 B5
Portile de Fier, *Europe* 38 E5
Portimão, *Portugal* 31 H2
Portland, *N.S.W., Australia* 91 E4
Portland, *Vic., Australia* 91 F3
Portland, *Canada* 107 B8
Portland, *Conn., U.S.A.* 107 E12
Portland, *Maine, U.S.A.* 99 D5
Portland, *Mich., U.S.A.* 104 D3
Portland, *Oreg., U.S.A.* 112 E4
Portland, I. of, *U.K.* 13 G5
Portland B., *Australia* 91 F3
Portland Bill, *U.K.* 13 G5
Portland Prom., *Canada* 97 C12
Portlands Roads, *Australia* 90 A3
Portneuf, *Canada* 99 C5
Pôrto, *Brazil* 122 B3
Porto, *France* 27 F12
Porto, *Portugal* 30 D2
Porto □, *Portugal* 30 D2
Porto, G. de, *France* 27 F12
Pôrto Acre, *Brazil* 124 B4
Pôrto Alegre, *Pará, Brazil* 121 D7
Pôrto Alegre, *Rio Grande do S., Brazil* 127 C5

Porto Amboim = Gunza, *Angola* **80 G2**
Porto Argentera, *Italy* **32 D4**
Porto Azzurro, *Italy* **32 F7**
Porto Botte, *Italy* **34 C1**
Pôrto Cajueiro, *Brazil* **125 C6**
Porto Civitanova, *Italy* **33 E10**
Porto Cristo, *Spain* **36 B10**
Pôrto da Fôlha, *Brazil* **122 C4**
Pôrto de Móz, *Brazil* **121 D7**
Pôrto de Pedras, *Brazil* **122 C4**
Pôrto des Meinacos, *Brazil* **125 C7**
Porto Empédocle, *Italy* **34 E6**
Pôrto Esperança, *Brazil* **125 D6**
Pôrto Esperidão, *Brazil* **125 D6**
Pôrto Franco, *Brazil* **122 C2**
Pôrto Garibaldi, *Italy* **33 D9**
Pôrto Grande, *Brazil* **121 C7**
Pôrto Jofre, *Brazil* **125 D6**
Pórto Lágo, *Greece* **39 J8**
Pôrto Mendes, *Brazil* **127 A5**
Porto Moniz, *Madeira* **36 D2**
Pôrto Murtinho, *Brazil* **125 E6**
Pôrto Nacional, *Brazil* **122 D2**
Porto Novo, *Benin* **79 D5**
Porto Petro, *Spain* **36 B10**
Porto Recanati, *Italy* **33 E10**
Porto San Giórgio, *Italy* **33 E10**
Pôrto Santana, *Brazil* **121 D7**
Porto Santo, *Madeira* **72 B1**
Porto Santo Stefano, *Italy* **32 F8**
Pôrto São José, *Brazil* **127 A5**
Pôrto Seguro, *Brazil* **123 E4**
Porto Tolle, *Italy* **33 D9**
Porto Tórres, *Italy* **34 B1**
Pôrto União, *Brazil* **127 B5**
Pôrto Válter, *Brazil* **124 B3**
Porto-Vecchio, *France* **27 G13**
Pôrto Velho, *Brazil* **125 B5**
Portobelo, *Panama* **116 E4**
Portoferráio, *Italy* **32 F7**
Portogruaro, *Italy* **33 C9**
Portola, *U.S.A.* **112 F6**
Portomaggiore, *Italy* **33 D8**
Portoscuso, *Italy* **34 C1**
Portovénere, *Italy* **32 D6**
Portovíejo, *Ecuador* **120 D1**
Portpatrick, *U.K.* **14 G3**
Portree, *U.K.* **14 D2**
Portrush, *U.K.* **15 A5**
Portsall, *France* **24 D2**
Portsmouth, *Domin.* **117 C7**
Portsmouth, *U.K.* **13 G6**
Portsmouth, *N.H., U.S.A.* **107 C14**
Portsmouth, *Ohio, U.S.A.* **104 F4**
Portsmouth, *R.I., U.S.A.* **107 E13**
Portsmouth, *Va., U.S.A.* **104 G7**
Portsoy, *U.K.* **14 D6**
Porttipahta, *Finland* **8 B19**
Portugal ■, *Europe* **30 F3**
Portugalete, *Spain* **28 B1**
Portuguesa □, *Venezuela* **120 B4**
Portuguese-Guinea = Guinea-Bissau ■, *Africa* **78 C2**
Portumna, *Ireland* **15 C3**
Portville, *U.S.A.* **106 D6**
Porvenir, *Bolivia* **124 C4**
Porvenir, *Chile* **128 D2**
Porvoo = Borgå, *Finland* **9 F18**
Porzuna, *Spain* **31 F6**
Posada →, *Italy* **34 B2**
Posadas, *Argentina* **127 B4**
Posadas, *Spain* **31 H5**
Poschiavo, *Switz.* **23 D10**
Posets, *Spain* **28 C5**
Poshan = Boshan, *China* **51 F9**
Posht-e-Badam, *Iran* **65 C7**
Posídhion, Ákra, *Greece* **39 K6**
Poso, *Indonesia* **57 E6**
Posoegroenoe, *Surinam* **121 C6**
Posong, *S. Korea* **51 G14**
Posse, *Brazil* **123 D2**
Possel, *C.A.R.* **80 C3**
Possession I., *Antarctica* **5 D11**
Pössneck, *Germany* **18 E7**
Post, *U.S.A.* **109 J4**
Post Falls, *U.S.A.* **110 C5**
Postavy, *Belorussia* **40 D5**
Poste Maurice Cortier, *Algeria* **75 D5**
Postmasburg, *S. Africa* **84 D3**
Postojna, *Slovenia* **33 C11**
Poston, *U.S.A.* **113 M12**
Potchefstroom, *S. Africa* **84 D4**
Poté, *Brazil* **123 E3**
Poteau, *U.S.A.* **109 H7**
Poteet, *U.S.A.* **109 L5**
Potelu, Lacul, *Romania* **38 F7**
Potenza, *Italy* **35 B8**
Potenza →, *Italy* **33 E10**
Potenza Picena, *Italy* **33 E10**
Poteriteri, L., *N.Z.* **87 M1**
Potes, *Spain* **30 B6**
Potgietersrus, *S. Africa* **85 C4**
Poti, *Georgia* **43 E9**
Potiraguá, *Brazil* **123 E4**
Potiskum, *Nigeria* **79 C7**
Potomac →, *U.S.A.* **104 F7**
Potosí, *Bolivia* **125 D4**
Potosí □, *Bolivia* **124 E4**
Potosi Mt., *U.S.A.* **113 K11**
Pototan, *Phil.* **55 F5**
Potrerillos, *Chile* **126 B2**
Potsdam, *Germany* **18 C9**
Potsdam, *U.S.A.* **107 B10**
Pottenstein, *Germany* **19 F7**
Potter, *U.S.A.* **108 E3**
Pottery Hill = Abû Ballas, *Egypt* **76 C2**
Pottstown, *U.S.A.* **107 F9**
Pottsville, *U.S.A.* **107 F8**
Pottuvil, *Sri Lanka* **60 R12**
Pouancé, *France* **24 E5**
Pouce Coupé, *Canada* **100 B4**
Poughkeepsie, *U.S.A.* **107 E11**
Pouilly-sur-Loire, *France* **25 E9**
Poulaphouca Res., *Ireland* **15 C5**
Poulsbo, *U.S.A.* **112 C4**
Pourri, Mt., *France* **27 C10**
Pouso Alegre, *Mato Grosso, Brazil* **125 C6**
Pouso Alegre, *Minas Gerais, Brazil* **127 A6**
Pouzauges, *France* **24 F6**
Povenets, *Russia* **44 C4**
Poverty B., *N.Z.* **87 H7**
Póvoa de Lanhosa, *Portugal* **30 D2**
Póvoa de Varzim, *Portugal* **30 D2**
Povorino, *Russia* **41 F13**
Powassan, *Canada* **98 C4**
Poway, *U.S.A.* **113 N9**
Powder →, *U.S.A.* **108 B2**
Powder River, *U.S.A.* **110 E10**
Powell, *U.S.A.* **110 D9**
Powell L., *U.S.A.* **111 H8**
Powell River, *Canada* **100 D4**
Powers, *Mich., U.S.A.* **104 C2**
Powers, *Oreg., U.S.A.* **110 E1**
Powers Lake, *U.S.A.* **108 A3**
Powys □, *U.K.* **13 E4**
Poxoreu, *Brazil* **125 D7**
Poyang Hu, *China* **53 C11**
Poyarkovo, *Russia* **45 E13**
Poza de la Sal, *Spain* **28 C1**
Poza Rica, *Mexico* **115 C5**
Pozanti, *Turkey* **66 E6**
Požarevac, *Serbia* **21 L11**
Pozi, *Taiwan* **53 F13**
Poznań, *Poland* **20 C6**
Pozo, *U.S.A.* **113 K6**
Pozo Alcón, *Spain* **29 H2**
Pozo Almonte, *Chile* **124 E4**
Pozo Colorado, *Paraguay* **126 A4**
Pozo del Dátil, *Mexico* **114 B2**
Pozoblanco, *Spain* **31 G6**
Pozuzo, *Peru* **124 C2**
Pozzallo, *Italy* **35 F7**
Pozzuoli, *Italy* **35 B7**
Pra →, *Ghana* **79 D4**
Prachin Buri, *Thailand* **58 E3**
Prachuap Khiri Khan, *Thailand* **59 G2**
Pradelles, *France* **26 D7**
Pradera, *Colombia* **120 C2**
Prades, *France* **26 F6**
Prado, *Brazil* **123 E4**
Prado del Rey, *Spain* **31 J5**
Præstø, *Denmark* **11 J6**
Pragersko, *Slovenia* **33 B12**
Prague = Praha, *Czech.* **20 E4**
Praha, *Czech.* **20 E4**
Prahecq, *France* **26 B3**
Prahova →, *Romania* **38 E8**
Prahovo, *Serbia* **21 L12**
Praid, *Romania* **38 C8**
Prainha, *Amazonas, Brazil* **125 B5**
Prainha, *Pará, Brazil* **121 D7**
Prairie, *Australia* **90 C3**
Prairie →, *U.S.A.* **109 H5**
Prairie City, *U.S.A.* **110 D4**
Prairie du Chien, *U.S.A.* **108 D9**
Prairies, *Canada* **96 C9**
Pramánda, *Greece* **39 K4**
Pran Buri, *Thailand* **58 F2**
Prang, *Ghana* **79 D4**
Prapat, *Indonesia* **56 D1**
Prasonísi, Ákra, *Greece* **37 D9**
Prata, *Brazil* **123 E2**
Pratapgarh, *India* **62 G6**
Prática di Mare, *Italy* **34 A5**
Prätigau, *Switz.* **23 C9**
Prato, *Italy* **32 E8**
Prátola Peligna, *Italy* **33 F10**
Pratovécchio, *Italy* **33 E8**
Prats-de-Mollo-la-Preste, *France* **26 F6**
Pratt, *U.S.A.* **109 G5**
Pratteln, *Switz.* **22 A5**
Prattville, *U.S.A.* **105 J2**
Pravdinsk, *Russia* **41 C13**
Pravia, *Spain* **30 B4**
Praya, *Indonesia* **56 F5**
Pré-en-Pail, *France* **24 D6**
Pré St. Didier, *Italy* **32 C4**
Precordillera, *Argentina* **126 C2**
Predáppio, *Italy* **33 D8**
Predazzo, *Italy* **33 B8**
Predejane, *Serbia* **21 N12**
Preeceville, *Canada* **101 C8**
Préfailles, *France* **24 E4**
Pregonero, *Venezuela* **120 B3**
Pregrada, *Croatia* **33 B12**
Preko, *Croatia* **33 D12**
Prelate, *Canada* **101 C7**
Prelog, *Croatia* **33 B13**
Premier, *Canada* **100 B3**
Premont, *U.S.A.* **109 M5**
Premuda, *Croatia* **33 D11**
Prenjasi, *Albania* **39 H3**
Prentice, *U.S.A.* **108 C9**
Prenzlau, *Germany* **18 B9**
Preobrazheniye, *Russia* **48 C6**
Prepansko Jezero, *Macedonia* **39 J4**
Preparis North Channel, *Ind. Oc.* **61 M18**
Preparis South Channel, *Ind. Oc.* **61 M18**
Přerov, *Czech.* **20 F7**
Presanella, *Italy* **32 B7**
Prescott, *Canada* **98 D4**
Prescott, *Ariz., U.S.A.* **111 J7**
Prescott, *Ark., U.S.A.* **109 J8**
Preservation Inlet, *N.Z.* **87 M1**
Preševo, *Serbia* **21 N11**
Presho, *U.S.A.* **108 D4**
Presicce, *Italy* **35 C11**
Presidencia de la Plaza, *Argentina* **126 B4**
Presidencia Roque Saenz Peña, *Argentina* **126 B3**
Presidente Epitácio, *Brazil* **123 F1**
Presidente Hayes □, *Paraguay* **126 A4**
Presidente Hermes, *Brazil* **125 C5**
Presidente Prudente, *Brazil* **127 A5**
Presidio, *Mexico* **114 B4**
Presidio, *U.S.A.* **109 L2**
Preslav, *Bulgaria* **38 F9**
Prešov, *Slovak Rep.* **20 F11**
Prespa, L. = Prepansko Jezero, *Macedonia* **39 J4**
Presque Isle, *U.S.A.* **99 C6**
Prestbury, *U.K.* **13 F5**
Prestea, *Ghana* **78 D4**
Presteigne, *U.K.* **13 E5**
Presto, *Bolivia* **125 D5**
Preston, *Canada* **106 C4**
Preston, *U.K.* **12 D5**
Preston, *Idaho, U.S.A.* **110 E8**
Preston, *Minn., U.S.A.* **108 D8**
Preston, *Nev., U.S.A.* **110 G6**
Preston, C., *Australia* **88 D2**
Prestonpans, *U.K.* **14 F6**
Prestwick, *U.K.* **14 F4**
Prêto →, *Amazonas, Brazil* **121 D5**
Prêto →, *Bahia, Brazil* **122 D3**
Prêto do Igapó-Açu →, *Brazil* **121 D6**
Pretoria, *S. Africa* **85 D4**
Preuilly-sur-Claise, *France* **24 F7**
Préveza, *Greece* **39 L3**
Priazovskoye, *Ukraine* **42 C6**
Pribilof Is., *Bering S.* **4 D17**
Priboj, *Serbia* **21 M9**
Příbram, *Czech.* **20 F4**
Price, *U.S.A.* **110 G8**
Price I., *Canada* **100 C3**
Prichalnaya, *Russia* **43 B11**
Prichard, *U.S.A.* **105 K1**
Priego, *Spain* **28 E2**
Priego de Córdoba, *Spain* **31 H6**
Priekule, *Latvia* **40 C2**
Prien, *Germany* **19 H8**
Prieska, *S. Africa* **84 D3**
Priest →, *U.S.A.* **110 B5**
Priest L., *U.S.A.* **110 B5**
Priest Valley, *U.S.A.* **112 J6**
Priestly, *Canada* **100 C3**
Prievidza, *Slovak Rep.* **20 G8**
Prijedor, *Bos.-H.* **33 D13**
Prikaspiyskaya Nizmennost, *Asia* **43 C13**
Prilep, *Macedonia* **39 H4**
Priluki, *Ukraine* **40 F8**
Prime Seal I., *Australia* **90 G4**
Primeira Cruz, *Brazil* **122 B3**
Primorsko-Akhtarsk, *Russia* **42 C8**
Primorskoye, *Ukraine* **42 C7**
Primrose L., *Canada* **101 C7**
Prince Albert, *Canada* **101 C7**
Prince Albert, *S. Africa* **84 E3**
Prince Albert Mts., *Antarctica* **5 D11**
Prince Albert Nat. Park, *Canada* **101 C7**
Prince Albert Pen., *Canada* **96 A8**
Prince Albert Sd., *Canada* **96 A8**
Prince Alfred, C., *Canada* **4 B1**
Prince Charles I., *Canada* **97 B12**
Prince Charles Mts., *Antarctica* **5 D6**
Prince Edward I. □, *Canada* **99 C7**
Prince Edward Is., *Ind. Oc.* **3 G11**
Prince George, *Canada* **100 C4**
Prince of Wales, C., *U.S.A.* **94 C3**
Prince of Wales I., *Australia* **90 A3**
Prince of Wales I., *Canada* **96 A10**
Prince of Wales I., *U.S.A.* **100 B2**
Prince Patrick I., *Canada* **4 B2**
Prince Regent Inlet, *Canada* **4 B3**
Prince Rupert, *Canada* **100 C2**
Princenhage, *Neths.* **17 F5**
Princesa Isabel, *Brazil* **122 C4**
Princess Charlotte B., *Australia* **90 A3**
Princess May Ras., *Australia* **88 C4**
Princess Royal I., *Canada* **100 C3**
Princeton, *Canada* **100 D4**
Princeton, *Calif., U.S.A.* **112 F4**
Princeton, *Ill., U.S.A.* **108 E10**
Princeton, *Ind., U.S.A.* **104 F2**
Princeton, *Ky., U.S.A.* **104 G2**
Princeton, *Mo., U.S.A.* **108 E8**
Princeton, *N.J., U.S.A.* **107 F10**
Princeton, *W. Va., U.S.A.* **104 G5**
Principe, I. de, *Atl. Oc.* **70 F4**
Principe Chan., *Canada* **100 C2**
Principe da Beira, *Brazil* **125 C5**
Prineville, *U.S.A.* **110 D3**
Prins Harald Kyst, *Antarctica* **5 D4**
Prinsesse Astrid Kyst, *Antarctica* **5 D3**
Prinsesse Ragnhild Kyst, *Antarctica* **5 D4**
Prinzapolca, *Nic.* **116 D3**
Prior, C., *Spain* **30 B2**
Pripet = Pripyat →, *Europe* **40 F7**
Pripet Marshes = Polesye, *Belorussia* **40 E6**
Pripyat →, *Europe* **40 F7**
Pripyat Marshes = Polesye, *Belorussia* **40 E6**
Prislop, Pasul, *Romania* **38 B8**
Pristen, *Russia* **41 F10**
Priština, *Serbia* **21 N11**
Pritzwalk, *Germany* **18 B8**
Privas, *France* **27 D8**
Priverno, *Italy* **34 A6**
Privolzhsk, *Russia* **41 C12**
Privolzhskaya Vozvyshennost, *Russia* **41 F15**
Privolzhskiy, *Russia* **41 F15**
Privolzhye, *Russia* **41 E16**
Priyutnoye, *Russia* **43 C10**
Prizren, *Serbia* **21 N10**
Prizzi, *Italy* **34 E6**
Prnjavor, *Bos.-H.* **21 L7**
Probolinggo, *Indonesia* **57 G15**
Procida, *Italy* **35 B7**
Proddatur, *India* **60 M11**
Prodhromos, *Cyprus* **37 E11**
Proença-a-Nova, *Portugal* **31 F3**
Prof. Van Blommestein Meer, *Surinam* **121 C6**
Profítis Ilías, *Greece* **37 C9**
Profondeville, *Belgium* **17 H5**
Progreso, *Mexico* **115 C7**
Prokhladnyy, *Russia* **43 E11**
Prokletije, *Albania* **38 G2**
Prokopyevsk, *Russia* **44 D9**
Prokuplje, *Serbia* **21 M11**
Proletarskaya, *Russia* **43 C9**
Prome = Pyè, *Burma* **61 K19**
Prophet →, *Canada* **100 B4**
Propriá, *Brazil* **122 D4**
Propriano, *France* **27 G12**
Proserpine, *Australia* **90 C4**
Prosser, *U.S.A.* **110 C4**
Prostějov, *Czech.* **20 F7**
Proston, *Australia* **91 D5**
Protection, *U.S.A.* **109 G5**
Próti, *Greece* **39 M4**
Provadiya, *Bulgaria* **38 F10**
Proven, *Belgium* **17 G1**
Provence, *France* **27 E9**
Providence, *Ky., U.S.A.* **104 G2**
Providence, *R.I., U.S.A.* **107 E13**
Providence Bay, *Canada* **98 C3**
Providence Mts., *U.S.A.* **111 J6**
Providencia, *Ecuador* **120 D2**
Providencia, I. de, *Colombia* **116 D3**
Provideniya, *Russia* **45 C19**
Provins, *France* **25 D10**
Provo, *U.S.A.* **110 F8**
Provost, *Canada* **101 C6**
Prozor, *Bos.-H.* **21 M7**
Prudentópolis, *Brazil* **123 G1**
Prud'homme, *Canada* **101 C7**
Prudnik, *Poland* **20 E7**
Prüm, *Germany* **19 E2**
Pruszcz Gdański, *Poland* **20 A8**
Pruszków, *Poland* **20 C10**
Prut →, *Romania* **38 D11**
Pruzhany, *Belorussia* **40 E4**
Prvič, *Croatia* **33 D11**
Prydz B., *Antarctica* **5 C6**
Pryluky = Priluki, *Ukraine* **40 F8**
Pryor, *U.S.A.* **109 G7**
Przasnysz, *Poland* **20 B10**
Przedbórz, *Poland* **20 D9**
Przemysl, *Poland* **20 F12**
Przeworsk, *Poland* **20 E12**
Przewóz, *Poland* **20 D4**
Przhevalsk, *Kirghizia* **44 E8**
Przysuchla, *Poland* **20 D10**
Psakhná, *Greece* **39 L6**
Psará, *Greece* **39 L8**
Psel →, *Ukraine* **42 B5**
Pserimos, *Greece* **39 N10**
Psíra, *Greece* **37 D7**
Pskov, *Russia* **40 C6**
Psunj, *Croatia* **21 K7**
Pszczyna, *Poland* **20 F8**
Pteleón, *Greece* **39 K5**
Ptich →, *Belorussia* **40 E6**
Ptolemaís, *Greece* **39 J4**
Ptuj, *Slovenia* **33 B12**
Ptujska Gora, *Slovenia* **33 B12**
Pu Xian, *China* **50 F6**
Pua, *Thailand* **58 C3**
Puán, *Argentina* **126 D3**
Pu'an, *China* **52 E5**
Puan, *S. Korea* **51 G14**
Pubei, *China* **52 F7**
Pucacuro →, *Peru* **120 D3**
Pucallpa, *Peru* **124 B3**
Pucará, *Bolivia* **125 D5**
Pucará, *Peru* **124 D3**
Pucarani, *Bolivia* **124 D4**
Pucheng, *China* **53 D12**
Pučišće, *Croatia* **33 E13**
Pucka, Zatoka, *Poland* **20 A8**
Puding, *China* **52 D5**
Pudukkottai, *India* **60 P11**
Puebla, *Mexico* **115 D5**
Puebla □, *Mexico* **115 D5**
Puebla de Alcocer, *Spain* **31 G5**
Puebla de Don Fadrique, *Spain* **29 H2**
Puebla de Don Rodrigo, *Spain* **31 F6**
Puebla de Guzmán, *Spain* **31 H3**
Puebla de Sanabria, *Spain* **30 C4**
Puebla de Trives, *Spain* **30 C3**
Puebla del Caramiñal, *Spain* **30 C2**
Pueblo, *U.S.A.* **108 F2**
Pueblo Hundido, *Chile* **126 B1**
Pueblo Nuevo, *Venezuela* **120 B3**
Puelches, *Argentina* **126 D2**
Puelén, *Argentina* **126 D2**
Puente Alto, *Chile* **126 C1**
Puente del Arzobispo, *Spain* **30 F5**
Puente-Genil, *Spain* **31 H6**
Puente la Reina, *Spain* **28 C3**
Puenteareas, *Spain* **30 C2**
Puentedeume, *Spain* **30 B2**
Puentes de Garcia Rodriguez, *Spain* **30 B3**
Pu'er, *China* **52 F3**
Puerco →, *U.S.A.* **111 J10**
Puerto, *Canary Is.* **36 F2**
Puerto Acosta, *Bolivia* **124 D4**
Puerto Aisén, *Chile* **128 C2**
Puerto Ángel, *Mexico* **115 D5**
Puerto Arista, *Mexico* **115 D6**
Puerto Armuelles, *Panama* **116 E3**
Puerto Ayacucho, *Venezuela* **120 B4**
Puerto Barrios, *Guatemala* **116 C2**
Puerto Bermejo, *Argentina* **126 B4**
Puerto Bermúdez, *Peru* **124 C3**
Puerto Bolívar, *Ecuador* **120 D2**
Puerto Cabello, *Venezuela* **120 A4**
Puerto Cabezas, *Nic.* **116 D3**
Puerto Cabo Gracias á Dios, *Nic.* **116 D3**
Puerto Capaz = Jebba, *Morocco* **74 A4**
Puerto Carreño, *Colombia* **120 B4**
Puerto Castilla, *Honduras* **116 C2**
Puerto Chicama, *Peru* **124 B2**
Puerto Coig, *Argentina* **128 D3**
Puerto Cortes, *Costa Rica* **116 E3**
Puerto Cortés, *Honduras* **116 C2**
Puerto Cumarebo, *Venezuela* **120 A4**
Puerto de Alcudia, *Spain* **36 B10**
Puerto de Andraitx, *Spain* **36 B9**
Puerto de Cabrera, *Spain* **36 B9**
Puerto de Gran Tarajal, *Canary Is.* **36 F5**
Puerto de la Cruz, *Canary Is.* **36 F3**
Puerto de Pozo Negro, *Canary Is.* **36 F6**
Puerto de Santa María, *Spain* **31 J4**
Puerto de Sóller, *Spain* **36 B9**
Pto. del Carmen, *Canary Is.* **36 F6**
Puerto del Rosario, *Canary Is.* **36 F6**
Puerto Deseado, *Argentina* **128 C3**
Puerto Guaraní, *Paraguay* **125 E6**
Puerto Heath, *Bolivia* **124 C4**
Puerto Huitoto, *Colombia* **120 C3**
Puerto Inca, *Peru* **124 B3**
Puerto Juárez, *Mexico* **115 C7**
Puerto La Cruz, *Venezuela* **121 A5**
Puerto Leguízamo, *Colombia* **120 D3**
Puerto Limón, *Colombia* **120 C3**
Puerto Lobos, *Argentina* **128 B3**
Puerto López, *Colombia* **120 C3**
Puerto Lumbreras, *Spain* **29 H3**
Puerto Madryn, *Argentina* **128 B3**
Puerto Maldonado, *Peru* **124 C4**
Puerto Manotí, *Cuba* **116 B4**
Puerto Mazarrón, *Spain* **29 H3**
Puerto Mercedes, *Colombia* **120 C3**
Puerto Miraña, *Colombia* **120 D3**
Puerto Montt, *Chile* **128 B2**
Puerto Morelos, *Mexico* **115 C7**
Puerto Nariño, *Colombia* **120 C4**
Puerto Natales, *Chile* **128 D2**
Puerto Nuevo, *Colombia* **120 B4**
Puerto Nutrias, *Venezuela* **120 B4**
Puerto Ordaz, *Venezuela* **121 B5**
Puerto Padre, *Cuba* **116 B4**
Puerto Páez, *Venezuela* **120 B4**
Puerto Peñasco, *Mexico* **114 A2**
Puerto Pinasco, *Paraguay* **126 A4**
Puerto Pirámides, *Argentina* **128 B4**

Puerto Plata, *Dom. Rep.* 117 C5
Puerto Pollensa, *Spain* 36 B10
Puerto Portillo, *Peru* 124 B3
Puerto Princesa, *Phil.* 55 G3
Puerto Quellón, *Chile* 128 B2
Puerto Quepos, *Costa Rica* 116 E3
Puerto Real, *Spain* 31 J4
Puerto Rico, *Bolivia* 124 C4
Puerto Rico, *Canary Is.* 36 G4
Puerto Rico ■, *W. Indies* 117 C6
Puerto Rico Trench, *Atl. Oc.* 117 C6
Puerto Saavedra, *Chile* 128 A2
Puerto Sastre, *Paraguay* 126 A4
Puerto Siles, *Bolivia* 125 C4
Puerto Suárez, *Bolivia* 125 D6
Puerto Tejada, *Colombia* 120 C2
Puerto Umbría, *Colombia* 120 C2
Puerto Vallarta, *Mexico* 114 C3
Puerto Varas, *Chile* 128 B2
Puerto Villazón, *Bolivia* 125 C5
Puerto Wilches, *Colombia* 120 B3
Puertollano, *Spain* 31 G6
Puertomarin, *Spain* 30 C3
Puesto Cunambo, *Peru* 120 D2
Pueyrredón, L., *Argentina* 128 C2
Pugachev, *Kazakhstan* 41 F16
Puge, *China* 52 D4
Puge, *Tanzania* 82 C3
Puget Sound, *U.S.A.* 110 C2
Puget-Théniers, *France* 27 E10
Púglia □, *Italy* 35 B9
Pugŏdong, *N. Korea* 51 C16
Pugu, *Tanzania* 82 D4
Pūgūnzī, *Iran* 65 E8
Pui, *Romania* 38 D6
Puica, *Peru* 124 C3
Puig Mayor, *Spain* 36 B9
Puigcerdá, *Spain* 28 C6
Puigmal, *Spain* 28 C7
Puigpuñent, *Spain* 36 B9
Puisaye, Collines de la, *France* 25 E10
Puiseaux, *France* 25 D9
Pujilí, *Ecuador* 120 D2
Pujon-chosuji, *N. Korea* 51 D14
Puka, *Albania* 38 G2
Pukaki L., *N.Z.* 87 L3
Pukapuka, *Cook Is.* 93 J11
Pukatawagan, *Canada* 101 B8
Pukchin, *N. Korea* 51 D13
Pukchŏng, *N. Korea* 51 D15
Pukekohe, *N.Z.* 87 G5
Pukou, *China* 53 A12
Pula, *Croatia* 33 D10
Pula, *Italy* 34 D2
Pulacayo, *Bolivia* 124 E4
Pulaski, *N.Y., U.S.A.* 107 C8
Pulaski, *Tenn., U.S.A.* 105 H2
Pulaski, *Va., U.S.A.* 104 G5
Pulawy, *Poland* 20 D11
Pulga, *U.S.A.* 112 F5
Pulicat, L., *India* 60 N12
Pullman, *U.S.A.* 110 C5
Pulog, *Phil.* 55 C4
Pułtusk, *Poland* 20 C11
Pülümür, *Turkey* 67 D8
Pumlumon Fawr, *U.K.* 13 E4
Puna, *Bolivia* 125 D4
Puná, I., *Ecuador* 120 D1
Punakha, *Bhutan* 61 F16
Punasar, *India* 62 F5
Punata, *Bolivia* 125 D4
Punch, *India* 63 C6
Pune, *India* 60 K8
Pungsan, *N. Korea* 51 D15
Pungue, Ponte de, *Mozam.* 83 F3
Puning, *China* 53 F11
Punjab □, *India* 62 D6
Punjab □, *Pakistan* 62 E6
Puno, *Peru* 124 D3
Punta Alta, *Argentina* 128 A4
Punta Arenas, *Chile* 128 D2
Punta Cardón, *Venezuela* 120 A3
Punta Coles, *Peru* 124 D3
Punta de Bombón, *Peru* 124 D3
Punta de Díaz, *Chile* 126 B1
Punta Delgado, *Argentina* 128 B4
Punta Gorda, *Belize* 115 D7
Punta Gorda, *U.S.A.* 105 M5
Punta Prieta, *Mexico* 114 B2
Punta Prima, *Spain* 36 B11
Puntabie, *Australia* 91 E1
Puntarenas, *Costa Rica* 116 E3
Punto Fijo, *Venezuela* 120 A3
Punxsatawney, *U.S.A.* 106 F5
Puqi, *China* 53 C9
Puquio, *Peru* 124 C3
Pur →, *Russia* 44 C8
Purace, Vol., *Colombia* 120 C2
Puralia = Puruliya, *India* 63 H12
Purbeck, Isle of, *U.K.* 13 G5
Purcell, *U.S.A.* 109 H6
Purchena Tetica, *Spain* 29 H2
Puri, *India* 61 K14
Purificación, *Colombia* 120 C3
Purmerend, *Neths.* 16 C5
Purnia, *India* 63 G12
Purukcahu, *Indonesia* 56 E4
Puruliya, *India* 63 H12
Purus →, *Brazil* 121 D5
Pŭrvomay, *Bulgaria* 38 G8
Purwakarta, *Indonesia* 57 G12
Purwodadi, *Jawa, Indonesia* 57 G14
Purwodadi, *Jawa, Indonesia* 57 G13
Purwokerto, *Indonesia* 57 G13
Purworejo, *Indonesia* 57 G14
Puryŏng, *N. Korea* 51 C15
Pusan, *S. Korea* 51 G15
Pushchino, *Russia* 45 D16
Pushkin, *Russia* 40 B7
Pushkino, *Russia* 41 F15
Pushkino, *Russia* 41 C10
Püspökladány, *Hungary* 21 H11
Pustoshka, *Russia* 40 C6
Putahow L., *Canada* 101 B8
Putao, *Burma* 61 F20
Putaruru, *N.Z.* 87 H5
Putbus, *Germany* 18 A9
Puthein Myit →, *Burma* 61 M19
Putian, *China* 53 E12
Putignano, *Italy* 35 B10
Putina, *Peru* 124 C4
Puting, Tanjung, *Indonesia* 56 E4
Putlitz, *Germany* 18 B8
Putna →, *Romania* 38 D10
Putnam, *U.S.A.* 107 E13
Putorana, Gory, *Russia* 45 C10
Putre, *Chile* 124 D4
Puttalam, *Sri Lanka* 60 Q11
Putte, *Neths.* 17 F4
Putten, *Neths.* 16 D7
Puttgarden, *Germany* 18 A7
Putumayo →, *S. Amer.* 120 D4
Putuo, *China* 53 C14
Putussibau, *Indonesia* 56 D4
Puurs, *Belgium* 17 F4
Puy-de-Dôme, *France* 26 C6
Puy-de-Dôme □, *France* 26 C7
Puy-Guillaume, *France* 26 C7
Puy-l'Évêque, *France* 26 D5
Puyallup, *U.S.A.* 112 C4
Puyang, *China* 50 G8
Puyehue, *Chile* 128 B2
Puylaurens, *France* 26 E6
Puyo, *Ecuador* 120 D2
Pūzeh Rīg, *Iran* 65 E8
Pwani □, *Tanzania* 82 D4
Pweto, *Zaïre* 83 D2
Pwllheli, *U.K.* 12 E3
Pyana →, *Russia* 41 D15
Pyapon, *Burma* 61 L19
Pyasina →, *Russia* 45 B9
Pyatigorsk, *Russia* 43 D10
Pyatykhatki, *Ukraine* 42 B5
Pyè, *Burma* 61 K19
Pyinmana, *Burma* 61 K20
Pyla, C., *Cyprus* 37 E12
Pyŏktong, *N. Korea* 51 D13
Pyŏnggang, *N. Korea* 51 E14
Pyŏngtaek, *S. Korea* 51 F14
P'yŏngyang, *N. Korea* 51 E13
Pyote, *U.S.A.* 109 K3
Pyramid L., *U.S.A.* 110 G4
Pyramid Pk., *U.S.A.* 113 J10
Pyramids, *Egypt* 76 J7
Pyrénées, *Europe* 26 F4
Pyrénées-Atlantiques □, *France* 26 E3
Pyrénées-Orientales □, *France* 26 F6
Pyrzyce, *Poland* 20 B4
Pyshchug, *Russia* 41 B14
Pytalovo, *Russia* 40 C5
Pyttegga, *Norway* 10 B1
Pyu, *Burma* 61 K20

Q

Qaanaaq = Thule, *Greenland* 4 B4
Qachasnek, *S. Africa* 85 E4
Qādib, *Yemen* 68 E5
Qa'el Jafr, *Jordan* 69 E5
Qa'emābād, *Iran* 65 D9
Qā'emshahr, *Iran* 65 B7
Qagan Nur, *China* 50 C8
Qahar Youyi Zhongqi, *China* 50 D7
Qahremānshahr = Bākhtarān, *Iran* 64 C5
Qaidam Pendi, *China* 54 C4
Qajarīyeh, *Iran* 65 D6
Qala, Ras il, *Malta* 37 C1
Qala-i-Jadid, *Afghan.* 62 D2
Qala Yangi, *Afghan.* 62 B2
Qal'at al Akhḑar, *Si. Arabia* 64 E3
Qal'at Sukkar, *Iraq* 64 D5
Qal'eh Darreh, *Iran* 64 B5
Qal'eh Shaharak, *Afghan.* 60 B4
Qalyūb, *Egypt* 76 H7
Qamar, Ghubbat al, *Yemen* 68 D5
Qamdo, *China* 52 B1
Qamruddin Karez, *Pakistan* 62 D3
Qandahār, *Afghan.* 60 D4
Qandahār □, *Afghan.* 60 D4
Qapān, *Iran* 65 B7
Qaqortoq = Julianehåb, *Greenland* 4 C5
Qâra, *Egypt* 76 B2
Qara Qash →, *India* 63 B8
Qaraghandy = Karaganda, *Kazakhstan* 44 E8
Qārah, *Si. Arabia* 64 D4
Qardud, *Sudan* 77 E2
Qareh →, *Iran* 64 B5
Qareh Tekān, *Iran* 65 B6
Qarqan, *China* 54 C3
Qarqan He →, *China* 54 C3
Qarrasa, *Sudan* 77 E3
Qarshi = Karshi, *Uzbekistan* 44 F7
Qartabā, *Lebanon* 69 A4
Qaryat al Gharab, *Iraq* 64 D5
Qaryat al 'Ulyā, *Si. Arabia* 64 E5
Qasr 'Amra, *Jordan* 64 D3
Qaşr-e Qand, *Iran* 65 E9
Qasr Farâfra, *Egypt* 76 B2
Qatanā, *Syria* 69 B5
Qatar ■, *Asia* 65 E6
Qatlīsh, *Iran* 65 B8
Qattâra, *Egypt* 76 A2
Qattâra, Munkhafed el, *Egypt* 76 B2
Qattâra Depression = Qattâra, Munkhafed el, *Egypt* 76 B2
Qawām al Ḩamzah, *Iraq* 64 D5
Qāyen, *Iran* 65 C8
Qazaqstan = Kazakhstan ■, *Asia* 44 E7
Qazvin, *Iran* 65 B6
Qena, *Egypt* 76 B3
Qena, Wadi →, *Egypt* 76 B3
Qeqertarsuag = Disko, *Greenland* 4 C5
Qeqertarsuaq = Godhavn, *Greenland* 4 C5
Qeshlāq, *Iran* 64 C5
Qeshm, *Iran* 65 E8
Qezi'ot, *Israel* 69 E3
Qi Xian, *China* 50 G8
Qian Gorlos, *China* 51 B13
Qian Xian, *China* 50 G5
Qiancheng, *China* 52 D7
Qianjiang, *Guangxi Zhuangzu, China* 52 F7
Qianjiang, *Hubei, China* 53 B9
Qianjiang, *Sichuan, China* 52 C7
Qianshan, *China* 53 B11
Qianwei, *China* 52 C4
Qianxi, *China* 52 D6
Qianyang, *Hunan, China* 53 D8
Qianyang, *Shaanxi, China* 50 G4
Qianyang, *Zhejiang, China* 53 B12
Qiaojia, *China* 52 D4
Qibā', *Si. Arabia* 64 E5
Qichun, *China* 53 B10
Qidong, *Hunan, China* 53 D9
Qidong, *Jiangsu, China* 53 B13
Qijiang, *China* 52 C6
Qila Safed, *Pakistan* 60 E2
Qila Saifullāh, *Pakistan* 62 D3
Qilian Shan, *China* 54 C4
Qimen, *China* 53 C11
Qin He →, *China* 50 G7
Qin Jiang →, *China* 53 D10
Qin Ling = Qinling Shandi, *China* 50 H5
Qin'an, *China* 50 G3
Qing Xian, *China* 50 E9
Qingcheng, *China* 51 F9
Qingdao, *China* 51 F11
Qingfeng, *China* 50 G8
Qinghai □, *China* 54 C4
Qinghai Hu, *China* 54 C5
Qinghecheng, *China* 51 D13
Qinghemen, *China* 51 D11
Qingjian, *China* 50 F6
Qingjiang, *Jiangsu, China* 51 H10
Qingjiang, *Jiangxi, China* 53 C10
Qingliu, *China* 53 D11
Qinglong, *China* 52 E5
Qingping, *China* 52 D6
Qingpu, *China* 53 B13
Qingshui, *China* 50 G4
Qingshuihe, *China* 50 E6
Qingtian, *China* 53 C13
Qingtongxia Shuiku, *China* 50 F3
Qingxi, *China* 52 D7
Qingxu, *China* 50 F7
Qingyang, *Anhui, China* 53 B11
Qingyang, *Gansu, China* 50 F4
Qingyi Jiang →, *China* 52 C4
Qingyuan, *Guangdong, China* 53 F9
Qingyuan, *Liaoning, China* 51 C13
Qingyuan, *Zhejiang, China* 53 D12
Qingyun, *China* 51 F9
Qingzhen, *China* 52 D6
Qinhuangdao, *China* 51 E10
Qinling Shandi, *China* 50 H5
Qinshui, *China* 50 G7
Qinyang, *China* 50 G7
Qinyuan, *China* 50 F7
Qinzhou, *China* 52 G7
Qionghai, *China* 58 C8
Qionglai, *China* 52 B4
Qionglai Shan, *China* 52 B4
Qiongshan, *China* 58 C8
Qiongzhou Haixia, *China* 58 B8
Qiqihar, *China* 45 E13
Qirâiya, W. →, *Egypt* 69 E3
Qiryat Ata, *Israel* 69 C4
Qiryat Gat, *Israel* 69 D3
Qiryat Mal'akhi, *Israel* 69 D3
Qiryat Shemona, *Israel* 69 B4
Qiryat Yam, *Israel* 69 C4
Qishan, *China* 50 G4
Qishan, *Taiwan* 53 F13
Qitai, *China* 54 B3
Qiubei, *China* 52 E5
Qixia, *China* 51 F11
Qiyang, *China* 53 D8
Qojūr, *Iran* 64 B5
Qom, *Iran* 65 C6
Qomsheh, *Iran* 65 D6
Qostanay = Kustanay, *Kazakhstan* 44 D7
Qu Jiang →, *China* 52 B6
Qu Xian, *Sichuan, China* 52 B6
Qu Xian, *Zhejiang, China* 53 C12
Quackenbrück, *Germany* 18 C3
Quairading, *Australia* 89 F2
Quakertown, *U.S.A.* 107 F9
Qualeup, *Australia* 89 F2
Quambatook, *Australia* 91 F3
Quambone, *Australia* 91 E4
Quamby, *Australia* 90 C3
Quan Long, *Vietnam* 59 H5
Quanah, *U.S.A.* 109 H5
Quandialla, *Australia* 91 E4
Quang Ngai, *Vietnam* 58 E7
Quang Yen, *Vietnam* 58 B6
Quannan, *China* 53 E10
Quantock Hills, *U.K.* 13 F4
Quanzhou, *Fujian, China* 53 E12
Quanzhou, *Guangxi Zhuangzu, China* 53 E8
Quaraí, *Brazil* 126 C4
Quarré-les-Tombes, *France* 25 E10
Quartu Sant' Elena, *Italy* 34 C2
Quartzsite, *U.S.A.* 113 M12
Quatsino, *Canada* 100 C3
Quatsino Sd., *Canada* 100 C3
Qūchān, *Iran* 65 B8
Queanbeyan, *Australia* 91 F4
Québec, *Canada* 99 C5
Québec □, *Canada* 99 B6
Quedlinburg, *Germany* 18 D7
Queen Alexandra Ra., *Antarctica* 5 E11
Queen Charlotte, *Canada* 100 C2
Queen Charlotte Bay, *Falk. Is.* 128 D4
Queen Charlotte Is., *Canada* 100 C2
Queen Charlotte Str., *Canada* 100 C3
Queen Elizabeth Is., *Canada* 94 B10
Queen Elizabeth Nat. Park, *Uganda* 82 C3
Queen Mary Land, *Antarctica* 5 D7
Queen Maud G., *Canada* 96 B9
Queen Maud Land, *Antarctica* 5 D3
Queen Maud Mts., *Antarctica* 5 E13
Queens Chan., *Australia* 88 C4
Queenscliff, *Australia* 91 F3
Queensland □, *Australia* 90 C3
Queenstown, *Australia* 90 G4
Queenstown, *N.Z.* 87 L2
Queenstown, *S. Africa* 84 E4
Queets, *U.S.A.* 112 C2
Queguay Grande →, *Uruguay* 126 C4
Queimadas, *Brazil* 122 D4
Quela, *Angola* 80 F3
Quelimane, *Mozam.* 83 F4
Quelpart = Cheju Do, *S. Korea* 51 H14
Quemado, *N. Mex., U.S.A.* 111 J9
Quemado, *Tex., U.S.A.* 109 L4
Quemú-Quemú, *Argentina* 126 D3
Quequén, *Argentina* 126 D4
Querco, *Peru* 124 C3
Querétaro, *Mexico* 114 C4
Querétaro □, *Mexico* 114 C5
Querfurt, *Germany* 18 D7
Quesada, *Spain* 29 H1
Queshan, *China* 50 H8
Quesnel, *Canada* 100 C4
Quesnel →, *Canada* 100 C4
Quesnel L., *Canada* 100 C4
Questa, *U.S.A.* 111 H11
Questembert, *France* 24 E4
Quetena, *Bolivia* 124 E4
Quetico Prov. Park, *Canada* 98 C1
Quetrequile, *Argentina* 128 B3
Quetta, *Pakistan* 62 D2
Quevedo, *Ecuador* 120 D2
Quezaltenango, *Guatemala* 116 D1
Quezon City, *Phil.* 55 D4
Qufār, *Si. Arabia* 64 E4
Qui Nhon, *Vietnam* 58 F7
Quibaxe, *Angola* 80 F2
Quibdo, *Colombia* 120 B2
Quiberon, *France* 24 E3
Quíbor, *Venezuela* 120 B4
Quick, *Canada* 100 C3
Quickborn, *Germany* 18 B5
Quiet L., *Canada* 100 A2
Quiévrain, *Belgium* 17 H3
Quiindy, *Paraguay* 126 B4
Quila, *Mexico* 114 C3
Quilán, C., *Chile* 128 B2
Quilcene, *U.S.A.* 112 C4
Quilengues, *Angola* 81 G2
Quilimarí, *Chile* 126 C1
Quilino, *Argentina* 126 C3
Quillabamba, *Peru* 124 C3
Quillacollo, *Bolivia* 124 D4
Quillagua, *Chile* 126 A2
Quillaicillo, *Chile* 126 C1
Quillan, *France* 26 F6
Quillebeuf-sur-Seine, *France* 24 C7
Quillota, *Chile* 126 C1
Quilmes, *Argentina* 126 C4
Quilon, *India* 60 Q10
Quilpie, *Australia* 91 D3
Quilpué, *Chile* 126 C1
Quilua, *Mozam.* 83 F4
Quime, *Bolivia* 124 D4
Quimilí, *Argentina* 126 B3
Quimper, *France* 24 D2
Quimperlé, *France* 24 E3
Quinault →, *U.S.A.* 112 C2
Quincemil, *Peru* 124 C3
Quincy, *Calif., U.S.A.* 112 F6
Quincy, *Fla., U.S.A.* 105 K3
Quincy, *Ill., U.S.A.* 108 F9
Quincy, *Mass., U.S.A.* 107 D14
Quincy, *Wash., U.S.A.* 110 C4
Quines, *Argentina* 126 C2
Quinga, *Mozam.* 83 F5
Quingey, *France* 25 E12
Quintana de la Serena, *Spain* 31 G5
Quintana Roo □, *Mexico* 115 D7
Quintanar de la Orden, *Spain* 28 F1
Quintanar de la Sierra, *Spain* 28 D2
Quintanar del Rey, *Spain* 29 F3
Quintero, *Chile* 126 C1
Quintin, *France* 24 D4
Quinto, *Spain* 28 D4
Quinyambie, *Australia* 91 E3
Quípar →, *Spain* 29 G3
Quipungo, *Angola* 81 G2
Quirihue, *Chile* 126 D1
Quirindi, *Australia* 91 E5
Quiroga, *Spain* 30 C3
Quiruvilca, *Peru* 124 B2
Quissac, *France* 27 E8
Quissanga, *Mozam.* 83 E5
Quitilipi, *Argentina* 126 B3
Quitman, *Ga., U.S.A.* 105 K4
Quitman, *Miss., U.S.A.* 105 J1
Quitman, *Tex., U.S.A.* 109 J7
Quito, *Ecuador* 120 D2
Quixadá, *Brazil* 122 B4
Quixaxe, *Mozam.* 83 F5
Quixeramobim, *Brazil* 122 C4
Qujing, *China* 52 E4
Qul'ân, Jazâ'ir, *Egypt* 76 C4
Qumbu, *S. Africa* 85 E4
Quneitra, *Syria* 69 B4
Quoin I., *Australia* 88 B4
Quoin Pt., *S. Africa* 84 E2
Quondong, *Australia* 91 E3
Quorn, *Australia* 91 E2
Quqon = Kokand, *Uzbekistan* 44 E8
Qurein, *Sudan* 77 E3
Qurnat as Sawdā', *Lebanon* 69 A5
Qûs, *Egypt* 76 B3
Qusaybah, *Iraq* 64 C4
Quseir, *Egypt* 76 B3
Qūshchī, *Iran* 64 B5
Quthing, *Lesotho* 85 E4
Qūţīābād, *Iran* 65 C6
Quwo, *China* 50 G6
Quyang, *China* 50 E8
Quynh Nhai, *Vietnam* 58 B4
Quzi, *China* 50 F4
Qytet Stalin, *Albania* 39 J2
Qyzylorda = Kzyl-Orda, *Kazakhstan* 44 E7

R

Ra, Ko, *Thailand* 59 H2
Råå, *Sweden* 11 J6
Raahe, *Finland* 8 D18
Raalte, *Neths.* 16 D8
Raamsdonksveer, *Neths.* 17 E5
Raasay, *U.K.* 14 D2
Raasay, Sd. of, *U.K.* 14 D2
Rab, *Croatia* 33 D11
Raba, *Indonesia* 57 F5
Rába →, *Hungary* 21 H7
Rabaçal →, *Portugal* 30 D3
Rabah, *Nigeria* 79 C6
Rabai, *Kenya* 82 C4
Rabastens, *France* 26 E5
Rabastens-de-Bigorre, *France* 26 E4
Rabat, *Malta* 37 D1
Rabat, *Morocco* 74 B3
Rabaul, *Papua N. G.* 92 H7
Rabbit →, *Canada* 100 B3
Rabbit Lake, *Canada* 101 C7
Rabbitskin →, *Canada* 100 A4
Rabka, *Poland* 20 F9
Rābor, *Iran* 65 D8
Răcale, *Italy* 35 C11
Racalmuto, *Italy* 34 E6
Racconigi, *Italy* 32 D4
Race, C., *Canada* 99 C9
Rach Gia, *Vietnam* 59 G5

Réunion

Raciąż, *Poland* 20 C10
Racibórz, *Poland* 20 E8
Racine, *U.S.A.* 104 D2
Rackerby, *U.S.A.* 112 F5
Radama, Nosy, *Madag.* 85 A8
Radama, Saikanosy, *Madag.* 85 A8
Rădăuţi, *Romania* 38 B8
Radbuza →, *Czech.* 20 F3
Radeburg, *Germany* 18 D9
Radeče, *Slovenia* 33 B12
Radekhov, *Ukraine* 40 F4
Radford, *U.S.A.* 104 G5
Radhanpur, *India* 62 H4
Radiska →, *Macedonia* 39 H3
Radisson, *Canada* 101 C7
Radium Hot Springs, *Canada* 100 C5
Radna, *Romania* 38 C4
Radnor Forest, *U.K.* 13 E4
Radolfzell, *Germany* 19 H4
Radom, *Poland* 20 D11
Radomir, *Bulgaria* 38 G6
Radomsko, *Poland* 20 D9
Radomyshl, *Ukraine* 40 F6
Radoviš, *Macedonia* 39 H5
Radovljica, *Slovenia* 33 B11
Radstock, *U.K.* 13 F5
Radstock, C., *Australia* 91 E1
Răducăneni, *Romania* 38 C10
Radviliškis, *Lithuania* 40 D3
Radville, *Canada* 101 D8
Rae, *Canada* 100 A5
Rae Bareli, *India* 63 F9
Rae Isthmus, *Canada* 97 B11
Raeren, *Belgium* 17 G8
Raeside, L., *Australia* 89 E3
Raetihi, *N.Z.* 87 H5
Rafaela, *Argentina* 126 C3
Rafah, *Egypt* 69 D3
Rafai, *C.A.R.* 82 B1
Raffadali, *Italy* 34 E6
Rafḩā, *Si. Arabia* 64 D4
Rafsanjān, *Iran* 65 D8
Raft Pt., *Australia* 88 C3
Ragag, *Sudan* 77 E1
Ragama, *Sri Lanka* 60 R11
Ragged, Mt., *Australia* 89 F3
Raglan, *Australia* 90 C5
Raglan, *N.Z.* 87 G5
Ragunda, *Sweden* 10 A10
Ragusa, *Italy* 35 F7
Raha, *Indonesia* 57 E6
Rahad, Nahr ed →, *Sudan* 77 E3
Rahad al Bardī, *Sudan* 73 F9
Rahaeng = Tak, *Thailand* 58 D2
Rahden, *Germany* 18 C4
Raheita, *Eritrea* 77 E5
Raḩīmah, *Si. Arabia* 65 E6
Rahimyar Khan, *Pakistan* 62 E4
Rāhjerd, *Iran* 65 C6
Raichur, *India* 60 L10
Raiganj, *India* 63 G13
Raigarh, *India* 61 J13
Raijua, *Indonesia* 57 F6
Railton, *Australia* 90 G4
Rainbow Lake, *Canada* 100 B5
Rainier, *U.S.A.* 112 D4
Rainier, Mt., *U.S.A.* 112 D5
Rainy L., *Canada* 101 D10
Rainy River, *Canada* 101 D10
Raipur, *India* 61 J12
Raj Nandgaon, *India* 61 J12
Raja, Ujung, *Indonesia* 56 D1
Raja Ampat, Kepulauan, *Indonesia* 57 E7
Rajahmundry, *India* 61 L12
Rajajooseppi, *Finland* 8 B20
Rajang →, *Malaysia* 56 D4
Rajapalaiyam, *India* 60 Q10
Rajasthan □, *India* 62 F5
Rajasthan Canal, *India* 62 E5
Rajauri, *India* 63 C6
Rajgarh, *Mad. P., India* 62 G7
Rajgarh, *Raj., India* 62 E6
Rajhenburg, *Slovenia* 33 B12
Rajkot, *India* 62 H4
Rajmahal Hills, *India* 63 G12
Rajpipla, *India* 60 J8
Rajpura, *India* 62 D7
Rajshahi, *Bangla.* 61 G16
Rajshahi □, *Bangla.* 63 G13
Rakaia, *N.Z.* 87 K4
Rakaia →, *N.Z.* 87 K4
Rakan, Ra's, *Qatar* 65 E6
Rakaposhi, *Pakistan* 63 A6
Rakata, Pulau, *Indonesia* 56 F3
Rakhni, *Pakistan* 62 D3
Rakitnoye, *Russia* 48 B7
Rakkestad, *Norway* 10 E5
Rakops, *Botswana* 84 C3
Rákospalota, *Hungary* 21 H9
Rakov, *Belorussia* 40 E5
Rakovica, *Croatia* 33 D12
Rakovník, *Czech.* 20 E3
Rakovski, *Bulgaria* 38 G7
Rakvere, *Estonia* 40 B5
Raleigh, *U.S.A.* 105 H6
Raleigh B., *U.S.A.* 105 H7
Ralja, *Serbia* 21 L10
Ralls, *U.S.A.* 109 J4
Ram →, *Canada* 100 A4
Rām Allāh, *Jordan* 69 D4
Ram Hd., *Australia* 91 F4
Rama, *Nic.* 116 D3
Ramacca, *Italy* 35 E7
Ramales de la Victoria, *Spain* 28 B1
Ramalho, Serra do, *Brazil* 123 D3
Raman, *Thailand* 59 J3
Ramanathapuram, *India* 60 Q11
Ramanetaka, B. de, *Madag.* 85 A8
Ramat Gan, *Israel* 69 C3
Ramatlhabama, *S. Africa* 84 D4
Ramban, *India* 63 C6
Rambervillers, *France* 25 D13
Rambipuji, *Indonesia* 57 H15
Rambouillet, *France* 25 D8
Ramea, *Canada* 99 C8
Ramechhap, *Nepal* 63 F12
Ramelau, *Indonesia* 57 F7
Ramenskoye, *Russia* 41 D11
Ramgarh, *Bihar, India* 63 H11
Ramgarh, *Raj., India* 62 F6
Ramgarh, *Raj., India* 62 F4
Rāmhormoz, *Iran* 65 D6
Ramīān, *Iran* 65 B7
Ramingining, *Australia* 90 A2
Ramla, *Israel* 69 D3
Ramlu, *Eritrea* 77 E5
Ramme, *Denmark* 11 H2
Ramnad = Ramanathapuram, *India* 60 Q11
Ramnagar, *India* 63 C6
Ramnäs, *Sweden* 10 E10
Ramon, *Russia* 41 F11
Ramona, *U.S.A.* 113 M10
Ramore, *Canada* 98 C3
Ramotswa, *Botswana* 84 C4
Rampur, *H.P., India* 62 D7
Rampur, *Mad. P., India* 62 H5
Rampur, *Ut. P., India* 63 E8
Rampur Hat, *India* 63 G12
Rampura, *India* 62 G6
Ramree I. = Ramree Kyun, *Burma* 61 K18
Ramree Kyun, *Burma* 61 K18
Rāmsar, *Iran* 65 B6
Ramsel, *Belgium* 17 F5
Ramsey, *Canada* 98 C3
Ramsey, *U.K.* 12 C3
Ramsgate, *U.K.* 13 F9
Ramsjö, *Sweden* 10 B9
Ramtek, *India* 60 J11
Ramvik, *Sweden* 10 B11
Ranaghat, *India* 63 H13
Ranahu, *Pakistan* 62 G3
Ranau, *Malaysia* 56 C5
Rancagua, *Chile* 126 C1
Rance, *Belgium* 17 H4
Rance →, *France* 24 D5
Rance, Barrage de la, *France* 24 D4
Rancharia, *Brazil* 123 F1
Rancheria →, *Canada* 100 A3
Ranchester, *U.S.A.* 110 D10
Ranchi, *India* 63 H11
Ranco, L., *Chile* 128 B2
Randan, *France* 26 B7
Randazzo, *Italy* 35 E7
Randers, *Denmark* 11 H4
Randers Fjord, *Denmark* 11 H4
Randfontein, *S. Africa* 85 D4
Randle, *U.S.A.* 112 D5
Randolph, *Mass., U.S.A.* 107 D13
Randolph, *N.Y., U.S.A.* 106 D6
Randolph, *Utah, U.S.A.* 110 F8
Randolph, *Vt., U.S.A.* 107 C12
Randsfjord, *Norway* 10 D4
Råne älv →, *Sweden* 8 D17
Rangae, *Thailand* 59 J3
Rangaunu B., *N.Z.* 87 F4
Rångedala, *Sweden* 11 G7
Rangeley, *U.S.A.* 107 B14
Rangely, *U.S.A.* 110 F9
Ranger, *U.S.A.* 109 J5
Rangia, *India* 61 F17
Rangiora, *N.Z.* 87 K4
Rangitaiki →, *N.Z.* 87 G6
Rangitata →, *N.Z.* 87 K3
Rangkasbitung, *Indonesia* 57 G12
Rangon →, *Burma* 61 L20
Rangoon, *Burma* 61 L20
Rangpur, *Bangla.* 61 G16
Rangsit, *Thailand* 58 F3
Ranibennur, *India* 60 M9
Raniganj, *India* 63 H12
Raniwara, *India* 60 G8
Rāniyah, *Iraq* 64 B5
Ranken →, *Australia* 90 C2
Rankin, *U.S.A.* 109 K4
Rankin Inlet, *Canada* 96 B10
Rankins Springs, *Australia* 91 E4
Rannoch, L., *U.K.* 14 E4
Rannoch Moor, *U.K.* 14 E4
Ranobe, Helodranon' i, *Madag.* 85 C7
Ranohira, *Madag.* 85 C8
Ranomafana, *Toamasina, Madag.* 85 B8
Ranomafana, *Toliara, Madag.* 85 C8
Ranong, *Thailand* 59 H2
Rānsa, *Iran* 65 C6
Ransiki, *Indonesia* 57 E8
Rantau, *Indonesia* 56 E5
Rantauprapat, *Indonesia* 56 D1
Rantekombola, *Indonesia* 57 E5
Rantoul, *U.S.A.* 104 E1
Ranum, *Denmark* 11 H3
Raon l'Étape, *France* 25 D13
Raoui, Erg er, *Algeria* 75 C4
Raoyang, *China* 50 E8
Rapa, *Pac. Oc.* 93 K13
Rapallo, *Italy* 32 D6
Rāpch, *Iran* 65 E8
Rapid →, *Canada* 100 B3
Rapid City, *U.S.A.* 108 D3
Rapid River, *U.S.A.* 104 C2
Rapides des Joachims, *Canada* 98 C4
Rapla, *Estonia* 40 B4
Rapperswil, *Switz.* 23 B7
Rapu Rapu I., *Phil.* 55 E6
Rarotonga, *Cook Is.* 93 K12
Ra's al' Ayn, *Syria* 64 B4
Ra's al Khaymah, *U.A.E.* 65 E8
Ra's al-Unuf, *Libya* 73 B8
Ra's an Naqb, *Jordan* 69 F4
Ras Bânâs, *Egypt* 76 C4
Ras Dashen, *Ethiopia* 77 E4
Ras el Ma, *Algeria* 75 B4
Ras Mallap, *Egypt* 76 J8
Râs Timirist, *Mauritania* 78 B1
Rasa, Punta, *Argentina* 128 B4
Rasca, Pta. de la, *Canary Is.* 36 G3
Raseiniai, *Lithuania* 40 D3
Rashad, *Sudan* 77 E3
Rashîd, *Egypt* 76 H7
Rashîd, Masabb, *Egypt* 76 H7
Rasht, *Iran* 65 B6
Rasi Salai, *Thailand* 58 E5
Raška, *Serbia* 21 M10
Rason L., *Australia* 89 E3
Raşova, *Romania* 38 E10
Rasra, *India* 63 G10
Rass el Oued, *Algeria* 75 A6
Rasskazovo, *Russia* 41 E12
Rastatt, *Germany* 19 G4
Rat Buri, *Thailand* 58 F2
Rat Islands, *U.S.A.* 96 C1
Rat River, *Canada* 100 A6
Ratangarh, *India* 62 E6
Raţāwī, *Iraq* 64 D5
Rath, *India* 63 G8
Rath Luirc, *Ireland* 15 D3
Rathdrum, *Ireland* 15 D5
Rathenow, *Germany* 18 C8
Rathkeale, *Ireland* 15 D3
Rathlin, *U.K.* 15 A5
Rathlin O'Birne I., *Ireland* 15 B3
Ratibor = Racibórz, *Poland* 20 E8
Ratlam, *India* 62 H6
Ratnagiri, *India* 60 L8
Raton, *U.S.A.* 109 G2
Rattaphum, *Thailand* 59 J3
Rattray Hd., *U.K.* 14 D7
Ratz, Mt., *Canada* 100 B2
Ratzeburg, *Germany* 18 B6
Raub, *Malaysia* 59 L3
Rauch, *Argentina* 126 D4
Raufarhöfn, *Iceland* 8 C6
Raufoss, *Norway* 10 D4
Raukumara Ra., *N.Z.* 87 H6
Raul Soares, *Brazil* 123 F3
Rauland, *Norway* 10 E2
Rauma, *Finland* 9 F16
Rauma →, *Norway* 10 B1
Raurkela, *India* 63 H11
Rausu-Dake, *Japan* 48 B12
Rava Russkaya, *Ukraine* 40 F3
Ravānsar, *Iran* 64 C5
Ravanusa, *Italy* 34 E6
Rāvar, *Iran* 65 D8
Ravels, *Belgium* 17 F6
Ravena, *U.S.A.* 107 D11
Ravenna, *Italy* 33 D9
Ravenna, *Nebr., U.S.A.* 108 E5
Ravenna, *Ohio, U.S.A.* 106 E3
Ravensburg, *Germany* 19 H5
Ravenshoe, *Australia* 90 B4
Ravenstein, *Neths.* 16 E7
Ravensthorpe, *Australia* 89 F3
Ravenswood, *Australia* 90 C4
Ravenswood, *U.S.A.* 104 F5
Ravi →, *Pakistan* 62 D4
Ravna Gora, *Croatia* 33 C11
Rawa Mazowiecka, *Poland* 20 D10
Rawalpindi, *Pakistan* 62 C5
Rawāndūz, *Iraq* 64 B5
Rawang, *Malaysia* 59 L3
Rawdon, *Canada* 98 C5
Rawene, *N.Z.* 87 F4
Rawicz, *Poland* 20 D6
Rawlinna, *Australia* 89 F4
Rawlins, *U.S.A.* 110 F10
Rawlinson Ra., *Australia* 89 D4
Rawson, *Argentina* 128 B3
Ray, *U.S.A.* 108 A3
Ray, C., *Canada* 99 C8
Rayadurg, *India* 60 M10
Rayagada, *India* 61 K13
Raychikhinsk, *Russia* 45 E13
Rāyen, *Iran* 65 D8
Raymond, *Canada* 100 D6
Raymond, *Calif., U.S.A.* 112 H7
Raymond, *Wash., U.S.A.* 112 D3
Raymondville, *U.S.A.* 109 M6
Raymore, *Canada* 101 C8
Rayne, *U.S.A.* 109 K8
Rayón, *Mexico* 114 B2
Rayong, *Thailand* 58 F3
Rayville, *U.S.A.* 109 J9
Raz, Pte. du, *France* 24 D2
Razan, *Iran* 65 C6
Ražana, *Serbia* 21 L9
Ražanj, *Serbia* 21 M11
Razdel'naya, *Ukraine* 42 C4
Razdolnoye, *Russia* 48 C5
Razdolnoye, *Ukraine* 42 D5
Razeh, *Iran* 65 C6
Razelm, Lacul, *Romania* 38 E12
Razgrad, *Bulgaria* 38 F9
Razmak, *Pakistan* 62 C3
Ré, I. de, *France* 26 B2
Reading, *U.K.* 13 F7
Reading, *U.S.A.* 107 F9
Real, Cordillera, *Bolivia* 124 D4
Realicó, *Argentina* 126 D3
Réalmont, *France* 26 E6
Reata, *Mexico* 114 B4
Rebais, *France* 25 D10
Rebecca, L., *Australia* 89 F3
Rebi, *Indonesia* 57 F8
Rebiana, *Libya* 73 D9
Rebun-Tō, *Japan* 48 B10
Recanati, *Italy* 33 E10
Recaş, *Romania* 38 D4
Recherche, Arch. of the, *Australia* 89 F3
Rechitsa, *Belorussia* 40 E7
Recht, *Belgium* 17 H8
Recife, *Brazil* 122 C5
Recklinghausen, *Germany* 17 E10
Reconquista, *Argentina* 126 B4
Recreio, *Brazil* 125 B6
Recreo, *Argentina* 126 B2
Recuay, *Peru* 124 B2
Red →, *La., U.S.A.* 109 K9
Red →, *N. Dak., U.S.A.* 108 A6
Red Bank, *U.S.A.* 107 F10
Red Bay, *Canada* 99 B8
Red Bluff, *U.S.A.* 110 F2
Red Bluff L., *U.S.A.* 109 K3
Red Cliffs, *Australia* 91 E3
Red Cloud, *U.S.A.* 108 E5
Red Deer, *Canada* 100 C6
Red Deer →, *Alta., Canada* 101 C6
Red Deer →, *Man., Canada* 101 C8
Red Deer L., *Canada* 101 C8
Red Indian L., *Canada* 99 C8
Red Lake, *Canada* 101 C10
Red Lake Falls, *U.S.A.* 108 B6
Red Lodge, *U.S.A.* 110 D9
Red Mountain, *U.S.A.* 113 K9
Red Oak, *U.S.A.* 108 E7
Red Rock, *Canada* 98 C2
Red Rock, L., *U.S.A.* 108 E8
Red Rocks Pt., *Australia* 89 F4
Red Sea, *Asia* 68 C2
Red Slate Mt., *U.S.A.* 112 H8
Red Sucker L., *Canada* 101 C10
Red Tower Pass = Turnu Rosu Pasul, *Romania* 38 D7
Red Wing, *U.S.A.* 108 C8
Rédange, *Lux.* 17 J7
Redbridge, *U.K.* 13 F8
Redcar, *U.K.* 12 C6
Redcliff, *Canada* 101 C6
Redcliffe, *Australia* 91 D5
Redcliffe, Mt., *Australia* 89 E3
Reddersburg, *S. Africa* 84 D4
Redding, *U.S.A.* 110 F2
Redditch, *U.K.* 13 E6
Redenção, *Brazil* 122 B4
Redfield, *U.S.A.* 108 C5
Redknife →, *Canada* 100 A5
Redlands, *U.S.A.* 113 M9
Redmond, *Australia* 89 F2
Redmond, *Oreg., U.S.A.* 110 D3
Redmond, *Wash., U.S.A.* 112 C4
Redon, *France* 24 E4
Redonda, *Antigua* 117 C7
Redondela, *Spain* 30 C2
Redondo, *Portugal* 31 G3
Redondo Beach, *U.S.A.* 113 M8
Redrock Pt., *Canada* 100 A5
Redruth, *U.K.* 13 G2
Redvers, *Canada* 101 D8
Redwater, *Canada* 100 C6
Redwood, *U.S.A.* 107 B9
Redwood City, *U.S.A.* 111 H2
Redwood Falls, *U.S.A.* 108 C7
Ree, L., *Ireland* 15 C4
Reed, L., *Canada* 101 C8
Reed City, *U.S.A.* 104 D3
Reeder, *U.S.A.* 108 B3
Reedley, *U.S.A.* 111 H4
Reedsburg, *U.S.A.* 108 D9
Reedsport, *U.S.A.* 110 E1
Reefton, *N.Z.* 87 K3
Refahiye, *Turkey* 67 D8
Refugio, *U.S.A.* 109 L6
Rega →, *Poland* 20 A5
Regalbuto, *Italy* 35 E7
Regen, *Germany* 19 G9
Regen →, *Germany* 19 F8
Regeneração, *Brazil* 122 C3
Regensburg, *Germany* 19 F8
Regensdorf, *Switz.* 23 B6
Réggio di Calábria, *Italy* 35 D8
Réggio nell' Emilia, *Italy* 32 D7
Regina, *Canada* 101 C8
Régina, *Fr. Guiana* 121 C7
Registro, *Brazil* 127 A6
Reguengos de Monsaraz, *Portugal* 31 G3
Rehar →, *India* 63 H10
Rehoboth, *Namibia* 84 C2
Rehovot, *Israel* 69 D3
Rei-Bouba, *Cameroon* 73 G7
Reichenbach, *Germany* 18 E8
Reichenbach, *Switz.* 22 C5
Reid, *Australia* 89 F4
Reid River, *Australia* 90 B4
Reiden, *Switz.* 22 B5
Reidsville, *U.S.A.* 105 G6
Reigate, *U.K.* 13 F7
Reillo, *Spain* 28 F3
Reims, *France* 25 C11
Reina Adelaida, Arch., *Chile* 128 D2
Reinach, *Aargau, Switz.* 22 B6
Reinach, *Basel, Switz.* 22 B5
Reinbeck, *U.S.A.* 108 D8
Reindeer →, *Canada* 101 B8
Reindeer I., *Canada* 101 C9
Reindeer L., *Canada* 101 B8
Reinga, C., *N.Z.* 87 F4
Reinosa, *Spain* 30 B6
Reinosa, Paso, *Spain* 30 C6
Reitdiep, *Neths.* 16 B8
Reitz, *S. Africa* 85 D4
Reivilo, *S. Africa* 84 D3
Rejmyre, *Sweden* 11 F9
Reka →, *Slovenia* 33 C11
Rekinniki, *Russia* 45 C17
Reliance, *Canada* 101 A7
Remad, Oued →, *Algeria* 75 B4
Rémalard, *France* 24 D7
Remarkable, Mt., *Australia* 91 E2
Rembang, *Indonesia* 57 G14
Remchi, *Algeria* 75 A4
Remedios, *Colombia* 120 B3
Remedios, *Panama* 116 E3
Remeshk, *Iran* 65 E8
Remich, *Lux.* 17 J8
Rémire, *Fr. Guiana* 121 C7
Remiremont, *France* 25 D13
Remo, *Ethiopia* 77 F5
Remontnoye, *Russia* 43 C10
Remoulins, *France* 27 E8
Remscheid, *Germany* 18 D3
Ren Xian, *China* 50 F8
Renascença, *Brazil* 120 D4
Rende, *Italy* 35 C9
Rendeux, *Belgium* 17 H7
Rendína, *Greece* 39 K4
Rendsburg, *Germany* 18 A5
Rene, *Russia* 45 C19
Renfrew, *Canada* 98 C4
Renfrew, *U.K.* 14 F4
Rengat, *Indonesia* 56 E2
Rengo, *Chile* 126 C1
Renhua, *China* 53 E9
Renhuai, *China* 52 D6
Reni, *Moldavia* 42 D3
Renk, *Sudan* 77 E3
Renkum, *Neths.* 16 E7
Renmark, *Australia* 91 E3
Rennell Sd., *Canada* 100 C2
Renner Springs T.O., *Australia* 90 B1
Rennes, *France* 24 D5
Rennes, Bassin de, *France* 24 E5
Reno, *U.S.A.* 112 F7
Reno →, *Italy* 33 D9
Renovo, *U.S.A.* 106 E7
Renqiu, *China* 50 E9
Rensselaer, *Ind., U.S.A.* 104 E2
Rensselaer, *N.Y., U.S.A.* 107 D11
Rentería, *Spain* 28 B3
Renton, *U.S.A.* 112 C4
Réo, *Burkina Faso* 78 C4
Reotipur, *India* 63 G10
Republic, *Mich., U.S.A.* 104 B2
Republic, *Wash., U.S.A.* 110 B4
Republican →, *U.S.A.* 108 F6
Republican City, *U.S.A.* 108 E5
Republiek, *Surinam* 121 B6
Repulse Bay, *Canada* 97 B11
Requena, *Peru* 124 B3
Requena, *Spain* 29 F3
Resadiye = Datça, *Turkey* 66 E2
Reşadiye, *Turkey* 66 C7
Resele, *Sweden* 10 A11
Reserve, *Canada* 101 C8
Reserve, *U.S.A.* 111 K9
Resht = Rasht, *Iran* 65 B6
Resistencia, *Argentina* 126 B4
Reşiţa, *Romania* 38 D4
Resolution I., *Canada* 97 B13
Resolution I., *N.Z.* 87 L1
Resplandes, *Brazil* 122 C2
Resplendor, *Brazil* 123 E3
Ressano Garcia, *Mozam.* 85 D5
Reston, *Canada* 101 D8
Retalhuleu, *Guatemala* 116 D1
Reteag, *Romania* 38 B7
Retenue, L. de, *Zaïre* 83 E2
Rethel, *France* 25 C11
Rethem, *Germany* 18 C5
Réthímnon, *Greece* 37 D6
Réthímnon □, *Greece* 37 D6
Retiche, Alpi, *Switz.* 23 D10
Retie, *Belgium* 17 F6
Retiers, *France* 24 E5
Retortillo, *Spain* 30 E4
Reuland, *Belgium* 17 H8
Réunion ■, *Ind. Oc.* 71 J9

Reus, *Spain* 28 D6
Reusel, *Neths.* 17 F6
Reuss →, *Switz.* 23 B6
Reutlingen, *Germany* 19 G5
Reutte, *Austria* 19 H6
Reuver, *Neths.* 17 F8
Reval = Tallinn, *Estonia* 40 B4
Revel, *France* 26 E6
Revelganj, *India* 63 G11
Revelstoke, *Canada* 100 C5
Reventazón, *Peru* 124 B1
Revigny-sur-Ornain, *France* 25 D11
Revilla Gigedo, Is., *Pac. Oc.* 93 F16
Revillagigedo I., *U.S.A.* 100 B2
Revin, *France* 25 C11
Revuè →, *Mozam.* 83 F3
Rewa, *India* 63 G9
Rewa →, *Guyana* 121 C6
Rewari, *India* 62 E7
Rexburg, *U.S.A.* 110 E8
Rey, *Iran* 65 C6
Rey, Rio del →, *Nigeria* 79 E6
Rey Malabo, *Eq. Guin.* 79 E6
Reyes, *Bolivia* 124 C4
Reyes, Pt., *U.S.A.* 112 H3
Reykjahlið, *Iceland* 8 D5
Reykjanes, *Iceland* 8 E2
Reykjavík, *Iceland* 8 D3
Reynolds, *Canada* 101 D9
Reynolds Ra., *Australia* 88 D5
Reynoldsville, *U.S.A.* 106 E6
Reynosa, *Mexico* 115 B5
Rēzekne, *Latvia* 40 C5
Rezvān, *Iran* 65 E8
Rharis, O. →, *Algeria* 75 C6
Rhayader, *U.K.* 13 E4
Rheden, *Neths.* 16 D8
Rhein, *Canada* 101 C8
Rhein →, *Europe* 16 E8
Rhein-Main-Donau-Kanal, *Germany* 19 F7
Rheinbach, *Germany* 18 E2
Rheine, *Germany* 18 C3
Rheineck, *Switz.* 23 B9
Rheinfelden, *Switz.* 22 A5
Rheinland-Pfalz □, *Germany* 19 E2
Rheinsberg, *Germany* 18 B8
Rheinwaldhorn, *Switz.* 23 D8
Rhenen, *Neths.* 16 E7
Rheriss, Oued →, *Morocco* 74 B4
Rheydt, *Germany* 18 D2
Rhin = Rhein →, *Europe* 16 E8
Rhinau, *France* 25 D14
Rhine = Rhein →, *Europe* 16 E8
Rhineland-Palatinate □ = Rheinland-Pfalz □, *Germany* 19 E2
Rhinelander, *U.S.A.* 108 C10
Rhino Camp, *Uganda* 82 B3
Rhir, Cap, *Morocco* 74 B3
Rhisnes, *Belgium* 17 G5
Rho, *Italy* 32 C6
Rhode Island □, *U.S.A.* 107 E13
Rhodes = Ródhos, *Greece* 37 C10
Rhodesia = Zimbabwe ■, *Africa* 83 F2
Rhodope Mts. = Rhodopi Planina, *Bulgaria* 39 H7
Rhodopi Planina, *Bulgaria* 39 H7
Rhön = Hohe Rhön, *Germany* 19 E5
Rhondda, *U.K.* 13 F4
Rhône □, *France* 27 C8
Rhône →, *France* 27 E8
Rhum, *U.K.* 14 E2
Rhyl, *U.K.* 12 D4
Rhymney, *U.K.* 13 F4
Ri-Aba, *Eq. Guin.* 79 E6
Riachão, *Brazil* 122 C2
Riacho de Santana, *Brazil* 123 D3
Rialma, *Brazil* 123 E2
Riaño, *Spain* 30 C5
Rians, *France* 27 E9
Riansares →, *Spain* 28 F1
Riasi, *India* 63 C6
Riau □, *Indonesia* 56 D2
Riau, Kepulauan, *Indonesia* 56 D2
Riau Arch. = Riau, Kepulauan, *Indonesia* 56 D2
Riaza, *Spain* 28 D1
Riaza →, *Spain* 28 D1
Riba de Saelices, *Spain* 28 E2
Ribadavia, *Spain* 30 C2
Ribadeo, *Spain* 30 B3
Ribadesella, *Spain* 30 B5
Ribamar, *Brazil* 122 B3
Ribas, *Spain* 28 C7
Ribas do Rio Pardo, *Brazil* 125 E7
Ribble →, *U.K.* 12 C5
Ribe, *Denmark* 11 J2
Ribeauvillé, *France* 25 D14
Ribécourt, *France* 25 C9
Ribeira, *Spain* 30 C2
Ribeira Brava, *Madeira* 36 D2
Ribeira do Pombal, *Brazil* 122 D4
Ribeirão Prêto, *Brazil* 127 A6
Ribeiro Gonçalves, *Brazil* 122 C2
Ribemont, *France* 25 C10
Ribera, *Italy* 34 E6
Ribérac, *France* 26 C4
Riberalta, *Bolivia* 125 C4
Ribnica, *Slovenia* 33 C11
Ribnitz-Damgarten, *Germany* 18 A8
Riccarton, *N.Z.* 87 K4
Riccia, *Italy* 35 A7
Riccione, *Italy* 33 D9
Rice, *U.S.A.* 113 L12
Rice L., *Canada* 106 B6
Rice Lake, *U.S.A.* 108 C9
Rich, *Morocco* 74 B4
Rich Hill, *U.S.A.* 109 F7
Richards Bay, *S. Africa* 85 D5
Richards L., *Canada* 101 B7
Richardson →, *Canada* 101 B6
Richardson Springs, *U.S.A.* 112 F5
Richardton, *U.S.A.* 108 B3
Riche, C., *Australia* 89 F2
Richelieu, *France* 24 E7
Richey, *U.S.A.* 108 B2
Richfield, *Idaho, U.S.A.* 110 E6
Richfield, *Utah, U.S.A.* 111 G8
Richford, *U.S.A.* 107 B12
Richibucto, *Canada* 99 C7
Richland, *Ga., U.S.A.* 105 J3
Richland, *Oreg., U.S.A.* 110 D5
Richland, *Wash., U.S.A.* 110 C4
Richland Center, *U.S.A.* 108 D9
Richlands, *U.S.A.* 104 G5
Richmond, *N.S.W., Australia* 91 E5
Richmond, *Queens., Australia* 90 C3
Richmond, *N.Z.* 87 J4
Richmond, *S. Africa* 85 D5
Richmond, *U.K.* 12 C6
Richmond, *Calif., U.S.A.* 112 H4
Richmond, *Ind., U.S.A.* 104 F3
Richmond, *Ky., U.S.A.* 104 G3
Richmond, *Mich., U.S.A.* 106 D2
Richmond, *Mo., U.S.A.* 108 F8
Richmond, *Tex., U.S.A.* 109 L7
Richmond, *Utah, U.S.A.* 110 F8
Richmond, *Va., U.S.A.* 104 G7
Richmond Ra., *Australia* 91 D5
Richmond-upon-Thames, *U.K.* 13 F7
Richterswil, *Switz.* 23 B7
Richton, *U.S.A.* 105 K1
Richwood, *U.S.A.* 104 F5
Ricla, *Spain* 28 D3
Ridder, *Kazakhstan* 44 D9
Ridderkerk, *Neths.* 16 E5
Riddes, *Switz.* 22 D4
Ridgecrest, *U.S.A.* 113 K9
Ridgedale, *Canada* 101 C8
Ridgefield, *U.S.A.* 112 E4
Ridgeland, *U.S.A.* 105 J5
Ridgelands, *Australia* 90 C5
Ridgetown, *Canada* 98 D3
Ridgewood, *U.S.A.* 107 F10
Ridgway, *U.S.A.* 106 E6
Riding Mountain Nat. Park, *Canada* 101 C8
Ridley, Mt., *Australia* 89 F3
Ried, *Austria* 21 G3
Riedlingen, *Germany* 19 G5
Riel, *Neths.* 17 E6
Rienza →, *Italy* 33 B8
Riesa, *Germany* 18 D9
Riesco, I., *Chile* 128 D2
Riesi, *Italy* 35 E7
Riet →, *S. Africa* 84 D3
Rieti, *Italy* 33 F9
Rieupeyroux, *France* 26 D6
Riez, *France* 27 E10
Riffe L., *U.S.A.* 112 D4
Rifle, *U.S.A.* 110 G10
Rifstangi, *Iceland* 8 C5
Rift Valley □, *Kenya* 82 B4
Rig Rig, *Chad* 73 F7
Riga, *Latvia* 40 C4
Riga, G. of = Rīgas Jūras Līcis, *Latvia* 40 C3
Rīgān, *Iran* 65 D8
Rīgas Jūras Līcis, *Latvia* 40 C3
Rigaud, *Canada* 107 A10
Rigby, *U.S.A.* 110 E8
Rīgestān □, *Afghan.* 60 D4
Riggins, *U.S.A.* 110 D5
Rignac, *France* 26 D6
Rigolet, *Canada* 99 B8
Riihimäki, *Finland* 9 F18
Riiser-Larsen-halvøya, *Antarctica* 5 C4
Rijau, *Nigeria* 79 C6
Rijeka, *Croatia* 33 C11
Rijen, *Neths.* 17 E5
Rijkevorsel, *Belgium* 17 F5
Rijn →, *Neths.* 16 D4
Rijnsberg, *Neths.* 16 D4
Rijsbergen, *Neths.* 17 E5
Rijssen, *Neths.* 16 D9
Rijswijk, *Neths.* 16 D4
Rike, *Ethiopia* 77 E4
Rikuzentakada, *Japan* 48 E10
Rila Planina, *Bulgaria* 38 G6
Riley, *U.S.A.* 110 E4
Rima →, *Nigeria* 79 C6
Rimah, Wadi ar →, *Si. Arabia* 64 E4
Rimavská Sobota, *Slovak Rep.* 21 G10
Rimbey, *Canada* 100 C6
Rimbo, *Sweden* 10 E12
Rimi, *Nigeria* 79 C6
Rímini, *Italy* 33 D9
Rîmnicu Sărat, *Romania* 38 D10
Rîmnicu Vîlcea, *Romania* 38 D7
Rimouski, *Canada* 99 C6
Rimrock, *U.S.A.* 112 D5
Rinca, *Indonesia* 57 F5
Rincón de Romos, *Mexico* 114 C4
Rinconada, *Argentina* 126 A2
Ringarum, *Sweden* 11 F10
Ringe, *Denmark* 11 J4
Ringim, *Nigeria* 79 C6
Ringkøbing, *Denmark* 11 H2
Ringling, *U.S.A.* 110 C8
Ringsaker, *Norway* 10 D4
Ringsted, *Denmark* 11 J5
Ringvassøy, *Norway* 8 B15
Rinjani, *Indonesia* 56 F5
Rinteln, *Germany* 18 C5
Río, Punta del, *Spain* 29 J2
Rio Branco, *Brazil* 124 B4
Río Branco, *Uruguay* 127 C5
Rio Brilhante, *Brazil* 127 A5
Río Bueno, *Chile* 128 B2
Río Chico, *Venezuela* 120 A4
Rio Claro, *Brazil* 127 A6
Rio Claro, *Trin. & Tob.* 117 D7
Río Colorado, *Argentina* 128 A4
Río Cuarto, *Argentina* 126 C3
Rio das Pedras, *Mozam.* 85 C6
Rio de Contas, *Brazil* 123 D3
Rio de Janeiro, *Brazil* 123 F3
Rio de Janeiro □, *Brazil* 123 F3
Rio do Prado, *Brazil* 123 E3
Rio do Sul, *Brazil* 127 B6
Río Gallegos, *Argentina* 128 D3
Río Grande, *Argentina* 128 D3
Río Grande, *Bolivia* 124 E4
Rio Grande, *Brazil* 127 C5
Río Grande, *Mexico* 114 C4
Río Grande, *Nic.* 116 D3
Rio Grande →, *U.S.A.* 109 N6
Rio Grande City, *U.S.A.* 109 M5
Río Grande del Norte →, *N. Amer.* 103 E7
Rio Grande do Norte □, *Brazil* 122 C4
Rio Grande do Sul □, *Brazil* 127 C5
Río Hato, *Panama* 116 E3
Río Lagartos, *Mexico* 115 C7
Rio Largo, *Brazil* 122 C4
Rio Maior, *Portugal* 31 F2
Rio Marina, *Italy* 32 F7
Río Mayo, *Argentina* 128 C2
Río Mulatos, *Bolivia* 124 D4
Río Muni = Mbini □, *Eq. Guin.* 80 D2
Rio Negro, *Brazil* 127 B6
Río Negro, *Chile* 128 B2
Rio Negro, Pantanal do, *Brazil* 125 D6
Rio Pardo, *Brazil* 127 C5
Río Pico, *Argentina* 128 B2
Rio Real, *Brazil* 123 D4
Río Segundo, *Argentina* 126 C3
Río Tercero, *Argentina* 126 C3
Rio Tinto, *Brazil* 122 C4
Rio Tinto, *Portugal* 30 D2
Rio Verde, *Brazil* 123 E1
Río Verde, *Mexico* 115 C5
Rio Verde de Mato Grosso, *Brazil* 125 D7
Rio Vista, *U.S.A.* 112 G5
Ríobamba, *Ecuador* 120 D2
Ríohacha, *Colombia* 120 A3
Rioja, *Peru* 124 B2
Riom, *France* 26 C7
Riom-ès-Montagnes, *France* 26 C6
Rion-des-Landes, *France* 26 E3
Rionegro, *Colombia* 120 B2
Rionero in Vúlture, *Italy* 35 B8
Rioni →, *Georgia* 43 E9
Rios, *Spain* 30 D3
Riosucio, *Caldas, Colombia* 120 B2
Riosucio, *Choco, Colombia* 120 B2
Riou L., *Canada* 101 B7
Rioz, *France* 25 E13
Riozinho →, *Brazil* 120 D4
Riparia, Dora →, *Italy* 32 C4
Ripatransone, *Italy* 33 F10
Ripley, *Canada* 106 B3
Ripley, *Calif., U.S.A.* 113 M12
Ripley, *N.Y., U.S.A.* 106 D5
Ripley, *Tenn., U.S.A.* 109 H10
Ripoll, *Spain* 28 C7
Ripon, *U.K.* 12 C6
Ripon, *Calif., U.S.A.* 112 H5
Ripon, *Wis., U.S.A.* 104 D1
Riposto, *Italy* 35 E8
Risalpur, *Pakistan* 62 B4
Risan, *Montenegro* 21 N8
Risaralda □, *Colombia* 120 B2
Riscle, *France* 26 E3
Rishā', W. ar →, *Si. Arabia* 64 E5
Rishiri-Tō, *Japan* 48 B10
Rishon le Ziyyon, *Israel* 69 D3
Risle →, *France* 24 C7
Rison, *U.S.A.* 109 J8
Risør, *Norway* 11 F3
Rissani, *Morocco* 74 B4
Riti, *Nigeria* 79 D6
Rittman, *U.S.A.* 106 F3
Ritzville, *U.S.A.* 110 C4
Riva Bella, *France* 24 C6
Riva del Garda, *Italy* 32 C7
Rivadavia, *Buenos Aires, Argentina* 126 D3
Rivadavia, *Mendoza, Argentina* 126 C2
Rivadavia, *Salta, Argentina* 126 A3
Rivadavia, *Chile* 126 B1
Rivarolo Canavese, *Italy* 32 C4
Rivas, *Nic.* 116 D2
Rive-de-Gier, *France* 27 C8
River Cess, *Liberia* 78 D3
Rivera, *Uruguay* 127 C4
Riverdale, *U.S.A.* 112 J7
Riverhead, *U.S.A.* 107 F12
Riverhurst, *Canada* 101 C7
Riverina, *Australia* 89 E3
Rivers, *Canada* 101 C8
Rivers □, *Nigeria* 79 E6
Rivers, L. of the, *Canada* 101 D7
Rivers Inlet, *Canada* 100 C3
Riversdale, *S. Africa* 84 E3
Riverside, *Calif., U.S.A.* 113 M9
Riverside, *Wyo., U.S.A.* 110 F10
Riversleigh, *Australia* 90 B2
Riverton, *Australia* 91 E2
Riverton, *Canada* 101 C9
Riverton, *N.Z.* 87 M1
Riverton, *U.S.A.* 110 E9
Riverton Heights, *U.S.A.* 112 C4
Rives, *France* 27 C9
Rivesaltes, *France* 26 F6
Riviera, *Europe* 32 E5
Rivière-à-Pierre, *Canada* 99 C5
Rivière-au-Renard, *Canada* 99 C7
Rivière-du-Loup, *Canada* 99 C6
Rivière-Pentecôte, *Canada* 99 C6
Rivière-Pilote, *Martinique* 117 D7
Rivne = Rovno, *Ukraine* 40 F5
Rívoli, *Italy* 32 C4
Rivoli B., *Australia* 91 F3
Rixensart, *Belgium* 17 G5
Riyadh = Ar Riyāḍ, *Si. Arabia* 64 E5
Rize, *Turkey* 67 C9
Rize □, *Turkey* 67 C9
Rizhao, *China* 51 G10
Rizokarpaso, *Cyprus* 37 D13
Rizzuto, C., *Italy* 35 D10
Rjukan, *Norway* 10 E2
Roa, *Norway* 10 D4
Roa, *Spain* 30 D7
Road Town, *Virgin Is.* 117 C7
Roag, L., *U.K.* 14 C2
Roanne, *France* 27 B8
Roanoke, *Ala., U.S.A.* 105 J3
Roanoke, *Va., U.S.A.* 104 G6
Roanoke →, *U.S.A.* 105 H7
Roanoke I., *U.S.A.* 105 H8
Roanoke Rapids, *U.S.A.* 105 G7
Roatán, *Honduras* 116 C2
Robbins I., *Australia* 90 G4
Robe →, *Australia* 88 D2
Robe →, *Ireland* 15 C2
Röbel, *Germany* 18 B8
Robert Lee, *U.S.A.* 109 K4
Roberts, *U.S.A.* 110 E7
Robertsganj, *India* 63 G10
Robertson, *S. Africa* 84 E2
Robertson I., *Antarctica* 5 C18
Robertson Ra., *Australia* 88 D3
Robertsport, *Liberia* 78 D2
Robertstown, *Australia* 91 E2
Roberval, *Canada* 99 C5
Robeson Chan., *Greenland* 4 A4
Robinson →, *Australia* 90 B2
Robinson Ra., *Australia* 89 E2
Robinson River, *Australia* 90 B2
Robinvale, *Australia* 91 E3
Roblin, *Canada* 101 C8
Roboré, *Bolivia* 125 D6
Robson, Mt., *Canada* 100 C5
Robstown, *U.S.A.* 109 M6
Roca, C. da, *Portugal* 6 H4
Roca Partida, I., *Mexico* 114 D2
Rocas, I., *Brazil* 122 B5
Rocca d'Aspidé, *Italy* 35 B8
Rocca San Casciano, *Italy* 33 D8
Roccalbegna, *Italy* 33 F8
Roccastrada, *Italy* 33 F8
Roccella Iónica, *Italy* 35 D9
Rocha, *Uruguay* 127 C5
Rochdale, *U.K.* 12 D5
Rochechouart, *France* 26 C4
Rochedo, *Brazil* 125 D7
Rochefort, *Belgium* 17 H6
Rochefort, *France* 26 C3
Rochefort-en-Terre, *France* 24 E4
Rochelle, *U.S.A.* 108 E10
Rocher River, *Canada* 100 A6
Rocherath, *Belgium* 17 H8
Rocheservière, *France* 24 F5
Rochester, *Canada* 100 C6
Rochester, *U.K.* 13 F8
Rochester, *Ind., U.S.A.* 104 E2
Rochester, *Minn., U.S.A.* 108 C8
Rochester, *N.H., U.S.A.* 107 C14
Rochester, *N.Y., U.S.A.* 106 C7
Rociana, *Spain* 31 H4
Rociu, *Romania* 38 E8
Rock →, *Canada* 100 A3
Rock Hill, *U.S.A.* 105 H5
Rock Island, *U.S.A.* 108 E9
Rock Rapids, *U.S.A.* 108 D6
Rock River, *U.S.A.* 110 F11
Rock Sound, *Bahamas* 116 B4
Rock Springs, *Mont., U.S.A.* 110 C10
Rock Springs, *Wyo., U.S.A.* 110 F9
Rock Valley, *U.S.A.* 108 D6
Rockall, *Atl. Oc.* 6 D3
Rockanje, *Neths.* 16 E4
Rockdale, *Tex., U.S.A.* 109 K6
Rockdale, *Wash., U.S.A.* 112 C5
Rockefeller Plateau, *Antarctica* 5 E14
Rockford, *U.S.A.* 108 D10
Rockglen, *Canada* 101 D7
Rockhampton, *Australia* 90 C5
Rockhampton Downs, *Australia* 90 B2
Rockingham, *Australia* 89 F2
Rockingham B., *Australia* 90 B4
Rockingham Forest, *U.K.* 13 E7
Rocklake, *U.S.A.* 108 A5
Rockland, *Canada* 107 A9
Rockland, *Idaho, U.S.A.* 110 E7
Rockland, *Maine, U.S.A.* 99 D6
Rockland, *Mich., U.S.A.* 108 B10
Rocklin, *U.S.A.* 112 G5
Rockmart, *U.S.A.* 105 H3
Rockport, *Mo., U.S.A.* 108 E7
Rockport, *Tex., U.S.A.* 109 L6
Rocksprings, *U.S.A.* 109 K4
Rockville, *Conn., U.S.A.* 107 E12
Rockville, *Md., U.S.A.* 104 F7
Rockwall, *U.S.A.* 109 J6
Rockwell City, *U.S.A.* 108 D7
Rockwood, *U.S.A.* 105 H3
Rocky Ford, *U.S.A.* 108 F3
Rocky Gully, *Australia* 89 F2
Rocky Lane, *Canada* 100 B5
Rocky Mount, *U.S.A.* 105 H7
Rocky Mountain House, *Canada* 100 C6
Rocky Mts., *N. Amer.* 100 C4
Rockyford, *Canada* 100 C6
Rocroi, *France* 25 C11
Rod, *Pakistan* 60 E3
Rødberg, *Norway* 10 D2
Rødby, *Denmark* 11 K5
Rødbyhavn, *Denmark* 11 K5
Roddickton, *Canada* 99 B8
Rødding, *Denmark* 11 J3
Rødekro, *Denmark* 11 J3
Roden, *Neths.* 16 B8
Rødenes, *Norway* 10 E5
Rodenkirchen, *Germany* 18 B4
Roderick I., *Canada* 100 C3
Rodez, *France* 26 D6
Rodholívas, *Greece* 39 J6
Rodhopoú, *Greece* 37 D5
Ródhos, *Greece* 37 C10
Rodi Garganico, *Italy* 35 A8
Rodna, *Romania* 38 B7
Rodney, *Canada* 106 D3
Rodney, C., *N.Z.* 87 G5
Rodniki, *Russia* 41 C12
Rodriguez, *Ind. Oc.* 3 E13
Roe →, *U.K.* 15 A5
Roebling, *U.S.A.* 107 F10
Roebourne, *Australia* 88 D2
Roebuck B., *Australia* 88 C3
Roebuck Plains, *Australia* 88 C3
Roer →, *Neths.* 17 F7
Roermond, *Neths.* 17 F7
Roes Welcome Sd., *Canada* 97 B11
Roeselare, *Belgium* 17 G2
Rœulx, *Belgium* 17 G4
Rogachev, *Belorussia* 40 E7
Rogagua, L., *Bolivia* 124 C4
Rogaland fylke □, *Norway* 9 G9
Rogaška Slatina, *Slovenia* 33 B12
Rogatec, *Slovenia* 33 B12
Rogatin, *Ukraine* 40 G4
Rogdhia, *Greece* 37 D7
Rogers, *U.S.A.* 109 G7
Rogers City, *U.S.A.* 104 C4
Rogerson, *U.S.A.* 110 E6
Rogersville, *U.S.A.* 105 G4
Roggan River, *Canada* 98 B4
Roggel, *Neths.* 17 F7
Roggeveldberge, *S. Africa* 84 E3
Roggiano Gravina, *Italy* 35 C9
Rogliano, *France* 27 F13
Rogliano, *Italy* 35 C9
Rogoaguado, L., *Bolivia* 125 C4
Rogue →, *U.S.A.* 110 E1
Rohan, *France* 24 D4
Róhda, *Greece* 37 A3
Rohnert Park, *U.S.A.* 112 G4
Rohrbach-lès-Bitche, *France* 25 C14
Rohri, *Pakistan* 62 F3
Rohri Canal, *Pakistan* 62 F3
Rohtak, *India* 62 E7
Roi Et, *Thailand* 58 D4
Roisel, *France* 25 C10
Rojas, *Argentina* 126 C3
Rojo, C., *Mexico* 115 C5
Rokan →, *Indonesia* 56 D2
Rokeby, *Australia* 90 A3
Rokiškis, *Lithuania* 40 D4
Rokitno, *Russia* 40 F9
Rolândia, *Brazil* 127 A5
Rolde, *Neths.* 16 C9
Rolette, *U.S.A.* 108 A5
Rolla, *Kans., U.S.A.* 109 G4
Rolla, *Mo., U.S.A.* 109 G9
Rolla, *N. Dak., U.S.A.* 108 A5
Rollag, *Norway* 10 D3
Rolle, *Switz.* 22 D2

Rolleston, *Australia* 90 C4
Rollingstone, *Australia* 90 B4
Rom, *Sudan* 77 F3
Roma, *Australia* 91 D4
Roma, *Italy* 34 A5
Roma, *Sweden* 9 H15
Roman, *Romania* 38 C9
Roman, *Russia* 45 C12
Roman-Kosh, Gora, *Ukraine* 42 D6
Romanche →, *France* 27 C9
Romang, *Indonesia* 57 F7
Românî, *Egypt* 69 E1
Romania ■, *Europe* 38 D8
Romano, Cayo, *Cuba* 116 B4
Romano di Lombardía, *Italy* 32 C6
Romanovka = Bessarabka, *Moldavia* 42 C3
Romans-sur-Isère, *France* 27 C9
Romanshorn, *Switz.* 23 A8
Romblon, *Phil.* 55 E5
Rombo □, *Tanzania* 82 C4
Rome = Roma, *Italy* 34 A5
Rome, *Ga., U.S.A.* 105 H3
Rome, *N.Y., U.S.A.* 107 C9
Romeleåsen, *Sweden* 11 J7
Romenay, *France* 27 B9
Romerike, *Norway* 10 D5
Romilly-sur-Seine, *France* 25 D10
Romîni, *Romania* 38 E7
Rommani, *Morocco* 74 B3
Romney, *U.S.A.* 104 F6
Romney Marsh, *U.K.* 13 F8
Romny, *Ukraine* 40 F8
Rømø, *Denmark* 11 J2
Romodan, *Ukraine* 40 G8
Romodanovo, *Russia* 41 D14
Romont, *Switz.* 22 C3
Romorantin-Lanthenay, *France* 25 E8
Romsdalen, *Norway* 10 B2
Ron, *Vietnam* 58 D6
Rona, *U.K.* 14 D3
Ronan, *U.S.A.* 110 C6
Roncador, Cayos, *Caribbean* 116 D3
Roncador, Serra do, *Brazil* 123 D1
Roncesvalles, Paso, *Spain* 28 B3
Ronceverte, *U.S.A.* 104 G5
Ronciglione, *Italy* 33 F9
Ronco →, *Italy* 33 D9
Ronda, *Spain* 31 J5
Ronda, Serranía de, *Spain* 31 J5
Rondane, *Norway* 10 C3
Rondón, *Colombia* 120 B3
Rondônia, *Brazil* 125 C5
Rondônia □, *Brazil* 125 C5
Rondonópolis, *Brazil* 125 D7
Rong Jiang →, *China* 52 E7
Rong Xian, *Guangxi Zhuangzu, China* 53 F8
Rong Xian, *Sichuan, China* 52 C5
Rong'an, *China* 52 E7
Rongchang, *China* 52 C5
Ronge, L. la, *Canada* 101 B7
Rongjiang, *China* 52 E7
Rongshui, *China* 52 E7
Ronne Ice Shelf, *Antarctica* 5 D18
Ronsard, C., *Australia* 89 D1
Ronse, *Belgium* 17 G3
Ronuro →, *Brazil* 125 C7
Roodepoort, *S. Africa* 85 D4
Roodeschool, *Neths.* 16 B9
Roof Butte, *U.S.A.* 111 H9
Roompot, *Neths.* 17 E3
Roorkee, *India* 62 E7
Roosendaal, *Neths.* 17 E4
Roosevelt, *Minn., U.S.A.* 108 A7
Roosevelt, *Utah, U.S.A.* 110 F8
Roosevelt →, *Brazil* 125 B5
Roosevelt, Mt., *Canada* 100 B3
Roosevelt I., *Antarctica* 5 D12
Roosevelt Res., *U.S.A.* 111 K8
Roper →, *Australia* 90 A2
Ropesville, *U.S.A.* 109 J3
Roque Pérez, *Argentina* 126 D4
Roquefort, *France* 26 D3
Roquemaure, *France* 27 D8
Roquetas, *Spain* 28 E5
Roquevaire, *France* 27 E9
Roraima □, *Brazil* 121 C5
Roraima, Mt., *Venezuela* 121 B5
Rorketon, *Canada* 101 C9
Røros, *Norway* 10 B5
Rorschach, *Switz.* 23 B8
Rosa, *Zambia* 83 D3
Rosa, C., *Algeria* 75 A6
Rosa, Monte, *Europe* 22 E5
Rosal, *Spain* 30 D2
Rosal de la Frontera, *Spain* 31 H3
Rosalia, *U.S.A.* 110 C5
Rosamond, *U.S.A.* 113 L8
Rosans, *France* 27 D9
Rosario, *Argentina* 126 C3
Rosário, *Brazil* 122 B3
Rosario, *Baja Calif. N., Mexico* 114 A1
Rosario, *Sinaloa, Mexico* 114 C3
Rosario, *Paraguay* 126 A4
Rosario, Villa del, *Venezuela* 120 A3
Rosario de la Frontera, *Argentina* 126 B3
Rosario de Lerma, *Argentina* 126 A2
Rosario del Tala, *Argentina* 126 C4
Rosário do Sul, *Brazil* 127 C5
Rosário Oeste, *Brazil* 125 C6
Rosarito, *Mexico* 113 N9
Rosarno, *Italy* 35 D8
Rosas, *Spain* 28 C8
Roscoe, *U.S.A.* 108 C5
Roscoff, *France* 24 D3
Roscommon, *Ireland* 15 C3
Roscommon, *U.S.A.* 104 C3
Roscommon □, *Ireland* 15 C3
Roscrea, *Ireland* 15 D4
Rose →, *Australia* 90 A2
Rose Blanche, *Canada* 99 C8
Rose Harbour, *Canada* 100 C2
Rose Pt., *Canada* 100 C2
Rose Valley, *Canada* 101 C8
Roseau, *Domin.* 117 C7
Roseau, *U.S.A.* 108 A7
Rosebery, *Australia* 90 G4
Rosebud, *U.S.A.* 109 K6
Roseburg, *U.S.A.* 110 E2
Rosedale, *Australia* 90 C5
Rosedale, *U.S.A.* 109 J9
Rosée, *Belgium* 17 H5
Roseland, *U.S.A.* 112 G4
Rosemary, *Canada* 100 C6
Rosenberg, *U.S.A.* 109 L7
Rosendaël, *France* 25 A9
Rosenheim, *Germany* 19 H8
Roseto degli Abruzzi, *Italy* 33 F11
Rosetown, *Canada* 101 C7
Rosetta = Rashîd, *Egypt* 76 H7
Roseville, *U.S.A.* 112 G5
Rosewood, *N. Terr., Australia* 88 C4
Rosewood, *Queens., Australia* 91 D5
Roshkhvār, *Iran* 65 C8
Rosières-en-Santerre, *France* 25 C9
Rosignano Marittimo, *Italy* 32 E7
Rosignol, *Guyana* 121 B6
Roşiori de Vede, *Romania* 38 E8
Rositsa, *Bulgaria* 38 F10
Rositsa →, *Bulgaria* 38 F8
Roskilde, *Denmark* 11 J6
Roskilde Amtskommune □, *Denmark* 11 J6
Roskilde Fjord, *Denmark* 11 J6
Roslavl, *Russia* 40 E8
Roslyn, *Australia* 91 E4
Rosmaninhal, *Portugal* 31 F3
Rosmead, *S. Africa* 84 E4
Røsnæs, *Denmark* 11 J4
Rosolini, *Italy* 35 F7
Rosporden, *France* 24 E3
Ross, *Australia* 90 G4
Ross, *N.Z.* 87 K3
Ross I., *Antarctica* 5 D11
Ross Ice Shelf, *Antarctica* 5 E12
Ross L., *U.S.A.* 110 B3
Ross-on-Wye, *U.K.* 13 F5
Ross Sea, *Antarctica* 5 D11
Rossa, *Switz.* 23 D8
Rossan Pt., *Ireland* 15 B3
Rossano Cálabro, *Italy* 35 C9
Rossburn, *Canada* 101 C8
Rosseau, *Canada* 106 A5
Rossignol, L., *Canada* 98 B5
Rossignol Res., *Canada* 99 D6
Rossland, *Canada* 100 D5
Rosslare, *Ireland* 15 D5
Rosslau, *Germany* 18 D8
Rosso, *Mauritania* 78 B1
Rossosh, *Russia* 43 A8
Rossport, *Canada* 98 C2
Rossum, *Neths.* 16 E6
Røssvatnet, *Norway* 8 D13
Rossville, *Australia* 90 B4
Rosthern, *Canada* 101 C7
Rostock, *Germany* 18 A8
Rostov, *Russia* 41 C11
Rostov, *Russia* 43 C8
Rostrenen, *France* 24 D3
Roswell, *U.S.A.* 109 J2
Rosyth, *U.K.* 14 E5
Rota, *Spain* 31 J4
Rotälven →, *Sweden* 10 C8
Rotan, *U.S.A.* 109 J4
Rotem, *Belgium* 17 F7
Rotenburg, *Germany* 18 B5
Roth, *Germany* 19 F7
Rothaargebirge, *Germany* 18 E4
Rothenburg, *Switz.* 23 B6
Rothenburg ob der Tauber, *Germany* 19 F6
Rother →, *U.K.* 13 G8
Rotherham, *U.K.* 12 D6
Rothes, *U.K.* 14 D5
Rothesay, *Canada* 99 C6
Rothesay, *U.K.* 14 F3
Rothrist, *Switz.* 22 B5
Roti, *Indonesia* 57 F6
Roto, *Australia* 91 E4
Rotondella, *Italy* 35 B9
Rotoroa, L., *N.Z.* 87 J4
Rotorua, *N.Z.* 87 H6
Rotorua, L., *N.Z.* 87 H6
Rotselaar, *Belgium* 17 G5
Rott →, *Germany* 19 G9
Rotten →, *Switz.* 22 D5
Rottenburg, *Germany* 19 G4
Rotterdam, *Neths.* 16 E5
Rottnest I., *Australia* 89 F2
Rottumeroog, *Neths.* 16 A9
Rottweil, *Germany* 19 G4
Rotuma, *Fiji* 92 J9
Roubaix, *France* 25 B10
Rouen, *France* 24 C8
Rouillac, *France* 26 C3
Rouleau, *Canada* 101 C8
Round Mt., *Australia* 91 E5
Round Mountain, *U.S.A.* 110 G5
Roundup, *U.S.A.* 110 C9
Roura, *Fr. Guiana* 121 C7
Rousay, *U.K.* 14 B5
Rouses Point, *U.S.A.* 107 B11
Roussillon, *Isère, France* 27 C8
Roussillon, *Pyrénées-Or., France* 26 F6
Rouveen, *Neths.* 16 C8
Rouxville, *S. Africa* 84 E4
Rouyn, *Canada* 98 C4
Rovaniemi, *Finland* 8 C18
Rovato, *Italy* 32 C7
Rovenki, *Ukraine* 43 B8
Rovereto, *Italy* 32 C8
Rovigo, *Italy* 33 C8
Rovinari, *Romania* 38 E6
Rovinj, *Croatia* 33 C10
Rovìra, *Colombia* 120 C2
Rovno, *Ukraine* 40 F5
Rovnoye, *Russia* 41 F15
Rovuma →, *Tanzania* 83 E5
Row'ān, *Iran* 65 C6
Rowena, *Australia* 91 D4
Rowley Shoals, *Australia* 88 C2
Roxa, *Guinea-Biss.* 78 C1
Roxas, *Capiz, Phil.* 55 F5
Roxas, *Isabela, Phil.* 55 C4
Roxas, *Mindoro, Phil.* 55 E4
Roxboro, *U.S.A.* 105 G6
Roxborough Downs, *Australia* 90 C2
Roxburgh, *N.Z.* 87 L2
Roxen, *Sweden* 11 F9
Roy, *Mont., U.S.A.* 110 C9
Roy, *N. Mex., U.S.A.* 109 H2
Roy Hill, *Australia* 88 D2
Roya, Peña, *Spain* 28 E4
Royal Leamington Spa, *U.K.* 13 E6
Royan, *France* 26 C2
Roye, *France* 25 C9
Røyken, *Norway* 10 E4
Rožaj, *Montenegro* 21 N10
Rozay-en-Brie, *France* 25 D9
Rozhishche, *Ukraine* 40 F4
Rožnava, *Slovak Rep.* 20 G10
Rozoy-sur-Serre, *France* 25 C11
Rtishchevo, *Russia* 41 D13
Rúa, *Spain* 30 C3
Ruacaná, *Angola* 84 B1
Ruahine Ra., *N.Z.* 87 H6
Ruapehu, *N.Z.* 87 H5
Ruapuke I., *N.Z.* 87 M2
Ruâq, W. →, *Egypt* 69 F2
Rub' al Khali, *Si. Arabia* 68 D4
Rubeho Mts., *Tanzania* 82 D4
Rubezhnoye, *Ukraine* 42 B8
Rubh a' Mhail, *U.K.* 14 F2
Rubha Hunish, *U.K.* 14 D2
Rubiataba, *Brazil* 123 E2
Rubicon →, *U.S.A.* 112 G5
Rubicone →, *Italy* 33 D9
Rubinéia, *Brazil* 123 F1
Rubino, *Ivory C.* 78 D4
Rubio, *Venezuela* 120 B3
Rubizhne = Rubezhnoye, *Ukraine* 42 B8
Rubtsovsk, *Russia* 44 D9
Ruby L., *U.S.A.* 110 F6
Ruby Mts., *U.S.A.* 110 F6
Rucava, *Latvia* 40 C2
Rucheng, *China* 53 E9
Rud, *Norway* 10 D4
Rūd Sar, *Iran* 65 B6
Ruda Śląska, *Poland* 20 E8
Rudall, *Australia* 91 E2
Rudall →, *Australia* 88 D3
Ruden, *Germany* 18 A9
Rüdersdorf, *Germany* 18 C9
Rudewa, *Tanzania* 83 E3
Rudkøbing, *Denmark* 11 K4
Rudnik, *Serbia* 21 L10
Rudnogorsk, *Russia* 45 D11
Rudnya, *Russia* 40 D7
Rudnyy, *Kazakhstan* 44 D7
Rudolf, Ostrov, *Russia* 44 A6
Rudolstadt, *Germany* 18 E7
Rudong, *China* 53 A13
Rudozem, *Bulgaria* 39 H7
Rudyard, *U.S.A.* 104 B3
Rue, *France* 25 B8
Ruelle, *France* 26 C4
Rufa'a, *Sudan* 77 E3
Ruffec, *France* 26 B4
Rufiji □, *Tanzania* 82 D4
Rufiji →, *Tanzania* 82 D4
Rufino, *Argentina* 126 C3
Rufisque, *Senegal* 78 C1
Rufunsa, *Zambia* 83 F2
Rugao, *China* 53 A13
Rugby, *U.K.* 13 E6
Rugby, *U.S.A.* 108 A5
Rügen, *Germany* 18 A9
Rugles, *France* 24 D7
Ruhengeri, *Rwanda* 82 C2
Ruhla, *Germany* 18 E6
Ruhland, *Germany* 18 D9
Ruhr →, *Germany* 18 D2
Ruhuhu →, *Tanzania* 83 E3
Rui Barbosa, *Brazil* 123 D3
Rui'an, *China* 53 D13
Ruichang, *China* 53 C10
Ruidosa, *U.S.A.* 109 L2
Ruidoso, *U.S.A.* 111 K11
Ruili, *China* 52 E1
Ruinen, *Neths.* 16 C8
Ruinerwold, *Neths.* 16 C8
Ruiten A Kanaal →, *Neths.* 16 C10
Ruivo, Pico, *Madeira* 36 D3
Rujm Tal'at al Jamā'ah, *Jordan* 69 E4
Ruk, *Pakistan* 62 F3
Rukwa □, *Tanzania* 82 D3
Rukwa L., *Tanzania* 82 D3
Rulhieres, C., *Australia* 88 B4
Rulles, *Belgium* 17 J7
Rum Cay, *Bahamas* 117 B5
Rum Jungle, *Australia* 88 B5
Ruma, *Serbia* 21 K9
Rumāḩ, *Si. Arabia* 64 E5
Rumania = Romania ■, *Europe* 38 D8
Rumaylah, *Iraq* 64 D5
Rumbalara, *Australia* 90 D1
Rumbêk, *Sudan* 77 F2
Rumbeke, *Belgium* 17 G2
Rumelange, *Lux.* 17 K8
Rumford, *U.S.A.* 107 B14
Rumilly, *France* 27 C9
Rumoi, *Japan* 48 C10
Rumonge, *Burundi* 82 C2
Rumsey, *Canada* 100 C6
Rumula, *Australia* 90 B4
Rumuruti, *Kenya* 82 B4
Runan, *China* 50 H8
Runanga, *N.Z.* 87 K3
Runaway, C., *N.Z.* 87 G6
Runcorn, *U.K.* 12 D5
Rungwa, *Tanzania* 82 D3
Rungwa →, *Tanzania* 82 D3
Rungwe, *Tanzania* 83 D3
Rungwe □, *Tanzania* 83 D3
Runka, *Nigeria* 79 C6
Runton Ra., *Australia* 88 D3
Ruoqiang, *China* 54 C3
Rupa, *India* 61 F18
Rupar, *India* 62 D7
Rupat, *Indonesia* 56 D2
Rupert →, *Canada* 98 B4
Rupert House = Fort Rupert, *Canada* 98 B4
Rupununi →, *Guyana* 121 C6
Rur →, *Germany* 18 E2
Rurrenabaque, *Bolivia* 124 C4
Rus →, *Spain* 29 F2
Rusambo, *Zimbabwe* 83 F3
Rusape, *Zimbabwe* 83 F3
Ruschuk = Ruse, *Bulgaria* 38 F8
Ruse, *Bulgaria* 38 F8
Ruşeţu, *Romania* 38 E10
Rushan, *China* 51 F11
Rushden, *U.K.* 13 E7
Rushford, *U.S.A.* 108 D9
Rushville, *Ill., U.S.A.* 108 E9
Rushville, *Ind., U.S.A.* 104 F3
Rushville, *Nebr., U.S.A.* 108 D3
Rushworth, *Australia* 91 F4
Russas, *Brazil* 122 B4
Russell, *Canada* 101 C8
Russell, *U.S.A.* 108 F5
Russell L., *Man., Canada* 101 B8
Russell L., *N.W.T., Canada* 100 A5
Russellkonda, *India* 61 K14
Russellville, *Ala., U.S.A.* 105 H2
Russellville, *Ark., U.S.A.* 109 H8
Russellville, *Ky., U.S.A.* 105 G2
Russi, *Italy* 33 D9
Russia ■, *Eurasia* 45 C11
Russian →, *U.S.A.* 112 G3
Russkaya Polyana, *Kazakhstan* 44 D8
Russkoye Ustie, *Russia* 4 B15
Rustam, *Pakistan* 62 B5
Rustam Shahr, *Pakistan* 62 F2
Rustavi, *Georgia* 43 F11
Rustenburg, *S. Africa* 84 D4
Ruston, *U.S.A.* 109 J8
Ruswil, *Switz.* 22 B6
Rutana, *Burundi* 82 C2
Rute, *Spain* 31 H6
Ruteng, *Indonesia* 57 F6
Ruth, *Mich., U.S.A.* 106 C2
Ruth, *Nev., U.S.A.* 110 G6
Rutherford, *U.S.A.* 112 G4
Rutherglen, *U.K.* 14 F4
Rüti, *Switz.* 23 B7
Rutigliano, *Italy* 35 A10
Rutland Plains, *Australia* 90 B3
Rutledge →, *Canada* 101 A6
Rutledge L., *Canada* 101 A6
Rutshuru, *Zaïre* 82 C2
Ruurlo, *Neths.* 16 D8
Ruvo di Púglia, *Italy* 35 A9
Ruvu, *Tanzania* 82 D4
Ruvu →, *Tanzania* 82 D4
Ruvuma □, *Tanzania* 83 E4
Ruwais, *U.A.E.* 65 E7
Ruwenzori, *Africa* 82 B2
Ruyigi, *Burundi* 82 C3
Ruyuan, *China* 53 E9
Ruzayevka, *Russia* 41 D14
Ružomberok, *Slovak Rep.* 20 F9
Rwanda ■, *Africa* 82 C3
Ry, *Denmark* 11 H3
Ryakhovo, *Bulgaria* 38 F9
Ryan, L., *U.K.* 14 G3
Ryazan, *Russia* 41 D11
Ryazhsk, *Russia* 41 E12
Rybache, *Kazakhstan* 44 E9
Rybinsk, *Russia* 41 B11
Rybinskoye Vdkhr., *Russia* 41 B11
Rybnik, *Poland* 20 E8
Rybnitsa, *Moldavia* 42 C3
Rybnoye, *Russia* 41 D11
Rychwał, *Poland* 20 C8
Ryde, *U.K.* 13 G6
Ryderwood, *U.S.A.* 112 D3
Rydöbruk, *Sweden* 11 H7
Rydułtowy, *Poland* 20 E8
Rye, *U.K.* 13 G8
Rye →, *U.K.* 12 C7
Rye Patch Reservoir, *U.S.A.* 110 F4
Ryegate, *U.S.A.* 110 C9
Rylsk, *Russia* 40 F9
Rylstone, *Australia* 91 E4
Ryōthu, *Japan* 48 E9
Rypin, *Poland* 20 B9
Ryūgasaki, *Japan* 49 G10
Ryūkyū Is. = Ryūkyū-rettō, *Japan* 49 M2
Ryūkyū-rettō, *Japan* 49 M2
Rzeszów, *Poland* 20 E11
Rzhev, *Russia* 40 C9

S

Sa, *Thailand* 58 C3
Sa Dec, *Vietnam* 59 G5
Sa'ādatābād, *Fārs, Iran* 65 D7
Sa'ādatābād, *Kermān, Iran* 65 D7
Saale →, *Germany* 18 D7
Saaler Bodden, *Germany* 18 A8
Saalfeld, *Germany* 18 E7
Saane →, *Switz.* 22 B4
Saar →, *Europe* 25 C13
Saarbrücken, *Germany* 19 F2
Saarburg, *Germany* 19 F2
Saaremaa, *Estonia* 40 B3
Saariselkä, *Finland* 8 B20
Saarland □, *Germany* 25 C13
Saarlouis, *Germany* 19 F2
Saas Fee, *Switz.* 22 D5
Sab 'Bi'ār, *Syria* 64 C3
Saba, *W. Indies* 117 C7
Šabac, *Serbia* 21 L9
Sabadell, *Spain* 28 D7
Sabah □, *Malaysia* 56 C5
Sabak Bernam, *Malaysia* 59 L3
Sábana de la Mar, *Dom. Rep.* 117 C6
Sábanalarga, *Colombia* 120 A3
Sabang, *Indonesia* 56 C1
Sabará, *Brazil* 123 E3
Sabarania, *Indonesia* 57 E9
Sabattis, *U.S.A.* 107 B10
Sabáudia, *Italy* 34 A6
Sabaya, *Bolivia* 124 D4
Sabhah, *Libya* 73 C7
Sabie, *S. Africa* 85 D5
Sabinal, *Mexico* 114 A3
Sabinal, *U.S.A.* 109 L5
Sabinal, Punta del, *Spain* 29 J2
Sabinas, *Mexico* 114 B4
Sabinas →, *Mexico* 114 B4
Sabinas Hidalgo, *Mexico* 114 B4
Sabine →, *U.S.A.* 109 L8
Sabine L., *U.S.A.* 109 L8
Sabine Pass, *U.S.A.* 109 L8
Sabinópolis, *Brazil* 123 E3
Sabinov, *Slovak Rep.* 20 F11
Sabirabad, *Azerbaijan* 43 F13
Sabkhet el Bardawîl, *Egypt* 69 D2
Sablayan, *Phil.* 55 E4
Sable, C., *U.S.A.* 103 E10
Sable, C., *Canada* 99 D6
Sable I., *Canada* 99 D8
Sablé-sur-Sarthe, *France* 24 E6
Saboeiro, *Brazil* 122 C4
Sabolev, *Russia* 45 D16
Sabor →, *Portugal* 30 D3
Sabou, *Burkina Faso* 78 C4
Sabrātah, *Libya* 75 B7
Sabria, *Tunisia* 75 B6
Sabrina Coast, *Antarctica* 5 C9
Sabugal, *Portugal* 30 E3
Sabulubek, *Indonesia* 56 E1
Sabzevār, *Iran* 65 B8
Sabzvārān, *Iran* 65 D8
Sac City, *U.S.A.* 108 D7
Sacedón, *Spain* 28 E2
Sachigo →, *Canada* 98 A2
Sachigo, L., *Canada* 98 B1
Sachkhere, *Georgia* 43 E10
Sachseln, *Switz.* 23 C6
Sachsen □, *Germany* 18 E9
Sachsen-Anhalt □, *Germany* 18 D8
Sacile, *Italy* 33 C9

Sackets Harbor, *U.S.A.* 107 C8
Saco, *Maine, U.S.A.* 105 D10
Saco, *Mont., U.S.A.* 110 B10
Sacramento, *Brazil* 123 E2
Sacramento, *U.S.A.* 112 G5
Sacramento →, *U.S.A.* 112 G5
Sacramento Mts., *U.S.A.* 111 K11
Sacramento Valley, *U.S.A.* 112 G5
Sacratif, C., *Spain* 29 J1
Săcueni, *Romania* 38 B5
Sada, *Spain* 30 B2
Sádaba, *Spain* 28 C3
Sadani, *Tanzania* 82 D4
Sadao, *Thailand* 59 J3
Sadd el Aali, *Egypt* 76 C3
Saddle Mt., *U.S.A.* 112 E3
Sade, *Nigeria* 79 C7
Sadimi, *Zaïre* 83 D1
Sado, *Japan* 48 E9
Sado →, *Portugal* 31 G2
Sadon, *Burma* 61 G20
Sadon, *Russia* 43 E10
Sæby, *Denmark* 11 G4
Saegerstown, *U.S.A.* 106 E4
Saelices, *Spain* 28 F2
Safaga, *Egypt* 76 B3
Şafājah, *Si. Arabia* 64 E3
Säffle, *Sweden* 9 G12
Safford, *U.S.A.* 111 K9
Saffron Walden, *U.K.* 13 E8
Safi, *Morocco* 74 B3
Şafīābād, *Iran* 65 B8
Safīd Dasht, *Iran* 65 C6
Safīd Kūh, *Afghan.* 60 B3
Safonovo, *Russia* 40 D8
Safranbolu, *Turkey* 42 F5
Safwān, *Iraq* 64 D5
Sag Harbor, *U.S.A.* 107 F12
Saga, *Indonesia* 57 E8
Saga, *Japan* 49 H5
Saga □, *Japan* 49 H5
Sagae, *Japan* 48 E10
Sagala, *Mali* 78 C3
Sagar, *India* 60 M9
Sagara, L., *Tanzania* 82 D3
Sagay, *Phil.* 55 F5
Sagil, *Mongolia* 54 A4
Saginaw, *U.S.A.* 104 D4
Saginaw B., *U.S.A.* 104 D4
Sagīr, Zab as →, *Iraq* 64 C4
Sagleipie, *Liberia* 78 D3
Saglouc, *Canada* 97 B12
Sagŏ-ri, *S. Korea* 51 G14
Sagone, *France* 27 F12
Sagone, G. de, *France* 27 F12
Sagres, *Portugal* 31 J2
Sagua la Grande, *Cuba* 116 B3
Saguache, *U.S.A.* 111 G10
Saguenay →, *Canada* 99 C5
Sagunto, *Spain* 28 F4
Sahaba, *Sudan* 76 D3
Sahagún, *Colombia* 120 B2
Sahagún, *Spain* 30 C5
Saḩam al Jawlān, *Syria* 69 C4
Sahand, Kūh-e, *Iran* 64 B5
Sahara, *Africa* 70 D4
Saharan Atlas = Saharien, Atlas, *Algeria* 75 B5
Saharanpur, *India* 62 E7
Saharien, Atlâs, *Algeria* 75 B5
Sahasinaka, *Madag.* 85 C8
Sahaswan, *India* 63 E8
Sahel, Canal du, *Mali* 78 C3
Sahibganj, *India* 63 G12
Sahiwal, *Pakistan* 62 D5
Şahneh, *Iran* 64 C5
Sahtaneh →, *Canada* 100 B4
Sahuaripa, *Mexico* 114 B3
Sahuarita, *U.S.A.* 111 L8
Sahuayo, *Mexico* 114 C4
Sahy, *Slovak Rep.* 21 G8
Sai Buri, *Thailand* 59 J3
Sai-Cinza, *Brazil* 125 B6
Sa'id Bundas, *Sudan* 73 G9
Saïda, *Algeria* 75 B5
Saïdābād, *Kermān, Iran* 65 D7
Sa'īdābād, *Semnān, Iran* 65 B7
Saïdia, *Morocco* 75 A4
Sa'idiyeh, *Iran* 65 B6
Saidpur, *Bangla.* 61 G16
Saidu, *Pakistan* 63 B5
Saignelégier, *Switz.* 22 B3
Saignes, *France* 26 C6
Saigon = Phanh Bho Ho Chi Minh, *Vietnam* 59 G6
Saijō, *Japan* 49 H6
Saikhoa Ghat, *India* 61 F19
Saiki, *Japan* 49 H5
Saillans, *France* 27 D9
Sailolof, *Indonesia* 57 E8
Saimbeyli, *Turkey* 66 E7
Şa'in Dezh, *Iran* 64 B5
St. Abb's Head, *U.K.* 14 F6
St. Aegyd, *Austria* 21 H5
St.-Affrique, *France* 26 E6
St.-Agrève, *France* 27 C8
St.-Aignan, *France* 24 E8
St. Alban's, *Canada* 99 C8
St. Albans, *U.K.* 13 F7
St. Albans, *Vt., U.S.A.* 107 B11
St. Albans, *W. Va., U.S.A.* 104 F5
St. Alban's Head, *U.K.* 13 G5
St. Albert, *Canada* 100 C6
St.-Amand-en-Puisaye, *France* 25 E10
St.-Amand-les-Eaux, *France* 25 B10
St.-Amand-Mont-Rond, *France* 26 B6
St.-Amarin, *France* 25 E14
St.-Amour, *France* 27 B9
St.-André-de-Cubzac, *France* 26 D3
St.-André-de-l'Eure, *France* 24 D8
St.-André-les-Alpes, *France* 27 E10
St. Andrew's, *Canada* 99 C8
St. Andrews, *U.K.* 14 E6
St-Anicet, *Canada* 107 A10
St. Ann B., *Canada* 99 C7
St. Anne, *U.K.* 24 C4
St. Ann's Bay, *Jamaica* 116 C4
St. Anthony, *Canada* 99 B8
St. Anthony, *U.S.A.* 110 E8
St.-Antonin-Noble-Val, *France* 26 D5
St. Arnaud, *Australia* 91 F3
St. Arthur, *Canada* 99 C6
St. Asaph, *U.K.* 12 D4
St.-Astier, *France* 26 C4
St.-Aubin, *Switz.* 22 C3
St.-Aubin-du-Cormier, *France* 24 D5
St-Augustin-Saguenay, *Canada* 99 B8
St. Augustine, *U.S.A.* 105 L5
St. Austell, *U.K.* 13 G3
St.-Avold, *France* 25 C13
St.-Barthélemy, I., *W. Indies* 117 C7
St. Bee's Hd., *U.K.* 12 C4
St.-Benoît-du-Sault, *France* 26 B5
St.-Bernard, Col du Grand, *Europe* 22 E4
St.-Bernard, Col du Petit, *France* 27 C10
St.-Blaise, *Switz.* 22 B3
St. Boniface, *Canada* 101 D9
St.-Bonnet, *France* 27 D10
St.-Brévin-les-Pins, *France* 24 E4
St.-Brice-en-Coglès, *France* 24 D5
St. Bride's, *Canada* 99 C9
St. Brides B., *U.K.* 13 F2
St.-Brieuc, *France* 24 D4
St.-Calais, *France* 24 E7
St.-Cast-le-Guildo, *France* 24 D4
St. Catharines, *Canada* 98 D4
St. Catherines I., *U.S.A.* 105 K5
St. Catherine's Pt., *U.K.* 13 G6
St.-Céré, *France* 26 D5
St.-Cergue, *Switz.* 22 D2
St.-Cernin, *France* 26 C6
St.-Chamond, *France* 27 C8
St. Charles, *Ill., U.S.A.* 104 E1
St. Charles, *Mo., U.S.A.* 108 F9
St.-Chély-d'Apcher, *France* 26 D7
St.-Chinian, *France* 26 E6
St. Christopher = St. Kitts, *W. Indies* 117 C7
St. Christopher-Nevis ■, *W. Indies* 117 C7
St.-Ciers-sur-Gironde, *France* 26 C3
St. Clair, *Mich., U.S.A.* 106 D2
St. Clair, *Pa., U.S.A.* 107 F8
St. Clair, L., *Canada* 98 D3
St. Clairsville, *U.S.A.* 106 F4
St.-Claud, *France* 26 C4
St. Claude, *Canada* 101 D9
St.-Claude, *France* 27 B9
St. Cloud, *Fla., U.S.A.* 105 L5
St. Cloud, *Minn., U.S.A.* 108 C7
St-Coeur de Marie, *Canada* 99 C5
St. Cricq, C., *Australia* 89 E1
St. Croix, *Virgin Is.* 117 C7
St. Croix →, *U.S.A.* 108 C8
St. Croix Falls, *U.S.A.* 108 C8
St.-Cyr-sur-Mer, *France* 27 E9
St. David's, *Canada* 99 C8
St. David's, *U.K.* 13 F2
St. David's Head, *U.K.* 13 F2
St.-Denis, *France* 25 D9
St.-Denis-d'Orques, *France* 24 D6
St.-Dié, *France* 25 D13
St.-Dizier, *France* 25 D11
St.-Égrève, *France* 27 C9
St. Elias, Mt., *U.S.A.* 96 B5
St. Elias Mts., *Canada* 100 A1
St.-Élie, *Fr. Guiana* 121 C7
St.-Eloy-les-Mines, *France* 26 B6
St.-Émilion, *France* 26 D3
St.-Étienne, *France* 27 C8
St.-Étienne-de-Tinée, *France* 27 D10
St. Eugène, *Canada* 107 A10
St. Eustatius, *W. Indies* 117 C7
St-Félicien, *Canada* 98 C5
St.-Florent, *France* 27 F13
St.-Florent-sur-Cher, *France* 25 F9
St.-Florentin, *France* 25 D10
St.-Flour, *France* 26 C7
St.-Fons, *France* 27 C8
St. Francis, *U.S.A.* 108 F4
St. Francis →, *U.S.A.* 109 H9
St. Francis, C., *S. Africa* 84 E3
St. Francisville, *U.S.A.* 109 K9
St-François, L., *Canada* 107 A10
St.-Fulgent, *France* 24 F5
St-Gabriel-de-Brandon, *Canada* 98 C5
St. Gallen = Sankt Gallen, *Switz.* 23 B8
St.-Gaudens, *France* 26 E4
St.-Gengoux-le-National, *France* 27 B8
St.-Geniez-d'Olt, *France* 26 D6
St. George, *Australia* 91 D4
St. George, *Canada* 99 C6
St. George, *S.C., U.S.A.* 105 J5
St. George, *Utah, U.S.A.* 111 H7
St. George, C., *Canada* 99 C8
St. George, C., *U.S.A.* 105 L3
St. George Ra., *Australia* 88 C4
St-Georges, *Belgium* 17 G6
St. George's, *Canada* 99 C8
St-Georges, *Canada* 99 C5
St.-Georges, *Fr. Guiana* 121 C7
St. George's, *Grenada* 117 D7
St. George's B., *Canada* 99 C8
St. Georges Basin, *Australia* 88 C4
St. George's Channel, *U.K.* 15 E6
St.-Georges-de-Didonne, *France* 26 C3
St. Georges Hd., *Australia* 91 F5
St.-Gérard, *Belgium* 17 H5
St.-Germain-de-Calberte, *France* 26 D7
St.-Germain-des-Fossés, *France* 26 B7
St.-Germain-du-Plain, *France* 25 F11
St.-Germain-en-Laye, *France* 25 D9
St.-Germain-Laval, *France* 27 C8
St.-Germain-Lembron, *France* 26 C7
St.-Gervais-d'Auvergne, *France* 26 B6
St.-Gervais-les-Bains, *France* 27 C10
St.-Gildas, Pte. de, *France* 24 E4
St.-Gilles, *France* 27 E8
St.-Gilles-Croix-de-Vie, *France* 26 B2
St.-Gingolph, *Switz.* 22 D3
St.-Girons, *France* 26 F5
St. Gotthard P. = San Gottardo, Paso del, *Switz.* 23 C7
St.-Gualtier, *France* 24 F8
St.-Guénolé, *France* 24 E2
St. Helena, *U.S.A.* 110 G2
St. Helena ■, *Atl. Oc.* 2 E9
St. Helena, Mt., *U.S.A.* 112 G4
St. Helena B., *S. Africa* 84 E2
St. Helens, *Australia* 90 G4
St. Helens, *U.K.* 12 D5
St. Helens, *U.S.A.* 112 E4
St. Helens, Mt., *U.S.A.* 112 D4
St. Helier, *U.K.* 13 H5
St.-Hilaire-du-Harcouët, *France* 24 D5
St.-Hippolyte, *France* 25 E13
St.-Hippolyte-du-Fort, *France* 26 E7
St.-Honoré-les-Bains, *France* 25 F10
St-Hubert, *Belgium* 17 H6
St-Hyacinthe, *Canada* 98 C5
St. Ignace, *U.S.A.* 104 C3
St. Ignace I., *Canada* 98 C2
St. Ignatius, *U.S.A.* 110 C6
St-Imier, *Switz.* 22 B3
St. Ives, *Cambs., U.K.* 13 E7
St. Ives, *Corn., U.K.* 13 G2
St.-James, *France* 24 D5
St. James, *U.S.A.* 108 D7
St-Jean, *Canada* 98 C5
St-Jean →, *Canada* 99 B7
St-Jean, L., *Canada* 99 C5
St. Jean Baptiste, *Canada* 101 D9
St.-Jean-d'Angély, *France* 26 C3
St.-Jean-de-Bournay, *France* 27 C9
St.-Jean-de-Luz, *France* 26 E2
St.-Jean-de-Maurienne, *France* 27 C10
St.-Jean-de-Monts, *France* 24 F4
St.-Jean-du-Gard, *France* 26 D7
St.-Jean-en-Royans, *France* 27 C9
St-Jean-Port-Joli, *Canada* 99 C5
St-Jérôme, *Qué., Canada* 98 C5
St-Jérôme, *Qué., Canada* 99 C5
St. John, *Canada* 99 C6
St. John, *Kans., U.S.A.* 109 G5
St. John, *N. Dak., U.S.A.* 108 A5
St. John →, *U.S.A.* 99 C6
St. John, C., *Canada* 99 B8
St. John's, *Antigua* 117 C7
St. John's, *Canada* 99 C9
St. Johns, *Ariz., U.S.A.* 111 J9
St. Johns, *Mich., U.S.A.* 104 D3
St. Johns →, *U.S.A.* 105 K5
St. Johnsbury, *U.S.A.* 107 B12
St. Johnsville, *U.S.A.* 107 C10
St. Joseph, *La., U.S.A.* 109 K9
St. Joseph, *Mich., U.S.A.* 104 D2
St. Joseph, *Mo., U.S.A.* 108 F7
St. Joseph →, *U.S.A.* 104 D2
St. Joseph, I., *Canada* 98 C3
St. Joseph, L., *Canada* 98 B1
St-Jovite, *Canada* 98 C5
St.-Juéry, *France* 26 E6
St.-Julien-Chapteuil, *France* 27 C8
St.-Julien-du-Sault, *France* 25 D10
St.-Julien-en-Genevois, *France* 27 B10
St.-Junien, *France* 26 C4
St.-Just-en-Chaussée, *France* 25 C9
St.-Just-en-Chevalet, *France* 26 C7
St.-Justin, *France* 26 E3
St. Kilda, *N.Z.* 87 L3
St. Kitts, *W. Indies* 117 C7
St. Kitts-Nevis = St. Christopher-Nevis ■, *W. Indies* 117 C7
St. Laurent, *Canada* 101 C9
St.-Laurent, *Fr. Guiana* 121 B7
St.-Laurent-du-Pont, *France* 27 C9
St.-Laurent-en-Grandvaux, *France* 27 B9
St. Lawrence, *Australia* 90 C4
St. Lawrence, *Canada* 99 C8
St. Lawrence →, *Canada* 99 C6
St. Lawrence, Gulf of, *Canada* 99 C7
St. Lawrence I., *U.S.A.* 96 B3
St.-Léger, *Belgium* 17 J7
St. Leonard, *Canada* 99 C6
St.-Léonard-de-Noblat, *France* 26 C5
St. Lewis →, *Canada* 99 B8
St.-Lô, *France* 24 C5
St-Louis, *Senegal* 78 B1
St. Louis, *Mich., U.S.A.* 104 D3
St. Louis, *Mo., U.S.A.* 108 F9
St. Louis →, *U.S.A.* 108 B8
St.-Loup-sur-Semouse, *France* 25 E13
St. Lucia ■, *W. Indies* 117 D7
St. Lucia, L., *S. Africa* 85 D5
St. Lucia Channel, *W. Indies* 117 D7
St. Lunaire-Griquet, *Canada* 99 B8
St. Maarten, *W. Indies* 117 C7
St.-Maixent-l'École, *France* 26 B3
St.-Malo, *France* 24 D4
St.-Malo, G. de, *France* 24 D4
St.-Mandrier-sur-Mer, *France* 27 E9
St-Marc, *Haiti* 117 C5
St.-Marcellin, *France* 27 C9
St.-Marcouf, Is., *France* 24 C5
St. Maries, *U.S.A.* 110 C5
St-Martin, *W. Indies* 117 C7
St. Martin, L., *Canada* 101 C9
St.-Martin-de-Ré, *France* 26 B2
St.-Martin-Vésubie, *France* 27 D11
St. Martins, *Canada* 99 C6
St. Martinville, *U.S.A.* 109 K9
St.-Martory, *France* 26 E4
St. Mary Pk., *Australia* 91 E2
St. Marys, *Australia* 90 G4
St. Marys, *Canada* 106 C3
St. Mary's, *U.K.* 13 H1
St. Marys, *U.S.A.* 106 E6
St. Mary's, C., *Canada* 99 C9
St. Mary's B., *Canada* 99 C9
St. Marys Bay, *Canada* 99 D6
St.-Mathieu, Pte., *France* 24 D2
St. Matthews, I. = Zadetkyi Kyun, *Burma* 59 H2
St.-Maur-des-Fossés, *France* 25 D9
St. Maurice, *Switz.* 22 D4
St-Maurice →, *Canada* 98 C5
St.-Médard-de-Guizières, *France* 26 C3
St.-Méen-le-Grand, *France* 24 D4
St. Michael's Mount, *U.K.* 13 G2
St.-Michel-de-Maurienne, *France* 27 C10
St.-Mihiel, *France* 25 D12
St.-Nazaire, *France* 24 E4
St. Neots, *U.K.* 13 E7
St.-Nicolas-de-Port, *France* 25 D13
St. Niklass = Sint Niklaas, *Belgium* 17 F4
St. Niklaus, *Switz.* 22 D5
St.-Omer, *France* 25 B9
St-Pacome, *Canada* 99 C6
St.-Palais-sur-Mer, *France* 26 C2
St-Pamphile, *Canada* 99 C6
St.-Pardoux-la-Rivière, *France* 26 C4
St. Pascal, *Canada* 99 C6
St. Paul, *Canada* 100 C6
St. Paul, *Minn., U.S.A.* 108 C8
St. Paul, *Nebr., U.S.A.* 108 E5
St. Paul, I., *Ind. Oc.* 3 F13
St.-Paul-de-Fenouillet, *France* 26 F6
St. Paul I., *Canada* 99 C7
St.-Paul-lès-Dax, *France* 26 E2
St.-Péray, *France* 27 D8
St.-Père-en-Retz, *France* 24 E4
St. Peter, *U.S.A.* 108 C8
St. Peter Port, *Chan. Is.* 13 H5
St. Peters, *N.S., Canada* 99 C7
St. Peters, *P.E.I., Canada* 99 C7
St. Petersburg = Sankt-Peterburg, *Russia* 40 B7
St. Petersburg, *U.S.A.* 105 M4
St.-Philbert-de-Grand-Lieu, *France* 24 E5
St.-Pierre, *St- P. & M.* 99 C8
St-Pierre, L., *Canada* 98 C5
St.-Pierre-d'Oléron, *France* 26 C2
St.-Pierre-Église, *France* 24 C5
St.-Pierre-en-Port, *France* 24 C7
St.-Pierre et Miquelon □, *St- P. & M.* 99 C8
St.-Pierre-le-Moûtier, *France* 25 F10
St.-Pierre-sur-Dives, *France* 24 C6
St.-Pieters Leew, *Belgium* 17 G4
St.-Pol-de-Léon, *France* 24 D2
St.-Pol-sur-Mer, *France* 25 A9
St.-Pol-sur-Ternoise, *France* 25 B9
St.-Pons, *France* 26 E6
St.-Pourçain-sur-Sioule, *France* 26 B7
St.-Quay-Portrieux, *France* 24 D4
St.-Quentin, *France* 25 C10
St.-Rambert-d'Albon, *France* 27 C8
St.-Raphaël, *France* 27 E10
St. Regis, *U.S.A.* 110 C6
St.-Rémy-de-Provence, *France* 27 E8
St.-Renan, *France* 24 D2
St.-Saëns, *France* 24 C8
St.-Sauveur-en-Puisaye, *France* 25 E10
St.-Sauveur-le-Vicomte, *France* 24 C5
St.-Savin, *France* 26 B4
St.-Savinien, *France* 26 C3
St. Sebastien, Tanjon' i, *Madag.* 85 A8
St.-Seine-l'Abbaye, *France* 25 E11
St.-Sernin-sur-Rance, *France* 26 E6
St.-Servan-sur-Mer, *France* 24 D4
St.-Sever, *France* 26 E3
St.-Sever-Calvados, *France* 24 D5
St-Siméon, *Canada* 99 C6
St. Stephen, *Canada* 99 C6
St.-Sulpice, *France* 26 E5
St.-Sulpice-Laurière, *France* 26 B5
St.-Syprien, *France* 26 F7
St.-Thégonnec, *France* 24 D3
St. Thomas, *Canada* 98 D3
St. Thomas I., *Virgin Is.* 117 C7
St-Tite, *Canada* 98 C5
St.-Tropez, *France* 27 E10
St. Troud = Sint Truiden, *Belgium* 17 G6
St.-Vaast-la-Hougue, *France* 24 C5
St.-Valéry-en-Caux, *France* 24 C7
St.-Valéry-sur-Somme, *France* 25 B8
St.-Vallier, *France* 27 C8
St.-Vallier-de-Thiey, *France* 27 E10
St.-Varent, *France* 24 F6
St. Vincent, *W. Indies* 117 D7
St. Vincent, G., *Australia* 91 F2
St. Vincent & the Grenadines ■, *W. Indies* 117 D7
St.-Vincent-de-Tyrosse, *France* 26 E2
St. Vincent Passage, *W. Indies* 117 D7
St-Vith, *Belgium* 17 H8
St.-Yrieix-la-Perche, *France* 26 C5
Ste.-Adresse, *France* 24 C7
Ste-Agathe-des-Monts, *Canada* 98 C5
Ste-Anne de Beaupré, *Canada* 99 C5
Ste-Anne-des-Monts, *Canada* 99 C6
Ste-Croix, *Switz.* 22 C3
Ste.-Enimie, *France* 26 D7
Ste.-Foy-la-Grande, *France* 26 D4
Ste. Genevieve, *U.S.A.* 108 G9
Ste.-Hermine, *France* 26 B2
Ste.-Livrade-sur-Lot, *France* 26 D4
Ste-Marguerite →, *Canada* 99 B6
Ste-Marie, *Martinique* 117 D7
Ste.-Marie-aux-Mines, *France* 25 D14
Ste-Marie de la Madeleine, *Canada* 99 C5
Ste.-Maure-de-Touraine, *France* 24 E7
Ste.-Maxime, *France* 27 E10
Ste.-Menehould, *France* 25 C11
Ste.-Mère-Église, *France* 24 C5
Ste.-Rose, *Guadeloupe* 117 C7
Ste. Rose du Lac, *Canada* 101 C9
Saintes, *France* 26 C3
Saintes, I. des, *Guadeloupe* 117 C7
Stes.-Maries-de-la-Mer, *France* 27 E8
Saintonge, *France* 26 C3
Saipan, *Pac. Oc.* 92 F6
Sairang, *India* 61 H18
Sairecábur, Cerro, *Bolivia* 126 A2
Saitama □, *Japan* 49 F9
Sajama, *Bolivia* 124 D4
Sajum, *India* 63 C8
Sak →, *S. Africa* 84 E3
Sakai, *Japan* 49 G7
Sakaide, *Japan* 49 G6
Sakaiminato, *Japan* 49 G6
Sakākah, *Si. Arabia* 64 D4
Sakakawea, L., *U.S.A.* 108 B3
Sakami, L., *Canada* 98 B4
Sâkâne, 'Erg i-n, *Mali* 74 D4
Sakania, *Zaïre* 83 E2

Sakarya = Adapazarı, *Turkey* 66 C4
Sakarya □, *Turkey* 66 C4
Sakarya →, *Turkey* 42 F4
Sakashima-Guntō, *Japan* 49 M2
Sakata, *Japan* 48 E9
Sakchu, *N. Korea* 51 D13
Sakeny →, *Madag.* 85 C8
Sakété, *Benin* 79 D5
Sakha = Yakut Republic □, *Russia* 45 C13
Sakhalin, *Russia* 45 D15
Sakhalinskiy Zaliv, *Russia* 45 D15
Saki, *Ukraine* 42 D5
Šakiai, *Lithuania* 40 D3
Sakon Nakhon, *Thailand* 58 D5
Sakrand, *Pakistan* 62 F3
Sakrivier, *S. Africa* 84 E3
Sakskøbing, *Denmark* 11 K5
Sakuma, *Japan* 49 G8
Sakurai, *Japan* 49 G7
Sal →, *Russia* 43 C9
Sala, *Sweden* 9 G14
Sala Consilina, *Italy* 35 B8
Sala-y-Gómez, *Pac. Oc.* 93 K17
Salaberry-de-Valleyfield, *Canada* 98 C5
Saladas, *Argentina* 126 B4
Saladillo, *Argentina* 126 D4
Salado →, *Buenos Aires, Argentina* 126 D4
Salado →, *La Pampa, Argentina* 128 A3
Salado →, *Río Negro, Argentina* 128 B3
Salado →, *Santa Fe, Argentina* 126 C3
Salado →, *Mexico* 114 B5
Salaga, *Ghana* 79 D4
Sālah, *Syria* 69 C5
Sálakhos, *Greece* 37 C9
Salala, *Liberia* 78 D2
Salala, *Sudan* 76 C4
Salālah, *Oman* 68 D5
Salamanca, *Chile* 126 C1
Salamanca, *Spain* 30 E5
Salamanca, *U.S.A.* 106 D6
Salamanca □, *Spain* 30 E5
Salāmatābād, *Iran* 64 C5
Salamina, *Colombia* 120 B2
Salamis, *Cyprus* 37 D12
Salamis, *Greece* 39 M6
Salar de Atacama, *Chile* 126 A2
Salar de Uyuni, *Bolivia* 124 E4
Sălard, *Romania* 38 B5
Salas, *Spain* 30 B4
Salas de los Infantes, *Spain* 28 C1
Salatiga, *Indonesia* 57 G14
Salaverry, *Peru* 124 B2
Salawati, *Indonesia* 57 E8
Salayar, *Indonesia* 57 F6
Salazar →, *Spain* 28 C3
Salbris, *France* 25 E9
Salcombe, *U.K.* 13 G4
Salda Gölü, *Turkey* 66 E3
Saldaña, *Spain* 30 C6
Saldanha, *S. Africa* 84 E2
Saldanha B., *S. Africa* 84 E2
Saldus, *Latvia* 40 C3
Sale, *Australia* 91 F4
Salé, *Morocco* 74 B3
Sale, *U.K.* 12 D5
Salekhard, *Russia* 44 C7
Salem, *India* 60 P11
Salem, *Ind., U.S.A.* 104 F2
Salem, *Mass., U.S.A.* 107 D14
Salem, *Mo., U.S.A.* 109 G9
Salem, *N.J., U.S.A.* 104 F8
Salem, *Ohio, U.S.A.* 106 F4
Salem, *Oreg., U.S.A.* 110 D2
Salem, *S. Dak., U.S.A.* 108 D6
Salem, *Va., U.S.A.* 104 G5
Salemi, *Italy* 34 E5
Salernes, *France* 27 E10
Salerno, *Italy* 35 B7
Salerno, G. di, *Italy* 35 B7
Salford, *U.K.* 12 D5
Salgir →, *Ukraine* 42 D6
Salgótarján, *Hungary* 21 G9
Salgueiro, *Brazil* 122 C4
Salida, *U.S.A.* 102 C5
Salies-de-Béarn, *France* 26 E3
Salihli, *Turkey* 66 D3
Salima, *Malawi* 81 G6
Salina, *Italy* 35 D7
Salina, *U.S.A.* 108 F6
Salina Cruz, *Mexico* 115 D5
Salinas, *Brazil* 123 E3
Salinas, *Chile* 126 A2
Salinas, *Ecuador* 120 D1
Salinas, *U.S.A.* 111 H3
Salinas →, *Guatemala* 115 D6
Salinas →, *U.S.A.* 111 H3
Salinas, B. de, *Nic.* 116 D2
Salinas, C. de, *Spain* 36 B10
Salinas, Pampa de las, *Argentina* 126 C2
Salinas Ambargasta, *Argentina* 126 B3
Salinas de Hidalgo, *Mexico* 114 C4
Salinas Grandes, *Argentina* 126 B2
Saline →, *Ark., U.S.A.* 109 J8
Saline →, *Kans., U.S.A.* 108 F6
Salines, *Spain* 36 B10
Salinópolis, *Brazil* 122 B2
Salins-les-Bains, *France* 25 F12
Salir, *Portugal* 31 H2
Salisbury = Harare, *Zimbabwe* 83 F3
Salisbury, *Australia* 91 E2
Salisbury, *U.K.* 13 F6
Salisbury, *Md., U.S.A.* 104 F8
Salisbury, *N.C., U.S.A.* 105 H5
Salisbury Plain, *U.K.* 13 F6
Săliște, *Romania* 38 D6
Salitre →, *Brazil* 122 C3
Salka, *Nigeria* 79 C5
Salkhad, *Jordan* 69 C5
Sallent, *Spain* 28 D6
Salles-Curan, *France* 26 D6
Salling, *Denmark* 11 H2
Sallisaw, *U.S.A.* 109 H7
Sallom Junction, *Sudan* 76 D4
Salmās, *Iran* 64 B5
Salmerón, *Spain* 28 E2
Salmo, *Canada* 100 D5
Salmon, *U.S.A.* 110 D7
Salmon →, *Canada* 100 C4
Salmon →, *U.S.A.* 110 D5
Salmon Arm, *Canada* 100 C5
Salmon Falls, *U.S.A.* 110 E6
Salmon Gums, *Australia* 89 F3
Salmon Res., *Canada* 99 C8
Salmon River Mts., *U.S.A.* 110 D6
Salo, *Finland* 9 F17
Salò, *Italy* 32 C7
Salobreña, *Spain* 31 J7
Salome, *U.S.A.* 113 M13
Salon-de-Provence, *France* 27 E9
Salonica = Thessaloníki, *Greece* 39 J5
Salonta, *Romania* 38 C4
Salor →, *Spain* 31 F3
Salou, C., *Spain* 28 D6
Salsacate, *Argentina* 126 C2
Salses, *France* 26 F6
Salsk, *Russia* 43 C9
Salso →, *Italy* 34 E6
Salsomaggiore, *Italy* 32 D6
Salt →, *Canada* 100 B6
Salt →, *U.S.A.* 111 K7
Salt Creek, *Australia* 91 F2
Salt Fork Arkansas →, *U.S.A.* 109 G6
Salt Lake City, *U.S.A.* 110 F8
Salt Range, *Pakistan* 62 C5
Salta, *Argentina* 126 A2
Salta □, *Argentina* 126 A2
Saltcoats, *U.K.* 14 F4
Saltee Is., *Ireland* 15 D5
Saltfjorden, *Norway* 8 C13
Saltholm, *Denmark* 11 J6
Salthólmavík, *Iceland* 8 D3
Saltillo, *Mexico* 114 B4
Salto, *Argentina* 126 C3
Salto, *Uruguay* 126 C4
Salto da Divisa, *Brazil* 123 E4
Salton City, *U.S.A.* 113 M11
Salton Sea, *U.S.A.* 113 M11
Saltpond, *Ghana* 79 D4
Saltsjöbaden, *Sweden* 10 E12
Saltville, *U.S.A.* 104 G5
Saluda →, *U.S.A.* 105 H5
Salûm, *Egypt* 76 A2
Salûm, Khâlig el, *Egypt* 76 A2
Salur, *India* 61 K13
Salut, Is. du, *Fr. Guiana* 121 B7
Saluzzo, *Italy* 32 D4
Salvación, B., *Chile* 128 D1
Salvador, *Brazil* 123 D4
Salvador, *Canada* 101 C7
Salvador, L., *U.S.A.* 109 L9
Salvaterra, *Brazil* 122 B2
Salvaterra de Magos, *Portugal* 31 F2
Sálvora, I., *Spain* 30 C2
Salween →, *Burma* 61 L20
Salyany, *Azerbaijan* 67 D13
Salyersville, *U.S.A.* 104 G4
Salza →, *Austria* 21 H4
Salzach →, *Austria* 21 G2
Salzburg, *Austria* 21 H3
Salzgitter, *Germany* 18 C6
Salzwedel, *Germany* 18 C7
Sam Neua, *Laos* 58 B5
Sam Ngao, *Thailand* 58 D2
Sam Rayburn Reservoir, *U.S.A.* 109 K7
Sam Son, *Vietnam* 58 C5
Sam Teu, *Laos* 58 C5
Sama, *Russia* 44 C7
Sama de Langreo, *Spain* 30 B5
Samagaltai, *Russia* 45 D10
Samaipata, *Bolivia* 125 D5
Samales Group, *Phil.* 55 J4
Samâlût, *Egypt* 76 J7
Samana, *India* 62 D7
Samana Cay, *Bahamas* 117 B5
Samandağı, *Turkey* 66 E6
Samanga, *Tanzania* 83 D4
Samangwa, *Zaïre* 82 C1
Samani, *Japan* 48 C11
Samar, *Phil.* 55 F6
Samara, *Russia* 41 E17
Samaria = Shōmrōn, *Jordan* 69 C4
Samariá, *Greece* 37 D5
Samarinda, *Indonesia* 56 E5
Samarkand, *Uzbekistan* 44 F7
Samarqand = Samarkand, *Uzbekistan* 44 F7
Sāmarrā, *Iraq* 64 C4
Samastipur, *India* 63 G11
Samatan, *France* 26 E4
Samaúma, *Brazil* 125 B5
Samba, *India* 63 C6
Samba, *Zaïre* 82 C2
Sambaíba, *Brazil* 122 C2
Sambalpur, *India* 61 J14
Sambar, Tanjung, *Indonesia* 56 E4
Sambas, *Indonesia* 56 D3
Sambava, *Madag.* 85 A9
Sambawizi, *Zimbabwe* 83 F2
Sambhal, *India* 63 E8
Sambhar, *India* 62 F6
Sambiase, *Italy* 35 D9
Sambonifacio, *Italy* 32 C8
Sambor, *Cambodia* 58 F6
Sambor, *Ukraine* 40 G3
Sambre →, *Europe* 17 H5
Sambuca di Sicilia, *Italy* 34 E6
Samburu □, *Kenya* 82 B4
Samchŏk, *S. Korea* 51 F15
Samchonpo, *S. Korea* 51 G15
Same, *Tanzania* 82 C4
Samedan, *Switz.* 23 C9
Samer, *France* 25 B8
Samfya, *Zambia* 83 E2
Sámi, *Greece* 39 L3
Samnah, *Si. Arabia* 64 E3
Samnaun, *Switz.* 23 C10
Samo Alto, *Chile* 126 C1
Samobor, *Croatia* 33 C12
Samoëns, *France* 27 B10
Samokov, *Bulgaria* 38 G6
Samoorombón, B., *Argentina* 126 D4
Samorogouan, *Burkina Faso* 78 C4
Sámos, *Greece* 39 M9
Samoš, *Serbia* 21 K10
Samos, *Spain* 30 C3
Samothráki, *Évros, Greece* 39 J8
Samothráki, *Kérkira, Greece* 37 A3
Samoylovka, *Russia* 41 F13
Sampa, *Ghana* 78 D4
Sampacho, *Argentina* 126 C3
Sampang, *Indonesia* 57 G15
Samper de Calanda, *Spain* 28 D4
Sampit, *Indonesia* 56 E4
Sampit, Teluk, *Indonesia* 56 E4
Samrée, *Belgium* 17 H7
Samrong, *Cambodia* 58 E4
Samrong, *Thailand* 58 E3
Samsø, *Denmark* 11 J4
Samsø Bælt, *Denmark* 11 J4
Samsun, *Turkey* 66 C7
Samtredia, *Georgia* 43 E10
Samui, Ko, *Thailand* 59 H3
Samun □, *Turkey* 66 C7
Samur →, *Azerbaijan* 43 F13
Samusole, *Zaïre* 83 E1
Samut Prakan, *Thailand* 58 F3
Samut Sakhon, *Thailand* 58 F3
Samut Songkhram →, *Thailand* 58 F3
Samwari, *Pakistan* 62 E2
San, *Mali* 78 C4
San →, *Cambodia* 58 F5
San →, *Poland* 20 E11
San Adrián, C. de, *Spain* 30 B2
San Agustín, *Colombia* 120 C2
San Agustin, C., *Phil.* 55 H7
San Agustín de Valle Fértil, *Argentina* 126 C2
San Ambrosio, *Pac. Oc.* 93 K20
San Andreas, *U.S.A.* 112 G6
San Andrés, I. de, *Caribbean* 116 D3
San Andres Mts., *U.S.A.* 111 K10
San Andrés Tuxtla, *Mexico* 115 D5
San Angelo, *U.S.A.* 109 K4
San Anselmo, *U.S.A.* 112 H4
San Antonio, *Belize* 115 D7
San Antonio, *Chile* 126 C1
San Antonio, *Phil.* 55 D4
San Antonio, *N. Mex., U.S.A.* 111 K10
San Antonio, *Tex., U.S.A.* 109 L5
San Antonio, *Venezuela* 120 C4
San Antonio →, *U.S.A.* 109 L6
San Antonio, C., *Argentina* 126 D4
San Antonio, C., *Cuba* 116 B3
San Antonio, C. de, *Spain* 29 G5
San Antonio, Mt., *U.S.A.* 113 L9
San Antonio Abad, *Spain* 36 C7
San Antonio de los Baños, *Cuba* 116 B3
San Antonio de los Cobres, *Argentina* 126 A2
San Antonio Oeste, *Argentina* 128 B4
San Arcángelo, *Italy* 35 B9
San Ardo, *U.S.A.* 112 J6
San Augustín, *Canary Is.* 36 G4
San Augustine, *U.S.A.* 109 K7
San Bartolomé, *Canary Is.* 36 F6
San Bartolomé de Tirajana, *Canary Is.* 36 G4
San Bartolomeo in Galdo, *Italy* 35 A8
San Benedetto, *Italy* 32 C7
San Benedetto del Tronto, *Italy* 33 F10
San Benedicto, I., *Mexico* 114 D2
San Benito, *U.S.A.* 109 M6
San Benito →, *U.S.A.* 112 J5
San Benito Mt., *U.S.A.* 112 J6
San Bernardino, *U.S.A.* 113 L9
San Bernardino, Paso del, *Switz.* 23 D8
San Bernardino Mts., *U.S.A.* 113 L10
San Bernardino Str., *Phil.* 55 E6
San Bernardo, *Chile* 126 C1
San Bernardo, I. de, *Colombia* 120 B2
San Blas, *Mexico* 114 B3
San Blas, Arch. de, *Panama* 116 E4
San Blas, C., *U.S.A.* 105 L3
San Borja, *Bolivia* 124 C4
San Buenaventura, *Bolivia* 124 C4
San Buenaventura, *Mexico* 114 B4
San Carlos = Butuku-Luba, *Eq. Guin.* 79 E6
San Carlos, *Argentina* 126 C2
San Carlos, *Bolivia* 125 D5
San Carlos, *Chile* 126 D1
San Carlos, *Mexico* 114 B4
San Carlos, *Nic.* 116 D3
San Carlos, *Negros, Phil.* 55 F5
San Carlos, *Pangasinan, Phil.* 55 D4
San Carlos, *Spain* 36 B8
San Carlos, *Uruguay* 127 C5
San Carlos, *U.S.A.* 111 K8
San Carlos, *Amazonas, Venezuela* 120 C4
San Carlos, *Cojedes, Venezuela* 120 B4
San Carlos de Bariloche, *Argentina* 128 B2
San Carlos de la Rápita, *Spain* 28 E5
San Carlos del Zulia, *Venezuela* 120 B3
San Carlos L., *U.S.A.* 111 K8
San Cataldo, *Italy* 34 E6
San Celoni, *Spain* 28 D7
San Clemente, *Chile* 126 D1
San Clemente, *Spain* 29 F2
San Clemente, *U.S.A.* 113 M9
San Clemente I., *U.S.A.* 113 N8
San Constanzo, *Italy* 33 E10
San Cristóbal, *Argentina* 126 C3
San Cristóbal, *Colombia* 120 D3
San Cristóbal, *Dom. Rep.* 117 C5
San Cristóbal, *Mexico* 115 D6
San Cristóbal, *Spain* 36 B11
San Cristóbal, *Venezuela* 120 B3
San Damiano d'Asti, *Italy* 32 D5
San Daniele del Friuli, *Italy* 33 B10
San Demétrio Corone, *Italy* 35 C9
San Diego, *Calif., U.S.A.* 113 N9
San Diego, *Tex., U.S.A.* 109 M5
San Diego, C., *Argentina* 128 D3
San Diego de la Unión, *Mexico* 114 C4
San Dimitri, Ras, *Malta* 37 C1
San Donà di Piave, *Italy* 33 C9
San Elpídio a Mare, *Italy* 33 E10
San Estanislao, *Paraguay* 126 A4
San Esteban de Gormaz, *Spain* 28 D1
San Felice sul Panaro, *Italy* 32 D8
San Felipe, *Chile* 126 C1
San Felipe, *Colombia* 120 C4
San Felipe, *Mexico* 114 A2
San Felipe, *Venezuela* 120 A4
San Felipe →, *U.S.A.* 113 M11
San Felíu de Guíxols, *Spain* 28 D8
San Felíu de Llobregat, *Spain* 28 D7
San Félix, *Pac. Oc.* 93 K20
San Fernando, *Chile* 126 C1
San Fernando, *Mexico* 114 B1
San Fernando, *La Union, Phil.* 55 C4
San Fernando, *Pampanga, Phil.* 55 D4
San Fernando, *Baleares, Spain* 36 C7
San Fernando, *Cádiz, Spain* 31 J4
San Fernando, *Trin. & Tob.* 117 D7
San Fernando, *U.S.A.* 113 L8
San Fernando →, *Mexico* 114 C5
San Fernando de Apure, *Venezuela* 120 B4
San Fernando de Atabapo, *Venezuela* 120 C4
San Fernando di Púglia, *Italy* 35 A9
San Francisco, *Argentina* 126 C3
San Francisco, *Bolivia* 125 D4
San Francisco, *U.S.A.* 111 H2
San Francisco →, *U.S.A.* 111 K9
San Francisco, Paso de, *S. Amer.* 126 B2
San Francisco de Macorís, *Dom. Rep.* 117 C5
San Francisco del Monte de Oro, *Argentina* 126 C2
San Francisco del Oro, *Mexico* 114 B3
San Francisco Javier, *Spain* 36 C7
San Francisco Solano, Pta., *Colombia* 120 B2
San Fratello, *Italy* 35 D7
San Gabriel, *Ecuador* 120 C2
San Gavino Monreale, *Italy* 34 C1
San Gil, *Colombia* 120 B3
San Gimignano, *Italy* 32 E8
San Giórgio di Nogaro, *Italy* 33 C10
San Giórgio Iónico, *Italy* 35 B10
San Giovanni Bianco, *Italy* 32 C6
San Giovanni in Fiore, *Italy* 35 C9
San Giovanni in Persiceto, *Italy* 33 D8
San Giovanni Rotondo, *Italy* 35 A8
San Giovanni Valdarno, *Italy* 33 E8
San Giuliano Terme, *Italy* 32 E7
San Gorgonio Mt., *U.S.A.* 113 L10
San Gottardo, Paso del, *Switz.* 23 C7
San Gregorio, *Uruguay* 127 C4
San Gregorio, *U.S.A.* 112 H4
San Guiseppe Iato, *Italy* 34 E6
San Ignacio, *Belize* 115 D7
San Ignacio, *Bolivia* 125 D5
San Ignacio, *Mexico* 114 B2
San Ignacio, *Paraguay* 126 B4
San Ignacio, L., *Mexico* 114 B2
San Ildefonso, C., *Phil.* 55 C5
San Isidro, *Argentina* 126 C4
San Jacinto, *Colombia* 120 B2
San Jacinto, *U.S.A.* 113 M10
San Jaime, *Spain* 36 B11
San Javier, *Misiones, Argentina* 127 B4
San Javier, *Santa Fe, Argentina* 126 C4
San Javier, *Beni, Bolivia* 125 C5
San Javier, *Santa Cruz, Bolivia* 125 D5
San Javier, *Chile* 126 D1
San Javier, *Spain* 29 H4
San Jerónimo, Sa. de, *Colombia* 120 B2
San Jeronimo Taviche, *Mexico* 115 D5
San Joaquín, *Bolivia* 125 C5
San Joaquin, *U.S.A.* 112 J6
San Joaquín, *Venezuela* 120 A4
San Joaquín →, *Bolivia* 125 C5
San Joaquin →, *U.S.A.* 111 G3
San Joaquin Valley, *U.S.A.* 112 J6
San Jordi, *Spain* 36 B9
San Jorge, *Argentina* 126 C3
San Jorge, *Spain* 36 C7
San Jorge, B. de, *Mexico* 114 A2
San Jorge, G., *Argentina* 128 C3
San Jorge, G. de, *Spain* 28 E4
San José, *Bolivia* 125 D5
San José, *Costa Rica* 116 E3
San José, *Guatemala* 116 D1
San José, *Mexico* 114 C2
San Jose, *Phil.* 55 D4
San José, *Spain* 36 C7
San Jose, *U.S.A.* 111 H3
San Jose →, *U.S.A.* 111 J10
San Jose de Buenovista, *Phil.* 55 E4
San José de Feliciano, *Argentina* 126 C4
San José de Jáchal, *Argentina* 126 C2
San José de Mayo, *Uruguay* 126 C4
San José de Ocune, *Colombia* 120 C3
San José de Uchapiamonas, *Bolivia* 124 C4
San José del Cabo, *Mexico* 114 C3
San José del Guaviare, *Colombia* 120 C3
San José do Anauá, *Brazil* 121 C5
San Juan, *Argentina* 126 C2
San Juan, *Colombia* 120 B2
San Juan, *Mexico* 114 C4
San Juan, *Ica, Peru* 124 D2
San Juan, *Puno, Peru* 124 C4
San Juan, *Phil.* 55 G7
San Juan, *Puerto Rico* 117 C6
San Juan □, *Argentina* 126 C2
San Juan →, *Argentina* 126 C2
San Juan →, *Bolivia* 125 E4
San Juan →, *Colombia* 120 C2
San Juan →, *Nic.* 116 D3
San Juan →, *U.S.A.* 111 H8
San Juan →, *Venezuela* 121 A5
San Juan, C., *Eq. Guin.* 80 D1
San Juan Bautista, *Paraguay* 126 B4
San Juan Bautista, *Spain* 36 B8
San Juan Bautista, *U.S.A.* 111 H3
San Juan Bautista Valle Nacional, *Mexico* 115 D5
San Juan Capistrano, *U.S.A.* 113 M9
San Juan Cr. →, *U.S.A.* 112 J5
San Juan de Guadalupe, *Mexico* 114 C4
San Juan de los Morros, *Venezuela* 120 B4
San Juan del César, *Colombia* 120 A3
San Juan del Norte, *Nic.* 116 D3
San Juan del Norte, B. de, *Nic.* 116 D3
San Juan del Puerto, *Spain* 31 H4
San Juan del Río, *Mexico* 115 C5

San Juan del Sur, *Nic.* 116 **D2**
San Juan I., *U.S.A.* 112 **B3**
San Juan Mts., *U.S.A.* ... 111 **H10**
San Julián, *Argentina* 128 **C3**
San Just, Sierra de, *Spain* . 28 **E4**
San Justo, *Argentina* 126 **C3**
San Kamphaeng, *Thailand* 58 **C2**
San Lázaro, C., *Mexico* .. 114 **C2**
San Lázaro, Sa., *Mexico* .. 114 **C3**
San Leandro, *U.S.A.* 111 **H2**
San Leonardo, *Spain* 28 **D1**
San Lorenzo, *Argentina* .. 126 **C3**
San Lorenzo, *Beni, Bolivia* 125 **D4**
San Lorenzo, *Tarija, Bolivia* 125 **E5**
San Lorenzo, *Ecuador* 120 **C2**
San Lorenzo, *Paraguay* ... 126 **B4**
San Lorenzo, *Spain* 36 **B10**
San Lorenzo, *Venezuela* .. 120 **B3**
San Lorenzo →, *Mexico* . 114 **C3**
San Lorenzo, I., *Mexico* .. 114 **B2**
San Lorenzo, I., *Peru* 124 **C2**
San Lorenzo, Mt., *Argentina* 128 **C2**
San Lorenzo de la Parrilla, *Spain* 28 **F2**
San Lorenzo de Morunys, *Spain* 28 **C6**
San Lucas, *Bolivia* 125 **E4**
San Lucas, *Baja Calif. S., Mexico* 114 **C3**
San Lucas, *Baja Calif. S., Mexico* 114 **B2**
San Lucas, *U.S.A.* 112 **J5**
San Lucas, C., *Mexico* ... 114 **C3**
San Lúcido, *Italy* 35 **C9**
San Luis, *Argentina* 126 **C2**
San Luis, *Cuba* 116 **B3**
San Luis, *Guatemala* 116 **C2**
San Luis, *U.S.A.* 111 **H11**
San Luis □, *Argentina* 126 **C2**
San Luis, I., *Mexico* 114 **B2**
San Luis, L. de, *Bolivia* .. 125 **C5**
San Luis, Sierra de, *Argentina* 126 **C2**
San Luis de la Paz, *Mexico* 114 **C4**
San Luis Obispo, *U.S.A.* .. 113 **K6**
San Luis Potosí, *Mexico* .. 114 **C4**
San Luis Potosí □, *Mexico* 114 **C4**
San Luis Reservoir, *U.S.A.* 112 **H5**
San Luis Río Colorado, *Mexico* 114 **A2**
San Marco Argentano, *Italy* 35 **C9**
San Marco dei Cavoti, *Italy* 35 **A7**
San Marco in Lámis, *Italy* 35 **A8**
San Marcos, *Colombia* ... 120 **B2**
San Marcos, *Guatemala* .. 116 **D1**
San Marcos, *Mexico* 114 **B2**
San Marcos, *U.S.A.* 109 **L6**
San Marino ■, *Europe* ... 33 **E9**
San Martín, *Argentina* 126 **C2**
San Martín, *Colombia* 120 **C3**
San Martin →, *Bolivia* ... 125 **C5**
San Martín, L., *Argentina* 128 **C2**
San Martin de los Andes, *Argentina* 128 **B2**
San Martín de Valdeiglesias, *Spain* 30 **E6**
San Martino de Calvi, *Italy* 32 **C6**
San Mateo, *Phil.* 55 **C4**
San Mateo, *Baleares, Spain* 36 **B7**
San Mateo, *Valencia, Spain* 28 **E5**
San Mateo, *U.S.A.* 111 **H2**
San Matías, *Bolivia* 125 **D6**
San Matías, G., *Argentina* 128 **B4**
San Miguel, *El Salv.* 116 **D2**
San Miguel, *Panama* 116 **E4**
San Miguel, *Spain* 36 **B7**
San Miguel, *U.S.A.* 111 **J3**
San Miguel, *Venezuela* ... 120 **B4**
San Miguel →, *Bolivia* ... 125 **C5**
San Miguel →, *S. Amer.* . 120 **C2**
San Miguel de Huachi, *Bolivia* 124 **D4**
San Miguel de Salinas, *Spain* 29 **H4**
San Miguel de Tucumán, *Argentina* 126 **B2**
San Miguel del Monte, *Argentina* 126 **D4**
San Miguel I., *U.S.A.* 113 **L6**
San Miniato, *Italy* 32 **E7**
San Narciso, *Phil.* 55 **D4**
San Nicolás, *Canary Is.* ... 36 **G4**
San Nicolas, *Phil.* 55 **B4**
San Nicolás de los Arroyas, *Argentina* 126 **C3**
San Nicolas I., *U.S.A.* 113 **M7**
San Onofre, *Colombia* 120 **B2**
San Onofre, *U.S.A.* 113 **M9**
San Pablo, *Bolivia* 126 **A2**
San Pablo, *Phil.* 55 **D4**
San Paolo di Civitate, *Italy* 35 **A8**
San Pedro, *Buenos Aires, Argentina* 127 **B5**
San Pedro, *Jujuy, Argentina* 126 **A3**
San Pedro, *Colombia* 120 **C3**
San-Pédro, *Ivory C.* 78 **E3**
San Pedro, *Mexico* 114 **C2**
San Pedro, *Peru* 124 **C3**
San Pedro □, *Paraguay* ... 126 **A4**
San Pedro →, *Chihuahua, Mexico* 114 **B3**
San Pedro →, *Michoacan, Mexico* 114 **D4**
San Pedro →, *Nayarit, Mexico* 114 **C3**
San Pedro →, *U.S.A.* 111 **K8**
San Pedro, Pta., *Chile* 126 **B1**
San Pedro, Sierra de, *Spain* 31 **F4**
San Pedro Channel, *U.S.A.* 113 **M8**
San Pedro de Arimena, *Colombia* 120 **C3**
San Pedro de Atacama, *Chile* 126 **A2**
San Pedro de Jujuy, *Argentina* 126 **A3**
San Pedro de las Colonias, *Mexico* 114 **B4**
San Pedro de Lloc, *Peru* .. 124 **B2**
San Pedro de Macorís, *Dom. Rep.* 117 **C6**
San Pedro del Norte, *Nic.* 116 **D3**
San Pedro del Paraná, *Paraguay* 126 **B4**
San Pedro del Pinatar, *Spain* 29 **H4**
San Pedro Mártir, Sierra, *Mexico* 114 **A1**
San Pedro Mixtepec, *Mexico* 115 **D5**
San Pedro Ocampo = Melchor Ocampo, *Mexico* 114 **C4**
San Pedro Sula, *Honduras* 116 **C2**
San Pietro, I., *Italy* 34 **C1**
San Pietro Vernótico, *Italy* 35 **B11**
San Quintín, *Mexico* 114 **A1**
San Rafael, *Argentina* 126 **C2**
San Rafael, *Calif., U.S.A.* 112 **H4**
San Rafael, *N. Mex., U.S.A.* 111 **J10**
San Rafael, *Venezuela* 120 **A3**
San Rafael Mt., *U.S.A.* ... 113 **L7**
San Rafael Mts., *U.S.A.* .. 113 **L7**
San Ramón, *Bolivia* 125 **C5**
San Ramón, *Peru* 124 **C2**
San Ramón de la Nueva Orán, *Argentina* 126 **A3**
San Remo, *Italy* 32 **E4**
San Román, C., *Venezuela* 120 **A3**
San Roque, *Argentina* 126 **B4**
San Roque, *Spain* 31 **J5**
San Rosendo, *Chile* 126 **D1**
San Saba, *U.S.A.* 109 **K5**
San Salvador, *Bahamas* ... 117 **B5**
San Salvador, *El Salv.* 116 **D2**
San Salvador, *Spain* 36 **B10**
San Salvador de Jujuy, *Argentina* 126 **A3**
San Salvador I., *Bahamas* . 117 **B5**
San Sebastián, *Argentina* . 128 **D3**
San Sebastián, *Spain* 28 **B3**
San Sebastián, *Venezuela* . 120 **B4**
San Sebastian de la Gomera, *Canary Is.* 36 **F2**
San Serra, *Spain* 36 **B10**
San Serverino Marche, *Italy* 33 **E10**
San Simeon, *U.S.A.* 112 **K5**
San Simon, *U.S.A.* 111 **K9**
San Stéfano di Cadore, *Italy* 33 **B9**
San Telmo, *Mexico* 114 **A1**
San Telmo, *Spain* 36 **B9**
San Tiburcio, *Mexico* 114 **C4**
San Valentin, Mte., *Chile* . 128 **C2**
San Vicente de Alcántara, *Spain* 31 **F3**
San Vicente de la Barquera, *Spain* 30 **B6**
San Vicente del Caguán, *Colombia* 120 **C3**
San Vincenzo, *Italy* 32 **E7**
San Vito, *Italy* 34 **C2**
San Vito, C., *Italy* 34 **D5**
San Vito al Tagliamento, *Italy* 33 **C9**
San Vito Chietino, *Italy* .. 33 **F11**
San Vito dei Normanni, *Italy* 35 **B10**
San Yanaro, *Colombia* ... 120 **C4**
San Ygnacio, *U.S.A.* 109 **M5**
Saña, *Peru* 124 **B2**
Sana', *Yemen* 68 **D3**
Sana →, *Bos.-H.* 33 **C13**
Sanaba, *Burkina Faso* 78 **C4**
Şanāfīr, *Si. Arabia* 76 **B3**
Sanaga →, *Cameroon* 79 **E6**
Sanaloa, Presa, *Mexico* ... 114 **C3**
Sanana, *Indonesia* 57 **E7**
Sanand, *India* 62 **H5**
Sanandaj, *Iran* 64 **C5**
Sanandita, *Bolivia* 126 **A3**
Sanary-sur-Mer, *France* ... 27 **E9**
Sanawad, *India* 62 **H7**
Sancellas, *Spain* 36 **B9**
Sancergues, *France* 25 **E9**
Sancerre, *France* 25 **E9**
Sancerrois, Collines du, *France* 25 **E9**
Sancha He →, *China* 52 **D6**
Sanchahe, *China* 51 **B14**
Sánchez, *Dom. Rep.* 117 **C6**
Sanchor, *India* 62 **G4**
Sanco Pt., *Phil.* 57 **C7**
Sancoins, *France* 25 **F9**
Sancti-Spíritus, *Cuba* 116 **B4**
Sancy, Puy de, *France* 26 **C6**
Sand →, *S. Africa* 85 **C5**
Sand Springs, *U.S.A.* 109 **G6**
Sanda, *Japan* 49 **G7**
Sandakan, *Malaysia* 56 **C5**
Sandan = Sambor, *Cambodia* 58 **F6**
Sandanski, *Bulgaria* 39 **H6**
Sandaré, *Mali* 78 **C2**
Sanday, *U.K.* 14 **B6**
Sandefjord, *Norway* 10 **E4**
Sanders, *U.S.A.* 111 **J9**
Sanderson, *U.S.A.* 109 **K3**
Sandfly L., *Canada* 101 **B7**
Sandgate, *Australia* 91 **D5**
Sandía, *Peru* 124 **C4**
Sandıklı, *Turkey* 66 **D4**
Sandnes, *Norway* 9 **G8**
Sandness, *U.K.* 14 **A7**
Sandoa, *Zaïre* 80 **F4**
Sandona, *Colombia* 120 **C2**
Sandover →, *Australia* 90 **C2**
Sandoway, *Burma* 61 **K19**
Sandpoint, *U.S.A.* 110 **B5**
Sandringham, *U.K.* 12 **E8**
Sandslån, *Sweden* 10 **A11**
Sandspit, *Canada* 100 **C2**
Sandstone, *Australia* 89 **E2**
Sandu, *China* 52 **E6**
Sandusky, *Mich., U.S.A.* . 98 **D3**
Sandusky, *Ohio, U.S.A.* .. 106 **E2**
Sandvig, *Sweden* 11 **J8**
Sandviken, *Sweden* 9 **F14**
Sandwich, C., *Australia* ... 90 **B4**
Sandwich B., *Canada* 99 **B8**
Sandwich B., *Namibia* 84 **C1**
Sandwip Chan., *Bangla.* .. 61 **H17**
Sandy, *Nev., U.S.A.* 113 **K11**
Sandy, *Oreg., U.S.A.* 112 **E4**
Sandy Bight, *Australia* 89 **F3**
Sandy C., *Queens., Australia* 90 **C5**
Sandy C., *Tas., Australia* . 90 **G3**
Sandy Cay, *Bahamas* 117 **B4**
Sandy Cr. →, *U.S.A.* 110 **F9**
Sandy L., *Canada* 98 **B1**
Sandy Lake, *Canada* 98 **B1**
Sandy Narrows, *Canada* .. 101 **B8**
Sanford, *Fla., U.S.A.* 105 **L5**
Sanford, *Maine, U.S.A.* .. 107 **C14**
Sanford, *N.C., U.S.A.* ... 105 **H6**
Sanford →, *Australia* 89 **E2**
Sanford, Mt., *U.S.A.* 96 **B5**
Sang-i-Masha, *Afghan.* ... 62 **C2**
Sanga, *Mozam.* 83 **E4**
Sanga →, *Congo* 80 **E3**
Sanga-Tolon, *Russia* 45 **C15**
Sangamner, *India* 60 **K9**
Sangar, *Afghan.* 62 **C1**
Sangar, *Russia* 45 **C13**
Sangar Sarai, *Afghan.* 62 **B4**
Sangasangadalam, *Indonesia* 56 **E5**
Sangay, *Ecuador* 120 **D2**
Sange, *Zaïre* 82 **D2**
Sangeang, *Indonesia* 57 **F5**
Sanger, *U.S.A.* 111 **H4**
Sangerhausen, *Germany* .. 18 **D7**
Sanggan He →, *China* 50 **E9**
Sanggau, *Indonesia* 56 **D4**
Sangihe, Kepulauan, *Indonesia* 57 **D7**
Sangihe, P., *Indonesia* 57 **D7**
Sangju, *S. Korea* 51 **F15**
Sangkapura, *Indonesia* ... 56 **F4**
Sangkhla, *Thailand* 58 **E2**
Sangli, *India* 60 **L9**
Sangmélina, *Cameroon* 79 **E7**
Sangonera →, *Spain* 29 **H3**
Sangre de Cristo Mts., *U.S.A.* 109 **G2**
Sangro →, *Italy* 33 **F11**
Sangudo, *Canada* 100 **C6**
Sangue →, *Brazil* 125 **C6**
Sangüesa, *Spain* 28 **C3**
Sanguinaires, Is., *France* .. 27 **G12**
Sangzhi, *China* 53 **C8**
Sanhala, *Ivory C.* 78 **C3**
Sāniyah, *Iraq* 64 **C4**
Sanje, *Uganda* 82 **C3**
Sanjiang, *China* 52 **E7**
Sanjo, *Japan* 48 **F9**
Sankt Antönien, *Switz.* 23 **C9**
Sankt Blasien, *Germany* .. 19 **H4**
Sankt Gallen, *Switz.* 23 **B8**
Sankt Gallen □, *Switz.* ... 23 **B8**
Sankt Goar, *Germany* 19 **E3**
Sankt Ingbert, *Germany* .. 19 **F3**
Sankt Margrethen, *Switz.* . 23 **B9**
Sankt Moritz, *Switz.* 23 **D9**
Sankt-Peterburg, *Russia* .. 40 **B7**
Sankt Pölten, *Austria* 21 **G5**
Sankt Valentin, *Austria* ... 21 **G4**
Sankt Veit, *Austria* 21 **J4**
Sankt Wendel, *Germany* .. 19 **F3**
Sankuru →, *Zaïre* 80 **E4**
Sanlúcar de Barrameda, *Spain* 31 **J4**
Sanlúcar la Mayor, *Spain* . 31 **H4**
Sanluri, *Italy* 34 **C1**
Sanmenxia, *China* 50 **G6**
Sanming, *China* 53 **D11**
Sannaspos, *S. Africa* 84 **D4**
Sannicandro Gargánico, *Italy* 35 **A8**
Sannidal, *Norway* 10 **F3**
Sannieshof, *S. Africa* 84 **D4**
Sannīn, J., *Lebanon* 69 **B4**
Sanok, *Poland* 20 **F12**
Sanquhar, *U.K.* 14 **F5**
Sansanding Dam, *Mali* ... 78 **C3**
Sansepolcro, *Italy* 33 **E9**
Sansha, *China* 53 **D13**
Sanshui, *China* 53 **F9**
Sanski Most, *Bos.-H.* 33 **D13**
Sansui, *China* 52 **D7**
Santa, *Peru* 124 **B2**
Sant' Ágata de Goti, *Italy* 35 **A7**
Sant' Ágata di Militello, *Italy* 35 **D7**
Santa Ana, *Beni, Bolivia* . 125 **C4**
Santa Ana, *Santa Cruz, Bolivia* 125 **D6**
Santa Ana, *Santa Cruz, Bolivia* 125 **D5**
Santa Ana, *Ecuador* 120 **D1**
Santa Ana, *El Salv.* 116 **D2**
Santa Ana, *Mexico* 114 **A2**
Santa Ana, *U.S.A.* 113 **M9**
Santa Ana →, *Venezuela* . 120 **B3**
Sant' Ángelo Lodigiano, *Italy* 32 **C6**
Sant' Antíoco, *Italy* 34 **C1**
Sant' Arcángelo di Romagna, *Italy* 33 **D9**
Santa Bárbara, *Colombia* . 120 **B2**
Santa Bárbara, *Honduras* . 116 **D2**
Santa Bárbara, *Mexico* ... 114 **B3**
Santa Bárbara, *Spain* 28 **E5**
Santa Barbara, *U.S.A.* ... 113 **L7**
Santa Bárbara, *Venezuela* . 120 **B3**
Santa Bárbara, Mt., *Spain* 29 **H2**
Santa Barbara Channel, *U.S.A.* 113 **L7**
Santa Barbara I., *U.S.A.* . 113 **M7**
Santa Catalina, *Colombia* . 120 **A2**
Santa Catalina, *Mexico* ... 114 **B2**
Santa Catalina, Gulf of, *U.S.A.* 113 **N9**
Santa Catalina I., *U.S.A.* . 113 **M8**
Santa Catarina □, *Brazil* . 127 **B6**
Santa Catarina, I. de, *Brazil* 127 **B6**
Santa Caterina Villarmosa, *Italy* 35 **E7**
Santa Cecília, *Brazil* 127 **B5**
Santa Clara, *Cuba* 116 **B4**
Santa Clara, *Calif., U.S.A.* 111 **H3**
Santa Clara, *Utah, U.S.A.* 111 **H7**
Santa Clara de Olimar, *Uruguay* 127 **C5**
Santa Clotilde, *Peru* 120 **D3**
Santa Coloma de Farners, *Spain* 28 **D7**
Santa Coloma de Gramanet, *Spain* 28 **D7**
Santa Comba, *Spain* 30 **B2**
Santa Croce Camerina, *Italy* 35 **F7**
Santa Croce di Magliano, *Italy* 35 **A7**
Santa Cruz, *Argentina* 128 **D3**
Santa Cruz, *Bolivia* 125 **D5**
Santa Cruz, *Brazil* 122 **C4**
Santa Cruz, *Chile* 126 **C1**
Santa Cruz, *Costa Rica* ... 116 **D2**
Santa Cruz, *Madeira* 36 **D3**
Santa Cruz, *Peru* 124 **B2**
Santa Cruz, *Phil.* 55 **D4**
Santa Cruz, *U.S.A.* 111 **H2**
Santa Cruz, *Venezuela* 121 **B5**
Santa Cruz □, *Argentina* .. 128 **C3**
Santa Cruz □, *Bolivia* 125 **D5**
Santa Cruz →, *Argentina* . 128 **D3**
Santa Cruz Cabrália, *Brazil* 123 **E4**
Santa Cruz de la Palma, *Canary Is.* 36 **F2**
Santa Cruz de Mudela, *Spain* 29 **G1**
Santa Cruz de Tenerife, *Canary Is.* 36 **F3**
Santa Cruz del Norte, *Cuba* 116 **B3**
Santa Cruz del Retamar, *Spain* 30 **E6**
Santa Cruz del Sur, *Cuba* . 116 **B4**
Santa Cruz do Rio Pardo, *Brazil* 127 **A6**
Santa Cruz do Sul, *Brazil* . 127 **B5**
Santa Cruz I., *Solomon Is.* 92 **J8**
Santa Cruz I., *U.S.A.* 113 **M7**
Santa Domingo, Cay, *Bahamas* 116 **B4**
Santa Elena, *Argentina* ... 126 **C4**
Santa Elena, *Ecuador* 120 **D1**
Santa Elena, C., *Costa Rica* 116 **D2**
Sant' Eufémia, G. di, *Italy* 35 **D9**
Santa Eugenia, Pta., *Mexico* 114 **B1**
Santa Eulalia, *Spain* 36 **C8**
Santa Fe, *Argentina* 126 **C3**
Santa Fe, *Spain* 31 **H7**
Santa Fe, *U.S.A.* 111 **J11**
Santa Fé □, *Argentina* 126 **C3**
Santa Filomena, *Brazil* ... 122 **C2**
Santa Galdana, *Spain* 36 **B10**
Santa Gertrudis, *Spain* ... 36 **B7**
Santa Helena, *Brazil* 122 **B2**
Santa Helena de Goiás, *Brazil* 123 **E1**
Santa Inês, *Brazil* 123 **D4**
Santa Inés, *Baleares, Spain* 36 **B7**
Santa Inés, *Extremadura, Spain* 31 **G5**
Santa Inés, I., *Chile* 128 **D2**
Santa Isabel = Rey Malabo, *Eq. Guin.* 79 **E6**
Santa Isabel, *Argentina* ... 126 **D2**
Santa Isabel, *Brazil* 123 **D1**
Santa Isabel, Pico, *Eq. Guin.* 79 **E6**
Santa Isabel do Araguaia, *Brazil* 122 **C2**
Santa Isabel do Morro, *Brazil* 123 **D1**
Santa Lucía, *Corrientes, Argentina* 126 **B4**
Santa Lucía, *San Juan, Argentina* 126 **C2**
Santa Lucía, *Spain* 29 **H4**
Santa Lucia, *Uruguay* 126 **C4**
Santa Lucia Range, *U.S.A.* 111 **J3**
Santa Magdalena, I., *Mexico* 114 **C2**
Santa Margarita, *Argentina* 126 **D3**
Santa Margarita, *Mexico* .. 114 **C2**
Santa Margarita, *Spain* ... 36 **B10**
Santa Margarita, *U.S.A.* .. 112 **K6**
Santa Margarita →, *U.S.A.* 113 **M9**
Santa Margherita, *Italy* ... 32 **D6**
Santa María, *Argentina* ... 126 **B2**
Santa Maria, *Brazil* 127 **B5**
Santa Maria, *Phil.* 55 **C4**
Santa Maria, *Spain* 36 **B9**
Santa Maria, *Switz.* 23 **C10**
Santa Maria, *U.S.A.* 113 **L6**
Santa María →, *Mexico* .. 114 **A3**
Santa María, B. de, *Mexico* 114 **B3**
Santa Maria, C. de, *Portugal* 31 **J3**
Santa Maria Capua Vetere, *Italy* 35 **A7**
Santa Maria da Vitória, *Brazil* 123 **D3**
Santa María de Ipire, *Venezuela* 121 **B4**
Santa Maria di Leuca, C., *Italy* 35 **C11**
Santa Maria do Suaçuí, *Brazil* 123 **E3**
Santa Maria dos Marmelos, *Brazil* 125 **B5**
Santa María la Real de Nieva, *Spain* 30 **D6**
Santa Marta, *Colombia* ... 120 **A3**
Santa Marta, *Spain* 31 **G4**
Santa Marta, Ría de, *Spain* 30 **B3**
Santa Marta, Sierra Nevada de, *Colombia* 120 **A3**
Santa Marta Grande, C., *Brazil* 127 **B6**
Santa Maura = Levkás, *Greece* 39 **L3**
Santa Monica, *U.S.A.* 113 **M8**
Santa Olalla, *Huelva, Spain* 31 **H4**
Santa Olalla, *Toledo, Spain* 30 **E6**
Sant' Onofrio, *Italy* 35 **D9**
Santa Pola, *Spain* 29 **G4**
Santa Ponsa, *Spain* 36 **B9**
Santa Quitéria, *Brazil* 122 **B3**
Santa Rita, *U.S.A.* 111 **K10**
Santa Rita, *Guarico, Venezuela* 120 **B4**
Santa Rita, *Zulia, Venezuela* 120 **A3**
Santa Rita do Araquaia, *Brazil* 125 **D7**
Santa Rosa, *La Pampa, Argentina* 126 **D3**
Santa Rosa, *San Luis, Argentina* 126 **C2**
Santa Rosa, *Bolivia* 124 **C4**
Santa Rosa, *Brazil* 127 **B5**
Santa Rosa, *Colombia* 120 **C4**
Santa Rosa, *Ecuador* 120 **D2**
Santa Rosa, *Peru* 124 **C3**
Santa Rosa, *Calif., U.S.A.* 112 **G4**
Santa Rosa, *N. Mex., U.S.A.* 109 **H2**
Santa Rosa, *Venezuela* ... 120 **C4**
Santa Rosa de Cabal, *Colombia* 120 **C2**
Santa Rosa de Copán, *Honduras* 116 **D2**
Santa Rosa de Osos, *Colombia* 120 **B2**
Santa Rosa de Río Primero, *Argentina* 126 **C3**
Santa Rosa de Viterbo, *Colombia* 120 **B3**
Santa Rosa del Palmar, *Bolivia* 125 **D5**
Santa Rosa I., *Calif., U.S.A.* 113 **M6**
Santa Rosa I., *Fla., U.S.A.* 105 **K2**
Santa Rosa Range, *U.S.A.* 110 **F5**
Santa Rosalía, *Mexico* 114 **B2**
Santa Sofia, *Italy* 33 **E8**
Santa Sylvina, *Argentina* .. 126 **B3**
Santa Tecla = Nueva San Salvador, *El Salv.* 116 **D2**
Santa Teresa, *Argentina* .. 126 **C3**
Santa Teresa, *Brazil* 123 **E3**
Santa Teresa, *Mexico* 115 **B5**
Santa Teresa, *Venezuela* .. 121 **C5**
Santa Teresa di Riva, *Italy* 35 **E8**
Santa Teresa Gallura, *Italy* 34 **A2**
Santa Vitória, *Brazil* 123 **E1**

Santa Vitória do Palmar, *Brazil* 127 C5
Santa Ynez →, *U.S.A.* 113 L6
Santa Ynez Mts., *U.S.A.* 113 L6
Santa Ysabel, *U.S.A.* 113 M10
Santadi, *Italy* 34 C1
Santai, *China* 52 B5
Santaluz, *Brazil* 122 D4
Santana, *Brazil* 123 D3
Santana, *Madeira* 36 D3
Santana, Coxilha de, *Brazil* 127 C4
Santana do Ipanema, *Brazil* 122 C4
Santana do Livramento, *Brazil* 127 C4
Santanayi, *Spain* 36 B10
Santander, *Colombia* 120 C2
Santander, *Spain* 30 B7
Santander Jiménez, *Mexico* 115 C5
Santaquin, *U.S.A.* 110 G8
Santarém, *Brazil* 121 D7
Santarém, *Portugal* 31 F2
Santarém □, *Portugal* 31 F2
Santaren Channel, *W. Indies* 116 B4
Santee, *U.S.A.* 113 N10
Santéramo in Colle, *Italy* 35 B9
Santerno →, *Italy* 33 D8
Santhia, *Italy* 32 C5
Santiago, *Bolivia* 125 D6
Santiago, *Brazil* 127 B5
Santiago, *Chile* 126 C1
Santiago, *Panama* 116 E3
Santiago, *Peru* 124 C2
Santiago, *Phil.* 55 C4
Santiago □, *Chile* 126 C1
Santiago →, *Peru* 120 D2
Santiago, C., *Chile* 128 D1
Santiago, Punta de, *Eq. Guin.* 79 E6
Santiago, Serranía de, *Bolivia* 125 D6
Santiago de Chuco, *Peru* 124 B2
Santiago de Compostela, *Spain* 30 C2
Santiago de Cuba, *Cuba* 116 C4
Santiago de los Cabelleros, *Dom. Rep.* 117 C5
Santiago del Estero, *Argentina* 126 B3
Santiago del Estero □, *Argentina* 126 B3
Santiago del Teide, *Canary Is.* 36 F3
Santiago do Cacém, *Portugal* 31 G2
Santiago Ixcuintla, *Mexico* 114 C3
Santiago Papasquiaro, *Mexico* 114 B3
Santiaguillo, L. de, *Mexico* 114 C4
Santillana del Mar, *Spain* 30 B6
Säntis, *Switz.* 23 B8
Santisteban del Puerto, *Spain* 29 G1
Santo →, *Peru* 124 B2
Santo Amaro, *Brazil* 123 D4
Santo Anastácio, *Brazil* 127 A5
Santo André, *Brazil* 127 A6
Santo Ângelo, *Brazil* 127 B5
Santo Antonio, *Brazil* 125 D6
Santo Antônio de Jesus, *Brazil* 123 D4
Santo Antônio do Içá, *Brazil* 120 D4
Santo Antônio do Leverger, *Brazil* 125 D6
Santo Corazón, *Bolivia* 125 D6
Santo Domingo, *Dom. Rep.* 117 C6
Santo Domingo, *Baja Calif. N., Mexico* 114 A1
Santo Domingo, *Baja Calif. S., Mexico* 114 B2
Santo Domingo, *Nic.* 116 D3
Santo Domingo de la Calzada, *Spain* 28 C2
Santo Domingo de los Colorados, *Ecuador* 120 D2
Santo Stéfano di Camastro, *Italy* 35 D7
Santo Stino di Livenza, *Italy* 33 C9
Santo Tirso, *Portugal* 30 D2
Santo Tomás, *Mexico* 114 A1
Santo Tomás, *Peru* 124 C3
Santo Tomé, *Argentina* 127 B4
Santo Tomé de Guayana = Ciudad Guayana, *Venezuela* 121 B5
Santoña, *Spain* 30 B7
Santos, *Brazil* 127 A6
Santos, Sierra de los, *Spain* 31 G5
Santos Dumont, *Brazil* 123 F3
Santpoort, *Neths.* 16 D5
Sanvignes-les-Mines, *France* 25 F11
Sanyuan, *China* 50 G5
Sanza Pombo, *Angola* 80 F3
São Anastácio, *Brazil* 127 A5
São Bartolomeu de Messines, *Portugal* 31 H2
São Benedito, *Brazil* 122 B3
São Bento, *Brazil* 122 B3
São Bento do Norte, *Brazil* 122 C4
São Bernado de Campo, *Brazil* 123 F2
São Borja, *Brazil* 127 B4
São Bras d'Alportel, *Portugal* 31 H3
São Caitano, *Brazil* 122 C4
São Carlos, *Brazil* 127 A6
São Cristóvão, *Brazil* 122 D4
São Domingos, *Brazil* 123 D2
São Domingos do Maranhão, *Brazil* 122 C3
São Félix, *Brazil* 123 D1
São Francisco, *Brazil* 123 E3
São Francisco →, *Brazil* 122 D4
São Francisco do Maranhão, *Brazil* 122 C3
São Francisco do Sul, *Brazil* 127 B6
São Gabriel, *Brazil* 127 C5
São Gabriel da Palha, *Brazil* 123 E3
São Gonçalo, *Brazil* 123 F3
São Gotardo, *Brazil* 123 E2
Sao Hill, *Tanzania* 83 D4
São João da Boa Vista, *Brazil* 127 A6
São João da Pesqueira, *Portugal* 30 D3
São João da Ponte, *Brazil* 123 E3
São João del Rei, *Brazil* 123 F3
São João do Araguaia, *Brazil* 122 C2
São João do Paraíso, *Brazil* 123 E3
São João do Piauí, *Brazil* 122 C3
São João dos Patos, *Brazil* 122 C3
São Joaquim da Barra, *Brazil* 123 F2
São Jorge, Pta. de, *Madeira* 36 D3
São José, B. de, *Brazil* 122 B3
São José da Laje, *Brazil* 122 C4
São José de Mipibu, *Brazil* 122 C4
São José do Peixe, *Brazil* 122 C3
São José do Rio Prêto, *Brazil* 127 A6
São José dos Campos, *Brazil* 127 A6
São Leopoldo, *Brazil* 127 B5
São Lourenço, *Brazil* 123 F2
São Lourenço →, *Brazil* 125 D6
São Lourenço, Pantanal do, *Brazil* 125 D6
São Lourenço, Pta. de, *Madeira* 36 D3
São Luís, *Brazil* 122 B3
São Luís do Curu, *Brazil* 122 B4
São Luís Gonzaga, *Brazil* 127 B5
São Marcos →, *Brazil* 123 E2
São Marcos, B. de, *Brazil* 122 B3
São Martinho, *Portugal* 30 E2
São Mateus, *Brazil* 123 E4
São Mateus →, *Brazil* 123 E4
São Miguel do Araguaia, *Brazil* 123 D1
São Miguel dos Campos, *Brazil* 122 C4
São Nicolau →, *Brazil* 122 C3
São Paulo, *Brazil* 127 A6
São Paulo □, *Brazil* 127 A6
São Paulo, I., *Atl. Oc.* 2 D8
São Paulo de Olivença, *Brazil* 120 D4
São Pedro do Sul, *Portugal* 30 E2
São Rafael, *Brazil* 122 C4
São Raimundo das Mangabeiras, *Brazil* 122 C2
São Raimundo Nonato, *Brazil* 122 C3
São Romão, *Brazil* 123 E2
São Roque, *Madeira* 36 D3
São Roque, C. de, *Brazil* 122 C4
São Sebastião, I. de, *Brazil* 127 A6
São Sebastião do Paraíso, *Brazil* 127 A6
São Simão, *Brazil* 123 E1
São Teotónio, *Portugal* 31 H2
São Tomé, *Atl. Oc.* 70 F4
São Tomé, *Brazil* 122 C4
São Tomé, C. de, *Brazil* 123 F3
São Tomé & Principe ■, *Africa* 71 F4
São Vicente, *Brazil* 127 A6
São Vicente, *Madeira* 36 D2
São Vicente, C. de, *Portugal* 31 H2
Saona, I., *Dom. Rep.* 117 C6
Saône →, *France* 27 C8
Saône-et-Loire □, *France* 25 F11
Saonek, *Indonesia* 57 E8
Saoura, O. →, *Algeria* 75 C4
Sapanca, *Turkey* 66 C4
Sapão →, *Brazil* 122 D2
Saparua, *Indonesia* 57 E7
Sapé, *Brazil* 122 C4
Sapele, *Nigeria* 79 D6
Sapelo I., *U.S.A.* 105 K5
Sapiéntza, *Greece* 39 N4
Sapone, *Burkina Faso* 79 C4
Saposoa, *Peru* 124 B2
Sapozhok, *Russia* 41 E12
Sappemeer, *Neths.* 16 B9
Sappho, *U.S.A.* 112 B2
Sapporo, *Japan* 48 C10
Sapri, *Italy* 35 B8
Sapudi, *Indonesia* 57 G16
Sapulpa, *U.S.A.* 109 G7
Saqqez, *Iran* 64 B5
Sar Dasht, *Iran* 65 C6
Sar Gachīneh, *Iran* 65 D6
Sar Planina, *Macedonia* 38 G4
Sara, *Burkina Faso* 78 C4
Sara, *Phil.* 55 F5
Sara Buri, *Thailand* 58 E3
Sarāb, *Iran* 64 B5
Sarabadi, *Iraq* 64 C5
Sarada →, *India* 61 F12
Saragossa = Zaragoza, *Spain* 28 D4
Saraguro, *Ecuador* 120 D2
Sarajevo, *Bos.-H.* 21 M8
Saramacca □, *Surinam* 121 C6
Saramacca →, *Surinam* 121 B6
Saran, G., *Indonesia* 56 E4
Saranac Lake, *U.S.A.* 107 B10
Saranda, *Tanzania* 82 D3
Sarandí del Yi, *Uruguay* 127 C4
Sarandí Grande, *Uruguay* 126 C4
Sarangani B., *Phil.* 55 J6
Sarangani Is., *Phil.* 55 J6
Sarangarh, *India* 61 J13
Saransk, *Russia* 41 D14
Sarapul, *Russia* 44 D6
Sarasota, *U.S.A.* 105 M4
Saratoga, *Calif., U.S.A.* 112 H4
Saratoga, *Wyo., U.S.A.* 110 F10
Saratoga Springs, *U.S.A.* 107 C11
Saratov, *Russia* 41 F15
Saravane, *Laos* 58 E6
Sarawak □, *Malaysia* 56 D4
Saray, *Turkey* 67 D11
Saraya, *Senegal* 78 C2
Sarayköy, *Turkey* 66 E3
Sarayönü, *Turkey* 66 D5
Sarbāz, *Iran* 65 E9
Sarbīsheh, *Iran* 65 C8
Sarca →, *Italy* 32 C7
Sarda → = Sarada →, *India* 61 F12
Sardalas, *Libya* 75 C7
Sardarshahr, *India* 62 E6
Sardegna, *Italy* 34 B2
Sardhana, *India* 62 E7
Sardina, Pta., *Canary Is.* 36 F4
Sardinata, *Colombia* 120 B3
Sardinia = Sardegna, *Italy* 34 B2
Sardis, *Turkey* 66 D3
Sārdūīyeh = Dar Mazār, *Iran* 65 D8
Saréyamou, *Mali* 78 B4
Sargent, *U.S.A.* 108 E5
Sargodha, *Pakistan* 62 C5
Sarh, *Chad* 73 G8
Sarhro, Djebel, *Morocco* 74 B3
Sārī, *Iran* 65 B7
Sária, *Greece* 39 P10
Sarıgöl, *Turkey* 66 D3
Sarikamiş, *Turkey* 67 C10
Sarıkaya, *Turkey* 66 D6
Sarikei, *Malaysia* 56 D4
Sarina, *Australia* 90 C4
Sariñena, *Spain* 28 D4
Sarita, *U.S.A.* 109 M6
Sariwŏn, *N. Korea* 51 E13
Sark, *Chan. Is.* 13 H5
Sarkad, *Hungary* 21 J11
Şarkışla, *Turkey* 66 D7
Şarköy, *Turkey* 66 C2
Sarlat-la-Canéda, *France* 26 D5
Sarles, *U.S.A.* 108 A5
Sărmaşu, *Romania* 38 C7
Sarmi, *Indonesia* 57 E9
Sarmiento, *Argentina* 128 C3
Särna, *Sweden* 10 C7
Sarnano, *Italy* 33 E10
Sarnen, *Switz.* 22 C6
Sarnia, *Canada* 98 D3
Sarno, *Italy* 35 B7
Sarny, *Ukraine* 40 F5
Särö, *Sweden* 11 G5
Sarolangun, *Indonesia* 56 E2
Saronikós Kólpos, *Greece* 39 M6
Saronno, *Italy* 32 C6
Saros Körfezi, *Turkey* 66 C2
Sárospatak, *Hungary* 21 G11
Sarova, *Russia* 41 D13
Sarpsborg, *Norway* 10 E5
Sarracín, *Spain* 28 C1
Sarralbe, *France* 25 D14
Sarre = Saar →, *Europe* 25 C13
Sarre-Union, *France* 25 D14
Sarrebourg, *France* 25 D14
Sarreguemines, *France* 25 C14
Sarriá, *Spain* 30 C3
Sarrión, *Spain* 28 E4
Sarro, *Mali* 78 C3
Sarstedt, *Germany* 18 C5
Sartène, *France* 27 G12
Sarthe □, *France* 24 E7
Sarthe →, *France* 24 E6
Sartilly, *France* 24 D5
Sartynya, *Russia* 44 C7
Sárvár, *Hungary* 21 H6
Sarvestān, *Iran* 65 D7
Särvfjället, *Sweden* 10 B7
Sárviz →, *Hungary* 21 J8
Sary-Tash, *Kirghizia* 44 F8
Sarych, Mys, *Ukraine* 42 D5
Saryshagan, *Kazakhstan* 44 E8
Sarzana, *Italy* 32 D6
Sarzeau, *France* 24 E4
Sas van Gent, *Neths.* 17 F3
Sasabeneh, *Ethiopia* 68 F3
Sasaram, *India* 63 G11
Sasebo, *Japan* 49 H4
Saser, *India* 63 B7
Saskatchewan □, *Canada* 101 C7
Saskatchewan →, *Canada* 101 C8
Saskatoon, *Canada* 101 C7
Saskylakh, *Russia* 45 B12
Sasnovka, *Russia* 41 C17
Sasolburg, *S. Africa* 85 D4
Sasovo, *Russia* 41 D12
Sassandra, *Ivory C.* 78 E3
Sassandra →, *Ivory C.* 78 E3
Sássari, *Italy* 34 B1
Sassenheim, *Neths.* 16 D5
Sassnitz, *Germany* 18 A9
Sasso Marconi, *Italy* 33 D8
Sassocorvaro, *Italy* 33 E9
Sassoferrato, *Italy* 33 E9
Sassuolo, *Italy* 32 D7
Sástago, *Spain* 28 D4
Sastown, *Liberia* 78 E3
Sasumua Dam, *Kenya* 82 C4
Sata-Misaki, *Japan* 49 J5
Satadougou, *Mali* 78 C2
Satanta, *U.S.A.* 109 G4
Satara, *India* 60 L8
Satilla →, *U.S.A.* 105 K5
Satipo, *Peru* 124 C3
Satmala Hills, *India* 60 J9
Satna, *India* 63 G9
Šator, *Bos.-H.* 33 D13
Sátoraljaújhely, *Hungary* 21 G11
Satpura Ra., *India* 62 J7
Satrup, *Germany* 18 A5
Satsuna-Shotō, *Japan* 49 K5
Sattahip, *Thailand* 58 F3
Satu Mare, *Romania* 38 B5
Satui, *Indonesia* 56 E5
Satun, *Thailand* 59 J3
Saturnina →, *Brazil* 125 C6
Sauce, *Argentina* 126 C4
Sauceda, *Mexico* 114 B4
Saucillo, *Mexico* 114 B3
Sauda, *Norway* 9 G9
Saúde, *Brazil* 122 D3
Sauðarkrókur, *Iceland* 8 D4
Saudi Arabia ■, *Asia* 68 B3
Sauer →, *Germany* 17 J9
Saugeen →, *Canada* 106 B3
Saugerties, *U.S.A.* 107 D11
Saugues, *France* 26 D7
Sauherad, *Norway* 10 E3
Saujon, *France* 26 C3
Sauk Centre, *U.S.A.* 108 C7
Sauk Rapids, *U.S.A.* 108 C7
Saül, *Fr. Guiana* 121 C7
Saulgau, *Germany* 19 G5
Saulieu, *France* 25 E11
Sault, *France* 27 D9
Sault Ste. Marie, *Canada* 98 C3
Sault Ste. Marie, *U.S.A.* 104 B3
Saumlaki, *Indonesia* 57 F8
Saumur, *France* 24 E6
Saunders C., *N.Z.* 87 L3
Saunders I., *Antarctica* 5 B1
Saunders Point, *Australia* 89 E4
Saurbær, *Borgarfjarðarsýsla, Iceland* 8 D3
Saurbær, *Eyjafjarðarsýsla, Iceland* 8 D4
Sauri, *Nigeria* 79 C6
Saurimo, *Angola* 80 F4
Sausalito, *U.S.A.* 112 H4
Sautatá, *Colombia* 120 B2
Sauveterre-de-Béarn, *France* 26 E3
Sauzé-Vaussais, *France* 26 B4
Savá, *Honduras* 116 C2
Sava →, *Serbia* 21 L10
Savage, *U.S.A.* 108 B2
Savage I. = Niue, *Cook Is.* 93 J11
Savai'i, *W. Samoa* 87 A12
Savalou, *Benin* 79 D5
Savane, *Mozam.* 83 F4
Savanna, *U.S.A.* 108 D9
Savanna la Mar, *Jamaica* 116 C4
Savannah, *Ga., U.S.A.* 105 J5
Savannah, *Mo., U.S.A.* 108 F7
Savannah, *Tenn., U.S.A.* 105 H1
Savannah →, *U.S.A.* 105 J5
Savannakhet, *Laos* 58 D5
Savant L., *Canada* 98 B1
Savant Lake, *Canada* 98 B1
Savanur, *India* 60 M9
Savé, *Benin* 79 D5
Save →, *France* 26 E5
Save →, *Mozam.* 85 C5
Sāveh, *Iran* 65 C6
Savelugu, *Ghana* 79 D4
Savenay, *France* 24 E5
Saverdun, *France* 26 E5
Saverne, *France* 25 D14
Savièse, *Switz.* 22 D4
Savigliano, *Italy* 32 D4
Savigny-sur-Braye, *France* 24 E7
Saviñao, *Spain* 30 C3
Savio →, *Italy* 33 D9
Savognin, *Switz.* 23 C9
Savoie □, *France* 27 C10
Savona, *Italy* 32 D5
Sawahlunto, *Indonesia* 56 E2
Sawai, *Indonesia* 57 E7
Sawai Madhopur, *India* 62 F7
Sawang Daen Din, *Thailand* 58 D4
Sawankhalok, *Thailand* 58 D2
Sawara, *Japan* 49 G10
Sawatch Mts., *U.S.A.* 111 G10
Sawel, *U.K.* 15 B4
Sawi, *Thailand* 59 G2
Sawmills, *Zimbabwe* 83 F2
Sawu, *Indonesia* 57 F6
Sawu Sea, *Indonesia* 57 F6
Saxby →, *Australia* 90 B3
Saxon, *Switz.* 22 D4
Saxony, Lower = Niedersachsen □, *Germany* 18 C5
Saxton, *U.S.A.* 106 F6
Say, *Niger* 79 C5
Saya, *Nigeria* 79 D5
Sayabec, *Canada* 99 C6
Sayaboury, *Laos* 58 C3
Sayán, *Peru* 124 C2
Sayan, Vostochnyy, *Russia* 45 D10
Sayan, Zapadnyy, *Russia* 45 D10
Sayasan, *Russia* 43 E12
Saydā, *Lebanon* 69 B4
Sayhan-Ovoo, *Mongolia* 50 B2
Sayhandulaan, *Mongolia* 50 B5
Sayḥut, *Yemen* 68 D5
Saynshand, *Mongolia* 50 B6
Sayre, *Okla., U.S.A.* 109 H5
Sayre, *Pa., U.S.A.* 107 E8
Sayula, *Mexico* 114 D4
Sazin, *Pakistan* 63 B5
Sazlika →, *Bulgaria* 39 H8
Sbeïtla, *Tunisia* 75 A6
Scaër, *France* 24 D3
Scafell Pikes, *U.K.* 12 C4
Scalea, *Italy* 35 C8
Scalpay, *U.K.* 14 D2
Scandia, *Canada* 100 C6
Scandiano, *Italy* 32 D7
Scandinavia, *Europe* 8 E12
Scansano, *Italy* 33 F8
Scapa Flow, *U.K.* 14 C5
Scappoose, *U.S.A.* 112 E4
Scarborough, *Trin. & Tob.* 117 D7
Scarborough, *U.K.* 12 C7
Scebeli, Wabi →, *Somali Rep.* 68 G3
Šćedro, *Croatia* 33 E13
Scenic, *U.S.A.* 108 D3
Schaal See, *Germany* 18 B6
Schaan, *Liech.* 23 B9
Schaesberg, *Neths.* 17 G8
Schaffen, *Belgium* 17 G6
Schaffhausen, *Switz.* 23 A7
Schaffhausen □, *Switz.* 23 A7
Schagen, *Neths.* 16 C5
Schaijk, *Neths.* 16 E7
Schalkhaar, *Neths.* 16 D8
Schalkwijk, *Neths.* 16 E6
Schangnau, *Switz.* 22 C5
Schänis, *Switz.* 23 B8
Schärding, *Austria* 20 G3
Scharhörn, *Germany* 18 B4
Scharnitz, *Austria* 19 H7
Scheessel, *Germany* 18 B5
Schefferville, *Canada* 99 B6
Schelde →, *Belgium* 17 F4
Schell Creek Ra., *U.S.A.* 110 G6
Schenectady, *U.S.A.* 107 D11
Scherfede, *Germany* 18 D5
Scherpenheuvel, *Belgium* 17 G5
Scherpenisse, *Neths.* 17 E4
Scherpenzeel, *Neths.* 16 D7
Schesaplana, *Switz.* 23 B9
Schesslitz, *Germany* 19 F7
Scheveningen, *Neths.* 16 D4
Schiedam, *Neths.* 16 E4
Schiermonnikoog, *Neths.* 16 B8
Schiers, *Switz.* 23 C9
Schifferstadt, *Germany* 19 F4
Schifflange, *Lux.* 17 K8
Schijndel, *Neths.* 17 E6
Schiltigheim, *France* 25 D14
Schio, *Italy* 33 C8
Schipbeek, *Neths.* 16 D8
Schipluiden, *Neths.* 16 E4
Schirmeck, *France* 25 D14
Schlei →, *Germany* 18 A5
Schleiden, *Germany* 18 E2
Schleiz, *Germany* 18 E7
Schleswig, *Germany* 18 A5
Schleswig-Holstein □, *Germany* 18 A5
Schlieren, *Switz.* 23 B6
Schlüchtern, *Germany* 19 E5
Schmalkalden, *Germany* 18 E6
Schmölln, *Brandenburg, Germany* 18 B10
Schmölln, *Thüringen, Germany* 18 E8
Schneeberg, *Austria* 21 H5
Schneeberg, *Germany* 18 E8
Schoenberg, *Belgium* 17 H8
Schofield, *U.S.A.* 108 C10
Scholls, *U.S.A.* 112 E4
Schönberg, *Mecklenburg-Vorpommern, Germany* 18 B6
Schönberg, *Schleswig-Holstein, Germany* 18 A6
Schönebeck, *Germany* 18 C7
Schönenwerd, *Switz.* 22 B5
Schongau, *Germany* 19 H6
Schöningen, *Germany* 18 C6
Schoondijke, *Neths.* 17 F3

Schoonebeek, Neths. 16 C9
Schoonhoven, Neths. 16 E5
Schoorl, Neths. 16 C5
Schortens, Germany 18 B3
Schoten, Belgium 17 F5
Schouten I., Australia 90 G4
Schouten Is. = Supriori, Kepulauan, Indonesia 57 E9
Schouwen, Neths. 17 E3
Schramberg, Germany 19 G4
Schrankogl, Austria 19 H7
Schreckhorn, Switz. 22 C6
Schreiber, Canada 98 C2
Schrobenhausen, Germany 19 G7
Schruns, Austria 19 H5
Schuler, Canada 101 C6
Schuls, Switz. 23 C10
Schumacher, Canada 98 C3
Schüpfen, Switz. 22 B4
Schüpfheim, Switz. 22 C6
Schurz, U.S.A. 110 G4
Schuyler, U.S.A. 108 E6
Schuylkill Haven, U.S.A. 107 F8
Schwabach, Germany 19 F7
Schwäbisch Gmünd, Germany 19 G5
Schwäbisch Hall, Germany 19 F5
Schwäbische Alb, Germany 19 G5
Schwabmünchen, Germany 19 G6
Schwanden, Switz. 23 C8
Schwandorf, Germany 19 F8
Schwaner, Pegunungan, Indonesia 56 E4
Schwarmstedt, Germany 18 C5
Schwärze, Germany 18 C9
Schwarze Elster →, Germany 18 D8
Schwarzenberg, Germany 18 E8
Schwarzenburg, Switz. 22 C4
Schwarzwald, Germany 19 H4
Schwaz, Austria 19 H7
Schwedt, Germany 18 B10
Schweinfurt, Germany 19 E6
Schweizer Mittelland, Switz. 22 C4
Schweizer-Reneke, S. Africa 84 D4
Schwenningen, Germany 19 G4
Schwerin, Germany 18 B7
Schweriner See, Germany 18 B7
Schwetzingen, Germany 19 F4
Schwyz, Switz. 23 B7
Schwyz □, Switz. 23 B7
Sciacca, Italy 34 E6
Scicli, Italy 35 F7
Scilla, Italy 35 D8
Scilly, Isles of, U.K. 13 H1
Ścinawa, Poland 20 D6
Scioto →, U.S.A. 104 F4
Scobey, U.S.A. 108 A2
Scone, Australia 91 E5
Scordia, Italy 35 E7
Scoresbysund, Greenland 4 B6
Scorno, Punta dello, Italy 34 A1
Scotia, Calif., U.S.A. 110 F1
Scotia, N.Y., U.S.A. 107 D11
Scotia Sea, Antarctica 5 B18
Scotland, U.S.A. 108 D6
Scotland □, U.K. 14 E5
Scotland Neck, U.S.A. 105 G7
Scott, C., Australia 88 B4
Scott City, U.S.A. 108 F4
Scott Glacier, Antarctica 5 C8
Scott I., Antarctica 5 C11
Scott Inlet, Canada 97 A12
Scott Is., Canada 100 C3
Scott L., Canada 101 B7
Scott Reef, Australia 88 B3
Scottburgh, S. Africa 85 E5
Scottdale, U.S.A. 106 F5
Scottsbluff, U.S.A. 108 E3
Scottsboro, U.S.A. 105 H2
Scottsburg, U.S.A. 104 F3
Scottsdale, Australia 90 G4
Scottsville, Ky., U.S.A. 105 G2
Scottsville, N.Y., U.S.A. 106 C7
Scottville, U.S.A. 104 D2
Scranton, U.S.A. 107 E9
Scugog, L., Canada 106 B6
Scunthorpe, U.K. 12 D7
Scuol, Switz. 23 C10
Scusciuban, Somali Rep. 68 E5
Scutari = Üsküdar, Turkey 39 H11
Seabra, Brazil 123 D3
Seabrook, L., Australia 89 F2
Seaford, U.S.A. 104 F8
Seaforth, Canada 98 D3
Seagraves, U.S.A. 109 J3
Seal →, Canada 101 B10
Seal Cove, Canada 99 C8
Seal L., Canada 99 B7
Sealy, U.S.A. 109 L6
Searchlight, U.S.A. 113 K12
Searcy, U.S.A. 109 H9
Searles L., U.S.A. 113 K9
Seaside, Calif., U.S.A. 112 J5
Seaside, Oreg., U.S.A. 112 E3
Seaspray, Australia 91 F4
Seattle, U.S.A. 112 C4
Seaview Ra., Australia 90 B4
Sebastián Vizcaíno, B., Mexico 114 B2
Sebastopol = Sevastopol, Ukraine 42 D5
Sebastopol, U.S.A. 112 G4
Sebderat, Eritrea 77 D4
Sebdou, Algeria 75 B4
Seben, Turkey 66 C4
Sebewaing, U.S.A. 104 D4
Sebezh, Russia 40 C6
Sebha = Sabhah, Libya 73 C7
Sébi, Mali 78 B4
Şebinkarahisar, Turkey 42 F8
Sebiş, Romania 38 C5
Sebkhet Te-n-Dghâmcha, Mauritania 78 B1
Sebkra Azzel Mati, Algeria 75 C5
Sebkra Mekerghene, Algeria 75 C5
Sebnitz, Germany 18 E10
Sebou, Oued →, Morocco 74 B3
Sebring, Fla., U.S.A. 105 M5
Sebring, Ohio, U.S.A. 106 F3
Sebringville, Canada 106 C3
Sebta = Ceuta, Morocco 74 A3
Sebuku, Indonesia 56 E5
Sebuku, Teluk, Malaysia 56 D5
Secchia →, Italy 32 C8
Sechelt, Canada 100 D4
Sechura, Peru 124 B1
Sechura, Desierto de, Peru 124 B1
Seclin, France 25 B10
Secondigny, France 24 F6
Secretary I., N.Z. 87 L1
Secunderabad, India 60 L11
Sécure →, Bolivia 125 D5
Sedalia, U.S.A. 108 F8
Sedan, Australia 91 E2
Sedan, France 25 C11
Sedan, U.S.A. 109 G6
Sedano, Spain 28 C1
Seddon, N.Z. 87 J5
Seddonville, N.Z. 87 J4
Sedeh, Fārs, Iran 65 D7
Sedeh, Khorāsān, Iran 65 C8
Sederot, Israel 69 D3
Sedgewick, Canada 100 C6
Sedhiou, Senegal 78 C1
Sedičany, Czech. 20 F4
Sedico, Italy 33 B9
Sedley, Canada 101 C8
Sedova, Pik, Russia 44 B6
Sedrata, Algeria 75 A6
Sedro-Woolley, U.S.A. 112 B4
Sedrun, Switz. 23 C7
Šeduva, Lithuania 40 D3
Seebad Ahlbeck, Germany 18 B10
Seehausen, Germany 18 C7
Seeheim, Namibia 84 D2
Seekoei →, S. Africa 84 E4
Seelaw, Germany 18 C10
Sées, France 24 D7
Seesen, Germany 18 D6
Sefadu, S. Leone 78 D2
Seferihisar, Turkey 66 D2
Séfeto, Mali 78 C3
Sefrou, Morocco 74 B4
Sefwi Bekwai, Ghana 78 D4
Segamat, Malaysia 59 L4
Segarcea, Romania 38 E6
Segbwema, S. Leone 78 D2
Seget, Indonesia 57 E8
Seggueur, O. →, Algeria 75 B5
Segonzac, France 26 C3
Segorbe, Spain 28 F4
Ségou, Mali 78 C3
Segovia = Coco →, Cent. Amer. 116 D3
Segovia, Colombia 120 B3
Segovia, Spain 30 E6
Segovia □, Spain 30 E6
Segré, France 24 E6
Segre →, Spain 28 D5
Séguéla, Ivory C. 78 D3
Seguin, U.S.A. 109 L6
Segundo →, Argentina 126 C3
Segura →, Spain 29 G4
Segura, Sierra de, Spain 29 G2
Seh Qal'eh, Iran 65 C8
Sehitwa, Botswana 84 C3
Sehore, India 62 H7
Sehwan, Pakistan 62 F2
Şeica Mare, Romania 38 C7
Seiland, Norway 8 A17
Seiling, U.S.A. 109 G5
Seille →, France 27 B8
Seilles, Belgium 17 G6
Sein, I. de, France 24 D2
Seinäjoki →, Finland 8 E17
Seine →, France 24 C7
Seine, B. de la, France 24 C6
Seine-et-Marne □, France 25 D9
Seine-Maritime □, France 24 C7
Seine-St.-Denis □, France 25 D9
Seistan, Iran 65 D9
Sejerø, Denmark 11 J5
Sejerø Bugt, Denmark 11 J5
Seka, Ethiopia 77 F4
Sekayu, Indonesia 56 E2
Seke, Tanzania 82 C3
Sekenke, Tanzania 82 C3
Sekken Veøy, Norway 10 B1
Sekondi-Takoradi, Ghana 78 E4
Sekuma, Botswana 84 C3
Selah, U.S.A. 110 C3
Selama, Malaysia 59 K3
Selárgius, Italy 34 C2
Selaru, Indonesia 57 F8
Selb, Germany 19 E8
Selby, U.K. 12 D6
Selby, U.S.A. 108 C4
Selca, Croatia 33 E13
Selçuk, Turkey 66 E2
Selden, U.S.A. 108 F4
Sele →, Italy 35 B7
Selemdzha →, Russia 45 D13
Selenga = Selenge Mörön →, Asia 54 A5
Selenge Mörön →, Asia 54 A5
Selenica, Albania 39 J2
Selenter See, Germany 18 A6
Sélestat, France 25 D14
Seletan, Tg., Indonesia 56 E4
Seletin, Romania 38 B8
Selfridge, U.S.A. 108 B4
Sélibabi, Mauritania 78 B2
Seliger, Oz., Russia 40 C8
Seligman, U.S.A. 111 J7
Şelim, Turkey 43 F10
Selîma, El Wâhât el, Sudan 76 C2
Selinda Spillway, Botswana 84 B3
Selinoús, Greece 39 M4
Selizharovo, Russia 40 C8
Seljord, Norway 10 E2
Selkirk, Canada 101 C9
Selkirk, U.K. 14 F6
Selkirk I., Canada 101 C9
Selkirk Mts., Canada 100 C5
Selles-sur-Cher, France 25 E8
Selliá, Greece 37 D6
Sellières, France 25 F12
Sells, U.S.A. 111 L8
Sellye, Hungary 21 K7
Selma, Ala., U.S.A. 105 J2
Selma, Calif., U.S.A. 111 H4
Selma, N.C., U.S.A. 105 H6
Selmer, U.S.A. 105 H1
Selongey, France 25 E12
Selowandoma Falls, Zimbabwe 83 G3
Selpele, Indonesia 57 E8
Selsey Bill, U.K. 13 G7
Seltz, France 25 D15
Selu, Indonesia 57 F8
Sélune →, France 24 D5
Selva, Argentina 126 B3
Selva, Italy 33 B8
Selva, Spain 28 D6
Selvas, Brazil 124 B4
Selwyn, Australia 90 C3
Selwyn L., Canada 101 A8
Selwyn Ra., Australia 90 C3
Seman →, Albania 39 J2
Semara, W. Sahara 74 C2
Semarang, Indonesia 57 G14
Semau, Indonesia 57 F6
Sembabule, Uganda 82 C3
Sémé, Senegal 78 B2
Semeih, Sudan 77 E3
Semenov, Russia 41 C14
Semenovka, Ukraine 40 E8
Semenovka, Ukraine 42 B5
Semeru, Indonesia 57 H15
Semey = Semipalatinsk, Kazakhstan 44 D9
Semiluki, Russia 41 F11
Seminoe Reservoir, U.S.A. 110 E10
Seminole, Okla., U.S.A. 109 H6
Seminole, Tex., U.S.A. 109 J3
Semiozernoye, Kazakhstan 44 D7
Semipalatinsk, Kazakhstan 44 D9
Semirara Is., Phil. 55 F4
Semisopochnoi I., U.S.A. 96 C2
Semitau, Indonesia 56 D4
Semiyarskoye, Kazakhstan 44 D8
Semmering Pass, Austria 21 H5
Semnān, Iran 65 C7
Semnān □, Iran 65 C7
Semois →, Europe 17 J5
Semporna, Malaysia 57 D5
Semuda, Indonesia 56 E4
Semur-en-Auxois, France 25 E11
Sena, Bolivia 124 C4
Senā, Iran 65 D6
Sena, Mozam. 83 F3
Sena →, Bolivia 124 C4
Sena Madureira, Brazil 124 B4
Senador Pompeu, Brazil 122 C4
Senaja, Malaysia 56 C5
Senaki, Georgia 43 E10
Senanga, Zambia 84 B3
Senatobia, U.S.A. 109 H10
Sendafa, Ethiopia 77 F4
Sendai, Kagoshima, Japan 49 J5
Sendai, Miyagi, Japan 48 E10
Sendai-Wan, Japan 48 E10
Sendenhorst, Germany 18 D3
Seneca, Oreg., U.S.A. 110 D4
Seneca, S.C., U.S.A. 105 H4
Seneca Falls, U.S.A. 107 D8
Seneca L., U.S.A. 106 D8
Seneffe, Belgium 17 G4
Senegal ■, W. Afr. 78 C2
Senegal →, W. Afr. 78 B1
Senegambia, Africa 70 E2
Senekal, S. Africa 85 D4
Senftenberg, Germany 18 D10
Senga Hill, Zambia 83 D3
Senge Khambab = Indus →, Pakistan 62 G2
Sengerema □, Tanzania 82 C3
Sengiley, Russia 41 E16
Sengkang, Indonesia 57 E6
Sengua →, Zimbabwe 83 F2
Senguerr →, Argentina 128 C3
Senhor-do-Bonfim, Brazil 122 D3
Senica, Slovak Rep. 20 G7
Senigállia, Italy 33 E10
Senio →, Italy 33 D9
Senirkent, Turkey 66 D4
Senise, Italy 35 B9
Senj, Croatia 33 D11
Senja, Norway 8 B14
Senlis, France 25 C9
Senmonorom, Cambodia 58 F6
Sennâr, Sudan 77 E3
Senne →, Belgium 17 G4
Senneterre, Canada 98 C4
Senniquelle, Liberia 78 D3
Senno, Belorussia 40 D6
Sennori, Italy 34 B1
Seno, Laos 58 D5
Senonches, France 24 D8
Senorbì, Italy 34 C2
Senožeče, Slovenia 33 C11
Sens, France 25 D10
Senta, Serbia 21 K10
Sentery, Zaïre 82 D2
Sentinel, U.S.A. 111 K7
Sentolo, Indonesia 57 G14
Senya Beraku, Ghana 79 D4
Seo de Urgel, Spain 28 C6
Seohara, India 63 E8
Seoni, India 63 H8
Seoul = Sŏul, S. Korea 51 F14
Separation Point, Canada 99 B8
Sepīdān, Iran 65 D7
Sepo-ri, N. Korea 51 E14
Sepone, Laos 58 D6
Sept-Îles, Canada 99 B6
Septemvri, Bulgaria 38 G7
Sepúlveda, Spain 30 D7
Sequeros, Spain 30 E4
Sequim, U.S.A. 112 B3
Sequoia National Park, U.S.A. 111 H4
Serafimovich, Russia 43 B10
Seraing, Belgium 17 G7
Seraja, Indonesia 59 L7
Serakhis →, Cyprus 37 D11
Seram, Indonesia 57 E7
Seram Laut, Kepulauan, Indonesia 57 E8
Seram Sea, Indonesia 57 E7
Serang, Indonesia 57 G12
Serasan, Indonesia 59 L7
Seravezza, Italy 32 E7
Serbia □, Yugoslavia 21 M11
Serdo, Ethiopia 77 E5
Serdobsk, Russia 41 E14
Serēdka, Russia 40 B6
Şereflikoçhisar, Turkey 66 D5
Seregno, Italy 32 C6
Seremban, Malaysia 59 L3
Serengeti □, Tanzania 82 C3
Serengeti Plain, Tanzania 82 C3
Serenje, Zambia 83 E3
Sereth = Siret →, Romania 38 D11
Sergach, Russia 41 D14
Serge →, Spain 28 D5
Sergino, Russia 44 C7
Sergipe □, Brazil 122 D4
Sergiyev Posad, Russia 41 C11
Seria, Brunei 56 D4
Serian, Malaysia 56 D4
Seriate, Italy 32 C6
Seribu, Kepulauan, Indonesia 56 F3
Sérifontaine, France 25 C8
Sérifos, Greece 39 M7
Sérignan, France 26 E7
Serik, Turkey 66 E4
Seringapatam Reef, Australia 88 B3
Sermaize-les-Bains, France 25 D11
Sermata, Indonesia 57 F7
Sérmide, Italy 33 C8
Sernovodsk, Russia 41 E17
Serny Zavod, Turkmenistan 44 F6
Serón, Spain 29 H2
Serós, Spain 28 D5
Serov, Russia 44 D7
Serowe, Botswana 84 C4
Serpa, Portugal 31 H3
Serpeddi, Punta, Italy 34 C2
Serpentara, Italy 34 C2
Serpentine, Australia 89 F2
Serpentine Lakes, Australia 89 E4
Serpis →, Spain 29 G4
Serpukhov, Russia 41 D10
Serra do Navio, Brazil 121 C7
Serra San Bruno, Italy 35 D9
Serra Talhada, Brazil 122 C4
Serracapriola, Italy 35 A8
Serradilla, Spain 30 F4
Sérrai, Greece 39 H6
Serramanna, Italy 34 C1
Serrat, C., Tunisia 75 A6
Serre-Ponçon, L. de, France 27 D10
Serres, France 27 D9
Serrezuela, Argentina 126 C2
Serrinha, Brazil 123 D4
Serrita, Brazil 122 C4
Sersale, Italy 35 C9
Sertã, Portugal 30 F2
Sertânia, Brazil 122 C4
Sertanópolis, Brazil 127 A5
Sêrtar, China 52 A3
Sertig, Switz. 23 C9
Serua, Indonesia 57 F8
Serui, Indonesia 57 E9
Serule, Botswana 84 C4
Sérvia, Greece 39 J4
Sese Is., Uganda 82 C3
Sesepe, Indonesia 57 E7
Sesfontein, Namibia 84 B1
Sesheke, Zambia 84 B3
Sesia →, Italy 32 C5
Sesimbra, Portugal 31 G1
Sessa Aurunca, Italy 34 A6
S'estañol, Spain 36 B9
Sesto San Giovanni, Italy 32 C6
Sestri Levante, Italy 32 D6
Sestrières, Italy 32 D3
Sestrunj, Croatia 33 D12
Sestu, Italy 34 C2
Sesvenna, Switz. 23 C10
Setana, Japan 48 C9
Sète, France 26 E7
Sete Lagôas, Brazil 123 E3
Sétif, Algeria 75 A6
Seto, Japan 49 G8
Setonaikai, Japan 49 G6
Settat, Morocco 74 B3
Setté-Cama, Gabon 80 E1
Séttimo Tor, Italy 32 C4
Setting L., Canada 101 B9
Settle, U.K. 12 C5
Settlement Pt., Bahamas 105 M6
Setto Calende, Italy 32 C5
Setúbal, Portugal 31 G2
Setúbal □, Portugal 31 G2
Setúbal, B. de, Portugal 31 G2
Seugne →, France 26 C3
Seulimeum, Indonesia 56 C1
Seuzach, Switz. 23 A7
Sevan, Armenia 43 F11
Sevan, Ozero, Armenia 43 F11
Sevastopol, Ukraine 42 D5
Sevelen, Switz. 23 B8
Seven Emu, Australia 90 B2
Seven Sisters, Canada 100 C3
Sevenum, Neths. 17 F8
Sever →, Spain 31 F3
Sévérac-le-Château, France 26 D7
Severn →, Canada 98 A2
Severn →, U.K. 13 F5
Severn L., Canada 98 B1
Severnaya Zemlya, Russia 45 B10
Severo-Kurilsk, Russia 45 D16
Severo-Yeniseyskiy, Russia 45 C10
Severodonetsk, Ukraine 43 B8
Severodvinsk, Russia 44 C4
Sevier, U.S.A. 111 G7
Sevier →, U.S.A. 111 G7
Sevier L., U.S.A. 110 G7
Sevilla, Colombia 120 C2
Sevilla, Spain 31 H5
Sevilla □, Spain 31 H5
Seville = Sevilla, Spain 31 H5
Sevnica, Slovenia 33 B12
Sèvre-Nantaise →, France 24 E5
Sèvre-Niortaise →, France 26 B3
Sevsk, Russia 40 E9
Seward, Alaska, U.S.A. 96 B5
Seward, Nebr., U.S.A. 108 E6
Seward Pen., U.S.A. 96 B3
Sewell, Chile 126 C1
Sewer, Indonesia 57 F8
Sewickley, U.S.A. 106 F4
Sexbierum, Neths. 16 B6
Sexsmith, Canada 100 B5
Seychelles ■, Ind. Oc. 47 K9
Seyðisfjörður, Iceland 8 D7
Seydvān, Iran 64 B5
Seyfe Gölü, Turkey 66 D6
Seyhan Barajı, Turkey 66 E6
Seyitgazi, Turkey 66 D4
Seym →, Ukraine 40 F8
Seymchan, Russia 45 C16
Seymour, Australia 91 F4
Seymour, S. Africa 85 E4
Seymour, Conn., U.S.A. 107 E11
Seymour, Ind., U.S.A. 104 F3
Seymour, Tex., U.S.A. 109 J5
Seymour, Wis., U.S.A. 104 C1
Seyne, France 27 D10
Seyssel, France 27 C9
Sežana, Slovenia 33 C10
Sézanne, France 25 D10
Sezze, Italy 34 A6
Sfax, Tunisia 75 B7
Sfîntu Gheorghe, Romania 38 D8
Sfîntu Gheorghe, Braţul →, Romania 38 E12
Sha Xi →, China 53 D12
Sha Xian, China 53 D11
Shaanxi □, China 50 G5
Shaba □, Zaïre 82 D2
Shabunda, Zaïre 82 C2
Shache, China 54 C2
Shackleton Ice Shelf, Antarctica 5 C8
Shackleton Inlet, Antarctica 5 E11
Shādegān, Iran 65 D6
Shadi, China 53 D10
Shadi, India 63 C7
Shadrinsk, Russia 44 D7
Shaffa, Nigeria 79 C7
Shafter, Calif., U.S.A. 113 K7
Shafter, Tex., U.S.A. 109 L2
Shaftesbury, U.K. 13 F5
Shagamu, Nigeria 79 D5

Shagram, *Pakistan* 63 A5
Shah Bunder, *Pakistan* 62 G2
Shahabad, *Punjab, India* 62 D7
Shahabad, *Raj., India* 62 G7
Shahabad, *Ut. P., India* 63 F8
Shahadpur, *Pakistan* 62 G3
Shahba, *Syria* 69 C5
Shahdād, *Iran* 65 D8
Shahdadkot, *Pakistan* 62 F2
Shahe, *China* 50 F8
Shahganj, *India* 63 F10
Shahgarh, *India* 60 F6
Shaḩḩāt, *Libya* 73 B9
Shahjahanpur, *India* 63 F8
Shahpur, *India* 62 H7
Shahpur, *Pakistan* 62 E3
Shahpura, *India* 63 H9
Shahr Kord, *Iran* 65 C6
Shāhrakht, *Iran* 65 C9
Shahrig, *Pakistan* 62 D2
Shahukou, *China* 50 D7
Shaikhabad, *Afghan.* 62 B3
Shajapur, *India* 62 H7
Shakargarh, *Pakistan* 62 C6
Shakawe, *Botswana* 84 B3
Shaker Heights, *U.S.A.* 106 E3
Shakhty, *Russia* 43 C9
Shakhunya, *Russia* 41 C15
Shaki, *Nigeria* 79 D5
Shakopee, *U.S.A.* 108 C8
Shala, L., *Ethiopia* 77 F4
Shallow Lake, *Canada* 106 B3
Shaluli Shan, *China* 52 B2
Shām, *Iran* 65 E8
Shamâl Dârfûr □, *Sudan* 77 D2
Shamâl Kordofân □, *Sudan* 77 D2
Shamattawa, *Canada* 101 B10
Shamattawa →, *Canada* 98 A2
Shambe, *Sudan* 77 F3
Shambu, *Ethiopia* 77 F4
Shamīl, *Iran* 65 E8
Shamkhor, *Azerbaijan* 43 F12
Shāmkūh, *Iran* 65 C8
Shamli, *India* 62 E7
Shamo = Gobi, *Asia* 50 C5
Shamo, L., *Ethiopia* 77 F4
Shamokin, *U.S.A.* 107 F8
Shamrock, *U.S.A.* 109 H4
Shamva, *Zimbabwe* 83 F3
Shan □, *Burma* 61 J21
Shan Xian, *China* 50 G9
Shanan →, *Ethiopia* 77 F5
Shanchengzhen, *China* 51 C13
Shāndak, *Iran* 65 D9
Shandon, *U.S.A.* 112 K6
Shandong □, *China* 51 F10
Shandong Bandao, *China* 51 F11
Shang Xian, *China* 50 H5
Shangalowe, *Zaïre* 83 E2
Shangani →, *Zimbabwe* 83 F2
Shangbancheng, *China* 51 D10
Shangcai, *China* 53 A10
Shangcheng, *China* 53 B10
Shangchuan Dao, *China* 53 G9
Shangdu, *China* 50 D7
Shanggao, *China* 53 C10
Shanghai, *China* 53 B13
Shanghang, *China* 53 E11
Shanghe, *China* 51 F9
Shangjin, *China* 53 A8
Shanglin, *China* 52 F7
Shangnan, *China* 50 H6
Shangqiu, *China* 50 G8
Shangrao, *China* 53 C11
Shangshui, *China* 50 H8
Shangsi, *China* 52 F6
Shangyou, *China* 53 E10
Shangzhi, *China* 51 B14
Shanhetun, *China* 51 B14
Shani, *Nigeria* 79 C7
Shaniko, *U.S.A.* 110 D3
Shannon, *Greenland* 4 B7
Shannon, *N.Z.* 87 J5
Shannon →, *Ireland* 15 D2
Shansi = Shanxi □, *China* 50 F7
Shantar, Ostrov Bolshoy, *Russia* 45 D14
Shantipur, *India* 63 H13
Shantou, *China* 53 F11
Shantung = Shandong □, *China* 51 F10
Shanxi □, *China* 50 F7
Shanyang, *China* 50 H5
Shanyin, *China* 50 E7
Shaoguan, *China* 53 E9
Shaowu, *China* 53 D11
Shaoxing, *China* 53 C13
Shaoyang, *Hunan, China* 53 D8
Shaoyang, *Hunan, China* 53 D8
Shapinsay, *U.K.* 14 B6
Shaqra', *Si. Arabia* 64 E5
Shaqrā', *Yemen* 68 E4
Sharafa, *Sudan* 77 E2
Sharbot Lake, *Canada* 107 B8
Shari, *Japan* 48 C12
Sharjah = Ash Shāriqah, *U.A.E.* 65 E7
Shark B., *Australia* 89 E1
Sharm el Sheikh, *Egypt* 76 B3
Sharon, *Mass., U.S.A.* 107 D13
Sharon, *Pa., U.S.A.* 106 E4
Sharon Springs, *U.S.A.* 108 F4
Sharp Pt., *Australia* 90 A3
Sharpe L., *Canada* 101 C10
Sharpsville, *U.S.A.* 106 E4
Sharq el Istiwa'iya □, *Sudan* 77 F3
Sharya, *Russia* 41 B14
Shasha, *Ethiopia* 77 F4
Shashemene, *Ethiopia* 77 F4
Shashi, *Botswana* 85 C4
Shashi, *China* 53 B9
Shashi →, *Africa* 83 G2
Shasta, Mt., *U.S.A.* 110 F2
Shasta L., *U.S.A.* 110 F2
Shatsk, *Russia* 41 D12
Shatt al'Arab →, *Iraq* 65 D6
Shattuck, *U.S.A.* 109 G5
Shatura, *Russia* 41 D11
Shaumyani, *Georgia* 43 F11
Shaunavon, *Canada* 101 D7
Shaver L., *U.S.A.* 112 H7
Shaw →, *Australia* 88 D2
Shaw I., *Australia* 90 C4
Shawan, *China* 54 B3
Shawanaga, *Canada* 106 A4
Shawano, *U.S.A.* 104 C1
Shawinigan, *Canada* 98 C5
Shawnee, *U.S.A.* 109 H6
Shaybārā, *Si. Arabia* 64 E3
Shayib el Banat, Gebel, *Egypt* 76 B3
Shaykh Sa'īd, *Iraq* 64 C5
Shchekino, *Russia* 41 D10
Shcherbakov = Rybinsk, *Russia* 41 B11
Shchigri, *Russia* 41 F10
Shchors, *Ukraine* 40 F7
Shchuchiosk, *Kazakhstan* 44 D8
She Xian, *Anhui, China* 53 C12
She Xian, *Hebei, China* 50 F7
Shea, *Guyana* 121 C6
Shebekino, *Russia* 41 F10
Shebele = Scebeli, Wabi →, *Somali Rep.* 68 G3
Sheboygan, *U.S.A.* 104 D2
Shediac, *Canada* 99 C7
Sheelin, L., *Ireland* 15 C4
Sheep Haven, *Ireland* 15 A4
Sheerness, *U.K.* 13 F8
Sheet Harbour, *Canada* 99 D7
Sheffield, *U.K.* 12 D6
Sheffield, *Ala., U.S.A.* 105 H2
Sheffield, *Mass., U.S.A.* 107 D11
Sheffield, *Pa., U.S.A.* 106 E5
Sheffield, *Tex., U.S.A.* 109 K4
Sheho, *Canada* 101 C8
Shehojele, *Ethiopia* 77 E4
Shehong, *China* 52 B5
Shehuen →, *Argentina* 128 C3
Sheikhpura, *India* 63 G11
Shek Hasan, *Ethiopia* 77 E4
Shekhupura, *Pakistan* 62 D5
Sheki, *Azerbaijan* 43 F12
Sheksna →, *Russia* 41 B11
Shelburne, *N.S., Canada* 99 D6
Shelburne, *Ont., Canada* 98 D3
Shelburne, *U.S.A.* 107 B11
Shelburne B., *Australia* 90 A3
Shelburne Falls, *U.S.A.* 107 D12
Shelby, *Mich., U.S.A.* 104 D2
Shelby, *Mont., U.S.A.* 110 B8
Shelby, *N.C., U.S.A.* 105 H5
Shelby, *Ohio, U.S.A.* 106 F2
Shelbyville, *Ill., U.S.A.* 108 F10
Shelbyville, *Ind., U.S.A.* 104 F3
Shelbyville, *Tenn., U.S.A.* 105 H2
Sheldon, *U.S.A.* 108 D7
Sheldrake, *Canada* 99 B7
Shelikhova, Zaliv, *Russia* 45 D16
Shell Lake, *Canada* 101 C7
Shell Lakes, *Australia* 89 E4
Shellbrook, *Canada* 101 C7
Shellharbour, *Australia* 91 E5
Shelling Rocks, *Ireland* 15 E1
Shelon →, *Russia* 40 B7
Shelton, *Conn., U.S.A.* 107 E11
Shelton, *Wash., U.S.A.* 112 C3
Shemakha, *Azerbaijan* 43 F13
Shen Xian, *China* 50 F8
Shenandoah, *Iowa, U.S.A.* 108 E7
Shenandoah, *Pa., U.S.A.* 107 F8
Shenandoah, *Va., U.S.A.* 104 F6
Shenandoah →, *U.S.A.* 104 F7
Shenchi, *China* 50 E7
Shendam, *Nigeria* 79 D6
Shendî, *Sudan* 77 D3
Sheng Xian, *China* 53 C13
Shengfang, *China* 50 E9
Shëngjergji, *Albania* 39 H3
Shëngjini, *Albania* 39 H2
Shenjingzi, *China* 51 B13
Shenmu, *China* 50 E6
Shennongjia, *China* 53 B8
Shenqiu, *China* 50 H8
Shenqiucheng, *China* 50 H8
Shensi = Shaanxi □, *China* 50 G5
Shenyang, *China* 51 D12
Sheopur Kalan, *India* 60 G10
Shepetovka, *Ukraine* 40 F5
Shepparton, *Australia* 91 F4
Sheqi, *China* 50 H7
Sher Qila, *Pakistan* 63 A6
Sherborne, *U.K.* 13 G5
Sherbro I., *S. Leone* 78 D2
Sherbrooke, *Canada* 99 C5
Shereik, *Sudan* 76 D3
Sheridan, *Ark., U.S.A.* 109 H8
Sheridan, *Wyo., U.S.A.* 110 D10
Sherkot, *India* 63 E8
Sherman, *U.S.A.* 109 J6
Sherridon, *Canada* 101 B8
Sherwood, *N. Dak., U.S.A.* 108 A4
Sherwood, *Tex., U.S.A.* 109 K4
Sherwood Forest, *U.K.* 12 D6
Sheslay, *Canada* 100 B2
Sheslay →, *Canada* 100 B2
Shethanei L., *Canada* 101 B9
Shetland □, *U.K.* 14 A7
Shetland Is., *U.K.* 14 A7
Shewa □, *Ethiopia* 77 F4
Shewa Gimira, *Ethiopia* 77 F4
Sheyenne, *U.S.A.* 108 B5
Sheyenne →, *U.S.A.* 108 B6
Shibām, *Yemen* 68 D4
Shibata, *Japan* 48 F9
Shibecha, *Japan* 48 C12
Shibetsu, *Japan* 48 B11
Shibîn el Kôm, *Egypt* 76 H7
Shibîn el Qanâtir, *Egypt* 76 H7
Shibing, *China* 52 D7
Shibogama L., *Canada* 98 B2
Shibushi, *Japan* 49 J5
Shicheng, *China* 53 D11
Shickshock Mts. = Chic-Chocs, Mts., *Canada* 99 C6
Shidao, *China* 51 F12
Shidian, *China* 52 E2
Shido, *Japan* 49 G7
Shiel, L., *U.K.* 14 E3
Shield, C., *Australia* 90 A2
Shiga □, *Japan* 49 G8
Shigaib, *Sudan* 73 E9
Shigu, *China* 52 D2
Shiguaigou, *China* 50 D6
Shihchiachuangi = Shijiazhuang, *China* 50 E8
Shijiazhuang, *China* 50 E8
Shijiu Hu, *China* 53 B12
Shikarpur, *India* 62 E8
Shikarpur, *Pakistan* 62 F3
Shikoku □, *Japan* 49 H6
Shikoku-Sanchi, *Japan* 49 H6
Shilabo, *Ethiopia* 68 F3
Shiliguri, *India* 61 F16
Shilka, *Russia* 45 D12
Shilka →, *Russia* 45 D13
Shillelagh, *Ireland* 15 D5
Shillong, *India* 61 G17
Shilo, *Jordan* 69 C4
Shilong, *China* 53 F9
Shilou, *China* 50 F6
Shilovo, *Russia* 41 D12
Shimabara, *Japan* 49 H5
Shimada, *Japan* 49 G9
Shimane □, *Japan* 49 G6
Shimanovsk, *Russia* 45 D13
Shimen, *China* 53 C8
Shimenjie, *China* 53 C11
Shimian, *China* 52 C4
Shimizu, *Japan* 49 G9
Shimodate, *Japan* 49 F9
Shimoga, *India* 60 N9
Shimoni, *Kenya* 82 C4
Shimonoseki, *Japan* 49 H5
Shimpuru Rapids, *Angola* 84 B2
Shimsk, *Russia* 40 B7
Shin, L., *U.K.* 14 C4
Shin-Tone →, *Japan* 49 G10
Shinan, *China* 52 F7
Shinano →, *Japan* 49 F9
Shīndand, *Afghan.* 60 C3
Shingleton, *U.S.A.* 98 C2
Shingū, *Japan* 49 H7
Shinjō, *Japan* 48 E10
Shinkafe, *Nigeria* 79 C6
Shinshār, *Syria* 69 A5
Shinyanga, *Tanzania* 82 C3
Shinyanga □, *Tanzania* 82 C3
Shiogama, *Japan* 48 E10
Shiojiri, *Japan* 49 F8
Ship I., *U.S.A.* 109 K10
Shipehenski Prokhod, *Bulgaria* 38 G8
Shiping, *China* 52 F4
Shipki La, *India* 60 D11
Shippegan, *Canada* 99 C7
Shippensburg, *U.S.A.* 106 F7
Shiprock, *U.S.A.* 111 H9
Shiqian, *China* 52 D7
Shiqma, N. →, *Israel* 69 D3
Shiquan, *China* 50 H5
Shīr Kūh, *Iran* 65 D7
Shiragami-Misaki, *Japan* 48 D10
Shirakawa, *Fukushima, Japan* 49 F10
Shirakawa, *Gifu, Japan* 49 F8
Shirane-San, *Gumma, Japan* 49 F9
Shirane-San, *Yamanashi, Japan* 49 G9
Shiraoi, *Japan* 48 C10
Shīrāz, *Iran* 65 D7
Shirbin, *Egypt* 76 H7
Shire →, *Africa* 83 F4
Shiretoko-Misaki, *Japan* 48 B12
Shirinab →, *Pakistan* 62 D2
Shiringushi, *Russia* 41 E13
Shiriya-Zaki, *Japan* 48 D10
Shiroishi, *Japan* 48 E10
Shīrvān, *Iran* 65 B8
Shirwa, L. = Chilwa, L., *Malawi* 83 F4
Shishou, *China* 53 C9
Shitai, *China* 53 B11
Shivpuri, *India* 62 G7
Shixian, *China* 51 C15
Shixing, *China* 53 E10
Shiyan, *China* 53 A8
Shiyata, *Egypt* 76 B2
Shizhu, *China* 52 C7
Shizong, *China* 52 E5
Shizuishan, *China* 50 E4
Shizuoka, *Japan* 49 G9
Shizuoka □, *Japan* 49 G9
Shklov, *Belorussia* 40 D7
Shkoder = Shkodra, *Albania* 38 G2
Shkodra, *Albania* 38 G2
Shkumbini →, *Albania* 39 H2
Shmidta, O., *Russia* 45 A10
Shō-Gawa →, *Japan* 49 F8
Shoal Lake, *Canada* 101 C8
Shōdo-Shima, *Japan* 49 G7
Shoeburyness, *U.K.* 13 F8
Sholapur = Solapur, *India* 60 L9
Shologontsy, *Russia* 45 C12
Shōmrōn, *Jordan* 69 C4
Shoshone, *Calif., U.S.A.* 113 K10
Shoshone, *Idaho, U.S.A.* 110 E6
Shoshone L., *U.S.A.* 110 D8
Shoshone Mts., *U.S.A.* 110 G5
Shoshong, *Botswana* 84 C4
Shoshoni, *U.S.A.* 110 E9
Shostka, *Ukraine* 40 F8
Shou Xian, *China* 53 A11
Shouchang, *China* 53 C12
Shouguang, *China* 51 F10
Shouning, *China* 53 D12
Shouyang, *China* 50 F7
Show Low, *U.S.A.* 111 J9
Shpola, *Ukraine* 42 B4
Shreveport, *U.S.A.* 109 J8
Shrewsbury, *U.K.* 12 E5
Shrirampur, *India* 63 H13
Shropshire □, *U.K.* 13 E5
Shuangbai, *China* 52 E3
Shuangcheng, *China* 51 B14
Shuangfeng, *China* 53 D9
Shuanggou, *China* 51 G9
Shuangjiang, *China* 52 F2
Shuangliao, *China* 51 C12
Shuangshanzi, *China* 51 D10
Shuangyang, *China* 51 C13
Shuangyashan, *China* 54 B8
Shucheng, *China* 53 B11
Shuguri Falls, *Tanzania* 83 D4
Shuicheng, *China* 52 D5
Shuiji, *China* 53 D12
Shuiye, *China* 50 F8
Shujalpur, *India* 62 H7
Shukpa Kunzang, *India* 63 B8
Shulan, *China* 51 B14
Shule, *China* 54 C2
Shumagin Is., *U.S.A.* 96 C4
Shumerlya, *Russia* 41 D15
Shumikha, *Russia* 44 D7
Shunchang, *China* 53 D11
Shunde, *China* 53 F9
Shungay, *Kazakhstan* 43 B12
Shungnak, *U.S.A.* 96 B4
Shuo Xian, *China* 50 E7
Shūr →, *Iran* 65 D7
Shūr Āb, *Iran* 65 C6
Shūr Gaz, *Iran* 65 D8
Shūrāb, *Iran* 65 C8
Shūrjestān, *Iran* 65 D7
Shurma, *Russia* 41 C17
Shurugwi, *Zimbabwe* 83 F3
Shūsf, *Iran* 65 D9
Shūshtar, *Iran* 65 D6
Shuswap L., *Canada* 100 C5
Shuya, *Russia* 41 C12
Shuyang, *China* 51 G10
Shūzū, *Iran* 65 D7
Shwebo, *Burma* 61 H19
Shwegu, *Burma* 61 G20
Shweli →, *Burma* 61 H20
Shymkent = Chimkent, *Kazakhstan* 44 E7
Shyok, *India* 63 B8
Shyok →, *Pakistan* 63 B6
Si Chon, *Thailand* 59 H2
Si Kiang = Xi Jiang →, *China* 53 F9
Si-ngan = Xi'an, *China* 50 G5
Si Prachan, *Thailand* 58 E3
Si Racha, *Thailand* 58 F3
Si Xian, *China* 51 H9
Siahan Range, *Pakistan* 60 F4
Siaksrindrapura, *Indonesia* 56 D2
Sialkot, *Pakistan* 62 C6
Siam = Thailand ■, *Asia* 58 E4
Siantan, P., *Indonesia* 59 L6
Siāpo →, *Venezuela* 120 C4
Sīāreh, *Iran* 65 D9
Siargao, *Phil.* 55 G7
Siari, *Pakistan* 63 B7
Siasi, *Phil.* 57 C6
Siasi I., *Phil.* 55 J4
Siátista, *Greece* 39 J4
Siau, *Indonesia* 57 D7
Šiauliai, *Lithuania* 40 D3
Siaya □, *Kenya* 82 B3
Siazan, *Azerbaijan* 43 F13
Sibâi, Gebel el, *Egypt* 76 B3
Sibari, *Italy* 35 C9
Sibasa, *S. Africa* 85 C5
Sibayi, L., *S. Africa* 85 D5
Šibenik, *Croatia* 33 E12
Siberia, *Russia* 4 D13
Siberut, *Indonesia* 56 E1
Sibi, *Pakistan* 62 E2
Sibil, *Indonesia* 57 E10
Sibiti, *Congo* 80 E2
Sibiu, *Romania* 38 D7
Sibley, *Iowa, U.S.A.* 108 D7
Sibley, *La., U.S.A.* 109 J8
Sibolga, *Indonesia* 56 D1
Sibret, *Belgium* 17 J7
Sibsagar, *India* 61 F19
Sibu, *Malaysia* 56 D4
Sibuco, *Phil.* 55 H5
Sibuguey B., *Phil.* 55 H5
Sibutu, *Phil.* 57 D5
Sibutu Group, *Phil.* 55 J3
Sibutu Passage, *E. Indies* 57 D5
Sibuyan, *Phil.* 55 E5
Sibuyan Sea, *Phil.* 55 E5
Sicamous, *Canada* 100 C5
Sichuan □, *China* 52 B5
Sicilia, *Italy* 35 E7
Sicilia □, *Italy* 35 E7
Sicilia, Canale di, *Italy* 34 E5
Sicilian Channel = Sicilia, Canale di, *Italy* 34 E5
Sicily = Sicilia, *Italy* 35 E7
Sicuani, *Peru* 124 C3
Siculiana, *Italy* 34 E6
Sidamo □, *Ethiopia* 77 G4
Sidaouet, *Niger* 79 B6
Sidári, *Greece* 37 A3
Siddeburen, *Neths.* 16 B9
Siddhapur, *India* 62 H5
Siddipet, *India* 60 K11
Side, *Turkey* 66 E4
Sidéradougou, *Burkina Faso* 78 C4
Siderno Marina, *Italy* 35 D9
Sídheros, Ákra, *Greece* 37 D8
Sidhirókastron, *Greece* 39 H6
Sîdi Abd el Rahmân, *Egypt* 76 H6
Sîdi Barrâni, *Egypt* 76 A2
Sidi-bel-Abbès, *Algeria* 75 A4
Sidi Bennour, *Morocco* 74 B3
Sidi Haneish, *Egypt* 76 A2
Sidi Kacem, *Morocco* 74 B3
Sidi Omar, *Egypt* 76 A1
Sidi Slimane, *Morocco* 74 B3
Sidi Smaïl, *Morocco* 74 B3
Sidlaw Hills, *U.K.* 14 E5
Sidley, Mt., *Antarctica* 5 D14
Sidmouth, *U.K.* 13 G4
Sidmouth, C., *Australia* 90 A3
Sidney, *Canada* 100 D4
Sidney, *Mont., U.S.A.* 108 B2
Sidney, *N.Y., U.S.A.* 107 D9
Sidney, *Nebr., U.S.A.* 108 E3
Sidney, *Ohio, U.S.A.* 104 E3
Sidoarjo, *Indonesia* 57 G15
Sidon = Saydā, *Lebanon* 69 B4
Sidra, G. of = Surt, Khalīj, *Libya* 73 B8
Siedlce, *Poland* 20 C12
Sieg →, *Germany* 18 E3
Siegburg, *Germany* 18 E3
Siegen, *Germany* 18 E4
Siem Pang, *Cambodia* 58 E6
Siem Reap, *Cambodia* 58 F4
Siena, *Italy* 33 E8
Sieradź, *Poland* 20 D8
Sierck-les-Bains, *France* 25 C13
Sierpc, *Poland* 20 C9
Sierpe, Bocas de la, *Venezuela* 121 B5
Sierra Blanca, *U.S.A.* 111 L11
Sierra Blanca Peak, *U.S.A.* 111 K11
Sierra City, *U.S.A.* 112 F6
Sierra Colorada, *Argentina* 128 B3
Sierra de Yeguas, *Spain* 31 H6
Sierra Gorda, *Chile* 126 A2
Sierra Grande, *Argentina* 128 B3
Sierra Leone ■, *W. Afr.* 78 D2
Sierra Madre, *Mexico* 115 D6
Sierra Mojada, *Mexico* 114 B4
Sierraville, *U.S.A.* 112 F6
Sierre, *Switz.* 22 D5
Sif Fatima, *Algeria* 75 B6
Sífnos, *Greece* 39 N7
Sifton, *Canada* 101 C8
Sifton Pass, *Canada* 100 B3
Sig, *Algeria* 75 A4
Sigdal, *Norway* 10 D3
Sigean, *France* 26 E6
Sighetu-Marmatiei, *Romania* 38 B6
Sighişoara, *Romania* 38 C7
Sigli, *Indonesia* 56 C1
Siglufjörður, *Iceland* 8 C4
Sigmaringen, *Germany* 19 G5
Signakhi, *Georgia* 43 F11
Signal, *U.S.A.* 113 L13
Signal Pk., *U.S.A.* 113 M12
Signau, *Switz.* 22 C5
Signy-l'Abbaye, *France* 25 C11
Sigsig, *Ecuador* 120 D2
Sigtuna, *Sweden* 10 E11
Sigüenza, *Spain* 28 D2
Siguiri, *Guinea* 78 C3
Sigulda, *Latvia* 40 C4
Sigurd, *U.S.A.* 111 G8
Sihanoukville = Kompong Som, *Cambodia* 59 G4
Sihaus, *Peru* 124 B2
Sihui, *China* 53 F9

Siirt, *Turkey* 67 E9
Siirt □, *Turkey* 67 E9
Sijarira Ra., *Zimbabwe* 83 F2
Sikao, *Thailand* 59 J2
Sikar, *India* 62 F6
Sikasso, *Mali* 78 C3
Sikeston, *U.S.A.* 109 G10
Sikhote Alin, Khrebet, *Russia* 45 E14
Sikhote Alin Ra. = Sikhote Alin, Khrebet, *Russia* 45 E14
Sikiá, *Greece* 39 J6
Síkinos, *Greece* 39 N8
Sikkani Chief →, *Canada* 100 B4
Sikkim □, *India* 61 F16
Sikotu-Ko, *Japan* 48 C10
Sil →, *Spain* 30 C3
Silacayoapan, *Mexico* 115 D5
Silandro, *Italy* 32 B7
Silay, *Phil.* 55 F5
Silba, *Croatia* 33 D11
Silchar, *India* 61 G18
Silcox, *Canada* 101 B10
Şile, *Turkey* 66 C3
Silenrieux, *Belgium* 17 H4
Siler City, *U.S.A.* 105 H6
Silesia = Sląsk, *Poland* 20 E6
Silet, *Algeria* 75 D5
Silgarhi Doti, *Nepal* 63 E9
Silghat, *India* 61 F18
Silifke, *Turkey* 66 E5
Siliguri = Shiliguri, *India* 61 F16
Siling Co, *China* 54 C3
Silíqua, *Italy* 34 C1
Silistra, *Bulgaria* 38 E10
Silivri, *Turkey* 66 C3
Siljan, *Sweden* 9 F13
Silkeborg, *Denmark* 11 H3
Sillajhuay, Cordillera, *Chile* 124 D4
Sillé-le-Guillaume, *France* 24 D6
Sillustani, *Peru* 124 D3
Siloam Springs, *U.S.A.* 109 G7
Silopi, *Turkey* 67 E10
Silsbee, *U.S.A.* 109 K7
Šilute, *Lithuania* 40 D2
Silva Porto = Kuito, *Angola* 81 G3
Silvan, *Turkey* 67 D9
Silvaplana, *Switz.* 23 D9
Silver City, *N. Mex., U.S.A.* 111 K9
Silver City, *Nev., U.S.A.* 110 G4
Silver Cr. →, *U.S.A.* 110 E4
Silver Creek, *U.S.A.* 106 D5
Silver L., *Calif., U.S.A.* 112 G6
Silver L., *Calif., U.S.A.* 113 K10
Silver Lake, *U.S.A.* 110 E3
Silver Streams, *S. Africa* 84 D3
Silverton, *Colo., U.S.A.* 111 H10
Silverton, *Tex., U.S.A.* 109 H4
Silves, *Portugal* 31 H2
Silvi, *Italy* 33 F11
Silvia, *Colombia* 120 C2
Silvies →, *U.S.A.* 110 E4
Silvolde, *Neths.* 16 E8
Silvretta-Gruppe, *Switz.* 23 C10
Silwa Bahari, *Egypt* 76 C3
Silz, *Austria* 19 H6
Sim, C., *Morocco* 74 B3
Simanggang, *Malaysia* 56 D4
Simao, *China* 52 F3
Simão Dias, *Brazil* 122 D4
Simard, L., *Canada* 98 C4
Simav, *Turkey* 66 D3
Simba, *Tanzania* 82 C4
Simbach, *Germany* 19 G9
Simbirsk, *Russia* 41 D16
Simbo, *Tanzania* 82 C2
Simcoe, *Canada* 98 D3
Simcoe, L., *Canada* 98 D4
Simenga, *Russia* 45 C11
Simeto →, *Italy* 35 E8
Simeulue, *Indonesia* 56 D1
Simferopol, *Ukraine* 42 D6
Sími, *Greece* 39 N10
Simi Valley, *U.S.A.* 113 L8
Simikot, *Nepal* 63 E9
Simití, *Colombia* 120 B3
Simla, *India* 62 D7
Şimleu-Silvaniei, *Romania* 38 B5
Simme →, *Switz.* 22 C4
Simmern, *Germany* 19 F3
Simmie, *Canada* 101 D7
Simmler, *U.S.A.* 113 K7
Simões, *Brazil* 122 C3
Simojärvi, *Finland* 8 C19
Simojoki →, *Finland* 8 D18
Simojovel, *Mexico* 115 D6
Simonette →, *Canada* 100 B5
Simonstown, *S. Africa* 84 E2
Simplício Mendes, *Brazil* 122 C3
Simplon, *Switz.* 22 D6
Simplon Pass = Simplonpass, *Switz.* 22 D6
Simplon Tunnel, *Switz.* 22 D6
Simplonpass, *Switz.* 22 D6
Simpson Desert, *Australia* 90 D2
Simpungdong, *N. Korea* 51 D15
Simunjan, *Malaysia* 56 D4
Simushir, Ostrov, *Russia* 45 E16
Sinabang, *Indonesia* 56 D1
Sinadogo, *Somali Rep.* 68 F4
Sinai = Es Sînâ', *Egypt* 76 J8
Sinai, Mt. = Mûsa, G., *Egypt* 76 J8
Sinai Peninsula, *Egypt* 69 F2
Sinaia, *Romania* 38 D8
Sinaloa □, *Mexico* 114 C3
Sinaloa de Levya, *Mexico* 114 B3
Sinalunga, *Italy* 33 E8
Sinan, *China* 52 D7
Sinarádhes, *Greece* 37 A3
Sīnāwan, *Libya* 75 B7
Sincé, *Colombia* 120 B2
Sincelejo, *Colombia* 120 B2
Sinchang, *N. Korea* 51 D15
Sinchang-ni, *N. Korea* 51 E14
Sinclair, *U.S.A.* 110 F10
Sinclair Mills, *Canada* 100 C4
Sincorá, Serra do, *Brazil* 123 D3
Sind, *Pakistan* 62 G3
Sind □, *Pakistan* 62 F3
Sind →, *India* 63 B6
Sind Sagar Doab, *Pakistan* 62 D4
Sindal, *Denmark* 11 G4
Sindangan, *Phil.* 55 G5
Sindangbarang, *Indonesia* 57 G12
Sinde, *Zambia* 83 F2
Sinegorski, *Russia* 43 C9
Sinelnikovo, *Ukraine* 42 B6
Sines, *Portugal* 31 H2
Sines, C. de, *Portugal* 31 H2
Sineu, *Spain* 36 B10
Sinfra, *Ivory C.* 78 D3
Sing Buri, *Thailand* 58 E3
Singa, *Sudan* 77 E3
Singapore ■, *Asia* 59 M4
Singapore, Straits of, *Asia* 59 M5
Singaraja, *Indonesia* 56 F5
Singen, *Germany* 19 H4
Singida, *Tanzania* 82 C3
Singida □, *Tanzania* 82 D3
Singitikós Kólpos, *Greece* 39 J6
Singkaling Hkamti, *Burma* 61 G19
Singkawang, *Indonesia* 56 D3
Singleton, *Australia* 91 E5
Singleton, Mt., *N. Terr., Australia* 88 D5
Singleton, Mt., *W. Austral., Australia* 89 E2
Singoli, *India* 62 G6
Singora = Songkhla, *Thailand* 59 J3
Singosan, *N. Korea* 51 E14
Sinhung, *N. Korea* 51 D14
Sînî □, *Egypt* 69 F2
Siniscóla, *Italy* 34 B2
Sinj, *Croatia* 33 E13
Sinjai, *Indonesia* 57 F6
Sinjār, *Iraq* 64 B4
Sinkat, *Sudan* 76 D4
Sinkiang Uighur = Xinjiang Uygur Zizhiqu □, *China* 54 B3
Sinmak, *N. Korea* 51 E14
Sinnai, *Italy* 34 C2
Sinni →, *Italy* 35 B9
Sinnuris, *Egypt* 76 J7
Sinoe, L., *Romania* 38 E11
Sinop, *Turkey* 42 E6
Sinop □, *Turkey* 66 C6
Sinpo, *N. Korea* 51 E15
Sins, *Switz.* 23 B6
Sinskoye, *Russia* 45 C13
Sint-Amandsberg, *Belgium* 17 F3
Sint Annaland, *Neths.* 17 E4
Sint Annaparoch, *Neths.* 16 B7
Sint-Denijs, *Belgium* 17 G2
Sint Eustatius, I., *Neth. Ant.* 117 C7
Sint-Genesius-Rode, *Belgium* 17 G4
Sint-Gillis-Waas, *Belgium* 17 F4
Sint-Huibrechts-Lille, *Belgium* 17 F6
Sint-Katelinje-Waver, *Belgium* 17 F5
Sint-Kruis, *Belgium* 17 F2
Sint-Laureins, *Belgium* 17 F3
Sint Maarten, I., *W. Indies* 117 C7
Sint-Michiels, *Belgium* 17 F2
Sint Nicolaasga, *Neths.* 16 C7
Sint Niklaas, *Belgium* 17 F4
Sint Oedenrode, *Neths.* 17 E6
Sint Pancras, *Neths.* 16 C5
Sint Philipsland, *Neths.* 17 E4
Sint Truiden, *Belgium* 17 G6
Sint Willebrord, *Neths.* 17 E5
Sîntana, *Romania* 38 C4
Sintang, *Indonesia* 56 D4
Sintjohannesga, *Neths.* 16 C7
Sinton, *U.S.A.* 109 L6
Sintra, *Portugal* 31 G1
Sinŭiju, *N. Korea* 51 D13
Sinyukha →, *Ukraine* 42 B4
Siocon, *Phil.* 55 H5
Siófok, *Hungary* 21 J8
Sioma, *Zambia* 84 B3
Sion, *Switz.* 22 D4
Sioux City, *U.S.A.* 108 D6
Sioux Falls, *U.S.A.* 108 D6
Sioux Lookout, *Canada* 98 B1
Sip Song Chau Thai, *Vietnam* 58 B4
Sipalay, *Phil.* 55 G5
Siping, *China* 51 C13
Sipiwesk L., *Canada* 101 B9
Sipora, *Indonesia* 56 E1
Siquia →, *Nic.* 116 D3
Siquijor, *Phil.* 55 G5
Siquirres, *Costa Rica* 116 D3
Siquisique, *Venezuela* 120 A4
Sir Edward Pellew Group, *Australia* 90 B2
Sir Graham Moore Is., *Australia* 88 B4
Siracusa, *Italy* 35 E8
Sirajganj, *Bangla.* 63 G13
Sirakoro, *Mali* 78 C3
Şiran, *Turkey* 67 C8
Sirasso, *Ivory C.* 78 D3
Sīrdān, *Iran* 65 B6
Sirer, *Spain* 36 C7
Siret, *Romania* 38 B9
Siret →, *Romania* 38 D11
Şiria, *Romania* 38 C4
Sirino, Monte, *Italy* 35 B8
Sírna, *Greece* 39 N9
Sirnach, *Switz.* 23 B7
Şirnak, *Turkey* 67 E10
Sirohi, *India* 62 G5
Sironj, *India* 62 G7
Síros, *Greece* 39 M7
Sirretta Pk., *U.S.A.* 113 K8
Sirsa, *India* 62 E6
Siruela, *Spain* 31 G5
Sisak, *Croatia* 33 C13
Sisaket, *Thailand* 58 E5
Sisante, *Spain* 29 F2
Sisargas, Is., *Spain* 30 B2
Sishen, *S. Africa* 84 D3
Sishui, *Henan, China* 50 G7
Sishui, *Shandong, China* 51 G9
Sisipuk L., *Canada* 101 B8
Sisophon, *Cambodia* 58 F4
Sissach, *Switz.* 22 B5
Sisseton, *U.S.A.* 108 C6
Sissonne, *France* 25 C10
Sīstān va Balūchestān □, *Iran* 65 E9
Sisteron, *France* 27 D9
Sisters, *U.S.A.* 110 D3
Sitamarhi, *India* 63 F11
Sitapur, *India* 63 F9
Siteki, *Swaziland* 85 D5
Sitges, *Spain* 28 D6
Sitía, *Greece* 37 D8
Sítio da Abadia, *Brazil* 123 D2
Sitka, *U.S.A.* 96 C6
Sitoti, *Botswana* 84 C3
Sitra, *Egypt* 76 B2
Sittang Myit →, *Burma* 61 L20
Sittard, *Neths.* 17 G7
Sittensen, *Germany* 18 B5
Sittona, *Eritrea* 77 E4
Sittwe, *Burma* 61 J18
Siuna, *Nic.* 116 D3
Siuri, *India* 63 H12
Sivana, *India* 62 E8
Sīvand, *Iran* 65 D7
Sivas, *Turkey* 66 D7
Sivas □, *Turkey* 66 D7
Siverek, *Turkey* 67 E8
Sivrihisar, *Turkey* 66 D4
Sivry, *Belgium* 17 H4
Sîwa, *Egypt* 76 B2
Sîwa, El Wâhât es, *Egypt* 76 B2
Siwalik Range, *Nepal* 63 F10
Siwan, *India* 63 F11
Siyâl, Jazâ'ir, *Egypt* 76 C4
Sizewell, *U.K.* 13 E9
Siziwang Qi, *China* 50 D6
Sjælland, *Denmark* 11 J5
Sjællands Odde, *Denmark* 11 J5
Själevad, *Sweden* 10 A12
Sjenica, *Serbia* 21 M10
Sjoa, *Norway* 10 C3
Sjöbo, *Sweden* 11 J7
Sjösa, *Sweden* 11 F11
Sjumen = Šumen, *Bulgaria* 38 F9
Skadovsk, *Ukraine* 42 C5
Skagafjörður, *Iceland* 8 D4
Skagastølstindane, *Norway* 9 F9
Skagen, *Denmark* 11 G4
Skagerrak, *Denmark* 11 G3
Skagit →, *U.S.A.* 112 B4
Skagway, *U.S.A.* 100 B1
Skaidi, *Norway* 8 A18
Skala Podolskaya, *Ukraine* 42 B2
Skalat, *Ukraine* 40 G4
Skalni Dol = Kamenyak, *Bulgaria* 38 F9
Skals, *Denmark* 11 H3
Skanderborg, *Denmark* 11 H3
Skanör, *Sweden* 11 J6
Skara, *Sweden* 9 G12
Skaraborgs län □, *Sweden* 9 G12
Skardu, *Pakistan* 63 B6
Skarrild, *Denmark* 11 J2
Skarzysko Kamienna, *Poland* 20 D10
Skebokvarn, *Sweden* 10 E10
Skeena →, *Canada* 100 C2
Skeena Mts., *Canada* 100 B3
Skegness, *U.K.* 12 D8
Skeldon, *Guyana* 121 B6
Skellefte älv →, *Sweden* 8 D16
Skellefteå, *Sweden* 8 D16
Skelleftehamn, *Sweden* 8 D16
Skender Vakuf, *Bos.-H.* 21 L7
Skene, *Sweden* 11 G6
Skerries, The, *U.K.* 12 D3
Skhoinoúsa, *Greece* 39 N8
Ski, *Norway* 10 E4
Skíathos, *Greece* 39 K6
Skibbereen, *Ireland* 15 E2
Skiddaw, *U.K.* 12 C4
Skien, *Norway* 10 E3
Skierniewice, *Poland* 20 D10
Skikda, *Algeria* 75 A6
Skilloura, *Cyprus* 37 D12
Skinári, Ákra, *Greece* 39 M3
Skipton, *Australia* 91 F3
Skipton, *U.K.* 12 D5
Skirmish Pt., *Australia* 90 A1
Skíros, *Greece* 39 L7
Skivarp, *Sweden* 11 J7
Skive, *Denmark* 11 H3
Skjálfandafljót →, *Iceland* 8 D5
Skjálfandi, *Iceland* 8 C5
Skjeberg, *Norway* 10 E5
Skjern, *Denmark* 11 J2
Škofja Loka, *Slovenia* 33 B11
Skoghall, *Sweden* 9 G12
Skole, *Ukraine* 40 G3
Skópelos, *Greece* 39 K6
Skopí, *Greece* 37 D8
Skopin, *Russia* 41 E11
Skopje, *Macedonia* 39 G4
Skórcz, *Poland* 20 B8
Skövde, *Sweden* 9 G12
Skovorodino, *Russia* 45 D13
Skowhegan, *U.S.A.* 99 D6
Skownan, *Canada* 101 C9
Skradin, *Croatia* 33 E12
Skreanäs, *Sweden* 11 H6
Skudeneshavn, *Norway* 9 G8
Skull, *Ireland* 15 E2
Skultorp, *Sweden* 11 F7
Skunk →, *U.S.A.* 108 E9
Skuodas, *Lithuania* 40 C2
Skurup, *Sweden* 11 J7
Skutskär, *Sweden* 10 D11
Skvira, *Ukraine* 42 B3
Skwierzyna, *Poland* 20 C5
Skye, *U.K.* 14 D2
Skykomish, *U.S.A.* 110 C3
Skyros = Skíros, *Greece* 39 L7
Slagelse, *Denmark* 11 J5
Slagharen, *Neths.* 16 C9
Slamet, *Indonesia* 56 F3
Slaney →, *Ireland* 15 D5
Slangerup, *Denmark* 11 J6
Slano, *Croatia* 21 N7
Slantsy, *Russia* 40 B6
Sląsk, *Poland* 20 E6
Slate Is., *Canada* 98 C2
Slatina, *Romania* 38 E7
Slaton, *U.S.A.* 109 J4
Slave →, *Canada* 100 A6
Slave Coast, *W. Afr.* 70 F4
Slave Lake, *Canada* 100 B6
Slave Pt., *Canada* 100 A5
Slavgorod, *Russia* 44 D8
Slavnoye, *Belorussia* 40 D6
Slavonska Požega, *Croatia* 21 K7
Slavonski Brod, *Croatia* 21 K8
Slavuta, *Ukraine* 40 F5
Slavyanka, *Russia* 48 C5
Slavyansk, *Ukraine* 42 B7
Slavyansk-na-Kubani, *Russia* 42 D8
Sławno, *Poland* 20 A6
Sławoborze, *Poland* 20 B5
Sleaford, *U.K.* 12 E7
Sleaford B., *Australia* 91 E2
Sleat, Sd. of, *U.K.* 14 D3
Sleeper Is., *Canada* 97 C11
Sleepy Eye, *U.S.A.* 108 C7
Sleidinge, *Belgium* 17 F3
Sleman, *Indonesia* 57 G14
Slemon L., *Canada* 100 A5
Slidell, *U.S.A.* 109 K10
Sliedrecht, *Neths.* 16 E5
Sliema, *Malta* 37 D2
Slieve Aughty, *Ireland* 15 C3
Slieve Bloom, *Ireland* 15 C4
Slieve Donard, *U.K.* 15 B6
Slieve Gullion, *U.K.* 15 B5
Slieve Mish, *Ireland* 15 D2
Slievenamon, *Ireland* 15 D4
Sligo, *Ireland* 15 B3
Sligo □, *Ireland* 15 B3
Sligo B., *Ireland* 15 B3
Slijpe, *Belgium* 17 F1
Slikkerveer, *Neths.* 16 E5
Slite, *Sweden* 9 H15
Sliven, *Bulgaria* 38 G9
Slivnitsa, *Bulgaria* 38 G6
Sljeme, *Croatia* 33 C12
Sloan, *U.S.A.* 113 K11
Sloansville, *U.S.A.* 107 D10
Slobodskoy, *Russia* 41 B17
Slobozia, *Romania* 38 E10
Slocan, *Canada* 100 D5
Slochteren, *Neths.* 16 B9
Slöinge, *Sweden* 11 H6
Slonim, *Belorussia* 40 E4
Slotermeer, *Neths.* 16 C7
Slough, *U.K.* 13 F7
Sloughhouse, *U.S.A.* 112 G5
Slovak Rep. ■, *Europe* 20 G9
Slovakia = Slovak Rep. ■, *Europe* 20 G9
Slovakian Ore Mts. = Slovenské Rudohorie, *Slovak Rep.* 20 G9
Slovenia ■, *Europe* 33 C11
Slovenija = Slovenia ■, *Europe* 33 C11
Slovenj Gradec, *Slovenia* 33 B12
Slovenska Bistrica, *Slovenia* 33 B12
Slovenská Republika = Slovak Rep. ■, *Europe* 20 G9
Slovenské Rudohorie, *Slovak Rep.* 20 G9
Slovyansk = Slavyansk, *Ukraine* 42 B7
Słubice, *Poland* 20 C4
Sluch →, *Ukraine* 40 F5
Sluis, *Neths.* 17 F2
Slunj, *Croatia* 33 C12
Słupca, *Poland* 20 C7
Słupsk, *Poland* 20 A7
Slurry, *S. Africa* 84 D4
Slutsk, *Belorussia* 40 E5
Slyne Hd., *Ireland* 15 C1
Slyudyanka, *Russia* 45 D11
Smålandsfarvandet, *Denmark* 11 J5
Smålandsstenar, *Sweden* 11 G7
Smalltree L., *Canada* 101 A7
Smara, *Morocco* 72 B3
Smarje, *Slovenia* 33 B12
Smartt Syndicate Dam, *S. Africa* 84 E3
Smartville, *U.S.A.* 112 F5
Smeaton, *Canada* 101 C8
Smederevo, *Serbia* 21 L10
Smederevska Palanka, *Serbia* 21 L10
Smela, *Ukraine* 42 B4
Smethport, *U.S.A.* 106 E6
Smidovich, *Russia* 45 E14
Smilde, *Neths.* 16 C8
Smiley, *Canada* 101 C7
Smith, *Canada* 100 B6
Smith →, *Canada* 100 B3
Smith Arm, *Canada* 96 B7
Smith Center, *U.S.A.* 108 F5
Smith Sund, *Greenland* 4 B4
Smithburne →, *Australia* 90 B3
Smithers, *Canada* 100 C3
Smithfield, *S. Africa* 85 E4
Smithfield, *N.C., U.S.A.* 105 H6
Smithfield, *Utah, U.S.A.* 110 F8
Smiths Falls, *Canada* 98 D4
Smithton, *Australia* 90 G4
Smithtown, *Australia* 91 E5
Smithville, *Canada* 106 C5
Smithville, *U.S.A.* 109 K6
Smoky →, *Canada* 100 B5
Smoky Bay, *Australia* 91 E1
Smoky Falls, *Canada* 98 B3
Smoky Hill →, *U.S.A.* 108 F6
Smoky Lake, *Canada* 100 C6
Smøla, *Norway* 10 A2
Smolensk, *Russia* 40 D8
Smolikas, Óros, *Greece* 39 J3
Smolník, *Slovak Rep.* 20 G10
Smolyan, *Bulgaria* 39 H7
Smooth Rock Falls, *Canada* 98 C3
Smoothstone L., *Canada* 101 C7
Smorgon, *Belorussia* 40 D5
Smyadovo, *Bulgaria* 38 F10
Smyrna = İzmir, *Turkey* 66 D2
Snaefell, *U.K.* 12 C3
Snæfellsjökull, *Iceland* 8 D2
Snake →, *U.S.A.* 110 C4
Snake I., *Australia* 91 F4
Snake L., *Canada* 101 B7
Snake Range, *U.S.A.* 110 G6
Snake River Plain, *U.S.A.* 110 E7
Snarum, *Norway* 10 D3
Snedsted, *Denmark* 11 H2
Sneek, *Neths.* 16 B7
Sneeker-meer, *Neths.* 16 B7
Sneeuberge, *S. Africa* 84 E3
Snejbjerg, *Denmark* 11 H2
Snelling, *U.S.A.* 112 H6
Snezhnoye, *Ukraine* 43 C8
Snežnik, *Slovenia* 33 C11
Snigirevka, *Ukraine* 42 C5
Snizort, L., *U.K.* 14 D2
Snøhetta, *Norway* 10 B3
Snohomish, *U.S.A.* 112 C4
Snoul, *Cambodia* 59 F6
Snow Hill, *U.S.A.* 104 F8
Snow Lake, *Canada* 101 C8
Snow Mt., *U.S.A.* 112 F4
Snowbird L., *Canada* 101 A8
Snowdon, *U.K.* 12 D3
Snowdrift, *Canada* 101 A6
Snowdrift →, *Canada* 101 A6
Snowflake, *U.S.A.* 111 J8
Snowshoe Pk., *U.S.A.* 110 B6
Snowtown, *Australia* 91 E2
Snowville, *U.S.A.* 110 F7
Snowy →, *Australia* 91 F4
Snowy Mts., *Australia* 91 F4
Snug Corner, *Bahamas* 117 B5
Snyatyn, *Ukraine* 42 B1
Snyder, *Okla., U.S.A.* 109 H5
Snyder, *Tex., U.S.A.* 109 J4
Soacha, *Colombia* 120 C3
Soahanina, *Madag.* 85 B7
Soalala, *Madag.* 85 B8
Soan →, *Pakistan* 62 C4
Soanierana-Ivongo, *Madag.* 85 B8
Soap Lake, *U.S.A.* 110 C4
Sobat, Nahr →, *Sudan* 77 F3
Sobhapur, *India* 62 H8
Sobinka, *Russia* 41 D12
Sobótka, *Poland* 20 E6
Sobrado, *Spain* 30 B2
Sobral, *Brazil* 122 B3

Sobreira Formosa, *Portugal* 31 F3
Soc Giang, *Vietnam* 58 A6
Soc Trang, *Vietnam* 59 H5
Soča →, *Europe* 33 B10
Sochaczew, *Poland* 20 C10
Soch'e = Shache, *China* 54 C2
Sochi, *Russia* 43 E8
Société, Is. de la, *Pac. Oc.* 93 J12
Society Is. = Société, Is. de la, *Pac. Oc.* 93 J12
Socompa, Portezuelo de, *Chile* 126 A2
Socorro, *Colombia* 120 B3
Socorro, *U.S.A.* 111 J10
Socorro, I., *Mexico* 114 D2
Socotra, *Ind. Oc.* 68 E5
Socúellmos, *Spain* 29 F2
Soda L., *U.S.A.* 111 J5
Soda Plains, *India* 63 B8
Soda Springs, *U.S.A.* 110 E8
Söderhamn, *Sweden* 9 F14
Söderköping, *Sweden* 9 G14
Södermanlands län □, *Sweden* 10 E10
Södertälje, *Sweden* 10 E11
Sodiri, *Sudan* 77 E2
Sodo, *Ethiopia* 77 F4
Sodražica, *Slovenia* 33 C11
Sodus, *U.S.A.* 106 C7
Soekmekaar, *S. Africa* 85 C4
Soest, *Germany* 18 D4
Soest, *Neths.* 16 D6
Soestdijk, *Neths.* 16 D6
Sofádhes, *Greece* 39 K5
Sofara, *Mali* 78 C4
Sofia = Sofiya, *Bulgaria* 38 G6
Sofia →, *Madag.* 85 B8
Sofievka, *Ukraine* 42 B5
Sofiiski, *Russia* 45 D14
Sofikón, *Greece* 39 M6
Sofiya, *Bulgaria* 38 G6
Sōfu-Gan, *Japan* 49 K10
Sogakofe, *Ghana* 79 D5
Sogamoso, *Colombia* 120 B3
Sogār, *Iran* 65 E8
Sögel, *Germany* 18 C3
Sogn og Fjordane fylke □, *Norway* 9 F9
Sogndalsfjøra, *Norway* 9 F9
Sognefjorden, *Norway* 9 F8
Söğüt, *Turkey* 66 C4
Söğüt Gölü, *Turkey* 66 E3
Sŏgwi-po, *S. Korea* 51 H14
Soh, *Iran* 65 C6
Sohâg, *Egypt* 76 B3
Sŏhori, *N. Korea* 51 D15
Soignies, *Belgium* 17 G4
Soira, *Eritrea* 77 E4
Soissons, *France* 25 C10
Sōja, *Japan* 49 G6
Sojat, *India* 62 G5
Sok →, *Russia* 41 E17
Sokal, *Ukraine* 40 F4
Söke, *Turkey* 66 E2
Sokelo, *Zaïre* 83 D1
Sokhumi = Sukhumi, *Georgia* 43 E9
Sokki, Oued In →, *Algeria* 75 C5
Sokna, *Norway* 10 D3
Soknedal, *Norway* 10 B4
Soko Banja, *Serbia* 21 M11
Sokodé, *Togo* 79 D5
Sokol, *Russia* 41 B12
Sokółka, *Poland* 20 B13
Sokolo, *Mali* 78 C3
Sokołów Małpolski, *Poland* 20 E12
Sokołów Podlaski, *Poland* 20 C12
Sokoto, *Nigeria* 79 C6
Sokoto □, *Nigeria* 79 C6
Sokoto →, *Nigeria* 79 C5
Sol Iletsk, *Russia* 44 D6
Solai, *Kenya* 82 B4
Solano, *Phil.* 55 C4
Solapur, *India* 60 L9
Solares, *Spain* 30 B7
Soléa □, *Cyprus* 37 D12
Solec Kujawski, *Poland* 20 B8
Soledad, *Colombia* 120 A3
Soledad, *U.S.A.* 111 H3
Soledad, *Venezuela* 121 B5
Solent, The, *U.K.* 13 G6
Solenzara, *France* 27 G13
Solesmes, *France* 25 B10
Solfonn, *Norway* 9 F9
Solhan, *Turkey* 67 D9
Soligalich, *Russia* 41 B13
Soligorsk, *Belorussia* 40 E5
Solikamsk, *Russia* 44 D6
Solila, *Madag.* 85 C8
Solimões = Amazonas →, *S. Amer.* 121 D7
Solingen, *Germany* 17 F10
Sollebrunn, *Sweden* 11 F6
Sollefteå, *Sweden* 10 A11
Sollentuna, *Sweden* 10 E11
Sóller, *Spain* 36 B9
Solling, *Germany* 18 D5
Solna, *Sweden* 10 E12
Solnechnogorsk, *Russia* 41 C10
Sologne, *France* 25 E8
Solok, *Indonesia* 56 E2
Sololá, *Guatemala* 116 D1
Solomon, N. Fork →, *U.S.A.* 108 F5
Solomon, S. Fork →, *U.S.A.* 108 F5
Solomon Is. ■, *Pac. Oc.* 92 H7
Solon, *China* 54 B7
Solon Springs, *U.S.A.* 108 B9
Solonópole, *Brazil* 122 C4
Solor, *Indonesia* 57 F6
Solotcha, *Russia* 41 D11
Solothurn, *Switz.* 22 B5
Solothurn □, *Switz.* 22 B5
Solsona, *Spain* 28 D6
Solta, *Croatia* 33 E13
Solṭānābād, *Khorāsān, Iran* 65 C8
Solṭānābād, *Khorāsān, Iran* 65 B8
Solṭānābād, *Markazī, Iran* 65 C6
Soltau, *Germany* 18 C5
Soltsy, *Russia* 40 B7
Solunska Glava, *Macedonia* 39 H4
Solvang, *U.S.A.* 113 L6
Solvay, *U.S.A.* 107 C8
Solway Firth, *U.K.* 12 C4
Solwezi, *Zambia* 83 E2
Sōma, *Japan* 48 F10
Soma, *Turkey* 66 D2
Somali Rep. ■, *Africa* 68 F4
Somalia ■ = Somali Rep. ■, *Africa* 68 F4
Sombernon, *France* 25 E11
Sombor, *Serbia* 21 K9
Sombra, *Canada* 106 D2
Sombrerete, *Mexico* 114 C4
Sombrero, *Anguilla* 117 C7
Someren, *Neths.* 17 F7
Somers, *U.S.A.* 110 B6
Somerset, *Canada* 101 D9
Somerset, *Colo., U.S.A.* 111 G10
Somerset, *Ky., U.S.A.* 104 G3
Somerset, *Mass., U.S.A.* 107 E13
Somerset, *Pa., U.S.A.* 106 F5
Somerset □, *U.K.* 13 F5
Somerset East, *S. Africa* 84 E4
Somerset I., *Canada* 96 A10
Somerset West, *S. Africa* 84 E2
Somerton, *U.S.A.* 111 K6
Somerville, *U.S.A.* 107 F10
Someş →, *Romania* 38 B5
Someşul Mare →, *Romania* 38 B7
Somma Lombardo, *Italy* 32 C5
Somma Vesuviana, *Italy* 35 B7
Sommariva, *Australia* 91 D4
Sommatino, *Italy* 34 E6
Somme □, *France* 25 C9
Somme →, *France* 25 B8
Somme, B. de la, *France* 24 B8
Sommelsdijk, *Neths.* 16 E4
Sommepy-Tahure, *France* 25 C11
Sömmerda, *Germany* 18 D7
Sommesous, *France* 25 D11
Sommières, *France* 27 E8
Somoto, *Nic.* 116 D2
Sompolno, *Poland* 20 C8
Somport, Paso, *Spain* 28 C4
Somport, Puerto de, *Spain* 28 C4
Somuncurá, Meseta de, *Argentina* 128 B3
Son, *Neths.* 17 E6
Son, *Norway* 10 E4
Son, *Spain* 30 C2
Son Ha, *Vietnam* 58 E7
Son Hoa, *Vietnam* 58 F7
Son La, *Vietnam* 58 B4
Son Tay, *Vietnam* 58 B5
Soná, *Panama* 116 E3
Sonamarg, *India* 63 B6
Sonamukhi, *India* 63 H12
Sŏnchŏn, *N. Korea* 51 E13
Soncino, *Italy* 32 C6
Sondags →, *S. Africa* 84 E4
Sóndalo, *Italy* 32 B7
Sondar, *India* 63 C6
Sønder Omme, *Denmark* 11 J2
Sønder Tornby, *Denmark* 11 G3
Sønderborg, *Denmark* 11 K3
Sønderjyllands Amtskommune □, *Denmark* 11 J3
Sondershausen, *Germany* 18 D6
Søndre Strømfjord, *Greenland* 97 B14
Sóndrio, *Italy* 32 B6
Sone, *Mozam.* 83 F3
Sonepur, *India* 61 J13
Song, *Thailand* 58 C3
Song Cau, *Vietnam* 58 F7
Song Xian, *China* 50 G7
Songchŏn, *N. Korea* 51 E14
Songea, *Tanzania* 83 E4
Songea □, *Tanzania* 83 E4
Songeons, *France* 25 C8
Songhua Hu, *China* 51 C14
Songhua Jiang →, *China* 54 B8
Songjiang, *China* 53 B13
Songjin, *N. Korea* 51 D15
Songjŏng-ni, *S. Korea* 51 G14
Songkan, *China* 52 C6
Songkhla, *Thailand* 59 J3
Songming, *China* 52 E4
Songnim, *N. Korea* 51 E13
Songpan, *China* 52 A4
Songtao, *China* 52 C7
Songwe, *Zaïre* 82 C2
Songwe →, *Africa* 83 D3
Songxi, *China* 53 D12
Songzi, *China* 53 B8
Sonid Youqi, *China* 50 C7
Sonipat, *India* 62 E7
Sonkovo, *Russia* 41 C10
Sonmiani, *Pakistan* 62 G2
Sonnino, *Italy* 34 A6
Sono →, *Goiás, Brazil* 122 C2
Sono →, *Minas Gerais, Brazil* 123 E2
Sonogno, *Switz.* 23 D7
Sonora, *Calif., U.S.A.* 111 H3
Sonora, *Tex., U.S.A.* 109 K4
Sonora □, *Mexico* 114 B2
Sonora →, *Mexico* 114 B2
Sonora Desert, *U.S.A.* 113 M12
Sonoyta, *Mexico* 114 A2
Sŏnsan, *S. Korea* 51 F15
Sonsonate, *El Salv.* 116 D2
Sonthofen, *Germany* 19 H6
Soochow = Suzhou, *China* 53 B13
Sop Hao, *Laos* 58 B5
Sop Prap, *Thailand* 58 D2
Sopachuy, *Bolivia* 125 D5
Sopi, *Indonesia* 57 D7
Sopo, Nahr →, *Sudan* 77 F2
Sopot, *Poland* 20 A8
Sopotnica, *Macedonia* 39 H4
Sopron, *Hungary* 21 H6
Sop's Arm, *Canada* 99 C8
Sopur, *India* 63 B6
Sør-Rondane, *Antarctica* 5 D4
Sør-Trøndelag fylke □, *Norway* 10 B3
Sora, *Italy* 34 A6
Sorah, *Pakistan* 62 F3
Söråker, *Sweden* 10 B11
Sorano, *Italy* 33 F8
Sorata, *Bolivia* 124 D4
Sorbas, *Spain* 29 H2
Sorel, *Canada* 98 C5
Sörenberg, *Switz.* 22 C6
Soreq, N. →, *Israel* 69 D3
Soresina, *Italy* 32 C6
Sorgono, *Italy* 34 B2
Sorgues, *France* 27 D8
Sorgun, *Turkey* 66 D6
Soria, *Spain* 28 D2
Soria □, *Spain* 28 D2
Soriano, *Uruguay* 126 C4
Soriano nel Cimino, *Italy* 33 F9
Sorkh, Kuh-e, *Iran* 65 C8
Sorø, *Denmark* 11 J5
Soro, *Guinea* 78 C3
Sorocaba, *Brazil* 127 A6
Soroki, *Moldavia* 42 B3
Soron, *India* 63 F8
Sorong, *Indonesia* 57 E8
Soroní, *Greece* 37 C10
Soroti, *Uganda* 82 B3
Sørøya, *Norway* 8 A17
Sørøysundet, *Norway* 8 A17
Sorraia →, *Portugal* 31 G2
Sorrento, *Australia* 91 F3
Sorrento, *Italy* 35 B7
Sorsele, *Sweden* 8 D14
Sorso, *Italy* 34 B1
Sorsogon, *Phil.* 55 E6
Sortino, *Italy* 35 E8
Sorvizhi, *Russia* 41 C16
Sos, *Spain* 28 C3
Sŏsan, *S. Korea* 51 F14
Soscumica, L., *Canada* 98 B4
Sosna →, *Russia* 41 E11
Sosnovka, *Russia* 41 E12
Sosnovka, *Russia* 45 D11
Sosnowiec, *Poland* 20 E9
Sospel, *France* 27 E11
Sostanj, *Slovenia* 33 B12
Sŏsura, *N. Korea* 51 C16
Soto la Marina →, *Mexico* 115 C5
Soto y Amío, *Spain* 30 C5
Sotteville-lès-Rouen, *France* 24 C8
Sotuta, *Mexico* 115 C7
Souanké, *Congo* 80 D2
Soúdha, *Greece* 37 D6
Soúdhas, Kólpos, *Greece* 37 D6
Sougne-Remouchamps, *Belgium* 17 H7
Souillac, *France* 26 D5
Souk-Ahras, *Algeria* 75 A6
Souk el Arba du Rharb, *Morocco* 74 B3
Soukhouma, *Laos* 58 E5
Sŏul, *S. Korea* 51 F14
Soulac-sur-Mer, *France* 26 C2
Soultz-sous-Forêts, *France* 25 D14
Soumagne, *Belgium* 17 G7
Sound, The = Øresund, *Europe* 11 J6
Sound, The, *U.K.* 13 G3
Soúnion, Ákra, *Greece* 39 M7
Sour el Ghozlane, *Algeria* 75 A5
Sources, Mt. aux, *Lesotho* 85 D4
Sourdeval, *France* 24 D6
Soure, *Brazil* 122 B2
Soure, *Portugal* 30 E2
Souris, *Man., Canada* 101 D8
Souris, *P.E.I., Canada* 99 C7
Souris →, *Canada* 108 A5
Sousa, *Brazil* 122 C4
Sousel, *Brazil* 122 B1
Sousel, *Portugal* 31 G3
Souss, O. →, *Morocco* 74 B3
Sousse, *Tunisia* 75 A7
Soustons, *France* 26 E2
South Africa ■, *Africa* 84 E3
South Aulatsivik I., *Canada* 99 A7
South Australia □, *Australia* 91 E2
South Baldy, *U.S.A.* 111 J10
South Bend, *Ind., U.S.A.* 104 E2
South Bend, *Wash., U.S.A.* 112 D3
South Boston, *U.S.A.* 105 G6
South Branch, *Canada* 99 C8
South Brook, *Canada* 99 C8
South Buganda □, *Uganda* 82 C3
South Carolina □, *U.S.A.* 105 J5
South Charleston, *U.S.A.* 104 F5
South China Sea, *Asia* 56 C4
South Dakota □, *U.S.A.* 108 C5
South Downs, *U.K.* 13 G7
South East C., *Australia* 90 G4
South East Is., *Australia* 89 F3
South Esk →, *U.K.* 14 E5
South Foreland, *U.K.* 13 F9
South Fork →, *U.S.A.* 110 C7
South Fork, American →, *U.S.A.* 112 G5
South Fork, Feather →, *U.S.A.* 112 F5
South Georgia, *Antarctica* 5 B1
South Glamorgan □, *U.K.* 13 F4
South Haven, *U.S.A.* 104 D2
South Henik, L., *Canada* 101 A9
South Honshu Ridge, *Pac. Oc.* 92 E6
South Horr, *Kenya* 82 B4
South I., *Kenya* 82 B4
South I., *N.Z.* 87 L3
South Invercargill, *N.Z.* 87 M2
South Knife →, *Canada* 101 B10
South Korea ■, *Asia* 51 F15
South Lake Tahoe, *U.S.A.* 112 G6
South Loup →, *U.S.A.* 108 E5
South Magnetic Pole, *Antarctica* 5 C9
South Milwaukee, *U.S.A.* 104 D2
South Molton, *U.K.* 13 F4
South Nahanni →, *Canada* 100 A4
South Natuna Is. = Natuna Selatan, Kepulauan, *Indonesia* 59 L7
South Negril Pt., *Jamaica* 116 C4
South Orkney Is., *Antarctica* 5 C18
South Pagai, I. = Pagai Selatan, P., *Indonesia* 56 E2
South Pass, *U.S.A.* 110 E9
South Pittsburg, *U.S.A.* 105 H3
South Platte →, *U.S.A.* 108 E4
South Pole, *Antarctica* 5 E
South Porcupine, *Canada* 98 C3
South River, *Canada* 98 C4
South River, *U.S.A.* 107 F10
South Ronaldsay, *U.K.* 14 C6
South Sandwich Is., *Antarctica* 5 B1
South Saskatchewan →, *Canada* 101 C7
South Seal →, *Canada* 101 B9
South Shetland Is., *Antarctica* 5 C18
South Shields, *U.K.* 12 C6
South Sioux City, *U.S.A.* 108 D6
South Taranaki Bight, *N.Z.* 87 H5
South Thompson →, *Canada* 100 C4
South Twin I., *Canada* 98 B4
South Tyne →, *U.K.* 12 C5
South Uist, *U.K.* 14 D1
South West Africa = Namibia ■, *Africa* 84 C2
South West C., *Australia* 90 G4
South Yorkshire □, *U.K.* 12 D6
Southampton, *Canada* 98 D3
Southampton, *U.K.* 13 G6
Southampton, *U.S.A.* 107 F12
Southampton I., *Canada* 97 B11
Southbridge, *N.Z.* 87 K4
Southbridge, *U.S.A.* 107 D12
Southend, *Canada* 101 B8
Southend-on-Sea, *U.K.* 13 F8
Southern □, *Malawi* 83 F4
Southern □, *S. Leone* 78 D2
Southern □, *Zambia* 83 F2
Southern Alps, *N.Z.* 87 K3
Southern Cross, *Australia* 89 F2
Southern Hills, *Australia* 89 F3
Southern Indian L., *Canada* 101 B9
Southern Ocean, *Antarctica* 5 C6
Southern Pines, *U.S.A.* 105 H6
Southern Uplands, *U.K.* 14 F5
Southington, *U.S.A.* 107 E12
Southold, *U.S.A.* 107 E12
Southport, *Australia* 91 D5
Southport, *U.K.* 12 D4
Southport, *U.S.A.* 105 J6
Southwest C., *N.Z.* 87 M1
Southwold, *U.K.* 13 E9
Soutpansberg, *S. Africa* 85 C4
Souvigny, *France* 26 B7
Sovetsk, *Russia* 40 D2
Sovetsk, *Russia* 41 C16
Sovetskaya Gavan, *Russia* 45 E15
Sovicille, *Italy* 33 E8
Soviet Union = Commonwealth of Independent States ■, *Eurasia* 45 D11
Sovra, *Croatia* 21 N7
Soweto, *S. Africa* 85 D4
Sōya-Kaikyō = La Perouse Str., *Asia* 48 B11
Sōya-Misaki, *Japan* 48 B10
Soyo, *Angola* 80 F2
Sozh →, *Belorussia* 40 F7
Sozopol, *Bulgaria* 38 G10
Spa, *Belgium* 17 H7
Spain ■, *Europe* 7 H5
Spakenburg, *Neths.* 16 D6
Spalding, *Australia* 91 E2
Spalding, *U.K.* 12 E7
Spalding, *U.S.A.* 108 E5
Spangler, *U.S.A.* 106 F6
Spaniard's Bay, *Canada* 99 C9
Spanish, *Canada* 98 C3
Spanish Fork, *U.S.A.* 110 F8
Spanish Town, *Jamaica* 116 C4
Sparks, *U.S.A.* 112 F7
Sparta = Spárti, *Greece* 39 M5
Sparta, *Ga., U.S.A.* 105 J4
Sparta, *Wis., U.S.A.* 108 D9
Spartanburg, *U.S.A.* 105 H4
Spartansburg, *U.S.A.* 106 E5
Spartel, C., *Morocco* 74 A3
Spárti, *Greece* 39 M5
Spartivento, C., *Calabria, Italy* 35 E9
Spartivento, C., *Sard., Italy* 34 D1
Spas-Demensk, *Russia* 40 D8
Spas-Klepiki, *Russia* 41 D12
Spassk-Dalniy, *Russia* 45 E14
Spassk-Ryazanskiy, *Russia* 41 D12
Spátha, Ákra, *Greece* 37 D5
Spatsizi →, *Canada* 100 B3
Spearfish, *U.S.A.* 108 C3
Spearman, *U.S.A.* 109 G4
Speer, *Switz.* 23 B8
Speers, *Canada* 101 C7
Speightstown, *Barbados* 117 D8
Speke Gulf, *Tanzania* 82 C3
Spekholzerheide, *Neths.* 17 G8
Spence Bay, *Canada* 96 B10
Spencer, *Idaho, U.S.A.* 110 D7
Spencer, *Iowa, U.S.A.* 108 D7
Spencer, *N.Y., U.S.A.* 107 D8
Spencer, *Nebr., U.S.A.* 108 D5
Spencer, *W. Va., U.S.A.* 104 F5
Spencer, C., *Australia* 91 F2
Spencer B., *Namibia* 84 D1
Spencer G., *Australia* 91 E2
Spencerville, *Canada* 107 B9
Spences Bridge, *Canada* 100 C4
Spenser Mts., *N.Z.* 87 K4
Sperkhiós →, *Greece* 39 L5
Sperrin Mts., *U.K.* 15 B5
Spessart, *Germany* 19 E5
Spétsai, *Greece* 39 M6
Spey →, *U.K.* 14 D5
Speyer, *Germany* 19 F4
Speyer →, *Germany* 19 F4
Spezzano Albanese, *Italy* 35 C9
Spiekeroog, *Germany* 18 B3
Spielfeld, *Austria* 33 B12
Spiez, *Switz.* 22 C5
Spijk, *Neths.* 16 B9
Spijkenisse, *Neths.* 16 E4
Spíli, *Greece* 37 D6
Spilimbergo, *Italy* 33 B9
Spin Baldak = Qala-i-Jadid, *Afghan.* 62 D2
Spinalónga, *Greece* 37 D7
Spinazzola, *Italy* 35 B9
Spirit Lake, *Idaho, U.S.A.* 110 C5
Spirit Lake, *Wash., U.S.A.* 112 D4
Spirit River, *Canada* 100 B5
Spiritwood, *Canada* 101 C7
Spišská Nová Ves, *Slovak Rep.* 20 G10
Spithead, *U.K.* 13 G6
Spittal, *Austria* 21 J3
Spitzbergen = Svalbard, *Arctic* 4 B8
Split, *Croatia* 33 E13
Split L., *Canada* 101 B9
Splitski Kanal, *Croatia* 33 E13
Splügen, *Switz.* 23 C8
Splügenpass, *Switz.* 23 C8
Spofford, *U.S.A.* 109 L4
Spokane, *U.S.A.* 110 C5
Spoleto, *Italy* 33 F9
Spooner, *U.S.A.* 108 C9
Sporyy Navolok, Mys, *Russia* 44 B7
Spragge, *Canada* 98 C3
Sprague, *U.S.A.* 110 C5
Sprague River, *U.S.A.* 110 E3
Spratly I., *S. China Sea* 56 C4
Spray, *U.S.A.* 110 D4
Spree →, *Germany* 18 C9
Spremberg, *Germany* 18 D10
Sprimont, *Belgium* 17 G7
Spring City, *U.S.A.* 110 G8
Spring Garden, *U.S.A.* 112 F6
Spring Mts., *U.S.A.* 111 H6
Spring Valley, *Calif., U.S.A.* 113 N10
Spring Valley, *Minn., U.S.A.* 108 D8
Springbok, *S. Africa* 84 D2
Springdale, *Canada* 99 C8
Springdale, *Ark., U.S.A.* 109 G7
Springdale, *Wash., U.S.A.* 110 B5
Springe, *Germany* 18 C5
Springer, *U.S.A.* 109 G2
Springerville, *U.S.A.* 111 J9
Springfield, *Canada* 106 D4
Springfield, *N.Z.* 87 K3
Springfield, *Colo., U.S.A.* 109 G3

Springfield

Springfield, *Ill., U.S.A.* ... 108 F10
Springfield, *Mass., U.S.A.* 107 D12
Springfield, *Mo., U.S.A.* . 109 G8
Springfield, *Ohio, U.S.A.* . 104 F4
Springfield, *Oreg., U.S.A.* 110 D2
Springfield, *Tenn., U.S.A.* 105 G2
Springfield, *Vt., U.S.A.* .. 107 C12
Springfontein, *S. Africa* .. 84 E4
Springhill, *Canada* 99 C7
Springhouse, *Canada* 100 C4
Springhurst, *Australia* 91 F4
Springs, *S. Africa* 85 D4
Springsure, *Australia* 90 C4
Springvale, *Queens., Australia* 90 C3
Springvale, *W. Austral., Australia* 88 C4
Springvale, *U.S.A.* 107 C14
Springville, *Calif., U.S.A.* 112 J8
Springville, *N.Y., U.S.A.* . 106 D6
Springville, *Utah, U.S.A.* . 110 F8
Springwater, *Canada* 101 C7
Spruce-Creek, *U.S.A.* 106 F6
Spur, *U.S.A.* 109 J4
Spurn Hd., *U.K.* 12 D8
Spuž, *Montenegro* 21 N9
Spuzzum, *Canada* 100 D4
Squam L., *U.S.A.* 107 C13
Squamish, *Canada* 100 D4
Square Islands, *Canada* ... 99 B8
Squillace, G. di, *Italy* 35 D9
Squinzano, *Italy* 35 B11
Squires, Mt., *Australia* 89 E4
Sragen, *Indonesia* 57 G14
Srbac, *Bos.-H.* 21 K7
Srbija = Serbia □, *Yugoslavia* 21 M11
Srbobran, *Serbia* 21 K9
Sre Khtum, *Cambodia* 59 F6
Sre Umbell, *Cambodia* ... 59 G4
Srebrnica, *Bos.-H.* 21 L9
Sredinny Ra. = Sredinnyy Khrebet, *Russia* 45 D16
Sredinnyy Khrebet, *Russia* 45 D16
Središče, *Slovenia* 33 B13
Sredna Gora, *Bulgaria* ... 38 G7
Sredne Tambovskoye, *Russia* 45 D14
Srednekolymsk, *Russia* ... 45 C16
Srednevilyuysk, *Russia* ... 45 C13
Śrem, *Poland* 20 C7
Sremska Mitrovica, *Serbia* 21 L9
Srepok →, *Cambodia* 58 F6
Sretensk, *Russia* 45 D12
Sri Lanka ■, *Asia* 60 R12
Srikakulam, *India* 61 K13
Srinagar, *India* 63 B6
Środa Wielkopolski, *Poland* 20 C7
Srpska Itabej, *Serbia* 21 K10
Staaten →, *Australia* 90 B3
Staberhuk, *Germany* 18 A7
Stabroek, *Belgium* 17 F4
Stad Delden, *Neths.* 16 D9
Stade, *Germany* 18 B5
Staden, *Belgium* 17 G2
Staðarhólskirkja, *Iceland* .. 8 D3
Städjan, *Sweden* 10 C6
Stadlandet, *Norway* 8 E8
Stadskanaal, *Neths.* 16 B9
Stadthagen, *Germany* 18 C5
Stadtlohn, *Germany* 18 D2
Stadtroda, *Germany* 18 E7
Stäfa, *Switz.* 23 B7
Stafafell, *Iceland* 8 D6
Staffa, *U.K.* 14 E2
Stafford, *U.K.* 12 E5
Stafford, *U.S.A.* 109 G5
Stafford Springs, *U.S.A.* .. 107 E12
Staffordshire □, *U.K.* 12 E5
Stagnone, *Italy* 34 E5
Staines, *U.K.* 13 F7
Stakhanov = Kadiyevka, *Ukraine* 43 B8
Stalden, *Switz.* 22 D5
Stalingrad = Volgograd, *Russia* 43 B11
Staliniri = Tskhinvali, *Georgia* 43 E11
Stalino = Donetsk, *Ukraine* 42 C7
Stalinogorsk = Novomoskovsk, *Russia* . 41 D11
Stalis, *Greece* 37 D7
Stalowa Wola, *Poland* 20 E12
Stalybridge, *U.K.* 12 D5
Stamford, *Australia* 90 C3
Stamford, *U.K.* 13 E7
Stamford, *Conn., U.S.A.* . 107 E11
Stamford, *Tex., U.S.A.* ... 109 J5
Stamps, *U.S.A.* 109 J8
Stanberry, *U.S.A.* 108 E7
Stančevo = Kalipetrovo, *Bulgaria* 38 E10
Standerton, *S. Africa* 85 D4
Standish, *U.S.A.* 104 D4
Stanford, *U.S.A.* 110 C8
Stange, *Norway* 10 D5
Stanger, *S. Africa* 85 D5
Stanislaus →, *U.S.A.* 112 H5
Stanislav = Ivano-Frankovsk, *Ukraine* 40 G4
Stanke Dimitrov, *Bulgaria* 38 G6
Stanley, *Australia* 90 G4
Stanley, *N.B., Canada* ... 99 C6
Stanley, *Sask., Canada* ... 101 B8
Stanley, *Falk. Is.* 128 D5
Stanley, *Idaho, U.S.A.* ... 110 D6
Stanley, *N. Dak., U.S.A.* . 108 A3
Stanley, *N.Y., U.S.A.* 106 D7
Stanley, *Wis., U.S.A.* 108 C9
Stanovoy Khrebet, *Russia* . 45 D13
Stanovoy Ra. = Stanovoy Khrebet, *Russia* 45 D13
Stans, *Switz.* 23 C6
Stansmore Ra., *Australia* . 88 D4
Stanthorpe, *Australia* 91 D5
Stanton, *U.S.A.* 109 J4
Stanwood, *U.S.A.* 112 B4
Staphorst, *Neths.* 16 C8
Staples, *U.S.A.* 108 B7
Stapleton, *U.S.A.* 108 E4
Star City, *Canada* 101 C8
Stara-minskaya, *Russia* 43 C8
Stara Moravica, *Serbia* 21 K9
Stara Planina, *Bulgaria* ... 38 F6
Stara Zagora, *Bulgaria* ... 38 G8
Starachowice, *Poland* 20 D11
Starashcherbinovskaya, *Russia* 43 C8
Staraya Russa, *Russia* 40 C7
Starbuck I., *Kiribati* 93 H12
Stargard Szczeciński, *Poland* 20 B5
Stari Trg, *Slovenia* 33 C12
Staritsa, *Russia* 40 C9
Starke, *U.S.A.* 105 K4
Starkville, *Colo., U.S.A.* . 109 G2
Starkville, *Miss., U.S.A.* . 105 J1
Starnberg, *Germany* 19 G7
Starnberger See, *Germany* 19 H7
Starobelsk, *Ukraine* 43 B8
Starodub, *Russia* 40 E8
Starogard, *Poland* 20 B8
Starokonstantinov, *Ukraine* 42 B2
Start Pt., *U.K.* 13 G4
Staryy Biryuzyak, *Russia* . 43 D12
Staryy Chartoriysk, *Ukraine* 40 F4
Staryy Kheydzhan, *Russia* 45 C15
Staryy Krym, *Ukraine* 42 D6
Staryy Oskol, *Russia* 41 F10
Stassfurt, *Germany* 18 D7
State College, *U.S.A.* 106 F7
Stateline, *U.S.A.* 112 G7
Staten, I. = Estados, I. de Los, *Argentina* 128 D4
Staten I., *U.S.A.* 107 F10
Statesboro, *U.S.A.* 105 J5
Statesville, *U.S.A.* 105 H5
Stauffer, *U.S.A.* 113 L7
Staunton, *Ill., U.S.A.* 108 F10
Staunton, *Va., U.S.A.* 104 F6
Stavanger, *Norway* 9 G8
Staveley, *N.Z.* 87 K3
Stavelot, *Belgium* 17 H7
Stavenhagen, *Germany* ... 18 B8
Stavenisse, *Neths.* 17 E4
Staveren, *Neths.* 16 C6
Stavern, *Norway* 10 F4
Stavre, *Sweden* 10 B9
Stavropol, *Russia* 43 D10
Stavros, *Cyprus* 37 D11
Stavrós, *Greece* 37 D6
Stavros, Ákra, *Greece* 37 D6
Stavroúpolis, *Greece* 39 H7
Stawell, *Australia* 91 F3
Stawell →, *Australia* 90 C3
Stawiszyn, *Poland* 20 D8
Stayner, *Canada* 106 B4
Steamboat Springs, *U.S.A.* 110 F10
Steckborn, *Switz.* 23 A7
Steele, *U.S.A.* 108 B5
Steelton, *U.S.A.* 106 F8
Steelville, *U.S.A.* 109 G9
Steen River, *Canada* 100 B5
Steenbergen, *Neths.* 17 E4
Steenkool = Bintuni, *Indonesia* 57 E8
Steenvoorde, *France* 25 B9
Steenwijk, *Neths.* 16 C8
Steep Pt., *Australia* 89 E1
Steep Rock, *Canada* 101 C9
Ştefăneşti, *Romania* 38 B10
Stefanie L. = Chew Bahir, *Ethiopia* 77 G4
Stefansson Bay, *Antarctica* 5 C5
Steffisburg, *Switz.* 22 C5
Stege, *Denmark* 11 K6
Steiermark □, *Austria* 21 H5
Steigerwald, *Germany* 19 F6
Steilacoom, *U.S.A.* 112 C4
Stein, *Neths.* 17 G7
Steinbach, *Canada* 101 D9
Steinfort, *Lux.* 17 J7
Steinfurt, *Germany* 18 C3
Steinheim, *Germany* 18 D5
Steinhuder Meer, *Germany* 18 C5
Steinkjer, *Norway* 8 E11
Steinkopf, *S. Africa* 84 D2
Stekene, *Belgium* 17 F4
Stellarton, *Canada* 99 C7
Stellenbosch, *S. Africa* ... 84 E2
Stellendam, *Neths.* 16 E4
Stelvio, Paso dello, *Italy* .. 23 C10
Stemshaug, *Norway* 10 A2
Stendal, *Germany* 18 C7
Stene, *Belgium* 17 F1
Stensele, *Sweden* 8 D14
Stenstorp, *Sweden* 11 F7
Stepanakert = Khankendy, *Azerbaijan* 67 D12
Stephen, *U.S.A.* 108 A6
Stephens Creek, *Australia* 91 E3
Stephens I., *Canada* 100 C2
Stephenville, *Canada* 99 C8
Stephenville, *U.S.A.* 109 J5
Stepnica, *Poland* 20 B4
Stepnoi = Elista, *Russia* .. 43 C11
Stepnyak, *Kazakhstan* 44 D8
Steppe, *Asia* 46 E9
Sterkstroom, *S. Africa* 84 E4
Sterling, *Colo., U.S.A.* ... 108 E3
Sterling, *Ill., U.S.A.* 108 E10
Sterling, *Kans., U.S.A.* ... 108 F5
Sterling City, *U.S.A.* 109 K4
Sterling Run, *U.S.A.* 106 E6
Sterlitamak, *Russia* 44 D6
Šternberg, *Germany* 18 B7
Šternberk, *Czech.* 20 F7
Stérnes, *Greece* 37 D6
Stettin = Szczecin, *Poland* 20 B4
Stettiner Haff, *Germany* .. 18 B10
Stettler, *Canada* 100 C6
Steubenville, *U.S.A.* 106 F4
Stevens Point, *U.S.A.* 108 C10
Stevenson, *U.S.A.* 112 E5
Stevenson L., *Canada* 101 C9
Stevns Klint, *Denmark* ... 11 J6
Stewart, *B.C., Canada* ... 100 B3
Stewart, *N.W.T., Canada* . 96 B6
Stewart, *U.S.A.* 112 F7
Stewart, C., *Australia* 90 A1
Stewart, I., *Chile* 128 D2
Stewart I., *N.Z.* 87 M1
Stewarts Point, *U.S.A.* ... 112 G3
Stewiacke, *Canada* 99 C7
Steynsburg, *S. Africa* 84 E4
Steyr, *Austria* 21 G4
Steytlerville, *S. Africa* 84 E3
Stia, *Italy* 33 E8
Stiens, *Neths.* 16 B7
Stigler, *U.S.A.* 109 H7
Stigliano, *Italy* 35 B9
Stigsnæs, *Denmark* 11 J5
Stigtomta, *Sweden* 11 F10
Stikine →, *Canada* 100 B2
Stilfontein, *S. Africa* 84 D4
Stilís, *Greece* 39 L5
Stillwater, *N.Z.* 87 K3
Stillwater, *Minn., U.S.A.* . 108 C8
Stillwater, *N.Y., U.S.A.* .. 107 D11
Stillwater, *Okla., U.S.A.* . 109 G6
Stillwater Range, *U.S.A.* . 110 G4
Stilwell, *U.S.A.* 109 H7
Štip, *Macedonia* 39 H5
Stíra, *Greece* 39 L7
Stirling, *Australia* 90 B3
Stirling, *Canada* 100 D6
Stirling, *U.K.* 14 E5
Stirling Ra., *Australia* 89 F2
Stittsville, *Canada* 107 A9
Stockach, *Germany* 19 H5
Stockerau, *Austria* 21 G6
Stockett, *U.S.A.* 110 C8
Stockholm, *Sweden* 10 E12
Stockholms län □, *Sweden* 10 E12
Stockhorn, *Switz.* 22 C5
Stockport, *U.K.* 12 D5
Stockton, *Calif., U.S.A.* .. 111 H3
Stockton, *Kans., U.S.A.* .. 108 F5
Stockton, *Mo., U.S.A.* ... 109 G8
Stockton-on-Tees, *U.K.* .. 12 C6
Stockvik, *Sweden* 10 B11
Stöde, *Sweden* 10 B10
Stogovo, *Macedonia* 39 H3
Stoke on Trent, *U.K.* 12 D5
Stokes Bay, *Canada* 98 C3
Stokes Pt., *Australia* 90 G3
Stokes Ra., *Australia* 88 C5
Stokkseyri, *Iceland* 8 E3
Stokksnes, *Iceland* 8 D6
Stolac, *Bos.-H.* 21 M7
Stolberg, *Germany* 18 E2
Stolbovaya, *Russia* 41 D10
Stolbovaya, *Russia* 45 C16
Stolbovoy, Ostrov, *Russia* 45 D17
Stolbtsy, *Belorussia* 40 E5
Stolin, *Belorussia* 40 F5
Stolwijk, *Neths.* 16 E5
Stomíon, *Greece* 37 D5
Ston, *Croatia* 21 N7
Stonehaven, *U.K.* 14 E6
Stonehenge, *Australia* 90 C3
Stonewall, *Canada* 101 C9
Stony L., *Man., Canada* .. 101 B9
Stony L., *Ont., Canada* .. 106 B6
Stony Rapids, *Canada* 101 B7
Stony Tunguska = Podkamennaya Tunguska →, *Russia* ... 45 C10
Stonyford, *U.S.A.* 112 F4
Stopnica, *Poland* 20 E10
Stora Lulevatten, *Sweden* . 8 C15
Stora Sjöfallet, *Sweden* ... 8 C15
Storavan, *Sweden* 8 D15
Store Bælt, *Denmark* 11 J5
Store Creek, *Australia* 91 E4
Store Heddinge, *Denmark* . 11 J6
Støren, *Norway* 10 A4
Storlulea = Stora Lulevatten, *Sweden* 8 C15
Storm B., *Australia* 90 G4
Storm Lake, *U.S.A.* 108 D7
Stormberge, *S. Africa* 84 E4
Stormsrivier, *S. Africa* ... 84 E3
Stornoway, *U.K.* 14 C2
Storozhinets, *Ukraine* 42 B1
Storsjö, *Sweden* 10 B7
Storsjøen, *Hedmark, Norway* 10 D5
Storsjøen, *Hedmark, Norway* 10 C5
Storsjön, *Sweden* 10 B7
Storstrøms Amt. □, *Denmark* 11 K5
Storuman, *Sweden* 8 D14
Stoughton, *Canada* 101 D8
Stour →, *Dorset, U.K.* ... 13 G5
Stour →, *Here. & Worcs., U.K.* 13 E5
Stour →, *Kent, U.K.* 13 F9
Stour →, *Suffolk, U.K.* .. 13 F9
Stourbridge, *U.K.* 13 E5
Stout, L., *Canada* 101 C10
Stove Pipe Wells Village, *U.S.A.* 113 J9
Stowmarket, *U.K.* 13 E9
Strabane, *U.K.* 15 B4
Strabane □, *U.K.* 15 B4
Stracin, *Macedonia* 38 G5
Stradella, *Italy* 32 C6
Strahan, *Australia* 90 G4
Strakonice, *Czech.* 20 F3
Straldzha, *Bulgaria* 38 G9
Stralsund, *Germany* 18 A9
Strand, *S. Africa* 84 E2
Strangford L., *U.K.* 15 B6
Strängnäs, *Sweden* 10 E11
Strangsville, *U.S.A.* 106 E3
Stranraer, *U.K.* 14 G3
Strasbourg, *Canada* 101 C8
Strasbourg, *France* 25 D14
Strasburg, *Germany* 18 B9
Strasburg, *U.S.A.* 108 B4
Strassen, *Lux.* 17 J8
Stratford, *Canada* 98 D3
Stratford, *N.Z.* 87 H5
Stratford, *Calif., U.S.A.* .. 111 H4
Stratford, *Conn., U.S.A.* . 107 E11
Stratford, *Tex., U.S.A.* ... 109 G3
Stratford-upon-Avon, *U.K.* 13 E6
Strath Spey, *U.K.* 14 D5
Strathalbyn, *Australia* 91 F2
Strathclyde □, *U.K.* 14 F4
Strathcona Prov. Park, *Canada* 100 D3
Strathmore, *Australia* 90 B3
Strathmore, *Canada* 100 C6
Strathmore, *U.K.* 14 E5
Strathmore, *U.S.A.* 112 J7
Strathnaver, *Canada* 100 C4
Strathpeffer, *U.K.* 14 D4
Strathroy, *Canada* 98 D3
Strathy Pt., *U.K.* 14 C4
Stratton, *U.S.A.* 108 F3
Straubing, *Germany* 19 G8
Straumnes, *Iceland* 8 C2
Strausberg, *Germany* 18 C9
Strawberry Reservoir, *U.S.A.* 110 F8
Strawn, *U.S.A.* 109 J5
Strážnice, *Czech.* 20 G7
Streaky B., *Australia* 91 E1
Streaky Bay, *Australia* 91 E1
Streator, *U.S.A.* 108 E10
Streé, *Belgium* 17 H4
Streeter, *U.S.A.* 108 B5
Streetsville, *Canada* 106 C5
Strehaia, *Romania* 38 E6
Strelcha, *Bulgaria* 38 G7
Strelka, *Russia* 45 D10
Streng →, *Cambodia* 58 F4
Strésa, *Italy* 32 C5
Strezhevoy, *Russia* 44 C8
Stříbro, *Czech.* 20 F3
Strijen, *Neths.* 16 E5
Strimón →, *Greece* 39 J6
Strimonikós Kólpos, *Greece* 39 J6
Stroeder, *Argentina* 128 B4
Strofádhes, *Greece* 39 M4
Strömbacka, *Sweden* 10 C10
Strómboli, *Italy* 35 D8
Stromeferry, *U.K.* 14 D3
Stromness, *U.K.* 14 C5
Ströms vattudal, *Sweden* .. 8 D13
Stromsburg, *U.S.A.* 108 E6
Strömstad, *Sweden* 9 G11
Strömsund, *Sweden* 8 E13
Stróngoli, *Italy* 35 C10
Stronsay, *U.K.* 14 B6
Stroud, *U.K.* 13 F5
Stroud Road, *Australia* ... 91 E5
Stroudsburg, *U.S.A.* 107 F9
Stroumbi, *Cyprus* 37 E11
Struer, *Denmark* 11 H2
Struga, *Macedonia* 39 H3
Strugi Krasnyye, *Russia* .. 40 B6
Strumica, *Macedonia* 39 H5
Strumica →, *Europe* 39 H6
Struthers, *Canada* 98 C2
Struthers, *U.S.A.* 106 E4
Stryi, *Ukraine* 40 G3
Stryker, *U.S.A.* 110 B6
Strzegom, *Poland* 20 E6
Strzelce Krajeńskie, *Poland* 20 C5
Strzelecki Cr. →, *Australia* 91 D2
Strzelin, *Poland* 20 E7
Strzelno, *Poland* 20 C8
Strzyżów, *Poland* 20 F11
Stuart, *Fla., U.S.A.* 105 M5
Stuart, *Nebr., U.S.A.* 108 D5
Stuart →, *Canada* 100 C4
Stuart Bluff Ra., *Australia* 88 D5
Stuart L., *Canada* 100 C4
Stuart Ra., *Australia* 91 D1
Stubbekøbing, *Denmark* .. 11 K6
Stugun, *Sweden* 10 A9
Stull, L., *Canada* 98 B1
Stung Treng, *Cambodia* .. 58 F5
Stupart →, *Canada* 101 B10
Stupino, *Russia* 41 D11
Sturgeon B., *Canada* 101 C9
Sturgeon Bay, *U.S.A.* 104 C2
Sturgeon Falls, *Canada* ... 98 C4
Sturgeon L., *Alta., Canada* 100 B5
Sturgeon L., *Ont., Canada* 106 B6
Sturgeon L., *Ont., Canada* 98 B1
Sturgis, *Mich., U.S.A.* 104 E3
Sturgis, *S. Dak., U.S.A.* .. 108 C3
Sturt Cr. →, *Australia* ... 88 C4
Sturt Creek, *Australia* 88 C4
Stutterheim, *S. Africa* 84 E4
Stuttgart, *Germany* 19 G5
Stuttgart, *U.S.A.* 109 H9
Stuyvesant, *U.S.A.* 107 D11
Stykkishólmur, *Iceland* ... 8 D2
Styr →, *Belorussia* 40 E5
Styria = Steiermark □, *Austria* 21 H5
Su Xian, *China* 50 H9
Suakin, *Sudan* 76 D4
Suan, *N. Korea* 51 E14
Suapure →, *Venezuela* ... 120 B4
Suaqui, *Mexico* 114 B3
Suatá →, *Venezuela* 121 B4
Subang, *Indonesia* 57 G12
Subansiri →, *India* 61 F18
Subayhah, *Si. Arabia* 64 D3
Subi, *Indonesia* 59 L7
Subiaco, *Italy* 33 G10
Subotica, *Serbia* 21 J9
Success, *Canada* 101 C7
Suceava, *Romania* 38 B9
Suceava →, *Romania* 38 B9
Sucha-Beskidzka, *Poland* . 20 F9
Suchan, *Poland* 20 B5
Suchan, *Russia* 48 C6
Suchitoto, *El Salv.* 116 D2
Suchou = Suzhou, *China* .. 53 B13
Süchow = Xuzhou, *China* 51 G9
Suchowola, *Poland* 20 B13
Sucio →, *Colombia* 120 B2
Suck →, *Ireland* 15 C3
Sucre, *Bolivia* 125 D4
Sucre, *Colombia* 120 B3
Sucre □, *Colombia* 120 B2
Sucre □, *Venezuela* 121 A5
Sucuaro, *Colombia* 120 C4
Sućuraj, *Croatia* 33 E14
Sucuriju, *Brazil* 122 A2
Sucuriú →, *Brazil* 125 E7
Sud, Pte., *Canada* 99 C7
Sud-Ouest, Pte. du, *Canada* 99 C7
Suda →, *Russia* 41 B10
Sudak, *Ukraine* 42 D6
Sudan, *U.S.A.* 109 H3
Sudan ■, *Africa* 77 E3
Suday, *Russia* 41 B13
Sudbury, *Canada* 98 C3
Sudbury, *U.K.* 13 E8
Sûdd, *Sudan* 77 F2
Suddie, *Guyana* 121 B6
Süderbrarup, *Germany* ... 18 A5
Süderlügum, *Germany* 18 A4
Süderoog-Sand, *Germany* . 18 A4
Sudeten Mts. = Sudety, *Europe* 20 E6
Sudety, *Europe* 20 E6
Sudi, *Tanzania* 83 E4
Sudirman, Pegunungan, *Indonesia* 57 E9
Sudogda, *Russia* 41 D12
Sudr, *Egypt* 76 J8
Sudzha, *Russia* 40 F9
Sueca, *Spain* 29 F4
Suedala, *Sweden* 11 J7
Suez = El Suweis, *Egypt* . 76 J8
Suez, G. of = Suweis, Khalîg el, *Egypt* 76 J8
Suez Canal = Suweis, Qanâ es, *Egypt* 76 H8
Suffield, *Canada* 101 C6
Suffolk, *U.S.A.* 104 G7
Suffolk □, *U.K.* 13 E9
Sugar City, *U.S.A.* 108 F3
Suğla Gölü, *Turkey* 66 E5
Sugluk = Saglouc, *Canada* 97 B12
Sugny, *Belgium* 17 J5
Suhaia, L., *Romania* 38 F8
Suhār, *Oman* 65 E8
Suhbaatar, *Mongolia* 54 A5
Sühbaatar □, *Mongolia* ... 50 B8
Suhl, *Germany* 18 E6
Suhr, *Switz.* 22 B6
Şuhut, *Turkey* 66 D4
Sui Xian, *Henan, China* .. 50 G8
Sui Xian, *Henan, China* .. 53 B9
Suiá Missu →, *Brazil* 125 C7
Suichang, *China* 53 C12
Suichuan, *China* 53 D10
Suide, *China* 50 F6
Suifenhe, *China* 51 B16
Suihua, *China* 54 B7
Suijiang, *China* 52 C4
Suining, *Hunan, China* ... 53 D8
Suining, *Jiangsu, China* .. 51 H9
Suining, *Sichuan, China* .. 52 B5

Suiping, *China* 50 H7
Suippes, *France* 25 C11
Suir →, *Ireland* 15 D4
Suixi, *China* 53 G8
Suiyang, *Guizhou, China* 52 D6
Suiyang, *Heilongjiang, China* 51 B16
Suizhong, *China* 51 D11
Sujangarh, *India* 62 F6
Sukabumi, *Indonesia* 57 G12
Sukadana, *Kalimantan, Indonesia* 56 E3
Sukadana, *Sumatera, Indonesia* 56 F3
Sukagawa, *Japan* 49 F10
Sukaraja, *Indonesia* 56 E4
Sukarnapura = Jayapura, *Indonesia* 57 E10
Sukchŏn, *N. Korea* 51 E13
Sukhinichi, *Russia* 40 D9
Sukhona →, *Russia* 44 D4
Sukhothai, *Thailand* 58 D2
Sukhumi, *Georgia* 43 E9
Sukkur, *Pakistan* 62 F3
Sukkur Barrage, *Pakistan* 62 F3
Sukumo, *Japan* 49 H6
Sukunka →, *Canada* 100 B4
Sul, Canal do, *Brazil* 122 B2
Sula →, *Ukraine* 40 G8
Sula, Kepulauan, *Indonesia* 57 E7
Sulaco →, *Honduras* 116 C2
Sulaiman Range, *Pakistan* 62 D3
Sulak →, *Russia* 43 E12
Sūlār, *Iran* 65 D6
Sulawesi □, *Indonesia* 57 E6
Sulawesi Sea, *Indonesia* 57 D6
Sulechów, *Poland* 20 C5
Sulejów, *Poland* 20 D9
Sulgen, *Switz.* 23 A8
Sulima, *S. Leone* 78 D2
Sulina, *Romania* 38 D12
Sulina, Braţul →, *Romania* 38 D12
Sulingen, *Germany* 18 C4
Sulitälma, *Sweden* 8 C14
Sulitjelma, *Norway* 8 C14
Sullana, *Peru* 124 A1
Sullivan, *Ill., U.S.A.* 108 F10
Sullivan, *Ind., U.S.A.* 104 F2
Sullivan, *Mo., U.S.A.* 108 F9
Sullivan Bay, *Canada* 100 C3
Sully-sur-Loire, *France* 25 E9
Sulmona, *Italy* 33 F10
Sulphur, *La., U.S.A.* 109 K8
Sulphur, *Okla., U.S.A.* 109 H6
Sulphur Pt., *Canada* 100 A6
Sulphur Springs, *U.S.A.* 109 J7
Sulphur Springs Draw →, *U.S.A.* 109 J4
Sultan, *Canada* 98 C3
Sultan, *U.S.A.* 112 C5
Sultanpur, *India* 63 F10
Sulu Arch., *Phil.* 55 J4
Sulu Sea, *E. Indies* 55 G4
Sülüklü, *Turkey* 66 D5
Sululta, *Ethiopia* 77 F4
Suluova, *Turkey* 66 C6
Suluq, *Libya* 73 B9
Sulzbach, *Germany* 19 F3
Sulzbach-Rosenberg, *Germany* 19 F7
Sulzberger Ice Shelf, *Antarctica* 5 D10
Sumalata, *Indonesia* 57 D6
Sumampa, *Argentina* 126 B3
Sumatera □, *Indonesia* 56 D2
Sumatra = Sumatera □, *Indonesia* 56 D2
Sumatra, *U.S.A.* 110 C10
Sumba, *Indonesia* 57 F5
Sumba, Selat, *Indonesia* 57 F5
Sumbawa, *Indonesia* 56 F5
Sumbawa Besar, *Indonesia* 56 F5
Sumbawanga □, *Tanzania* 82 D3
Sumbe, *Angola* 80 G2
Sumburgh Hd., *U.K.* 14 B7
Sumdo, *India* 63 B8
Sumé, *Brazil* 122 C4
Sumedang, *Indonesia* 57 G12
Šumen, *Bulgaria* 38 F9
Sumenep, *Indonesia* 57 G15
Sumgait, *Azerbaijan* 43 F13
Sumiswald, *Switz.* 22 B5
Summer L., *U.S.A.* 110 E3
Summerland, *Canada* 100 D5
Summerside, *Canada* 99 C7
Summerville, *Ga., U.S.A.* 105 H3
Summerville, *S.C., U.S.A.* 105 J5
Summit Lake, *Canada* 100 C4
Summit Peak, *U.S.A.* 111 H10
Sumner, *Iowa, U.S.A.* 108 D8
Sumner, *Wash., U.S.A.* 112 C4
Sumoto, *Japan* 49 G7
Sumqayit = Sumgait, *Azerbaijan* 43 F13
Sumter, *U.S.A.* 105 J5
Sumy, *Ukraine* 40 F9
Sun City, *Ariz., U.S.A.* 111 K7
Sun City, *Calif., U.S.A.* 113 M9
Sunagawa, *Japan* 48 C10
Sunan, *N. Korea* 51 E13
Sunart, L., *U.K.* 14 E3
Sunburst, *U.S.A.* 110 B8
Sunbury, *Australia* 91 F3
Sunbury, *U.S.A.* 107 F8
Sunchales, *Argentina* 126 C3
Suncho Corral, *Argentina* 126 B3
Sunchon, *S. Korea* 51 G14
Suncook, *U.S.A.* 107 C13
Sunda, Selat, *Indonesia* 56 F3
Sunda Is., *Indonesia* 46 K14
Sunda Str. = Sunda, Selat, *Indonesia* 56 F3
Sundance, *U.S.A.* 108 C2
Sundarbans, The, *Asia* 61 J16
Sundargarh, *India* 61 H14
Sundays = Sondags →, *S. Africa* 84 E4
Sundbyberg, *Sweden* 10 E11
Sunderland, *Canada* 106 B5
Sunderland, *U.K.* 12 C6
Sundre, *Canada* 100 C6
Sundridge, *Canada* 98 C4
Sunds, *Denmark* 11 H3
Sundsjö, *Sweden* 10 B9
Sundsvall, *Sweden* 10 B11
Sung Hei, *Vietnam* 59 G6
Sungai Kolok, *Thailand* 59 J3
Sungai Lembing, *Malaysia* 59 L4
Sungai Patani, *Malaysia* 59 K3
Sungaigerong, *Indonesia* 56 E2
Sungailiat, *Indonesia* 56 E3
Sungaipakning, *Indonesia* 56 D2
Sungaipenuh, *Indonesia* 56 E2
Sungaitiram, *Indonesia* 56 E5
Sungari = Songhua Jiang →, *China* 54 B8
Sungguminasa, *Indonesia* 57 F5
Sunghua Chiang = Songhua Jiang →, *China* 54 B8
Sungikai, *Sudan* 77 E2
Sungurlu, *Turkey* 42 F6
Sunja, *Croatia* 33 C13
Sunnyside, *Utah, U.S.A.* 110 G8
Sunnyside, *Wash., U.S.A.* 110 C3
Sunnyvale, *U.S.A.* 111 H2
Sunray, *U.S.A.* 109 G4
Suntar, *Russia* 45 C12
Sunyani, *Ghana* 78 D4
Supai, *U.S.A.* 111 H7
Supamo →, *Venezuela* 121 B5
Supaul, *India* 63 F12
Supe, *Peru* 124 C2
Superior, *Ariz., U.S.A.* 111 K8
Superior, *Mont., U.S.A.* 110 C6
Superior, *Nebr., U.S.A.* 108 E5
Superior, *Wis., U.S.A.* 108 B8
Superior, L., *U.S.A.* 98 C2
Supetar, *Croatia* 33 E13
Suphan Buri, *Thailand* 58 E3
Suphan Dağı, *Turkey* 67 D10
Supriori, Kepulauan, *Indonesia* 57 E9
Supung Sk., *China* 51 D13
Sūq Suwayq, *Si. Arabia* 64 E3
Suqian, *China* 51 H10
Sūr, *Lebanon* 69 B4
Sur, Pt., *U.S.A.* 111 H3
Sura →, *Russia* 41 C15
Surab, *Pakistan* 62 E2
Surabaja = Surabaya, *Indonesia* 57 G15
Surabaya, *Indonesia* 57 G15
Suraia, *Romania* 38 D10
Surakarta, *Indonesia* 57 G14
Surakhany, *Azerbaijan* 43 F14
Surat, *Australia* 91 D4
Surat, *India* 60 J8
Surat Thani, *Thailand* 59 H2
Suratgarh, *India* 62 E5
Surazh, *Belorussia* 40 D7
Surazh, *Russia* 40 E8
Surduc Pasul, *Romania* 38 D6
Surdulica, *Serbia* 21 N12
Sûre = Sauer →, *Germany* 17 J9
Surendranagar, *India* 62 H4
Surf, *U.S.A.* 113 L6
Surgères, *France* 26 B3
Surgut, *Russia* 44 C8
Surhuisterveen, *Neths.* 16 B8
Suriapet, *India* 60 L11
Surigao, *Phil.* 55 G6
Surigao Strait, *Phil.* 55 F6
Surin, *Thailand* 58 E4
Surin Nua, Ko, *Thailand* 59 H1
Surinam ■, *S. Amer.* 121 C6
Suriname □, *Surinam* 121 B6
Suriname ■ = Surinam ■, *S. Amer.* 121 C6
Suriname →, *Surinam* 121 B6
Sūrmaq, *Iran* 65 D7
Sürmene, *Turkey* 43 F9
Surovikino, *Russia* 43 B10
Surprise L., *Canada* 100 B2
Surrey □, *U.K.* 13 F7
Sursee, *Switz.* 22 B6
Sursk, *Russia* 41 E14
Surt, *Libya* 73 B8
Surt, Khalīj, *Libya* 73 B8
Surtsey, *Iceland* 8 E3
Surubim, *Brazil* 122 C4
Sürüç, *Turkey* 67 E8
Suruga-Wan, *Japan* 49 G9
Surumu →, *Brazil* 121 C5
Susa, *Italy* 32 C4
Suså →, *Denmark* 11 J5
Sušac, *Croatia* 33 F13
Susak, *Croatia* 33 D11
Susaki, *Japan* 49 H6
Sūsangerd, *Iran* 65 D6
Susanino, *Russia* 45 D15
Susanville, *U.S.A.* 110 F3
Susch, *Switz.* 23 C10
Suşehri, *Turkey* 67 C8
Susong, *China* 53 B11
Susquehanna →, *U.S.A.* 107 G8
Susquehanna Depot, *U.S.A.* 107 E9
Susques, *Argentina* 126 A2
Sussex, *Canada* 99 C6
Sussex, *U.S.A.* 107 E10
Sussex, E. □, *U.K.* 13 G8
Sussex, W. □, *U.K.* 13 G7
Susteren, *Neths.* 17 F7
Sustut →, *Canada* 100 B3
Susuman, *Russia* 45 C15
Susunu, *Indonesia* 57 E8
Susurluk, *Turkey* 66 D3
Susuz, *Turkey* 67 C10
Sütçüler, *Turkey* 66 E4
Sutherland, *S. Africa* 84 E3
Sutherland, *U.S.A.* 108 E4
Sutherland Falls, *N.Z.* 87 L1
Sutherlin, *U.S.A.* 110 E2
Sutivan, *Croatia* 33 E13
Sutlej →, *Pakistan* 62 E4
Sutter, *U.S.A.* 112 F5
Sutter Creek, *U.S.A.* 112 G6
Sutton, *Canada* 107 A12
Sutton, *U.S.A.* 108 E6
Sutton →, *Canada* 98 A3
Sutton in Ashfield, *U.K.* 12 D6
Suttor →, *Australia* 90 C4
Suttsu, *Japan* 48 C10
Suva, *Fiji* 87 D8
Suva Reka, *Serbia* 21 N10
Suvo Rudište, *Serbia* 21 M10
Suvorov, *Russia* 41 D10
Suvorov Is. = Suwarrow Is., *Cook Is.* 93 J11
Suwałki, *Poland* 20 A12
Suwannaphum, *Thailand* 58 E4
Suwannee →, *U.S.A.* 105 L4
Suwanose-Jima, *Japan* 49 K4
Suwarrow Is., *Cook Is.* 93 J11
Suwayq aş Şuqban, *Iraq* 64 D5
Suweis, Khalîg el, *Egypt* 76 J8
Suweis, Qanâl es, *Egypt* 76 H8
Suwŏn, *S. Korea* 51 F14
Suzdal, *Russia* 41 C12
Suzhou, *China* 53 B13
Suzu, *Japan* 49 F8
Suzu-Misaki, *Japan* 49 F8
Suzuka, *Japan* 49 G8
Suzzara, *Italy* 32 C7
Svalbard, *Arctic* 4 B8
Svalbarð, *Iceland* 8 C6
Svalöv, *Sweden* 11 J7
Svanvik, *Norway* 8 B21
Svappavaara, *Sweden* 8 C16
Svarstad, *Norway* 10 E3
Svartisen, *Norway* 8 C12
Svartvik, *Sweden* 10 B11
Svatovo, *Ukraine* 42 B8
Svay Chek, *Cambodia* 58 F4
Svay Rieng, *Cambodia* 59 G5
Svealand □, *Sweden* 9 G13
Sveg, *Sweden* 9 E13
Svendborg, *Denmark* 11 J4
Svene, *Norway* 10 E3
Svenljunga, *Sweden* 11 G7
Svenstrup, *Denmark* 11 H3
Sverdlovsk = Yekaterinburg, *Russia* 44 D7
Sverdlovsk, *Ukraine* 43 B8
Sverdrup Is., *Canada* 4 B3
Svetac, *Croatia* 33 E12
Sveti Ivan Zelina, *Croatia* 33 C13
Sveti Jurij, *Slovenia* 33 B12
Sveti Lenart, *Slovenia* 33 B12
Sveti Nikole, *Macedonia* 39 H4
Sveti Trojica, *Slovenia* 33 B12
Svetlaya, *Russia* 48 A9
Svetlogorsk, *Belorussia* 40 E6
Svetlograd, *Russia* 43 D10
Svetlovodsk, *Ukraine* 40 G8
Svetozarevo, *Serbia* 21 L11
Svidník, *Slovak Rep.* 20 F11
Svilaja Planina, *Croatia* 33 E13
Svilengrad, *Bulgaria* 39 H9
Svir →, *Russia* 6 C12
Svishtov, *Bulgaria* 38 F8
Svisloch, *Belorussia* 40 E4
Svitava →, *Czech.* 20 F6
Svitavy, *Czech.* 20 F6
Svobodnyy, *Russia* 45 D13
Svolvær, *Norway* 8 B13
Svratka →, *Czech.* 20 F6
Svrljig, *Serbia* 21 M12
Swabian Alps = Schwäbische Alb, *Germany* 19 G5
Swainsboro, *U.S.A.* 105 J4
Swakopmund, *Namibia* 84 C1
Swale →, *U.K.* 12 C6
Swalmen, *Neths.* 17 F8
Swan Hill, *Australia* 91 F3
Swan Hills, *Canada* 100 C5
Swan Is., *W. Indies* 116 C3
Swan L., *Canada* 101 C8
Swan River, *Canada* 101 C8
Swanage, *U.K.* 13 G6
Swansea, *Australia* 91 E5
Swansea, *U.K.* 13 F4
Swar →, *Pakistan* 63 B5
Swartberge, *S. Africa* 84 E3
Swartmodder, *S. Africa* 84 D3
Swartruggens, *S. Africa* 84 D4
Swarzędz, *Poland* 20 C7
Swastika, *Canada* 98 C3
Swatow = Shantou, *China* 53 F11
Swaziland ■, *Africa* 85 D5
Sweden ■, *Europe* 9 H13
Swedru, *Ghana* 79 D4
Sweet Home, *U.S.A.* 110 D2
Sweetwater, *Nev., U.S.A.* 112 G7
Sweetwater, *Tex., U.S.A.* 109 J4
Sweetwater →, *U.S.A.* 110 E10
Swellendam, *S. Africa* 84 E3
Świdnica, *Poland* 20 E6
Świdnik, *Poland* 20 D12
Świdwin, *Poland* 20 B5
Świebodzin, *Poland* 20 C5
Świecie, *Poland* 20 B8
Świętokrzyskie, Góry, *Poland* 20 E10
Swift Current, *Canada* 101 C7
Swiftcurrent →, *Canada* 101 C7
Swilly, L., *Ireland* 15 A4
Swindle, I., *Canada* 100 C3
Swindon, *U.K.* 13 F6
Swinemünde = Świnoujście, *Poland* 20 B4
Świnoujście, *Poland* 20 B4
Switzerland ■, *Europe* 22 D6
Swords, *Ireland* 15 C5
Syasstroy, *Russia* 40 A8
Sychevka, *Russia* 40 D9
Sydney, *Australia* 91 E5
Sydney, *Canada* 99 C7
Sydney Mines, *Canada* 99 C7
Sydprøven, *Greenland* 4 C5
Sydra G. of = Surt, Khalīj, *Libya* 73 B8
Syke, *Germany* 18 C4
Syktyvkar, *Russia* 44 C6
Sylacauga, *U.S.A.* 105 J2
Sylarna, *Sweden* 8 E12
Sylhet, *Bangla.* 61 G17
Sylt, *Germany* 18 A4
Sylvan Lake, *Canada* 100 C6
Sylvania, *U.S.A.* 105 J5
Sylvester, *U.S.A.* 105 K4
Sym, *Russia* 44 C9
Symón, *Mexico* 114 C4
Synnott Ra., *Australia* 88 C4
Syracuse, *Kans., U.S.A.* 109 F4
Syracuse, *N.Y., U.S.A.* 107 C8
Syrdarya →, *Kazakhstan* 44 E7
Syria ■, *Asia* 64 C3
Syul'dzhyukyor, *Russia* 45 C12
Syzran, *Russia* 41 E16
Szaraz →, *Hungary* 21 J10
Szarvas, *Hungary* 21 J10
Szczebrzeszyn, *Poland* 20 E12
Szczecin, *Poland* 20 B4
Szczecinek, *Poland* 20 B6
Szczekocimy, *Poland* 20 E9
Szczytno, *Poland* 20 B11
Szechwan = Sichuan □, *China* 52 B5
Szeged, *Hungary* 21 J10
Szeghalom, *Hungary* 21 H11
Székesfehérvár, *Hungary* 21 H8
Szekszárd, *Hungary* 21 J8
Szendrö, *Hungary* 21 G10
Szentendre, *Hungary* 21 H9
Szentes, *Hungary* 21 J10
Szentgotthárd, *Hungary* 21 J6
Szentlörinc, *Hungary* 21 J8
Szigetvár, *Hungary* 21 J7
Szolnok, *Hungary* 21 H10
Szombathely, *Hungary* 21 H6
Szprotawa, *Poland* 20 D5
Szydłowiec, *Poland* 20 D10
Szypliszki, *Poland* 20 A13

T

't Harde, *Neths.* 16 D7
't Zandt, *Neths.* 16 B9
Ta Khli Khok, *Thailand* 58 E3
Ta Lai, *Vietnam* 59 G6
Tabacal, *Argentina* 126 A3
Tabaco, *Phil.* 55 E5
Tabagné, *Ivory C.* 78 D4
Ţābah, *Si. Arabia* 64 E4
Tabajara, *Brazil* 125 B5
Tabalos, *Peru* 124 B2
Tabarca, I. de, *Spain* 29 G4
Tabarka, *Tunisia* 75 A6
Ţabas, *Khorāsān, Iran* 65 C9
Ţabas, *Khorāsān, Iran* 65 C8
Tabasará, Serranía de, *Panama* 116 E3
Tabasco □, *Mexico* 115 D6
Tabatinga, Serra da, *Brazil* 122 D3
Tabāzīn, *Iran* 65 D8
Tabelbala, Kahal de, *Algeria* 75 C4
Taber, *Canada* 100 D6
Tabernas, *Spain* 29 H2
Tabernes de Valldigna, *Spain* 29 F4
Tabira, *Brazil* 122 C4
Tablas, *Phil.* 55 E5
Tablas Strait, *Phil.* 55 E4
Table B. = Tafelbaai, *S. Africa* 84 E2
Table B., *Canada* 99 B8
Table Mt., *S. Africa* 84 E2
Tableland, *Australia* 88 C4
Tabletop, Mt., *Australia* 90 C4
Tábor, *Czech.* 20 F4
Tabora, *Tanzania* 82 D3
Tabora □, *Tanzania* 82 D3
Tabou, *Ivory C.* 78 E3
Tabrīz, *Iran* 64 B5
Tabuaeran, *Pac. Oc.* 93 G12
Tabuelan, *Phil.* 55 F5
Tabuenca, *Spain* 28 D3
Tabūk, *Si. Arabia* 64 D3
Tacámbaro de Codallos, *Mexico* 114 D4
Tacheng, *China* 54 B3
Tach'ing Shan = Daqing Shan, *China* 50 D6
Táchira □, *Venezuela* 120 B3
Tácina →, *Italy* 35 D9
Tacloban, *Phil.* 55 F6
Tacna, *Peru* 124 D3
Tacna □, *Peru* 124 D3
Tacoma, *U.S.A.* 112 C4
Tacuarembó, *Uruguay* 127 C4
Tacutu →, *Brazil* 121 C5
Tademaït, Plateau du, *Algeria* 75 C5
Tadent, O. →, *Algeria* 75 D6
Tadjerdjeri, O. →, *Algeria* 75 C6
Tadjerouna, *Algeria* 75 B5
Tadjettaret, O. →, *Algeria* 75 D6
Tadjmout, *Oasis, Algeria* 75 B5
Tadjmout, *Saoura, Algeria* 75 C5
Tadjoura, *Djibouti* 68 E3
Tadjoura, Golfe de, *Djibouti* 77 E5
Tadmor, *N.Z.* 87 J4
Tadoule, L., *Canada* 101 B9
Tadoussac, *Canada* 99 C6
Tadzhikistan = Tajikistan ■, *Asia* 44 F8
Taechŏn-ni, *S. Korea* 51 F14
Taegu, *S. Korea* 51 G15
Taegwan, *N. Korea* 51 D13
Taejŏn, *S. Korea* 51 F14
Tafalla, *Spain* 28 C3
Tafar, *Sudan* 77 F2
Tafassasset, O. →, *Algeria* 75 D6
Tafelbaai, *S. Africa* 84 E2
Tafelney, C., *Morocco* 74 B3
Tafermaar, *Indonesia* 57 F8
Taffermit, *Morocco* 74 C3
Tafí Viejo, *Argentina* 126 B2
Tafīhān, *Iran* 65 D7
Tafiré, *Ivory C.* 78 D3
Tafnidilt, *Morocco* 74 C2
Tafraoute, *Morocco* 74 C3
Taft, *Iran* 65 D7
Taft, *Phil.* 55 F6
Taft, *Calif., U.S.A.* 113 K7
Taft, *Tex., U.S.A.* 109 M6
Taga Dzong, *Bhutan* 61 F16
Taganrog, *Russia* 43 C8
Taganrogskiy Zaliv, *Russia* 42 C8
Tagânt, *Mauritania* 78 B2
Tagatay, *Phil.* 55 D4
Tagbilaran, *Phil.* 55 G5
Tàggia, *Italy* 32 E4
Taghzout, *Morocco* 74 B4
Tagish, *Canada* 100 A2
Tagish L., *Canada* 100 A2
Tagliacozzo, *Italy* 33 F10
Tagliamento →, *Italy* 33 C10
Tàglio di Po, *Italy* 33 D9
Tagna, *Colombia* 120 D3
Tago, *Phil.* 55 G7
Tagomago, I. de, *Spain* 36 B8
Taguatinga, *Brazil* 123 D3
Tagudin, *Phil.* 55 C4
Tagum, *Phil.* 55 H6
Tagus = Tejo →, *Europe* 31 G1
Tahakopa, *N.Z.* 87 M2
Tahala, *Morocco* 74 B4
Tahan, Gunong, *Malaysia* 59 K4
Tahat, *Algeria* 75 D6
Tāherī, *Iran* 65 E7
Tahiti, *Pac. Oc.* 93 J13
Tahoe, L., *U.S.A.* 112 G6
Tahoe City, *U.S.A.* 112 F6
Taholah, *U.S.A.* 112 C2
Tahoua, *Niger* 79 C6
Tahta, *Egypt* 76 B3
Tahtali Dağları, *Turkey* 66 D6
Tahuamanu →, *Bolivia* 124 C4
Tahulandang, *Indonesia* 57 D7
Tahuna, *Indonesia* 57 D7
Taï, *Ivory C.* 78 D3
Tai Hu, *China* 54 C7
Tai Shan, *China* 51 F9
Tai Xian, *China* 53 A13
Tai'an, *China* 51 F9
Taibei, *Taiwan* 53 E13
Taibique, *Canary Is.* 36 G2
Taibus Qi, *China* 50 D8
T'aichung = Taizhong, *Taiwan* 53 E13
Taidong, *Taiwan* 53 F13
Taieri →, *N.Z.* 87 M3
Taigu, *China* 50 F7
Taihang Shan, *China* 50 G7
Taihape, *N.Z.* 87 H5
Taihe, *Anhui, China* 50 H8
Taihe, *Jiangxi, China* 53 D10
Taihu, *China* 53 B11
Taijiang, *China* 52 D7
Taikang, *China* 50 G8

Tailem Bend

Tailem Bend, *Australia* 91 F2
Tailfingen, *Germany* 19 G5
Taimyr Peninsula = Taymyr, Poluostrov, *Russia* 45 B11
Tain, *U.K.* 14 D4
Tainan, *Taiwan* 53 F13
Taínaron, Ákra, *Greece* 39 N5
Taining, *China* 53 D11
Taintignies, *Belgium* 17 G2
Taiobeiras, *Brazil* 123 E3
T'aipei = Taibei, *Taiwan* 53 E13
Taiping, *China* 53 B12
Taiping, *Malaysia* 59 K3
Taipingzhen, *China* 50 H6
Taipu, *Brazil* 122 C4
Taishan, *China* 53 F9
Taishun, *China* 53 D12
Taita □, *Kenya* 82 C4
Taita Hills, *Kenya* 82 C4
Taitao, C., *Chile* 128 C1
Taitao, Pen. de, *Chile* 128 C2
Taivalkoski, *Finland* 8 D20
Taiwan ■, *Asia* 53 F13
Taiwan Shan, *Taiwan* 53 F13
Taixing, *China* 53 A13
Taïyetos Óros, *Greece* 39 N5
Taiyiba, *Israel* 69 C4
Taiyuan, *China* 50 F7
Taizhong, *Taiwan* 53 E13
Taizhou, *China* 53 A12
Taizhou Liedao, *China* 53 C13
Ta'izz, *Yemen* 68 E3
Tājābād, *Iran* 65 D7
Tajapuru, Furo do, *Brazil* 122 B1
Tajikistan ■, *Asia* 44 F8
Tajima, *Japan* 49 F9
Tajo = Tejo →, *Europe* 31 G1
Tajrīsh, *Iran* 65 C6
Tājūrā, *Libya* 73 B7
Tak, *Thailand* 58 D2
Takāb, *Iran* 64 B5
Takachiho, *Japan* 49 H5
Takada, *Japan* 49 F9
Takahagi, *Japan* 49 F10
Takaka, *N.Z.* 87 J4
Takamatsu, *Japan* 49 G7
Takaoka, *Japan* 49 F8
Takapuna, *N.Z.* 87 G5
Takasaki, *Japan* 49 F9
Takatsuki, *Japan* 49 G7
Takaungu, *Kenya* 82 C4
Takayama, *Japan* 49 F8
Take-Shima, *Japan* 49 J5
Takefu, *Japan* 49 G8
Takengon, *Indonesia* 56 D1
Takeo, *Cambodia* 59 G5
Takeo, *Japan* 49 H5
Tåkern, *Sweden* 11 F8
Tākestān, *Iran* 65 C6
Taketa, *Japan* 49 H5
Takh, *India* 63 C7
Takhman, *Cambodia* 59 G5
Takikawa, *Japan* 48 C10
Takla L., *Canada* 100 B3
Takla Landing, *Canada* 100 B3
Takla Makan = Taklamakan Shamo, *China* 54 C3
Taklamakan Shamo, *China* 54 C3
Taku →, *Canada* 100 B2
Takum, *Nigeria* 79 D6
Takutu →, *Guyana* 121 C5
Tal Halāl, *Iran* 65 D7
Tala, *Uruguay* 127 C4
Talacogan, *Phil.* 55 G6
Talagante, *Chile* 126 C1
Talaint, *Morocco* 74 C3
Talak, *Niger* 79 B6
Talamanca, Cordillera de, *Cent. Amer.* 116 E3
Talara, *Peru* 124 A1
Talas, *Kirghizia* 44 E8
Talas, *Turkey* 66 D6
Talâta, *Egypt* 69 E1
Talata Mafara, *Nigeria* 79 C6
Talaud, Kepulauan, *Indonesia* 57 D7
Talaud Is. = Talaud, Kepulauan, *Indonesia* 57 D7
Talavera de la Reina, *Spain* 30 F6
Talawana, *Australia* 88 D3
Talayan, *Phil.* 55 H6
Talbert, Sillon de, *France* 24 D3
Talbot, C., *Australia* 88 B4
Talbragar →, *Australia* 91 E4
Talca, *Chile* 126 D1
Talca □, *Chile* 126 D1
Talcahuano, *Chile* 126 D1
Talcher, *India* 61 J14
Talcho, *Niger* 79 C5
Taldy Kurgan, *Kazakhstan* 44 E8
Taldyqorghan = Taldy Kurgan, *Kazakhstan* 44 E8
Talesh, *Iran* 65 B6
Ţalesh, Kūhhā-ye, *Iran* 65 B6
Talguharai, *Sudan* 76 D4
Tali Post, *Sudan* 77 F3
Taliabu, *Indonesia* 57 E6
Talibon, *Phil.* 57 B6
Talibong, Ko, *Thailand* 59 J2
Talihina, *U.S.A.* 109 H7
Talisayan, *Phil.* 55 G6
Taliwang, *Indonesia* 56 F5
Tall 'Asūr, *Jordan* 69 D4
Tall Kalakh, *Syria* 69 A5
Talla, *Egypt* 76 J7
Talladega, *U.S.A.* 105 J2
Tallahassee, *U.S.A.* 105 K3
Tallangatta, *Australia* 91 F4
Tallarook, *Australia* 91 F4
Tallering Pk., *Australia* 89 E2
Tallinn, *Estonia* 40 B4
Tallulah, *U.S.A.* 109 J9
Talmest, *Morocco* 74 B3
Talmont, *France* 26 B2
Talnoye, *Ukraine* 42 B4
Talodi, *Sudan* 77 E3
Talovaya, *Russia* 41 F12
Talpa de Allende, *Mexico* 114 C4
Talsi, *Latvia* 40 C3
Talsinnt, *Morocco* 75 B4
Taltal, *Chile* 126 B1
Taltson →, *Canada* 100 A6
Talwood, *Australia* 91 D4
Talyawalka Cr. →, *Australia* 91 E3
Tam Chau, *Vietnam* 59 G5
Tam Ky, *Vietnam* 58 E7
Tam Quan, *Vietnam* 58 E7
Tama, *U.S.A.* 108 E8
Tamala, *Australia* 89 E1
Tamalameque, *Colombia* 120 B3
Tamale, *Ghana* 79 D4
Taman, *Russia* 42 D7
Tamanar, *Morocco* 74 B3
Tamano, *Japan* 49 G6
Tamanrasset, *Algeria* 75 D6
Tamanrasset, O. →, *Algeria* 75 D5
Tamaqua, *U.S.A.* 107 F9
Tamar →, *U.K.* 13 G3
Támara, *Colombia* 120 B3
Tamarang, *Australia* 91 E5
Tamarinda, *Spain* 36 B10
Tamarite de Litera, *Spain* 28 D5
Tamashima, *Japan* 49 G6
Tamaské, *Niger* 79 C6
Tamaulipas □, *Mexico* 115 C5
Tamaulipas, Sierra de, *Mexico* 115 C5
Tamazula, *Mexico* 114 C3
Tamazunchale, *Mexico* 115 C5
Tamba-Dabatou, *Guinea* 78 C2
Tambacounda, *Senegal* 78 C2
Tambelan, Kepulauan, *Indonesia* 56 D3
Tambellup, *Australia* 89 F2
Tambo, *Australia* 90 C4
Tambo, *Peru* 124 C3
Tambo →, *Peru* 124 C3
Tambo de Mora, *Peru* 124 C2
Tambobamba, *Peru* 124 C3
Tambohorano, *Madag.* 85 B7
Tambopata →, *Peru* 124 C4
Tambora, *Indonesia* 56 F5
Tambov, *Russia* 41 E12
Tambre →, *Spain* 30 C2
Tambuku, *Indonesia* 57 G15
Tamburâ, *Sudan* 77 F2
Tâmchekket, *Mauritania* 78 B2
Tame, *Colombia* 120 B3
Tamega →, *Portugal* 30 D2
Tamelelt, *Morocco* 74 B3
Tamenglong, *India* 61 G18
Tamerza, *Tunisia* 75 B6
Tamgak, Mts., *Niger* 72 E6
Tamiahua, L. de, *Mexico* 115 C5
Tamil Nadu □, *India* 60 P10
Tamines, *Belgium* 17 H5
Tamis →, *Serbia* 38 E3
Tamluk, *India* 63 H12
Tammerfors = Tampere, *Finland* 9 F17
Tammisaari, *Finland* 9 F17
Tamo Abu, Pegunungan, *Malaysia* 56 D5
Tampa, *U.S.A.* 105 M4
Tampa B., *U.S.A.* 105 M4
Tampere, *Finland* 9 F17
Tampico, *Mexico* 115 C5
Tampin, *Malaysia* 59 L4
Tamri, *Morocco* 74 B3
Tamrida = Qādib, *Yemen* 68 E5
Tamsagbulag, *Mongolia* 54 B6
Tamsalu, *Estonia* 40 B5
Tamu, *Burma* 61 G19
Tamuja →, *Spain* 31 F4
Tamworth, *Australia* 91 E5
Tamworth, *U.K.* 13 E6
Tamyang, *S. Korea* 51 G14
Tan An, *Vietnam* 59 G6
Tan-tan, *Morocco* 74 C2
Tana, *Norway* 8 A20
Tana →, *Kenya* 82 C5
Tana →, *Norway* 8 A20
Tana, L., *Ethiopia* 77 E4
Tana River, *Kenya* 82 C4
Tanabe, *Japan* 49 H7
Tanabi, *Brazil* 123 F2
Tanafjorden, *Norway* 8 A20
Tanaga, Pta., *Canary Is.* 36 G1
Tanagro →, *Italy* 35 B8
Tanahbala, *Indonesia* 56 E1
Tanahgrogot, *Indonesia* 56 E5
Tanahjampea, *Indonesia* 57 F6
Tanahmasa, *Indonesia* 56 E1
Tanahmerah, *Indonesia* 57 F10
Tanakura, *Japan* 49 F10
Tanami, *Australia* 88 C4
Tanami Desert, *Australia* 88 C5
Tanana, *U.S.A.* 96 B4
Tanana →, *U.S.A.* 96 B4
Tananarive = Antananarivo, *Madag.* 85 B8
Tanannt, *Morocco* 74 B3
Tánaro →, *Italy* 32 C5
Tanaunella, *Italy* 34 B2
Tanbar, *Australia* 90 D3
Tancarville, *France* 24 C7
Tancheng, *China* 51 G10
Tanchŏn, *N. Korea* 51 D15
Tanda, *Ut. P., India* 63 F10
Tanda, *Ut. P., India* 63 E8
Tanda, *Ivory C.* 78 D4
Tandag, *Phil.* 55 G7
Tandaia, *Tanzania* 83 D3
Tăndărei, *Romania* 38 E10
Tandaué, *Angola* 84 B2
Tandil, *Argentina* 126 D4
Tandil, Sa. del, *Argentina* 126 D4
Tandlianwala, *Pakistan* 62 D5
Tando Adam, *Pakistan* 62 G3
Tandou L., *Australia* 91 E3
Tandsbyn, *Sweden* 10 A8
Tane-ga-Shima, *Japan* 49 J5
Taneatua, *N.Z.* 87 H6
Tanen Tong Dan, *Burma* 58 D2
Tanezrouft, *Algeria* 75 D5
Tang, Koh, *Cambodia* 59 G4
Tang Krasang, *Cambodia* 58 F5
Tanga, *Tanzania* 82 D4
Tanga □, *Tanzania* 82 D4
Tanganyika, L., *Africa* 82 D2
Tanger, *Morocco* 74 A3
Tangerang, *Indonesia* 57 G12
Tangerhütte, *Germany* 18 C7
Tangermünde, *Germany* 18 C7
Tanggu, *China* 51 E9
Tanggula Shan, *China* 54 C4
Tanghe, *China* 50 H7
Tangier = Tanger, *Morocco* 74 A3
Tangorin P.O., *Australia* 90 C3
Tangshan, *China* 51 E10
Tangtou, *China* 51 G10
Tanguiéta, *Benin* 79 C5
Tangxi, *China* 53 C12
Tangyan He →, *China* 52 C7
Tanimbar, Kepulauan, *Indonesia* 57 F8
Tanimbar Is. = Tanimbar, Kepulauan, *Indonesia* 57 F8
Taninges, *France* 27 B10
Tanjay, *Phil.* 55 G5
Tanjong Malim, *Malaysia* 59 L3
Tanjore = Thanjavur, *India* 60 P11
Tanjung, *Indonesia* 56 E5
Tanjungbalai, *Indonesia* 56 D1
Tanjungbatu, *Indonesia* 56 D5
Tanjungkarang Telukbetung, *Indonesia* 56 F3
Tanjungpandan, *Indonesia* 56 E3
Tanjungpinang, *Indonesia* 56 D2
Tanjungpriok, *Indonesia* 57 G12
Tanjungredeb, *Indonesia* 56 D5
Tanjungselor, *Indonesia* 56 D5
Tank, *Pakistan* 62 C4
Tänndalen, *Sweden* 10 B6
Tannis Bugt, *Denmark* 11 G4
Tannu-Ola, *Russia* 45 D10
Tano →, *Ghana* 78 D4
Tanon Str., *Phil.* 55 F5
Tanout, *Niger* 79 C6
Tanquinho, *Brazil* 123 D4
Tanta, *Egypt* 76 H7
Tantoyuca, *Mexico* 115 C5
Tantung = Dandong, *China* 51 D13
Tanumshede, *Sweden* 11 F5
Tanunda, *Australia* 91 E2
Tanus, *France* 26 D6
Tanyeri, *Turkey* 67 D8
Tanzania ■, *Africa* 82 D3
Tanzilla →, *Canada* 100 B2
Tao Ko, *Thailand* 59 G2
Tao'an, *China* 51 B12
Tao'er He →, *China* 51 B13
Taohua Dao, *China* 53 C14
Taolanaro, *Madag.* 85 D8
Taole, *China* 50 E4
Taormina, *Italy* 35 E8
Taos, *U.S.A.* 111 H11
Taoudenni, *Mali* 74 D4
Taoudrart, Adrar, *Algeria* 75 D5
Taounate, *Morocco* 74 B4
Taourirt, *Algeria* 75 C5
Taourirt, *Morocco* 75 B4
Taouz, *Morocco* 74 B4
Taoyuan, *China* 53 C8
Taoyuan, *Taiwan* 53 E13
Tapa, *Estonia* 40 B4
Tapa Shan = Daba Shan, *China* 52 B7
Tapachula, *Mexico* 115 E6
Tapah, *Malaysia* 59 K3
Tapajós →, *Brazil* 121 D7
Tapaktuan, *Indonesia* 56 D1
Tapanahoni →, *Surinam* 121 C7
Tapanui, *N.Z.* 87 L2
Tapauá, *Brazil* 125 B5
Tapauá →, *Brazil* 125 B5
Tapeta, *Liberia* 78 D3
Taphan Hin, *Thailand* 58 D3
Tapi →, *India* 60 J8
Tapia, *Spain* 30 B4
Tápiószele, *Hungary* 21 H9
Tapiraí, *Brazil* 123 E2
Tapirapé →, *Brazil* 122 D1
Tapirapecó, Serra, *Venezuela* 121 C5
Tapirapuã, *Brazil* 125 C6
Tapoeripa, *Surinam* 121 B6
Tapolca, *Hungary* 21 J7
Tappahannock, *U.S.A.* 104 G7
Tapuaenuku, Mt., *N.Z.* 87 J4
Tapul Group, *Phil.* 55 J4
Tapurucuará, *Brazil* 121 D4
Taqīābād, *Iran* 65 C8
Ţaqţaq, *Iraq* 64 C5
Taquara, *Brazil* 127 B5
Taquari →, *Brazil* 125 D6
Taquaritinga, *Brazil* 123 F2
Tara, *Australia* 91 D5
Tara, *Canada* 106 B3
Tara, *Russia* 44 D8
Tara, *Zambia* 83 F2
Tara →, *Russia* 44 D8
Taraba □, *Nigeria* 79 D7
Tarabagatay, Khrebet, *Kazakhstan* 44 E9
Tarabuco, *Bolivia* 125 D5
Tarābulus, *Lebanon* 69 A4
Tarābulus, *Libya* 75 B7
Tarahouahout, *Algeria* 75 D6
Tarajalejo, *Canary Is.* 36 F5
Tarakan, *Indonesia* 56 D5
Tarakit, Mt., *Kenya* 82 B4
Taralga, *Australia* 91 E4
Tarama-Jima, *Japan* 49 M2
Taranagar, *India* 62 E6
Taranaki □, *N.Z.* 87 H5
Tarancón, *Spain* 28 E1
Taranga, *India* 62 H5
Taranga Hill, *India* 62 H5
Táranto, *Italy* 35 B10
Táranto, G. di, *Italy* 35 B10
Tarapacá, *Colombia* 120 D4
Tarapacá □, *Chile* 126 A2
Tarapoto, *Peru* 124 B2
Taraquá, *Brazil* 120 C4
Tarare, *France* 27 C8
Tararua Ra., *N.Z.* 87 J5
Tarascon, *France* 27 E8
Tarascon-sur-Ariège, *France* 26 F5
Tarashcha, *Ukraine* 42 B4
Tarata, *Peru* 124 D3
Tarauacá, *Brazil* 124 B3
Tarauacá →, *Brazil* 124 B4
Taravo →, *France* 27 G12
Tarawera, *N.Z.* 87 H6
Tarawera L., *N.Z.* 87 H6
Tarazona, *Spain* 28 D3
Tarazona de la Mancha, *Spain* 29 F3
Tarbat Ness, *U.K.* 14 D5
Tarbela Dam, *Pakistan* 62 B5
Tarbert, *Strath., U.K.* 14 F3
Tarbert, *W. Isles, U.K.* 14 D2
Tarbes, *France* 26 E4
Tarboro, *U.S.A.* 105 H7
Tarbrax, *Australia* 90 C3
Tarcento, *Italy* 33 B10
Tarcoola, *Australia* 91 E1
Tarcoon, *Australia* 91 E4
Tardets-Sorholus, *France* 26 E3
Tardoire →, *France* 26 C4
Taree, *Australia* 91 E5
Tarentaise, *France* 27 C10
Tarf, Ras, *Morocco* 74 A3
Tarfa, Wadi el →, *Egypt* 76 J7
Tarfaya, *Morocco* 74 C2
Targon, *France* 26 D3
Targuist, *Morocco* 74 B4
Tarhbalt, *Morocco* 74 B3
Tarhit, *Algeria* 75 B4
Táriba, *Venezuela* 120 B3
Tarifa, *Spain* 31 J5
Tarija, *Bolivia* 126 A3
Tarija □, *Bolivia* 126 A3
Tariku →, *Indonesia* 57 E9
Tarim Basin = Tarim Pendi, *China* 54 C3
Tarim He →, *China* 54 C3
Tarim Pendi, *China* 54 C3
Tarime □, *Tanzania* 82 C3
Taritatu →, *Indonesia* 57 E9
Tarka →, *S. Africa* 84 E4
Tarkastad, *S. Africa* 84 E4
Tarkhankut, Mys, *Ukraine* 42 D5
Tarko Sale, *Russia* 44 C8
Tarkwa, *Ghana* 78 D4
Tarlac, *Phil.* 55 D4
Tarlton Downs, *Australia* 90 C2
Tarm, *Denmark* 11 J2
Tarma, *Peru* 124 C2
Tarn □, *France* 26 E6
Tarn →, *France* 26 D5
Tarn-et-Garonne □, *France* 26 D5
Tarna →, *Hungary* 21 H9
Tårnby, *Denmark* 11 J6
Tarnobrzeg, *Poland* 20 E11
Tarnów, *Poland* 20 F11
Táro →, *Italy* 32 D7
Taroom, *Australia* 91 D4
Taroudannt, *Morocco* 74 B3
Tarp, *Germany* 18 A5
Tarpon Springs, *U.S.A.* 105 L4
Tarquínia, *Italy* 33 F8
Tarragona, *Spain* 28 D6
Tarragona □, *Spain* 28 D6
Tarrasa, *Spain* 28 D7
Tárrega, *Spain* 28 D6
Tarrytown, *U.S.A.* 107 E11
Tarshiha = Me'ona, *Israel* 69 B4
Tarso Emissi, *Chad* 73 D8
Tarsus, *Turkey* 66 E6
Tartagal, *Argentina* 126 A3
Tartas, *France* 26 E3
Tartu, *Estonia* 40 B5
Ţarţūs, *Syria* 64 C2
Tarumirim, *Brazil* 123 E3
Tarumizu, *Japan* 49 J5
Tarussa, *Russia* 41 D10
Tarutao, Ko, *Thailand* 59 J2
Tarutung, *Indonesia* 56 D1
Tarvisio, *Italy* 33 B10
Tarz Ulli, *Libya* 75 C7
Tasāwah, *Libya* 73 C7
Taschereau, *Canada* 98 C4
Taseko →, *Canada* 100 C4
Tash-Kumyr, *Kirghizia* 44 E8
Tashauz, *Turkmenistan* 44 E6
Tashi Chho Dzong = Thimphu, *Bhutan* 61 F16
Tashkent, *Uzbekistan* 44 E7
Tashtagol, *Russia* 44 D9
Tasikmalaya, *Indonesia* 57 G13
Tåsjön, *Sweden* 8 D13
Taskan, *Russia* 45 C16
Taşköprü, *Turkey* 42 F6
Tasman B., *N.Z.* 87 J4
Tasman Mts., *N.Z.* 87 J4
Tasman Pen., *Australia* 90 G4
Tasman Sea, *Pac. Oc.* 92 L8
Tasmania □, *Australia* 90 G4
Tăşnad, *Romania* 38 B5
Tassil Tin-Rerhoh, *Algeria* 75 D5
Tassili n-Ajjer, *Algeria* 75 C6
Tassili-Oua-n-Ahaggar, *Algeria* 75 D6
Tasu Sd., *Canada* 100 C2
Tata, *Morocco* 74 C3
Tatabánya, *Hungary* 21 H8
Tatahouine, *Tunisia* 75 B7
Tatar Republic □, *Russia* 44 D6
Tatarbunary, *Ukraine* 42 D3
Tatarsk, *Russia* 44 D8
Tateyama, *Japan* 49 G9
Tathlina L., *Canada* 100 A5
Tathra, *Australia* 91 F4
Tatinnai L., *Canada* 101 A9
Tatnam, C., *Canada* 101 B10
Tatra = Tatry, *Slovak Rep.* 20 F9
Tatry, *Slovak Rep.* 20 F9
Tatsuno, *Japan* 49 G7
Tatta, *Pakistan* 62 G2
Tatuī, *Brazil* 127 A6
Tatum, *U.S.A.* 109 J3
Tat'ung = Datong, *China* 50 D7
Tatvan, *Turkey* 67 D10
Tauá, *Brazil* 122 C3
Taubaté, *Brazil* 127 A6
Tauberbischofsheim, *Germany* 19 F5
Taucha, *Germany* 18 D8
Taufikia, *Sudan* 77 F3
Taumarunui, *N.Z.* 87 H5
Taumaturgo, *Brazil* 124 B3
Taung, *S. Africa* 84 D3
Taungdwingyi, *Burma* 61 J19
Taunggyi, *Burma* 61 J20
Taungup, *Burma* 61 K19
Taungup Pass, *Burma* 61 K19
Taungup Taunggya, *Burma* 61 K18
Taunsa Barrage, *Pakistan* 62 D4
Taunton, *U.K.* 13 F4
Taunton, *U.S.A.* 107 E13
Taunus, *Germany* 19 E4
Taupo, *N.Z.* 87 H6
Taupo, L., *N.Z.* 87 H5
Taurage, *Lithuania* 40 D3
Tauranga, *N.Z.* 87 G6
Tauranga Harb., *N.Z.* 87 G6
Taurianova, *Italy* 35 D9
Taurus Mts. = Toros Dağları, *Turkey* 66 E5
Tauste, *Spain* 28 D3
Tauz, *Azerbaijan* 43 F11
Tavannes, *Switz.* 22 B4
Tavda, *Russia* 44 D7
Tavda →, *Russia* 44 D7
Taverny, *France* 25 C9
Taveta, *Tanzania* 82 C4
Taveuni, *Fiji* 87 C9
Tavignano →, *France* 27 F13
Tavira, *Portugal* 31 H3
Tavistock, *Canada* 106 C4
Tavistock, *U.K.* 13 G3
Tavolara, *Italy* 34 B2
Távora →, *Portugal* 30 D3
Tavoy, *Burma* 58 E2
Tavşanlı, *Turkey* 66 D3
Taw →, *U.K.* 13 F3
Tawas City, *U.S.A.* 104 C4
Tawau, *Malaysia* 56 D5
Tawitawi, *Phil.* 55 J4
Taxila, *Pakistan* 62 C5
Tay →, *U.K.* 14 E5
Tay, Firth of, *U.K.* 14 E5
Tay, L., *Australia* 89 F3
Tay, L., *U.K.* 14 E4
Tay Ninh, *Vietnam* 59 G6
Tayabamba, *Peru* 124 B2
Tayabas Bay, *Phil.* 55 E4
Taylakovy, *Russia* 44 D8
Taylor, *Canada* 100 B4
Taylor, *Nebr., U.S.A.* 108 E5
Taylor, *Pa., U.S.A.* 107 E9
Taylor, *Tex., U.S.A.* 109 K6

Taylor, Mt., *U.S.A.* 111 J10
Taylorville, *U.S.A.* 108 F10
Taymā, *Si. Arabia* 64 E3
Taymyr, Oz., *Russia* 45 B11
Taymyr, Poluostrov, *Russia* 45 B11
Tayport, *U.K.* 14 E6
Tayshet, *Russia* 45 D10
Tayside □, *U.K.* 14 E5
Taytay, *Phil.* 55 F3
Taz →, *Russia* 44 C8
Taza, *Morocco* 74 B4
Tāzah Khurmātū, *Iraq* 64 C5
Tazawa-Ko, *Japan* 48 E10
Tazenakht, *Morocco* 74 B3
Tazin L., *Canada* 101 B7
Tazoult, *Algeria* 75 A6
Tazovskiy, *Russia* 44 C8
Tbilisi, *Georgia* 43 F11
Tchad = Chad ■, *Africa* 73 E8
Tchad, L., *Chad* 73 F7
Tchaourou, *Benin* 79 D5
Tch'eng-tou = Chengdu, *China* 52 B5
Tchentlo L., *Canada* 100 B4
Tchibanga, *Gabon* 80 E2
Tchien, *Liberia* 78 D3
Tchin Tabaraden, *Niger* 79 B6
Tch'ong-k'ing = Chongqing, *China* 52 C6
Tczew, *Poland* 20 A8
Te Anau, L., *N.Z.* 87 L1
Te Aroha, *N.Z.* 87 G5
Te Awamutu, *N.Z.* 87 H5
Te Kuiti, *N.Z.* 87 H5
Te Puke, *N.Z.* 87 G6
Te Waewae B., *N.Z.* 87 M1
Tea →, *Brazil* 120 D4
Tea Tree, *Australia* 90 C1
Teague, *U.S.A.* 109 K6
Teano, *Italy* 35 A7
Teapa, *Mexico* 115 D6
Teba, *Spain* 31 J6
Tebakang, *Malaysia* 56 D4
Teberda, *Russia* 43 E9
Tébessa, *Algeria* 75 A6
Tebicuary →, *Paraguay* 126 B4
Tebingtinggi, *Indonesia* 56 D1
Tébourba, *Tunisia* 75 A6
Téboursouk, *Tunisia* 75 A6
Tebulos, *Russia* 43 E11
Tecate, *Mexico* 113 N10
Tecer Daği, *Turkey* 66 D7
Tech →, *France* 26 F7
Techiman, *Ghana* 78 D4
Tecka, *Argentina* 128 B2
Tecomán, *Mexico* 114 D4
Tecopa, *U.S.A.* 113 K10
Tecoripa, *Mexico* 114 B3
Tecuala, *Mexico* 114 C3
Tecuci, *Romania* 38 D10
Tecumseh, *U.S.A.* 104 D4
Tedzhen, *Turkmenistan* 44 F7
Tees →, *U.K.* 12 C6
Teesside, *U.K.* 12 C6
Teeswater, *Canada* 106 C3
Tefé, *Brazil* 121 D5
Tefé →, *Brazil* 121 D5
Tefenni, *Turkey* 66 E3
Tegal, *Indonesia* 57 G13
Tegelen, *Neths.* 17 F8
Tegernsee, *Germany* 19 H7
Teggiano, *Italy* 35 B8
Teghra, *India* 63 G11
Tegid, L. = Bala, L., *U.K.* 12 E4
Tegina, *Nigeria* 79 C6
Tegucigalpa, *Honduras* 116 D2
Tehachapi, *U.S.A.* 113 K8
Tehachapi Mts., *U.S.A.* 113 L8
Tehamiyam, *Sudan* 76 D4
Tehilla, *Sudan* 76 D4
Téhini, *Ivory C.* 78 D4
Tehrān, *Iran* 65 C6
Tehuacán, *Mexico* 115 D5
Tehuantepec, *Mexico* 115 D5
Tehuantepec, G. de, *Mexico* 115 D5
Tehuantepec, Istmo de, *Mexico* 115 D6
Teide, *Canary Is.* 36 F3
Teifi →, *U.K.* 13 E3
Teign →, *U.K.* 13 G4
Teignmouth, *U.K.* 13 G4
Teixeira, *Brazil* 122 C4
Teixeira Pinto, *Guinea-Biss.* 78 C1
Tejo →, *Europe* 31 G1
Tejon Pass, *U.S.A.* 113 L8
Tekamah, *U.S.A.* 108 E6
Tekapo, L., *N.Z.* 87 K3
Tekax, *Mexico* 115 C7
Tekeli, *Kazakhstan* 44 E8
Tekeze →, *Ethiopia* 77 E4
Tekija, *Serbia* 21 L12
Tekirdağ, *Turkey* 66 C2
Tekirdağ □, *Turkey* 66 C2
Tekkali, *India* 61 K14
Tekke, *Turkey* 66 C7
Tekman, *Turkey* 67 D9
Tekoa, *U.S.A.* 110 C5
Tekouiât, O. →, *Algeria* 75 D5
Tel Aviv-Yafo, *Israel* 69 C3
Tel Lakhish, *Israel* 69 D3
Tel Megiddo, *Israel* 69 C4
Tela, *Honduras* 116 C2
Télagh, *Algeria* 75 B4
Telanaipura = Jambi, *Indonesia* 56 E2
Telavi, *Georgia* 43 F11
Telde, *Canary Is.* 36 G4
Telegraph Creek, *Canada* 100 B2
Telekhany, *Belorussia* 40 E4
Telemark fylke □, *Norway* 10 E2
Telén, *Argentina* 126 D2
Teleng, *Iran* 65 E9
Teleño, *Spain* 30 C4
Teleorman →, *Romania* 38 E8
Teles Pires →, *Brazil* 125 B6
Telescope Pk., *U.S.A.* 113 J9
Teletaye, *Mali* 79 B5
Telford, *U.K.* 12 E5
Telfs, *Austria* 19 H7
Télimélé, *Guinea* 78 C2
Telkwa, *Canada* 100 C3
Tell City, *U.S.A.* 104 G2
Tellicherry, *India* 60 P9
Tellin, *Belgium* 17 H6
Telluride, *U.S.A.* 111 H10
Teloloapán, *Mexico* 115 D5
Telpos Iz, *Russia* 6 C17
Telsen, *Argentina* 128 B3
Telšiai, *Lithuania* 40 D3
Teltow, *Germany* 18 C9
Teluk Anson, *Malaysia* 59 K3
Teluk Betung = Tanjungkarang Telukbetung, *Indonesia* 56 F3
Teluk Intan = Teluk Anson, *Malaysia* 59 K3
Telukbutun, *Indonesia* 59 K7
Telukdalem, *Indonesia* 56 D1
Tema, *Ghana* 79 D5
Temanggung, *Indonesia* 57 G14
Temapache, *Mexico* 115 C5
Temax, *Mexico* 115 C7
Temba, *S. Africa* 85 D4
Tembe, *Zaïre* 82 C2
Temblador, *Venezuela* 121 B5
Tembleque, *Spain* 28 F1
Temblor Range, *U.S.A.* 113 K7
Teme →, *U.K.* 13 E5
Temecula, *U.S.A.* 113 M9
Temerloh, *Malaysia* 59 L4
Temir, *Kazakhstan* 44 E6
Temirtau, *Kazakhstan* 44 D8
Temirtau, *Russia* 44 D9
Témiscaming, *Canada* 98 C4
Temma, *Australia* 90 G3
Temnikov, *Russia* 41 D13
Temo →, *Italy* 34 B1
Temora, *Australia* 91 E4
Temosachic, *Mexico* 114 B3
Tempe, *U.S.A.* 111 K8
Tempe Downs, *Australia* 88 D5
Témpio Pausania, *Italy* 34 B2
Tempiute, *U.S.A.* 112 H11
Temple, *U.S.A.* 109 K6
Temple B., *Australia* 90 A3
Templemore, *Ireland* 15 D4
Templeton, *U.S.A.* 112 K6
Templeton →, *Australia* 90 C2
Templeuve, *Belgium* 17 G2
Templin, *Germany* 18 B9
Tempoal, *Mexico* 115 C5
Temryuk, *Russia* 42 D7
Temse, *Belgium* 17 F4
Temska →, *Serbia* 21 M12
Temuco, *Chile* 128 A2
Temuka, *N.Z.* 87 L3
Ten Boer, *Neths.* 16 B9
Tena, *Ecuador* 120 D2
Tenabo, *Mexico* 115 C6
Tenaha, *U.S.A.* 109 K7
Tenali, *India* 60 L12
Tenancingo, *Mexico* 115 D5
Tenango, *Mexico* 115 D5
Tenasserim, *Burma* 59 F2
Tenasserim □, *Burma* 58 F2
Tenay, *France* 27 C9
Tenby, *U.K.* 13 F3
Tenda, Col di, *France* 27 D11
Tendaho, *Ethiopia* 68 E3
Tende, *France* 27 D11
Tendelti, *Sudan* 77 E3
Tendjedi, Adrar, *Algeria* 75 D6
Tendrara, *Morocco* 75 B4
Tendre, Mt., *Switz.* 22 C2
Teneida, *Egypt* 76 B2
Tenente Marques →, *Brazil* 125 C6
Ténéré, *Niger* 79 B7
Tenerife, *Canary Is.* 36 F3
Tenerife, Pico, *Canary Is.* 36 G1
Ténès, *Algeria* 75 A5
Teng Xian, *Guangxi Zhuangzu, China* 53 F8
Teng Xian, *Shandong, China* 51 G9
Tengah □, *Indonesia* 57 E6
Tengah Kepulauan, *Indonesia* 56 F5
Tengchong, *China* 52 E2
Tengchowfu = Penglai, *China* 51 F11
Tenggara □, *Indonesia* 57 E6
Tenggarong, *Indonesia* 56 E5
Tenggol, P., *Malaysia* 59 K4
Tengiz, Ozero, *Kazakhstan* 44 D7
Tenigerbad, *Switz.* 23 C7
Tenino, *U.S.A.* 112 D4
Tenkasi, *India* 60 Q10
Tenke, *Shaba, Zaïre* 83 E2
Tenke, *Shaba, Zaïre* 83 E2
Tenkodogo, *Burkina Faso* 79 C4
Tenna →, *Italy* 33 E10
Tennant Creek, *Australia* 90 B1
Tennessee □, *U.S.A.* 105 H2
Tennessee →, *U.S.A.* 104 G1
Tenneville, *Belgium* 17 H7
Tennille, *U.S.A.* 105 J4
Tennsift, Oued →, *Morocco* 74 B3
Teno, Pta. de, *Canary Is.* 36 F3
Tenom, *Malaysia* 56 C5
Tenosique, *Mexico* 115 D6
Tenryū-Gawa →, *Japan* 49 G8
Tent L., *Canada* 101 A7
Tenterfield, *Australia* 91 D5
Teófilo Otoni, *Brazil* 123 E3
Teotihuacán, *Mexico* 115 D5
Tepa, *Indonesia* 57 F7
Tepalcatepec →, *Mexico* 114 D4
Tepehuanes, *Mexico* 114 B3
Tepequem, Serra, *Brazil* 121 C5
Tepetongo, *Mexico* 114 C4
Tepic, *Mexico* 114 C4
Tepoca, C., *Mexico* 114 A2
Tequila, *Mexico* 114 C4
Ter →, *Spain* 28 C8
Ter Apel, *Neths.* 16 C10
Téra, *Niger* 79 C5
Tera →, *Spain* 30 D5
Teraina, *Kiribati* 93 G11
Téramo, *Italy* 33 F10
Terang, *Australia* 91 F3
Terborg, *Neths.* 16 E8
Tercan, *Turkey* 67 D9
Tercero →, *Argentina* 126 C3
Terebovlya, *Ukraine* 40 G4
Terek →, *Russia* 43 E12
Terenos, *Brazil* 125 E7
Tereshka →, *Russia* 41 F15
Teresina, *Brazil* 122 C3
Teresinha, *Brazil* 121 C7
Terewah, L., *Australia* 91 D4
Terges →, *Portugal* 31 H3
Tergnier, *France* 25 C10
Terhazza, *Mali* 74 D3
Terheijden, *Neths.* 17 E5
Teridgerie Cr. →, *Australia* 91 E4
Terlizzi, *Italy* 35 A9
Terme, *Turkey* 42 F7
Termez, *Uzbekistan* 44 F7
Términi Imerese, *Italy* 34 E6
Términos, L. de, *Mexico* 115 D6
Térmoli, *Italy* 33 F12
Ternate, *Indonesia* 57 D7
Terneuzen, *Neths.* 17 F3
Terney, *Russia* 45 E14
Terni, *Italy* 33 F9
Ternitz, *Austria* 21 H6
Ternopol, *Ukraine* 42 B1
Terowie, *N.S.W., Australia* 91 E4
Terowie, *S. Austral., Australia* 91 E2
Terra Bella, *U.S.A.* 113 K7
Terrace, *Canada* 100 C3
Terrace Bay, *Canada* 98 C2
Terracina, *Italy* 34 A6
Terralba, *Italy* 34 C1
Terranova = Ólbia, *Italy* 34 B2
Terranuova Bracciolini, *Italy* 33 E8
Terrasini Favarotta, *Italy* 34 D6
Terrassa = Tarrasa, *Spain* 28 D7
Terrasson-la-Villedieu, *France* 26 C5
Terre Haute, *U.S.A.* 104 F2
Terrebonne B., *U.S.A.* 109 L9
Terrecht, *Mali* 75 D4
Terrell, *U.S.A.* 109 J6
Terrenceville, *Canada* 99 C9
Terrick Terrick, *Australia* 90 C4
Terry, *U.S.A.* 108 B2
Terschelling, *Neths.* 16 B6
Terter →, *Azerbaijan* 43 F12
Teruel, *Spain* 28 E3
Teruel □, *Spain* 28 E4
Tervel, *Bulgaria* 38 F10
Tervola, *Finland* 8 C18
Teryaweyna L., *Australia* 91 E3
Tešanj, *Bos.-H.* 21 L7
Teseney, *Eritrea* 77 D4
Tesha →, *Russia* 41 D13
Teshio, *Japan* 48 B10
Teshio-Gawa →, *Japan* 48 B10
Tesiyn Gol →, *Mongolia* 54 A4
Teslin, *Canada* 100 A2
Teslin →, *Canada* 100 A2
Teslin L., *Canada* 100 A2
Tesouro, *Brazil* 125 D7
Tessalit, *Mali* 79 A5
Tessaoua, *Niger* 79 C6
Tessenderlo, *Belgium* 17 F6
Tessin, *Germany* 18 A8
Tessit, *Mali* 79 B5
Test →, *U.K.* 13 F6
Testa del Gargano, *Italy* 35 A9
Têt →, *France* 26 F7
Tetachuck L., *Canada* 100 C3
Tetas, Pta., *Chile* 126 A1
Tete, *Mozam.* 83 F3
Tete □, *Mozam.* 83 F3
Teterev →, *Ukraine* 40 F7
Teteringen, *Neths.* 17 E5
Teterow, *Germany* 18 B8
Teteven, *Bulgaria* 38 G7
Tethul →, *Canada* 100 A6
Tetiyev, *Ukraine* 42 B3
Teton →, *U.S.A.* 110 C8
Tétouan, *Morocco* 74 A3
Tetovo, *Macedonia* 38 G4
Tetuán = Tétouan, *Morocco* 74 A3
Tetyukhe Pristan, *Russia* 48 B7
Tetyushi, *Russia* 41 D16
Teuco →, *Argentina* 126 B3
Teufen, *Switz.* 23 B8
Teulada, *Italy* 34 D1
Teulon, *Canada* 101 C9
Teun, *Indonesia* 57 F7
Teutoburger Wald, *Germany* 18 C4
Tevere →, *Italy* 33 G9
Teverya, *Israel* 69 C4
Teviot →, *U.K.* 14 F6
Tewantin, *Australia* 91 D5
Tewkesbury, *U.K.* 13 F5
Texada I., *Canada* 100 D4
Texarkana, *Ark., U.S.A.* 109 J8
Texarkana, *Tex., U.S.A.* 109 J7
Texas, *Australia* 91 D5
Texas □, *U.S.A.* 109 K5
Texas City, *U.S.A.* 109 L7
Texel, *Neths.* 16 B5
Texhoma, *U.S.A.* 109 G4
Texline, *U.S.A.* 109 G3
Texoma, L., *U.S.A.* 109 J6
Teykovo, *Russia* 41 C12
Teza →, *Russia* 41 C12
Tezin, *Afghan.* 62 B3
Teziutlán, *Mexico* 115 D5
Tezpur, *India* 61 F18
Tezzeron L., *Canada* 100 C4
Tha-anne →, *Canada* 101 A10
Tha Deua, *Laos* 58 D4
Tha Deua, *Laos* 58 C3
Tha Pla, *Thailand* 58 D3
Tha Rua, *Thailand* 58 E3
Tha Sala, *Thailand* 59 H2
Tha Song Yang, *Thailand* 58 D1
Thaba Nchu, *S. Africa* 84 D4
Thaba Putsoa, *Lesotho* 85 D4
Thabana Ntlenyana, *Lesotho* 85 D4
Thabazimbi, *S. Africa* 85 C4
Thai Binh, *Vietnam* 58 B6
Thai Hoa, *Vietnam* 58 C5
Thai Muang, *Thailand* 59 H2
Thai Nguyen, *Vietnam* 58 B5
Thailand ■, *Asia* 58 E4
Thailand, G. of, *Asia* 59 G3
Thakhek, *Laos* 58 D5
Thal, *Pakistan* 62 C4
Thal Desert, *Pakistan* 62 D4
Thala, *Tunisia* 75 A6
Thala La, *Burma* 61 E20
Thalabarivat, *Cambodia* 58 F5
Thalkirch, *Switz.* 23 C8
Thallon, *Australia* 91 D4
Thalwil, *Switz.* 23 B7
Thame →, *U.K.* 13 F6
Thames, *N.Z.* 87 G5
Thames →, *Canada* 98 D3
Thames →, *U.K.* 13 F8
Thames →, *U.S.A.* 107 E12
Thamesford, *Canada* 106 C3
Thamesville, *Canada* 106 D3
Than Uyen, *Vietnam* 58 B4
Thane, *India* 60 K8
Thanesar, *India* 62 D7
Thanet, I. of, *U.K.* 13 F9
Thangoo, *Australia* 88 C3
Thangool, *Australia* 90 C5
Thanh Hoa, *Vietnam* 58 C5
Thanh Hung, *Vietnam* 59 H5
Thanh Pho Ho Chi Minh = Phanh Bho Ho Chi Minh, *Vietnam* 59 G6
Thanh Thuy, *Vietnam* 58 A5
Thanjavur, *India* 60 P11
Thann, *France* 25 E14
Thaon-les-Vosges, *France* 25 D13
Thap Sakae, *Thailand* 59 G2
Thap Than, *Thailand* 58 E2
Thar Desert, *India* 62 F4
Tharad, *India* 62 G4
Thargomindah, *Australia* 91 D3
Tharrawaddy, *Burma* 61 L19
Tharthar, W. →, *Iraq* 64 C4
Thásos, *Greece* 39 J7
That Khe, *Vietnam* 58 A6
Thatcher, *Ariz., U.S.A.* 111 K9
Thatcher, *Colo., U.S.A.* 109 G2
Thaton, *Burma* 61 L20
Thau, Bassin de, *France* 26 E7
Thaungdut, *Burma* 61 G19
Thayer, *U.S.A.* 109 G9
Thayetmyo, *Burma* 61 K19
Thayngen, *Switz.* 23 A7
Thazi, *Burma* 61 J20
The Alberga →, *Australia* 91 D2
The Bight, *Bahamas* 117 B4
The Coorong, *Australia* 91 F2
The Dalles, *U.S.A.* 110 D3
The English Company's Is., *Australia* 90 A2
The Frome →, *Australia* 91 D2
The Grampians, *Australia* 91 F3
The Great Divide = Great Dividing Ra., *Australia* 90 C4
The Hague = 's-Gravenhage, *Neths.* 16 D4
The Hamilton →, *Australia* 91 D2
The Macumba →, *Australia* 91 D2
The Neales →, *Australia* 91 D2
The Officer →, *Australia* 89 E5
The Pas, *Canada* 101 C8
The Range, *Zimbabwe* 83 F3
The Rock, *Australia* 91 F4
The Salt L., *Australia* 91 E3
The Stevenson →, *Australia* 91 D2
The Warburton →, *Australia* 91 D2
Thebes = Thívai, *Greece* 39 L6
Thebes, *Egypt* 76 B3
Thedford, *Canada* 106 C3
Thedford, *U.S.A.* 108 E4
Theebine, *Australia* 91 D5
Thekulthili L., *Canada* 101 A7
Thelon →, *Canada* 101 A8
Thénezay, *France* 24 F6
Thenia, *Algeria* 75 A5
Thenon, *France* 26 C5
Theodore, *Australia* 90 C5
Thepha, *Thailand* 59 J3
Thérain →, *France* 25 C9
Theresa, *U.S.A.* 107 B9
Thermaïkos Kólpos, *Greece* 39 J5
Thermopolis, *U.S.A.* 110 E9
Thermopylae P., *Greece* 39 L5
Thessalía □, *Greece* 39 L4
Thessalon, *Canada* 98 C3
Thessaloníki, *Greece* 39 J5
Thessaloniki, Gulf of = Thermaïkos Kólpos, *Greece* 39 J5
Thessaly = Thessalía □, *Greece* 39 L4
Thetford, *U.K.* 13 E8
Thetford Mines, *Canada* 99 C5
Theun →, *Laos* 58 C5
Theunissen, *S. Africa* 84 D4
Theux, *Belgium* 17 G7
Thevenard, *Australia* 91 E1
Thiámis →, *Greece* 39 K3
Thiberville, *France* 24 C7
Thibodaux, *U.S.A.* 109 L9
Thicket Portage, *Canada* 101 B9
Thief River Falls, *U.S.A.* 108 A6
Thiel Mts., *Antarctica* 5 E16
Thiene, *Italy* 33 C8
Thiérache, *France* 25 C10
Thiers, *France* 26 C7
Thies, *Senegal* 78 C1
Thiet, *Sudan* 77 F2
Thika, *Kenya* 82 C4
Thikombia, *Fiji* 87 B9
Thille-Boubacar, *Senegal* 78 B1
Thimphu, *Bhutan* 61 F16
þingvallavatn, *Iceland* 8 D3
Thionville, *France* 25 C13
Thíra, *Greece* 39 N8
Thirasía, *Greece* 39 N8
Thirsk, *U.K.* 12 C6
Thisted, *Denmark* 9 H10
Thistle I., *Australia* 91 F2
Thívai, *Greece* 39 L6
Thiviers, *France* 26 C4
Thizy, *France* 27 B8
þjórsá →, *Iceland* 8 E3
Thlewiaza →, *Man., Canada* 101 B8
Thlewiaza →, *N.W.T., Canada* 101 A10
Thmar Puok, *Cambodia* 58 F4
Tho Vinh, *Vietnam* 58 C5
Thoa →, *Canada* 101 A7
Thoen, *Thailand* 58 D2
Thoeng, *Thailand* 58 C3
Thoissey, *France* 27 B8
Tholdi, *Pakistan* 63 B7
Tholen, *Neths.* 17 E4
Thomas, *Okla., U.S.A.* 109 H5
Thomas, *W. Va., U.S.A.* 104 F6
Thomas, L., *Australia* 91 D2
Thomaston, *U.S.A.* 105 J3
Thomasville, *Ala., U.S.A.* 105 K2
Thomasville, *Ga., U.S.A.* 105 K3
Thomasville, *N.C., U.S.A.* 105 H5
Thommen, *Belgium* 17 H8
Thompson, *Canada* 101 B9
Thompson, *U.S.A.* 111 G9
Thompson →, *Canada* 100 C4
Thompson →, *U.S.A.* 108 F8
Thompson Falls, *U.S.A.* 110 C6
Thompson Landing, *Canada* 101 A6
Thompson Pk., *U.S.A.* 110 F2
Thomson's Falls = Nyahururu, *Kenya* 82 B4
Thon Buri, *Thailand* 59 F3
Thônes, *France* 27 C10
Thonon-les-Bains, *France* 27 B10
Thorez, *Ukraine* 43 B8
þórisvatn, *Iceland* 8 D4
þorlákshöfn, *Iceland* 8 E3
Thornaby on Tees, *U.K.* 12 C6
Thornbury, *Canada* 106 B4
Thorold, *Canada* 106 C5
þórshöfn, *Iceland* 8 C6
Thouarcé, *France* 24 E6
Thouars, *France* 24 F6
Thouin, C., *Australia* 88 D2
Thousand Oaks, *U.S.A.* 113 L8

Thrace, *Turkey* 66 C2
Thrakikón Pélagos, *Greece* 39 J8
Three Forks, *U.S.A.* 110 D8
Three Hills, *Canada* 100 C6
Three Hummock I., *Australia* 90 G3
Three Lakes, *U.S.A.* 108 C10
Three Points, C., *Ghana* 78 E4
Three Rivers, *Australia* 89 E2
Three Rivers, *Calif., U.S.A.* 112 J8
Three Rivers, *Tex., U.S.A.* 109 L5
Three Sisters, *U.S.A.* 110 D3
Throssell, L., *Australia* 89 E3
Throssell Ra., *Australia* 88 D3
Thuan Hoa, *Vietnam* 59 H5
Thubun Lakes, *Canada* 101 A6
Thueyts, *France* 27 D8
Thuillies, *Belgium* 17 H4
Thuin, *Belgium* 17 H4
Thuir, *France* 26 F6
Thule, *Greenland* 4 B4
Thun, *Switz.* 22 C5
Thundelarra, *Australia* 89 E2
Thunder B., *U.S.A.* 106 B1
Thunder Bay, *Canada* 98 C2
Thunersee, *Switz.* 22 C5
Thung Song, *Thailand* 59 H2
Thunkar, *Bhutan* 61 F17
Thuong Tra, *Vietnam* 58 D6
Thur →, *Switz.* 23 A8
Thurgau □, *Switz.* 23 A8
Thüringen □, *Germany* 18 E7
Thüringer Wald, *Germany* 18 E7
Thurles, *Ireland* 15 D4
Thurloo Downs, *Australia* 91 D3
Thurn P., *Austria* 19 H8
Thursday I., *Australia* 90 A3
Thurso, *Canada* 98 C4
Thurso, *U.K.* 14 C5
Thurston I., *Antarctica* 5 D16
Thury-Harcourt, *France* 24 D6
Thusis, *Switz.* 23 C8
Thutade L., *Canada* 100 B3
Thyborøn, *Denmark* 11 H2
Thylungra, *Australia* 91 D3
Thyolo, *Malawi* 83 F4
Thysville = Mbanza Ngungu, *Zaïre* 80 F2
Ti-n-Barraouene, O. →, *Africa* 79 B5
Ti-n-Medjerdam, O. →, *Algeria* 75 C5
Ti-n-Tarabine, O. →, *Algeria* 75 D6
Ti-n-Zaouatène, *Algeria* 75 E5
Tia, *Australia* 91 E5
Tiahuanacu, *Bolivia* 124 D4
Tian Shan, *China* 54 B3
Tianchang, *China* 53 A12
Tiandong, *China* 52 F6
Tian'e, *China* 52 E6
Tianguá, *Brazil* 122 B3
Tianhe, *China* 52 E7
Tianjin, *China* 51 E9
Tiankoura, *Burkina Faso* 78 C4
Tianlin, *China* 52 E6
Tianmen, *China* 53 B9
Tianquan, *China* 52 B4
Tianshui, *China* 50 G3
Tiantai, *China* 53 C13
Tianyang, *China* 52 F6
Tianzhen, *China* 50 D8
Tianzhu, *China* 52 D7
Tianzhuangtai, *China* 51 D12
Tiaret, *Algeria* 75 A5
Tiassalé, *Ivory C.* 78 D4
Tibagi, *Brazil* 127 A5
Tibagi →, *Brazil* 127 A5
Tibati, *Cameroon* 79 D7
Tiber = Tevere →, *Italy* 33 G9
Tiber Reservoir, *U.S.A.* 110 B8
Tiberias = Teverya, *Israel* 69 C4
Tiberias, L. = Yam Kinneret, *Israel* 69 C4
Tibesti, *Chad* 73 D8
Tibet = Xizang □, *China* 54 C3
Tibiao, *Phil.* 55 F5
Tibiri, *Niger* 79 C6
Ţibleş, *Romania* 38 B7
Tibnī, *Syria* 64 C3
Tibooburra, *Australia* 91 D3
Tibro, *Sweden* 11 F8
Tibugá, G. de, *Colombia* 120 B2
Tiburón, *Mexico* 114 B2
Ticao I., *Phil.* 55 E5
Tichît, *Mauritania* 78 B3
Tichla, *Mauritania* 74 D2
Ticho, *Ethiopia* 77 F4
Ticino □, *Switz.* 23 D7
Ticino →, *Italy* 32 C6
Ticonderoga, *U.S.A.* 107 C11
Ticul, *Mexico* 115 C7
Tidaholm, *Sweden* 11 F7
Tiddim, *Burma* 61 H18
Tideridjaouine, Adrar, *Algeria* 75 D5
Tidikelt, *Algeria* 75 C5
Tidjikja, *Mauritania* 78 B2
Tidore, *Indonesia* 57 D7
Tiébissou, *Ivory C.* 78 D3
Tiefencastel, *Switz.* 23 C9
Tiel, *Neths.* 16 E6
Tiel, *Senegal* 78 C1
Tieling, *China* 51 C12
Tielt, *Belgium* 17 F2
Tien Shan, *Asia* 46 E11
Tien-tsin = Tianjin, *China* 51 E9
Tien Yen, *Vietnam* 58 B6
T'ienching = Tianjin, *China* 51 E9
Tienen, *Belgium* 17 G5
Tiénigbé, *Ivory C.* 78 D3
Tientsin = Tianjin, *China* 51 E9
Tierra Amarilla, *Chile* 126 B1
Tierra Amarilla, *U.S.A.* 111 H10
Tierra Colorada, *Mexico* 115 D5
Tierra de Barros, *Spain* 31 G4
Tierra de Campos, *Spain* 30 C6
Tierra del Fuego □, *Argentina* 128 D3
Tierra del Fuego, I. Gr. de, *Argentina* 128 D3
Tierralta, *Colombia* 120 B2
Tiétar →, *Spain* 30 F4
Tieté →, *Brazil* 127 A5
Tieyon, *Australia* 91 D1
Tifarati, *W. Sahara* 74 C2
Tiffin, *U.S.A.* 104 E4
Tiflèt, *Morocco* 74 B3
Tiflis = Tbilisi, *Georgia* 43 F11
Tifton, *U.S.A.* 105 K4
Tifu, *Indonesia* 57 E7
Tigil, *Russia* 45 D16
Tignish, *Canada* 99 C7
Tigray □, *Ethiopia* 77 E4
Tigre →, *Peru* 120 D3
Tigre →, *Venezuela* 121 B5
Tigris = Dijlah, Nahr →, *Asia* 64 D5
Tiguentourine, *Algeria* 75 C6
Tigyaing, *Burma* 61 H20
Tigzerte, O. →, *Morocco* 74 C3
Tîh, Gebel el, *Egypt* 76 J8
Tihodaine, Dunes de, *Algeria* 75 C6
Tijesno, *Croatia* 33 E12
Tījī, *Libya* 75 B7
Tijuana, *Mexico* 113 N9
Tikal, *Guatemala* 116 C2
Tikamgarh, *India* 63 G8
Tikhoretsk, *Russia* 43 D9
Tikhvin, *Russia* 40 B8
Tikkadouine, Adrar, *Algeria* 75 D5
Tiko, *Cameroon* 79 E6
Tikrīt, *Iraq* 64 C4
Tiksi, *Russia* 45 B13
Tilamuta, *Indonesia* 57 D6
Tilburg, *Neths.* 17 E6
Tilbury, *Canada* 98 D3
Tilbury, *U.K.* 13 F8
Tilcara, *Argentina* 126 A2
Tilden, *Nebr., U.S.A.* 108 D6
Tilden, *Tex., U.S.A.* 109 L5
Tilemses, *Niger* 79 B5
Tilemsi, Vallée du, *Mali* 79 B5
Tilhar, *India* 63 F8
Tilia, O. →, *Algeria* 75 C5
Tilichiki, *Russia* 45 C17
Tiligul →, *Ukraine* 42 C4
Tililane, *Algeria* 75 C4
Tílissos, *Greece* 37 D7
Till →, *U.K.* 12 B5
Tillabéri, *Niger* 79 C5
Tillamook, *U.S.A.* 110 D2
Tillberga, *Sweden* 10 E10
Tillia, *Niger* 79 B5
Tillsonburg, *Canada* 98 D3
Tillyeria □, *Cyprus* 37 D11
Tílos, *Greece* 39 N10
Tilpa, *Australia* 91 E3
Tilrhemt, *Algeria* 75 B5
Tilsit = Sovetsk, *Russia* 40 D2
Tilt →, *U.K.* 14 E5
Tilton, *U.S.A.* 107 C13
Timagami L., *Canada* 98 C3
Timaru, *N.Z.* 87 L3
Timashevsk, *Russia* 43 D8
Timau, *Italy* 33 B10
Timau, *Kenya* 82 B4
Timbákion, *Greece* 37 D6
Timbaúba, *Brazil* 122 C4
Timbedgha, *Mauritania* 78 B3
Timber Lake, *U.S.A.* 108 C4
Timber Mt., *U.S.A.* 112 H10
Timbío, *Colombia* 120 C2
Timbiqui, *Colombia* 120 C2
Timboon, *Australia* 91 F3
Timbuktu = Tombouctou, *Mali* 78 B4
Timellouline, *Algeria* 75 C6
Timétrine Montagnes, *Mali* 79 B4
Timfristós, Óros, *Greece* 39 L4
Timhadit, *Morocco* 74 B3
Timi, *Cyprus* 37 E11
Tîmia, *Niger* 79 B6
Timimoun, *Algeria* 75 C5
Timiş = Tamis →, *Serbia* 38 E3
Timişoara, *Romania* 38 D4
Timmins, *Canada* 98 C3
Timok →, *Serbia* 21 L12
Timon, *Brazil* 122 C3
Timor, *Indonesia* 57 F7
Timor □, *Indonesia* 57 F7
Timor Sea, *Ind. Oc.* 88 B4
Tin Alkoum, *Algeria* 75 D7
Tin Gornai, *Mali* 79 B4
Tin Mt., *U.S.A.* 112 J9
Tîna, Khalîg el, *Egypt* 76 H8
Tinaca Pt., *Phil.* 55 J6
Tinaco, *Venezuela* 120 B4
Tinafak, O. →, *Algeria* 75 C6
Tinajo, *Canary Is.* 36 E6
Tinaquillo, *Venezuela* 120 B4
Tinca, *Romania* 38 C4
Tinchebray, *France* 24 D6
Tindouf, *Algeria* 74 C3
Tinée →, *France* 27 E11
Tineo, *Spain* 30 B4
Tinerhir, *Morocco* 74 B3
Tinfouchi, *Algeria* 74 C3
Ting Jiang →, *China* 53 E11
Tinggi, Pulau, *Malaysia* 59 L5
Tinglev, *Denmark* 11 K3
Tingo Maria, *Peru* 124 B2
Tinh Bien, *Vietnam* 59 G5
Tinharé, I. de, *Brazil* 123 D4
Tinjoub, *Algeria* 72 C3
Tinkurrin, *Australia* 89 F2
Tinnevelly = Tirunelveli, *India* 60 Q10
Tinnoset, *Norway* 10 E3
Tinnsjø, *Norway* 10 E2
Tinogasta, *Argentina* 126 B2
Tínos, *Greece* 39 M8
Tiñoso, C., *Spain* 29 H3
Tinta, *Peru* 124 C3
Tintigny, *Belgium* 17 J7
Tintina, *Argentina* 126 B3
Tintinara, *Australia* 91 F3
Tinto →, *Spain* 31 H4
Tioga, *U.S.A.* 106 E7
Tioman, Pulau, *Malaysia* 59 L5
Tione di Trento, *Italy* 32 B7
Tionesta, *U.S.A.* 106 E5
Tior, *Sudan* 77 F3
Tioulilin, *Algeria* 75 C4
Tipongpani, *India* 61 F19
Tipperary, *Ireland* 15 D3
Tipperary □, *Ireland* 15 D4
Tipton, *U.K.* 13 E5
Tipton, *Calif., U.S.A.* 111 H4
Tipton, *Ind., U.S.A.* 104 E2
Tipton, *Iowa, U.S.A.* 108 E9
Tipton Mt., *U.S.A.* 113 K12
Tiptonville, *U.S.A.* 109 G10
Tiquié →, *Brazil* 120 C4
Tiracambu, Serra do, *Brazil* 122 B2
Tīrān, *Iran* 65 C6
Tīrān, *Si. Arabia* 76 B3
Tirana, *Albania* 39 H2
Tiranë = Tirana, *Albania* 39 H2
Tirano, *Italy* 32 B7
Tiraspol, *Moldavia* 42 C3
Tirat Karmel, *Israel* 69 C3
Tiratimine, *Algeria* 75 C5
Tirdout, *Mali* 79 B4
Tire, *Turkey* 66 D2
Tirebolu, *Turkey* 67 C8
Tiree, *U.K.* 14 E2
Tîrgovişte, *Romania* 38 E8
Tîrgu Frumos, *Romania* 38 B10
Tîrgu-Jiu, *Romania* 38 D6
Tîrgu Mureş, *Romania* 38 C7
Tîrgu Neamţ, *Romania* 38 B9
Tîrgu Ocna, *Romania* 38 C9
Tîrgu Secuiesc, *Romania* 38 D9
Tirich Mir, *Pakistan* 60 A7
Tiriola, *Italy* 35 D9
Tiririca, Serra da, *Brazil* 123 E2
Tiris, *W. Sahara* 74 D2
Tîrnava Mare →, *Romania* 38 C7
Tîrnava Mică →, *Romania* 38 C7
Tîrnăveni, *Romania* 38 C7
Tírnavos, *Greece* 39 K5
Tirodi, *India* 60 J11
Tiros, *Brazil* 123 E2
Tirschenreuth, *Germany* 19 F8
Tirso →, *Italy* 34 C1
Tirso, L. del, *Italy* 34 B1
Tiruchchirappalli, *India* 60 P11
Tirunelveli, *India* 60 Q10
Tirupati, *India* 60 N11
Tiruppur, *India* 60 P10
Tiruvannamalai, *India* 60 N11
Tisa →, *Hungary* 21 J10
Tisa →, *Serbia* 21 K10
Tisdale, *Canada* 101 C8
Tishomingo, *U.S.A.* 109 H6
Tisnaren, *Sweden* 10 F9
Tisovec, *Slovak Rep.* 20 G9
Tissemsilt, *Algeria* 75 A5
Tissint, *Morocco* 74 C3
Tissø, *Denmark* 11 J5
Tisza = Tisa →, *Hungary* 21 J10
Tiszafüred, *Hungary* 21 H10
Tiszavasvári, *Hungary* 21 H11
Tit, *Ahaggar, Algeria* 75 D6
Tit, *Tademait, Algeria* 75 C5
Tit-Ary, *Russia* 45 B13
Titaguas, *Spain* 28 F3
Titel, *Serbia* 21 K10
Tithwal, *Pakistan* 63 B5
Titicaca, L., *S. Amer.* 124 D4
Titiwa, *Nigeria* 79 C7
Titlis, *Switz.* 23 C6
Titograd = Podgorica, *Montenegro* 21 N9
Titov Veles, *Macedonia* 39 H4
Titova Korenica, *Croatia* 33 D12
Titovo Užice, *Serbia* 21 M9
Titule, *Zaïre* 82 B2
Titumate, *Colombia* 120 B2
Titusville, *Fla., U.S.A.* 105 L5
Titusville, *Pa., U.S.A.* 106 E5
Tivaouane, *Senegal* 78 C1
Tiveden, *Sweden* 11 F8
Tiverton, *U.K.* 13 G4
Tívoli, *Italy* 33 G9
Tiyo, *Eritrea* 77 E5
Tizga, *Morocco* 74 B3
Ti'zi N'Isli, *Morocco* 74 B3
Tizi-Ouzou, *Algeria* 75 A5
Tizimín, *Mexico* 115 C7
Tiznados →, *Venezuela* 120 B4
Tiznit, *Morocco* 74 C3
Tjeggelvas, *Sweden* 8 C14
Tjeukemeer, *Neths.* 16 C7
Tjirebon = Cirebon, *Indonesia* 57 G13
Tjøme, *Norway* 10 E4
Tjonger Kanaal, *Neths.* 16 C7
Tjörn, *Sweden* 11 G5
Tkibuli, *Georgia* 43 E10
Tkvarcheli, *Georgia* 43 E9
Tlacotalpan, *Mexico* 115 D5
Tlahualilo, *Mexico* 114 B4
Tlaquepaque, *Mexico* 114 C4
Tlaxcala, *Mexico* 115 D5
Tlaxcala □, *Mexico* 115 D5
Tlaxiaco, *Mexico* 115 D5
Tlell, *Canada* 100 C2
Tlemcen, *Algeria* 75 B4
Tleta Sidi Bouguedra, *Morocco* 74 B3
Tlumach, *Ukraine* 42 B1
Tlyarata, *Russia* 43 E12
Tmassah, *Libya* 73 C8
Tnine d'Anglou, *Morocco* 74 C3
To Bong, *Vietnam* 58 F7
Toad →, *Canada* 100 B4
Toamasina, *Madag.* 85 B8
Toamasina □, *Madag.* 85 B8
Toay, *Argentina* 126 D3
Toba, *Japan* 49 G8
Toba Kakar, *Pakistan* 62 D3
Toba Tek Singh, *Pakistan* 62 D5
Tobago, *W. Indies* 117 D7
Tobarra, *Spain* 29 G3
Tobelo, *Indonesia* 57 D7
Tobermorey, *Australia* 90 C2
Tobermory, *Canada* 98 C3
Tobermory, *U.K.* 14 E2
Tobin, *U.S.A.* 112 F5
Tobin, L., *Australia* 88 D4
Tobin L., *Canada* 101 C8
Toboali, *Indonesia* 56 E3
Tobol, *Kazakhstan* 44 D7
Tobol →, *Russia* 44 D7
Toboli, *Indonesia* 57 E6
Tobolsk, *Russia* 44 D7
Tobruk = Tubruq, *Libya* 73 B9
Tobyhanna, *U.S.A.* 107 E9
Tocache Nuevo, *Peru* 124 B2
Tocantínia, *Brazil* 122 C2
Tocantinópolis, *Brazil* 122 C2
Tocantins →, *Brazil* 122 B2
Toccoa, *U.S.A.* 105 H4
Toce →, *Italy* 32 C5
Tochigi, *Japan* 49 F9
Tochigi □, *Japan* 49 F9
Tocina, *Spain* 31 H5
Tocopilla, *Chile* 126 A1
Tocumwal, *Australia* 91 F4
Tocuyo →, *Venezuela* 120 A4
Tocuyo de la Costa, *Venezuela* 120 A4
Todd →, *Australia* 90 C2
Todeli, *Indonesia* 57 E6
Todenyang, *Kenya* 82 B4
Todi, *Italy* 33 F9
Tödi, *Switz.* 23 C7
Todos os Santos, B. de, *Brazil* 123 D4
Todos Santos, *Mexico* 114 C2
Todtnau, *Germany* 19 H3
Toecé, *Burkina Faso* 79 C4
Tofield, *Canada* 100 C6
Tofino, *Canada* 100 D3
Töfsingdalens nationalpark, *Sweden* 10 B6
Toftlund, *Denmark* 11 J3
Tofua, *Tonga* 87 D11
Tōgane, *Japan* 49 G10
Togba, *Mauritania* 78 B2
Toggenburg, *Switz.* 23 B8
Togian, Kepulauan, *Indonesia* 57 E6
Togliatti, *Russia* 41 E16
Togo ■, *W. Afr.* 79 D5
Togtoh, *China* 50 D6
Tohma →, *Turkey* 67 D8
Tōhoku □, *Japan* 48 E10
Toinya, *Sudan* 77 F2
Tojikiston = Tajikistan ■, *Asia* 44 F8
Tojo, *Indonesia* 57 E6
Tōjō, *Japan* 49 G6
Toka, *Guyana* 121 C6
Tokachi-Dake, *Japan* 48 C11
Tokachi-Gawa →, *Japan* 48 C11
Tokaj, *Hungary* 21 G11
Tokala, *Indonesia* 57 E6
Tōkamachi, *Japan* 49 F9
Tokanui, *N.Z.* 87 M2
Tokar, *Sudan* 76 D4
Tokara-Rettō, *Japan* 49 K4
Tokarahi, *N.Z.* 87 L3
Tokashiki-Shima, *Japan* 49 L3
Tokat, *Turkey* 66 C7
Tokat □, *Turkey* 66 C7
Tökchŏn, *N. Korea* 51 E14
Tokeland, *U.S.A.* 112 D3
Tokelau Is., *Pac. Oc.* 92 H10
Tokmak, *Kirghizia* 44 E8
Toko Ra., *Australia* 90 C2
Tokoro-Gawa →, *Japan* 48 B12
Tokuno-Shima, *Japan* 49 L4
Tokushima, *Japan* 49 G7
Tokushima □, *Japan* 49 H7
Tokuyama, *Japan* 49 G5
Tōkyō, *Japan* 49 G9
Tolaga Bay, *N.Z.* 87 H7
Tolbukhin, *Bulgaria* 38 F10
Toledo, *Spain* 30 F6
Toledo, *Ohio, U.S.A.* 104 E4
Toledo, *Oreg., U.S.A.* 110 D2
Toledo, *Wash., U.S.A.* 110 C2
Toledo, Montes de, *Spain* 31 F6
Tolentino, *Italy* 33 E10
Tolga, *Algeria* 75 B6
Tolga, *Norway* 10 B5
Toliara, *Madag.* 85 C7
Toliara □, *Madag.* 85 C8
Tolima, *Colombia* 120 C2
Tolima □, *Colombia* 120 C2
Tolitoli, *Indonesia* 57 D6
Tolkamer, *Neths.* 16 E8
Tolleson, *U.S.A.* 111 K7
Tollhouse, *U.S.A.* 112 H7
Tolmachevo, *Russia* 40 B6
Tolmezzo, *Italy* 33 B10
Tolmin, *Slovenia* 33 B10
Tolo, *Zaïre* 80 E3
Tolo, Teluk, *Indonesia* 57 E6
Tolochin, *Belorussia* 40 D6
Tolosa, *Spain* 28 B2
Tolox, *Spain* 31 J6
Toltén, *Chile* 128 A2
Toluca, *Mexico* 115 D5
Tom Burke, *S. Africa* 85 C4
Tom Price, *Australia* 88 D2
Tomah, *U.S.A.* 108 D9
Tomahawk, *U.S.A.* 108 C10
Tomakomai, *Japan* 48 C10
Tomales, *U.S.A.* 112 G4
Tomales B., *U.S.A.* 112 G3
Tomar, *Portugal* 31 F2
Tomarza, *Turkey* 66 D6
Tomás Barrón, *Bolivia* 124 D4
Tomaszów Mazowiecki, *Poland* 20 D9
Tomatlán, *Mexico* 114 D3
Tombador, Serra do, *Brazil* 125 C6
Tombé, *Sudan* 77 F3
Tombigbee →, *U.S.A.* 105 K2
Tombouctou, *Mali* 78 B4
Tombstone, *U.S.A.* 111 L8
Tombua, *Angola* 84 B1
Tomé, *Chile* 126 D1
Tomé-Açu, *Brazil* 122 B2
Tomelilla, *Sweden* 11 J7
Tomelloso, *Spain* 29 F1
Tomingley, *Australia* 91 E4
Tomini, *Indonesia* 57 D6
Tomini, Teluk, *Indonesia* 57 E6
Tominian, *Mali* 78 C4
Tomiño, *Spain* 30 D2
Tomkinson Ras., *Australia* 89 E4
Tommot, *Russia* 45 D13
Tomnavoulin, *U.K.* 14 D5
Tomnop Ta Suos, *Cambodia* 59 G5
Tomo, *Colombia* 120 C4
Tomo →, *Colombia* 120 B4
Toms Place, *U.S.A.* 112 H8
Toms River, *U.S.A.* 107 G10
Tomsk, *Russia* 44 D9
Tonalá, *Mexico* 115 D6
Tonale, Passo del, *Italy* 32 B7
Tonalea, *U.S.A.* 111 H8
Tonantins, *Brazil* 120 D4
Tonasket, *U.S.A.* 110 B4
Tonate, *Fr. Guiana* 121 C7
Tonawanda, *U.S.A.* 106 D6
Tonbridge, *U.K.* 13 F8
Tondano, *Indonesia* 57 D6
Tondela, *Portugal* 30 E2
Tønder, *Denmark* 11 K2
Tondi Kiwindi, *Niger* 79 C5
Tondibi, *Mali* 79 B4
Tonekābon, *Iran* 65 B6
Tong Xian, *China* 50 E9
Tonga ■, *Pac. Oc.* 87 D11
Tonga Trench, *Pac. Oc.* 92 J10
Tongaat, *S. Africa* 85 D5
Tong'an, *China* 53 E12
Tongareva, *Cook Is.* 93 H12
Tongatapu, *Tonga* 87 E11
Tongbai, *China* 53 A9
Tongcheng, *Anhui, China* 53 B11
Tongcheng, *Hubei, China* 53 C9
Tongchŏn-ni, *N. Korea* 51 E14
Tongchuan, *China* 50 G5
Tongdao, *China* 52 D7
Tongeren, *Belgium* 17 G6
Tonggu, *China* 53 C10
Tongguan, *China* 50 G6
Tonghai, *China* 52 E4
Tonghua, *China* 51 D13
Tongjiang, *Heilongjiang, China* 54 B8
Tongjiang, *Sichuan, China* 52 B6
Tongjosŏn Man, *N. Korea* 51 E14
Tongking, G. of = Tonkin, G. of, *Asia* 58 B7
Tongliang, *China* 52 C6
Tongliao, *China* 51 C12
Tongling, *China* 53 B11
Tonglu, *China* 53 C12

Tongnae, *S. Korea* 51 G15
Tongnan, *China* 52 B5
Tongobory, *Madag.* 85 C7
Tongoy, *Chile* 126 C1
Tongren, *China* 52 D7
Tongres = Tongeren, *Belgium* 17 G6
Tongsa Dzong, *Bhutan* 61 F17
Tongue, *U.K.* 14 C4
Tongue →, *U.S.A.* 108 B2
Tongwei, *China* 50 G3
Tongxin, *China* 50 F3
Tongyang, *N. Korea* 51 E14
Tongyu, *China* 51 B12
Tongzi, *China* 52 C6
Tonj, *Sudan* 77 F2
Tonk, *India* 62 F6
Tonkawa, *U.S.A.* 109 G6
Tonkin = Bac Phan, *Vietnam* 58 B5
Tonkin, G. of, *Asia* 58 B7
Tonlé Sap, *Cambodia* 58 F4
Tonnay-Charente, *France* 26 C3
Tonneins, *France* 26 D4
Tonnerre, *France* 25 E10
Tönning, *Germany* 18 A4
Tono, *Japan* 48 E10
Tonopah, *U.S.A.* 111 G5
Tonosí, *Panama* 116 E3
Tønsberg, *Norway* 10 E4
Tooele, *U.S.A.* 110 F7
Toompine, *Australia* 91 D3
Toonpan, *Australia* 90 B4
Toora, *Australia* 91 F4
Toora-Khem, *Russia* 45 D10
Toowoomba, *Australia* 91 D5
Topalu, *Romania* 38 E11
Topaz, *U.S.A.* 112 G7
Topeka, *U.S.A.* 108 F7
Topki, *Russia* 44 D9
Topl'a →, *Slovak Rep.* 20 G11
Topley, *Canada* 100 C3
Toplica →, *Serbia* 21 M11
Toplița, *Romania* 38 C8
Topocalma, Pta., *Chile* 126 C1
Topock, *U.S.A.* 113 L12
Topola, *Serbia* 21 L10
Topoľčany, *Slovak Rep.* 20 G8
Topoli, *Kazakhstan* 43 C14
Topolnitsa →, *Bulgaria* 38 G7
Topolobampo, *Mexico* 114 B3
Topolovgrad, *Bulgaria* 38 G9
Toppenish, *U.S.A.* 110 C3
Topusko, *Croatia* 33 C12
Toquepala, *Peru* 124 D3
Torá, *Spain* 28 D6
Tora Kit, *Sudan* 77 E3
Toraka Vestale, *Madag.* 85 B7
Torata, *Peru* 124 D3
Torbalı, *Turkey* 66 D2
Torbay, *Canada* 99 C9
Torbay, *U.K.* 13 G4
Tørdal, *Norway* 10 E2
Tordesillas, *Spain* 30 D6
Tordoya, *Spain* 30 B2
Töreboda, *Sweden* 11 F8
Torfajökull, *Iceland* 8 E4
Torgau, *Germany* 18 D8
Torgelow, *Germany* 18 B9
Torhout, *Belgium* 17 F2
Tori, *Ethiopia* 77 F3
Tori-Shima, *Japan* 49 J10
Torigni-sur-Vire, *France* 24 C6
Torija, *Spain* 28 E1
Torin, *Mexico* 114 B2
Toriñana, C., *Spain* 30 B1
Torino, *Italy* 32 C4
Torit, *Sudan* 77 G3
Torkovichi, *Russia* 40 B7
Tormes →, *Spain* 30 D4
Tornado Mt., *Canada* 100 D6
Torne älv →, *Sweden* 8 D18
Torneå = Tornio, *Finland* 8 D18
Torneträsk, *Sweden* 8 B15
Tornio, *Finland* 8 D18
Tornionjoki →, *Finland* 8 D18
Tornquist, *Argentina* 126 D3
Toro, *Baleares, Spain* 36 B11
Toro, *Zamora, Spain* 30 D5
Torö, *Sweden* 11 F11
Toro, Cerro del, *Chile* 126 B2
Toro Pk., *U.S.A.* 113 M10
Törökszentmiklós, *Hungary* 21 H10
Toronios Kólpos, *Greece* 39 J6
Toronto, *Australia* 91 E5
Toronto, *Canada* 98 D4
Toronto, *U.S.A.* 106 F4
Toropets, *Russia* 40 C7
Tororo, *Uganda* 82 B3
Toros Dağları, *Turkey* 66 E5
Torotoro, *Bolivia* 125 D4
Torpshammar, *Sweden* 10 B10
Torquay, *Canada* 101 D8
Torquay, *U.K.* 13 G4
Torquemada, *Spain* 30 C6
Torralba de Calatrava, *Spain* 31 F7
Torrance, *U.S.A.* 113 M8
Torrão, *Portugal* 31 G2
Torre Annunziata, *Italy* 35 B7
Tôrre de Moncorvo, *Portugal* 30 D3
Torre del Greco, *Italy* 35 B7
Torre del Mar, *Spain* 31 J6
Torre-Pacheco, *Spain* 29 H4
Torre Pellice, *Italy* 32 D4
Torreblanca, *Spain* 28 E5
Torrecampo, *Spain* 31 G6
Torrecilla en Cameros, *Spain* 28 C2
Torredembarra, *Spain* 28 D6
Torredonjimeno, *Spain* 31 H7
Torrejoncillo, *Spain* 30 F4
Torrelaguna, *Spain* 28 E1
Torrelavega, *Spain* 30 B6
Torremaggiore, *Italy* 35 A8
Torremolinos, *Spain* 31 J6
Torrens, L., *Australia* 91 E2
Torrens Cr. →, *Australia* 90 C4
Torrens Creek, *Australia* 90 C4
Torrente, *Spain* 29 F4
Torrenueva, *Spain* 29 G1
Torreón, *Mexico* 114 B4
Torreperogil, *Spain* 29 G1
Torres, *Mexico* 114 B2
Torres Novas, *Portugal* 31 F2
Torres Strait, *Australia* 92 H6
Torres Vedras, *Portugal* 31 F1
Torrevieja, *Spain* 29 H4
Torrey, *U.S.A.* 111 G8
Torridge →, *U.K.* 13 G3
Torridon, L., *U.K.* 14 D3
Torrijos, *Spain* 30 F6
Torrington, *Conn., U.S.A.* 107 E11
Torrington, *Wyo., U.S.A.* 108 D2
Torroella de Montgri, *Spain* 28 C8
Torrox, *Spain* 31 J7
Torsö, *Sweden* 11 F7
Tortola, *Virgin Is.* 117 C7
Tórtoles de Esgueva, *Spain* 30 D6
Tortona, *Italy* 32 D5
Tortoreto, *Italy* 33 F10
Tortorici, *Italy* 35 D7
Tortosa, *Spain* 28 E5
Tortosa, C., *Spain* 28 E5
Tortosendo, *Portugal* 30 E3
Tortue, I. de la, *Haiti* 117 B5
Tortum, *Turkey* 67 C9
Ţorūd, *Iran* 65 C7
Torul, *Turkey* 67 C8
Toruń, *Poland* 20 B8
Torup, *Denmark* 11 G3
Torup, *Sweden* 11 H7
Tory I., *Ireland* 15 A3
Torysa →, *Slovak Rep.* 20 G11
Torzhok, *Russia* 40 C9
Tosa, *Japan* 49 H6
Tosa-Shimizu, *Japan* 49 H6
Tosa-Wan, *Japan* 49 H6
Toscana, *Italy* 32 E8
Toscano, Arcipelago, *Italy* 32 F7
Toshkent = Tashkent, *Uzbekistan* 44 E7
Tosno, *Russia* 40 B7
Tossa, *Spain* 28 D7
Tostado, *Argentina* 126 B3
Tostedt, *Germany* 18 B5
Tostón, Pta. de, *Canary Is.* 36 F5
Tosu, *Japan* 49 H5
Tosya, *Turkey* 66 C6
Totana, *Spain* 29 H3
Toten, *Norway* 10 D4
Toteng, *Botswana* 84 C3
Tôtes, *France* 24 C8
Tótkomlós, *Hungary* 21 J10
Totma, *Russia* 41 B13
Totnes, *U.K.* 13 G4
Totness, *Surinam* 121 B6
Totonicapán, *Guatemala* 116 D1
Totora, *Bolivia* 125 D4
Totten Glacier, *Antarctica* 5 C8
Tottenham, *Australia* 91 E4
Tottenham, *Canada* 106 B5
Tottori, *Japan* 49 G7
Tottori □, *Japan* 49 G7
Touat, *Algeria* 75 C5
Touba, *Ivory C.* 78 D3
Toubkal, Djebel, *Morocco* 74 B3
Toucy, *France* 25 E10
Tougan, *Burkina Faso* 78 C4
Touggourt, *Algeria* 75 B6
Tougué, *Guinea* 78 C2
Toukmatine, *Algeria* 75 D6
Toul, *France* 25 D12
Toulepleu, *Ivory C.* 78 D3
Toulon, *France* 27 E9
Toulouse, *France* 26 E5
Toummo, *Niger* 73 D7
Toumodi, *Ivory C.* 78 D3
Tounassine, Hamada, *Algeria* 74 C3
Toungoo, *Burma* 61 K20
Touques →, *France* 24 C7
Touraine, *France* 24 E7
Tourane = Da Nang, *Vietnam* 58 D7
Tourcoing, *France* 25 B10
Tourine, *Mauritania* 74 D2
Tournai, *Belgium* 17 G2
Tournan-en-Brie, *France* 25 D9
Tournay, *France* 26 E4
Tournon, *France* 27 C8
Tournon-St.-Martin, *France* 24 F7
Tournus, *France* 27 B8
Touros, *Brazil* 122 C4
Tours, *France* 24 E7
Touwsrivier, *S. Africa* 84 E3
Tovar, *Venezuela* 120 B3
Tovarkovskiy, *Russia* 41 E11
Tovdal, *Norway* 11 F2
Tovdalselva →, *Norway* 11 F2
Towada, *Japan* 48 D10
Towada-Ko, *Japan* 48 D10
Towamba, *Australia* 91 F4
Towanda, *U.S.A.* 107 E8
Towang, *India* 61 F17
Tower, *U.S.A.* 108 B8
Towerhill Cr. →, *Australia* 90 C3
Towner, *U.S.A.* 108 A4
Townsend, *U.S.A.* 110 C8
Townshend I., *Australia* 90 C5
Townsville, *Australia* 90 B4
Towson, *U.S.A.* 104 F7
Toya-Ko, *Japan* 48 C10
Toyah, *U.S.A.* 109 K3
Toyahvale, *U.S.A.* 109 K3
Toyama, *Japan* 49 F8
Toyama □, *Japan* 49 F8
Toyama-Wan, *Japan* 49 F8
Toyohashi, *Japan* 49 G8
Toyokawa, *Japan* 49 G8
Toyonaka, *Japan* 49 G7
Toyooka, *Japan* 49 G7
Toyota, *Japan* 49 G8
Tozeur, *Tunisia* 75 B6
Tra On, *Vietnam* 59 H5
Trabancos →, *Spain* 30 D5
Traben Trarbach, *Germany* 19 F3
Trabzon, *Turkey* 42 F8
Trabzon □, *Turkey* 67 C8
Tracadie, *Canada* 99 C7
Tracy, *Calif., U.S.A.* 111 H3
Tracy, *Minn., U.S.A.* 108 C7
Tradate, *Italy* 32 C5
Tradovoye, *Russia* 48 C6
Trafalgar, C., *Spain* 31 J4
Traiguén, *Chile* 128 A2
Trail, *Canada* 100 D5
Trainor L., *Canada* 100 A4
Traíra →, *Brazil* 120 D4
Trákhonas, *Cyprus* 37 D12
Tralee, *Ireland* 15 D2
Tralee B., *Ireland* 15 D2
Tramelan, *Switz.* 22 B4
Tramore, *Ireland* 15 D4
Tran Ninh, Cao Nguyen, *Laos* 58 C4
Tranås, *Sweden* 9 G13
Trancas, *Argentina* 126 B2
Trancoso, *Portugal* 30 E3
Tranebjerg, *Denmark* 11 J4
Tranemo, *Sweden* 11 G7
Trang, *Thailand* 59 J2
Trangahy, *Madag.* 85 B7
Trangan, *Indonesia* 57 F8
Trangie, *Australia* 91 E4
Trångsviken, *Sweden* 10 A8
Trani, *Italy* 35 A9
Tranoroa, *Madag.* 85 C8
Tranqueras, *Uruguay* 127 C4
Trans Nzoia □, *Kenya* 82 B3
Transantarctic Mts., *Antarctica* 5 E12
Transcaucasia = Zakavkazye, *Asia* 43 F11
Transcona, *Canada* 101 D9
Transilvania, *Romania* 38 D8
Transkei □, *S. Africa* 85 E4
Transvaal □, *S. Africa* 84 D4
Transylvania = Transilvania, *Romania* 38 D8
Transylvanian Alps, *Romania* 6 F10
Trápani, *Italy* 34 D5
Trapper Pk., *U.S.A.* 110 D6
Traralgon, *Australia* 91 F4
Trarza, *Mauritania* 78 B2
Trasacco, *Italy* 33 G10
Trăscău, Munții, *Romania* 38 C6
Trasimeno, L., *Italy* 33 E9
Trat, *Thailand* 59 F4
Traun, *Austria* 21 G4
Traunstein, *Germany* 19 H8
Trâvad, *Sweden* 11 F7
Traveller's L., *Australia* 91 E3
Travemünde, *Germany* 18 B6
Travers, Mt., *N.Z.* 87 K4
Traverse City, *U.S.A.* 104 C3
Travnik, *Bos.-H.* 21 L7
Trayning, *Australia* 89 F2
Trazo, *Spain* 30 B2
Trbovlje, *Slovenia* 33 B12
Trébbia →, *Italy* 32 C6
Trebel →, *Germany* 18 B9
Trebinje, *Bos.-H.* 21 N8
Trebisacce, *Italy* 35 C9
Trebišnica →, *Bos.-H.* 21 N8
Trebišov, *Slovak Rep.* 20 G11
Trebižat →, *Bos.-H.* 21 M7
Trebnje, *Slovenia* 33 C12
Třeboň, *Czech.* 20 G4
Trebujena, *Spain* 31 J4
Trecate, *Italy* 32 C5
Trece Martires, *Phil.* 55 D4
Tredegar, *U.K.* 13 F4
Tregaron, *U.K.* 13 E4
Trégastel-Plage, *France* 24 D3
Tregnago, *Italy* 33 C8
Tregrosse Is., *Australia* 90 B5
Tréguier, *France* 24 D3
Trégunc, *France* 24 E3
Treherne, *Canada* 101 D9
Tréia, *Italy* 33 E10
Treignac, *France* 26 C5
Treinta y Tres, *Uruguay* 127 C5
Treis, *Germany* 19 E3
Trekveld, *S. Africa* 84 E2
Trelde Næs, *Denmark* 11 J3
Trelew, *Argentina* 128 B3
Trélissac, *France* 26 C4
Trelleborg, *Sweden* 11 J7
Trélon, *France* 25 B11
Tremiti, *Italy* 33 F12
Tremonton, *U.S.A.* 110 F7
Tremp, *Spain* 28 C5
Trenche →, *Canada* 98 C5
Trenčín, *Slovak Rep.* 20 G8
Trenggalek, *Indonesia* 57 H14
Trenque Lauquen, *Argentina* 126 D3
Trent →, *U.K.* 12 D7
Trentino-Alto Adige □, *Italy* 32 B8
Trento, *Italy* 32 B8
Trenton, *Canada* 98 D4
Trenton, *Mo., U.S.A.* 108 E8
Trenton, *N.J., U.S.A.* 107 F10
Trenton, *Nebr., U.S.A.* 108 E4
Trenton, *Tenn., U.S.A.* 109 H10
Trepassey, *Canada* 99 C9
Trepuzzi, *Italy* 35 B11
Tres Arroyos, *Argentina* 126 D3
Três Corações, *Brazil* 123 F2
Três Lagoas, *Brazil* 123 F1
Tres Lagos →, *Argentina* 128 C2
Tres Marías, *Mexico* 114 C3
Três Marias, Reprêsa, *Brazil* 123 E2
Tres Montes, C., *Chile* 128 C1
Tres Pinos, *U.S.A.* 112 J5
Três Pontas, *Brazil* 123 F2
Tres Puentes, *Chile* 126 B1
Tres Puntas, C., *Argentina* 128 C3
Três Rios, *Brazil* 123 F3
Tres Valles, *Mexico* 115 D5
Treska →, *Macedonia* 39 H4
Trespaderne, *Spain* 28 C1
Trets, *France* 27 E9
Treuchtlingen, *Germany* 19 G6
Treuenbrietzen, *Germany* 18 C8
Treungen, *Norway* 9 G10
Treviglio, *Italy* 32 C6
Trevinca, Peña, *Spain* 30 C4
Treviso, *Italy* 33 C9
Trévoux, *France* 27 C8
Treysa, *Germany* 18 E5
Trgovište, *Serbia* 21 N12
Triabunna, *Australia* 90 G4
Triánda, *Greece* 37 C10
Triang, *Malaysia* 59 L4
Triaucourt-en-Argonne, *France* 25 D12
Tribsees, *Germany* 18 A8
Tribulation, C., *Australia* 90 B4
Tribune, *U.S.A.* 108 F4
Tricárico, *Italy* 35 B9
Tricase, *Italy* 35 C11
Trichinopoly = Tiruchchirappalli, *India* 60 P11
Trichur, *India* 60 P10
Trida, *Australia* 91 E4
Trier, *Germany* 19 F2
Trieste, *Italy* 33 C10
Trieste, G. di, *Italy* 33 C10
Trieux →, *France* 24 D3
Triggiano, *Italy* 35 A9
Triglav, *Slovenia* 33 B10
Trigno →, *Italy* 33 F11
Trigueros, *Spain* 31 H4
Trikhonis, Límni, *Greece* 39 L4
Tríkkala, *Greece* 39 K4
Trikomo, *Cyprus* 37 D12
Trikora, Puncak, *Indonesia* 57 E9
Trilj, *Croatia* 33 E13
Trillo, *Spain* 28 E2
Trim, *Ireland* 15 C5
Trincomalee, *Sri Lanka* 60 Q12
Trindade, *Brazil* 123 E2
Trindade, I., *Atl. Oc.* 2 F8
Trinidad, *Bolivia* 125 C5
Trinidad, *Colombia* 120 B3
Trinidad, *Cuba* 116 B3
Trinidad, *Uruguay* 126 C4
Trinidad, *U.S.A.* 109 G2
Trinidad, *W. Indies* 117 D7
Trinidad →, *Mexico* 115 D5
Trinidad, G., *Chile* 128 C1
Trinidad, I., *Argentina* 128 A4
Trinidad & Tobago ■, *W. Indies* 117 D7
Trinitápoli, *Italy* 35 A9
Trinity, *Canada* 99 C9
Trinity, *U.S.A.* 109 K7
Trinity →, *Calif., U.S.A.* 110 F2
Trinity →, *Tex., U.S.A.* 109 L7
Trinity B., *Canada* 99 C9
Trinity Range, *U.S.A.* 110 F4
Trinkitat, *Sudan* 76 D4
Trino, *Italy* 32 C5
Trion, *U.S.A.* 105 H3
Trionto, C., *Italy* 35 C9
Triora, *Italy* 32 E4
Tripoli = Tarābulus, *Lebanon* 69 A4
Tripoli = Tarābulus, *Libya* 75 B7
Tripp, *U.S.A.* 108 D6
Tripura □, *India* 61 H17
Tripylos, *Cyprus* 37 E11
Trischen, *Germany* 18 A4
Tristan da Cunha, *Atl. Oc.* 2 F9
Trivandrum, *India* 60 Q10
Trivento, *Italy* 35 A7
Trnava, *Slovak Rep.* 21 G7
Trochu, *Canada* 100 C6
Trodely I., *Canada* 98 B4
Trogir, *Croatia* 33 E13
Troglav, *Croatia* 33 E13
Trøgstad, *Norway* 10 E5
Tróia, *Italy* 35 A8
Troilus, L., *Canada* 98 B5
Troina, *Italy* 35 E7
Trois Fourches, Cap des, *Morocco* 75 A4
Trois-Pistoles, *Canada* 99 C6
Trois-Rivières, *Canada* 98 C5
Troisvierges, *Belgium* 17 H8
Troitsk, *Russia* 44 D7
Troitsko Pechorsk, *Russia* 44 C6
Trölladyngja, *Iceland* 8 D5
Trollhättan, *Sweden* 11 F6
Trollheimen, *Norway* 10 B3
Trombetas →, *Brazil* 121 D6
Troms fylke □, *Norway* 8 B15
Tromsø, *Norway* 8 B15
Trona, *U.S.A.* 113 K9
Tronador, *Argentina* 128 B2
Trondheim, *Norway* 10 A4
Trondheimsfjorden, *Norway* 8 E11
Trönninge, *Sweden* 11 H6
Trönö, *Sweden* 10 C10
Tronto →, *Italy* 33 F10
Troodos, *Cyprus* 37 E11
Troon, *U.K.* 14 F4
Tropea, *Italy* 35 D8
Tropic, *U.S.A.* 111 H7
Tropoja, *Albania* 38 G3
Trossachs, The, *U.K.* 14 E4
Trostan, *U.K.* 15 A5
Trostberg, *Germany* 19 G8
Trostyanets, *Ukraine* 40 F9
Trotternish, *U.K.* 14 D2
Troup, *U.S.A.* 109 J7
Trout →, *Canada* 100 A5
Trout L., *N.W.T., Canada* 100 A4
Trout L., *Ont., Canada* 101 C10
Trout Lake, *Mich., U.S.A.* 98 C2
Trout Lake, *Wash., U.S.A.* 112 E5
Trout River, *Canada* 99 C8
Trouville-sur-Mer, *France* 24 C7
Trowbridge, *U.K.* 13 F5
Troy, *Turkey* 66 D2
Troy, *Ala., U.S.A.* 105 K3
Troy, *Idaho, U.S.A.* 110 C5
Troy, *Kans., U.S.A.* 108 F7
Troy, *Mo., U.S.A.* 108 F9
Troy, *Mont., U.S.A.* 110 B6
Troy, *N.Y., U.S.A.* 107 D11
Troy, *Ohio, U.S.A.* 104 E3
Troyan, *Bulgaria* 38 G7
Troyes, *France* 25 D11
Trpanj, *Croatia* 21 M7
Trstena, *Slovak Rep.* 20 F9
Trstenik, *Serbia* 21 M10
Trubchevsk, *Russia* 40 E8
Trucial States = United Arab Emirates ■, *Asia* 65 F7
Truckee, *U.S.A.* 112 F6
Trujillo, *Colombia* 120 C2
Trujillo, *Honduras* 116 C2
Trujillo, *Peru* 124 B2
Trujillo, *Spain* 31 F5
Trujillo, *U.S.A.* 109 H2
Trujillo, *Venezuela* 120 B3
Trujillo □, *Venezuela* 120 B3
Truk, *Pac. Oc.* 92 G7
Trumann, *U.S.A.* 109 H9
Trumbull, Mt., *U.S.A.* 111 H7
Trun, *France* 24 D7
Trun, *Switz.* 23 C7
Trundle, *Australia* 91 E4
Trung-Phan, *Vietnam* 58 E7
Truro, *Canada* 99 C7
Truro, *U.K.* 13 G2
Truslove, *Australia* 89 F3
Trustrup, *Denmark* 11 H4
Truth or Consequences, *U.S.A.* 111 K10
Trutnov, *Czech.* 20 E5
Truyère →, *France* 26 D6
Tryavna, *Bulgaria* 38 G8
Tryon, *U.S.A.* 105 H4
Tryonville, *U.S.A.* 106 E5
Trzcianka, *Poland* 20 B6
Trzebiatów, *Poland* 20 A5
Trzebiez, *Poland* 20 B4
Trzebinia-Siersza, *Poland* 20 E9
Trzebnica, *Poland* 20 D7
Tržič, *Slovenia* 33 B11
Tsageri, *Georgia* 43 E10
Tsaratanana, *Madag.* 85 B8
Tsaratanana, Mt. de, *Madag.* 85 A8
Tsarevo = Michurin, *Bulgaria* 38 G10
Tsarichanka, *Ukraine* 42 B6
Tsau, *Botswana* 84 C3
Tsebrikovo, *Ukraine* 42 C4
Tselinograd, *Kazakhstan* 44 D8
Tsetserleg, *Mongolia* 54 B5
Tshabong, *Botswana* 84 D3
Tshane, *Botswana* 84 C3
Tshela, *Zaïre* 80 E2
Tshesebe, *Botswana* 85 C4
Tshibeke, *Zaïre* 82 C2
Tshibinda, *Zaïre* 82 C2
Tshikapa, *Zaïre* 80 F4
Tshilenge, *Zaïre* 82 D1
Tshinsenda, *Zaïre* 83 E2
Tshofa, *Zaïre* 82 D2

Tshwane

Tshwane, *Botswana* 84 C3
Tsigara, *Botswana* 84 C4
Tsihombe, *Madag.* 85 D8
Tsimlyansk, *Russia* 43 C10
Tsimlyansk Res. = Tsimlyanskoye Vdkhr., *Russia* 43 B10
Tsimlyanskoye Vdkhr., *Russia* 43 B10
Tsinan = Jinan, *China* 50 F9
Tsineng, *S. Africa* 84 D3
Tsinghai = Qinghai □, *China* 54 C4
Tsingtao = Qingdao, *China* 51 F11
Tsinjomitondraka, *Madag.* 85 B8
Tsiroanomandidy, *Madag.* 85 B8
Tsivilsk, *Russia* 41 D15
Tsivory, *Madag.* 85 C8
Tskhinvali, *Georgia* 43 E11
Tsna →, *Russia* 41 D12
Tso Moriri, L., *India* 63 C8
Tsodilo Hill, *Botswana* 84 B3
Tsogttsetsiy, *Mongolia* 50 C3
Tsolo, *S. Africa* 85 E4
Tsomo, *S. Africa* 85 E4
Tsu, *Japan* 49 G8
Tsu L., *Canada* 100 A6
Tsuchiura, *Japan* 49 F10
Tsugaru-Kaikyō, *Japan* 48 D10
Tsumeb, *Namibia* 84 B2
Tsumis, *Namibia* 84 C2
Tsuruga, *Japan* 49 G8
Tsurugi-San, *Japan* 49 H7
Tsuruoka, *Japan* 48 E9
Tsushima, *Gifu, Japan* 49 G8
Tsushima, *Nagasaki, Japan* 49 G4
Tsvetkovo, *Ukraine* 42 B4
Tua →, *Portugal* 30 D3
Tual, *Indonesia* 57 F8
Tuam, *Ireland* 15 C3
Tuamotu Arch. = Tuamotu Is., *Pac. Oc.* 93 J13
Tuamotu Is., *Pac. Oc.* 93 J13
Tuamotu Ridge, *Pac. Oc.* 93 K14
Tuanfeng, *China* 53 B10
Tuanxi, *China* 52 D6
Tuao, *Phil.* 55 C4
Tuapse, *Russia* 43 D8
Tuatapere, *N.Z.* 87 M1
Tuba City, *U.S.A.* 111 H8
Tuban, *Indonesia* 57 G15
Tubarão, *Brazil* 127 B6
Tūbās, *Jordan* 69 C4
Tubau, *Malaysia* 56 D4
Tubbergen, *Neths.* 16 D9
Tübingen, *Germany* 19 G5
Tubize, *Belgium* 17 G4
Tubruq, *Libya* 73 B9
Tubuai Is., *Pac. Oc.* 93 K12
Tuc Trung, *Vietnam* 59 G6
Tucacas, *Venezuela* 120 A4
Tucano, *Brazil* 122 D4
Tuchang, *Taiwan* 53 E13
Tuchodi →, *Canada* 100 B4
Tuchola, *Poland* 20 B7
Tucson, *U.S.A.* 111 K8
Tucumán □, *Argentina* 126 B2
Tucumcari, *U.S.A.* 109 H3
Tucunaré, *Brazil* 125 B6
Tucupido, *Venezuela* 120 B4
Tucupita, *Venezuela* 121 B5
Tucuruí, *Brazil* 122 B2
Tudela, *Spain* 28 C3
Tudela de Duero, *Spain* 30 D6
Tudmur, *Syria* 64 C3
Tudor, L., *Canada* 99 A6
Tudora, *Romania* 38 B9
Tuella →, *Portugal* 30 D3
Tuen, *Australia* 91 D4
Tueré →, *Brazil* 122 B1
Tugela →, *S. Africa* 85 D5
Tuguegarao, *Phil.* 55 C4
Tugur, *Russia* 45 D14
Tuineje, *Canary Is.* 36 F5
Tukangbesi, Kepulauan, *Indonesia* 57 F6
Tukarak I., *Canada* 98 A4
Tukayyid, *Iraq* 64 D5
Tûkh, *Egypt* 76 H7
Tukobo, *Ghana* 78 D4
Tūkrah, *Libya* 73 B9
Tuktoyaktuk, *Canada* 96 B6
Tukums, *Latvia* 40 C3
Tukuyu, *Tanzania* 83 D3
Tula, *Hidalgo, Mexico* 115 C5
Tula, *Tamaulipas, Mexico* 115 C5
Tula, *Nigeria* 79 D7
Tula, *Russia* 41 D10
Tulancingo, *Mexico* 115 C5
Tulare, *U.S.A.* 111 H4
Tulare Lake Bed, *U.S.A.* 111 J4
Tularosa, *U.S.A.* 111 K10
Tulbagh, *S. Africa* 84 E2
Tulcán, *Ecuador* 120 C2
Tulcea, *Romania* 38 D11
Tulchin, *Ukraine* 42 B3
Tūleh, *Iran* 65 C7
Tulemalu L., *Canada* 101 A9
Tuli, *Indonesia* 57 E6
Tuli, *Zimbabwe* 83 G2
Tulia, *U.S.A.* 109 H4
Ţūlkarm, *Jordan* 69 C4
Tullahoma, *U.S.A.* 105 H2
Tullamore, *Australia* 91 E4
Tullamore, *Ireland* 15 C4
Tulle, *France* 26 C5
Tullibigeal, *Australia* 91 E4
Tullins, *France* 27 C9
Tulln, *Austria* 21 G6
Tullow, *Ireland* 15 D4
Tullus, *Sudan* 77 E1
Tully, *Australia* 90 B4
Ţulmaythah, *Libya* 73 B9
Tulmur, *Australia* 90 C3
Tulnici, *Romania* 38 D9
Tulovo, *Bulgaria* 38 G8
Tulsa, *U.S.A.* 109 G7
Tulsequah, *Canada* 100 B2
Tulu Milki, *Ethiopia* 77 F4
Tulu Welel, *Ethiopia* 77 F3
Tulua, *Colombia* 120 C2
Tulun, *Russia* 45 D11
Tulungagung, *Indonesia* 56 F4
Tum, *Indonesia* 57 E8
Tuma, *Russia* 41 D12
Tuma →, *Nic.* 116 D3
Tumaco, *Colombia* 120 C2
Tumaco, Ensenada, *Colombia* 120 C2
Tumatumari, *Guyana* 121 B6
Tumba, *Sweden* 10 E11
Tumba, L., *Zaïre* 80 E3
Tumbarumba, *Australia* 91 F4
Tumbaya, *Argentina* 126 A2
Túmbes, *Peru* 124 A1
Tumbes □, *Peru* 124 A1
Tumbwe, *Zaïre* 83 E2
Tumby Bay, *Australia* 91 E2
Tumd Youqi, *China* 50 D6
Tumen, *China* 51 C15
Tumen Jiang →, *China* 51 C16
Tumeremo, *Venezuela* 121 B5
Tumiritinga, *Brazil* 123 E3
Tumkur, *India* 60 N10
Tummel, L., *U.K.* 14 E5
Tump, *Pakistan* 60 F3
Tumpat, *Malaysia* 59 J4
Tumu, *Ghana* 78 C4
Tumucumaque, Serra, *Brazil* 121 C7
Tumupasa, *Bolivia* 124 C4
Tumut, *Australia* 91 F4
Tumwater, *U.S.A.* 110 C2
Tunas de Zaza, *Cuba* 116 B4
Tunbridge Wells, *U.K.* 13 F8
Tunceli, *Turkey* 67 D8
Tunceli □, *Turkey* 67 D8
Tuncurry, *Australia* 91 E5
Tunduru, *Tanzania* 83 E4
Tunduru □, *Tanzania* 83 E4
Tundzha →, *Bulgaria* 39 H9
Tunga Pass, *India* 61 E19
Tungabhadra →, *India* 60 M11
Tungaru, *Sudan* 77 E3
Tungla, *Nic.* 116 D3
Tungnafellsjökull, *Iceland* 8 D5
Tungsten, *Canada* 100 A3
Tungurahua □, *Ecuador* 120 D2
Tunguska, Nizhnyaya →, *Russia* 45 C9
Tunia, *Colombia* 120 C2
Tunica, *U.S.A.* 109 H9
Tunis, *Tunisia* 75 A7
Tunis, Golfe de, *Tunisia* 75 A7
Tunisia ■, *Africa* 75 B6
Tunja, *Colombia* 120 B3
Tunkhannock, *U.S.A.* 107 E9
Tunliu, *China* 50 F7
Tunnsjøen, *Norway* 8 D12
Tunungayualok I., *Canada* 99 A7
Tunuyán, *Argentina* 126 C2
Tunuyán →, *Argentina* 126 C2
Tunxi, *China* 53 C12
Tuo Jiang →, *China* 52 C5
Tuolumne, *U.S.A.* 111 H3
Tuolumne →, *U.S.A.* 112 H5
Tuoy-Khaya, *Russia* 45 C12
Tūp Āghāj, *Iran* 64 B5
Tupã, *Brazil* 127 A5
Tupaciguara, *Brazil* 123 E2
Tupelo, *U.S.A.* 105 H1
Tupik, *Russia* 40 D8
Tupik, *Russia* 45 D12
Tupinambaranas, *Brazil* 121 D6
Tupirama, *Brazil* 122 C2
Tupiratins, *Brazil* 122 C2
Tupiza, *Bolivia* 126 A2
Tupman, *U.S.A.* 113 K7
Tupper, *Canada* 100 B4
Tupper Lake, *U.S.A.* 107 B10
Tupungato, Cerro, *S. Amer.* 126 C2
Tuquan, *China* 51 B11
Túquerres, *Colombia* 120 C2
Tura, *Russia* 45 C11
Turabah, *Si. Arabia* 64 D4
Turagua, Serranía, *Venezuela* 121 B5
Tūrān, *Iran* 65 C8
Turan, *Russia* 45 D10
Turayf, *Si. Arabia* 64 D3
Turbenthal, *Switz.* 23 B7
Turégano, *Spain* 30 D6
Turek, *Poland* 20 C8
Turen, *Venezuela* 120 B4
Turfan = Turpan, *China* 54 B3
Turfan Depression = Turpan Hami, *China* 54 B3
Tŭrgovishte, *Bulgaria* 38 F9
Turgutlu, *Turkey* 66 D2
Turhal, *Turkey* 42 F7
Turia →, *Spain* 29 F4
Turiaçu, *Brazil* 122 B2
Turiaçu →, *Brazil* 122 B2
Turin = Torino, *Italy* 32 C4
Turin, *Canada* 100 D6
Turka, *Ukraine* 40 G3
Turkana □, *Kenya* 82 B4
Turkana, L., *Africa* 82 B4
Turkestan, *Kazakhstan* 44 E7
Túrkeve, *Hungary* 21 H10
Turkey ■, *Eurasia* 66 D7
Turkey Creek, *Australia* 88 C4
Turki, *Russia* 41 F13
Turkmenistan ■, *Asia* 44 F6
Türkoğlu, *Turkey* 66 E7
Turks & Caicos Is. ■, *W. Indies* 117 B5
Turks Island Passage, *W. Indies* 117 B5
Turku, *Finland* 9 F17
Turkwe →, *Kenya* 82 B4
Turlock, *U.S.A.* 111 H3
Turnagain →, *Canada* 100 B3
Turnagain, C., *N.Z.* 87 J6
Turneffe Is., *Belize* 115 D7
Turner, *Australia* 88 C4
Turner, *U.S.A.* 110 B9
Turner Pt., *Australia* 90 A1
Turner Valley, *Canada* 100 C6
Turners Falls, *U.S.A.* 107 D12
Turnhout, *Belgium* 17 F5
Turnor L., *Canada* 101 B7
Tŭrnovo, *Bulgaria* 38 F8
Turnu Măgurele, *Romania* 38 F7
Turnu Rosu Pasul, *Romania* 38 D7
Turon, *U.S.A.* 109 G5
Turpan, *China* 54 B3
Turpan Hami, *China* 54 B3
Turriff, *U.K.* 14 D6
Tursāq, *Iraq* 64 C5
Tursha, *Russia* 41 C15
Tursi, *Italy* 35 B9
Turtle Head I., *Australia* 90 A3
Turtle L., *Canada* 101 C7
Turtle Lake, *N. Dak., U.S.A.* 108 B4
Turtle Lake, *Wis., U.S.A.* 108 C8
Turtleford, *Canada* 101 C7
Turukhansk, *Russia* 45 C9
Turun ja Porin lääni □, *Finland* 9 F17
Turzovka, *Slovak Rep.* 20 F8
Tuscaloosa, *U.S.A.* 105 J2
Tuscánia, *Italy* 33 F8
Tuscany = Toscana, *Italy* 32 E8
Tuscola, *Ill., U.S.A.* 104 F1
Tuscola, *Tex., U.S.A.* 109 J5
Tuscumbia, *U.S.A.* 105 H2
Tuskar Rock, *Ireland* 15 D5
Tuskegee, *U.S.A.* 105 J3
Tustna, *Norway* 10 A2
Tutak, *Turkey* 67 D10
Tutayev, *Russia* 41 C11
Tuticorin, *India* 60 Q11
Tutin, *Serbia* 21 N10
Tutóia, *Brazil* 122 B3
Tutong, *Brunei* 56 D4
Tutova →, *Romania* 38 C10
Tutrakan, *Bulgaria* 38 E9
Tutshi L., *Canada* 100 B2
Tuttle, *U.S.A.* 108 B5
Tuttlingen, *Germany* 19 H4
Tutuala, *Indonesia* 57 F7
Tutuila, *Amer. Samoa* 87 B13
Tututepec, *Mexico* 115 D5
Tuva Republic □, *Russia* 45 D10
Tuvalu ■, *Pac. Oc.* 92 H9
Tuxpan, *Mexico* 115 C5
Tuxtla Gutiérrez, *Mexico* 115 D6
Tuy, *Spain* 30 C2
Tuy An, *Vietnam* 58 F7
Tuy Duc, *Vietnam* 59 F6
Tuy Hoa, *Vietnam* 58 F7
Tuy Phong, *Vietnam* 59 G7
Tuya L., *Canada* 100 B2
Tuyen Hoa, *Vietnam* 58 D6
Tuyen Quang, *Vietnam* 58 B5
Tūysarkān, *Iran* 65 C6
Tuz Gölü, *Turkey* 66 D5
Ţūz Khurmātū, *Iraq* 64 C5
Tuzla, *Bos.-H.* 21 L8
Tuzla Gölü, *Turkey* 66 D6
Tuzlov →, *Russia* 43 C8
Tvååker, *Sweden* 11 G6
Tvedestrand, *Norway* 11 F2
Tver, *Russia* 41 C9
Tvŭrditsa, *Bulgaria* 38 G8
Twain, *U.S.A.* 112 E5
Twain Harte, *U.S.A.* 112 G6
Tweed, *Canada* 106 B7
Tweed →, *U.K.* 14 F7
Tweed Heads, *Australia* 91 D5
Tweedsmuir Prov. Park, *Canada* 100 C3
Twello, *Neths.* 16 D8
Twentynine Palms, *U.S.A.* 113 L10
Twillingate, *Canada* 99 C9
Twin Bridges, *U.S.A.* 110 D7
Twin Falls, *U.S.A.* 110 E6
Twin Valley, *U.S.A.* 108 B6
Twisp, *U.S.A.* 110 B3
Twistringen, *Germany* 18 C4
Two Harbors, *U.S.A.* 108 B9
Two Hills, *Canada* 100 C6
Two Rivers, *U.S.A.* 104 C2
Twofold B., *Australia* 91 F4
Tychy, *Poland* 20 E8
Tykocin, *Poland* 20 B12
Tyldal, *Norway* 10 B4
Tyler, *U.S.A.* 103 D7
Tyler, *Minn., U.S.A.* 108 C6
Tyler, *Tex., U.S.A.* 109 J7
Týn nad Vltavou, *Czech.* 20 F4
Tynda, *Russia* 45 D13
Tyne →, *U.K.* 12 C6
Tyne & Wear □, *U.K.* 12 C6
Tynemouth, *U.K.* 12 B6
Tynset, *Norway* 10 B4
Tyre = Sūr, *Lebanon* 69 B4
Tyrifjorden, *Norway* 10 D4
Tyringe, *Sweden* 11 H7
Tyristrand, *Norway* 10 D4
Tyrnyauz, *Russia* 43 E10
Tyrone, *U.S.A.* 106 F6
Tyrrell →, *Australia* 91 F3
Tyrrell, L., *Australia* 91 F3
Tyrrell Arm, *Canada* 101 A9
Tyrrell L., *Canada* 101 A7
Tyrrhenian Sea, *Europe* 34 B5
Tysfjorden, *Norway* 8 B14
Tystberga, *Sweden* 11 F11
Tyub Karagan, Mys, *Kazakhstan* 43 D14
Tyuleniy, *Russia* 43 D12
Tyumen, *Russia* 44 D7
Tywi →, *U.K.* 13 F3
Tywyn, *U.K.* 13 E3
Tzaneen, *S. Africa* 85 C5
Tzermiádhes, *Greece* 37 D7
Tzermíadhes Neápolis, *Greece* 39 P8
Tzoumérka, Óros, *Greece* 39 K4
Tzukong = Zigong, *China* 52 C5
Tzummarum, *Neths.* 16 B7

U

U Taphao, *Thailand* 58 F3
U.S.A. = United States of America ■, *N. Amer.* 102 C7
Uachadi, Sierra, *Venezuela* 121 C4
Uainambi, *Colombia* 120 C4
Uanda, *Australia* 90 C3
Uarsciek, *Somali Rep.* 68 G4
Uasin □, *Kenya* 82 B4
Uato-Udo, *Indonesia* 57 F7
Uatumã →, *Brazil* 121 D6
Uauá, *Brazil* 122 C4
Uaupés, *Brazil* 120 D4
Uaupés →, *Brazil* 120 C4
Uaxactún, *Guatemala* 116 C2
Ubá, *Brazil* 123 F3
Ubaitaba, *Brazil* 123 D4
Ubangi = Oubangi →, *Zaïre* 80 E3
Ubaté, *Colombia* 120 B3
Ubauro, *Pakistan* 62 E3
Ubaye →, *France* 27 D10
Ube, *Japan* 49 H5
Ubeda, *Spain* 29 G1
Uberaba, *Brazil* 123 E2
Uberaba, L., *Brazil* 125 D6
Uberlândia, *Brazil* 123 E2
Überlingen, *Germany* 19 H5
Ubiaja, *Nigeria* 79 D6
Ubolratna Res., *Thailand* 58 D4
Ubombo, *S. Africa* 85 D5
Ubon Ratchathani, *Thailand* 58 E5
Ubondo, *Zaïre* 82 C2
Ubort →, *Belorussia* 40 E6
Ubrique, *Spain* 31 J5
Ubundu, *Zaïre* 82 C2
Ucayali →, *Peru* 124 A3
Uccle, *Belgium* 17 G4
Uchi Lake, *Canada* 101 C10
Uchiura-Wan, *Japan* 48 C10
Uchiza, *Peru* 124 B2
Uchte, *Germany* 18 C4
Uchur →, *Russia* 45 D14
Ucluelet, *Canada* 100 D3
Ucuriş, *Romania* 38 C4
Uda →, *Russia* 45 D14
Udaipur, *India* 62 G5
Udaipur Garhi, *Nepal* 63 F12
Udbina, *Croatia* 33 D12
Uddel, *Neths.* 16 D7
Uddevalla, *Sweden* 11 F5
Uddjaur, *Sweden* 8 D16
Uden, *Neths.* 17 E7
Udgir, *India* 60 K10
Udhampur, *India* 63 C6
Udi, *Nigeria* 79 D6
Údine, *Italy* 33 B10
Udmurt Republic □, *Russia* 44 D6
Udon Thani, *Thailand* 58 D4
Udupi, *India* 60 N9
Udvoy Balkan, *Bulgaria* 38 G9
Udzungwa Range, *Tanzania* 83 D4
Ueckermünde, *Germany* 18 B10
Ueda, *Japan* 49 F9
Uedineniya, Os., *Russia* 4 B12
Uele →, *Zaïre* 80 D4
Uelen, *Russia* 45 C19
Uelzen, *Germany* 18 C6
Uetendorf, *Switz.* 22 C5
Ufa, *Russia* 44 D6
Uffenheim, *Germany* 19 F6
Ugab →, *Namibia* 84 C1
Ugalla →, *Tanzania* 82 D3
Uganda ■, *Africa* 82 B3
Ugchelen, *Neths.* 16 D7
Ugento, *Italy* 35 C11
Ugep, *Nigeria* 79 D6
Ugie, *S. Africa* 85 E4
Ugijar, *Spain* 29 J1
Ugine, *France* 27 C10
Uglegorsk, *Russia* 45 E15
Uglich, *Russia* 41 C11
Ugljane, *Croatia* 33 E13
Ugolyak, *Russia* 45 C13
Ugra →, *Russia* 41 D10
Ugûn Mûsa, *Egypt* 69 F1
Ugûrchin, *Bulgaria* 38 F7
Uh →, *Slovak Rep.* 21 G11
Uherske Hradiště, *Czech.* 20 F7
Uhrichsville, *U.S.A.* 106 F3
Uíge, *Angola* 80 F2
Uijŏngbu, *S. Korea* 51 F14
Ŭiju, *N. Korea* 51 D13
Uinta Mts., *U.S.A.* 110 F8
Uitenhage, *S. Africa* 84 E4
Uitgeest, *Neths.* 16 C5
Uithoorn, *Neths.* 16 D5
Uithuizen, *Neths.* 16 B9
Uitkerke, *Belgium* 17 F2
Újfehértó, *Hungary* 21 H11
Ujhani, *India* 63 F8
Uji-guntō, *Japan* 49 J4
Ujjain, *India* 62 H6
Újpest, *Hungary* 21 H9
Újszász, *Hungary* 21 H10
Ujung Pandang, *Indonesia* 57 F5
Uka, *Russia* 45 D17
Ukara I., *Tanzania* 82 C3
Uke-Shima, *Japan* 49 K4
Ukerewe □, *Tanzania* 82 C3
Ukerewe I., *Tanzania* 82 C3
Ukholovo, *Russia* 41 E12
Ukhrul, *India* 61 G19
Ukhta, *Russia* 44 C6
Ukiah, *U.S.A.* 112 F3
Ukki Fort, *India* 63 C7
Ukmerge, *Lithuania* 40 D4
Ukraine ■, *Europe* 42 B4
Ukwi, *Botswana* 84 C3
Ulaanbaatar, *Mongolia* 45 E11
Ulaangom, *Mongolia* 54 A4
Ulamba, *Zaïre* 83 D1
Ulan Bator = Ulaanbaatar, *Mongolia* 45 E11
Ulan Ude, *Russia* 45 D11
Ulanga □, *Tanzania* 83 D4
Ulanów, *Poland* 20 E12
Ulaş, *Turkey* 66 D7
Ulaya, *Morogoro, Tanzania* 82 D4
Ulaya, *Tabora, Tanzania* 82 C3
Ulcinj, *Montenegro* 39 H2
Ulco, *S. Africa* 84 D3
Ulfborg, *Denmark* 11 H2
Ulft, *Neths.* 16 E8
Ulhasnagar, *India* 60 K8
Uljma, *Serbia* 21 K11
Ulla →, *Spain* 30 C2
Ulladulla, *Australia* 91 F5
Ullånger, *Sweden* 10 B12
Ullapool, *U.K.* 14 D3
Ullared, *Sweden* 11 G6
Ulldecona, *Spain* 28 E5
Ullswater, *U.K.* 12 C5
Ullung-do, *S. Korea* 51 F16
Ulm, *Germany* 19 G5
Ulmarra, *Australia* 91 D5
Ulmeni, *Romania* 38 D9
Ulonguè, *Mozam.* 83 E3
Ulricehamn, *Sweden* 9 H12
Ulrum, *Neths.* 16 B8
Ulsan, *S. Korea* 51 G15
Ulsberg, *Norway* 10 B3
Ulster □, *U.K.* 15 B5
Ulubaria, *India* 63 H13
Ulubat Gölü, *Turkey* 66 C3
Ulubey, *Turkey* 66 D3
Uluborlu, *Turkey* 66 D4
Uludağ, *Turkey* 66 C3
Uludere, *Turkey* 67 E10
Uluguru Mts., *Tanzania* 82 D4
Ulukışla, *Turkey* 66 E6
Ulungur He →, *China* 54 B3
Ulutau, *Kazakhstan* 44 E7
Ulvenhout, *Neths.* 17 E5
Ulverston, *U.K.* 12 C4
Ulverstone, *Australia* 90 G4
Ulya, *Russia* 45 D15
Ulyanovsk = Simbirsk, *Russia* 41 D16
Ulyasutay, *Mongolia* 54 B4
Ulysses, *U.S.A.* 109 G4
Umag, *Croatia* 33 C10
Umala, *Bolivia* 124 D4
Uman, *Ukraine* 42 B4
Umaria, *India* 61 H12
Umarkot, *Pakistan* 60 G6
Umatilla, *U.S.A.* 110 D4
Umba, *Russia* 44 C4
Umbertide, *Italy* 33 E9
Umbrella Mts., *N.Z.* 87 L2
Umbria □, *Italy* 33 F9
Ume älv →, *Sweden* 8 E16
Umeå, *Sweden* 8 E16
Umera, *Indonesia* 57 E7
Umfuli →, *Zimbabwe* 83 F2

Umgusa, *Zimbabwe* 83 F2
Umka, *Serbia* 21 L10
Umkomaas, *S. Africa* 85 E5
Umm ad Daraj, J., *Jordan* 69 C4
Umm al Qaywayn, *U.A.E.* 65 E7
Umm al Qittayn, *Jordan* 69 C5
Umm Arda, *Sudan* 77 D3
Umm Bāb, *Qatar* 65 E6
Umm Bel, *Sudan* 77 E2
Umm Dubban, *Sudan* 77 D3
Umm el Fahm, *Israel* 69 C4
Umm Koweika, *Sudan* 77 E3
Umm Lajj, *Si. Arabia* 64 E3
Umm Merwa, *Sudan* 76 D3
Umm Ruwaba, *Sudan* 77 E3
Umm Sidr, *Sudan* 77 E2
Ummanz, *Germany* 18 A9
Umnak I., *U.S.A.* 96 C3
Umniati →, *Zimbabwe* 83 F2
Umpqua →, *U.S.A.* 110 E1
Umreth, *India* 62 H5
Umtata, *S. Africa* 85 E4
Umuahia, *Nigeria* 79 D6
Umuarama, *Brazil* 127 A5
Umvukwe Ra., *Zimbabwe* 83 F3
Umzimvubu = Port St. Johns, *S. Africa* 85 E4
Umzingwane →, *Zimbabwe* 83 G2
Umzinto, *S. Africa* 85 E5
Una, *India* 62 J4
Una →, *Bos.-H.* 33 C13
Unac →, *Bos.-H.* 33 D13
Unadilla, *U.S.A.* 107 D9
Unalaska, *U.S.A.* 96 C3
Uncastillo, *Spain* 28 C3
Uncía, *Bolivia* 124 D4
Uncompahgre Peak, *U.S.A.* 111 G10
Unden, *Sweden* 11 F8
Underberg, *S. Africa* 85 D4
Underbool, *Australia* 91 F3
Undersaker, *Sweden* 10 A7
Undersvik, *Sweden* 10 C10
Unecha, *Russia* 40 E8
Uneiuxi →, *Brazil* 120 D4
Ungarie, *Australia* 91 E4
Ungarra, *Australia* 91 E2
Ungava B., *Canada* 97 C13
Ungava Pen., *Canada* 97 C12
Ungeny, *Moldavia* 42 C2
Unggi, *N. Korea* 51 C16
Ungwatiri, *Sudan* 77 D4
Uni, *Russia* 41 C17
União da Vitória, *Brazil* 127 B5
União dos Palmares, *Brazil* 122 C4
Unije, *Croatia* 33 D11
Unimak I., *U.S.A.* 96 C3
Unini →, *Brazil* 121 D5
Union, *Miss., U.S.A.* 109 J10
Union, *Mo., U.S.A.* 108 F9
Union, *S.C., U.S.A.* 105 H5
Union, Mt., *U.S.A.* 111 J7
Union City, *Calif., U.S.A.* 112 H4
Union City, *N.J., U.S.A.* 107 F10
Union City, *Pa., U.S.A.* 106 E5
Union City, *Tenn., U.S.A.* 109 G10
Union Gap, *U.S.A.* 110 C3
Union of Soviet Socialist Republics = Commonwealth of Independent States ■, *Eurasia* 45 D11
Union Springs, *U.S.A.* 105 J3
Uniondale, *S. Africa* 84 E3
Uniontown, *U.S.A.* 104 F6
Unionville, *U.S.A.* 108 E8
United Arab Emirates ■, *Asia* 65 F7
United Kingdom ■, *Europe* 7 E5
United States of America ■, *N. Amer.* 102 C7
Unity, *Canada* 101 C7
Universales, Mtes., *Spain* 28 E3
Unjha, *India* 62 H5
Unnao, *India* 63 F9
Uno, Ilha, *Guinea-Biss.* 78 C1
Unst, *U.K.* 14 A8
Unstrut →, *Germany* 18 D7
Unter-engadin, *Switz.* 23 C10
Unterägeri, *Switz.* 23 B7
Unterkulm, *Switz.* 22 B6
Unterseen, *Switz.* 22 C5
Unterwaldner Alpen, *Switz.* 23 C6
Unuk →, *Canada* 100 B2
Ünye, *Turkey* 42 F7
Unzha, *Russia* 41 B14
Unzha →, *Russia* 41 C13
Uors, *Switz.* 23 C8
Uozu, *Japan* 49 F8
Upa →, *Czech.* 20 E6
Upata, *Venezuela* 121 B5
Upemba, L., *Zaïre* 83 D2
Upernavik, *Greenland* 4 B5
Upington, *S. Africa* 84 D3
Upleta, *India* 62 J4
Upolu, *W. Samoa* 87 A13
Upper Alkali Lake, *U.S.A.* 110 F3
Upper Arrow L., *Canada* 100 C5
Upper Foster L., *Canada* 101 B7
Upper Hutt, *N.Z.* 87 J5
Upper Klamath L., *U.S.A.* 110 E3
Upper Lake, *U.S.A.* 112 F4
Upper Musquodoboit, *Canada* 99 C7
Upper Red L., *U.S.A.* 108 A7
Upper Sandusky, *U.S.A.* 104 E4
Upper Volta = Burkina Faso ■, *Africa* 78 C4
Upphärad, *Sweden* 11 F6
Uppsala, *Sweden* 10 E11
Uppsala län □, *Sweden* 9 G14
Upshi, *India* 63 C7
Upstart, C., *Australia* 90 B4
Upton, *U.S.A.* 108 C2
Ur, *Iraq* 64 D5
Urabá, G. de, *Colombia* 120 B2
Uracara, *Brazil* 121 D6
Urad Qianqi, *China* 50 D5
Urakawa, *Japan* 48 C11
Ural, *Australia* 91 E4
Ural →, *Kazakhstan* 43 C14
Ural Mts. = Uralskie Gory, *Russia* 44 D6
Uralla, *Australia* 91 E5
Uralsk, *Kazakhstan* 44 D6
Uralskie Gory, *Russia* 44 D6
Urambo, *Tanzania* 82 D3
Urambo □, *Tanzania* 82 D3
Urandangi, *Australia* 90 C2
Uranium City, *Canada* 101 B7
Uranquinty, *Australia* 91 F4
Uraricaá →, *Brazil* 121 C5
Uraricuera →, *Brazil* 121 C5
Urawa, *Japan* 49 G9
Uray, *Russia* 44 C7
'Uray'irah, *Si. Arabia* 65 E6
Urbana, *Ill., U.S.A.* 104 E1
Urbana, *Ohio, U.S.A.* 104 E4
Urbánia, *Italy* 33 E9
Urbano Santos, *Brazil* 122 B3
Urbel →, *Spain* 28 C1
Urbino, *Italy* 33 E9
Urbión, Picos de, *Spain* 28 C2
Urcos, *Peru* 124 C3
Urda, *Kazakhstan* 43 B12
Urda, *Spain* 31 F7
Urdinarrain, *Argentina* 126 C4
Urdos, *France* 26 F3
Urdzhar, *Kazakhstan* 44 E9
Ure →, *U.K.* 12 C6
Uren, *Russia* 41 C14
Ures, *Mexico* 114 B2
Urfa, *Turkey* 67 E8
Urfa □, *Turkey* 67 E8
Urfahr, *Austria* 21 G4
Urganch = Urgench, *Uzbekistan* 44 E7
Urgench, *Uzbekistan* 44 E7
Uri, *India* 63 B6
Uri □, *Switz.* 23 C7
Uribante →, *Venezuela* 120 B3
Uribe, *Colombia* 120 C3
Uribia, *Colombia* 120 A3
Uriondo, *Bolivia* 126 A3
Urique, *Mexico* 114 B3
Urique →, *Mexico* 114 B3
Urirotstock, *Switz.* 23 C7
Urk, *Neths.* 16 C7
Urla, *Turkey* 66 D2
Urlati, *Romania* 38 E9
Urmia = Orūmīyeh, *Iran* 64 B5
Urmia, L. = Orūmīyeh, Daryācheh-ye, *Iran* 64 B5
Urner Alpen, *Switz.* 23 C7
Uroševac, *Serbia* 21 N11
Urrao, *Colombia* 120 B2
Ursus, *Poland* 20 C10
Uruaçu, *Brazil* 123 D2
Uruana, *Brazil* 123 E2
Uruapan, *Mexico* 114 D4
Uruará →, *Brazil* 121 D7
Urubamba, *Peru* 124 C3
Urubamba →, *Peru* 124 C3
Urubaxi →, *Brazil* 121 D5
Urubu →, *Brazil* 121 D6
Uruçara, *Brazil* 121 D6
Uruçuí, *Brazil* 122 C3
Uruçuí, Serra do, *Brazil* 122 C3
Uruçuí Prêto →, *Brazil* 122 C3
Urucuia →, *Brazil* 123 E2
Urucurituba, *Brazil* 121 D6
Uruguai →, *Brazil* 127 B5
Uruguaiana, *Brazil* 126 B4
Uruguay ■, *S. Amer.* 126 C4
Uruguay →, *S. Amer.* 126 C4
Urumchi = Ürümqi, *China* 44 E9
Ürümqi, *China* 44 E9
Urup →, *Russia* 43 D9
Urup, Os., *Russia* 45 E16
Urutaí, *Brazil* 123 E2
Uryung-Khaya, *Russia* 45 B12
Uryupinsk, *Russia* 41 F12
Urzhum, *Russia* 41 C16
Urziceni, *Romania* 38 E9
Uşak, *Turkey* 66 D3
Uşak □, *Turkey* 66 D3
Usakos, *Namibia* 84 C2
Usborne, Mt., *Falk. Is.* 128 D5
Ušće, *Serbia* 21 M10
Usedom, *Germany* 18 B9
'Usfān, *Si. Arabia* 76 C4
Ush-Tobe, *Kazakhstan* 44 E8
Ushakova, Os., *Russia* 4 A12
Ushant = Ouessant, I. d', *France* 24 D1
Ushashi, *Tanzania* 82 C3
Ushat, *Sudan* 77 F2
Ushibuka, *Japan* 49 H5
Ushuaia, *Argentina* 128 D3
Ushumun, *Russia* 45 D13
Usk →, *U.K.* 13 F5
Üsküdar, *Turkey* 39 H11
Uslar, *Germany* 18 D5
Usman, *Russia* 41 E11
Usoke, *Tanzania* 82 D3
Usolye Sibirskoye, *Russia* 45 D11
Usoro, *Nigeria* 79 D6
Uspallata, P. de, *Argentina* 126 C2
Uspenskiy, *Kazakhstan* 44 E8
Usquert, *Neths.* 16 B9
Ussel, *France* 26 C6
Ussuri →, *Asia* 48 A7
Ussuriysk, *Russia* 45 E14
Ussurka, *Russia* 48 B6
Ust-Aldan = Batamay, *Russia* 45 C13
Ust Amginskoye = Khandyga, *Russia* 45 C14
Ust-Bolsheretsk, *Russia* 45 D16
Ust Buzulukskaya, *Russia* 41 F13
Ust Chaun, *Russia* 45 C18
Ust-Donetskiy, *Russia* 43 C9
Ust'-Ilga, *Russia* 45 D11
Ust Ilimpeya = Yukti, *Russia* 45 C11
Ust-Ilimsk, *Russia* 45 D11
Ust Ishim, *Russia* 44 D8
Ust-Kamchatsk, *Russia* 45 D17
Ust-Kamenogorsk, *Kazakhstan* 44 E9
Ust-Karenga, *Russia* 45 D12
Ust Khayryuzova, *Russia* 45 D16
Ust-Kut, *Russia* 45 D11
Ust Kuyga, *Russia* 45 B14
Ust-Labinsk, *Russia* 43 D8
Ust Luga, *Russia* 40 B6
Ust Maya, *Russia* 45 C14
Ust-Mil, *Russia* 45 D14
Ust-Nera, *Russia* 45 C15
Ust-Nyukzha, *Russia* 45 D13
Ust Olenek, *Russia* 45 B12
Ust-Omchug, *Russia* 45 C15
Ust Port, *Russia* 44 C9
Ust Tsilma, *Russia* 44 C6
Ust-Tungir, *Russia* 45 D13
Ust Urt = Ustyurt, Plato, *Kazakhstan* 44 E6
Ust Vorkuta, *Russia* 44 C7
Ustaoset, *Norway* 10 D2
Ustaritz, *France* 26 E2
Uste, *Russia* 41 B11
Uster, *Switz.* 23 B7
Ústí nad Labem, *Czech.* 20 E4
Ústí nad Orlicí, *Czech.* 20 F6
Ustica, *Italy* 34 D6
Ustinov = Izhevsk, *Russia* 44 D6
Ustka, *Poland* 20 A6
Ustrzyki Dolne, *Poland* 20 F12
Ustye, *Russia* 45 D10
Ustyurt, Plato, *Kazakhstan* 44 E6
Ustyuzhna, *Russia* 41 B10
Usu, *China* 54 B3
Usuki, *Japan* 49 H5
Usulután, *El Salv.* 116 D2
Usumacinta →, *Mexico* 115 D6
Usumbura = Bujumbura, *Burundi* 82 C2
Usure, *Tanzania* 82 C3
Uta, *Indonesia* 57 E9
Utah □, *U.S.A.* 110 G8
Utah, L., *U.S.A.* 110 F8
Ute Creek →, *U.S.A.* 109 H3
Utena, *Lithuania* 40 D4
Ütersen, *Germany* 18 B5
Utete, *Tanzania* 82 D4
Uthai Thani, *Thailand* 58 E3
Uthal, *Pakistan* 62 G2
Utiariti, *Brazil* 125 C6
Utica, *N.Y., U.S.A.* 107 C9
Utica, *Ohio, U.S.A.* 106 F2
Utiel, *Spain* 28 F3
Utik L., *Canada* 101 B9
Utikuma L., *Canada* 100 B5
Utinga, *Brazil* 123 D3
Utrecht, *Neths.* 16 D6
Utrecht, *S. Africa* 85 D5
Utrecht □, *Neths.* 16 D6
Utrera, *Spain* 31 H5
Utsjoki, *Finland* 8 B19
Utsunomiya, *Japan* 49 F9
Uttar Pradesh □, *India* 63 F9
Uttaradit, *Thailand* 58 D3
Uttoxeter, *U.K.* 12 E6
Ütze, *Germany* 18 C6
Uudenmaan lääni □, *Finland* 9 F18
Uusikaarlepyy, *Finland* 8 E17
Uusikaupunki, *Finland* 9 F16
Uva, *Russia* 41 C18
Uvá →, *Colombia* 120 C3
Uvalde, *U.S.A.* 109 L5
Uvarovo, *Russia* 41 F13
Uvat, *Russia* 44 D7
Uvinza, *Tanzania* 82 D3
Uvira, *Zaïre* 82 C2
Uvs Nuur, *Mongolia* 54 A4
Uwajima, *Japan* 49 H6
Uweinat, Jebel, *Sudan* 76 C1
Uxbridge, *Canada* 106 B5
Uxin Qi, *China* 50 E5
Uxmal, *Mexico* 115 C7
Uyandi, *Russia* 45 C15
Uyo, *Nigeria* 79 D6
Uyuni, *Bolivia* 124 E4
Uzbekistan ■, *Asia* 44 E7
Uzen, Bol. →, *Kazakhstan* 41 G16
Uzen, Mal. →, *Kazakhstan* 41 G16
Uzerche, *France* 26 C5
Uzès, *France* 27 D8
Uzh →, *Ukraine* 40 F7
Uzhgorod, *Ukraine* 40 G3
Uzlovaya, *Russia* 41 E11
Uzunköprü, *Turkey* 39 H9
Uzwil, *Switz.* 23 B8

V

Vaal →, *S. Africa* 84 D3
Vaal Dam, *S. Africa* 85 D4
Vaals, *Neths.* 17 G8
Vaalwater, *S. Africa* 85 C4
Vaasa, *Finland* 8 E16
Vaasan lääni □, *Finland* 8 E17
Vaassen, *Neths.* 16 D7
Vabre, *France* 26 E6
Vác, *Hungary* 21 H9
Vacaria, *Brazil* 127 B5
Vacaville, *U.S.A.* 112 G5
Vaccarès, Étang de, *France* 27 E8
Vach →, *Russia* 44 C8
Vache, I.-à-, *Haiti* 117 C5
Vadnagar, *India* 62 H5
Vado Lígure, *Italy* 32 D5
Vadodara, *India* 62 H5
Vadsø, *Norway* 8 A20
Vadstena, *Sweden* 11 F8
Vaduz, *Liech.* 23 B9
Værøy, *Norway* 8 C12
Vagnhärad, *Sweden* 10 F11
Vagos, *Portugal* 30 E2
Váh →, *Slovak Rep.* 21 H8
Vahsel B., *Antarctica* 5 D1
Vái, *Greece* 37 D8
Vaigach, *Russia* 44 B6
Vaiges, *France* 24 D6
Vaihingen, *Germany* 19 G4
Vailly-sur-Aisne, *France* 25 C10
Vaison-la-Romaine, *France* 27 D9
Vakfikebir, *Turkey* 67 C8
Val-de-Marne □, *France* 25 D9
Val-d'Oise □, *France* 25 C9
Val d'Or, *Canada* 98 C4
Val Marie, *Canada* 101 D7
Valadares, *Portugal* 30 D2
Valahia, *Romania* 38 E8
Valais □, *Switz.* 22 D5
Valais, Alpes du, *Switz.* 22 D5
Valandovo, *Macedonia* 39 H5
Valcheta, *Argentina* 128 B3
Valdagno, *Italy* 33 C8
Valday, *Russia* 40 C8
Valdayskaya Vozvyshennost, *Russia* 40 C8
Valdeazogues →, *Spain* 31 G6
Valdemarsvik, *Sweden* 11 F10
Valdepeñas, *Ciudad Real, Spain* 31 G7
Valdepeñas, *Jaén, Spain* 31 H7
Valderaduey →, *Spain* 30 D5
Valderrobres, *Spain* 28 E5
Valdés, Pen., *Argentina* 128 B4
Valdez, *Ecuador* 120 C2
Valdez, *U.S.A.* 96 B5
Valdivia, *Chile* 128 A2
Valdivia, *Colombia* 120 B2
Valdivia □, *Chile* 128 B2
Valdobbiádene, *Italy* 33 C9
Valdosta, *U.S.A.* 105 K4
Valdoviño, *Spain* 30 B2
Valdres, *Norway* 10 D3
Vale, *Georgia* 43 F10
Vale, *U.S.A.* 110 E5
Valea lui Mihai, *Romania* 38 B5
Valença, *Brazil* 123 D4
Valença, *Portugal* 30 C2
Valença do Piauí, *Brazil* 122 C3
Valençay, *France* 25 E8
Valence, *Drôme, France* 27 D8
Valence, *Tarn-et-Garonne, France* 26 D4
Valencia, *Spain* 29 F4
Valencia, *Venezuela* 120 A4
Valencia □, *Spain* 29 F4
Valencia, Albufera de, *Spain* 29 F4
Valencia, G. de, *Spain* 29 F5
Valencia de Alcántara, *Spain* 31 F3
Valencia de Don Juan, *Spain* 30 C5
Valencia del Ventoso, *Spain* 31 G4
Valenciennes, *France* 25 B10
Valensole, *France* 27 E9
Valentia Harbour, *Ireland* 15 E1
Valentia I., *Ireland* 15 E1
Valentim, Sa. do, *Brazil* 122 C3
Valentin, *Russia* 48 C7
Valentine, *Nebr., U.S.A.* 108 D4
Valentine, *Tex., U.S.A.* 109 K2
Valenza, *Italy* 32 C5
Valera, *Venezuela* 120 B3
Valguarnera Caropepe, *Italy* 35 E7
Valier, *U.S.A.* 110 B7
Valinco, G. de, *France* 27 G12
Valjevo, *Serbia* 21 L9
Valka, *Estonia* 40 C5
Valkeakoski, *Finland* 9 F18
Valkenburg, *Neths.* 17 G7
Valkenswaard, *Neths.* 17 F6
Vall de Uxó, *Spain* 28 F4
Valla, *Sweden* 10 E10
Valladolid, *Mexico* 115 C7
Valladolid, *Spain* 30 D6
Valladolid □, *Spain* 30 D6
Vallata, *Italy* 35 A8
Valldemosa, *Spain* 36 B9
Valle d'Aosta □, *Italy* 32 C4
Valle de Arán, *Spain* 28 C5
Valle de Cabuérniga, *Spain* 30 B6
Valle de la Pascua, *Venezuela* 120 B4
Valle de las Palmas, *Mexico* 113 N10
Valle de Santiago, *Mexico* 114 C4
Valle de Suchil, *Mexico* 114 C4
Valle de Zaragoza, *Mexico* 114 B3
Valle del Cauca □, *Colombia* 120 C2
Valle Fértil, Sierra del, *Argentina* 126 C2
Valle Hermoso, *Mexico* 115 B5
Vallecas, *Spain* 30 E7
Valledupar, *Colombia* 120 A3
Vallehermoso, *Canary Is.* 36 F2
Vallejo, *U.S.A.* 112 G4
Vallenar, *Chile* 126 B1
Valleraugue, *France* 26 D7
Vallet, *France* 24 E5
Valletta, *Malta* 37 D2
Valley Center, *U.S.A.* 113 M9
Valley City, *U.S.A.* 108 B6
Valley Falls, *U.S.A.* 110 E3
Valley Springs, *U.S.A.* 112 G6
Valley Wells, *U.S.A.* 113 K11
Valleyview, *Canada* 100 B5
Valli di Comácchio, *Italy* 33 D9
Vallimanca, Arroyo, *Argentina* 126 D4
Vallo della Lucánia, *Italy* 35 B8
Vallon-Pont-d'Arc, *France* 27 D8
Vallorbe, *Switz.* 22 C2
Valls, *Spain* 28 D6
Vallsta, *Sweden* 10 C10
Valmaseda, *Spain* 28 B1
Valmiera, *Latvia* 40 C4
Valmont, *France* 24 C7
Valmontone, *Italy* 34 A5
Valmy, *France* 25 C11
Valnera, Mte., *Spain* 28 B1
Valognes, *France* 24 C5
Valona = Vlóra, *Albania* 39 J2
Valongo, *Portugal* 30 D2
Valpaços, *Portugal* 30 D3
Valparaíso, *Chile* 126 C1
Valparaíso, *Mexico* 114 C4
Valparaiso, *U.S.A.* 104 E2
Valparaíso □, *Chile* 126 C1
Valpovo, *Croatia* 21 K8
Valréas, *France* 27 D8
Vals, *Switz.* 23 C8
Vals →, *S. Africa* 84 D4
Vals, Tanjung, *Indonesia* 57 F9
Vals-les-Bains, *France* 27 D8
Valsad, *India* 60 J8
Valskog, *Sweden* 10 E9
Válta, *Greece* 39 J6
Valtellina, *Italy* 32 B6
Valuyki, *Russia* 41 F11
Valverde, *Canary Is.* 36 G2
Valverde del Camino, *Spain* 31 H4
Valverde del Fresno, *Spain* 30 E4
Vama, *Romania* 38 B8
Vámos, *Greece* 37 D6
Van, *Turkey* 67 D10
Van □, *Turkey* 67 D10
Van, L. = Van Gölü, *Turkey* 67 D10
Van Alstyne, *U.S.A.* 109 J6
Van Bruyssel, *Canada* 99 C5
Van Buren, *Canada* 99 C6
Van Buren, *Ark., U.S.A.* 109 H7
Van Buren, *Maine, U.S.A.* 105 B11
Van Buren, *Mo., U.S.A.* 109 G9
Van Canh, *Vietnam* 58 F7
Van Diemen, C., *N. Terr., Australia* 88 B5
Van Diemen, C., *Queens., Australia* 90 B2
Van Diemen G., *Australia* 88 B5
Van Gölü, *Turkey* 67 D10
Van Horn, *U.S.A.* 109 K2
Van Ninh, *Vietnam* 58 F7
Van Reenen P., *S. Africa* 85 D4
Van Rees, Pegunungan, *Indonesia* 57 E9
Van Tassell, *U.S.A.* 108 D2
Van Wert, *U.S.A.* 104 E3
Van Yen, *Vietnam* 58 B5
Vanavara, *Russia* 45 C11
Vancouver, *Canada* 100 D4
Vancouver, *U.S.A.* 112 E4
Vancouver, C., *Australia* 89 G2
Vancouver I., *Canada* 100 D3
Vandalia, *Ill., U.S.A.* 108 F10
Vandalia, *Mo., U.S.A.* 108 F9
Vandenburg, *U.S.A.* 113 L6
Vanderbijlpark, *S. Africa* 85 D4
Vandergrift, *U.S.A.* 106 F5
Vanderhoof, *Canada* 100 C4
Vanderlin I., *Australia* 90 B2
Vandyke, *Australia* 90 C4
Vänern, *Sweden* 11 F7
Vänersborg, *Sweden* 11 F6
Vang Vieng, *Laos* 58 C4

Vanga, *Kenya* 82 C4
Vangaindrano, *Madag.* 85 C8
Vanguard, *Canada* 101 D7
Vanier, *Canada* 98 C4
Vankarem, *Russia* 45 C18
Vankleek Hill, *Canada* 98 C5
Vanna, *Norway* 8 A15
Vännäs, *Sweden* 8 E15
Vannes, *France* 24 E4
Vanoise, Massif de la, *France* 27 C10
Vanrhynsdorp, *S. Africa* 84 E2
Vanrook, *Australia* 90 B3
Vansbro, *Sweden* 9 F13
Vansittart B., *Australia* 88 B4
Vanthli, *India* 62 J4
Vanua Levu, *Fiji* 87 C8
Vanua Mbalavu, *Fiji* 87 C9
Vanuatu ■, *Pac. Oc.* 92 J8
Vanwyksvlei, *S. Africa* 84 E3
Vanzylsrus, *S. Africa* 84 D3
Vapnyarka, *Ukraine* 42 B3
Var □, *France* 27 E10
Var →, *France* 27 E11
Vara, *Sweden* 11 F6
Varades, *France* 24 E5
Varaita →, *Italy* 32 D4
Varallo, *Italy* 32 C5
Varanasi, *India* 63 G10
Varangerfjorden, *Norway* 8 A20
Varaždin, *Croatia* 33 B13
Varazze, *Italy* 32 D5
Varberg, *Sweden* 11 G6
Vardar = Axiós →, *Greece* 39 J5
Varde, *Denmark* 11 J2
Varde Å →, *Denmark* 11 J2
Varel, *Germany* 18 B4
Varella, Mui, *Vietnam* 58 F7
Varena, *Lithuania* 40 D4
Varennes-sur-Allier, *France* 26 B7
Vareš, *Bos.-H.* 21 L8
Varese, *Italy* 32 C5
Varese Lígure, *Italy* 32 D6
Vårgårda, *Sweden* 11 F6
Vargem Bonita, *Brazil* 123 F2
Vargem Grande, *Brazil* 122 B3
Varginha, *Brazil* 127 A6
Vargön, *Sweden* 11 F6
Variadero, *U.S.A.* 109 H2
Varillas, *Chile* 126 A1
Väring, *Sweden* 11 F8
Värmlands län □, *Sweden* 9 G12
Varna, *Bulgaria* 38 F10
Värnamo, *Sweden* 9 H13
Värö, *Sweden* 11 G6
Vars, *Canada* 107 A9
Varsseveld, *Neths.* 16 E8
Varto, *Turkey* 67 D9
Varvarin, *Serbia* 21 M11
Varzaneh, *Iran* 65 C7
Várzea Alegre, *Brazil* 122 C4
Várzea da Palma, *Brazil* 123 E3
Várzea Grande, *Brazil* 125 D6
Varzi, *Italy* 32 D6
Varzo, *Italy* 32 B5
Varzy, *France* 25 E10
Vasa, *Finland* 8 E16
Vasa Barris →, *Brazil* 122 D4
Vascâo →, *Portugal* 31 H3
Vaşcău, *Romania* 38 C5
Vascongadas = País Vasco □, *Spain* 28 C2
Vasht = Khāsh, *Iran* 60 E2
Vasilevichi, *Belorussia* 40 E6
Vasilikón, *Greece* 39 L6
Vasilkov, *Ukraine* 40 F7
Vaslui, *Romania* 38 C10
Vassar, *Canada* 101 D9
Vassar, *U.S.A.* 104 D4
Västeräs, *Sweden* 10 E10
Västerbottens län □, *Sweden* 8 D14
Västernorrlands län □, *Sweden* 10 A11
Västervik, *Sweden* 9 H14
Västmanlands län □, *Sweden* 9 G14
Vasto, *Italy* 33 F11
Vasvár, *Hungary* 21 H6
Vatan, *France* 25 E8
Vathí, *Greece* 39 M10
Váthia, *Greece* 39 N5
Vatican City ■, *Europe* 33 G9
Vaticano, C., *Italy* 35 D8
Vatili, *Cyprus* 37 D12
Vatnajökull, *Iceland* 8 D5
Vatnås, *Norway* 10 E3
Vatneyri, *Iceland* 8 D2
Vatoa, *Fiji* 87 D9
Vatólakkos, *Greece* 37 D5
Vatoloha, *Madag.* 85 B8
Vatomandry, *Madag.* 85 B8
Vatra-Dornei, *Romania* 38 B8
Vättern, *Sweden* 11 F8
Vättis, *Switz.* 23 C8
Vaucluse □, *France* 27 E9
Vaucouleurs, *France* 25 D12
Vaud □, *Switz.* 22 C2
Vaughn, *Mont., U.S.A.* 110 C8
Vaughn, *N. Mex., U.S.A.* 111 J11
Vaulruz, *Switz.* 22 C3
Vaupés = Uaupés →, *Brazil* 120 C4
Vaupes □, *Colombia* 120 C3
Vauvert, *France* 27 E8
Vauxhall, *Canada* 100 C6
Vava'u, *Tonga* 87 D11
Vavoua, *Ivory C.* 78 D3
Vaxholm, *Sweden* 10 E12
Växjö, *Sweden* 9 H13
Vaygach, Ostrov, *Russia* 44 C6
Váyia, Ákra, *Greece* 37 C10
Veadeiros, *Brazil* 123 D2
Vechta, *Germany* 18 C4
Vechte →, *Neths.* 16 C8
Vecsés, *Hungary* 21 H9
Veddige, *Sweden* 11 G6
Vedea →, *Romania* 38 F8
Vedia, *Argentina* 126 C3
Vedra, I. del, *Spain* 36 C7
Vedrin, *Belgium* 17 G5
Veendam, *Neths.* 16 B9
Veenendaal, *Neths.* 16 D7
Veerle, *Belgium* 17 F5
Vefsna →, *Norway* 8 D12
Vega, *Norway* 8 D11
Vega, *U.S.A.* 109 H3
Vegadeo, *Spain* 30 B3
Vegafjorden, *Norway* 8 D12
Veghel, *Neths.* 17 E7
Vegorritis, Límni, *Greece* 39 J4
Vegreville, *Canada* 100 C6
Vegusdal, *Norway* 11 F2
Veii, *Italy* 33 F9
Vejen, *Denmark* 11 J3
Vejer de la Frontera, *Spain* 31 J5
Vejle, *Denmark* 11 J3
Vejle Fjord, *Denmark* 11 J3
Vela Luka, *Croatia* 33 F13
Velas, C., *Costa Rica* 116 D2
Velasco, Sierra de, *Argentina* 126 B2
Velay, Mts. du, *France* 26 D7
Velddrif, *S. Africa* 84 E2
Veldegem, *Belgium* 17 F2
Velden, *Neths.* 17 F8
Veldhoven, *Neths.* 17 F6
Velebit Planina, *Croatia* 33 D12
Velebitski Kanal, *Croatia* 33 D11
Veleka →, *Bulgaria* 38 G10
Velenje, *Slovenia* 33 B12
Velestínon, *Greece* 39 K5
Vélez, *Colombia* 120 B3
Vélez Blanco, *Spain* 29 H2
Vélez Málaga, *Spain* 31 J6
Vélez Rubio, *Spain* 29 H2
Velhas →, *Brazil* 123 E3
Velika, *Croatia* 21 K7
Velika Gorica, *Croatia* 33 C13
Velika Kapela, *Croatia* 33 C12
Velika Kladuša, *Bos.-H.* 33 C12
Velika Morava →, *Serbia* 21 L11
Velikaya →, *Russia* 40 C6
Velikaya Kema, *Russia* 48 B8
Velikaya Lepetikha, *Ukraine* 42 C5
Velike Lašče, *Slovenia* 33 C11
Velikiye Luki, *Russia* 40 C7
Velikonda Range, *India* 60 M11
Velikoye, Oz., *Russia* 41 D12
Velingrad, *Bulgaria* 39 G6
Velino, Mte., *Italy* 33 F10
Velizh, *Russia* 40 D7
Velké Meziřící, *Czech.* 20 F6
Velletri, *Italy* 34 A5
Vellinge, *Sweden* 11 J7
Vellore, *India* 60 N11
Velp, *Neths.* 16 D7
Velsen-Noord, *Neths.* 16 D5
Velten, *Germany* 18 C9
Veluwe Meer, *Neths.* 16 D7
Velva, *U.S.A.* 108 A4
Veme, *Norway* 10 D4
Ven, *Sweden* 11 J6
Venaco, *France* 27 F13
Venado Tuerto, *Argentina* 126 C3
Venafro, *Italy* 35 A7
Venarey-les-Laumes, *France* 25 E11
Venaria, *Italy* 32 C4
Venčane, *Serbia* 21 L10
Vence, *France* 27 E11
Venda □, *S. Africa* 85 C5
Vendas Novas, *Portugal* 31 G2
Vendée □, *France* 24 F5
Vendée →, *France* 24 F5
Vendéen, Bocage, *France* 26 B2
Vendeuvre-sur-Barse, *France* 25 D11
Vendôme, *France* 24 E8
Vendrell, *Spain* 28 D6
Vendsyssel, *Denmark* 11 G4
Véneta, L., *Italy* 33 C9
Véneto □, *Italy* 33 C8
Venev, *Russia* 41 D11
Venézia, *Italy* 33 C9
Venézia, G. di, *Italy* 33 C10
Venezuela ■, *S. Amer.* 120 B4
Venezuela, G. de, *Venezuela* 120 A3
Vengurla, *India* 60 M8
Venice = Venézia, *Italy* 33 C9
Venkatapuram, *India* 61 K12
Venlo, *Neths.* 17 F8
Venraij, *Neths.* 17 E7
Venta de Cardeña, *Spain* 31 G6
Venta de San Rafael, *Spain* 30 E6
Ventana, Punta de la, *Mexico* 114 C3
Ventana, Sa. de la, *Argentina* 126 D3
Ventersburg, *S. Africa* 84 D4
Venterstad, *S. Africa* 84 E4
Ventimíglia, *Italy* 32 E4
Ventnor, *U.K.* 13 G6
Ventotene, *Italy* 34 B6
Ventoux, Mt., *France* 27 D9
Ventspils, *Latvia* 9 H16
Ventuarí →, *Venezuela* 120 C4
Ventucopa, *U.S.A.* 113 L7
Ventura, *U.S.A.* 113 L7
Venus B., *Australia* 91 F4
Vera, *Argentina* 126 B3
Vera, *Spain* 29 H3
Veracruz, *Mexico* 115 D5
Veracruz □, *Mexico* 115 D5
Veraval, *India* 62 J4
Verbánia, *Italy* 32 C5
Verbicaro, *Italy* 35 C8
Verbier, *Switz.* 22 D4
Vercelli, *Italy* 32 C5
Verchovchevo, *Ukraine* 42 B6
Verdalsøra, *Norway* 8 E11
Verde →, *Argentina* 128 B3
Verde →, *Goiás, Brazil* 123 E1
Verde →, *Goiás, Brazil* 123 E1
Verde →, *Mato Grosso, Brazil* 125 E7
Verde →, *Mato Grosso, Brazil* 125 C6
Verde →, *Chihuahua, Mexico* 114 B3
Verde →, *Oaxaca, Mexico* 115 D5
Verde →, *Veracruz, Mexico* 114 C4
Verde →, *Paraguay* 126 A4
Verde, Cay, *Bahamas* 116 B4
Verde Grande →, *Brazil* 123 E3
Verde Island Pass, *Phil.* 55 E4
Verde Pequeno →, *Brazil* 123 D3
Verden, *Germany* 18 C5
Verdi, *U.S.A.* 112 F7
Verdigre, *U.S.A.* 108 D5
Verdon →, *France* 27 E9
Verdun, *France* 25 C12
Verdun-sur-le-Doubs, *France* 25 F12
Vereeniging, *S. Africa* 85 D4
Vérendrye, Parc Prov. de la, *Canada* 98 C4
Verga, C., *Guinea* 78 C2
Vergato, *Italy* 32 D8
Vergemont, *Australia* 90 C3
Vergemont Cr. →, *Australia* 90 C3
Vergennes, *U.S.A.* 107 B11
Vergt, *France* 26 C4
Verín, *Spain* 30 D3
Veriña, *Spain* 30 B5
Verkhnedvinsk, *Belorussia* 40 D5
Verkhnevilyuysk, *Russia* 45 C13
Verkhneye Kalinino, *Russia* 45 D11
Verkhniy Baskunchak, *Russia* 43 B12
Verkhovye, *Russia* 41 E10
Verkhoyansk, *Russia* 45 C14
Verkhoyansk Ra. = Verkhoyanskiy Khrebet, *Russia* 45 C13
Verkhoyanskiy Khrebet, *Russia* 45 C13
Verlo, *Canada* 101 C7
Verma, *Norway* 10 B2
Vermenton, *France* 25 E10
Vermilion, *Canada* 101 C6
Vermilion →, *Alta., Canada* 101 C6
Vermilion →, *Qué., Canada* 98 C5
Vermilion, B., *U.S.A.* 109 L9
Vermilion Bay, *Canada* 101 D10
Vermilion Chutes, *Canada* 100 B6
Vermilion L., *U.S.A.* 108 B8
Vermillion, *U.S.A.* 108 D6
Vermont □, *U.S.A.* 107 C12
Vernal, *U.S.A.* 110 F9
Vernalis, *U.S.A.* 112 H5
Vernayaz, *Switz.* 22 D4
Verner, *Canada* 98 C3
Verneuil-sur-Avre, *France* 24 D7
Verneukpan, *S. Africa* 84 D3
Vernier, *Switz.* 22 D2
Vernon, *Canada* 100 C5
Vernon, *France* 24 C8
Vernon, *U.S.A.* 109 H5
Vernonia, *U.S.A.* 112 E3
Vero Beach, *U.S.A.* 105 M5
Véroia, *Greece* 39 J5
Verolanuova, *Italy* 32 C7
Véroli, *Italy* 34 A6
Verona, *Italy* 32 C8
Veropol, *Russia* 45 C17
Versailles, *France* 25 D9
Versalles, *Bolivia* 125 C5
Versoix, *Switz.* 22 D2
Vert, C., *Senegal* 78 C1
Vertou, *France* 24 E5
Vertus, *France* 25 D11
Verulam, *S. Africa* 85 D5
Verviers, *Belgium* 17 G7
Vervins, *France* 25 C10
Verzej, *Slovenia* 33 B13
Vescavoto, *France* 27 F13
Vesdre →, *Belgium* 17 G7
Veselí nad Lužnicí, *Czech.* 20 F4
Veselovskoye Vdkhr., *Russia* 43 C9
Veshenskaya, *Russia* 43 B9
Vesle →, *France* 25 C10
Vesoul, *France* 25 E13
Vessigebro, *Sweden* 11 H6
Vest-Agder fylke □, *Norway* 9 G9
Vesterålen, *Norway* 8 B13
Vestersche Veld, *Neths.* 16 C8
Vestfjorden, *Norway* 8 C13
Vestfold fylke □, *Norway* 9 G11
Vestmannaeyjar, *Iceland* 8 E3
Vestmarka, *Norway* 10 E5
Vestone, *Italy* 32 C7
Vestsjællands Amtskommune □, *Denmark* 11 J5
Vestspitsbergen, *Svalbard* 4 B8
Vestvågøy, *Norway* 8 B12
Vesuvio, *Italy* 35 B7
Vesuvius, Mt. = Vesuvio, *Italy* 35 B7
Vesyegonsk, *Russia* 41 B10
Veszprém, *Hungary* 21 H7
Vésztö, *Hungary* 21 J11
Vetlanda, *Sweden* 9 H13
Vetluga, *Russia* 41 C14
Vetlugu →, *Russia* 41 C15
Vetluzhskiy, *Russia* 41 C14
Vetovo, *Bulgaria* 38 F9
Vetralia, *Italy* 33 F9
Vettore, Monte, *Italy* 33 F10
Veurne, *Belgium* 17 F1
Vevey, *Switz.* 22 D3
Veynes, *France* 27 D9
Veys, *Iran* 65 D6
Vézelise, *France* 25 D13
Vézère →, *France* 26 D4
Vezirköprü, *Turkey* 66 C6
Vi Thanh, *Vietnam* 59 H5
Viacha, *Bolivia* 124 D4
Viadana, *Italy* 32 D7
Viamão, *Brazil* 127 C5
Viana, *Brazil* 122 B3
Viana, *Spain* 28 C2
Viana del Bollo, *Spain* 30 C3
Viana do Alentejo, *Portugal* 31 G3
Viana do Castelo, *Portugal* 30 D2
Vianden, *Belgium* 17 J8
Vianen, *Neths.* 16 E6
Vianna do Castelo □, *Portugal* 30 D2
Vianópolis, *Brazil* 123 E2
Viar →, *Spain* 31 H5
Viaréggio, *Italy* 32 E7
Viaur →, *France* 26 D5
Vibank, *Canada* 101 C8
Vibo Valéntia, *Italy* 35 D9
Viborg, *Denmark* 11 H3
Vibraye, *France* 24 D7
Vic-en-Bigorre, *France* 26 E4
Vic-Fézensac, *France* 26 E4
Vic-sur-Cère, *France* 26 D6
Vicenza, *Italy* 33 C8
Vich, *Spain* 28 D7
Vichada □, *Colombia* 120 C4
Vichada →, *Colombia* 120 C4
Vichuga, *Russia* 41 C12
Vichy, *France* 26 B7
Vicksburg, *Ariz., U.S.A.* 113 M13
Vicksburg, *Mich., U.S.A.* 104 D3
Vicksburg, *Miss., U.S.A.* 109 J9
Vico, L. di, *Italy* 33 F9
Vico del Gargaro, *Italy* 35 A8
Viçosa, *Brazil* 122 C4
Viçosa do Ceará, *Brazil* 122 B3
Vicosoprano, *Switz.* 23 D9
Victor, *India* 62 J4
Victor, *Colo., U.S.A.* 108 F2
Victor, *N.Y., U.S.A.* 106 D7
Victor Harbor, *Australia* 91 F2
Victoria, *Argentina* 126 C3
Victoria, *Canada* 100 D4
Victoria, *Chile* 128 A2
Victoria, *Guinea* 78 C2
Victoria, *Malaysia* 56 C5
Victoria, *Malta* 37 C1
Victoria, *Phil.* 55 D4
Victoria, *Kans., U.S.A.* 108 F5
Victoria, *Tex., U.S.A.* 109 L6
Victoria □, *Australia* 91 F3
Victoria →, *Australia* 88 C4
Victoria, Grand L., *Canada* 98 C4
Victoria, L., *Africa* 82 C3
Victoria, L., *Australia* 91 E3
Victoria Beach, *Canada* 101 C9
Victoria de Durango, *Mexico* 114 C4
Victoria de las Tunas, *Cuba* 116 B4
Victoria Falls, *Zimbabwe* 83 F2
Victoria Harbour, *Canada* 98 D4
Victoria I., *Canada* 96 A8
Victoria Ld., *Antarctica* 5 D11
Victoria Nile →, *Uganda* 82 B3
Victoria Res., *Canada* 99 C8
Victoria River Downs, *Australia* 88 C5
Victoria Taungdeik, *Burma* 61 J18
Victoria West, *S. Africa* 84 E3
Victorias, *Phil.* 55 F5
Victoriaville, *Canada* 99 C5
Victorica, *Argentina* 126 D2
Victorville, *U.S.A.* 113 L9
Vicuña, *Chile* 126 C1
Vicuña Mackenna, *Argentina* 126 C3
Vidal, *U.S.A.* 113 L12
Vidal Junction, *U.S.A.* 113 L12
Vidalia, *U.S.A.* 105 J4
Vidauban, *France* 27 E10
Vídho, *Greece* 37 A3
Vidigueira, *Portugal* 31 G3
Vidin, *Bulgaria* 38 F5
Vidio, C., *Spain* 30 B4
Vidisha, *India* 62 H7
Vidzy, *Belorussia* 40 D5
Viechtach, *Germany* 19 F8
Viedma, *Argentina* 128 B4
Viedma, L., *Argentina* 128 C2
Vieira, *Portugal* 30 D2
Viella, *Spain* 28 C5
Vielsalm, *Belgium* 17 H7
Vienenburg, *Germany* 18 D6
Vieng Pou Kha, *Laos* 58 B3
Vienna = Wien, *Austria* 21 G6
Vienna, *U.S.A.* 109 G10
Vienne, *France* 27 C8
Vienne □, *France* 26 B4
Vienne →, *France* 24 E7
Vientiane, *Laos* 58 D4
Vientos, Paso de los, *Caribbean* 117 C5
Vierlingsbeek, *Neths.* 17 E8
Viersen, *Germany* 18 D2
Vierwaldstättersee, *Switz.* 23 C7
Vierzon, *France* 25 E9
Vieste, *Italy* 35 A9
Vietnam ■, *Asia* 58 C5
Vieux-Boucau-les-Bains, *France* 26 E2
Vif, *France* 27 C9
Vigan, *Phil.* 55 C4
Vigévano, *Italy* 32 C5
Vigia, *Brazil* 122 B2
Vigía Chico, *Mexico* 115 D7
Víglas, Ákra, *Greece* 37 D9
Vignemale, Pic du, *France* 26 F3
Vigneulles-lès-Hattonchâtel, *France* 25 D12
Vignola, *Italy* 32 D8
Vigo, *Spain* 30 C2
Vigo, Ría de, *Spain* 30 C2
Vihiers, *France* 24 E6
Vijayawada, *India* 61 L12
Vijfhuizen, *Neths.* 16 D5
Viken, *Sweden* 11 F8
Viking, *Canada* 100 C6
Vikna, *Norway* 8 D11
Viksjö, *Sweden* 10 B11
Vikulovo, *Russia* 44 D8
Vila da Maganja, *Mozam.* 83 F4
Vila de João Belo = Xai-Xai, *Mozam.* 85 D5
Vila de Rei, *Portugal* 31 F2
Vila do Bispo, *Portugal* 31 H2
Vila do Chibuto, *Mozam.* 85 C5
Vila do Conde, *Portugal* 30 D2
Vila Franca de Xira, *Portugal* 31 G2
Vila Gamito, *Mozam.* 83 E3
Vila Gomes da Costa, *Mozam.* 85 C5
Vila Machado, *Mozam.* 83 F3
Vila Mouzinho, *Mozam.* 83 E3
Vila Nova de Foscôa, *Portugal* 30 D3
Vila Nova de Ourém, *Portugal* 31 F2
Vila Novo de Gaia, *Portugal* 30 D2
Vila Pouca de Aguiar, *Portugal* 30 D3
Vila Real, *Portugal* 30 D3
Vila Real de Santo António, *Portugal* 31 H3
Vila Vasco da Gama, *Mozam.* 83 E3
Vila Velha, *Amapá, Brazil* 121 C7
Vila Velha, *Espírito Santo, Brazil* 123 F3
Vila Viçosa, *Portugal* 31 G3
Vilaboa, *Spain* 30 C2
Vilaine →, *France* 24 E4
Vilanandro, Tanjona, *Madag.* 85 B7
Vilanculos, *Mozam.* 85 C6
Vilar Formosa, *Portugal* 30 E4
Vilareal □, *Portugal* 30 D3
Vilaseca-Salou, *Spain* 28 D6
Vilcabamba, Cordillera, *Peru* 124 C3
Vilcanchos, *Peru* 124 C3
Vileyka, *Belorussia* 40 D5
Vilhelmina, *Sweden* 8 D14
Vilhena, *Brazil* 125 C5
Viliga, *Russia* 45 C16
Viliya →, *Lithuania* 40 D3
Viljandi, *Estonia* 40 B4
Vilkovo, *Ukraine* 42 D3
Villa Abecia, *Bolivia* 126 A2
Villa Ahumada, *Mexico* 114 A3
Villa Ana, *Argentina* 126 B4
Villa Ángela, *Argentina* 126 B3
Villa Bella, *Bolivia* 125 C4
Villa Bens = Tarfaya, *Morocco* 74 C2
Villa Cañás, *Argentina* 126 C3
Villa Carlos, *Spain* 36 B11
Villa Cisneros = Dakhla, *W. Sahara* 74 D1
Villa Colón, *Argentina* 126 C2
Villa Constitución, *Argentina* 126 C3

Waddy Pt.

Villa de Cura, *Venezuela* 120 A4
Villa de María, *Argentina* 126 B3
Villa del Rosario, *Venezuela* 120 A3
Villa Dolores, *Argentina* 126 C2
Villa Frontera, *Mexico* 114 B4
Villa Guillermina, *Argentina* 126 B4
Villa Hayes, *Paraguay* 126 B4
Villa Iris, *Argentina* 126 D3
Villa Juárez, *Mexico* 114 B4
Villa María, *Argentina* 126 C3
Villa Mazán, *Argentina* 126 B2
Villa Minozzo, *Italy* 32 D7
Villa Montes, *Bolivia* 126 A3
Villa Ocampo, *Argentina* 126 B4
Villa Ocampo, *Mexico* 114 B3
Villa Ojo de Agua, *Argentina* 126 B3
Villa San Giovanni, *Italy* 35 D8
Villa San José, *Argentina* 126 C4
Villa San Martín, *Argentina* 126 B3
Villa Santina, *Italy* 33 B9
Villa Unión, *Mexico* 114 C3
Villablino, *Spain* 30 C4
Villacañas, *Spain* 28 F1
Villacarriedo, *Spain* 28 B1
Villacarrillo, *Spain* 29 G1
Villacastín, *Spain* 30 E6
Villach, *Austria* 21 J3
Villaciado, *Italy* 34 C1
Villada, *Spain* 30 C6
Villadiego, *Spain* 30 C6
Villadóssola, *Italy* 32 B5
Villafeliche, *Spain* 28 D3
Villafranca, *Spain* 28 C3
Villafranca de los Barros, *Spain* 31 G4
Villafranca de los Caballeros, *Spain* 29 F1
Villafranca de los Caballeros, *Spain* 36 B10
Villafranca del Bierzo, *Spain* 30 C4
Villafranca del Cid, *Spain* 28 E4
Villafranca del Panadés, *Spain* 28 D6
Villafranca di Verona, *Italy* 32 C7
Villagarcía de Arosa, *Spain* 30 C2
Villagrán, *Mexico* 115 C5
Villaguay, *Argentina* 126 C4
Villaharta, *Spain* 31 G6
Villahermosa, *Mexico* 115 D6
Villahermosa, *Spain* 29 G2
Villaines-la-Juhel, *France* 24 D6
Villajoyosa, *Spain* 29 G4
Villalba, *Spain* 30 B3
Villalba de Guardo, *Spain* 30 C6
Villalcampo, Pantano de, *Spain* 30 D4
Villalón de Campos, *Spain* 30 C5
Villalpando, *Spain* 30 D5
Villaluenga, *Spain* 30 E7
Villamanán, *Spain* 30 C5
Villamartín, *Spain* 31 J5
Villamayor, *Spain* 28 F2
Villamblard, *France* 26 C4
Villanova Monteleone, *Italy* 34 B1
Villanueva, *Colombia* 120 A3
Villanueva, *U.S.A.* 111 J11
Villanueva de Castellón, *Spain* 29 F4
Villanueva de Córdoba, *Spain* 31 G6
Villanueva de la Fuente, *Spain* 29 G2
Villanueva de la Serena, *Spain* 31 G5
Villanueva de la Sierra, *Spain* 30 E4
Villanueva de los Castillejos, *Spain* 31 H3
Villanueva del Arzobispo, *Spain* 29 G1
Villanueva del Duque, *Spain* 31 G5
Villanueva del Fresno, *Spain* 31 G3
Villanueva y Geltrú, *Spain* 28 D6
Villaodrid, *Spain* 30 B3
Villaputzu, *Italy* 34 C2
Villar del Arzobispo, *Spain* 28 F4
Villar del Rey, *Spain* 31 F4
Villarcayo, *Spain* 28 C1
Villard-Bonnot, *France* 27 C9
Villard-de-Lans, *France* 27 C9
Villarino de los Aires, *Spain* 30 D4
Villarosa, *Italy* 35 E7
Villarramiel, *Spain* 30 C6
Villarreal, *Spain* 28 F4
Villarrica, *Chile* 128 A2
Villarrica, *Paraguay* 126 B4
Villarrobledo, *Spain* 29 F2
Villarroya de la Sierra, *Spain* 28 D3
Villarrubia de los Ojos, *Spain* 29 F1
Villars-les-Dombes, *France* 27 B9
Villarta de San Juan, *Spain* 29 F1
Villasayas, *Spain* 28 D2
Villaseca de los Gamitos, *Spain* 30 D4
Villastar, *Spain* 28 E3
Villatobas, *Spain* 28 F1
Villavicencio, *Argentina* 126 C2
Villavicencio, *Colombia* 120 C3
Villaviciosa, *Spain* 30 B5
Villazón, *Bolivia* 126 A2
Ville-Marie, *Canada* 98 C4
Ville Platte, *U.S.A.* 109 K8
Villedieu-les-Poêlles, *France* 24 D5
Villefort, *France* 26 D7
Villefranche-de-Lauragais, *France* 26 E5
Villefranche-de-Rouergue, *France* 26 D6
Villefranche-du-Périgord, *France* 26 D5
Villefranche-sur-Cher, *France* 25 E8
Villefranche-sur-Saône, *France* 27 C8
Villegrande, *Bolivia* 125 D5
Villel, *Spain* 28 E3
Villemaur-sur-Vanne, *France* 25 D10
Villemur-sur-Tarn, *France* 26 E5
Villena, *Spain* 29 G4
Villenauxe-la-Grande, *France* 25 D10
Villenave-d'Ornon, *France* 26 D3
Villeneuve, *Italy* 32 C4
Villeneuve, *Switz.* 22 D3
Villeneuve-l'Archevêque, *France* 25 D10
Villeneuve-lès-Avignon, *France* 27 E8
Villeneuve-St.-Georges, *France* 25 D9
Villeneuve-sur-Allier, *France* 26 B7
Villeneuve-sur-Lot, *France* 26 D4
Villeréal, *France* 26 D4
Villers-Bocage, *France* 24 C6
Villers-Bretonneux, *France* 25 C9
Villers-Cotterêts, *France* 25 C10
Villers-le-Bouillet, *Belgium* 17 G6
Villers-le-Gambon, *Belgium* 17 H5
Villers-sur-Mer, *France* 24 C6
Villersexel, *France* 25 E13
Villerupt, *France* 25 C12
Villerville, *France* 24 C7
Villiers, *S. Africa* 85 D4
Villingen, *Germany* 19 G4
Villisca, *U.S.A.* 108 E7
Vilna, *Canada* 100 C6
Vilnius, *Lithuania* 40 D4
Vils →, *Germany* 19 G9
Vilsbiburg, *Germany* 19 G8
Vilshofen, *Germany* 19 G9
Vilskutskogo, Proliv, *Russia* 45 B11
Vilusi, *Montenegro* 21 N8
Vilvoorde, *Belgium* 17 G4
Vilyuy →, *Russia* 45 C13
Vilyuysk, *Russia* 45 C13
Vimercate, *Italy* 32 C6
Vimiosa, *Portugal* 30 D4
Vimoutiers, *France* 24 D7
Vimperk, *Czech.* 20 F3
Viña del Mar, *Chile* 126 C1
Vinaroz, *Spain* 28 E5
Vincennes, *U.S.A.* 104 F2
Vincent, *U.S.A.* 113 L8
Vinces, *Ecuador* 120 D2
Vinchina, *Argentina* 126 B2
Vindel älven →, *Sweden* 8 E15
Vindeln, *Sweden* 8 D15
Vinderup, *Denmark* 11 H2
Vindhya Ra., *India* 62 H7
Vineland, *U.S.A.* 104 F8
Vinga, *Romania* 38 D4
Vingnes, *Norway* 10 C4
Vinh, *Vietnam* 58 C5
Vinh Linh, *Vietnam* 58 D6
Vinh Long, *Vietnam* 59 G5
Vinh Yen, *Vietnam* 58 B5
Vinhais, *Portugal* 30 D3
Vinica, *Croatia* 33 B13
Vinica, *Slovenia* 33 C12
Vinita, *U.S.A.* 109 G7
Vinkeveen, *Neths.* 16 D5
Vinkovci, *Croatia* 21 K8
Vinnitsa, *Ukraine* 42 B3
Vinnytsya = Vinnitsa, *Ukraine* 42 B3
Vinstra, *Norway* 10 C3
Vinton, *Calif., U.S.A.* 112 F6
Vinton, *Iowa, U.S.A.* 108 D8
Vinton, *La., U.S.A.* 109 K8
Vinţu de Jos, *Romania* 38 D6
Viöl, *Germany* 18 A5
Vipava, *Slovenia* 33 C10
Vipiteno, *Italy* 33 B8
Viqueque, *Indonesia* 57 F7
Vir, *Croatia* 33 D12
Virac, *Phil.* 55 E6
Virachei, *Cambodia* 58 F6
Virago Sd., *Canada* 100 C2
Viramgam, *India* 62 H5
Viranşehir, *Turkey* 67 E8
Virden, *Canada* 101 D8
Vire, *France* 24 D6
Vire →, *France* 24 C5
Virgem da Lapa, *Brazil* 123 E3
Vírgenes, C., *Argentina* 128 D3
Virgin →, *Canada* 101 B7
Virgin →, *U.S.A.* 111 H6
Virgin Gorda, *Virgin Is.* 117 C7
Virgin Is. (British) ■, *W. Indies* 117 C7
Virgin Is. (U.S.) ■, *W. Indies* 117 C7
Virginia, *S. Africa* 84 D4
Virginia, *U.S.A.* 108 B8
Virginia □, *U.S.A.* 104 G7
Virginia Beach, *U.S.A.* 104 G8
Virginia City, *Mont., U.S.A.* 110 D8
Virginia City, *Nev., U.S.A.* 112 F7
Virginia Falls, *Canada* 100 A3
Virginiatown, *Canada* 98 C4
Virieu-le-Grand, *France* 27 C9
Viroqua, *U.S.A.* 108 D9
Virovitica, *Croatia* 21 K7
Virton, *Belgium* 17 J7
Virtsu, *Estonia* 40 B3
Virú, *Peru* 124 B2
Virudunagar, *India* 60 Q10
Vis, *Croatia* 33 E13
Vis Kanal, *Croatia* 33 E13
Visalia, *U.S.A.* 111 H4
Visayan Sea, *Phil.* 55 F5
Visby, *Sweden* 9 H15
Viscount Melville Sd., *Canada* 4 B2
Visé, *Belgium* 17 G7
Višegrad, *Bos.-H.* 21 M9
Viseu, *Brazil* 122 B2
Viseu, *Portugal* 30 E3
Viseu □, *Portugal* 30 E3
Vişeu de Sus, *Romania* 38 B7
Vishakhapatnam, *India* 61 L13
Viskafors, *Sweden* 11 G6
Visnagar, *India* 62 H5
Višnja Gora, *Slovenia* 33 C11
Viso, Mte., *Italy* 32 D4
Viso del Marqués, *Spain* 29 G1
Visoko, *Bos.-H.* 21 M8
Visokoi I., *Antarctica* 5 B1
Visp, *Switz.* 22 D5
Vispa →, *Switz.* 22 D5
Visselhövede, *Germany* 18 C5
Vissoie, *Switz.* 22 D5
Vista, *U.S.A.* 113 M9
Vistula = Wisła →, *Poland* 20 A8
Vit →, *Bulgaria* 38 F7
Vitanje, *Slovenia* 33 B12
Vitebsk, *Belorussia* 40 D7
Viterbo, *Italy* 33 F9
Viti Levu, *Fiji* 87 C7
Vitigudino, *Spain* 30 D4
Vitim, *Russia* 45 D12
Vitim →, *Russia* 45 D12
Vitória, *Brazil* 123 F3
Vitoria, *Spain* 28 C2
Vitória da Conquista, *Brazil* 123 D3
Vitória de São Antão, *Brazil* 122 C4
Vitorino Friere, *Brazil* 122 B2
Vitré, *France* 24 D5
Vitry-le-François, *France* 25 D11
Vitsi, Óros, *Greece* 39 J4
Vitsyebsk = Vitebsk, *Belorussia* 40 D7
Vitteaux, *France* 25 E11
Vittel, *France* 25 D12
Vittória, *Italy* 35 F7
Vittório Véneto, *Italy* 33 C9
Vivario, *France* 27 F13
Vivegnis, *Belgium* 17 G7
Viver, *Spain* 28 F4
Vivero, *Spain* 30 B3
Viviers, *France* 27 D8
Vivonne, *France* 26 B4
Vizcaíno, Desierto de, *Mexico* 114 B2
Vizcaíno, Sierra, *Mexico* 114 B2
Vizcaya □, *Spain* 28 B2
Vize, *Turkey* 66 C2
Vizianagaram, *India* 61 K13
Vizille, *France* 27 C9
Viziñada, *Croatia* 33 C10
Viziru, *Romania* 38 E10
Vizovice, *Czech.* 20 F7
Vizzini, *Italy* 35 E7
Vlaardingen, *Neths.* 16 E4
Vlădeasa, *Romania* 38 C5
Vladikavkaz, *Russia* 43 E11
Vladimir, *Russia* 41 C12
Vladimir Volynskiy, *Ukraine* 40 F4
Vladimirovac, *Serbia* 21 K10
Vladimirovka, *Russia* 43 B12
Vladimirovka, *Russia* 43 D11
Vladislavovka, *Ukraine* 42 D6
Vladivostok, *Russia* 45 E14
Vlamertinge, *Belgium* 17 G1
Vlasenica, *Bos.-H.* 21 L8
Vlasinsko Jezero, *Serbia* 21 N12
Vleuten, *Neths.* 16 D6
Vlieland, *Neths.* 16 B5
Vliestroom, *Neths.* 16 B6
Vlijmen, *Neths.* 17 E6
Vlissingen, *Neths.* 17 F3
Vlóra, *Albania* 39 J2
Vlorës, Gjiri i, *Albania* 39 J2
Vltava →, *Czech.* 20 E4
Vo Dat, *Vietnam* 59 G6
Vobarno, *Italy* 32 C7
Voćin, *Croatia* 21 K7
Vodice, *Croatia* 33 E12
Vodnjan, *Croatia* 33 D10
Vogelkop = Doberai, Jazirah, *Indonesia* 57 E8
Vogelsberg, *Germany* 18 E5
Voghera, *Italy* 32 D6
Vohibinany, *Madag.* 85 B8
Vohimarina, *Madag.* 85 A9
Vohimena, Tanjon' i, *Madag.* 85 D8
Vohipeno, *Madag.* 85 C8
Voi, *Kenya* 82 C4
Void, *France* 25 D12
Voiron, *France* 27 C9
Voisey B., *Canada* 99 A7
Voitsberg, *Austria* 21 H5
Voiviïs Límni, *Greece* 39 K5
Vojens, *Denmark* 11 J3
Vojmsjön, *Sweden* 8 D14
Vojnić, *Croatia* 33 C12
Vojnik, *Italy* 33 B12
Vokhma, *Russia* 41 B15
Vokhma →, *Russia* 41 C15
Vokhtoga, *Russia* 41 B12
Volborg, *U.S.A.* 108 C2
Volcano Is. = Kazan-Rettō, *Pac. Oc.* 92 E6
Volchansk, *Ukraine* 42 A7
Volchayevka, *Russia* 45 E14
Volchya →, *Ukraine* 42 C7
Volda, *Norway* 8 E9
Volendam, *Neths.* 16 D6
Volga, *Russia* 41 C11
Volga →, *Russia* 43 C13
Volga Hts. = Privolzhskaya Vozvyshennost, *Russia* 41 F15
Volgodonsk, *Russia* 43 C10
Volgograd, *Russia* 43 B11
Volgogradskoye Vdkhr., *Russia* 41 F14
Volgorechensk, *Russia* 41 C12
Volkach, *Germany* 19 F6
Volkerak, *Neths.* 17 E4
Volkhov, *Russia* 40 B8
Volkhov →, *Russia* 40 A8
Völklingen, *Germany* 19 F2
Volkovysk, *Belorussia* 40 E4
Volksrust, *S. Africa* 85 D4
Vollenhove, *Neths.* 16 C7
Vol'n'ansk, *Ukraine* 42 C6
Volnovakha, *Ukraine* 42 C7
Volochanka, *Russia* 45 B10
Volodarsk, *Russia* 41 C13
Vologda, *Russia* 41 B11
Volokolamsk, *Russia* 41 C9
Volokonovka, *Russia* 41 F10
Vólos, *Greece* 39 K5
Volosovo, *Russia* 40 B6
Volozhin, *Belorussia* 40 D5
Volsk, *Russia* 41 E15
Volta →, *Ghana* 70 F4
Volta, L., *Ghana* 79 D5
Volta Blanche = White Volta →, *Ghana* 79 D4
Volta Redonda, *Brazil* 123 F3
Voltaire, C., *Australia* 88 B4
Volterra, *Italy* 32 E7
Voltri, *Italy* 32 D5
Volturara Áppula, *Italy* 35 A8
Volturno →, *Italy* 34 A6
Volubilis, *Morocco* 74 B3
Volvo, *Australia* 91 E3
Volzhsk, *Russia* 41 D16
Volzhskiy, *Russia* 43 B11
Vondrozo, *Madag.* 85 C8
Voorburg, *Neths.* 16 D4
Voorne Putten, *Neths.* 16 E4
Voorst, *Neths.* 16 D8
Voorthuizen, *Neths.* 16 D7
Vopnafjörður, *Iceland* 8 D6
Vóras Óros, *Greece* 39 J4
Vorbasse, *Denmark* 11 J3
Vorden, *Neths.* 16 D8
Vorderrhein →, *Switz.* 23 C8
Vordingborg, *Denmark* 11 K5
Voreppe, *France* 27 C9
Voríai Sporádhes, *Greece* 39 K6
Vórios Evvoïkos Kólpos, *Greece* 39 L6
Vorkuta, *Russia* 44 C7
Vorma →, *Norway* 10 D5
Vorona →, *Russia* 41 F13
Voronezh, *Russia* 41 F11
Voronezh, *Ukraine* 40 F8
Voronezh →, *Russia* 41 F10
Vorontsovo-Aleksandrovskoye = Zelenokumsk, *Russia* 43 D10
Voroshilovgrad = Lugansk, *Ukraine* 43 B8
Voroshilovsk = Kommunarsk, *Ukraine* 43 B8
Vorovskoye, *Russia* 45 D16
Vorselaar, *Belgium* 17 F5
Vorskla →, *Ukraine* 42 B6
Võru, *Estonia* 40 C5
Vorupør, *Denmark* 11 H2
Vosges, *France* 25 D14
Vosges □, *France* 25 D13
Voskopoja, *Albania* 39 J3
Voskresensk, *Russia* 41 D11
Voskresenskoye, *Russia* 41 C14
Voss, *Norway* 9 F9
Vosselaar, *Belgium* 17 F5
Vostok I., *Kiribati* 93 J12
Vouga →, *Portugal* 30 E2
Vouillé, *France* 24 F7
Vouvray, *France* 24 E7
Vouvry, *Switz.* 22 D3
Voúxa, Ákra, *Greece* 37 D5
Vouzela, *Portugal* 30 E2
Vouziers, *France* 25 C11
Voves, *France* 25 D8
Voxna, *Sweden* 10 C9
Vozhgaly, *Russia* 41 B17
Voznesenka, *Russia* 45 D10
Voznesensk, *Ukraine* 42 C4
Voznesenye, *Russia* 44 C4
Vrådal, *Norway* 10 E2
Vrakhnéïka, *Greece* 39 L4
Vrancei, Munţii, *Romania* 38 D9
Vrangelya, Ostrov, *Russia* 45 B19
Vranica, *Bos.-H.* 21 M7
Vranje, *Serbia* 21 N11
Vransko, *Slovenia* 33 B11
Vratsa, *Bulgaria* 38 F6
Vrbas, *Serbia* 21 K9
Vrbas →, *Bos.-H.* 21 K7
Vrbnik, *Croatia* 33 C11
Vrbovec, *Croatia* 33 C13
Vrbovsko, *Croatia* 33 C12
Vrchlabí, *Czech.* 20 E5
Vrede, *S. Africa* 85 D4
Vredefort, *S. Africa* 84 D4
Vredenburg, *S. Africa* 84 E2
Vredendal, *S. Africa* 84 E2
Vreeswijk, *Neths.* 16 D6
Vrena, *Sweden* 11 F10
Vrgorac, *Croatia* 21 M7
Vrhnika, *Slovenia* 33 C11
Vridi, *Ivory C.* 78 D4
Vries, *Neths.* 16 B9
Vriezenveen, *Neths.* 16 D9
Vrindavan, *India* 62 F7
Vrises, *Greece* 37 D6
Vrnograč, *Bos.-H.* 33 C12
Vroomshoop, *Neths.* 16 D9
Vršac, *Serbia* 21 K11
Vrsacki Kanal, *Serbia* 21 K11
Vryburg, *S. Africa* 84 D3
Vryheid, *S. Africa* 85 D5
Vsetín, *Czech.* 20 F8
Vu Liet, *Vietnam* 58 C5
Vucha →, *Bulgaria* 39 G7
Vught, *Neths.* 17 E6
Vukovar, *Croatia* 21 K8
Vulcan, *Canada* 100 C6
Vulcan, *U.S.A.* 104 C2
Vulcano, *Italy* 35 D7
Vŭlchedruma, *Bulgaria* 38 F6
Vulci, *Italy* 33 F8
Vulkaneshty, *Moldavia* 42 D3
Vunduzi →, *Mozam.* 83 F3
Vung Tau, *Vietnam* 59 G6
Vŭrbitsa, *Bulgaria* 38 G9
Vyasniki, *Russia* 41 C13
Vyatka, *Russia* 41 B16
Vyatka →, *Russia* 41 C17
Vyatskiye Polyany, *Russia* 41 C17
Vyazemskiy, *Russia* 45 E14
Vyazma, *Russia* 40 D9
Vyborg, *Russia* 44 C3
Vychegda →, *Russia* 44 C5
Vychodné Beskydy, *Europe* 20 F11
Vyksa, *Russia* 41 D13
Vyrnwy, L., *U.K.* 12 E4
Vyshniy Volochek, *Russia* 40 C9
Vyškov, *Czech.* 20 F6
Vysoké Mýto, *Czech.* 20 F6
Vysokovsk, *Russia* 41 C10
Vysotsk, *Ukraine* 40 F5

W

W.A.C. Bennett Dam, *Canada* 100 B4
Wa, *Ghana* 78 C4
Waal →, *Neths.* 16 E6
Waalwijk, *Neths.* 17 E6
Waarschoot, *Belgium* 17 F3
Waasmunster, *Belgium* 17 F4
Wabakimi L., *Canada* 98 B2
Wabana, *Canada* 99 C9
Wabasca, *Canada* 100 B6
Wabash, *U.S.A.* 104 E3
Wabash →, *U.S.A.* 104 G1
Wabeno, *U.S.A.* 104 C1
Wabi →, *Ethiopia* 77 F5
Wabigoon L., *Canada* 101 D10
Wabowden, *Canada* 101 C9
Wąbrzeźno, *Poland* 20 B8
Wabu Hu, *China* 53 A11
Wabuk Pt., *Canada* 98 A2
Wabush, *Canada* 99 B6
Wabuska, *U.S.A.* 110 G4
Wachtebeke, *Belgium* 17 F3
Wächtersbach, *Germany* 19 E5
Waco, *U.S.A.* 109 K6
Waconichi, L., *Canada* 98 B5
Wad Ban Naqa, *Sudan* 77 D3
Wad Banda, *Sudan* 77 E2
Wad el Haddad, *Sudan* 77 E3
Wad en Nau, *Sudan* 77 E3
Wad Hamid, *Sudan* 77 D3
Wâd Medanî, *Sudan* 77 E3
Wad Thana, *Pakistan* 62 F2
Wadayama, *Japan* 49 G7
Waddeneilanden, *Neths.* 16 B6
Waddenzee, *Neths.* 16 B6
Wadderin Hill, *Australia* 89 F2
Waddington, *U.S.A.* 107 B9
Waddington, Mt., *Canada* 100 C3
Waddinxveen, *Neths.* 16 D5
Waddy Pt., *Australia* 91 C5

Wadena, Canada 101 C8
Wadena, U.S.A. 108 B7
Wädenswil, Switz. 23 B7
Wadesboro, U.S.A. 105 H5
Wadhams, Canada 100 C3
Wādī as Sīr, Jordan 69 D4
Wadi Gemâl, Egypt 76 C4
Wadi Halfa, Sudan 76 C3
Wadian, China 53 A9
Wadowice, Poland 20 F9
Wadsworth, U.S.A. 110 G4
Waegwan, S. Korea 51 G15
Wafrah, Si. Arabia 64 D5
Wagenberg, Neths. 17 E5
Wageningen, Neths. 16 E7
Wageningen, Surinam 121 B6
Wager B., Canada 97 B11
Wager Bay, Canada 97 B10
Wagga Wagga, Australia 91 F4
Waghete, Indonesia 57 E9
Wagin, Australia 89 F2
Wağon Mound, U.S.A. 109 G2
Wagoner, U.S.A. 109 G7
Wagrowiec, Poland 20 C7
Wah, Pakistan 62 C5
Wahai, Indonesia 57 E7
Wahiawa, U.S.A. 102 H15
Wâḥid, Egypt 69 E1
Wahnai, Afghan. 62 C1
Wahoo, U.S.A. 108 E6
Wahpeton, U.S.A. 108 B6
Wai, Koh, Cambodia 59 H4
Waiau →, N.Z. 87 K4
Waibeem, Indonesia 57 E8
Waiblingen, Germany 19 G5
Waidhofen, Niederösterreich, Austria 20 G5
Waidhofen, Niederösterreich, Austria 21 H4
Waigeo, Indonesia 57 E8
Waihi, N.Z. 87 G5
Waihou →, N.Z. 87 G5
Waika, Zaïre 82 C2
Waikabubak, Indonesia 57 F5
Waikari, N.Z. 87 K4
Waikato →, N.Z. 87 G5
Waikerie, Australia 91 E2
Waikokopu, N.Z. 87 H6
Waikouaiti, N.Z. 87 L3
Waimakariri →, N.Z. 87 K4
Waimate, N.Z. 87 L3
Waimes, Belgium 17 H8
Wainganga →, India 60 K11
Waingapu, Indonesia 57 F6
Waini →, Guyana 121 B6
Wainwright, Canada 101 C6
Wainwright, U.S.A. 96 A3
Waiouru, N.Z. 87 H5
Waipara, N.Z. 87 K4
Waipawa, N.Z. 87 H6
Waipiro, N.Z. 87 H7
Waipu, N.Z. 87 F5
Waipukurau, N.Z. 87 J6
Wairakei, N.Z. 87 H6
Wairarapa, L., N.Z. 87 J5
Wairoa, N.Z. 87 H6
Waitaki →, N.Z. 87 L3
Waitara, N.Z. 87 H5
Waitsburg, U.S.A. 110 C5
Waiuku, N.Z. 87 G5
Wajima, Japan 49 F8
Wajir, Kenya 82 B5
Wajir □, Kenya 82 B5
Wakasa, Japan 49 G7
Wakasa-Wan, Japan 49 G7
Wakatipu, L., N.Z. 87 L2
Wakaw, Canada 101 C7
Wakayama, Japan 49 G7
Wakayama-ken □, Japan 49 H7
Wake Forest, U.S.A. 105 H6
Wake I., Pac. Oc. 92 F8
Wakefield, N.Z. 87 J4
Wakefield, U.K. 12 D6
Wakefield, Mass., U.S.A. 107 D13
Wakefield, Mich., U.S.A. 108 B10
Wakeham Bay = Maricourt, Canada 97 C12
Wakema, Burma 61 L19
Wakkanai, Japan 48 B10
Wakkerstroom, S. Africa 85 D5
Wakool, Australia 91 F3
Wakool →, Australia 91 F3
Wakre, Indonesia 57 E8
Wakuach L., Canada 99 A6
Walamba, Zambia 83 E2
Wałbrzych, Poland 20 E6
Walbury Hill, U.K. 13 F6
Walcha, Australia 91 E5
Walcheren, Neths. 17 E3
Walcott, U.S.A. 110 F10
Wałcz, Poland 20 B6
Wald, Switz. 23 B7
Waldbröl, Germany 18 E3
Waldburg Ra., Australia 88 D2
Waldeck, Germany 18 D5
Walden, Colo., U.S.A. 110 F10
Walden, N.Y., U.S.A. 107 E10
Waldenburg, Switz. 22 B5
Waldport, U.S.A. 110 D1
Waldron, U.S.A. 109 H7
Waldshut, Germany 19 H4
Walembele, Ghana 78 C4
Walensee, Switz. 23 B8
Walenstadt, Switz. 23 B8
Wales □, U.K. 13 E4
Walewale, Ghana 79 C4
Walgett, Australia 91 E4
Walgreen Coast, Antarctica 5 D15
Walhalla, Australia 91 F4
Walhalla, U.S.A. 101 D9
Walker, U.S.A. 108 B7
Walker L., Man., Canada 101 C9
Walker L., Qué., Canada 99 B6
Walker L., U.S.A. 110 G4
Walkerston, Australia 90 C4
Walkerton, Canada 106 B3
Wall, U.S.A. 108 C3
Walla Walla, U.S.A. 110 C4
Wallabadah, Australia 90 B3
Wallace, Idaho, U.S.A. 110 C6
Wallace, N.C., U.S.A. 105 H7
Wallace, Nebr., U.S.A. 108 E4
Wallaceburg, Canada 98 D3
Wallachia = Valahia, Romania 38 E8
Wallal, Australia 91 D4
Wallal Downs, Australia 88 C3
Wallambin, L., Australia 89 F2
Wallaroo, Australia 91 E2
Wallasey, U.K. 12 D4
Walldürn, Germany 19 F5
Wallerawang, Australia 91 E5
Wallhallow, Australia 90 B2
Wallingford, U.S.A. 107 E12
Wallis & Futuna, Is., Pac. Oc. 92 J10
Wallisellen, Switz. 23 B7
Wallowa, U.S.A. 110 D5
Wallowa Mts., U.S.A. 110 D5
Wallsend, Australia 91 E5
Wallsend, U.K. 12 C6
Wallula, U.S.A. 110 C4
Wallumbilla, Australia 91 D4
Walmsley, L., Canada 101 A7
Walney, I. of, U.K. 12 C4
Walnut Creek, U.S.A. 112 H4
Walnut Ridge, U.S.A. 109 G9
Walsall, U.K. 13 E6
Walsenburg, U.S.A. 109 G2
Walsh, U.S.A. 109 G3
Walsh →, Australia 90 B3
Walsh P.O., Australia 90 B3
Walshoutem, Belgium 17 G6
Walsrode, Germany 18 C5
Walterboro, U.S.A. 105 J5
Walters, U.S.A. 109 H5
Waltershausen, Germany 18 E6
Waltham, U.S.A. 107 D13
Waltham Station, Canada 98 C4
Waltman, U.S.A. 110 E10
Walton, U.S.A. 107 D9
Walvisbaai, S. Africa 84 C1
Wamba, Kenya 82 B4
Wamba, Zaïre 82 B2
Wamego, U.S.A. 108 F6
Wamena, Indonesia 57 E9
Wamsasi, Indonesia 57 E7
Wan Xian, China 50 E8
Wana, Pakistan 62 C3
Wanaaring, Australia 91 D3
Wanaka, N.Z. 87 L2
Wanaka L., N.Z. 87 L2
Wan'an, China 53 D10
Wanapiri, Indonesia 57 E9
Wanapitei L., Canada 98 C3
Wanbi, Australia 91 E3
Wandaik, Guyana 121 C6
Wandarrie, Australia 89 E2
Wanderer, Zimbabwe 83 F3
Wandoan, Australia 91 D4
Wandre, Belgium 17 G7
Wanfercée-Baulet, Belgium 17 H5
Wanfu, China 51 D12
Wang →, Thailand 58 D2
Wang Kai, Sudan 77 F2
Wang Noi, Thailand 58 E3
Wang Saphung, Thailand 58 D3
Wang Thong, Thailand 58 D3
Wanga, Zaïre 82 B2
Wangal, Indonesia 57 F8
Wanganella, Australia 91 F3
Wanganui, N.Z. 87 H5
Wangaratta, Australia 91 F4
Wangary, Australia 91 E2
Wangcang, China 52 A6
Wangdu, China 50 E8
Wangerooge, Germany 18 B3
Wangi, Kenya 82 C5
Wangiwangi, Indonesia 57 F6
Wangjiang, China 53 B11
Wangmo, China 52 E6
Wangqing, China 51 C15
Wankaner, India 62 H4
Wanless, Canada 101 C8
Wannian, China 53 C11
Wanon Niwat, Thailand 58 D4
Wanquan, China 50 D8
Wanrong, China 50 G6
Wanshan, China 52 D7
Wanshengchang, China 52 C6
Wanssum, Neths. 17 E8
Wanxian, China 52 B7
Wanyuan, China 52 A7
Wanzai, China 53 C10
Wanze, Belgium 17 G6
Wapakoneta, U.S.A. 104 E3
Wapato, U.S.A. 110 C3
Wapawekka L., Canada 101 C8
Wapikopa L., Canada 98 B2
Wappingers Falls, U.S.A. 107 E11
Wapsipinicon →, U.S.A. 108 E9
Warangal, India 60 L11
Waratah, Australia 90 G4
Waratah B., Australia 91 F4
Warburg, Germany 18 D5
Warburton, Vic., Australia 91 F4
Warburton, W. Austral., Australia 89 E4
Warburton Ra., Australia 89 E4
Ward, N.Z. 87 J5
Ward →, Australia 91 D4
Ward Cove, U.S.A. 100 B2
Ward Mt., U.S.A. 112 H8
Warden, S. Africa 85 D4
Wardha, India 60 J11
Wardha →, India 60 K11
Wardlow, Canada 100 C6
Ware, Canada 100 B3
Ware, U.S.A. 107 D12
Waregem, Belgium 17 G2
Wareham, U.S.A. 107 E14
Waremme, Belgium 17 G6
Waren, Germany 18 B8
Warendorf, Germany 18 D3
Warialda, Australia 91 D5
Wariap, Indonesia 57 E8
Warin Chamrap, Thailand 58 E5
Warkopi, Indonesia 57 E8
Warley, U.K. 13 E6
Warm Springs, U.S.A. 111 G5
Warman, Canada 101 C7
Warmbad, Namibia 84 D2
Warmbad, S. Africa 85 C4
Warmenhuizen, Neths. 16 C5
Warmeriville, France 25 C11
Warmond, Neths. 16 D5
Warnambool Downs, Australia 90 C3
Warnemünde, Germany 18 A8
Warner, Canada 100 D6
Warner Mts., U.S.A. 110 F3
Warner Robins, U.S.A. 105 J4
Warnes, Bolivia 125 D5
Warneton, Belgium 17 G1
Warnow →, Germany 18 A8
Warnsveld, Neths. 16 D8
Waroona, Australia 89 F2
Warracknabeal, Australia 91 F3
Warragul, Australia 91 F4
Warrawagine, Australia 88 D3
Warrego →, Australia 91 E4
Warrego Ra., Australia 90 C4
Warren, Australia 91 E4
Warren, Ark., U.S.A. 109 J8
Warren, Mich., U.S.A. 104 D4
Warren, Minn., U.S.A. 108 A6
Warren, Ohio, U.S.A. 106 E4
Warren, Pa., U.S.A. 106 E5
Warrenpoint, U.K. 15 B5
Warrensburg, U.S.A. 108 F8
Warrenton, S. Africa 84 D3
Warrenton, U.S.A. 112 D3
Warrenville, Australia 91 D4
Warri, Nigeria 79 D6
Warrina, Australia 91 D2
Warrington, U.K. 12 D5
Warrington, U.S.A. 105 K2
Warrnambool, Australia 91 F3
Warroad, U.S.A. 108 A7
Warsa, Indonesia 57 E9
Warsaw = Warszawa, Poland 20 C11
Warsaw, Ind., U.S.A. 104 E3
Warsaw, N.Y., U.S.A. 106 D6
Warsaw, Ohio, U.S.A. 106 F2
Warstein, Germany 18 D4
Warszawa, Poland 20 C11
Warta →, Poland 20 C4
Warthe = Warta →, Poland 20 C4
Waru, Indonesia 57 E8
Warwick, Australia 91 D5
Warwick, U.K. 13 E6
Warwick, U.S.A. 107 E13
Warwickshire □, U.K. 13 E6
Wasaga Beach, Canada 106 B4
Wasatch Ra., U.S.A. 110 F8
Wasbank, S. Africa 85 D5
Wasco, Calif., U.S.A. 113 K7
Wasco, Oreg., U.S.A. 110 D3
Waseca, U.S.A. 108 C8
Wasekamio L., Canada 101 B7
Wash, The, U.K. 12 E8
Washago, Canada 106 B5
Washburn, N. Dak., U.S.A. 108 B4
Washburn, Wis., U.S.A. 108 B9
Washim, India 60 J10
Washington, D.C., U.S.A. 104 F7
Washington, Ga., U.S.A. 105 J4
Washington, Ind., U.S.A. 104 F2
Washington, Iowa, U.S.A. 108 E9
Washington, Mo., U.S.A. 108 F9
Washington, N.C., U.S.A. 105 H7
Washington, N.J., U.S.A. 107 F10
Washington, Pa., U.S.A. 106 F4
Washington, Utah, U.S.A. 111 H7
Washington □, U.S.A. 110 C3
Washington, Mt., U.S.A. 107 B13
Washington I., U.S.A. 104 C2
Washougal, U.S.A. 112 E4
Wasian, Indonesia 57 E8
Wasior, Indonesia 57 E8
Waskaiowaka, L., Canada 101 B9
Waskesiu Lake, Canada 101 C7
Wasmes, Belgium 17 H3
Waspik, Neths. 17 E5
Wassen, Switz. 23 C7
Wassenaar, Neths. 16 D4
Wasserburg, Germany 19 G8
Wasserkuppe, Germany 18 E5
Wassy, France 25 D11
Waswanipi, Canada 98 C4
Waswanipi, L., Canada 98 C4
Watangpone, Indonesia 57 E6
Water Park Pt., Australia 90 C5
Water Valley, U.S.A. 109 H10
Waterberge, S. Africa 85 C4
Waterbury, Conn., U.S.A. 107 E11
Waterbury, Vt., U.S.A. 107 B12
Waterbury L., Canada 101 B8
Waterdown, Canada 106 C5
Waterford, Canada 106 D4
Waterford, Ireland 15 D4
Waterford, U.S.A. 112 H6
Waterford □, Ireland 15 D4
Waterford Harbour, Ireland 15 D5
Waterhen L., Man., Canada 101 C9
Waterhen L., Sask., Canada 101 C7
Wateringen, Neths. 16 D4
Waterloo, Belgium 17 G4
Waterloo, Ont., Canada 98 D3
Waterloo, Qué., Canada 107 A12
Waterloo, S. Leone 78 D2
Waterloo, Ill., U.S.A. 108 F9
Waterloo, Iowa, U.S.A. 108 D8
Waterloo, N.Y., U.S.A. 106 D8
Watermeal-Boitsford, Belgium 17 G4
Watersmeet, U.S.A. 108 B10
Waterton-Glacier International Peace Park, U.S.A. 110 B7
Watertown, Conn., U.S.A. 107 E11
Watertown, N.Y., U.S.A. 107 C9
Watertown, S. Dak., U.S.A. 108 C6
Watertown, Wis., U.S.A. 108 D10
Waterval-Boven, S. Africa 85 D5
Waterville, Canada 107 A13
Waterville, Maine, U.S.A. 99 D6
Waterville, N.Y., U.S.A. 107 D9
Waterville, Pa., U.S.A. 106 E7
Waterville, Wash., U.S.A. 110 C3
Watervliet, Belgium 17 F3
Watervliet, U.S.A. 107 D11
Wates, Indonesia 57 G14
Watford, Canada 106 D3
Watford, U.K. 13 F7
Watford City, U.S.A. 108 B3
Wathaman →, Canada 101 B8
Watheroo, Australia 89 F2
Wating, China 50 G4
Watkins Glen, U.S.A. 106 D8
Watling I. = San Salvador, Bahamas 117 B5
Watonga, U.S.A. 109 H5
Watou, Belgium 17 G1
Watrous, Canada 101 C7
Watrous, U.S.A. 109 H2
Watsa, Zaïre 82 B2
Watseka, U.S.A. 104 E2
Watson, Australia 89 F5
Watson, Canada 101 C8
Watson Lake, Canada 100 A3
Watsonville, U.S.A. 111 H3
Wattenwil, Switz. 22 C5
Wattiwarriganna Cr. →, Australia 91 D2
Wattwil, Switz. 23 B8
Watuata = Batuata, Indonesia 57 F6
Watubela, Kepulauan, Indonesia 57 E8
Watubela Is. = Watubela, Kepulauan, Indonesia 57 E8
Waubach, Neths. 17 G8
Waubamik, Canada 106 A4
Waubay, U.S.A. 108 C6
Waubra, Australia 91 F3
Wauchope, Australia 91 E5
Wauchula, U.S.A. 105 M5
Waugh, Canada 101 D9
Waukarlycarly, L., Australia 88 D3
Waukegan, U.S.A. 104 D2
Waukesha, U.S.A. 104 D1
Waukon, U.S.A. 108 D9
Wauneta, U.S.A. 108 E4
Waupaca, U.S.A. 108 C10
Waupun, U.S.A. 108 D10
Waurika, U.S.A. 109 H6
Wausau, U.S.A. 108 C10
Wautoma, U.S.A. 108 C10
Wauwatosa, U.S.A. 104 D2
Wave Hill, Australia 88 C5
Waveney →, U.K. 13 E9
Waverley, N.Z. 87 H5
Waverly, Iowa, U.S.A. 108 D8
Waverly, N.Y., U.S.A. 107 D8
Wavre, Belgium 17 G5
Wavreille, Belgium 17 H6
Wâw, Sudan 77 F2
Wāw al Kabīr, Libya 73 C8
Wawa, Canada 98 C3
Wawa, Nigeria 79 D5
Wawa, Sudan 76 C3
Wawanesa, Canada 101 D9
Wawona, U.S.A. 112 H7
Waxahachie, U.S.A. 109 J6
Way, L., Australia 89 E3
Wayabula Rau, Indonesia 57 D7
Wayatinah, Australia 90 G4
Waycross, U.S.A. 105 K4
Wayi, Sudan 77 F3
Wayne, Nebr., U.S.A. 108 D6
Wayne, W. Va., U.S.A. 104 F4
Waynesboro, Ga., U.S.A. 105 J4
Waynesboro, Miss., U.S.A. 105 K1
Waynesboro, Pa., U.S.A. 104 F7
Waynesboro, Va., U.S.A. 104 F6
Waynesburg, U.S.A. 104 F5
Waynesville, U.S.A. 105 H4
Waynoka, U.S.A. 109 G5
Wāzin, Libya 75 B7
Wazirabad, Pakistan 62 C6
We, Indonesia 56 C1
Weald, The, U.K. 13 F8
Wear →, U.K. 12 C6
Weatherford, Okla., U.S.A. 109 H5
Weatherford, Tex., U.S.A. 109 J6
Weaverville, U.S.A. 110 F2
Webb City, U.S.A. 109 G7
Webo = Nyaake, Liberia 78 E3
Webster, Mass., U.S.A. 107 D13
Webster, N.Y., U.S.A. 106 C7
Webster, S. Dak., U.S.A. 108 C6
Webster, Wis., U.S.A. 108 C8
Webster City, U.S.A. 108 D8
Webster Green, U.S.A. 108 F9
Webster Springs, U.S.A. 104 F5
Weda, Indonesia 57 D7
Weda, Teluk, Indonesia 57 D7
Weddell I., Falk. Is. 128 D4
Weddell Sea, Antarctica 5 D1
Wedderburn, Australia 91 F3
Wedgeport, Canada 99 D6
Wedza, Zimbabwe 83 F3
Wee Waa, Australia 91 E4
Weed, U.S.A. 110 F2
Weed Heights, U.S.A. 112 G7
Weedsport, U.S.A. 107 C8
Weedville, U.S.A. 106 E6
Weemelah, Australia 91 D4
Weenen, S. Africa 85 D5
Weener, Germany 18 B3
Weert, Neths. 17 F7
Weesp, Neths. 16 D6
Weggis, Switz. 23 B6
Węgliniec, Poland 20 D5
Węgorzewo, Poland 20 A11
Węgrów, Poland 20 C12
Wehl, Neths. 16 E8
Wei He →, Hebei, China 50 F8
Wei He →, Shaanxi, China 50 G6
Weichang, China 51 D9
Weichuan, China 50 G7
Weida, Germany 18 E8
Weiden, Germany 19 F8
Weifang, China 54 C6
Weifang, Shandong, China 51 F10
Weihai, China 51 F12
Weilburg, Germany 18 E4
Weilheim, Germany 19 H7
Weimar, Germany 18 E7
Weinan, China 50 G5
Weinfelden, Switz. 23 A8
Weingarten, Germany 19 H5
Weinheim, Germany 19 F4
Weining, China 52 D5
Weipa, Australia 90 A3
Weir →, Australia 91 D4
Weir →, Canada 101 B10
Weir River, Canada 101 B10
Weirton, U.S.A. 106 F4
Weisen, Switz. 23 C9
Weiser, U.S.A. 110 D5
Weishan, Shandong, China 51 G9
Weishan, Yunnan, China 52 E3
Weissenburg, Germany 19 F6
Weissenfels, Germany 18 D8
Weisshorn, Switz. 22 D5
Weissmies, Switz. 22 D6
Weisstannen, Switz. 23 C8
Weisswasser, Germany 18 D10
Weiswampach, Belgium 17 H8
Weixi, China 52 D2
Weixin, China 52 D5
Weiyuan, China 50 G3
Weiz, Austria 21 H5
Weizhou Dao, China 52 G7
Wejherowo, Poland 20 A8
Wekusko L., Canada 101 C9
Welbourn Hill, Australia 91 D1
Welch, U.S.A. 104 G5
Weldya, Ethiopia 77 E4
Welega □, Ethiopia 77 F3
Welkenraedt, Belgium 17 G7
Welkite, Ethiopia 77 F4
Welkom, S. Africa 84 D4
Welland, Canada 98 D4
Welland →, U.K. 12 E7
Wellen, Belgium 17 G6
Wellesley Is., Australia 90 B2
Wellin, Belgium 17 H6
Wellingborough, U.K. 13 E7
Wellington, Australia 91 E4
Wellington, Canada 98 D4
Wellington, N.Z. 87 J5
Wellington, S. Africa 84 E2
Wellington, Shrops., U.K. 12 E5
Wellington, Somst., U.K. 13 G4
Wellington, Colo., U.S.A. 108 E2
Wellington, Kans., U.S.A. 109 G6
Wellington, Nev., U.S.A. 112 G7
Wellington, Ohio, U.S.A. 106 E2
Wellington, Tex., U.S.A. 109 H4

Wellington, I., *Chile* 128 C2
Wellington, L., *Australia* .. 91 F4
Wells, *Norfolk, U.K.* 12 E8
Wells, *Somst., U.K.* 13 F5
Wells, *Maine, U.S.A.* 107 C14
Wells, *Minn., U.S.A.* 108 D8
Wells, *Nev., U.S.A.* 110 F6
Wells, L., *Australia* 89 E3
Wells Gray Prov. Park,
    Canada 100 C4
Wells River, *U.S.A.* 107 B12
Wellsboro, *U.S.A.* 106 E7
Wellsburg, *U.S.A.* 106 F4
Wellsville, *Mo., U.S.A.* ... 108 F8
Wellsville, *N.Y., U.S.A.* .. 106 D7
Wellsville, *Ohio, U.S.A.* .. 106 F4
Wellsville, *Utah, U.S.A.* .. 110 F8
Wellton, *U.S.A.* 111 K6
Welmel →, *Ethiopia* 77 F5
Welo □, *Ethiopia* 77 E4
Wels, *Austria* 21 G4
Welshpool, *U.K.* 13 E4
Wem, *U.K.* 12 E5
Wembere →, *Tanzania* 82 C3
Wemmel, *Belgium* 17 G4
Wen Xian, *Gansu, China* .. 50 H3
Wen Xian, *Henan, China* .. 50 G7
Wenatchee, *U.S.A.* 110 C3
Wenchang, *China* 58 C8
Wencheng, *China* 53 D13
Wenchi, *Ghana* 78 D4
Wenchow = Wenzhou,
    China 53 C13
Wenchuan, *China* 52 B4
Wendell, *U.S.A.* 110 E6
Wenden, *U.S.A.* 113 M13
Wendeng, *China* 51 F12
Wendesi, *Indonesia* 57 E8
Wendo, *Ethiopia* 77 F4
Wendover, *U.S.A.* 110 F6
Wenduine, *Belgium* 17 F2
Weng'an, *China* 52 D6
Wengcheng, *China* 53 E9
Wengen, *Switz.* 22 C5
Wengyuan, *China* 53 E10
Wenjiang, *China* 52 B4
Wenling, *China* 53 C13
Wenlock →, *Australia* 90 A3
Wenshan, *China* 52 F5
Wenshang, *China* 50 G9
Wenshui, *Guizhou, China* . 52 C6
Wenshui, *Shanxi, China* .. 50 F7
Wensu, *China* 54 B3
Wentworth, *Australia* 91 E3
Wenut, *Indonesia* 57 E8
Wenxi, *China* 50 G6
Wenzhou, *China* 53 C13
Weott, *U.S.A.* 110 F2
Wepener, *S. Africa* 84 D4
Werbomont, *Belgium* 17 H7
Werda, *Botswana* 84 D3
Werdau, *Germany* 18 E8
Werder, *Ethiopia* 68 F4
Werder, *Germany* 18 C8
Werdohl, *Germany* 18 D3
Wereilu, *Ethiopia* 77 E4
Weri, *Indonesia* 57 E8
Werkendam, *Neths.* 16 E5
Werne, *Germany* 18 D3
Werneck, *Germany* 19 F6
Wernigerode, *Germany* ... 18 D6
Werra →, *Germany* 18 D5
Werribee, *Australia* 91 F3
Werrimull, *Australia* 91 E3
Werris Creek, *Australia* .. 91 E5
Wersar, *Indonesia* 57 E8
Wertach →, *Germany* 19 G6
Wertheim, *Germany* 19 F5
Wertingen, *Germany* 19 G6
Wervershoof, *Neths.* 16 C6
Wervik, *Belgium* 17 G2
Weser →, *Germany* 18 B4
Wesiri, *Indonesia* 57 F7
Wesley Vale, *U.S.A.* 111 J10
Wesleyville, *Canada* 99 C9
Wesleyville, *U.S.A.* 106 D4
Wessel, C., *Australia* 90 A2
Wessel Is., *Australia* 90 A2
Wesselburen, *Germany* ... 18 A4
Wessem, *Neths.* 17 F7
Wessington, *U.S.A.* 108 C5
Wessington Springs, *U.S.A.* 108 C5
West, *U.S.A.* 109 K6
West B., *U.S.A.* 109 L10
West Baines →, *Australia* . 88 C4
West Bend, *U.S.A.* 104 D1
West Bengal □, *India* 63 H12
West Beskids = Západné
    Beskydy, *Europe* 20 F9
West Branch, *U.S.A.* 104 C3
West Bromwich, *U.K.* 13 E5
West Cape Howe, *Australia* 89 G2
West Chazy, *U.S.A.* 107 B11
West Chester, *U.S.A.* 104 F8
West Columbia, *U.S.A.* .. 109 L7
West Covina, *U.S.A.* 113 L9
West Des Moines, *U.S.A.* . 108 E8
West End, *Bahamas* 116 A4
West Falkland, *Falk. Is.* .. 128 D4
West Fjord = Vestfjorden,
    Norway 8 C3
West Frankfort, *U.S.A.* ... 108 G10
West Glamorgan □, *U.K.* . 13 F4
West Hartford, *U.S.A.* ... 107 E12
West Haven, *U.S.A.* 107 E12

West Helena, *U.S.A.* 109 H9
West Ice Shelf, *Antarctica* . 5 C7
West Indies, *Cent. Amer.* . 117 C7
West Lorne, *Canada* 106 D3
West Lunga →, *Zambia* .. 83 E1
West Memphis, *U.S.A.* ... 109 H9
West Midlands □, *U.K.* ... 13 E6
West Mifflin, *U.S.A.* 106 F5
West Monroe, *U.S.A.* 109 J8
West Newton, *U.S.A.* 106 F5
West Nicholson, *Zimbabwe* 83 G2
West Palm Beach, *U.S.A.* . 105 M5
West Plains, *U.S.A.* 109 G9
West Pt. = Ouest, Pte.,
    Canada 99 C7
West Pt., *Australia* 91 F2
West Point, *Ga., U.S.A.* .. 105 J3
West Point, *Miss., U.S.A.* . 105 J1
West Point, *Nebr., U.S.A.* . 108 E6
West Point, *Va., U.S.A.* .. 104 G7
West Pokot □, *Kenya* 82 B4
West Road →, *Canada* ... 100 C4
West Rutland, *U.S.A.* 107 C11
West Schelde =
    Westerschelde →, *Neths.* 17 F2
West Seneca, *U.S.A.* 106 D6
West Siberian Plain, *Russia* 46 C11
West Sussex □, *U.K.* 13 G7
West-Terschelling, *Neths.* . 16 B6
West Virginia □, *U.S.A.* .. 104 F5
West-Vlaanderen □,
    Belgium 17 G2
West Walker →, *U.S.A.* .. 112 G7
West Wyalong, *Australia* . 91 E4
West Yellowstone, *U.S.A.* . 110 D8
West Yorkshire □, *U.K.* .. 12 D6
Westall Pt., *Australia* 91 E1
Westbrook, *Maine, U.S.A.* 105 D10
Westbrook, *Tex., U.S.A.* . 109 J4
Westbury, *Australia* 90 G4
Westby, *U.S.A.* 108 A2
Westend, *U.S.A.* 113 K9
Westerbork, *Neths.* 16 C9
Westerland, *Germany* 18 A4
Western □, *Kenya* 82 B3
Western □, *Uganda* 82 B3
Western □, *Zambia* 83 F1
Western Australia □,
    Australia 89 E2
Western Ghats, *India* 60 N9
Western Isles □, *U.K.* 14 D1
Western Sahara ■, *Africa* . 74 D2
Western Samoa ■,
    Pac. Oc. 87 A13
Westernport, *U.S.A.* 104 F6
Westerschelde →, *Neths.* . 17 F2
Westerstede, *Germany* ... 18 B3
Westervoort, *Neths.* 16 E7
Westerwald, *Germany* 18 E4
Westfield, *Mass., U.S.A.* . 107 D12
Westfield, *N.Y., U.S.A.* .. 106 D5
Westfield, *Pa., U.S.A.* ... 106 E7
Westgat, *Neths.* 17 E3
Westhope, *U.S.A.* 108 A4
Westkapelle, *Belgium* 17 F2
Westkapelle, *Neths.* 17 E2
Westland Bight, *N.Z.* 87 K3
Westlock, *Canada* 100 C6
Westmalle, *Belgium* 17 F5
Westmeath □, *Ireland* ... 15 C4
Westminster, *U.S.A.* 104 F7
Westmorland, *U.S.A.* 111 K6
Weston, *Malaysia* 56 C5
Weston, *Oreg., U.S.A.* ... 110 D4
Weston, *W. Va., U.S.A.* .. 104 F5
Weston I., *Canada* 98 B4
Weston-super-Mare, *U.K.* . 13 F5
Westport, *Canada* 107 B8
Westport, *Ireland* 15 C2
Westport, *N.Z.* 87 J3
Westport, *Oreg., U.S.A.* .. 112 D3
Westport, *Wash., U.S.A.* . 110 C1
Westray, *Canada* 101 C8
Westray, *U.K.* 14 B6
Westree, *Canada* 98 C3
Westville, *Calif., U.S.A.* .. 112 F6
Westville, *Ill., U.S.A.* 104 E2
Westville, *Okla., U.S.A.* .. 109 G7
Westwood, *U.S.A.* 110 F3
Wetar, *Indonesia* 57 F7
Wetaskiwin, *Canada* 100 C6
Wethersfield, *U.S.A.* 107 E12
Wetteren, *Belgium* 17 G3
Wettingen, *Switz.* 23 B6
Wetzikon, *Switz.* 23 B7
Wetzlar, *Germany* 18 E4
Wevelgem, *Belgium* 17 G2
Wewoka, *U.S.A.* 109 H6
Wexford, *Ireland* 15 D5
Wexford □, *Ireland* 15 D5
Wexford Harbour, *Ireland* 15 D5
Weyburn, *Canada* 101 D8
Weyburn L., *Canada* 100 A5
Weyer, *Austria* 21 H4
Weyib →, *Ethiopia* 77 F5
Weymouth, *Canada* 99 D6
Weymouth, *U.K.* 13 G5
Weymouth, *U.S.A.* 107 D14
Weymouth, C., *Australia* . 90 A3
Wezemaal, *Belgium* 17 G5
Wezep, *Neths.* 16 D7
Whakatane, *N.Z.* 87 G6
Whale →, *Canada* 99 A6
Whale Cove, *Canada* 101 A10
Whales, B. of, *Antarctica* . 5 D12
Whalsay, *U.K.* 14 A7

Whangamomona, *N.Z.* ... 87 H5
Whangarei, *N.Z.* 87 F5
Whangarei Harb., *N.Z.* ... 87 F5
Wharfe →, *U.K.* 12 D6
Wharfedale, *U.K.* 12 C5
Wharton, *N.J., U.S.A.* ... 107 F10
Wharton, *Pa., U.S.A.* 106 E6
Wharton, *Tex., U.S.A.* ... 109 L6
Wheatland, *Calif., U.S.A.* . 112 F5
Wheatland, *Wyo., U.S.A.* . 108 D2
Wheatley, *Canada* 106 D2
Wheaton, *U.S.A.* 108 C6
Wheelbarrow Pk., *U.S.A.* . 112 H10
Wheeler, *Oreg., U.S.A.* .. 110 D2
Wheeler, *Tex., U.S.A.* ... 109 H4
Wheeler →, *Canada* 101 B7
Wheeler Pk., *N. Mex.,*
    U.S.A. 111 H11
Wheeler Pk., *Nev., U.S.A.* 111 G6
Wheeler Ridge, *U.S.A.* ... 113 L8
Wheeling, *U.S.A.* 106 F4
Whernside, *U.K.* 12 C5
Whidbey I., *U.S.A.* 100 D4
Whiskey Gap, *Canada* 100 D6
Whiskey Jack L., *Canada* . 101 B8
Whistleduck Cr. →,
    Australia 90 C2
Whitby, *Canada* 106 C6
Whitby, *U.K.* 12 C7
White →, *Ark., U.S.A.* ... 109 J9
White →, *Ind., U.S.A.* ... 104 F2
White →, *S. Dak., U.S.A.* 108 D5
White →, *Utah, U.S.A.* .. 110 F9
White →, *Wash., U.S.A.* . 112 C4
White, L., *Australia* 88 D4
White B., *Canada* 99 B8
White Bear Res., *Canada* . 99 C8
White Bird, *U.S.A.* 110 D5
White Butte, *U.S.A.* 108 B3
White City, *U.S.A.* 108 F6
White Cliffs, *Australia* ... 91 E3
White Deer, *U.S.A.* 109 H4
White Hall, *U.S.A.* 108 F9
White Haven, *U.S.A.* 107 E9
White I., *N.Z.* 87 G6
White L., *Canada* 107 A8
White L., *U.S.A.* 109 L8
White Mts., *Calif., U.S.A.* 111 H4
White Mts., *N.H., U.S.A.* 107 B13
White Nile = Nîl el
    Abyad →, *Sudan* 77 D3
White Nile Dam =
    Khazzân Jabal el Awliyâ,
    Sudan 77 D3
White Otter L., *Canada* .. 98 C1
White Pass, *Canada* 100 B1
White Pass, *U.S.A.* 112 D5
White Plains, *U.S.A.* 107 E11
White River, *Canada* 98 C2
White River, *S. Africa* ... 85 D5
White River, *U.S.A.* 108 D4
White Russia =
    Belorussia ■, *Europe* . 40 E5
White Sea = Beloye More,
    Russia 44 C4
White Sulphur Springs,
    Mont., U.S.A. 110 C8
White Sulphur Springs,
    W. Va., U.S.A. 104 G5
White Swan, *U.S.A.* 112 D6
White Volta →, *Ghana* .. 79 D4
Whitecliffs, *N.Z.* 87 K3
Whitecourt, *Canada* 100 C5
Whiteface, *U.S.A.* 109 J3
Whitefield, *U.S.A.* 107 B13
Whitefish, *U.S.A.* 110 B6
Whitefish L., *Canada* 101 A7
Whitefish Point, *U.S.A.* .. 104 B3
Whitegull, L., *Canada* ... 99 A7
Whitehall, *Mich., U.S.A.* . 104 D2
Whitehall, *Mont., U.S.A.* 110 D7
Whitehall, *N.Y., U.S.A.* . 107 C11
Whitehall, *Wis., U.S.A.* . 108 C9
Whitehaven, *U.K.* 12 C4
Whitehorse, *Canada* 100 A1
Whitehorse, Vale of, *U.K.* 13 F6
Whitemark, *Australia* 90 G4
Whitemouth, *Canada* 101 D9
Whiteplains, *Liberia* 78 D2
Whitesboro, *N.Y., U.S.A.* 107 C9
Whitesboro, *Tex., U.S.A.* 109 J6
Whiteshell Prov. Park,
    Canada 101 C9
Whiteside, Canal, *Chile* .. 128 D2
Whitetail, *U.S.A.* 108 A2
Whiteville, *U.S.A.* 105 H6
Whitewater, *U.S.A.* 104 D1
Whitewater Baldy, *U.S.A.* 111 K9
Whitewater L., *Canada* .. 98 B2
Whitewood, *Australia* ... 90 C3
Whitewood, *Canada* 101 C8
Whitfield, *Australia* 91 F4
Whithorn, *U.K.* 14 G4
Whitianga, *N.Z.* 87 G5
Whitman, *U.S.A.* 107 D14
Whitmire, *U.S.A.* 105 H5
Whitney, *Canada* 98 C4
Whitney, Mt., *U.S.A.* ... 111 H4
Whitney Point, *U.S.A.* ... 107 D9
Whitstable, *U.K.* 13 F9
Whitsunday I., *Australia* . 90 C4
Whittier, *U.S.A.* 113 M8
Whittlesea, *Australia* 91 F4
Whitwell, *U.S.A.* 105 H3
Wholdaia L., *Canada* 101 A8
Whyalla, *Australia* 91 E2

Whyjonta, *Australia* 91 D3
Wiarton, *Canada* 98 D3
Wiawso, *Ghana* 78 D4
Wibaux, *U.S.A.* 108 B2
Wichabai, *Guyana* 121 C6
Wichian Buri, *Thailand* .. 58 E3
Wichita, *U.S.A.* 109 G6
Wichita Falls, *U.S.A.* 109 J5
Wick, *U.K.* 14 C5
Wickenburg, *U.S.A.* 111 K7
Wickepin, *Australia* 89 F2
Wickham, C., *Australia* .. 90 F3
Wickliffe, *U.S.A.* 106 E3
Wicklow, *Ireland* 15 D5
Wicklow □, *Ireland* 15 D5
Wicklow Hd., *Ireland* 15 D5
Widgiemooltha, *Australia* 89 F3
Widnes, *U.K.* 12 D5
Wiedenbrück, *Germany* .. 18 D4
Wiek, *Germany* 18 A9
Wielbark, *Poland* 20 B10
Wieliczka, *Poland* 20 F10
Wieluń, *Poland* 20 D8
Wien, *Austria* 21 G6
Wiener Neustadt, *Austria* 21 H6
Wieprz →, *Koszalin,*
    Poland 20 A6
Wieprz →, *Lublin, Poland* 20 D11
Wierden, *Neths.* 16 D9
Wiers, *Belgium* 17 H3
Wiesbaden, *Germany* 19 E4
Wiesental, *Germany* 19 F4
Wigan, *U.K.* 12 D5
Wiggins, *Colo., U.S.A.* ... 108 E2
Wiggins, *Miss., U.S.A.* .. 109 K10
Wight, I. of □, *U.K.* 13 G6
Wigston, *U.K.* 14 G4
Wigtown, *U.K.* 14 G4
Wigtown B., *U.K.* 14 G4
Wijchen, *Neths.* 16 E7
Wijhe, *Neths.* 16 D8
Wijk bij Duurstede, *Neths.* 16 E6
Wil, *Switz.* 23 B8
Wilber, *U.S.A.* 108 E6
Wilberforce, *Canada* 106 A6
Wilberforce, C., *Australia* 90 A2
Wilburton, *U.S.A.* 109 H7
Wilcannia, *Australia* 91 E3
Wilcox, *U.S.A.* 106 E6
Wildbad, *Germany* 19 G4
Wildervank, *Neths.* 16 B9
Wildeshausen, *Germany* . 18 C4
Wildhorn, *Switz.* 22 D4
Wildrose, *Calif., U.S.A.* .. 113 J9
Wildrose, *N. Dak., U.S.A.* 108 A3
Wildspitze, *Austria* 19 J6
Wildstrubel, *Switz.* 22 D5
Wildwood, *U.S.A.* 104 F8
Wilge →, *S. Africa* 85 D4
Wilhelm II Coast,
    Antarctica 5 C7
Wilhelm-Pieck-Stadt
    Guben, *Germany* 18 D10
Wilhelmina, Geb., *Surinam* 121 C6
Wilhelmina Kanaal, *Neths.* 17 E6
Wilhelmsburg, *Austria* ... 21 G5
Wilhelmshaven, *Germany* 18 B4
Wilhelmstal, *Namibia* 84 C2
Wilkes-Barre, *U.S.A.* 107 E9
Wilkesboro, *U.S.A.* 105 G5
Wilkie, *Canada* 101 C7
Wilkinsburg, *U.S.A.* 106 F5
Wilkinson Lakes, *Australia* 89 E5
Willamina, *U.S.A.* 110 D2
Willandra Billabong
    Creek →, *Australia* ... 91 E4
Willapa B., *U.S.A.* 110 C2
Willapa Hills, *U.S.A.* 112 D3
Willard, *N. Mex., U.S.A.* 111 J10
Willard, *Utah, U.S.A.* ... 110 F7
Willcox, *U.S.A.* 111 K9
Willebroek, *Belgium* 17 F4
Willemstad, *Neth. Ant.* .. 117 D6
Willeroo, *Australia* 88 C5
William →, *Canada* 101 B7
William Creek, *Australia* . 91 D2
Williambury, *Australia* ... 89 D2
Williams, *Australia* 89 F2
Williams, *Ariz., U.S.A.* .. 111 J7
Williams, *Calif., U.S.A.* .. 112 F4
Williams Lake, *Canada* .. 100 C4
Williamsburg, *Ky., U.S.A.* 105 G3
Williamsburg, *Pa., U.S.A.* 106 F6
Williamsburg, *Va., U.S.A.* 104 G7
Williamson, *N.Y., U.S.A.* 106 C7
Williamson, *W. Va.,*
    U.S.A. 104 G4
Williamsport, *U.S.A.* 106 E7
Williamston, *U.S.A.* 105 H7
Williamstown, *Australia* . 91 F3
Williamstown, *Mass.,*
    U.S.A. 107 D11
Williamstown, *N.Y.,*
    U.S.A. 107 C9
Williamsville, *U.S.A.* 109 G9
Willimantic, *U.S.A.* 107 E12
Willis Group, *Australia* .. 90 B5
Willisau, *Switz.* 22 B6
Williston, *Fla., U.S.A.* ... 105 L4
Williston, *N. Dak., U.S.A.* 108 A3
Williston L., *Canada* 100 B4
Willits, *U.S.A.* 110 G2
Willmar, *U.S.A.* 108 C7
Willoughby, *U.S.A.* 106 E3
Willow Bunch, *Canada* .. 101 D7
Willow L., *Canada* 100 A5

Willow Lake, *U.S.A.* 108 C6
Willow Springs, *U.S.A.* .. 109 G8
Willow Wall, The, *China* . 51 C12
Willowlake →, *Canada* .. 100 A4
Willowmore, *S. Africa* ... 84 E3
Willows, *Australia* 90 C4
Willows, *U.S.A.* 112 F4
Willowvale = Gatyana,
    S. Africa 85 E4
Wills, L., *Australia* 88 D4
Wills Cr. →, *Australia* ... 90 C3
Wills Point, *U.S.A.* 109 J7
Willunga, *Australia* 91 F2
Wilmette, *U.S.A.* 104 D2
Wilmington, *Australia* ... 91 E2
Wilmington, *Del., U.S.A.* 104 F8
Wilmington, *Ill., U.S.A.* . 104 E1
Wilmington, *N.C., U.S.A.* 105 H7
Wilmington, *Ohio, U.S.A.* 104 F4
Wilpena Cr. →, *Australia* 91 E2
Wilrijk, *Belgium* 17 F4
Wilsall, *U.S.A.* 110 D8
Wilson, *U.S.A.* 105 H7
Wilson →, *Queens.,*
    Australia 91 D3
Wilson →, *W. Austral.,*
    Australia 88 C4
Wilson Bluff, *Australia* ... 89 F4
Wilsons Promontory,
    Australia 91 F4
Wilster, *Germany* 18 B5
Wilton, *U.K.* 13 F6
Wilton, *U.S.A.* 108 B4
Wilton →, *Australia* 90 A1
Wiltshire □, *U.K.* 13 F6
Wiltz, *Lux.* 17 J7
Wiluna, *Australia* 89 E3
Wimereux, *France* 25 B8
Wimmera →, *Australia* .. 91 F3
Winam G., *Kenya* 82 C3
Winburg, *S. Africa* 84 D4
Winchendon, *U.S.A.* 107 D12
Winchester, *U.K.* 13 F6
Winchester, *Conn., U.S.A.* 107 E11
Winchester, *Idaho, U.S.A.* 110 C5
Winchester, *Ind., U.S.A.* 104 E3
Winchester, *Ky., U.S.A.* . 104 G3
Winchester, *N.H., U.S.A.* 107 D12
Winchester, *Nev., U.S.A.* 113 J11
Winchester, *Tenn., U.S.A.* 105 H2
Winchester, *Va., U.S.A.* . 104 F6
Wind →, *U.S.A.* 110 E9
Wind River Range, *U.S.A.* 110 E9
Windau = Ventspils, *Latvia* 9 H16
Windber, *U.S.A.* 106 F6
Windermere, L., *U.K.* ... 12 C5
Windfall, *Canada* 100 C5
Windflower L., *Canada* .. 100 A5
Windhoek, *Namibia* 84 C2
Windom, *U.S.A.* 108 D7
Windorah, *Australia* 90 D3
Window Rock, *U.S.A.* ... 111 J9
Windrush →, *U.K.* 13 F6
Windsor, *Australia* 91 E5
Windsor, *N.S., Canada* .. 99 D7
Windsor, *Nfld., Canada* .. 99 C8
Windsor, *Ont., Canada* .. 98 D3
Windsor, *U.K.* 13 F7
Windsor, *Colo., U.S.A.* .. 108 E2
Windsor, *Conn., U.S.A.* . 107 E12
Windsor, *Mo., U.S.A.* ... 108 F8
Windsor, *N.Y., U.S.A.* .. 107 D9
Windsor, *Vt., U.S.A.* 107 C12
Windsorton, *S. Africa* ... 84 D3
Windward Is., *W. Indies* . 117 D7
Windward Passage =
    Vientos, Paso de los,
    Caribbean 117 C5
Windy L., *Canada* 101 A8
Winefred L., *Canada* 101 B6
Winejok, *Sudan* 77 F2
Winfield, *U.S.A.* 109 G6
Wingate Mts., *Australia* . 88 B5
Wingen, *Australia* 91 E5
Wingene, *Belgium* 17 F2
Wingham, *Australia* 91 E5
Wingham, *Canada* 98 D3
Winifred, *U.S.A.* 110 C9
Winisk, *Canada* 98 A2
Winisk →, *Canada* 98 A2
Winisk L., *Canada* 98 B2
Wink, *U.S.A.* 109 K3
Winkler, *Canada* 101 D9
Winlock, *U.S.A.* 112 D4
Winneba, *Ghana* 79 D4
Winnebago, *U.S.A.* 108 D7
Winnebago, L., *U.S.A.* .. 104 D1
Winnecke Cr. →, *Australia* 88 C5
Winnemucca, *U.S.A.* 110 F5
Winnemucca L., *U.S.A.* . 110 F4
Winner, *U.S.A.* 108 D5
Winnett, *U.S.A.* 110 C9
Winnfield, *U.S.A.* 109 K8
Winnibigoshish, L., *U.S.A.* 108 B7
Winning, *Australia* 88 D1
Winnipeg, *Canada* 101 D9
Winnipeg →, *Canada* ... 101 C9
Winnipeg, L., *Canada* ... 101 C9
Winnipeg Beach, *Canada* 101 C9
Winnipegosis, *Canada* ... 101 C9
Winnipegosis L., *Canada* . 101 C9
Winnipesaukee, L., *U.S.A.* 107 C13
Winnsboro, *La., U.S.A.* .. 109 J9
Winnsboro, *S.C., U.S.A.* . 105 H5
Winnsboro, *Tex., U.S.A.* . 109 J7
Winokapau, L., *Canada* .. 99 B7

Winona, *Minn., U.S.A.* 108 C9
Winona, *Miss., U.S.A.* 109 J10
Winooski, *U.S.A.* 107 B11
Winschoten, *Neths.* 16 B10
Winsen, *Germany* 18 B6
Winslow, *Ariz., U.S.A.* 111 J8
Winslow, *Wash., U.S.A.* 112 C4
Winsted, *U.S.A.* 107 E11
Winston-Salem, *U.S.A.* 105 G5
Winsum, *Neths.* 16 B9
Winter Garden, *U.S.A.* 105 L5
Winter Haven, *U.S.A.* 105 M5
Winter Park, *U.S.A.* 105 L5
Winterberg, *Germany* 18 D4
Winterhaven, *U.S.A.* 113 N12
Winters, *Calif., U.S.A.* 112 G5
Winters, *Tex., U.S.A.* 109 K5
Winterset, *U.S.A.* 108 E7
Wintersville, *U.S.A.* 106 F4
Winterswijk, *Neths.* 16 E9
Winterthur, *Switz.* 23 B7
Winthrop, *Minn., U.S.A.* 108 C7
Winthrop, *Wash., U.S.A.* 110 B3
Winton, *Australia* 90 C3
Winton, *N.Z.* 87 M2
Winton, *U.S.A.* 105 G7
Wintzenheim, *France* 25 D14
Wipper →, *Germany* 18 D7
Wirral, *U.K.* 12 D4
Wirrulla, *Australia* 91 E1
Wisbech, *U.K.* 12 E8
Wisconsin □, *U.S.A.* 108 C10
Wisconsin →, *U.S.A.* 108 D9
Wisconsin Dells, *U.S.A.* 108 D10
Wisconsin Rapids, *U.S.A.* 108 C10
Wisdom, *U.S.A.* 110 D7
Wishaw, *U.K.* 14 F5
Wishek, *U.S.A.* 108 B5
Wisła, *Poland* 20 F8
Wisła →, *Poland* 20 A8
Wisłok →, *Poland* 20 E12
Wisłoka →, *Poland* 20 E11
Wismar, *Germany* 18 B7
Wismar, *Guyana* 121 B6
Wisner, *U.S.A.* 108 E6
Wissant, *France* 25 B8
Wissembourg, *France* 25 C14
Wissenkerke, *Neths.* 17 E3
Witbank, *S. Africa* 85 D4
Witdraai, *S. Africa* 84 D3
Witham →, *U.K.* 12 D7
Withernsea, *U.K.* 12 D8
Witmarsum, *Neths.* 16 B6
Witney, *U.K.* 13 F6
Witnossob →, *Namibia* 84 D3
Wittdün, *Germany* 18 A4
Witten, *Germany* 17 F10
Wittenberg, *Germany* 18 D8
Wittenberge, *Germany* 18 B7
Wittenburg, *Germany* 18 B7
Wittenoom, *Australia* 88 D2
Wittingen, *Germany* 18 C6
Wittlich, *Germany* 19 F2
Wittmund, *Germany* 18 B3
Wittow, *Germany* 18 A9
Wittstock, *Germany* 18 B8
Witzenhausen, *Germany* 18 D5
Wlingi, *Indonesia* 57 H15
Włocławek, *Poland* 20 C9
Włodawa, *Poland* 20 D13
Włoszczowa, *Poland* 20 E9
Woburn, *U.S.A.* 107 D13
Wodian, *China* 50 H7
Wodonga, *Australia* 91 F4
Woerden, *Neths.* 16 D5
Woerth, *France* 25 D14
Woëvre, *France* 25 C12
Wognum, *Neths.* 16 C6
Wohlen, *Switz.* 23 B6
Woinbogoin, *China* 52 A2
Wokam, *Indonesia* 57 F8
Wolbrom, *Poland* 20 E9
Woldegk, *Germany* 18 B9
Wolf →, *Canada* 100 A2
Wolf Creek, *U.S.A.* 110 C7
Wolf L., *Canada* 100 A2
Wolf Point, *U.S.A.* 108 A2
Wolfe I., *Canada* 98 D4
Wolfenbüttel, *Germany* 18 C6
Wolfheze, *Neths.* 16 D7
Wolfsberg, *Austria* 21 J4
Wolfsburg, *Germany* 18 C6
Wolgast, *Germany* 18 A9
Wolhusen, *Switz.* 22 B6
Wolin, *Poland* 20 B4
Wollaston, Is., *Chile* 128 E3
Wollaston L., *Canada* 101 B8
Wollaston Pen., *Canada* 96 B8
Wollogorang, *Australia* 90 B2
Wollongong, *Australia* 91 E5
Wolmaransstad, *S. Africa* 84 D4
Wolmirstedt, *Germany* 18 C7
Wolseley, *Australia* 91 F3
Wolseley, *Canada* 101 C8
Wolseley, *S. Africa* 84 E2
Wolstenholme, C., *Canada* 94 C12
Wolsztyn, *Poland* 20 C6
Wolvega, *Neths.* 16 C7
Wolverhampton, *U.K.* 13 E5
Wommels, *Neths.* 16 B7
Wonarah, *Australia* 90 B2
Wonck, *Belgium* 17 G7
Wondai, *Australia* 91 D5
Wondelgem, *Belgium* 17 F3
Wongalarroo L., *Australia* 91 E3
Wongan Hills, *Australia* 89 F2
Wongawol, *Australia* 89 E3
Wŏnju, *S. Korea* 51 F14
Wonosari, *Indonesia* 57 G14
Wŏnsan, *N. Korea* 51 E14
Wonthaggi, *Australia* 91 F4
Woocalla, *Australia* 91 E2
Wood Buffalo Nat. Park, *Canada* 100 B6
Wood Is., *Australia* 88 C3
Wood L., *Canada* 101 B8
Wood Lake, *U.S.A.* 108 D4
Woodah I., *Australia* 90 A2
Woodanilling, *Australia* 89 F2
Woodbridge, *Canada* 106 C5
Woodburn, *Australia* 91 D5
Woodenbong, *Australia* 91 D5
Woodend, *Australia* 91 F3
Woodfords, *U.S.A.* 112 G7
Woodgreen, *Australia* 90 C1
Woodlake, *U.S.A.* 112 J7
Woodland, *U.S.A.* 112 G5
Woodlands, *Australia* 88 D2
Woodpecker, *Canada* 100 C4
Woodridge, *Canada* 101 D9
Woodroffe, Mt., *Australia* 89 E5
Woodruff, *Ariz., U.S.A.* 111 J8
Woodruff, *Utah, U.S.A.* 110 F8
Woods, L., *Australia* 90 B1
Woods, L., *Canada* 99 B6
Woods, L. of the, *Canada* 101 D10
Woodstock, *Queens., Australia* 90 B4
Woodstock, *W. Austral., Australia* 88 D2
Woodstock, *N.B., Canada* 99 C6
Woodstock, *Ont., Canada* 98 D3
Woodstock, *U.K.* 13 F6
Woodstock, *Ill., U.S.A.* 108 D10
Woodstock, *Vt., U.S.A.* 107 C12
Woodsville, *U.S.A.* 107 B13
Woodville, *N.Z.* 87 J5
Woodville, *U.S.A.* 109 K7
Woodward, *U.S.A.* 109 G5
Woody, *U.S.A.* 113 K8
Woolamai, C., *Australia* 91 F4
Woolgoolga, *Australia* 91 E5
Woombye, *Australia* 91 D5
Woomera, *Australia* 91 E2
Woonsocket, *R.I., U.S.A.* 107 D13
Woonsocket, *S. Dak., U.S.A.* 108 C5
Wooramel, *Australia* 89 E1
Wooramel →, *Australia* 89 E1
Wooroloo, *Australia* 89 F2
Wooster, *U.S.A.* 106 F3
Worb, *Switz.* 22 C5
Worcester, *S. Africa* 84 E2
Worcester, *U.K.* 13 E5
Worcester, *Mass., U.S.A.* 107 D13
Worcester, *N.Y., U.S.A.* 107 D10
Wörgl, *Austria* 19 H8
Workington, *U.K.* 12 C4
Worksop, *U.K.* 12 D6
Workum, *Neths.* 16 C6
Worland, *U.S.A.* 110 D10
Wormerveer, *Neths.* 16 D5
Wormhoudt, *France* 25 B9
Worms, *Germany* 19 F4
Wörth, *Germany* 19 F8
Wortham, *U.S.A.* 109 K6
Wörther See, *Austria* 21 J4
Worthing, *U.K.* 13 G7
Worthington, *U.S.A.* 108 D7
Wosi, *Indonesia* 57 E7
Wou-han = Wuhan, *China* 53 B10
Woubrugge, *Neths.* 16 D5
Woudenberg, *Neths.* 16 D6
Woudsend, *Neths.* 16 C7
Wour, *Chad* 73 D8
Wousi = Wuxi, *China* 53 B13
Wouw, *Neths.* 17 E4
Wowoni, *Indonesia* 57 E6
Woy Woy, *Australia* 91 E5
Wrangel I. = Vrangelya, Ostrov, *Russia* 45 B19
Wrangell, *U.S.A.* 96 C6
Wrangell I., *U.S.A.* 100 B2
Wrangell Mts., *U.S.A.* 96 B5
Wrath, C., *U.K.* 14 C3
Wray, *U.S.A.* 108 E3
Wrekin, The, *U.K.* 12 E5
Wrens, *U.S.A.* 105 J4
Wrexham, *U.K.* 12 D4
Wriezen, *Germany* 18 C10
Wright, *Canada* 100 C4
Wright, *Phil.* 55 F6
Wrightson Mt., *U.S.A.* 111 L8
Wrightwood, *U.S.A.* 113 L9
Wrigley, *Canada* 96 B7
Wrocław, *Poland* 20 D7
Września, *Poland* 20 C7
Wschowa, *Poland* 20 D6
Wu Jiang →, *China* 52 C6
Wu'an, *China* 50 F8
Wubin, *Australia* 89 F2
Wubu, *China* 50 F6
Wuchang, *China* 51 B14
Wucheng, *China* 50 F9
Wuchuan, *Guangdong, China* 53 G8
Wuchuan, *Guizhou, China* 52 C7
Wuchuan, *Nei Mongol Zizhiqu, China* 50 D6
Wudi, *China* 51 F9
Wuding, *China* 52 E4
Wuding He →, *China* 50 F6
Wudu, *China* 50 H3
Wufeng, *China* 53 B8
Wugang, *China* 53 D8
Wugong Shan, *China* 53 D9
Wuhan, *China* 53 B10
Wuhe, *China* 51 H9
Wuhsi = Wuxi, *China* 53 B13
Wuhu, *China* 53 B12
Wujiang, *China* 53 B13
Wukari, *Nigeria* 79 D6
Wulajie, *China* 51 B14
Wulanbulang, *China* 50 D6
Wulehe, *Ghana* 79 D5
Wulian, *China* 51 G10
Wuliang Shan, *China* 52 E3
Wuliaru, *Indonesia* 57 F8
Wulumuchi = Ürümqi, *China* 44 E9
Wum, *Cameroon* 79 D7
Wuming, *China* 52 F7
Wuning, *China* 53 C10
Wunnummin L., *Canada* 98 B2
Wunsiedel, *Germany* 19 E8
Wunstorf, *Germany* 18 C5
Wuntho, *Burma* 61 H19
Wuping, *China* 53 E11
Wuppertal, *Germany* 18 D3
Wuppertal, *S. Africa* 84 E2
Wuqing, *China* 51 E9
Würenlingen, *Switz.* 23 A6
Wurung, *Australia* 90 B3
Würzburg, *Germany* 19 F5
Wurzen, *Germany* 18 D8
Wushan, *Gansu, China* 50 G3
Wushan, *Sichuan, China* 52 B7
Wusuli Jiang = Ussuri →, *Asia* 48 A7
Wutach →, *Germany* 19 H4
Wutai, *China* 50 E7
Wuting = Huimin, *China* 51 F9
Wutong, *China* 53 E8
Wutonghaolai, *China* 51 C11
Wutongqiao, *China* 52 C4
Wuustwezel, *Belgium* 17 F5
Wuwei, *Anhui, China* 53 B11
Wuwei, *Gansu, China* 54 C5
Wuxi, *Jiangsu, China* 53 B13
Wuxi, *Sichuan, China* 52 B7
Wuxiang, *China* 50 F7
Wuxing, *China* 53 B13
Wuxuan, *China* 52 F7
Wuyang, *China* 50 H7
Wuyi, *Hebei, China* 50 F8
Wuyi, *Zhejiang, China* 53 C12
Wuyi Shan, *China* 53 D11
Wuyo, *Nigeria* 79 C7
Wuyuan, *Jiangxi, China* 53 C11
Wuyuan, *Nei Mongol Zizhiqu, China* 50 D5
Wuzhai, *China* 50 E6
Wuzhi Shan, *China* 54 E5
Wuzhong, *China* 50 E4
Wuzhou, *China* 53 F8
Wyaaba Cr. →, *Australia* 90 B3
Wyalkatchem, *Australia* 89 F2
Wyalusing, *U.S.A.* 107 E8
Wyandotte, *U.S.A.* 104 D4
Wyandra, *Australia* 91 D4
Wyangala Res., *Australia* 91 E4
Wyara, L., *Australia* 91 D3
Wycheproof, *Australia* 91 F3
Wye →, *U.K.* 13 F5
Wyemandoo, *Australia* 89 E2
Wyk, *Germany* 18 A4
Wymondham, *U.K.* 13 E7
Wymore, *U.S.A.* 108 E6
Wynbring, *Australia* 91 E1
Wyndham, *Australia* 88 C4
Wyndham, *N.Z.* 87 M2
Wyndmere, *U.S.A.* 108 B6
Wynne, *U.S.A.* 109 H9
Wynnum, *Australia* 91 D5
Wynyard, *Australia* 90 G4
Wynyard, *Canada* 101 C8
Wyola, L., *Australia* 89 E5
Wyoming □, *U.S.A.* 110 E10
Wyong, *Australia* 91 E5
Wyszków, *Poland* 20 C11
Wyszogród, *Poland* 20 C10
Wytheville, *U.S.A.* 104 G5

X

Xai-Xai, *Mozam.* 85 D5
Xainza, *China* 54 C3
Xambioá, *Brazil* 122 C2
Xangongo, *Angola* 84 B2
Xanten, *Germany* 18 D2
Xánthi, *Greece* 39 H7
Xanthos, *Turkey* 66 E3
Xapuri, *Brazil* 124 C4
Xar Moron He →, *China* 51 C11
Xau, L., *Botswana* 84 C3
Xavantina, *Brazil* 127 A5
Xenia, *U.S.A.* 104 F4
Xeropotamos →, *Cyprus* 37 E11
Xhora, *S. Africa* 85 E4
Xhumo, *Botswana* 84 C3
Xi Jiang →, *China* 53 F9
Xi Xian, *Henan, China* 53 A10
Xi Xian, *Shanxi, China* 50 F6
Xia Xian, *China* 50 G6
Xiachengzi, *China* 51 B16
Xiachuan Dao, *China* 53 G9
Xiaguan, *China* 52 E3
Xiajiang, *China* 53 D10
Xiajin, *China* 50 F8
Xiamen, *China* 53 E12
Xi'an, *China* 50 G5
Xian Xian, *China* 50 E9
Xianfeng, *China* 52 C7
Xiang Jiang →, *China* 53 C9
Xiangcheng, *Henan, China* 50 H8
Xiangcheng, *Henan, China* 50 H7
Xiangcheng, *Sichuan, China* 52 C2
Xiangdu, *China* 52 F6
Xiangfan, *China* 53 A9
Xianghuang Qi, *China* 50 C7
Xiangning, *China* 50 G6
Xiangquan, *China* 50 F7
Xiangshan, *China* 53 C13
Xiangshui, *China* 51 G10
Xiangtan, *China* 53 D9
Xiangxiang, *China* 53 D9
Xiangyin, *China* 53 C9
Xiangyun, *China* 52 E3
Xiangzhou, *China* 52 F7
Xianju, *China* 53 C13
Xianning, *China* 53 C10
Xianshui He →, *China* 52 B3
Xianyang, *China* 50 G5
Xianyou, *China* 53 E12
Xiao Hinggan Ling, *China* 54 B7
Xiao Xian, *China* 50 G9
Xiaofeng, *China* 53 B12
Xiaogan, *China* 53 B9
Xiaojin, *China* 52 B4
Xiaolan, *China* 53 F9
Xiaoshan, *China* 53 B13
Xiaoyi, *China* 50 F6
Xiapu, *China* 53 D12
Xiawa, *China* 51 C11
Xiayi, *China* 50 G9
Xichang, *China* 52 D4
Xichong, *China* 52 B5
Xichuan, *China* 50 H6
Xiemahe, *China* 53 B8
Xieng Khouang, *Laos* 58 C4
Xifei He →, *China* 50 H9
Xifeng, *Guizhou, China* 52 D6
Xifeng, *Liaoning, China* 51 C13
Xifengzhen, *China* 50 G4
Xigazê, *China* 54 D3
Xihe, *China* 50 G3
Xihua, *China* 50 H8
Xiliao He →, *China* 51 C12
Xilin, *China* 52 E5
Xilókastron, *Greece* 39 L5
Xin Jiang →, *China* 53 C11
Xin Xian, *China* 50 E7
Xinavane, *Mozam.* 85 D5
Xinbin, *China* 51 D13
Xincai, *China* 53 A10
Xinchang, *China* 53 C13
Xincheng, *Guangxi Zhuangzu, China* 52 E7
Xincheng, *Jiangxi, China* 53 D10
Xinfeng, *Guangdong, China* 53 E10
Xinfeng, *Jiangxi, China* 53 D11
Xinfeng, *Jiangxi, China* 53 E10
Xing Xian, *China* 50 E6
Xing'an, *Guangxi Zhuangzu, China* 53 E8
Xingan, *Jiangxi, China* 53 D10
Xingcheng, *China* 51 D11
Xingguo, *China* 53 D10
Xinghe, *China* 50 D7
Xinghua, *China* 51 H10
Xinghua Wan, *China* 53 E12
Xinglong, *China* 51 D9
Xingning, *China* 53 E10
Xingping, *China* 50 G5
Xingren, *China* 52 E5
Xingshan, *China* 53 B8
Xingtai, *China* 50 F8
Xingu →, *Brazil* 121 D7
Xingyang, *China* 50 G7
Xinhe, *China* 50 F8
Xinhua, *China* 53 D8
Xinhuang, *China* 52 D7
Xinhui, *China* 53 F9
Xining, *China* 54 C5
Xinjiang, *China* 50 G6
Xinjiang Uygur Zizhiqu □, *China* 54 B3
Xinjie, *China* 52 D3
Xinjin, *Liaoning, China* 51 E11
Xinjin, *Sichuan, China* 52 B4
Xinkai He →, *China* 51 C12
Xinle, *China* 50 E8
Xinlitun, *China* 51 D12
Xinlong, *China* 52 B3
Xinmin, *China* 51 D12
Xinning, *China* 53 D8
Xinping, *China* 52 E3
Xinshao, *China* 53 D8
Xintai, *China* 51 G9
Xintian, *China* 53 E9
Xinxiang, *China* 50 G7
Xinxing, *China* 53 F9
Xinyang, *China* 53 A10
Xinye, *China* 53 A9
Xinyi, *China* 53 F8
Xinyu, *China* 53 D10
Xinzhan, *China* 51 C14
Xinzheng, *China* 50 G7
Xinzhou, *China* 53 B10
Xinzhu, *Taiwan* 53 E13
Xiong Xian, *China* 50 E9
Xiongyuecheng, *China* 51 D12
Xiping, *Henan, China* 50 H8
Xiping, *Henan, China* 50 H6
Xiping, *Zhejiang, China* 53 C12
Xique-Xique, *Brazil* 122 D3
Xiruá →, *Brazil* 124 B4
Xisha Qundao = Hsisha Chuntao, *Pac. Oc.* 56 A4
Xishui, *China* 53 B10
Xituozhen, *China* 52 B7
Xiuning, *China* 53 C12
Xiuren, *China* 53 E8
Xiushan, *China* 52 C7
Xiushui, *China* 53 C10
Xiuwen, *China* 52 D6
Xiuyan, *China* 51 D12
Xixabangma Feng, *China* 61 E14
Xixia, *China* 50 H6
Xixiang, *China* 50 H4
Xiyang, *China* 50 F7
Xizang □, *China* 54 C3
Xlendi, *Malta* 37 C1
Xu Jiang →, *China* 53 D11
Xuan Loc, *Vietnam* 59 G6
Xuancheng, *China* 53 B12
Xuan'en, *China* 52 C7
Xuanhan, *China* 52 B6
Xuanhua, *China* 50 D8
Xuchang, *China* 50 G7
Xuefeng Shan, *China* 53 D8
Xuejiaping, *China* 53 B8
Xun Jiang →, *China* 53 F8
Xun Xian, *China* 50 G8
Xundian, *China* 52 E4
Xunwu, *China* 53 E10
Xunyang, *China* 50 H5
Xunyi, *China* 50 G5
Xupu, *China* 53 D8
Xushui, *China* 50 E8
Xuwen, *China* 53 G8
Xuyen Moc, *Vietnam* 59 G6
Xuyong, *China* 52 C5
Xuzhou, *China* 51 G9
Xylophagou, *Cyprus* 37 E12

Y

Ya Xian, *China* 58 C7
Yaamba, *Australia* 90 C5
Ya'an, *China* 52 C4
Yaapeet, *Australia* 91 F3
Yabassi, *Cameroon* 79 E6
Yabelo, *Ethiopia* 77 G4
Yablonovy Khrebet, *Russia* 45 D12
Yablonovy Ra. = Yablonovy Khrebet, *Russia* 45 D12
Yabrai Shan, *China* 50 E2
Yabrūd, *Syria* 69 B5
Yacuiba, *Bolivia* 126 A3
Yacuma →, *Bolivia* 125 C4
Yadgir, *India* 60 L10
Yadkin →, *U.S.A.* 105 H5
Yadrin, *Russia* 41 D15
Yagaba, *Ghana* 79 C4
Yagodnoye, *Russia* 45 C15
Yagoua, *Cameroon* 80 B3
Yaguas →, *Peru* 120 D3
Yaha, *Thailand* 59 J3
Yahila, *Zaïre* 82 B1
Yahk, *Canada* 100 D5
Yahuma, *Zaïre* 80 D4
Yahyalı, *Turkey* 66 D6
Yaita, *Japan* 49 F9
Yaiza, *Canary Is.* 36 F6
Yajiang, *China* 52 B3
Yajua, *Nigeria* 79 C7
Yakima, *U.S.A.* 110 C3
Yakima →, *U.S.A.* 110 C3
Yako, *Burkina Faso* 78 C4
Yakoruda, *Bulgaria* 39 G6
Yakovlevka, *Russia* 48 B6
Yaku-Shima, *Japan* 49 J5
Yakut Republic □, *Russia* 45 C13
Yakutat, *U.S.A.* 96 C6
Yakutsk, *Russia* 45 C13
Yala, *Thailand* 59 J3
Yalbalgo, *Australia* 89 E1
Yalboroo, *Australia* 90 C4
Yale, *U.S.A.* 106 C2
Yalgoo, *Australia* 89 E2
Yalinga, *C.A.R.* 73 G9
Yalkubul, Punta, *Mexico* 115 C7
Yalleroi, *Australia* 90 C4
Yalobusha →, *U.S.A.* 109 J9
Yalong Jiang →, *China* 52 D3
Yalova, *Turkey* 66 C3
Yalpukh, Oz., *Ukraine* 38 D11
Yalta, *Ukraine* 42 D6
Yalu Jiang →, *China* 51 E13
Yalutorovsk, *Russia* 44 D7
Yalvaç, *Turkey* 66 D4
Yam Ha Melaḥ = Dead Sea, *Asia* 69 D4
Yam Kinneret, *Israel* 69 C4
Yamada, *Japan* 49 H5
Yamagata, *Japan* 48 E10

Yamagata □, *Japan* 48 E10
Yamaguchi, *Japan* 49 G5
Yamaguchi □, *Japan* 49 G5
Yamal, Poluostrov, *Russia* 44 B8
Yamal Pen. = Yamal, Poluostrov, *Russia* 44 B8
Yamanashi □, *Japan* 49 G9
Yamantau, Gora, *Russia* 44 D6
Yamba, *N.S.W., Australia* 91 D5
Yamba, *S. Austral., Australia* 91 E3
Yambah, *Australia* 90 C1
Yambarran Ra., *Australia* 88 C5
Yâmbiô, *Sudan* 77 G2
Yambol, *Bulgaria* 38 G9
Yamdena, *Indonesia* 57 F8
Yame, *Japan* 49 H5
Yamethin, *Burma* 61 J20
Yamil, *Nigeria* 79 C6
Yamma-Yamma, L., *Australia* 91 D3
Yamoussoukro, *Ivory C.* 78 D3
Yampa →, *U.S.A.* 110 F9
Yampi Sd., *Australia* 88 C3
Yampol, *Ukraine* 42 B3
Yamrat, *Nigeria* 79 C6
Yamrukchal, *Bulgaria* 38 G7
Yamuna →, *India* 63 G9
Yamzho Yumco, *China* 54 D4
Yan, *Nigeria* 79 C7
Yana →, *Russia* 45 B14
Yanac, *Australia* 91 F3
Yanagawa, *Japan* 49 H5
Yanai, *Japan* 49 H6
Yan'an, *China* 50 F5
Yanbian, *China* 52 D3
Yanbu 'al Baḩr, *Si. Arabia* 64 F3
Yancannia, *Australia* 91 E3
Yanchang, *China* 50 F6
Yancheng, *Henan, China* 50 H7
Yancheng, *Jiangsu, China* 51 H11
Yanchi, *China* 50 F4
Yanchuan, *China* 50 F6
Yanco Cr. →, *Australia* 91 F4
Yandal, *Australia* 89 E3
Yandanooka, *Australia* 89 E2
Yandaran, *Australia* 90 C5
Yandoon, *Burma* 61 L19
Yanfeng, *China* 52 E3
Yanfolila, *Mali* 78 C3
Yang Xian, *China* 50 H4
Yangambi, *Zaïre* 82 B1
Yangbi, *China* 52 E2
Yangcheng, *China* 50 G7
Yangch'ü = Taiyuan, *China* 50 F7
Yangchun, *China* 53 F8
Yanggao, *China* 50 D7
Yanggu, *China* 50 F8
Yangi-Yer, *Kazakhstan* 44 E7
Yangjiang, *China* 53 G8
Yangliuqing, *China* 51 E9
Yangon = Rangoon, *Burma* 61 L20
Yangping, *China* 53 B8
Yangpingguan, *China* 50 H4
Yangquan, *China* 50 F7
Yangshan, *China* 53 E9
Yangshuo, *China* 53 E8
Yangtze Kiang = Chang Jiang →, *China* 53 B13
Yangxin, *China* 53 C10
Yangyang, *S. Korea* 51 E15
Yangyuan, *China* 50 D8
Yangzhou, *China* 53 A12
Yanhe, *China* 52 C7
Yanji, *China* 51 C15
Yanjin, *China* 52 C5
Yanjing, *China* 52 C2
Yankton, *U.S.A.* 108 D6
Yanna, *Australia* 91 D4
Yanonge, *Zaïre* 82 B1
Yanqi, *China* 54 B3
Yanqing, *China* 50 D8
Yanshan, *Hebei, China* 51 E9
Yanshan, *Jiangxi, China* 53 C11
Yanshan, *Yunnan, China* 52 F5
Yanshou, *China* 51 B15
Yantabulla, *Australia* 91 D4
Yantai, *China* 51 F11
Yanting, *China* 52 B5
Yantra →, *Bulgaria* 38 F8
Yanwa, *China* 52 D2
Yanyuan, *China* 52 D3
Yanzhou, *China* 50 G9
Yao, *Chad* 73 F8
Yao Xian, *China* 50 G5
Yao Yai, Ko, *Thailand* 59 J2
Yao'an, *China* 52 E3
Yaodu, *China* 52 A5
Yaoundé, *Cameroon* 79 E7
Yaowan, *China* 51 G10
Yap I., *Pac. Oc.* 92 G5
Yapen, *Indonesia* 57 E9
Yapen, Selat, *Indonesia* 57 E9
Yappar →, *Australia* 90 B3
Yaqui →, *Mexico* 114 B2
Yar, *Russia* 41 B18
Yar-Sale, *Russia* 44 C8
Yaracuy □, *Venezuela* 120 A4
Yaracuy →, *Venezuela* 120 A4
Yaraka, *Australia* 90 C3
Yarangüme, *Turkey* 66 E3
Yaransk, *Russia* 41 C15
Yaratishky, *Belorussia* 40 D4
Yardea P.O., *Australia* 91 E2
Yare →, *U.K.* 13 E9
Yarensk, *Russia* 44 C5
Yarí →, *Colombia* 120 D3
Yaritagua, *Venezuela* 120 A4
Yarkand = Shache, *China* 54 C2
Yarker, *Canada* 107 B8
Yarkhun →, *Pakistan* 63 A5
Yarmouth, *Canada* 99 D6
Yarmūk →, *Syria* 69 C4
Yaroslavl, *Russia* 41 C11
Yarqa, W. →, *Egypt* 69 F2
Yarra Yarra Lakes, *Australia* 89 E2
Yarraden, *Australia* 90 A3
Yarraloola, *Australia* 88 D2
Yarram, *Australia* 91 F4
Yarraman, *Australia* 91 D5
Yarranvale, *Australia* 91 D4
Yarras, *Australia* 91 E5
Yarrowmere, *Australia* 90 C4
Yartsevo, *Russia* 40 D8
Yartsevo, *Russia* 45 C10
Yarumal, *Colombia* 120 B2
Yasawa Group, *Fiji* 87 C7
Yaselda →, *Belorussia* 40 E5
Yashi, *Nigeria* 79 C6
Yasin, *Pakistan* 63 A5
Yasinovataya, *Ukraine* 42 B7
Yasinski, L., *Canada* 98 B4
Yasothon, *Thailand* 58 E5
Yass, *Australia* 91 E4
Yata →, *Bolivia* 125 C4
Yatağan, *Turkey* 66 E3
Yates Center, *U.S.A.* 109 G7
Yathkyed L., *Canada* 101 A9
Yatsushiro, *Japan* 49 H5
Yatta Plateau, *Kenya* 82 C4
Yauca, *Peru* 124 D3
Yauya, *Peru* 124 B2
Yauyos, *Peru* 124 C2
Yavari →, *Peru* 124 A3
Yavatmal, *India* 60 J11
Yavne, *Israel* 69 D3
Yavorov, *Ukraine* 40 G3
Yavuzeli, *Turkey* 67 E7
Yawatahama, *Japan* 49 H6
Yawri B., *S. Leone* 78 D2
Yaxi, *China* 52 D6
Yayama-Rettō, *Japan* 49 M1
Yazd, *Iran* 65 D7
Yazd □, *Iran* 65 D7
Yazoo →, *U.S.A.* 109 J9
Yazoo City, *U.S.A.* 109 J9
Yding Skovhøj, *Denmark* 9 J10
Ye Xian, *Henan, China* 50 H7
Ye Xian, *Shandong, China* 51 F10
Yealering, *Australia* 89 F2
Yebyu, *Burma* 61 M21
Yechŏn, *S. Korea* 51 F15
Yecla, *Spain* 29 G3
Yécora, *Mexico* 114 B3
Yedintsy, *Moldavia* 42 B2
Yeeda, *Australia* 88 C3
Yeelanna, *Australia* 91 E2
Yefremov, *Russia* 41 E11
Yegorlyk →, *Russia* 43 C9
Yegorlykskaya, *Russia* 43 C9
Yegoryevsk, *Russia* 41 D11
Yegros, *Paraguay* 126 B4
Yehuda, Midbar, *Israel* 69 D4
Yei, *Sudan* 77 G3
Yei, Nahr →, *Sudan* 77 F3
Yekaterinburg, *Russia* 44 D7
Yekaterinodar = Krasnodar, *Russia* 43 D8
Yelan, *Russia* 41 F13
Yelan-Kolenovskiy, *Russia* 41 F12
Yelanskoye, *Russia* 45 C13
Yelarbon, *Australia* 91 D5
Yelatma, *Russia* 41 D12
Yelcho, L., *Chile* 128 B2
Yelets, *Russia* 41 E11
Yélimané, *Mali* 78 B2
Yelizavetgrad = Kirovograd, *Ukraine* 42 B5
Yell, *U.K.* 14 A7
Yell Sd., *U.K.* 14 A7
Yellow Sea, *China* 51 G12
Yellowhead Pass, *Canada* 100 C5
Yellowknife, *Canada* 100 A6
Yellowknife →, *Canada* 100 A6
Yellowstone →, *U.S.A.* 108 B3
Yellowstone L., *U.S.A.* 110 D8
Yellowstone National Park, *U.S.A.* 110 D8
Yellowtail Res., *U.S.A.* 110 D9
Yelnya, *Russia* 40 D8
Yelsk, *Belorussia* 40 F6
Yelvertoft, *Australia* 90 C2
Yelwa, *Nigeria* 79 C5
Yemen ■, *Asia* 68 E3
Yen Bai, *Vietnam* 58 B5
Yenakiyevo, *Ukraine* 42 B8
Yenangyaung, *Burma* 61 J19
Yenbo = Yanbu 'al Baḩr, *Si. Arabia* 64 F3
Yenda, *Australia* 91 E4
Yendéré, *Ivory C.* 78 C4
Yendi, *Ghana* 79 D4
Yenice, *Turkey* 66 D2
Yenice →, *Turkey* 66 E6
Yenisaía, *Greece* 39 H7
Yenişehir, *Turkey* 66 C3
Yenisey →, *Russia* 44 B9
Yeniseysk, *Russia* 45 D10
Yeniseyskiy Zaliv, *Russia* 44 B9
Yennádhi, *Greece* 37 C9
Yenne, *France* 27 C9
Yenotayevka, *Russia* 43 C12
Yenyuka, *Russia* 45 D13
Yeo, L., *Australia* 89 E3
Yeola, *India* 60 J9
Yeoryioúpolis, *Greece* 37 D6
Yeovil, *U.K.* 13 G5
Yepes, *Spain* 28 F1
Yeppoon, *Australia* 90 C5
Yeráki, *Greece* 39 N4
Yerbent, *Turkmenistan* 44 F6
Yerbogachen, *Russia* 45 C11
Yerevan, *Armenia* 43 F11
Yerilla, *Australia* 89 E3
Yerköy, *Turkey* 66 D6
Yermak, *Kazakhstan* 44 D8
Yermakovo, *Russia* 45 D13
Yermo, *U.S.A.* 113 L10
Yerofey Pavlovich, *Russia* 45 D13
Yerólakkos, *Cyprus* 37 D12
Yeropótamos →, *Greece* 37 D6
Yeroskipos, *Cyprus* 37 E11
Yerseke, *Neths.* 17 F4
Yershov, *Russia* 41 F16
Yerunaja, Cerro, *Peru* 124 C2
Yerushalayim = Jerusalem, *Israel* 69 D4
Yerville, *France* 24 C7
Yes Tor, *U.K.* 13 G4
Yesan, *S. Korea* 51 F14
Yeşilhisar, *Turkey* 66 D6
Yeşilırmak →, *Turkey* 66 C7
Yesilkent, *Turkey* 66 E7
Yesnogorsk, *Russia* 41 D10
Yeso, *U.S.A.* 109 H2
Yessentuki, *Russia* 43 D10
Yessey, *Russia* 45 C11
Yeste, *Spain* 29 G2
Yeu, I. d', *France* 24 F4
Yevlakh, *Azerbaijan* 43 F12
Yevpatoriya, *Ukraine* 42 D5
Yevstratovskiy, *Russia* 41 F11
Yeya →, *Russia* 43 C8
Yeysk, *Russia* 42 C8
Yezd = Yazd, *Iran* 65 D7
Yhati, *Paraguay* 126 B4
Yhú, *Paraguay* 127 B4
Yi →, *Uruguay* 126 C4
Yi 'Allaq, G., *Egypt* 69 E2
Yi He →, *China* 51 G10
Yi Xian, *Anhui, China* 53 C11
Yi Xian, *Hebei, China* 50 E8
Yi Xian, *Liaoning, China* 51 D11
Yialí, *Greece* 39 N10
Yialiás →, *Cyprus* 37 D12
Yi'allaq, G., *Egypt* 76 H8
Yialousa, *Cyprus* 37 D13
Yiáltra, *Greece* 39 L5
Yianisádhes, *Greece* 37 D8
Yiannitsa, *Greece* 39 J5
Yibin, *China* 52 C5
Yichang, *China* 53 B8
Yicheng, *Henan, China* 53 B9
Yicheng, *Shanxi, China* 50 G6
Yichuan, *China* 50 F6
Yichun, *Heilongjiang, China* 54 B7
Yichun, *Jiangxi, China* 53 D10
Yidu, *Hubei, China* 53 B8
Yidu, *Shandong, China* 51 F10
Yidun, *China* 52 B2
Yihuang, *China* 53 D11
Yijun, *China* 50 G5
Yilan, *Taiwan* 53 E13
Yıldızeli, *Turkey* 66 D7
Yiliang, *Yunnan, China* 52 D5
Yiliang, *Yunnan, China* 52 E4
Yilong, *China* 52 B6
Yimen, *China* 52 E4
Yimianpo, *China* 51 B15
Yinchuan, *China* 50 E4
Yindarlgooda, L., *Australia* 89 F3
Ying He →, *China* 50 H9
Ying Xian, *China* 50 E7
Yingcheng, *China* 53 B9
Yingde, *China* 53 E9
Yingjiang, *China* 52 E1
Yingjing, *China* 52 C4
Yingkou, *China* 51 D12
Yingshan, *Henan, China* 53 B9
Yingshan, *Hubei, China* 53 B10
Yingshan, *Sichuan, China* 52 B6
Yingshang, *China* 53 A11
Yingtan, *China* 54 D6
Yining, *China* 44 E9
Yinjiang, *China* 52 C7
Yinmabin, *Burma* 61 H19
Yinnietharra, *Australia* 88 D2
Yiofiros →, *Greece* 37 D7
Yioúra, *Greece* 39 K7
Yipinglang, *China* 52 E3
Yirga Alem, *Ethiopia* 77 F4
Yishan, *China* 52 E7
Yishui, *China* 51 G10
Yíthion, *Greece* 39 N5
Yitiaoshan, *China* 50 F3
Yitong, *China* 51 C13
Yiwu, *China* 53 C13
Yixing, *China* 53 B12
Yiyang, *Henan, China* 50 G7
Yiyang, *Hunan, China* 53 C9
Yiyang, *Jiangxi, China* 53 C11
Yizhang, *China* 53 E9
Yizheng, *China* 53 A12
Ylitornio, *Finland* 8 C17
Ylivieska, *Finland* 8 D18
Yngaren, *Sweden* 11 F10
Ynykchanskiy, *Russia* 45 C14
Yoakum, *U.S.A.* 109 L6
Yobe □, *Nigeria* 79 C7
Yog Pt., *Phil.* 57 B6
Yogan, *Togo* 79 D5
Yogyakarta, *Indonesia* 57 G14
Yoho Nat. Park, *Canada* 100 C5
Yojoa, L. de, *Honduras* 116 D2
Yŏju, *S. Korea* 51 F14
Yokadouma, *Cameroon* 80 D2
Yokkaichi, *Japan* 49 G8
Yoko, *Cameroon* 79 D7
Yokohama, *Japan* 49 G9
Yokosuka, *Japan* 49 G9
Yokote, *Japan* 48 E10
Yola, *Nigeria* 79 D7
Yolaina, Cordillera de, *Nic.* 116 D3
Yonago, *Japan* 49 G6
Yonaguni-Jima, *Japan* 49 M1
Yŏnan, *N. Korea* 51 F14
Yonezawa, *Japan* 48 F10
Yong Peng, *Malaysia* 59 L4
Yong Sata, *Thailand* 59 J2
Yongampo, *N. Korea* 51 E13
Yong'an, *China* 53 E11
Yongcheng, *China* 50 H9
Yŏngchŏn, *S. Korea* 51 G15
Yongchuan, *China* 52 C5
Yongchun, *China* 53 E12
Yongdeng, *China* 50 F2
Yongding, *China* 53 E11
Yŏngdŏk, *S. Korea* 51 F15
Yŏngdŭngpo, *S. Korea* 51 F14
Yongfeng, *China* 53 D10
Yongfu, *China* 52 E7
Yonghe, *China* 50 F6
Yŏnghŭng, *N. Korea* 51 E14
Yongji, *China* 50 G6
Yŏngju, *S. Korea* 51 F15
Yongkang, *Yunnan, China* 52 E2
Yongkang, *Zhejiang, China* 53 C13
Yongnian, *China* 50 F8
Yongning, *Guangxi Zhuangzu, China* 52 F7
Yongning, *Ningxia Huizu, China* 50 E4
Yongping, *China* 52 E2
Yongqing, *China* 50 E9
Yongren, *China* 52 D3
Yongshan, *China* 52 C4
Yongsheng, *China* 52 D3
Yongshun, *China* 52 C7
Yongtai, *China* 53 E12
Yŏngwŏl, *S. Korea* 51 F15
Yongxin, *China* 53 D10
Yongxing, *China* 53 D9
Yongxiu, *China* 53 C10
Yonibana, *S. Leone* 78 D2
Yonkers, *U.S.A.* 107 F11
Yonne □, *France* 25 E10
Yonne →, *France* 25 D9
York, *Australia* 89 F2
York, *U.K.* 12 D6
York, *Ala., U.S.A.* 105 J1
York, *Nebr., U.S.A.* 108 E6
York, *Pa., U.S.A.* 104 F7
York, C., *Australia* 90 A3
York, Kap, *Greenland* 4 B4
York Sd., *Australia* 88 B4
Yorke Pen., *Australia* 91 E2
Yorkshire Wolds, *U.K.* 12 D7
Yorkton, *Canada* 101 C8
Yorktown, *U.S.A.* 109 L6
Yorkville, *U.S.A.* 112 G3
Yornup, *Australia* 89 F2
Yoro, *Honduras* 116 C2
Yoron-Jima, *Japan* 49 L4
Yos Sudarso, Pulau, *Indonesia* 57 F9
Yosemite National Park, *U.S.A.* 111 H4
Yosemite Village, *U.S.A.* 112 H7
Yoshkar Ola, *Russia* 41 C15
Yŏsu, *S. Korea* 51 G14
Yotala, *Bolivia* 125 D4
Yotvata, *Israel* 69 F4
You Xian, *China* 53 D9
Youbou, *Canada* 100 D4
Youghal, *Ireland* 15 E4
Youghal B., *Ireland* 15 E4
Youkounkoun, *Guinea* 78 C2
Young, *Australia* 91 E4
Young, *Canada* 101 C7
Young, *Uruguay* 126 C4
Younghusband, L., *Australia* 91 E2
Younghusband Pen., *Australia* 91 F2
Youngstown, *Canada* 101 C6
Youngstown, *N.Y., U.S.A.* 106 C5
Youngstown, *Ohio, U.S.A.* 106 E4
Youngsville, *U.S.A.* 106 E5
Youssoufia, *Morocco* 74 B3
Youxi, *China* 53 D12
Youyang, *China* 52 C7
Youyu, *China* 50 D7
Yoweragabbie, *Australia* 89 E2
Yozgat, *Turkey* 66 D6
Yozgat □, *Turkey* 66 D6
Ypané →, *Paraguay* 126 A4
Yport, *France* 24 C7
Ypres = Ieper, *Belgium* 17 G1
Ypsilanti, *U.S.A.* 104 D4
Yreka, *U.S.A.* 110 F2
Ysleta, *U.S.A.* 111 L10
Yssingeaux, *France* 27 C8
Ystad, *Sweden* 11 J7
Ysyk-Köl = Issyk-Kul, Ozero, *Kirghizia* 44 E8
Ythan →, *U.K.* 14 D7
Ytterhogdal, *Sweden* 10 B8
Ytyk-Kel, *Russia* 45 C14
Yu Jiang →, *China* 54 D6
Yu Shan, *Taiwan* 53 F13
Yu Xian, *Hebei, China* 50 E8
Yu Xian, *Henan, China* 50 G7
Yu Xian, *Shanxi, China* 50 E7
Yuan Jiang →, *Hunan, China* 53 C8
Yuan Jiang →, *Yunnan, China* 52 F4
Yuan'an, *China* 53 B8
Yuanjiang, *Hunan, China* 53 C9
Yuanjiang, *Yunnan, China* 52 F4
Yuanli, *Taiwan* 53 E13
Yuanlin, *Taiwan* 53 F13
Yuanling, *China* 53 C8
Yuanmou, *China* 52 E3
Yuanqu, *China* 50 G6
Yuanyang, *Henan, China* 50 G7
Yuanyang, *Yunnan, China* 52 F4
Yuba →, *U.S.A.* 112 F5
Yuba City, *U.S.A.* 112 F5
Yūbari, *Japan* 48 C10
Yūbetsu, *Japan* 48 B11
Yucatán □, *Mexico* 115 C7
Yucatán, Canal de, *Caribbean* 116 B2
Yucatan Str. = Yucatán, Canal de, *Caribbean* 116 B2
Yucca, *U.S.A.* 113 L12
Yucca Valley, *U.S.A.* 113 L10
Yucheng, *China* 50 F9
Yuci, *China* 50 F7
Yudino, *Russia* 41 D16
Yudino, *Russia* 44 D7
Yudu, *China* 53 E10
Yuendumu, *Australia* 88 D5
Yueqing, *China* 53 C13
Yueqing Wan, *China* 53 C13
Yuexi, *Anhui, China* 53 B11
Yuexi, *Sichuan, China* 52 C4
Yueyang, *China* 53 C9
Yugan, *China* 53 C11
Yugoslavia ■, *Europe* 21 M10
Yuhuan, *China* 53 C13
Yujiang, *China* 53 C11
Yukhnov, *Russia* 40 D9
Yukon →, *U.S.A.* 96 B3
Yukon Territory □, *Canada* 96 B6
Yüksekova, *Turkey* 67 E11
Yukti, *Russia* 45 C11
Yukuhashi, *Japan* 49 H5
Yule →, *Australia* 88 D2
Yuli, *Nigeria* 79 D7
Yulin, *Guangxi Zhuangzu, China* 53 F8
Yulin, *Shaanxi, China* 50 E5
Yuma, *Ariz., U.S.A.* 113 N12
Yuma, *Colo., U.S.A.* 108 E3
Yuma, B. de, *Dom. Rep.* 117 C6
Yumbe, *Uganda* 82 B3
Yumbi, *Zaïre* 82 C2
Yumbo, *Colombia* 120 C2
Yumen, *China* 54 C4
Yumurtalık, *Turkey* 66 E6
Yun Ho →, *China* 51 E9
Yun Xian, *Hubei, China* 53 A8
Yun Xian, *Yunnan, China* 52 E3
Yunak, *Turkey* 66 D4
Yunan, *China* 53 F8
Yuncheng, *Henan, China* 50 G8
Yuncheng, *Shanxi, China* 50 G6
Yundamindra, *Australia* 89 E3
Yunfu, *China* 53 F9
Yungas, *Bolivia* 125 D4
Yungay, *Chile* 126 D1
Yungay, *Peru* 124 B2
Yunhe, *China* 53 C12
Yunlin, *Taiwan* 53 F13
Yunling, *China* 52 D2
Yunlong, *China* 52 E2
Yunmeng, *China* 53 B9
Yunnan □, *China* 52 E4
Yunquera de Henares, *Spain* 28 E1
Yunta, *Australia* 91 E2
Yunxi, *China* 50 H6
Yunxiao, *China* 53 F11
Yunyang, *China* 52 B7
Yuping, *China* 52 D7
Yupukarri, *Guyana* 121 C6
Yupyongdong, *N. Korea* 51 D15
Yuqing, *China* 52 D6
Yur, *Russia* 45 D14
Yurgao, *Russia* 44 D9
Yuribei, *Russia* 44 B8
Yurimaguas, *Peru* 124 B2
Yurya, *Russia* 41 B16
Yuryev-Polskiy, *Russia* 41 C11
Yuryevets, *Russia* 41 C13
Yuscarán, *Honduras* 116 D2
Yushanzhen, *China* 52 C7
Yushe, *China* 50 F7
Yushu, *Jilin, China* 51 B14
Yushu, *Qinghai, China* 54 C4
Yutai, *China* 50 G9
Yutian, *China* 51 E9

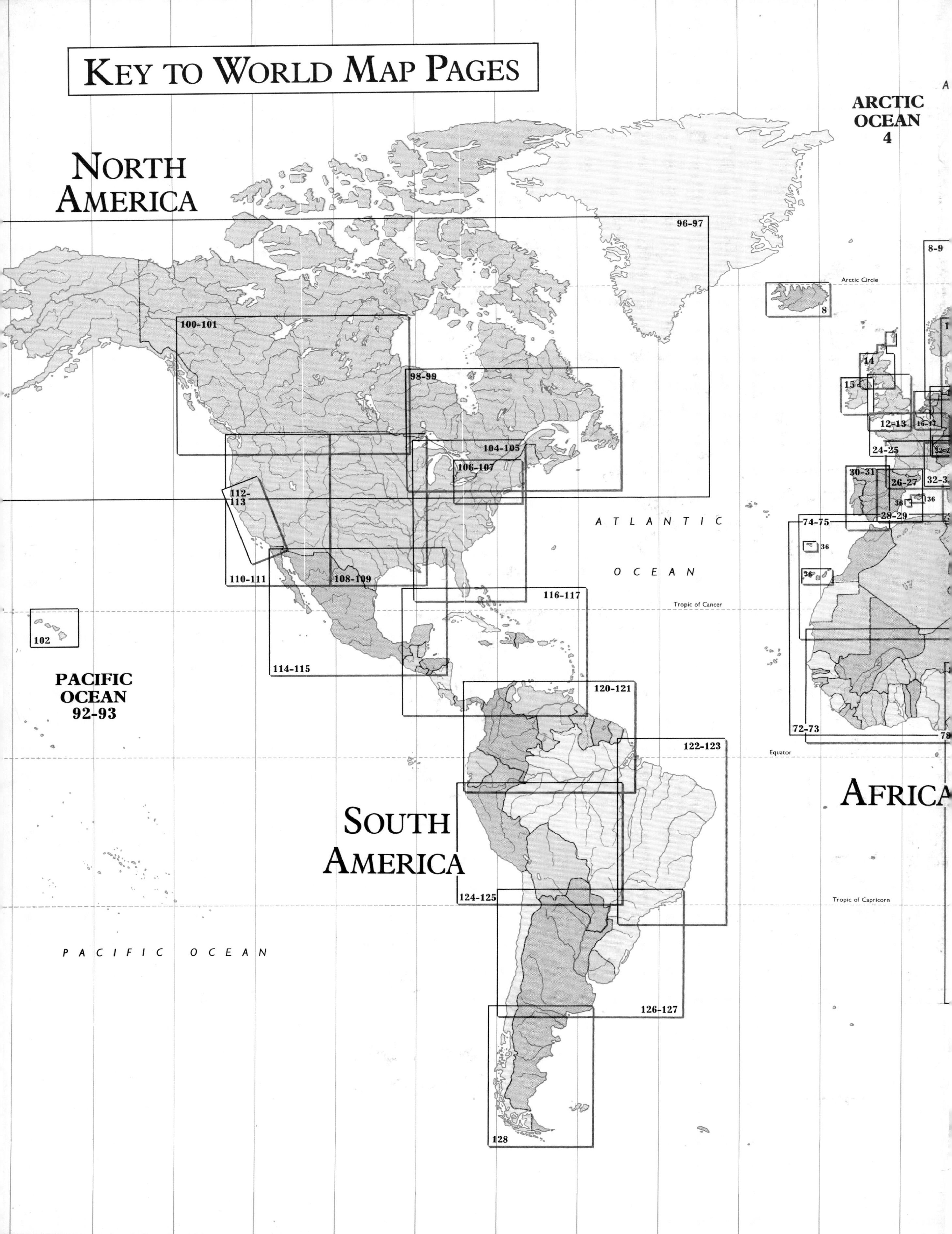

KEY TO WORLD MAP PAGES

NORTH AMERICA

ARCTIC OCEAN 4

Arctic Circle

96–97

8–9

8

100–101

98–99

14

15

12–13   16–17

24–25

104–105

106–107

30–31

26–27   32–33

112–113

ATLANTIC

36   36

74–75

28–29

110–111

108–109

OCEAN

36

116–117

Tropic of Cancer

36

102

114–115

PACIFIC OCEAN 92–93

72–73

78

120–121

122–123

Equator

AFRICA

SOUTH AMERICA

124–125

Tropic of Capricorn

PACIFIC OCEAN

126–127

128